THE
HARBRACE
ANTHOLOGY
OF
LITERATURE

P9-BBN-287

PREFACE

"**W**e imagine ourselves, we create ourselves, we touch ourselves into being with words, words that are important to us," writes Native North American author Gerald Vizenor. One means by which we imagine or create ourselves is through the reading of literature.

The Harbrace Anthology of Literature uses three approaches to encourage its readers in this activity. First, it presents significant and representative works from the increasingly widening canon of literature in English. Second, it provides strategies to assist readers in their appreciation of works of literature. Third, by introducing readers to the language of literature, both simple and complex, and by suggesting methods for articulating responses, it provides opportunities to explore literature and to respond to language in its rich and varied forms.

Although no anthology can include all of its readers' favourite works, the editors have attempted to make their selections as varied and diverse as possible. Thus, The Harbrace Anthology of Literature offers many contemporary poems, plays, and short stories, by men and women alike, from a variety of cultures and backgrounds, in addition to many of those works that have always formed an integral part of the accepted canon of literature in English. It also includes a large sampling of English-Canadian literature in the belief that Canadian students should have the opportunity to experience the major works of their literary tradition both on their own terms and within the larger context of literature written in English.

Individual works in The Harbrace Anthology of Literature mirror the diversity of backgrounds and interests of Canadian students as well as reflecting an expanded canon. The poems, plays, and short stories reveal many of the characteristic themes and artistic techniques of their authors; they also reflect the cultural and social contexts in which they were written. In particular, they embody, as the eighteenth-century poet Alexander Pope observed, "what oft was thought but ne'er so well expressed." Most readers of this anthology will find its works speaking directly to them and addressing their most deeply felt concerns.

The Harbrace Anthology of Literature is organized by genre, beginning with poetry. Its poetry selections span eleven hundred years, the longest period of the three genres presented in the anthology. It continues with drama and concludes with short stories, the most recent of the three genres to develop. Selections within each genre are chronological, according to the birth dates of their authors. Following a selection, its date of publication is printed in parentheses on the right; when it differs significantly and is known, the date of composition appears in parentheses on the left. Such an organizational pattern, based on chronology rather than on pedagogical or theoretical concerns, invites a broad range of responses to a work, unencumbered by artificial or purely technical groupings based on content or theme. It does, of course, implicitly suggest a historical continuity in literature: that works from a specific period often have technical and thematic similarities; and that earlier works and authors can influence later ones.

The book's Introduction considers the reading of literature both as a personal, necessary lifelong activity and as a discipline. It explores how reading poems, plays, and short stories allows individuals to understand their own lives and responses to literature in relation to those of other people. It also demonstrates how readers can engage more deeply with a text, experiencing it more fully and relating it more completely to their own lives.

The introduction to each genre focuses directly on the characteristics and conventions of the genre, using examples from the literature presented in *The Harbrace Anthology of Literature*. Discussions of individual characteristics are intended not to offer explanations or explications, but to indicate ways in which authors have used the various elements of the genre. For the reader, an awareness of these characteristics may assist in engagement with the text and lead to a broader range of responses.

Each work or, in the case of poetry, each group of poems by the same author, is prefaced by a brief headnote establishing a biographical and literary context. The headnote may also touch on technique or theme. Explanatory footnotes identify historical, fictional, and mythological personages; literary and artistic works; real and fictional places; and terms not usually found in standard dictionaries. This material provides resources to assist readers in the personal creation of meaning — not to impose a critical viewpoint or to force interpretation in a specific, narrow direction.

Reading literature invites writing about it. The chapter entitled "Writing Essays about Literature" explores some of the challenges that writing about literature poses, without prescribing a recipe or rigid format for writing. It offers constructive suggestions to assist readers and writers in articulating responses — intellectual, aesthetic, or emotional — to works of literature.

The Glossary offers definitions of key terms, providing for readers both an awareness of essential concepts and a standard vocabulary for use in discussing literature.

ACKNOWLEDGEMENTS

The compilation of this anthology was a co-operative venture of the seven colleagues whose names appear on the title page; however, no book, even one developed by seven people, is ever created in a vacuum. During the planning, compiling, writing, and editing stages of *The Harbrace Anthology of Literature*, many people offered suggestions and made valuable comments. We wish to acknowledge the contributions and suggestions of reviewers from universities across Canada.

As well, we thank Anne Williams, Martina van de Velde, Shefali Mehta, Gil Adamson, Faith Gildenhuys, and Cindy Howard. These people have made this a better anthology; the responsibility for its limitations is our own.

A Note from the Publisher

Thank you for selecting *The Harbrace Anthology of Literature*, Third Edition, edited by Jon C. Stott, Raymond E. Jones, and Rick Bowers. The editors and publisher have devoted considerable time and care to the development of this book. We appreciate your recognition of this effort and accomplishment.

A Note to the Reader

We would like to draw your attention to two elements of this text:

1. *Dates at the end of poems:* One or two dates follow each poem in the poetry section. The date on the left is the date of the poem's original composition, and the date on the right is the date of the poem's first publication. Where the date of the poem's creation is unknown or where it is the same as the date of the poem's first publication, the date on the left has been omitted.

2. *Stanza continuation symbol (⟶):* We have introduced a unique feature in the poetry section of this text. Because stanzas often flow onto a new page, it is sometimes difficult for the reader to establish whether a stanza ends at the bottom of the page or continues on the next page. Stanza breaks often have significant implications for the interpretation of poems. To avoid confusion about where stanzas end or continue, we have placed the symbol " ⟶ " below the last line on a page to indicate that a stanza continues on the next page. We hope this will assist your reading of the poetry.

CONTENTS

DRAMA

SHORT FICTION

INTRODUCTION

"Part of the beauty of all literature," commented novelist and short story writer F. Scott Fitzgerald, is that "you discover that your longings are universal longings, that you're not lonely and isolated from anyone. You belong." Sharing experience through the creation and reception of stories, poems, and plays is a very old, basic, and necessary human activity, as necessary to human existence as food, shelter, and clothing. The literary critic Northrop Frye further emphasized the importance of literature, observing that "whenever a society is reduced to the barest primary requirements of food and sex and shelter, the arts, including poetry, stand out sharply in relief as ranking with those primary requirements." The need to bring order, through language and stories, to human experience seems to be fundamental to all societies and cultures.

While some literature may simply entertain or allow escape from everyday lives, the works that ultimately stay with their readers are those that challenge, engage, or make demands. Well-crafted literature invites its readers to laugh, to cry, to wonder, to analyze, to explore, to understand.

Throughout our lives, we seek to understand ourselves, our emotions, our experiences, and our relationships with others. We also attempt to define our connections to larger social and cultural institutions. One way that we can do so is through literature, for works of literature are the records of individual response to the world in which we live.

Because of our own experiences, we are able to understand the self-doubts and uncertainties expressed in T.S. Eliot's "The Love Song of J. Alfred Prufrock," the wonder of first love experienced by Ferdinand and Miranda in William Shakespeare's *The Tempest*, the disillusionment and disappointment of returning to a family home after a prolonged absence in Greg Hollingshead's "The Naked Man," and the anguish of Phyllis Webb's "Treblinka Gas Chamber." The specific experiences may be different from our own, but we recognize similarities in the thoughts and emotions of the characters; examination and reflection may lead to clearer insights into our own lives.

Because works of literature are often demanding, they offer great rewards. Readers come to fuller awareness of themselves and others. They discover both the uniqueness and the universality of human experience; they explore both their own world and worlds they may never otherwise see. Through critical response to literature, readers question a work, examine their relationship to the author, consider the author's role, and develop an appreciation of the work, both on its own terms and as an expression of the author's vision of life. Readers may also explore a work in the context of its times, whether social, historical, or ideological.

Until fairly recently, much of the literature studied in English courses was chosen from a list of works deemed important by a majority of critics and scholars, a list referred to as the canon of English literature. Like most of these

1

critics and scholars, most of the writers were white, male, and British or of British descent. The list usually began with the anonymous creator of the Anglo-Saxon epic "Beowulf" and ended with such earlier twentieth-century writers as T.S. Eliot, W.H. Auden, and Dylan Thomas. Because it included very few works by women, members of ethnic minorities, or writers from the British colonies, however, it could not be said to reflect the diversity of writing in English.

The past 30 years have seen a remarkable change in our society as a whole: the recognition of the equal place of all people in it, regardless of gender or ethnic origin. As a consequence, many literary scholars and critics have vigorously sought to expand the canon so that it speaks to everyone. They have demanded the inclusion of the many voices whose stories, poems, and dramas are worthy of study, both on their own merits and because of the insights they offer into a very large segment of the population of the English-speaking world. Such critics have argued that literature should certainly present universal human concerns but should also help readers understand how gender, cultural background, and social position influence responses to life. The works in this anthology reflect this expanded canon.

Reading and reflecting on works of literature reveal human similarities as well as differences. Aphra Behn's drama *The Rover* makes us aware of the position of women in the male-dominated upper-class English society of the late seventeenth century. Tennessee Williams's *Cat on a Hot Tin Roof* presents intense family conflicts as these take place within the culture of the rural American south in the middle of the twentieth century. The poetry of Oodgeroo Noonuccal (Kath Walker) reveals a modern Australian aboriginal woman examining her people's past and its troubled relationships with both government and newcomers.

Readers who come actively to such works with an open, questioning mind will be able to join with their authors in making explicit the implicit. They will appreciate that an author has used language connotatively, choosing words that, in addition to their dictionary meanings, suggest a range of emotions, ideas, or associations. They will recognize the symbolic nature of actions, characters, and objects. As the German literary critic Wolfgang Iser has commented, literary texts are incomplete; they contain gaps that readers fill in or bridge to create meaning. Readers anticipate, make inferences, draw conclusions; in short, they actively work with the language of a piece of literature to arrive at meaning.

Reading for meaning is a very personal act. It is not simply a matter of paraphrasing or summarizing a story or play, of transforming poetry into prose, or of examining literary technique or metaphorical language. Each reader is unique and will, therefore, respond differently — perhaps slightly, perhaps dramatically — to a work. A Dubliner will no doubt react differently to James Joyce's "Araby" than will a Winnipegger; a man about to retire will react differently to Shakespeare's *The Tempest* than will a young woman who has just left home for first-year college or university; a woman will react differently to Margaret Atwood's "The Resplendent Quetzal" than will a man. People who have read widely in each of these three authors or who have a well-developed knowledge of literature would likely have a different and broader interpretation of these three works than someone who seldom reads. Readers draw on personal experience, knowledge, and awareness of both specific literature and literary techniques to appreciate and interpret a literary work.

There is no one simple process for interpreting literature; different readers develop different approaches, some of which will be more useful for some works than for others. That said, interpretation of a literary work begins with the words of the text themselves. Readers question the choice and arrangement of details and ponder their significance. Such active inquiry may commence on reading the title or during a first reading. Individual interpretation will change with each rereading as readers observe more details, acquire more information about them, and perceive new relationships among them.

Readers bring their own experiences to their interpretation of literature. Basing interpretation on the words of the text, they can compare and contrast their own responses to life with those of authors and characters. Readers who have had intense family conflicts will be able to make inferences about the domestic arguments in Eudora Welty's "Why I Live at the P.O." Reciprocally, interpretation of literature can enrich experiences of life. Younger readers will not have had the experiences of the middle-aged women in Jane Rule's "Inland Passage," but a reading of that story may bring empathy for problems different from theirs. Recalling personal experience while reading a work for the first time can assist in its interpretation.

Readers also bring considerable literary experience to their reading of literature: an understanding of the ways in which authors use language and the general patterns of the major literary genres (poetry, drama, and fiction), awareness of important themes, and, frequently, familiarity with other works by the same writer. For example, knowledge of Shakespeare's use of blank verse, his creation of patterns of imagery, and the structure of his earlier comedies will make a study of The Tempest more rewarding. Reflection on the myths surrounding men and women will aid in the interpretation of Adrienne Rich's "Diving into the Wreck." Readers draw on what they already know and on critical literature to expand their interpretation of a literary work.

While readers bring considerable knowledge and experience to a literary work, they must also be conscious of the creative intelligence behind the selection and arrangement of its elements. General techniques and genre characteristics, as well as cultural or other forces at play during the writing, may influence some of the selection and arrangement, but most choices arise from the author's purpose in writing the work. Although readers may not find this purpose apparent on first reading, speculation on purpose, based on attention to details and their sequence, may reveal potentially deeper meanings in a work.

Understanding is enhanced as readers acquire more relevant background information and apply it to the text. Knowledge of the actual people and literary or mythological characters mentioned in the text, of allusions to historical events and episodes in other works, and of geographical or architectural settings will clarify their function in a work. In "Fogbound in Avalon," for example, Annie, the narrator, reads a magazine article about the painter Edvard Munch. Examining that artist's works may reveal a clearer picture of Annie's state of mind.

Literary works often reflect events and conflicts in the lives of their authors; awareness of such personal details can enhance a reader's understanding of how and why authors have written as they have. For example, James Joyce, in "Araby," William Wordsworth, in "Lines Composed a Few Miles Above Tintern Abbey," and Amy Tan, in "Two Kinds," drew on facts from their own lives. What is perhaps most interesting is the way in which an author has taken such raw materials of life and shaped them to meet the needs of the work.

Literary works are also products of the times in which they were written, for nearly all writers have been sensitive to and influenced by the literary, intellectual, political, and social forces around them. Ernest Hemingway's attitude toward the rejection by many of traditional moral and religious values during and after World War I helps to explain the actions of the two waiters and the elderly man in "A Clean, Well-Lighted Place." Familiarity with Margaret Atwood's musings on being a woman writer will enrich interpretations of her poetry and such short stories as "The Resplendent Quetzal."

Finally, readers should remember that just as it is impossible to understand completely another person or even oneself, so there is no such thing as a final, complete, or totally correct interpretation of a work of literature. To successive readings of a work readers bring different frames of mind, other personal experiences, new literary or other factual knowledge, and greater familiarity with the work. Thus, with each reading, fuller, more rewarding, and potentially new interpretations are possible.

To assist readers in the creation of meaning, the introductions to the three genres in this anthology — poetry, drama, and short stories — discuss technical aspects of literary works. Headnotes and footnotes provide information about authors and their works and about names, places, and obscure terms mentioned in the texts. The Glossary defines terms frequently used in discussing literature.

Critical response to literature often involves writing about poems, stories, and dramas. Through writing, readers explore the parts and the whole of a work, examine their previous interpretations and test their validity, evaluate the significance of relationships among parts of a work, and create new meanings. Of course, new interpretations may not be final ones; indeed, they may be modified several times during the writing process. Exploration of apparently contradictory information may provide fresh insights into a work. If, in creating an interpretation, the writer has based the statements on the text, has provided evidence and not ignored contradictory evidence, and has argued logically and clearly, then the interpretation is valid. For those seeking assistance in the writing of interpretive essays, the chapter entitled "Writing Essays about Literature" offers a number of suggestions and guidelines.

What are the rewards of becoming active readers and interpreters? An answer can be found by returning to this introduction's opening discussion of essential human needs. Poems, plays, and short stories are artistic and articulate responses to life that offer emotional, intellectual, and imaginative nourishment to their readers. Anthologies such as this provide exposure to literature that enhances the readers' knowledge of themselves and the world outside of themselves. Such experiences can lead to self-discovery and a lifelong love of reading.

INTRODUCTION

DEFINING POETRY

No one can state definitely how poetry began, but we know that it existed as an oral medium long before writing developed. Perhaps it originated in primitive religious rituals; people probably used rhythmical, repetitive chants to placate angry gods, to beseech them for success in the hunt or in battle, or to honour them for food and victories received. Furthermore, the rhythm of these chants probably exercised an almost hypnotic power, arousing the appropriate feelings of awe or fear in those who listened. Even today, poetry continues to arouse and express religious feelings, for it is prominent in the sacred texts and hymns of many religions.

Poetry, however, has served many other purposes. It instilled pride in nations, celebrating in the lofty language of epics the great deeds of their heroes. Poetry also became a major feature of important public ceremonies, such as coronations, inaugurations, and victory celebrations. Poetry was not, of course, limited to official and public events. Primarily in the form of **ballads** and other songs, poetry has entertained and expressed the feelings of ordinary people, the "folk." As well, the development of a tradition of writing poetry, either instead of or in addition to reciting it, allowed poetry to serve even more functions because it was now available whenever anyone wanted to read it, and not only when a bard recited it. Poetry could, among other things, entertain and inform in printed collections, express gratitude in dedications to books, celebrate passion in love letters, and honour the memory of the dead on monuments and tombstones. In short, throughout history, whenever people have wanted to give elevated verbal expression to deeds or ideas, whenever they have wanted to make memorable their thoughts, whenever they have wanted to convey their feelings, they have turned to poetry.

Poetry was once a major form of entertainment, providing stories, jokes, descriptions, and reflections. Novels, movies, and television have now replaced many of its storytelling functions, but poetry is everywhere in the modern world. Parents continue to recite it to their children, who delight in the rollicking metres of nursery rhymes. Teenagers and adults who listen to music often listen to poetry, which exists in the lyrics of many popular songs. They also meet poetry in commercials on television and radio, for advertisers rely on its ability to linger in the memory when they devise slogans to sell products. People still mark special occasions with it, expressing their feelings through greeting-card verse that ranges in mood from the sentimental to the humorously bawdy. Of course, numerous magazines still include poetry, and book publishers prominently display it in their catalogues. What is more, in an age that often demands elaborate spectacles in its public entertainments, poetry readings enjoy remarkable popularity.

Defining poetry, however, is like wrestling with Proteus: just when we think we have pinned it into submission, it changes shape, like the ancient Greek god, and eludes us. Poetry, that is, is so varied in form and content that comprehensive definitions always seem inadequate. Nevertheless, some of the most accomplished poets have tried to identify the essence of their art. Many have emphasized the emotional and intellectual depth of poetry. William Wordsworth said that "poetry is the spontaneous overflow of powerful feelings" and that "poetry is the breath and finer spirit of all knowledge. . . ." Emily Dickinson emphasized emotional response: "If I read a book and it makes my whole body so cold no fire can ever warm me I know that is poetry. If I feel physically as if the top of my head were taken off, I know that is poetry." Percy Bysshe Shelley defined poetry as "the record of the best and happiest moments of the happiest and best minds." Similarly, Matthew Arnold declared: "Poetry is simply the most beautiful, impressive and wisely effective mode of saying things, and hence its importance." Twentieth-century poets have given their own cast to such ideas. Wallace Stevens stressed the metaphysical: "Poetry is a search for the inexplicable." Adrienne Rich has emphasized poetry's power, its ability to condense and communicate significant meaning: "Poetry is above all a concentration of the *power* of language, which is the power of our ultimate relationship to everything in the universe. It is as if forces we can lay claim to in no other way, [sic] become present to us in sensuous form." Robert Frost was more colourful: "Poetry is a way of taking life by the throat." The Canadian poet Irving Layton has described it as a way of bridging the gap between mundane reality and the world of imagination, a process that creates a separate world: "Mercifully, all poetry, in the final analysis, is about poetry itself; creating through its myriad forms a world in which the elements of reality are sundered; are, as it were, preserved for a time in suspension."

Instead of defining poetry through its connections to feelings, ideas, and actions, however, some writers have tried to look at the aesthetic and technical elements of the craft. Edgar Allan Poe called poetry "*the Rhythmical Creation of Beauty.*" Samuel Taylor Coleridge avoided both the emphasis on refined feelings or ideas and the insistence on beauty when he stressed verbal craftsmanship in this equation: "poetry = the best words in their best order." Throughout the twentieth century, writers have returned to this concept of craftsmanship in their definitions. Dylan Thomas, for instance, described the task of creating poetry as "constructing a formally watertight compartment of words." Frost defined poetry even more simply as "a performance in words." Wallace Stevens probably went as far as possible in dissociating the poet's task from that described in definitions stressing ethical thought, declaring: "Poetry is poetry, and one's objective as a poet is to achieve poetry precisely as one's objective in music is to achieve music."

The precise nature of the poetic achievement is, as these disparate definitions suggest, very much open to debate. Poetry does not seem to depend upon content: poems may be about beauty or ugliness, refined feelings or base ones, matters of perpetual importance or of transient interest. Neither is any single technical feature, such as rhyme, rhythm, or division into lines with ragged right margins, the determinant: it is possible for a good poem to exhibit none of these features. Probably the best we can do is to describe poetry as a concentrated form of literary expression. Poetry employs evocative, often rhythmical language that describes or comments on ideas and experiences and that evokes feelings about them. In poetry the manner of expression is as important as the matter.

POETRY AND LITERARY READING

Because each word in a poem is charged with meaning and feeling to a degree rarely possible in prose, reading poetry may require patience. One reading is simply not sufficient to allow readers to engage with the text, to sense all of its intellectual, emotional, and aesthetic resources. Literary reading demands rereading. As the general Introduction makes clear, no single reading procedure is adequate in all circumstances. In fact, theorists do not agree on how poems work and how they should be read. Competing theories emphasize different elements of the relationships among poet, reader, and poem. Nevertheless, readers who are aware of the various biographical, historical, and theoretical contexts may find their reading of a poem more meaningful and, therefore, more enjoyable.

Understanding biographical and cultural contexts may at first seem to be a separate area of study, but these contexts can be vital in constructing meaning. Many critics and theorists, that is, insist that poems do not exist in isolation from the poets who wrote them or apart from the societies in which the poets lived. Personal feelings and experiences shape what poets write and how they write. In turn, their feelings and experiences, if not directly shaped by cultural situations, have often been influenced by the social and moral assumptions of their societies. No one argues that readers must know everything about a poet's life to enjoy a poem. Many critics do suggest, however, that an understanding of a poet's life and artistic ideas may provide information that will help readers to understand the mind and verbal habits of the poet and thus better to construct meaning when reading poetry. The poet's gender and attitudes to gender, for example, may be crucial. The American poet Adrienne Rich says, "I had been taught that poetry should be 'universal,' which meant, of course, nonfemale." In her own poems, therefore, she seeks to express her feelings as a female whose views and experiences may be distinct from those previously celebrated as universal.

Similarly, some critics claim that an understanding of cultural history is sometimes essential. First, literary conventions and habits of expression change from generation to generation; understanding these may help in the understanding of works written during an earlier period. Second, what people of any age write reflects their connection to the dominant culture of their time. Literature may thus openly express attitudes officially sanctioned by a given society. This is the belief of Thomas Carlyle, who saw poetry as a mirror of the spirit of an age: "The history of a nation's poetry is the essence of its history, political, scientific, religious." Of course, as Marxist and other theorists concerned with class and economic factors note, poetry may also seek, often covertly, to subvert the dominant culture. In developing meaning, the contemporary reader may thus require an understanding of the sometimes latent assumptions within a poem.

Many other theorists downplay the significance of such contexts. For some of these, poetry is an artifact, like a Greek vase, that exists separate from the reader and must be understood on its own terms. For others, poetry is more of a tool kit or an Erector set that the reader plays with, constructing and reconstructing meaning. One group argues for the realization of a final meaning inherent in the work; the other argues that no single meaning can be inherent in the work and, instead, stresses the process of reading rather than the results. The more traditional theorists point out that the word *poetry* comes from a Greek root meaning "thing made" and that a poet is a "maker." They see poems as carefully constructed, unified artifacts, and they argue that the reader needs to note the contribution of all of the parts of a work to discover its inherent meaning. For example, some of these theorists argue that a poem's basic structure is a set of binary oppositions, such as life and death or virtue and sin, and that meaning comes when the poem "privileges," or gives approval to, one set of these oppositions. They believe that the reader's task in understanding a poem is to locate the structure of binary oppositions. Those who look at poetry more as the tool kit that the reader uses take differing approaches. Some have extended this notion of binary oppositions, arguing that every literary work actually contains not only oppositions but also contradictions and that, therefore, no poem can have a determinate meaning. They contend that a work "deconstructs" itself, saying two contradictory things at once. Finally, another group of theorists concentrates on the reader's involvement with poems, arguing that the work itself contains no meaning: a poem is simply a series of squiggles on the page until the reader engages with the text and actively creates meaning from it. The reader not only "decodes" individual words — deciding, for example, that the letters *d-o-g* refer to a particular kind of animal — but also, because of previous personal and literary experiences, associates particular ideas and attitudes with each word decoded: when faced with the word *dog*, some readers will envisage a slavering attack beast, whereas others will envisage a friendly lapdog. Although many poems use what Wolfgang Iser calls "response-inviting structures," devices that encourage readers to read in particular ways, these devices cannot possibly limit readers to one single response. Because each person's experiences and associations are different, each will read a given poem differently.

Although the competition between rival theories may suggest to some readers that a poem means anything a given reader thinks it means, all theories imply that literary understanding begins with close attention to words. Many theories stress that poetry is a playful use of language, even in poems about serious matters, and that a playful attitude in reading, an attitude that brings all of a person's associations and experiences to bear on each word, makes it easier to discover or construct meaning.

In truth, few readers are concerned about competing theories when first reading a poem; instead, most readers ordinarily want to construct at least a provisional meaning as soon as possible. Such readers may find some guidelines useful as the basis for beginning a significant reading of a work.

Because poetry is an art that depends upon achieving the maximum effect from each word, readers need to understand both the **denotations**, or dictionary meanings, of words and the **connotations**, or implications, of these words. Some words, that is, carry extra meaning: they have negative or positive associations that may influence interpretation. We may think positively about an adult who is *childlike*, but negatively about one who is *childish*. We may also have different attitudes about speakers who use colloquial language and speakers who consistently use elaborate, formal language. Sensitivity to words and their nuances is an important step in meaningful reading.

Traditionally, readers have also found useful a number of basic questions about the content and form of a poem. The first questions focus on the speaker in the poem: Who is the speaker? To whom is he or she speaking? What are the circumstances? These questions may not be very important in a poem like Tennyson's "The Eagle," but they are crucial considerations in dramatic monologues such as Browning's "The Bishop Orders His Tomb at Saint Praxed's Church," in which an understanding of the speaker's character and the context in which he or she is speaking is necessary to make the poem meaningful. Another question concerns the arrangement of content: How is the poem organized to develop its ideas? The order in which details are presented can influence our attitudes toward them and our understanding of the development of major ideas within the poem. In Browning's "My Last Duchess," the duke's description of the fate of his last wife precedes his discussion of arrangements for a new bride, making him seem especially arrogant, cynical, and brutal. In Sonnet 73, Shakespeare emphasizes both the narrator's age and the brevity of time by arranging images that imply death: he creates a sequence that moves from larger to smaller measures of time, from a season, to a day, to the moment when a fire is dying out.

Readers may also find it useful to ask questions about the technical elements of a poem: How do techniques or elements such as rhythm, sound devices, images, and diction influence our understanding? The purpose of examining techniques is not to catalogue them but to understand their role in shaping our ideas and feelings within the poem as a whole. For example, readers who notice the difference in rhythm in the first and final sections of Marvell's "To His Coy Mistress" can determine how it influences their understanding of the narrator's attitudes toward traditional ideals of courtship and his own growing sense of urgency. Finally, readers often find it useful to consider literary contexts: How does this poem compare to other poems, especially those with similar forms, those from the same period, and those about similar subjects? An understanding of conventions of form or subject matter and of literary "schools" or literary periods enables readers to place the work in a literary and historical context that can be helpful in understanding the poem. Shakespeare's Sonnet 130, "My mistress' eyes are nothing like the sun," for instance, is far more meaningful to readers who understand something of the Petrarchan tradition of love sonnets and have read some English love sonnets by such poets as Wyatt, Surrey, and Constable.

FIGURATIVE LANGUAGE (1): IMAGERY, SIMILE, METAPHOR, CONCEIT

Poetry is a sensual medium. Sound, discussed later, and imagery, the subject of this section, appeal to the senses, stimulating an imaginative body of impressions, feelings, and ideas. These may be new, or they may be familiar, but the sensory appeals of poetry give them an immediacy that directly involves readers.

At its most basic level, **imagery** is language that creates images, or pictures, in the imagination. Some poems, like "The Red Wheelbarrow," by William Carlos Williams, rely almost exclusively on verbal pictures. Most poems, however, use imagery to develop statements about feelings and ideas. The opening section of Wordsworth's "Lines Composed a Few Miles above Tintern Abbey" creates a picture of the scene, describing such things as "These hedge-rows, hardly hedge-rows, little lines / Of sportive wood run wild. . . ." In this way, the narrator impresses on readers the power the setting holds over him as a scene of "beauteous forms." Although the roots of the word suggest a visual element, imagery is not exclusively visual; it frequently makes appeals to touch, taste, and sound. In the final stanza of "To Autumn," for example, Keats describes the "music" of autumn, with such sound images as "Then in a wailful choir the small gnats mourn / Among the river sallows. . . ." In "Dover Beach," Arnold uses sound imagery to convey "The eternal note of sadness": he describes "the grating roar / Of pebbles" flung back and forth by the waves.

Images, like all appeals to the senses, can evoke emotional reactions. Because they can give concrete form to ideas by forcing readers to understand one idea in terms of another, they also can be a medium of intellectual discourse. This linking of objects or ideas is the basis of most figurative language, language that goes beyond the literal denotation of the words by imaginatively extending their meanings.

The most common figures of speech are similes and metaphors. Both tend to give concrete form to abstract ideas or to make the unfamiliar clearer and more forceful by linking it to something familiar. **Simile** expresses similarity between things and always uses such linking terms as *like*, *as*, *than*, or *as if*. Keats, in "On First Looking into Chapman's Homer," conveys the magnitude of his feelings of discovery with a simile that connects his reactions upon reading a book to a rarer but more public experience: "Then felt I like some watcher of the skies / When a new planet swims into his ken." In the opening simile of T.S. Eliot's "The Love Song of J. Alfred Prufrock," the narrator pro-vides a clue to his own emotional numbness by saying that "the evening is spread out against the sky / Like a patient etherised upon a table." P.K. Page does much the same thing when she describes the secretaries in "The Stenographers" as being "taut as net curtains / stretched upon frames." **Metaphor** compares by equating things. In Shakespeare's Sonnet 73, the metaphor in which the boughs become "Bare ruin'd choirs" creates a sense of collapse and destruction because it implicitly equates the trees in late autumn and abandoned, ruined churches. In "The Flea," John Donne's narrator uses metaphor as part of his strategy of seduction, aggrandizing the flea: "This flea is you and I, and this / Our marriage bed, and marriage temple is."

Not every comparison is as brief as those just discussed. More elaborate and extended comparisons, whether similes or metaphors, are called **con-ceits**. The **Petrarchan conceit**, developed by those who followed the example of the Italian Petrarch, the poet who popularized the sonnet form, uses rather conventional extended comparisons, as in Wyatt's "My galley . . . ," which compares the lover to a ship at sea, or Surrey's "Love that doth reign . . . ," which personifies love as a military leader. More original and startling comparisons are called **metaphysical conceits** because they were developed by the so-called **metaphysical poets** of the seventeenth century, who linked physical with metaphysical or spiritual elements in their images. John Donne's "A Valediction: Forbidding Mourning" contains the most famous of these, his comparison of separated lovers to "stiff twin compasses."

FIGURATIVE LANGUAGE (2): PERSONIFICATION, APOSTROPHE, METONYMY, SYNECDOCHE, SYMBOL, MOTIF

Other figurative devices also link ideas. **Personification** gives human qualities to abstractions or to things that do not possess them. Thus, William Wordsworth, in "The world is too much with us," suggests the sensuousness of nature through personification: "This Sea that bares her bosom to the moon." In one of his odes, John Keats personifies an object, an ancient Greek urn, as a "Sylvan historian," suggesting that it can tell much about life. Personification often develops through **apostrophe**, a direct address to a thing or abstraction, as in Shelley's "O wild West Wind, thou breath of Autumn's being" or Donne's "Death be not proud." Apostrophe is not always part of personification because the device also includes direct addresses to an absent or dead person, as in Wordsworth's "Milton! thou shouldst be living at this hour." In either case, it gives immediacy and concreteness to people, events, and ideas.

Two other linking devices are frequently used to condense complex experiences into images. **Metonymy**, or "substitute naming," uses an associated idea to name something. In "London, 1802," for example, Wordsworth talks of "altar, sword, and pen," instead of the clergy, soldiers, and authors, in order to suggest concretely both the people and the function of those people. A related device is **synecdoche**, in which a part stands for the whole, or the whole stands for the part. It is most evident in such expressions as "All hands on deck!" in which *hands* stands for *sailors*, and in the prayer for "daily bread," in which *bread* stands for all food. In Eliot's "Prufrock," synecdoche, evident in the naming of a part instead of the whole crab or lobster, suggests the narrator's lack of a fully developed identity: "I should have been a pair of ragged claws / Scuttling across the floors of silent seas." Synecdoche is most shockingly apparent, however, in the vision of death in Marvell's "To His Coy Mistress," which reduces the woman's morality to sexual organs: "... then worms shall try / That long preserved virginity, / And your quaint honour turn to dust."

The linking device that many readers find most difficult to grasp is **symbolism**. *Symbol* comes from the Greek "to throw together." A symbol throws together objects, people, or actions and a meaning that is not necessarily inherent in them. Symbols fall into two major categories, conventional symbols and contextual symbols. **Conventional symbols** are those that traditionally carry a particular meaning. Sometimes, the symbol is conventional only within a given culture. A cross, for example, means something quite different to Christians in North America than to Buddhists in China. The rose, to cite another example, traditionally suggests love or beauty in Western culture. Such conventional symbols may be the basis of relatively simple ideas: "Gather ye rose-buds while ye may," the opening line of Herrick's "To the Virgins, To Make Much of Time," develops the *carpe diem* ("seize the day") idea of living for the moment because, like the rose, youth and beauty fade. They may also develop more complex and even ambiguous ideas, as in William Blake's "The Sick Rose," in which the rose suggests ideas of love but leaves open to speculation the exact nature of that love and of the worm that destroys it. Not all conventional symbols are limited to a specific culture. Some seem to be universal, having appeared so frequently and for such a long time in the literatures of various cultures that their meanings seem to be natural. These are known as **archetypes**. One such archetype is the description of the sun's movement from sunrise to sunset to symbolize aging in human beings. This archetype appears in such different works as Herrick's "To the Virgins, To Make Much of Time," where it reinforces the idea that youth must live for the moment, and Earle Birney's "Bushed," where it suggests the rapidly approaching death of the trapper.

Readers acquire understanding of conventional symbols by familiarity with a large number of works using them. In Frost's "Stopping by Woods on a Snowy Evening," for example, repetition of the last line, "And miles to go before I sleep," puts such additional stress on both *miles* and *sleep* that these words imply more than they literally say. Readers familiar with other poems that use either a journey or sleep as a symbol can see this poem as using the conventional archetypal symbol of a journey toward death, an additional implication that co-exists with its surface meaning of a journey on a winter's night.

Contextual symbols, however, become symbolic only within the context of a given work; they may not have the same symbolic meaning, or even any symbolic meaning, in a different work. For example, the tiger symbolizes, among other things, fierceness and destructiveness in Blake's "The Tyger," but it symbolizes the repressed dreams of a conventional woman in Adrienne Rich's "Aunt Jennifer's Tigers." Sometimes the accumulation of details creates a contextual symbol, as it does in Shelley's "Ozymandias," in which the ruined statue of the pharaoh gradually becomes a general symbol of mutability and the vanity of human desires. Such contextual symbols are not always obvious: during an initial reading, they may seem to be simply a part of the concrete description or narrative movement of the poem. This is why rereading is important. With each rereading, a poem becomes more familiar, and its details, patterns, and emphases — the elements that create contextual symbols — become more apparent.

With each rereading, as well, the links to other poems and the connecting links within the poem itself become more apparent. Any poem using an archetype, for example, is using an element that occurs in many works. Understanding the archetype in one poem thus helps in understanding others. Archetypes and symbols are not the only recurring elements, of course. Images, characters, objects, settings, situations, or themes may recur in many works; these recurring elements are called **motifs**. The *carpe diem* theme, for example, is a thematic motif, whether or not it is expressed by the archetype of the setting sun. Elements can also be repeated to link the parts of an individual work. For example, Margaret Atwood's "Progressive Insanities of a Pioneer" contains several references to water and to terms associated with measurement and enclosure. Such recurring elements within an individual work, whether recurring words, phrases, images, situations, or themes, are also sometimes called motifs, although they are more generally called **leitmotifs**. Readers who note such recurring devices will be able to respond more completely to the poem, to link together its various parts, to connect the poem to other works and to situations outside the poem itself, and to construct more meaning.

IRONY, PARADOX, OXYMORON, ZEUGMA

Simile, metaphor, symbol, and other devices of figurative language discussed above link images to feelings and ideas, but they do not always forge their links in the way that we may at first expect. Sometimes another device, irony, twists the connections. **Irony** is a discrepancy between appearance and reality, expectation and result, or surface meaning and implied meaning. Traditionally, critics have described three major kinds of irony: dramatic irony, situational irony, and verbal irony. Dramatic irony, a device found more frequently in drama and fiction than in poetry, is the discrepancy between what a character says or does and what the reader knows to be the truth of the situation. Situational irony, which is also inherent in dramatic irony, presents a situation in which the result is the reverse of what a character or speaker expected. Verbal irony reverses the denotation of words so that a given statement actually means the opposite of what it says literally, as when we call "graceful" someone who has just tripped.

Whatever its form, irony is a device that is often integral to the **theme**, the central idea developed by a poem. In "Ozymandias," for example, both verbal irony, the boast that Ozymandias makes about his greatness, and situational irony, the image of a shattered statue upon whose base the boastful words are carved, reverse the pharaoh's intention: instead of celebrating glorious, lasting achievements, both the words and the statue make a moving statement about mutability and the impermanence of human achievement. Similarly, in Margaret Atwood's "Progressive Insanities of a Pioneer," the language of measurement and geometry, normally a sign of logic and control, reverses itself to reveal the mad egocentricity of the pioneer. Unable to recognize nature for what it is, he tries to impose his vision on it and stands "a point / on a sheet of green paper / proclaiming himself the centre." His failure of vision eventually leads to his defeat by the very forces he sought to dominate. Irony can also be a powerful device for political comment and protest. Wilfred Owen deliberately uses the juxtaposition of the title phrase in *"Dulce et Decorum Est"* and the scene of a soldier dying in a gas attack to reverse the wartime propaganda that called it glorious for the young to die for their country.

Two other devices found frequently in poetry depend upon an unusual link of expression and idea. **Paradox** is a statement that seems contradictory on the surface but contains a truth on deeper examination. Among the most famous of paradoxes is Wordsworth's statement that "The Child is father of the Man," a claim that is biologically absurd but psychologically profound: the statement concisely expresses the idea that the experiences of childhood shape adult lives. Paradox often serves to convey complex spiritual and psychological truths, as in Donne's Holy Sonnet XIV ("Batter my heart"), which concludes with a notable and shocking set of paradoxes about the narrator's relationship with God:

> Take me to you, imprison me, for I
> Except you enthral me, never shall be free,
> Nor ever chaste, except you ravish me.

A related device is **oxymoron**, a word whose Greek roots imply "sharp stupidity" or "wise foolishness." Oxymoron contains a contradiction: it links opposites in the surface expression in order to defamiliarize or make unusual the connections we expect. Thus, Milton describes hell as having "darkness visible."

Although found less frequently than paradox and oxymoron, another notable device also twists connections for comical or critical effect. **Zeugma** grammatically links a term to two words, but the linkage is logically appropriate in a different way for each word. One of the most famous examples is in Pope's *The Rape of the Lock*: "Or stain her Honour, or her new Brocade." With its first object, "Honour," the verb "stain" indicates the ruin of a woman's virtue; with its second, "Brocade," it merely points to the soiling of a gown. By linking these two incompatible meanings in one sentence, Pope succinctly and wittily implies that women in high society do not discriminate between realms of morality and fashion, that both are equally trivial, or equally important, to them. Zeugma does not, however, have to be a comic device. In "The Devil's Language," for example, Marilyn Dumont speaks of the mother who "fed you bannock and tea / and syllables." By linking food and language, zeugma here stresses that language is part of nurture and that it thus has both cultural and emotional significance.

LINE LENGTH, METRE, AND RHYTHM

Two things immediately distinguish poetry from prose: the look upon the page and the sound when read aloud. The distinctive look of most poetry comes from its organization into lines. In most English poems written before the twentieth century, the line lengths were dependent upon **metre**. English, with its stressed syllables (indicated by ´) and unstressed syllables (indicated by ˘), naturally creates rhythm, the flow of rising and falling sounds, but poetry organizes rhythm, as prose and common speech do not. Metre, a word derived from the Greek "to measure," measures the organization of repeated stressed and unstressed syllables, giving names to the rhythmic patterns within a poem.

At various times and in various places, different systems of measurement have been used. French poetry, for example, counts only syllables. The same is true of the Japanese haiku, a form sometimes adopted by writers in English: it contains three lines of five, seven, and five syllables, respectively. Anglo-Saxon, or Old English, poetry, on the other hand, is accentual: it measures only the stresses in a given line and does not count the unstressed syllables. Furthermore, it organizes the stresses by placing two in each half, or hemistich, of a line, by having three stresses share an **alliterative** sound, and by separating each half with a **caesura**, or pause. A few poets have tried to use this form with modern English. In "Anglosaxon Street," for example, Earle Birney graphically indicates the hemistiches by using a wide space for each caesura:

Dáwndrízzle ended   dámpness stéams from

blótching bríck and   blánk plásterwaste

The most common system for measuring poetry in modern English, however, considers both the **accents** and the number of syllables in a line. The base of the system is the **foot**, a unit consisting of one or more syllables, usually with one stressed. Repetition of the pattern of stressed and unstressed syllables found within a given foot creates a regular **rhythm**, and each of the various regular rhythms has a name based on the pattern within the foot and the number of feet composing the line. Table 1 lists the names and shows the patterns of the metrical feet. The dominant rhythm in a poem will probably be one of the first four patterns: the others are normally variations within a regular rhythm. Table 2 names the various line lengths according to the number of feet in each. A process called **scansion** indicates graphically the metre of a poem. This process requires the marking of all stressed and unstressed syllables and the clear division of feet from each other by means of a vertical line. Scansion graphically shows, for example, that the opening line of Shakespeare's Sonnet 73 is iambic pentameter, a pattern formed from five iambic feet:

Thăt tíme | ŏf yéar | thŏu máyst | ĭn mé | bĕhóld

Table 1 The Metrical Feet

Noun	Adjective	Pattern	Example
iamb	iambic	˘ ´	remote
trochee	trochaic	´ ˘	joker
anapest	anapestic	˘ ˘ ´	interrupt
dactyl	dactylic	´ ˘ ˘	heavenly
spondee	spondaic	´ ´	heartbreak
pyrrhic	pyrrhic	˘ ˘	in the
amphibrach	amphibrachic	˘ ´ ˘	soprano
amphimacer (or cretic)	amphimacric	´ ˘ ´	first and last

Table 2 Line Lengths

Number of Feet in Line	Name of Line Length
1	monometer
2	dimeter
3	trimeter
4	tetrameter
5	pentameter
6	hexameter
7	heptameter
8	octameter

Rhythmic Variation

Poets do not always write according to strict metre. They frequently introduce variations within their lines not only to avoid the potential monotony of a regular metre but also to emphasize particular words or ideas. For example, in the last line of Sonnet 73, Shakespeare substitutes a spondee for the iamb in the final foot:

To lŏve | thăt wéll | whĭch thóu | mŭst léave | ĕre lóng

This substitution creates three stressed syllables in a row. Generally, a sequence of stressed syllables slows the movement of a line, whereas a sequence of unaccented syllables quickens the flow. Here, the rhythmic flow slows down, emphasizing these last words, which summarize the idea of the brief time remaining to the narrator.

While it is common to vary rhythm within lines by using metrical feet that deviate from the dominant pattern and by adding extra feet or extra syllables to a line, poets can affect the flow of their lines in other ways. One is by judicious use of the caesura, or pause (indicated in scansion by two vertical lines). Because the most emphatic positions in any unit of expression (line, phrase, sentence, paragraph) are first, at the end, and second, at the beginning, the caesura creates emphasis by increasing the number of these positions. In Tennyson's "Ulysses," for example, the caesura effectively halts the flow of the lines to emphasize tedium:

Hŏw dúll | ĭt ís | tŏ páuse, ‖ tŏ máke | ăn énd.

Tŏ rúst | ŭnbúrn|ĭsh'd, ‖ nót | tŏ shíne | ĭn úse!

In the first line, "pause" immediately precedes a pause, and "end" comes at the end of the line, the meaning of both words thus being effectively reinforced by their position. In the second line, the caesura comes in the middle of a foot, disrupting the regular flow and creating an oral counterpoint to it. Strictly speaking, that is, metre expresses the division into feet according to the stresses of syllables, and this line is a perfectly regular iambic line. Dramatic reading of it, however, provides a different sense of how the line flows. If we consider the caesura as creating a pause that divides this line into two units, we would scan this line for reading by marking it as consisting of an iamb, amphibrach, amphimacer, and iamb:

> Tŏ rúst | ŭnbúrnĭsh'd, ‖ nŏt tŏ shíne | ĭn úse!

The dramatic, interpretive rhythm exists simultaneously with the regular metre. The interpretive rhythm insists on a pause, accentuating the contrast between the sedentary state and the active one that follows; the conventional metre pulls the reader forward in expectation of completing the iambic pattern. Interpretive rhythm could also make the contrast between the two parts of the line even more emphatic: when "not to shine" is read as an anapest, the two unaccented syllables quicken the pace, indicating joy, and place an even more meaningful and emphatic stress on *shine*.

In the lines just quoted, Tennyson uses **end-stopped lines**, lines that terminate with a natural pause. Such lines are usually indicated by punctuation, which reinforces this pause. Poets often vary the flow of their lines by using run-on lines, or **enjambment** (from the French for "striding over"). Tennyson uses enjambment throughout "Ulysses":

> Ĭ cán | nŏt rést | frŏm tráv | ĕl; ‖ Í | wĭll drínk
>
> Lífe tŏ | thĕ lées.

Because of the caesura in the middle of a foot in the first line and the shift to trochee in the first foot of the second line, the key words *I*, *drink*, *Life*, and *lees* are all accented and are all visually, grammatically, or by strict measure in positions of emphasis, at the beginning or end of a unit. The enjambment, however, creates a variation in the rhythmic flow, linking the last part of the first line to the first part of the second line: although the iambic pentameter pattern is completed with *drink*, the reader cannot pause at the end of the line because the idea is incomplete; instead, the reader must continue until the completion of the idea in the middle of the second line.

Beyond Scansion: Free Verse And Shaped Verse

Not every poem displays a dominant rhythm that can be scanned like those in the preceding examples. Some poems are written in **free verse** or **vers libre**, terms popularized by Ezra Pound, among others. Pound compared the conventional patterns of regularly repeated metrical feet to the monotonous beat of a metronome. He argued that the lines of a poem should be free from the conventional system, that, instead, lines should follow the more natural patterns evident in spoken language and music. (Incidentally, free verse should not be confused with **blank verse**, a form popular in Elizabethan England, which usually means an unrhymed line of iambic pentameter.) Other writers, however, may organize lines by meaning. In "The Country North of Belleville," for example, Al Purdy intensifies the irony of defeat by placing each stage of the farmers' recognition of futility in a separate line:

> without grandeur or self deception in
> > noble struggle
> of being a fool —

Margaret Atwood is even subtler in her description of the man standing in a field in "Progressive Insanities of a Pioneer":

> with no walls, no borders
> anywhere; the sky no height
> above him, totally un-
> enclosed

She divides the lines to place words suggesting measurement and logical calculation in emphatic positions. Furthermore, she breaks up the word "unenclosed" to emphasize the ironic discrepancy between the pioneer's perception that he is "enclosed," which leads him to shout insanely that he wants out, and the reader's understanding that nothing actually encloses him.

Line length may also graphically reflect meaning. George Herbert's "The Altar" arranges lines to form a picture that represents the central idea of the poem. Lines in such shaped verse convey meaning, but they must be seen on the page to be fully appreciated. Much the same is true of concrete poetry, a form popular in the 1960s and early 1970s. In some concrete poems, however, the lines forming the picture may be letters or other typographical elements that can have no meaning on their own. Meaning exists entirely in the picture as a whole.

RHYME AND STANZA FORM

Many poems, especially those written before the twentieth century, link lines by more than subject matter and rhythm: they use **rhyme**, the repetition of accented vowels and all syllables following the accented vowel. **Single rhymes**, or **masculine rhymes**, repeat only the last syllable of words: *know, go; delight, fight*. **Double rhymes**, also called **feminine rhymes** or **trochaic rhymes**, repeat identical sounds in both an accented syllable and the following unaccented syllable: *kissing, missing; seasons, reasons*. **Triple rhymes**, or **dactylic rhymes**, also occur: *tenderly, slenderly; scornfully, mournfully*. Rhymes most frequently occur as **end rhymes**, in which the rhyming words are at the end of lines. **Internal rhymes** operate within lines, as in this example from "The Rime of the Ancient Mariner": "And every *day*, for food or *play*."

All the examples so far have been **exact rhymes** or **true rhymes**. In some cases, poets use **near rhyme** (also known as **slant**, **off**, **imperfect**, or **oblique** rhyme), a rhyme that approximates rather than exactly repeats a sound: *bridge, hedge; still, wheel; tucker, supper*. Slant rhyme usually depends on similarity of the final consonant, but it can include such imperfect rhymes as *flew* and *boot*, which rhyme the vowel but not the consonant. Another form is **eye rhyme**, or **sight rhyme**, in which words spelled similarly but pronounced differently are treated as rhymes. In some cases, as with Shakespeare's rhyming of *proved* and *loved*, the words may have been pronounced similarly at the time the poem was written. In other cases, such as Coleridge's rhyming of *prow* and *blow* in "The Rime of the Ancient Mariner," the rhymes are purely visual.

Rhyme can be a mnemonic device, something that helps poets, listeners, and readers to remember a work; it is also an important structural device that helps to group lines into meaningful sections. The normal grouping of lines is called the **stanza**. Table 3 provides the general names for stanzas according to the number of lines they contain. Stanzas are infinitely variable, but a number of poetic forms specify the precise number of lines the stanza can contain and the pattern of rhymes, known as the rhyme scheme, that those lines must follow.

Table 3 Names of Stanzas and Line Groupings

Number of Lines	Name
2	couplet
3	tercet (triplet when all three lines rhyme together)
4	quatrain
5	quintet
6	sestet
7	septet
8	octave

Table 4 names and describes the most notable of these fixed forms. We describe rhyme schemes by using a separate letter for each end rhyme. Thus, we indicate a stanza in which the first and fourth lines and the second and third lines rhyme by the formula *a b b a*. Sometimes, however, we must resort to a more complex description because line lengths vary. In these cases, we describe a stanza by indicating its predominant rhythm and by noting with each letter of the rhyme scheme the number of feet in that line. Consider the opening stanza of "Sir Patrick Spens," which we could describe as predominantly iambic with a rhyme scheme of 4*a*, 3*b*, 4*c*, 3*b*:

The king | sits in | Dumfer | ling toune,   *a* (4 feet)

Drinking | the blude- | reid wine: *b* (3 feet)

"Ŏ whar | will Ĭ get | guid | sailŏr,   *c* (4 feet)

To sail | this schip | of mine?"   *b* (3 feet)

This pattern is known as ballad measure; many other patterns also have names, and knowing these can simplify the description.

Stanzas depend upon a few basic patterns in their rhymes. **Couplets** are pairs of rhyming lines: *a a b b*. Heroic couplets are in iambic pentameter. If the idea expressed by the couplet is completed within the compass of the two lines, the couplet is a **closed couplet**. **Triplets** or **tercets** consist of three lines, rhymed or unrhymed. A **quatrain** is any group of four lines, rhymed or unrhymed; it is the most common form in English poetry. A **sestet** is a unit of six lines, whereas an **octave** is one of eight lines.

These last three — the quatrain, the sestet, and the octave — are important terms in describing one of the most pervasive and highly controlled of poetic forms, the **sonnet**. The **Italian** or **Petrarchan sonnet** is a fourteen-line iambic pentameter form usually rhyming *abba abba cdecde* (but the last six lines have many variations in rhyme scheme). The Italian sonnet develops an idea in the octave, and then uses a **volta**, or turn (often signalled by such words as "yet" or "but"), before concluding that idea in the sestet. The **English** or **Shakespearean sonnet** is an iambic pentameter poem rhyming *abab cdcd efef gg*. It consists of three quatrains and a heroic couplet. Its turn of thought occurs in the couplet and must be more compressed and concentrated than that in an Italian sonnet. A Spenserian sonnet is similar, except that it rhymes *abab bcbc cdcd ee*. A fourth variation is the **Miltonic sonnet**. It follows the Italian form, but it does not pause after the octave.

Table 4 Notable Fixed and Complex Forms

Number of Lines in Poem or Stanza	Name and Description
3	TERZA RIMA: tercets of iambic pentameter with linked rhymes (*aba bcb cdc*...)
4	COMMON MEASURE: a quatrain in iambic metre, with the first and third lines having four iambic feet and the second and fourth having three iambic feet (*abcb*)
	BALLAD STANZA: similar to common measure but the four lines can be in any metre, with four metrical feet in the first and third and three in the second and fourth lines (*abcb*)
6	ITALIAN SESTET: six lines of iambic pentameter (*abcabc*)
	SICILIAN SESTET: six lines of iambic pentameter (*ababab*)
	HEROIC SESTET: six lines of iambic pentameter (*ababcc*)
7	RIME ROYAL: seven lines of iambic pentameter (*ababbcc*)
8	OTTAVA RIMA: eight lines of iambic pentameter (*abababcc*)
	ITALIAN OCTAVE: eight lines of iambic pentameter (*abbaabba*)
	SICILIAN OCTAVE: eight lines of iambic pentameter (*abababab*)
9	SPENSERIAN STANZA: nine lines rhyming *ababbcbcc* with the first eight in iambic pentameter and the last in iambic hexameter (which is called an Alexandrine)

(continued)

Table 4 Notable Fixed and Complex Forms *(continued)*

Number of Lines in Poem or Stanza	Name and Description
10	ENGLISH (KEATSIAN) ODE: Three ten-line iambic pentameter stanzas, each with the same rhyme scheme (*ababcdecde*)
14	SONNET: fourteen iambic pentameter lines ENGLISH (SHAKESPEAREAN) SONNET: (*abab cdcd efef gg*) SPENSERIAN SONNET (*abab bcbc cdcd ee*) PETRARCHAN (ITALIAN) SONNET (*abba abba cde cde* or *abba abba cdcdcd*)
19	VILLANELLE: nineteen lines of any length, divided into five tercets and one quatrain; built on two rhymes and two refrains (shown by superscripts ^{R1} and ^{R2}, both of which end with the *a* rhyme ($a^{R1}ba^{R2}aba^{R1}aba^{R2}aba^{R1}aba^{R2}aba^{R1}a^{R2}$)

Some stanzaic forms can be very complicated, requiring the poet to possess exceptional skill in order both to meet the technical requirements of the form and to produce a work that is moving or interesting. For example, Dylan Thomas's "Do Not Go Gentle into That Good Night" and Theodore Roethke's "The Waking" are built on a medieval French form called the **villanelle**: this nineteen-line form requires five tercets and one quatrain, contains only two rhymes, and uses two refrains that must appear in a specified order.

Line length, rhythm, rhyme, and stanzaic form contribute to the development of thought and feeling. Whether the work is in free verse or follows a restrictive form like that of the villanelle, these elements emphasize certain words and create links between words and groups of lines. Readers who note these emphases are not only better able to appreciate the craft of the poet, but they are better able to understand the textures of a poem's ideas and to feel its emotional shadings.

SOUND AND SOUND DEVICES

The rhythmic flow of a line of poetry is not entirely a matter of rhythm patterns, caesurae, and run-on lines; the choice of words, their very sounds, can make a line flow more swiftly or slowly. In "An Essay on Criticism," a work not included in this anthology, Alexander Pope argued that "the sound must seem an echo to the sense," and illustrated how word choice and placement can make a strict iambic rhythm seem ponderously slow or light and quick:

> When Ajax strives some rock's vast weight to throw,
> The line too labors, and the words move slow;
> Not so, when swift Camilla scours the plain,
> Flies o'er th' unbending corn and skims along the main.

In the first of these lines, Pope slows the reading of the line by using a number of monosyllabic words and cacophony, harsh or unpleasant-sounding language, produced here by a sequence of consonants that are relatively difficult to pronounce together. In the third and fourth lines, he quickens the pace with a careful placement of polysyllabic words and the use of euphony, or pleasant-sounding language with pleasing combinations of vowels and consonants.

Several other sound devices affect a poem's pace and meaning; sometimes these are instrumental in conveying the tone, which is the speaker's attitude toward the subject and the audience (both the audience implied by the context, as in a dramatic monologue, and the audience actually reading or listening to the poem). One of the most notable of these is **alliteration**, the repetition of initial consonants. In Donne's Holy Sonnet XIV, for example, the *b* sound is repeated when the speaker pleads that God "bend / Your force, to break, blow, burn, and make me new." Alliteration tends to emphasize words, giving them extra force and linking them as a unit. Here, the *b* sound emphasizes the violence of the action Donne requests of God and suggests that it will require all of God's force to save the speaker. Alliteration, therefore, suggests both the difficulty of the task and the intensity of the speaker's desire for renewal. It can, of course, be used for gentler effects, as in Christina Rossetti's "Song": "When I am dead, my dearest, / Sing no sad songs for me." In this case, the heaviness of the *d* sounds in the first line suggests the sadness normally associated with death, but the softness of the *s* sounds in the second line lightens the mood to indicate the speaker's contrary feeling. Furthermore, the alliteration surrounds the word *no*, a word that in scansion receives an accent, or heavy beat, creating a contrast that emphasizes the word and its idea even more.

Repetition of sound is also central to assonance and consonance. **Assonance** is the repetition of vowel sounds, as in the *i* sound of "swift Camilla" and "skims" in Pope's lines quoted above. **Consonance** is the repetition of consonant sounds within or at the end of words, as with the repeated *l* sounds in the last line of Archibald Lampman's "Winter Evening": "Glittering and still shall come the awful night."

One other important device is **onomatopoeia**, or imitative harmony, in which a word imitates or echoes a sound, as in "clip clop" to suggest the movement of horses, or as in the word *break* in Donne's alliterative "break, blow, bend" quoted above, or as in this famous example from a long poem that does not appear in this anthology, Tennyson's *The Princess* (1847): "The moan of doves in immemorial elms, / And murmuring of innumerable bees." Here *moan* and *murmur* imitate natural sounds, and alliteration of the *m* heightens and extends the effect throughout both lines.

Although it has been necessary to examine them separately, sound devices most frequently work together. In the final line of Shakespeare's Sonnet 73, "To love that well which thou must leave ere long," discussed earlier to show meaningful variation in metre, alliteration links *love, leave,* and *long,* emphasizing these three important words. Moreover, the two major terms, *love* and *leave,* are further linked and intensified by internal slant rhyme. Finally, consonance links *love* and *well,* uniting these words into a single concept. Readers who notice such uses of sound gain a greater appreciation of the resources and technical demands of the craft of poetry, but they also gain something personally enriching. Sensitivity to sound enables readers to respond more fully to the nuances of language and, thus, to be more open to both emotional stimulation and intellectual meaning in their reading.

POETRY AND PLEASURE

The preceding sections have explored only the major technical elements that make poetry such a complex literary form. Poems can use these techniques in inexhaustible combinations. Poems, however, are much more than compilations of techniques, and reading poetry is more than cataloguing techniques. Poems express the deepest feelings, the most moving thoughts, the heartiest laughter, the most scathing denunciations that people throughout the ages have felt. Poems are expressions of unique personalities and bear the marks of originating in particular social, cultural, and historical contexts, but poems are open to all readers who take the time to open themselves to them, who listen to the rhythms and the sounds, who imaginatively perceive the imagery. The more readers discover about a poem, its context, and literature and poetry in general, the more they can extend their appreciation and enjoyment of poetry. The key to such appreciation and enjoyment, however, is to forget that a poem is a work of "serious literature" that must be studied. Readers need to approach the poem in the same way they approach music, plays, short stories, and novels; they should, that is, be willing to be entertained, be open to new sensations and ideas, be ready to be teased and puzzled, be eager to enter into the imaginative life of the poem. This willingness allows readers to experience an array of emotions and ideas they may not otherwise have. Reading poetry in this way can thus become an act of self-revelation that makes readers more deeply aware of their own humanity. Such reading does not, however, lock us into ourselves. Because poetry originates in another's mind and voice and because it touches on nearly universal experiences and feelings, such reading can connect us to other human beings. It can also make the moments of reading moments of pleasure. That, in itself, is a worthwhile reason for reading poetry.

Anonymous Medieval Lyrics and Ballads

Medieval lyrics and ballads may be remnants of the popular entertainment of the twelfth to fifteenth centuries. In the case of the lyrics, it is unlikely that the polished poems recorded in manuscripts are unaltered compositions of the common people. Their history is not clear, but lyrics probably began among the common people as songs. The conventions of this folk poetry probably influenced the art of the minstrels and educated poets, whose compositions have been preserved. In any case, from its beginnings as oral poetry to its later manifestation as written compositions, the medieval lyric remained relatively unaltered in form and content. Its very conventionality in constantly returning to such themes as the joy of spring, the sorrow of lost love, the inevitability of death, and the sacrifice of Christ suggests that these lyrics represent direct expression of ideas that the medieval world considered to be of compelling universal importance.

Many ballads also originated in the medieval period, but they were not recorded until the eighteenth century, being preserved for centuries almost entirely through oral performances. Unlike the lyrics, which express feelings, these anonymous songs concentrate on events. Ballads are not, however, fully developed narratives. Usually, that is, they focus on a climactic episode, often involving murder, tragic death, or supernatural phenomena. Events leading to the climax typically function as a series of condensed scenes, and the events that link them are omitted or swiftly passed over. The narrator seldom offers interpretations or judgements, allowing the story to advance through a spare recitation of events and a heavy reliance on dialogue. Because they are set to music, ballads have a simple stanzaic structure and rhythm: they usually consist of quatrains in which each line has four stresses or in which lines of four stresses and three stresses alternate. They also commonly employ refrains, or repeated phrases, some of which contain nonsense phrases. As a kind of common man's romance, ballads offer evidence of the intense passions, the fears, and the heroism that have entertained and inspired people for hundreds of years and that continue to do so in some contemporary songs.

Anonymous Lyrics

Western Wind

Western wind, when will thou blow,
    The small rain down can rain?
Christ, if my love were in my arms
    And I in my bed again!

Sumer is icumen in (The Cuckoo Song)

Sumer is icumen in,
 Lhude[1] sing cuccu;
Groweth sed and bloweth[2] med[3]
 And springth the wode[4] nu.[5]
5 Sing cuccu!
Awe[6] bleteth after lamb,
 Lhouth[7] after calve cu[8]
Bulluc sterteth,[9] bucke verteth[10]
 Murie[11] sing cuccu.
10 Cuccu, Cuccu,
 Wel singes thu, cuccu,
 Ne swik[12] thu[13] never nu.

 Sing cuccu nu! Sing cuccu!
 Sing cuccu! Sing cuccu nu!

I sing of a maiden

I sing of a maiden
 That is makeles,[1]
King of all kinges
 To[2] her sone sche ches.[3]
5 He cam also stille[4]
 There[5] his moder was
As dew in Aprille
 That falleth on the grass.
He cam also stille
10 To his moderes bour,[6]
As dew in Aprille
 That falleth on the flour.
He cam also stille
 There his moder lay,
15 As dew in April
 That falleth on the spray.

   ⟶

1 loud. 2 blows, or blooms, into flower. 3 meadow. 4 wood. 5 now. 6 ewe. 7 loweth. 8 cow.
9 the bullock starts, or leaps. 10 farteth; eating fresh green grass causes flatulence. 11 merry, merrily.
12 nor cease. 13 thou.
1 both matchless (incomparable) and mateless. 2 as, for. 3 chose. 4 as quietly or gently. 5 where.
6 bower; boudoir.

Moder and maiden
    Was never non but sche
Well may swich a lady
20   Godes[7] moder be.

Anonymous Popular Ballads

Sir Patrick Spens

The king sits in Dumferling toune,[1]
    Drinking the blude-reid wine:[2]
"O whar will I get guid sailor,
    To sail this schip of mine?"

5 Up and spak an eldern knicht,
    Sat at the kings richt kne:
"Sir Patrick Spens is the best sailor
    That sails upon the se."

The king has written a braid[3] letter,
10   And signed it wi' his hand,
And sent it to Sir Patrick Spens,
    Was walking on the sand.

The first line that Sir Patrick red,
    A loud lauch[4] lauched he;
15 The next line that Sir Patrick red,
    The teir blinded his ee.[5]

"O wha is this has don this deid,
    This ill deid don to me,
To send me out this time o' the yeir,
20   To sail upon the se?"

"Mak haste, mak haste, my mirry men all,
    Our guid schip sails the morne."

$\longrightarrow$

7 God's.
1 Dunfermline, in eastern Scotland, was a favourite residence of Scottish kings. 2 blood-red. 3 broad.
4 laugh. 5 eye.

"O say na sae,[6] my master deir,
 For I feir a deadlie storme.

25 "Late late yestreen I saw the new moone
  Wi' the auld moone in her arme;
 And I feir, I feir, my deir master,
  That we will come to harme."

O our Scots nobles were richt laith[7]
30 To weet[8] their cork-heild schoone;[9]
 Bot lang owre[10] a' the play were played,
  Their hats they swam aboone.[11]

O lang, lang may their ladies sit
  Wi' their fans into their hand,
35 Or eir they see Sir Patrick Spens
  Come sailing to the land.

O lang, lang may the ladies stand
  Wi' their gold kems[12] in their hair,
 Waiting for their ain[13] deir lords,
40 For they'll see thame na mair.[14]

Haf owre, haf owre[15] to Aberdour,[16]
  It's fiftie fadom[17] deip:
 And there lies guid Sir Patrick Spens
  Wi' the Scots lords at his feit.

The Three Ravens

There were three ravens sat on a tree,
 Downe a downe, hay down, hay downe
There were three ravens sat on a tree,
 With a downe
5 There were three ravens sat on a tree,
They were as blacke as they might be.
 With a downe derrie, derrie, derrie, downe, downe.

---

6 not so. 7 loath. 8 wet. 9 cork-healed shoes. 10 ere; before. 11 above. 12 combs. 13 own.
14 no more. 15 half(way) over. 16 Aberdeen. 17 fathoms.

The one of them said to his mate,
"Where shall we our breakefast take?"

10   "Downe in yonder greene field,
There lies a knight slain under his shield.

"His hounds they lie downe at his feete,
So well they can their master keepe.

"His hawkes they fly so eagerly,
15   There's no fowle dare him come nie."

Downe there comes a fallow[1] doe,
As great with yong as she might goe.

She lift up his bloudy hed,
And kist his wounds that were so red.

20   She got him up upon her backe,
And carried him to earthen lake.

She buried him before the prime,[2]
She was dead herselfe ere even-song[3] time.

God send every gentleman,
25   Such hawkes, such hounds, and such a leman.[4]

Bonny Barbara Allan

It was in and about the Martinmas time,[1]
    When the green leaves were a falling,
That Sir John Graeme, in the West Country,
    Fell in love with Barbara Allan.

1 light brown, dun. 2 the first hour after dawn in canonical system. 3 vespers, the sixth of seven canonical hours, a period of worship in the late afternoon or early evening. 4 mistress, sweetheart, lover.
1 November 11, the feast day of Saint Martin of Tours.

5   He sent his men down through the town
        To the place where she was dwelling:
    "O haste and come to my master dear,
        Gin ye be Barbara Allan."

    O hooly,[2] hooly rose she up,
10   To the place where he was lying,
    And when she drew the curtain by,
        "Young man, I think you're dying."

    "O it's I'm sick, and very, very sick,
        And 't is a' for Barbara Allan."
15   "O the better for me ye 's[3] never be,
        Tho your heart's blood were a spilling.

    "O dinna, ye mind, young man," said she,
        "When ye was in the tavern a drinking,
    That ye made the healths gae round and round,
20   And slighted Barbara Allan?"

    He turned his face unto the wall,
        And death was with him dealing:
    "Adieu, adieu, my dear friends all,
        And be kind to Barbara Allan."

25   And slowly, slowly raise she up,
        And slowly, slowly left him,
    And sighing said, she could not stay,
        Since death of life had reft[4] him.

    She had not gane a mile but twa,
30   When she heard the dead-bell ringing,
    And every jow[5] that the dead-bell geid,[6]
        It cried, Woe to Barbara Allan!

    "O mother, mother, make my bed!
        O make it saft and narrow!
35   Since my love died for me to-day,
        I'll die for him to-morrow."

2 cautiously, slowly.   3 ye shall.   4 torn from; robbed.   5 ring or toll.   6 gave or made.

The Renaissance Sonnet

The sonnet originated in thirteenth-century Italy, but the sonnet sequences of Dante (1265–1321) and Petrarch (1304–74) made the form popular throughout Europe during the fifteenth and sixteenth centuries. In every country, the topics and attitudes of the sonnet were quite conventional. The Platonic love themes developed by the Italian masters created a pattern of contemplation, love, and rejection: the Lover begs acceptance of the Lady through various metaphors of agony, disenchantment, and bliss; she, with studied disregard, rebuffs or ignores his advances; such rejection only intensifies his next attempt. Even when it did not speak of unrequited love, however, the sonnet was frequently artificial in its expression. Compare, for example, Constable's "My lady's presence makes the roses red," a conventional celebration of the beloved, with Shakespeare's biting satire of such formulaic comparisons in Sonnet 130 ("My mistress' eyes are nothing like the sun"), which is included among the sonnets printed in the author entry for Shakespeare. The six poems in this section represent various approaches to the love sonnet that dominated the Renaissance. For sonnets on other topics, see the author entries for John Donne and John Milton.

Although the sonnet is rigid in length, it can be remarkably varied in structure and rhyme. Sir Thomas Wyatt, who introduced the sonnet to England through free English translations of Petrarch, preserved the rhyming of the Italian octave (*abba abba*), but he concluded the sestet with the couplet, a device that became characteristic of the English sonnet. His contemporary, Henry Howard, Earl of Surrey, established the division into three quatrains and a couplet (*abab cdcd efef gg*). This structural change altered the Italian conception of the sonnet as a poem divided into two parts: an eight-line exposition of the problem or an observation and a six-line statement of conclusion or resolution. The English sonnet allows greater repetition and development of the problem while forcing a concentrated resolution in the epigrammatic couplet. Furthermore, because English is harder to rhyme than Italian, this structure gave greater freedom by permitting seven instead of the conventional five rhymes. Note, however, that variations in the three-quatrain scheme are possible: Surrey's "Love that doth reign," for example, contains only six rhymes. Edmund Spenser made a further adaptation, linking quatrains through the couplet created when one quatrain begins with the rhyme with which the previous one ends (*abab bcbc cdcd ee*). Sir Philip Sidney, although he usually followed Wyatt in using the Italian pattern in his octaves and a closing couplet in his sestet, also experimented with alternating rhyme in "Loving in truth" (*abab abab cdcd ee*). The last great poet of the Renaissance, John Milton, followed the true Italian pattern (*abba abba cdecde*), but he intensified the unity of his sonnets by having the octave run into the sestet. After Milton's death, the sonnet lost favour, but it was revived as a powerful lyrical force by the Romantics, notably Wordsworth and Keats (see their author entries).

Sir Thomas Wyatt (1503–1542)

My galley charged with forgetfulness

*The lover compareth his state to a ship in perilous storm
tossed on the sea.*

My galley charged with forgetfulness,
Through sharp seas, in winter nights, doth pass
'Tween rock and rock; and eke[1] my foe, alas,
That is my lord,[2] steereth with cruelness:
5   And every hour, a thought in readiness,
As though that death were light in such a case.
An endless wind doth tear the sail apace
Of forced sighs and trusty fearfulness;
A rain of tears, a cloud of dark disdain,
10   Have done the wearied cords great hinderance:
Wreathed with error, and with ignorance;
The stars[3] be hid that lead me to this pain;
    Drown'd is reason that should be my comfort,
    And I remain, despairing of the port.

(1520–30?)   (1557)

Henry Howard, Earl of Surrey (1517–1547)

Love that doth reign

Love that doth reign and live within my thought,
And built his seat within my captive breast,
Clad in the arms wherein with me he fought,
Oft in my face he doth his banner rest.
5   But she that taught me love and suffer pain,
My doubtful hope and eke[1] my hot desire
With shamefast[2] look to shadow and refrain,

$\longrightarrow$

1 also. 2 i.e., Cupid. 3 i.e., the lady's eyes.
1 also. 2 shamefaced.

Her smiling grace converteth straight to ire.
And coward love then to the heart apace
10   Taketh his flight, where he doth lurk and plain[3]
His purpose lost, and dare not show his face.
For my lord's guilt thus faultless bide I pain;
Yet from my lord shall not my foot remove.
Sweet is the death that taketh end by love.

(1542?)   (1557)

Edmund Spenser (1552–1599)

One day I wrote her name upon the strand

One day I wrote her name upon the strand;[1]
But came the waves, and washed it away:
Agayne, I wrote it with a second hand;
But came the tyde, and made my paynes his pray.
5   Vayne man, sayd she, that doest in vaine assay
A mortall thing so to immortalize;
For I my selve shall lyke to this decay,
And eke[2] my name bee wyped out lykewize.
Not so, quod I; let baser things devize
10   To dy in dust, but you shall live by fame:
My verse your vertues rare shall eternize,
And in the hevens wryte your glorious name.
        Where, when as death shall all the world subdew,
        Our love shall live, and later life renew.

(1595)

Sir Philip Sidney (1554–1586)

Who will in fairest book of nature know

Who will in fairest book of nature know,
How virtue may best lodged in beauty be,

——→

3 complain.
1 beach. 2 also .

Let him but learn of love to read in thee
Stella, those fair lines which true Beauty show.
5   There shall he find all vices' overthrow;
Not by rude force, but sweetest sovereignty
Of reason, from whose light, the night birds fly;
That inward sun in thine eyes shineth so.
And not content to be perfection's heir
10   Thyself, dost strive all minds that way to move,
Who mark in thee what is in thee most fair.
So while thy beauty drives my heart to love,
As fast thy virtue bends that love to good:
"But ah," desire still cries, "give me some food."

(1581–83?)   (1591)

Henry Constable (1562–1613)

My lady's presence makes the roses red

My lady's presence makes the roses red
Because to see her lips they blush for shame.
The lilies leaves for envy pale became,
And her white hands in them this envy bred.
5   The marigold the leaves abroad doth spread
Because the sun's and her power is the same.
The violet of purple colour came,
Dyed in the blood she made my heart to shed.
In brief, all flowers from her their virtue take;
10   From her sweet breath their sweet smells do proceed;
The living heat which her eyebeams doth make
Warmeth the ground and quickeneth the seed.
    The rain wherewith she watereth the flowers
    Falls from mine eyes which she dissolves in showers.

(1594)

Michael Drayton (1563–1631)

Since there's no help, come let us kiss and part

Since there's no help, come let us kiss and part,
Nay, I have done: you get no more of me,
And I am glad, yea glad with all my heart,
That thus so cleanly I myself can free;
5   Shake hands forever, cancel all our vows,
And when we meet at any time again,
Be it not seen in either of our brows
That we one jot of former love retain.
Now at the last gasp of love's latest breath,
10 When his pulse failing, passion speechless lies,
When faith is kneeling by his bed of death,
and innocence is closing up his eyes,
  Now if thou would'st, when all have given him over,
  From death to life, thou might'st him yet recover.

(1619)

Sir Walter Ralegh (c. 1552–1618)

Ralegh is perhaps best known for his colonization of Virginia and for popularizing the use of tobacco in England. He was also friend and patron to Edmund Spenser. Notoriously proud, ambitious, and ostentatious, he commanded extremes of loyalty and hatred through the power of his public personality. Though he was a favourite of Queen Elizabeth in the 1580s, Ralegh spent most of the final fifteen years of his life imprisoned in the Tower by James I. While in the Tower, Ralegh wrote the bulk of his voluminous *History of the World*. But he was a poet as well as a man of action and confirmed sceptic. His is a hard-minded poetic vision that rejects easy idealizations. Released from prison in 1616 to lead the ill-fated Guiana expedition in search of gold for the English treasury, Ralegh was tried on charges of reopening hostilities with Spain and beheaded.

The Nymph's Reply [1]

If all the world and love were young,
And truth in every shepherd's tongue,
These pretty pleasures might me move
To live with thee and be thy love.

1 reply to Christopher Marlowe's "The Passionate Shepherd to His Love" (see page 38).

5   But time drives flocks from field to fold,
    When rivers rage and rocks grow cold;
    And Philomel[2] becometh dumb;
    The rest complains of cares to come.

    The flowers do fade, and wanton fields
10   To wayward winter reckoning yields:
    A honey tongue, a heart of gall,
    Is fancy's spring, but sorrow's fall.

    Thy gowns, thy shoes, thy beds of roses,
    Thy cap, thy kirtle, and thy posies,
15   Soon break, soon wither, soon forgotten, —
    In folly ripe, in reason rotten.

    Thy belt of straw and ivy buds,
    Thy coral clasps and amber studs, —
    All those in me no means can move
20   To come to thee and be thy love.

    But could youth last, and love still breed;
    Had joys no date, nor age no need;
    Then those delights my mind might move
    To live with thee and be thy love.

(1600)

Christopher Marlowe (1564–1593)

Born the son of a Canterbury shoemaker, Christopher Marlowe received the M.A. degree from Cambridge in 1587. Best known as a dramatic poet using blank verse, he demonstrated technical virtuosity in translating such classics as Ovid's *Amores* and the first book of Lucan's *Pharsalia*. His unfinished erotic narrative *Hero and Leander* is written in ironic and smooth rhyming couplets. Thus, the short pastoral verse entitled "The Passionate Shepherd to His Love" seems somewhat uncharacteristic. And yet, since at least the seventeenth century, it has been celebrated, and linked with Sir Walter Ralegh's sceptical "answer."

    Marlowe's mercurial career saw him gain prominence very early with the introduction of his "mighty line": the blank verse metre of *Tamburlaine* (1587), which was to become the poetic medium of Shakespearean and Renaissance drama, as well as the measure of Milton's *Paradise Lost*. Surrey had used

2 nightingale (mythological).

unrhymed decasyllables in translating the *Aeneid* some 35 years before, but his verse was meant to be stately and Latinate. It was Marlowe who made the measure distinctly English by demonstrating its directness, versatility, and power.

The Passionate Shepherd to His Love

Come live with me, and be my love;
And we will all the pleasures prove[1]
That hills and valleys, dales and fields,
Woods, or steepy mountain yields.

5 And we will sit upon the rocks,
Seeing the shepherds feed their flocks
By shallow rivers, to whose falls
Melodious birds sing madrigals.

And I will make thee beds of roses,
10 And a thousand fragrant posies;
A cap of flowers, and a kirtle[2]
Embroidered all with leaves of myrtle;

A gown made of the finest wool
Which from our pretty lambs we pull;
15 Fair-lined slippers for the cold,
With buckles of the purest gold;

A belt of straw and ivy-buds,
With coral clasps and amber-studs:
And if these pleasures may thee move,
20 Come live with me, and be my love.

The shepherd-swains shall dance and sing
For thy delight each May-morning;
If these delights thy mind may move,
Then live with me, and be my love.

(1599)

1 try. 2 a skirt or loose gown.

William Shakespeare   (1564–1616)

Shakespeare was born in Stratford-upon-Avon, probably a day or two previous to his christening on April 26, 1564. It is traditional that his birthday be celebrated on April 23, which is the feast day of St. George, England's patron saint. Much of Shakespeare's adult life was spent in London as an actor and playwright with the Globe Theatre.

Although celebrated as the foremost dramatist in the language, Shakespeare is also a sonneteer. His 154 sonnets were published in 1609 but were noted previously by Francis Meres, who in 1598 made mention of Shakespeare's "sugared sonnets among his private friends." The sonnets, however, are far from sugary. They are profound moral and aesthetic contemplations that adapt metaphors from the theatrical world and from the world of human emotions. Investigators have been fascinated by the biographical possibilities of Shakespeare's sonnets, but they are primarily metaphorical contemplations that probe the complexities of love, death, fame, and mutability.

Sonnets

18

Shall I compare thee to a summer's day?
Thou art more lovely and more temperate:
Rough winds do shake the darling buds of May,
And summer's lease hath all too short a date:
5   Sometime too hot the eye of heaven shines,
And often is his gold complexion dimm'd;
And every fair from fair sometime declines
By chance or nature's changing course untrimm'd;
But thy eternal summer shall not fade
10   Nor lose possession of that fair thou ow'st;[1]
Nor shall Death brag thou wander'st in his shade,
When in eternal lines to time thou grow'st:
   So long as men can breathe or eyes can see,
   So long lives this and this gives life to thee.

(1609)

---

1 ownest.

55

Not marble, nor the gilded monuments
Of princes, shall outlive this powerful rime;
But you shall shine more bright in these contents
Than unswept stone besmear'd with sluttish time.
5 When wasteful war shall statues overturn,
And broils root out the work of masonry,
Nor Mars his sword nor war's quick fire shall burn
The living record of your memory.
'Gainst death and all-oblivious enmity
10 Shall you pace forth: your praise shall still find room
Even in the eyes of all posterity
That wear this world out to the ending doom.
    So, till the judgement that yourself arise,[1]
    You live in this, and dwell in lovers' eyes.

(1609)

73

That time of year thou mayst in me behold
When yellow leaves, or none, or few, do hang
Upon those boughs which shake against the cold,
Bare ruin'd choirs where late the sweet birds sang.
5 In me thou see'st the twilight of such day
As after sunset fadeth in the west;
Which by and by black night doth take away,
Death's second self, that seals up all in rest.
In me thou see'st the glowing of such fire
10 That on the ashes of his youth doth lie,
As the death-bed whereon it must expire,
Consumed with that which it was nourish'd by.
    This thou perceiv'st, which makes thy love more strong,
    To love that well which thou must leave ere long.

(1609)

---

1 i.e., "So until you arise from the dead on Judgement Day."

116

Let me not to the marriage of true minds
Admit impediments. Love is not love
Which alters when it alteration finds,
Or bends with the remover to remove:
5   O, no! it is an ever-fixed mark,
That looks on tempests and is never shaken;
It is the star to every wandering bark,[1]
Whose worth's unknown, although his height be taken.
Love's not Time's fool,[2] though rosy lips and cheeks
10 Within his bending sickle's compass come;
Love alters not with his brief hours and weeks,
But bears it out even to the edge of doom.
    If this be error and upon me proved,
    I never writ, nor no man ever loved.

(1609)

130

My mistress' eyes are nothing like the sun;
Coral is far more red than her lips' red:
If snow be white, why then her breasts are dun;
If hairs be wires, black wires grow on her head.
5   I have seen roses damask'd,[1] red and white,
But no such roses see I in her cheeks;
And in some perfumes is there more delight
Than in the breath that from my mistress reeks.
I love to hear her speak, yet well I know
10 That music hath a far more pleasing sound:
I grant I never saw a goddess go;
My mistress, when she walks, treads on the ground:
    And yet, by heaven, I think my love as rare
    As any she belied[2] with false compare.

(1609)

1 sailing ship. 2 i.e., victim.
1 mingled, variegated. 2 misrepresented.

John Donne   (1572–1631)

John Donne was a talented young man hopeful of worldly advancement. Appointed private secretary to Sir Thomas Egerton in 1598, Donne ruined hope of further preferment in that household when his secret marriage to Sir Thomas's seventeen-year-old niece became public. But Donne's gifts of learning, intelligence, and social grace would not let him fade away from the public eye. On the encouragement of King James himself, Donne took holy orders and was appointed Dean of St. Paul's Cathedral, London, in 1621.

Next to nothing of Donne's literary output was published during his own lifetime. (The first edition of his collected poems appeared in 1633.) His brilliance as a "metaphysical" poet is a virtual rediscovery by twentieth-century criticism, and he is now recognized as one of the greatest English love poets. Donne's forceful exposition and bold metaphorical style also made him one of the greatest preachers of the seventeenth century, as well as a significant religious poet. He seemed singularly adept at uniting passion and intellect. And the two periods of "Jack Donne," lyrical poet, and "Doctor Donne," learned divine, into which Donne himself separated his life might not seem all that irreconcilable in light of the powerful rhetoric and deep meditational technique common to both.

Song

Go, and catch a falling star,
    Get with child a mandrake root,
Tell me where all past years are,
    Or who cleft the Devil's foot,
5   Teach me to hear Mermaids singing,
Or to keep off envy's stinging,
            And find
            What wind
Serves to advance an honest mind.

10   If thou be'st born to strange sights,
    Things invisible to see,
Ride ten thousand days and nights,
    Till age snow white hairs on thee,
Thou, when thou return'st, wilt tell me
15   All strange wonders that befell thee,

———→

And swear
No where
Lives a woman true, and fair.

If thou find'st one, let me know,
20   Such a Pilgrimage were sweet;
Yet do not, I would not go,
     Though at next door we might meet,
Though she were true, when you met her,
And last, till you write your letter,
25   Yet she
     Will be
False, ere I come, to two, or three.

          (1633)

The Bait [1]

Come live with me, and be my love,
And we will some new pleasures prove [2]
Of golden sands, and crystal brooks,
With silken lines, and silver hooks.

5 There will the river whispering run
Warm'd by thy eyes, more than the Sun.
And there th' enamour'd fish will stay,
Begging themselves they may betray.

When thou wilt swim in that live bath,
10 Each fish, which every channel hath,
Will amorously to thee swim,
Gladder to catch thee, than thou him.

If thou, to be so seen, be'st loth,
By Sun, or Moon, thou dark'nest both,
15 And if myself have leave to see,
I need not their light, having thee.

---

1 reply to Marlowe's "The Passionate Shepherd to His Love" (see page 38).   2 try.

Let others freeze with angling reeds,
And cut their legs, with shells and weeds,
Or treacherously poor fish beset,
20   With strangling snare, or windowy net:

Let coarse bold hands, from slimy nest
The bedded fish in banks out-wrest,
Or curious traitors, sleeve-silk flies
Bewitch poor fishes' wand'ring eyes.

25   For thee, thou need'st no such deceit,
For thou thyself art thine own bait;
That fish, that is not catch'd thereby,
Alas, is wiser far than I.

(1633)

A Valediction: Forbidding Mourning

As virtuous men pass mildly away,
    And whisper to their souls, to go,
Whilst some of their sad friends do say,
    The breath goes now, and some say, no:

5   So let us melt, and make no noise,
    No tear-floods, nor sigh-tempests move,
'Twere profanation of our joys
    To tell the laity our love.

Moving of th' earth brings harms and fears,
10   Men reckon what it did and meant,
But trepidation of the spheres,[1]
    Though greater far, is innocent.

Dull sublunary lovers' love
    (Whose soul is sense) cannot admit
15   Absence, because it doth remove
    Those things which elemented it.

1 in pre-Copernican cosmology, the shaking of the nine concentric spheres around the earth.

But we by a love, so much refin'd,
    That ourselves know not what it is,
Inter-assured of the mind,
20   Care less eyes, lips, and hands to miss.

Our two souls therefore, which are one,
    Though I must go, endure not yet
A breach, but an expansion,
    Like gold to aery thinness beat.

25 If they be two, they are two so
    As stiff twin compasses are two,
Thy soul the fixed foot, makes no show
    To move, but doth, if th' other do.

And though it in the centre sit,
30   Yet when the other far doth roam,
It leans, and hearkens after it,
    And grows erect, as that comes home.
Such wilt thou be to me, who must
    Like th' other foot, obliquely run;
35 Thy firmness draws my circle just,
    And makes me end, where I begun.

(1633)

The Canonization

For God's sake hold your tongue, and let me love;
    Or chide my palsy, or my gout,
My five grey hairs, or ruin'd fortune flout;
    With wealth your state, your mind with arts improve,
5   Take you a course, get you a place,
      Observe his Honour, or his Grace,
Or the King's real, or his stamped face
    Contemplate; what you will, approve,
    So you will let me love.
10 Alas, alas, who's injur'd by my love?
    What merchant's ships have my sighs drown'd?

—→

Who says my tears have overflow'd his ground?
　　When did my colds a forward spring remove?
　　When did the heats which my veins fill
15　　　Add one more to the plaguy bill?[1]
Soldiers find wars, and lawyers find out still
　　Litigious men, which quarrels move,
　　Though she and I do love.

Call us what you will, we are made such by love;
20　　Call her one, me another fly,
We're tapers too, and at our own cost die,
　　And we in us find the Eagle and the Dove.
　　　The Phœnix riddle hath more wit
　　　By us; we two being one, are it.
25 So to one neutral thing both sexes fit,
　　We die and rise the same, and prove
　　Mysterious by this love.

We can die by it, if not live by love,
　　And if unfit for tombs and hearse
30 Our legend be, it will be fit for verse;
　　And if no piece of Chronicle we prove,
　　　We'll build in sonnets pretty rooms;
　　　As well a well-wrought urn becomes
The greatest ashes, as half-acre tombs,
35　　And by these hymns, all shall approve
　　Us canonized for Love:

And thus invoke us; You whom reverend love
　　Made one another's hermitage;
You, to whom love was peace, that now is rage;
40　　Who did the whole world's soul contract, and drove
　　　Into the glasses of your eyes
　　　(So made such mirrors, and such spies,
That they did all to you epitomize,)
　　Countries, Towns, Courts: beg from above
45　　A pattern of your love!

　　　　　　　　　　　　　　　　　(1633)

---

1 i.e., add one more name to the weekly list (bill) of plague victims.

The Flea

Mark but this flea, and mark in this,
How little that which thou deny'st me is;
It suck'd me first, and now sucks thee,
And in this flea, our two bloods mingled be;
5   Thou know'st that this cannot be said
A sin, nor shame, nor loss of maidenhead,
     Yet this enjoys before it woo,
     And pamper'd swells with one blood made of two,
     And this, alas, is more than we would do.

10   Oh stay, three lives in one flea spare,
Where we almost, yea more than married are.
This flea is you and I, and this
Our marriage bed, and marriage temple is;
Though parents grudge, and you, we're met,
15   And cloistered in these living walls of jet.
     Though use make you apt to kill me,
     Let not to that, self murder added be,
     And sacrilege, three sins in killing three.

Cruel and sudden, hast thou since
20   Purpled thy nail, in blood of innocence?
Wherein could this flea guilty be,
Except in that drop which it suck'd from thee?
Yet thou triumph'st, and say'st that thou
Find'st not thyself, nor me, the weaker now;
25   'Tis true, then learn how false, fears be;
     Just so much honour, when thou yield'st to me,
     Will waste, as this flea's death took life from thee.

(1633)

Holy Sonnet X

Death be not proud, though some have called thee
Mighty and dreadful, for, thou art not so,
For, those, whom thou think'st, thou dost overthrow,
Die not, poor death, nor yet canst thou kill me.
5 From rest and sleep, which but thy pictures be,
Much pleasure, then from thee, much more must flow,
And soonest our best men with thee do go,
Rest of their bones, and soul's delivery.
Thou art slave to Fate, Chance, kings, and desperate men,
10 And dost with poison, war, and sickness dwell,
And poppy, or charms can make us sleep as well,
And better than thy stroke; why swell'st thou then?
One short sleep past, we wake eternally,
And death shall be no more; death, thou shalt die.

(1633)

Holy Sonnet XIV

Batter my heart, three-person'd God; for, you
As yet but knock, breathe, shine, and seek to mend;
That I may rise, and stand, o'erthrow me, and bend
Your force, to break, blow, burn and make me new.
5 I, like an usurp'd town, to another due,
Labour to admit you, but Oh, to no end,
Reason your viceroy in me, me should defend,
But is captiv'd, and proves weak or untrue.
Yet dearly I love you, and would be loved fain,
10 But am betroth'd unto your enemy:
Divorce me, untie, or break that knot again,
Take me to you, imprison me, for I
Except you enthral me, never shall be free,
Nor ever chaste, except you ravish me.

(1633)

Ben Jonson (1572–1637)

Scholar, poet, playwright, classicist, and controversialist — Jonson's career consolidates the emergence of professional letters in the English Renaissance. He was the first English poet to publish his own works, in 1616, and his first play, *Every Man in His Humour* (1598), included actor William Shakespeare in the cast. Master of the English plain style, Jonson, whose output was voluminous and various, held pride of place at the Mermaid Tavern where he presided over a club of aspiring poets known as the "sons of Ben."

Jonson was also a man of action who, while a soldier in Flanders, killed an enemy champion in hand-to-hand combat — a biographical fact that he gloried in relating to his host, William Drummond of Hawthornden. Argumentative, satirical, and pugnacious, Jonson was a professional writer who took his business seriously enough to insist on its critical appreciation in both the public playhouse and the private masquing house where he also triumphed as author. With stage architect Inigo Jones (a detested rival), Jonson prepared many lavish ceremonial masques for the court of James I, and he was still a significant cultural spokesperson in the reign of Charles I.

Song: To Celia

Drink to me only with thine eyes,
    And I will pledge with mine;
Or leave a kiss within the cup,
    And I'll not look for wine.
5 The thirst that from the soul doth rise,
    Doth ask a drink divine;
But might I of Jove's nectar sup,
    I would not change for thine.

I sent thee late a rosy wreath,
10   Not so much honouring thee,
As giving it a hope that there
    It could not withered be.
But thou thereon didst only breathe,
    And sent'st it back to me;
15 Since when it grows, and smells, I swear,
    Not of itself, but thee.

(1616)

On My First Son

Farewell, thou child of my right hand, and joy;
My sin was too much hope of thee, lov'd boy:
Seven years thou wert lent to me, and I thee pay,
Exacted by thy fate, on the just day.
5   O, could I lose all father,[1] now! for why,
Will man lament the state he should envy?
To have so soon scaped world's, and flesh's rage,
And, if no other misery, yet age!
Rest in soft peace, and ask'd, say here doth lie
10   BEN JONSON his best piece of poetry:
For whose sake henceforth all his vows be such,
As what he loves may never like too much.

(1603?)   (1616)

Robert Herrick (1591–1674)

Herrick was a clergyman from London who found himself at the age of 38
posted to the tiny vicarage of Dean Prior, Devonshire. There he performed
the social and religious rituals for a largely illiterate population, all the while
recording his own witty poetic observations on his flock. But his observations
are never condescending. His rural themes are consistently simple, often
playful, but seldom trivial: beauty, love, art, natural splendour, religious devotion. And his speaking voice or persona — somewhat risqué for a bachelor
country parson — no doubt occasioned the final couplet in the first part of
his collection: "To his book's end this last line he'd have placed: / Jocund his
Muse was, but his life was chaste."

Expelled from his vicarage in 1647 as a Royalist sympathizer, Herrick went
back to London where he published his verses in a single volume, *Hesperides*
(1648), comprising over fourteen hundred sacred and secular lyrics. After the
Puritan interregnum, Herrick was reinstated under Charles II and lived out the
end of his long life in Dean Prior.

---

1 i.e., give up all gentle, fatherly thoughts.

To the Virgins, To Make Much of Time

Gather ye rose-buds while ye may,
    Old time is still a flying,
And this same flower that smiles to-day,
    To-morrow will be dying.

5   The glorious lamp of Heaven, the sun,
      The higher he's a getting,
The sooner will his race be run,
    And neerer he's to setting.

That age is best which is the first,
10   When youth and blood are warmer;
But being spent, the worse, and worst
    Times still succeed the former.

Then be not coy, but use your time,
    And while ye may, go marry;
15   For having lost but once your prime,
    You may for ever tarry.

                                          (1648)

Upon Julia's Clothes

Whenas in silks my Julia goes,
Then, then, me thinks, how sweetly flows
That liquefaction of her clothes.

Next, when I cast mine eyes and see
5   That brave vibration, each way free,
O how that glittering taketh me!

                                          (1648)

George Herbert (1593–1633)

George Herbert was born into an ancient and respected Welsh family. His brother Edward was the philosopher-statesman Lord Herbert of Cherbury, and another brother, Sir Henry, was Master of the Revels in England, whose job it was to censor and approve public entertainment during the Stuart reign. George was more private, if (it seems) no less ambitious. A scholar and ecclesiastic, he attained the position of Public Orator at Cambridge University but never received the place at court that he must surely have coveted. Instead, in 1629 he accepted a minor church living at Bemerton near Salisbury, where he lived out the rest of his short life in good works, holy contemplation, and poetic composition.

Herbert's poetry is sharply expressed, richly imaginative, and concrete. Here, a poem's shape expresses meaning, souls have voices, love speaks. Consistently devotional, his verse has an artistic originality and cleverness that mark it as among the most exalted of the "metaphysical" mode.

The Altar

A broken ALTAR, Lord, thy servant rears,
Made of a heart, and cemented with tears:
Whose parts are as thy hand did frame;
No workman's tool hath touch'd the same.
5   A   HEART   alone
Is   such   a   stone,
As   nothing   but
Thy power doth cut.
Wherefore each part
10   Of my hard heart
Meets in this frame,
To praise thy name:
That, if I chance to hold my peace,
These stones to praise thee may not cease.
15   O   let   thy   blessed   SACRIFICE   be   mine,
And   sanctify   this   ALTAR   to   be   thine.

(1633)

Easter Wings

LORD, who createdst man in wealth and store,[1]
Though foolishly he lost the same,
Decaying more and more,
Till he became
5   Most poor:

With Thee
O let me rise
As larks, harmoniously,
And sing this day Thy victories:
10   Then shall the fall further the flight in me.

My tender age in sorrow did begin:
And still with sicknesses and shame
Thou didst so punish sin,
That I became
15   Most thin.

With Thee
Let me combine,
And feel this day Thy victory,
For, if I imp[2] my wing on Thine,
20   Affliction shall advance the flight in me.

(1633)

John Milton (1608–1674)

Milton was born into a middle-class London family. Prodigiously intellectual, he received a thorough education at St. Paul's School, London, and in Christ's College, Cambridge. Later, he travelled on the Continent where he met the aged and broken Galileo. Milton, too, would later survey the heavens, but as a blind poet with a self-proclaimed mandate to "justify the ways of God to men" (*Paradise Lost* I.26).

---

1 abundance. 2 to graft a feather on a falcon's wing or tail, either to repair a deficiency or to improve its power of flight.

Milton was also a public figure who held the position of Latin Secretary to Oliver Cromwell during the Puritan interregnum. His journalism on topical matters such as divorce, church government, and censorship, in addition to diplomatic and political matters, was prolific. He lived out his final days after the restoration of Charles II in humble circumstances. But it was during this time that Milton gained his immortal reputation as a poet. His poetry is celebrated for its profound spiritual and metaphorical sense of inquiry. Considered by many as the highest achievement in English non-dramatic verse, his epic *Paradise Lost* stands as testament to his genius.

Lycidas [1]

In this Monody the Author bewails a learned Friend,[2] unfortunately drowned in his passage from Chester on the Irish Sea, 1637; and, by occasion, foretells the ruin of our corrupted Clergy, then in their height.

Yet once more, O ye laurels, and once more,
Ye myrtles brown, with ivy never sere,[3]
I come to pluck your berries harsh and crude,
And with forced fingers rude
5   Shatter your leaves before the mellowing year.
Bitter constraint and sad occasion dear
Compels me to disturb your season due;
For Lycidas is dead, dead ere his prime,
Young Lycidas, and hath not left his peer.
10   Who would not sing for Lycidas? he knew
Himself to sing, and build the lofty rhyme.
He must not float upon his watery bier
Unwept, and welter to the parching wind,
Without the meed[4] of some melodious tear.
15   Begin, then, Sisters of the sacred well[5]
That from beneath the seat of Jove doth spring;
Begin, and somewhat loudly sweep the string.
Hence with denial vain and coy excuse:
So may some gentle Muse
20   With lucky words favour my destined urn,
And as he passes turn,
And bid fair peace to be my sable shroud!

———→

1 traditional pastoral name for a shepherd. 2 Edward King, a fellow student of Milton's acquaintance at Cambridge. 3 laurels, myrtles, ivy: evergreens associated with poetic inspiration and honour. 4 reward.
5 i.e., the nine sister Muses responsible for the flow of poetic inspiration.

For we were nursed upon the self-same hill,
Fed the same flock, by fountain, shade, and rill;
25   Together both, ere the high lawns appeared
Under the opening eyelids of the morn,
We drove a-field, and both together heard
What time the grey-fly winds her sultry horn,
Battening our flocks with the fresh dews of night,
30 Oft till the star that rose at evening bright
Toward heaven's descent had sloped his westering wheel.
Meanwhile the rural ditties were not mute;
Tempered to the oaten flute,
Rough Satyrs danced, and Fauns with cloven heel
35 From the glad sound would not be absent long;
And old Damœtas[6] loved to hear our song.

    But O! the heavy change, now thou art gone,
Now thou art gone and never must return!
Thee, Shepherd, thee the woods and desert caves,
40 With wild thyme and the gadding vine o'ergrown,
And all their echoes, mourn.
The willows, and the hazel copses green,
Shall now no more be seen
Fanning their joyous leaves to thy soft lays.
45 As killing as the canker to the rose,
Or taint-worm to the weanling herds that graze,
Or frost to flowers, that their gay wardrobe wear,
When first the white-thorn blows;
Such, Lycidas, thy loss to shepherd's ear.
50   Where were ye, Nymphs,[7] when the remorseless deep
Closed o'er the head of your loved Lycidas?
For neither were ye playing on the steep
Where your old bards, the famous Druids,[8] lie,
Nor on the shaggy top of Mona high,
55 Nor yet where Deva spreads her wizard stream.[9]
Ay me! I fondly dream
"Had ye been there," — for what could that have done?
What could the Muse herself that Orpheus[10] bore,
The Muse herself, for her enchanting son,
60 Whom universal nature did lament,

                ——→

6 traditional pastoral name which perhaps refers to a specific Cambridge don known to both Milton and King. 7 female nature spirits. 8 priestly class in ancient Britain. 9 Mona: isle of Anglesey; Deva: the river Dee in Cheshire that empties into the Irish Sea. 10 archetypal poet born of the muse Calliope.

When, by the rout that made the hideous roar,
His gory visage down the stream was sent,
Down the swift Hebrus to the Lesbian shore?[11]
    Alas! what boots[12] it with uncessant care
65 To tend the homely, slighted, shepherd's trade,
And strictly meditate the thankless Muse?
Were it not better done, as others use,
To sport with Amaryllis in the shade,
Or with the tangles of Neæra's hair?[13]
70 Fame is the spur that the clear spirit doth raise
(That last infirmity of noble mind)
To scorn delights and live laborious days;
But the fair guerdon[14] when we hope to find,
And think to burst out into sudden blaze,
75 Comes the blind Fury with the abhorred shears,[15]
And slits the thin-spun life. "But not the praise,"
Phœbus[16] replied, and touched my trembling ears:
    "Fame is no plant that grows on mortal soil,
Nor in the glistering foil
80 Set off to the world, nor in broad rumour lies
But lives and spreads aloft by those pure eyes
And perfect witness of all-judging Jove;
As he pronounces lastly on each deed,
Of so much fame in heaven expect thy meed."
85   O fountain Arethuse, and thou honoured flood,
Smooth-sliding Mincius, crowned with vocal reeds,[17]
That strain I heard was of a higher mood.
But now my oat[18] proceeds,
And listens to the Herald of the Sea,[19]
90 That came in Neptune's plea.
He asked the waves, and asked the felon winds,
What hard mishap hath doomed this gentle swain?
And questioned every gust of rugged wings
That blows from off each beaked promontory.
95 They knew not of his story;
And sage Hippotades[20] their answer brings,
That not a blast was from his dungeon strayed:

                    →

11 decapitated by angered and overzealous celebrants, Orpheus's head floated down the river Hebrus to
the isle of Lesbos. 12 profits. 13 Amaryllis, Neæra: pastoral names for pretty shepherdesses. 14 reward.
15 i.e., Atropos, the Fate who finally cuts off the thread of life. 16 i.e., Phoebus Apollo, god of poetry.
17 Arethuse, a spring; Mincius, a river: Italian locations associated respectively with the great pastoral
poets Theocritus and Virgil. 18 i.e., "oaten flute" (line 33). 19 Triton is Neptune's "herald of the sea."
20 god of winds.

The air was calm, and on the level brine
Sleek Panope[21] with all her sisters played.
100 It was that fatal and perfidious bark,
Built in the eclipse, and rigged with curses dark,
That sunk so low that sacred head of thine.
 Next, Camus,[22] reverend sire, went footing slow,
His mantle hairy, and his bonnet sedge,
105 Inwrought with figures dim, and on the edge
Like to that sanguine flower inscribed with woe.
 "Ah! who hath reft," quoth he, "my dearest pledge?"
Last came, and last did go,
The Pilot of the Galilean Lake;[23]
110 Two massy keys he bore of metals twain
(The golden opes, the iron shuts amain).
He shook his mitred locks, and stern bespake:—
"How well could I have spared for thee, young swain,
Enow of such as, for their bellies' sake,
115 Creep, and intrude, and climb into the fold!
Of other care they little reckoning make
Than how to scramble at the shearers' feast,
And shove away the worthy bidden guest.
Blind mouths! that scarce themselves know how to hold
120 A sheep-hook, or have learnt aught else the least
That to the faithful herdman's art belongs!
What recks it them? What need they? They are sped;
And, when they list, their lean and flashy songs
Grate on their scrannel[24] pipes of wretched straw;
125 The hungry sheep look up, and are not fed,
But, swoln with wind and the rank mist they draw,
Rot inwardly, and foul contagion spread;
Besides what the grim wolf with privy paw
Daily devours apace, and nothing said.
130 But that two-handed engine at the door
Stands ready to smite once, and smite no more."
 Return, Alpheus;[25] the dread voice is past
That shrunk thy streams; return Sicilian Muse,
And call the vales, and bid them hither cast
135 Their bells and flowerets of a thousand hues.
Ye valleys low, where the mild whispers use

⟶

21 sea nymph: one of 50 sisters who were daughters of Nereus. 22 god of the river Cam, upon which
Cambridge University is situated. 23 i.e., St. Peter. 24 thin, meagre. 25 Arcadian river, symbol for gentle
pastoral verse.

Of shades, and wanton winds, and gushing brooks,
On whose fresh lap the swart star[26] sparely looks,
Throw hither all your quaint enamelled eyes,
140   That on the green turf suck the honeyed showers,
And purple all the ground with vernal flowers.
Bring the rathe[27] primrose that forsaken dies,
The tufted crow-toe, and pale jessamine,
The white pink, and the pansy freaked[28] with jet,
145   The glowing violet,
The musk-rose, and the well-attired woodbine,
With cowslips wan that hang the pensive head,
And every flower that sad embroidery wears;
Bid amaranthus[29] all his beauty shed,
150   And daffadillies fill their cups with tears,
To strew the laureate hearse where Lycid lies.
For so, to interpose a little ease,
Let our frail thoughts dally with false surmise,
Ay me! whilst thee the shores and sounding seas
155   Wash far away, where'er thy bones are hurled;
Whether beyond the stormy Hebrides,[30]
Where thou perhaps under the whelming tide
Visit'st the bottom of the monstrous world;
Or whether thou, to our moist vows denied,
160   Sleep'st by the fable of Bellerus[31] old,
Where the great Vision of the guarded mount
Looks toward Namancos and Bayona's hold.[32]
Look homeward, Angel, now, and melt with ruth:
And, O ye dolphins, waft the hapless youth.
165   Weep no more, woeful shepherds, weep no more,
For Lycidas, your sorrow, is not dead,
Sunk though he be beneath the watery floor.
So sinks the day-star[33] in the ocean bed,
And yet anon repairs his drooping head,
170   And tricks his beams, and with new-spangled ore
Flames in the forehead of the morning sky:
So Lycidas sunk low, but mounted high,
Through the dear might of Him that walked the waves,
Where, other groves and other streams along,

—————▶

---

26 Sirius, the Dog Star of late summer. 27 early. 28 freckled. 29 imaginary flower that is always in bloom.
30 islands off the coast of Scotland that mark the northern boundary of the Irish Sea. 31 imaginary giant
supposed to be buried at Land's End, Cornwall. 32 Namancos, Bayona: locations on the coast of Spain,
imagined as visible from St. Michael's Mount, Cornwall. 33 i.e., the sun.

175 With nectar pure his oozy locks he laves,
And hears the unexpressive nuptial song,
In the blest kingdoms meek of joy and love.
There entertain him all the Saints above,
In solemn troops, and sweet societies,
180 That sing, and singing in their glory move,
And wipe the tears for ever from his eyes.
Now, Lycidas, the shepherds weep no more;
Henceforth thou art the Genius [34] of the shore,
In thy large recompense, and shalt be good
185 To all that wander in that perilous flood.

   Thus sang the uncouth swain to the oaks and rills,
While the still morn went out with sandals grey:
He touched the tender stops of various quills,
With eager thought warbling his Doric lay: [35]
190 And now the sun had stretched out all the hills,
And now was dropt into the western bay.
At last he rose, and twitched his mantle blue:
To-morrow to fresh woods, and pastures new.

(1638)

How soon hath Time

How soon hath Time, the subtle thief of youth,
    Stol'n on his wing my three-and-twentieth year!
    My hasting days fly on with full career,
    But my late spring no bud or blossom shew'th.
5 Perhaps my semblance might deceive the truth
    That I to manhood am arrived so near;
    And inward ripeness doth much less appear,
    That some more timely-happy spirits endu'th.[1]
Yet, be it less or more, or soon or slow,
10   It shall be still in strictest measure even
    To that same lot, however mean or high,
Toward which Time leads me, and the will of Heaven,
    All is, if I have grace to use it so,
    As ever in my great Task-Master's eye.

(1631–32)   (1645)

34 i.e., protective local deity.   35 i.e., simple song.
1 endoweth.

When I consider how my light is spent

When I consider how my light is spent
    Ere half my days in this dark world and wide,
    And that one talent which is death to hide
 · Lodged with me useless, though my soul more bent
5 To serve therewith my Maker, and present
    My true account, lest He returning chide,
    "Doth God exact day-labour, light denied?"
  I fondly ask. But Patience, to prevent
That murmur, soon replies, "God doth not need
10 Either man's work or his own gifts. Who best
    Bear his mild yoke, they serve him best. His state
Is kingly: thousands at his bidding speed,
    And post o'er land and ocean without rest;
    They also serve who only stand and wait."

(1652?)   (1673)

On the Late Massacre in Piedmont[1]

Avenge, O Lord, thy slaughtered saints, whose bones
    Lie scattered on the Alpine mountains cold;
    Even them who kept thy truth so pure of old,
    When all our fathers worshiped stocks and stones,
5 Forget not: in thy book record their groans
    Who were thy sheep, and in their ancient fold
    Slain by the bloody Piemontese, that rolled
    Mother with infant down the rocks. Their moans
The vales redoubled to the hills, and they
10 To heaven. Their martyred blood and ashes sow
    O'er all the Italian fields, where still doth sway
The triple Tyrant;[2] that from these may grow
    A hundredfold, who, having learnt thy way,
    Early may fly the Babylonian woe.[3]

(1655)   (1673)

---

1 the Piedmont region of northwestern Italy, bounded by France and Switzerland. On April 24, 1655, Italian troops massacred the Protestant Piedmontese for their dissenting views. 2 i.e., the pope, identified by his triple crown. 3 apocalyptic destruction; see Revelation 18.

Anne Bradstreet (c. 1612–1672)

Born in Northampton, England, Anne Bradstreet, unlike most young women of her day, read widely in classical and English poetry. When she was eighteen years old, she came to Massachusetts with her family and husband. While taking care of the family's frequent moves and raising eight children, she wrote a great deal of poetry and is recognized as one of the first important American poets. Although she wrote many long, complex works on theological subjects, she is best remembered for those poems that sensitively communicate her feelings and observations about her home and family.

To my Dear and loving Husband

If ever two were one, then surely we.
If ever man were lov'd by wife, then thee;
If ever wife was happy in a man,
Compare with me ye women if you can.
5   I prize thy love more than whole Mines of gold,
Or all the riches that the East doth hold.
My love is such that Rivers cannot quench,
Nor ought but love from thee, give recompence.
Thy love is such I can no way repay,
10   The heavens reward thee manifold I pray.
Then while we live, in love lets so persever,[1]
That when we live no more, we may live ever.

(1678)

Upon the burning of our house, July 10, 1666

In silent night when rest I took,
For sorrow neer I did not look,
I waken'd was with thundring nois
And Piteous shreiks of dreadfull voice.
5   That fearfull sound of fire and fire,
Let no man know is my Desire.

1 persevere.

I, starting up, the light did spye,
And to my God my heart did cry
To strengthen me in my Distresse
And not to leave me succourlesse.[1]
Then coming out beheld a space,
The flame consume my dwelling place.

And, when I could no longer look,
I blest his Name that gave and took,
That layd my goods now in the dust:
Yea so it was, and so 'twas just.
It was his own: it was not mine;
Far be it that I should repine.

He might of All justly bereft,
But yet sufficient for us left.
When by the Ruines oft I past,
My sorrowing eyes aside did cast,
And here and there the places spye
Where oft I sate, and long did lye.

Here stood that Trunk, and there that chest;
There lay that store I counted best:
My pleasant things in ashes lye,
And them behold no more shall I.
Under thy roof no guest shall sitt,
Nor at thy Table eat a bitt.

No pleasant tale shall e'er be told,
Nor things recounted done of old.
No Candle e'er shall shine in Thee,
Nor bridegroom's voice e'er heard shall bee.
In silence ever shalt thou lye;
Adeiu, Adeiu; All's vanity.

Then streight I gin my heart to chide,
And did thy wealth on earth abide?
Didst fix thy hope on mouldring dust,
The arm of flesh didst make thy trust?
Raise up thy thoughts above the skye
That dunghill mists away may flie.

1 without help.

Thou hast an house on high erect
Fram'd by that mighty Architect,
45 With glory richly furnished,
Stands permanent tho' this bee fled.
It's purchaséd, and paid for too
By him who hath enough to doe.

A Prise so vast as is unknown,
50 Yet, by his Gift, is made thine own.
Ther's wealth enough, I need no more;
Farewell my Pelf,² farewell my Store.
The world no longer let me Love,
My hope and Treasure lyes Above.

(1678)

Andrew Marvell (1621–1678)

Andrew Marvell was the son of a Yorkshire clergyman. He obtained his B.A. at Trinity College, Cambridge, and proceeded to travel widely on the Continent. Adept at learning, he absorbed French, Italian, Dutch, and Spanish — languages important for an Englishman bent on a career in public service and diplomacy. He was appointed assistant to Cromwell's Latin secretary, John Milton, in 1658, and was later elected M.P. for Hull. It seems Marvell brought some influence to bear upon securing the release and safety of Milton at the Restoration. Throughout his career in public life, Marvell was prudent, honest, and committedly faithful to Puritan politics during and after the time of Cromwell's administration.

But he was also a poet. His verses are smooth and urbane with a metaphysical quality of irony and control that reinvests conventional images with freshness. Although overshadowed in reputation by Milton, Marvell creates lucid images of nature and time with wit and precision. None of his poems was published in his own lifetime.

2 property, earthly possessions.

To His Coy Mistress

Had we but world enough, and time,
This coyness, lady, were no crime.
We would sit down, and think which way
To walk, and pass our long love's day.
Thou by the Indian Ganges' side
Should'st rubies find: I by the tide
Of Humber[1] would complain. I would
Love you ten years before the flood,
And you should, if you please, refuse
Till the conversion of the Jews;[2]
My vegetable[3] love should grow
Vaster than empires, and more slow;
An hundred years should go to praise
Thine eyes, and on thy forehead gaze;
Two hundred to adore each breast,
But thirty thousand to the rest;
An age at least to every part,
And the last age should show your heart.
For, lady, you deserve this state,
Nor would I love at lower rate.
    But at my back I always hear
Time's winged chariot hurrying near,
And yonder all before us lie
Deserts of vast eternity.
Thy beauty shall no more be found,
Nor, in thy marble vault, shall sound
My echoing song: then worms shall try
That long preserved virginity,
And your quaint[4] honour turn to dust,
And into ashes all my lust:
The grave's a fine and private place,
But none, I think, do there embrace.
    Now therefore, while the youthful hue
Sits on thy skin like morning dew,
And while thy willing soul transpires
At every pore with instant fires,

———→

---

1 a river flowing through Hull, Marvell's home town. 2 an event expected at the end of time. 3 following
Aristotle, Renaissance scientists saw humans as possessing three qualities: the rational, the sensitive, and the
vegetative; the vegetative provided only life and growth. 4. fastidious, prim, with a vulgar pun on the female
sexual organ.

Now let us sport us while we may,
And now, like amorous birds of prey
Rather at once our time devour,
40 Than languish in his slow chapped[5] power.
Let us roll all our strength and all
Our sweetness up into one ball,
And tear our pleasures with rough strife,
Thorough[6] the iron gates of life;
45 Thus, though we cannot make our sun
Stand still, yet we will make him run.

(1650–58?)   (1681)

The Garden

How vainly men themselves amaze,[1]
To win the palm, the oak, or bays,[2]
And their incessant labours see
Crowned from some single herb, or tree,
5 Whose short and narrow-verged shade
Does prudently their toils upbraid,
While all the flowers, and trees, do close
To weave the garlands of repose!

   Fair Quiet, have I found thee here,
10 And Innocence, thy sister dear?
Mistaken long, I sought you then
In busy companies of men.
Your sacred plants, if here below,
Only among the plants will grow;
15 Society is all but rude
To this delicious solitude.

   No white nor red was ever seen
So amorous as this lovely green.
Fond lovers, cruel as their flame,
20 Cut in these trees their mistress' name:

                               ⟶

5 i.e., slow-jawed, slow-chewing. 6 through.
1 bewilder, perplex. 2 classical trophies for military, civic, or poetic achievement.

Little, alas! they know or heed,
How far these beauties her exceed!
Fair trees! where'er your barks I wound,
No name shall but your own be found.

25   When we have run our passion's heat,
Love hither makes his best retreat.
The gods, who mortal beauty chase,
Still in a tree did end their race;
Apollo hunted Daphne so,
30   Only that she might laurel grow;
And Pan did after Syrinx speed,
Not as a nymph, but for a reed.[3]

What wond'rous life is this I lead!
Ripe apples drop about my head;
35   The luscious clusters of the vine
Upon my mouth do crush their wine;
The nectarine, and curious peach,
Into my hands themselves do reach;
Stumbling on melons, as I pass,
40   Insnared with flowers, I fall on grass.

Meanwhile the mind, from pleasure less,
Withdraws into its happiness; —
The mind, that ocean where each kind
Does straight its own resemblance find;[4]—
45   Yet it creates, transcending these,
Far other worlds, and other seas,
Annihilating all that's made
To a green thought in a green shade.

Here at the fountain's sliding foot,
50   Or at some fruit-tree's mossy root,
Casting the body's vest aside,
My soul into the boughs does glide:
There, like a bird, it sits and sings,
Then whets and combs its silver wings,

————▶

3 Marvell here alters the motivation of the gods in Ovid's *Metamorphoses*, in which the nymphs Daphne and Syrinx elude pursuit by the lustful gods Apollo and Pan by turning themselves into a laurel tree and a reed, respectively.   4 the sea was supposed to contain creatures corresponding to all those on land.

55 And, till prepared for longer flight,
Waves in its plumes the various light.

Such was that happy garden-state,
While man there walked without a mate:
After a place so pure and sweet,
60 What other help could yet be meet!
But 'twas beyond a mortal's share
To wander solitary there:
Two paradises 'twere in one,
To live in paradise alone.

65 How well the skilful gardener drew
Of flowers, and herbs, this dial[2] new,
Where, from above, the milder sun
Does through a fragrant zodiac run,
And, as it works, the industrious bee
70 Computes its time as well as we!
How could such sweet and wholesome hours
Be reckoned but with herbs and flowers?

(1650–58?)   (1681)

Alexander Pope (1688–1744)

Pope dominated English poetry during the first half of the eighteenth century. His greatest poems were satires, public statements that had the power to change the course of public events. Like most poets of his own and the previous age, Pope wrote primarily in heroic couplets (i.e., closed iambic pentameter couplets); unlike others, however, Pope lived on his earnings as a poet. He had to, since he faced two devastating handicaps. He was born into a Roman Catholic family, which meant that he was forbidden by law from attending university, holding public office, or even living in London. Even worse, when he was a boy he contracted tuberculosis of the spine, which stunted his growth (he was never more than about four-foot-eight in height), made his body crooked, and gave him almost constant pain during his adult life. Fortunately, however, he had kindly and well-to-do parents, who raised him just outside London and saw that he had a thorough education in classical literature. Pope's poetic career falls into three distinct phases. His early poems, up to about 1713, were witty and playful satires; *The Rape of the Lock*, first published in 1712, is the gem of these early poems and still his best-known work. During a middle

2 sundial.

period, from roughly 1713 to 1726, he devoted himself to translating Homer's two great epics, the *Iliad* (completed in 1720) and the *Odyssey* (completed in 1726), and to producing an edition of Shakespeare's plays (1725). These projects gave him financial security, and from 1727 onward Pope again wrote his own poetry, but now of a much more sober nature: satires, including the autobiographical *Epistle to Dr. Arbuthnot* (1735) and *The Dunciad* (1728–43), a mock-epic celebrating the triumph of duncedom in contemporary Britain; moral essays in verse upon such topics as the proper use of riches; and his philosophical poem *An Essay on Man*, published anonymously in 1733–34.

The Rape of the Lock;
An Heroi-Comical Poem[1]

Nolueram, Belinda, tuos violare capillos,
Sed juvat hoc precibus me tribuisse tuis.
　　　　　　　— Martial[2]

TO
Mrs.[3] *ARABELLA FERMOR.*

MADAM,

It will be in vain to deny that I have some Regard for this Piece, since I Dedicate it to You. Yet You may bear me Witness, it was intended only to divert a few young Ladies, who have good Sense and good Humour enough, to laugh not only at their Sex's little unguarded Follies, but at their own. But as it was communicated with the Air of a Secret, it soon found its Way into the World. An imperfect Copy having been offer'd to a Bookseller, You had the Good-Nature for my Sake to consent to the Publication of one more correct: This I was forc'd to before I had executed half my Design, for the *Machinery* was entirely wanting to compleat it.[4]

---

1 Pope's title alludes to the poem's origin. A quarrel had developed between two prominent Roman Catholic families when Robert, Lord Petre, cut off a lock from the head of Arabella Fermor, a celebrated beauty known as "Belle." John Caryll, Pope's friend, urged Pope to write a poem that would restore good feelings. Pope's subtitle alludes to the poem's genre: it is a mock-epic, and the well-known features of epic poems are comically transformed. The combat of heroic warriors becomes the drawing-room war between the sexes; the rape of Helen becomes that of a lock of hair; the arming of the hero for combat becomes the heroine's dressing and beautification for a social engagement, and so on. 2 Pope's epigraph is slightly altered from the Roman satirist Martial: "I did not wish, Belinda, to profane your locks, but it pleases me to have granted this to your prayers." 3 "Mrs." was used for ladies, whether married or single. 4 in its original (1712) form, the poem consisted of two cantos of 334 lines; as Pope explains, he expanded the poem to five cantos in 1714 by adding the "machinery" (the supernatural agents found in epic poems).

The *Machinery*, Madam, is a Term invented by the Criticks, to signify that Part which the Deities, Angels, or Dæmons, are made to act in a Poem: For the ancient Poets are in one respect like many modern Ladies; Let an Action be never so trivial in it self, they always make it appear of the utmost Importance. These Machines I determin'd to raise on a very new and odd Foundation, the *Rosicrucian*[5] Doctrine of Spirits.

I know how disagreeable it is to make use of hard Words before a Lady; but 'tis so much the Concern of a Poet to have his Works understood, and particularly by your Sex, that You must give me leave to explain two or three difficult Terms.

The *Rosicrucians* are a People I must bring You acquainted with. The best Account I know of them is in a French Book call'd *Le Comte de Gabalis*, which both in its Title and Size is so like a *Novel*, that many of the Fair Sex have read it for one by Mistake.[6] According to these Gentlemen, the four Elements[7] are inhabited by Spirits, which they call *Sylphs, Gnomes, Nymphs*, and *Salamanders*. The *Gnomes*, or Dæmons of Earth, delight in Mischief; but the *Sylphs*, whose Habitation is in the Air, are the best-condition'd Creatures imaginable. For they say, any Mortals may enjoy the most intimate Familiarities with these gentle Spirits, upon a Condition very easie to all true *Adepts*, an inviolate Preservation of Chastity.

As to the following Canto's, all the Passages of them are as Fabulous, as the Vision at the Beginning, or the Transformation at the End; (except the Loss of your Hair, which I always mention with Reverence.) The Human Persons are as Fictitious as the Airy ones; and the Character of *Belinda*, as it is now manag'd, resembles You in nothing but in Beauty.

If this Poem had as many Graces as there are in Your Person, or in Your Mind, yet I could never hope it should pass thro' the World half so Uncensured as You have done. But let its Fortune be what it will, mine is happy enough, to have given me this Occasion of assuring You that I am, with the truest Esteem,

Madam,
Your Most Obedient
Humble Servant.
A. POPE

---

5 eccentric occult religion that originated in Germany early in the seventeenth century. 6 in fact, *Le Comte de Gabalis* (1670), written by the Abbé de Montfaucon de Villars, is a facetious and largely fictitious summary of Rosicrucianism that had been published as a novel when translated into English in 1680. 7 air, earth, water, and fire, according to traditional science.

CANTO I.

What dire Offence from am'rous Causes springs,
What mighty Contests rise from trivial Things,[8]
I sing — This Verse to *Caryll*, Muse! is due;
This, ev'n *Belinda* may vouchsafe to view:
5 Slight is the Subject, but not so the Praise,
If She inspire, and He approve my Lays.
       Say what strange Motive, Goddess! cou'd compel
A well-bred *Lord* t'assault a gentle *Belle*?[9]
Oh say what stranger Cause, yet unexplor'd,
10 Cou'd make a gentle *Belle* reject a *Lord*?
In Tasks so bold, can Little Men engage,
And in soft Bosoms dwells such mighty Rage?
       Sol thro' white Curtains shot a tim'rous Ray,
And Op'd those Eyes that must eclipse the Day;
15 Now Lapdogs give themselves the rowzing Shake,
And sleepless Lovers, just at Twelve, awake:
Thrice rung the Bell, the Slipper knock'd the Ground,[10]
And the press'd Watch return'd a silver Sound.[11]
Belinda still her downy Pillow prest,
20 Her Guardian *Sylph* prolong'd the balmy Rest.
'Twas he had summon'd to her silent Bed
The Morning-Dream that hover'd o'er her Head.[12]
A Youth more glitt'ring than a *Birth-night Beau*,[13]
(That ev'n in Slumber caus'd her Cheek to glow)
25 Seem'd to her Ear his winning Lips to lay,
And thus in Whispers said, or seem'd to say.
       Fairest of Mortals, thou distinguish'd Care
Of thousand bright Inhabitants of Air!
If e'er one Vision touch'd thy infant Thought,
30 Of all the Nurse and all the Priest have taught,[14]
Of airy Elves by Moonlight Shadows seen,
The silver Token,[15] and the circled Green,[16]

⟶

8 like Homer, Virgil, and Milton, Pope begins his poem with a concise statement of its theme, immediately followed by an invocation of the Muse. 9 again, like Virgil and Milton, before plunging into the action of his poem Pope asks questions about the causes of all that will follow. 10 ladies summoned their maids by ringing a hand-bell or by knocking on the floor with a high-heeled shoe. 11 England was famous for its "repeater" watches; when the stem was pressed, the watch chimed the most recent hour and quarter-hour. 12 epic heroes often receive warnings about coming events from the gods in dreams; cf. Eve's dream in *Paradise Lost* V.28–93. 13 courtier splendidly dressed for the royal birthday. 14 the traditional promulgators of superstitions. 15 fairies were believed to skim off the cream from jugs of milk left standing overnight, leaving a coin as payment. 16 "fairy rings" (withered circles in grass) were thought to be caused by fairies dancing.

Or Virgins visited by Angel-Pow'rs,[17]
With Golden Crowns and Wreaths of heav'nly Flow'rs,
35 Hear and believe! thy own Importance know,
Nor bound thy narrow Views to Things below.
Some secret Truths from Learned Pride conceal'd,
To Maids alone and Children are reveal'd:
What tho' no Credit doubting Wits may give?
40 The Fair and Innocent shall still believe.
Know then, unnumber'd Spirits round thee fly,
The light *Militia* of the lower Sky;
These, tho' unseen, are ever on the Wing,
Hang o'er the *Box*,[18] and hover round the *Ring*.[19]
45 Think what an Equipage[20] thou hast in Air,
And view with scorn *Two Pages* and a *Chair*.[21]
As now your own, our Beings were of old,
And once inclos'd in Woman's beauteous Mold;
Thence, by a soft Transition, we repair
50 From earthly Vehicles[22] to these of Air.
Think not, when Woman's transient Breath is fled,
That all her Vanities at once are dead:
Succeeding Vanities she still regards,
And tho' she plays no more, o'erlooks the Cards.
55 Her Joy in gilded Chariots, when alive,
And Love of *Ombre*,[23] after Death survive.
For when the Fair in all their Pride expire,
To their first Elements[24] their Souls retire:
The Sprights[25] of fiery Termagants[26] in Flame
60 Mount up, and take a *Salamander*'s[27] Name.
Soft yielding Minds to Water glide away,
And sip with *Nymphs*, their Elemental Tea.
The graver Prude sinks downward to a *Gnome*,
In search of Mischief still on Earth to roam.
65 The light Coquettes in *Sylphs* aloft repair,
And sport and flutter in the Fields of Air.

——→

17 many saints were virgins to whom angels appeared in mystic visions (St. Theresa of Avila, for instance).
18 the theatre box, where the elite among playgoers sat. 19 a fashionable circular drive in Hyde Park.
20 carriage with horses and footmen. 21 sedan-chair, in which passengers were carried. 22 meaning both
carriages and bodies (the body is the vehicle of the soul). 23 popular card game (see note 73). 24 traditionally, the four elements of all matter (earth, air, fire, water) had their counterparts in the four "humours"
or fluids of the human body (black bile, yellow bile, blood, phlegm); one of these humours was supposed to
dominate each person, determining his or her temperament. 25 spirits. 26 shrews. 27 salamanders were
believed able to live in fire.

Know farther yet; Whoever fair and chaste
Rejects Mankind, is by some *Sylph* embrac'd:
For Spirits, freed from mortal Laws, with ease
70   Assume what Sexes and what Shapes they please.[28]
What guards the Purity of melting Maids,
In Courtly Balls, and Midnight Masquerades,[29]
Safe from the treach'rous Friend, the daring Spark,[30]
The Glance by Day, the Whisper in the Dark;
75   When kind Occasion prompts their warm Desires,
When Musick softens, and when Dancing fires?
'Tis but their *Sylph*, the wise Celestials know,
Tho' *Honour* is the Word with Men below.
      Some Nymphs there are, too conscious of their Face,
80   For Life predestin'd to the *Gnomes'* Embrace.
These swell their Prospects and exalt their Pride,
When Offers are disdain'd, and Love deny'd.
Then gay Ideas crowd the vacant Brain;
While Peers and Dukes, and all their sweeping Train,
85   And Garters, Stars, and Coronets[31] appear,
And in soft Sounds, *Your Grace*[32] salutes their Ear.
'Tis these that early taint the Female Soul,
Instruct the Eyes of young *Coquettes* to roll,
Teach Infant-Cheeks a bidden Blush to know,
90   And little Hearts to flutter at a *Beau*.
      Oft when the World imagine Women stray,
The *Sylphs* thro' mystick Mazes guide their Way,
Thro' all the giddy Circle they pursue,
And old Impertinence expel by new.
95   What tender Maid but must a Victim fall
To one Man's Treat,[33] but for another's Ball?
When *Florio* speaks, what Virgin could withstand,
If gentle *Damon* did not squeeze her Hand?
With varying Vanities, from ev'ry Part,
100   They shift the moving Toyshop of their Heart;
Where Wigs with Wigs, with Sword-knots[34] Sword-knots strive,
Beaus banish Beaus, and Coaches Coaches drive.
This erring Mortals Levity may call,
Oh blind to Truth! the *Sylphs* contrive it all.

                              ⟶

28 as Milton had explained in *Paradise Lost* I.423–31. 29 masked balls. 30 fop or beau. 31 garters, stars, and coronets are all insignia of noble rank. 32 the courtesy title used to address a duke or duchess. 33 feast, entertainment. 34 ribbons tied to the hilt of a sword.

105   Of these am I, who thy Protection claim,
         A watchful Sprite, and *Ariel* is my Name.
         Late, as I rang'd the Crystal Wilds of Air,
         In the clear Mirror of thy ruling *Star*
         I saw, alas! some dread Event impend,
110   Ere to the Main this Morning Sun descend.
         But Heav'n reveals not what, or how, or where:
         Warn'd by thy *Sylph*, oh Pious Maid beware!
         This to disclose is all thy Guardian can.
         Beware of all, but most beware of Man!
115   He said; when *Shock*,[35] who thought she slept too long,
         Leapt up, and wak'd his Mistress with his Tongue.
         'Twas then *Belinda*! if Report say true,
         Thy Eyes first open'd on a *Billet-doux*;[36]
         Wounds, *Charms*, and *Ardors*, were no sooner read,
120   But all the Vision vanish'd from thy Head.
         And now, unveil'd, the *Toilet*[37] stands display'd,
         Each Silver Vase in mystic Order laid.
         First, rob'd in White, the Nymph intent adores
         With Head uncover'd, the *Cosmetic* Pow'rs.
125   A heavn'ly Image in the Glass appears,
         To that she bends, to that her Eyes she rears;
         Th'inferior Priestess,[38] at her Altar's side,
         Trembling, begins the sacred Rites of Pride.
         Unnumber'd Treasures ope at once, and here
130   The various Off'rings of the World appear;
         From each she nicely[39] culls with curious[40] Toil,
         And decks the Goddess with the glitt'ring Spoil.
         This Casket *India*'s glowing Gems unlocks,
         And all *Arabia* breathes from yonder Box.
135   The Tortoise here and Elephant unite,
         Transform'd to *Combs*, the speckled and the white.
         Here Files of Pins extend their shining Rows,
         Puffs, Powders, Patches, Bibles, Billet-doux.
         Now awful[41] Beauty puts on all its Arms;
140   The Fair each moment rises in her Charms,
         Repairs her Smiles, awakens ev'ry Grace,
         And calls forth all the Wonders of her Face;

                              ⟶

---

35 Belinda's lap dog. 36 love letter. 37 dressing table. 38 Belinda's maid Betty. 39 fastidiously.
40 careful. 41 awe-inspiring.

Sees by Degrees a purer Blush arise,
And keener Lightnings quicken in her Eyes.
145 The busy *Sylphs* surround their darling Care;
These set the Head, and those divide the Hair,
Some fold the Sleeve, whilst others plait the Gown;
And *Betty's* prais'd for Labours not her own.

CANTO II.

Not with more Glories, in th' Etherial Plain,
The Sun first rises o'er the purpled Main,
Than issuing forth, the Rival of his Beams
Lanch'd on the Bosom of the Silver *Thames*.[42]
5 Fair Nymphs, and well-drest Youths around her shone,
But ev'ry Eye was fix'd on her alone.
On her white Breast a sparkling *Cross* she wore,
Which *Jews* might kiss, and Infidels adore.[43]
Her lively Looks a sprightly Mind disclose,
10 Quick as her Eyes, and as unfix'd as those:
Favours to none, to all she Smiles extends,
Oft she rejects, but never once offends.
Bright as the Sun, her Eyes the Gazers strike,
And, like the Sun, they shine on all alike.
15 Yet graceful Ease, and Sweetness void of Pride,
Might hide her Faults, if *Belles* had Faults to hide:
If to her share some Female Errors fall,
Look on her Face, and you'll forget 'em all.
    This Nymph, to the Destruction of Mankind,
20 Nourish'd two Locks, which graceful hung behind
In equal Curls, and well conspir'd to deck
With shining Ringlets the smooth Iv'ry Neck.
Love in these Labyrinths his Slaves detains,
And mighty Hearts are held in slender Chains.
25 With hairy Sprindges[44] we the Birds betray,
Slight Lines of Hair surprize the Finny Prey,
Fair Tresses Man's Imperial Race insnare,
And Beauty draws us with a single Hair.
    Th' Adventrous *Baron* the bright Locks admir'd,
30 He saw, he wish'd, and to the Prize aspir'd:

———→

42 Belinda travels by boat up the Thames from London to Hampton Court Palace, the royal palace some
ten kilometres upstream. 43 kissing or adoration of the cross marked conversion to Christianity.
44 snares, traps; pronounced *sprin-jez*.

Resolv'd to win, he meditates the way,
By Force to ravish, or by Fraud betray;
For when Success a Lover's Toil attends,
Few ask, if Fraud or Force attain'd his Ends.
35   For this, ere *Phœbus*[45] rose, he had implor'd
Propitious Heav'n, and ev'ry Pow'r ador'd,
But chiefly *Love* — to *Love* an Altar built,
Of twelve vast *French* Romances,[46] neatly gilt.
There lay three Garters, half a Pair of Gloves;
40   And all the Trophies of his former Loves.
With tender *Billet-doux* he lights the Pyre,
And breathes three am'rous Sighs to raise the Fire.
Then prostrate falls, and begs with ardent Eyes
Soon to obtain, and long possess the Prize:
45   The Pow'rs gave Ear, and granted half his Pray'r,
The rest, the Winds dispers'd in empty Air.[47]
       But now secure[48] the painted Vessel glides,
The Sun-beams trembling on the floating Tydes,
While melting Musick steals upon the Sky,
50   And soften'd Sounds along the Waters die.
Smooth flow the Waves, the Zephyrs[49] gently play,
Belinda smil'd, and all the World was gay.
All but the *Sylph* — With careful Thoughts opprest,
Th'impending Woe sate heavy on his Breast.
55   He summons strait his Denizens of Air;
The lucid Squadrons round the Sails repair:[50]
Soft o'er the Shrouds[51] Aerial Whispers breathe,
That seem'd but *Zephyrs* to the Train beneath.
Some to the Sun their Insect-Wings unfold,
60   Waft on the Breeze, or sink in Clouds of Gold.
Transparent Forms, too fine for mortal Sight,
Their fluid Bodies half dissolv'd in Light.
Loose to the Wind their airy Garments flew,
Thin glitt'ring Textures of the filmy Dew;
65   Dipt in the richest Tincture of the Skies,
Where Light disports in ever-mingling Dies,
While ev'ry Beam new transient Colours flings,
Colours that change whene'er they wave their Wings.

⟶

45 the sun. 46 notoriously long and idealized love stories, written by seventeenth-century French aristocrats
and set in ancient Greece and Rome. 47 in epics, the gods frequently grant only half of a character's prayer,
with the other half being abandoned to the winds. 48 free from care. 49 gentle breezes. 50 gather.
51 ropes.

Amid the Circle, on the gilded Mast,
70 Superior by the Head,[52] was *Ariel* plac'd;
His Purple Pinions opening to the Sun,
He rais'd his Azure Wand, and thus begun.
   Ye *Sylphs* and *Sylphids*,[53] to your Chief give Ear,
Fays, Fairies, Genii, Elves, and *Dæmons* hear![54]
75 Ye know the Spheres and various Tasks assign'd,
By Laws Eternal, to th' Aerial Kind.
Some in the Fields of purest *aether*[55] play,
And bask and whiten in the Blaze of Day.
Some guide the Course of wandring Orbs on high,
80 Or roll the Planets thro' the boundless Sky.
Some less refin'd, beneath the Moon's pale Light
Pursue the Stars that shoot athwart the Night,
Or suck the Mists in grosser Air below,
Or dip their Pinions in the painted Bow,
85 Or brew fierce Tempests on the wintry Main,
Or o'er the Glebe[56] distill the kindly Rain.
Others on Earth o'er human Race preside,
Watch all their Ways, and all their Actions guide:
Of these the Chief the Care of Nations own,
90 And guard with Arms Divine the *British Throne*.
   Our humbler Province is to tend the Fair,
Not a less pleasing, tho' less glorious Care.
To save the Powder from too rude a Gale,
Nor let th' imprison'd Essences[57] exhale,
95 To draw fresh Colours from the vernal[58] Flow'rs,
To steal from Rainbows ere they drop in Show'rs
A brighter Wash;[59] to curl their waving Hairs,
Assist their Blushes, and inspire their Airs;
Nay oft, in Dreams, Invention we bestow,
100 To change a *Flounce*, or add a *Furbelo*.[60]
   This Day, black Omens threat the brightest Fair
That e'er deserv'd a watchful Spirit's Care;
Some dire Disaster, or by Force, or Slight,[61]
But what, or where, the Fates have wrapt in Night.

⟶

52 epic heroes are usually taller than their followers. 53 female sylphs. 54 the epic hero normally rallies his
forces for action by a stirring speech that begins by addressing each of the ranks present in turn. 55 the air
above the moon was considered pure and was known as the aether. 56 farmland. 57 perfumes. 58 spring.
59 lotion, rinse. 60 ruffle. 61 sleight, trick.

105 Whether the Nymph shall break *Diana's*[62] Law,
Or some frail *China* Jar receive a Flaw,
Or stain her Honour, or her new Brocade,
Forget her Pray'rs, or miss a Masquerade,
Or lose her Heart, or Necklace, at a Ball;
110 Or whether Heav'n has doom'd that *Shock* must fall.
Haste then ye Spirits! to your Charge repair;
The flutt'ring Fan be *Zephyretta's* Care;
The Drops[63] to thee, *Brillante*, we consign;
And, *Momentilla*, let the Watch be thine;
115 Do thou, *Crispissa*, tend her fav'rite Lock;
Ariel himself shall be the Guard of *Shock*.
        To Fifty chosen *Sylphs*, of special Note,
We trust th'important Charge, the *Petticoat*:
Oft have we known that sev'nfold Fence to fail,
120 Tho' stiff with Hoops, and arm'd with Ribs of Whale.
Form a strong Line about the Silver Bound,
And guard the wide Circumference around.
        Whatever Spirit, careless of his Charge,
His Post neglects, or leaves the Fair at large,
125 Shall feel sharp Vengeance soon o'ertake his Sins,
Be stopt in *Vials*, or transfixt with *Pins*;
Or plung'd in Lakes of bitter *Washes* lie,
Or wedg'd whole Ages in a *Bodkin's*[64] Eye:
Gums and *Pomatums*[65] shall his Flight restrain,
130 While clog'd he beats his silken Wings in vain;
Or Alom-*Stypticks*[66] with contracting Power
Shrink his thin Essence like a rivell'd[67] Flower.
Or as *Ixion*[68] fix'd, the Wretch shall feel
The giddy Motion of the whirling Mill,[69]
135 In Fumes of burning Chocolate shall glow,
And tremble at the Sea that froaths below!
        He spoke; the Spirits from the Sails descend;
Some, Orb in Orb, around the Nymph extend,
Some thrid the mazy Ringlets of her Hair,
140 Some hang upon the Pendants of her Ear;
With beating Hearts the dire Event they wait,
Anxious, and trembling for the Birth of Fate.

62 Diana was the Roman goddess of the hunt and the protector of chastity. 63 diamond earrings. 64 needle's. 65 ointments. 66 astringents to stop bleeding. 67 shrivelled, wrinkled. 68 in Greek mythology, Ixion was a king whose punishment for his attempt to seduce the goddess Hera was to be bound in hell to a perpetually turning wheel. 69 for beating chocolate.

CANTO III.

Close by those Meads for ever crown'd with Flow'rs,
Where *Thames* with Pride surveys his rising Tow'rs,
There stands a Structure of Majestick Frame,[70]
Which from the neighb'ring *Hampton* takes it Name.
5 Here *Britain's* Statesmen oft the Fall foredoom
Of Foreign Tyrants, and of Nymphs at home;
Here Thou, Great *Anna!*[71] whom three Realms obey,
Dost sometimes Counsel take — and sometimes *Tea*.
    Hither the Heroes and the Nymphs resort,
10 To taste awhile the Pleasures of a Court;
In various Talk th' instructive hours they past,
Who gave the *Ball*, or paid the *Visit* last:
One speaks the Glory of the *British Queen*,
And one describes a charming *Indian Screen*;
15 A third interprets Motions, Looks, and Eyes;
At ev'ry Word a Reputation dies.
Snuff, or the *Fan*, supply each Pause of Chat,
With singing, laughing, ogling, and all that.
    Mean while declining from the Noon of Day,
20 The Sun obliquely shoots his burning Ray;
The hungry Judges soon the Sentence sign,
And Wretches hang that Jury-men may Dine;
The Merchant from th'*Exchange*[72] returns in Peace,
And the long Labours of the *Toilette* cease —
25 *Belinda* now, whom Thirst of Fame invites,
Burns to encounter two adventrous Knights,
At *Ombre*[73] singly to decide their Doom;
And swells her Breast with Conquests yet to come.
Strait the three Bands prepare in Arms to join,
30 Each Band the number of the Sacred Nine.
Soon as she spreads her Hand, th' Aerial Guard
Descend, and sit on each important Card:
First *Ariel* perch'd upon a *Matadore*,[74]
Then each, according to the Rank they bore;

→

70 Hampton Court Palace, largest of the royal palaces. 71 Queen Anne, ruler of England, Scotland, and Ireland. 72 the Royal Exchange in London's financial district, where merchants, bankers, and stockbrokers met to do business. 73 Belinda's card game mimics the epic games at which warriors relax and at the same time celebrate their heroic code; see Homer's *Iliad*, Book XXIII. Ombre (pronounced *om-ber*, from the Spanish *hombre*, meaning man) is played by three persons with 40 cards, the eights, nines, and tens being removed from the deck. Nine cards are dealt to each player, and nine tricks are played, with the highest card winning each. One player, called the "Ombre," undertakes to win more tricks than either of the other two and chooses which suit will be trumps. 74 one of the three cards of highest value; they are, in order, the ace of spades, the two of the trump suit (when, as here, a black suit is trumps), the ace of clubs.

35   For *Sylphs*, yet mindful of their ancient Race,
    Are, as when Women, wondrous fond of Place.[75]
        Behold, four *Kings* in Majesty rever'd,
    With hoary Whiskers and a forky Beard;
    And four fair *Queens* whose hands sustain a Flow'r,
40   Th' expressive Emblem of their softer Pow'r;
    Four *Knaves* in Garbs succinct,[76] a trusty Band,
    Caps on their heads, and Halberds[77] in their hand;
    And Particolour'd Troops, a shining Train,
    Draw forth to Combat on the Velvet Plain.
45   The skilful Nymph reviews her Force with Care;
    Let Spades be Trumps! she said, and Trumps they were.[78]
        Now move to War her Sable *Matadores*,
    In Show like Leaders of the swarthy *Moors*.
    Spadillio[79] first, unconquerable Lord!
50   Led off two captive Trumps, and swept the Board.
    As many more *Manillio*[80] forc'd to yield,
    And march'd a Victor from the verdant Field.
    Him *Basto*[81] follow'd, but his Fate more hard
    Gain'd but one Trump and one *Plebeian* Card.
55   With his broad Sabre next, a Chief in Years,
    The hoary Majesty of *Spades* appears;
    Puts forth one manly Leg, to sight reveal'd;
    The rest of his many-colour'd Robe conceal'd.
    The Rebel-*Knave*, who dares his Prince engage,
60   Proves the just Victim of his Royal Rage.
    Ev'n mighty *Pam*[82] that Kings and Queens o'erthrew,
    And mow'd down Armies in the Fights of *Lu*,
    Sad Chance of War! now, destitute of Aid,
    Falls undistinguish'd by the Victor *Spade*!
65   Thus far both Armies to *Belinda* yield;
    Now to the *Baron* Fate inclines the Field.
    His warlike *Amazon*[83] her Host invades,
    Th' Imperial Consort of the Crown of *Spades*.
    The *Club*'s black Tyrant first her Victim dy'd,
70   Spite of his haughty Mien, and barb'rous Pride:
    What boots the Regal Circle on his Head,
    His Giant Limbs in State unwieldy spread?

                    ⟶

---

75 rank. 76 girded up. 77 battle-axes attached to long spears. 78 cf. Genesis 1:3: "And God said, Let there be light; and there was light." 79 the ace of spades. 80 the two of spades. 81 the ace of clubs. 82 the knave of clubs, highest card in the game of Loo, or Lu. 83 the queen of spades.

That long behind he trails his pompous Robe,
And of all Monarchs only grasps the Globe?
75   The *Baron* now his *Diamonds* pours apace;
Th' embroider'd *King* who shows but half his Face,
And his refulgent[84] *Queen*, with Pow'rs combin'd,
Of broken Troops an easie Conquest find.
Clubs, Diamonds, Hearts, in wild Disorder seen,
80 With Throngs promiscuous strow the level Green.
Thus when dispers'd a routed Army runs,
Of *Asia*'s Troops, and *Africk*'s Sable Sons,
With like Confusion different Nations fly,
Of various Habit and of various Dye,
85 The pierc'd Battalions dis-united fall,
In Heaps on Heaps; one Fate o'erwhelms them all.
      The *Knave* of *Diamonds* tries his wily Arts,
And wins (oh shameful Chance!) the *Queen* of *Hearts*.
At this, the Blood the Virgin's Cheek forsook,
90 A livid Paleness spreads o'er all her Look;
She sees, and trembles at th' approaching Ill,
Just in the Jaws of Ruin, and *Codille*.[85]
And now, (as oft in some distemper'd State)
On one nice[86] *Trick* depends the gen'ral Fate.
95 An *Ace* of Hearts steps forth: The *King* unseen
Lurk'd in her Hand, and mourn'd his captive *Queen*.
He springs to Vengeance with an eager pace,
And falls like Thunder on the prostrate *Ace*.[87]
The Nymph exulting fills with Shouts the Sky,
100 The Walls, the Woods, and long Canals reply.
      Oh thoughtless Mortals! ever blind to Fate,
Too soon dejected, and too soon elate!
Sudden these Honours shall be snatch'd away,
And curs'd for ever this Victorious Day.
105   For lo! the Board with Cups and Spoons is crown'd,
The Berries crackle, and the Mill[88] turns round.
On shining Altars of *Japan*[89] they raise
The silver Lamp; the fiery Spirits[90] blaze.

—————→

84 shining, glorious. 85 if the Ombre failed to win more tricks than one of the other players, he or she was said to be given "codille" (from the Spanish for elbow). 86 precise. 87 when a black suit is trumps, the king, queen, and knave of a red suit outrank the ace; Belinda thus wins the trick and the game. 88 the coffee mill, which grinds coffee beans (the "Berries"). 89 japanned or lacquered tables. 90 in spirit-lamps.

From silver Spouts the grateful [91] Liquors glide,
110 While *China*'s Earth [92] receives the smoking Tyde.
At once they gratify their Scent and Taste,
And frequent Cups prolong the rich Repast.
Strait hover round the Fair her Airy Band;
Some, as she sip'd the fuming Liquor fann'd,
115 Some, o'er her Lap their careful Plumes display'd,
Trembling, and conscious of the rich Brocade.
Coffee, (which makes the Politician wise,
And see thro' all things with his half-shut Eyes)
Sent up in Vapours to the *Baron*'s Brain
120 New Stratagems, the radiant Lock to gain.
Ah cease rash Youth! desist ere 'tis too late,
Fear the just Gods, and think of *Scylla*'s [93] Fate!
Chang'd to a Bird, and sent to flit in Air,
She dearly pays for *Nisus*' injur'd Hair!
125 But when to Mischief Mortals bend their Will,
How soon they find fit Instruments of Ill!
Just then, *Clarissa* drew with tempting Grace
A two-edg'd Weapon from her shining Case;
So Ladies in Romance assist their Knight,
130 Present the Spear, and arm him for the Fight.
He takes the Gift with rev'rence, and extends
The little Engine on his Fingers' Ends,
This just behind *Belinda*'s Neck he spread,
As o'er the fragrant Steams she bends her Head:
135 Swift to the Lock a thousand Sprights repair,
A thousand Wings, by turns, blow back the Hair,
And thrice they twitch'd the Diamond in her Ear,
Thrice she look'd back, and thrice the Foe drew near.
Just in that instant, anxious *Ariel* sought
140 The close Recesses of the Virgin's Thought;
As on the Nosegay [94] in her Breast reclin'd,
He watch'd th' Ideas rising in her Mind,
Sudden he view'd, in spite of all her Art,
An Earthly Lover lurking at her Heart.
145 Amaz'd, confus'd, he found his Pow'r expir'd,
Resign'd to Fate, and with a Sigh retir'd.

———▶

91 pleasing. 92 cups of china, i.e., fine earthenware. 93 according to legend, Scylla was the daughter of King Nisus, whose life and kingdom depended on a purple hair growing on his head. Scylla fell in love with King Minos, who was besieging her father's kingdom, and plucked out the hair and took it to Minos; he rejected it with horror, and she was turned into a sea bird. 94 corsage of flowers.

The Peer now spreads the glitt'ring *Forfex*[95] wide,
T'inclose the Lock; now joins it, to divide.
Ev'n then, before the fatal Engine clos'd,
150   A wretched *Sylph* too fondly interpos'd;
Fate urg'd the Sheers, and cut the *Sylph* in twain,
(But Airy Substance soon unites again)[96]
The meeting Points the sacred Hair dissever
From the fair Head, for ever and for ever!
155   Then flash'd the living Lightning from her Eyes,
And Screams of Horror rend th' affrighted Skies.
Not louder Shrieks to pitying Heav'n are cast,
When Husbands or when Lap-dogs breathe their last,
Or when rich *China* Vessels, fal'n from high,
160   In glittring Dust and painted Fragments lie!
      Let Wreaths of Triumph now my Temples twine,
(The Victor cry'd) the glorious Prize is mine!
While Fish in Streams, or Birds delight in Air,
Or in a Coach and Six the *British* Fair,
165   As long as *Atalantis*[97] shall be read,
Or the small Pillow grace a Lady's Bed,
While *Visits* shall be paid on solemn Days,
When numerous Wax-lights in bright Order blaze,
While Nymphs take Treats, or Assignations give,
170   So long my Honour, Name, and Praise shall live!
      What Time wou'd spare, from Steel receives its date,
And Monuments, like Men, submit to Fate!
Steel cou'd the Labour of the Gods[98] destroy,
And strike to Dust th' Imperial Tow'rs of *Troy*;
175   Steel cou'd the Works of mortal Pride confound,
And hew Triumphal Arches to the Ground.
What Wonder then, fair Nymph! thy Hairs shou'd feel
The conqu'ring Force of unresisted Steel?

CANTO IV.

But anxious Cares the pensive Nymph opprest,
And secret Passions labour'd in her Breast.

———→

---

95 the Latin word for scissors. 96 just as Milton's Satan does when pierced by Michael's sword (*Paradise Lost* VI.330–31). 97 *The New Atalantis* (1709), by Delarivier Manley, a popular novel consisting largely of thinly veiled accounts of scandals in high life. 98 Troy was believed to have been built by two gods, Apollo and Poseidon.

Not youthful Kings in Battel seiz'd alive,
Not scornful Virgins who their Charms survive,
5   Not ardent Lovers robb'd of all their Bliss,
Not ancient Ladies when refus'd a Kiss,
Not Tyrants fierce that unrepenting die,
Not *Cynthia* when her *Manteau's* [99] pinn'd awry,
E'er felt such Rage, Resentment and Despair,
10 As Thou, sad Virgin! for thy ravish'd Hair.

For, that sad moment, when the *Sylphs* withdrew,
And *Ariel* weeping from *Belinda* flew,
Umbriel, [100] a dusky melancholy Spright,
As ever sully'd the fair face of Light,
15 Down to the Central Earth, his proper Scene, [101]
Repair'd to search the gloomy Cave of *Spleen.* [102]

Swift on his sooty Pinions flitts the *Gnome,*
And in a Vapour [103] reach'd the dismal Dome.
No cheerful Breeze this sullen Region knows,
20 The dreadful *East* [104] is all the Wind that blows.
Here, in a Grotto, sheltred close from Air,
And screen'd in Shades from Day's detested Glare,
She sighs for ever on her pensive Bed,
Pain at her Side, and *Megrim* [105] at her Head.

25 Two Handmaids wait the Throne: Alike in Place,
But diff'ring far in Figure and in Face.
Here stood *Ill-nature* like an *ancient* Maid,
Her wrinked Form in *Black* and *White* array'd;
With store of Pray'rs, for Mornings, Nights, and Noons,
30 Her Hand is fill'd; her Bosom with Lampoons.

There *Affectation* with a sickly Mien
Shows in her Cheek the Roses of Eighteen,
Practis'd to Lisp, and hang the Head aside,
Faints into Airs, and languishes with Pride;
35 On the rich Quilt sinks with becoming Woe,
Wrapt in a Gown, for Sickness, and for Show. [106]

———→

99 loose robe or cloak. 100 a Gnome (see I.63–64); his name is from the Latin word *umbra,* meaning
shadow. 101 Umbriel's journey to the cave of Spleen imitates the epic hero's visit to the underworld in
search of knowledge unavailable on earth; see Homer's *Odyssey,* Book XI, and Virgil's *Aeneid,* Book VI.
102 the spleen, thought to be the seat of the emotions in traditional medicine, became the name of a fashionable psychosomatic ailment of the rich and leisured; it consisted of ill temper, depression, and hypochon-
dria. 103 suitably, since the disease known as "the spleen" was also called "the vapours" (see lines 39 and 59
of this canto). 104 the east wind was considered unhealthy; it was thought to provoke the spleen.
105 migraine headache. 106 ladies often received formal visits in bed.

The Fair-ones feel such Maladies as these,
When each new Night-Dress gives a new Disease.
    A constant *Vapour* o'er the Palace flies;
40   Strange Phantoms rising as the Mists arise;
Dreadful, as Hermit's Dreams in haunted Shades,
Or bright as Visions of expiring Maids.
Now glaring Fiends, and Snakes on rolling Spires,[107]
Pale Spectres, gaping Tombs and Purple Fires:
45   Now Lakes of liquid Gold, *Elysian*[108] Scenes,
And Crystal Domes, and Angels in Machines.[109]
    Unnumber'd Throngs on ev'ry side are seen
Of Bodies chang'd to various Forms by *Spleen*.[110]
Here living *Teapots* stand, one Arm held out,
50   One bent; the Handle this, and that the Spout:
A Pipkin[111] there like *Homer*'s *Tripod*[112] walks;
Here sighs a Jar, and there a Goose-pye talks;
Men prove with Child, as powr'ful Fancy works,
And Maids turn'd Bottels, call aloud for Corks.
55   Safe past the *Gnome* thro' this fantastick Band,
A Branch of healing *Spleenwort*[113] in his hand.
Then thus addrest the Pow'r — Hail wayward Queen!
Who rule the Sex to Fifty from Fifteen,
Parents of Vapours and of Female Wit,
60   Who give th' *Hysteric* or *Poetic* Fit,
On various Tempers act by various ways,
Make some take Physick,[114] others scribble Plays;
Who cause the Proud their Visits to delay,
And send the Godly in a Pett, to pray.
65   A Nymph there is, that all thy Pow'r disdains,
And thousands more in equal Mirth maintains.
But oh! if e'er thy *Gnome* could spoil a Grace,
Or raise a Pimple on a beauteous Face,
Like Citron-Waters[115] Matrons' Cheeks inflame,
70   Or change Complexions at a losing Game;
If e'er with airy Horns[116] I planted Heads,
Or rumpled Petticoats, or tumbled Beds,

                    ⟶

107 spirals. 108 Elysium in Greek mythology was the abode of the blessed after death, and so a place of ideal happiness. 109 stage machinery. 110 one symptom of the spleen was suffering from hallucinations. 111 small earthen pot. 112 in the *Iliad* (XVIII.439 ff.), Homer tells how Hephaistos made walking tripods (three-legged stools). 113 just as Aeneas carries a golden bough to guarantee safe passage through the under-world in the *Aeneid*, Umbriel carries a branch of spleenwort, a fern believed to protect one against the spleen. 114 medicine. 115 brandy flavoured with lemon peel. 116 the traditional emblem of the cuckold.

Or caus'd Suspicion when no Soul was rude,
Or discompos'd the Head-dress of a Prude,
75 Or e'er to costive [117] Lap-Dog gave Disease,
Which not the Tears of brightest Eyes could ease:
Hear me, and touch *Belinda* with Chagrin;
That single Act gives half the World the Spleen.
    The Goddess with a discontented Air
80 Seems to reject him, tho' she grants his Pray'r.
A wondrous Bag with both her Hands she binds,
Like that where once *Ulysses* held the Winds; [118]
There she collects the Force of Female Lungs,
Sighs, Sobs, and Passions, and the War of Tongues.
85 A Vial next she fills with fainting Fears,
Soft Sorrows, melting Griefs, and flowing Tears.
The *Gnome* rejoicing bears her Gifts away,
Spreads his black Wings, and slowly mounts to Day.
    Sunk in *Thalestris'* [119] Arms the Nymph he found,
90 Her Eyes dejected and her Hair unbound.
Full o'er their Heads the swelling Bag he rent,
And all the Furies issued at the Vent.
Belinda burns with more than mortal Ire,
And fierce *Thalestris* fans the rising Fire.
95 O wretched Maid! she spread her Hands, and cry'd,
(While *Hampton's* Ecchos, wretched Maid! reply'd)
Was it for this you took such constant Care
The *Bodkin*, [120] *Comb*, and *Essence* to prepare;
For this your Locks in Paper-Durance [121] bound,
100 For this with tort'ring Irons wreath'd around?
For this with Fillets [122] strain'd your tender Head,
And bravely bore the double Loads of Lead? [123]
Gods! shall the Ravisher display your Hair,
While the Fops envy, and the Ladies Stare!
105 *Honour* forbid! at whose unrival'd Shrine
Ease, Pleasure, Virtue, All, our Sex resign.
Methinks already I your Tears survey,
Already hear the horrid things they say,

                ⟶

117 constipated. 118 Aeolus, god of winds, gave Odysseus, or Ulysses, a bag containing all the winds that could prevent him from returning home; Odysseus's men opened the bag when he was asleep and the ensuing storms drove them far away (*Odyssey* X.19 ff.). 119 the name of a legendary warrior-queen of the Amazons. 120 needle used as a hairpin. 121 inflated epic diction for curling papers, the papers that were wrapped around curling irons (the "tort'ring" of line 100) to prepare the elaborate coiffures worn by women. 122 headbands. 123 the elaborate upright coiffures of ladies were arranged upon a wooden frame; strips of pliant lead attached to the frame kept the curls in place.

Already see you a degraded Toast,[124]
110 And all your Honour in a Whisper lost!
How shall I, then, your helpless Fame defend?
'Twill then be Infamy to seem your Friend!
And shall this Prize, th' inestimable Prize,
Expos'd thro' Crystal to the gazing Eyes,
115 And heighten'd by the Diamond's circling Rays,
On that Rapacious Hand for ever blaze?
Sooner shall Grass in *Hide*-Park *Circus*[125] grow,
And Wits take Lodgings in the Sound of *Bow*;[126]
Sooner let Earth, Air, Sea, to *Chaos* fall,
120 Men, Monkies, Lap-dogs, Parrots, perish all!
　　She said; then raging to *Sir Plume*[127] repairs,
And bids her *Beau* demand the precious Hairs:
(*Sir Plume*, of *Amber Snuff-box* justly vain,
And the nice Conduct of a *clouded*[128] *Cane*)
125 With earnest Eyes, and round unthinking Face,
He first the Snuff-box open'd, then the Case,
And thus broke out — "My Lord, why, what the Devil?
"Z — ds![129] damn the Lock! 'fore Gad, you must be civil!
"Plague on't! 'tis past a Jest — nay prithee, Pox!
130 "Give her the Hair" — he spoke, and rapp'd his Box.
　　It grieves me much (reply'd the Peer again)
Who speaks so well shou'd ever speak in vain.
But by this Lock, this sacred Lock I swear,
(Which never more shall join its parted Hair,
135 Which never more its Honours[130] shall renew,
Clipt from the lovely Head where late it grew)
That while my Nostrils draw the vital Air,
This Hand, which won it, shall for ever wear.
He spoke, and speaking, in proud Triumph spread
140 The long-contended Honours of her Head.
　　But *Umbriel*, hateful *Gnome*! forbears not so;
He breaks the Vial whence the Sorrows flow.
Then see! the *Nymph* in beauteous Grief appears,
Her Eyes half-languishing, half-drown'd in Tears;

　　　　　　　　　　　　　　　　　→

124 woman whose health is often drunk by men. 125 the Ring (see I.44), where carriages kept the grass
from growing. 126 within the sound of St. Mary-le-Bow in Cheapside, the unfashionable commercial
quarter of London. 127 Sir George Browne, Arabella's kinsman, who chiefly fomented the quarrel.
128 mottled. 129 Zounds, a corrupted version of "God's wounds" — an oath expressing indignation.
130 beauties, graces (as well as honours); see also line 140 of this canto.

145　On her heav'd Bosom hung her drooping Head,
　　　Which, with a Sigh, she rais'd; and thus she said.
　　　　　For ever curs'd be this detested Day,[131]
　　　Which snatch'd my best, my fav'rite Curl away!
　　　Happy! ah ten times happy, had I been,
150　If *Hampton-Court* these Eyes had never seen!
　　　Yet am not I the first mistaken Maid,
　　　By Love of *Courts* to num'rous Ills betray'd.
　　　Oh had I rather un-admir'd remain'd
　　　In some lone Isle, or distant *Northern* Land;
155　Where the gilt *Chariot* never marks the Way,
　　　Where none learn *Ombre*, none e'er taste *Bohea*![132]
　　　There kept my Charms conceal'd from mortal Eye,
　　　Like Roses that in Desarts bloom and die.
　　　What mov'd my Mind with youthful Lords to rome?
160　O had I stay'd, and said my Pray'rs at home!
　　　'Twas this, the Morning *Omens* seem'd to tell;
　　　Thrice from my trembling hand the *Patch-box* fell;
　　　The tott'ring *China* shook without a Wind,
　　　Nay, *Poll* sate mute, and *Shock* was most Unkind!
165　A *Sylph* too warn'd me of the Threats of Fate,
　　　In mystic Visions, now believ'd too late!
　　　See the poor Remnants of these slighted Hairs!
　　　My hands shall rend what ev'n thy Rapine spares:
　　　These, in two sable Ringlets taught to break,
170　Once gave new Beauties to the snowie Neck.
　　　The Sister-Lock now sits uncouth, alone,
　　　And in its Fellow's Fate foresees its own;
　　　Uncurl'd it hangs, the fatal Sheers demands;
　　　And tempts once more thy sacrilegious Hands.
175　Oh hadst thou, Cruel! been content to seize
　　　Hairs less in sight, or any Hairs but these!

CANTO V.

She said: the pitying Audience melt in Tears,
But *Fate* and *Jove* had stopp'd the *Baron's* Ears.
In Vain *Thalestris* with Reproach assails,
For who can move when fair *Belinda* fails?

———→

131 imitation of Achilles's lament for Patroclus in the *Iliad* (XVIII.107 ff.).　132 costly kind of tea.

Not half so fixt the *Trojan* cou'd remain,
While *Anna* begg'd and *Dido* rag'd in vain.[133]
Then grave *Clarissa* graceful wav'd her Fan;
Silence ensu'd, and thus the Nymph began.[134]
    Say, why are Beauties prais'd and honour'd most,
The wise Man's Passion, and the vain Man's Toast?
Why deck'd with all that Land and Sea afford,
Why Angels call'd, and Angel-like ador'd?
Why round our Coaches crowd the white-glov'd Beaus,
Why bows the Side-box[135] from its inmost Rows?
How vain are all these Glories, all our Pains,
Unless good Sense preserve what Beauty gains:
That Men may say, when we the Front-box grace,
Behold the first in Virtue, as in Face!
Oh! if to dance all Night, and dress all Day,
Charm'd the Small-pox,[136] or chas'd old Age away;
Who would not scorn what Huswife's Cares produce,
Or who would learn one earthly Thing of Use?
To patch, nay ogle, might become a Saint,
Nor could it sure be such a Sin to paint.
But since, alas! frail Beauty must decay,
Curl'd or uncurl'd, since Locks will turn to grey,
Since painted, or not painted, all shall fade,
And she who scorns a Man, must die a Maid;
What then remains, but well our Pow'r to use,
And keep good Humour still whate'er we lose?
And trust me, Dear! good Humour can prevail,
When Airs, and Flights, and Screams, and Scolding fail.
Beauties in vain their pretty Eyes may roll;
Charms strike the Sight, but Merit wins the Soul.
    So spoke the Dame, but no Applause ensu'd;
Belinda frown'd, *Thalestris* call'd her Prude.
To Arms, to Arms! the fierce Virago[137] cries,
And swift as Lightning to the Combate flies.

→

133 Aeneas, burdened with his divine mission of founding a new Troy, left Carthage and Queen Dido, despite her furious reproaches and the prayers of her sister Anna (*Aeneid* IV.296–449). 134 when Pope published his collected early poetry in 1717, he added Clarissa's speech to the five-canto *Rape* of 1714 in order, as he explained, "to open the moral of the poem, in a parody of the speech of Sarpedon to Glaucus in Homer"; Sarpedon's speech is an appeal to his comrade to earn in battle the honour they both enjoy as leaders (*Iliad* XII.371–96). 135 gentlemen preferred the side boxes at the theatre, ladies the front boxes facing the stage (see line 17 of this canto). 136 before vaccination, smallpox was common and deadly; the Lord Petre of this poem died of smallpox in 1713. 137 man-like woman, female warrior.

All side in Parties, and begin th' Attack;
40 Fans clap, Silks russle, and tough Whalebones crack;
Heroes' and Heroins' Shouts confus'dly rise,
And base, and treble Voices strike the Skies.
No common Weapons in their Hands are found,
Like Gods they fight, nor dread a mortal Wound.
45   So when bold *Homer* makes the Gods engage,[138]
And heavn'ly Breasts with human Passions rage;
'Gainst *Pallas*,[139] Mars; *Latona*,[140] Hermes arms;
And all *Olympus* rings with loud Alarms.
Jove's Thunder roars, Heav'n trembles all around;
50 Blue *Neptune* storms, the bellowing Deeps resound;
Earth shakes her nodding Tow'rs, the Ground gives way;
And the pale Ghosts start at the Flash of Day!
        Triumphant *Umbriel* on a Sconce's [141] Height
Clapt his glad Wings, and sate to view the Fight:
55 Propt on their Bodkin Spears, the Sprights survey
The growing Combat, or assist the Fray.
        While thro' the Press enrag'd *Thalestris* flies,
And scatters Deaths around from both her Eyes,
A *Beau* and *Witling* [142] perish'd in the Throng,
60 One dy'd in *Metaphor*, and one in *Song*.
O cruel Nymph! a living Death I bear,
Cry'd *Dapperwit*,[143] and sunk beside his Chair.
A mournful Glance Sir *Fopling* upwards cast,
Those Eyes are made so killing — was his last:
65 Thus on *Meander*'s [144] flow'ry Margin lies
Th' expiring Swan, and as he sings he dies.[145]
        When bold Sir *Plume* had drawn *Clarissa* down,
Chloe stept in, and kill'd him with a Frown;
She smil'd to see the doughty Hero slain,
70 But at her Smile, the Beau reviv'd again.
        Now *Jove* suspends his golden Scales in Air,[146]
Weighs the Men's Wits against the Lady's Hair;
The doubtful Beam long nods from side to side;
At length the Wits mount up, the Hairs subside.

⎯⎯→

138 see the *Iliad* XX.91 ff. 139 Pallas Athena, the Greek goddess of war (also the goddess of wisdom).
140 the mother of the Greek deities Apollo and Artemis. 141 candlestick attached to the wall. 142 tiny
wit. 143 like "Sir Fopling" in the next line, a type-name for a fop and would-be wit in Restoration comic
plays. 144 celebrated winding river in Asia Minor. 145 swans were believed to sing beautifully only as they
died. 146 epic convention when a decisive battle is about to take place; see the *Iliad* VIII.87 ff. and the
Aeneid XII.725 ff.

75   See fierce *Belinda* on the *Baron* flies,
With more than usual Lightning in her Eyes;
Nor fear'd the Chief th'unequal Fight to try,
Who sought no more than on his Foe to die.
But this bold Lord, with manly Strength indu'd,
80 She with one Finger and a Thumb subdu'd:
Just where the Breath of Life his Nostrils drew,
A Charge of *Snuff* the wily Virgin threw;
The *Gnomes* direct, to ev'ry Atome just,
The pungent Grains of titillating Dust.
85 Sudden, with starting Tears each Eye o'erflows,
And the high Dome re-ecchoes to his Nose.
     Now meet thy Fate, incens'd *Belinda* cry'd,
And drew a deadly *Bodkin* from her Side.
(The same,[147] his ancient Personage to deck,
90 Her great great Grandsire wore about his Neck
In three *Seal-Rings*; which after, melted down,
Form'd a vast *Buckle* for his Widow's Gown:
Her infant Grandame's *Whistle* next it grew,
The *Bells* she gingled,[148] and the *Whistle* blew;
95 Then in a *Bodkin* grac'd her Mother's Hairs,
Which long she wore, and now *Belinda* wears.)
     Boast not my Fall (he cry'd) insulting Foe!
Thou by some other shalt be laid as low.
Nor think, to die dejects my lofty Mind;
100 All that I dread, is leaving you behind!
Rather than so, ah let me still survive,
And burn in *Cupid*'s Flames, — but burn alive.
     Restore the Lock! she cries; and all around
Restore the Lock! the vaulted Roofs rebound.
105 Not fierce *Othello* in so loud a Strain
Roar'd for the Handkerchief that caus'd his Pain.
But see how oft Ambitious Aims are cross'd,
And Chiefs contend 'till all the Prize is lost!
The Lock, obtain'd with Guilt, and kept with Pain,
110 In ev'ry place is sought, but sought in vain:
With such a Prize no Mortal must be blest,
So Heav'n decrees! with Heav'n who can contest?

                                  —→

---

147 what follows is a parody of epic descriptions of a hero's armour and its descent through the generations in his family. 148 jingled.

Some thought it mounted to the Lunar Sphere,
Since all things lost on Earth, are treasur'd there.[149]
115 There Heroes' Wits are kept in pondrous Vases,
And Beaus' in *Snuff-boxes* and *Tweezer-Cases*.
There broken Vows, and Death-bed Alms are found,
And Lovers' Hearts with Ends of Riband[150] bound;
The Courtier's Promises, and Sick Man's Pray'rs,
120 The Smiles of Harlots, and the Tears of Heirs,
Cages for Gnats, and Chains to Yoak a Flea;
Dry'd Butterflies, and Tomes of Casuistry.[151]
But trust the Muse — she saw it upward rise,
Tho' mark'd by none but quick Poetic Eyes:
125 (So *Rome*'s great Founder to the Heav'ns withdrew,
To *Proculus* alone confess'd in view.)[152]
A sudden Star, it shot thro' liquid[153] Air,
And drew behind a radiant *Trail of Hair*.
Not *Berenice*'s[154] Locks first rose so bright,
130 The Heav'ns bespangling with dishevel'd Light.
The *Sylphs* behold it kindling as it flies,
And pleas'd pursue its Progress thro' the Skies.
This the *Beau-monde*[155] shall from the *Mall*[156] survey,
And hail with Musick its propitious Ray.
135 This, the blest Lover shall for *Venus* take,
And send up Vows from *Rosamonda*'s Lake.[157]
This *Partridge*[158] soon shall view in cloudless Skies,
When next he looks thro' *Galileo*'s Eyes;[159]
And hence th' Egregious Wizard shall foredoom
140 The Fate of *Louis*, and the Fall of *Rome*.
Then cease, bright Nymph! to mourn thy ravish'd Hair
Which adds new Glory to the shining Sphere!

⟶

149 in a striking episode in *Orlando Furioso* (1532), the chivalric epic by the Italian poet Ariosto, the hero's lost wits are found on the moon, where all things that are lost on earth may be found. 150 ribbon. 151 casuistry, the branch of theology that studies the application of general ethical rules to particular cases, had become a synonym for hair-splitting rationalization. 152 Romulus, the founder and first king of Rome, disappeared from earth in the midst of a storm; the senator Proculus affirmed that Romulus had ascended to the heavens. 153 clear, transparent. 154 Berenice, wife of King Ptolemy III of ancient Egypt, vowed to sacrifice her hair to the gods if her husband returned safe from battle; upon his return, she placed her hair in the temple of Aphrodite, but the next day it had disappeared and was believed to have become a constellation. 155 fashionable world. 156 Pall Mall, a walk laid out by Charles II in St. James's Park. 157 pond in St. James's Park considered to be the haunt of unhappy lovers; it was named after Rosamund Clifford (died 1177), known as "Fair Rosamond," mistress of Henry II, who was, according to legend, made to drink poison by his queen. 158 quack astrologer of the time, who predicted every year that the pope and King Louis XIV of France would fall from power that year (see line 140). 159 i.e., telescope; Galileo constructed the first telescope in 1609.

Not all the Tresses that fair Head can boast
Shall draw such Envy as the Lock you lost.
145   For, after all the Murders of your Eye,
When, after Millions slain, your self shall die;
When those fair Suns shall sett, as sett they must,
And all those Tresses shall be laid in Dust;
This Lock, the Muse shall consecrate to Fame,
150   And mid'st the Stars inscribe *Belinda*'s Name!

(1714)

Thomas Gray (1716–1771)

Thomas Gray, a shy scholar, wrote very few poems—but among them is one of the best-known and most-loved poems in the language, his *Elegy Written in a Country Church-Yard* (or, as it is usually called, Gray's *Elegy*). Gray spent his entire adult life as a scholar at Cambridge University; he was known as one of the most learned men in Europe, and helped create scholarly interest in Welsh, Old Norse, and medieval English poetry. Gray published his *Elegy* in 1751. His shyness led him to turn down the position of Poet Laureate when he was offered it in 1757; although named Professor of Modern History at Cambridge, he was unable to deliver a single lecture. Nevertheless, as soon as his *Elegy* was published, he became recognized as the greatest lyric poet of the age. His contemporary Samuel Johnson memorably sums up the poem's appeal: "The *Church-Yard* abounds with images which find a mirror in every mind, and with sentiments to which every bosom returns an echo."

Elegy Written in a Country Church-Yard

The Curfew tolls the knell of parting day,
The lowing herd wind slowly o'er the lea,[1]
The plowman homeward plods his weary way,
And leaves the world to darkness and to me.

5   Now fades the glimmering landscape on the sight,
And all the air a solemn stillness holds,
Save where the beetle wheels his droning flight,
And drowsy tinklings lull the distant folds;

---

1 open field, grassland.

Save that from yonder ivy-mantled tow'r
10 The mopeing owl does to the moon complain
Of such, as wand'ring near her secret bow'r,
Molest her ancient solitary reign.

Beneath those rugged elms, that yew-tree's shade,
Where heaves the turf in many a mould'ring heap,
15 Each in his narrow cell for ever laid,
The rude² Forefathers of the hamlet sleep.

The breezy call of incense-breathing Morn,
The swallow twitt'ring from the straw-built shed,
The cock's shrill clarion, or the echoing horn,
20 No more shall rouse them from their lowly bed.

For them no more the blazing hearth shall burn,
Or busy houswife ply her evening care:
No children run to lisp their sire's return,
Or climb his knees the envied kiss to share.

25 Oft did the harvest to their sickle yield,
Their furrow oft the stubborn glebe³ has broke;
How jocund did they drive their team afield!
How bow'd the woods beneath their sturdy stroke!

Let not Ambition mock their useful toil,
30 Their homely joys, and destiny obscure;
Nor Grandeur hear with a disdainful smile,
The short and simple annals of the poor.

The boast of heraldry, the pomp of pow'r,
And all that beauty, all that wealth e'er gave,
35 Awaits alike th' inevitable hour.
The paths of glory lead but to the grave.

Nor you, ye Proud, impute to These the fault,
If Mem'ry o'er their Tomb no Trophies raise,
Where thro' the long-drawn isle⁴ and fretted vault
40 The pealing anthem swells the note of praise.

2 uneducated. 3 soil. 4 aisle.

Can storied urn or animated bust
Back to its mansion call the fleeting breath?
Can Honour's voice provoke the silent dust,
Or Flatt'ry sooth the dull cold ear of Death?

45 Perhaps in this neglected spot is laid
Some heart once pregnant with celestial fire,
Hands, that the rod of empire might have sway'd,
Or wak'd to extasy the living lyre.

But Knowledge to their eyes her ample page
50 Rich with the spoils of time did ne'er unroll;
Chill Penury repress'd their noble rage,[5]
And froze the genial[6] current of the soul.

Full many a gem of purest ray serene,
The dark unfathom'd caves of ocean bear:
55 Full many a flower is born to blush unseen,
And waste its sweetness on the desert air.

Some village-Hampden,[7] that with dauntless breast
The little Tyrant of his fields withstood;
Some mute inglorious Milton here may rest,
60 Some Cromwell guiltless of his country's blood.

Th' applause of list'ning senates to command,
The threats of pain and ruin to despise,
To scatter plenty o'er a smiling land,
And read their hist'ry in a nation's eyes

65 Their lot forbad: nor circumscrib'd alone
Their growing virtues, but their crimes confin'd;
Forbad to wade through slaughter to a throne,
And shut the gates of mercy on mankind,

The struggling pangs of conscious truth to hide,
70 To quench the blushes of ingenuous shame,
Or heap the shrine of Luxury and Pride
With incense kindled at the Muse's flame.

---

5 rapture, ardour. 6 creative. 7 John Hampden (1594–1643), member of Parliament who defended the
rights of the people against Charles I and became a leader of the Puritan cause in the Civil War.

Far from the madding[8] crowd's ignoble strife,
Their sober wishes never learn'd to stray;
75   Along the cool sequester'd vale of life
They kept the noiseless tenor of their way.

Yet ev'n these bones from insult to protect
Some frail memorial still erected nigh,
With uncouth rhimes and shapeless sculpture deck'd,
80   Implores the passing tribute of a sigh.

Their name, their years, spelt by th' unletter'd muse,
The place of fame and elegy supply:
And many a holy text around she strews,
That teach the rustic moralist to die.

85   For who to dumb Forgetfulness a prey,
This pleasing anxious being e'er resign'd,
Left the warm precincts of the chearful day,
Nor cast one longing ling'ring look behind?

On some fond breast the parting soul relies,
90   Some pious drops the closing eye requires;
Ev'n from the tomb the voice of Nature cries,
Ev'n in our Ashes live their wonted Fires.

For thee, who mindful of th' unhonour'd Dead
Dost in these lines their artless tale relate;
95   If chance,[9] by lonely contemplation led,
Some kindred Spirit shall inquire thy fate,

Haply some hoary-headed Swain[10] may say,
"Oft have we seen him at the peep of dawn
Brushing with hasty steps the dews away
100   To meet the sun upon the upland lawn.

"There at the foot of yonder nodding beech
That wreathes its old fantastic roots so high,
His listless length at noontide wou'd he stretch,
And pore upon the brook that babbles by.

8 frenzied, maddened. 9 by chance. 10 shepherd.

105   "Hard by yon wood, now smiling as in scorn,
      Mutt'ring his wayward fancies he wou'd rove,
      Now drooping, woeful wan, like one forlorn,
      Or craz'd with care, or cross'd in hopeless love.

      "One morn I miss'd him on the custom'd hill,
110   Along the heath and near his fav'rite tree;
      Another came; nor yet beside the rill,
      Nor up the lawn, nor at the wood was he;

      "The next with dirges due in sad array
      Slow thro' the church-way path we saw him borne.
115   Approach and read (for thou can'st read) the lay,
      Grav'd on the stone beneath yon aged thorn."

The EPITAPH.

HERE rests his head upon the lap of Earth
A Youth to Fortune and to Fame unknown,
Fair Science [11] *frown'd not on his humble birth,*
120   *And Melancholy mark'd him for her own.*

Large was his bounty, and his soul sincere,
Heav'n did a recompence as largely send:
He gave to Mis'ry all he had, a tear,
He gain'd from Heav'n ('twas all he wish'd) a friend.

125   *No farther seek his merits to disclose,*
      Or draw his frailties from their dread abode,
      (There they alike in trembling hope repose)
      The bosom of his Father and his God.

                                              (1751)

William Blake (1757–1827)

Born in London, William Blake studied art at the Royal Academy as a boy before serving an apprenticeship to an engraver. His first collection of poems, *Poetic Sketches* (1783), indicated his departure from the neoclassical conventions that had dominated the eighteenth century. However, *Songs of Innocence and Experience* (1794), illustrated by his own hand-painted engravings, marked the

11 learning.

first flowering of his genius. Lyrics revealing the influence of Elizabethan and seventeenth-century English poetry, they present "two contrasting states of the human mind." Many are companion poems, using the lives and views of children to symbolize innocence and experience. During the 1790s, Blake was influenced by radical political, religious, and philosophical currents prevalent in England and wrote in his poems about tyranny and oppression, the power of "God & his Priest & King," as they affected the lives of common people, especially children. He celebrated the visionary powers of the imagination in a series of "Prophetic Books" written after the publication of the *Songs*. Complex and often obscure, they develop a philosophy in which human life is seen as progressing from the initial innocence of childhood, to the complexity and pain of experience, and finally to a higher, more fulfilled innocence. Relatively ignored during his lifetime and in the 50 years after his death, Blake's works have been studied seriously during the twentieth century, and he is now recognized as one of the greatest Romantic poets.

The Lamb

    Little Lamb who made thee
    Dost thou know who made thee
Gave thee life & bid thee feed,
By the stream & o'er the mead;[1]
Gave thee clothing of delight,
Softest clothing wooly bright;
Gave thee such a tender voice,
Making all the vales rejoice!
    Little Lamb who made thee
    Dost thou know who made thee

    Little Lamb I'll tell thee,
    Little Lamb I'll tell thee!
He is called by thy name,
For he calls himself a Lamb:
He is meek & he is mild,
He became a little child:
I a child & thou a lamb,
We are called by his name.
    Little Lamb God bless thee.
    Little Lamb God bless thee.

(1789)

---

1 meadow.

The Little Black Boy

My mother bore me in the southern wild,
And I am black, but O! my soul is white;
White as an angel is the English child:
But I am black as if bereav'd[1] of light.

5   My mother taught me underneath a tree
And sitting down before the heat of day,
She took me on her lap and kissed me,
And pointing to the east began to say.

Look on the rising sun: there God does live
10   And gives his light, and gives his heat away.
And flowers and trees and beasts and men receive
Comfort in morning joy in the noon day.

And we are put on earth a little space,
That we may learn to bear the beams of love,
15   And these black bodies and this sun-burnt face
Is but a cloud, and like a shady grove.

For when our souls have learn'd the heat to bear
The cloud will vanish we shall hear his voice.
Saying: come out from the grove my love & care,
20   And round my golden tent like lambs rejoice.

Thus did my mother say and kissed me,
And thus I say to little English boy.
When I from black and he from white cloud free,
And round the tent of God like lambs we joy:

25   I'll shade him from the heat till he can bear,
To lean in joy upon our fathers knee.
And then I'll stand and stroke his silver hair,
And be like him and he will then love me.

(1789)

1 deprived.

The Chimney Sweeper I

When my mother died I was very young,
And my father sold me while yet my tongue,
Could scarcely cry weep weep weep weep.
So your chimneys I sweep & in soot I sleep.

5   There's little Tom Dacre, who cried when his head
That curl'd like a lambs back, was shav'd, so I said.
Hush Tom never mind it, for when your head's bare,
You know that the soot cannot spoil your white hair.

And so he was quiet, & that very night,
10   As Tom was a sleeping he had such a sight,
That thousands of sweepers, Dick, Joe, Ned & Jack,
Were all of them lock'd up in coffins of black,

And by came an Angel who had a bright key,
And he open'd the coffins & set them all free.
15   Then down a green plain leaping laughing they run
And wash in a river and shine in the Sun.

Then naked & white, all their bags left behind,
They rise upon clouds, and sport in the wind.
And the Angel told Tom if he'd be a good boy,
20   He'd have God for his father & never want joy.

And so Tom awoke and we rose in the dark
And got with our bags & our brushes to work.
Tho' the morning was cold, Tom was happy & warm,
So if all do their duty, they need not fear harm.

(1789)

Holy Thursday [1]

Twas on a Holy Thursday their innocent faces clean
The children walking two & two in red & blue & green
Grey headed beadles walkd before with wands as white as snow
Till into the high dome of Pauls [2] they like Thames waters flow

---

1 in the Anglican tradition, the Thursday 40 days after Easter, when Christ is said to have ascended to heaven.
2 St. Paul's Cathedral, London.

5 O what a multitude they seemd these flowers of London town
   Seated in companies they sit with radiance all their own
   The hum of multitudes was there but multitudes of lambs
   Thousands of little boys & girls raising their innocent hands

   Now like a mighty wind they raise to heaven the voice of song
10 Or like harmonious thunderings the seats of heaven among
   Beneath them sit the aged men wise guardians of the poor
   Then cherish pity, lest you drive an angel from your door

                                                    (1789)

Nurse's[1] Song

   When the voices of children are heard on the green
   And laughing is heard on the hill,
   My heart is at rest within my breast
   And every thing else is still

5 Then come home my children, the sun is gone down
   And the dews of night arise
   Come come leave off play, and let us away
   Till the morning appears in the skies

   No no let us play, for it is yet day
10 And we cannot go to sleep
   Besides in the sky, the little birds fly
   And the hills are all covered with sheep

   Well well go & play till the light fades away
   And then go home to bed
15 The little ones leaped & shouted & laugh'd
   And all the hills ecchoed

   (c. 1784)   (1789)

1 woman hired to care for a young child.

The Tyger

Tyger Tyger, burning bright,
In the forests of the night;
What immortal hand or eye,
Could frame thy fearful symmetry?

5   In what distant deeps or skies!
Burnt the fire of thine eyes?
On what wings dare he aspire?
What the hand, dare seize the fire?

And what shoulder, & what art,
10   Could twist the sinews of thy heart?
And when thy heart began to beat,
What dread hand? & what dread feet?

What the hammer? what the chain?
In what furnace was thy brain?
15   What the anvil? what dread grasp,
Dare its deadly terrors clasp?

When the stars threw down their spears
And water'd heaven with their tears;
Did he smile his work to see?
20   Did he who made the Lamb make thee?

Tyger Tyger, burning bright,
In the forests of the night;
What immortal hand or eye,
Dare frame thy fearful symmetry?

(1790–92)   (1794)

The Chimney Sweeper

A little black thing among the snow:
Crying weep, weep, in notes of woe!
Where are thy father & mother? say?
They are both gone up to the church to pray.

5   Because I was happy upon the heath,[1]
    And smil'd among the winters snow:
    They clothed me in the clothes of death,
    And taught me to sing the notes of woe.

    And because I am happy, & dance & sing,
10   They think they have done me no injury:
    And are gone to praise God & his Priest & King
    Who make up a heaven of our misery.

(1790–92)   (1794)

Holy Thursday

    Is this a holy thing to see,
    In a rich and fruitful land,
    Babes reducd to misery,
    Fed with cold and usurous hand?

5   Is that trembling cry a song?
    Can it be a song of joy?
    And so many children poor?
    It is a land of poverty!

    And their sun does never shine.
10 And their fields are bleak & bare.
    And their ways are fill'd with thorns.
    It is eternal winter there.

    For where-e'er the sun does shine,
    And where-e'er the rain does fall:
15 Babe can never hunger there,
    Nor poverty the mind appall.

(1794)

---

1 open countryside containing scrubby vegetation.

Nurse's Song

When the voices of children are heard on the green
And whisprings are in the dale:
The days of my youth rise fresh in my mind,
My face turns green and pale.

5   Then come home my children, the sun is gone down
And the dews of night arise
Your spring & your day are wasted in play
And your winter and night in disguise.

(1794)

The Sick Rose

O Rose thou art sick.
The invisible worm,
That flies in the night
In the howling storm:

5   Has found out thy bed
Of crimson joy:
And his dark secret love
Does thy life destroy.

(1794)

London

I wander thro' each charter'd[1] street,
Near where the charter'd Thames does flow.
And mark in every face I meet
Marks of weakness, marks of woe.

5   In every cry of every Man,
In every Infants cry of fear,
In every voice; in every ban,
The mind-forg'd manacles I hear

1 protected as private property.

How the Chimney-sweepers cry
10   Every blackning Church appalls,
And the hapless Soldiers sigh
Runs in blood down Palace walls

But most thro' midnight streets I hear
How the youthful Harlots curse
15   Blasts the new-born Infants tear
And blights with plagues the Marriage hearse.

(1794)

William Wordsworth   (1770–1850)

Born in Cockermouth, near the English Lake District, William Wordsworth attended Cambridge University and then travelled widely in Europe, spending a year in France during the Revolution. There he fathered an illegitimate child, Caroline, referred to indirectly in his sonnet "It is a beauteous evening." In 1798, with his friend Samuel Taylor Coleridge, he published *Lyrical Ballads*, a collection in which, as Coleridge stated, Wordsworth gave "the charm of novelty to things of everyday." In the Preface to the 1800 edition, written in response to criticism of the first edition, Wordsworth explained the theory underlying his poems. Reacting in part against the dominant poetic tastes and conventions of the eighteenth century, he stated that the poems were created from "emotion recollected in tranquillity," an idea illustrated in "Lines Composed a Few Miles above Tintern Abbey," and later in "I wandered lonely as a cloud." As seen in "Michael," he chose as his subjects "incidents and situations of common life," presented in "language really used by men." In 1802, influenced in part by his reading of John Milton, who is addressed in "London, 1802," Wordsworth wrote a number of sonnets considered by many critics to be the finest to have appeared since the seventeenth century. Wordsworth's reputation increased steadily during his lifetime, and, in 1843, he was appointed Poet Laureate. He is now recognized not only as one of the greatest of the Romantics and a major English poet, but as one who, in his portrayal of common people and nature, radically altered the course of English poetry in the nineteenth century.

Lines

COMPOSED A FEW MILES ABOVE TINTERN ABBEY, [1] ON REVISITING THE BANKS
OF THE WYE DURING A TOUR. JULY 13, 1798

Five years have past; five summers, with the length
Of five long winters! and again I hear
These waters, rolling from their mountain-springs
With a soft inland murmur. — Once again
5 Do I behold these steep and lofty cliffs,
That on a wild secluded scene impress
Thoughts of more deep seclusion; and connect
The landscape with the quiet of the sky.
The day is come when I again repose
10 Here, under this dark sycamore, and view
These plots of cottage-ground, these orchard-tufts,
Which at this season, with their unripe fruits,
Are clad in one green hue, and lose themselves
'Mid groves and copses. Once again I see
15 These hedge-rows, hardly hedge-rows, little lines
Of sportive wood run wild: these pastoral farms,
Green to the very door; and wreaths of smoke
Sent up, in silence, from among the trees!
With some uncertain notice, as might seem
20 Of vagrant dwellers in the houseless woods,
Or of some Hermit's cave, where by his fire
The Hermit sits alone.
               These beauteous forms,
Through a long absence, have not been to me
As is a landscape to a blind man's eye:
25 But oft, in lonely rooms, and 'mid the din
Of towns and cities, I have owed to them
In hours of weariness, sensations sweet,
Felt in the blood, and felt along the heart;
And passing even into my purer mind,
30 With tranquil restoration: — feelings too
Of unremembered pleasure: such, perhaps,
As have no slight or trivial influence
On that best portion of a good man's life,
His little, nameless, unremembered, acts

———→

1 ruined Cistercian abbey located on the Wye River, Wales.

35   Of kindness and of love. Nor less, I trust,
To them I may have owed another gift,
Of aspect more sublime; that blessed mood,
In which the burthen of the mystery,
In which the heavy and the weary weight
40   Of all this unintelligible world,
Is lightened: — that serene and blessed mood,
In which the affections gently lead us on, —
Until the breath of this corporeal frame
And even the motion of our human blood
45   Almost suspended, we are laid asleep
In body, and become a living soul:
While with an eye made quiet by the power
Of harmony, and the deep power of joy,
We see into the life of things.
                            If this
50   Be but a vain belief, yet, oh! how oft —
In darkness and amid the many shapes
Of joyless daylight; when the fretful stir
Unprofitable, and the fever of the world,
Have hung upon the beatings of my heart —
55   How oft, in spirit, have I turned to thee,
O sylvan Wye! thou wanderer thro' the woods,
How often has my spirit turned to thee!
    And now, with gleams of half-extinguished thought,
With many recognitions dim and faint,
60   And somewhat of a sad perplexity,
The picture of the mind revives again:
While here I stand, not only with the sense
Of present pleasure, but with pleasing thoughts
That in this moment there is life and food
65   For future years. And so I dare to hope,
Though changed, no doubt, from what I was when first
I came among these hills; when like a roe
I bounded o'er the mountains, by the sides
Of the deep rivers, and the lonely streams,
70   Wherever nature led: more like a man
Flying from something that he dreads than one
Who sought the thing he loved. For nature then

                                ⟶

(The coarser pleasures of my boyish days,
And their glad animal movements all gone by)
75   To me was all in all.— I cannot paint
What then I was. The sounding cataract
Haunted me like a passion: the tall rock,
The mountain, and the deep and gloomy wood,
Their colours and their forms, were then to me
80   An appetite; a feeling and a love,
That had no need of a remoter charm,
By thought supplied, nor any interest
Unborrowed from the eye.— That time is past,
And all its aching joys are now no more,
85   And all its dizzy raptures. Not for this
Faint I, nor mourn nor murmur; other gifts
Have followed; for such loss, I would believe,
Abundant recompense. For I have learned
To look on nature, not as in the hour
90   Of thoughtless youth; but hearing oftentimes
The still, sad music of humanity,
Nor harsh nor grating, though of ample power
To chasten and subdue. And I have felt
A presence that disturbs me with the joy
95   Of elevated thoughts; a sense sublime
Of something far more deeply interfused,
Whose dwelling is the light of setting suns,
And the round ocean and the living air,
And the blue sky, and in the mind of man:
100   A motion and a spirit, that impels
All thinking things, all objects of all thought,
And rolls through all things. Therefore am I still
A lover of the meadows and the woods,
And mountains; and of all that we behold
105   From this green earth; of all the mighty world
Of eye, and ear,— both what they half create,
And what perceive; well pleased to recognise
In nature and the language of the sense
The anchor of my purest thoughts, the nurse,
110   The guide, the guardian of my heart, and soul
Of all my moral being.

———→

                         Nor perchance,
If I were not thus taught, should I the more
Suffer my genial spirits to decay:
For thou art with me here upon the banks
115 Of this fair river; thou my dearest Friend,[2]
My dear, dear Friend; and in thy voice I catch
The language of my former heart, and read
My former pleasures in the shooting lights
Of thy wild eyes. Oh! yet a little while
120 May I behold in thee what I was once,
My dear, dear Sister! and this prayer I make,
Knowing that Nature never did betray
The heart that loved her; 'tis her privilege,
Through all the years of this our life, to lead
125 From joy to joy: for she can so inform
The mind that is within us, so impress
With quietness and beauty, and so feed
With lofty thoughts, that neither evil tongues,
Rash judgments, nor the sneers of selfish men,
130 Nor greetings where no kindness is, nor all
The dreary intercourse of daily life,
Shall e'er prevail against us, or disturb
Our cheerful faith, that all which we behold
Is full of blessings. Therefore let the moon
135 Shine on thee in thy solitary walk;
And let the misty mountain-winds be free
To blow against thee: and, in after years,
When these wild ecstasies shall be matured
Into a sober pleasure; when thy mind
140 Shall be a mansion for all lovely forms,
Thy memory be as a dwelling-place
For all sweet sounds and harmonies; oh! then,
If solitude, or fear, or pain, or grief,
Should be thy portion, with what healing thoughts
145 Of tender joy wilt thou remember me,
And these my exhortations! Nor, perchance —
If I should be where I no more can hear
Thy voice, nor catch from thy wild eyes these gleams
Of past existence — wilt thou then forget
150 That on the banks of this delightful stream

                         ⟶

2 Wordsworth's sister, Dorothy.

We stood together; and that I, so long
A worshipper of Nature, hither came
Unwearied in that service: rather say
With warmer love — oh! with far deeper zeal
155   Of holier love. Nor wilt thou then forget
That after many wanderings, many years
Of absence, these steep woods and lofty cliffs,
And this green pastoral landscape, were to me
More dear, both for themselves and for thy sake!

(1798)

Nutting

It seems a day
(I speak of one from many singled out)
One of those heavenly days that cannot die;
When, in the eagerness of boyish hope,
5   I left our cottage-threshold, sallying forth
With a huge wallet[1] o'er my shoulders slung,
A nutting-crook[2] in hand; and turned my steps
Tow'rd some far-distant wood, a Figure quaint,
Tricked out in proud disguise of cast-off weeds
10   Which for that service had been husbanded,
By exhortation of my frugal Dame[3]—
Motley accoutrement, of power to smile
At thorns, and brakes, and brambles, — and in truth
More ragged than need was! O'er pathless rocks,
15   Through beds of matted fern, and tangled thickets,
Forcing my way, I came to one dear nook
Unvisited, where not a broken bough
Drooped with its withered leaves, ungracious sign
Of devastation; but the hazels rose
20   Tall and erect, with tempting clusters hung,
A virgin scene! — A little while I stood,
Breathing with such suppression of the heart
As joy delights in; and with wise restraint
———→

1 a knapsack. 2 a pole with a curved end used to pull down nut-laden branches. 3 Anne Tyson, with whom Wordsworth boarded while attending Hawkshead School in the Lake District.

Voluptuous, fearless of a rival, eyed
25   The banquet; — or beneath the trees I sate
Among the flowers, and with the flowers I played;
A temper known to those who, after long
And weary expectation, have been blest
With sudden happiness beyond all hope.
30   Perhaps it was a bower beneath whose leaves
The violets of five seasons re-appear
And fade, unseen by any human eye;
Where fairy water-breaks do murmur on
For ever; and I saw the sparkling foam,
35   And — with my cheek on one of those green stones
That, fleeced with moss, under the shady trees,
Lay round me, scattered like a flock of sheep —
I heard the murmur and the murmuring sound,
In that sweet mood when pleasure loves to pay
40   Tribute to ease; and, of its joy secure,
The heart luxuriates with indifferent things,
Wasting its kindliness on stocks and stones,
And on the vacant air. Then up I rose,
And dragged to earth both branch and bough, with crash
45   And merciless ravage: and the shady nook
Of hazels, and the green and mossy bower,
Deformed and sullied, patiently gave up
Their quiet being: and unless I now
Confound my present feelings with the past,
50   Ere from the mutilated bower I turned
Exulting, rich beyond the wealth of kings,
I felt a sense of pain when I beheld
The silent trees, and saw the intruding sky. —
Then, dearest Maiden, [4] move along these shades
55   In gentleness of heart; with gentle hand
Touch — for there is a spirit in the woods.

(1798)   (1800)

---

4 probably his sister, Dorothy.

She dwelt among the untrodden ways

She dwelt among the untrodden ways
    Beside the springs of Dove,[1]
A Maid whom there were none to praise
    And very few to love:

5   A violet by a mossy stone
    Half hidden from the eye!
— Fair as a star, when only one
    Is shining in the sky.

She lived unknown, and few could know
10   When Lucy ceased to be;
But she is in her grave, and, oh,
    The difference to me!

(1799)   (1800)

It is a beauteous evening, calm and free

It is a beauteous evening, calm and free,
The holy time is quiet as a Nun
Breathless with adoration; the broad sun
Is sinking down in its tranquillity;
5   The gentleness of heaven broods o'er the Sea:
Listen! the mighty Being is awake,
And doth with his eternal motion make
A sound like thunder — everlastingly.
Dear Child![1] dear Girl! that walkest with me here,
10   If thou appear untouched by solemn thought,
Thy nature is not therefore less divine:
Thou liest in Abraham's bosom[2] all the year;
And worshipp'st at the Temple's inner shrine,
God being with thee when we know it not.

(1802)   (1807)

---

1 one of several rivers and streams named Dove is in Wordworth's Lake District, in the northwest of England.
1 Wordsworth's illegitimate daughter, Caroline. 2 heavenly rest, peace. Cf. Luke 16:22–23.

London, 1802

Milton! thou shouldst be living at this hour:
England hath need of thee: she is a fen
Of stagnant waters: altar, sword, and pen,
Fireside, the heroic wealth of hall and bower,
5   Have forfeited their ancient English dower
Of inward happiness. We are selfish men;
Oh! raise us up, return to us again;
And give us manners, virtue, freedom, power.
Thy soul was like a Star, and dwelt apart;
10   Thou hadst a voice whose sound was like the sea:
Pure as the naked heavens, majestic, free,
So didst thou travel on life's common way,
In cheerful godliness; and yet thy heart
The lowliest duties on herself did lay.

(1802)   (1807)

The world is too much with us

The world is too much with us; late and soon,
Getting and spending, we lay waste our powers:
Little we see in Nature that is ours;
We have given our hearts away, a sordid boon!
5   This Sea that bares her bosom to the moon;
The winds that will be howling at all hours,
And are up-gathered now like sleeping flowers;
For this, for everything, we are out of tune;
It moves us not. — Great God! I'd rather be
10   A Pagan suckled in a creed outworn;
So might I, standing on this pleasant lea,
Have glimpses that would make me less forlorn;
Have sight of Proteus[1] rising from the sea;
Or hear old Triton[2] blow his wreathèd horn.

(c. 1802)   (1807)

---

1 Greek sea deity who had the power of prophecy. 2 Greek sea deity who was half-man and half-fish and who had the power to calm the ocean.

I wandered lonely as a cloud

I wandered lonely as a cloud
That floats on high o'er vales and hills,
When all at once I saw a crowd,
A host, of golden daffodils;
5   Beside the lake, beneath the trees,
Fluttering and dancing in the breeze.

Continuous as the stars that shine
And twinkle on the milky way,
They stretched in never-ending line
10   Along the margin of a bay:
Ten thousand saw I at a glance,
Tossing their heads in sprightly dance.

The waves beside them danced; but they
Out-did the sparkling waves in glee:
15   A poet could not but be gay,
In such a jocund company:
I gazed — and gazed — but little thought
What wealth the show to me had brought:

For oft, when on my couch I lie
20   In vacant or in pensive mood,
They flash upon that inward eye
Which is the bliss of solitude;
And then my heart with pleasure fills,
And dances with the daffodils.

(1804)   (1807)

Samuel Taylor Coleridge (1772–1834)

Born in the small town of Ottery St. Mary, Devonshire, Samuel Taylor Coleridge grew up in London, an intelligent, but very lonely, unhappy child. He studied at Cambridge, spent a year in the army, and interested himself in radical politics. In 1797, he met William Wordsworth, and a year later the two published *Lyrical Ballads.* Coleridge's contributions were poems written on supernatural or romantic subjects, designed to create in the reader what he called "that willing suspension of disbelief for the moment, which constitutes poetic faith." Of these poems, the best known is "The Rime of the Ancient Mariner." Adapting the traditional ballad stanza, which had become popular during the last half of the eighteenth century, he drew on his voluminous reading in folklore and science to create the account of the title figure's symbolic journey of sin, guilt, repentance, and redemption, and the effect its retelling has on the somewhat self-satisfied wedding guest. Also written during this period was "Kubla Khan," which Coleridge said was based on an opium-induced dream. "Frost at Midnight" expresses his intense longing as well as his hope that nature would provide his son with the opportunities and satisfactions that he himself had been denied. Although Coleridge continued to write poetry throughout his life, his most noted later work is *Biographia Literaria* (1817), a combination of autobiography, philosophy, and literary criticism.

Kubla Khan[1]

In Xanadu[2] did Kubla Khan
A stately pleasure-dome decree:
Where Alph, the sacred river, ran
Through caverns measureless to man
5   Down to a sunless sea.
So twice five miles of fertile ground
With walls and towers were girdled round:
And there were gardens bright with sinuous rills,
Where blossomed many an incense-bearing tree;
10   And here were forests ancient as the hills,
Enfolding sunny spots of greenery.

But oh! that deep romantic chasm which slanted
Down the green hill athwart a cedarn cover![3]
A savage place! as holy and enchanted
15   As e'er beneath a waning moon was haunted
By woman wailing for her demon-lover!
And from this chasm, with ceaseless turmoil seething,

———→

1 thirteenth-century emperor of China. He was the grandson of Genghis Khan and a patron of the arts.
2 Shang-tu, a city founded by Kubla Khan, on the site of modern Beijing. 3 covered by cedar trees.

As if this earth in fast thick pants were breathing,
A mighty fountain momently was forced:
20   Amid whose swift half-intermitted burst
Huge fragments vaulted like rebounding hail,
Or chaffy grain beneath the thresher's flail:
And 'mid these dancing rocks at once and ever
It flung up momently the sacred river.
25   Five miles meandering with a mazy motion
Through wood and dale the sacred river ran,
Then reached the caverns measureless to man,
And sank in tumult to a lifeless ocean:
And 'mid this tumult Kubla heard from far
30   Ancestral voices prophesying war!
    The shadow of the dome of pleasure
    Floated midway on the waves
    Where was heard the mingled measure
    From the fountain and the caves.
35   It was a miracle of rare device,
A sunny pleasure-dome with caves of ice!

    A damsel with a dulcimer
    In a vision once I saw:
    It was an Abyssinian maid,
40   And on her dulcimer she played,
    Singing of Mount Abora.[4]
    Could I revive within me
    Her symphony and song,
    To such a deep delight 'twould win me,
45   That with music loud and long,
I would build that dome in air,
That sunny dome! those caves of ice!
And all who heard should see them there,
And all should cry, Beware! Beware!
50   His flashing eyes, his floating hair!
Weave a circle round him thrice,
And close your eyes with holy dread,
For he on honey-dew hath fed,
And drunk the milk of Paradise.

(1797)   (1816)

---

4 possibly Mt. Amara, in Abyssinia, now Ethiopia.

The Rime of the Ancient Mariner

PART I

It is an ancient Mariner,
And he stoppeth one of three.
"By thy long grey beard and glittering eye,
Now wherefore stopp'st thou me?

An ancient Mariner meeteth three Gallants bidden to a wedding feast, and detaineth one.

5   The Bridegroom's doors are opened wide,
And I am next of kin;
The guests are met, the feast is set:
May'st hear the merry din."

He holds him with his skinny hand,
10   "There was a ship," quoth he.
"Hold off! unhand me, grey-beard loon!"
Eftsoons[1] his hand dropt he.

He holds him with his glittering eye —
The Wedding-Guest stood still,
15   And listens like a three years' child:
The Mariner hath his will.

The Wedding-Guest is spellbound by the eye of the old seafaring man, and constrained to hear his tale.

The Wedding-Guest sat on a stone:
He cannot choose but hear;
And thus spake on that ancient man,
20   The bright-eyed Mariner.

"The ship was cheered, the harbour cleared,
Merrily did we drop
Below the kirk,[2] below the hill,
Below the lighthouse top.

25   The Sun came up upon the left,
Out of the sea came he!
And he shone bright, and on the right
Went down into the sea.

The Mariner tells how the ship sailed southward with a good wind and fair weather, till it reached the Line.

1 immediately. 2 church.

Higher and higher every day,
30   Till over the mast at noon —"
The Wedding-Guest here beat his breast,
For he heard the loud bassoon.

The bride hath paced into the hall,   *The Wedding-Guest heareth*
Red as a rose is she;   *the bridal music; but the*
                                          Mariner continueth his tale.
35   Nodding their heads before her goes
The merry minstrelsy.³

The Wedding-Guest he beat his breast,
Yet he cannot choose but hear;
And thus spake on that ancient man,
40   The bright-eyed Mariner.

"And now the STORM-BLAST came, and he   *The ship driven by a storm*
Was tyrannous and strong: *toward the South Pole.*
He struck with his o'ertaking wings,
And chased us south along.

45   With sloping masts and dipping prow,
As who pursued with yell and blow
Still treads the shadow of his foe,
And forward bends his head,
The ship drove fast, loud roared the blast,
50   And southward aye we fled.

And now there came both mist and snow,
And it grew wondrous cold:
And ice, mast-high, came floating by,
As green as emerald.

                                          The land of ice, and of
                                          fearful sounds where no
                                          living thing was to be seen.
55   And through the drifts the snowy clifts
Did send a dismal sheen:
Nor shapes of men nor beasts we ken —⁴
The ice was all between.

3 group of minstrels. 4 know.

The ice was here, the ice was there,
60 The ice was all around:
It cracked and growled, and roared and howled,
Like noises in a swound!⁵

At length did cross an Albatross,
Thorough the fog it came;
65 As if it had been a Christian soul,
We hailed it in God's name.

Till a great sea-bird, called the Albatross, came through the snow-fog, and was received with great joy and hospitality.

It ate the food it ne'er had eat,
And round and round it flew.
The ice did split with a thunder-fit;
70 The helmsman⁶ steered us through!

And a good south wind sprung up behind;
The Albatross did follow,
And every day, for food or play,
Came to the mariners' hollo!

And lo! the Albatross proveth a bird of good omen, and followeth the ship as it returned northward through fog and floating ice.

75 In mist or cloud, on mast or shroud,
It perched for vespers⁷ nine;
Whiles all the night, through fog-smoke white,
Glimmered the white Moon-shine."

"God save thee, ancient Mariner!
80 From the fiends, that plague thee thus! —
Why look'st thou so?" — "With my cross-bow
I shot the ALBATROSS.

The ancient Mariner inhospitably killeth the pious bird of good omen.

PART II

The Sun now rose upon the right:
Out of the sea came he,
85 Still hid in mist, and on the left
Went down into the sea.

5 swoon. 6 person who steers the ship. 7 evening worship; i.e., the bird remained for nine evenings.

And the good south wind still blew behind,
But no sweet bird did follow,
Nor any day for food or play
90   Came to the mariners' hollo!

And I had done a hellish thing,
And it would work 'em woe:
For all averred, I had killed the bird
That made the breeze to blow.
95   Ah wretch! said they, the bird to slay,
That made the breeze to blow!

*His shipmates cry out against
the ancient Mariner, for
killing the bird of good luck.*

Nor dim nor red, like God's own head,
The glorious Sun uprist:
Then all averred, I had killed the bird
100   That brought the fog and mist.
'Twas right, said they, such birds to slay,
That bring the fog and mist.

*But when the fog cleared off,
they justify the same, and
thus make themselves accomplices in the crime.*

The fair breeze blew, the white foam flew,
The furrow followed free;
105   We were the first that ever burst
Into that silent sea.

*The fair breeze continues;
the ship enters the Pacific
Ocean, and sails northward,
even till it reaches the Line.*

Down dropt the breeze, the sails dropt down,
'Twas sad as sad could be;
And we did speak only to break
110   The silence of the sea!

*The ship hath been suddenly
becalmed.*

All in a hot and copper sky,
The bloody Sun, at noon,
Right up above the mast did stand,
No bigger than the Moon.

115   Day after day, day after day,
We stuck, nor breath nor motion;
As idle as a painted ship
Upon a painted ocean.

Water, water, every where,
120   And all the boards did shrink;
Water, water, every where,
Nor any drop to drink.

The very deep did rot: O Christ!
That ever this should be!
125   Yea, slimy things did crawl with legs
Upon the slimy sea.

About, about, in reel and rout
The death-fires danced at night;
The water, like a witch's oils,
130   Burnt green, and blue and white.

And some in dreams assuréd were
Of the Spirit that plagued us so;
Nine fathom deep he had followed us
From the land of mist and snow.

135   And every tongue, through utter drought,
Was withered at the root;
We could not speak, no more than if
We had been choked with soot.

Ah! well a-day! what evil looks
140   Had I from old and young!
Instead of the cross, the Albatross
About my neck was hung.

PART III

There passed a weary time. Each throat
Was parched, and glazed each eye.
145   A weary time! a weary time!
How glazed each weary eye,
When looking westward, I beheld
A something in the sky.

And the Albatross begins to be avenged.

A Spirit had followed them; one of the invisible inhabitants of this planet, neither departed souls nor angels; concerning whom the learned Jew, Josephus, and the Platonic Constantinopolitan, Michael Psellus, may be consulted. They are very numerous, and there is no climate or element without one or more.

The shipmates, in their sore distress, would fain throw the whole guilt on the ancient Mariner: in sign whereof they hang the dead sea-bird round his neck.

The ancient Mariner beholdeth a sign in the element afar off.

At first it seemed a little speck,
150 And then it seemed a mist;
It moved and moved, and took at last
A certain shape, I wist.

A speck, a mist, a shape, I wist!
And still it neared and neared:
155 As if it dodged a water-sprite,[8]
It plunged and tacked and veered.

With throats unslaked, with black lips baked,
We could nor laugh nor wail:
Through utter drought all dumb we stood!
160 I bit my arm, I sucked the blood,
And cried, A sail! a sail!

At its nearer approach, it seemeth him to be a ship; and at a dear ransom he freeth his speech from the bonds of thirst.

With throats unslaked, with black lips baked,
Agape they heard me call:
Gramercy![9] they for joy did grin,
165 And all at once their breath drew in,
As they were drinking all.

A flash of joy;

See! see! (I cried) she tacks no more!
Hither to work us weal;
Without a breeze, without a tide,
170 She steadies with upright keel!

And horror follows. For can it be a ship that comes onward without wind or tide?

The western wave was all a-flame.
The day was well nigh done!
Almost upon the western wave
Rested the broad bright Sun;
175 When that strange shape drove suddenly
Betwixt us and the Sun.

And straight the Sun was flecked with bars,
(Heaven's Mother send us grace!)
As if through a dungeon-grate he peered
180 With broad and burning face.

It seemeth him but the skeleton of a ship.

8 spirit living in water. 9 expression of surprise or gratitude, literally, "Great thanks."

Alas! (thought I, and my heart beat loud)
How fast she nears and nears!
Are those *her* sails that glance in the Sun,
Like restless gossameres? [10]

185   Are those *her* ribs through which the Sun
Did peer, as through a grate?
And is that Woman all her crew?
Is that a DEATH? and are there two?
Is DEATH that woman's mate?

And the ribs are seen as bars on the face of the setting Sun. The Spectre-Woman and her Death-mate, and no other on board the skeleton ship.

190   *Her* lips were red, *her* looks were free,
Her locks were yellow as gold:
Her skin was as white as leprosy,
The Night-mare LIFE-IN-DEATH was she,
Who thicks man's blood with cold.

Like vessel, like crew!

Death and Life-in-Death have diced for the ship's crew, and she (the latter) winneth the ancient Mariner.

195   The naked hulk alongside came,
And the twain were casting dice;
'The game is done! I've won! I've won!'
Quoth she, and whistles thrice.

The Sun's rim dips; the stars rush out:
200   At one stride comes the dark;
With far-heard whisper, o'er the sea,
Off shot the spectre-bark. [11]

No twilight within the courts of the Sun.

We listened and looked sideways up!
Fear at my heart, as at a cup,
205   My life-blood seemed to sip!
The stars were dim, and thick the night,
The steersman's face by his lamp gleamed white;
From the sails the dew did drip —
Till clomb above the eastern bar
210   The hornéd Moon, [12] with one bright star
Within the nether tip.

At the rising of the Moon,

One after one, by the star-dogged [13] Moon,
Too quick for groan or sigh,
Each turned his face with a ghastly pang,
215   And cursed me with his eye.

One after another,

10 cobwebs. 11 phantom ship. 12 crescent moon. 13 followed by a star.

Four times fifty living men,
(And I heard nor sigh nor groan)
With heavy thump, a lifeless lump,
They dropped down one by one.

His shipmates drop down dead.

220 The souls did from their bodies fly, —
They fled to bliss or woe!
And every soul, it passed me by,
Like the whizz of my cross-bow!"

But Life-in-Death begins her work on the ancient Mariner.

PART IV

"I fear thee, ancient Mariner!
225 I fear thy skinny hand!
And thou art long, and lank, and brown,
As is the ribbed sea-sand.

The Wedding-Guest feareth that a Spirit is talking to him;

I fear thee and thy glittering eye,
And thy skinny hand, so brown." —
230 "Fear not, fear not, thou Wedding-Guest!
This body dropt not down.

But the ancient Mariner assureth him of his bodily life, and proceedeth to relate his horrible penance.

Alone, alone, all, all alone,
Alone on a wide wide sea!
And never a saint took pity on
235 My soul in agony.

The many men, so beautiful!
And they all dead did lie:
And a thousand thousand slimy things
Lived on; and so did I.

He despiseth the creatures of the calm,

240 I looked upon the rotting sea,
And drew my eyes away;
I looked upon the rotting deck,
And there the dead men lay.

And envieth that they should live, and so many lie dead.

I looked to heaven, and tried to pray;
245 But or ever a prayer had gusht,
A wicked whisper came, and made
My heart as dry as dust.

I closed my lids, and kept them close,
And the balls like pulses beat;
250 For the sky and the sea, and the sea and the sky
Lay like a load on my weary eye,
And the dead were at my feet.

The cold sweat melted from their limbs,
Nor rot nor reek did they:
255 The look with which they looked on me
Had never passed away.

But the curse liveth for him in the eye of the dead men.

An orphan's curse would drag to hell
A spirit from on high;
But oh! more horrible than that
260 Is the curse in a dead man's eye!
Seven days, seven nights, I saw that curse,
And yet I could not die.

The moving Moon went up the sky,
And no where did abide:
265 Softly she was going up,
And a star or two beside —

In his loneliness and fixedness he yearneth towards the journeying Moon, and the stars that still sojourn, yet still move onward; and every where the blue sky belongs to them, and is their appointed rest, and their native country and their own natural homes, which they enter unannounced, as lords that are certainly expected and yet there is a silent joy at their arrival.

Her beams bemocked the sultry main,[14]
Like April hoar-frost spread;
But where the ship's huge shadow lay,
270 The charméd water burnt alway
A still and awful red.

Beyond the shadow of the ship,
I watched the water-snakes:
They moved in tracks of shining white,
275 And when they reared, the elfish light
Fell off in hoary flakes.

By the light of the Moon he beholdeth God's creatures of the great calm.

Within the shadow of the ship
I watched their rich attire:
Blue, glossy green, and velvet black,
280 They coiled and swam; and every track
Was a flash of golden fire.

14 sea.

O happy living things! no tongue
Their beauty might declare:
A spring of love gushed from my heart,
285 And I blessed them unaware:
Sure my kind saint took pity on me,
And I blessed them unaware.

The self-same moment I could pray;
And from my neck so free
290 The Albatross fell off, and sank
Like lead into the sea.

PART V

Oh sleep! it is a gentle thing,
Beloved from pole to pole!
To Mary Queen[15] the praise be given!
295 She sent the gentle sleep from Heaven,
That slid into my soul.

The silly buckets on the deck,
That had so long remained,
I dreamt that they were filled with dew;
300 And when I awoke, it rained.

My lips were wet, my throat was cold,
My garments all were dank;
Sure I had drunken in my dreams,
And still my body drank.

305 I moved, and could not feel my limbs:
I was so light — almost
I thought that I had died in sleep,
And was a blesséd ghost.

And soon I heard a roaring wind:
310 It did not come anear;
But with its sound it shook the sails,
That were so thin and sere.

Their beauty and their happiness.

He blesseth them in his heart.

The spell begins to break.

By grace of the holy Mother, the ancient Mariner is refreshed with rain.

He heareth sound and seeth strange sights and commotions in the sky and the element.

15 the Virgin Mary, queen of Heaven.

The upper air burst into life!
And a hundred fire-flags sheen,[16]
315 To and fro they were hurried about!
And to and fro, and in and out,
The wan stars danced between.

And the coming wind did roar more loud,
And the sails did sigh like sedge;
320 And the rain poured down from one black cloud;
The Moon was at its edge.

The thick black cloud was cleft, and still
The Moon was at its side:
Like waters shot from some high crag,
325 The lightning fell with never a jag,
A river steep and wide.

The loud wind never reached the ship,
Yet now the ship moved on!
Beneath the lightning and the Moon
330 The dead men gave a groan.

The bodies of the ship's crew are inspired and the ship moves on;

They groaned, they stirred, they all uprose,
Nor spake, nor moved their eyes;
It had been strange, even in a dream,
To have seen those dead men rise.

335 The helmsman steered, the ship moved on;
Yet never a breeze up-blew;
The mariners all 'gan work the ropes,
Where they were wont to do;
They raised their limbs like lifeless tools —
340 We were a ghastly crew.

The body of my brother's son
Stood by me, knee to knee:
The body and I pulled at one rope,
But he said nought to me."

16 meteors shone.

345   "I fear thee, ancient Mariner!"
   "Be calm, thou Wedding-Guest!
   'Twas not those souls that fled in pain,
   Which to their corses [17] came again,
   But a troop of spirits blest:

But not by the souls of the men, nor by demons of earth or middle air, but by a blessed troop of angelic spirits, sent down by the invocation of the guardian saint.

350   For when it dawned — they dropped their arms,
   And clustered round the mast;
   Sweet sounds rose slowly through their mouths,
   And from their bodies passed.

   Around, around, flew each sweet sound,
355   Then darted to the Sun;
   Slowly the sounds came back again,
   Now mixed, now one by one.

   Sometimes a-dropping from the sky
   I heard the sky-lark sing;
360   Sometimes all little birds that are,
   How they seemed to fill the sea and air
   With their sweet jargoning!

   And now 'twas like all instruments,
   Now like a lonely flute;
365   And now it is an angel's song,
   That makes the heavens be mute.

   It ceased; yet still the sails made on
   A pleasant noise till noon,
   A noise like of a hidden brook
370   In the leafy month of June,
   That to the sleeping woods all night
   Singeth a quiet tune.

   Till noon we quietly sailed on,
   Yet never a breeze did breathe:
375   Slowly and smoothly went the ship,
   Moved onward from beneath.

17 corpses.

Under the keel nine fathom deep,
From the land of mist and snow,
The spirit slid: and it was he
380 That made the ship to go.
The sails at noon left off their tune,
And the ship stood still also.

The lonesome Spirit from the South Pole carries on the ship as far as the Line, in obedience to the angelic troop, but still requireth vengeance.

The Sun, right up above the mast,
Had fixed her to the ocean:
385 But in a minute she 'gan stir,
With a short uneasy motion —
Backwards and forwards half her length
With a short uneasy motion.

Then like a pawing horse let go,
390 She made a sudden bound:
It flung the blood into my head,
And I fell down in a swound.

How long in that same fit I lay,
I have not to declare;
395 But ere my living life returned,
I heard and in my soul discerned
Two voices in the air.

The Polar Spirit's fellow-demons, the invisible inhabitants of the element, take part in his wrong; and two of them relate, one to the other, that penance long and heavy for the ancient Mariner hath been accorded to the Polar Spirit, who returneth southward.

'Is it he?' quoth one, 'Is this the man?
By him who died on cross,[18]
400 With his cruel bow he laid full low
The harmless Albatross.

The spirit who bideth by himself
In the land of mist and snow,
He loved the bird that loved the man
405 Who shot him with his bow.'

The other was a softer voice,
As soft as honey-dew:
Quoth he, 'The man hath penance done,
And penance more will do.'

18 Christ, who was crucified on a cross.

PART VI

FIRST VOICE

410 'But tell me, tell me! speak again,
Thy soft response renewing —
What makes that ship drive on so fast?
What is the ocean doing?'

SECOND VOICE

'Still as a slave before his lord,
415 The ocean hath no blast;
His great bright eye most silently
Up to the Moon is cast —

If he may know which way to go;
For she guides him smooth or grim.
420 See, brother, see! how graciously
She looketh down on him.'

FIRST VOICE

'But why drives on that ship so fast,
Without or wave or wind?'

SECOND VOICE

'The air is cut away before,
425 And closes from behind.

Fly, brother, fly! more high, more high!
Or we shall be belated:
For slow and slow that ship will go,
When the Mariner's trance is abated.'

430 I woke, and we were sailing on
As in a gentle weather:
'Twas night, calm night, the moon was high;
The dead men stood together.

All stood together on the deck,
435 For a charnel-dungeon[19] fitter:
All fixed on me their stony eyes,
That in the Moon did glitter.

The Mariner hath been cast into a trance; for the angelic power causeth the vessel to drive northward faster than human life could endure.

The supernatural motion is retarded; the Mariner awakes, and his penance begins anew.

19 burial house, or prison in which people are left to die.

The pang, the curse, with which they died,
Had never passed away:
I could not draw my eyes from theirs,
Nor turn them up to pray.

And now this spell was snapt: once more
I viewed the ocean green,
And looked far forth, yet little saw
Of what had else been seen —

The curse is finally expiated.

Like one that on a lonesome road
Doth walk in fear and dread,
And having once turned round walks on,
And turns no more his head;
Because he knows, a frightful fiend
Doth close behind him tread.

But soon there breathed a wind on me,
Nor sound nor motion made:
Its path was not upon the sea,
In ripple or in shade.

It raised my hair, it fanned my cheek
Like a meadow-gale of spring —
It mingled strangely with my fears,
Yet it felt like a welcoming.

Swiftly, swiftly flew the ship,
Yet she sailed softly too:
Sweetly, sweetly blew the breeze —
On me alone it blew.

Oh! dream of joy! is this indeed
The light-house top I see?
Is this the hill? is this the kirk?
Is this mine own countree?

And the ancient Mariner
beholdeth his native country.

We drifted o'er the harbour-bar,[20]
And I with sobs did pray —
O let me be awake, my God!
Or let me sleep alway.

20 breakwater or sandbar protecting a harbour.

The harbour-bay was clear as glass,
So smoothly it was strewn!
And on the bay the moonlight lay,
475   And the shadow of the Moon.

The rock shone bright, the kirk no less,
That stands above the rock:
The moonlight steeped in silentness
The steady weathercock.

480   And the bay was white with silent light,
Till rising from the same,
Full many shapes, that shadows were,
In crimson colours came.

*The angelic spirits leave the
dead bodies,*

A little distance from the prow
485   Those crimson shadows were:
I turned my eyes upon the deck —
Oh, Christ! what saw I there!

*And appear in their own
forms of light.*

Each corse lay flat, lifeless and flat,
And, by the holy rood! [21]
490   A man all light, a seraph-man, [22]
On every corse there stood.

This seraph-band, each waved his hand:
It was a heavenly sight!
They stood as signals to the land,
495   Each one a lovely light;

This seraph-band, each waved his hand,
No voice did they impart —
No voice; but oh! the silence sank
Like music on my heart.

500   But soon I heard the dash of oars,
I heard the Pilot's [23] cheer;
My head was turned perforce away,
And I saw a boat appear.

---

21 the cross on which Christ was crucified. 22 fiery angel. 23 person who steers ships into harbour.

The Pilot and the Pilot's boy,
505 I heard them coming fast:
Dear Lord in Heaven! it was a joy
The dead men could not blast.

I saw a third — I heard his voice:
It is the Hermit good!
510 He singeth loud his godly hymns
That he makes in the wood.
He'll shrieve[24] my soul, he'll wash away
The Albatross's blood.

PART VII

This Hermit good lives in that wood   *The Hermit of the Wood,*
515 Which slopes down to the sea.
How loudly his sweet voice he rears!
He loves to talk with marineres
That come from a far countree.

He kneels at morn, and noon, and eve —
520 He hath a cushion plump:
It is the moss that wholly hides
The rotted old oak-stump.

The skiff-boat neared: I heard them talk,
'Why, this is strange, I trow!
525 Where are those lights so many and fair,
That signal made but now?'

'Strange, by my faith!' the Hermit said —   *Approacheth the ship with*
'And they answered not our cheer!   *wonder.*
The planks looked warped! and see those sails,
530 How thin they are and sere!
I never saw aught like to them,
Unless perchance it were

Brown skeletons of leaves that lag
My forest-brook along;
535 When the ivy-tod is heavy with snow,
And the owlet whoops to the wolf below,
That eats the she-wolf's young.'

24 administer spiritual absolution.

'Dear Lord! it hath a fiendish look —
(The Pilot made reply)
540   I am a-feared' —'Push on, push on!'
Said the Hermit cheerily.

The boat came closer to the ship,
But I nor spake nor stirred;
The boat came close beneath the ship,
545   And straight a sound was heard.

Under the water it rumbled on,   *The ship suddenly sinketh.*
Still louder and more dread:
It reached the ship, it split the bay;
The ship went down like lead.

550   Stunned by that loud and dreadful sound,   *The ancient Mariner is saved*
Which sky and ocean smote,   *in the Pilot's boat.*
Like one that hath been seven days drowned
My body lay afloat;
But swift as dreams, myself I found
555   Within the Pilot's boat.

Upon the whirl, where sank the ship,
The boat spun round and round;
And all was still, save that the hill
Was telling of the sound.

560   I moved my lips — the Pilot shrieked
And fell down in a fit;
The holy Hermit raised his eyes,
And prayed where he did sit.

I took the oars: the Pilot's boy,
565   Who now doth crazy go,
Laughed loud and long, and all the while
His eyes went to and fro.
'Ha! ha!' quoth he, 'full plain I see,
The Devil knows how to row.'

570   And now, all in my own countree,
I stood on the firm land!
The Hermit stepped forth from the boat,
And scarcely he could stand.

'O shrieve me, shrieve me, holy man!'
575 The Hermit crossed his brow.
'Say quick,' quoth he, 'I bid thee say —
What manner of man art thou?'

*The ancient Mariner
earnestly entreateth the
Hermit to shrieve him;
and the penance of life falls
on him.*

Forthwith this frame of mine was wrenched
With a woful agony,
580 Which forced me to begin my tale;
And then it left me free.

Since then, at an uncertain hour,
That agony returns:
And till my ghastly tale is told,
585 This heart within me burns.

*And ever and anon through-
out his future life an agony
constraineth him to travel
from land to land;*

I pass, like night, from land to land;
I have strange power of speech;
That moment that his face I see,
I know the man that must hear me:
590 To him my tale I teach.

What loud uproar bursts from that door!
The wedding-guests are there:
But in the garden-bower the bride
And bride-maids singing are:
595 And hark the little vesper bell,[25]
Which biddeth me to prayer!

O Wedding-Guest! this soul hath been
Alone on a wide wide sea:
So lonely 'twas, that God himself
600 Scarce seeméd there to be.

O sweeter than the marriage-feast,
'Tis sweeter far to me,
To walk together to the kirk
With a goodly company! —

25 bell calling people to evening worship.

605 To walk together to the kirk,
    And all together pray,
    While each to his great Father bends,
    Old men, and babes, and loving friends
    And youths and maidens gay!

610 Farewell, farewell! but this I tell
    To thee, thou Wedding-Guest!
    He prayeth well, who loveth well
    Both man and bird and beast.

    And to teach, by his own example, love and reverence to all things that God made and loveth.

    He prayeth best, who loveth best
615 All things both great and small;
    For the dear God who loveth us,
    He made and loveth all."

    The Mariner, whose eye is bright,
    Whose beard with age is hoar,[26]
620 Is gone: and now the Wedding-Guest
    Turned from the bridegroom's door.

    He went like one that hath been stunned,
    And is of sense forlorn:
    A sadder and a wiser man,
625 He rose the morrow morn.

(1798)

Frost at Midnight

The Frost performs its secret ministry,
Unhelped by any wind. The owlet's cry
Came loud — and hark, again! loud as before.
The inmates of my cottage, all at rest,
5 Have left me to that solitude, which suits
Abstruser musings: save that at my side
My cradled infant[1] slumbers peacefully.
'Tis calm indeed! so calm, that it disturbs
And vexes meditation with its strange

→

26 greyish-white
1 his son Hartley.

10   And extreme silentness. Sea, hill, and wood,
     This populous village! Sea, and hill, and wood,
     With all the numberless goings-on of life,
     Inaudible as dreams! the thin blue flame
     Lies on my low-burnt fire, and quivers not;
15   Only that film, [2] which fluttered on the grate,
     Still flutters there, the sole unquiet thing.
     Methinks, its motion in this hush of nature
     Gives it dim sympathies with me who live,
     Making it a companionable form,
20   Whose puny flaps and freaks the idling Spirit
     By its own moods interprets, everywhere
     Echo or mirror seeking of itself,
     And makes a toy of Thought.

                         But O! how oft,
25   How oft, at school, [3] with most believing mind,
     Presageful, have I gazed upon the bars,
     To watch that fluttering *stranger*! and as oft
     With unclosed lids, already had I dreamt
     Of my sweet birth-place, [4] and the old church-tower,
30   Whose bells, the poor man's only music, rang
     From morn to evening, all the hot Fair-day,
     So sweetly, that they stirred and haunted me
     With a wild pleasure, falling on mine ear
     Most like articulate sounds of things to come!
35   So gazed I, till the soothing things I dreamt,
     Lulled me to sleep, and sleep prolonged my dreams!
     And so I brooded all the following morn,
     Awed by the stern preceptor's[5] face, mine eye
     Fixed with mock study on my swimming book:
40   Save if the door half opened, and I snatched
     A hasty glance, and still my heart leaped up,
     For still I hoped to see the *stranger's* face,
     Townsman, or aunt, or sister more beloved,
     My playmate when we both were clothed alike! [6]

---

2 flake of soot or ash; in his note to the poem, Coleridge wrote, "In all parts of the kingdom these films are called *strangers* and supposed to portend the arrival of some absent friend." 3 the grammar school, Christ's Hospital, London. 4 Ottery St. Mary, Devonshire. 5 Rev. James Boyer, whom Coleridge describes in the first chapter of his *Biographia Litereria* (1817). 6 until they reached a certain age, Coleridge and his sister Ann would have been dressed in infant clothing, which was the same for males and females.

45   Dear Babe, that sleepest cradled by my side,
        Whose gentle breathings, heard in this deep calm,
        Fill up the interspersed vacancies
        And momentary pauses of the thought!
        My babe so beautiful! it thrills my heart
50   With tender gladness, thus to look at thee,
        And think that thou shalt learn far other lore
        And in far other scenes! For I was reared
        In the great city, pent 'mid cloisters dim,
        And saw nought lovely but the sky and stars.
55   But *thou*, my babe! shalt wander like a breeze
        By lakes and sandy shores, beneath the crags
        Of ancient mountain, and beneath the clouds,
        Which image in their bulk both lakes and shores
        And mountain crags: so shalt thou see and hear
60   The lovely shapes and sounds intelligible
        Of that eternal language, which thy God
        Utters, who from eternity doth teach
        Himself in all, and all things in himself.
        Great universal Teacher! he shall mould
65   Thy spirit, and by giving make it ask.

        Therefore all seasons shall be sweet to thee,
        Whether the summer clothe the general earth
        With greenness, or the redbreast sit and sing
        Betwixt the tufts of snow on the bare branch
70   Of mossy apple-tree, while the nigh thatch
        Smokes in the sun-thaw; whether the eave-drops fall
        Heard only in the trances of the blast,
        Or if the secret ministry of frost
        Shall hang them up in silent icicles,
        Quietly shining to the quiet Moon.

                                                    (1798)

George Gordon, Lord Byron (1788–1824)

Raised in Aberdeen, Scotland, George Gordon became Lord Byron at age ten, after the death of his uncle. While a student at Cambridge, he became notorious for his flamboyant life. His first major work, *Childe Harold*, cantos I and II (1812), was based in part on his own European travels. An advocate of liberal causes as a member of the House of Lords, he died in Greece while training soldiers for that country's fight for independence. During his life and after, he was regarded as an almost legendary figure: handsome, athletic, proud, talented, but often filled with guilt and remorse. An accomplished craftsman, his works range from the beautiful lyric "She Walks in Beauty," to the long, satirical, and humorous *Don Juan* (1819–24). In "On This Day I Complete My Thirty-Sixth Year," written shortly before his death, Byron portrays himself as a world-weary individual seeking to find meaning in his life through involvement in the political and military struggles of Greece.

She Walks in Beauty

I.

She walks in beauty, like the night
    Of cloudless climes and starry skies;
And all that's best of dark and bright
    Meet in her aspect and her eyes:
5   Thus mellow'd to that tender light
    Which heaven to gaudy day denies.

II.

One shade the more, one ray the less,
    Had half impair'd the nameless grace
Which waves in every raven tress,
10   Or softly lightens o'er her face;
Where thoughts serenely sweet express
    How pure, how dear their dwelling-place.

III.

And on that cheek, and o'er that brow,
    So soft, so calm, yet eloquent,
15 The smiles that win, the tints that glow,
    But tell of days in goodness spent,
A mind at peace with all below,
    A heart whose love is innocent!

(1814)   (1815)

On This Day I Complete My Thirty-Sixth Year

Missolonghi, Jan. 22, 1824.

'Tis time this heart should be unmoved,
    Since others it hath ceased to move:
Yet, though I cannot be beloved,
      Still let me love!

5   My days are in the yellow leaf;
    The flowers and fruits of love are gone;
The worm, the canker, and the grief
      Are mine alone!

The fire that on my bosom preys
10   Is lone as some volcanic isle;
No torch is kindled at its blaze —
      A funeral pile.

The hope, the fear, the jealous care,
    The exalted portion of the pain
15   And power of love, I cannot share,
      But wear the chain.

But 'tis not *thus* — and 'tis not *here* —
    Such thoughts should shake my soul, nor *now*,
Where glory decks the hero's bier,
20   Or binds his brow.

The sword, the banner, and the field,
    Glory and Greece, around me see!
The Spartan, borne upon his shield,
      Was not more free.

25   Awake! (not Greece — she *is* awake!)
    Awake, my spirit! Think through *whom*
Thy life-blood tracks its parent lake,
      And then strike home!

Tread those reviving passions down,
30   Unworthy manhood! — unto thee
Indifferent should the smile or frown
      Of beauty be.

If thou regrett'st thy youth, *why live?*
   The land of honourable death
35 Is here: — up to the field, and give
     Away thy breath!

Seek out — less often sought than found —
   A soldier's grave, for thee the best;
Then look around, and choose thy ground,
40   And take thy rest.

                                          (1824)

Percy Bysshe Shelley (1792–1822)

Born in Field Place, Sussex, Percy Bysshe Shelley lived a stormy life. Expelled from Oxford for writing a pamphlet on atheism, he eloped with sixteen-year-old Harriet Westbrook, whom he later abandoned for Mary Godwin, the daughter of the political radical William Godwin and author of the novel *Frankenstein*. In 1818, he moved permanently to Italy, but never settled in one place. He drowned after his sailboat was swamped in a squall. Frequently condemned during his life for his highly unconventional moral, political, and anti-religious beliefs, Shelley has been praised for his careful craftsmanship as a poet. In "Ozymandias," the words of the pharaoh are juxtaposed with a description of the desert setting and the present condition of the pharaoh's statue to create an implicit satirical comment on the vainglory of tyrants. "Ode to the West Wind" and "To a Skylark" illustrate the various ways in which Shelley used his observations of nature to present his themes. The West Wind becomes a complex symbol representing, among other things, the interrelationship between life and death and the forces of revolution which may create a better world (a new spring) for people. Like John Keats in "Ode to a Nightingale" and Gerard Manley Hopkins in "The Windhover," Shelley, in "To a Skylark," contrasts the freedom of the bird with the limitations of his own life.

Ozymandias[1]

I met a traveller from an antique land
Who said: Two vast and trunkless legs of stone
Stand in the desert. . . Near them, on the sand,
Half sunk, a shattered visage lies, whose frown,

                         →

1 Greek variant of the name of the thirteenth-century B.C. Egyptian pharaoh, Ramses II.

5   And wrinkled lip, and sneer of cold command,
Tell that its sculptor well those passions read
Which yet survive, stamped on these lifeless things,
The hand that mocked them, and the heart that fed:
And on the pedestal these words appear:
10 "My name is Ozymandias, king of kings:
Look on my works, ye Mighty, and despair!"
Nothing beside remains. Round the decay
Of that colossal wreck, boundless and bare
The lone and level sands stretch far away.

(1817)   (1818)

Ode to the West Wind

I

O wild West Wind, thou breath of Autumn's being,
Thou, from whose unseen presence the leaves dead
Are driven, like ghosts from an enchanter fleeing,

Yellow, and black, and pale, and hectic red,
5   Pestilence-stricken multitudes: O thou,
Who chariotest to their dark wintry bed

The wingèd seeds, where they lie cold and low,
Each like a corpse within its grave, until
Thine azure sister of the Spring shall blow

10 Her clarion o'er the dreaming earth, and fill
(Driving sweet buds like flocks to feed in air)
With living hues and odours plain and hill:

Wild Spirit, which art moving everywhere;
Destroyer and preserver; hear, Oh hear!

II

15 Thou on whose stream, 'mid the steep sky's commotion,
Loose clouds like earth's decaying leaves are shed,
Shook from the tangled boughs of Heaven and Ocean,

Angels of rain and lightning: there are spread
On the blue surface of thine airy surge,
20 Like the bright hair uplifted from the head

Of some fierce Mænad,[1] even from the dim verge
Of the horizon to the zenith's height
The locks of the approaching storm. Thou dirge[2]

Of the dying year, to which this closing night
25　Will be the dome of a vast sepulchre,
Vaulted with all thy congregated might

Of vapours, from whose solid atmosphere
Black rain, and fire, and hail will burst: Oh hear!

III

Thou who didst waken from his summer dreams
30　The blue Mediterranean, where he lay,
Lulled by the coil of his crystàlline streams,

Beside a pumice isle in Baiæ's bay,[3]
And saw in sleep old palaces and towers
Quivering within the wave's intenser day,

35　All overgrown with azure moss and flowers
So sweet, the sense faints picturing them! Thou
For whose path the Atlantic's level powers

Cleave themselves into chasms, while far below
The sea-blooms and the oozy woods which wear
40　The sapless foliage of the ocean, know

Thy voice, and suddenly grow gray with fear,
And tremble and despoil themselves: Oh hear!

IV

If I were a dead leaf thou mightest bear;
If I were a swift cloud to fly with thee;
45　A wave to pant beneath thy power, and share

The impulse of thy strength, only less free
Than thou, O uncontrollable! If even
I were as in my boyhood, and could be

The comrade of thy wanderings over Heaven,
50　As then, when to outstrip thy skiey speed
Scarce seemed a vision; I would ne'er have striven

---

1 female worshippers of Dionysus, the Greek god of wine. 2 song of mourning. 3 city in southwestern Italy.

As thus with thee in prayer in my sore need.
Oh, lift me as a wave, a leaf, a cloud!
I fall upon the thorns of life! I bleed!

55 A heavy weight of hours has chained and bowed
One too like thee: tameless, and swift, and proud.

V

Make me thy lyre, even as the forest is:
What if my leaves are falling like its own!
The tumult of thy mighty harmonies

60 Will take from both a deep, autumnal tone,
Sweet though in sadness. Be thou, Spirit fierce,
My spirit! be thou me, impetuous one!

Drive my dead thoughts over the universe
Like withered leaves to quicken a new birth!
65 And, by the incantation of this verse,

Scatter, as from an unextinguished hearth
Ashes and sparks, my words among mankind!
Be through my lips to unawakened earth

The trumpet of a prophecy! O, Wind,
70 If Winter comes, can Spring be far behind?

(1819)   (1820)

To a Skylark

Hail to thee, blithe spirit!
    Bird thou never wert,
That from heaven, or near it,
    Pourest thy full heart
5 In profuse strains of unpremeditated art.

Higher still and higher
    From the earth thou springest
Like a cloud of fire;
    The blue deep thou wingest,
10 And singing still dost soar, and soaring ever singest.

In the golden lightning
   Of the sunken sun,
O'er which clouds are brightning,
   Thou dost float and run;
15 Like an unbodied joy whose race is just begun.

The pale purple even
   Melts around thy flight;
Like a star of heaven,
   In the broad daylight
20 Thou art unseen, but yet I hear thy shrill delight,

Keen as are the arrows
   Of that silver sphere,
Whose intense lamp narrows
   In the white dawn clear,
25 Until we hardly see, we feel that it is there.

All the earth and air
   With thy voice is loud,
As, when night is bare,
   From one lonely cloud
30 The moon rains out her beams, and heaven is overflowed.

What thou art we know not;
   What is most like thee?
From rainbow clouds there flow not
   Drops so bright to see,
35 As from thy presence showers a rain of melody.

Like a poet hidden
   In the light of thought,
Singing hymns unbidden,
   Till the world is wrought
40 To sympathy with hopes and fears it heeded not:

Like a high-born maiden
   In a palace-tower,
Soothing her love-laden
   Soul in secret hour
45 With music sweet as love, which overflows her bower:

Like a glow-worm golden
 In a dell of dew,
Scattering unbeholden
 Its aërial hue
50 Among the flowers and grass, which screen it from the view:

Like a rose embowered
 In its own green leaves,
By warm winds deflowered,
 Till the scent it gives
55 Makes faint with too much sweet these heavy-wingèd thieves:

Sound of vernal showers
 On the twinkling grass,
Rain-awakened flowers,
 All that ever was
60 Joyous, and clear, and fresh, thy music doth surpass:

Teach us, sprite or bird,
 What sweet thoughts are thine:
I have never heard
 Praise of love or wine
65 That panted forth a flood of rapture so divine.

Chorus Hymeneal,[1]
 Or triumphal chaunt,
Matched with thine would be all
 But an empty vaunt,
70 A thing wherein we feel there is some hidden want.

What objects are the fountains
 Of thy happy strain?
What fields, or waves, or mountains?
 What shapes of sky or plain?
75 What love of thine own kind? what ignorance of pain?

With thy clear keen joyance
 Languor cannot be:
Shadow of annoyance
 Never came near thee:
80 Thou lovest; but ne'er knew love's sad satiety.

1 marriage hymn.

Waking or asleep,
 Thou of death must deem
Things more true and deep
 Than we mortals dream,
85   Or how could thy notes flow in such a crystal stream?

We look before and after,
 And pine for what is not:
Our sincerest laughter
 With some pain is fraught;
90   Our sweetest songs are those that tell of saddest thought.

Yet if we could scorn
 Hate, and pride, and fear;
If we were things born
 Not to shed a tear,
95   I know not how thy joy we ever should come near.

Better than all measures
 Of delightful sound,
Better than all treasures
 That in books are found,
100   Thy skill to poet were, thou scorner of the ground!

Teach me half the gladness
 That thy brain must know,
Such harmonious madness
 From my lips would flow,
105   The world should listen then, as I am listening now.

(1820)   (1824)

John Keats   (1795–1821)

Born in London, John Keats was orphaned at age fourteen. Although he trained
as an apothecary-surgeon, he chose to devote his life to the writing of poetry;
in his sonnet "On First Looking into Chapman's Homer," he described the inspiration he received on reading the sixteenth-century translation of Homer's *Odyssey*.
His talents matured rapidly, and in 1819, at the age of twenty-four, he wrote his
greatest works, "La Belle Dame sans Merci," his six famous odes, and several
sonnets that, along with those of William Wordsworth, are considered the finest

of the Romantic era. In "When I have fears," his rich, concrete imagery reflects his deep appreciation for the physical world and his awareness that his worsening health would probably result in his dying before he had fulfilled his love for his fiancée, Fanny Brawne, and his poetic ambitions. The theme of the destructive power of death appears again in "La Belle Dame sans Merci," in which Keats used the form and imagery of medieval ballads. "Ode to a Nightingale," "Ode on a Grecian Urn," and "To Autumn," three of his best-known poems, reveal Keats's poetic talents at their fullest. The melancholy song of the nightingale, a traditional symbol of suffering transformed into beauty; the burial urn decorated with scenes of life; and the physical splendour of autumn are symbols used to evoke meditations on the nature of art, life and death, and permanence and transience. Imagery that evokes several senses, skilful portrayal of the shifting emotions of the speaker of each poem, the penetrating questions and observations, and the tightly unified stanzas are superb vehicles for Keats's themes. Although he died before his pen had gleaned his "teeming brain," the quality of the works Keats did write marks him as one of the greatest of English poets.

On First Looking into Chapman's Homer

Much have I travell'd in the realms of gold,
    And many goodly states and kingdoms seen;
    Round many western islands have I been
Which bards in fealty to Apollo[1] hold.
5 Oft of one wide expanse had I been told
    That deep-brow'd Homer[2] ruled as his demesne;
    Yet did I never breathe its pure serene
Till I heard Chapman[3] speak out loud and bold:
Then felt I like some watcher of the skies
10   When a new planet swims into his ken;
Or like stout Cortez[4] when with eagle eyes
    He star'd at the Pacific — and all his men
Look'd at each other with a wild surmise —
    Silent, upon a peak in Darien.[5]

(1816)

1 Greek god of music and poetry; also the sun. 2 ninth-century B.C. Greek poet, author of the *Iliad* and the *Odyssey*. 3 George Chapman, late-sixteenth-century English translator of Homer. 4 sixteenth-century Spanish conquerer of Mexico whom Keats confused with Balboa, the first European to see the Pacific Ocean. 5 former name of the Isthmus of Panama.

When I have fears

When I have fears that I may cease to be
   Before my pen has glean'd my teeming brain,
Before high-piled books, in charact'ry,[1]
   Hold like rich garners the full-ripen'd grain;
5 When I behold, upon the night's starr'd face,
   Huge cloudy symbols of a high romance,
And think that I may never live to trace
   Their shadows, with the magic hand of chance;
And when I feel, fair creature of an hour!
10 That I shall never look upon thee more,
Never have relish in the faery power
   Of unreflecting love! — then on the shore
Of the wide world I stand alone, and think
Till love and fame to nothingness do sink.

(1818)   (1848)

Ode to a Nightingale

1

My heart aches, and a drowsy numbness pains
   My sense, as though of hemlock[1] I had drunk,
Or emptied some dull opiate to the drains
   One minute past, and Lethe-wards[2] had sunk:
5 'Tis not through envy of thy happy lot,
   But being too happy in thine happiness, —
     That thou, light-winged Dryad[3] of the trees,
      In some melodious plot
   Of beechen green, and shadows numberless,
10   Singest of summer in full-throated ease.

2

O, for a draught of vintage! that hath been
   Cool'd a long age in the deep-delved earth,

$\longrightarrow$

---

1 printed letters.
1 poison derived from a parsnip-like root, not the common hemlock. 2 toward Lethe, in Greek mythology,
a river in Hades. Drinking its water caused one to forget the past. 3 tree nymph.

Tasting of Flora[4] and the country green,
    Dance, and Provençal song,[5] and sunburnt mirth!
15 O for a beaker full of the warm South,
    Full of the true, the blushful Hippocrene,[6]
        With beaded bubbles winking at the brim,
          And purple-stained mouth;
    That I might drink, and leave the world unseen,
20   And with thee fade away into the forest dim:

3

Fade far away, dissolve, and quite forget
    What thou among the leaves hast never known,
The weariness, the fever, and the fret
    Here, where men sit and hear each other groan;
25 Where palsy shakes a few, sad, last gray hairs,
    Where youth grows pale, and spectre-thin, and dies;
        Where but to think is to be full of sorrow
          And leaden-eyed despairs,
    Where Beauty cannot keep her lustrous eyes,
30   Or new Love pine at them beyond to-morrow.

4

Away! away! for I will fly to thee,
    Not charioted by Bacchus[7] and his pards,
But on the viewless wings of Poesy,
    Though the dull brain perplexes and retards:
35 Already with thee! tender is the night,
    And haply the Queen-Moon is on her throne,
        Cluster'd around by all her starry Fays;[8]
          But here there is no light,
    Save what from heaven is with the breezes blown
40   Through verdurous glooms and winding mossy ways.

5

I cannot see what flowers are at my feet,
    Nor what soft incense hangs upon the boughs,
But, in embalmed darkness, guess each sweet
    Wherewith the seasonable month endows

⟶

4 Roman goddess of flowers. 5 in the Middle Ages, Provence, in southern France, was famous for its poets and singers. 6 in Greek mythology, the sacred fountain of the muses of poetry. 7 Roman god of wine, whose chariot was pulled by leopards (pards). 8 fairies.

45 The grass, the thicket, and the fruit-tree wild;
    White hawthorn, and the pastoral eglantine;
      Fast fading violets cover'd up in leaves;
        And mid-May's eldest child,
    The coming musk-rose, full of dewy wine,
50   The murmurous haunt of flies on summer eves.

6

Darkling[9] I listen; and, for many a time
    I have been half in love with easeful Death,
Call'd him soft names in many a mused rhyme,
    To take into the air my quiet breath;
55 Now more than ever seems it rich to die,
    To cease upon the midnight with no pain,
      While thou art pouring forth thy soul abroad
        In such an ecstasy!
    Still wouldst thou sing, and I have ears in vain —
60   To thy high requiem[10] become a sod.

7

Thou wast not born for death, immortal Bird!
    No hungry generations tread thee down;
The voice I hear this passing night was heard
    In ancient days by emperor and clown:
65 Perhaps the self-same song that found a path
    Through the sad heart of Ruth,[11] when, sick for home,
      She stood in tears amid the alien corn;
        The same that oft-times hath
    Charm'd magic casements, opening on the foam
70   Of perilous seas, in faery lands forlorn.

8

Forlorn! the very word is like a bell
    To toll me back from thee to my sole self!
Adieu! the fancy cannot cheat so well
    As she is fam'd to do, deceiving elf.

⟶

9 in the dark. 10 mass performed for the souls of the dead. 11 in the Old Testament, Ruth was a foreigner who gleaned corn in the fields of ancient Israel; see Ruth 2:3.

75   Adieu! adieu! thy plaintive anthem fades
        Past the near meadows, over the still stream,
           Up the hill-side; and now 'tis buried deep
             In the next valley-glades.
        Was it a vision, or a waking dream?
80   Fled is that music:— Do I wake or sleep?

(1819)   (1820)

Ode on a Grecian Urn

1

Thou still unravish'd bride of quietness,
    Thou foster-child of silence and slow time,
Sylvan[1] historian, who canst thus express
    A flowery tale more sweetly than our rhyme:
5   What leaf-fring'd legend haunts about thy shape
        Of deities or mortals, or of both,
           In Tempe[2] or the dales of Arcady?[3]
What men or gods are these? What maidens loth?
    What mad pursuit? What struggle to escape?
10   What pipes and timbrels?[4] What wild ecstasy?

2

Heard melodies are sweet, but those unheard
    Are sweeter; therefore, ye soft pipes, play on;
Not to the sensual ear, but, more endear'd,
    Pipe to the spirit ditties of no tone:
15   Fair youth, beneath the trees, thou canst not leave
        Thy song, nor ever can those trees be bare;
           Bold Lover, never, never canst thou kiss,
Though winning near the goal — yet, do not grieve;
    She cannot fade, though thou hast not thy bliss,
20   For ever wilt thou love, and she be fair!

---

1 belonging to the woods or forests. 2 quiet valley in Greece, noted for its beauty. 3 mountainous area in Greece, symbol of an ideal rural area. 4 tambourine-like musical instrument.

3

Ah, happy, happy boughs! that cannot shed
   Your leaves, nor ever bid the Spring adieu;
And, happy melodist, unwearied,
   For ever piping songs for ever new;
25 More happy love! more happy, happy love!
   For ever warm and still to be enjoy'd,
      For ever panting, and for ever young;
All breathing human passion far above,
   That leaves a heart high-sorrowful and cloy'd,
30   A burning forehead, and a parching tongue.

4

Who are these coming to the sacrifice?
   To what green altar, O mysterious priest,
Lead'st thou that heifer lowing at the skies,
   And all her silken flanks with garlands drest?
35 What little town by river or sea shore,
   Or mountain-built with peaceful citadel,
      Is emptied of this folk, this pious morn?
And, little town, thy streets for evermore
   Will silent be; and not a soul to tell
40   Why thou art desolate, can e'er return.

5

O Attic[5] shape! Fair attitude! with brede[6]
   Of marble men and maidens overwrought,
With forest branches and the trodden weed;
   Thou, silent form, dost tease us out of thought
45 As doth eternity: Cold Pastoral!
   When old age shall this generation waste,
      Thou shalt remain, in midst of other woe
Than ours, a friend to man, to whom thou say'st,
   "Beauty is truth, truth beauty," — that is all
50   Ye know on earth, and all ye need to know.

(1819)   (1820)

5 belonging to or relating to Attica, whose capital was Athens. 6 pattern of interwoven designs.

To Autumn

1

Season of mists and mellow fruitfulness,
   Close bosom-friend of the maturing sun;
Conspiring with him how to load and bless
   With fruit the vines that round the thatch-eves run;
5 To bend with apples the moss'd cottage-trees,
    And fill all fruit with ripeness to the core;
      To swell the gourd, and plump the hazel shells
With a sweet kernel; to set budding more,
    And still more, later flowers for the bees,
10   Until they think warm days will never cease,
      For Summer has o'er-brimm'd their clammy cells.

2

Who hath not seen thee oft amid thy store?
   Sometimes whoever seeks abroad may find
Thee sitting careless on a granary floor,
15   Thy hair soft-lifted by the winnowing wind;
Or on a half-reap'd furrow sound asleep,
    Drows'd with the fume of poppies, while thy hook
      Spares the next swath and all its twined flowers:
And sometimes like a gleaner thou dost keep
20   Steady thy laden head across a brook;
    Or by a cyder-press, with patient look,
      Thou watchest the last oozings hours by hours.

3

Where are the songs of Spring? Ay, where are they?
   Think not of them, thou hast thy music too,—
25 While barred clouds bloom the soft-dying day,
    And touch the stubble-plains with rosy hue;
Then in a wailful choir the small gnats mourn
    Among the river sallows, borne aloft
      Or sinking as the light wind lives or dies;
30 And full-grown lambs loud bleat from hilly bourn;
    Hedge-crickets sing; and now with treble soft
    The red-breast whistles from a garden-croft;
      And gathering swallows twitter in the skies.

(1819)   (1820)

La Belle Dame sans Merci[1]

A BALLAD

I

O what can ail thee, knight-at-arms,
    Alone and palely loitering?
The sedge has wither'd from the lake,
    And no birds sing.

II

5 O what can ail thee, knight-at-arms!
    So haggard and so woe-begone?
The squirrel's granary is full,
    And the harvest's done.

III

I see a lilly on thy brow,
10   With anguish moist and fever dew,
And on thy cheeks a fading rose
    Fast withereth too.

IV

I met a lady in the meads,[2]
    Full beautiful — a faery's child,
15 Her hair was long, her foot was light,
    And her eyes were wild.

V

I made a garland for her head,
    And bracelets too, and fragrant zone;[3]
She look'd at me as she did love,
20   And made sweet moan.

VI

I set her on my pacing steed,
    And nothing else saw all day long,
For sidelong would she bend, and sing
    A faery's song.

---

1 the beautiful lady without pity. 2 meadows. 3 belt.

VII

25 She found me roots of relish sweet,
 And honey wild, and manna dew,[4]
And sure in language strange she said —
 "I love thee true.")

VIII

She took me to her elfin grot,[5]
30 And there she wept, and sigh'd full sore,
And there I shut her wild wild eyes
 With kisses four.

IX

And there she lulled me asleep,
 And there I dream'd — Ah! woe betide!
35 The latest dream I ever dream'd
 On the cold hill side.

X

I saw pale kings and princes too,
 Pale warriors, death-pale were they all;
They cried — 'La Belle Dame sans Merci
40 Hath thee in thrall!'[6]

XI

I saw their starved lips in the gloam,[7]
 With horrid warning gaped wide,
And I awoke and found me here,
 On the cold hill's side.

XII

45 And this is why I sojourn here,
 Alone and palely loitering,
Though the sedge has wither'd from the lake,
 And no birds sing.

(1819)   (1820)

---

4 food that miraculously fell from heaven. 5 grotto: a cave or cavern. 6 in bondage or slavery. 7 twilight.

Elizabeth Barrett Browning (1806–1861)

Barrett Browning, a self-educated classical scholar and poet, was an invalid for much of her life. At the age of forty she left her notoriously tyrannical father and her home in Wimpole Street, London, and eloped with Robert Browning to Italy, where she lived for the remaining fifteen years of her life. The story of this courtship and her gradual growth toward a belief in and an acceptance of love, transformed into poetry, resulted in the sequence of love poems called the *Sonnets from the Portuguese*, the work for which she is still most popularly known, and which, in its adaptation of the sonnet for the female voice, is still considered one of her most notable achievements. Critical interest now, however, focuses more on *Aurora Leigh* (1857), her verse novel exploring the problems faced by Victorian women generally and the Victorian woman poet in particular. Barrett Browning's extensive body of work reveals a wide thematic range and an innovative use of genre. "Hiram Powers's Greek Slave" contains one of her many protests against injustice with an attack on slavery, whereas "A Musical Instrument" explores the nature of poetic creativity, linking this creativity with pain and isolation. In such works as these, Barrett Browning expands upon the territory traditionally allocated to women poets, replacing the emphasis on love and sensibility with an uncompromising exploration of social and political power.

from Sonnets from the Portuguese[1]

XLIII

How do I love thee? Let me count the ways.
I love thee to the depth and breadth and height
My soul can reach, when feeling out of sight
For the ends of Being and ideal Grace.
5   I love thee to the level of everyday's
Most quiet need, by sun and candle-light.
I love thee freely, as men strive for Right;
I love thee purely, as they turn from Praise.
I love thee with the passion put to use
10   In my old griefs, and with my childhood's faith.
I love thee with a love I seemed to lose
With my lost saints, — I love thee with the breath,
Smiles, tears, of all my life! — and, if God choose,
I shall but love thee better after death.

(1850)

---

1 the title was an attempt to disguise the personal nature of the sonnets by suggesting that they were translations.

Hiram Powers's Greek Slave[1]

They say Ideal Beauty cannot enter
The house of anguish. On the threshold stands
An alien Image with the shackled hands,
Called the Greek Slave: as if the artist meant her,
5   (That passionless perfection which he lent her,
Shadowed, not darkened, where the sill expands)
To, so, confront man's crimes in different lands,
With man's ideal sense. Pierce to the centre,
Art's fiery finger! — and break up ere long
10   The serfdom of this world! Appeal, fair stone,
From God's pure heights of beauty, against man's wrong!
Catch up in thy divine face, not alone
East griefs but west, — and strike and shame the strong,
By thunders of white silence, overthrown.

(1850)

A Musical Instrument

What was he doing, the great god Pan,[1]
   Down in the reeds by the river?
Spreading ruin and scattering ban,
Splashing and paddling with hoofs of a goat,
5   And breaking the golden lilies afloat
   With the dragon-fly on the river.

He tore out a reed, the great god Pan,
   From the deep cool bed of the river:
The limpid water turbidly ran,
10   And the broken lilies a-dying lay,
And the dragon-fly had fled away,
   Ere he brought it out of the river.

1 the American sculptor Hiram Powers (1805–73) first exhibited "The Greek Slave" at the Great
Exhibition in London in 1851; it represents a Greek Christian woman captured by the Turks in the Greek
war of independence (1821–26).
1 half animal and half god, Pan combines the creative and destructive forces. In Ovid's *Metamorphoses*,
he chases the nymph Syrinx, who prays for help and is transformed into reeds. Pan takes these reeds and
produces pipes from them.

High on the shore sat the great god Pan,
    While turbidly flowed the river;
15 And hacked and hewed as a great god can,
With his hard bleak steel at the patient reed,
Till there was not a sign of a leaf indeed
    To prove it fresh from the river.

He cut it short, did the great god Pan,
20   (How tall it stood in the river!)
Then drew the pith, like the heart of a man,
Steadily from the outside ring,
And notched the poor dry empty thing
    In holes, as he sat by the river.

25 "This is the way," laughed the great god Pan,
    (Laughed while he sat by the river,)
"The only way, since gods began
To make sweet music, they could succeed."
Then, dropping his mouth to a hole in the reed,
30   He blew in power by the river.

Sweet, sweet, sweet, O Pan!
    Piercing sweet by the river!
Blinding sweet, O great god Pan!
The sun on the hill forgot to die,
35 And the lilies revived, and the dragon-fly
    Came back to dream on the river.

Yet half a beast is the great god Pan,
    To laugh as he sits by the river,
Making a poet out of a man:
40 The true gods sigh for the cost and pain —
For the reed which grows nevermore again
    As a reed with the reeds in the river.

(1860)

Alfred, Lord Tennyson (1809–1892)

Tennyson, the son of a clergyman, was born in Lincolnshire and educated at Cambridge. Here he joined a group of young intellectuals called the Apostles and formed the friendship with Arthur Hallam that had such an influence upon his work. In May of 1850 Tennyson published *In Memoriam*—the elegy prompted by Hallam's death in 1833—which comprised a cycle of 131 linked poems and which established his reputation. In June of the same year Tennyson married Emily Sellwood, and in November he succeeded Wordsworth as Poet Laureate. His other major works include *The Princess* (1847), an extended narrative, interspersed with lyric, on the question of women's proper sphere, and the *Idylls of the King* (1859–74), a reworking of the Arthurian legends. The languorous, flowing rhythms, which led W.H. Auden to conclude that Tennyson possessed the "finest ear, perhaps, of any English poet," are frequently undercut by sharp dramatic irony. Like Browning, Tennyson is interested in the depiction of varying, sometimes abnormal, psychological states, and often, as in "Ulysses" and "Tithonus," he uses the vehicle of the dramatic monologue to capture these states. And like Arnold, Tennyson repeatedly provides evidence of a divided self; "The Lady of Shalott," probably his best-known and most anthologized work, contains one of the earliest explorations of the dilemma that would continue to trouble him throughout his poetic career: the tension between the artist's desire for aesthetic withdrawal and the recognition of the need for responsible commitment to society.

The Eagle. Fragment

He clasps the crag with crooked hands;
Close to the sun in lonely lands,
Ring'd with the azure world, he stands.

The wrinkled sea beneath him crawls;
5 He watches from his mountain walls,
And like a thunderbolt he falls.

(1851)

The Lady of Shalott

PART I

On either side the river lie
Long fields of barley and of rye,
That clothe the wold and meet the sky;
And thro' the field the road runs by
To many-tower'd Camelot;[1]
And up and down the people go,
Gazing where the lilies blow
Round an island there below,
The island of Shalott.

Willows whiten,[2] aspens quiver,
Little breezes dusk and shiver
Thro' the wave that runs for ever
By the island in the river
Flowing down to Camelot.
Four gray walls, and four gray towers,
Overlook a space of flowers,
And the silent isle imbowers
The Lady of Shalott.

By the margin, willow-veil'd,
Slide the heavy barges trail'd
By slow horses; and unhail'd
The shallop flitteth silken-sail'd
Skimming down to Camelot:
But who hath seen her wave her hand?
Or at the casement seen her stand?
Or is she known in all the land,
The Lady of Shalott?

Only reapers, reaping early
In among the bearded barley,
Hear a song that echoes cheerly
From the river winding clearly,
Down to tower'd Camelot:

———→

1 legendary seat of King Arthur's court. 2 the wind reveals the white underside of the leaves.

And by moon the reaper weary,
Piling sheaves in uplands airy,
35   Listening, whispers, "'Tis the fairy
        Lady of Shalott."

PART II

There she weaves by night and day
A magic web with colours gay.
She has heard a whisper say,
40   A curse is on her if she stay
        To look down to Camelot.
She knows not what the curse may be,
And so she weaveth steadily,
And little other care hath she,
45   The Lady of Shalott.

And moving thro' a mirror clear
That hangs before her all the year,
Shadows of the world appear.
There she sees the highway near
50   Winding down to Camelot:
There the river eddy whirls,
And there the surly village-churls,
And the red cloaks of market girls,
        Pass onward from Shalott.

55   Sometimes a troop of damsels glad,
An abbot on an ambling pad,
Sometimes a curly shepherd-lad,
Or long-hair'd page in crimson clad,
        Goes by to tower'd Camelot;
60   And sometimes thro' the mirror blue
The knights come riding two and two:
She hath no loyal knight and true,
        The Lady of Shalott.

But in her web she still delights
65   To weave the mirror's magic sights,
For often thro' the silent nights
A funeral, with plumes and lights
        And music, went to Camelot:

Or when the moon was overhead,
70 Came two young lovers lately wed;
"I am half sick of shadows," said
        The Lady of Shalott.

PART III

A bow-shot from her bower-eaves,
He rode between the barley-sheaves,
75 The sun came dazzling thro' the leaves,
And flamed upon the brazen greaves
        Of bold Sir Lancelot.
A red-cross knight[3] for ever kneel'd
To a lady in his shield,
80 That sparkled on the yellow field,
        Beside remote Shalott.

The gemmy bridle glitter'd free,
Like to some branch of stars we see
Hung in the golden Galaxy.[4]
85 The bridle bells rang merrily
        As he rode down to Camelot:
And from his blazon'd baldric[5] slung
A mighty silver bugle hung,
And as he rode his armour rung,
90   Beside remote Shalott.

All in the blue unclouded weather
Thick-jewell'd shone the saddle-leather,
The helmet and the helmet-feather
Burn'd like one burning flame together,
95 As he rode down to Camelot.
As often thro' the purple night,
Below the starry clusters bright,
Some bearded meteor, trailing light,
        Moves over still Shalott.

100 His broad clear brow in sunlight glow'd;
On burnished hooves his war-horse trode;

→

3 an allusion to the hero in the first book of Spenser's *Faerie Queene*, who shows his Christian devotion by wearing on his chest a red cross. 4 Milky Way. 5 a decorated belt worn over the shoulder and across the chest.

From underneath his helmet flow'd
His coal-black curls as on he rode,
    As he rode down to Camelot.
105 From the bank and from the river
He flash'd into the crystal mirror,
"Tirra lirra," by the river
    Sang Sir Lancelot.

She left the web, she left the loom,
110 She made three paces thro' the room,
She saw the water-lily bloom,
She saw the helmet and the plume,
    She look'd down to Camelot.
Out flew the web and floated wide;
115 The mirror crack'd from side to side;
"The curse is come upon me," cried
    The Lady of Shalott.

PART IV

In the stormy east-wind straining,
The pale yellow woods were waning,
120 The broad stream in his banks complaining,
Heavily the low sky raining
    Over tower'd Camelot;
Down she came and found a boat
Beneath a willow left afloat,
125 And round about the prow she wrote
    The Lady of Shalott.

And down the river's dim expanse
Like some bold seër in a trance,
Seeing all his own mischance —
130 With a glassy countenance
    Did she look to Camelot.
And at the closing of the day
She loosed the chain, and down she lay;
The broad stream bore her far away,
135   The Lady of Shalott.

Lying, robed in snowy white
That loosely flew to left and right —
The leaves upon her falling light —
Thro' the noises of the night
140   She floated down to Camelot:
And as the boat-head wound along
The willowy hills and fields among,
They heard her singing her last song,
      The Lady of Shalott.

145 Heard a carol, mournful, holy,
Chanted loudly, chanted lowly,
Till her blood was frozen slowly,
And her eyes were darken'd wholly,
      Turn'd to tower'd Camelot.
150 For ere she reach'd upon the tide
The first house by the water-side,
Singing in her song she died,
      The Lady of Shalott.

Under tower and balcony,
155 By garden-wall and gallery,
A gleaming shape she floated by,
Dead-pale between the houses high,
      Silent into Camelot.
Out upon the wharfs they came,
160 Knight and burgher, lord and dame,
And round the prow they read her name,
      The Lady of Shalott.

Who is this? and what is here?
And in the lighted palace near
165 Died the sound of royal cheer;
And they cross'd themselves for fear,
      All the knights at Camelot:
But Lancelot mused a little space;
He said, "She has a lovely face;
170 God in his mercy lend her grace,
      The Lady of Shalott."

(1833)   (1842)

Ulysses [1]

It little profits that an idle king,
By this still hearth, among these barren crags,
Match'd with an aged wife, I mete and dole
Unequal laws unto a savage race,
5   That hoard, and sleep, and feed, and know not me.
I cannot rest from travel; I will drink
Life to the lees. All times I have enjoy'd
Greatly, have suffer'd greatly, both with those
That loved me, and alone; on shore, and when
10   Thro' scudding drifts the rainy Hyades [2]
Vext the dim sea. I am become a name;
For always roaming with a hungry heart
Much have I seen and known, — cities of men
And manners, climates, councils, governments,
15   Myself not least, but honor'd of them all, —
And drunk delight of battle with my peers,
Far on the ringing plains of windy Troy.
I am a part of all that I have met;
Yet all experience is an arch wherethro'
20   Gleams that untravell'd world whose margin fades
For ever and for ever when I move.
How dull it is to pause, to make an end.
To rust unburnish'd, not to shine in use!
As tho' to breathe were life! Life piled on life
25   Were all too little, and of one to me
Little remains; but every hour is saved
From that eternal silence, something more,
A bringer of new things; and vile it were
For some three suns to store and hoard myself,
30   And this gray spirit yearning in desire
To follow knowledge like a sinking star,
Beyond the utmost bound of human thought.

---

1 Ulysses (Greek Odysseus) wandered for ten years following the fall of Troy before returning to his island kingdom of Ithaca and to his wife, Penelope, and son, Telemachus. For Tennyson's sources, see particularly Homer's Odyssey XI.100–37 and Dante's Inferno XXVI. 2 cluster of stars in the constellation Taurus that are associated with the rainy season.

This is my son, mine own Telemachus,
To whom I leave the sceptre and the isle,—
35   Well-loved of me, discerning to fulfil
This labor, by slow prudence to make mild
A rugged people, and thro' soft degrees
Subdue them to the useful and the good.
Most blameless is he, centred in the sphere
40   Of common duties, decent not to fail
In offices of tenderness, and pay
Meet adoration to my household gods,
When I am gone. He works his work, I mine.

There lies the port; the vessel puffs her sail;
45   There gloom the dark, broad seas. My mariners,
Souls that have toil'd, and wrought, and thought with me,—
That ever with a frolic welcome took
The thunder and the sunshine, and opposed
Free hearts, free foreheads,— you and I are old;
50   Old age hath yet his honor and his toil.
Death closes all; but something ere the end,
Some work of noble note, may yet be done,
Not unbecoming men that strove with Gods.
The lights begin to twinkle from the rocks;
55   The long day wanes; the slow moon climbs; the deep
Moans round with many voices. Come, my friends.
'Tis not too late to seek a newer world.
Push off, and sitting well in order smite
The sounding furrows; for my purpose holds
60   To sail beyond the sunset, and the baths
Of all the western stars, until I die.
It may be that the gulfs will wash us down;
It may be we shall touch the Happy Isles,[3]
And see the great Achilles,[4] whom we knew.
65   Tho' much is taken, much abides; and tho'
We are not now that strength which in old days
Moved earth and heaven, that which we are, we are,—
One equal temper of heroic hearts,
Made weak by time and fate, but strong in will
70   To strive, to seek, to find, and not to yield.

(1833)   (1842)

3 the abode of dead heroes, also known as Elysium. 4 Greek hero who fought at Troy. Homer's *Iliad* revolves
around the wrath of Achilles.

Tithonus[1]

The woods decay, the woods decay and fall,
The vapours weep their burthen to the ground,
Man comes and tills the fields and lies beneath,
And after many a summer dies the swan.
5 Me only cruel immortality
Consumes; I wither slowly in thine arms,
Here at the quiet limit of the world,
A white-hair'd shadow roaming like a dream
The ever-silent spaces of the East,
10 Far-folded mists, and gleaming halls of morn.

    Alas! for this gray shadow, once a man —
So glorious in his beauty and thy choice,
Who madest him thy chosen, that he seem'd
To his great heart none other than a God!
15 I ask'd thee, "Give me immortality."
Then didst thou grant mine asking with a smile,
Like wealthy men who care not how they give.
But thy strong Hours indignant work'd their wills,
And beat me down, and marr'd and wasted me,
20 And tho' they could not end me, left me maim'd
To dwell in presence of immortal youth,
Immortal age beside immortal youth,
And all I was, in ashes. Can thy love,
Thy beauty, make amends, tho' even now,
25 Close over us, the silver star,[2] thy guide,
Shines in those tremulous eyes that fill with tears
To hear me? Let me go; take back thy gift:
Why should a man desire in any way
To vary from the kindly race of men,
30 Or pass beyond the goal of ordinance[3]
Where all should pause, as is most meet for all?

    A soft air fans the cloud apart; there comes
A glimpse of that dark world where I was born.
Once more the old mysterious glimmer steals

—————→

1 Eos, goddess of the dawn, loved the mortal Tithonus and begged Zeus to grant him eternal life; she forgot to ask also for eternal youth. 2 the morning star. 3 appointed limit.

35　From thy pure brows, and from thy shoulders pure,
　　And bosom beating with a heart renew'd.
　　Thy cheek begins to redden thro' the gloom,
　　Thy sweet eyes brighten slowly close to mine,
　　Ere yet they blind the stars, and the wild team[4]
40　Which love thee, yearning for thy yoke, arise,
　　And shake the darkness from their loosen'd manes,
　　And beat the twilight into flakes of fire.

　　Lo! ever thus thou growest beautiful
　　In silence, then before thine answer given
45　Departest, and thy tears are on my cheek.

　　Why wilt thou ever scare me with thy tears,
　　And make me tremble lest a saying learnt,
　　In days far-off, on that dark earth, be true?
　　"The Gods themselves cannot recall their gifts."

50　Ay me! ay me! with what another heart
　　In days far-off, and with what other eyes
　　I used to watch — if I be he that watch'd —
　　The lucid outline forming round thee; saw
　　The dim curls kindle into sunny rings;
55　Changed with thy mystic change, and felt my blood
　　Glow with the glow that slowly crimson'd all
　　Thy presence and thy portals, while I lay,
　　Mouth, forehead, eyelids, growing dewy-warm
　　With kisses balmier than half-opening buds
60　Of April, and could hear the lips that kiss'd
　　Whispering I knew not what of wild and sweet,
　　Like that strange song I heard Apollo sing,
　　While Ilion like a mist rose into towers.[5]
　　Yet hold me not for ever in thine East:
65　How can my nature longer mix with thine?
　　Coldly thy rosy shadows bathe me, cold
　　Are all thy lights, and cold my wrinkled feet
　　Upon thy glimmering thresholds, when the steam
　　Floats up from those dim fields about the homes
70　Of happy men that have the power to die,
　　And grassy barrows of the happier dead.
　　Release me, and restore me to the ground;

———→

4 horses that draw the chariot of dawn. 5 Troy (Ilion) was supposedly built to the music of Apollo's lyre.

Thou seëst all things, thou wilt see my grave:
Thou wilt renew thy beauty morn by morn;
75 I earth in earth forget these empty courts,
And thee returning on thy silver wheels.

(1833)   (1860)

Robert Browning   (1812–1889)

Born in London and educated mostly at home, Browning eloped with Elizabeth Barrett to Italy in 1846 and did not return to live in England until after her death. When his first significant work, *Pauline* (1833), prompted the philosopher and critic J.S. Mill to remark on his "intense and morbid self-consciousness," Browning turned to the objective dramatic mode. He is best known for his development of the dramatic monologue, a form that focuses on a single character whose personality is exposed— often indirectly and ironically— through his or her speech. The culmination of Browning's experiments with this form is *The Ring and the Book* (1869), ten long monologues focusing on a single event, in which he suggests that the only way of knowing "truth" may be through art. His attempt to give this "truth broken into prismatic hues" is represented here by such ironic works as "The Bishop Orders His Tomb at Saint Praxed's Church" (1845) and by the surrealistic psychological study " 'Childe Roland to the Dark Tower Came'." His dramatic monologues, along with his notably "unpoetic" language and his interests in psychology, philosophy, and arcane learning, had a great influence on modern poetic movements and particularly upon the poetry of Ezra Pound and T.S. Eliot.

My Last Duchess

Ferrara[1]

That's my last Duchess painted on the wall,
Looking as if she were alive. I call
That piece a wonder, now: Frà Pandolf's[2] hands
Worked busily a day, and there she stands.
5   Will't please you sit and look at her? I said
"Frà Pandolf" by design, for never read
Strangers like you that pictured countenance,
The depth and passion of its earnest glance,

———→

1 an Italian town. The Duke of Ferrara's first wife died under suspicious circumstances in 1561. Soon after, he began to negotiate for the hand of the niece of the Count of Tyrol.
2 Brother Pandolf, an imaginary painter.

But to myself they turned (since none puts by
10   The curtain I have drawn for you, but I)
And seemed as they would ask me, if they durst,
How such a glance came there; so, not the first
Are you to turn and ask thus. Sir, 'twas not
Her husband's presence only, called that spot
15   Of joy into the Duchess' cheek: perhaps
Frà Pandolf chanced to say 'Her mantle laps
Over my lady's wrist too much,' or 'Paint
Must never hope to reproduce the faint
Half-flush that dies along her throat': such stuff
20   Was courtesy, she thought, and cause enough
For calling up that spot of joy. She had
A heart — how shall I say? — too soon made glad,
Too easily impressed; she liked whate'er
She looked on, and her looks went everywhere.
25   Sir, 'twas all one! My favour at her breast,
The dropping of the daylight in the West,
The bough of cherries some officious fool
Broke in the orchard for her, the white mule
She rode with round the terrace — all and each
30   Would draw from her alike the approving speech,
Or blush, at least. She thanked men, — good! but thanked
Somehow — I know not how — as if she ranked
My gift of a nine-hundred-years-old name
With anybody's gift. Who'd stoop to blame
35   This sort of trifling? Even had you skill
In speech — (which I have not) — to make your will
Quite clear to such an one, and say, "Just this
Or that in you disgusts me; here you miss,
Or there exceed the mark" — and if she let
40   Herself be lessoned so, nor plainly set
Her wits to yours, forsooth, and made excuse,
— E'en then would be some stooping; and I choose
Never to stoop. Oh sir, she smiled, no doubt,
Whene'er I passed her; but who passed without
45   Much the same smile? This grew; I gave commands;
Then all smiles stopped together. There she stands
As if alive. Will't please you rise? We'll meet
The company below, then. I repeat,
The Count your master's known munificence
50   Is ample warrant that no just pretence

———→

Of mine for dowry will be disallowed;
Though his fair daughter's self, as I avowed
At starting, is my object. Nay, we'll go
Together down, sir. Notice Neptune, though,
55   Taming a sea-horse, thought a rarity,
Which Claus of Innsbruck[3] cast in bronze for me!

(1842)

The Bishop Orders His Tomb at Saint Praxed's Church[1]

Rome, 15 —

Vanity, saith the preacher, vanity![2]
Draw round my bed: is Anselm keeping back?
Nephews[3] — sons of mine...ah God, I know not! Well —
She, men would have to be your mother once,
5   Old Gandolf envied me, so fair she was!
What's done is done, and she is dead beside,
Dead long ago, and I am Bishop since,
And as she died so must we die ourselves,
And thence ye may perceive the world's a dream.
10   Life, how and what is it? As here I lie
In this state-chamber, dying by degrees,
Hours and long hours in the dead night, I ask
"Do I live, am I dead?" Peace, peace seems all.
Saint Praxed's ever was the church for peace;
15   And so, about this tomb of mine. I fought
With tooth and nail to save my niche, ye know:
— Old Gandolf cozened me, despite my care;
Shrewd was that snatch from out the corner South
He graced his carrion with, God curse the same!
20   Yet still my niche is not so cramped but thence
One sees the pulpit o' the epistle-side,[4]
And somewhat of the choir, those silent seats,
And up into the airy dome where live
The angels, and a sunbeam's sure to lurk:

———→

3 imaginary sculptor.
1 Church of Santa Prassede, in Rome. 2 Ecclesiastes 1:2. "Vanity of vanities, saith the Preacher, vanity of vanities." 3 conventional euphemism for illegitimate sons. 4 the right-hand side as one faces the altar.

25 And I shall fill my slab of basalt there,
    And 'neath my tabernacle[5] take my rest,
    With those nine columns round me, two and two,
    The odd one at my feet where Anselm stands:
    Peach-blossom marble all, the rare, the ripe
30 As fresh-poured red wine of a mighty pulse.
    — Old Gandolf with his paltry onion-stone,[6]
    Put me where I may look at him! True peach,
    Rosy and flawless: how I earned the prize!
    Draw close: that conflagration of my church
35 — What then? So much was saved if aught were missed!
    My sons, ye would not be my death? Go dig
    The white-grape vineyard where the oil-press stood,
    Drop water gently till the surface sink,
    And if ye find ... Ah God, I know not, I! ...
40 Bedded in store of rotten fig-leaves soft,
    And corded up in a tight olive-frail,[7]
    Some lump, ah God, of *lapis lazuli*,
    Big as a Jew's head cut off at the nape,
    Blue as a vein o'er the Madonna's breast ...
45 Sons, all have I bequeathed you, villas, all,
    That brave Frascati[8] villa with its bath,
    So, let the blue lump poise between my knees,
    Like God the Father's globe on both his hands
    Ye worship in the Jesu Church[9] so gay,
50 For Gandolf shall not choose but see and burst!
    Swift as a weaver's shuttle fleet our years:
    Man goeth to the grave, and where is he?
    Did I say basalt for my slab, sons? Black —
    'Twas ever antique-black I meant! How else
55 Shall ye contrast my frieze to come beneath?
    The bas-relief in bronze ye promised me,
    Those Pans and Nymphs ye wot of, and perchance
    Some tripod, thyrsus,[10] with a vase or so,
    The Saviour at his sermon on the mount,
60 Saint Praxed in a glory,[11] and one Pan
    Ready to twitch the Nymph's last garment off,
    And Moses with the tables ... but I know

                                    ———→

---

5 canopy over his tomb. 6 inferior grade of marble. 7 olive basket. 8 fashionable resort town in the mountains. 9 Church of Il Gesu in Rome. 10 classical and pagan ornamentation. The tripod is associated with the priestess of Apollo at Delphi; the thyrsus is the staff carried by Dionysus. 11 with a halo.

Ye mark me not! What do they whisper thee,
Child of my bowels, Anselm? Ah, ye hope
65 To revel down my villas while I gasp
Bricked o'er with beggar's mouldy travertine[12]
Which Gandolf from his tomb-top chuckles at!
Nay, boys, ye love me — all of jasper, then!
'Tis jasper ye stand pledged to, lest I grieve
70 My bath must needs be left behind, alas!
One block, pure green as a pistachio-nut,
There's plenty jasper somewhere in the world —
And have I not Saint Praxed's ear to pray
Horses for ye, and brown Greek manuscripts,
75 And mistresses with great smooth marbly limbs?
— That's if ye carve my epitaph aright,
Choice Latin, picked phrase, Tully's[13] every word,
No gaudy ware like Gandolf's second line —
Tully, my masters? Ulpian[14] serves his need!
80 And then how I shall lie through centuries,
And hear the blessed mutter of the mass,
And see God made and eaten all day long,[15]
And feel the steady candle-flame, and taste
Good strong thick stupefying incense-smoke!
85 For as I lie here, hours of the dead night,
Dying in state and by such slow degrees,
I fold my arms as if they clasped a crook,
And stretch my feet forth straight as stone can point,
And let the bedclothes, for a mortcloth,[16] drop
90 Into great laps and folds of sculptor's-work:
And as yon tapers dwindle, and strange thoughts
Grow, with a certain humming in my ears,
About the life before I lived this life,
And this life too, popes, cardinals and priests,
95 Saint Praxed at his sermon on the mount,[17]
Your tall pale mother with her talking eyes,
And new-found agate urns as fresh as day,
And marble's language, Latin pure, discreet,
— Aha, ELUCESCEBAT[18] quoth our friend?

                                        ⟶

12 ordinary limestone. 13 Cicero. 14 the decadent Latin of Ulpianus was far inferior to that of Cicero.
15 reference to doctrine of transubstantiation, the conversion of bread and wine into the body and blood of
Christ which is thought to occur during mass. 16 funeral pall. 17 the Bishop is confusing Praxed with
Christ. 18 "He was illustrious." Phrase in Ulpianus's Latin, which is part of the inscription on Gandolf's
tomb. The Ciceronian form would be *elucebat*.

100　No Tully, said I, Ulpian at the best!
　　　Evil and brief hath been my pilgrimage.
　　　All *lapis*, all, sons! Else I give the Pope
　　　My villas! Will ye ever eat my heart?
　　　Ever your eyes were as a lizard's quick,
105　They glitter like your mother's for my soul,
　　　Or ye would heighten my impoverished frieze,
　　　Piece out its starved design, and fill my vase
　　　With grapes, and add a vizor and a Term,[19]
　　　And to the tripod ye would tie a lynx
110　That in his struggle throws the thyrsus down,
　　　To comfort me on my entablature
　　　Whereon I am to lie till I must ask
　　　"Do I live, am I dead?" There, leave me, there!
　　　For ye have stabbed me with ingratitude
115　To death — ye wish it — God, ye wish it! Stone —
　　　Gritstone,[20] a-crumble! Clammy squares which sweat
　　　As if the corpse they keep were oozing through —
　　　And no more *lapis* to delight the world!
　　　Well go! I bless ye. Fewer tapers there,
120　But in a row: and, going, turn your backs
　　　— Ay, like departing altar-ministrants,
　　　And leave me in my church, the church for peace,
　　　That I may watch at leisure if he leers —
　　　Old Gandolf, at me, from his onion-stone,
125　As still he envied me, so fair she was!

(1845)

"Childe Roland to the Dark Tower Came"[1]

I

My first thought was, he lied in every word,
　　　That hoary cripple, with malicious eye
　　　Askance to watch the working of his lie

⟶

---

19 a vizor is the eye covering of a helmet; *Term* is an abbreviation of *Terminus*, the Roman god of boundaries, and thus, a common symbol of mortality. A term was also the tapered pedestal on which a bust, such as that of Terminus, would be placed.　20 sandstone.

1 see Edgar's mad song in Shakespeare's *King Lear* 3.4:171–73. "Child Rowland to the dark tower came, / His word was still — Fie, foh, and fum! / I smell the blood of a British man." A childe is a young knight who has not yet proved himself.

On mine, and mouth scarce able to afford
5   Suppression of the glee, that pursed and scored
     Its edge, at one more victim gained thereby.

II

What else should he be set for, with his staff?
    What, save to waylay with his lies, ensnare
    All travellers who might find him posted there,
10   And ask the road? I guessed what skull-like laugh
Would break, what crutch 'gin write my epitaph
    For pastime in the dusty thoroughfare,

III

If at his counsel I should turn aside
    Into that ominous tract which, all agree,
15   Hides the Dark Tower. Yet acquiescingly
I did turn as he pointed: neither pride
Nor hope rekindling at the end descried,
    So much as gladness that some end might be.

IV

For, what with my whole world-wide wandering,
20   What with my search drawn out through years, my hope
    Dwindled into a ghost not fit to cope
With that obstreperous joy success would bring, —
I hardly tried now to rebuke the spring
    My heart made, finding failure in its scope.

V

25 As when a sick man very near to death
    Seems dead indeed, and feels begin and end
    The tears and takes the farewell of each friend,
And hears one bid the other go, draw breath
Freelier outside, ("since all is o'er," he saith,
30   "And the blow fallen no grieving can amend";)

VI

While some discuss if near the other graves
    Be room enough for this, and when a day
    Suits best for carrying the corpse away,

——→

With care about the banners, scarves and staves:
35 And still the man hears all, and only craves
    He may not shame such tender love and stay.

VII

Thus, I had so long suffered in this quest,
    Heard failure prophesied so oft, been writ
    So many times among "The Band" — to wit,
40 The knights who to the Dark Tower's search addressed
Their steps — that just to fail as they, seemed best,
    And all the doubt was now — should I be fit?

VIII

So, quiet as despair, I turned from him,
    That hateful cripple, out of his highway
45   Into the path he pointed. All the day
Had been a dreary one at best, and dim
Was settling to its close, yet shot one grim
    Red leer to see the plain catch its estray.[2]

IX

For mark! no sooner was I fairly found
50   Pledged to the plain, after a pace or two,
    Than, pausing to throw backward a last view
O'er the safe road, 'twas gone; grey plain all around:
Nothing but plain to the horizon's bound.
    I might go on; naught else remained to do.

X

55 So, on I went. I think I never saw
    Such starved ignoble nature; nothing throve:
    For flowers — as well expect a cedar grove!
But cockle, spurge,[3] according to their law
Might propagate their kind, with none to awe,
60   You'd think; a burr had been a treasure-trove.

2 someone who has strayed. 3 cockle is any of several weeds that grow in wheat fields; some of the varieties belong to the spurge family and have an acrid milky juice with purgative properties.

XI

No! penury, inertness and grimace,
    In some strange sort, were the land's portion. "See
    Or shut your eyes," said Nature peevishly,
"It nothing skills: I cannot help my case:
65   'Tis the Last Judgement's fire must cure this place,
    Calcine [4] its clods and set my prisoners free."

XII

If there pushed any ragged thistle-stalk
    Above its mates, the head was chopped; the bents
    Were jealous else. What made those holes and rents
70   In the dock's harsh swarth leaves, bruised as to balk
All hope of greenness? 'tis a brute must walk
    Pashing their life out, with a brute's intents.

XIII

As for the grass, it grew as scant as hair
    In leprosy; thin dry blades pricked the mud
75   Which underneath looked kneaded up with blood.
One stiff blind horse, his every bone a-stare,
Stood stupefied, however he came there:
    Thrust out past service from the devil's stud!

XIV

Alive? he might be dead for aught I know,
80   With that red gaunt and colloped [5] neck a-strain,
    And shut eyes underneath the rusty mane;
Seldom went such grotesqueness with such woe;
I never saw a brute I hated so;
    He must be wicked to deserve such pain.

XV

85   I shut my eyes and turned them on my heart.
    As a man calls for wine before he fights,
    I asked one draught of earlier, happier sights,
Ere fitly I could hope to play my part.
Think first, fight afterwards — the soldier's art:
90   One taste of the old time sets all to rights.

4 pulverize by heat. 5 in folds or ridges.

XVI

Not it! I fancied Cuthbert's reddening face
   Beneath its garniture of curly gold,
   Dear fellow, till I almost felt him fold
An arm in mine to fix me to the place,
95 That way he used. Alas, one night's disgrace!
   Out went my heart's new fire and left it cold.

XVII

Giles then, the soul of honour — there he stands
   Frank as ten years ago when knighted first.
   What honest man should dare (he said) he durst.
100 Good — but the scene shifts — faugh! what hangman-hands
Pin to his breast a parchment? His own bands
   Read it. Poor traitor, spit upon and curst!

XVIII

Better this present than a past like that;
   Back therefore to my darkening path again!
105   No sound, no sight as far as eye could strain.
Will the night send a howler[6] or a bat?
I asked: when something on the dismal flat
   Came to arrest my thoughts and change their train.

XIX

A sudden little river crossed my path
110   As unexpected as a serpent comes.
   No sluggish tide congenial to the glooms;
This, as it frothed by, might have been a bath
For the fiend's glowing hoof — to see the wrath
   Of its black eddy bespate with flakes and spumes.

XX

115 So petty yet so spiteful! All along,
   Low scrubby alders kneeled down over it;
   Drenched willows flung them headlong in a fit
Of mute despair, a suicidal throng:
The river which had done them all the wrong,
120   Whate'er that was, rolled by, deterred no whit.

6 owl.

XXI

Which, while I forded, — good saints, how I feared
   To set my foot upon a dead man's cheek,
   Each step, or feel the spear I thrust to seek
For hollows, tangled in his hair or beard!
125   — It may have been a water-rat I speared,
   But, ugh! it sounded like a baby's shriek.

XXII

Glad was I when I reached the other bank.
   Now for a better country. Vain presage!
   Who were the strugglers; what war did they wage,
130   Whose savage trample thus could pad the dank
Soil to a plash? Toads in a poisoned tank,
   Or wild cats in a red-hot iron cage —

XXIII

The fight must so have seemed in that fell cirque.
   What penned them there, with all the plain to choose?
135   No foot-print leading to that horrid mews,
None out of it. Mad brewage set to work
Their brains, no doubt, like galley-slaves the Turk
   Pits for his pastime, Christians against Jews.

XXIV

And more than that — a furlong on — why, there!
140   What bad use was that engine for, that wheel,
   Or brake,[7] not wheel — that harrow fit to reel
Men's bodies out like silk? with all the air
Of Tophet's tool,[8] on earth left unaware,
   Or brought to sharpen its rusty teeth of steel.

XXV

145   Then came a bit of stubbed ground, once a wood,
   Next a marsh, it would seem, and now mere earth
   Desperate and done with; (so a fool finds mirth,
Makes a thing and then mars it, till his mood
Changes and off he goes!) within a rood[9]—
150   Bog, clay and rubble, sand and stark black dearth.

7 a machine with teeth used for breaking up flax or hemp to separate the fibre; here used as a device of torture. 8 hell's tool. 9 approximately a quarter of an acre.

XXVI

Now blotches rankling, coloured gay and grim,
    Now patches where some leanness of the soil's
    Broke into moss or substances like boils;
Then came some palsied oak, a cleft in him
155 Like a distorted mouth that splits its rim
    Gaping at death, and dies while it recoils.

XXVII

And just as far as ever from the end!
    Naught in the distance but the evening, naught
    To point my footsteps further! At the thought,
160 A great black bird, Apollyon's bosom-friend,[10]
Sailed past, nor beat his wide wing dragon-penned[11]
    That brushed my cap — perchance the guide I sought.

XXVIII

For, looking up, aware I somehow grew,
    'Spite of the dusk, the plain had given place
165   All round to mountains — with such name to grace
Mere ugly heights and heaps now stolen in view.
How thus they had surprised me, — solve it, you!
    How to get from them was no clearer case.

XXIX

Yet half I seemed to recognize some trick
170   Of mischief happened to me, God knows when —
    In a bad dream perhaps. Here ended, then,
Progress this way. When, in the very nick
Of giving up, one time more, came a click
    As when a trap shuts — you're inside the den!

XXX

175 Burningly it came on me all at once,
    This was the place! those two hills on the right,
    Crouched like two bulls locked horn in horn in fight;
While to the left, a tall scalped mountain . . . Dunce,
Dotard, a-dozing at the very nonce,
180   After a life spent training for the sight!

10 in Revelations 9:11, the devil is called Apollyon, the destroyer. 11 with pinions like a dragon.

XXXI

What in the midst lay but the Tower itself?
    The round squat turret, blind as the fool's heart,
    Built of brown stone, without a counterpart
In the whole world. The tempest's mocking elf
185   Points to the shipman thus the unseen shelf
    He strikes on, only when the timbers start.

XXXII

Not see? because of night perhaps?— why, day
    Came back again for that! before it left,
    The dying sunset kindled through a cleft:
190   The hills, like giants at a hunting, lay,
Chin upon hand, to see the game at bay, —
    "Now stab and end the creature — to the heft!"[12]

XXXIII

Not hear? when noise was everywhere! it tolled
    Increasing like a bell. Names in my ears
195   Of all the lost adventurers my peers, —
How such a one was strong, and such was bold,
And such was fortunate, yet each of old
    Lost, lost! one moment knelled the woe of years.

XXXIV

There they stood, ranged along the hill-sides, met
200   To view the last of me, a living frame
    For one more picture! in a sheet of flame
I saw them and I knew them all. And yet
Dauntless the slug-horn[13] to my lips I set,
    And blew. *"Childe Roland to the Dark Tower came."*

(1855)

---

12 handle of a dagger. 13 trumpet.

Walt Whitman (1819–1892)

Born on Long Island, New York (referred to by its Native name, Paumanok, in many of his poems), Walt Whitman worked as a labourer, teacher, printer, journalist, and, during the American Civil War, as a nurse. *Leaves of Grass,* first published in 1855 and revised and expanded several times during his life, was the first major collection by an American poet, and influenced such twentieth-century American poets as Hart Crane and Allen Ginsberg. Celebrating the diversity of the United States and the dignity of the common person, the poems were praised by the poet-essayist Ralph Waldo Emerson, but often criticized by reviewers for what they considered obscene passages. Their central figure is a speaker who embodies the diversity and greatness of American life. While many of Whitman's poems have justly been described as massive and formless, others, such as "When Lilacs Last in the Dooryard Bloom'd," in which the death and funeral procession of Abraham Lincoln are the occasion for an elegy examining the interrelationships between life, death, and love, are tightly knit and intricately developed.

When Lilacs Last in the Dooryard Bloom'd

1

When lilacs last in the dooryard bloom'd,
And the great star early droop'd in the western sky in the night,
I mourn'd, and yet shall mourn with ever-returning spring.
Ever-returning spring, trinity sure to me you bring,
5 Lilac blooming perennial and drooping star in the west,
And thought of him[1] I love.

2

O powerful western fallen star!
O shades of night — O moody, tearful night!
O great star disappear'd — O the black murk that hides the star!
10 O cruel hands that hold me powerless — O helpless soul of me!
O harsh surrounding cloud that will not free my soul.

1 Abraham Lincoln, American president assassinated April 14, 1865.

3

In the dooryard fronting an old farm-house near the white-wash'd palings,
Stands the lilac-bush tall-growing with heart-shaped leaves of rich green,
With many a pointed blossom rising delicate, with the perfume strong I love,
15   With every leaf a miracle — and from this bush in the dooryard,
With delicate-color'd blossoms and heart-shaped leaves of rich green,
A sprig with its flower I break.

4

In the swamp in secluded recesses,
A shy and hidden bird is warbling a song.
20   Solitary the thrush,[2]
The hermit withdrawn to himself, avoiding the settlements,
Sings by himself a song.

Song of the bleeding throat,
Death's outlet song of life, (for well dear brother I know,
25   If thou wast not granted to sing thou would'st surely die.)

5

Over the breast of the spring, the land, amid cities,
Amid lanes and through old woods, where lately the violets peep'd from the
      ground, spotting the gray debris,
Amid the grass in the fields each side of the lanes, passing the endless grass,
Passing the yellow-spear'd wheat, every grain from its shroud in the
      dark-brown fields uprisen,
30   Passing the apple-tree blows of white and pink in the orchards,
Carrying a corpse to where it shall rest in the grave,
Night and day journeys a coffin.[3]

6

Coffin that passes through lanes and streets,
Through day and night with the great cloud darkening the land,

⟶

2 thrush, seldom seen, but whose beautiful song is often heard in the spring. 3 Lincoln's coffin was carried
from Washington, D.C., to Springfield, Illinois.

35 With the pomp of the inloop'd flags with the cities draped in black,
    With the show of the States themselves as of crape-veil'd women standing,
    With processions long and winding and the flambeaus of the night,
    With the countless torches lit, with the silent sea of faces and the
        unbared heads,
    With the waiting depot, the arriving coffin, and the sombre faces,
40 With dirges through the night, with the thousand voices rising strong
        and solemn,
    With all the mournful voices of the dirges pour'd around the coffin,
    The dim-lit churches and the shuddering organs — where amid these
        you journey,
    With the tolling tolling bells' perpetual clang,
    Here, coffin that slowly passes,
45 I give you my sprig of lilac.

7

(Nor for you, for one alone,
Blossoms and branches green to coffins all I bring,
For fresh as the morning, thus would I chant a song for you O sane and
    sacred death.

All over bouquets of roses,
50 O death, I cover you over with roses and early lilies,
But mostly and now the lilac that blooms the first,
Copious I break, I break the sprigs from the bushes,
With loaded arms I come, pouring for you,
For you and the coffins all of you O death.)

8

55 O western orb sailing the heaven,
    Now I know what you must have meant as a month since I walk'd,
    As I walk'd in silence the transparent shadowy night,
    As I saw you had something to tell as you bent to me night after night,
    As you droop'd from the sky low down as if to my side, (while the other
        stars all look'd on,)
60 As we wander'd together the solemn night, (for something I know not what

—————▶

kept me from sleep,)
As the night advanced, and I saw on the rim of the west how full you
    were of woe,
As I stood on the rising ground in the breeze in the cool transparent night,
As I watch'd where you pass'd and was lost in the netherward black
    of the night,
As my soul in its trouble dissatisfied sank, as where you sad orb,
65   Concluded, dropt in the night, and was gone.

9

Sing on there in the swamp,
O singer bashful and tender, I hear your notes, I hear your call,
I hear, I come presently, I understand you,
But a moment I linger, for the lustrous star has detain'd me,
70   The star my departing comrade holds and detains me.

10

O how shall I warble myself for the dead one there I loved?
And how shall I deck my song for the large sweet soul that has gone?
And what shall my perfume be for the grave of him I love?

Sea-winds blown from east and west,
75   Blown from the Eastern sea and blown from the Western sea, till there on
    the prairies meeting,
These and with these and the breath of my chant,
I'll perfume the grave of him I love.

11

O what shall I hang on the chamber walls?
And what shall the pictures be that I hang on the walls,
80   To adorn the burial-house of him I love?

Pictures of growing spring and farms and homes,
With the Fourth-month[4] eve at sundown, and the gray smoke lucid
    and bright,

      ——→

---

4 Quaker name for April.

With floods of the yellow gold of the gorgeous, indolent, sinking sun,
    burning, expanding the air,
With the fresh sweet herbage under foot, and the pale green leaves of the
    trees prolific,
In the distance the flowing glaze, the breast of the river, with a wind-dapple
    here and there,
With ranging hills on the banks, with many a line against the sky, and
    shadows,
And the city at hand with dwellings so dense, and stacks of chimneys,
And all the scenes of life and the workshops, and the workmen homeward
    returning.

12

Lo, body and soul — this land,
My own Manhattan with spires, and the sparkling and hurrying tides, and
    the ships,
The varied and ample land, the South and the North in the light,
    Ohio's shores and flashing Missouri,
And ever the far-spreading prairies cover'd with grass and corn.

Lo, the most excellent sun so calm and haughty,
The violet and purple morn with just-felt breezes,
The gentle soft-born measureless light,
The miracle spreading bathing all, the fulfill'd noon,
The coming eve delicious, the welcome night and the stars,
Over my cities shining all, enveloping man and land.

13

Sing on, sing on you gray-brown bird,
Sing from the swamps, the recesses, pour your chant from the bushes,
Limitless out of the dusk, out of the cedars and pines.

Sing on dearest brother, warble your reedy song,
Loud human song, with voice of uttermost woe.

O liquid and free and tender!
O wild and loose to my soul — O wondrous singer!
You only I hear — yet the star holds me, (but will soon depart,)
Yet the lilac with mastering odor holds me.

14

Now while I sat in the day and look'd forth,
In the close of the day with its light and the fields of spring, and the farmers preparing their crops,
In the large unconscious scenery of my land with its lakes and forests,
In the heavenly aerial beauty, (after the perturb'd winds and the storms,)
Under the arching heavens of the afternoon swift passing, and the voices of children and women,
The many-moving sea-tides, and I saw the ships how they sail'd,
And the summer approaching with richness, and the fields all busy with labor,
And the infinite separate houses, how they all went on, each with its meals and minutia of daily usages,
And the streets how their throbbings throbb'd, and the cities pent — lo, then and there,
Falling upon them all and among them all, enveloping me with the rest,
Appear'd the cloud, appear'd the long black trail,
And I knew death, its thought, and the sacred knowledge of death.

Then with the knowledge of death as walking one side of me,
And the thought of death close-walking the other side of me,
And I in the middle as with companions, and as holding the hands of companions,
I fled forth to the hiding receiving night that talks not,
Down to the shores of the water, the path by the swamp in the dimness,
To the solemn shadowy cedars and ghostly pines so still.

And the singer so shy to the rest receiv'd me,
The gray-brown bird I know receiv'd us comrades three,
And he sang the carol of death, and a verse for him I love.

From deep secluded recesses,
From the fragrant cedars and the ghostly pines so still,
Came the carol of the bird.

And the charm of the carol rapt me,
As I held as if by their hands my comrades in the night,
And the voice of my spirit tallied the song of the bird.

135   Come lovely and soothing death,
Undulate round the world, serenely arriving, arriving,
In the day, in the night, to all, to each,
Sooner or later delicate death.

Prais'd be the fathomless universe,
140   For life and joy, and for objects and knowledge curious,
And for love, sweet love — but praise! praise! praise!
For the sure-enwinding arms of cool-enfolding death.

Dark mother always gliding near with soft feet,
Have none chanted for thee a chant of fullest welcome?
145   Then I chant it for thee, I glorify thee above all,
I bring thee a song that when thou must indeed come, come unfalteringly.

Approach strong deliveress,
When it is so, when thou hast taken them I joyously sing the dead,
Lost in the loving floating ocean of thee,
150   Laved in the flood of thy bliss O death.

From me to thee glad serenades,
Dances for thee I propose saluting thee, adornments and feastings for thee,
And the sights of the open landscape and the high-spread sky are fitting,
And life and the fields, and the huge and thoughtful night.

155   The night in silence under many a star,
The ocean shore and the husky whispering wave whose voice I know,
And the soul turning to thee O vast and well-veil'd death,
And the body gratefully nestling close to thee.

Over the tree-tops I float thee a song,
160   Over the rising and sinking waves, over the myriad fields and the prairies wide,
Over the dense-pack'd cities all and the teeming wharves and ways,
I float this carol with joy, with joy to thee O death.

15

To the tally[5] of my soul,
Loud and strong kept up the gray-brown bird,
165   With pure deliberate notes spreading filling the night.

5 record or account.

Loud in the pines and cedars dim,
Clear in the freshness moist and the swamp-perfume,
And I with my comrades there in the night.

170 While my sight that was bound in my eyes unclosed,
As to long panoramas of visions.

And I saw askant the armies,[6]
I saw as in noiseless dreams hundreds of battle-flags,
Borne through the smoke of the battles and pierc'd with missiles I saw them,
And carried hither and yon through the smoke, and torn and bloody,
175 And at last but a few shreds left on the staffs, (and all in silence,)
And the staffs all splinter'd and broken.

I saw battle-corpses, myriads of them,
And the white skeletons of young men, I saw them,
I saw the debris and debris of all the slain soldiers of the war,
180 But I saw they were not as was thought,
They themselves were fully at rest, they suffer'd not,
The living remain'd and suffer'd, the mother suffer'd,
And the wife and the child and the musing comrade suffer'd,
And the armies that remain'd suffer'd.

16

185 Passing the visions, passing the night,
Passing, unloosing the hold of my comrades' hands,
Passing the song of the hermit bird and the tallying song of my soul,
Victorious song, death's outlet song, yet varying ever-altering song,
As low and wailing, yet clear the notes, rising and falling, flooding the night,
190 Sadly sinking and fainting, as warning and warning, and yet again bursting
with joy,
Covering the earth and filling the spread of the heaven,
As that powerful psalm in the night I heard from recesses,
Passing, I leave thee lilac with heart-shaped leaves,
I leave thee there in the door-yard, blooming, returning with spring.

195 I cease from my song for thee,
From my gaze on thee in the west, fronting the west, communing with thee,
O comrade lustrous with silver face in the night.

6 armies of the American Civil War.

Yet each to keep and all, retrievements out of the night,
The song, the wondrous chant of the gray-brown bird,
200   And the tallying chant, the echo arous'd in my soul,
With the lustrous and drooping star with the countenance full of woe,
With the holders holding my hand nearing the call of the bird,
Comrades mine and I in the midst, and their memory ever to keep, for the
    dead I loved so well,
For the sweetest, wisest soul of all my days and lands — and this for his
    dear sake,
205   Lilac and star and bird twined with the chant of my soul,
There in the fragrant pines and the cedars dusk and dim.

(1865–66)   (1881)

One's-Self I Sing

One's-Self I sing, a simple separate person,
Yet utter the word Democratic, the word En-Masse.[1]

Of physiology from top to toe I sing,
Not physiognomy[2] alone nor brain alone is worthy for the Muse, I say the
    Form complete is worthier far,
5   The Female equally with the Male I sing.

Of Life immense in passion, pulse, and power,
Cheerful, for freest action form'd under the laws divine,
The Modern Man I sing.

(1867)   (1871)

Matthew Arnold   (1822–1888)

Arnold, the eldest son of Thomas Arnold, headmaster of Rugby, was educated at Oxford, stayed on as professor of poetry for ten years, and was subsequently appointed an inspector of schools in 1851. He became one of the leading social and literary critics of the age, and such critical works as *Culture and Anarchy* (1869), an investigation into the question of whether the anarchy of individualism should be checked by the authority of culture, are now often considered to be of greater significance than his poetical works. The two genres

1 in a group.   2 facial features.

of poetry and criticism come together in his once-influential theory of critical "touchstones" in "The Study of Poetry" (1888), an attempt to establish standards for distinguishing poetry of "high seriousness." Frequently referred to as the poet of alienation, Arnold is preoccupied with the isolation of the individual and the difficulty of knowing the self. His work is suffused with a sense of frustration, a sharp awareness of the failings of his age, and a poignant nostalgia for a basically illusory earlier age when questions of faith and moral integrity were more easily answered. At the same time, Arnold reveals an unfailing optimistic belief in the efficacy of cultural institutions in bringing about change. The resulting self-division is aptly captured in the haunting lyricism of "Dover Beach." In looking back to a better time and yet still believing in human progress, Arnold is quintessentially Victorian, a man, as he so memorably says in "Stanzas from the Grande Chartreuse" (1855), "Wandering between two worlds, one dead, / The other powerless to be born."

Dover Beach

The sea is calm to-night.
The tide is full, the moon lies fair,
Upon the straits; — on the French coast the light
Gleams and is gone; the cliffs of England stand,
5   Glimmering and vast, out in the tranquil bay.
Come to the window, sweet is the night-air!
Only, from the long line of spray
Where the sea meets the moon-blanch'd land,
Listen! you hear the grating roar
10   Of pebbles which the waves draw back, and fling,
At their return, up the high strand,
Begin, and cease, and then again begin,
With tremulous cadence slow, and bring
The eternal note of sadness in.

15   Sophocles long ago
Heard it on the Ægæan, and it brought
Into his mind the turbid ebb and flow
Of human misery;[1] we
Find also in the sound a thought,
20   Hearing it by this distant northern sea.

---

1 see Sophocles, *Antigone* 2.583ff.

The Sea of Faith
Was once, too, at the full, and round earth's shore
Lay like the folds of a bright girdle furl'd.
But now I only hear
25   Its melancholy, long, withdrawing roar,
Retreating, to the breath
Of the night-wind, down the vast edges drear
And naked shingles[2] of the world.

Ah, love, let us be true
30   To one another! for the world, which seems
To lie before us like a land of dreams,
So various, so beautiful, so new,
Hath really neither joy, nor love, nor light,
Nor certitude, nor peace, nor help for pain;
35   And we are here as on a darkling plain
Swept with confused alarms of struggle and flight,
Where ignorant armies clash by night.

(1867)

Christina Rossetti (1830–1894)

Rossetti, younger sister of the poet-painter Dante Gabriel Rossetti, was educated at home and lived with her family in London for most of her life. Like
her mother and sister, she was a devout High Anglican with a great interest in
the Oxford Movement, which attempted to merge Catholic doctrine and ritual
with the Anglican faith. In 1862 she established her reputation as a poet with
the publication of her most famous work, "Goblin Market." Rossetti was the only
woman in the Pre-Raphaelite circle to achieve recognition for her own work, to
be the creative rather than simply the inspirational force, and she is also the only
British woman poet of the nineteenth century to have consistently drawn critical acclaim right up to the present day. She wrote much religious poetry and
many children's rhymes, as well as numerous ballads and lyrics that reveal a deep
ambivalence toward romantic love and the conventional roles of women; they
have a strong critical subtext rejecting the limitations imposed upon women by
society. Unhappy or frustrated love between men and the women they betray
is often the focus of her frequently melancholy works, and the women she
depicts find their only consolation in resignation, postponement, and the love
of God.

2 pebbled beaches.

Song

When I am dead, my dearest,
    Sing no sad songs for me;
Plant thou no roses at my head,
    Nor shady cypress tree:
5 Be the green grass above me
    With showers and dewdrops wet;
And if thou wilt, remember,
    And if thou wilt, forget.

I shall not see the shadows,
10   I shall not feel the rain;
I shall not hear the nightingale
    Sing on as if in pain:
And dreaming through the twilight
    That doth not rise nor set,
15 Haply I may remember,
    And haply may forget.

(1848)   (1862)

The World

By day she woos me, soft, exceeding fair:
    But all night as the moon so changeth she;
    Loathsome and foul with hideous leprosy,
And subtle serpents gliding in her hair.
5 By day she woos me to the outer air,
    Ripe fruits, sweet flowers, and full satiety:
    But thro' the night a beast she grins at me,
A very monster void of love and prayer.
By day she stands a lie: by night she stands
10   In all the naked horror of the truth,
With pushing horns and clawed and clutching hands.
Is this a friend indeed, that I should sell
    My soul to her, give her my life and youth,
Till my feet, cloven too, take hold on hell?

(1854)   (1862)

Goblin Market

Morning and evening
Maids heard the goblins cry:
"Come buy our orchard fruits,
Come buy, come buy:
5   Apples and quinces,
Lemons and oranges,
Plump unpecked cherries,
Melons and raspberries,
Bloom-down-cheeked peaches,
10   Swart-headed mulberries,
Wild free-born cranberries,
Crab-apples, dewberries,
Pine-apples, blackberries,
Apricots, strawberries; —
15   All ripe together
In summer weather, —
Morns that pass by,
Fair eves that fly;
Come buy, come buy:
20   Our grapes fresh from the vine,
Pomegranates full and fine,
Dates and sharp bullaces,[1]
Rare pears and greengages,
Damsons and bilberries,
25   Taste them and try:
Currants and gooseberries,
Bright-fire-like barberries,[2]
Figs to fill your mouth,
Citrons from the South,
30   Sweet to tongue and sound to eye;
Come buy, come buy."

Evening by evening
Among the brookside rushes,
Laura bowed her head to hear,
35   Lizzie veiled her blushes:
Crouching close together

          →

---

1 plums, as are the greengages and damsons mentioned in the following lines. 2 red berries from the berberis, a thorny shrub.

In the cooling weather,
With clasping arms and cautioning lips,
With tingling cheeks and finger tips.
40 "Lie close," Laura said,
Pricking up her golden head:
"We must not look at goblin men,
We must not buy their fruits:
Who knows upon what soil they fed
45 Their hungry thirsty roots?"
"Come buy," call the goblins
Hobbling down the glen.
"Oh," cried Lizzie, "Laura, Laura,
You should not peep at goblin men."
50 Lizzie covered up her eyes,
Covered close lest they should look;
Laura reared her glossy head,
And whispered like the restless brook:
"Look, Lizzie, look, Lizzie,
55 Down the glen tramp little men.
One hauls a basket,
One bears a plate,
One lugs a golden dish
Of many pounds' weight.
60 How fair the vine must grow
Whose grapes are so luscious;
How warm the wind must blow
Through those fruit bushes."
"No," said Lizzie: "No, no, no;
65 Their offers should not charm us,
Their evil gifts would harm us."
She thrust a dimpled finger
In each ear, shut eyes and ran:
Curious Laura chose to linger
70 Wondering at each merchant man.
One had a cat's face,
One whisked a tail,
One tramped at a rat's pace,
One crawled like a snail,
75 One like a wombat[3] prowled obtuse and furry,
One like a ratel[4] tumbled hurry skurry.

$\longrightarrow$

3 Australian marsupial like a small bear. 4 nocturnal, carnivorous, burrowing mammal found in India and Africa.

She heard a voice like voice of doves
Cooing all together:
They sounded kind and full of loves
80   In the pleasant weather.

Laura stretched her gleaming neck
Like a rush-imbedded swan,
Like a lily from the beck,[5]
Like a moonlit poplar branch,
85   Like a vessel at the launch
When its last restraint is gone.

Backwards up the mossy glen
Turned and trooped the goblin men,
With their shrill repeated cry,
90   "Come buy, come buy."
When they reached where Laura was
They stood stock still upon the moss,
Leering at each other,
Brother with queer brother;
95   Signalling each other,
Brother with sly brother.
One set his basket down,
One reared his plate;
One began to weave a crown
100   Of tendrils, leaves, and rough nuts brown
(Men sell not such in any town);
One heaved the golden weight
Of dish and fruit to offer her:

"Come buy, come buy," was still their cry.
105   Laura stared but did not stir,
Longed but had no money.
The whisk-tailed merchant bade her taste
In tones as smooth as honey,
The cat-faced purr'd,
110   The rat-paced spoke a word
Of welcome, and the snail-paced even was heard;
One parrot-voiced and jolly
Cried "Pretty Goblin" still for "Pretty Polly";
One whistled like a bird.

5 brook.

115 But sweet-tooth Laura spoke in haste:
"Good Folk, I have no coin;
To take were to purloin:
I have no copper in my purse,
I have no silver either,
120 And all my gold is on the furze
That shakes in windy weather
Above the rusty heather."
"You have much gold upon your head,"
They answered all together:
125 "Buy from us with a golden curl."
She clipped a precious golden lock,
She dropped a tear more rare than pearl,
Then sucked their fruit globes fair or red.
Sweeter than honey from the rock,
130 Stronger than man-rejoicing wine,
Clearer than water flowed that juice;
She never tasted such before,
How should it cloy with length of use?
She sucked and sucked and sucked the more
135 Fruits which that unknown orchard bore;
She sucked until her lips were sore;
Then flung the emptied rinds away
But gathered up one kernel stone,
And knew not was it night or day
140 As she turned home alone.

Lizzie met her at the gate
Full of wise upbraidings:
"Dear, you should not stay so late,
Twilight is not good for maidens;
145 Should not loiter in the glen
In the haunts of goblin men.
Do you not remember Jeanie,
How she met them in the moonlight,
Took their gifts both choice and many,
150 Ate their fruits and wore their flowers
Plucked from bowers
Where summer ripens at all hours?
But ever in the noonlight

——→

She pined and pined away;
155   Sought them by night and day,
Found them no more, but dwindled and grew grey;
Then fell with the first snow,
While to this day no grass will grow
Where she lies low:
160   I planted daisies there a year ago
That never blow.
You should not loiter so."
"Nay, hush," said Laura:
"Nay, hush, my sister:
165   I ate and ate my fill,
Yet my mouth waters still:
To-morrow night I will
Buy more;" and kissed her.
"Have done with sorrow;
170   I'll bring you plums to-morrow
Fresh on their mother twigs,
Cherries worth getting;
You cannot think what figs
My teeth have met in,
175   What melons icy-cold
Piled on a dish of gold
Too huge for me to hold,
What peaches with a velvet nap,
Pellucid grapes without one seed:
180   Odorous indeed must be the mead
Whereon they grow, and pure the wave they drink
With lilies at the brink,
And sugar-sweet their sap."

Golden head by golden head,
185   Like two pigeons in one nest
Folded in each other's wings,
They lay down in their curtained bed:
Like two blossoms on one stem,
Like two flakes of new-fall'n snow,
190   Like two wands of ivory
Tipped with gold for awful kings.
Moon and stars gazed in at them,
Wind sang to them lullaby,
Lumbering owls forebore to fly,

→

195 Not a bat flapped to and fro
Round their nest:
Cheek to cheek and breast to breast
Locked together in one nest.

Early in the morning
200 When the first cock crowed his warning,
Neat like bees, as sweet and busy,
Laura rose with Lizzie:
Fetched in honey, milked the cows,
Aired and set to rights the house,
205 Kneaded cakes of whitest wheat,
Cakes for dainty mouths to eat,
Next churned butter, whipped up cream,
Fed their poultry, sat and sewed;
Talked as modest maidens should:
210 Lizzie with an open heart,
Laura in an absent dream,
One content, one sick in part;
One warbling for the mere bright day's delight,
One longing for the night.

215 At length slow evening came:
They went with pitchers to the reedy brook;
Lizzie most placid in her look,
Laura most like a leaping flame.
They drew the gurgling water from its deep.
220 Lizzie plucked purple and rich golden flags,
Then turning homeward said: "The sunset flushes
Those furthest loftiest crags;
Come, Laura, not another maiden lags.
No wilful squirrel wags,
225 The beasts and birds are fast asleep."
But Laura loitered still among the rushes,
And said the bank was steep.

And said the hour was early still,
The dew not fall'n, the wind not chill;
230 Listening ever, but not catching
The customary cry,
"Come buy, come buy,"
With its iterated jingle

———→

Of sugar-baited words:
235   Not for all her watching
Once discerning even one goblin
Racing, whisking, tumbling, hobbling;
Let alone the herds
That used to tramp along the glen,
240   In groups or single,
Of brisk fruit-merchant men.

Till Lizzie urged, "O Laura, come;
I hear the fruit-call, but I dare not look:
You should not loiter longer at this brook:
245   Come with me home.
The stars rise, the moon bends her arc,
Each glow-worm winks her spark,
Let us get home before the night grows dark:
For clouds may gather
250   Though this is summer weather,
Put out the lights and drench us through;
Then if we lost our way what should we do?"

Laura turned cold as stone
To find her sister heard that cry alone,
255   That goblin cry,
"Come buy our fruits, come buy."
Must she then buy no more such dainty fruit?
Must she no more such succous pasture find,
Gone deaf and blind?
260   Her tree of life drooped from the root:
She said not one word in her heart's sore ache:
But peering thro' the dimness, nought discerning,
Trudged home, her pitcher dripping all the way;
So crept to bed, and lay
265   Silent till Lizzie slept;
Then sat up in a passionate yearning,
And gnashed her teeth for baulked desire, and wept
As if her heart would break.

Day after day, night after night,
270   Laura kept watch in vain
In sullen silence of exceeding pain.

⟶

She never caught again the goblin cry,
"Come buy, come buy;" —
She never spied the goblin men
275 Hawking their fruits along the glen:
But when the noon waxed bright
Her hair grew thin and grey;
She dwindled, as the fair full moon doth turn
To swift decay and burn
280 Her fire away.

One day remembering her kernel-stone
She set it by a wall that faced the south;
Dewed it with tears, hoped for a root,
Watched for a waxing shoot,
285 But there came none.
It never saw the sun,
It never felt the trickling moisture run:
While with sunk eyes and faded mouth
She dreamed of melons, as a traveller sees
290 False waves in desert drouth
With shade of leaf-crowned trees,
And burns the thirstier in the sandful breeze.

She no more swept the house,
Tended the fowls or cows,
295 Fetched honey, kneaded cakes of wheat,
Brought water from the brook:
But sat down listless in the chimney-nook
And would not eat.

Tender Lizzie could not bear
300 To watch her sister's cankerous care,
Yet not to share.
She night and morning
Caught the goblins' cry:
"Come buy our orchard fruits,
305 Come buy, come buy:" —
Beside the brook, along the glen,
She heard the tramp of goblin men,
The voice and stir
Poor Laura could not hear;

310 Longed to buy fruit to comfort her,
But feared to pay too dear.
She thought of Jeanie in her grave,
Who should have been a bride;
But who for joys brides hope to have
315 Fell sick and died
In her gay prime,
In earliest winter time,
With the first glazing rime,
With the first snow-fall of crisp winter time.

320 Till Laura dwindling
Seemed knocking at Death's door.
Then Lizzie weighed no more
Better and worse;
But put a silver penny in her purse,
325 Kissed Laura, crossed the heath with clumps of furze
At twilight, halted by the brook:
And for the first time in her life
Began to listen and look.

Laughed every goblin
330 When they spied her peeping:
Came towards her hobbling,
Flying, running, leaping,
Puffing and blowing,
Chuckling, clapping, crowing,
335 Clucking and gobbling,
Mopping and mowing,
Full of airs and graces,
Pulling wry faces,
Demure grimaces,
340 Cat-like and rat-like,
Ratel- and wombat-like,
Snail-paced in a hurry,
Parrot-voiced and whistler,
Helter skelter, hurry skurry,
345 Chattering like magpies,
Fluttering like pigeons,
Gliding like fishes, —

⟶

Hugged her and kissed her:
Squeezed and caressed her:
350 Stretched up their dishes,
Panniers,[6] and plates:
"Look at our apples
Russet and dun,
Bob at our cherries,
355 Bite at our peaches,
Citrons and dates,
Grapes for the asking,
Pears red with basking
Out in the sun,
360 Plums on their twigs;
Pluck them and suck them,—
Pomegranates, figs."

"Good folk," said Lizzie,
Mindful of Jeanie:
365 "Give me much and many:"
Held out her apron,
Tossed them her penny.
"Nay, take a seat with us,
Honour and eat with us,"
370 They answered grinning:
"Our feast is but beginning.
Night yet is early,
Warm and dew-pearly,
Wakeful and starry:
375 Such fruits as these
No man can carry;
Half their bloom would fly,
Half their dew would dry,
Half their flavour would pass by.
380 Sit down and feast with us,
Be welcome guest with us,
Cheer you and rest with us."—
"Thank you," said Lizzie: "But one waits
At home alone for me:
385 So without further parleying,
If you will not sell me any

———➤

6 baskets.

Of your fruits though much and many,
Give me back my silver penny
I tossed you for a fee."—
390   They began to scratch their pates,
No longer wagging, purring,
But visibly demurring,
Grunting and snarling.
One called her proud,
395   Cross-grained, uncivil;
Their tones waxed loud,
Their looks were evil.
Lashing their tails
They trod and hustled her,
400   Elbowed and jostled her,
Clawed with their nails,
Barking, mewing, hissing, mocking,
Tore her gown and soiled her stocking,
Twitched her hair out by the roots,
405   Stamped upon her tender feet,
Held her hands and squeezed their fruits
Against her mouth to make her eat.

White and golden Lizzie stood,
Like a lily in a flood,—
410   Like a rock of blue-veined stone
Lashed by tides obstreperously,—
Like a beacon left alone
In a hoary roaring sea,
Sending up a golden fire,—
415   Like a fruit-crowned orange-tree
White with blossoms honey-sweet
Sore beset by wasp and bee,—
Like a royal virgin town
Topped with gilded dome and spire
420   Close beleaguered by a fleet
Mad to tug her standard down.

One may lead a horse to water,
Twenty cannot make him drink.
Though the goblins cuffed and caught her,
425   Coaxed and fought her,
Bullied and besought her,

———→

Scratched her, pinched her black as ink,
Kicked and knocked her,
Mauled and mocked her,
430   Lizzie uttered not a word;
Would not open lip from lip
Lest they should cram a mouthful in:
But laughed in heart to feel the drip
Of juice that syruped all her face,
435   And lodged in dimples of her chin,
And streaked her neck which quaked like curd.
At last the evil people,
Worn out by her resistance,
Flung back her penny, kicked their fruit
440   Along whichever road they took,
Not leaving root or stone or shoot;
Some writhed into the ground,
Some dived into the brook
With ring and ripple,
445   Some scudded on the gale without a sound,
Some vanished in the distance.

In a smart, ache, tingle,
Lizzie went her way;
Knew not was it night or day;
450   Sprang up the bank, tore thro' the furze,
Threaded copse and dingle,
And heard her penny jingle
Bouncing in her purse, —
Its bounce was music to her ear.
455   She ran and ran
As if she feared some goblin man
Dogged her with gibe or curse
Or something worse:
But not one goblin skurried after,
460   Nor was she pricked by fear;
The kind heart made her windy-paced
That urged her home quite out of breath with haste
And inward laughter.

She cried, "Laura," up the garden,
465   "Did you miss me?
Come and kiss me.

Never mind my bruises,
Hug me, kiss me, suck my juices
Squeezed from goblin fruits for you,
470 Goblin pulp and goblin dew.
Eat me, drink me, love me;
Laura, make much of me;
For your sake I have braved the glen
And had to do with goblin merchant men."

475 Laura started from her chair,
Flung her arms up in the air,
Clutched her hair:
"Lizzie, Lizzie, have you tasted
For my sake the fruit forbidden?
480 Must your light like mine be hidden,
Your young life like mine be wasted,
Undone in mine undoing,
And ruined in my ruin,
Thirsty, cankered, goblin-ridden?"—
485 She clung about her sister,
Kissed and kissed and kissed her:
Tears once again
Refreshed her shrunken eyes,
Dropping like rain
490 After long sultry drouth;
Shaking with anguish fear, and pain,
She kissed and kissed her with a hungry mouth.

Her lips began to scorch,
That juice was wormwood[7] to her tongue,
495 She loathed the feast:
Writhing as one possessed she leaped and sung,
Rent all her robe, and wrung
Her hands in lamentable haste,
And beat her breast.
500 Her locks streamed like the torch
Borne by a racer at full speed,
Or like the mane of horses in their flight,
Or like an eagle when she stems the light
Straight toward the sun,

———→

7 bitter herb.

505 Or like a caged thing freed,
    Or like a flying flag when armies run.

    Swift fire spread through her veins, knocked at her heart,
    Met the fire smouldering there
    And overbore its lesser flame;
510 She gorged on bitterness without a name:
    Ah fool, to choose such part
    Of soul-consuming care!
    Sense failed in the mortal strife:
    Like the watch-tower of a town
515 Which an earthquake shatters down,
    Like a lightning-stricken mast,
    Like a wind-uprooted tree
    Spun about,
    Like a foam-topped waterspout
520 Cast down headlong in the sea,
    She fell at last;
    Pleasure past and anguish past,
    Is it death or is it life?

    Life out of death.
525 That night long Lizzie watched by her,
    Counted her pulse's flagging stir,
    Felt for her breath,
    Held water to her lips, and cooled her face
    With tears and fanning leaves.
530 But when the first birds chirped about their eaves,
    And early reapers plodded to the place
    Of golden sheaves,
    And dew-wet grass
    Bowed in the morning winds so brisk to pass,
535 And new buds with new day
    Opened of cup-like lilies on the stream,
    Laura awoke as from a dream,
    Laughed in the innocent old way,
    Hugged Lizzie but not twice or thrice;
540 Her gleaming locks showed not one thread of grey,
    Her breath was sweet as May,
    And light danced in her eyes.

Days, weeks, months, years
Afterwards, when both were wives
545 With children of their own;
Their mother-hearts beset with fears,
Their lives bound up in tender lives;
Laura would call the little ones
And tell them of her early prime,
550 Those pleasant days long gone
Of not-returning time:
Would talk about the haunted glen,
The wicked quaint fruit-merchant men,
Their fruits like honey to the throat
555 But poison in the blood
(Men sell not such in any town):
Would tell them how her sister stood
In deadly peril to do her good,
And win the fiery antidote:
560 Then joining hands to little hands
Would bid them cling together,—
"For there is no friend like a sister
In calm or stormy weather;
To cheer one on the tedious way,
565 To fetch one if one goes astray,
To lift one if one totters down,
To strengthen whilst one stands."

(1859)   (1862)

Emily Dickinson (1830–1886)

Born in Amherst, Massachusetts, where she lived all her life, Emily Dickinson spent her last twenty-five years, those of her greatest poetic creativity, a relative recluse. For several decades after her death she was regarded as a timid hermit. However, recent studies reveal that, while she seldom ventured outside the family home, she read widely in the classics, contemporary philosophy, and particularly the works of major nineteenth-century women poets and novelists. At a time when intellectual activity was considered detrimental to the emotional and physical health of women and their greatest fulfilment was believed to be found in domestic life, Emily Dickinson was a truly radical woman in her attitudes about religion, society, and art. Although she thought, as she said, "New Englandly," her ideas anticipate by nearly a century those of many modern feminists. During her lifetime, only a handful of her more than seventeen hundred poems were published. Today, she is one of the most widely read and studied American writers. None of her poems is long; most are written within a pattern resembling the four-line stanza characteristic of New England hymns, with alternating lines containing 4, 3, 4, and 3 strong beats. Yet within this limitation, Dickinson achieved tremendous variety of poetic effect and complexity of theme. Using dashes to indicate breath pauses, incomplete and inverted syntax, startling images of nature, and homely domestic images, she depicted the individual consciousness questioning itself in relation to other people, society at large, nature, and death.

288

I'm Nobody! Who are you?
Are you — Nobody — Too?
Then there's a pair of us?
Don't tell! they'd advertise — you know!
How dreary — to be — Somebody!
How public — like a Frog —
To tell one's name — the livelong June —
To an admiring Bog!

(c. 1861)   (1891)

303

The Soul selects her own Society —
Then — shuts the Door —
To her divine Majority —
Present no more —

Unmoved — she notes the Chariots — pausing —
At her low Gate —
Unmoved — and Emperor be kneeling
Upon her Mat —

I've known her — from an ample nation —
Choose One —
Then — close the Valves of her attention —
Like Stone —

(c. 1862)   (1890)

328

A Bird came down the Walk —
He did not know I saw —
He bit an Angleworm in halves
And ate the fellow, raw,

5 And then he drank a Dew
From a convenient Grass —
And then hopped sidewise to the Wall
To let a Beetle pass —

He glanced with rapid eyes
10 That hurried all around —
They looked like frightened Beads, I thought —
He stirred his Velvet Head

Like one in danger, Cautious,
I offered him a Crumb
15 And he unrolled his feathers
And rowed him softer home —

Than Oars divide the Ocean,
Too silver for a seam —
Or Butterflies, off Banks of Noon
20 Leap, plashless as they swim.

(c. 1862)   (1891)

465

I heard a Fly buzz — when I died —
The Stillness in the Room
Was like the Stillness in the Air —
Between the Heaves of Storm —

5 The Eyes around — had wrung them dry —
And Breaths were gathering firm

———→

For that last Onset — when the King
Be witnessed — in the Room —

I willed my Keepsakes — Signed away
10 What portion of me be
Assignable — and then it was
There interposed a Fly —

With Blue — uncertain stumbling Buzz —
Between the light — and me —
15 And then the Windows failed — and then
I could not see to see —

(c. 1862)   (1896)

520

I started Early — Took my Dog —
And visited the Sea —
The Mermaids in the Basement
Came out to look at me —

5 And Frigates[1] — in the Upper Floor
Extended Hempen Hands —
Presuming Me to be a Mouse —
Aground — upon the Sands —

But no Man moved Me — till the Tide
10 Went past my simple Shoe —
And past my Apron — and my Belt
And past my Bodice[2] — too —

And made as He would eat me up —
As wholly as a Dew
15 Upon a Dandelion's Sleeve —
And then — I started — too —

---

1 armed naval vessels. 2 laced garment that fits over a blouse.

And He — He followed — close behind —
I felt His Silver Heel
Upon my Ankle — Then my Shoes
20   Would overflow with Pearl —

Until We met the Solid Town —
No One He seemed to know —
And bowing — with a Mighty look —
At me — The Sea withdrew —

(c. 1862)   (1891)

712

Because I could not stop for Death —
He kindly stopped for me —
The Carriage held but just Ourselves —
And Immortality.

5   We slowly drove — He knew no haste
And I had put away
My labor and my leisure too,
For His Civility —

We passed the School, where Children strove
10   At Recess — in the Ring —
We passed the Fields of Gazing Grain —
We passed the Setting Sun —

Or rather — He passed Us —
The Dews drew quivering and chill —
15   For only Gossamer, my Gown —
My Tippet[1] — only Tulle[2] —

We paused before a House that seemed
A Swelling of the Ground —
The Roof was scarcely visible —
20   The Cornice — in the Ground —

1 a covering for the shoulders, like a stole. 2 a fine netting.

Since then —'tis Centuries — and yet
Feels shorter than the Day
I first surmised the Horses' Heads
Were toward Eternity —

(c. 1863)   (1890)

Gerard Manley Hopkins (1844–1889)

Hopkins was born near London and educated at Oxford during a time of violent religious controversy. He converted to Catholicism in 1866, became a Jesuit priest, and spent the remainder of his life serving the order. Hopkins is generally considered one of the most powerful of the religious poets and one of the most daring innovators in poetic technique. Two notions central to his work are what he calls "inscape," the unique quality that distinguishes one thing from every other, and "instress," the response evoked by the perception of inscape. The attempt to capture these elements in his work can be seen in the lyrically powerful "The Windhover." Hopkins was also one of the most effective practitioners of the sonnet during this age, and in the articulation of his struggles with his faith in the "dark" or "terrible" sonnets, including "No worst, there is none," he is typically Victorian.

Pied Beauty [1]

Glory be to God for dappled things —
        For skies of couple-colour as a brinded[2] cow;
                For rose-moles all in stipple[3] upon trout that swim;
Fresh-firecoal chestnut-falls;[4] finches' wings;
5   Landscape plotted and pieced — fold, fallow, and plough;
                And áll trádes, their gear and tackle and trim.

All things counter, original, spare, strange;
        Whatever is fickle, freckled (who knows how?)
                With swift, slow; sweet, sour; adazzle, dim;
10   He fathers-forth whose beauty is past change:
                                        Praise him.

(1877)   (1918)

1 having two or more colours; in patches or blotches. 2 streaked. 3 method in painting of applying colour in dots. 4 chestnuts dappling the dark ground like bright coals.

God's Grandeur

The world is charged with the grandeur of God.
   It will flame out, like shining from shook foil;[1]
   It gathers to a greatness, like the ooze of oil
Crushed.[2] Why do men then now not reck his rod?
5 Generations have trod, have trod, have trod;
   And all is seared with trade; bleared, smeared with toil;
   And wears man's smudge and shares man's smell: the soil
Is bare now, nor can foot feel, being shod.

And for all this, nature is never spent;
10   There lives the dearest freshness deep down things;
And though the last lights off the black West went
   Oh, morning, at the brown brink eastward, springs —
Because the Holy Ghost over the bent
   World broods with warm breast and with ah! bright wings.

(1877)   (1917)

The Windhover[1]

TO CHRIST OUR LORD

I caught this morning morning's minion,[2] king-
   dom of daylight's dauphin,[3] dapple-dawn-drawn Falcon, in his riding
   Of the rolling level underneath him steady air, and striding
High there, how he rung upon the rein of a wimpling wing[4]
5 In his ecstasy! then off, off forth on swing,
   As a skate's heel sweeps smooth on a bow-bend: the hurl and gliding
   Rebuffed the big wind. My heart in hiding
Stirred for a bird, — the achieve of, the mastery of the thing!

Brute beauty and valour and act, oh, air, pride, plume, here
10   Buckle![5] AND the fire that breaks from thee then, a billion
Times told lovelier, more dangerous, O my chevalier![6]

---

1 foil leaf or tinsel. 2 like oil crushed out of olives or seeds.
1 small hawk. 2 favourite. 3 name given to the heir to the French throne. 4 in falconry, to ring means to
rise in the air spirally. 5 *buckle* has many possible meanings: fasten, join, enclose, grapple, submit, bend, and
crumple. 6 knight, nobleman, champion.

No wonder of it: shéer plód makes plough down sillion[7]
Shine, and blue-bleak embers, ah my dear,
    Fall, gall themselves, and gash gold-vermilion.

(1877)   (1918)

A.E. Housman   (1859–1936)

Born in Worcestershire and educated at Oxford, Housman failed his final exam-
inations and subsequently worked for ten years as a civil servant before becoming professor of Latin at University College, London. *A Shropshire Lad* (1896),
from which the following selections are taken, initially met with little interest,
but became immensely popular during World War I, probably because of the
recurrent intermingled themes of mutability, pessimism, and patriotism, and the
recurrent theme of doomed youth. Housman's output was limited: he published only two small volumes during his lifetime, *A Shropshire Lad* and *Last
Poems* (1922), and another, *More Poems* (1936), appeared after his death.
Housman is important as a link between the Victorian and the modern world,
and he is at his best when he avoids the rather artificial, decadent style that influenced him in his youth and produces the finely crafted, concentrated poems
marked by a vigorous, deceptive simplicity for which he is best known. Revealing
the influence of the classical lyric and the popular ballad, these works skillfully
exploit balance and opposition and frequently close with a pervasive gentle
melancholy undercut by the sudden introduction of irony or bathos.

Loveliest of trees, the cherry now

Loveliest of trees, the cherry now
Is hung with bloom along the bough,
And stands about the woodland ride
Wearing white for Eastertide.

5   Now, of my threescore years and ten,
Twenty will not come again,
And take from seventy springs a score,
It only leaves me fifty more.

7 the ridge between two furrows.

And since to look at things in bloom
10 Fifty springs are little room
About the woodlands I will go
To see the cherry hung with snow.

(1896)

When I was one-and-twenty

When I was one-and-twenty
    I heard a wise man say,
"Give crowns and pounds and guineas
    But not your heart away;
5   Give pearls away and rubies
    But keep your fancy free."
But I was one-and-twenty,
    No use to talk to me.

When I was one-and-twenty
10   I heard him say again,
"The heart out of the bosom
    Was never given in vain;
'Tis paid with sighs a plenty
    And sold for endless rue."
15 And I am two-and-twenty,
    And oh, 'tis true, 'tis true.

(1896)

To an Athlete Dying Young

The time you won your town the race
We chaired you through the market-place;
Man and boy stood cheering by,
And home we brought you shoulder-high.

5   To-day, the road all runners come,
Shoulder-high we bring you home,
And set you at your threshold down,
Townsman of a stiller town.

Smart lad, to slip betimes away
10 From fields where glory does not stay
And early though the laurel[1] grows
It withers quicker than the rose.[2]

Eyes the shady night has shut
Cannot see the record cut,
15 And silence sounds no worse than cheers
After earth has stopped the ears:

Now you will not swell the rout
Of lads that wore their honours out,
Runners whom renown outran
20 And the name died before the man.

So set, before its echoes fade,
The fleet foot on the sill of shade,
And hold to the low lintel up
The still-defended challenge-cup.

25 And round that early-laurelled head
Will flock to gaze the strengthless dead
And find unwithered on its curls
The garland briefer than a girl's.

(1896)

---

1 symbol of victory, traditionally awarded by the Greeks to the victor in the Pythian Games. 2 symbol of
beauty.

Sir Charles G.D. Roberts   (1860–1943)

Credited with creating the first truly Canadian literary form, the realistic animal tale, Charles George Douglas Roberts also played a significant role in the development of Canadian poetry. His first volume, *Orion and Other Poems* (1880), inspired both his cousin, Bliss Carman, and Archibald Lampman, who, together with Duncan Campbell Scott and Roberts, formed the Confederation Poets, a group that consciously sought to create a distinctive Canadian poetry. Born in Douglas, New Brunswick, Roberts worked as an editor and then an English professor, but after 1897 he earned his living by writing prose, living in New York, London, and Europe until his return to Canada in 1925. Paradoxically, his most enduring and universal poems are not the obtrusively moralizing ones in which he deliberately tried to be universal, but the early ones in which he was most regional in subject. These poems show three major influences: his classical training, in the highly organized form and choice of allusions; the English Romantics, especially Wordsworth, in the presentation of sharply detailed landscapes in language that avoids consciously poetic diction; and the Victorian intellectual poets, particularly Matthew Arnold, in the probing for spiritual or philosophical significance. These poems support his claim in "The Poetry of Nature" that "nature-poetry is not mere description of landscape in metrical form, but the expression of one or another of many vital relationships between external nature and 'the deep heart of man.'"

Tantramar[1] Revisited

Summers and summers have come, and gone with the flight of the swallow;
Sunshine and thunder have been, storm, and winter, and frost;
Many and many a sorrow has all but died from remembrance,
Many a dream of joy fall'n in the shadow of pain.
5   Hands of chance and change have marred, or moulded, or broken,
Busy with spirit or flesh, all I most have adored;
Even the bosom of Earth is strewn with heavier shadows,—
Only in these green hills, aslant to the sea, no change!
Here where the road that has climbed from the inland valleys and woodlands,
10   Dips from the hill-tops down, straight to the base of the hills,—
Here, from my vantage-ground, I can see the scattering houses,
Stained with time, set warm in orchards, meadows, and wheat,
Dotting the broad bright slopes outspread to southward and eastward,
Wind-swept all day long, blown by the south-east wind.

---

1 saltwater tidal marshes along the New Brunswick coast of the Bay of Fundy, where Roberts spent his childhood. Minudie (line 25) is across the bay in Nova Scotia.

15   Skirting the sunbright uplands stretches a riband² of meadow,
     Shorn of the labouring grass, bulwarked well from the sea,
     Fenced on its seaward border with long clay dikes from the turbid
     Surge and flow of the tides vexing the Westmoreland shores.
     Yonder, toward the left, lie broad the Westmoreland marshes, —
20   Miles on miles they extend, level, and grassy, and dim,
     Clear from the long red sweep of flats to the sky in the distance,
     Save for the outlying heights, green-rampired³ Cumberland Point;
     Miles on miles outrolled, and the river-channels divide them, —
     Miles on miles of green, barred by the hurtling gusts.

25   Miles on miles beyond the tawny bay is Minudie.
     There are the low blue hills; villages gleam at their feet.
     Nearer a white sail shines across the water, and nearer
     Still are the slim, grey masts of fishing boats dry on the flats.
     Ah, how well I remember those wide red flats, above tide-mark
30   Pale with scurf⁴ of the salt, seamed and baked in the sun!
     Well I remember the piles of blocks and ropes, and the net-reels
     Wound with the beaded nets, dripping and dark from the sea!
     Now at this season the nets are unwound; they hang from the rafters
     Over the fresh-stowed hay in upland barns, and the wind
35   Blows all day through the chinks, with the streaks of sunlight, and sways them
     Softly at will; or they lie heaped in the gloom of a loft.

     Now at this season the reels are empty and idle; I see them
     Over the lines of the dikes, over the gossiping grass,
     Now at this season they swing in the long strong wind, thro' the lonesome
40   Golden afternoon, shunned by the foraging gulls.
     Near about sunset the crane will journey homeward above them;
     Round them, under the moon, all the calm night long,
     Winnowing soft grey wings of marsh-owls wander and wander,
     Now to the broad, lit marsh, now to the dusk of the dike.
45   Soon, thro' their dew-wet frames, in the live keen freshness of morning,
     Out of the teeth of the dawn blows back the awakening wind.
     Then, as the blue day mounts, and the low-shot shafts of the sunlight
     Glance from the tide to the shore, gossamers jewelled with dew
     Sparkle and wave, where late sea-spoiling fathoms of drift-net
50   Myriad-meshed, uploomed sombrely over the land.

2 ribbon. 3 containing ramparts (protective embankments). 4 scales.

Well I remember it all. The salt, raw scent of the margin;
While, with men at the windlass, groaned each reel, and the net,
Surging in ponderous lengths, uprose and coiled in its station;
Then each man to his home, — well I remember it all!

55   Yet, as I sit and watch, this present peace of the landscape, —
Stranded boats, these reels empty and idle, the hush,
One grey hawk slow-wheeling above yon cluster of haystacks, —
More than the old-time stir this stillness welcomes me home.
Ah, the old-time stir, how once it stung me with rapture, —
60   Old-time sweetness, the winds freighted with honey and salt!
Yet will I stay my steps and not go down to the marshland, —
Muse and recall far off, rather remember than see, —
Lest on too close sight I miss the darling illusion,
Spy at their task even here the hands of chance and change.

(1883)

The Potato Harvest

A high bare field, brown from the plough, and borne
    Aslant from sunset; amber wastes of sky
    Washing the ridge; a clamour of crows that fly
In from the wide flats where the spent tides mourn
5   To yon their rocking roosts in pines wind-torn;
    A line of grey snake-fence that zigzags by
    A pond and cattle; from the homestead nigh
The long deep summonings of the supper horn.

Black on the ridge, against that lonely flush,
10   A cart, and stoop-necked oxen; ranged beside
    Some barrels; and the day-worn harvest-folk,
Here emptying their baskets, jar the hush
    With hollow thunders. Down the dusk hillside
    Lumbers the wain;[1] and day fades out like smoke.

(1886)

1 wagon.

The Winter Fields

Winds here, and sleet, and frost that bites like steel.
   The low bleak hill rounds under the low sky.
   Naked of flock and fold the fallows lie,
Thin streaked with meagre drift. The gusts reveal
5 By fits the dim grey snakes of fence, that steal
   Through the white dusk. The hill-foot poplars sigh,
   While storm and death with winter trample by,
And the iron fields ring sharp, and blind lights reel.
Yet in the lonely ridges, wrenched with pain,
10 Harsh solitary hillocks, bound and dumb,
Grave glebes[1] close-lipped beneath the scourge and chain,
   Lurks hid the germ of ecstasy — the sum
Of life that waits on summer, till the rain
   Whisper in April and the crocus come.

(1890)

The Herring Weir[1]

Back to the green deeps of the outer bay
   The red and amber currents glide and cringe,
   Diminishing behind a luminous fringe
Of cream-white surf and wandering wraiths of spray.
5 Stealthily, in the old reluctant way,
   The red flats are uncovered, mile on mile,
   To glitter in the sun a golden while.
Far down the flats, a phantom sharply grey,
The herring weir emerges, quick with spoil.
10 Slowly the tide forsakes it. Then draws near,
   Descending from the farm-house on the height,
A cart, with gaping tubs. The oxen toil
   Sombrely o'er the level to the weir,
   And drag a long black trail across the light.

(1893)

1 fields.
1 fence of stakes erected to catch fish.

Archibald Lampman   (1861–1899)

Born in 1861 in Morpeth, Canada West (Ontario), Lampman graduated from the University of Toronto in 1882 and spent his working life as a clerk with the Post Office Department, Ottawa. The most accomplished of the Confederation Poets — a group of literary nationalists intent on developing a distinctive Canadian literature — he had a talent for precise observation of nature. Lampman refined his knowledge of nature with walking tours in the country-side and canoe trips into the wilderness with his friend and fellow poet, Duncan Campbell Scott. Not surprisingly, perhaps, his poetry was heavily influenced by the English Romantics, who recorded in poetry their responses to similar excursions. The influence of Keats is especially prominent in Lampman's characteristic device: a detailed description of nature leads to the focus on a solitary observer who begins to "dream," to experience a state of transcendent harmony. It is also evident in his concern for exploiting the musical possibilities of language. Romantic reverie represents only one side of Lampman's poetry, however. He sometimes shows an ambivalence about Canadian nature, presenting it as both beautiful and frightening. In darker poems, he completely replaces the dream of romantic harmony with a vision of modern industrial society as a dehumanizing nightmare.

Heat

From plains that reel to southward, dim,
    The road runs by me white and bare;
Up the steep hill it seems to swim
    Beyond, and melt into the glare.
5 Upward half-way, or it may be
    Nearer the summit, slowly steals
A hay-cart, moving dustily
    With idly clacking wheels.

By his cart's side the wagoner
10   Is slouching slowly at his ease,
Half-hidden in the windless blur
    Of white dust puffing to his knees.
This wagon on the height above,
    From sky to sky on either hand,
15 Is the sole thing that seems to move
    In all the heat-held land.

Beyond me in the fields the sun
   Soaks in the grass and hath his will;
I count the marguerites one by one;
20   Even the buttercups are still.
On the brook yonder not a breath
   Disturbs the spider or the midge.
The water-bugs draw close beneath
   The cool gloom of the bridge.

25 Where the far elm-tree shadows flood
   Dark patches in the burning grass,
The cows, each with her peaceful cud,
   Lie waiting for the heat to pass.
From somewhere on the slope near by
30   Into the pale depth of the noon
A wandering thrush slides leisurely
   His thin revolving tune.

In intervals of dreams I hear
   The cricket from the droughty ground;
35 The grasshoppers spin into mine ear
   A small innumerable sound.
I lift mine eyes sometimes to gaze:
   The burning sky-line blinds my sight:
The woods far off are blue with haze:
40   The hills are drenched in light.

And yet to me not this or that
   Is always sharp or always sweet;
In the sloped shadow of my hat
   I lean at rest, and drain the heat;
45 Nay more, I think some blessèd power
   Hath brought me wandering idly here:
In the full furnace of this hour
   My thoughts grow keen and clear.

(1888)

In November

With loitering step and quiet eye,
Beneath the low November sky,
I wandered in the woods, and found
A clearing, where the broken ground
Was scattered with black stumps and briers,
And the old wreck of forest fires.
It was a bleak and sandy spot,
And, all about, the vacant plot,
Was peopled and inhabited
By scores of mulleins[1] long since dead.
A silent and forsaken brood
In that mute opening of the wood,
So shrivelled and so thin they were,
So gray, so haggard, and austere,
Not plants at all they seemed to me,
But rather some spare company
Of hermit folk, who long ago,
Wandering in bodies to and fro,
Had chanced upon this lonely way,
And rested thus, till death one day
Surprised them at their compline[2] prayer,
And left them standing lifeless there.

There was no sound about the wood
Save the wind's secret stir. I stood
Among the mullein-stalks as still
As if myself had grown to be
One of their sombre company,
A body without wish or will.
And as I stood, quite suddenly,
Down from a furrow in the sky
The sun shone out a little space
Across that silent sober place,
Over the sand heaps and brown sod,
The mulleins and dead goldenrod,

—————→

1 tall plants with coarse, woolly leaves and dense spikes of flowers. 2 the last of seven canonical hours; the last service of the day.

35 And passed beyond the thickets gray,
    And lit the fallen leaves that lay,
    Level and deep within the wood,
    A rustling yellow multitude.

    All around me the thin light,
40 So sere, so melancholy bright,
    Fell like the half-reflected gleam
    Or shadow of some former dream;
    A moment's golden reverie
    Poured out on every plant and tree
45 A semblance of weird joy, or less,
    A sort of spectral happiness;
    And I, too, standing idly there,
    With muffled hands in the chill air,
    Felt the warm glow about my feet,
50 And shuddering betwixt cold and heat,
    Drew my thoughts closer, like a cloak,
    While something in my blood awoke,
    A nameless and unnatural cheer,
    A pleasure secret and austere.

                                        (1895)

Winter Evening

    To-night the very horses springing by
    Toss gold from whitened nostrils. In a dream
    The streets that narrow to the westward gleam
    Like rows of golden palaces; and high
5   From all the crowded chimneys tower and die
    A thousand aureoles. Down in the west
    The brimming plains beneath the sunset rest,
    One burning sea of gold. Soon, soon shall fly
    The glorious vision, and the hours shall feel
10 A mightier master; soon from height to height,
    With silence and the sharp unpitying stars,
    Stern creeping frosts, and winds that touch like steel,
    Out of the depth beyond the eastern bars,
    Glittering and still shall come the awful night.

                                        (1899)

The City of the End of Things

Beside the pounding cataracts
Of midnight streams unknown to us
'Tis builded in the leafless tracts
And valleys huge of Tartarus.[1]
5   Lurid and lofty and vast it seems;
It hath no rounded name that rings,
But I have heard it called in dreams
The City of the End of Things.

Its roofs and iron towers have grown
10   None knoweth how high within the night,
But in its murky streets far down
A flaming terrible and bright
Shakes all the stalking shadows there,
Across the walls, across the floors,
15   And shifts upon the upper air
From out a thousand furnace doors;
And all the while an awful sound
Keeps roaring on continually,
And crashes in the ceaseless round
20   Of a gigantic harmony.
Through its grim depths re-echoing
And all its weary height of walls,
With measured roar and iron ring,
The inhuman music lifts and falls.
25   Where no thing rests and no man is,
And only fire and night hold sway;
The beat, the thunder and the hiss
Cease not, and change not, night nor day.
And moving at unheard commands,
30   The abysses and vast fires between,
Flit figures that with clanking hands
Obey a hideous routine;
They are not flesh, they are not bone,
They see not with the human eye,

———→

---

1 the lowest, gloomiest region of Hades, into which Zeus hurled the Titans and Giants; hell.

35   And from their iron lips is blown
A dreadful and monotonous cry;
And whoso of our mortal race
Should find that city unaware,
Lean Death would smite him face to face,
40   And blanch him with its venomed air:
Or caught by the terrific spell,
Each thread of memory snapt and cut,
His soul would shrivel and its shell
Go rattling like an empty nut.

45   It was not always so, but once,
In days that no man thinks upon,
Fair voices echoed from its stones,
The light above it leaped and shone:
Once there were multitudes of men,
50   That built that city in their pride,
Until its might was made, and then
They withered age by age and died.
But now of that prodigious race,
Three only in an iron tower,
55   Set like carved idols face to face,
Remain the masters of its power;
And at the city gate a fourth,
Gigantic and with dreadful eyes,
Sits looking toward the lightless north,
60   Beyond the reach of memories;
Fast rooted to the lurid floor,
A bulk that never moves a jot,
In his pale body dwells no more,
Or mind or soul, — an idiot!
65   But sometime in the end those three
Shall perish and their hands be still,
And with the master's touch shall flee
Their incommunicable skill.
A stillness absolute as death
70   Along the slacking wheels shall lie,
And, flagging at a single breath,

—————→

The fires that moulder out and die.
The roar shall vanish at its height,
And over that tremendous town
75   The silence of eternal night
Shall gather close and settle down.
All its grim grandeur, tower and hall,
Shall be abandoned utterly,
And into rust and dust shall fall
80   From century to century;
Nor ever living thing shall grow,
Nor trunk of tree, nor blade of grass;
No drop shall fall, no wind shall blow,
Nor sound of any foot shall pass:
85   Alone of its accursèd state,
One thing the hand of Time shall spare,
For the grim Idiot at the gate
Is deathless and eternal there.

(1899)

Duncan Campbell Scott (1862–1947)

One of the Confederation Poets, a group inspired by the success of Charles G.D. Roberts to work toward a distinctly Canadian poetry, Duncan Campbell Scott often substituted for the pastoral subjects that characterized the work of his colleagues portraits of the indigenous peoples and of wilderness landscapes. Born in Ottawa, Scott was a lifelong civil servant who rose to be deputy superintendent general in the Department of Indian Affairs. As a consequence of his duties, which enabled him to travel throughout the Canadian North and West, he came to believe that the Native peoples were doomed to extinction as separate peoples, a belief evident in a number of his poems. His experiences also developed in him a deep feeling for the wilderness, which he described as a replacement for the church of his youth. Scott was both lyrical and intellectual. He declared in "An Autobiographical Note" that "Everything I write starts with its rhythmical life . . ." and that "I value brain power at the bottom of everything." As a lyric poet, he organized this "rhythmical life" through carefully developed metres, rhymes, and repetition; as an intellectual poet, he characteristically exercised "brain power" by organizing poems according to dialectic oppositions or paired terms.

The Forsaken

I

Once in the winter
Out on a lake
In the heart of the north-land,
Far from the Fort
5 And far from the hunters,
A Chippewa woman
With her sick baby,
Crouched in the last hours
Of a great storm.
10 Frozen and hungry,
She fished through the ice
With a line of the twisted
Bark of the cedar,
And a rabbit-bone hook
15 Polished and barbed;
Fished with the bare hook
All through the wild day,
Fished and caught nothing;
While the young chieftain
20 Tugged at her breasts,
Or slept in the lacings
Of the warm *tikanagan*.[1]
All the lake-surface
Streamed with the hissing
25 Of millions of iceflakes
Hurled by the wind;
Behind her the round
Of a lonely island
Roared like a fire
30 With the voice of the storm
In the deeps of the cedars.
Valiant, unshaken,
She took of her own flesh,

——→

1 cradle-board to which is fastened a moss-bag for carrying an infant.

Baited the fish-hook,
35   Drew in a gray-trout,
Drew in his fellows,
Heaped them beside her,
Dead in the snow.
Valiant, unshaken,
40   She faced the long distance,
Wolf-haunted and lonely,
Sure of her goal
And the life of her dear one:
Tramped for two days,
45   On the third in the morning,
Saw the strong bulk
Of the Fort by the river,
Saw the wood-smoke
Hang soft in the spruces,
50   Heard the keen yelp
Of the ravenous huskies
Fighting for whitefish:
Then she had rest.

II

Years and years after,
55   When she was old and withered,
When her son was an old man
And his children filled with vigour,
They came in their northern tour on the verge of winter,
To an island in a lonely lake.
60   There one night they camped, and on the morrow
Gathered their kettles and birch-bark
Their rabbit-skin robes and their mink-traps,
Launched their canoes and slunk away through the islands,
Left her alone forever,
65   Without a word of farewell,
Because she was old and useless,
Like a paddle broken and warped,
Or a pole that was splintered.

                        ⟶

Then, without a sigh,
70   Valiant, unshaken,
She smoothed her dark locks under her kerchief,
Composed her shawl in state,
Then folded her hands rigid with sinews and corded with veins,
Folded them across her breasts spent with the nourishing of children,
75   Gazed at the sky past the tops of the cedars,
Saw two spangled nights arise out of the twilight,
Saw two days go by filled with the tranquil sunshine,
Saw, without pain, or dread, or even a moment of longing:
Then on the third great night there came thronging and thronging
80   Millions of snowflakes out of a windless cloud;
They covered her close with a beautiful crystal shroud,
Covered her deep and silent.
But in the frost of the dawn,
Up from the life below,
85   Rose a column of breath
Through a tiny cleft in the snow,
Fragile, delicately drawn,
Wavering with its own weakness,
In the wilderness a sign of the spirit,
90   Persisting still in the sight of the sun
Till day was done.
Then all light was gathered up by the hand of God and hid in His breast,
Then there was born a silence deeper than silence,
Then she had rest.

(1905)

Night Hymns on Lake Nipigon

Here in the midnight, where the dark mainland and island
Shadows mingle in shadow deeper, profounder,
Sing we the hymns of the churches, while the dead water
    Whispers before us.

5   Thunder is travelling slow on the path of the lightning;
One after one the stars and the beaming planets
Look serene in the lake from the edge of the storm-cloud,
    Then have they vanished.

While our canoe, that floats dumb in the bursting thunder,
10   Gathers her voice in the quiet and thrills and whispers,
Presses her prow in the star-gleam, and all her ripple
    Lapses in blackness.

Sing we the sacred ancient hymns of the churches,
Chanted first in old-world nooks of the desert,
15   While in the wild, pellucid Nipigon reaches
    Hunted the savage.

Now have the ages met in the Northern midnight,
And on the lonely, loon-haunted Nipigon reaches
Rises the hymn of triumph and courage and comfort,
20   Adeste Fideles.[1]

Tones that were fashioned when the faith brooded in darkness,
Joined with sonorous vowels in the noble Latin,
Now are married with the long-drawn Ojibwa,
    Uncouth and mournful.

25   Soft with the silver drip of the regular paddles
Falling in rhythm, timed with the liquid, plangent
Sounds from the blades where the whirlpools break and are carried
    Down into darkness;

Each long cadence, flying like a dove from her shelter
30   Deep in the shadow, wheels for a throbbing moment,
Poises in utterance, returning in circles of silver
    To nest in the silence.

1 "O Come All Ye Faithful."

All wild nature stirs with the infinite, tender
Plaint of a bygone age whose soul is eternal,
35   Bound in the lonely phrases that thrill and falter
       Back into quiet.

Back they falter as the deep storm overtakes them,
Whelms them in splendid hollows of booming thunder,
Wraps them in rain, that, sweeping, breaks and on-rushes
40   Ringing like cymbals.

(1905)

William Butler Yeats (1865–1939)

Born and raised in Dublin, Ireland, William Butler Yeats became one of the leaders in the Irish nationalist movement in the late nineteenth and early twentieth centuries, and was influential in the formation of the Irish Literary Society and the Irish National Theatre Company. Many of his poems and plays are based on Irish legends and folklore. Yeats rejected conventional religious beliefs and studied a variety of religious and philosophical systems, out of which he developed his own poetic mythology, published in *A Vision* (1925, revised in 1937). He believed that history was divided into 2000-year cycles. As he implied in "Leda and the Swan," the classical age had begun with the union of the god Zeus (who assumed the form of a swan) and a human being, Leda. The Christian age, which ended the classical, commenced with the union of the Holy Spirit (in the form of a dove) and the Virgin Mary. The period of the Byzantine Empire, between the fifth and fifteenth centuries, represented the Christian age's era of greatest artistic achievement, while the twentieth century marked the final phase of its destruction. Many of the ideas in his system are complex and obscure and are dismissed by some as muddle-headed and foolish; however, it provided him with a number of symbols that, in "The Second Coming," "Sailing to Byzantium," and "Among School Children," are used to present the individual's quest for meaning in the chaotic modern world. In such poems as "Easter 1916," Yeats commented on the tumultuous and often tragic conflicts between the Irish and the British. "Crazy Jane Talks with the Bishop" embodies his belief that great wisdom can be found in the words of old, common, or apparently crazy people.

Easter 1916 [1]

I have met them at close of day
Coming with vivid faces
From counter or desk among grey
Eighteenth-century houses.
5   I have passed with a nod of the head
Or polite meaningless words,
Or have lingered awhile and said
Polite meaningless words,
And thought before I had done
10   Of a mocking tale or a gibe
To please a companion
Around the fire at the club,
Being certain that they and I
But lived where motley [2] is worn:
15   All changed, changed utterly:
A terrible beauty is born.

That woman's days were spent
In ignorant good-will,
Her nights in argument
20   Until her voice grew shrill.
What voice more sweet than hers
When, young and beautiful,
She rode to harriers? [3]
This man had kept a school
25   And rode our wingèd horse; [4]
This other his helper and friend
Was coming into his force;
He might have won fame in the end,
So sensitive his nature seemed,
30   So daring and sweet his thought.
This other man I had dreamed
A drunken, vainglorious lout.
He had done most bitter wrong
To some who are near my heart,
35   Yet I number him in the song;
He, too, has resigned his part

——————→

1 at Easter 1916, Irish nationalists unsuccessfully rebelled against the British government. Many nationalists
were executed. 2 many-coloured cloth often used in the clothing of court jesters. 3 i.e., on a hunt with
hounds. 4 Pegasus, the winged horse associated with poetry in Greek mythology.

In the casual comedy;
He, too, has been changed in his turn,
Transformed utterly:
40   A terrible beauty is born.

Hearts with one purpose alone
Through summer and winter seem
Enchanted to a stone
To trouble the living stream.
45   The horse that comes from the road,
The rider, the birds that range
From cloud to tumbling cloud,
Minute by minute they change;
A shadow of cloud on the stream
50   Changes minute by minute;
A horse-hoof slides on the brim,
And a horse plashes within it;
The long-legged moor-hens dive,
And hens to moor-cocks call;
55   Minute by minute they live:
The stone's in the midst of all.

Too long a sacrifice
Can make a stone of the heart.
O when may it suffice?
60   That is Heaven's part, our part
To murmur name upon name,
As a mother names her child
When sleep at last has come
On limbs that had run wild.
65   What is it but nightfall?
No, no, not night but death;
Was it needless death after all?
For England may keep faith
For all that is done and said.
70   We know their dream; enough
To know they dreamed and are dead;
And what if excess of love
Bewildered them till they died?
I write it out in a verse —
75   MacDonagh and MacBride

→

And Connolly and Pearse[5]
Now and in time to be,
Wherever green is worn,
Are changed, changed utterly:
80   A terrible beauty is born.

(1916)   (1921)

The Second Coming[1]

Turning and turning in the widening gyre[2]
The falcon cannot hear the falconer;
Things fall apart; the centre cannot hold;
Mere anarchy is loosed upon the world,
5   The blood-dimmed tide is loosed, and everywhere
The ceremony of innocence is drowned;
The best lack all conviction, while the worst
Are full of passionate intensity.

Surely some revelation is at hand;
10   Surely the Second Coming is at hand.
The Second Coming! Hardly are those words out
When a vast image out of *Spiritus Mundi*[3]
Troubles my sight; somewhere in sands of the desert
A shape with lion body and the head of a man,
15   A gaze blank and pitiless as the sun,
Is moving its slow thighs, while all about it
Reel shadows of the indignant desert birds.
The darkness drops again; but now I know
That twenty centuries of stony sleep
20   Were vexed to nightmare by a rocking cradle,
And what rough beast, its hour come round at last,
Slouches towards Bethlehem[4] to be born?

(1919)   (1920)

---

5 four Irish patriots who were executed by the British after the Easter uprising.
1 traditionally, the coming of Jesus Christ on the Day of Judgement. 2 spiral. 3 the Spirit of the Universe.
4 birthplace of Jesus Christ.

Leda and the Swan [1]

A sudden blow: the great wings beating still
Above the staggering girl, her thighs caressed
By the dark webs, her nape caught in his bill,
He holds her helpless breast upon his breast.

5   How can those terrified vague fingers push
The feathered glory from her loosening thighs?
And how can body, laid in that white rush,
But feel the strange heart beating where it lies?

A shudder in the loins engenders there
10   The broken wall, the burning roof and tower [2]
And Agamemnon dead. [3]
               Being so caught up,
So mastered by the brute blood of the air,
Did she put on his knowledge with his power
Before the indifferent beak could let her drop?

(1923)
                                     (1924)

Sailing to Byzantium [1]

I

That is no country for old men. The young
In one another's arms, birds in the trees
— Those dying generations — at their song,
The salmon-falls, the mackerel-crowded seas,
5   Fish, flesh, or fowl, commend all summer long
Whatever is begotten, born, and dies.
Caught in that sensual music all neglect
Monuments of unageing intellect.

1 Zeus, in the form of a swan, raped Leda, a Spartan Queen, who subsequently gave birth to Helen and
Clytemnestra. 2 Helen, the most beautiful woman in the world, married Menelaus, but Paris abducted her,
thus causing the war that ended in the destruction of Troy. 3 Agamemnon, the leader of the Greek forces
attacking Troy, was murdered by Clytemnestra, his wife, when he returned from the Trojan War.
1 Greek city on whose site was built the city of Constantinople (now known as Istanbul), noted for its
exceptional art.

II

An aged man is but a paltry thing,
A tattered coat upon a stick, unless
Soul clap its hands and sing, and louder sing
For every tatter in its mortal dress,
Nor is there singing school but studying
Monuments of its own magnificence;
And therefore I have sailed the seas and come
To the holy city of Byzantium.

III

O sages standing in God's holy fire
As in the gold mosaic of a wall,
Come from the holy fire, perne in a gyre,[2]
And be the singing-masters of my soul.
Consume my heart away; sick with desire
And fastened to a dying animal
It knows not what it is; and gather me
Into the artifice of eternity.

IV

Once out of nature I shall never take
My bodily form from any natural thing,
But such a form as Grecian goldsmiths make
Of hammered gold and gold enamelling
To keep a drowsy Emperor awake;
Or set upon a golden bough to sing
To lords and ladies of Byzantium
Of what is past, or passing, or to come.

(1926)   (1927)

Among School Children

I

I walk through the long schoolroom questioning;
A kind old nun in a white hood replies;

→

2 spin in a spiral motion.

The children learn to cipher and to sing,
To study reading-books and histories,
5   To cut and sew, be neat in everything
In the best modern way — the children's eyes
In momentary wonder stare upon
A sixty-year-old smiling public man.

II

I dream of a Ledaean[1] body, bent
10 Above a sinking fire, a tale that she
Told of a harsh reproof, or trivial event
That changed some childish day to tragedy —
Told, and it seemed that our two natures blent
Into a sphere from youthful sympathy,
15 Or else, to alter Plato's parable,[2]
Into the yolk and white of the one shell.

III

And thinking of that fit of grief or rage
I look upon one child or t'other there
And wonder if she stood so at that age —
20 For even daughters of the swan can share
Something of every paddler's heritage —
And had that colour upon cheek or hair,
And thereupon my heart is driven wild:
She stands before me as a living child.

IV

25 Her present image floats into the mind —
Did Quattrocento[3] finger fashion it
Hollow of cheek as though it drank the wind
And took a mess of shadows for its meat?
And I though never of Ledaean kind
30 Had pretty plumage once — enough of that,
Better to smile on all that smile, and show
There is a comfortable kind of old scarecrow.

1 like Leda, a beautiful woman in Greek mythology. 2 in this legend, human beings originally had four legs,
four arms, and two faces. This body later split into two. The embrace of love was an attempt to become
reunified. 3 fifteenth century. The term usually refers to Italian painting of the period.

V

What youthful mother, a shape upon her lap
Honey of generation had betrayed,
35 And that must sleep, shriek, struggle to escape
As recollection or the drug decide,
Would think her son, did she but see that shape
With sixty or more winters on its head,
A compensation for the pang of his birth,
40 Or the uncertainty of his setting forth?

VI

Plato thought nature but a spume that plays
Upon a ghostly paradigm of things;
Solider Aristotle played the taws
Upon the bottom of a king of kings;
45 World-famous golden-thighed Pythagoras [4]
Fingered upon a fiddle-stick or strings
What a star sang and careless Muses heard:
Old clothes upon old sticks to scare a bird.

VII

Both nuns and mothers worship images,
50 But those the candles light are not as those
That animate a mother's reveries,
But keep a marble or a bronze repose.
And yet they too break hearts — O Presences
That passion, piety or affection knows,
55 And that all heavenly glory symbolise —
O self-born mockers of man's enterprise;

VIII

Labour is blossoming or dancing where
The body is not bruised to pleasure soul,
Nor beauty born out of its own despair,
60 Nor blear-eyed wisdom out of midnight oil.
O chestnut-tree, great-rooted blossomer,
Are you the leaf, the blossom or the bole?
O body swayed to music, O brightening glance,
How can we know the dancer from the dance?

(1926)   (1927)

4 Plato, Aristotle, and Pythagoras were ancient Greek philosophers.

Crazy Jane Talks with the Bishop

I met the Bishop on the road
And much said he and I.
"Those breasts are flat and fallen now,
Those veins must soon be dry;
5   Live in a heavenly mansion,
Not in some foul sty."

"Fair and foul are near of kin,
And fair needs foul," I cried.
"My friends are gone, but that's a truth
10   Nor grave nor bed denied,
Learned in bodily lowliness
And in the heart's pride.

"A woman can be proud and stiff
When on love intent;
15   But Love has pitched his mansion in
The place of excrement;
For nothing can be sole or whole
That has not been rent."

(1931)   (1932)

Robert Frost (1874–1963)

Though born in California, Robert Frost wrote most of his poetry about life in New England, where his family originated and where he moved at age eleven with his widowed mother. Frost had the ability, rare in modern times, to appeal to both sophisticated and unsophisticated audiences with the same poems, and he eventually became the most popular serious poet of his country. But success did not come easily. He wrote in obscurity until middle age, supporting his family mainly by farming and teaching, and received recognition in his own country only after his first two books, *A Boy's Will* (1913) and *North of Boston* (1914), had been published and praised in England.

Although Frost was learned and intellectual, and taught in various universities after 1915, he preferred to present himself as a rustic sage whose wisdom was derived from common sense and the everyday experiences he explored in his poetry. Despite its wide appeal, this public persona, together with Frost's reliance on traditional forms and his treatment of homely subjects, gives many of his best-known poems the deceptive appearance of slightness, but Frost confronts the darkness and philosophical uncertainty of modern life as honestly as any of his contemporaries, and his work is highly innovative in its use of vernacular speech and conversational rhythms.

After Apple-Picking

My long two-pointed ladder's sticking through a tree
Toward heaven still,
And there's a barrel that I didn't fill
Beside it, and there may be two or three
5   Apples I didn't pick upon some bough.
But I am done with apple-picking now.
Essence of winter sleep is on the night,
The scent of apples: I am drowsing off.
I cannot rub the strangeness from my sight
10   I got from looking through a pane of glass
I skimmed this morning from the drinking trough
And held against the world of hoary grass.
It melted, and I let it fall and break.
But I was well
15   Upon my way to sleep before it fell,
And I could tell
What form my dreaming was about to take.
Magnified apples appear and disappear,
Stem end and blossom end,
20   And every fleck of russet showing clear.
My instep arch not only keeps the ache,
It keeps the pressure of a ladder-round.
I feel the ladder sway as the boughs bend.
And I keep hearing from the cellar bin
25   The rumbling sound
Of load on load of apples coming in.
For I have had too much
Of apple-picking: I am overtired
Of the great harvest I myself desired.
30   There were ten thousand thousand fruit to touch,
Cherish in hand, lift down, and not let fall.
For all
That struck the earth,
No matter if not bruised or spiked with stubble,
35   Went surely to the cider-apple heap
As of no worth.
One can see what will trouble

——→

This sleep of mine, whatever sleep it is.
Were he not gone,
40   The woodchuck could say whether it's like his
Long sleep, as I describe its coming on,
Or just some human sleep.

(1914)

An Old Man's Winter Night

All out-of-doors looked darkly in at him
Through the thin frost, almost in separate stars,
That gathers on the pane in empty rooms.
What kept his eyes from giving back the gaze
5   Was the lamp tilted near them in his hand.
What kept him from remembering what it was
That brought him to that creaking room was age.
He stood with barrels round him — At a loss.
And having scared the cellar under him
10   In clomping here, he scared it once again
In clomping off; — and scared the outer night,
Which has its sounds, familiar, like the roar
Of trees and crack of branches, common things,
But nothing so like beating on a box.
15   A light he was to no one but himself
Where now he sat, concerned with he knew what,
A quiet light, and then not even that.
He consigned to the moon, such as she was,
So late-arising, to the broken moon
20   As better than the sun in any case
For such a charge, his snow upon the roof,
His icicles along the wall to keep;
And slept. The log that shifted with a jolt
Once in the stove, disturbed him and he shifted,
25   And eased his heavy breathing, but still slept.
One aged man — one man — can't keep a house,
A farm, a countryside, or if he can,
It's thus he does it of a winter night.

(1916)

Stopping by Woods on a Snowy Evening

Whose woods these are I think I know.
His house is in the village though;
He will not see me stopping here
To watch his woods fill up with snow.

5   My little horse must think it queer
To stop without a farmhouse near
Between the woods and frozen lake
The darkest evening of the year.

He gives his harness bells a shake
10   To ask if there is some mistake.
The only other sound's the sweep
Of easy wind and downy flake.

The woods are lovely, dark and deep,
But I have promises to keep,
15   And miles to go before I sleep,
And miles to go before I sleep.

(1923)

Acquainted with the Night

I have been one acquainted with the night.
I have walked out in rain — and back in rain.
I have outwalked the furthest city light.

I have looked down the saddest city lane.
5   I have passed by the watchman on his beat
And dropped my eyes, unwilling to explain.

I have stood still and stopped the sound of feet
When far away an interrupted cry
Came over houses from another street,

10 But not to call me back or say good-by;
And further still at an unearthly height,
One luminary clock against the sky

Proclaimed the time was neither wrong nor right.
I have been one acquainted with the night.

(1928)

Design

I found a dimpled spider, fat and white,
On a white heal-all,[1] holding up a moth
Like a white piece of rigid satin cloth —
Assorted characters of death and blight
5 Mixed ready to begin the morning right,
Like the ingredients of a witches' broth —
A snow-drop spider, a flower like a froth,
And dead wings carried like a paper kite.

What had that flower to do with being white,
10 The wayside blue and innocent heal-all?
What brought the kindred spider to that height,
Then steered the white moth thither in the night?
What but design of darkness to appall?—
If design govern in a thing so small.

(1936)

1 plant (*Prunella vulgaris*, also called woundwort), normally with blue flowers, thought to have healing power.

Wallace Stevens (1879–1955)

Born in Pennsylvania and educated at Harvard and the New York Law School, Wallace Stevens lived most of his adult life in Hartford, Connecticut, where he advanced to the rank of vice-president with the Hartford Accident and Indemnity Company. Although Stevens began writing poetry seriously when at university, he devoted much of his energy to law and business in the years that followed and was forty-four when his first collection of poems, *Harmonium* (1923), was published. From late middle age on, having become financially secure, Stevens devoted himself increasingly to his poetry. Although he is a philosophical poet, much concerned with ideas of order and the relationship between imagination and reality, Stevens is also a master at evoking complex sensuous experience; his poems are distinguished by the originality of their opulent, intricate images and their subtle, deftly controlled rhythms.

Thirteen Ways of Looking at a Blackbird

I

Among twenty snowy mountains,
The only moving thing
Was the eye of the blackbird.

II

I was of three minds,
Like a tree
In which there are three blackbirds.

III

The blackbird whirled in the autumn winds.
It was a small part of the pantomime.

IV

A man and a woman
Are one.
A man and a woman and a blackbird
Are one.

V

I do not know which to prefer,
The beauty of inflections
15 Or the beauty of innuendoes,
The blackbird whistling
Or just after.

VI

Icicles filled the long window
With barbaric glass.
20 The shadow of the blackbird
Crossed it, to and fro.
The mood
Traced in the shadow
An indecipherable cause.

VII

25 O thin men of Haddam,[1]
Why do you imagine golden birds?
Do you not see how the blackbird
Walks around the feet
Of the women about you?

VIII

30 I know noble accents
And lucid, inescapable rhythms;
But I know, too,
That the blackbird is involved
In what I know.

IX

35 When the blackbird flew out of sight,
It marked the edge
Of one of many circles.

1 town in Connecticut.

X

At the sight of blackbirds
Flying in a green light,
40   Even the bawds of euphony
Would cry out sharply.

XI

He rode over Connecticut
In a glass coach.
Once, a fear pierced him,
45   In that he mistook
The shadow of his equipage
For blackbirds.

XII

The river is moving.
The blackbird must be flying.

XIII

50   It was evening all afternoon.
It was snowing
And it was going to snow.
The blackbird sat
In the cedar-limbs.

(1931)

The Idea of Order at Key West

She sang beyond the genius of the sea.
The water never formed to mind or voice,
Like a body wholly body, fluttering
Its empty sleeves; and yet its mimic motion
5   Made constant cry, caused constantly a cry,
That was not ours although we understood,
Inhuman, of the veritable ocean.

The sea was not a mask. No more was she.
The song and water were not medleyed sound

10 Even if what she sang was what she heard,
Since what she sang was uttered word by word.
It may be that in all her phrases stirred
The grinding water and the gasping wind;
But it was she and not the sea we heard.

15 For she was the maker of the song she sang.
The ever-hooded, tragic-gestured sea
Was merely a place by which she walked to sing.
Whose spirit is this? we said, because we knew
It was the spirit that we sought and knew

20 That we should ask this often as she sang.

If it was only the dark voice of the sea
That rose, or even colored by many waves;
If it was only the outer voice of sky
And cloud, of the sunken coral water-walled,

25 However clear, it would have been deep air,
The heaving speech of air, a summer sound
Repeated in a summer without end
And sound alone. But it was more than that,
More even than her voice, and ours, among

30 The meaningless plungings of water and the wind,
Theatrical distances, bronze shadows heaped
On high horizons, mountainous atmospheres
Of sky and sea.
                        It was her voice that made
The sky acutest at its vanishing.

35 She measured to the hour its solitude.
She was the single artificer of the world
In which she sang. And when she sang, the sea,
Whatever self it had, became the self
That was her song, for she was the maker. Then we,

40 As we beheld her striding there alone,
Knew that there never was a world for her
Except the one she sang and, singing, made.

Ramon Fernandez,[1] tell me, if you know,
Why, when the singing ended and we turned
45 Toward the town, tell why the glassy lights,
The lights in the fishing boats at anchor there,
As the night descended, tilting in the air,
Mastered the night and portioned out the sea,
Fixing emblazoned zones and fiery poles,
50 Arranging, deepening, enchanting night.
Oh! Blessed rage for order, pale Ramon,
The maker's rage to order words of the sea,
Words of the fragrant portals, dimly-starred,
And of ourselves and of our origins,
55 In ghostlier demarcations, keener sounds.

(1935)

E.J. Pratt   (1882–1964)

Edwin John Pratt, son of a Methodist minister, was born in Western Bay, Newfoundland. After graduating from St. John's Methodist College and serving as both a teacher and a preacher in several outport villages, he attended Victoria College, University of Toronto, receiving his B.A. (1911), M.A. (1912), B.D. (1913), and Ph.D. (1917). Although ordained in 1913, Pratt never served as a minister. Instead, he became a member of the Victoria College English Department in 1920. He is best known for his lengthy narratives, such as *The Titanic* (1935), *Brébeuf and His Brethren* (1940), and *Towards the Last Spike* (1952), the latter two of which won Governor General's Awards. Pratt's concern for scientific and technological matters, ranging from evolution to communication, is evident throughout his work. His religious background and ethical ideas are embodied in biblical references and images of individuals sacrificing themselves for the common good or enduring inevitable suffering.

The Shark

He seemed to know the harbour,
So leisurely he swam;
His fin,
Like a piece of sheet-iron,
5 Three-cornered,
And with knife-edge,

---

1 Stevens said he simply made this name up with no actual person in mind.

Stirred not a bubble
As it moved
With its base-line on the water.

10   His body was tubular
And tapered
And smoke-blue,
And as he passed the wharf
He turned,
15   And snapped at a flat-fish
That was dead and floating.
And I saw the flash of a white throat,
And a double row of white teeth,
And eyes of metallic grey,
20   Hard and narrow and slit.

Then out of the harbour,
With that three-cornered fin
Shearing without a bubble the water
Lithely,
25   Leisurely,
He swam —
That strange fish,
Tubular, tapered, smoke-blue,
Part vulture, part wolf,
30   Part neither — for his blood was cold.

(1923)

From Stone to Steel

From stone to bronze, from bronze to steel
Along the road-dust of the sun,
Two revolutions of the wheel
From Java[1] to Geneva[2] run.

5   The snarl Neanderthal[3] is worn
Close to the smiling Aryan[4] lips,
The civil polish of the horn
Gleams from our praying finger tips.

The evolution of desire
10   Has but matured a toxic wine,
Drunk long before its heady fire
Reddened Euphrates or the Rhine.[5]

Between the temple and the cave
The boundary lies tissue-thin:
15   The yearlings still the altars crave
As satisfaction for a sin.

The road goes up, the road goes down —
Let Java or Geneva be —
But whether to the cross or crown,
20   The path lies through Gethsemane.[6]

(1932)

---

1 the site of the discovery in 1891 of the fossil remains of an early type of human, Pithecanthropus, or, as he was popularly called, "Java Ape Man." 2 a city long identified with advocating humane and reasonable conduct — the Geneva Convention of 1864 codified rules of war, for example — it was chosen as headquarters for the League of Nations in 1919. 3 cave-dwelling early human of the Upper Pleistocene Age, whose remains were first located in sites in Europe. 4 even before Hitler assumed power in 1933, the term, originally describing a prehistoric group of peoples whose language was presumed to be the basis of most Indo-European languages, was being used to refer to non-Jews of European, especially Nordic, descent. 5 the Euphrates, a major river in southwest Asia, and the Rhine, the principal waterway of Europe, were influential in developing civilizations and were sites of numerous wars. 6 a garden outside the walls of Jerusalem, it was the site of what is known as the agony of Christ: the sorrowing Christ prayed that his coming trials might be removed, yet also resigned himself, saying that God's will, not his own, should prevail. Shortly afterward, Judas betrayed Christ in this garden.

The Truant

"What have you there?" the great Panjandrum[1] said
To the Master of the Revels who had led
A bucking truant with a stiff backbone
Close to the foot of the Almighty's throne.

5   "Right Reverend, most adored,
And forcibly acknowledged Lord
By the keen logic of your two-edged sword!
This creature has presumed to classify
Himself — a biped, rational, six feet high
10 And two feet wide; weighs fourteen stone;[2]
Is guilty of a multitude of sins.
He has abjured his choric origins,
And like an undomesticated slattern,
Walks with tangential step unknown
15 Within the weave of the atomic pattern.
He has developed concepts, grins
Obscenely at your Royal bulletins,
Possesses what he calls a will
Which challenges your power to kill."

20 "What is his pedigree?"

"The base is guaranteed, your Majesty —
Calcium, carbon, phosphorus, vapour
And other fundamentals spun
From the umbilicus of the sun,
25 And yet he says he will not caper
Around your throne, nor toe the rules
For the ballet of the fiery molecules."
"His concepts and denials — scrap them, burn them —
To the chemists with them promptly."
                      "Sire,
30 The stuff is not amenable to fire.
Nothing but their own kind can overturn them.

⟶

---

1 coined by the English dramatist Samuel Foote (1720–77), this is a mock title for a pompous official of exaggerated importance or power. 2 British unit of weight equal to fourteen pounds or about six kilograms.

The chemists have sent back the same old story —
'With our extreme gelatinous apology,
We beg to inform your Imperial Majesty,
Unto whom be dominion and power and glory,
There still remains that strange precipitate
Which has the quality to resist
Our oldest and most trusted catalyst.
It is a substance we cannot cremate
By temperatures known to our Laboratory.'"

And the great Panjandrum's face grew dark —
"I'll put those chemists to their annual purge,
And I myself shall be the thaumaturge[3]
To find the nature of this fellow's spark.
Come, bring him nearer by yon halter rope:
I'll analyse him with the cosmoscope."

Pulled forward with his neck awry,
The little fellow six feet short,
Aware he was about to die,
Committed grave contempt of court
By answering with a flinchless stare
The Awful Presence seated there.

The ALL HIGH swore until his face was black.
He called him a coprophagite,[4]
A genus *homo*, egomaniac,
Third cousin to the family of worms,
A sporozoan[5] from the ooze of night,
Spawn of a spavined[6] troglodyte:[7]
He swore by all the catalogue of terms
Known since the slang of carboniferous[8] Time.
He said that he could trace him back
To pollywogs and earwigs in the slime.
And in his shrillest tenor he began
Reciting his indictment of the man,
Until he closed upon this capital crime —

⟶

35

40

45

50

55

60

65

---

3 worker of miracles or wonders. 4 one who eats dung. 5 class of parasitic protozoans. 6 suffering from
spavin, a disease of horses in which the hock joint becomes inflamed; by extension, lame or broken down.
7 cave-dweller. 8 geological period, beginning about 315 million years ago, during which conditions produced a lush growth of vegetation, the remains of which formed the great coal beds.

"You are accused of singing out of key,
(A foul unmitigated dissonance)
Of shuffling in the measures of the dance,
Then walking out with that defiant, free
70 Toss of your head, banging the doors,
Leaving a stench upon the jacinth[9] floors.
You have fallen like a curse
On the mechanics of my Universe.

"Herewith I measure out your penalty —
75 Hearken while you hear, look while you see:
I send you now upon your homeward route
Where you shall find
Humiliation for your pride of mind.
I shall make deaf the ear, and dim the eye,
80 Put palsy in your touch, make mute
Your speech, intoxicate your cells and dry
Your blood and marrow, shoot
Arthritic needles through your cartilage,
And having parched you with old age,
85 I'll pass you wormwise through the mire;
And when your rebel will
Is mouldered, all desire
Shrivelled, all your concepts broken,
Backward in dust I'll blow you till
90 You join my spiral festival of fire.
Go, Master of the Revels — I have spoken."

And the little genus *homo*, six feet high,
Standing erect, countered with this reply —
"You dumb insouciant invertebrate,
95 You rule a lower than a feudal state —
A realm of flunkey decimals that run,
Return; return and run; again return,
Each group around its little sun,
And every sun a satellite.
100 There they go by day and night,
Nothing to do but run and burn,
Taking turn and turn about,
Light-year in and light-year out,

———→

9 reddish-orange gem.

Dancing, dancing in quadrillions,
105   Never leaving their pavilions.

"Your astronomical conceit
Of bulk and power is anserine.[10]
Your ignorance so thick,
You did not know your own arithmetic.
110   We flung the graphs about your flying feet;
We measured your diameter —
Merely a line
Of zeros prefaced by an integer.
Before we came
115   You had no name.
You did not know direction or your pace;
We taught you all you ever knew
Of motion, time and space.
We healed you of your vertigo
120   And put you in our kindergarten show,
Perambulated you through prisms, drew
Your mileage through the Milky Way,
Lassoed your comets when they ran astray,
Yoked Leo, Taurus, and your team of Bears[11]
125   To pull our kiddy cars of inverse squares.

"Boast not about your harmony,
Your perfect curves, your rings
Of *pure and endless light*[12] —'Twas we
Who pinned upon your Seraphim[13] their wings,
130   And when your brassy heavens rang
With joy that morning while the planets sang
Their choruses of archangelic lore,
'Twas we who ordered the notes upon their score
Out of our winds and strings.
135   Yes! all your shapely forms
Are ours — parabolas of silver light,
Those blueprints of your spiral stairs
From nadir depth to zenith height,
Coronas, rainbows after storms,

——→

10 goose-like; thus, stupid or foolish. 11 constellations: Leo, the lion; Taurus, the bull; and Ursa Major and Ursa Minor, the big bear and little bear, respectively. 12 phrase from the opening of "The World" (1650) by Henry Vaughan (1621–95):
>   I saw eternity the other night
>   Like a great ring of pure and endless light.
13 one of the highest orders of angels.

140 Auroras on your eastern tapestries
     And constellations over western seas.

     "And when, one day, grown conscious of your age,
     While pondering an eolith,[14]
     We turned a human page
145 And blotted out a cosmic myth
     With all its baby symbols to explain
     The sunlight in Apollo's eyes,[15]
     Our rising pulses and the birth of pain,
     Fear, and that fern-and-fungus breath
150 Stalking our nostrils to our caves of death —
     That day we learned how to anatomize
     Your body, calibrate your size
     And set a mirror up before your face
     To show you what you really were — a rain
155 Of dull Lucretian atoms[16] crowding space,
     A series of concentric waves which any fool
     Might make by dropping stones within a pool,
     Or an exploding bomb forever in flight
     Bursting like hell through Chaos and Old Night.[17]

160 "You oldest of the hierarchs
     Composed of electronic sparks,
     We grant you speed,
     We grant you power, and fire
     That ends in ash, but we concede
165 To you no pain nor joy nor love nor hate,
     No final tableau of desire,
     No causes won or lost, no free
     Adventure at the outposts — only
     The degradation of your energy[18]
170 When at some late
     Slow number of your dance your sergeant-major Fate

                              ⟶

14 roughly shaped tool from the earliest stone age. 15 Apollo, the Greek god of music, poetry, archery, healing, and prophecy, was often identified with Helios, the sun god, and given the epithet Phoebus ("Shining One"). 16 in *De rerum natura* (*On the Nature of Things*), the Roman poet and philosopher Lucretius (c. 96–55 B.C.) sought to provide a reasonable explanation for natural phenomena. He argued that, since nothing can come from nothing, all being has its source in minuscule seeds of matter that rain down from a void. 17 in *Paradise Lost* (I.541–43), Milton says of the fallen angels:
     ... the universal host up sent
     A shout that tore Hell's concave, and beyond
     Frighted the reign of Chaos and Old Night.
In Milton's schema, Chaos and Old Night represent the first materials of the cosmos. 18 entropy, one of the concepts of thermodynamics, suggests that the universe must eventually lose all of its energy.

Will catch you blind and groping and will send
You reeling on that long and lonely
Lockstep of your wave-lengths towards your end.

175   "We who have met
With stubborn calm the dawn's hot fusillades;[19]
Who have seen the forehead sweat
Under the tug of pulleys on the joints,
Under the liquidating tally
180   Of the cat-and-truncheon bastinades;[20]
Who have taught our souls to rally
To mountain horns and the sea's rockets
When the needle ran demented through the points;
We who have learned to clench
185   Our fists and raise our lightless sockets
To morning skies after the midnight raids,
Yet cocked our ears to bugles on the barricades,
And in cathedral rubble found a way to quench
A dying thirst within a Galilean valley — [21]
190   No! by the Rood,[22] we will not join your ballet."

(1943)

William Carlos Williams   (1883–1963)

A medical doctor as well as a writer, William Carlos Williams spent most of his life in Rutherford, New Jersey, where he maintained a busy practice as a pediatrician. Williams worked in various genres, producing more than two dozen volumes of poetry, fiction, essays, plays, and autobiography, but he was most influential as a poet. While studying at the University of Pennsylvania, he developed a lasting friendship with Ezra Pound, and through Pound was influenced by imagism, an Anglo-American poetic movement stressing concentration, freedom in form and subject matter, and especially precise, concrete images. Working from imagism, Williams developed a distinctive style of free verse, characterized by careful observation, vivid images, and a reliance on the rhythms and diction of common American speech. Although initially overshadowed by other modernist poets, Williams's influence on American poets since World War II has equalled that of any of his contemporaries.

19 simultaneous discharge of firearms. 20 beatings with whips (cat-o'-nine-tails) and sticks or clubs (truncheons). 21 Galilee was a Roman province in northern Palestine during the time of Christ, who began his ministry there and was sometimes called the Galilean. 22 the cross upon which Christ died.

Tract

I will teach you my townspeople
how to perform a funeral —
for you have it over a troop
of artists —
5   unless one should scour the world —
you have the ground sense necessary.

See! the hearse leads.
I begin with a design for a hearse.
For Christ's sake not black —
10   nor white either — and not polished!
Let it be weathered — like a farm wagon —
with gilt wheels (this could be
applied fresh at small expense)
or no wheels at all:
15   a rough dray to drag over the ground.

Knock the glass out!
My God — glass, my townspeople!
For what purpose? Is it for the dead
to look out or for us to see
20   how well he is housed or to see
the flowers or the lack of them —
or what?
To keep the rain and snow from him?
He will have a heavier rain soon:
25   pebbles and dirt and what not.
Let there be no glass —
and no upholstery, phew!
and no little brass rollers
and small easy wheels on the bottom —
30   my townspeople what are you thinking of?

A rough plain hearse then
with gilt wheels and no top at all.
On this the coffin lies
by its own weight.

           No wreaths please —
35 especially no hot-house flowers.
Some common memento is better,
something he prized and is known by:
his old clothes — a few books perhaps —
God knows what! You realize
40 how we are about these things,
my townspeople —
something will be found — anything —
even flowers if he had come to that.
So much for the hearse.

45 For heaven's sake though see to the driver!
Take off the silk hat! In fact
that's no place at all for him
up there unceremoniously
dragging our friend out to his own dignity!
50 Bring him down — bring him down!
Low and inconspicuous! I'd not have him ride
on the wagon at all — damn him —
the undertaker's understrapper![1]
Let him hold the reins
55 and walk at the side
and inconspicuously too!

Then briefly as to yourselves:
Walk behind — as they do in France,
seventh class, or if you ride
60 Hell take curtains! Go with some show
of inconvenience; sit openly —
to the weather as to grief.

Or do you think you can shut grief in?
What — from us? We who have perhaps
65 nothing to lose? Share with us
share with us — it will be money
in your pockets.
           Go now
I think you are ready.

                                 (1917)

---

1 subordinate; underling.

The Red Wheelbarrow

so much depends
upon

a red wheel
barrow

5   glazed with rain
water

beside the white
chickens.

(1923)

D.H. Lawrence (1885–1930)

The son of a miner, David Herbert Lawrence was born in Eastwood, Nottinghamshire, and was educated at Nottingham University, where he obtained a teacher's certificate in 1908. He gave up teaching in 1912 after falling in love with Frieda von Richthofen, the wife of one of his former professors. They went to Germany and, after her divorce, married in 1914. Lawrence returned to England during World War I, but he travelled extensively during the rest of his life, living for varying periods in Italy, Ceylon, Australia, the United States, Mexico, and France. Frequently ill, he died of tuberculosis in southern France. Lawrence is one of the twentieth century's greatest novelists, a rebel against conformity whose books were often attacked for their frank treatment of sexuality. His first published works, however, were poems printed in the *English Review* in 1909. Although not as obviously an innovator in his poetry, Lawrence rejected traditional forms, believing that each poem should find its own form. Lawrence celebrated the free expression of emotions as a natural part of human identity; he believed that modern civilization was artificial, that it had separated humanity from nature, and that it sought to repress natural and healthy feelings.

Snake

A snake came to my water-trough
On a hot, hot day, and I in pyjamas for the heat,
To drink there.

In the deep, strange-scented shade of the great dark carob-tree
5   I came down the steps with my pitcher
And must wait, must stand and wait, for there he was at the trough
          before me.

He reached down from a fissure in the earth-wall in the gloom
And trailed his yellow-brown slackness soft-bellied down, over the edge
          of the stone trough
And rested his throat upon the stone bottom,
10   And where the water had dripped from the tap, in a small clearness,
He sipped with his straight mouth,
Softly drank through his straight gums, into his slack long body,
Silently.

Someone was before me at my water-trough,
15   And I, like a second comer, waiting.

He lifted his head from his drinking, as cattle do,
And looked at me vaguely, as drinking cattle do,
And flickered his two-forked tongue from his lips, and mused a moment,
And stooped and drank a little more,
20   Being earth-brown, earth-golden from the burning bowels of the earth
On the day of Sicilian July, with Etna smoking.

The voice of my education said to me
He must be killed,
For in Sicily the black, black snakes are innocent, the gold are venomous.

25   And voices in me said, If you were a man
You would take a stick and break him now, and finish him off.

But must I confess how I liked him,
How glad I was he had come like a guest in quiet, to drink at my water-trough
And depart peaceful, pacified, and thankless,
30   Into the burning bowels of this earth?

Was it cowardice, that I dared not kill him?
Was it perversity, that I longed to talk to him?
Was it humility, to feel so honoured?
I felt so honoured.

35 And yet those voices:
If you were not afraid, you would kill him!

And truly I was afraid, I was most afraid,
But even so, honoured still more
That he should seek my hospitality
40 From out of the dark door of the secret earth.

He drank enough
And lifted his head, dreamily, as one who has drunken,
And flickered his tongue like a forked night on the air, so black,
Seeming to lick his lips,
45 And looked around like a god, unseeing, into the air,
And slowly turned his head,
And slowly, very slowly, as if thrice adream,
Proceeded to draw his slow length curving round
And climb again the broken bank of my wall-face.

50 And as he put his head into that dreadful hole,
And as he slowly drew up, snake-easing his shoulders, and entered farther,
A sort of horror, a sort of protest against his withdrawing into that horrid
    black hole,
Deliberately going into the blackness, and slowly drawing himself after,
Overcame me now his back was turned.

55 I looked round, I put down my pitcher,
I picked up a clumsy log
And threw it at the water-trough with a clatter.

I think it did not hit him,
But suddenly that part of him that was left behind convulsed
    in undignified haste,
60 Writhed like lightning, and was gone
Into the black hole, the earth-lipped fissure in the wall-front,
At which, in the intense still noon, I stared with fascination.

And immediately I regretted it.
I thought how paltry, how vulgar, what a mean act!
65   I despised myself and the voices of my accursed human education.

And I thought of the albatross,[1]
And I wished he would come back, my snake.

For he seemed to me again like a king,
Like a king in exile, uncrowned in the underworld,
70   Now due to be crowned again.

And so, I missed my chance with one of the lords
Of life.
And I have something to expiate;
A pettiness.

(1923)

Ezra Pound   (1885–1972)

Ezra Pound was born in Idaho but grew up in Pennsylvania. He specialized in Romance languages and literature at the University of Pennsylvania and received an M.A. in 1906. Considering his native country intellectually oppressive, Pound lived most of the rest of his life in Europe. A leader in the modernist revolution in literature, Pound influenced and assisted dozens of modern writers, including James Joyce, W.B. Yeats, Ernest Hemingway, and T.S. Eliot, whose famous poem "The Waste Land" he edited. Early in his poetic career, he advocated the concentration, free forms, and precise, concrete images of the imagist movement, and while he soon moved away from imagism to write erudite, esoterically allusive poems that all but specialists find daunting, his early insistence on unforced rhythms and clear detail had a pervasive, lasting effect on twentieth-century poetry.

Critical opinion of Pound's own work is divided, partly because it varies in quality and is sometimes extremely difficult, and partly because it reflects his unpopular social and political views. Living in Italy between the world wars and increasingly convinced that art prospered in stable societies with strong leaders, Pound actively supported Italian dictator Benito Mussolini. He became stridently anti-Semitic and attacked the American political and economic system in both writing and radio broadcasts. Charged with treason at the end of World

---

1 see Coleridge's "The Rime of the Ancient Mariner" (page 116), in which the mariner wantonly slays an albatross, which is then hung around his neck as a symbol of his guilt.

War II, he was confined at Pisa and brought to the United States only after his mental condition had deteriorated to the point where he was judged unfit to stand trial. He was confined at St. Elizabeth's Hospital for the criminally insane in Washington until efforts by American writers led to his release in 1958, after which he lived the remainder of his life in Italy.

The River-Merchant's Wife: A Letter[1]

While my hair was still cut straight across my forehead
I played about the front gate, pulling flowers.
You came by on bamboo stilts, playing horse,
You walked about my seat, playing with blue plums.
5   And we went on living in the village of Chokan:[2]
Two small people, without dislike or suspicion.

At fourteen I married My Lord you.
I never laughed, being bashful.
Lowering my head, I looked at the wall.
10   Called to, a thousand times, I never looked back.

At fifteen I stopped scowling,
I desired my dust to be mingled with yours
Forever and forever and forever.
Why should I climb the look out?

15   At sixteen you departed,
You went into far Ku-to-yen,[3] by the river of swirling eddies,
And you have been gone five months.
The monkeys make sorrowful noise overhead.

You dragged your feet when you went out.
20   By the gate now, the moss is grown, the different mosses,
Too deep to clear them away!
The leaves fall early this autumn, in wind.
The paired butterflies are already yellow with August
Over the grass in the West garden;
25   They hurt me. I grow older.
If you are coming down through the narrows of the river Kiang,

——————▶

---

1 adapted from a translation of the Chinese poet Li Po (701?–62), called Rihaku in Japanese. 2 suburb of Nanjing, China. 3 island hundreds of miles up the Kiang River from Nanjing.

Please let me know beforehand,
And I will come out to meet you
           As far as Cho-fu-Sa.[4]

                                  (1915)

In a Station of the Metro

The apparition of these faces in the crowd;
Petals on a wet, black bough.

                                  (1916)

Ancient Music [1]

Winter is icummen in,
Lhude sing Goddamm,
Raineth drop and staineth slop,
And how the wind doth ramm!
5   Sing: Goddamm.
Skiddeth bus and sloppeth us,
An ague hath my ham.
Freezeth river, turneth liver,
            Damn you, sing: Goddamm.
10 Goddamm, Goddamm, 'tis why I am, Goddamm.
            So 'gainst the winter's balm.
Sing goddamm, damm, sing Goddamm,
Sing goddamm, sing goddamm, DAMM.

                                  (1917)

4 beach on the Kiang River not far from Ku-to-yen.
1 parody of the medieval lyric "The Cuckoo Song" (see page 27).

T.S. Eliot (1888–1965)

Thomas Stearns Eliot grew up in St. Louis, Missouri, where his grandfather had founded Washington University. His parents were well-to-do; his mother wrote poetry and supported cultural activities. Eliot attended Harvard, from which he received an M.A., the Sorbonne in Paris, and Oxford. After 1914, he lived mainly in England and became a British subject in 1927. While he first made his living as a teacher, then from 1917 to 1925 as a banker, and later as an editor with the British publisher Faber and Faber, Eliot also devoted himself to writing criticism. In his essays, no less than in his poetry, he had an immense influence on the literature of his time.

The development of Eliot's poetry reflects his personal struggle to find meaning and order in an age that seemed to many to deny them. Such early poems as "The Love Song of J. Alfred Prufrock" and "The Waste Land" captured the mood of doubt, the loss of confidence in Western traditions and religion, that followed World War I. *The Four Quartets* and his verse plays, written after his conversion to Anglo-Catholicism in the late 1920s, reflect his personal solutions to this earlier doubt. Despite its changing perspective, however, most of Eliot's poetry, early and late, shows his concern with literary and religious tradition, which is reflected in a wealth of allusions; his interest in symbols, not only as literary devices but as manifestations of culture as well; and his facility for capturing speaking voices. Eliot's achievements were recognized with the Nobel Prize for literature in 1948.

The Love Song of J. Alfred Prufrock

S'io credesse che mia risposta fosse
A persona che mai tornasse al mondo,
Questa fiamma staria senza piu scosse.
Ma perciocche giammai di questo fondo
Non torno vivo alcun, s'i'odo il vero,
Senza tema d'infamia ti rispondo.[1]

Let us go then, you and I,
When the evening is spread out against the sky
Like a patient etherised upon a table;
Let us go, through certain half-deserted streets,
5   The muttering retreats

———→

---

1 in Dante's *Inferno* XXXVII.61–66, Guido da Montefeltro answers Dante through the tongue of flame that imprisons him: "If I thought I were answering someone who could ever return to the world, this flame would be still; but since no one has returned alive from this depth, if what I hear is true, I respond without fear of ill repute."

Of restless nights in one-night cheap hotels
And sawdust restaurants with oyster-shells:
Streets that follow like a tedious argument
Of insidious intent
10 To lead you to an overwhelming question . . .
Oh, do not ask, "What is it?"
Let us go and make our visit.

In the room the women come and go
Talking of Michelangelo.

15 The yellow fog that rubs its back upon the window-panes,
The yellow smoke that rubs its muzzle on the window-panes
Licked its tongue into the corners of the evening,
Lingered upon the pools that stand in drains,
Let fall upon its back the soot that falls from chimneys,
20 Slipped by the terrace, made a sudden leap,
And seeing that it was a soft October night,
Curled once about the house, and fell asleep.

And indeed there will be time
For the yellow smoke that slides along the street,
25 Rubbing its back upon the window-panes;
There will be time, there will be time
To prepare a face to meet the faces that you meet;
There will be time to murder and create,
And time for all the works and days of hands
30 That lift and drop a question on your plate;
Time for you and time for me,
And time yet for a hundred indecisions,
And for a hundred visions and revisions,
Before the taking of a toast and tea.

35 In the room the women come and go
Talking of Michelangelo.

And indeed there will be time
To wonder, "Do I dare?" and, "Do I dare?"
Time to turn back and descend the stair,
40 With a bald spot in the middle of my hair —
[They will say: "How his hair is growing thin!"]

⟶

My morning coat, my collar mounting firmly to the chin,
My necktie rich and modest, but asserted by a simple pin —
[They will say: "But how his arms and legs are thin!"]
45   Do I dare
Disturb the universe?
In a minute there is time
For decisions and revisions which a minute will reverse.

For I have known them all already, known them all —
50   Have known the evenings, mornings, afternoons,
I have measured out my life with coffee spoons;
I know the voices dying with a dying fall
Beneath the music from a farther room.
        So how should I presume?

55   And I have known the eyes already, known them all —
The eyes that fix you in a formulated phrase,
And when I am formulated, sprawling on a pin,
When I am pinned and wriggling on the wall,
Then how should I begin
60   To spit out all the butt-ends of my days and ways?
        And how should I presume?

And I have known the arms already, known them all —
Arms that are braceleted and white and bare
[But in the lamplight, downed with light brown hair!]
65   Is it perfume from a dress
That makes me so digress?
Arms that lie along a table, or wrap about a shawl.
        And should I then presume?
        And how should I begin?

                    . . . . .

70   Shall I say, I have gone at dusk through narrow streets
And watched the smoke that rises from the pipes
Of lonely men in shirt-sleeves, leaning out of windows?...

I should have been a pair of ragged claws
Scuttling across the floors of silent seas.

                    . . . . .

75 And the afternoon, the evening, sleeps so peacefully!
Smoothed by long fingers,
Asleep — tired — or it malingers,
Stretched on the floor, here beside you and me.
Should I, after tea and cakes and ices,
80 Have the strength to force the moment to its crisis?
But though I have wept and fasted, wept and prayed,
Though I have seen my head [grown slightly bald] brought in upon a platter, [2]
I am no prophet — and here's no great matter;
I have seen the moment of my greatness flicker,
85 And I have seen the eternal Footman hold my coat, and snicker,
And in short, I was afraid.

And would it have been worth it, after all,
After the cups, the marmalade, the tea,
Among the porcelain, among some talk of you and me,
90 Would it have been worth while,
To have bitten off the matter with a smile,
To have squeezed the universe into a ball
To roll it toward some overwhelming question,
To say: "I am Lazarus, come from the dead, [3]
95 Come back to tell you all, I shall tell you all" —
If one, settling a pillow by her head,
       Should say: "That is not what I meant at all.
       That is not it, at all."

And would it have been worth it, after all,
100 Would it have been worth while,
After the sunsets and the dooryards and the sprinkled streets,
After the novels, after the teacups, after the skirts that trail along the floor —
And this, and so much more? —
It is impossible to say just what I mean!
105 But as if a magic lantern threw the nerves in patterns on a screen:
Would it have been worth while
If one, settling a pillow or throwing off a shawl,
And turning toward the window, should say:
       "That is not it at all,
110   That is not what I meant, at all."

. . . . .

2 the head of John the Baptist was presented on a platter to Queen Herodias (see Matthew 14; Mark 6).
3 Christ raised Lazarus from the dead. See John 11.

No! I am not Prince Hamlet, nor was meant to be;
Am an attendant lord, one that will do
To swell a progress, start a scene or two,
Advise the prince; no doubt, an easy tool,
115 Deferential, glad to be of use,
Politic, cautious, and meticulous;
Full of high sentence, but a bit obtuse;
At times, indeed, almost ridiculous —
Almost, at times, the Fool.

120 I grow old ... I grow old ...
I shall wear the bottoms of my trousers rolled.

Shall I part my hair behind? Do I dare to eat a peach?
I shall wear white flannel trousers, and walk upon the beach.
I have heard the mermaids singing, each to each.

125 I do not think that they will sing to me.

I have seen them riding seaward on the waves
Combing the white hair of the waves blown back
When the wind blows the water white and black.

We have lingered in the chambers of the sea
130 By sea-girls wreathed with seaweed red and brown
Till human voices wake us, and we drown.

(1915)

The Hollow Men

Mistah Kurtz — he dead.[1]

A penny for the Old Guy[2]

I

We are the hollow men
We are the stuffed men
Leaning together
Headpiece filled with straw. Alas!
5   Our dried voices, when
We whisper together
Are quiet and meaningless
As wind in dry grass
Or rats' feet over broken glass
10 In our dry cellar

Shape without form, shade without colour,
Paralysed force, gesture without motion;

Those who have crossed
With direct eyes, to death's other Kingdom
15 Remember us — if at all — not as lost
Violent souls, but only
As the hollow men
The stuffed men.

II

Eyes I dare not meet in dreams
20 In death's dream kingdom
These do not appear:
There, the eyes are
Sunlight on a broken column
There, is a tree swinging
25 And voices are
In the wind's singing

$\longrightarrow$

---

1 in Joseph Conrad's *Heart of Darkness*, Kurtz's European cultural values fail him in the African jungle
and he dies insane. 2 refers to an English children's custom of begging on Guy Fawkes Day (November 5),
the anniversary of the execution of the leading conspirator in the plot to blow up the Houses of Parliament
in 1605.

More distant and more solemn
Than a fading star.

Let me be no nearer
30   In death's dream kingdom
Let me also wear
Such deliberate disguises
Rat's coat, crowskin, crossed staves
In a field
35   Behaving as the wind behaves
No nearer —

Not that final meeting
In the twilight kingdom

III

This is the dead land
40   This is cactus land
Here the stone images
Are raised, here they receive
The supplication of a dead man's hand
Under the twinkle of a fading star.

45   Is it like this
In death's other kingdom
Waking alone
At the hour when we are
Trembling with tenderness
50   Lips that would kiss
Form prayers to broken stone.

IV

The eyes are not here
There are no eyes here
In this valley of dying stars
55   In this hollow valley
This broken jaw of our lost kingdoms

In this last of meeting places
We grope together

———→

And avoid speech
60 Gathered on this beach of the tumid river

Sightless, unless
The eyes reappear
As the perpetual star
Multifoliate rose
65 Of death's twilight kingdom
The hope only
Of empty men.

V

Here we go round the prickly pear
Prickly pear prickly pear
70 *Here we go round the prickly pear*
At five o'clock in the morning.

Between the idea
And the reality
Between the motion
75 And the act
Falls the Shadow
                    For Thine is the Kingdom

Between the conception
And the creation
80 Between the emotion
And the response
Falls the Shadow
                    Life is very long

Between the desire
85 And the spasm
Between the potency
And the existence
Between the essence
And the descent
90 Falls the Shadow
                    For Thine is the Kingdom
For Thine is

⎯⎯→

Life is
For Thine is the

95   *This is the way the world ends*
This is the way the world ends
This is the way the world ends
Not with a bang but a whimper.

(1925)

Journey of the Magi[1]

"A cold coming we had of it,
Just the worst time of the year
For a journey, and such a long journey:
The ways deep and the weather sharp,
5   The very dead of winter."[2]
And the camels galled, sore-footed, refractory,
Lying down in the melting snow.
There were times we regretted
The summer palaces on slopes, the terraces,
10   And the silken girls bringing sherbet.
Then the camel men cursing and grumbling
And running away, and wanting their liquor and women,
And the night-fires going out, and the lack of shelters,
And the cities hostile and the towns unfriendly
15   And the villages dirty and charging high prices:
A hard time we had of it.
At the end we preferred to travel all night,
Sleeping in snatches,
With the voices singing in our ears, saying
20   That this was all folly.

Then at dawn we came down to a temperate valley,
Wet, below the snow line, smelling of vegetation;
With a running stream and a water-mill beating the darkness,
And three trees on the low sky,

———▶

1 the wise men who brought gifts to the infant Jesus (see Matthew 2). 2 adapted from a Christmas sermon
by Bishop Lancelot Andrewes (1555–1626), who helped prepare the 1611 King James version of the Bible.

25 And an old white horse galloped away in the meadow.
Then we came to a tavern with vine-leaves over the lintel,
Six hands at an open door dicing for pieces of silver,
And feet kicking the empty wine-skins.
But there was no information, and so we continued
30 And arrived at evening, not a moment too soon
Finding the place; it was (you may say) satisfactory.

    All this was a long time ago, I remember,
And I would do it again, but set down
This set down
35 This: were we led all that way for
Birth or Death? There was a Birth, certainly,
We had evidence and no doubt. I had seen birth and death,
But had thought they were different; this Birth was
Hard and bitter agony for us, like Death, our death.
40 We returned to our places, these Kingdoms,
But no longer at ease here, in the old dispensation,
With an alien people clutching their gods.
I should be glad of another death.

                                                                (1927)

Wilfred Owen (1893–1918)

Although his best poems were written in the year before his death in action during World War I, Wilfred Owen had decided to become a poet while a boy in Shropshire, England. He was critical of conventional religious beliefs before the war and had written many war poems before his 1917 meeting with Siegfried Sassoon; however, the meeting was the catalyst for the creation of the works for which he is now remembered, many of which were included in the libretto of composer Benjamin Britten's *War Requiem* (1962). In the Preface to his *Collected Poems*, Owen stated: "My subject is War, and the pity of War. The Poetry is in the pity." He achieves his startling, moving effects through the sharp contrasts of his language and the careful modulation of rhythms, rhyme schemes, and sound patterns. In "*Dulce et Decorum Est*," the Latin motto, with its conventional notions of glorious, patriotic death, is set against vivid, realistic details of a gas attack. "Anthem for Doomed Youth" juxtaposes the noises of war with the quietness of mourning. In "Strange Meeting," the speaker escapes from the terrors of war into a place marked by the muted sadness of lives ended before their time.

Anthem[1] for Doomed Youth

What passing-bells[2] for these who die as cattle?
   — Only the monstrous anger of the guns.
   Only the stuttering rifles' rapid rattle
Can patter out their hasty orisons.[3]
5 No mockeries now for them; no prayers nor bells;
   Nor any voice of mourning save the choirs, —
The shrill, demented choirs of wailing shells;
   And bugles calling for them from sad shires.[4]

What candles may be held to speed them all?
10   Not in the hands of boys but in their eyes
Shall shine the holy glimmers of goodbyes.
   The pallor of girls' brows shall be their pall;
Their flowers the tenderness of patient minds,
And each slow dusk a drawing-down of blinds.

(1917)   (1920)

Dulce et Decorum Est[1]

Bent double, like old beggars under sacks,
Knock-kneed, coughing like hags, we cursed through sludge,
Till on the haunting flares we turned our backs
And towards our distant rest began to trudge.
5 Men marched asleep. Many had lost their boots
But limped on, blood-shod. All went lame; all blind;
Drunk with fatigue; deaf even to the hoots
Of tired, outstripped Five-Nines[2] that dropped behind.

Gas! GAS! Quick, boys! — An ecstasy of fumbling,
10 Fitting the clumsy helmets just in time;
But someone still was yelling out and stumbling,
And flound'ring like a man in fire or lime . . .
Dim, through the misty panes and thick green light,
As under a green sea, I saw him drowning.

                                        ⟶

---

1 song of praise. 2 church bells rung to announce a death. 3 prayers. 4 districts, counties.
1 "It is sweet and fitting [to die for one's country]" (Horace *Odes* III.2.13). 2 shells that are 5.9 inches
(or 150 mm) in diameter.

15 In all my dreams, before my helpless sight,
  He plunges at me, guttering, choking, drowning.

  If in some smothering dreams you too could pace
  Behind the wagon that we flung him in,
  And watch the white eyes writhing in his face,
20 His hanging face, like a devil's sick of sin;
  If you could hear, at every jolt, the blood
  Come gargling from the froth-corrupted lungs,
  Obscene as cancer, bitter as the cud
  Of vile, incurable sores on innocent tongues, —
25 My friend, you would not tell with such high zest
  To children ardent for some desperate glory,
  The old Lie: Dulce et decorum est
  Pro patria mori.

  (1917)   (1920)

Strange Meeting

  It seemed that out of battle I escaped
  Down some profound dull tunnel, long since scooped
  Through granites which titanic wars had groined.

  Yet also there encumbered sleepers groaned,
5 Too fast in thought or death to be bestirred.
  Then, as I probed them, one sprang up, and stared
  With piteous recognition in fixed eyes,
  Lifting distressful hands, as if to bless.
  And by his smile, I knew that sullen hall,
10 By his dead smile I knew we stood in Hell.

  With a thousand pains that vision's face was grained;
  Yet no blood reached there from the upper ground,
  And no guns thumped, or down the flues made moan.
  "Strange friend," I said, "here is no cause to mourn,"
15 "None," said that other, "save the undone years,
  The hopelessness. Whatever hope is yours,
  Was my life also; I went hunting wild
  After the wildest beauty in the world,

      ⟶

Which lies not calm in eyes, or braided hair,
20 But mocks the steady running of the hour,
And if it grieves, grieves richlier than here.
For by my glee might many men have laughed,
And of my weeping something had been left,
Which must die now. I mean the truth untold,
25 The pity of war, the pity war distilled.
Now men will go content with what we spoiled,
Or, discontent, boil bloody, and be spilled.
They will be swift with swiftness of the tigress.
None will break ranks, though nations trek from progress.
30 Courage was mine, and I had mystery,
Wisdom was mine, and I had mastery:
To miss the march of this retreating world
Into vain citadels that are not walled.
Then, when much blood had clogged their chariot-wheels,
35 I would go up and wash them from sweet wells,
Even with truths that lie too deep for taint.
I would have poured my spirit without stint
But not through wounds; not on the cess of war.
Foreheads of men have bled where no wounds were.

40 "I am the enemy you killed, my friend.
I knew you in this dark: for so you frowned
Yesterday through me as you jabbed and killed.
I parried; but my hands were loath and cold.
Let us sleep now...."

(1918)   (1920)

E.E. Cummings (1894–1962)

Born in Cambridge, Massachusetts, and educated at Harvard, Edward Estlin
Cummings became one of the most unconventional of modern American poets.
Cummings was a successful painter and wrote both fiction and drama, but his
greatest artistic achievement was his poetry. Sometimes lyric, sometimes satirical, Cummings's poetry celebrates spontaneous feeling, individualism, the love
of nature, and erotic love; it attacks institutions, formality, and stuffiness generally. He has sometimes been criticized for being exhibitionist and overly playful
in his manipulations of diction, syntax, stanzaic forms, and typography, but,
notwithstanding his eccentricities, Cummings was always a careful craftsman and

serious artist. His ardent rebellion against both poetic conventions and what he considered the complacent, middle-class narrowness of his country gave him considerable influence with poets after World War II.

in Just-   spring

in Just-
spring   when the world is mud-
luscious the little
lame balloonman

5   whistles   far   and wee

and eddieandbill come
running from marbles and
piracies and it's
spring

10   when the world is puddle-wonderful

the queer
old balloonman whistles
far   and   wee
and bettyandisbel come dancing

15   from hop-scotch and jump-rope and

it's
spring
and
         the

20   goat-footed

balloonMan   whistles
far
and
wee

(1923)

next to of course god america i

"next to of course god america i
love you land of the pilgrims' and so forth oh
say can you see by the dawn's early my
country 'tis of centuries come and go
and are no more what of it we should worry
in every language even deafanddumb
thy sons acclaim your glorious name by gorry
by jingo by gee by gosh by gum
why talk of beauty what could be more beautiful than these heroic happy dead
who rushed like lions to the roaring slaughter
they did not stop to think they died instead
then shall the voice of liberty be mute?"

He spoke.   And drank rapidly a glass of water

(1926)

1(a

1(a

le
af
fa

ll

s)
one
l

iness

(1958)

F.R. Scott   (1899–1985)

The son of Frederick George Scott (1861–1944), an Anglican clergyman and minor poet of the Confederation group, Francis Reginald Scott made remarkable contributions to Canadian life in several areas. Born in Quebec City, he was educated at Bishop's College, Oxford University, where he was a Rhodes Scholar, and McGill University, where he eventually became dean of the law school. As a social reformer, he was active in founding the Co-operative Commonwealth Federation, the forerunner of the New Democratic Party. As a lawyer, he defended civil liberties in several important court cases. As a professor of constitutional law, he promoted the cause of social justice and served as a member of the Royal Commission on Bilingualism and Biculturalism. As a poet and anthologist, he was a leader in the fight against romantic and traditional poetry as outmoded and insincere forms of verse. He began writing while still a student, but his first collection was not published until 1945. His *Collected Poems* (1981) won the Governor General's Award. Often sharply satirical, his poetry is notable for its precision and grace of expression, its unpretentious allusions, and its wit.

The Canadian Authors Meet[1]

Expansive puppets percolate self-unction
Beneath a portrait of the Prince of Wales.[2]
Miss Crotchet's muse has somehow failed to function,
Yet she's a poetess. Beaming, she sails

5   From group to chattering group, with such a dear
Victorian saintliness, as is her fashion,
Greeting the other unknowns with a cheer —
Virgins of sixty who still write of passion.

The air is heavy with Canadian topics,
10   And Carman, Lampman, Roberts, Campbell, Scott,
Are measured for their faith and philanthropics,
Their zeal for God and King, their earnest thought.

The cakes are sweet, but sweeter is the feeling
That one is mixing with the *literati*;[3]

———⟶

1 an earlier version of this poem appeared in the *McGill Fortnightly Review* in April 1927, shortly after Scott had attended a meeting of the Canadian Authors' Association. Scott viewed the CAA as a group smugly content with the clichés and forms of the past and incapable of appreciating or promoting meaningful writing of the present. 2 Edward, Prince of Wales when the poem was written, became King Edward VIII on January 21, 1936, and abdicated on December 11, 1936, in order to marry an American divorcée, Wallis Warfield Simpson. 3 people of letters; the learned.

15   It warms the old, and melts the most congealing.
       Really, it is a most delightful party.

       Shall we go round the mulberry bush, or shall
       We gather at the river, or shall we
       Appoint a Poet Laureate this fall,
20   Or shall we have another cup of tea?

       O Canada, O Canada, Oh can
       A day go by without new authors springing
       To paint the native maple, and to plan
       More ways to set the selfsame welkin[4] ringing?

(1927)   (1945)

Trans Canada

       Pulled from our ruts by the made-to-order gale
       We sprang upward into a wider prairie
       And dropped Regina below like a pile of bones.[1]

       Sky tumbled upon us in waterfalls,
5   But we were smarter than a Skeena[2] salmon
       And shot our silver body over the lip of air
       To rest in a pool of space
       On the top storey of our adventure.

       A solar peace
10   And a six-way choice.

       Clouds, now, are the solid substance,
       A floor of wool roughed by the wind
       Standing in waves that halt in their fall.
       A still of troughs.

15   The plane, our planet,
       Travels on roads that are not seen or laid
       But sound in instruments on pilots' ears,

——→

4 sky, or vault of heaven; a poetic archaism.
1 because of a huge pile of bones left after buffalo hunts, Regina was originally known as Pile of Bones Creek.
2 the Skeena River, which empties into the Pacific Ocean near Prince Rupert, British Columbia, has been
an important salmon fishery for well over a hundred years.

While underneath
The sure wings
20   Are the everlasting arms of science.

Man, the lofty worm, tunnels his latest clay,
And bores his new career.

This frontier, too, is ours.
This everywhere whose life can only be led
25   At the pace of a rocket
Is common to man and man,
And every country below is an I land.

The sun sets on its top shelf,
And stars seem farther from our nearer grasp.

30   I have sat by night beside a cold lake
And touched things smoother than moonlight on still water,
But the moon on this cloud sea is not human,
And here is no shore, no intimacy,
Only the start of space, the road to suns.

(1945)

Laurentian Shield

Hidden in wonder and snow, or sudden with summer,
This land stares at the sun in a huge silence
Endlessly repeating something we cannot hear.
Inarticulate, arctic,
5   Not written on by history, empty as paper,
It leans away from the world with songs in its lakes
Older than love, and lost in the miles.

This waiting is wanting.
It will choose its language
10   When it has chosen its technic,
A tongue to shape the vowels of its productivity.
A *language of flesh and of roses.*[1]

1 line from Stephen Spender's "The Making of a Poem," an essay in which Spender discusses the landscape
of an English mining region as a kind of language expressing human thoughts and wishes; Spender argues
that humans aspire to "a language of flesh and roses."

Now there are pre-words,
Cabin syllables,
15   Nouns of settlement
Slowly forming, with steel syntax,
The long sentence of its exploitation.

The first cry was the hunter, hungry for fur,
And the digger for gold, nomad, no-man, a particle;
20   Then the bold commands of monopoly, big with machines,
Carving its kingdoms out of the public wealth;
And now the drone of the plane, scouting the ice,
Fills all the emptiness with neighbourhood
And links our future over the vanished pole.

25   But a deeper note is sounding, heard in the mines,
The scattered camps and the mills, a language of life,
And what will be written in the full culture of occupation
Will come, presently, tomorrow,
From millions whose hands can turn this rock into children.

(1954)

For Bryan Priestman

(Drowned while attempting to save a child.)

The child fell, turning slowly with arms outstretched like a doll,
One shrill cry dying under the arches,
And floated away, her time briefer than foam.

Nothing was changed on the summer's day. The birds sang,
5   The busy insects followed their fixed affairs.
Only a Professor of Chemistry, alone on the bridge,
Suddenly awoke from his reverie, into the intense moment,
Saw all the elements of his life compounded for testing,
And plunged with searching hands into his last experiment.
10   This was a formula he had carried from childhood,
That can work but once in the life of a man.
His were the labels of an old laboratory,
And the long glass tubes of the river.

(1954)

Earle Birney (1904–1995)

Born in Calgary, Birney grew up on a farm in the British Columbia interior and in Banff. He studied at British Columbia and Toronto before completing a Ph.D. on Chaucer's irony at the University of Toronto in 1938. He spent most of his academic career at the University of British Columbia. Twice winner of the Governor General's Award, for his first volume, *David and Other Poems* (1942), and for *Now Is Time* (1945), he also wrote two novels, the first of which, *Turvey* (1949), won the Leacock Medal for humour.

Literally and figuratively, Birney was a peripatetic poet. For much of his life he travelled throughout the world, writing poems about his observations. He also journeyed widely through poetic forms, producing everything from poems based on Anglo-Saxon metrics (see "Anglosaxon Street") to concrete poetry mobiles. Not surprisingly, journeys of various kinds are prominent thematic elements in much of his poetry. In fact, Birney saw life itself as a journey, and his poems are "signals out of the loneliness into which all of us are born and in which we die, affirmations of kinship with other wayfarers...."

Vancouver Lights

About me the night   moonless   wimples[1] the mountains
wraps ocean   land   air   and mounting
sucks at the stars   The city   throbbing below
webs the sable peninsula   The golden
5   strands overleap the seajet   by bridge and buoy
vault the shears of the inlet   climb the woods
toward me   falter   and halt   Across to the firefly
haze of a ship on the gulf's erased horizon
roll the lambent spokes of a lighthouse

10   Through the feckless years we have come to the time
when to look on this quilt of lamps is a troubling delight
Welling from Europe's bog   through Africa flowing
and Asia   drowning the lonely lumes[2] on the oceans
tiding up over Halifax   now to this winking
15   outpost comes flooding the primal ink[3]

On this mountain's brutish forehead with terror of space
I stir   of the changeless night and the stark ranges
of nothing   pulsing down from beyond and between

                   ⟶

1 veils. 2 lights. 3 in *The Cow Jumped Over the Moon* (1972), Birney explains that this stanza describes the spreading of blackouts during World War II.

the fragile planets   We are a spark beleaguered
20 by darkness   this twinkle we make in a corner of emptiness
how shall we utter our fear that the black Experimentress
will never in the range of her microscope find it?   Our Phoebus [1]
himself is a bubble that dries on Her slide   while the Nubian [5]
wears for an evening's whim a necklace of nebulae

25 Yet we must speak   we the unique glowworms
Out of the waters and rocks of our little world
we conjured these flames   hooped these sparks
by our will   From blankness and cold we fashioned stars
to our size   and signalled Aldebaran [6]
30 This must we say   whoever may be to hear us
if murk devour   and none weave again in gossamer:

            These rays were ours
we made and unmade them   Not the shudder of continents
doused us   the moon's passion   nor crash of comets
35 In the fathomless heat of our dwarfdom   our dream's combustion
we contrived the power   the blast that snuffed us
No one bound Prometheus   Himself he chained
and consumed his own bright liver [7]   O stranger
Plutonian [8]   descendant   or beast in the stretching night —
40 there was light

(1941)   (1942)

Anglosaxon Street

Dawndrizzle ended   dampness steams from
blotching brick and   blank plasterwaste
Faded housepatterns   hoary and finicky
unfold stuttering   stick like a phonograph

5 Here is a ghetto   gotten for goyim [1]
O with care denuded   of nigger and kike

              ⟶

4 Phoebus Apollo, the sun. 5 black native from Nubia, in northeastern Africa. 6 the brightest star in the constellation Taurus. 7 Prometheus stole fire for mankind, and Zeus punished him by chaining him to a rock, where every day an eagle ate his liver, which was renewed each night. 8 pertaining to Pluto, god of the dead, or to the dark lower world where the souls of the dead lived.
1 Gentiles; non-Jews.

No coonsmell rankles   reeks only cellarrot
attar of carexhaust   catcorpse and cookinggrease
Imperial hearts   heave in this haven
10   Cracks across windows   are welded with slogans
There'll Always Be An England   enhances geraniums
and V's for Victory   vanquish the housefly

Ho! with climbing sun   march the bleached beldames
festooned with shopping bags   farded² flatarched
15   bigthewed Saxonwives³   stepping over buttrivers
waddling back wienerladen   to suckle smallfry

Hoy! with sunslope   shrieking over hydrants
flood from learninghall   the lean fingerlings
Nordic nobblecheeked⁴   not all clean of nose
20   leaping Commandowise   into leprous lanes

What! after whistleblow!   spewed from wheelboat
after daylong doughtiness   dire handplay
in sewertrench or sandpit   come Saxonthegns⁵
Junebrown Jutekings   jawslack for meat

25   Sit after supper   on smeared doorsteps
not humbly swearing   hatedeeds on Huns⁶
profiteers politicians   pacifists Jews

Then by twobit magic   to muse in movie
unlock picturehoard   or lope to alehall
30   soaking bleakly   in beer skittleless

Home again to hotbox   and humid husbandhood
in slumbertrough adding   sleepily to Anglekin
Alongside the lanenooks   carling⁷ and leman⁸
caterwaul and clip   careless of Saxonry
35   with moonglow and haste   and a higher heartbeat

Slumbers now slumtrack   unstinks cooling
waiting brief for milkmaid   mornstar and worldrise

(*Toronto 1942*)   (1966)

2 painted, here with cosmetics. 3 the Saxons were one of three Germanic tribes, the others — mentioned later in the poem — being the Jutes and the Angles, who conquered Britain in the fifth century. 4 ulcerous or pimpled. 5 a thegn was a freeman who held land by virtue of military service. 6 fierce Asiatic tribe of nomads who conquered much of eastern and central Europe; a derogatory appellation for Germans during the two world wars. 7 woman. 8 lover.

Bushed

He invented a rainbow but lightning struck it
shattered it into the lake-lap of a mountain
so big his mind slowed when he looked at it

Yet he built a shack on the shore
5 learned to roast porcupine belly and
wore the quills on his hatband

At first he was out with the dawn
whether it yellowed bright as wood-columbine
or was only a fuzzed moth in a flannel of storm
10 But he found the mountain was clearly alive
sent messages whizzing down every hot morning
boomed proclamations at noon and spread out
a white guard of goat
before falling asleep on its feet at sundown

15 When he tried his eyes on the lake   ospreys
would fall like valkyries [1]
choosing the cut-throat [2]
He took then to waiting
till the night smoke rose from the boil of the sunset

20 But the moon carved unknown totems
out of the lakeshore
owls in the beardusky woods derided him
moosehorned cedars circled his swamps and tossed
their antlers up to the stars
25 then he knew   though the mountain slept   the winds
were shaping its peak to an arrowhead
poised

And now he could only
bar himself in and wait
30 for the great flint to come singing into his heart

(*Wreck Beach 1951*)   (1952)

---

1 in Norse mythology, the Valkyries (Choosers of the Slain) were handmaidens of Odin who hovered over battlefields in order to choose the heroes killed in battle and escort them to Valhalla. 2 this pun points to both the slain warriors awaiting the Valkyries and a kind of large trout found in the Rocky Mountain region.

The Bear on the Delhi Road

Unreal   tall as a myth
by the road the Himalayan bear
is beating the brilliant air
with his crooked arms
5   About him two men   bare
spindly as locusts   leap

One pulls on a ring
in the great soft nose   His mate
flicks   flicks with a stick
10   up at the rolling eyes

They have not led him here
down from the fabulous hills
to this bald alien plain
and the clamorous world   to kill
15   but simply to teach him to dance

They are peaceful both   these spare
men of Kashmir   and the bear
alive is their living   too
If   far on the Delhi way
20   around him galvanic they dance
it is merely to wear   wear
from his shaggy body the tranced
wish forever to stay
only an ambling bear
25   four-footed in berries

It is no more joyous for them
in this hot dust to prance
out of reach of the praying claws
sharpened to paw for ants
30   in the shadows of deodars[1]
It is not easy to free
myth from reality

⟶

1 the deodar, or "tree of the gods," is a cedar native to the Western Himalayas.

or rear this fellow up
to lurch   lurch with them
35   in the tranced dancing of men

(*Srinagar 1958/Île des Porquerolles 1959*)   (1962)

W.H. Auden (1907–1973)

Though born in Britain and educated at Oxford, Wystan Hugh Auden lived in the United States much of the time after 1939 and became an American citizen in 1946. He began writing poetry in school, revealed a remarkable talent for handling various styles, and established himself as a leader among the younger poets in Britain while he was still in his twenties. Early in his career, Auden was influenced by Marxism and was much concerned with satirizing the British middle class. Later, however, while still showing an ironic bent, his work became more generally philosophical as it explored the need for meaning in modern life. Typically less personal and more analytical than most modern poets, Auden demonstrated an unsurpassed gift for capturing the political and intellectual temper of the times in which he lived.

Primarily a poet, Auden also produced a body of non-poetic work, including travel literature, philosophical writings, plays, and criticism, that is impressive both in its extent and its variety.

The Unknown Citizen

(*To JS/07/M/378*
This Marble Monument
Is Erected by the State)

He was found by the Bureau of Statistics to be
One against whom there was no official complaint,
And all the reports on his conduct agree
That, in the modern sense of an old-fashioned word, he was a saint,
5   For in everything he did he served the Greater Community.
Except for the War till the day he retired
He worked in a factory and never got fired,
But satisfied his employers, Fudge Motors Inc.
Yet he wasn't a scab or odd in his views,
10   For his Union reports that he paid his dues,

——→

(Our report on his Union shows it was sound)
And our Social Psychology workers found
That he was popular with his mates and liked a drink.
The Press are convinced that he bought a paper every day
15   And that his reactions to advertisements were normal in every way.
Policies taken out in his name prove that he was fully insured,
And his Health-card shows he was once in hospital but left it cured.
Both Producers Research and High-Grade Living declare
He was fully sensible to the advantages of the Instalment Plan
20   And had everything necessary to the Modern Man,
A phonograph, a radio, a car and a frigidaire.
Our researchers into Public Opinion are content
That he held the proper opinions for the time of year;
When there was peace, he was for peace; when there was war, he went.
25   He was married and added five children to the population,
Which our Eugenist says was the right number for a parent of his generation,
And our teachers report that he never interfered with their education.
Was he free? Was he happy? The question is absurd:
Had anything been wrong, we should certainly have heard.

(1939)

In Memory of W.B. Yeats

(D. Jan. 1939)

I

He disappeared in the dead of winter:
The brooks were frozen, the airports almost deserted,
And snow disfigured the public statues;
The mercury sank in the mouth of the dying day.
5   What instruments we have agree
The day of his death was a dark cold day.

Far from his illness
The wolves ran on through the evergreen forests,
The peasant river was untempted by the fashionable quays;
10   By mourning tongues
The death of the poet was kept from his poems.

But for him it was his last afternoon as himself,
An afternoon of nurses and rumours;
The provinces of his body revolted,
15 The squares of his mind were empty,
Silence invaded the suburbs,
The current of his feeling failed; he became his admirers.

Now he is scattered among a hundred cities
And wholly given over to unfamiliar affections,
20 To find his happiness in another kind of wood
And be punished under a foreign code of conscience.
The words of a dead man
Are modified in the guts of the living.

But in the importance and noise of to-morrow
25 When the brokers are roaring like beasts on the floor of the Bourse,[1]
And the poor have the sufferings to which they are fairly accustomed,
And each in the cell of himself is almost convinced of his freedom,
A few thousand will think of this day
As one thinks of a day when one did something slightly unusual.
30 What instruments we have agree
The day of his death was a dark cold day.

II

You were silly like us; your gift survived it all:
The parish of rich women, physical decay,
Yourself. Mad Ireland hurt you into poetry.
35 Now Ireland has her madness and her weather still,
For poetry makes nothing happen: it survives
In the valley of its making where executives
Would never want to tamper, flows on south
From ranches of isolation and the busy griefs,
40 Raw towns that we believe and die in; it survives,
A way of happening, a mouth.

III

Earth, receive an honoured guest:
William Yeats is laid to rest.
Let the Irish vessel lie
45 Emptied of its poetry.[2]

1 French Stock Exchange. 2 in the original version written in 1939, Auden included three more stanzas here
in which Time, while indifferent to other gifts and virtues, is said to pardon the failings of those who write well.

In the nightmare of the dark
All the dogs of Europe bark,
And the living nations wait,
Each sequestered in its hate;

50   Intellectual disgrace
Stares from every human face,
And the seas of pity lie
Locked and frozen in each eye.

Follow, poet, follow right
55   To the bottom of the night,
With your unconstraining voice
Still persuade us to rejoice;

With the farming of a verse
Make a vineyard of the curse,
60   Sing of human unsuccess
In a rapture of distress;

In the deserts of the heart
Let the healing fountain start,
In the prison of his days
65   Teach the free man how to praise.

(1939)   (1966)

Musée des Beaux Arts[1]

About suffering they were never wrong,
The Old Masters: how well they understood
Its human position; how it takes place
While someone else is eating or opening a window or just walking dully along;
5   How, when the aged are reverently, passionately waiting
For the miraculous birth, there always must be
Children who did not specially want it to happen, skating
On a pond at the edge of the wood:

---

1 refers to the Museum of Fine Arts in Brussels, Belgium, where The Fall of Icarus, a painting by Flemish
painter Pieter Brueghel the Elder (c. 1525–69), still hangs.

10   They never forgot
That even the dreadful martyrdom must run its course
Anyhow in a corner, some untidy spot
Where the dogs go on with their doggy life and the torturer's horse
Scratches its innocent behind on a tree.

15   In Brueghel's *Icarus*,[2] for instance: how everything turns away
Quite leisurely from the disaster; the ploughman may
Have heard the splash, the forsaken cry,
But for him it was not an important failure; the sun shone
As it had to on the white legs disappearing into the green
Water; and the expensive delicate ship that must have seen
20   Something amazing, a boy falling out of the sky,
Had somewhere to get to and sailed calmly on.

(1940)

Theodore Roethke   (1908–1963)

Theodore Roethke's family operated greenhouses in Saginaw, Michigan, and, growing up surrounded by plants, he developed the almost mystical sympathy with primitive life that characterized his early nature lyrics. He received an M.A. from the University of Michigan, did graduate work at Harvard, and devoted his working life to college teaching as well as writing poetry.

During much of his adult life, Roethke suffered from alcoholism and mental illness, which caused him to experience alternating bouts of manic energy and depression. He managed to turn these problems to poetic advantage, however, by exploring his changing mental states as poetic journeys through interior psychic landscapes.

Root Cellar

Nothing would sleep in that cellar, dank as a ditch,
Bulbs broke out of boxes hunting for chinks in the dark,
Shoots dangled and drooped,
Lolling obscenely from mildewed crates,
5   Hung down long yellow evil necks, like tropical snakes.

———→

2 in Greek myth, the skilled craftsman Daedalus made wings of wax and feathers in order to escape with Icarus, his son, from the Cretan labyrinth, which he himself had designed. When Icarus flew too near the sun, the wax melted and he fell into the sea.

And what a congress of stinks! —
Roots ripe as old bait,
Pulpy stems, rank, silo-rich,
Leaf-mold, manure, lime, piled against slippery planks.
10 Nothing would give up life:
Even the dirt kept breathing a small breath.

(1948)

My Papa's Waltz

The whiskey on your breath
Could make a small boy dizzy;
But I hung on like death:
Such waltzing was not easy.

5 We romped until the pans
Slid from the kitchen shelf;
My mother's countenance
Could not unfrown itself.

The hand that held my wrist
10 Was battered on one knuckle;
At every step you missed
My right ear scraped a buckle.

You beat time on my head
With a palm caked hard by dirt,
15 Then waltzed me off to bed
Still clinging to your shirt.

(1948)

The Waking

I wake to sleep, and take my waking slow.
I feel my fate in what I cannot fear.
I learn by going where I have to go.

We think by feeling. What is there to know?
5   I hear my being dance from ear to ear.
I wake to sleep, and take my waking slow.

Of those so close beside me, which are you?
God bless the Ground! I shall walk softly there,
And learn by going where I have to go.

10   Light takes the Tree; but who can tell us how?
The lowly worm climbs up a winding stair;
I wake to sleep, and take my waking slow.

Great Nature has another thing to do
To you and me; so take the lively air,
15   And, lovely, learn by going where to go.

This shaking keeps me steady. I should know.
What falls away is always. And is near.
I wake to sleep, and take my waking slow.
I learn by going where I have to go.

(1953)

A.M. Klein (1909–1972)

Abraham Moses Klein was born in Ratno, Ukraine, and came to Montreal with his parents in 1910. After receiving a B.A. from McGill University in 1930, he studied law at the Université de Montréal and was admitted to the bar in 1933. A mental breakdown and several suicide attempts forced his retirement in 1956. Klein became reclusive and completely abandoned all writing, but he had already made a permanent literary contribution as one of the leading figures in the development of modern poetry in Canada.

Jewish themes dominate Klein's writing: his first book, *Hath Not a Jew...* (1940), celebrates the rich heritage and customs of the Jewish people, and much of his later work treats Jewish suffering. *The Rocking Chair* (1948), winner of the Governor General's Award for poetry, contained poems about Quebec, as well as his finest work, "Portrait of the Poet as Landscape." He returned to Jewish themes in his complex visionary novel, *The Second Scroll* (1951). Klein's poetry is both intellectual and witty; it is characterized by learned allusions, metaphors, puns, archaisms, and words derived from several languages.

Heirloom

My father bequeathed me no wide estates;
No keys and ledgers were my heritage;
Only some holy books with *yahrzeit* dates[1]
Writ mournfully upon a blank front page —

5   Books of the Baal Shem Tov,[2] and of his wonders;
Pamphlets upon the devil and his crew;
Prayers against road demons, witches, thunders;
And sundry other tomes for a good Jew.

Beautiful: though no pictures on them, save
10 The scorpion crawling on a printed track;
The Virgin floating on a scriptural wave,
Square letters twinkling in the Zodiac.[3]

The snuff left on this page, now brown and old,
The tallow stains of midnight liturgy —
15 These are my coat of arms, and these unfold
My noble lineage, my proud ancestry!

And my tears, too, have stained this heirloomed ground,
When reading in these treatises some weird
Miracle, I turned a leaf and found
20 A white hair fallen from my father's beard.

(1940)

1 anniversary dates of the death of ancestors. 2 the eighteenth-century rabbi who founded Hasidism, a Jewish movement that emphasizes communion with God through joyful prayer, encourages religious expression in song and dance, and values the experience of the natural world and a simple delight in service to God more than the legal dialectic of traditional study of the Torah. 3 in a letter to A.J.M. Smith dated January 21, 1943, Klein explained that "Hebrew prayer books are never illustrated. The only drawings that appear in the liturgy are the signs of the Zodiac illustrating the prayers for rain and fertility."

Portrait of the Poet as Landscape

i

Not an editorial-writer, bereaved with bartlett,[1]
mourns him, the shelved Lycidas.[2]
No actress squeezes a glycerine[3] tear for him.
The radio broadcast lets his passing pass.
5 And with the police, no record. Nobody, it appears,
either under his real name or his alias,
missed him enough to report.

It is possible that he is dead, and not discovered.
It is possible that he can be found some place
10 in a narrow closet, like the corpse in a detective story,
standing, his eyes staring, and ready to fall on his face.
It is also possible that he is alive
and amnesiac, or mad, or in retired disgrace,
or beyond recognition lost in love.

15 We are sure only that from our real society
he has disappeared; he simply does not count,
except in the pullulation[4] of vital statistics —
somebody's vote, perhaps, an anonymous taunt
of the Gallup poll, a dot in a government table —
20 but not felt, and certainly far from eminent —
in a shouting mob, somebody's sigh.

O, he who unrolled our culture from his scroll —
the prince's quote, the rostrum-rounding roar —
who under one name made articulate
25 heaven, and under another the seven-circled air,[5]
is, if he is at all, a number, an x,
a Mr. Smith in a hotel register, —
incognito, lost, lacunal.[6]

---

1 *Familiar Quotations*, first published in 1855 by John Bartlett and frequently updated. 2 "Lycidas" (1638),
a pastoral elegy by John Milton, mourns the drowning of Edward King, a young poet (see page 54).
3 used to simulate tears on stage. 4 teeming; rapid sprouting or breeding. 5 before Nicolaus Copernicus
(1473–1543), people believed that the earth was the fixed centre of the universe and that it was surrounded
by seven concentric circles. 6 a lacuna is a blank space or missing portion.

ii

The truth is he's not dead, but only ignored —
30   like the mirroring lenses forgotten on a brow
that shine with the guilt of their unnoticed world.
The truth is he lives among neighbours, who, though they will allow
him a passable fellow, think him eccentric, not solid,
a type that one can forgive, and for that matter, forgo.

35   Himself he has his moods, just like a poet.
Sometimes, depressed to nadir,[7] he will think all lost,
will see himself as throwback, relict,[8] freak,
his mother's miscarriage, his great-grandfather's ghost,
and he will curse his quintuplet senses, and their tutors
40   in whom he put, as he should not have put, his trust.

Then he will remember his travels over that body —
the torso verb, the beautiful face of the noun,
and all those shaped and warm auxiliaries!
A first love it was, the recognition of his own.
45   Dear limbs adverbial, complexion of adjective,
dimple and dip of conjugation!

And then remember how this made a change in him
affecting for always the glow and growth of his being;
how suddenly was aware of the air, like shaken tinfoil,[9]
50   of the patents of nature, the shock of belated seeing,
the loneliness peering from the eyes of crowds;
the integers of thought; the cube-roots of feeling.

Thus, zoomed to zenith, sometimes he hopes again,
and sees himself as a character, with a rehearsed role:
55   the Count of Monte Cristo,[10] come for his revenges;
the unsuspecting heir, with papers; the risen soul;
or the chloroformed prince awakening from his flowers;
or — deflated again — the convict on parole.

7 the lowest point; the point opposite the zenith. 8 plant or animal surviving from a previous age. 9 see line 2 of "God's Grandeur," by Gerard Manley Hopkins (page 214). 10 in *The Count of Monte Cristo* (1844–45), by Alexandre Dumas *père* (1802–70), Edmond Dantes elaborately plots the ruin of those whose false accusations led to his prolonged imprisonment.

iii

He is alone; yet not completely alone.
Pins on a map of a colour similar to his,
each city has one, sometimes more than one;
here, caretakers of art, in colleges;
in offices, there, with arm-bands, and green-shaded;
and there, pounding their catalogued beats in libraries, —

everywhere menial, a shadow's shadow.
And always for their egos — their outmoded art.
Thus, having lost the bevel[11] in the ear,
they know neither up nor down, mistake the part
for the whole, curl themselves in a comma,
talk technics, make a colon their eyes. They distort —
such is the pain of their frustration — truth
to something convolute and cerebral.
How they do fear the slap of the flat of the platitude!
Now Pavlov's victims[12] their mouths water at bell,
the platter empty.
                    See they set twenty-one jewels
into their watches; the time they do not tell!

Some, patagonian[13] in their own esteem,
and longing for the multiplying word,
join party and wear pins, now have a message,
an ear, and the convention-hall's regard.
Upon the knees of ventriloquists, they own,
of their dandled[14] brightness, only the paint and board.

And some go mystical, and some go mad.
One stares at a mirror all day long, as if
to recognize himself; another courts
angels, — for here he does not fear rebuff;
and a third, alone, and sick with sex, and rapt,
doodles him symbols convex and concave.

11 instrument for determining angles; thus, the sense of balance. 12 Ivan Petrovich Pavlov (1849–1936), a Russian physiologist, studied conditioned reflexes by ringing a bell when he provided food to dogs. Later, even if he did not serve them food, the dogs salivated when he rang the bell. 13 the natives of Patagonia, at the extreme southern tip of South America, were reputed to be the tallest people in the world; figuratively, patagonian means gigantic. 14 to be moved up and down on one's knee, as with a child.

O schizoid solitudes! O purities
90   curdling upon themselves! Who live for themselves,
or for each other, but for nobody else;
desire affection, private and public loves;
are friendly, and then quarrel and surmise
the secret perversions of each other's lives.

iv

95   He suspects that something has happened, a law
been passed, a nightmare ordered. Set apart,
he finds himself, with special haircut and dress,
as on a reservation. Introvert.
He does not understand this; sad conjecture
100   muscles and palls thrombotic on his heart.

He thinks an impostor, having studied his personal biography,
his gestures, his moods, now has come forward to pose
in the shivering vacuums his absence leaves.
Wigged with his laurel, that other, and faked with his face,
105   he pats the heads of his children, pecks his wife,
and is at home, and slippered, in his house.

So he guesses at the impertinent silhouette
that talks to his phone-piece and slits open his mail.
Is it the local tycoon who for a hobby
110   plays poet, he so epical in steel?
The orator, making a pause? Or is that man
he who blows his flash of brass in the jittering hall?

Or is he cuckolded by the troubadour
rich and successful out of celluloid?
115   Or by the don who unrhymes atoms? Or
the chemist death built up? Pride, lost impostor'd pride,
it is another, another, whoever he is,
who rides where he should ride.

v

Fame, the adrenalin:[15] to be talked about;
to be a verb; to be introduced as *The*:
to smile with endorsement from slick paper; make
caprices anecdotal; to nod to the world; to see
one's name like a song upon the marquees played;
to be forgotten with embarrassment; to be —
to be.

It has its attractions, but is not the thing;
nor is it the ape mimesis[16] who speaks from the tree
ancestral; nor the merkin[17] joy...
Rather it is stark infelicity
which stirs him from his sleep, undressed, asleep
to walk upon roofs and window-sills and defy
the gape of gravity.

vi

Therefore he seeds illusions. Look, he is
the nth Adam taking a green inventory
in world[18] but scarcely uttered, naming, praising,
the flowering fiats in the meadow, the
syllabled fur, stars aspirate, the pollen
whose sweet collusion sounds eternally.
For to praise

the world — he, solitary man — is breath
to him. Until it has been praised, that part
has not been. Item by exciting item —
air to his lungs, and pressured blood to his heart —
they are pulsated, and breathed, until they map,
not the world's, but his own body's chart!

And now in imagination he has climbed
another planet, the better to look
with single camera view upon this earth —
its total scope, and each afflated[19] tick,
its talk, its trick, its tracklessness — and this,
this, he would like to write down in a book!

15 Milton's "Lycidas" also argues about a poet's motivation, first declaring that "Fame is the spur" (line 70) and then rejecting this notion. 16 imitation. 17 false hairpiece for the female genitalia. 18 in Genesis 2:19–20, Adam names the animals. 19 inspired.

To find a new function for the *déclassé*[20] craft
archaic like the fletcher's;[21] to make a new thing;
to say the word that will become sixth sense;
perhaps by necessity and indirection bring
new forms to life, anonymously, new creeds —
O, somehow pay back the daily larcenies of the lung!

These are not mean ambitions. It is already something
merely to entertain them. Meanwhile, he
makes of his status as zero a rich garland,
a halo of his anonymity,
and lives alone, and in his secret shines
like phosphorus. At the bottom of the sea.

(1948)

Dorothy Livesay   (1909–1996)

Dorothy Livesay's poetry developed through a number of distinct phases. Born in Winnipeg, Livesay began her career while an undergraduate at the University of Toronto. Thematically, her first book, *Green Pitcher* (1928), displayed her sensitivity to nature and its relationship to people; technically, it showed the influence of the imagists. After studying at the Sorbonne and returning to Toronto for a degree in social work, she joined the Communist Party and was active as an organizer. Her poetry during the Depression and war years was dominated by political issues and her concern for workers' rights. Two collections of her leftist poetry won the Governor General's Award — *Day and Night* (1944) and *Poems for People* (1947). Livesay served as a teacher in Zambia (1960–63) and earned her M.Ed. at the University of British Columbia in 1964. After this, her career entered a new phase. With the publication of *The Unquiet Bed* (1967), she established herself as a lyric poet capable of giving fresh, sensitive, and forceful expression to issues of female identity and sexuality.

Bartok[1] and the Geranium

She lifts her green umbrellas
Towards the pane
Seeking her fill of sunlight

———→

---

20 outmoded. 21 arrow-maker's.
1 Béla Bartók (1881–1945), a Hungarian composer of intense, passionate music, exerted a profound influence on modern music through his efforts to free himself from strict tonality and the bar-measure system.

Or of rain;
5 Whatever falls
She has no commentary
Accepts, extends,
Blows out her furbelows,[2]
Her bustling boughs;

10 And all the while he whirls
Explodes in space,
Never content with this small room:
Not even can he be
Confined to sky
15 But must speed high and higher still
From galaxy to galaxy,
Wrench from the stars their momentary notes
Steal music from the moon.

She's daylight
20 He is dark
She's heaven-held breath
He storms and crackles
Spits with hell's own spark.

Yet in this room, this moment now
25 These together breathe and be:
She, essence of serenity,
He in a mad intensity
Soars beyond sight
Then hurls, lost Lucifer,
30 From heaven's height.

And when he's done, he's out:
She leans a lip against the glass
And preens herself in light.

(1955)

2 ornamental pleats or flounces.

The Three Emilys [1]

These women crying in my head
Walk alone, uncomforted:
The Emilys, these three
Cry to be set free —
5   And others whom I will not name
Each different, each the same.

Yet they had liberty!
Their kingdom was the sky:
They batted clouds with easy hand,
10   Found a mountain for their stand;
From wandering lonely they could catch
The inner magic of a heath —
A lake their palette, any tree
Their brush could be.

15   And still they cry to me
As in reproach —
I, born to hear their inner storm
Of separate man in woman's form,
I yet possess another kingdom, barred
20   To them, these three, this Emily. [2]
I move as mother in a frame,
My arteries
Flow the immemorial way
Towards the child, the man;
25   And only for brief span
Am I an Emily on mountain snows
And one of these.

And so the whole that I possess
Is still much less —
30   They move triumphant through my head:
I am the one
Uncomforted.

(1953)   (1972)

1 a note identifying the three as Emily Brontë, Emily Dickinson, and Emily Carr appeared with first publication of this poem in *The Canadian Forum* (September 1953). Emily Brontë (1818–48) was a British poet and
author of the novel *Wuthering Heights* (1848); Emily Dickinson (1830–86) was an American poet (see pages
208–212); Emily Carr (1871–1945) was a Canadian painter and author. 2 none of the three Emilys married
or gave birth, whereas Livesay married and raised two children.

Irving Layton (b. 1912)

Born in Romania, Layton (originally Lazarovitch) came to Montreal as an infant. He was educated at Macdonald College and McGill University, taught parochial school in Montreal, and eventually became an English professor at York University. A prolific writer, he published his first book in 1945. *A Red Carpet for the Sun* (1959) won the Governor General's Award. Layton is probably as well known for his controversial attacks on those who disagree with him or criticize him as he is for his poetry. The guardians of official morality, intellectuals, women resistant to his charms, and Christians — all of whom he has grouped among the forces of repression — have felt his deliberately outrageous assaults. In spite of the provocations and bombast in his public statements, his poetry is not always acerbic: it can express tenderness, pathos, humour, and complex ideas, often in elegantly memorable language. Furthermore, Layton has a lofty vision of his calling, which he expresses in terms of his Jewish heritage. He believes that the true poet is, like the Hebrew prophets, one who knows truth, one whose work is of extreme importance: "Poetry, by giving dignity and utterance to our distress, enables us to hope, makes compassion reasonable."

The Birth of Tragedy[1]

And me happiest when I compose poems.
　　　　Love, power, the huzza of battle
　　　　are something, are much;
yet a poem includes them like a pool
5　　　　water and reflection.
In me, nature's divided things —
　　　　tree, mould on tree —
　　　　have their fruition;
I am their core. Let them swap,
10　bandy, like a flame swerve
I am their mouth; as a mouth I serve.

And I observe how the sensual moths
　　　　big with odour and sunshine
　　　　dart into the perilous shrubbery;
15　or drop their visiting shadows
　　　　upon the garden I one year made

———→

1 in *The Birth of Tragedy* (1872), the German philosopher Friedrich Nietzsche (1844–1900) sought to explain the origins of Greek tragedy in a fusion of opposite tendencies. One, the Apollonian, stood for order and idealism; the other, the Dionysian, represented energy and actual experience.

of flowering stone to be a footstool
   for the perfect gods:
    who, friends to the ascending orders,
20 sustain all passionate meditations
and call down pardons
for the insurgent blood.

A quiet madman, never far from tears,
   I lie like a slain thing
25   under the green air the trees
inhabit, or rest upon a chair
    towards which the inflammable air
tumbles on many robins' wings;
    noting how seasonably
30   leaf and blossom uncurl
and living things arrange their death,
while someone from afar off
blows birthday candles for the world.

            (1954)

Keine Lazarovitch 1870–1959

When I saw my mother's head on the cold pillow,
Her white waterfalling hair in the cheeks' hollows,
I thought, quietly circling my grief, of how
She had loved God but cursed extravagantly his creatures.

5 For her final mouth was not water but a curse,
A small black hole, a black rent in the universe,
Which damned the green earth, stars and trees in its stillness
And the inescapable lousiness of growing old.

And I record she was comfortless, vituperative,
10 Ignorant, glad, and much else besides; I believe
She endlessly praised her black eyebrows, their thick weave,
Till plagiarizing Death leaned down and took them for his mould.

And spoiled a dignity I shall not again find,
And the fury of her stubborn limited mind;

         ⟶

15   Now none will shake her amber beads and call God blind,
     Or wear them upon a breast so radiantly.

     O fierce she was, mean and unaccommodating,
     But I think now of the toss of her gold earrings,
     Their proud carnal assertion, and her youngest sings
20   While all the rivers of her red veins move into the sea.

                                                        (1961)

Douglas LePan   (b. 1914)

Winner of the Governor General's Award for both poetry and fiction, Douglas
LePan has been a professor and a member of the diplomatic service. Born in
Toronto, he was educated at the University of Toronto and Oxford. His first
published volume, *The Wounded Prince* (1948), contains some of his best-known
and most important work, including "A Country without a Mythology." A significant contribution to the tradition that stretches at least as far back as Charles
G.D. Roberts and the Confederation Poets — the attempt to create a distinctly
Canadian poetry through treatment of the Canadian landscape — this poem
contains sharply rendered scenes of external nature. It is not, however, simply
another romantic landscape poem: its concern with myth transforms it into a
compelling mental landscape and gives it an ironic edge as a comment on the
traditions and possibilities of Canadian poetry.

A Country without a Mythology

No monuments or landmarks guide the stranger
Going among this savage people, masks
Taciturn or babbling out an alien jargon
And moody as barbaric skies are moody.

5   Berries must be his food. Hurriedly
    He shakes the bushes, plucks pickerel from the river,
    Forgetting every grace and ceremony,
    Feeds like an Indian, and is on his way.

    And yet, for all his haste, time is worth nothing.
10 The abbey clock, the dial in the garden,
    Fade like saint's days and festivals.
    Months, years, are here unbroken virgin forests.

There is no law — even no atmosphere
To smooth the anger of the flagrant sun.
15   November skies sting sting like icicles.
The land is open to all violent weathers.

Passion is not more quick. Lightnings in August
Stagger, rocks split, tongues in the forest hiss,
As fire drinks up the lovely sea-dream coolness.
20   This is the land the passionate man must travel.

Sometimes — perhaps at the tentative fall of twilight —
A belief will settle that waiting around the bend
Are sanctities of childhood, that melting birds
Will sing him into a limpid gracious Presence.

25   The hills will fall in folds, the wilderness
Will be a garment innocent and lustrous
To wear upon a birthday, under a light
That curls and smiles, a golden-haired Archangel.

And now the channel opens. But nothing alters.
30   Mile after mile of tangled struggling roots,
Wild-rice, stumps, weeds, that clutch at the canoe,
Wild birds hysterical in tangled trees.

And not a sign, no emblem in the sky
Or boughs to friend him as he goes; for who
35   Will stop where, clumsily constructed, daubed
With war-paint, teeters some lust-red manitou?[1]

(1948)

Dylan Thomas (1914–1953)

Gifted with a richly expressive voice, Dylan Thomas attracted many who had never previously felt the beauty and emotional power of poetry. At the same time, he often repelled those who met him because of his excessive drinking and blunt, irreverent wit. Born in Swansea, Wales, Thomas earned fame with his first collection, *Eighteen Poems* (1934). Later collections, such as *The Map of*

1 the spirit worshipped as a force of nature by Algonquin Indians.

Love (1939) and Deaths and Entrances (1946), consolidated his reputation as the leading lyric poet of his generation. Thomas, who worked at the beginning of his career as a script-writer and broadcaster for the BBC, was also an accomplished prose writer, his best-known works being the novel Portrait of the Artist as a Young Dog (1940), the radio drama Under Milk Wood (1954), and his reminiscence, A Child's Christmas in Wales (1954). Much of his popularity, however, came because of performances — readings of poems by himself and others, phonograph recordings, and three American tours. His readings stressed the musical and oral qualities of the poetry. His own poems are distinctive in employing a profusion of sonorous images, for, as he once said, "A poem by myself needs a host of images, because its centre is a host of images." Although his sequences of images can sometimes seem an incoherent, surrealistic jumble, his best work unifies the abundant imagery through theme. His major themes are childhood experience, the cycle of nature, religious sensibility, sex, and death.

And Death Shall Have No Dominion [1]

And death shall have no dominion.
Dead men naked they shall be one
With the man in the wind and the west moon;
When their bones are picked clean and the clean bones gone,
5   They shall have stars at elbow and foot;
Though they go mad they shall be sane,
Though they sink through the sea they shall rise again;
Though lovers be lost love shall not;
And death shall have no dominion.

10   And death shall have no dominion.
Under the windings of the sea
They lying long shall not die windily;
Twisting on racks when sinews give way,
Strapped to a wheel, yet they shall not break;
15   Faith in their hands shall snap in two,
And the unicorn evils run them through;
Split all ends up they shan't crack;
And death shall have no dominion.

And death shall have no dominion.
20   No more may gulls cry at their ears
Or waves break loud on the seashores;

———→

1 an echo of Romans 6:9: "Knowing that Christ being raised from the dead dieth no more; death hath no more dominion over him."

Where blew a flower may a flower no more
Lift its head to the blows of the rain;
Though they be mad and dead as nails,
25 Heads of the characters hammer through daisies;
Break in the sun till the sun breaks down,
And death shall have no dominion.

(1934)

The Force That Through the
Green Fuse Drives the Flower

The force that through the green fuse drives the flower
Drives my green age; that blasts the roots of trees
Is my destroyer.
And I am dumb to tell the crooked rose
5 My youth is bent by the same wintry fever.

The force that drives the water through the rocks
Drives my red blood; that dries the mouthing streams
Turns mine to wax.
And I am dumb to mouth unto my veins
10 How at the mountain spring the same mouth sucks.

The hand that whirls the water in the pool
Stirs the quicksand; that ropes the blowing wind
Hauls my shroud sail.
And I am dumb to tell the hanging man
15 How of my clay is made the hangman's lime.

The lips of time leech to the fountain head;
Love drips and gathers, but the fallen blood
Shall calm her sores.
And I am dumb to tell a weather's wind
20 How time has ticked a heaven round the stars.

And I am dumb to tell the lover's tomb
How at my sheet goes the same crooked worm.

(1934)

Fern Hill [1]

Now as I was young and easy under the apple boughs
About the lilting house and happy as the grass was green,
   The night above the dingle [2] starry,
    Time let me hail and climb
5   Golden in the heydays of his eyes,
And honoured among wagons I was prince of the apple towns
And once below a time I lordly had the trees and leaves
    Trail with daisies and barley
  Down the rivers of the windfall [3] light.

10 And as I was green and carefree, famous among the barns
About the happy yard and singing as the farm was home,
   In the sun that is young once only,
    Time let me play and be
  Golden in the mercy of his means,
15 And green and golden I was huntsman and herdsman, the calves
Sang to my horn, the foxes on the hills barked clear and cold,
    And the sabbath rang slowly
  In the pebbles of the holy streams.

All the sun long it was running, it was lovely, the hay
20 Fields high as the house, the tunes from the chimneys, it was air
   And playing, lovely and watery
    And fire green as grass.
    And nightly under the simple stars
As I rode to sleep the owls were bearing the farm away,
25 All the moon long I heard, blessed among stables, the nightjars [4]
   Flying with the ricks, [5] and the horses
    Flashing into the dark.

And then to awake, and the farm, like a wanderer white
With the dew, come back, the cock on his shoulder: it was all
30 Shining, it was Adam and maiden,
    The sky gathered again
  And the sun grew round that very day.

→

1 the Welsh farm of Ann Jones, the aunt with whom Thomas spent holidays away from Swansea. 2 deep
dell or hollow, usually wooded. 3 a transferred epithet: windfall apples are those blown down by the wind.
4 common nocturnal bird. 5 stacks of hay.

So it must have been after the birth of the simple light
In the first, spinning place, the spellbound horses walking warm
35   Out of the whinnying green stable
         On to the fields of praise.

And honoured among foxes and pheasants by the gay house
Under the new made clouds and happy as the heart was long,
    In the sun born over and over,
40   I ran my heedless ways,
    My wishes raced through the house high hay
And nothing I cared, at my sky blue trades, that time allows
In all his tuneful turning so few and such morning songs
    Before the children green and golden
45   Follow him out of grace,

Nothing I cared, in the lamb white days, that time would take me
Up to the swallow thronged loft by the shadow of my hand,
    In the moon that is always rising,
      Nor that riding to sleep
50   I should hear him fly with the high fields
And wake to the farm forever fled from the childless land.
Oh as I was young and easy in the mercy of his means,
      Time held me green and dying
    Though I sang in my chains like the sea.

                        (1946)

Do Not Go Gentle into That Good Night[1]

Do not go gentle into that good night,
Old age should burn and rave at close of day;
Rage, rage against the dying of the light.

Though wise men at their end know dark is right,
5 Because their words had forked no lightning they
Do not go gentle into that good night.

Good men, the last wave by, crying how bright
Their frail deeds might have danced in a green bay,
Rage, rage against the dying of the light.

1 written in 1951 and addressed to his dying father.

10   Wild men who caught and sang the sun in flight,
And learn, too late, they grieved it on its way,
Do not go gentle into that good night.

Grave men, near death, who see with blinding sight
Blind eyes could blaze like meteors and be gay,
15   Rage, rage against the dying of the light.

And you, my father, there on the sad height,
Curse, bless, me now with your fierce tears, I pray.
Do not go gentle into that good night.
Rage, rage against the dying of the light.

(1952)

P.K. Page   (b. 1916)

Patricia Kathleen Page was born in Swanage, England, but came to Red Deer, Alberta, when she was two. She began her career as a poet in Montreal, where she was associated with the founders of *Preview*, a literary journal that championed formally sophisticated and intellectually demanding poetry. Her first collection, published in 1946, showed concern with both social issues and psychology. Page is also a graphic artist, and the abundant imagery and profusion of metaphors in her poetry are signs of her intensely visual sensibility. Nevertheless, Page tries to present more than surface appearance. In doing so, especially in her later work, she has been influenced by Sufism. Thus in her poetry, Page is a mystic, seeking, with what she calls her "two-dimensional consciousness," a glimpse of the three-dimensional unity beyond mundane appearances.

The Stenographers

After the brief bivouac of Sunday,
their eyes, in the forced march of Monday to Saturday,
hoist the white flag, flutter in the snow-storm of paper,
haul it down and crack in the mid-sun of temper.

5   In the pause between the first draft and the carbon
they glimpse the smooth hours when they were children —

———→

the ride in the ice-cart, the ice-man's name,
the end of the route and the long walk home;

remember the sea where floats at high tide
10   were sea marrows growing on the scatter-green vine
or spools of grey toffee, or wasps' nests on water;
remember the sand and the leaves of the country.

Bell rings and they go and the voice draws their pencil
like a sled across snow; when its runners are frozen
15   rope snaps and the voice then is pulling no burden
but runs like a dog on the winter of paper.

Their climates are winter and summer — no wind
for the kites of their hearts — no wind for a flight;
a breeze at the most, to tumble them over
20   and leave them like rubbish — the boy-friends of blood.

In the inch of the noon as they move they are stagnant.
The terrible calm of the noon is their anguish;
the lip of the counter, the shapes of the straws
like icicles breaking their tongues, are invaders.

25   Their beds are their oceans — salt water of weeping
the waves that they know — the tide before sleep;
and fighting to drown they assemble their sheep
in columns and watch them leap desks for their fences
and stare at them with their own mirror-worn faces.

30   In the felt of the morning the calico-minded,
sufficiently starched, insert papers, hit keys,
efficient and sure as their adding machines;
yet they weep in the vault, they are taut as net curtains
stretched upon frames. In their eyes I have seen
35   the pin men of madness in marathon trim
race round the track of the stadium pupil.

(1946)

Stories of Snow

Those in the vegetable rain retain
an area behind their sprouting eyes
held soft and rounded with the dream of snow
precious and reminiscent as those globes —
5 souvenir of some never-nether land —
which hold their snow-storms circular, complete,
high in a tall and teakwood cabinet.

In countries where the leaves are large as hands
where flowers protrude their fleshy chins
10 and call their colours,
an imaginary snow-storm sometimes falls
among the lilies.
And in the early morning one will waken
to think the glowing linen of his pillow
15 a northern drift, will find himself mistaken
and lie back weeping.
And there the story shifts from head to head,
of how in Holland, from their feather beds
hunters arise and part the flakes and go
20 forth to the frozen lakes in search of swans —
the snow-light falling white along their guns,
their breath in plumes.
While tethered in the wind like sleeping gulls
ice-boats wait the raising of their wings
25 to skim the electric ice at such a speed
they leap jet strips of naked water,
and how these flying, sailing hunters feel
air in their mouths as terrible as ether.
And on the story runs that even drinks
30 in that white landscape dare to be no colour;
how flasked and water clear, the liquor slips
silver against the hunters' moving hips.
And of the swan in death these dreamers tell
of its last flight and how it falls, a plummet,
35 pierced by the freezing bullet
and how three feathers, loosened by the shot,
descend like snow upon it.
While hunters plunge their fingers in its down
deep as a drift, and dive their hands

40 up to the neck of the wrist
in that warm metamorphosis of snow
as gentle as the sort that woodsmen know
who, lost in the white circle, fall at last
and dream their way to death.

45 And stories of this kind are often told
in countries where great flowers bar the roads
with reds and blues which seal the route to snow —
as if, in telling, raconteurs unlock
the colour with its complement and go
50 through to the area behind the eyes
where silent, unrefractive whiteness lies.

(1946)

The Landlady

Through sepia air the boarders come and go,
impersonal as trains. Pass silently
the craving silence swallowing her speech;
click doors like shutters on her camera eye.

5 Because of her their lives become exact:
their entrances and exits are designed;
phone calls are cryptic. Oh, her ticklish ears
advance and fall back stunned.

Nothing is unprepared. They hold the walls
10 about them as they weep or laugh. Each face
is dialled to zero publicly. She peers
stippled with curious flesh;

pads on the patient landing like a pulse,
unlocks their keyholes with the wire of sight,
15 searches their rooms for clues when they are out,
pricks when they come home late.

Wonders when they are quiet, jumps when they move,
dreams that they dope or drink, trembles to know
the traffic of their brains, jaywalks their street
20 in clumsy shoes.

Yet knows them better than their closest friends:
their cupboards and the secrets of their drawers,
their books, their private mail, their photographs
are theirs and hers.

25   Knows when they wash, how frequently their clothes
go to the cleaners, what they like to eat,
their curvature of health, but even so
is not content.

And like a lover must know all, all, all.
30   Prays she may catch them unprepared at last
and palm the dreadful riddle of their skulls —
hoping the worst.

(1974)

Al Purdy   (1918–2000)

Born in Wooler, Ontario, Alfred Purdy left school after Grade 10, riding freight trains to Vancouver, where he worked in a mattress factory and at other manual labour. Purdy published his first book in 1944 and won the Governor General's Award for *The Cariboo Horses* (1965). Much of his early poetry relies upon his experiences as a labourer and uses the voice of a "common person." Combining colloquial expressions, vulgarity, and poetic sentimentality, this conversational voice is frequently an effective vehicle for philosophic thought and social criticism because it casts ideas into unexpected forms. Purdy has travelled widely and written about his travels throughout Canada, including the Arctic, and such places as Cuba, Mexico, South America, Greece, and Japan. Nevertheless, he is quintessentially the poet of a single place, the area around his home of Ameliasburg, Ontario. Purdy conveys his love of Canada, of ordinary working people, and of tradition in these poems, which mingle past and present and thereby transform the area into a mythic landscape.

The Country North of Belleville

Bush land scrub land —
        Cashel Township and Wollaston
Elzevir McClure and Dungannon
green lands of Weslemkoon Lake
5   where a man might have some

      opinion of what beauty
is and none deny him
                 for miles —

Yet this is the country of defeat
10   where Sisyphus[1] rolls a big stone
year after year up the ancient hills
picnicking glaciers have left strewn
with centuries' rubble
                 backbreaking days
15   in the sun and rain
when realization seeps slow in the mind
without grandeur or self deception in
                noble struggle
of being a fool —

20   A country of quiescence and still distance
lean land
              not like the fat south
with inches of black soil on
              earth's round belly —
25   And where the farms are
              it's as if a man stuck
both thumbs in the stony earth and pulled

                 it apart
                 to make room
30   enough between the trees
for a wife
               and maybe some cows and
               room for some
of the more easily kept illusions —
35   And where the farms have gone back
to forest
              are only soft outlines
              shadowy differences —

Old fences drift vaguely among the trees
40   a pile of moss-covered stones

1 king of Corinth whose punishment in Hades was to roll a heavy stone up a hill, only to have it roll down
again when it neared the top.

gathered for some ghost purpose
has lost meaning under the meaningless sky
      — they are like cities under water
and the undulating green waves of time
45   are laid on them —

This is the country of our defeat
        and yet
during the fall plowing a man
might stop and stand in a brown valley of the furrows
50   and shade his eyes to watch for the same
         red patch mixed with gold
         that appears on the same
         spot in the hills
         year after year
55   and grow old
plowing and plowing a ten-acre field until
the convolutions run parallel with his own brain —

And this is a country where the young
        leave quickly
60 unwilling to know what their fathers know
or think the words their mothers do not say —

Herschel Monteagle and Faraday
lakeland rockland and hill country
a little adjacent to where the world is
65 a little north of where the cities are and
sometime
we may go back there
        to the country of our defeat
Wollaston Elzevir and Dungannon
70 and Weslemkoon lake land
where the high townships of Cashel
        McClure and Marmora once were —
But it's been a long time since
and we must enquire the way
75   of strangers —

(1965)   (1972)

Trees at the Arctic Circle
(Salix Cordifolia — Ground Willow)

They are 18 inches long
or even less
crawling under rocks
grovelling among the lichens
5   bending and curling to escape
making themselves small
finding new ways to hide
Coward trees
I am angry to see them
10   like this
not proud of what they are
bowing to weather instead
careful of themselves
worried about the sky
15   afraid of exposing their limbs
like a Victorian married couple

I call to mind great Douglas Firs
I see tall maples waving green
and oaks like gods in autumn gold
the whole horizon jungle dark
20   and I crouched under that continual night
But these
even the dwarf shrubs of Ontario
mock them
Coward trees

25   And yet — and yet —
their seed pods glow
like delicate grey earrings
their leaves are veined and intricate
like tiny parkas
30   They have about three months
to ensure the species does not die
and that's how they spend their time
unbothered by any human opinion
just digging in here and now

⟶

35 sending their roots down down down
And you know it occurs to me
        about 2 feet under
those roots must touch permafrost
ice that remains ice forever
40 and they use it for their nourishment
use death to remain alive

I see that I've been carried away
in my scorn of the dwarf trees
most foolish in my judgements
45 To take away the dignity
        of any living thing
even tho it cannot understand
        the scornful words
is to make life itself trivial
50 and yourself the Pontifex Maximus[1]
        of nullity
I have been stupid in a poem
I will not alter the poem
but let the stupidity remain permanent
55 as the trees are
in a poem
the dwarf trees of Baffin Island

Pangnirtung   (1967)

Lament for the Dorsets

(Eskimos extinct in the 14th century A.D.*)* [1]

Animal bones and some mossy tent rings
scrapers and spearheads   carved ivory swans
all that remains of the Dorset giants
who drove the Vikings back to their long ships
5 talked to spirits of earth and water

→

1 highest priest of the Roman religion and chief administrator of religious affairs.
1 in about A.D. 1000, the Dorset people were displaced from most of the Arctic regions by Thule Inuit
from Alaska, but they continued to live in northern Quebec and Labrador until about A.D. 1500, when
they disappeared.

— a picture of terrifying old men
so large they broke the backs of bears
so small they lurk behind bone rafters
in the brain of modern hunters
10   among good thoughts and warm things
and come out at night
to spit on the stars

The big men with clever fingers
who had no dogs and hauled their sleds
15   over the frozen northern oceans
awkward giants
     killers of seal
they couldn't compete with little men
who came from the west with dogs
20   Or else in a warm climatic cycle
the seals went back to cold waters
and the puzzled Dorsets scratched their heads
with hairy thumbs around 1350 A.D.
— couldn't figure it out
25   went around saying to each other
plaintively
    "What's wrong? What happened?
    Where are the seals gone?"
And died

30   Twentieth-century people
apartment dwellers
executives of neon death
warmakers with things that explode
— they have never imagined us in their future
35   how could we imagine them in the past
squatting among the moving glaciers
six hundred years ago
with glowing lamps?
As remote or nearly
40   as the trilobites and swamps
when coal became
or the last great reptile hissed
at a mammal the size of a mouse
that squeaked and fled

     ⟶

45   Did they ever realize at all
    what was happening to them?
    Some old hunter with one lame leg
    a bear had chewed
    sitting in a caribou-skin tent
50   — the last Dorset?
    Let's say his name was Kudluk
    and watch him sitting there
    carving 2-inch ivory swans
    for a dead grand-daughter
55   taking them out of his mind
    the places in his mind
    where pictures are
    He selects a sharp stone tool
    to gouge a parallel pattern of lines
60   on both sides of the swan
    holding it with his left hand
    bearing down and transmitting
    his body's weight
    from brain to arm and right hand
65   and one of his thoughts
    turns to ivory
    The carving is laid aside
    in beginning darkness
    at the end of hunger
70   and after a while wind
    blows down the tent and snow
    begins to cover him

    After 600 years
    the ivory thought
75   is still warm

                                                    (1968)

Wilderness Gothic

Across Roblin Lake, two shores away,
they are sheathing the church spire
with new metal. Someone hangs in the sky

                         ⟶

over there from a piece of rope,
5   hammering and fitting God's belly-scratcher,
working his way up along the spire
until there's nothing left to nail on —
Perhaps the workman's faith reaches beyond:
touches intangibles, wrestles with Jacob,[1]
10   replacing rotten timber with pine thews,
pounds hard in the blue cave of the sky,
contends heroically with difficult problems of
gravity, sky navigation and mythopeia,
his volunteer time and labour donated to God,
15   minus sick benefits of course on a non-union job —

Fields around are yellowing into harvest,
nestling and fingerling are sky and water borne,
death is yodelling quiet in green woodlots,
and bodies of three young birds have disappeared
20   in the sub-surface of the new county highway —

That picture is incomplete, part left out
that might alter the whole Dürer[2] landscape:
gothic ancestors peer from medieval sky,
dour faces trapped in photograph albums escaping
25   to clop down iron roads with matched greys:
work-sodden wives groping inside their flesh
for what keeps moving and changing and flashing
beyond and past the long frozen Victorian day.
A sign of fire and brimstone? A two-headed calf
30   born in the barn last night? A sharp female agony?
An age and a faith moving into transition,
the dinner cold and new-baked bread a failure,
deep woods shiver and water drops hang pendant,
double yolked eggs and the house creaks a little —
35   Something is about to happen. Leaves are still.
Two shores away, a man hammering in the sky.
Perhaps he will fall.

(1968)

---

1 Jacob wrestled with an angel, refusing to release him until the angel gave him a blessing;
see Genesis 32:24–29. 2 landscapes in many paintings and engravings by German artist Albrecht Dürer
(1471–1528) are elaborate, often gloomy combinations of realistic details and visionary symbolism.

Oodgeroo Noonuccal
(Kath Walker) (1920–1993)

The first prominent Aboriginal poet and protest writer in Australia, Kath Walker, who used her Aboriginal name, Oodgeroo Noonuccal, was born on Stradbroke Island, off the Queensland coast near Brisbane. At the age of thirteen, she began work as a domestic servant. When she was sixteen, she encountered a powerful example of official discrimination: because she was part Aboriginal, she was denied admission to nursing studies. A leading advocate of Aboriginal rights, she was involved in the campaign that led to the 1967 repeal of constitutional discrimination against Aborigines. The title of her first volume of poetry, *We Are Going* (1964), she has said, was "a warning to the white people: we can go out of existence, or with proper help we could also go on and live in this world in peace and harmony. . . ." She has also said that her poems are "sloganistic, civil rightish, plain and simple." At their best, however, they are powerfully emotional presentations of the culture and history of the Aborigines; they clearly portray the abuses whites have inflicted, the dignity of Aborigines, and the value of an ancient way of life lived close to the land.

We Are Going

For Grannie Coolwell

They came in to the little town
A semi-naked band subdued and silent,
All that remained of their tribe.
They came here to the place of their old bora ground[1]
5 Where now the many white men hurry about like ants.
Notice of estate agent reads: "Rubbish May Be Tipped Here."
Now it half covers the traces of the old bora ring.
They sit and are confused, they cannot say their thoughts:
"We are as strangers here now, but the white tribe are the strangers.
10 We belong here, we are of the old ways.
We are the corroboree[2] and the bora ground,
We are the old sacred ceremonies, the laws of the elders.
We are the wonder tales of Dream Time,[3] the tribal legends told.
We are the past, the hunts and the laughing games, the wandering camp fires.

———▶

1 the term *bora* is applied both to the most solemn of Aboriginal rites, in which a young boy is admitted to the rights of manhood, and to the site of the ceremony. The bora ground is usually called a bora ring because it is most often a circular earthen bank or an area marked off by a ring of stones.   2 Aboriginal dance ceremony, sometimes sacred and sometimes secular, involving singing and rhythmical musical accompaniment. 3 the time of mythic events; the time of the first ancestors or the time, beyond living memory, in which the physical, spiritual, and moral world was developed.

15   We are the lightning-bolt over Gaphembah Hill[4]
Quick and terrible,
And the Thunderer[5] after him, that loud fellow.
We are the quiet daybreak paling the dark lagoon.
We are the shadow-ghosts creeping back as the camp fires burn low.
20   We are nature and the past, all the old ways
Gone now and scattered.
The scrubs are gone, the hunting and the laughter.
The eagle is gone, the emu[6] and the kangaroo are gone from this place.
The bora ring is gone.
25   The corroboree is gone.
And we are going."

(1964)

Philip Larkin (1922–1985)

Born at Coventry and educated at Oxford, Larkin led a quiet and unremarkable life. He worked as a librarian in several places, completing his career as head librarian at the University of Hull, a post he took up in 1955. His first poetry collection was *The North Ship* (1945), but it was *The Less Deceived* (1955) that established him as one of the most popular British poets of the postwar era. Larkin was opposed to what he considered the overly complex techniques of modernist and academic poetry, such as that written by Eliot and Pound. Instead, he favoured carefully crafted works that speak directly to people who may not have a specialized understanding of literature and literary tradition. Poetry should be, he said, "emotional in nature and theatrical in operation, a skilled re-creation of emotion in other people." Therefore, like Thomas Hardy, whose poems obviously influenced him, he used traditional forms and techniques, employed the language of ordinary people, and used his own experiences, rather than other poetry or works of art, as the basis for most of his poems. Larkin's range was narrow, but people responded favourably because his poetry was both witty and accessible.

4 on Stradbroke Island, behind Myora Springs and near Moongalba, where the author, also known as Oodgeroo Noonuccal Moongalba, lives. 5 thunder; Aboriginal beliefs tend to be localized, rather than universal among the various tribes, and mythic figures, such as Thunderer, are often attached to specific sites or regions. 6 large, flightless bird that can run at a speed of approximately 50 kilometres per hour.

Next, Please

Always too eager for the future, we
Pick up bad habits of expectancy.
Something is always approaching; every day
Till then we say,

5   Watching from a bluff the tiny, clear,
Sparkling armada[1] of promises draw near.
How slow they are! And how much time they waste,
Refusing to make haste!

Yet still they leave us holding wretched stalks
10 Of disappointment, for, though nothing balks,
Each big approach, leaning with brasswork prinked,[2]
Each rope distinct,

Flagged, and the figurehead with golden tits
Arching our way, it never anchors; it's
15 No sooner present than it turns to past.
Right to the last

We think each one will heave to and unload
All good into our lives, all we are owed
For waiting so devoutly and so long.
20 But we are wrong:

Only one ship is seeking us, a black-
Sailed unfamiliar, towing at her back
A huge and birdless silence. In her wake
No waters breed or break.

(1955)

1 large fleet. 2 spruced up, shined.

Church Going

Once I am sure there's nothing going on
I step inside, letting the door thud shut.
Another church: matting, seats, and stone,
And little books; sprawlings of flowers, cut
5   For Sunday, brownish now; some brass and stuff
Up at the holy end; the small neat organ;
And a tense, musty, unignorable silence,
Brewed God knows how long. Hatless, I take off
My cycle-clips in awkward reverence,

10   Move forward, run my hand around the font.
From where I stand, the roof looks almost new —
Cleaned, or restored? Someone would know: I don't.
Mounting the lectern, I peruse a few
Hectoring large-scale verses, and pronounce
15   'Here endeth' much more loudly than I'd meant.
The echoes snigger briefly. Back at the door
I sign the book, donate an Irish sixpence,
Reflect the place was not worth stopping for.

Yet stop I did: in fact I often do,
20   And always end much at a loss like this,
Wondering what to look for; wondering, too,
When churches fall completely out of use
What we shall turn them into, if we shall keep
A few cathedrals chronically on show,
25   Their parchment, plate and pyx[1] in locked cases,
And let the rest rent-free to rain and sheep.
Shall we avoid them as unlucky places?

Or, after dark, will dubious women come
To make their children touch a particular stone;
30   Pick simples[2] for a cancer; or on some
Advised night see walking a dead one?
Power of some sort or other will go on
In games, in riddles, seemingly at random;

⎯⎯⎯→

---

1 vessel in which the consecrated Host is reserved. 2 herbs or plants used for medicinal purposes.

But superstition, like belief, must die,
35   And what remains when disbelief has gone?
Grass, weedy pavement, brambles, buttress, sky,

A shape less recognisable each week,
A purpose more obscure. I wonder who
Will be the last, the very last, to seek
40   This place for what it was; one of the crew
That tap and jot and know what rood-lofts[3] were?
Some ruin-bibber,[4] randy for antique,
Or Christmas-addict, counting on a whiff
Of gowns-and-bands and organ-pipes and myrrh?
45   Or will he be my representative,

Bored, uninformed, knowing the ghostly silt
Dispersed, yet tending to this cross of ground
Through suburb scrub because it held unspilt
So long and equably what since is found
50   Only in separation — marriage, and birth,
And death, and thoughts of these — for which was built
This special shell? For, though I've no idea
What this accoutred frowsty[5] barn is worth,
It pleases me to stand in silence here;

55   A serious house on serious earth it is,
In whose blent air all our compulsions meet,
Are recognised, and robed as destinies.
And that much never can be obsolete,
Since someone will forever be surprising
60   A hunger in himself to be more serious,
And gravitating with it to this ground,
Which, he once heard, was proper to grow wise in,
If only that so many dead lie round.

(1955)

---

3 loft or gallery over a rood-screen, a screen with a cross on top separating the nave from the choir or chancel. 4 a bibber is one who drinks frequently; hence, a ruin-bibber frequents ruins or antiquities.
5 musty, or stale-smelling.

Toads

Why should I let the toad *work*
    Squat on my life?
Can't I use my wit as a pitchfork
    And drive the brute off?

5   Six days of the week it soils
    With its sickening poison —
Just for paying a few bills!
    That's out of proportion.

Lots of folk live on their wits:
10   Lecturers, lispers,
Losels, loblolly-men,[1] louts —
    They don't end as paupers;

Lots of folk live up lanes
    With fires in a bucket,
15 Eat windfalls and tinned sardines —
    They seem to like it.

Their nippers[2] have got bare feet,
    Their unspeakable wives
Are skinny as whippets[3]— and yet
20   No one actually *starves*.

Ah, were I courageous enough
    To shout *Stuff your pension!*
But I know, all too well, that's the stuff
    That dreams are made on:

25 For something sufficiently toad-like
    Squats in me, too;
Its hunkers are heavy as hard luck,
    And cold as snow,

1 losels are worthless persons, scoundrels, or rakes; loblolly-men are bumpkins or rustics.   2 children.
3 short-haired dogs, resembling but smaller than greyhounds, that are bred for speed.

And will never allow me to blarney
30   My way to getting
The fame and the girl and the money
      All at one sitting.

I don't say, one bodies the other
      One's spiritual truth;
35   But I do say it's hard to lose either,
      When you have both.

(1955)

Phyllis Webb   (b. 1927)

Born in Victoria, B.C., Phyllis Webb received her B.A. from the University of British Columbia and studied briefly at McGill. She has taught at UBC and the University of Victoria and was writer in residence at the University of Alberta. She has also been a producer for the Canadian Broadcasting Corporation. Her first book of poetry was *Trio* (1954), which also featured the work of two other poets. *The Vision Tree: Selected Poems* (1982) won the Governor General's Award. An intellectual with an often bleak vision of the world, Webb develops ideas carefully through complex structures and careful arrangements of sounds, creating what she calls "the dance of the intellect in the syllables."

Marvell's Garden [1]

Marvell's garden, that place of solitude,
is not where I'd choose to live
yet is the fixed sundial
that turns me round
5   unwillingly
in a hot glade
as closer, closer I come to contradiction
to the shade green within the green shade. [2]

---

1 see Andrew Marvell's "The Garden" (page 65), in which a garden symbolizes the solitary contemplative life.   2 in "The Garden," Marvell speaks of "a green thought in a green shade" (line 48). Green symbolizes a cool detachment from human concerns.

The garden where Marvell scorned love's solicitude —
10   that dream — and played instead an arcane solitaire,
shuffling his thoughts like shadowy chance
across the shrubs of ecstasy,
and cast the myths away to flowering hours[3]
as yes, his mind, that sea,[4] caught at green
15   thoughts shadowing a green infinity.

And yet Marvell's garden was not Plato's[5]
garden — and yet — he did care more for the form
of things than for the thing itself —
ideas and visions,
20   resemblances and echoes,
things seeming and being
not quite what they were.

That was his garden, a kind of attitude
struck out of an earth too carefully attended,
25   wanting to be left alone.
And I don't blame him for that.
God knows, too many fences fence us out
and his garden closed in on Paradise.[6]

On Paradise! When I think of his hymning
30   Puritans in the Bermudas, the bright oranges
lighting up that night![7] When I recall
his rustling tinsel hopes
beneath the cold decree of steel,
Oh, I have wept for some new convulsion
35   to tear together this world and his.[8]

---

3 the fourth stanza of "The Garden" recounts the stories of Daphne and Syrinx, maidens who escaped seduction when they were transformed into, respectively, a laurel and a reed. 4 Marvell's poem (lines 43–44) refers to the mind as an ocean because, like the ocean, which was thought to contain a form of everything on land, the mind contains a resemblance of everything on earth. 5 Plato argued that any earthly thing was but a pale reflection or shadow of the ideal form or idea of that thing. 6 Marvell compared his garden, a solitary place — and thus free from sexual passion — to Eden before the creation of Eve: "Two paradises 'twere in one, / To live in paradise alone" (lines 63–64). 7 in "Bermudas" (1681), Marvell wrote of Puritans seeking refuge from English bishops in a land "far kinder than our own." In praising God, who gave the Puritans such a beautiful refuge, he says God "hangs in shades the orange bright, / Like golden lamps in a green night." 8 in "The Definition of Love" (1681), a poem about a lover's despair because he can never consummate his love, Marvell speaks of "feeble hope," which "vainly flapped its tinsel wing." Fate's "decrees of steel" separate the lovers as if they were the poles of the earth. He declares that they will remain apart "Unless the giddy heaven fall, / And earth some new convulsion tear," joining the lovers by flattening the globe.

But then I saw his luminous plumèd Wings
prepared for flight,
and then I heard him singing glory
in a green tree,
40   and then I caught the vest he'd laid aside
all blest with fire.[9]

And I have gone walking slowly in
his garden of necessity
leaving brothers, lovers, Christ
45   outside my walls
where they have wept without
and I within.

(1956)

Treblinka[1] Gas Chamber

Klostermayer ordered another count of the children.
Then their stars were snipped off and thrown into
the center of the courtyard. It looked like a field of
buttercups.
        — Joseph Hyams, A Field of Buttercups

fallingstars
       "a field of
            buttercups"

       yellow stars
5   of David
               falling
the prisoners
      ⟶

9 in the seventh stanza of "The Garden," Marvell speaks of his soul casting off "the body's vest" to fly like a bird into the trees.
1 extermination camp in Poland where the Nazis gassed thousands of Jews during World War II.

                    the children
                              falling

          in heaps
                         on one another
                                        they go down
Thanatos[2]
              showers
                    his dirty breath
                                   they must breathe
                                                  him in
                    they see stars
                              behind their
                                        eyes
David's
          "a field of
                    buttercups"

          a metaphor
                         where all that's
                                   left lies down

                                                  (1980)

Adrienne Rich (b. 1929)

Adrienne Rich grew up in Baltimore, Maryland, where she began writing poetry as a girl. While formal and restrained compared with her later work, her first book, *A Change of World* (1951), showed remarkable maturity of thought and technique for a 22-year-old and won the Yale Series of Younger Poets award. Only after marrying early and having three sons in quick succession did Rich begin breaking away from stereotypical female roles. Beginning with her third book, *Snapshots of a Daughter-in-Law* (1963), her forms are freer, her voice is more personal, and her growing resentment of the limitations she sees imposed on her in a male-dominated society is made plain. Beginning with her opposition to the Vietnam War in the 1960s, Rich — guided always by a strong feminist commitment — has become increasingly involved in various liberal political movements. In 1986, she became professor of English and feminist studies at Stanford University.

2 the ancient Greek personification of Death.

Aunt Jennifer's Tigers

Aunt Jennifer's tigers prance across a screen,
Bright topaz denizens of a world of green.
They do not fear the men beneath the tree;
They pace in sleek chivalric certainty.

5   Aunt Jennifer's fingers fluttering through her wool
Find even the ivory needle hard to pull.
The massive weight of Uncle's wedding band
Sits heavily upon Aunt Jennifer's hand.

When Aunt is dead, her terrified hands will lie
10   Still ringed with ordeals she was mastered by.
The tigers in the panel that she made
Will go on prancing, proud and unafraid.

(1951)

Diving into the Wreck

First having read the book of myths,
and loaded the camera,
and checked the edge of the knife-blade,
I put on
5   the body-armor of black rubber
the absurd flippers
the grave and awkward mask.
I am having to do this
not like Cousteau[1] with his
10   assiduous team
aboard the sun-flooded schooner
but here alone.
There is a ladder.
The ladder is always there
15   hanging innocently
close to the side of the schooner.
We know what it is for,
we who have used it.

———→

1 Jacques Cousteau (1910–97), French author, filmmaker, and underwater explorer.

Otherwise
20   it's a piece of maritime floss
some sundry equipment.

I go down.
Rung after rung and still
the oxygen immerses me
25   the blue light
the clear atoms
of our human air.
I go down.
My flippers cripple me,
30   I crawl like an insect down the ladder
and there is no one
to tell me when the ocean
will begin.

First the air is blue and then
35   it is bluer and then green and then
black I am blacking out and yet
my mask is powerful
it pumps my blood with power
the sea is another story
40   the sea is not a question of power
I have to learn alone
to turn my body without force
in the deep element.

And now: it is easy to forget
45   what I came for
among so many who have always
lived here
swaying their crenellated fans
between the reefs
50   and besides
you breathe differently down here.

I came to explore the wreck.
The words are purposes.
The words are maps.

⟶

55 I came to see the damage that was done
    and the treasures that prevail.
    I stroke the beam of my lamp
    slowly along the flank
    of something more permanent
60 than fish or weed.

    the thing I came for:
    the wreck and not the story of the wreck
    the thing itself and not the myth
    the drowned face always staring
65 toward the sun
    the evidence of damage
    worn by salt and sway into this threadbare beauty
    the ribs of the disaster
    curving their assertion
70 among the tentative haunters.

    This is the place.
    And I am here, the mermaid whose dark hair
    streams black, the merman in his armored body
    We circle silently
75 about the wreck
    we dive into the hold.
    I am she: I am he

    whose drowned face sleeps with open eyes
    whose breasts still bear the stress
80 whose silver, copper, vermeil cargo lies
    obscurely inside barrels
    half-wedged and left to rot
    we are the half-destroyed instruments
    that once held to a course
85 the water-eaten log
    the fouled compass

    We are, I am, you are
    by cowardice or courage
    the one who find our way

                    ⟶

90   back to this scene
        carrying a knife, a camera
        a book of myths
        in which
        our names do not appear.

                                                                    (1973)

What Kind of Times Are These[1]

There's a place between two stands of trees where the grass grows uphill
and the old revolutionary road breaks off into shadows
near a meeting-house abandoned by the persecuted
who disappeared into those shadows.

5   I've walked there picking mushrooms at the edge of dread, but don't be fooled,
        this isn't a Russian poem, this is not somewhere else but here,
        our country moving closer to its own truth and dread,[2]
        its own ways of making people disappear.

        I won't tell you where the place is, the dark mesh of the woods
10   meeting the unmarked strip of light —
        ghost-ridden crossroads, leafmold paradise:
        I know already who wants to buy it, sell it, make it disappear.

        And I won't tell you where it is, so why do I tell you
        anything? Because you still listen, because in times like these
15   to have you listen at all, it's necessary
        to talk about trees.

        (1991)   (1995)

1 in her note to this poem, Rich says, "The title is from Bertolt Brecht's poem 'An Die Nachgeborenen' ('For Those Born Later'): *What kind of times are these / When it's almost a crime to talk about trees / Because it means keeping still about so many evil deeds?*"   2 Rich explains that this line "echoes Osip Mandelstam's 1921 poem that begins *I was washing outside in the darkness* and ends *The earth's moving closer to truth and to dread....* Mandelstam was forbidden to publish, then exiled and sentenced to five years of hard labor for a poem caricaturing Stalin; he died in a transit camp in 1938."

In Those Years

In those years, people will say, we lost track
of the meaning of *we*, of *you*
we found ourselves
reduced to *I*
5   and the whole thing became
silly, ironic, terrible:
we were trying to live a personal life
and, yes, that was the only life
we could bear witness to

10   But the great dark birds of history screamed and plunged
into our personal weather
They were headed somewhere else but their beaks and pinions drove
along the shore, through the rags of fog
where we stood, saying *I*

(1991)   (1995)

Derek Walcott   (b. 1930)

Recipient of the Nobel Prize for literature in 1992, Derek Walcott was born in
Castries on the Caribbean island of St. Lucia. He proved to be a precocious
writer, publishing his first collection of poems when he was only eighteen
and seeing his first play produced when he was just twenty. After he graduated from the University College of the West Indies, Jamaica, in 1953, Walcott
moved to Trinidad, where he worked full-time as a writer, art critic, and
theatre director. He took up a position as a professor of creative writing at
Boston University in 1981. In poems characterized by wit, passion, and learning, Walcott presents the Caribbean as a region in which the landscape and
the memories it triggers keep alive a history of oppression. At the same time,
as a person whose education has taught him to value European culture and
whose own ancestry is racially mixed (see the final note to "A Far Cry from
Africa"), he expresses deeply divided feelings about the conflicts between
colonialists and native populations.

A Far Cry from Africa

A wind is ruffling the tawny pelt
Of Africa. Kikuyu,[1] quick as flies,
Batten upon the bloodstreams of the veldt.[2]
Corpses are scattered through a paradise.
5   Only the worm, colonel of carrion, cries:
"Waste no compassion on these separate dead!"
Statistics justify and scholars seize
The salients of colonial policy.
What is that to the white child hacked in bed?
10   To savages, expendable as Jews?

Threshed out by beaters,[3] the long rushes break
In a white dust of ibises[4] whose cries
Have wheeled since civilization's dawn
From the parched river or beast-teeming plain.
15   The violence of beast on beast is read
As natural law, but upright man
Seeks his divinity by inflicting pain.
Delirious as these worried beasts, his wars
Dance to the tightened carcass of a drum,
20   While he calls courage still that native dread
Of the white peace contracted by the dead.

Again brutish necessity wipes its hands
Upon the napkin of a dirty cause, again
A waste of our compassion, as with Spain,[5]
25   The gorilla wrestles with the superman.
I who am poisoned with the blood of both,[6]
Where shall I turn, divided to the vein?

---

1 tribe from the highlands of south-central Kenya whose members formed the Mau Mau, a secret revolutionary organization that employed terrorist activities in order to drive out British colonialists. 2 open country covered with grass and bushes, but having few trees. 3 natives hired to drive game birds and animals from cover. 4 wading birds notable for their long, downward-curving bills. 5 in the Spanish Civil War (1936–39), the Loyalists, supported by liberal intellectuals and Soviet Communists, were defeated by the insurgents of Generalissmo Francisco Franco (1892–1975), who were supported by Nazi Germany and Fascist Italy. 6 Walcott is of mixed ancestry: both of his grandfathers were white, and both of his grandmothers were black.

I who have cursed
The drunken officer of British rule, how choose
30   Between this Africa and the English tongue I love?
Betray them both, or give back what they give?
How can I face such slaughter and be cool?
How can I turn from Africa and live?

(1962)

Ruins of a Great House [1]

though our longest sun sets at right declensions and
makes but winter arches, it cannot be long before we
lie down in darkness, and have our light in ashes…
— Browne, *Urn Burial* [2]

Stones only, the disjecta membra [3] of this Great House,
Whose moth-like girls are mixed with candledust,
Remain to file the lizard's dragonish claws.
The mouths of those gate cherubs shriek with stain;
5   Axle and coach wheel silted under the muck
Of cattle droppings.
                          Three crows flap for the trees
And settle, creaking the eucalyptus boughs.
A smell of dead limes quickens in the nose
The leprosy of empire.
                          "Farewell, green fields,
10   Farewell, ye happy groves!"
Marble like Greece, like Faulkner's [4] South in stone,
Deciduous beauty prospered and is gone,
But where the lawn breaks in a rash of trees
A spade below dead leaves will ring the bone
15   Of some dead animal or human thing
Fallen from evil days, from evil times.

---

1 the main house on a plantation, usually the residence of the owner or manager. 2 *Hydriotaphia, Urne-Buriall* (1658) is a meditation on death and burial practices that Sir Thomas Browne (1605–82), an English physician, wrote after viewing old funeral urns excavated in Norwich. 3 scattered limbs or parts; from "disjecti membra poetae," "the scattered limbs of the poet" (*Satires* of Horace). 4 William Faulkner (1897–1962), an American novelist and winner of the Nobel Prize for literature (1949), wrote about the collapse of the aristocratic South and the guilt its slave-holding culture bequeathed to future generations.

It seems that the original crops were limes
Grown in the silt that clogs the river's skirt;
The imperious rakes are gone, their bright girls gone,
20 The river flows, obliterating hurt.
I climbed a wall with the grille ironwork
Of exiled craftsmen protecting that great house
From guilt, perhaps, but not from the worm's rent
Nor from the padded cavalry of the mouse.
25 And when a wind shook in the limes I heard
What Kipling[5] heard, the death of a great empire, the abuse
Of ignorance by Bible and by sword.

A green lawn, broken by low walls of stone,
Dipped to the rivulet, and pacing, I thought next
30 Of men like Hawkins, Walter Raleigh, Drake,[6]
Ancestral murderers and poets, more perplexed
In memory now by every ulcerous crime.
The world's green age then was a rotting lime
Whose stench became the charnel galleon's text.
35 The rot remains with us, the men are gone.
But, as dead ash is lifted in a wind
That fans the blackening ember of the mind,
My eyes burned from the ashen prose of Donne.[7]

Ablaze with rage I thought,
40 Some slave is rotting in this manorial lake,
But still the coal of my compassion fought
That Albion too was once
A colony like ours, "part of the continent, piece of the main,"
Nook-shotten, rook o'erblown, deranged
45 By foaming channels and the vain expense
Of bitter faction.

All in compassion ends
So differently from what the heart arranged:
"as well as if a manor of thy friend's . . ."

(1962)

5 Rudyard Kipling (1865–1936), an Indian-born English author, was famous for the imperialistic sentiments he expressed in many of his works. 6 Sir John Hawkins (1532–95), Sir Walter Raleigh (1552–1618), and Sir Francis Drake (c. 1540–96) were English explorers and adventurers, who sailed to the West Indies. 7 John Donne (1572–1631), English metaphysical poet and clergyman; phrases from a famous passage in "Meditation XVII" of his Devotions upon Emergent Occasions (1624) are quoted, somewhat incorrectly, in lines 43 and 48: "No man is an island, entire of itself; every man is a piece of the continent, a part of the main. If a clod be washed away by the sea, Europe is the less, as well as if a promontory were, as well as if a manor of thy friend's or thine own were."

The Virgins [1]

Down the dead streets of sun-stoned Frederiksted,[2]
the first freeport [3] to die for tourism,
strolling at funeral pace, I am reminded
of life not lost to the American dream;
5   but my small-islander's [4] simplicities
can't better our new empire's civilized
exchange of cameras, watches, perfumes, brandies
for the good life, so cheaply underpriced
that only the crime rate is on the rise
10   in streets blighted with sun, stone arches
and plazas blown dry by the hysteria
of rumour. A condominium drowns
in vacancy; its bargains are dusted,
but only a jewelled housefly drones
15   over the bargains. The roulettes spin
rustily to the wind; the vigorous trade [5]
that every morning would begin afresh
by revving up green water round the pierhead
heading for where the banks of silver thresh.

(1976)

Ted Hughes (1930–1998)

Born in the small Yorkshire town of Mytholmroyd, Hughes received B.A. and
M.A. degrees from Cambridge. His first wife was the American poet Sylvia
Plath. Hughes, who was appointed England's Poet Laureate in 1984, achieved
critical respect with his very first volume of poems, *The Hawk in the Rain* (1957),
which introduced one of his dominant subjects, animal life. Although some
critics contend that Hughes celebrates raw power and brutality in his animal
poems, even accusing him of presenting the figure of a fascist in "Hawk
Roosting," Hughes contends that he is presenting "Nature thinking. Simply
Nature." Hughes says: "What excites my imagination is the war between vitality and death, and my poems may be said to celebrate the exploits of the warriors of either side." For him, animals combine "the arrogance of blood and
bone" with "an energy too strong for death." Hughes compares his poetic
technique to that of a composer. He says that he turns each of his combatants
"into a bit of music" and then resolves "the whole uproar into as formal and balanced a figure of melody and rhythm as I can."

1 the Virgin Islands lie east of Puerto Rico in the Caribbean. 2 the largest port in St. Croix, the American
Virgin Islands. 3 port that does not charge customs taxes. 4 St. Lucia, Walcott's birthplace, is smaller than
St. Croix. 5 trade winds, nearly constant easterly winds that dominate in tropical regions.

Pike

Pike, three inches long, perfect
Pike in all parts, green tigering the gold.
Killers from the egg: the malevolent aged grin.
They dance on the surface among the flies.

5   Or move, stunned by their own grandeur,
Over a bed of emerald, silhouette
Of submarine delicacy and horror.
A hundred feet long in their world.

In ponds, under the heat-struck lily pads —
10   Gloom of their stillness:
Logged on last year's black leaves, watching upwards.
Or hung in an amber cavern of weeds

The jaws' hooked clamp and fangs
Not to be changed at this date;
15   A life subdued to its instrument;
The gills kneading quietly, and the pectorals.

Three we kept behind glass,
Jungled in weed: three inches, four,
And four and a half: fed fry to them —
20   Suddenly there were two. Finally one.

With a sag belly and the grin it was born with.
And indeed they spare nobody.
Two, six pounds each, over two feet long,
High and dry and dead in the willow-herb —

25   One jammed past its gills down the other's gullet:
The outside eye stared: as a vice locks —
The same iron in this eye
Though its film shrank in death.

A pond I fished, fifty yards across,
30   Whose lilies and muscular tench[1]

———→

1 fresh-water fish that inhabits still, deep waters.

Had outlasted every visible stone
Of the monastery that planted them —

Stilled legendary depth:
It was as deep as England. It held
35   Pike too immense to stir, so immense and old
That past nightfall I dared not cast

But silently cast and fished
With the hair frozen on my head
For what might move, for what eye might move.
40   The still splashes on the dark pond,

Owls hushing the floating woods
Frail on my ear against the dream
Darkness beneath night's darkness had freed,
That rose slowly towards me, watching.

(1960)

Hawk Roosting

I sit in the top of the wood, my eyes closed.
Inaction, no falsifying dream
Between my hooked head and hooked feet:
Or in sleep rehearse perfect kills and eat.

5   The convenience of the high trees!
The air's buoyancy and the sun's ray
Are of advantage to me;
And the earth's face upward for my inspection.

My feet are locked upon the rough bark.
10   It took the whole of Creation
To produce my foot, my each feather:
Now I hold Creation in my foot

Or fly up, and revolve it all slowly —
I kill where I please because it is all mine.
15   There is no sophistry in my body:
My manners are tearing off heads —

The allotment of death.
For the one path of my flight is direct
Through the bones of the living.
20   No arguments assert my right:

The sun is behind me.
Nothing has changed since I began.
My eye has permitted no change.
I am going to keep things like this.

(1960)

Sylvia Plath (1932–1963)

The daughter of German and Austrian parents who taught at Boston University, Sylvia Plath was both precocious and ambitious. She excelled at school and college, began writing as a child, and was publishing in popular magazines while still in her teens. She was also manic-depressive and suffered emotionally from the pressure she felt to succeed at everything. Married to English poet Ted Hughes and living in England with her two young children, she committed suicide at age thirty.

Plath's early poems are deftly controlled but fairly conventional, and it is mainly to her later work, most of which appeared in book form only after her death, that she owes her reputation. In her later poems, Plath turned inward to confront the darker side of her psyche — her anger at her parents, her resentment at the cost to her art of motherhood, her sense of evil in modern society, and her obsession with self-destruction as a means of escape — in powerful, highly original, intensely disturbing poems.

Daddy[1]

You do not do, you do not do
Any more, black shoe
In which I have lived like a foot
For thirty years, poor and white,
5   Barely daring to breathe or Achoo.

Daddy, I have had to kill you.
You died before I had time —

———→

1 Plath's father was of German descent but came to America from Poland at age fifteen. He was an expert on bees and taught at Boston University until his early death in 1940.

Marble-heavy, a bag full of God,
Ghastly statue with one gray toe[2]
10   Big as a Frisco seal

And a head in the freakish Atlantic
Where it pours bean green over blue
In the waters off beautiful Nauset.
I used to pray to recover you.
15   Ach, du.[3]

In the German tongue, in the Polish town
Scraped flat by the roller
Of wars, wars, wars.
But the name of the town is common.
20   My Polack friend

Says there are a dozen or two.
So I never could tell where you
Put your foot, your root,
I never could talk to you.
25   The tongue stuck in my jaw.

It stuck in a barb wire snare.
Ich, ich, ich, ich,[4]
I could hardly speak.
I thought every German was you.
30   And the language obscene

An engine, an engine
Chuffing me off like a Jew.
A Jew to Dachau, Auschwitz, Belsen.[5]
I began to talk like a Jew.
35   I think I may well be a Jew.

The snows of the Tyrol, the clear beer of Vienna
Are not very pure or true.
With my gipsy ancestress and my weird luck
And my Taroc pack and my Taroc pack
40   I may be a bit of a Jew.

2 Plath's father died of blood poisoning when his diabetes led to gangrene in a toe. 3 Ah, you (German).
4 I, I, I, I (German). 5 Nazi concentration camps.

I have always been scared of *you*,
With your Luftwaffe, your gobbledygoo.
And your neat mustache
And your Aryan eye, bright blue.
45   Panzer-man, panzer-man, O You —

Not God but a swastika
So black no sky could squeak through.
Every woman adores a Fascist,
The boot in the face, the brute
50   Brute heart of a brute like you.

You stand at the blackboard, daddy,
In the picture I have of you,
A cleft in your chin instead of your foot
But no less a devil for that, no not
55   Any less the black man who

Bit my pretty red heart in two.
I was ten when they buried you.
At twenty I tried to die
And get back, back, back to you.
60   I thought even the bones would do.

But they pulled me out of the sack,
And they stuck me together with glue.
And then I knew what to do.
I made a model of you,
65   A man in black with a Meinkampf[6] look

And a love of the rack and the screw.
And I said I do, I do.
So daddy, I'm finally through.
The black telephone's off at the root,
70   The voices just can't worm through.

---

6 before coming to power, Adolf Hitler (1889–1945) outlined his plans for world domination in *Mein Kampf*, "my struggle" in German.

If I've killed one man, I've killed two —
The vampire who said he was you
And drank my blood for a year,
Seven years, if you want to know.
75   Daddy, you can lie back now.

There's a stake in your fat black heart
And the villagers never liked you.
They are dancing and stamping on you.
They always *knew* it was you.
80   Daddy, daddy, you bastard, I'm through.

(1965)

Mirror

I am silver and exact. I have no preconceptions.
Whatever I see I swallow immediately
Just as it is, unmisted by love or dislike.
I am not cruel, only truthful —
5   The eye of a little god, four-cornered.
Most of the time I meditate on the opposite wall.
It is pink, with speckles. I have looked at it so long
I think it is a part of my heart. But it flickers.
Faces and darkness separate us over and over.

10   Now I am a lake. A woman bends over me,
Searching my reaches for what she really is.
Then she turns to those liars, the candles or the moon.
I see her back, and reflect it faithfully.
She rewards me with tears and an agitation of hands.
15   I am important to her. She comes and goes.
Each morning it is her face that replaces the darkness.
In me she has drowned a young girl, and in me an old woman
Rises toward her day after day, like a terrible fish.

(1961)

(1971)

Lady Lazarus[1]

I have done it again.
One year in every ten
I manage it —

A sort of walking miracle, my skin
5   Bright as a Nazi lampshade,
My right foot

A paperweight,
My face a featureless, fine
Jew linen.

10   Peel off the napkin
O my enemy.
Do I terrify?—

The nose, the eye pits, the full set of teeth?
The sour breath
15   Will vanish in a day.

Soon, soon the flesh
The grave cave ate will be
At home on me

And I a smiling woman.
20   I am only thirty.
And like the cat I have nine times to die.

This is Number Three.
What a trash
To annihilate each decade.

25   What a million filaments.
The peanut-crunching crowd
Shoves in to see

Them unwrap me hand and foot —
The big strip tease.
30   Gentlemen, ladies

1 Lazarus was brought back from death by Jesus (John 11).

These are my hands
My knees.
I may be skin and bone,

Nevertheless, I am the same, identical woman.
35 The first time it happened I was ten.
It was an accident.

The second time I meant
To last it out and not come back at all.
I rocked shut

40 As a seashell.
They had to call and call
And pick the worms off me like sticky pearls.

Dying
Is an art, like everything else.
45 I do it exceptionally well.

I do it so it feels like hell.
I do it so it feels real.
I guess you could say I've a call.

It's easy enough to do it in a cell.
50 It's easy enough to do it and stay put.
It's the theatrical

Comeback in broad day
To the same place, the same face, the same brute
Amused shout:

55 "A miracle!"
That knocks me out.
There is a charge

For the eyeing of my scars, there is a charge
For the hearing of my heart —
60 It really goes.

And there is a charge, a very large charge
For a word or a touch
Or a bit of blood

Or a piece of my hair or my clothes.
65   So, so, Herr Doktor.
So, Herr Enemy.

I am your opus,
I am your valuable,
The pure gold baby

70   That melts to a shriek.
I turn and burn.
Do not think I underestimate your great concern.

Ash, ash —
You poke and stir.
75   Flesh, bone, there is nothing there —

A cake of soap,
A wedding ring,
A gold filling.

Herr God, Herr Lucifer
80   Beware
Beware.

Out of the ash
I rise with my red hair
And I eat men like air.

(1965)

Wole Soyinka (b. 1934)

A poet, playwright, novelist, essayist, filmmaker, and academic, Wole Soyinka won the Nobel Prize for literature in 1986, becoming the first African to do so. Born in Abeokuta, Nigeria, Soyinka was educated at the University College, Ibadan, and at Leeds University, where he took a degree in English. A passionate defender of human freedom, Soyinka has had several brushes with Nigerian authorities. During the Nigerian Civil War, he was imprisoned by the military government, an experience that produced some of his most powerful prose and poetry. After he protested the cancellation of election results in 1993, the government seized his passport. Soyinka was forced to live in exile, travelling on a U.N. passport. Nevertheless, the Nigerian government charged him with treason in March 1997, claiming that he and other dissidents were instrumental in a series of bombings of army installations. In 1999, the year after the charges were dropped, Soyinka visited Nigeria. He also published *The Burden of Memory, the Muse of Forgiveness*, about African crimes against humanity and the problems of reconciliation.

Although he can write biting satire, such as "Telephone Conversation," Soyinka tends to be a profound and complex writer, drawing on sources as disparate as Yoruba culture, the Bible, and Greek mythology. He can evoke a sense of the African landscape as a physical and psychological setting, but his dominant concerns are universal: a respect for life and a desire for a society in which individuals can live in dignity and freedom.

Telephone Conversation

The price seemed reasonable, location
Indifferent. The landlady swore she lived
Off premises. Nothing remained
But self-confession. "Madam," I warned,
5   "I hate a wasted journey — I am African."
Silence. Silenced transmission of
Pressurized good-breeding. Voice, when it came,
Lipstick coated, long gold-rolled
Cigarette-holder pipped. Caught I was, foully.
10 "HOW DARK?" ... I had not misheard ... "ARE YOU LIGHT
OR VERY DARK?" Button B. Button A.[1] Stench
Of rancid breath of public hide-and-speak.

———————→

1 at the time the poem was written, on coin-operated telephones in England the caller pressed Button A to make a connection and Button B to cancel the call and to retrieve coins if the number was busy or if no one answered.

Red booth. Red pillar-box.[2] Red double-tiered
Omnibus squelching tar. It *was* real! Shamed
15   By ill-mannered silence, surrender
Pushed dumbfoundment to beg simplification.
Considerate she was, varying the emphasis —
"ARE YOU DARK? OR VERY LIGHT?" Revelation came.
"You mean — like plain or milk chocolate?"
20   Her assent was clinical, crushing in its light
Impersonality. Rapidly, wave-length adjusted,
I chose. "West African sepia"— and as afterthought,
"Down in my passport." Silence for spectroscopic[3]
Flight of fancy, till truthfulness clanged her accent
25   Hard on the mouthpiece. "WHAT'S THAT?" conceding
"DON'T KNOW WHAT THAT IS." "Like brunette."
"THAT'S DARK, ISN'T IT?" "Not altogether.
Facially, I am brunette, but madam, you should see
The rest of me. Palm of my hand, soles of my feet
30   Are a peroxide blonde. Friction, caused —
Foolishly madam — by sitting down, has turned
My bottom raven black — One moment madam!"— sensing
Her receiver rearing on the thunderclap
About my ears — "Madam," I pleaded, "wouldn't you rather
35   See for yourself?"

(1960)

I Think It Rains

I think it rains
That tongues may loosen from the parch
Uncleave roof-tops of the mouth, hang
Heavy with knowledge

5   I saw it raise
The sudden cloud, from ashes. Settling
They joined in a ring of grey; within,
The circling spirit

---

2 cylindrical postal box. 3 a spectroscope is an instrument that enables analysis of a range of colours.

Oh it must rain
10 These closures on the mind, binding us
In strange despairs, teaching
Purity of sadness

And how it beats
Skeined transparencies on wings
15 Of our desires, searing dark longings
In cruel baptisms

Rain-reeds, practised in
The grace of yielding, yet unbending
From afar, this your conjugation with my earth
20 Bares crouching rocks.

(1967)

Procession I: Hanging Day

Hanging day. A hollow earth
Echoes footsteps of the grave procession
Walls in sunspots
Lean to shadows of the shortening morn

5 Behind, an eyepatch lushly blue.
The wall of prayer[1] has taken refuge
In a peace of blindness, closed
Its grey recessive deeps. Fretful limbs

And glances that would sometimes
10 Conjure up a drawbridge
Raised but never lowered between
Their gathering and my sway

Withdraw, as all the living world
Belie their absence in a feel of eyes
15 Barred and secret in the empty home
Of shuttered windows. I know the heart
Has journeyed far from present

1 prison wall where the inmates prayed and sang hymns.

Tread. Drop. Dread Drop. Dead

What may I tell you? What reveal?
20   I who before them peered unseen
Who stood one-legged on the untrodden
Verge — lest I should not return.

That I received them? That I
Wheeled above and flew beneath them
25   And brought them on their way
And came to mine, even to the edge
Of the unspeakable encirclement?
What may I tell you of the five
Bell-ringers on the ropes to chimes
30   Of silence?
What tell you of rigors of the law?
From watchtowers on stunted walls,
Raised to stay a siege of darkness
What whisper to their football thunders
35   Vanishing to shrouds of sunlight?

Let no man speak of justice, guilt.
Far away, blood-stained in their
Tens of thousands, hands that damned
These wretches to the pit triumph
40   But here, alone the solitary deed.

(1972)

Alden Nowlan   (1933–1983)

Although he had a limited formal education — he left school after Grade 5 — Nowlan became one of the leading literary figures in Atlantic Canada. Born in Windsor, Nova Scotia, he held various jobs as a manual labourer until he moved to New Brunswick to work as a journalist. He began his literary career as a poet, publishing his first collection in 1958. *Bread, Wine and Salt* (1967) won the Governor General's Award. Later, he turned his hand to other genres, producing plays, stories, and a novel. Although he is a regionalist, painting relatively realistic pictures of nature and society in Atlantic Canada, Nowlan infuses his poems with universal significance. He can also, like a backwoods storyteller, be by turns sentimental and ironic. "The Bull Moose," his most famous poem, shows his characteristic attitudes; he evokes sympathy for victims and imbues even mundane events with religious or spiritual importance.

The Bull Moose

Down from the purple mist of trees on the mountain,
lurching through forests of white spruce and cedar,
stumbling through tamarack swamps,
came the bull moose
5   to be stopped at last by a pole-fenced pasture.

Too tired to turn or, perhaps, aware
there was no place left to go, he stood with the cattle.
They, scenting the musk of death, seeing his great head
like the ritual mask of a blood god, moved to the other end
10   of the field, and waited.

The neighbours heard of it, and by afternoon
cars lined the road. The children teased him
with alder switches and he gazed at them
like an old, tolerant collie. The women asked
15   if he could have escaped from a Fair.

The oldest man in the parish remembered seeing
a gelded moose yoked with an ox for plowing.
The young men snickered and tried to pour beer
down his throat, while their girlfriends took their pictures.

20   And the bull moose let them stroke his tick-ravaged flanks,
let them pry open his jaws with bottles, let a giggling girl
plant a little purple cap
of thistles on his head.

When the wardens came, everyone agreed it was a shame
25   to shoot anything so shaggy and cuddlesome.
He looked like the kind of pet
women put to bed with their sons.

So they held their fire. But just as the sun dropped in the river
the bull moose gathered his strength
30   like a scaffolded king, straightened and lifted his horns
so that even the wardens backed away as they raised their rifles.
When he roared, people ran to their cars. All the young men
leaned on their automobile horns as he toppled.

(1962)

Leonard Cohen   (b. 1934)

Born into a wealthy Montreal family, Cohen received a B.A. from McGill University in 1955. Since then, he has moved freely between literature and popular culture, becoming an internationally successful poet and singer, and a controversial experimental novelist. He won, but refused to accept, the Governor General's Award for *Selected Poems* (1968). Cohen has received three Juno Awards for his recordings, and in 1993 he was honoured for his lifetime achievement with a Governor General's Performing Arts Award.

In much of Cohen's work, traditional poetic elements contrast with the contemporary subject matter. That is to say, their lush imagery and abundant musical qualities mark his poems as conventionally romantic and deliberately "poetic" works. However, their bleakness and shocking assaults on conventional moral assumptions make them thoroughly modern. Cohen frequently combines images from classical mythology or religion (drawing on both his own Jewish heritage and that of the dominant Catholic culture of Quebec) with images of sex, suffering, violence, and death. In this way he attempts to create an informal mythology to replace what he considers the worn-out myths of the past. The exact meaning of Cohen's poems is often elusive, but one figure is central. The "saint" renounces the ordinary world, enduring consequent suffering and even destruction of the self in order to achieve the purity necessary to attain a higher state. In Cohen's mythic world, the only winners are beautiful losers.

A Kite Is a Victim

A kite is a victim you are sure of.
You love it because it pulls
gentle enough to call you master,
strong enough to call you fool;
5   because it lives
like a trained falcon
in the high sweet air,
and you can always haul it down
to tame it in your drawer.

10   A kite is a fish you have already caught
      in a pool where no fish come,
      so you play him carefully and long,
      and hope he won't give up,
      or the wind die down.

15   A kite is the last poem you've written,
      so you give it to the wind,
      but you don't let it go
      until someone finds you
      something else to do.

20   A kite is a contract of glory
      that must be made with the sun,
      so you make friends with the field
      the river and the wind,
      then you pray the whole cold night before,
25   under the travelling cordless moon,
      to make you worthy and lyric and pure.

                                  (1961)

For E.J.P. [1]

I once believed a single line
    in a Chinese poem could change
      forever how blossoms fell
and that the moon itself climbed on
5   the grief of concise weeping men
      to journey over cups of wine
I thought invasions were begun for crows
    to pick at a skeleton
      dynasties sown and spent

             ⟶

1 E.J. Pratt (see page 250).

10 to serve the language of a fine lament
  I thought governors ended their lives
   as sweetly drunken monks
telling time by rain and candles
  instructed by an insect's pilgrimage
15   across the page — all this
so one might send an exile's perfect letter
to an ancient home-town friend

I chose a lonely country
  broke from love
20   scorned the fraternity of war
I polished my tongue against the pumice moon
  floated my soul in cherry wine
   a perfumed barge for Lords of Memory
to languish on to drink to whisper out
25 their store of strength
   as if beyond the mist along the shore
their girls their power still obeyed
  like clocks wound for a thousand years
I waited until my tongue was sore

30 Brown petals wind like fire around my poems
  I aimed them at the stars but
   like rainbows they were bent
before they sawed the world in half
  Who can trace the canyoned paths
35   cattle have carved out of time
wandering from meadowlands to feasts
  Layer after layer of autumn leaves
   are swept away
Something forgets us perfectly

(1964)

Suzanne Takes You Down

Suzanne takes you down
to her place near the river,
you can hear the boats go by
you can stay the night beside her.

⟶

5   And you know that she's half crazy
but that's why you want to be there
and she feeds you tea and oranges
that come all the way from China.
Just when you mean to tell her
10   that you have no gifts to give her,
she gets you on her wave-length
and she lets the river answer
that you've always been her lover.
     And you want to travel with her,
15   you want to travel blind
     and you know that she can trust you
     because you've touched her perfect body
     with your mind.

Jesus was a sailor
20   when he walked upon the water
and he spent a long time watching
from a lonely wooden tower
and when he knew for certain
only drowning men could see him
25   he said All men will be sailors then
until the sea shall free them,
but he himself was broken
long before the sky would open,
forsaken, almost human,
30   he sank beneath your wisdom like a stone.
     And you want to travel with him,
     you want to travel blind
     and you think maybe you'll trust him
     because he touched your perfect body
35   with his mind.

Suzanne takes your hand
and she leads you to the river,
she is wearing rags and feathers
from Salvation Army counters.
40   The sun pours down like honey
on our lady of the harbour
as she shows you where to look
among the garbage and the flowers,
there are heroes in the seaweed

⟶

45   there are children in the morning,
they are leaning out for love
they will lean that way forever
while Suzanne she holds the mirror.
    And you want to travel with her
50   and you want to travel blind
and you're sure that she can find you
because she's touched her perfect body
with her mind.

(1966)

Closing Time

So we're drinking and we're dancing
and the band is really happening
and the Johnny Walker[1] wisdom running high
And my very sweet companion
5   she's the Angel of Compassion
and she's rubbing half the world against her thigh
Every drinker, every dancer
lifts a happy face to thank her
and the fiddler fiddles something so sublime
10   All the women tear their blouses off
and the men they dance on the polka-dots
and it's partner found and it's partner lost
and it's hell to pay when the fiddler stops
It's closing time

15   We're lonely, we're romantic
and the cider's laced with acid[2]
and the Holy Spirit's crying, "Where's the beef?"[3]
And the moon is swimming naked
and the summer night is fragrant
20   with a mighty expectation of relief
So we struggle and we stagger
down the snakes and up the ladder

———→

1 brand of Scotch whisky.   2 lysergic acid diethylamide (LSD), a hallucinogenic drug.   3 slogan made
popular by commercials for a hamburger chain.

to the tower where the blessed hours chime
And I swear it happened just like this:
25   a sigh, a cry, a hungry kiss
the Gates of Love they budged an inch
I can't say much has happened since
but closing time

I loved you for your beauty
30   but that doesn't make a fool of me —
you were in it for your beauty too
I loved you for your body
there's a voice that sounds like G-d to me
declaring that your body's really you
35   I loved you when our love was blessed
and I love you now there's nothing left
but sorrow and a sense of overtime
And I miss you since our place got wrecked
I just don't care what happens next
40   looks like freedom but it feels like death
it's something in between, I guess
it's closing time

And I miss you since the place got wrecked
by the winds of change and the weeds of sex
45   looks like freedom but it feels like death
it's something in between, I guess
it's closing time

We're drinking and we're dancing
but there's nothing really happening
50   the place is dead as Heaven on a Saturday night
And my very close companion
gets me fumbling, gets me laughing
she's a hundred but she's wearing something tight
And I lift my glass to the Awful Truth
55   which you can't reveal to the Ears of Youth
except to say it isn't worth a dime
And the whole damn place goes crazy twice
and it's once for the Devil and it's once for Christ
but the Boss don't like these dizzy heights —
60   we're busted in the blinding lights
of closing time.

(1992)

Seamus Heaney (b. 1939)

Winner of the 1995 Nobel Prize for literature, Seamus Heaney has been praised for his evocative language and for the integrity of his treatment of the troubles in Northern Ireland. Born in County Derry in Northern Ireland, he graduated from Queen's University, Belfast, in 1961 and obtained a teacher's diploma the next year. He has held a number of teaching appointments, including positions at his alma mater and at Harvard University. He published his first full-length collection, *Death of a Naturalist*, to critical acclaim in 1966. A Roman Catholic increasingly upset by the conflict in Northern Ireland, Heaney moved to the Irish Republic in 1972 in order, he said, "to put the practice of poetry more deliberately at the centre of my life." Ireland — its traditions, its rural landscape, and its political and religious difficulties — is at the centre of Heaney's poetry, but he also explores universal themes, such as the role of the poet and the nature of art. A poet whose unobtrusive craftsmanship produces works that are immediately accessible but also deeply moving and memorable, he has described poetry "as a point of entry into the buried life of the feelings or as a point of exit for it."

Death of a Naturalist

All year the flax-dam festered in the heart
Of the townland; green and heavy headed
Flax had rotted there, weighted down by huge sods.
Daily it sweltered in the punishing sun.
5 Bubbles gargled delicately, bluebottles
Wove a strong gauze of sound around the smell.
There were dragon-flies, spotted butterflies,
But best of all was the warm thick slobber
Of frogspawn that grew like clotted water
10 In the shade of the banks. Here, every spring
I would fill jampotfuls of the jellied
Specks to range on window-sills at home,
On shelves at school, and wait and watch until
The fattening dots burst into nimble-
15 Swimming tadpoles. Miss Walls would tell us how
The daddy frog was called a bullfrog
And how he croaked and how the mammy frog
Laid hundreds of little eggs and this was
Frogspawn. You could tell the weather by frogs too
20 For they were yellow in the sun and brown
In rain.

Then one hot day when fields were rank
With cowdung in the grass the angry frogs
Invaded the flax-dam; I ducked through hedges
25 To a coarse croaking that I had not heard
Before. The air was thick with a bass chorus.
Right down the dam gross-bellied frogs were cocked
On sods; their loose necks pulsed like sails. Some hopped:
The slap and plop were obscene threats. Some sat
30 Poised like mud grenades, their blunt heads farting.
I sickened, turned, and ran. The great slime kings
Were gathered there for vengeance and I knew
That if I dipped my hand the spawn would clutch it.

(1966)

The Singer's House

When they said *Carrickfergus*[1] I could hear
the frosty echo of saltminers' picks.
I imagined it, chambered and glinting,
a township built of light.

5 What do we say any more
to conjure the salt of our earth?
So much comes and is gone
that should be crystal and kept

and amicable weathers
10 that bring up the grain of things,
their tang of season and store,
are all the packing we'll get.

So I say to myself *Gweebarra*[2]
and its music hits off the place
15 like water hitting off granite.
I see the glittering sound

---

1 Northern Irish salt-mining area and seaport, the subject of a popular Irish folksong. 2 the bay in County
Donegal in the Irish Republic.

framed in your window,
knives and forks set on oilcloth,
and the seals' heads, suddenly outlined,
20 scanning everything.

People here used to believe
that drowned souls lived in the seals.
At spring tides they might change shape.
They loved music and swam in for a singer

25 who might stand at the end of summer
in the mouth of a whitewashed turf-shed,
his shoulder to the jamb, his song
a rowboat far out in evening.

When I came here first you were always singing,
30 a hint of the clip of the pick
in your winnowing climb and attack.
Raise it again, man. We still believe what we hear.

(1979)

The Harvest Bow

As you plaited the harvest bow
You implicated the mellowed silence in you
In wheat that does not rust
But brightens as it tightens twist by twist
5   Into a knowable corona,
A throwaway love-knot of straw.

Hands that aged round ashplants and cane sticks
And lapped the spurs on a lifetime of game cocks
Harked to their gift and worked with fine intent
10 Until your fingers moved somnambulant:
I tell and finger it like braille,
Gleaning the unsaid off the palpable,

And if I spy into its golden loops
I see us walk between the railway slopes
15 Into an evening of long grass and midges,
Blue smoke straight up, old beds and ploughs in hedges,
An auction notice on an outhouse wall —
You with a harvest bow in your lapel,

Me with the fishing rod, already homesick
20 For the big lift of these evenings, as your stick
Whacking the tips off weeds and bushes
Beats out of time, and beats, but flushes
Nothing: that original townland
Still tongue-tied in the straw tied by your hand.

25 *The end of art is peace*
Could be the motto of this frail device
That I have pinned up on our deal dresser —
Like a drawn snare
Slipped lately by the spirit of the corn
30 Yet burnished by its passage, and still warm.

(1979)

Casualty [1]

I

He would drink by himself
And raise a weathered thumb
Towards the high shelf,
Calling another rum
5 And blackcurrant, without
Having to raise his voice,
Or order a quick stout
By a lifting of the eyes
And a discreet dumb-show

——→

1 Heaney has identified the subject of this poem as Louis O'Neill, who frequented a pub owned by Heaney's father-in-law in County Tyrone. An alcoholic, O'Neill defied a curfew imposed by Catholics who were mourning the thirteen men shot dead by British soldiers on "Bloody Sunday," January 30, 1972. The men were killed after violence erupted during an illegal march organized by the Derry Civil Rights Association. As Heaney noted, O'Neill was killed by a bomb "planted by his own people."

10   Of pulling off the top;
At closing time would go
In waders and peaked cap
Into the showery dark,
A dole-kept[2] breadwinner
15   But a natural for work.
I loved his whole manner,
Sure-footed but too sly,
His deadpan sidling tact,
His fisherman's quick eye
20   And turned observant back.

Incomprehensible
To him, my other life.
Sometimes, on his high stool,
Too busy with his knife
25   At a tobacco plug
And not meeting my eye,
In the pause after a slug
He mentioned poetry.
We would be on our own
30   And, always politic
And shy of condescension,
I would manage by some trick
To switch the talk to eels
Or lore of the horse and cart
35   Or the Provisionals.[3]

But my tentative art
His turned back watches too:
He was blown to bits
Out drinking in a curfew
40   Others obeyed, three nights
After they shot dead
The thirteen men in Derry.
PARAS THIRTEEN, the walls said,

———————>

---

2 one who lives on social assistance payments "doled out" by the government. 3 the Provisional Irish
Republican Army, a militant group that split off from the IRA in December 1969 when the IRA decided to
give at least token recognition to three parliaments: Westminster, Dublin, and Stormont.

BOGSIDE NIL.[4] That Wednesday
45 Everybody held
His breath and trembled.

II

It was a day of cold
Raw silence, wind-blown
Surplice and soutane:[5]
50 Rained-on, flower-laden
Coffin after coffin
Seemed to float from the door
Of the packed cathedral
Like blossoms on slow water.
55 The common funeral
Unrolled its swaddling band,
Lapping, tightening
Till we were braced and bound
Like brothers in a ring.

60 But he would not be held
At home by his own crowd
Whatever threats were phoned,
Whatever black flags waved.
I see him as he turned
65 In that bombed offending place,
Remorse fused with terror
In his still knowable face,
His cornered outfaced stare
Blinding in the flash.

70 He had gone miles away
For he drank like a fish
Nightly, naturally
Swimming towards the lure
Of warm lit-up places,
75 The blurred mesh and murmur

⟶

4 the slogan on the wall is like a football score. Paras are the members of the First Parachute Regiment, who
had killed the thirteen men on Bloody Sunday; Bogside is the working-class Catholic district in which the
killings occurred. 5 a soutane, or cassock, is a long, loose-fitting garment worn by priests, altar boys, and
choristers; a surplice is a loose-fitting, wide-sleeved white vestment worn over the soutane.

Drifting among glasses
In the gregarious smoke.
How culpable was he
That last night when he broke
80 Our tribe's complicity?
"Now you're supposed to be
An educated man,"
I hear him say. "Puzzle me
The right answer to that one."

III

85 I missed his funeral,
Those quiet walkers
And sideways talkers
Shoaling out of his lane
To the respectable
90 Purring of the hearse...
They move in equal pace
With the habitual
Slow consolation
Of a dawdling engine,
95 The line lifted, hand
Over fist, cold sunshine
On the water, the land
Banked under fog: that morning
I was taken in his boat,
100 The screw purling,[6] turning
Indolent fathoms white,
I tasted freedom with him.
To get out early, haul
Steadily off the bottom,
105 Dispraise the catch, and smile
As you find a rhythm
Working you, slow mile by mile,
Into your proper haunt
Somewhere, well out, beyond...

110 Dawn-sniffing revenant,[7]
Plodder through midnight rain,
Question me again.

(1979)

6 the boat's propeller, or screw, is making a murmuring sound. 7 one who returns, such as a ghost or spirit
after death.

Margaret Atwood   (b. 1939)

Internationally successful as both a poet and a novelist, Margaret Atwood was born in Ottawa and educated at the University of Toronto and Radcliffe College, Harvard. She has worked as a book editor, has taught English at several universities, and has been a university writer in residence. Her first book was a thin volume of poems, *Double Persephone* (1961). Her second collection, *The Circle Game* (1966), won the Governor General's Award. Her novels include *Surfacing* (1972) and *The Handmaid's Tale* (1985), winner of the Governor General's Award for fiction. *Survival* (1972) is a controversial study of Canadian literature in which she expands upon Northrop Frye's analysis of the "garrison mentality" and argues that Canadian literature is dominated by images of victims. In her own poetry, she often explores victimization and liberation, dissecting the personal, psychological, cultural, political, and sexual ideas or myths confining the individual. This exploration frequently challenges both conventional perceptions of reality and conventional logic. Although she has said that sound and phrasing are important elements in her poetry, Atwood does not indulge in verbal pyrotechnics. Typically, her narrators employ startlingly provocative and often violent images, but they make thematic pronouncements in a flat, unemotional voice. In this way, she conveys both the violence of the modern world and the alienation of its victims.

Progressive Insanities of a Pioneer

i

He stood, a point
on a sheet of green paper
proclaiming himself the centre,

with no walls, no borders
5   anywhere; the sky no height
above him, totally un-
enclosed
and shouted:
Let me out!

ii

10   He dug the soil in rows,
imposed himself with shovels
He asserted
into the furrows, I
am not random.

———▶

15   The ground
replied with aphorisms:

a tree-sprout, a nameless
weed, words
he couldn't understand.

iii

20   The house pitched
the plot staked
in the middle of nowhere.

At night the mind
inside, in the middle
25   of nowhere.

The idea of an animal
patters across the roof.

In the darkness the fields
defend themselves with fences
30   in vain:
        everything
        is getting in.

iv

By daylight he resisted.
He said, disgusted
35   with the swamp's clamourings and the outbursts
of rocks,
        This is not order
        but the absence
        of order.

40   He was wrong, the unanswering
forest implied:

        It was
        an ordered absence

v

For many years
45   he fished for a great vision,
dangling the hooks of sown
roots under the surface
of the shallow earth.

It was like
50   enticing whales with a bent
pin. Besides he thought

in that country
only the worms were biting.

vi

If he had known unstructured
55   space is a deluge
and stocked his log house-
boat with all the animals

even the wolves,

he might have floated.

60   But obstinate he
stated, The land is solid
and stamped,

watching his foot sink
down through stone
65   up to the knee.

vii

Things
refused to name themselves; refused
to let him name them.

The wolves hunted
70   outside.

On his beaches, his clearings,
by the surf of under-
growth breaking
at his feet, he foresaw
75   disintegration
                    and in the end
through eyes
made ragged by his
effort, the tension
80   between subject and object,

the green
vision, the unnamed
whale invaded.

(1968)

The Animals in That Country

In that country the animals
have the faces of people:

the ceremonial
cats possessing the streets

5   the fox run
politely to earth, the huntsmen
standing around him, fixed
in their tapestry of manners

the bull, embroidered
10   with blood and given
an elegant death, trumpets, his name
stamped on him, heraldic brand
because

(when he rolled
15   on the sand, sword in his heart, the teeth
in his blue mouth were human)

he is really a man

even the wolves, holding resonant
conversations in their
20   forests thickened with legend.

In this country the animals
have the faces of
animals.

Their eyes
25   flash once in car headlights
and are gone.

Their deaths are not elegant.

They have the faces of
no-one.

(1968)

Further Arrivals[1]

After we had crossed the long illness
that was the ocean, we sailed up-river

On the first island
the immigrants threw off their clothes
5   and danced like sandflies

We left behind one by one
the cities rotting with cholera,
one by one our civilized
distinctions

10   and entered a large darkness.

---

1 the speaker in this poem is Susanna Moodie (1803–85), a pioneer settler and author. Atwood based
events in this and the other poems in The Journals of Susanna Moodie (1970) on Mrs. Moodie's accounts of
her life in Roughing It in the Bush (1852) and Life in the Clearings (1853).

It was our own
ignorance we entered.

I have not come out yet

My brain gropes nervous
15 tentacles in the night, sends out
fears hairy as bears,
demands lamps; or waiting

for my shadowy husband, hears
malice in the trees' whispers.

20 I need wolf's eyes to see
the truth.

I refuse to look in a mirror.

Whether the wilderness is
real or not
25 depends on who lives there.

(1970)

you fit into me

you fit into me
like a hook into an eye

a fish hook
an open eye

(1973)

Siren Song[1]

This is the song everyone
would like to learn: the song
that is irresistible:

the song that forces men
5   to leap overboard in squadrons
even though they see the beached skulls

the song nobody knows
because anyone who has heard it
is dead, and the others can't remember.

10   Shall I tell you the secret
and if I do, will you get me
out of this bird suit?

I don't enjoy it here
squatting on this island
15   looking picturesque and mythical

with these two feathery maniacs,
I don't enjoy singing
this trio, fatal and valuable.

I will tell the secret to you,
20   to you, only to you.
Come closer. This song

is a cry for help: Help me!
Only you, only you can,
you are unique

25   at last. Alas
it is a boring song
but it works every time.

(1974)

---

1 in Greek mythology, the three sirens, who were half woman and half bird, lured sailors to destruction with enchanting songs.

Variations on the Word *Love*

This is a word we use to plug
holes with. It's the right size for those warm
blanks in speech, for those red heart-
shaped vacancies on the page that look nothing
5   like real hearts. Add lace
and you can sell
it. We insert it also in the one empty
space on the printed form
that comes with no instructions. There are whole
10   magazines with not much in them
but the word *love*, you can
rub it all over your body and you
can cook with it too. How do we know
it isn't what goes on at the cool
15   debaucheries of slugs under damp
pieces of cardboard? As for the weed-
seedlings nosing their tough snouts up
among the lettuces, they shout it.
Love! Love! sing the soldiers, raising
20   their glittering knives in salute.

Then there's the two
of us. This word
is far too short for us, it has only
four letters, too sparse
25   to fill those deep bare
vacuums between the stars
that press on us with their deafness.
It's not love we don't wish
to fall into, but that fear.
30   This word is not enough but it will
have to do. It's a single
vowel in this metallic
silence, a mouth that says
O again and again in wonder
35   and pain, a breath, a finger-
grip on a cliffside. You can
hold on or let go.

(1981)

A Women's Issue

The woman in the spiked device
that locks around the waist and between
the legs, with holes in it like a tea strainer
is Exhibit A.

5   The woman in black with a net window
to see through and a four-inch
wooden peg jammed up
between her legs so she can't be raped
is Exhibit B.

10   Exhibit C is the young girl
dragged into the bush by the midwives
and made to sing while they scrape the flesh
from between her legs, then tie her thighs
till she scabs over and is called healed.

15   Now she can be married.
For each childbirth they'll cut her
open, then sew her up.
Men like tight women.
The ones that die are carefully buried.

20   The next exhibit lies flat on her back
while eighty men a night
move through her, ten an hour.
She looks at the ceiling, listens
to the door open and close.
25   A bell keeps ringing.
Nobody knows how she got here.

You'll notice that what they have in common
is between the legs. Is this
why wars are fought?
30   Enemy territory, no man's
land, to be entered furtively,
fenced, owned but never surely,
scene of these desperate forays
at midnight, captures

———→

35   and sticky murders, doctors' rubber gloves
greasy with blood, flesh made inert, the surge
of your own uneasy power.

This is no museum.
Who invented the word *love*?

(1981)

Helen of Troy[1] Does Counter Dancing

The world is full of women
who'd tell me I should be ashamed of myself
if they had the chance. Quit dancing.
Get some self-respect
5   and a day job.
Right. And minimum wage,
and varicose veins, just standing
in one place for eight hours
behind a glass counter
10   bundled up to the neck, instead of
naked as a meat sandwich.
Selling gloves, or something.
Instead of what I do sell.
You have to have talent
15   to peddle a thing so nebulous
and without material form.
Exploited, they'd say. Yes, any way
you cut it, but I've a choice
of how, and I'll take the money.

20   I do give value.
Like preachers, I sell vision,
like perfume ads, desire
or its facsimile. Like jokes
or war, it's all in the timing.

———→

1 according to Greek legend, Helen was the most beautiful woman in the world and the cause of the
Trojan War. Her mother was Leda, and her father was Zeus, who assumed the form of a swan and raped
Leda. Helen, who had many suitors, married Menelaus, but Paris seduced her and carried her off to Troy.
Menelaus and her Greek suitors then waged war on Troy to recover her. (See also Yeats's "Leda and the
Swan," page 261.)

25 I sell men back their worst suspicions:
that everything's for sale,
and piecemeal. They gaze at me and see
a chain-saw murder just before it happens,
when thigh, ass, inkblot, crevice, tit, and nipple
30 are still connected.
Such hatred leaps in them,
my beery worshippers! That, or a bleary
hopeless love. Seeing the rows of heads
and upturned eyes, imploring
35 but ready to snap at my ankles,
I understand floods and earthquakes, and the urge
to step on ants. I keep the beat,
and dance for them because
they can't. The music smells like foxes,
40 crisp as heated metal
searing the nostrils
or humid as August, hazy and languorous
as a looted city the day after,
when all the rape's been done
45 already, and the killing,
and the survivors wander around
looking for garbage
to eat, and there's only a bleak exhaustion.

Speaking of which, it's the smiling
50 tires me out the most.
This, and the pretence
that I can't hear them.
And I can't, because I'm after all
a foreigner to them.
55 The speech here is all warty gutturals,
obvious as a slab of ham,
but I come from the province of the gods
where meanings are lilting and oblique.
I don't let on to everyone,
60 but lean close, and I'll whisper:
My mother was raped by a holy swan.
You believe that? You can take me out to dinner.
That's what we tell all the husbands.
There sure are a lot of dangerous birds around.

65 Not that anyone here
    but you would understand.
    The rest of them would like to watch me
    and feel nothing. Reduce me to components
    as in a clock factory or abattoir.
70 Crush out the mystery.
    Wall me up alive
    in my own body.
    They'd like to see through me,
    but nothing is more opaque
75 than absolute transparency.
    Look — my feet don't hit the marble!
    Like breath or a balloon, I'm rising,
    I hover six inches in the air
    in my blazing swan-egg of light.
80 You think I'm not a goddess?
    Try me.
    This is a torch song.[2]
    Touch me and you'll burn.

(1995)

Tom Dawe (b. 1940)

Born in Long Pond, Manuels, Conception Bay, Tom Dawe graduated from Memorial University, St. John's, Newfoundland. After teaching for seven years at outport schools, he became a member of Memorial's English Department in 1969. Dawe's first collection of poems was *Connections* (1972), which also contains work by Tom Moore. *Hemlock Cove and After* (1975) was the first book devoted solely to his own poems. Dawe has been active in promoting Newfoundland literature, being one of the founding members of Breakwater Books and a founding editor of *TickleAce*. A respected painter as well as a poet, Dawe brings a sharp visual sense to his writing, often capturing outport scenes in crisp, imagistic phrases.

---

2 song concerned with failure in love.

The Bear

Once in a long gone night
before any people came
and the island's trees
were spears of ice
5   against the frosty stars
he came ashore
and used the land
as a stepping stone
in miles of polar ice.
10   His great tracks
in a long cryptic chain
from shore to shore
were there for days and nights
before another snowfall
15   filled them in
and trees waved in resonance
as a rising surf
rolled the ice offshore.

Years later when a few people lived here
20   there was once
a long winter famine
with the fish all gone
and a grave-digger worked hard
getting below the snow and earth
25   on energy from his last meal
of potato peels.
One day in this starvation spell
he came back again
walking out of a blizzard
30   like some misty giant
from the children's books
walking towards the village guns
and bringing the famine to an end.

In another age
35   when only the old remembered
the hungry times
he came ashore one day

→

from the loose ice-pans
unlocking from the shoreline
40   in the south-west wind.
Some people saw him
and watched him cross the beach
on his way past flakes and stages
and low root-cellars.
45   Others came with spears and guns
and tracked him to the tree-line.

Later, in a sea-port town
they charged people ten cents
to look at him
50   propped up with ropes
against the wall of a merchant's shed.

Years later with the island abandoned
two boys returned one spring
to fish for salmon
55   in the land of their ancestors
and in a night
with pebbles rolling
in the land-wash moonlight
the bear returned
60   brushing by their tent
on his way down the river bank.

Next morning they found his body
stiff under fly-buzzing
on the warm beach stones.
65   They saw the swollen head
that had starved for some time
with a tin-can stuck
on the gangrene tongue.

Tonight in the glow from televisions
70   descendants of the island people
half-listen to somebody
reading late news
linked across a nation
and near the end

———→

75   just before the Late Show
        they hear of another large bear
        roaming dangerously close
        to some town dump
        where concerned officials
80   are on the way
        with a sleeping-drug
        on the tips of gun-powered needles.
        They will do their best
        to fly him far back somewhere
85   from any civilized community.

(1975)

The Naked Man

In a wet August day
with salt wind on the berry leaves,
he loomed in the close fog
across the cape
5   and bog meadows slanting down
to the ocean's roar.
Around him, dim cattle stood
still as rock piles
in the driftwood light.
10   Above him gulls screamed
down the dark tide
and gannets darted
in the herring shine.

I asked him to come with me
15   down through wet marshes
where the pond was hidden
but he had fences to mend
and cattle to tend
and a sure way for me
20   to find the pond myself.
His face was granite smiling
and offering warm pipes
and chairs by a cracking stove
and brown china mugs

$\longrightarrow$

25   where kitchen-saints smiled down
through kettle steam.

Later, in the half-gone morning,
I found his marker to the pond:
"the naked man"
30   of weathered, wind-honed stones
and snakes of juniper stumps,
a clumsy rock man
leaning back from the sea wind.

Still later, returning in twilight,
35   I crept by the man of stones
silently watching me
returning to my road-sign world
with small trout in a plastic bag,
silently watching me
40   wander on wet, pathless moss,
groping in metamorphic shadows
in bog-sucking footsteps
away from those cryptic rocks,
me, the most naked man of all.

(1978)   (1981)

Gwendolyn MacEwen (1941–1987)

Born in Toronto, Gwendolyn MacEwen grew up there and in Winnipeg. She discovered her calling as a writer early: at the age of seventeen she published her first poem, and she left school the next year to pursue her career. In addition to poetry, MacEwen wrote two novels, a collection of short stories, two children's books, and a number of radio plays and documentaries. Her books of poetry include *A Breakfast for Barbarians* (1966), *The Shadow-Maker* (1969), winner of the Governor General's Award, and *The T.E. Lawrence Poems* (1982). MacEwen said of her work: "I write basically to communicate joy, mystery, passion... not the joy that naïvely exists without knowledge of pain, but that joy which arises out of and conquers pain. I want to construct a myth." MacEwen constructs her myth, which celebrates the triumph of the human spirit, with materials borrowed from a variety of traditions. Lush, even exotic, imagery establishes the dualities that are central to her mythic vision. Throughout her poetry, she explores meaningful relationships between spiritual and physical worlds, archetypal and mundane experience, waking and dreaming consciousness, past and present times, painful and joyful events, and male and female lives.

A Breakfast for Barbarians

my friends, my sweet barbarians,
there is that hunger which is not for food —
but an eye at the navel turns the appetite
round
5   with visions of some fabulous sandwich,
the brain's golden breakfast
               eaten with beasts
               with books on plates

let us make an anthology of recipes,
10   let us edit for breakfast
our most unspeakable appetites —
let us pool spoons, knives
and all cutlery in a cosmic cuisine,
let us answer hunger
15   with boiled chimera [1]
and apocalyptic tea,
an arcane salad of spiced bibles,
tossed dictionaries —
               (O my barbarians
20   we will consume our mysteries)

and can we, can we slake the gaping eye of our desires?
we will sit around our hewn wood table
until our hair is long and our eyes are feeble,
eating, my people, O my insatiates,
25   eating until we are no more able
to jack up the jaws any longer —

to no more complain of the soul's vulgar cavities,
to gaze at each other over the rust-heap of cutlery,
drinking a coffee that takes an eternity —
30   till, bursting, bleary,
we laugh, barbarians, and rock the universe —
and exclaim to each other over the table

                    ——→

---

1 in Greek mythology, a fire-breathing monster with a lion's head, a goat's body, and a serpent's tail; also used figuratively to indicate an absurdly fanciful or impossible idea.

over the table of bones and scrap metal
over the gigantic junk-heaped table:

35   by God that was a meal

(1966)

Dark Pines under Water

This land like a mirror turns you inward
And you become a forest in a furtive lake;
The dark pines of your mind reach downward,
You dream in the green of your time,
5   Your memory is a row of sinking pines.

Explorer, you tell yourself this is not what you came for
Although it is good here, and green;
You had meant to move with a kind of largeness,
You had planned a heavy grace, an anguished dream.

10   But the dark pines of your mind dip deeper
And you are sinking, sinking, sleeper
In an elementary world;
There is something down there and you want it told.

(1969)

Suniti Namjoshi (b. 1941)

Born in Bombay, Namjoshi worked as an officer in the Indian Administrative Service before coming to Canada to pursue a Ph.D. at McGill University. After teaching for several years in Toronto, she took up an academic post in Devon, England, where she now lives. Namjoshi has had a peripatetic career, but she locates her cultural and artistic roots in India. For instance, she notes that she derives her interest in fables, evident in such volumes as *Feminist Fables* (1981) and *The Blue Donkey Fables* (1988), from India's heritage of myth-making and storytelling. At once mythical and autobiographical, Namjoshi's work examines the matrices of desire that determine her diasporic, feminist, and lesbian perspectives. Although issues of gender and sexuality dominate much of her work, Namjoshi is pursuing an interest in cultural formation and artistic collaboration in her latest book, *Building Babel* (1996), which has an electronic component that allows readers to contribute to the architectural blueprint of a structured but everchanging culture.

Look, Medusa![1]

Medusa living on a remote shore
troubled no one: fish swam, birds flew, and the sea
did not turn to glass. All was as before.
A few broken statues lay untidily
5   on the lonely beach, but other than these
there was nothing wrong with that peaceful scene.
And so, when the hero Perseus[2] came to seize
the Gorgon's head, he thought he might have been
mistaken. He watched for a while, but she turned
10   nothing to stone. The waves roared as waves will,
till at last the hidden hero burned
to be seen by her whom he had come to kill.
"Look, Medusa, I am Perseus!" he cried,
thus gaining recognition before he died.

(1988)

Poem Against Poets

I fall upon the thorns of life,
          I weep, I bleed,[1]
but to what purpose?
        There was once a poet
5   who thought she was a nightingale,[2]
        and another
who thought she was a rose —
          charming perhaps,
able certainly, having found at least
10   a way to cope.
Would the nightingale's entrails

        ⟶

---

1 in Greek legend, a Gorgon whose hair was composed of snakes and whose face could turn the viewer to stone. 2 semi-divine hero who managed to behead Medusa by looking at her reflection in his shield.
1 see line 54 of Percy Bysshe Shelley's "Ode to the West Wind" (page 141). 2 like the rose in line 7, a conventional Romantic poetic symbol. Namjoshi told the editors of this anthology that she did not have any actual women poets in mind in these examples but that she referred to female poets "simply because of the reference to Philomel, and also, I suppose, because I tend to make the heroes (and anti-heroes) female whenever possible."

           have been more powerful
(as emblematic objects)
           laid out on the floor
15   of a room that you came to, and then
                    withdrew from,
startled and amazed?
           Oh the rose is bloodless,
she is white with pain;
20   and Philomel[3] wails
in the woods again.
           But there are the other
more ordinary animals.
           They are not literary.
25   They own their pain.

                                     (1988)

Michael Ondaatje (b. 1943)

Born in Colombo, Ceylon (now Sri Lanka), Ondaatje moved to England when he was eleven and came to Canada in 1962. He received a B.A. from the University of Toronto and an M.A. from Queen's University. He currently teaches at York University. Ondaatje began his career as a poet, publishing his first book in 1967. He has also produced novels, films, criticism, and anthologies. Two of his poetry collections have won the Governor General's Award: *The Collected Works of Billy the Kid* (1970), in which he combined poetry and prose, and *There's a Trick with a Knife I'm Learning to Do: Poems 1973–1978* (1979). He also received the Governor General's Award and the Booker Prize for his novel *The English Patient* (1992). His complex novel about civil unrest in Sri Lanka, *Anil's Ghost* (2000), was co-winner of the Giller Prize. Ondaatje most frequently explores the tensions between the subjective inner vision and the supposedly objective and logical realm of outward reality. Dissatisfied with traditional classifications and methods, he challenges both conventional perceptions and literary forms by mixing prose and poetry, fact and fiction, realism and surrealism, lyricism and violence.

---

3 in Greek mythology, Philomel, or Philomela, avenges her violation by her brother-in-law, Tereus, and then turns herself into a tongueless swallow and her sister, Procne, into a nightingale. The later, more influential Latin version of the story reverses the sisters' roles.

Elizabeth[1]

Catch, my Uncle Jack[2] said
and oh I caught this huge apple
red as Mrs Kelly's[3] bum.
It's red as Mrs Kelly's bum, I said
5   and Daddy[4] roared
and swung me on his stomach with a heave.
Then I hid the apple in my room
till it shrunk like a face
growing eyes and teeth ribs.

10   Then Daddy took me to the zoo
he knew the man there
they put a snake around my neck
and it crawled down the front of my dress.
I felt its flicking tongue
15   dripping onto me like a shower.
Daddy laughed and said Smart Snake
and Mrs Kelly with us scowled.

In the pond where they kept the goldfish
Philip[5] and I broke the ice with spades
20   and tried to spear the fishes;
we killed one and Philip ate it,
then he kissed me
with raw saltless fish in his mouth.

My sister Mary's got bad teeth
25   and said I was lucky, then she said
I had big teeth, but Philip said I was pretty.
He had big hands that smelled.

I would speak of Tom,[6] soft laughing,
who danced in the mornings round the sundial

———→

1 the speaker is Elizabeth I (1533–1603). 2 fictitious character, probably not an actual uncle but a man given that title because of familiarity with the child. 3 fictitious character, probably a nurse. 4 Elizabeth's father, Henry VIII (1491–1547). 5 Philip II of Spain (1527–98) married Elizabeth's sister, Mary Tudor (1515–58), in 1554. After Mary's death, he unsuccessfully sought to marry Elizabeth. 6 Lord Thomas Seymour of Sudeley (c. 1508–49) was executed for intriguing against his brother, Edward, Duke of Somerset, Lord Protector of the Realm. He vainly sought the hand of Elizabeth, having treated her with marked indelicacy when she stayed at his house.

30   teaching me the steps from France, turning
with the rhythm of the sun on the warped branches,
who'd hold my breast and watch it move like a snail
leaving his quick urgent love in my palm.
And I kept his love in my palm till it blistered.

35   When they axed his shoulders and neck
the blood moved like a branch into the crowd.
And he staggered with his hanging shoulder
cursing their thrilled cry, wheeling,
waltzing in the French style to his knees
40   holding his head with the ground,
blood settling on his clothes like a blush;
this way
when they aimed the thud into his back.

And I find cool entertainment now
45   with white young Essex,[7] and my nimble rhymes.[8]

(1967)

Letters & Other Worlds

"for there was no more darkness for him and, no doubt
like Adam before the fall, he could see in the dark"[1]

My father's body was a globe of fear
His body was a town we never knew
He hid that he had been where we were going
His letters were a room he seldom lived in
5   In them the logic of his love could grow

My father's body was a town of fear
He was the only witness to its fear dance
He hid where he had been that we might lose him
His letters were a room his body scared

---

7 Robert Devereux (1566–1601), the second Earl of Essex and one of Elizabeth's confidants, was
executed for attempting to raise a rebellion. 8 Elizabeth wrote lyric poetry.
1 from "*Descendit ad infernos*" (He Descends to the Underworld), a chapter for Alfred Jarry's *La dragonne*
(1943), quoted in Roger Shattuck's *The Banquet Years: The Arts in France, 1885–1918* (1955). The clause
immediately preceding the section Ondaatje quotes is "But soon he could drink no more."

10   He came to death with his mind drowning.
      On the last day he enclosed himself
      in a room with two bottles of gin, later
      fell the length of his body
      so that brain blood moved
15   to new compartments
      that never knew the wash of fluid
      and he died in minutes of a new equilibrium.

      His early life was a terrifying comedy
      and my mother divorced him again and again.
20   He would rush into tunnels magnetized
      by the white eye of trains
      and once, gaining instant fame,
      managed to stop a Perahara² in Ceylon
      — the whole procession of elephants dancers
25   local dignitaries — by falling
      dead drunk onto the street.

      As a semi-official, and semi-white at that,
      the act was seen as a crucial
      turning point in the Home Rule Movement
30   and led to Ceylon's independence in 1948.

      (My mother had done her share too —
      her driving so bad
      she was stoned by villagers
      whenever her car was recognized)

35   For 14 years of marriage
      each of them claimed he or she
      was the injured party.
      Once on the Colombo docks
      saying goodbye to a recently married couple
40   my father, jealous
      at my mother's articulate emotion,
      dove into the waters of the harbour
      and swam after the ship waving farewell.
      My mother pretending no affiliation
45   mingled with the crowd back to the hotel.

2 Sinhalese for *procession*; a *perahara* was most frequently associated with a religious celebration or marriage.

Once again he made the papers
though this time my mother
with a note to the editor
corrected the report — saying he was drunk
50 rather than broken hearted at the parting of friends.
The married couple received both editions
of *The Ceylon Times* when their ship reached Aden.[3]

And then in his last years
he was the silent drinker,
55 the man who once a week
disappeared into his room with bottles
and stayed there until he was drunk
and until he was sober.

There speeches, head dreams, apologies,
60 the gentle letters, were composed.
With the clarity of architects
he would write of the row of blue flowers
his new wife had planted,
the plans for electricity in the house,
65 how my half-sister fell near a snake
and it had awakened and not touched her.
Letters in a clear hand of the most complete empathy
his heart widening and widening and widening
to all manner of change in his children and friends
70 while he himself edged
into the terrible acute hatred
of his own privacy
till he balanced and fell
the length of his body
75 the blood screaming in
the empty reservoir of bones
the blood searching in his head without metaphor

(1973)

3 the capital of the British colony of Aden and later the capital of the People's Democratic Republic of
Yemen; port of call on voyages through the Suez Canal.

The Cinnamon Peeler [1]

If I were a cinnamon peeler
I would ride your bed
and leave the yellow bark dust
on your pillow.

5   Your breasts and shoulders would reek
you could never walk through markets
without the profession of my fingers
floating over you. The blind would
stumble certain of whom they approached
10   though you might bathe
under rain gutters, monsoon.

Here on the upper thigh
at this smooth pasture
neighbour to your hair
15   or the crease
that cuts your back. This ankle.
You will be known among strangers
as the cinnamon peeler's wife.

I could hardly glance at you
20   before marriage
never touch you
— your keen nosed mother, your rough brothers.
I buried my hands
in saffron, disguised them
25   over smoking tar,
helped the honey gatherers...

. . . . .

When we swam once
I touched you in water
and our bodies remained free,
30   you could hold me and be blind of smell.
You climbed the bank and said

---

1 one who peels from the cinnamon tree the bark whose inner layer provides the aromatic spice.

this is how you touch other women
the grass cutter's wife, the lime burner's daughter.
And you searched your arms
35 for the missing perfume
and knew

what good is it
to be the lime burner's daughter
left with no trace
40 as if not spoken to in the act of love
as if wounded without the pleasure of a scar.

You touched
your belly to my hands
in the dry air and said
45 I am the cinnamon
peeler's wife. Smell me.

(1982)

To a Sad Daughter

All night long the hockey pictures
gaze down at you
sleeping in your tracksuit.
Belligerent goalies are your ideal.

5 Threats of being traded
cuts and wounds
— all this pleases you.
O my god! you say at breakfast
reading the sports page over the Alpen[1]
10 as another player breaks his ankle
or assaults the coach.

When I thought of daughters
I wasn't expecting this
but I like this more.

——————▶

---

1 a brand of breakfast cereal.

15 I like all your faults
even your purple moods
when you retreat from everyone
to sit in bed under a quilt.
And when I say "like"
20 I mean of course "love"
but that embarrasses you.
You who feel superior to black and white movies
(coaxed for hours to see *Casablanca*)²
though you were moved
25 by *Creature from the Black Lagoon*.³

One day I'll come swimming
beside your ship or someone will
and if you hear the siren⁴
listen to it. For if you close your ears
30 only nothing happens. You will never change.

I don't care if you risk
your life to angry goalies
creatures with webbed feet.
You can enter their caves and castles
35 their glass laboratories. Just
don't be fooled by anyone but yourself.

This is the first lecture I've given you.
You're "sweet sixteen" you said.
I'd rather be your closest friend
40 than your father. I'm not good at advice
you know that, but ride
the ceremonies
until they grow dark.

Sometimes you are so busy
45 discovering your friends
I ache with a loss
— but that is greed.

   ———→

---

2 celebrated 1942 film starring Humphrey Bogart and Ingrid Bergman. 3 1954 monster film starring Richard
Carlson. 4 sirens were mythical creatures, half-woman and half-bird, who used their sweet song to lure
sailors. In the *Odyssey*, Odysseus (Ulysses) escaped by stopping the ears of the members of his crew with wax
and then lashing himself to the ship's mast.

And sometimes I've gone
into *my* purple world
50   and lost you.

One afternoon I stepped
into your room. You were sitting
at the desk where I now write this.
Forsythia outside the window
55   and sun spilled over you
like a thick yellow miracle
as if another planet
was coaxing you out of the house
— all those possible worlds! —
60   and you, meanwhile, busy with mathematics.

I cannot look at forsythia now
without loss, or joy for you.
You step delicately
into the wild world
65   and your real prize will be
the frantic search.
Want everything. If you break
break going out not in.
How you live your life I don't care
70   but I'll sell my arms for you,
hold your secrets forever.

If I speak of death
which you fear now, greatly,
it is without answers,
75   except that each
one we know is
in our blood.
Don't recall graves.
Memory is permanent.
80   Remember the afternoon's
yellow suburban annunciation.
Your goalie
in his frightening mask
dreams perhaps
85   of gentleness.

(1984)

Leona Gom (b. 1946)

Born in the Peace River district of Alberta, Gom lived for twenty years on an isolated farm. She received a B.Ed. and M.A. from the University of Alberta, where she taught for two years before taking up posts in English and creative writing at U.B.C. and at Douglas/Kwantlen College (Surrey, B.C.), where she was editor of the literary magazine *Event* for almost a decade. Gom has published five novels, the first of which, *Housebroken* (1986), won the Ethel Wilson Fiction Prize. The third of her six books of poetry, *Land of the Peace* (1980), won the Canadian Authors' Association Award for Best Book of Poetry. Gom's poetry is particularly notable for her ability to invest commonplace details and events with both emotion and broad significance.

Metamorphosis

Something is happening
to this girl.

She stands on one leg
on the third block
5   of her hopscotch game,
lifts herself forward
to the next double squares,
and, as she jumps,
something changes.

10   Her straight child's body
curls slowly in the air,
the legs that assert themselves
apart on the squares
curve in calf and thigh,
15   angles become arches;
her arms pumping slowly
to her sides adjust
to a new centre of gravity,
the beginnings of breasts
20   push at her sweater,
her braids have come undone
and her hair flies loose around her.

Behind her
the schoolhouse blurs,
25   becomes insubstantial
and meaningless,
and the boys in the playground
move toward her,
something sure and sinister
30   in their languid circling.

Slowly she picks up the beanbag.
When she straightens,
her face gathers
the bewildered awareness
35   of the body's betrayal,
the unfamiliar feel
of the child's toy
in her woman's hand.

(1980)

Marlene Nourbese Philip (b. 1947)

Born in Moriah, Tobago, Philip spent much of her youth in Trinidad. After a residence in Jamaica, she received her B.Sc. in economics from the University of the West Indies. Moving to Canada, she earned both an M.A. in political science and an LL.B. at the University of Western Ontario. Philip then practised law for seven years, writing the entire time. Since 1982, she has devoted herself to writing professionally, and has also been a part-time academic. Philip published her first collection of poetry, *Thorns*, in 1980, and her second, *Salmon Courage*, in 1983. In 1988, she won the *Casa del las Americas* prize for the manuscript version of *She Tries Her Tongue; Her Silence Softly Breaks* (1989). Exploring the same cultural grounds as her previous collections, Philip's third book comprises grouped series of poetic utterances, grammar lessons, multiple choice questions, aphorisms, fictional excerpts, bibilical allusions, and linguistic violence. In her essay, "Managing the Unmanagable" (1990), Philip suggests that such formal and linguistic experimentation is necessary for a historically colonized voice to emerge authentically from within the confines of the colonizer's language. By juxtaposing Western and African mythology, standard and demotic English, and male and female sexuality, Philip repeatedly attempts to subvert the hegemonic, white, male construction of history and to give voice to the "mother-tongue," the racial consciousness connecting the diasporic poet to her African ancestors. A relentlessly political artist, Philip is a founding member of Vision 21, a collective dedicated to fighting racism in the arts.

Blackman Dead

The magnum pistol barked
its last command
broke his chest —
red words of silence erupt
5   silken ribbons of death
wreathe the sullen Sunday morning madness.

A magnum pistol broke the secret
Sunday morning pact,
red roads of silence
10   lead us
nowhere

but to bury him
bury him
in a plain pine coffin
15   and repeat after me
how bad he was because,
because he was
just another immigrant
I say repeat
20   after me
how he deserved to die
because he didn't learn our ways
the ways of death
repeat
25   after me blackman dead, blackman dead
blackman dead.

as we dress dong
in we tree piece suit

——→

we disco dress
30   an' we fancy wheels —
dere is a magnum fe each one a we.

Listen me, listen me,
dey say every man palace is 'is 'ome
dat no man is
35   one hisland honto 'imself
dat if yuh mark one crass
pon yuh door
in blood
all we fus born is safe,

40   I say repeat
after me
how he deserved to die
because he didn't learn our ways
the ways of death
45   repeat
after me
blackman dead, blackman dead
blackman dead.

Toronto has no silk cotton trees
50   strong enough to bear
one blackman's neck
the only crosses that burn
are those upon our souls
and the lynch mobs meet
55   at Winstons[1]....

Blackman dead, blackman dead,
blood seeps beneath
the subterfuged lie
living as men
60   how can we die as niggers,
red roads of silence
lead us where
no birds sing

———→

1 an upscale restaurant, now defunct.

65   blackman dead
      blackman dead
      black roses for blackman dead.

(1980)

Meditations on the Declension of Beauty by the Girl with the Flying Cheek-bones

    If not   If not   If
    Not
    If not in yours
               In whose
5   In whose language
    Am I
    If not in yours
               In whose
    In whose language
10   Am I   I am
               If not in yours
    In whose
        Am I
    (if not in yours)
15   I am yours
    In whose language
               Am I not
    Am I not   I am yours
    If not in yours
    If not in yours
20   In whose
    In whose language
               Am I...

    Girl with the flying cheek-bones:
    She is
25   I am
    Woman with the behind that drives men mad
    And if not in yours

⟶

Where is the woman with a nose broad
As her strength
30   If not in yours
In whose language
Is the man with the full-moon lips
Carrying the midnight of colour
Split by the stars — a smile
35   If not in yours
        In whose

In whose language
        Am I
        Am I not
40   Am I   I am yours
        Am I not   I am yours

        Am I   I am
If not in yours
        In whose
45   In whose language
        Am I
If not in yours
        Beautiful

                      (1989)

Dionne Brand (b. 1953)

Born in Guayguayare, Trinidad, Dionne Brand moved to Toronto in 1970 to study at the University of Toronto, where she earned an honours degree in English and drama, and an M.A. in the philosophy of education. She published her first volume of poetry, 'Fore Day Morning, in 1978. Chronicles of the Hostile Sun (1984) records her experiences in Grenada in the months leading up to the American invasion in October 1983. One of the major concerns of No Language Is Neutral (1990) is the living presence of the past. In Land to Light On (1997), winner of the Governor General's Literary Award, Brand mingles prose and poetry to investigate her status as an outsider. A vocal feminist and advocate for black rights, Brand frequently attacks imperialism and patriarchy in her poetry. Impassioned and allusive, these poems focus on the abuses suffered and the heroism displayed by both blacks and women.

Blues Spiritual for Mammy Prater

On looking at "the photograph of Mammy Prater an ex-slave,
115 years old when her photograph was taken"

she waited for her century to turn
she waited until she was one hundred and fifteen
years old to take a photograph
to take a photograph and to put those eyes in it
5   she waited until the technique of photography was
suitably developed
to make sure the picture would be clear
to make sure no crude daguerreotype[1] would lose
her image
10 would lose her lines and most of all her eyes
and her hands
she knew the patience of one hundred and fifteen years
she knew that if she had the patience,
to avoid killing a white man
15 that I would see this photograph
she waited until it suited her
to take this photograph and to put those eyes in it.

in the hundred and fifteen years which it took her to
wait for this photograph she perfected this pose
20 she sculpted it over a shoulder of pain,
a thing like despair which she never called
this name for she would not have lasted
the fields, the ones she ploughed
on the days that she was a mule, left
25 their etching on the gait of her legs
deliberately and unintentionally
she waited, not always silently, not always patiently,
for this self portrait
by the time she sat in her black dress, white collar,
30 white handkerchief, her feet had turned to marble,
her heart burnished red,
and her eyes.

---

1 picture produced by a method invented in 1839 by Louis Daguerre (1789–1851); the image was taken
upon a silver-coated copper plate sensitized by iodine and was developed by being treated with vapour of
mercury.

she waited one hundred and fifteen years
until the science of photography passed tin and
35   talbotype[2] for a surface sensitive enough
to hold her eyes
she took care not to lose the signs
to write in those eyes what her fingers could not script
a pact of blood across a century, a decade and more
40   she knew then that it would be me who would find
her will, her meticulous account, her eyes,
her days when waiting for this photograph
was all that kept her sane
she planned it down to the day,
45   the light,
the superfluous photographer
her breasts,
her hands
this moment of
50   my turning the leaves of a book,
noticing, her eyes.

(1990)

Louise Bernice Halfe (b.1953)

Also known as Sky Dancer, Halfe was born in Two Hill, Alberta, and raised on the Saddle Lake Indian Reserve. Interested in improving the social and psychological conditions of Native Canadians, Halfe earned a bachelor of social work from the University of Regina and a certificate in drugs and alcohol counselling from from the Nechi Institute (St. Albert, Alberta). Though she had been keeping a journal since high school, it was during a six-year residency in Saskatchewan that Halfe first collected her journal writings into a book of poetry, *Bear Bones & Feathers* (1994). Shortlisted for both the Spirit of Saskatchewan Award and the Gerald Lambert Award, this collection won the Milton Acorn People's Poetry Award in 1996. Her second collection, *Blue Marrow* (1998), which was nominated for the Governor General's Award for Poetry, combines prose, poetry, and journal entries to express the polyphonic voices of her Native ancestors and their spiritual inheritors. The poems reprinted below show a distinctive feature of Halfe's talent: her ability to use dialect and humour for pointed social comment.

2 a tintype, also known as a ferrotype, is a photograph taken as a positive image on a sheet of coated tin or iron; the talbotype (originally called the callotype) was named after its inventor, William Henry Fox Talbot (1800–77), who, in 1841, patented a process for producing photographic images on paper sensitized with iodide of silver.

My Ledders

dear popo
i no, i no, you tired of my ledders
i couldn't let dis one go
i dought you could do somedin 'bout it.
5   years ago you stopped *nōkhom* and *nimosōm*[1]
from prayin in da sweatlodge and sundance,
drummin, singin and dancin.
you even stopped dem from Indian speakin
and storydellin.
10   well you must have some kind of bower
cuz da govment sure listen.

well, pope
last night on DV
i watched some whitemen
15   sweat in da lodge, and at
dinner dime on da radio
i heard dat man dell us
dat some darafist was havin a retreat
and to register.
20   what dat mean, i not sure
anyway he is buildin' a sweatlodge.
i never hear anybody before on da radio
dell da whole world dat.
i sure surprise and kinda made me mad.

25   i wonder if you could dell da govment
to make dem laws dat stop dat
whiteman from dakin our *isistāwina*[2]
cuz i dell you pope
i don't dink you like it
30   if i dook you
gold cup and wine
pass it 'round our circles
cuz i don't have you drainin
from doze schools.

———>

1 my grandmother and my grandfather. 2 a word that can have deep, sacred implications, but essentially
meaning customs, rites, or beliefs.

35 i haven't married you jeesuz
and i don't kneel to him,
cuz he ain't my god.

dese men, pope, don't know what
tobacco mean, what suffer mean,
40 alls dey no is you jeesuz die for dem
dey don't no what fastin' mean
dey jist dake and gobble our *mātotsān*[3]
as if dey own it.
dey don't no what it mean to dake
45 from da earth and give somedin' back
i so dired of all dis *kimoti*,[4] pope
deach your children.
eat your jeesuz body.
drink his blood.
50 dell dem to go back to dere own deachings,
pope.

(1994)

Body Politics

Mama said,

Real woman
don't steal
from the sky and wear clouds
5 on their eyelids.

Real woman
eat rabbit well-done
not left half-raw
on their mouth.

10 Real woman
have lots of meat
on their bones.
They're not starving,

———>

3 sweat lodges. 4 theft.

15   hobbled horses
with bony, grinding hips.

Real woman caress
with featherstone hands
not with falcon fingernails
that have never worked.

20   When she was finished talking
she clicked her teeth
lifted her arse
and farted
at the passing
25   city women.

(1994)

Erin Mouré (b. 1955)

A supervisor for VIA Rail, Erin Mouré is notable as one of the few working-class female poets to have earned critical respect in Canada. Born and educated in Calgary, she published her first book, *Empire, York Street*, in 1979. In 1982 she won the DuMaurier Award for Poetry. The railroad, current events, and social issues figure prominently in her poems, which often develop themes of social and political criticism. Whether looking at the way popular culture and economic forces shape individual lives, especially those of women, or portraying universal experiences such as love and loneliness, Mouré typically moves from physical perception and emotion to an attempt at intellectual comprehension.

Miss Chatelaine[1]

In the movie, the horse almost dies.
A classic for children, where the small girl pushes a thin
knife into the horse's side.
Later I am sitting in brightness with the women
5   I went to high school with in Calgary,
fifteen years later we are all feminist, talking of the girl
in the film.

———→

1 *Miss Chatelaine* (now published as *Flare*) was a magazine of fashion, beauty, and lifestyles for young Canadian women.

The horse who has some parasite & is afraid of the storm,
& the girl who goes out to save him.

10 We are in a baggage car on VIA Rail around a huge table,
its varnish light & cold,
as if inside the board rooms of the corporation;
the baggage door is open
to the smell of dark prairie,

15 we are fifteen years older, serious
about women, these images:
the girl running at night between the house & the barn,
& the noise of the horse's fear mixed in with the rain.

Finally there are no men between us.

20 Finally none of us are passing or failing according to
Miss Chatelaine.
I wish I could tell you how much I love you,
my friends with your odd looks, our odd looks,
our nervousness with each other,

25 the girl crying out as she runs in the darkness,
our decoration we wore, so many years ago, high school
boys watching from another table.

Finally I can love you.
Wherever you have gone to, in your secret marriages.

30 When the knife goes so deeply into the horse's side, a
few seconds & the rush of air.
In the morning, the rain is over.
The space between the house & barn is just a space again.
Finally I can meet with you & talk this over.

35 Finally I can see us meeting, & our true tenderness, emerge.

(1988)

The Producers

What the producers do to meat, you pay for in your cells.
It is your cells I have come to speak about.
Only a certain thickness separates me from the air in this room.
Density. Its whirligig[1] spinning
5   to the tune of bouzouki[2] music.
My body the street fair offers you the altered clothing of the cells.
It offers you the chance to read a novel by a famous woman
in which other women reproduce, & their
value is this:
10   reproduction.

It is because of this I have come to speak to you:
because it is possible that
the meaning of a woman is the meaning of a single cell.

A certain thickness prevents me from saying what I might say.
15   The difference between a human cell & the atoms in this table.
I lean my head against the wood.
Where are you, I want to speak to you.
What the producers do to lettuce, you pay for in your cells.
Everything they do, you will pay for.
20   Your cells will not recognize what they are to become.
It is on behalf of your cells.
I speak to you without election because the cells know nothing
of democracy.
They think not of the good of the whole, but of themselves.
25   They think of their thin unguarded border.
The illusion of wholeness captivates us, as a kind of slavery.
I asked a woman with cancer, who told me.
Now she has died because some cells wanted to go
someplace else.
30   Before she died, she thought about the producers
of x-rays,
& how we once believed we could see thru anything,
we humans.

(1988)

---

1 spinning toy, such as a top. 2 fretted musical instrument, something like a mandolin, having three or
four courses of double metal strings and traditionally used in Greece to play music for dancing and social
entertainment.

Marilyn Dumont (b. 1955)

Born in Olds, Alberta, Dumont received a B.A. from the University of Alberta and an M.F.A. from the University of British Columbia. A descendent of the legendary Gabriel Dumont, who led Métis military forces during the Northwest Resistance of 1885, Dumont has long been a Native educator and rights activist. Her first collection of poetry, *A Really Good Brown Girl* (1996), winner of the Gerald Lampert Award, examines the manifest ways that western hegemonic society, or "White Noise," distorts and does violence to Native and Métis notions of self and culture. In particular, these poems show the debilitating self-consciousness that develops because white society constantly sits in judgement of people outside of the pale of the main culture. By juxtaposing images of her Cree/Métis heritage with images showing the dominant culture debasing or suppressing that heritage, especially its verbal heritage, these poems are also self-conscious in a more positive way. Dumont's poems, that is, do more than protest victimization: they express consciousness of an identity formed by both oppression and by traditions and family relationships of which the oppressors lack understanding; they thus celebrate the vitality and persistence of the outsider. See the interview with Dumont, pages 417–421.

Letter to Sir John A. Macdonald[1]

Dear John: I'm still here and halfbreed,
after all these years
you're dead, funny thing,
that railway you wanted so badly,
5   there was talk a year ago
of shutting it down
and part of it was shut down,
the dayliner at least,
"from sea to shining sea,"
10 and you know, John,
after all that shuffling us around to suit the settlers,
we're still here and Métis.

We're still here
after Meech Lake[2] and

-------->

1 Sir John Alexander Macdonald (1815–1891), the first prime minister of Canada (1867–1873, 1878–1891), promoted construction of the transcontinental railway, using it before it was even completed to send troops to suppress Louis Riel's last rebellion (see note 4). 2 a proposed amendment to the Constitution Act, agreed to in principle by Prime Minister Brian Mulroney and ten provincial premiers in meetings at Meech Lake, Quebec, on April 30, 1987. The final proposal was issued in Ottawa on June 3, 1987. Because it would have granted Quebec designation as a "distinct society," objectors, notably Manitoba MLA Elijah Harper, an Ojibway Cree, successfully campaigned against ratification of the Meech Lake Accord.

15   one no-good-for-nothin-Indian
       holdin-up-the-train,
       stalling the "Cabin syllables / Nouns of settlement,
       /... steel syntax | and | / The long sentence of its exploitation"[3]
       and John, that goddamned railroad never made this a great nation,
20   cause the railway shut down
       and this country is still quarreling over unity,
       and Riel[4] is dead
       but he just keeps coming back
       in all the Bill Wilsons[5] yet to speak out of turn or favour
25   because you know as well as I
       that we were railroaded
       by some steel tracks that didn't last
       and some settlers who wouldn't settle
       and it's funny we're still here and callin ourselves halfbreed.

                                                                    (1996)

The Devil's Language

1. I have since reconsidered Eliot[1]
    and the Great White way of writing English
    standard that is
    the great white way
5   has measured, judged and assessed me   all my life
    by its
    lily white words
    its picket fence sentences
    and manicured paragraphs
10   one wrong sound and you're shelved in the Native Literature section
    resistance writing
    a mad Indian
    unpredictable

    ⎯⎯⎯→

3 F.R. Scott, "Laurentian Shield" [Dumont's note]. 4 Louis Riel (1844–1885), leader of Métis uprisings over land rights in the Red River valley (1869) and in Saskatchewan (1884–85). Despite legends of his madness and his official execution for treason, Riel embodies for many native and other Canadians a national revolutionary ideal. 5 Wilson (Hemas Ka-lee-lee-kla), member of the Cape Mudge Indian Band of Comox, B.C., became an important national representative for Native rights, especially through his involvement in the Assembly of First Nations.
1 T.S. Eliot (1888–1965), influential American-born English poet, dramatist and critic (see pages 267–276), wrote learned, allusive poetry. He expressed his reverence for tradition in his essay "Tradition and the Individual Talent" (1922), which envisions literary history as shaped by the unique talents of great poets, the examples of whom are white males.

on the war path
15   native ethnic protest
the Great White way could silence us all
if we let it
it's had its hand over my mouth since my first day of school
since Dick and Jane, ABC's and fingernail checks
20   syntactic laws: use the wrong order or
register and you're a dumb Indian
dumb, drunk or violent
my father doesn't read or write
the King's English says he's
25   dumb but he speaks Cree
how many of you speak Cree?
correct Cree not correct English
grammatically correct Cree
is there one?

30   2. is there a Received Pronunciation of Cree, is there
a Modern Cree Usage?
the Chief's Cree not the King's English

as if violating God the Father and standard English
is like talking back(wards)

35   as if speaking the devil's language is
talking back
back(words)
back to your mother's sound, your mother's tongue, your mother's language
back to that clearing in the bush
40   in the tall black spruce

3. near the sound of horses and wind
where you sat on her knee in a canvas tent
and she fed you bannock and tea
and syllables
45   that echo in your mind now, now
that you can't make the sound
of that voice that rocks you and sings you to sleep
in the devil's language.

(1996)

INTERVIEW
with Marilyn Dumont

Q. *Why are you a poet?*

A. I guess because I'm obsessed with words. I guess I was always looking for the exact word, which led me to metaphor and simile, because I could never find the exact word.

Q. *When did you first become aware of your interest in language and thus in poetry?*

A. I probably became aware at university in the 80s when I was taking some poetry courses. It seemed to me that poetry had an ineffable quality to it. I liked the different levels that poetry worked on. I liked that it was also philosophy and music and — I don't really want to say theology — perhaps spirituality, too.

Q. *Poetry doesn't make the bestseller lists, so it is not reaching massive audiences. What is the role or function of poetry today? Why should students care about it?*

A. I think it's our conscience, and I think that is why students should care about it. A lot of poets ask questions that, maybe because of our societal norms or taboos, we are not supposed to ask. For me, that is what is important. Poets have been the ones who have resisted conformity, and lots of poets have been revolutionaries. That's why it's important.

Q. *Your poems play with various line lengths. How do you decide on the length of lines in a poem?*

A. To me a line is like breath. It's the length of my breath when I conceive it. To me it's how much verbal impact, intensity, power you need to deliver this particular message. Most of the time I try to work towards my poems being music so that when people hear them, first of all, as with music, they're engaged by a sound or rhythm that piques their interest, and then they give over to content. It has a lot to do with sound and rhythm. In working with words and line lengths, I go by the sound and by how the sound relates to all the other lines. For example, I think about whether I want contrast or symmetry between the lines. It's like creating a musical score. I've always envied musicians. I've never been able to be a musician, so in a way, poetry is a way of expressing my musical side.

Q. *In your poem "For Bruce: The Night We Sat Studying Cree," one not included in this anthology, you say that "*Cree Language Structures *and* Common Errors in English *book-end / my life." To what extent do you feel caught between two cultures, a double outsider?*

A. That question is hard for me to answer. I guess I just feel that I've been between all my life. Sometimes I wish I could identify with being treaty or status or just one thing, but I realize that my life is in the middle. That's the way I have been looking at the world ever since I can remember. I think that it has actually given me strength as a writer, as a poet.

Q. *Were you able to borrow from both traditions?*

A. Yes, I borrow from both, but because I stand on the outside of both, I can criticize both of them. It gives me a sense of distance or dissonance. By that I mean that, if you're always on the outside, there's always a sense of bitterness. You know you're not inside the circle; you're outside, and that's where you'll always be.

Q. *What prompted you to address a "Letter to Sir John A. Macdonald"?*

A. Part of it was tongue in cheek because of my heritage. Gabriel Dumont is a third great-uncle. Writing that poem was a way of speaking of that hegemony, that oppression in history, of the Métis people. It was a way of talking back to that hegemony, to say, "I am still here; we are still here," even though we were seen as being "the other," and the other was always seen as being a problem. It was sarcasm. Being sarcastic is an angry way of being funny. Sarcasm comes from a place where one feels powerless, and is a way of biting back.

Q. *So it is an expression of power within powerlessness, an ironic state itself?*

A. Yes.

Q. *Do you think that your protests and your revelations of differences of view in such poems as "The Devil's Language" will change anything?*

A. Native people have come up to me and said that they are glad that I said that. I think that the situation is that I give them permission to at least have those feelings and to express that resentment, those feelings of hostility, that they might have but weren't able to articulate. It may also be that they sense that I am pointing to language — or any kind of rule — as a way of assimilating people. I think that it may have made a difference, but maybe not as much as I wanted it to. Poets aren't read a heck of a lot, but I still write, hoping that somebody will read and be affected by my poems.

Q. *You (or the persona through whom you speak in your poems) are obviously self-conscious, intensely aware of yourself as an object of observation and judgement because of your racial background. you are also self-conscious in a second, more positive sense, in that you are intensely aware of who you are and what you feel as both a member of a racial group and as a woman. Is poetry a way of insisting on a complex identity as both a victim of history and an aggressive racial other?*

A. I never quite thought of it in those terms, but you really hit the nail on the head when you said the word *judgement* because that has been a large part of my life. This was internalized racism that was passed on to me by my parents, who got it from their parents, and on and on and on. We felt that we always had to prove that we were good enough. That whole sense of judgement was always there and I was aware of it. There is that sense of self-awareness.

Q. *Is there also a sense in which you are trying to show that this self-aware person has not been victimized or trodden down?*

A. Yes, again, it's a way of feeling a sense of power.

Q. *Are you thumbing your nose at the official culture?*

A. Oh, yeah; in fact, any culture that has colonized any other culture; it's not just white.

Q. *What is "the Great White way of writing" that you reject in the opening lines of "The Devil's Language"?*

A. The Great White way of writing is the perpetuation of the sexist, racist, and classist underpinnings in the subtext of the English language. Languages are not just neutral forms of communication. All languages are ways of perceiving the world and one's place in it. Languages inhabit and define ways of being in the world, and "the Great White way of writing" is one way of seeing the world. Because Canada's aboriginal people were colonized by the British and the French, those languages have imposed their belief systems on all of us, but particularly aboriginal people in Canada.

Q. *How are you resisting that way in your writing?*

A. I am resisting through the content, rather than the form. I have tried to subvert the socio-political forces that labeled me woman, aboriginal, and poor. Of course, the most pernicious force of all is one's own internalized sexism, racism, and classism. In my writing, I try to raise the awareness of these issues in all of us, myself included.

Q. *At the end of "The Devil's Language," you move in tone from what we might call the stridency of protest to a romantic nostalgia, looking back in lyrical tenderness on memories of a Cree mother and her child, who when grown, lovingly remembers the native language that she herself cannot speak. How does this change in tone and rhythm illustrate your opposition to "the Great White way"?*

A. In one sense I am feeling angry at and resistant to the English language, but at the same time I feel sorrow and loss, and probably in some ways, a sense of resignation that I'm going to have to live with my feelings because the English language is not going to go away, nor are the accessories that go along with it — values, for example. I'm part of that now.

Q. *What, specifically, are you rejecting?*

A. The sense that certain people are better because they are more powerful. Again, going back to the judgement thing, I was aware early on that my parents felt very uncomfortable in certain situations because their English was different from, say, the English that a doctor may have spoken, the English that a school principal may have spoken, or the English that a priest may have spoken. I was always aware of that discomfort and the apology that they spoke Cree. Ideas of hierarchy are inherent in language. English has gendered pronouns (he and she), but Cree has animate and inanimate words: to me that's a good illustration of a difference in world view. I always felt at a loss in not being able to speak Cree. One of the forces that stopped me from acquiring the Cree language was that people thought that it was primitive, that it wasn't of any use in this day and age, that its ideas of animate and inanimate were heathen. I want people to acknowledge difference without believing that one way is inferior just because it's different; I want people to consider that Aboriginal language is as important, as powerful, as the English language. The English language is being used worldwide because of political reasons; it's a weapon.

Q. *If you could preserve only one of your poems, which would it be?*

A. "The Devil's Language." I think that in ten or twenty years it's still going to make an impact on people. In fact, I know a lot of Asian students respond to this poem in classes, and maybe it's because of their multi-linguistic backgrounds. They know what I'm talking about. I think the kind of linguistic issues to which I refer are still going to be around.

Robert Crawford (b. 1959)

A scholar, an editor, and a poet, Robert Crawford was born in 1959 at Bellshill, near Glasgow. After receiving an M.A from Glasgow University, he studied at Oxford University, earning the degree of D.Phil. He is now Professor of Modern Scottish Literature at the University of St Andrews. As an academic, Crawford has explored, in such books as *Devolving English Literature* (1992) and *The Scottish Invention of English Literature* (1998), the attempts of Scottish writers to maintain their distinctive culture in spite of the dominance of English political and cultural institutions. As co-editor of the international poetry magazine *Verses* and of *The Penguin Book of Poetry since 1945 from Britain and Ireland* (1998), he has been instrumental in bringing the work of younger poets to critical attention. Crawford himself has published four collections of poetry: *A Scottish Assembly* (1990), *Talkies* (1992), *Masculinity* (1996), and *Spirit Machines* (1999). This poetry is regional in the best sense of the term, displaying a profound understanding of the ways in which history, social conditions, and rugged landscape have affected the character of the Scottish people. Although they are always evident, even if it is just in the mention of setting, the regional concerns are not always foremost; Crawford also explores deeply personal issues, such as the emotions that arise in modern relationships. In all of his poems, however, Crawford tends to make his points more through implication, through wit and verbal restraint, than through overt pronouncements of ideas.

Anne of Green Gables[1]

Short moneyless summers at West Kilbride[2] you sat out
On the back steps with a view of the outside toilet
Reading the Anne books, one after the datestamped next,

Anne of Windy Willows, Anne of Avonlea,
5   *Anne of the Island, Anne's House of Dreams.*
No books were ever as good as these

From West Kilbride Public Library
That always had to go back.
When we got married, one by one

10   You bought the whole set, reading them through. At first
I was jealous when you sat not speaking,
Then put the books away on your own shelf.

" 'How white the moonlight is tonight,' said Anne
Blythe to herself." [3] At first
15   I was jealous. Not now.

(1992)

Mary Shelley on Broughty Ferry Beach[1]

One small boat tugs the enormous corpse inshore
Towards waiting locals. A lad opens up its mouth
And wades inside, clutching a flensing tool
For blubber. Piece by hacked-off piece

1 Anne Shirley, the central character of *Anne of Green Gables* (1908), by Lucy Maud Montgomery
(1874–1942), is an orphan who displays a romantic love of nature and beauty. She is adopted by an elderly
brother and sister, who live on a Prince Edward Island farm called Green Gables. Her story continues in a
number of sequels, including *Anne of Windy Poplars* (1936), which was released in the United Kingdom as
Anne of Windy Willows, Anne of Avonlea (1909), *Anne of the Island* (1915), *Anne's House of Dreams* (1917).
In this last title, she marries her one-time school rival, Gilbert Blythe. 2 coastal town in Ayrshire, southwest
of Glasgow. 3 first part of the opening sentence of *Anne of Ingleside* (1939).
1 Broughty Ferry is a Scottish coastal town just east of Dundee on the Firth of Tay. Mary Shelley
(1797–1851), author of *Frankenstein* (1818), a novel about a scientist who creates a monster from parts of
corpses, stayed in Dundee with the Baxters, friends of her father, in 1812-13, returning a few times later
about 1814.

5   Men deconstruct the outcast zeppelin body,
    Carting lumps back to beachfront cottages —
    Sturdy food and good oil for the winter.
    Harpoons glint in the candlelight.

    Safe home, the men of Broughty Ferry take
10   Their sweet uncorseted wives to bed, or croon
    Shanties to bairns beside toys made of teeth.
    The Tay flows quiet. Dundee's lights wink their yellow.

    A sad girl walks from the beach, carefully picking
    Her steps as she sneaks past a leftover eye
15   Flung on the sand, and other small last bits
    Of monster littering the promenade.

(1992)

George Elliot Clarke (b. 1960)

Born in Windsor Plains, Nova Scotia, Clarke was raised in Halifax. Clarke, who holds a Ph.D. from Queen's University, taught English and Canadian studies at Duke University and was the third Seagram Visiting Chair of Canadian Studies at McGill (1998-99). Now a professor at the University of Toronto, he has published numerous critical articles in creative and scholarly journals. He has also edited *Fire on the Water: An Anthology of Black Nova Scotian Writing* (1991-92) and *Eyeing the North Star: Directions in African-Canadian Literature* (1997). Clarke's first published collection, *Saltwater Spirituals and Deeper Blues* (1983), nominated for the Bliss Carman Award for poetry, explores the aesthetic and spiritual concerns of Nova Scotia's black citizens. In *Whylah Falls* (1990), winner of the Archibald Lampman Award for poetry, Clarke attempts to "remap" Nova Scotia by tracing the spiritual geography of the black community, one that has often been exiled from Canadian historical and political writing. In *Lush Dreams, Blue Exile: Fugitive Poems, 1978-1993* (1994), Clarke coined the term "Africadian" to describe his community. Throughout his poetry and other writings, he has sought make readers aware of the unique Africadian perspective on aesthetic and political values.

Salvation Army Blues

Seeking after hard things —
muscular work or sweat-swagger action —
I rip wispy, Help Wanted ads,
dream of water-coloured sailors
5   pulling apart insect wings of maps,
stagger down saxophone blues avenues
where blackbirds cry for crumbs.
I yearn to be Ulyssean[1], to roam
foaming oceans or wrest
10   a wage from tough, mad adventure.
    For now, I labour language,
earn a cigarette
for a poem, a coffee
for a straight answer,
15   and stumble, punch-drunk,
down these drawn-and-quartered streets,
tense hands manacled
to snarling pockets.

(1983)

Blank Sonnet

The air smells of rhubarb, occasional
Roses, or first birth of blossoms, a fresh,
Undulant hurt, so body snaps and curls
Like flower. I step through snow as thin as script,
5   Watch white stars spin dizzy as drunks, and yearn
To sleep beneath a patchwork quilt of rum.
I want the slow, sure collapse of language
Washed out by alcohol. Lovely Shelley,[1]
I have no use for measured, cadenced verse
10   If you won't read. Icarus-like,[2] I'll fall
Against this page of snow, tumble blackly
Across vision to drown in the white sea
That closes every poem — the white reverse
That cancels the blackness of each image.

(1990)

---

1 Ulysses, the Roman name for Odysseus, was a Trojan war hero and legendary wanderer.
1 Shelley Clemence, a female resident of the fictional Whylah Falls, is the beloved of the narrator, known as
X. 2 in Greek mythology, Icarus, son of Daedalus, escaped from Crete on wings his father had made for him.
He flew so close to the sun, however, that the wax holding together the wings melted, and he fell into the
Aegean Sea.

Evelyn Lau   (b. 1971)

A teenage prostitute and drug abuser, Evelyn Lau became the youngest person ever nominated for the Governor General's Award for poetry. Born in Vancouver, Lau was unable to tolerate the strict routine her parents imposed on her, especially because they forbade her to do any kind of writing. At the age of fourteen, she therefore ran away. Although she felt hurt and confused — she even attempted suicide — her sordid experiences had one positive value: they provided the dramatic material that enabled her to fulfil her dream of becoming a writer. *Runaway: Diary of a Street Kid* (1989), an autobiography seething with rage, made her a literary celebrity, especially after the CBC turned it into a movie. Lau has since published three collections of poetry, a volume of short stories, and a novel. Lau's work is autobiographical and emotional, but she says, "When I'm translating personal experiences onto the page, there is very much a writerly presence at work, so that it's not just spilling my guts." Lau portrays a night-time world of illicit sex and drugs that most readers have never experienced, but she suggests that the desperate role-playing, constant deceptions, and chronic sensual excesses that characterize that world are really expressions of a universal longing for acceptance and love.

What We Do in the Name of Money

heavy feet on the back stairs announce
300 lbs. of stock promoter
you wonder what it's like to drive across town at midnight
for a blow job[1]
5 guess it's no different than going out for a hamburger

every time you see a father now
in real life or on TV
you see you're young enough to be their daughter
instead you've become the girl they visit
10 on nights like these
you caress their faces differently
than a daughter's hands
it changes the way you watch happy families in the sitcoms

---

1 slang term for oral sex.

tug the sash of your silk robe tighter
15   walk fast to the door
his mouth opens as if to swallow you
like the boxes of shortbread cookies he consumes
in his unconfessed loneliness
you know him well, 2 years and enough conversations
20   but tonight the history doesn't show
you light his cigarettes, put on coffee
exaggerate the slavery he hands you with the folded bills

the robe falls like water down a rock
he sprawls on your bed
25   the fan in the bathroom whirs for the next hour
the apartment lights burn your brain into white metal
your thighs straddle his shoulders like run-on sentences
his hands clench the edges of the comforter
brown and defenseless
30   he raises them to cover his face
his mindless words are lost to you, the expletives
forced out between lubricated lips
your bed is awash with his sweat
you will wrap yourself in its smell for days
35   its acridity relieved by cologne

memo: don't brush your teeth for 15 minutes afterwards
when you should be licking your lips
he watches you now with that cool reservation
only guilt can bring
40   on the slow painful descent down the back stairs
he puckers his lips
whistles at the sightless constellations.

(1990)

Nineteen

the men file home with flowers in their hands
rubbery petals scent the rain, it is late
the hours pass in dreams, you wake •
after the shade of night is tugged down
5   the men walk past in white trenchcoats, asking directions.
it is February and the flowers in the grocery stores
are dying in their white pails, the grocer is bending down
and picking them up, taking them inside,
taking them away.

10   the men say they love you, your hair
falls over their alcoholic faces in slick blue curls
you kiss them randomly. oh, the men:
precious as ivory,
dead flowers uprooted in their hands.
15   all you have to show for them is a few roses,
a smattering of pills in the green glass ashtray,
but he calls you Baby Girl and you watch porn movies together
on the white leather sectional, pop antibiotics and drink scotch
when there's nothing else around.
20   you know he's your last chance.

he keeps pictures of you in his drawer
your artificial hair whipping against the camera
your model's pout damp with hunger
your eyes like tombstones, black and white.
25   upstairs the beds are quiet.
at three AM you smash the twisted iron gate and run to the cab
to a driver who assaults you with hard hands
you say nothing, tell no one

is it not enough that you got away?
30   four AM and you sit in the hallway listening to the rain
emptying out through the drains in the balcony
a stench in the bathroom
knees drawn up in that classic position, you're alive
which should be enough for anybody, but already
35   you've begun to stop wanting
and more and more men in their ivory skins pass you
in the increasing night, carrying away flowers til all is dark.

(1992)

DRAMA

INTRODUCTION

DRAMA, ACTION, AND LIFE

The very word *drama* comes from a Greek root meaning "to do," "to perform." Thus the word means essentially what it is: action. Drama is action. But more: drama is communication between human beings that conveys meaning through language, gesture, position, costume, expression. In fact, the Greek root for *theatre* has to do with *seeing*, and so a dramatic text comprises a set of directions for theatrical completion. The action can be visualized in the reader's imagination or realized on the actor's stage. In both cases the drama is seen and interpreted, and a spectator or reader is necessary for the communication of meaning. A reader of drama thus constitutes an audience that collaborates with the script in actively interpreting action and meaning; the reader becomes an actor/director of the mind.

Drama communicates at a human level that is at once primitive and profound. It is pre-philosophical, pre-literate, even pre-structural. Before the first stories were told, before the first songs were sung, human beings had enacted drama. Their physical gestures and movements were themselves a kind of dramatic language that represented where the hunt was held, re-created acts of bravery and heroism, celebrated the blessings of a benign spirit, expressed pleasure, disappointment, outrage, and loss. These enactments, codified and performed as ritual, explain a society in terms of its social action. And the actions that are performed are the actions and orientations of human life: birth, death, maturity, sexual interaction, seasonal change, societal history, criticism, and accomplishment. These actions and social perspectives, celebrated through ritual, communicate unifying truths about a people. At their essence, they state: "Our tribe 'acts' in this manner; this is the way we 'do' things."

At another, conscious, level, we humans discover that we can imagine ourselves as other than what we really *are*. This dramatic realization sets humans apart as a species. We celebrate and indulge our imaginations, mythologies, and aesthetic impulses because they are fundamental to our human nature and provide the metaphorical nourishment that only human beings can appreciate. We thus enact rituals to order our lives and reinforce our mythologies. Rituals, however, while they do not feed us or physically protect us, do something equally important: they represent us as we believe or wish ourselves to be, as people with social structures and spiritual insights that have meaning beyond animal instinct and physical sensation. In primitive societies, costumed performers assume the form of benign and malevolent gods: the performers represent the gods in relation to themselves and to their society; they actively develop the mythology of the people. In such religious representation, performers and audience are mutually involved social participants. When performers and audience perceive that there is a distinct difference between

431

them, ritual has become drama. And yet the shared experience of human creativity, meaning, and assertion remains. Drama represents the insights of human beliefs and social interaction.

In the English experience, drama grew out of the rituals of the early Christian church. The *Regularis Concordia* (c. A.D. 970) of St. Ethelwold, Bishop of Winchester, includes directions for an interaction between priests at the end of matins on Easter Sunday. Known as the *Quem Quaeritis* ("Whom do you seek?") play, the dialogue dramatizes the information of the angel and the joy of the three Marys at news of the resurrection of Christ reported in the gospels of the New Testament. Medieval mystery plays (so called because they were performed by various civic "mysteries" or trade groups such as carpenters, bakers, or drapers) emphasized social involvement and expression on a larger scale. Popular from about 1380 to the second half of the sixteenth century, these plays involved entire cities in the annual performance of biblical stories. These enactments celebrated and communicated the sacred history of an early European society, from the creation of the world by an all-powerful deity to the human action of that deity in the person of Christ, to the resurrection of all human souls at the end of time.

Actively ignored if not suppressed, Catholic church drama under Henry VIII eventuated in allegorical moral dramas that enacted themes of sin, wickedness, repentance, faith, and human conduct in general. The way was already prepared for them before Henry's break with Rome: such titles as *Youth* (c. 1513), *Magnificence* (c. 1516), and *The World and the Child* (c. 1520) suggest stereotyped conflict between figures with indicative names such as Pride, Riot, Humility, Sad Circumspection, Conscience, and Perseverance. The performers of such plays were no longer participants in the civic ritual, but actors practising a craft whose venues included the feast halls of the nobility and the public market square.

A production such as Christopher Marlowe's *Doctor Faustus* in 1592 could reach back to earlier morality representations for such action as the dance of the Seven Deadly Sins, the high jinks of asinine irreverence, or the torment of spiritual suffering in general. But Marlowe's drama also looked forward to more fully psychologized human conflicts of hope, doubt, delusion, achievement, betrayal, and grief. The standard medieval prop representing hell as a monstrous mouth emitting fire and smoke can be suggested through a stage trap, but Marlowe also makes it clear that hell is a state of mind. Good and Bad Angels represent moral stereotypes in Faustus's conscience, but the title character also seeks power, significance, meaning. This early play represents human possibility and striving in the character of Faustus, but it also expresses the misery of failure and damnation as understood in the context of Christian Renaissance Europe.

Drama, in fact, always expresses active human orientation. And we need not speculate exclusively on the performance possibilities of Renaissance plays or on the mists of spiritual impulse. Everywhere today, drama is a medium of expression that orders reality for the human mind. A ritual warm-up and introduction precedes hockey games and orchestral performances alike; royal coronations, ribbon-cutting ceremonies, graduation exercises, and funerals proceed according to script; advertising and news reportage on television owe much to dramatic techniques; the wedding party in the centre aisle, dancers on the dance floor, and fashion models on the runway all conform to a loose spatial pattern in the service of dramatization. A classroom or public meeting often reflects a spectator–performer orientation. Business, political, and military strategists all proceed according to "scenarios." Children learn "roles" through which their social and emotional development is patterned by dramatic improvisation, and which they call "play." It is also a dramatically suggestive coincidence that some modern social and philosophical thinkers such as Sartre, Beckett, Shaw, and Brecht are also playwrights; that Shakespeare is a word for literary and cultural significance as much as it is the name of a Renaissance actor and playwright; that one of Plato's contributions to philosophy is titled *Dialogues*; that Freudian psychology sees the plot of the ancient Greek play *Oedipus the King* as pattern and paradigm for modern subconscious reality. Drama explains and drama entertains; it concretizes, represents, and translates the complexities of human nature and existence.

CONFLICT, CHARACTER, AND EXPOSITION

Because drama "means" action, it needs, at all points, dramatic **conflict**. Life itself can be seen as a competitive struggle for physical, emotional, and spiritual survival, and drama represents such struggle through conflict and its resolution. Adversarial forces within a character or between characters provide the stress and tension that keep the action interesting. **Dialogue**, as a struggle for meaning between diverse, often antagonistic, points of view, is also a kind of conflict. Such struggle goes beyond the simple Antagonist versus Protagonist opposition of the Villain and the Hero. All the characters of *Sled* relate to one another in terms of overt or insidious conflict. One might say that Brick in *Cat on a Hot Tin Roof* is in conflict with himself as much as he is with Maggie, Big Daddy, and the hypocrisy of the situation in general on Big Daddy's birthday. Dramatic conflict suggests a variety of differences in attitude, allegiance, situation, opinion, and expression. Characters in drama argue, deny, insult, reject, and insinuate. They also try to resolve conflict when they embrace one another, take sides, share knowledge, or face the future.

The oppositions in character and action that ensure conflict are also basic elements of dramatic exposition. **Exposition** is the background information about characters, situations, and relationships that acts as a starting point for understanding the drama that ensues. Expository information establishes aspects of character at the same time as it explains the situation at the beginning of the play. In *Blood Relations*, Miss Lizzie and the Actress enter into a conversational and retrospective game of "painting the background" which provides expository details about Lizzie's notorious reputation. Prospero, by lecturing in turn to Miranda and Ariel in the second scene of *The Tempest*, actually sets forth the exposition of family and island history. Exposition can occur later in a play, too, and can be just as revealing, as in *The Shipbuilder* (Act 2, Scene 2), where Jukka describes Karkulainen's early love life back in Finland. Expository information "fills in the blanks"; it provides past details of character and situation that are relevant if the audience is to understand the present action.

"Who are these people? What are they doing?" These are basic questions concerning character; good exposition provides clues to their answers. But a character is more than just a name in the *dramatis personae*. **Characters** in drama are agents of action. They signify the attitudes, psychological impulses, and moral conditions of separate human minds as well as the actions for which their minds are agent. They can be complex and unpredictable, though credible, as Lizzie is in *Blood Relations*, or relatively simple, flat, and unsurprising, as is Mae in *Cat on a Hot Tin Roof*. Mae, however, is a character important for her antagonistic relationship to the complex characters of Maggie and Big Daddy. Annie, Evangeline, and Kevin in *Sled* are complex characters with highly developed intuitive, emotional, and personal relationships.

Characters in drama reveal their characteristics through interaction with others, but are further exposed through their own words and actions. Every line, every word, even every pause in the text says something about the character involved. Algernon's cheerful character and nonchalant attitude is reinforced by nearly his every utterance in *The Importance of Being Earnest*. In *Cat on a Hot Tin Roof*, Maggie's nervous intensity is signalled from the beginning, her voice described in an early stage direction as "both rapid and drawling," her lines as "almost sung, always continuing a little beyond her breath so she has to gasp for another." Character is exposed and intensified not only by *what* is said, but throughout by *how* things are said. This represents the linguistic and motivational essence of acting. The script provokes questions at every point about why and how things are said and performed. Consequently, an active reader of drama must pose, consider, and respond to such questions at every point in the play.

PLOT AND SETTING

The **plot** of the play is the sequence of events through which the action proceeds. It represents the playwright's selection of actions to be staged and the order in which they are staged. Thus the plot of a play, as a moment-by-moment occurrence in time, conforms to an overall pattern. The **action** moves forward in time, complicated by various interactions of character and situation, as well as by happenings of subplot and the ideas that stem from these interactions and secondary plots. Then, after a **climax** of recognition, revelation, or discovery, the play draws itself rhetorically to a satisfying conclusion. This standard pattern is usually outlined in terms of the **Freytag Pyramid**, a structural diagram devised by the nineteenth-century German playwright and critic Gustav Freytag. His terms correspond to the five-act structure:

3. Climax

2. Rising Action   4. Falling Action

1. Exposition   5. Resolution

This pattern, however, is rarely a simple one. The plot of a play is usually more lateral and complicated than the rising-and-falling movement suggested by Freytag's diagram. In *Sled*, the plot moves through violent actions of murder and exploitation punctuated by lyrical monologues and song as well as flashbacks and ghost sequences. The relatively simple plot of Florinda's desire for Belvile in *The Rover* is countered and thwarted throughout by various subplots, misalliances, and misrepresentations. One might say that the "climax" of *Blood Relations* occurs in the very last line spoken.

The plot of a play always acts as commentary on the play itself, whether tightly drawn to an unassailable conclusion, as in *The Importance of Being Earnest*, or rendered through the more tacit gambits of conversation, confrontation, meaningful pauses, and desperate hopes of *Cat on a Hot Tin Roof*. Often, aspects of exposure and discovery are foreshadowed through plot for dramatic effect. In *Blood Relations*, Harry makes early reference to cutting kindling; he re-enters with the hatchet and hands it to Mr. Borden, who slams the weapon into the table at the end of the first act while resolving to decapitate all of Lizzie's pet birds: these are significant plotted actions in a play about the social and ethical complications surrounding a famous axe murder.

Drama occurs in an eternally present tense of representation that makes plot a kind of unifying tendency for the action. Thus, the reader takes active part in reconstructing the plot of a drama. In *Blood Relations*, the "plot" of Lizzie Borden's alleged parricide is perceived, patterned, and developed through an actress playing an actress who is playing Lizzie's part. The activity of playing Lizzie is the actual plot of the play. The reader must visualize an actress *now* playing the part of an actress in 1902, who is performing what had actually happened some ten years earlier. Similarly, in terms of space, the plot of *The Shipbuilder* moves through Karkulainen's actions in Saskatchewan, Minnesota, and beyond.

A plot contains a variety of actions and situations that need an environment in which to occur. This environment, at once physical and psychological, is known as the **setting**. It is a background, context, or location that contributes much to the plot. The setting can be simple and suggestive as it is at the beginning of *The Importance of Being Earnest*:

> *Morning-room in Algernon's flat in Half-Moon Street. The room is luxuriously and artistically furnished. The sound of a piano is heard in the adjoining room.*
> *(LANE is arranging afternoon tea on the table and, after the music has ceased, ALGERNON enters.)*

A reader or audience begins immediately to work with the play in terms of luxurious setting, cultivated character, and attention-getting musical introduction. The setting can also be expressed within the play as time and place, as in *Blood Relations*: "*The time proper is late Sunday afternoon and evening, late fall, in Fall River, 1902.*" The audience thus has a concrete setting to consider in terms of prevailing social mores and expectations. But setting can also be attentive to the nuances and subtleties of atmosphere, as indicated in Tennessee Williams's "Notes for the Designer," prefixed to *Cat on a Hot Tin Roof*: "The room must evoke some ghosts; it is gently and poetically haunted by a relationship that must have involved a tenderness which was uncommon." He continues:

I once saw a reproduction of a faded photograph of the verandah of Robert Louis Stevenson's home on that Samoan Island where he spent his last years, and there was a quality of tender light on weathered wood, such as porch furniture made of bamboo and wicker, exposed to tropical suns and tropical rains, which came to mind when I thought about the set for this play, bringing also to mind the grace and comfort of light, the reassurance it gives, on a late and fair afternoon in summer, the way that no matter what, even dread of death, is gently touched and soothed by it.

This certainly suggests a mood and atmosphere in which the characters of the drama can move within the reader's imagination. But it also raises technical and aesthetic questions: How would such a setting be realized onstage? Why? What is it supposed to evoke for reader and audience? for actor? director? character?

IRONY AND CHARACTER

In a sense, drama is an extended **irony** of representation. Character, plot, setting — none of it "exists" except on the stage as a patterned imitative enactment, or in the imagination of a sensitive reader. Dramatic irony occurs when the reader or audience knows more about a situation than the characters in that situation do. Such irony occurs in the first meeting between Prospero and the shipwrecked nobles. Shakespeare crafts the scene so that Prospero and the reader/audience are aware of the situation while the others are not. The audience relishes the comic irony of belated understanding. But the irony of withheld information can also work in an opposite way, as in *Sled* when Evangeline experiences a loving reunion with her lost brother, Kevin. Irony always heightens suspense and emphasizes, for this play, terrible emotional pain.

But comic irony of representation occurs for characters within a play, too. Their self-deception and mistaken identity are features of irony pleasing to an audience. Thus, an extended comic irony of withheld information virtually constitutes the plot of *The Importance of Being Earnest*. It also informs the role-play of Jack — representing himself as Ernest — and Algernon, who also represents himself as Ernest. The character "Ernest," of course, does not really exist, but the other characters of the play do not know this. The climactic visual irony of the play follows in Act 2, as Jack enters in mourning for the supposedly dead Ernest, while Algernon — very much alive — is impersonating Ernest in another part of the garden. Such ironic disguise and role-play is a comic staple of television sitcoms and popular film. It also heightens the irony of characters in their disguises, misrepresentations, and mistaken identities throughout *The Rover*. In *Blood Relations*, however, role-play is a grimly ironic basis of character as the Actress portrays Lizzie, and Lizzie herself portrays Bridget.

Irony occurs in plot, too, as circumstances twist themselves and turn out to be quite different from what a character — or sometimes the audience — expects. Irony operates in the gap between expectation and actuality, between what is said and what is meant, between what is intended and what occurs. In

Cat on a Hot Tin Roof, Big Daddy considers himself cured, looks forward to many years of vigorous life ahead. But then he learns the truth about his condition. And then Maggie makes a surprise announcement about hers. Throughout *The Shipbuilder*, one must consider the deep irony of building an ocean-going vessel in the middle of land-locked Saskatchewan. In *The Tempest*, Miranda's marvellous insight, "O brave new world / That has such people in 't!" is under-cut by the irony of Prospero's response: "'Tis new to thee" (5.1.183–84). The audience intellectually savours the added significance, incongruity, compli-cation, and paradox that irony constantly presents in drama.

THEME, SYMBOL, AND EFFECT

It might be said that drama lacks narration because it proceeds primarily through dialogue. As noted in the section on exposition, however, characters do sometimes narrate. Most often, though, narrative, as the story of the plot in time, is assembled in the imagination of the reader or audience. And inas-much as drama is a participatory theatrical script, it is also a literary text with features of figurative language to be considered. Just as the plot is a per-ceived chain of events in the play, so the **theme** is an interpretation sug-gested by the plot. Basically, the plot of *The Tempest* concerns Prospero's return to power as Duke of Milan and the marriage of his daughter to the heir of the Kingdom of Naples. But issues of imperialism, political logic, and benign despotism inevitably suggest themselves, as do overall themes of love, education, and growth of awareness. The title *Sled* suggests powerful the-matic forces of northern solidity, emotional endurance, and unsentimental accommodation. In *The Importance of Being Earnest*, by contrast, the plot involves a rather trivial farce of deception but suggests thematic complexity in terms of how people actually represent themselves to others and to them-selves. The enduring freshness of drama as a form is due in large part to its active assembly, destruction, or consideration of situation through thematic and metaphorical suggestiveness.

Theme is conveyed powerfully through **symbol** and **metaphor** in the drama. Consider the symbolic visual significance of the hatchet in *Blood Relations*, along with the image of Lizzie's decapitated birds. Irrational vio-lence? Sudden terror? Freedom destroyed? All three, and more, suggest them-selves. In *The Rover*, the masks and disguises which the characters continually put on signify physical deception as a controlling theme of the play. Brick, in *Cat on a Hot Tin Roof*, moves around on a crutch, suggesting other "crutches" on which he desperately depends. In terms of language, notice the clipped, unmetaphorical efficiency of the fearful lines that Caliban speaks in *The Tempest* when in Prospero's presence:

> I must obey. His art is of such pow'r
> It would control my dam's god, Setebos,
> And make a vassal of him.

(1.2.372–74)

Compare Caliban's richer emotional and poetic complexity as he later describes his island in terms of comfort, beauty, and love:

> Be not afeard. The isle is full of noises,
> Sounds and sweet airs that give delight and hurt not.
> Sometimes a thousand twangling instruments
> Will hum about mine ears; and sometime voices
> That, if I then had wak'd after long sleep,
> Will make me sleep again; and then, in dreaming,
> The clouds methought would open and show riches
> Ready to drop upon me, that, when I wak'd,
> I cried to dream again.

(3.2.119–27)

SCRIPT AND MEANING

In drama, the time is always *now*, the mood is always imperative. The script is a set of textual instructions to be followed, interpreted, and performed. A reader mediates in the manner of an actor or director to construct meaning from the text. Drama involves plot, but there is no first-person or third-person narrative guide with a ready-made **point of view** for the reader's consideration. Instead, the reader of drama must discern general themes from a multiplicity of points of view provided by the words and actions of various characters. Thus, a reader of drama provides narration mentally in terms of plot, and performs the play imaginatively in terms of action. As a result, the reading of drama can never be passive. There is too much to do and consider: Imagine yourself performing a specific character or two. Read an especially emotional speech or dialogue aloud, and listen to what is created by the words. Consider yourself a director, and imagine how you would stage a specific scene in terms of movement, timing, costume. How do these various effects relate to each other? to character, action, and theme? The reading of drama, as opposed to the theatrical performance of it, allows a reader time to analyze, time to reread, reconsider, and reinterpret dramatic possibilities. In fact — as every actor and director knows — no drama can be performed without a complex variety of interpretive prior "readings."

Variety, possibility, and surprise combine to make drama an eternally vital medium of communication. The script exists as a recipe and a suggestion because nothing is finalized; everything must be interpreted and created. This form of mental construction is a fundamental activity of the human mind and explains the enduring importance of drama to human beings. It represents the way we are. It expresses our social interactions as well as our deepest personal fears and hopes. We live our lives in a variety of roles and contexts as daughters, sons, students, parents, spectators, activists. In every one of our daily roles we must create a context in which to speak and act, and then we must perform. We must also interpret the performances of others. This is not to say that everything is illusion — not at all. Everything is action. Drama is human action. To read drama effectively is to re-create and interpret human social activity in order to broaden our understanding, refine our sympathy, and inform our prejudices about what it means to be human.

William Shakespeare (1564–1616)

Although little is known for certain about Shakespeare's early life and education, his entire professional life as actor and playwright was spent with the Lord Chamberlain's Men, who were renamed the King's Men in 1604 upon the accession of James I. He was thus, along with his colleagues, under direct patronage of the royal household. The King's Men were the pre-eminent performing company of the day. They acted plays by Ben Jonson, John Fletcher, and others, but Shakespeare was their most sustained playwright.

Shakespeare retired in comfort after 1611, having made a substantial living as actor, playwright, and investor in the Globe Theatre. His plays were first collected after his death by fellow actors John Heminges and Henry Condell into *Mr. William Shakespeare's Comedies, Histories, and Tragedies*, better known as the First Folio of 1623. Half of the texts (including *The Tempest*) had never been previously published.

INTRODUCTION TO *THE TEMPEST*

By the time Shakespeare came to write *The Tempest* (in late 1610 or early 1611), he had already penned the four great tragedies *Hamlet*, *Othello*, *Macbeth*, and *King Lear*. His comic ventures such as *Twelfth Night* and *A Midsummer Night's Dream* were behind him, as were the problematic dramas *Troilus and Cressida* and *Measure for Measure*. He was clearly at the height of his power as a playwright. Having been connected with the professional London theatre for some twenty years, Shakespeare knew both the power and the limitations of the stage. He would put both to work in achieving the political, magical, and yet intimately emotional quality of *The Tempest*.

A record shows that *The Tempest* was produced at court on November 1, 1611, and was likely quite new at that point. Two topical pamphlets of the year before have a clear bearing on the play: *A Discovery of the Bermudas* by Sylvester Jourdain, and *The True Declaration of the Estate of the Colony of Virginia* issued by the Virginia Company, which was then headed by the earls of Pembroke and Southampton, Shakespeare's patrons. These reports, along with a testamentary letter dated July 15, 1610, tell of the wreck and survival of an English crew off the Bermudas in 1609. The survivors fashioned crude sailing vessels and arrived in Jamestown, Virginia, a year after being lost. Their experience was an unprecedented one of survival and endurance, but what was even more noteworthy was their report of Bermuda as an island paradise. Shakespeare seems to have drawn a measure of inspiration from these pamphlets in crafting the utopian island of *The Tempest* — a fantastic place in which to explore comic themes such as discovery, good government, love, freedom, and reconciliation.

No clear source exists for the plot of *The Tempest*, but the pattern is a virtual archetype for comedy: the challenged paradise adapted to social needs, the triumphant but sad return home after self-discovery, the hopes that reside in a new generation of people. The plot thus shares many characteristics with mythologies, romances, folktales, and sophisticated children's stories: testing the fidelity of character, revealing unsuspected evil, asserting self-discovery, moving from trepidation to safety through shades of good and evil and their sub-sequent realignment after testing. Here, all is not quite as it seems: Prospero is not the inflexible, overbearing father that Ferdinand takes him to be; Miranda is not merely an island beauty; the shipwrecked European nobles are far from noble; Caliban himself is "savage and deformed" only when judged by the standards of European civilization. And yet all is resolved at the conclusion, in a comic understanding that goes beyond the trite "happily-ever-after" notion to express a sense of human value and endurance.

In plotting his drama, Shakespeare had no way of knowing about the 300 years of colonialism and emigration that were to follow the New World's dis-covery, but he did know of aboriginal people in Africa and the Americas. Caliban is suggestive of just such a native whose land has been taken away, and David Suchet triumphed in interpreting the character thus in the 1978 season of the Royal Shakespeare Company. Fiercely hateful of his oppressors, Caliban can also be lyrically sensitive and touched by beauty, as when he describes his island to the drunks whom he has mistaken for supernaturals. The isle is indeed "full of noises," along with countless other possibilities in effecting comic resolution in terms of survival, reintegration, and restored stability.

Good government — personal and political — is itself a key issue of the play. Prospero is the deposed Duke of Milan, and the survivors of the wreck are mostly his political enemies: his usurping brother Antonio, Alonso, King of Naples, and Sebastian, Alonso's ambitious brother. But the trusty councillor Gonzalo is also a member of the survivors, and his good-natured fantasies about the ideal state in Act 2, Scene 1 are roundly lampooned through the literalism and dim hopes of the others. This, at the same time as Antonio counsels Sebastian on the merits of assassinating his brother and usurping his throne. In another part of the island, Caliban, Stephano, and Trinculo drunkenly plan to assassinate Prospero and take over the island. Prospero, of course, sees all — through closed-circuit TV, in the 1950s production of the Yale Dramatic Association — and achieves political reconciliation through reuniting all the victims of the shipwreck and effecting the marriage of Miranda and Ferdinand. Their love, and the survival of the others, is both a discovery and an effect of Prospero's gov-ernment. Prospero himself has come a long way politically and personally from the arm's-length ineffectuality that saw him deposed back in Milan.

In a sense, satisfied isolation on the island has allowed Prospero the freedom to effect desirable political change. For him, however, this change is belated. Not so for the others in the play who achieve their personal and political freedom. Ariel, in his first exchange with Prospero, demands his liberty and has it granted to him at the play's conclusion. For Ferdinand and Miranda, freedom is found in their love-at-first-sight togetherness. Caliban is aware of his lack of freedom, as he declares to Prospero: "I am all the subjects that you have, / Which first was mine own king" (1.2.341–42), and in his euphoric drunken slogan: "Freedom, high-day! high-day, freedom!" (2.2.154). Like Prospero in a way, who recovers his dukedom, Caliban gets his island back and he is free to chart its future. Prospero himself, in the tender epi-logue that concludes the play, asks the audience for freedom.

The dominating effect of Prospero's character has led to allegorical inter-pretations of the play which see him as a figure for Shakespeare himself at the end of his dramatic career. Some of his lines on the nature of art and drama are richly suggestive, but to locate Prospero as a direct mouthpiece for the playwright simplifies his power within the play. This strategy also simplifies the play in terms of strict causality in order to explain the rich aesthetic effect that the play communicates. And yet the play itself, through amorphous themes of love, embitterment, magical possibility, and human forgiveness, resists such reductive interpretation.

In *The Tempest* everything is forgiven; anything is possible; comic reintegration ties all the loose ends of the play together. And yet confusion, at once blissful and disturbing, is suggested and sustained throughout by the sheer theatricality of the play. The variety of music, dance, and special effects constantly interrupts the plot and varies the pace. There is much room for costume, pageantry, and farce. The "happy" ending of the play, however, is not a transparent theatrical victory: Prospero's desire for revenge is tempered by the extra-human plea of Ariel; Ferdinand must labour like a peasant and prove his kingly love through abstinence; Caliban learns the folly of uncritical trust once more. All three face their futures with varying measures of hope and resolve at the conclusion, a conclusion that signifies hope and possibility for every character involved.

THE TEMPEST

NAMES OF THE ACTORS

ALONSO, King of Naples
SEBASTIAN, his brother
PROSPERO, the right Duke of Milan
ANTONIO, his brother, the usurping Duke of Milan
FERDINAND, son to the King of Naples
GONZALO, an honest old councillor
ADRIAN and FRANCISCO, lords
CALIBAN, a salvage[1] and deformed slave
TRINCULO, a jester
STEPHANO, a drunken butler
MASTER OF A SHIP, BOATSWAIN, MARINERS
MIRANDA, daughter to PROSPERO
ARIEL, an airy spirit
IRIS
CERES
JUNO   [presented by spirits]
NYMPHS
REAPERS
[Other SPIRITS attending on PROSPERO]

1 savage, uncivilized.

THE SCENE. — [On board a ship at sea; afterwards] an uninhabited island.

ACT ONE

SCENE 1. [On board a ship at sea.]

(A tempestuous noise of thunder and lightning heard.
Enter a SHIPMASTER and a BOATSWAIN.)

MASTER: Boatswain!

BOATSWAIN: Here, master. What cheer?

MASTER: Good, speak to th' mariners! Fall to 't — yarely,[1] or we run ourselves aground! Bestir, bestir! (Exit.)

(Enter MARINERS.)

BOATSWAIN: Heigh, my hearts! Cheerly, cheerly, my hearts! Yare, yare! Take in the topsail! Tend to th' master's whistle! Blow till thou burst thy wind, if room enough!

(Enter ALONSO, SEBASTIAN, ANTONIO, FERDINAND, GONZALO, and others.)

ALONSO: Good boatswain, have care. Where's the master? Play the men.

BOATSWAIN: I pray now, keep below.

10   ANTONIO: Where is the master, bos'n?

BOATSWAIN: Do you not hear him? You mar our labour. Keep your cabins! You do assist the storm.

GONZALO: Nay, good, be patient.

BOATSWAIN: When the sea is. Hence! What cares these roarers for the name of king? To cabin! Silence! Trouble us not!

GONZALO: Good, yet remember whom thou hast aboard.

BOATSWAIN: None that I more love than myself. You are a councillor. If you can command these elements to silence and work the peace of the present, we will not hand a rope more; use your authority. If you cannot, give

20   thanks you have liv'd so long, and make yourself ready in your cabin for the mischance of the hour, if it so hap. — Cheerly, good hearts! — Out of our way, I say. (Exit.)

GONZALO: I have great comfort from this fellow. Methinks he hath no drowning mark upon him; his complexion[2] is perfect gallows.[3] Stand fast, good Fate, to his hanging! Make the rope of his destiny our cable, for our own doth little advantage. If he be not born to be hang'd, our case is miserable. (Exeunt.)

(Enter BOATSWAIN.)

BOATSWAIN: Down with the topmast! Yare! Lower, lower! Bring her to try with maincourse![4] (A cry within.) A plague upon this howling! They are louder than the weather or our office.

1 smartly, briskly. 2 attitude. 3 proverbial: he that is born to be hanged need have no fear of drowning.
4 mainsail.

(*Enter* SEBASTIAN, ANTONIO, *and* GONZALO.)

30   Yet again? What do you here? Shall we give o'er and drown? Have you a
mind to sink!

SEBASTIAN: A pox o' your throat, you bawling, blasphemous, incharitable dog!

BOATSWAIN: Work you then.

ANTONIO: Hang, cur, hang, you whoreson, insolent noisemaker! We are less
afraid to be drown'd than thou art.

GONZALO: I'll warrant[5] him for drowning, though the ship were no stronger than
a nutshell and as leaky as an unstanched wench.

BOATSWAIN: Lay her ahold, ahold! Set her two courses! Off to sea again! Lay
her off!

(*Enter* MARINERS *wet.*)

40 MARINERS: All lost! To prayers, to prayers! All lost! [*Exeunt.*]

BOATSWAIN: What, must our mouths be cold?

GONZALO: The King and Prince at prayers! Let's assist them,
For our case is as theirs.

SEBASTIAN: I am out of patience.

ANTONIO: We are merely cheated of our lives by drunkards.
This wide-chopp'd[6] rascal — would thou mightst lie drowning
The washing of ten tides!

GONZALO: He'll be hang'd yet,
Though every drop of water swear against it
And gape at wid'st to glut him.
    (*A confused noise within:*) "Mercy on us! —
50   We split, we split! — Farewell, my wife and children! —
Farewell, brother! — We split, we split, we split!"

[*Exit* BOATSWAIN]

ANTONIO: Let's all sink with th' King.

SEBASTIAN: Let's take leave of him.

(*Exeunt* [ANTONIO *and* SEBASTIAN].)

GONZALO: Now would I give a thousand furlongs of sea for an acre of barren
ground — long heath, brown furze, anything. The wills above be done!
but I would fain die a dry death. (*Exit.*)

SCENE 2. [*The island. Before* PROSPERO'S *cell.*]

(*Enter* PROSPERO *and* MIRANDA.)

MIRANDA: If by your art, my dearest father, you have
Put the wild waters in this roar, allay them.
The sky, it seems, would pour down stinking pitch
But that the sea, mounting to th' welkin's[1] cheek,
Dashes the fire out. O, I have suffered

5 guarantee against.   6 bigmouthed.
1 sky's.

With those that I saw suffer! a brave vessel
(Who had no doubt some noble creature in her)
Dash'd all to pieces! O, the cry did knock
Against my very heart! Poor souls, they perish'd!
Had I been any god of power, I would
Have sunk the sea within the earth or ere
It should the good ship so have swallow'd and
The fraughting[2] souls within her.

PROSPERO: Be collected.
No more amazement. Tell your piteous heart
There's no harm done.

MIRANDA: O, woe the day!

PROSPERO: No harm.
I have done nothing but in care of thee,
Of thee my dear one, thee my daughter, who
Art ignorant of what thou art, naught knowing
Of whence I am; nor that I am more better
Than Prospero, master of a full poor cell,
And thy no greater father.

MIRANDA: More to know
Did never meddle with my thoughts.

PROSPERO: 'Tis time
I should inform thee farther. Lend thy hand
And pluck my magic garment from me. So,

[*Lays down his robe.*]

Lie there, my art. Wipe thou thine eyes; have comfort.
The direful spectacle of the wrack,[3] which touch'd
The very virtue of compassion in thee,
I have with such provision in mine art
So safely ordered that there is no soul —
No, not so much perdition[4] as an hair
Betid[5] to any creature in the vessel
Which thou heard'st cry, which thou saw'st sink. Sit down;
For thou must now know farther.

MIRANDA: You have often
Begun to tell me what I am; but stopp'd
And left me to a bootless[6] inquisition,
Concluding, "Stay! Not yet."

PROSPERO: The hour's now come;
The very minute bids thee ope thine ear.
Obey, and be attentive. Canst thou remember
A time before we came unto this cell?
I do not think thou canst, for then thou wast not
Out three years old.

MIRANDA: Certainly, sir, I can.

2 freighted. 3 wreck. 4 loss, damage. 5 happened. 6 pointless.

PROSPERO: By what? By any other house or person?
    Of any thing the image tell me that
    Hath kept with thy remembrance.
MIRANDA: 'Tis far off,
    And rather like a dream than an assurance
    That my remembrance warrants. Had I not
    Four or five women once that tended me?
PROSPERO: Thou hadst, and more, Miranda. But how is it
    That this lives in thy mind? What seest thou else
50   In the dark backward and abysm of time?
    If thou rememb'rest aught ere thou cam'st here,
    How thou cam'st here thou mayst.
MIRANDA: But that I do not.
PROSPERO: Twelve year since, Miranda, twelve year since,
    Thy father was the Duke of Milan and
    A prince of power.
MIRANDA: Sir, are not you my father?
PROSPERO: Thy mother was a piece of virtue, and
    She said thou wast my daughter; and thy father
    Was Duke of Milan; and his only heir
    A princess — no worse issued.
MIRANDA: O the heavens!
60   What foul play had we that we came from thence?
    Or blessed was't we did?
PROSPERO: Both, both, my girl!
    By foul play, as thou say'st, were we heav'd thence,
    But blessedly holp[7] hither.
MIRANDA: O, my heart bleeds
    To think o' th' teen[8] that I have turn'd you to,
    Which is from my remembrance! Please you, farther.
PROSPERO: My brother, and thy uncle, call'd Antonio —
    I pray thee mark me — that a brother should
    Be so perfidious! — he whom next thyself
    Of all the world I lov'd, and to him put
70   The manage of my state, as at that time
    Through all the signories[9] it was the first,
    And Prospero the prime duke, being so reputed
    In dignity, and for the liberal arts
    Without a parallel; those being all my study,
    The government I cast upon my brother
    And to my state grew stranger, being transported
    And rapt in secret studies — thy false uncle —
    Dost thou attend me?
MIRANDA: Sir, most heedfully.
PROSPERO: Being once perfected how to grant suits,
80   How to deny them, who t' advance, and who

7 helped. 8 trouble. 9 dukedoms, city states.

To trash for over-topping, new created
The creatures that were mine, I say, or chang'd 'em,
Or else new-form'd 'em; having both the key
Of officer and office, set all hearts i' th' state
To what tune pleas'd his ear, that now he was
The ivy which had hid my princely trunk
And suck'd my verdure[10] out on 't. Thou attend'st not!

MIRANDA: O, good sir, I do.

PROSPERO: I pray thee mark me.
I thus neglecting worldly ends, all dedicated
90 To closeness, and the bettering of my mind
With that which, but by being so retir'd,
O'er-priz'd all popular rate,[11] in my false brother
Awak'd an evil nature, and my trust,
Like a good parent, did beget of him
A falsehood in its contrary as great
As my trust was, which had indeed no limit,
A confidence sans[12] bound. He being thus lorded,
Not only with what my revenue yielded
But what my power might else exact, like one
100 Who having unto truth, by telling of it,
Made such a sinner of his memory
To credit his own lie, he did believe
He was indeed the Duke, out o' th' substitution
And executing th' outward face of royalty
With all prerogative. Hence his ambition growing —
Dost thou hear?

MIRANDA: Your tale, sir, would cure deafness.

PROSPERO: To have no screen between this part he play'd
And him he play'd it for, he needs will be
Absolute Milan.[13] Me (poor man) my library
110 Was dukedom large enough! Of temporal royalties
He thinks me now incapable; confederates[14]
(So dry he was for sway)[15] with th' King of Naples
To give him annual tribute, do him homage,
Subject his coronet to his crown, and bend
The dukedom yet unbow'd (alas, poor Milan!)
To most ignoble stooping.

MIRANDA: O, the heavens!

PROSPERO: Mark his condition,[16] and th' event; then tell me
If this might be a brother.

MIRANDA: I should sin
To think but nobly of my grandmother.
Good wombs have borne bad sons.

120 PROSPERO: Now the condition.
This King of Naples, being an enemy

10 vitality, strength. 11 i.e., overran all usual interests in state and politics. 12 without. 13 i.e., the actual
Duke of Milan. 14 makes alliance. 15 power, influence. 16 terms of agreement.

To me inveterate, hearkens my brother's suit;
Which was, that he, in lieu o' th' premises,
Of homage and I know not how much tribute,
Should presently extirpate me and mine
Out of the dukedom and confer fair Milan,
With all the honours, on my brother. Whereon,
A treacherous army levied, one midnight
Fated to th' purpose, did Antonio open
130   The gates of Milan; and, i' th' dead of darkness,
The ministers[17] for th' purpose hurried thence
Me and thy crying self.

MIRANDA: Alack, for pity!
I, not rememb'ring how I cried out then,
Will cry it o'er again. It is a hint[18]
That wrings mine eyes to 't.

PROSPERO: Hear a little further,
And then I'll bring thee to the present business
Which now 's upon 's; without the which this story
Were most impertinent.[19]

MIRANDA: Wherefore did they not
That hour destroy us?

PROSPERO: Well demanded, wench.
140   My tale provokes that question. Dear, they durst not,
So dear the love my people bore me; nor set
A mark so bloody on the business; but
With colours fairer painted their foul ends.
In few, they hurried us aboard a bark,
Bore us some leagues to sea; where they prepar'd
A rotten carcass of a butt,[20] not rigg'd,
Nor tackle, sail, nor mast; the very rats
Instinctively have quit it. There they hoist us,
To cry to th' sea, that roar'd to us; to sigh
150   To th' winds, whose pity, sighing back again,
Did us but loving wrong.

MIRANDA: Alack, what trouble
Was I then to you!

PROSPERO: O, a cherubin
Thou wast that did preserve me! Thou didst smile,
Infused with a fortitude from heaven,
When I have deck'd the sea with drops[21] full salt,
Under my burden groan'd; which rais'd in me
An undergoing stomach, to bear up
Against what should ensue.

MIRANDA: How came we ashore?

PROSPERO: By providence divine.
160   Some food we had, and some fresh water, that

17 agents. 18 occasion. 19 inappropriate, irrelevant. 20 tub; small, barely seaworthy boat.
21 tears.

A noble Neapolitan, Gonzalo,
Out of his charity, who being then appointed
Master of this design, did give us, with
Rich garments, linens, stuffs, and necessaries
Which since have steaded[22] much. So, of his gentleness,
Knowing I lov'd my books, he furnish'd me
From mine own library with volumes that
I prize above my dukedom.

MIRANDA: Would I might
But ever see that man!

PROSPERO: Now I arise.
170   Sit still, and hear the last of our sea-sorrow.
Here in this island we arriv'd; and here
Have I, thy schoolmaster, made thee more profit
Than other princess can, that have more time
For vainer hours, and tutors not so careful.

MIRANDA: Heavens thank you for 't! And now I pray you, sir, —
For still 'tis beating in my mind, — your reason
For raising this sea-storm?

PROSPERO: Know thus far forth.
By accident most strange, bountiful Fortune
(Now my dear lady) hath mine enemies
180   Brought to this shore; and by my prescience
I find my zenith[23] doth depend upon
A most auspicious star, whose influence
If now I court not, but omit,[24] my fortunes
Will ever after droop. Here cease more questions.
Thou art inclin'd to sleep. 'Tis a good dullness,
And give it way. I know thou canst not choose.

[MIRANDA *sleeps*.]

Come away, servant, come! I am ready now.
Approach, my Ariel. Come!

(*Enter* ARIEL.)

ARIEL: All hail, great master! Grave sir, hail! I come
190   To answer thy best pleasure; be 't to fly,
To swim, to dive into the fire, to ride
On the curl'd clouds. To thy strong bidding task
Ariel and all his quality.

PROSPERO: Hast thou, spirit,
Perform'd to point the tempest that I bade thee?

ARIEL: To every article.
I boarded the King's ship. Now on the beak,

---

22 helped; benefited. 23 i.e., highest point of good fortune. 24 ignore.

Now in the waist, the deck, in every cabin,
I flam'd amazement. Sometime I'd divide
And burn in many places; on the topmast,
200 The yards, and boresprit would I flame distinctly,
Then meet and join. Jove's lightnings, the precursors
O' th' dreadful thunderclaps, more momentary
And sight-outrunning were not. The fire and cracks
Of sulphurous roaring the most mighty Neptune
Seem to besiege and make his bold waves tremble;
Yea, his dread trident shake.

PROSPERO: My brave spirit!
Who was so firm, so constant, that this coil[25]
Would not infect his reason?

ARIEL: Not a soul
But felt a fever of the mad and play'd
210 Some tricks of desperation. All but mariners
Plung'd in the foaming brine and quit the vessel,
Then all afire with me. The King's son Ferdinand,
With hair up-staring[26] (then like reeds, not hair),
Was the first man that leapt; cried "Hell is empty,
And all the devils are here!"

PROSPERO: Why, that's my spirit!
But was not this nigh shore?

ARIEL: Close by, my master.

PROSPERO: But are they, Ariel, safe?

ARIEL: Not a hair perish'd.
On their sustaining[27] garments not a blemish,
But fresher than before; and as thou bad'st me,
220 In troops I have dispers'd them 'bout the isle.
The King's son have I landed by himself,
Whom I left cooling of the air with sighs
In an odd angle of the isle, and sitting,
His arms in this sad knot.

PROSPERO: Of the King's ship
The mariners say how thou hast dispos'd,
And all the rest o' th' fleet.

ARIEL: Safely in harbour
Is the King's ship; in the deep nook where once
Thou call'dst me up at midnight to fetch dew
From the still-vex'd Bermoothes,[28] there she's hid;
230 The mariners all under hatches stow'd,
Who, with a charm join'd to their suff'red labour,
I have left asleep; and for the rest o' th' fleet,
Which I dispers'd, they all have met again,
And are upon the Mediterranean flote[29]

25 uproar, excitement. 26 i.e., standing on end. 27 buoying. 28 Bermudas. 29 sea.

Bound sadly home for Naples,
Supposing that they saw the King's ship wrack'd
And his great person perish.

PROSPERO: Ariel, thy charge
Exactly is perform'd; but there's more work.
What is the time o' th' day?

ARIEL: Past the mid season.

240 PROSPERO: At least two glasses.[30] The time 'twixt six and now
Must by us both be spent most preciously.

ARIEL: Is there more toil? Since thou dost give me pains,
Let me remember[31] thee what thou hast promis'd,
Which is not yet perform'd me.

PROSPERO: How now? moody?
What is 't thou canst demand?

ARIEL: My liberty.

PROSPERO: Before the time be out? No more!

ARIEL: I prithee,
Remember I have done thee worthy service,
Told thee no lies, made no mistakings, serv'd
Without or grudge or grumblings. Thou didst promise
To bate[32] me a full year.

250 PROSPERO: Dost thou forget
From what a torment I did free thee?

ARIEL: No.

PROSPERO: Thou dost; and think'st it much to tread the ooze
Of the salt deep,
To run upon the sharp wind of the North,
To do me business in the veins o' th' earth
When it is bak'd with frost.

ARIEL: I do not, sir.

PROSPERO: Thou liest, malignant thing! Hast thou forgot
The foul witch Sycorax, who with age and envy
Was grown into a hoop? Hast thou forgot her?

ARIEL: No, sir.

260 PROSPERO: Thou hast. Where was she born? Speak! Tell me!

ARIEL: Sir, in Argier.[33]

PROSPERO: O, was she so? I must
Once in a month recount what thou hast been,
Which thou forget'st. This damn'd witch Sycorax,
For mischiefs manifold, and sorceries terrible
To enter human hearing, from Argier
Thou know'st was banish'd. For one thing she did
They would not take her life. Is not this true?

ARIEL: Ay, sir.

PROSPERO: This blue-ey'd hag was hither brought with child
270   And here was left by th' sailors. Thou, my slave,

30 i.e., 2:00 P.M. 31 remind. 32 rebate. 33 Algiers.

As thou report'st thyself, wast then her servant;
And, for thou wast a spirit too delicate
To act her earthy and abhorr'd commands,
Refusing her grand hests,[34] she did confine thee,
By help of her more potent ministers,
And in her most unmitigable rage,
Into a cloven pine; within which rift
Imprison'd thou didst painfully remain
A dozen years; within which space she died
280   And left thee there; where thou didst vent thy groans
As fast as millwheels strike. Then was this island
(Save for the son that she did litter here,
A freckled whelp, hag-born) not honour'd with
A human shape.
ARIEL: Yes, Caliban her son.
PROSPERO: Dull thing, I say so! He, that Caliban
Whom now I keep in service. Thou best know'st
What torment I did find thee in. Thy groans
Did make wolves howl and penetrate the breasts
Of ever-angry bears. It was a torment
290   To lay upon the damn'd, which Sycorax
Could not again undo. It was mine art,
When I arriv'd and heard thee, that made gape
The pine, and let thee out.
ARIEL: I thank thee, master.
PROSPERO: If thou more murmur'st, I will rend an oak
And peg thee in his knotty entrails till
Thou hast howl'd away twelve winters.
ARIEL: Pardon, master.
I will be correspondent[35] to command
And do my spriting gently.
PROSPERO: Do so; and after two days
I will discharge thee.
ARIEL: That's my noble master!
300   What shall I do? Say what! What shall I do?
PROSPERO: Go make thyself like a nymph o' th' sea. Be subject
To no sight but thine and mine; invisible
To every eyeball else. Go take this shape
And hither come in't. Go! Hence with diligence!

(*Exit* [ARIEL].)

Awake, dear heart, awake! Thou hast slept well.
Awake!
MIRANDA: The strangeness of your story put
Heaviness in me.

34 behests. 35 obedient.

PROSPERO: Shake it off. Come on.
　　We'll visit Caliban, my slave, who never
　　Yields us kind answer.
MIRANDA: 'Tis a villain, sir,
　　I do not love to look on.
310　PROSPERO: But as 'tis,
　　We cannot miss him. He does make our fire,
　　Fetch in our wood, and serves in offices
　　That profit us. What, ho! slave! Caliban!
　　Thou earth, thou! Speak!
CALIBAN: (within)   There's wood enough within.
PROSPERO: Come forth, I say! There's other business for thee.
　　Come, thou tortoise! When?[36]

　　(Enter ARIEL like a water nymph.)

　　Fine apparition! My quaint Ariel,
　　Hark in thine ear. [whispers]
ARIEL: My lord, it shall be done. (Exit.)
PROSPERO: Thou poisonous slave, got by the devil himself
320　Upon thy wicked dam, come forth!

　　(Enter CALIBAN.)

CALIBAN: As wicked dew as e'er my mother brush'd
　　With raven's feather from unwholesome fen
　　Drop on you both! A south-west blow on ye
　　And blister you all o'er!
PROSPERO: For this, be sure, to-night thou shalt have cramps,
　　Side-stitches that shall pen thy breath up; urchins
　　Shall, for that vast of night that they may work,
　　All exercise on thee; thou shalt be pinch'd
　　As thick as honeycomb, each pinch more stinging
　　Than bees that made 'em.
330　CALIBAN: I must eat my dinner.
　　This island's mine by Sycorax my mother,
　　Which thou tak'st from me. When thou camest first,
　　Thou strok'dst me and mad'st much of me; wouldst give me
　　Water with berries in 't; and teach me how
　　To name the bigger light, and how the less,
　　That burn by day, and night; and then I lov'd thee
　　And show'd thee all the qualities o' th' isle,
　　The fresh springs, brine-pits, barren place and fertile.
　　Cursed be I that did so! All the charms
340　Of Sycorax — toads, beetles, bats light on you!
　　For I am all the subjects that you have,
　　Which first was mine own king; and here you sty me
　　In this hard rock, whiles you do keep from me
　　The rest o' th' island.

36 Hurry up; Come on (an expression of impatience).

PROSPERO: Thou most lying slave,
Whom stripes[37] may move, not kindness! I have us'd thee,
(Filth as thou art) with humane care, and lodg'd thee
In mine own cell till thou didst seek to violate
The honour of my child.

CALIBAN: O ho, O ho! Would 't had been done!
350 Thou didst prevent me; I had peopled else
This isle with Calibans.

MIRANDA: Abhorred slave,
Which any print of goodness wilt not take,
Being capable of all ill! I pitied thee,
Took pains to make thee speak, taught thee each hour
One thing or other. When thou didst not, savage,
Know thine own meaning, but wouldst gabble like
A thing most brutish, I endow'd thy purposes
With words that made them known. But thy vile race,
Though thou didst learn, had that in 't which good natures
360 Could not abide to be with. Therefore wast thou
Deservedly confin'd into this rock, who hadst
Deserv'd more than a prison.

CALIBAN: You taught me language, and my profit on 't
Is, I know how to curse. The red plague rid you
For learning me your language!

PROSPERO: Hag-seed, hence!
Fetch us in fuel; and be quick, thou'rt best,[38]
To answer other business. Shrug'st thou, malice?
If thou neglect'st or dost unwillingly
What I command, I'll rack thee with old cramps,
370 Fill all thy bones with achës, make thee roar
That beasts shall tremble at thy din.

CALIBAN: No, pray thee.
[Aside] I must obey. His art is of such pow'r
It would control my dam's god, Setebos,
And make a vassal of him.

PROSPERO: So, slave; hence!

(Exit CALIBAN.)

(Enter FERDINAND; and ARIEL, invisible, playing and singing.)

Ariel's song.

Come unto these yellow sands,
And then take hands.
Curtsied when you have and kiss'd,
The wild waves whist,
Foot it featly here and there;
380 And, sweet sprites, the burden[39] bear.

37 lashes. 38 i.e., you'd better (a warning). 39 refrain.

Hark, hark!
> (*Burden, dispersedly.*) [40] Bowgh, wawgh!
The watchdogs bark.
> (*Burden, dispersedly.*) Bowgh, wawgh.
Hark, hark! I hear
The strain of strutting chanticleer
> Cry, cock-a-diddle-dowe.

FERDINAND: Where should this music be? I' th' air, or th' earth?
It sounds no more; and sure it waits upon
390   Some god o' th' island. Sitting on a bank,
Weeping again the King my father's wrack,
This music crept by me upon the waters,
Allaying both their fury and my passion[41]
With its sweet air. Thence I have follow'd it,
Or it hath drawn me rather; but 'tis gone.
No, it begins again.

> *Ariel's song.*

Full fathom five thy father lies;
> Of his bones are coral made;
Those are pearls that were his eyes;
400   > Nothing of him that doth fade
But doth suffer a sea-change
Into something rich and strange.
Sea nymphs hourly ring his knell;
> (*Burden.*) Ding-dong.
Hark! now I hear them — Ding-dong bell.

FERDINAND: The ditty does remember my drown'd father.
This is no mortal business, nor no sound
That the earth owes.[42] I hear it now above me.
PROSPERO: The fringed curtains of thine eye advance[43]
And say what thou seest yond.
410   MIRANDA: What is 't? a spirit?
Lord, how it looks about! Believe me, sir,
It carries a brave form. But 'tis a spirit.
PROSPERO: No, wench. It eats, and sleeps, and hath such senses
As we have, such. This gallant which thou seest
Was in the wrack; and, but he's something stain'd
With grief (that's beauty's canker), thou mightst call him
A goodly person. He hath lost his fellows
And strays about to find 'em.
MIRANDA: I might call him
A thing divine; for nothing natural
I ever saw so noble.

---

40 coming from various directions. 41 sorrow, grief. 42 owns. 43 raise.

420   PROSPERO: [*aside*]   It goes on, I see,
        As my soul prompts it. Spirit, fine spirit! I'll free thee
        Within two days for this.
        FERDINAND: Most sure, the goddess
        On whom these airs attend! Vouchsafe my pray'r
        May know if you remain upon this island,
        And that you will some good instruction give
        How I may bear me here. My prime request,
        Which I do last pronounce, is (O you wonder!)
        If you be maid or no?
        MIRANDA: No wonder, sir,
        But certainly a maid.
        FERDINAND: My language? Heavens!
430   I am the best of them that speak this speech,
        Were I but where 'tis spoken.
        PROSPERO: How? the best?
        What wert thou if the King of Naples heard thee?
        FERDINAND: A single thing, as I am now, that wonders
        To hear thee speak of Naples. He does hear me;
        And that he does I weep. Myself am Naples,
        Who with mine eyes, never since at ebb, beheld
        The King my father wrack'd.
        MIRANDA: Alack, for mercy!
        FERDINAND: Yes, faith, and all his lords, the Duke of Milan
        And his brave son being twain.
        PROSPERO: [*aside*]   The Duke of Milan
440   And his more braver daughter could control thee,
        If now 'twere fit to do 't. At the first sight
        They have chang'd eyes.[44] Delicate Ariel,
        I'll set thee free for this! — A word, good sir.
        I fear you have done yourself some wrong.[45] A word!
        MIRANDA: Why speaks my father so ungently? This
        Is the third man that e'er I saw; the first
        That e'er I sigh'd for. Pity move my father
        To be inclin'd my way!
        FERDINAND: O, if a virgin,
        And your affection not gone forth, I'll make you
        The Queen of Naples.
450   PROSPERO: Soft, sir! one word more.
        [*Aside*] They are both in either's pow'rs. But this swift business
        I must uneasy make, lest too light winning
        Make the prize light. — One word more! I charge thee
        That thou attend me. Thou dost here usurp
        The name thou ow'st[46] not, and hast put thyself
        Upon this island as a spy, to win it
        From me, the lord on 't.

---

44 i.e., exchanged loving glances. 45 i.e., done (or said) something mistaken. 46 ownest.

FERDINAND: No, as I am a man!

MIRANDA: There's nothing ill can dwell in such a temple.
If the ill spirit have so fair a house,
Good things will strive to dwell with 't.

460 PROSPERO: Follow me. —
Speak not you for him; he's a traitor. — Come!
I'll manacle thy neck and feet together;
Sea water shalt thou drink; thy food shall be
The fresh-brook mussels, wither'd roots, and husks
Wherein the acorn cradled. Follow.

FERDINAND: No.
I will resist such entertainment till
Mine enemy has more power.

(He draws, and is charmed from moving.)

MIRANDA: O dear father,
Make not too rash a trial of him, for
He's gentle, and not fearful.

PROSPERO: What, I say,
470 My foot[47] my tutor? — Put thy sword up, traitor!
Who mak'st a show but dar'st not strike, thy conscience
Is so possess'd with guilt. Come, from thy ward![48]
For I can here disarm thee with this stick
And make thy weapon drop.

MIRANDA: Beseech you, father!

PROSPERO: Hence! Hang not on my garments.

MIRANDA: Sir, have pity.
I'll be his surety.

PROSPERO: Silence! One word more
Shall make me chide thee, if not hate thee. What,
An advocate for an impostor? Hush!
Thou think'st there is no more such shapes as he,
480 Having seen but him and Caliban. Foolish wench!
To th' most of men this is a Caliban,
And they to him are angels.

MIRANDA: My affections
Are then most humble. I have no ambition
To see a goodlier man.

PROSPERO: [*To* FERDINAND] Come on, obey!
Thy nerves[49] are in their infancy again
And have no vigour in them.

FERDINAND: So they are.
My spirits, as in a dream, are all bound up.
My father's loss, the weakness which I feel,
The wrack of all my friends, nor this man's threats
490 To whom I am subdu'd, are but light to me,

---

47 inferior. 48 defensive posture; this is the challenge, "On guard!" 49 sinews.

Might I but through my prison once a day
Behold this maid. All corners else o' th' earth
Let liberty make use of. Space enough
Have I in such a prison.
PROSPERO: [aside]   It works. [To FERDINAND] Come on.—
Thou hast done well, fine Ariel! [To FERDINAND] Follow me.—
[To ARIEL] Hark what thou else shalt do me.
MIRANDA: Be of comfort.
My father's of a better nature, sir,
Than he appears by speech. This is unwonted
Which now came from him.
PROSPERO: Thou shalt be as free
500 As mountain winds; but then exactly do
All points of my command.
ARIEL: To th' syllable.
PROSPERO: Come, follow.— Speak not for him.

(Exeunt.)

ACT TWO

SCENE 1. [*Another part of the island.*]

(*Enter* ALONSO, SEBASTIAN, ANTONIO, GONZALO, ADRIAN, FRANCISCO, *and others.*)

GONZALO: Beseech you, sir, be merry. You have cause
(So have we all) of joy; for our escape
Is much beyond our loss. Our hint of woe
Is common. Every day some sailor's wife,
The masters of some merchant,[1] and the merchant,
Have just our theme of woe; but for the miracle,
I mean our preservation, few in millions
Can speak like us. Then wisely, good sir, weigh
Our sorrow with our comfort.
ALONSO: Prithee peace.
10 SEBASTIAN: He receives comfort like cold porridge.
ANTONIO: The visitor[2] will not give him o'er so.
SEBASTIAN: Look, he's winding up the watch of his wit; by and by it will strike.
GONZALO: Sir —
SEBASTIAN: One. Tell.[3]
GONZALO: When every grief is entertain'd,
    That's offer'd comes to th' entertainer —
SEBASTIAN: A dollar.
GONZALO: Dolour comes to him, indeed. You have spoken truer than you
    purpos'd.

---

1 i.e., merchant ship. 2 spiritual adviser (sarcastic reference to Gonzalo). 3 count.

20 SEBASTIAN: You have taken it wiselier than I meant you should.

GONZALO: Therefore, my lord —

ANTONIO: Fie, what a spendthrift is he of his tongue!

ALONSO: I prithee spare.

GONZALO: Well, I have done. But yet —

SEBASTIAN: He will be talking.

ANTONIO: Which, of he or Adrian, for a good wager, first begins to crow?

SEBASTIAN: The old cock.[4]

ANTONIO: The cock'rel.[5]

SEBASTIAN: Done! The wager?

30 ANTONIO: A laughter.

SEBASTIAN: A match!

ADRIAN: Though this island seem to be desert —

ANTONIO: Ha, ha, ha!

SEBASTIAN: So, you're paid.

ADRIAN: Uninhabitable and almost inaccessible —

SEBASTIAN: Yet —

ADRIAN: Yet —

ANTONIO: He could not miss 't.

ADRIAN: It must needs be of subtle, tender, and delicate temperance.

40 ANTONIO: Temperance was a delicate wench.

SEBASTIAN: Ay, and a subtle, as he most learnedly deliver'd.

ADRIAN: The air breathes upon us here most sweetly.

SEBASTIAN: As if it had lungs, and rotten ones.

ANTONIO: Or as 'twere perfum'd by a fen.

GONZALO: Here is everything advantageous to life.

ANTONIO: True; save means to live.

SEBASTIAN: Of that there's none, or little.

GONZALO: How lush and lusty the grass looks! how green!

ANTONIO: The ground indeed is tawny.

50 SEBASTIAN: With an eye[6] of green in 't.

ANTONIO: He misses not much.

SEBASTIAN: No; he doth but mistake the truth totally.

GONZALO: But the rarity of it is — which is indeed almost beyond credit —

SEBASTIAN: As many vouch'd rarities are.

GONZALO: That our garments, being, as they were, drench'd in the sea, hold, notwithstanding, their freshness and glosses, being rather new-dy'd than stain'd with salt water.

ANTONIO: If but one of his pockets could speak, would it not say he lies?

SEBASTIAN: Ay, or very falsely pocket up his report.

60 GONZALO: Methinks our garments are now as fresh as when we put them on first in Afric, at the marriage of the King's fair daughter Claribel to the King of Tunis.

SEBASTIAN: 'Twas a sweet marriage, and we prosper well in our return.

ADRIAN: Tunis was never grac'd before with such a paragon to their queen.

GONZALO: Not since widow Dido's time.

---

4 i.e., Gonzalo. 5 i.e., Adrian. 6 spot.

ANTONIO: Widow? A pox o' that! How came that "widow" in?
　Widow Dido![7]

SEBASTIAN: What if he had said "widower Aeneas" too? Good Lord, how you
　take it!

70　ADRIAN: "Widow Dido," said you? You make me study of that. She was of
　Carthage, not of Tunis.

GONZALO: This Tunis, sir, was Carthage.

ADRIAN: Carthage?

GONZALO: I assure you, Carthage.

ANTONIO: His word is more than the miraculous harp.[8]

SEBASTIAN: He hath rais'd the wall, and houses too.

ANTONIO: What impossible matter will he make easy next?

SEBASTIAN: I think he will carry this island home in his pocket and give it his
　son for an apple.

80　ANTONIO: And, sowing the kernels of it in the sea, bring forth more islands.

GONZALO: Ay!

ANTONIO: Why, in good time!

GONZALO: Sir, we were talking that our garments seem now as fresh as when we
　were at Tunis at the marriage of your daughter, who is now Queen.

ANTONIO: And the rarest that e'er came there.

SEBASTIAN: Bate,[9] I beseech you, widow Dido.

ANTONIO: O, widow Dido? Ay, widow Dido!

GONZALO: Is not, sir, my doublet as fresh as the first day I wore it?
　I mean, in a sort.

90　ANTONIO: That "sort" was well fish'd for.

GONZALO: When I wore it at your daughter's marriage.

ALONSO: You cram these words into mine ears against
　The stomach[10] of my sense. Would I had never
　Married my daughter there! for, coming thence,
　My son is lost; and, in my rate,[11] she too,
　Who is so far from Italy remov'd
　I ne'er again shall see her. O thou mine heir
　Of Naples and of Milan, what strange fish
　Hath made his meal on thee?

FRANCISCO:　　　　　　　　　　　Sir, he may live.

100　I saw him beat the surges under him
　And ride upon their backs. He trod the water,
　Whose enmity he flung aside, and breasted
　The surge most swol'n that met him. His bold head
　'Bove the contentious waves he kept, and oar'd
　Himself with his good arms in lusty stroke
　To th' shore, that o'er his wave-worn basis bow'd,
　As stooping to relieve him. I not doubt
　He came alive to land.

7 Dido, queen of Carthage and lover of Aeneas, is not usually thought of as widow of Sichaeus.
8 in mythology, the music of the harp of Amphion rebuilt the walls of Thebes. (Antonio and Sebastian make
fun of Gonzalo's error in associating modern Tunis with ancient Carthage.) 9 except. 10 desire. 11 opinion.

ALONSO: No, no, he's gone.
SEBASTIAN: Sir, you may thank yourself for this great loss,
110   That would not bless our Europe with your daughter,
           But rather loose her to an African,
           Where she, at least, is banish'd from your eye
           Who hath cause to wet the grief on 't.
ALONSO: Prithee peace.
SEBASTIAN: You were kneel'd to and importun'd otherwise
           By all of us; and the fair soul herself
           Weigh'd, between loathness and obedience, at
           Which end o' th' beam should bow. We have lost your son,
           I fear, for ever. Milan and Naples have
           Moe [12] widows in them of this business' making
120   Than we bring men to comfort them.
           The fault's your own.
ALONSO: So is the dear'st o' th' loss.
GONZALO: My Lord Sebastian,
           The truth you speak doth lack some gentleness,
           And time to speak it in. You rub the sore
           When you should bring the plaster.
SEBASTIAN: Very well.
ANTONIO: And most chirurgeonly. [13]
GONZALO: It is foul weather in us all, good sir,
           When you are cloudy.
SEBASTIAN: Foul weather?
ANTONIO: Very foul.
GONZALO: Had I plantation of this isle, my lord —
ANTONIO: He'd sow 't with nettle seed.
130 SEBASTIAN: Or docks, or mallows.
GONZALO: And were the king on 't, what would I do?
SEBASTIAN: Scape being drunk, for want of wine.
GONZALO: I' th' commonwealth I would by contraries [14]
           Execute all things; for no kind of traffic [15]
           Would I admit; no name of magistrate;
           Letters should not be known; riches, poverty,
           And use of service, [16] none; contract, succession,
           Bourn, [17] bound of land, tilth, [18] vineyard, none;
           No use of metal, corn, or wine, or oil;
140   No occupation; all men idle, all;
           And women too, but innocent and pure;
           No sovereignty.
SEBASTIAN: Yet he would be king on 't.
ANTONIO: The latter end of his commonwealth forgets the beginning.
GONZALO: All things in common nature should produce
           Without sweat or endeavour. Treason, felony,

---

12 more. 13 like a surgeon. 14 i.e., by the opposite of customary practices. 15 business, trade. 16 servants.
17 division of land among individual owners. 18 tillage, agriculture.

Sword, pike, knife, gun, or need of any engine
Would I not have; but nature should bring forth,
Of its own kind, all foison,[19] all abundance,
To feed my innocent people.

150 SEBASTIAN: No marrying mong his subjects?

ANTONIO: None, man! All idle — whores and knaves.

GONZALO: I would with such perfection govern, sir,
    T' excel the golden age.

SEBASTIAN: Save his Majesty!

ANTONIO: Long live Gonzalo!

GONZALO: And — do you mark me, sir?

ALONSO: Prithee no more. Thou dost talk nothing to me.

GONZALO: I do well believe your Highness; and did it to minister[20] occasion to
    these gentlemen, who are of such sensible and nimble lungs that they
    always use to laugh at nothing.

ANTONIO: 'Twas you we laugh'd at.

160 GONZALO: Who in this kind of merry fooling am nothing to you. So you may
    continue, and laugh at nothing still.

ANTONIO: What a blow was there given!

SEBASTIAN: An[21] it had not fall'n flatlong.[22]

GONZALO: You are gentlemen of brave metal. You would lift the moon out of
    her sphere if she would continue in it five weeks without changing.

(Enter ARIEL, *[invisible,] playing solemn music.)*

SEBASTIAN: We would so, and then go a-batfowling.[23]

ANTONIO: Nay, good my lord, be not angry.

GONZALO: No, I warrant you. I will not adventure my discretion so weakly.
    Will you laugh me asleep, for I am very heavy?

170 ANTONIO: Go sleep, and hear us.

[All sleep except ALONSO, SEBASTIAN, *and* ANTONIO.]

ALONSO: What, all so soon asleep? I wish mine eyes
    Would, with themselves, shut up my thoughts. I find
    They are inclin'd to do so.

SEBASTIAN: Please you, sir,
    Do not omit[24] the heavy offer of it.
    It seldom visits sorrow; when it doth,
    It is a comforter.

ANTONIO: We two, my lord,
    Will guard your person while you take your rest,
    And watch your safety.

ALONSO: Thank you. Wondrous heavy.

*[*ALONSO *sleeps. Exit* ARIEL.]

SEBASTIAN: What a strange drowsiness possesses them!

---

19 plenty. 20 provide. 21 if. 22 along the flat of the blade (as opposed to the slicing edge). 23 knocking
birds out of the air after attracting them with a light. 24 neglect.

ANTONIO: It is the quality o' th' climate.

180 SEBASTIAN: Why
Doth it not then our eyelids sink? I find not
Myself dispos'd to sleep.

ANTONIO: Nor I. My spirits are nimble.
They fell together all, as by consent.
They dropp'd as by a thunder-stroke. What might,
Worthy Sebastian — O, what might? — No more!
And yet methinks I see it in thy face,
What thou shouldst be. Th' occasion speaks thee, and
My strong imagination sees a crown
Dropping upon thy head.

SEBASTIAN: What? Art thou waking?

ANTONIO: Do you not hear me speak?

190 SEBASTIAN: I do; and surely
It is a sleepy language, and thou speak'st
Out of thy sleep. What is it thou didst say?
This is a strange repose, to be asleep
With eyes wide open; standing, speaking, moving —
And yet so fast asleep.

ANTONIO: Noble Sebastian,
Thou let'st thy fortune sleep — die, rather; wink'st
Whiles thou art waking.

SEBASTIAN: Thou dost snore distinctly;
There's meaning in thy snores.

ANTONIO: I am more serious than my custom. You

200 Must be so too, if heed me; which to do
Trebles[25] thee o'er.

SEBASTIAN: Well, I am standing water.

ANTONIO: I'll teach you how to flow.

SEBASTIAN: Do so. To ebb
Hereditary sloth instructs me.

ANTONIO: O,
If you but knew how you the purpose[26] cherish
Whiles thus you mock it; how, in stripping it,
You more invest it! Ebbing men indeed
(Most often) do so near the bottom run
By their own fear or sloth.

SEBASTIAN: Prithee say on.
The setting of thine eye and cheek proclaim

210 A matter from thee; and a birth, indeed,
Which throes[27] thee much to yield.

ANTONIO: Thus, sir:
Although this lord[28] of weak remembrance, this
Who shall be of as little memory
When he is earth'd,[29] hath here almost persuaded

---

25 triples (in influence, prestige over Antonio, Ferdinand, Alonso).   26 i.e., the gaining of political power.
27 pains, discomforts.   28 i.e., Gonzalo.   29 buried.

(For he's a spirit of persuasion, only
Professes to persuade) the King his son's alive,
'Tis as impossible that he's undrown'd
As he that sleeps here swims.

SEBASTIAN: I have no hope
That he's undrown'd.

ANTONIO: O, out of that no hope
220   What great hope have you! No hope that way is
Another way so high a hope that even
Ambition cannot pierce a wink beyond,
But doubt discovery there. Will you grant with me
That Ferdinand is drown'd?

SEBASTIAN: He's gone.

ANTONIO: Then tell me,
Who's the next heir of Naples?

SEBASTIAN: Claribel.

ANTONIO: She that is Queen of Tunis; she that dwells
Ten leagues beyond man's life; she that from Naples
Can have no note, unless the sun were post[30]—
The man i' th' moon 's too slow — till new-born chins
230   Be rough and razorable; she that from whom
We all were sea-swallow'd, though some cast[31] again,
And, by that destiny, to perform an act
Whereof what's past is prologue, what to come,
In yours and my discharge.[32]

SEBASTIAN: What stuff is this? How say you?
'Tis true my brother's daughter's Queen of Tunis;
So is she heir of Naples; 'twixt which regions
There is some space.

ANTONIO: A space whose ev'ry cubit
Seems to cry out "How shall that Claribel
Measure us back to Naples? Keep in Tunis,
240   And let Sebastian wake!" Say this were death
That now hath seiz'd them, why, they were no worse
Than now they are. There be that can rule Naples
As well as he that sleeps; lords that can prate
As amply and unnecessarily
As this Gonzalo. I myself could make
A chough[33] of as deep chat. O, that you bore
The mind that I do! What a sleep were this
For your advancement! Do you understand me?

SEBASTIAN: Methinks I do.

ANTONIO: And how does your content[34]
Tender your own good fortune?

250   SEBASTIAN: I remember
You did supplant your brother Prospero.

---

30 messenger. 31 cast upon shore, cast for performance. 32 action, performance. 33 member of the crow
family; birds that can be taught to mimic a few words. 34 inclination.

ANTONIO: True.
    And look how well my garments sit upon me,
    Much feater[35] than before! My brother's servants
    Were then my fellows; now they are my men.

SEBASTIAN: But, for your conscience —

ANTONIO: Ay, sir! Where lies that? If 'twere a kibe,[36]
    'Twould put me to my slipper; but I feel not
    This deity in my bosom. Twenty consciences
    That stand 'twixt me and Milan, candied be they

260   And melt, ere they molest! Here lies your brother,
    No better than the earth he lies upon
    If he were that which now he's like — that's dead;
    Whom I with this obedient steel (three inches of it)
    Can lay to bed for ever; whiles you, doing thus,
    To the perpetual wink[37] for aye might put
    This ancient morsel, this Sir Prudence, who
    Should not upbraid our course. For all the rest,
    They'll take suggestion as a cat laps milk;
    They'll tell the clock to any business that
    We say befits the hour.

270 SEBASTIAN: Thy case, dear friend,
    Shall be my precedent. As thou got'st Milan,
    I'll come by Naples. Draw thy sword. One stroke
    Shall free thee from the tribute which thou payest,
    And I the King shall love thee.

ANTONIO: Draw together;
    And when I rear my hand, do you the like,
    To fall it on Gonzalo. [*They draw.*]

SEBASTIAN: O, but one word!

    [*They converse apart.*]

    (*Enter* ARIEL, [*invisible,*] *with music and song.*)

ARIEL: My master through his art foresees the danger
    That you, his friend, are in, and sends me forth
    (For else his project dies) to keep them living.

    (*Sings in* GONZALO's *ear.*)

280   While you here do snoring lie,
    Open-ey'd conspiracy
       His time doth take.
    If of life you keep a care,
    Shake off slumber and beware.
       Awake, Awake!

ANTONIO: Then let us both be sudden.

---

35 better, more appropriately. 36 chilblain. 37 sleep.

GONZALO: [*wakes*]   Now good angels
    Preserve the King! [*The others wake.*]
ALONSO: Why, how now? Ho, awake!—Why are you drawn?
    Wherefore this ghastly looking?
GONZALO: What's the matter?
290   SEBASTIAN: Whiles we stood here securing your repose,
    Even now, we heard a hollow burst of bellowing
    Like bulls, or rather lions. Did 't not wake you?
    It struck mine ear most terribly.
ALONSO: I heard nothing.
ANTONIO: O, 'twas a din to fright a monster's ear,
    To make an earthquake! Sure it was the roar
    Of a whole herd of lions.
ALONSO: Heard you this, Gonzalo?
GONZALO: Upon mine honour, sir, I heard a humming,
    And that a strange one too, which did awake me.
    I shak'd you, sir, and cried. As mine eyes open'd,
300   I saw their weapons drawn. There was a noise;
    That's verily.[38] 'Tis best we stand upon our guard,
    Or that we quit this place. Let's draw our weapons.
ALONSO: Lead off this ground, and let's make further search
    For my poor son.
GONZALO: Heavens keep him from these beasts!
    For he is sure i' th' island.
ALONSO: Lead away.
ARIEL: Prospero my lord shall know what I have done.
    So, King, go safely on to seek thy son. (*Exeunt.*)

SCENE 2. [*Another part of the island.*]

(*Enter* CALIBAN *with a burden of wood. A noise of thunder heard.*)

CALIBAN: All the infections that the sun sucks up
    From bogs, fens, flats, on Prosper fall and make him
    By inchmeal[1] a disease! His spirits hear me,
    And yet I needs must curse. But they'll nor pinch,
    Fright me with urchin-shows,[2] pitch me i' th' mire,
    Nor lead me, like a firebrand,[3] in the dark
    Out of my way, unless he bid 'em; but
    For every trifle are they set upon me;
    Sometime like apes that mow[4] and chatter at me,
10   And after bite me; then like hedgehogs which
    Lie tumbling in my barefoot way and mount
    Their pricks at my footfall; sometime am I
    All wound with adders, who with cloven tongues

38 true.
1 i.e., inch by inch. 2 goblin-like hallucinations. 3 will-o'-the-wisp, *ignis fatuus*—bizarre light effects of swamp gas. 4 scowl, grimace.

Do hiss me into madness.

(*Enter* TRINCULO.)

> Lo, now, lo!
> Here comes a spirit of his, and to torment me
> For bringing wood in slowly. I'll fall flat.
> Perchance he will not mind me. [*Lies down.*]

TRINCULO: Here's neither bush nor shrub to bear[5] off any weather at all, and another storm brewing. I hear it sing i' th' wind. Yond same black cloud, yond huge one, looks like a foul bombard[6] that would shed his liquor. If it should thunder as it did before, I know not where to hide my head. Yond same cloud cannot choose but fall by pailfuls. What have we here? a man or a fish? dead or alive? A fish: he smells like a fish; a very ancient and fishlike smell; a kind of, not of the newest, poor-John.[7] A strange fish! Were I in England now, as once I was, and had but this fish painted, not a holiday fool there but would give a piece of silver. There would this monster make a man. Any strange beast there makes a man. When they will not give a doit[8] to relieve a lame beggar, they will lay out ten to see a dead Indian. Legg'd like a man! and his fins like arms! Warm, o' my troth! I do now let loose my opinion, hold it no longer: this is no fish, but an islander, that hath lately suffered by a thunderbolt. [*Thunder.*] Alas, the storm is come again! My best way is to creep under his gaberdine. There is no other shelter hereabout. Misery acquaints a man with strange bedfellows. I will here shroud till the dregs of the storm be past. [*Creeps under* CALIBAN'S *garment.*]

(*Enter* STEPHANO, *singing*; [*a bottle in his hand*].)

STEPHANO: I shall no more to sea, to sea;
Here shall I die ashore.
This is a very scurvy tune to sing at a man's funeral.
Well, here's my comfort. (*Drinks.*)

> The master, the swabber, the boatswain, and I,
>   The gunner, and his mate,
> Lov'd Mall, Meg, and Marian, and Margery,
>   But none of us car'd for Kate.
>   For she had a tongue with a tang,
>   Would cry to a sailor "Go hang!"
> She lov'd not the savour of tar nor of pitch;
>   Yet a tailor might scratch her where'er she did itch.
>   Then to sea, boys, and let her go hang!

This is a scurvy tune too; but here's my comfort. (*Drinks.*)

CALIBAN: Do not torment me! O!

STEPHANO: What's the matter? Have we devils here? Do you put tricks upon 's with salvages and men of Inde, ha? I have not scap'd drowning to be afeared now of your four legs; for it hath been said, "As proper a man as ever went

---

5 ward. 6 leather jug. 7 dried cod or hake. 8 coin.

on four legs cannot make him give ground"; and it shall be said so again, while Stephano breathes at' nostrils.

CALIBAN: The spirit torments me. O!

STEPHANO: This is some monster of the isle, with four legs, who hath got, as I take it, an ague.[9] Where the devil should he learn our language? I will give him some relief, if it be but for that. If I can recover him, and keep him tame, and get to Naples with him, he's a present for any emperor that ever trod on neat's leather.[10]

CALIBAN: Do not torment me prithee! I'll bring my wood home faster.

STEPHANO: He's in his fit now and does not talk after the wisest. He shall taste of my bottle. If he have never drunk wine afore, it will go near to remove his fit. If I can recover him and keep him tame, I will not take too much for him; he shall pay for him that hath him, and that soundly.

CALIBAN: Thou dost me yet but little hurt.
Thou wilt anon;[11] I know it by thy trembling.
Now Prosper works upon thee.

STEPHANO: Come on your ways. Open your mouth. Here is that which will give language to you, cat. Open your mouth. This will shake your shaking, I can tell you, and that soundly. [*Gives* CALIBAN *drink.*] You cannot tell who's your friend. Open your chaps[12] again.

TRINCULO: I should know that voice. It should be — but he is drown'd; and these are devils. O, defend me!

STEPHANO: Four legs and two voices — a most delicate monster! His forward voice now is to speak well of his friend; his backward voice is to utter foul speeches and to detract. If all the wine in my bottle will recover him, I will help his ague. Come! [*Gives drink.*] Amen! I will pour some in thy other mouth.

TRINCULO: Stephano!

STEPHANO: Doth thy other mouth call me? Mercy, mercy! This is a devil, and no monster. I will leave him; I have no long spoon.[13]

TRINCULO: Stephano! If thou beest Stephano, touch me and speak to me; for I am Trinculo — be not afeard — thy good friend Trinculo.

STEPHANO: If thou beest Trinculo, come forth. I'll pull thee by the lesser legs. If any be Trinculo's legs, these are they. [*Draws him out from under* CALIBAN'S *garment.*] Thou art very Trinculo indeed! How cam'st thou to be the siege[14] of this mooncalf? Can he vent Trinculos?

TRINCULO: I took him to be kill'd with a thunderstroke. But art thou not drown'd, Stephano? I hope now thou art not drown'd. Is the storm overblown? I hid me under the dead mooncalf's gaberdine for fear of the storm. And art thou living, Stephano? O Stephano, two Neapolitans scap'd?

STEPHANO: Prithee do not turn me about. My stomach is not constant.

CALIBAN: [*aside*] These be fine things, an if they be not sprites.
That's a brave god and bears celestial liquor.
I will kneel to him.

STEPHANO: How didst thou scape? How cam'st thou hither? Swear by this bottle how thou cam'st hither. I escap'd upon a butt of sack which the

---

9 fever. 10 cowhide. 11 soon. 12 chops, jaws. 13 proverbial: He who eats with the Devil must have a long spoon. 14 excrement.

100   sailor's heaved o'erboard, by this bottle! which I made of the bark of a tree with mine own hands since I was cast ashore.

CALIBAN: I'll swear upon that bottle to be thy true subject, for the liquor is not earthly.

STEPHANO: Here! Swear then how thou escap'dst.

TRINCULO: Swum ashore, man, like a duck. I can swim like a duck, I'll be sworn.

STEPHANO: Here, kiss the book. [*Gives him drink.*] Though thou canst swim like a duck, thou art made like a goose.

TRINCULO: O Stephano, hast any more of this?

110   STEPHANO: The whole butt, man. My cellar is in a rock by th' seaside, where my wine is hid. How now, mooncalf? How does thine ague?

CALIBAN: Hast thou not dropp'd from heaven?

STEPHANO: Out o' th' moon, I do assure thee. I was the Man i' th' Moon when time was.[15]

CALIBAN: I have seen thee in her, and I do adore thee.
    My mistress show'd me thee, and thy dog, and thy bush.[16]

STEPHANO: Come, swear to that; kiss the book. I will furnish it anon with new contents. Swear. [CALIBAN *drinks.*]

TRINCULO: By this good light, this is a very shallow monster! I afeard of him?
    A very weak monster! The Man i' th' Moon? A most poor credulous monster!

120   Well drawn,[17] monster, in good sooth.

CALIBAN: I'll show thee every fertile inch o' th' island;
    And I will kiss thy foot. I prithee be my god.

TRINCULO: By this light, a most perfidious and drunken monster!
    When's god's asleep he'll rob his bottle.

CALIBAN: I'll kiss thy foot. I'll swear myself thy subject.

STEPHANO: Come on then. Down, and swear!

TRINCULO: I shall laugh myself to death at this puppy-headed monster. A most scurvy monster! I could find in my heart to beat him —

STEPHANO: Come, kiss.

130   TRINCULO: But that the poor monster 's in drink. An abominable monster!

CALIBAN: I'll show thee the best springs; I'll pluck thee berries;
    I'll fish for thee, and get thee wood enough.
    A plague upon the tyrant that I serve!
    I'll bear him no more sticks, but follow thee,
    Thou wondrous man.

TRINCULO: A most ridiculous monster, to make a wonder of a poor drunkard!

CALIBAN: I prithee let me bring thee where crabs[18] grow;
    And I with my long nails will dig thee pignuts,[19]
    Show thee a jay's nest, and instruct thee how

140   To snare the nimble marmoset; I'll bring thee
    To clust'ring filberts, and sometimes I'll get thee
    Young scamels[20] from the rock. Wilt thou go with me?

---

15 i.e., once upon a time. 16 legendary: The Man in the Moon, along with his dog and some brushwood, was banished from earth for gathering firewood on Sunday. 17 drunk. 18 crab apples. 19 peanuts. 20 sea birds (perhaps shellfish).

STEPHANO: I prithee now lead the way without any more talking. Trinculo, the King and all our company else being drown'd, we will inherit here. Here, bear my bottle. Fellow Trinculo, we'll fill him by-and-by again.

(CALIBAN *sings drunkenly.*)

CALIBAN: Farewell, master; farewell, farewell!
TRINCULO: A howling monster! a drunken monster!
CALIBAN: No more dams I'll make for fish,
    Nor fetch in firing
150   At requiring,
    Nor scrape trenchering,[21] nor wash dish.
    'Ban, 'Ban, Ca — Caliban
    Has a new master. Get a new man.

Freedom, high-day! high-day, freedom! freedom, high-day, freedom!
STEPHANO: O brave monster! lead the way. (*Exeunt.*)

ACT THREE

SCENE 1. [*Before* PROSPERO'S *cell.*]

(*Enter* FERDINAND, *bearing a log.*)

FERDINAND: There be some sports are painful, and their labour
    Delight in them sets off; some kinds of baseness
    Are nobly undergone, and most poor matters
    Point to rich ends. This my mean task
    Would be as heavy to me as odious, but
    The mistress which I serve quickens[1] what's dead
    And makes my labours pleasures. O, she is
    Ten times more gentle than her father's crabbed;
    And he's compos'd of harshness! I must remove
10   Some thousands of these logs and pile them up,
    Upon a sore injection.[2] My sweet mistress
    Weeps when she sees me work, and says such baseness
    Had never like executor. I forget;
    But these sweet thoughts do even refresh my labours
    Most busy, least when I do it.

(*Enter* MIRANDA; *and* PROSPERO [*behind, unseen*].)

MIRANDA: Alas, now pray you
    Work not so hard! I would the lightning had
    Burnt up those logs that you are enjoin'd to pile!
    Pray set it down and rest you. When this burns,

---

21 wooden plates and bowls.
1 enlivens. 2 harsh command.

'Twill weep[3] for having wearied you. My father
20   Is hard at study. Pray now rest yourself.
He's safe for these three hours.

FERDINAND: O most dear mistress,
The sun will set before I shall discharge
What I must strive to do.

MIRANDA: If you'll sit down,
I'll bear your logs the while. Pray give me that.
I'll carry it to the pile.

FERDINAND: No, precious creature.
I had rather crack my sinews, break my back,
Than you should such dishonour undergo
While I sit lazy by.

MIRANDA: It would become me
As well as it does you; and I should do it
30   With much more ease; for my good will is to it,
And yours it is against.

PROSPERO: [*aside*]   Poor worm, thou art infected!
This visitation shows it.

MIRANDA: You look wearily.

FERDINAND: No, noble mistress. 'Tis fresh morning with me
When you are by at night. I do beseech you,
Chiefly that I might set it in my prayers,
What is your name?

MIRANDA: Miranda. O my father,
I have broke your hest[4] to say so!

FERDINAND: Admir'd Miranda!
Indeed the top of admiration, worth
What's dearest to the world! Full many a lady
40   I have ey'd with best regard, and many a time
Th' harmony of their tongues hath into bondage
Brought my too diligent ear; for several virtues
Have I lik'd several women; never any
With so full soul but some defect in her
Did quarrel with the noblest grace she ow'd,[5]
And put it to the foil; but you, O you,
So perfect and so peerless, are created
Of every creature's best!

MIRANDA: I do not know
One of my sex; no woman's face remember,
50   Save, from my glass, mine own; nor have I seen
More that I may call men than you, good friend,
And my dear father. How features are abroad
I am skilless[6] of; but, by my modesty
(The jewel in my dower), I would not wish
Any companion in the world but you;

3 i.e., run sap. 4 behest, command. 5 owned. 6 ignorant.

Nor can imagination form a shape,
Besides yourself, to like of.[7] But I prattle
Something too wildly, and my father's precepts
I therein do forget.

FERDINAND: I am, in my condition,
60   A prince, Miranda; I do think, a king
(I would not so!), and would no more endure
This wooden slavery than to suffer
The flesh-fly blow my mouth. Hear my soul speak!
The very instant that I saw you, did
My heart fly to your service; there resides,
To make me slave to it; and for your sake
Am I this patient log-man.

MIRANDA: Do you love me?

FERDINAND: O heaven, O earth, bear witness to this sound,
And crown what I profess with kind event[8]
70   If I speak true! if hollowly, invert
What best is boded[9] me to mischief! I,
Beyond all limit of what else i' th' world,
Do love, prize, honour you.

MIRANDA: I am a fool
To weep at what I am glad of.

PROSPERO: [aside]   Fair encounter
Of two most rare affections! Heavens rain grace
On that which breeds between 'em!

FERDINAND: Wherefore weep you?

MIRANDA: At mine unworthiness, that dare not offer
What I desire to give, and much less take
What I shall die to want. But this is trifling;
80   And all the more it seeks to hide itself,
The bigger bulk it shows. Hence, bashful cunning!
And prompt me plain and holy innocence!
I am your wife, if you will marry me;
If not, I'll die your maid. To be your fellow[10]
You may deny me; but I'll be your servant,
Whether you will or no.

FERDINAND: My mistress, dearest!
And I thus humble ever.

MIRANDA: My husband then?

FERDINAND: Ay, with a heart as willing
As bondage e'er of freedom. Here's my hand.
90   MIRANDA: And mine, with my heart in't; and now farewell
Till half an hour hence.

FERDINAND: A thousand thousand!

(Exeunt [FERDINAND and MIRANDA severally[11]].)

---

7 i.e., to like, admire. 8 outcome. 9 destined, promised by fate. 10 friend. 11 i.e., in different directions.

PROSPERO: So glad of this as they I cannot be,
    Who are surpris'd withal; but my rejoicing
    At nothing can be more. I'll to my book;
    For yet ere supper time must I perform
    Much business appertaining.

    (Exit.)

SCENE 2. [*Another part of the island.*]

    (Enter CALIBAN, STEPHANO, *and* TRINCULO.*)*

STEPHANO: Tell not me! When the butt is out, we will drink water; not a drop before. Therefore bear up and board 'em![1] Servant monster, drink to me.

TRINCULO: Servant monster? The folly of this island! They say there's but five upon this isle. We are three of them. If th' other two be brain'd like us, the state totters.

STEPHANO: Drink, servant monster, when I bid thee. Thy eyes are almost set in thy head.

TRINCULO: Where should they be set else? He were a brave monster indeed if they were set in his tail.

10 STEPHANO: My man-monster hath drown'd his tongue in sack. For my part, the sea cannot drown me. I swam, ere I could recover the shore, five-and-thirty leagues off and on, by this light. Thou shalt be my lieutenant, monster, or my standard.[2]

TRINCULO: Your lieutenant, if you list; he's no standard.

STEPHANO: We'll not run, Monsieur Monster.

TRINCULO: Nor go neither; but you'll lie like dogs, and yet say nothing neither.

STEPHANO: Mooncalf, speak once in thy life, if thou beest a good mooncalf.

CALIBAN: How does thy honour? Let me lick thy shoe.
    I'll not serve him; he is not valiant.

20 TRINCULO: Thou liest, most ignorant monster! I am in case[3] to justle a constable. Why, thou debosh'd fish thou, was there ever man a coward that hath drunk so much sack as I to-day? Wilt thou tell a monstrous lie, being but half a fish and half a monster?

CALIBAN: Lo, how he mocks me! Wilt thou let him, my lord?

TRINCULO: "Lord" quoth he? That a monster should be such a natural![4]

CALIBAN: Lo, lo, again! Bite him to death I prithee.

STEPHANO: Trinculo, keep a good tongue in your head. If you prove a mutineer — the next tree! The poor monster's my subject, and he shall not suffer indignity.

30 CALIBAN: I thank my noble lord. Wilt thou be pleas'd
    to hearken once again to the suit I made to thee?

STEPHANO: Marry,[5] will I. Kneel and repeat it; I will stand, and so shall Trinculo.

    (Enter ARIEL, *invisible.)*

---

1 i.e., Drink up! 2 standard-bearer. 3 shape, fit condition. 4 congenital idiot. 5 i.e., By the Virgin Mary (a common expletive).

CALIBAN: As I told thee before, I am subject to a tyrant,
    A sorcerer, that by his cunning hath
    Cheated me of the island.
ARIEL: Thou liest.
CALIBAN: Thou liest, thou jesting monkey thou!
    I would my valiant master would destroy thee.
    I do not lie.
STEPHANO: Trinculo, if you trouble him any more in 's tale, by this hand, I will
40   supplant some of your teeth.
TRINCULO: Why, I said nothing.
STEPHANO: Mum then, and no more. — Proceed.
CALIBAN: I say by sorcery he got this isle;
    From me he got it. If thy greatness will
    Revenge it on him — for I know thou dar'st,
    But this thing[6] dare not —
STEPHANO: That's most certain.
CALIBAN: Thou shalt be lord of it, and I'll serve thee.
STEPHANO: How now shall this be compass'd?
50   Canst thou bring me to the party?
CALIBAN: Yea, yea, my lord! I'll yield him thee asleep,
    Where thou mayst knock a nail into his head.
ARIEL: Thou liest; thou canst not.
CALIBAN: What a pied[7] ninny's this! Thou scurvy patch![8]
    I do beseech thy greatness give him blows
    And take his bottle from him. When that's gone,
    He shall drink naught but brine, for I'll not show him
    Where the quick freshes[9] are.
STEPHANO: Trinculo, run into no further danger. Interrupt the monster one
60   word further and, by this hand, I'll turn my mercy out o' doors and make
        a stockfish[10] of thee.
TRINCULO: Why, what did I? I did nothing. I'll go farther off.
STEPHANO: Didst thou not say he lied?
ARIEL: Thou liest.
STEPHANO: Do I so? Take thou that! [*Strikes* TRINCULO.] As you like this, give
    me the lie another time.
TRINCULO: I did not give the lie. Out o' your wits, and hearing too? A pox o'
    your bottle! This can sack and drinking do. A murrain[11] on your monster,
    and the devil take your fingers!
70 CALIBAN: Ha, ha, ha!
STEPHANO: Now forward with your tale. — Prithee stand further off.
CALIBAN: Beat him enough. After a little time
    I'll beat him too.
STEPHANO: Stand farther. — Come, proceed.
CALIBAN: Why, as I told thee, 'tis a custom with him
    I' th' afternoon to sleep. There thou mayst brain him,

6 i.e., Trinculo. 7 particoloured. 8 jester. 9 freshwater springs. 10 dried, pulverized fish. 11 disease
(especially of cattle).

Having first seiz'd his books, or with a log
Batter his skull, or paunch him with a stake,
Or cut his wesand[12] with thy knife. Remember
First to possess his books; for without them
80   He's but a sot, as I am, nor hath not
One spirit to command. They all do hate him
As rootedly as I. Burn but his books.
He has brave utensils (for so he calls them)
Which, when he has a house, he'll deck withal.
And that most deeply to consider is
The beauty of his daughter. He himself
Calls her a nonpareil. I never saw a woman
But only Sycorax my dam and she;
But she as far surpasseth Sycorax
As great'st does least.

90   STEPHANO: Is it so brave a lass?

CALIBAN: Ay, lord. She will become thy bed, I warrant,
And bring thee forth brave brood.

STEPHANO: Monster, I will kill this man. His daughter and I will be king and
Queen, save our Graces! and Trinculo and thyself shall be viceroys. Dost
thou like the plot, Trinculo?

TRINCULO: Excellent.

STEPHANO: Give me thy hand. I am sorry I beat thee; but while thou liv'st, keep
a good tongue in thy head.

CALIBAN: Within this half hour will he be asleep.
Wilt thou destroy him then?

100   STEPHANO: Ay, on mine honour.

ARIEL: This will I tell my master.

CALIBAN: Thou mak'st me merry; I am full of pleasure.
Let us be jocund. Will you troll[13] the catch[14]
You taught me but whilere?[15]

STEPHANO: At thy request, monster, I will do reason, any reason. Come on,
Trinculo, let us sing. (*Sings.*)

Flout 'em and scout[16] 'em
And scout 'em and flout 'em!
Thought is free.

110   CALIBAN: That's not the tune.

(ARIEL *plays the tune on a tabor*[17] *and pipe.*)

STEPHANO: What is this same?

TRINCULO: This is the tune of our catch, play'd by the picture of Nobody.

STEPHANO: If thou beest a man, show thyself in thy likeness. If thou beest a
devil, take't as thou list.

TRINCULO: O, forgive me my sins!

---

12 windpipe. 13 sing. 14 three-part song. 15 a while ago. 16 jeer, scoff. 17 small drum.

STEPHANO: He that dies pays all debts. I defy thee. Mercy upon us!

CALIBAN: Art thou afeard?

STEPHANO: No, monster, not I.

CALIBAN: Be not afeard. The isle is full of noises,
120   Sounds and sweet airs that give delight and hurt not.
      Sometimes a thousand twangling instruments
      Will hum about mine ears; and sometime voices
      That, if I then had wak'd after long sleep,
      Will make me sleep again; and then, in dreaming,
      The clouds methought would open and show riches
      Ready to drop upon me, that, when I wak'd,
      I cried to dream again.

STEPHANO: This will prove a brave kingdom to me, where I shall have my music for nothing.

130 CALIBAN: When Prospero is destroy'd.

STEPHANO: That shall be by and by. I remember the story.

TRINCULO: The sound is going away. Let's follow it, and after do our work.

STEPHANO: Lead, monster; we'll follow. I would I could see this taborer! He lays it on.

TRINCULO: Wilt come? I'll follow, Stephano. (*Exeunt.*)

SCENE 3. [*Another part of the island.*]

(*Enter* ALONSO, SEBASTIAN, ANTONIO, GONZALO, ADRIAN, FRANCISCO, *etc.*)

GONZALO: By'r Lakin,[1] I can go no further, sir!
      My old bones ache. Here's a maze trod indeed
      Through forthrights[2] and meanders. By your patience,
      I needs must rest me.

ALONSO: Old lord, I cannot blame thee,
      Who am myself attach'd with weariness
      To th' dulling of my spirits. Sit down and rest.
      Even here I will put off my hope, and keep it
      No longer for my flatterer. He is drown'd
      Whom thus we stray to find; and the sea mocks
10   Our frustrate search on land. Well, let him go.

ANTONIO: [*aside to* SEBASTIAN] I am right glad that he's so out of hope.
      Do not for one repulse forgo the purpose
      That you resolv'd t' effect.

SEBASTIAN: [*aside to* ANTONIO] The next advantage
      We will take throughly.[3]

ANTONIO: [*aside to* SEBASTIAN] Let it be tonight;
      For, now they are oppress'd with travel, they
      Will not nor cannot use such vigilance
      As when they are fresh.

SEBASTIAN: [*aside to* ANTONIO] I say tonight. No more.

1 By our Lady. 2 straight paths. 3 thoroughly.

(*Solemn and strange music; and* PROSPERO *on the top,*[4] *invisible.*)

ALONSO: What harmony is this? My good friends, hark!
GONZALO: Marvellous sweet music!

(*Enter several strange* SHAPES, *bringing in a banquet; and dance about it with gentle actions of salutations; and, inviting the* KING, *etc., to eat, they depart.*)

20 ALONSO: Give us kind keepers,[5] heavens! What were these?
SEBASTIAN: A living drollery.[6] Now I will believe
    That there are unicorns; that in Arabia
    There is one tree, the phoenix' throne; one phoenix
    At this hour reigning there.
ANTONIO: I'll believe both;
    And what does else want credit,[7] come to me,
    And I'll be sworn 'tis true. Travellers ne'er did lie,
    Though fools at home condemn 'em.
GONZALO: If in Naples
    I should report this now, would they believe me?
    If I should say, I saw such islanders
30   (For certes[8] these are people of the island),
    Who, though they are of monstrous shape, yet, note,
    Their manners are more gentle, kind, than of
    Our human generation you shall find
    Many — nay, almost any.
PROSPERO: [*aside*]   Honest lord,
    Thou hast said well; for some of you there present
    Are worse than devils.
ALONSO: I cannot too much muse[9]
    Such shapes, such gesture, and such sound, expressing
    (Although they want the use of tongue) a kind
    Of excellent dumb discourse.
PROSPERO: [*aside*]   Praise in departing.
FRANCISCO: They vanish'd strangely.
40 SEBASTIAN: No matter, since
    They have left their viands behind; for we have stomachs.
    Will 't please you taste of what is here?
ALONSO: Not I.
GONZALO: Faith, sir, you need not fear. When we were boys,
    Who would believe that there were mountaineers
    Dewlapp'd like bulls, whose throats had hanging at 'em
    Wallets of flesh?[10] or that there were such men
    Whose heads stood in their breasts? which now we find
    Each putter-out of five for one[11] will bring us
    Good warrant of.

---

4 upper stage. 5 guardian angels. 6 puppet show. 7 belief. 8 certainly. 9 wonder at. 10 i.e., goitre (from which Swiss mountaineers especially were said to suffer). 11 a traveller, whose insured deposit was repaid fivefold if alive upon return to collect it.

ALONSO: I will stand to, and feed;

50 Although my last, no matter, since I feel
The best is past. Brother, my lord the Duke,
Stand to, and do as we.

(Thunder and lightning. Enter ARIEL, *like a harpy; claps his wings upon the table; and with a quaint device the banquet vanishes.)*

ARIEL: You are three men of sin, whom destiny —
That hath to instrument[12] this lower world
And what is in 't — the never-surfeited sea
Hath caus'd to belch up you, and on this island,
Where man doth not inhabit — you 'mongst men
Being most unfit to live. I have made you mad;
And even with such-like valour men hang and drown
Their proper selves.

[ALONSO, SEBASTIAN, *etc., draw their swords.*]

60   You fools! I and my fellows
Are ministers of Fate. The elements,
Of whom your swords are temper'd, may as well
Wound the loud winds, or with bemock'd-at stabs
Kill the still-closing waters, as diminish
One dowle[13] that's in my plume. My fellow ministers
Are like invulnerable. If you could hurt,
Your swords are now too massy for your strengths
And will not be uplifted. But remember
(For that's my business to you) that you three

70 From Milan did supplant good Prospero;
Expos'd unto the sea, which hath requit it,[14]
Him and his innocent child; for which foul deed
The powers, delaying (not forgetting), have
Incens'd the seas and shores, yea, all the creatures,
Against your peace. Thee of thy son, Alonso,
They have bereft; and do pronounce by me
Ling'ring perdition (worse than any death
Can be at once) shall step by step attend
You and your ways; whose[15] wraths to guard you from,

80 Which here, in this most desolate isle, else falls
Upon your heads, is nothing but heart's sorrow[16]
And a clear life ensuing.

(He vanishes in thunder; then, to soft music, enter the SHAPES *again, and dance, with mocks and mows,*[17] *and carrying out the table.)*

PROSPERO: [*aside*] Bravely the figure of this harpy hast thou
Perform'd, my Ariel; a grace it had, devouring.[18]

---

12 i.e., as its instrument. 13 downy feather. 14 i.e., repaid the crime of supplanting Prospero. 15 i.e., the "powers" of line 73. 16 repentance. 17 mocking gestures and grimaces. 18 i.e., making the banquet disappear.

Of my instruction hast thou nothing bated[19]
In what thou hadst to say. So, with good life
And observation strange,[20] my meaner ministers[21]
Their several kinds[22] have done. My high charms work,
And these, mine enemies, are all knit up
In their distractions. They now are in my pow'r;
And in these fits I leave them, while I visit
Young Ferdinand, whom they suppose is drown'd,
And his and mine lov'd darling. [*Exit above.*]

GONZALO: I' th' name of something holy, sir, why stand you
In this strange stare?

ALONSO: O, it is monstrous, monstrous!
Methought the billows spoke and told me of it;
The winds did sing it to me; and the thunder,
That deep and dreadful organ pipe, pronounc'd
The name of Prosper. It did bass my trespass.
Therefore my son i' th' ooze is bedded; and
I'll seek him deeper than e'er plummet sounded
And with him there lie mudded. (*Exit.*)

SEBASTIAN: But one fiend at a time,
I'll fight their legions o'er![23]

ANTONIO: I'll be thy second.

(*Exeunt* [SEBASTIAN *and* ANTONIO].)

GONZALO: All three of them are desperate. Their great guilt,
Like poison given to work a great time after,
Now 'gins to bite the spirits. I do beseech you,
That are of suppler joints, follow them swiftly
And hinder them from what this ecstasy[24]
May now provoke them to.

ADRIAN: Follow, I pray you.

(*Exeunt omnes.*)

ACT FOUR

SCENE 1. [*Before* PROSPERO'S *cell.*]

(*Enter* PROSPERO, FERDINAND, *and* MIRANDA.)

PROSPERO: If I have too austerely punish'd you,
Your compensation makes amends; for I
Have given you here a third of mine own life,
Or that for which I live; who once again
I tender to thy hand. All thy vexations
Were but my trials of thy love, and thou

19 omitted. 20 i.e., close observance. 21 spirits (inferior to Ariel). 22 duties. 23 i.e., to the last. 24 madness.

Hast strangely[1] stood the test. Here, afore heaven,
I ratify this my rich gift. O Ferdinand,
Do not smile at me that I boast her off,
For thou shalt find she will outstrip all praise
And make it halt behind her.
FERDINAND: I do believe it
Against an oracle.[2]
PROSPERO: Then, as my gift, and thine own acquisition
Worthily purchas'd, take my daughter. But
If thou dost break her virgin-knot before
All sanctimonious ceremonies may
With full and holy rite be minist'red,
No sweet aspersion[3] shall the heavens let fall
To make this contract grow; but barren hate,
Sour-ey'd disdain, and discord shall bestrew
The union of your bed with weeds so loathly
That you shall hate it both. Therefore take heed,
As Hymen's[4] lamps shall light you!
FERDINAND: As I hope
For quiet days, fair issue, and long life,
With such love as 'tis now, the murkiest den,
The most opportune place, the strong'st suggestion[5]
Our worser genius can,[6] shall never melt
Mine honour into lust, to take away
The edge of that day's celebration
When I shall think or Phoebus'[7] steeds are founder'd[8]
Or Night kept chain'd below.
PROSPERO: Fairly spoke.
Sit then and talk with her; she is thine own.
What, Ariel! my industrious servant, Ariel!

(*Enter* ARIEL.)

ARIEL: What would my potent master? Here I am.
PROSPERO: Thou and thy meaner fellows your last service
Did worthily perform; and I must use you
In such another trick. Go bring the rabble,[9]
O'er whom I give thee pow'r, here to this place.
Incite them to quick motion; for I must
Bestow upon the eyes of this young couple
Some vanity of mine art. It is my promise,
And they expect it from me.
ARIEL: Presently?
PROSPERO: Ay, with a twink.
ARIEL: Before you can say "Come" and "Go,"
And breathe twice and cry, "So, so,"

---

1 wonderfully, remarkably. 2 i.e., even though an oracle declared otherwise. 3 blessing. 4 god of marriage.
5 temptation. 6 i.e., can offer. 7 sun god. 8 lamed. 9 lesser spirits ("thy meaner fellows," line 35).

Each one, tripping on his toe,
Will be here with mop and mow.[10]
Do you love me, master? No?

PROSPERO: Dearly, my delicate Ariel. Do not approach
Till thou dost hear me call.

50 ARIEL: Well! I conceive. (*Exit.*)

PROSPERO: Look thou be true. Do not give dalliance
Too much the rein. The strongest oaths are straw
To th' fire i' th' blood. Be more abstemious,
Or else good night your vow!

FERDINAND: I warrant you, sir.
The white cold virgin snow upon my heart
Abates the ardour of my liver.[11]

PROSPERO: Well.
Now come, my Ariel! Bring a corollary[12]
Rather than want a spirit. Appear, and pertly!
No tongue! All eyes! Be silent. (*Soft music.*)

(*Enter* IRIS.[13])

60 IRIS: Ceres,[14] most bounteous lady, thy rich leas[15]
Of wheat, rye, barley, fetches,[16] oats, and pease;
Thy turfy mountains, where live nibbling sheep,
And flat meads thatch'd with stover,[17] them to keep;
Thy banks with pioned[18] and twilled[19] brims,
Which spongy April at thy hest betrims
To make cold nymphs chaste crowns; and thy broom groves,
Whose shadow the dismissed bachelor loves,
Being lasslorn; thy pole-clipt[20] vineyard;
And thy sea-marge, sterile and rocky-hard,
70 Where thou thyself dost air — the queen o' th' sky,[21]
Whose wat'ry arch and messenger am I,
Bids thee leave these, and with her sovereign grace,
Here on this grass-plot, in this very place,
To come and sport. Her peacocks fly amain.[22]
Approach, rich Ceres, her to entertain.

(*Enter* CERES.)

CERES: Hail, many-coloured messenger, that ne'er
Dost disobey the wife of Jupiter,
Who, with thy saffron wings, upon my flow'rs
Diffusest honey drops, refreshing show'rs,
80 And with each end of thy blue bow dost crown
My bosky[23] acres and my unshrubb'd down,

---

10 mocking gestures and grimaces. 11 supposed internal organ of passion. 12 extra. 13 goddess of the
rainbow and messenger of Juno. 14 goddess of agriculture. 15 meadows. 16 vetches, fodder. 17 hay.
18 trenched. 19 ridged. 20 pruned or pole-clinging. 21 i.e., Juno. 22 swiftly. 23 wooded.

Rich scarf to my proud earth — why hath thy queen
Summon'd me hither to this short-grass'd green?
IRIS: A contract of true love to celebrate
And some donation freely to estate[24]
On the bless'd lovers.
CERES: Tell me, heavenly bow,
If Venus or her son,[25] as thou dost know,
Do now attend the Queen. Since they did plot
The means that dusky Dis[26] my daughter got,
90   Her and her blind boy's scandal'd company
I have forsworn.
IRIS: Of her society
Be not afraid. I met her Deity
Cutting the clouds towards Paphos,[27] and her son
Dove-drawn with her. Here thought they to have done
Some wanton charm upon this man and maid,
Whose vows are, that no bed-right shall be paid
Till Hymen's torch be lighted; but in vain.
Mars's hot minion[28] is return'd again;
Her waspish-headed son has broke his arrows,
100   Swears he will shoot no more, but play with sparrows
And be a boy right out.[29]

[*Enter* JUNO.]

CERES: Highest queen of state,
Great Juno, comes; I know her by her gait.
JUNO: How does my bounteous sister? Go with me
To bless this twain, that they may prosperous be
And honour'd in their issue.

(*They sing.*)

JUNO: Honour, riches, marriage blessing,
Long continuance, and increasing,
Hourly joys be still upon you!
Juno sings her blessings on you.
110   CERES: Earth's increase, foison[30] plenty,
Barns and garners never empty,
Vines with clust'ring bunches growing,
Plants with goodly burden bowing;
Spring come to you at the farthest
In the very end of harvest!
Scarcity and want shall shun you,
Ceres' blessing so is on you.

---

24 grant, bestow. 25 Cupid. 26 Pluto, who abducted Ceres's daughter Proserpine with the complicity of
Venus and Cupid. 27 a town in Cyprus; a centre of Venus-worship. 28 mistress (i.e., Venus). 29 outright
(i.e., an ordinary boy). 30 abundance.

FERDINAND: This is a most majestic vision, and
    Harmonious charmingly. May I be bold
    To think these spirits?
120 PROSPERO: Spirits, which by mine art
    I have from their confines call'd to enact
    My present fancies.
FERDINAND: Let me live here ever!
    So rare a wond'red [31] father and a wife
    Makes this place Paradise.

(JUNO *and* CERES *whisper, and send* IRIS *on employment.*)

PROSPERO: Sweet now, silence!
    Juno and Ceres whisper seriously.
    There's something else to do. Hush and be mute,
    Or else our spell is marr'd.
IRIS: You nymphs, call'd Naiades, of the wand'ring brooks,
    With your sedg'd crowns and ever-harmless looks,
130   Leave your crisp [32] channels, and on this green land
    Answer your summons. Juno does command.
    Come, temperate nymphs, and help to celebrate
    A contract of true love. Be not too late.

(*Enter certain* NYMPHS.)

You sunburn'd sicklemen, of August weary,
Come hither from the furrow and be merry.
Make holiday. Your rye-straw hats put on,
And these fresh nymphs encounter every one
In country footing. [33]

(*Enter certain* REAPERS, *properly habited. They join with the* NYMPHS *in a graceful dance; towards the end whereof* PROSPERO *starts suddenly and speaks; after which, to a strange, hollow, and confused noise, they heavily* [34] *vanish.*)

PROSPERO: [*aside*] I had forgot that foul conspiracy
140   Of the beast Caliban and his confederates
    Against my life. The minute of their plot
    Is almost come.— [*To the* SPIRITS] Well done! Avoid! [35] No more!
FERDINAND: This is strange. Your father's in some passion
    That works him strongly.
MIRANDA: Never till this day
    Saw I him touch'd with anger so distemper'd.
PROSPERO: You do look, my son, in a mov'd sort,
    As if you were dismay'd. Be cheerful, sir.
    Our revels now are ended. These our actors,
    As I foretold you, were all spirits and
150   Are melted into air, into thin air;

---

31 wondrous, wonderful. 32 rippling. 33 dancing. 34 reluctantly, mopingly. 35 Begone!

And, like the baseless fabric of this vision,
The cloud-capp'd towers, the gorgeous palaces,
The solemn temples, the great globe itself,
Yea, all which it inherit,[36] shall dissolve,
And, like this insubstantial pageant faded,
Leave not a rack[37] behind. We are such stuff
As dreams are made on, and our little life
Is rounded with a sleep. Sir, I am vex'd.
Bear with my weakness. My old brain is troubled.
160   Be not disturb'd with my infirmity.
If you be pleas'd, retire into my cell
And there repose. A turn or two I'll walk
To still my beating mind.

FERDINAND, MIRANDA: We wish your peace. (*Exeunt.*)

(*Enter* ARIEL.)

PROSPERO: Come with a thought! I thank thee, Ariel. Come.
ARIEL: Thy thoughts I cleave to. What's thy pleasure?
PROSPERO: Spirit,
   We must prepare to meet with Caliban.
ARIEL: Ay, my commander. When I presented Ceres,
   I thought to have told thee of it, but I fear'd
   Lest I might anger thee.
170   PROSPERO: Say again, where didst thou leave these varlets?
ARIEL: I told you, sir, they were red-hot with drinking;
   So full of valour that they smote the air
   For breathing in their faces, beat the ground
   For kissing of their feet; yet always bending
   Towards their project.[38] Then I beat my tabor;
   At which like unback'd[39] colts they prick'd their ears,
   Advanc'd their eyelids, lifted up their noses
   As they smelt music. So I charm'd their ears
   That calf-like they my lowing follow'd through
180   Tooth'd briers, sharp furzes, pricking goss,[40] and thorns,
   Which ent'red their frail shins. At last I left them
   I' th' filthy mantled[41] pool beyond your cell,
   There dancing up to th' chins, that the foul lake
   O'erstunk their feet.
PROSPERO: This was well done, my bird.
   Thy shape invisible retain thou still.
   The trumpery[42] in my house, go bring it hither
   For stale[43] to catch these thieves.
ARIEL: I go, I go. (*Exit.*)
PROSPERO: A devil, a born devil, on whose nature
   Nurture can never stick! on whom my pains,

---

36 occupies, possesses. 37 shred, wisp of cloud. 38 i.e., the murder of Prospero. 39 unbroken, unridden.
40 gorse. 41 scummed. 42 finery (the *glistering apparel* of the next stage direction). 43 bait.

190 Humanely taken, all, all lost, quite lost!
And as with age his body uglier grows,
So his mind cankers. I will plague them all,
Even to roaring.

(Enter ARIEL, *loaden with glistering apparel, etc.)*

Come, hang them on this line.

[PROSPERO *and* ARIEL *remain, invisible*]

(Enter CALIBAN, STEPHANO, *and* TRINCULO, *all wet.)*

CALIBAN: Pray you tread softly, that the blind mole may not
Hear a foot fall. We now are near his cell.
STEPHANO: Monster, your fairy, which you say is a harmless fairy, has done
little better than play'd the Jack[44] with us.
TRINCULO: Monster, I do smell all horse-piss, at which my nose is in great
indignation.
200 STEPHANO: So is mine. Do you hear, monster? If I should take a displeasure
against you, look you —
TRINCULO: Thou wert but a lost monster.
CALIBAN: Good my lord, give me thy favour still.
Be patient, for the prize I'll bring thee to
Shall hoodwink[45] this mischance. Therefore speak softly.
All's hush'd as midnight yet.
TRINCULO: Ay, but to lose our bottles in the pool —
STEPHANO: There is not only disgrace and dishonour in that, monster, but an
infinite loss.
210 TRINCULO: That's more to me than my wetting. Yet this is your harmless fairy,
monster.
STEPHANO: I will fetch off my bottle, though I be o'er ears for my labour.
CALIBAN: Prithee, my king, be quiet. Seest thou here?
This is the mouth o' th' cell. No noise, and enter.
Do that good mischief which may make this island
Thine own for ever, and I, thy Caliban,
For aye thy foot-licker.
STEPHANO: Give me thy hand. I do begin to have bloody thoughts.
TRINCULO: O King Stephano! O peer! O worthy Stephano, look what a
220 wardrobe here is for thee!
CALIBAN: Let it alone, thou fool! It is but trash.
TRINCULO: O, ho, monster! we know what belongs to a frippery.[46] O King
Stephano!
STEPHANO: Put off that gown, Trinculo. By this hand, I'll have that gown!
TRINCULO: Thy Grace shall have it.
CALIBAN: The dropsy drown this fool! What do you mean
To dote thus on such luggage?[47] Let 't alone,

---

44 knave. 45 put out of sight (and mind). 46 second-hand clothing store. 47 bulky encumbrance.

And do the murder first. If he awake,
From toe to crown he'll fill our skins with pinches,
230   Make us strange stuff.

STEPHANO: Be you quiet, monster. Mistress line, is not this my jerkin?[48] [*Takes*
it down.] Now is the jerkin under the line.[49] Now, jerkin, you are like to lose
your hair and prove a bald jerkin.

TRINCULO: Do, do! We steal by line and level,[50] an 't like your Grace.

STEPHANO: I thank thee for that jest. Here's a garment for 't. Wit shall not go
unrewarded while I am king of this country. "Steal by line and level" is
an excellent pass of pate.[51] There's another garment for 't.

TRINCULO: Monster, come put some lime[52] upon your fingers, and away with
the rest!

240 CALIBAN: I will have none on 't. We shall lose our time
And all be turn'd to barnacles, or to apes
With foreheads villainous low.

STEPHANO: Monster, lay-to your fingers. Help to bear this away where my
hogshead of wine is, or I'll turn you out of my kingdom. Go to, carry this.

TRINCULO: And this.

STEPHANO: Ay, and this.

(*A noise of hunters heard. Enter divers*[53] SPIRITS *in shape of dogs and
hounds, hunting them about*, PROSPERO *and* ARIEL *setting them on*.)

PROSPERO: Hey, Mountain, hey!
ARIEL: Silver! there it goes, Silver!
PROSPERO: Fury, Fury! There, Tyrant, there! Hark, Hark!

[CALIBAN, STEPHANO, *and* TRINCULO *are driven out*.]

250 Go, charge my goblins that they grind their joints
With dry convulsions, shorten up their sinews
With aged cramps, and more pinch-spotted make them
Than pard[54] or cat o' mountain.
ARIEL: Hark, they roar.
PROSPERO: Let them be hunted soundly. At this hour
Lie at my mercy all mine enemies.
Shortly shall all my labours end, and thou
Shalt have the air at freedom. For a little
Follow, and do me service. (*Exeunt*.)

48 jacket. 49 clothes line, tree, equator. The joke that follows involves the popular understanding that
tropical diseases contracted south of the equator involved loss of hair. 50 plumb line and carpenter's level;
i.e., with professional skill. 51 wit. 52 sticky substance. 53 diverse. 54 leopard.

ACT FIVE

SCENE 1. [*Before the cell of* PROSPERO.]

(*Enter* PROSPERO *in his magic robes, and* ARIEL.)

PROSPERO: Now does my project gather to a head.
    My charms crack not, my spirits obey, and time
    Goes upright with his carriage. How's the day?
ARIEL: On the sixth hour, at which time, my lord,
    You said our work should cease.
PROSPERO: I did say so
    When first I rais'd the tempest. Say, my spirit,
    How fares the King and 's followers?
ARIEL: Confin'd together
    In the same fashion as you gave in charge,
    Just as you left them — all prisoners, sir,
10   In the line grove which weather-fends[1] your cell.
    They cannot budge till your release.[2] The King,
    His brother, and yours abide all three distracted,
    And the remainder mourning over them,
    Brimful of sorrow and dismay; but chiefly
    Him that you term'd, sir, the good old Lord Gonzalo.
    His tears run down his beard like winter's drops
    From eaves of reeds.[3] Your charm so strongly works 'em,
    That if you now beheld them, your affections
    Would become tender.
PROSPERO: Dost thou think so, spirit?
ARIEL: Mine would, sir, were I human.
20 PROSPERO: And mine shall.
    Hast thou, which art but air, a touch, a feeling
    Of their afflictions, and shall not myself,
    One of their kind, that relish all as sharply
    Passion as they, be kindlier mov'd than thou art?
    Though with their high wrongs I am struck to th' quick,
    Yet with my nobler reason 'gainst my fury
    Do I take part. The rarer action is
    In virtue than in vengeance. They being penitent,
    The sole drift of my purpose doth extend
30   Not a frown further. Go, release them, Ariel.
    My charms I'll break, their senses I'll restore,
    And they shall be themselves.
ARIEL: I'll fetch them, sir. (*Exit.*)
PROSPERO: [*makes a magic circle with his staff*] Ye elves of hills, brooks, standing
        lakes, and groves,
    And ye that on the sands with printless foot
    Do chase the ebbing Neptune, and do fly him

---

1 acts as windbreak. 2 i.e., released by you. 3 i.e., thatched roofs.

When he comes back; you demi-puppets that
By moonshine do the green sour ringlets[4] make,
Whereof the ewe not bites; and you whose pastime
Is to make midnight mushrumps,[5] that rejoice
40   To hear the solemn curfew; by whose aid
(Weak masters though ye be) I have bedimm'd
The noontide sun, call'd forth the mutinous winds,
And 'twixt the green sea and the azur'd vault
Set roaring war; to the dread rattling thunder
Have I given fire and rifted Jove's stout oak
With his own bolt; the strong-bas'd promontory
Have I made shake and by the spurs[6] pluck'd up
The pine and cedar; graves at my command
Have wak'd their sleepers, op'd, and let 'em forth
50   By my so potent art. But this rough magic
I here abjure; and when I have requir'd
Some heavenly music (which even now I do)
To work mine end upon their senses that
This airy charm is for, I'll break my staff,
Bury it certain fathoms in the earth,
And deeper than did ever plummet sound
I'll drown my book. (*Solemn music.*)

(*Here enters* ARIEL *before; then* ALONSO, *with a frantic gesture, attended by*
GONZALO; SEBASTIAN *and* ANTONIO *in like manner, attended by* ADRIAN
and FRANCISCO. *They all enter the circle which* PROSPERO *had made, and
there stand charm'd; which* PROSPERO *observing, speaks.*)

A solemn air, and the best comforter
To an unsettled fancy, cure thy brains,
60   Now useless, boil'd within thy skull! There stand,
For you are spell-stopp'd.
Holy Gonzalo, honourable man,
Mine eyes, ev'n sociable to the show of thine,
Fall fellowly drops.[7] The charm dissolves apace;
And as the morning steals upon the night,
Melting the darkness, so their rising senses
Begin to chase the ignorant fumes that mantle
Their clearer reason. O good Gonzalo,
My true preserver, and a loyal sir
70   To him thou follow'st! I will pay thy graces
Home[8] both in word and deed. Most cruelly
Didst thou, Alonso, use me and my daughter.
Thy brother was a furtherer in the act.
Thou art pinch'd for 't now, Sebastian. Flesh and blood,
You, brother mine, that entertain'd ambition,
Expell'd remorse and nature; who, with Sebastian

4 fairy rings. 5 mushrooms. 6 roots. 7 sympathetic tears. 8 i.e., thoroughly, completely.

(Whose inward pinches therefore are most strong),
Would here have kill'd your king, I do forgive thee,
Unnatural though thou art. Their understanding
80   Begins to swell, and the approaching tide
Will shortly fill the reasonable shore,
That now lies foul and muddy. Not one of them
That yet looks on me or would know me. Ariel,
Fetch me the hat and rapier in my cell.
I will discase⁹ me, and myself present
As I was sometime Milan.¹⁰ Quickly, spirit!
Thou shalt ere long be free.

[*Exit* ARIEL *and returns immediately.*]

(ARIEL *sings and helps to attire him.*)

ARIEL: Where the bee sucks, there suck I;
                In a cowslip's bell I lie;
90   There I couch when owls do cry.
                On the bat's back I do fly
                After summer merrily.
            Merrily, merrily shall I live now
            Under the blossom that hangs on the bough.

PROSPERO: Why, that's my dainty Ariel! I shall miss thee,
        But yet thou shalt have freedom. So, so, so.
        To the King's ship, invisible as thou art!
        There shalt thou find the mariners asleep
        Under the hatches. The master and the boatswain
100   Being awake, enforce them to this place,
        And presently,¹¹ I prithee.
ARIEL: I drink the air before me, and return
        Or ere your pulse twice beat. (*Exit.*)
GONZALO: All torment, trouble, wonder, and amazement
        Inhabits here. Some heavenly power guide us
        Out of this fearful country!
PROSPERO: Behold, sir King,
        The wronged Duke of Milan, Prospero.
        For more assurance that a living prince
        Does now speak to thee, I embrace thy body,
110   And to thee and thy company I bid
        A hearty welcome.
ALONSO: Whe'r¹² thou be'st he or no,
        Or some enchanted trifle¹³ to abuse me,
        As late I have been, I not know. Thy pulse
        Beats, as of flesh and blood; and, since I saw thee,
        Th' affliction of my mind amends, with which,
        I fear, a madness held me. This must crave¹⁴

9 disrobe.   10 i.e., the former Duke of Milan.   11 immediately.   12 whether.   13 trick, apparition.   14 require.

(An if this be at all) a most strange story.
Thy dukedom I resign and do entreat
Thou pardon me my wrongs. But how should Prospero
Be living and be here?

120 PROSPERO: First, noble friend,
Let me embrace thine age, whose honour cannot
Be measur'd or confin'd.

GONZALO: Whether this be
Or be not, I'll not swear.

PROSPERO: You do yet taste
Some subtleties o' th' isle, that will not let you
Believe things certain. Welcome, my friends all.
[*Aside to* SEBASTIAN *and* ANTONIO] But you, my brace of lords, were I so
        minded,
I here could pluck his Highness' frown upon you,
And justify[15] you traitors. At this time
I will tell no tales.

SEBASTIAN: [*aside*]   The devil speaks in him.

PROSPERO: No.
130 For you, most wicked sir, whom to call brother
Would even infect my mouth, I do forgive
Thy rankest fault — all of them; and require
My dukedom of thee, which perforce I know
Thou must restore.

ALONSO: If thou beest Prospero,
Give us particulars of thy preservation;
How thou hast met us here, who three hours since
Were wrack'd upon this shore; where I have lost
(How sharp the point of this remembrance is!)
My dear son Ferdinand.

PROSPERO: I am woe[16] for 't, sir.
140 ALONSO: Irreparable is the loss, and patience
Says it is past her cure.

PROSPERO: I rather think
You have not sought her help, of whose soft grace
For the like loss I have her sovereign aid
And rest myself content.

ALONSO: You the like loss?

PROSPERO: As great to me as late;[17] and, supportable
To make the dear[18] loss, have I means much weaker
Than you may call to comfort you; for I
Have lost my daughter.

ALONSO: A daughter?
O heavens, that they were living both in Naples,
150 The King and Queen there! That they were, I wish
Myself were mudded in that oozy bed
Where my son lies. When did you lose your daughter?

15 prove. 16 sorry. 17 recent. 18 deeply felt, intensified.

PROSPERO: In this last tempest. I perceive these lords
    At this encounter do so much admire[19]
    That they devour their reason, and scarce think
    Their eyes do offices of truth, their words
    Are natural breath. But, howsoev'r you have
    Been justled from your senses, know for certain
    That I am Prospero, and that very duke
160   Which was thrust forth of Milan, who most strangely
    Upon this shore, where you were wrack'd, was landed
    To be the lord on 't. No more yet of this;
    For 'tis a chronicle of day by day,
    Not a relation for a breakfast, nor
    Befitting this first meeting. Welcome, sir.
    This cell's my court. Here have I few attendants,
    And subjects none abroad.[20] Pray you look in.
    My dukedom since you have given me again,
    I will requite you with as good a thing,
170   At least bring forth a wonder to content ye
    As much as me my dukedom.

(*Here* PROSPERO *discovers*[21] FERDINAND *and* MIRANDA *playing at chess.*)

MIRANDA: Sweet lord, you play me false.
FERDINAND: No, my dearest love,
    I would not for the world.
MIRANDA: Yes, for a score of kingdoms you should wrangle,
    And I would call it fair play.
ALONSO: If this prove
    A vision of the island, one dear son
    Shall I twice lose.
SEBASTIAN: A most high miracle!
FERDINAND: Though the seas threaten, they are merciful.
    I have curs'd them without cause. [*Kneels.*]
ALONSO: Now all the blessings
180   Of a glad father compass thee about!
    Arise, and say how thou cam'st here.
MIRANDA: O, wonder!
    How many goodly creatures are there here!
    How beauteous mankind is! O brave new world
    That has such people in 't!
PROSPERO: 'Tis new to thee.
ALONSO: What is this maid with whom thou wast at play?
    Your eld'st[22] acquaintance cannot be three hours.
    Is she the goddess that hath sever'd us
    And brought us thus together?
FERDINAND: Sir, she is mortal;
    But by immortal providence she's mine.

19 wonder, marvel. 20 i.e., on the rest of the island. 21 reveals. 22 longest.

190   I chose her when I could not ask my father
    For his advice, nor thought I had one. She
    Is daughter to this famous Duke of Milan,
    Of whom so often I have heard renown
    But never saw before; of whom I have
    Receiv'd a second life; and second father
    This lady makes him to me.
ALONSO: I am hers.
    But, O, how oddly will it sound that I
    Must ask my child forgiveness!
PROSPERO: There, sir, stop.
    Let us not burden our remembrance with
    A heaviness that's gone.
200 GONZALO: I have inly wept,
    Or should have spoke ere this. Look down, you gods,
    And on this couple drop a blessed crown!
    For it is you that have chalk'd forth the way
    Which brought us hither.
ALONSO: I say amen, Gonzalo.
GONZALO: Was Milan thrust from Milan that his issue
    Should become kings of Naples? O, rejoice
    Beyond a common joy, and set it down
    With gold on lasting pillars: In one voyage
    Did Claribel her husband find at Tunis,
210   And Ferdinand her brother found a wife
    Where he himself was lost; Prospero his dukedom
    In a poor isle; and all of us ourselves
    When no man was his own.
ALONSO: [to FERDINAND and MIRANDA] Give me your hands.
    Let grief and sorrow still[23] embrace his heart
    That doth not wish you joy.
GONZALO: Be it so! Amen!

    (Enter ARIEL, with the MASTER and BOATSWAIN amazedly following.)

    O, look, sir; look, sir! Here is more of us!
    I prophesied, if a gallows were on land,
    This fellow could not drown. Now, blasphemy,[24]
    That swear'st grace o'erboard, not an oath on shore?
220   Hast thou no mouth by land? What is the news?
BOATSWAIN: The best news is that we have safely found
    Our king and company; the next, our ship,
    Which, but three glasses[25] since, we gave out split,
    Is tight and yare[26] and bravely rigg'd as when
    We first put out to sea.
ARIEL: [aside to PROSPERO] Sir, all this service
    Have I done since I went.

23 always, forever. 24 i.e., blasphemous fellow. 25 hours. 26 shipshape.

PROSPERO: [*aside to* ARIEL]   My tricksy spirit!

ALONSO: These are not natural events; they strengthen
From strange to stranger. Say, how came you hither?

BOATSWAIN: If I did think, sir, I were well awake,
230   I'd strive to tell you. We were dead of sleep
And (how we know not) all clapp'd under hatches;
Where, but even now, with strange and several noises
Of roaring, shrieking, howling, jingling chains,
And moe[27] diversity of sounds, all horrible,
We were awak'd; straightway at liberty;
Where we, in all her trim, freshly beheld
Our royal, good, and gallant ship; our master
Cap'ring[28] to eye her. On a trice, so please you,
Even in a dream, were we divided from them
And were brought moping[29] hither.

240   ARIEL: [*aside to* PROSPERO]   Was 't well done?

PROSPERO: [*aside to* ARIEL] Bravely, my diligence. Thou shalt be free.

ALONSO: This is as strange a maze as e'er men trod,
And there is in this business more than nature
Was ever conduct[30] of. Some oracle
Must rectify our knowledge.

PROSPERO: Sir, my liege,
Do not infest your mind with beating on
The strangeness of this business. At pick'd leisure,
Which shall be shortly, single I'll resolve you
(Which to you shall seem probable) of every
250   These happen'd accidents; till when, be cheerful
And think of each thing well. [*Aside to* ARIEL] Come hither, spirit.
Set Caliban and his companions free.
Untie the spell. [*Exit* ARIEL.] How fares my gracious sir?
There are yet missing of your company
Some few odd lads that you remember not.

(*Enter* ARIEL, *driving in* CALIBAN, STEPHANO, *and* TRINCULO, *in their stol'n
apparel.*)

STEPHANO: Every man shift for all the rest, and let no man take care for himself;
for all is but fortune. Coragio,[31] bully-monster, coragio!

TRINCULO: If these be true spies which I wear in my head, here's a goodly sight.

CALIBAN: O Setebos, these be brave spirits indeed!
260   How fine my master is! I am afraid
He will chastise me.

SEBASTIAN: Ha, ha!
What things are these, my Lord Antonio?
Will money buy 'em?

ANTONIO: Very like. One of them
Is a plain fish and no doubt marketable.

---

27 more. 28 i.e., dancing with joy. 29 dazed. 30 conductor. 31 courage.

PROSPERO: Mark but the badges[32] of these men, my lords,
   Then say if they be true.[33] This misshapen knave,
   His mother was a witch, and one so strong
   That could control the moon, make flows and ebbs,
   And deal in her[34] command without[35] her power.
270 These three have robb'd me, and this demi-devil
   (For he's a bastard one) had plotted with them
   To take my life. Two of these fellows you
   Must know and own; this thing of darkness I
   Acknowledge mine.
CALIBAN: I shall be pinch'd to death.
ALONSO: Is not this Stephano, my drunken butler?
SEBASTIAN: He is drunk now. Where had he wine?
ALONSO: And Trinculo is reeling ripe. Where should they
   Find this grand liquor that hath gilded 'em?
   How cam'st thou in this pickle?
280 TRINCULO: I have been in such a pickle, since I saw you last, that I fear me will
   never out of my bones. I shall not fear fly-blowing.[36]
SEBASTIAN: Why, how now, Stephano?
STEPHANO: O, touch me not! I am not Stephano, but a cramp.
PROSPERO: You'd be king o' the isle, sirrah?[37]
STEPHANO: I should have been a sore one then.
ALONSO: This is as strange a thing as e'er I look'd on.
PROSPERO: He is as disproportion'd in his manners
   As in his shape. Go, sirrah, to my cell;
   Take with you your companions. As you look
290 To have my pardon, trim it handsomely.
CALIBAN: Ay, that I will; and I'll be wise hereafter,
   And seek for grace. What a thrice-double ass
   Was I to take this drunkard for a god
   And worship this dull fool!
PROSPERO: Go to! Away!
ALONSO: Hence, and bestow your luggage where you found it.
SEBASTIAN: Or stole it rather.

   [*Exeunt* CALIBAN, STEPHANO, *and* TRINCULO.]

PROSPERO: Sir, I invite your Highness and your train
   To my poor cell, where you shall take your rest
   For this one night; which, part of it, I'll waste[38]
300 With such discourse as, I not doubt, shall make it
   Go quick away — the story of my life,
   And the particular accidents[39] gone by
   Since I came to this isle; and in the morn
   I'll bring you to your ship, and so to Naples,

---

32 insignia indicating the allegiance of a servant (in this case, stolen clothes indicate untrustworthiness and rascality). 33 honest. 34 i.e., the moon's. 35 beyond. 36 rotting (he is well pickled). 37 sir (addressed to an inferior). 38 spend. 39 incidents, occurrences.

Where I have hope to see the nuptial
Of these our dear-belov'd solemnized;
And thence retire me to my Milan, where
Every third thought shall be my grave.
ALONSO: I long
To hear the story of your life, which must
Take the ear strangely.
310 PROSPERO: I'll deliver[40] all;
And promise you calm seas, auspicious gales,
And sail[41] so expeditious that shall catch
Your royal fleet far off. [*Aside to* ARIEL] My Ariel, chick,
That is thy charge. Then to the elements
Be free, and fare thou well — Please you draw near.

(*Exeunt omnes.*)

EPILOGUE

(*Spoken by* PROSPERO.)

Now my charms are all o'erthrown,
And what strength I have's mine own,
Which is most faint. Now 'tis true
I must be here confin'd by you,
Or sent to Naples. Let me not,
Since I have my dukedom got
And pardon'd the deceiver, dwell
In this bare island by your spell;
But release me from my bands[42]
10 With the help of your good hands.[43]
Gentle breath[44] of yours my sails
Must fill, or else my project fails,
Which was to please. Now I want[45]
Spirits to enforce, art to enchant;
And my ending is despair
Unless I be reliev'd by prayer,[46]
Which pierces so that it assaults
Mercy itself and frees all faults.
As you from crimes would pardon'd be,
20 Let your indulgence set me free.

(*Exit.*)

40 tell, report. 41 course, voyage. 42 bonds. 43 i.e., applause. 44 commentary, acclaim. 45 lack.
46 i.e., this epilogue, petition.

Aphra Behn (1640–1689)

Little is known for sure about Aphra Behn's early life. Born in Kent in south-east England, her original surname may have been Johnson but definite family origins are uncertain. At a young age she travelled to the South American English colony of Surinam, returning to England in 1664. By this time referring to herself as "Mrs. Behn," she gained widowed social respectability and a chance at an independent life. Doubtless, such independence proved useful in her commission as a spy in the Netherlands for Charles II in 1666.

In 1670 she emerged as a playwright, producing *The Forc'd Marriage* for the Duke's Company at Lincoln's Inn Fields. Over a long and successful writing career, she penned some eighteen plays, including *The Rover* (1677), *The Roundheads* (1681), and *The Lucky Chance* (1686). Her plays typically combine fast pacing, innovative stagecraft, satirical wit, and empowerment of female characters. Her career also involved a collection of poems (1684), a short novel, *Oroonoko* (1688), and translations of scientific writing and French fiction. A committed Stuart royalist, Behn publicly satirized both the hypocritical mercantilism of Whigs and the moralism of Puritans. At her death, as befits the first professional English woman writer, Aphra Behn was buried in Westminster Abbey.

INTRODUCTION TO *THE ROVER*

The Rover (1677) was Behn's most successful play and one of the very few plays written by a woman to be acted frequently on the English stage. First performed in the presence of King Charles II (who was highly amused by it), it was very popular; Behn produced a sequel, *The Second Part of the Rover*, in 1681. *The Rover* was frequently performed until 1760. By then, tastes had grown more fastidious, and the play was dropped from the repertoire of the English acting companies; in 1790, the actor and manager John Philip Kemble produced an adaptation, entitled *Love in Many Masks*, which, he claimed, "purified" the play of its earthy action and racy language. After falling out of favour in the nineteenth century and the first half of the twentieth, it is once again enjoying popularity.

Though the play was first performed in 1677, it is set in the years before 1660, the date when the English people rejected the Puritan austerity of the Commonwealth, which had come to power under Oliver Cromwell in 1649, and restored the monarchy, in the person of Charles II. The leading men in the play are, as the play's subtitle and opening scenes make clear, "banished cavaliers"— royalist supporters of Charles II whose estates have been seized and who are thus social and economic freebooters. The Puritans, who had suppressed most forms of amusement, including public theatres, had become hated by the time they were driven out; Behn's play celebrates the aristocratic, pleasure-loving, anti-Puritan rule of Charles II, "the Merry Monarch." By setting her play in Naples (like most of Italy, part of the Spanish Empire in the seventeenth century) and during carnival time, Behn accentuates her play's uninhibited, anti-Puritanical world.

More than simply the monarchy was restored in 1660. The Church of England, rule by Parliament, and the public theatres also returned to British life. But the new British stage was very different from what it had been: female roles were now played by actresses instead of by young boys, and the proscenium stage replaced the Elizabethan and Jacobean thrust stage. Even more importantly, the Restoration stage was primarily a court amusement. Whereas there had been about seventeen theatres in Shakespeare's London, the much larger city of Behn's time had only two theatres; whereas Shakespeare's Globe Theatre held about 3000 people and was attended by people from all walks of life, Behn's Dorset Garden Theatre held 500 to 600 and was dominated by the aristocracy. Significantly, the Prologue to Behn's play was written by "a Person of Quality" (that is, one of rank), and there is an opposition throughout between aristocratic and commercial values — between "quality" and money. Moreover, The Rover exemplifies the kind of play dominant in the cavalier and hedonistic Restoration theatre: the sex-comedy. Characterized by complex and interwoven intrigues, tough-minded inquiry into conventional sexual ethics, and an attempt to harmonize the claims of impulse and morality (as Willmore and Hellena eventually do), these plays present a world in which prose is the norm and poetry a departure from that norm.

As a woman, Behn handles this standard form distinctively. Her leading man, Willmore, like other heroes of Restoration comedy, is gallant, generous, scheming, unscrupulous, sexually predatory: his name says it all. Behn's heroine, Hellena, however, is a striking departure. She is like other comic heroines in that she is witty and intelligent, high-spirited, and independent-minded; what makes her different is Behn's emphasis upon her struggle to find a way of life that expresses her active energies, one that is socially acceptable and yet avoids the two obvious (and equally passive) alternatives — chaste retirement from the world as a nun, or an arranged marriage that amounts to prostitution. Even more indicative of Behn's female perspective are the acts of violence, real and threatened, directed against women in the play and the sympathetic portrayal of Angelica Bianca, the prostitute. In fact, Angelica's sign, a huge image of herself as a commodity, dominates the stage when the play is performed, and the problems that she raises have hardly been resolved by the play's conclusion. To a very large degree, it is Behn's special perspective as a woman writer that makes The Rover so significant for readers and playgoers of our age.

THE ROVER
or THE BANISHED CAVALIERS

DRAMATIS PERSONAE

MEN
DON ANTONIO, the Vice-Roy's Son
DON PEDRO, a Noble Spaniard, his Friend
BELVILE, an English Colonel in love with FLORINDA
WILLMORE, the Rover

FREDERICK, an English Gentleman, and Friend to BELVILE and BLUNT
BLUNT, an English Country Gentleman
STEPHANO, Servant to DON PEDRO
PHILIPPO, LUCETTA's Gallant
SANCHO, Pimp to LUCETTA
BISKY and SEBASTIAN, two Bravoes[1] to ANGELICA
DIEGO, Page to DON ANTONIO
PAGE to HELLENA
BOY, Page to BELVILE
BLUNT'S MAN
OFFICERS and SOLDIERS

WOMEN
FLORINDA, Sister to DON PEDRO
HELLENA, a gay young Woman design'd for a Nun, and Sister to FLORINDA
VALERIA, a Kinswoman to FLORINDA
ANGELICA BIANCA, a famous Curtezan[2]
MORETTA, her Woman
CALLIS, Governess to FLORINDA and HELLENA
LUCETTA, a jilting Wench

THE SCENE — *Naples, in Carnival-time.*

PROLOGUE

Written by a Person of Quality

> *WITS, like Physicians, never can agree,*
> *When of a different Society;*
> *And Rabel's Drops[1] were never more cry'd down*
> *By all the Learned Doctors of the Town,*
> *Than a new Play, whose Author is unknown:*
> *Nor can those Doctors with more Malice sue*
> *(And powerful Purses) the dissenting Few,*
> *Than those with an insulting Pride do rail*
> *At all who are not of their own Cabal.[2]*
> *If a Young Poet hit your Humour right,*
> *You judge him then out of Revenge and Spite;*
> *So amongst Men there are ridiculous Elves,[3]*
> *Who Monkeys hate for being too like themselves:*
> *So that the Reason of the Grand Debate,*
> *Why Wit so oft is damn'd, when good Plays take,*
> *Is, that you censure as you love or hate.*

10

1 hired ruffians, desperadoes. 2 courtesan.
1 popular patent medicine. 2 secret group. 3 devils, malicious persons.

Thus, like a learned Conclave, Poets sit
Catholick Judges both of Sense and Wit,
And damn or save, as they themselves think fit.
20 *Yet those who to others Faults are so severe,*
Are not so perfect, but themselves may err.
Some write correct indeed, but then the whole
(Bating[4] *their own dull Stuff i' th' Play) is stole:*
As Bees do suck from Flowers their Honey-dew,
So they rob others, striving to please you.

    Some write their Characters genteel and fine,
But then they do so toil for every Line,
That what to you does easy seem, and plain,
Is the hard issue of their labouring Brain.
30 *And some th' Effects of all their Pains we see,*
Is but to mimick good Extempore.
Others by long Converse about the Town,
Have Wit enough to write a leud Lampoon,
But their chief Skill lies in a Baudy Song.
In short, the only Wit that's now in Fashion
Is but the Gleanings of good Conversation.
As for the Author of this coming Play,
I ask'd him what he thought fit I should say,
In thanks for your good Company to day:
40 *He call'd me Fool, and said it was well known,*
You came not here for our sakes, but your own.
New Plays are stuff'd with Wits, and with Debauches,
That crowd and sweat like Cits[5] *in May-day Coaches.*[6]

ACT ONE

SCENE 1. (*A chamber.*)

(*Enter* FLORINDA *and* HELLENA.)

FLORINDA: What an impertinent thing is a young Girl bred in a Nunnery!
How full of Questions! Prithee no more, *Hellena*; I have told thee more than
thou understand'st already.

HELLENA: The more's my Grief; I wou'd fain know as much as you, which
makes me so inquisitive; nor is't enough to know you're a Lover, unless
you tell me too, who 'tis you sigh for.

FLORINDA: When you are a Lover, I'll think you fit for a Secret of that nature.

HELLENA: 'Tis true, I was never a Lover yet — but I begin to have a shreud Guess,
what 'tis to be so, and fancy it very pretty to sigh, and sing, and blush and wish,
10 and dream and wish, and long and wish to see the Man; and when I do,
look pale and tremble; just as you did when my Brother brought home the
fine *English* Colonel to see you — what do you call him? Don *Belvile*.

FLORINDA: Fie, *Hellena*.

---

4 excepting. 5 middle-class citizens. 6 on May Day (May 1), Londoners paraded around Hyde Park.

HELLENA: That Blush betrays you — I am sure 'tis so — or is it Don *Antonio* the Vice-Roy's Son? — or perhaps the rich old Don *Vincentio*, whom my father designs for your Husband? — Why do you blush again?

FLORINDA: With Indignation; and how near soever my Father thinks I am to marrying that hated Object, I shall let him see I understand better what's due to my Beauty, Birth and Fortune, and more to my Soul, than to obey those unjust Commands.

HELLENA: Now hang me, if I don't love thee for that dear Disobedience. I love Mischief strangely, as most of our Sex do, who are come to love nothing else — But tell me, dear *Florinda*, don't you love that fine *Anglese*?[1] — for I vow next to loving him my self, 'twill please me most that you do so, for he is so gay and so handsome.

FLORINDA: *Hellena*, a Maid design'd for a Nun ought not to be so curious in a Discourse of Love.

HELLENA: And dost thou think that ever I'll be a Nun? Or at least till I'm so old, I'm fit for nothing else. Faith no, Sister; and that which makes me long to know whether you love *Belvile*, is because I hope he has some mad Companion or other, that will spoil my Devotion; nay I'm resolv'd to provide my self this Carnival, if there be e'er a handsome Fellow of my Humour above Ground, tho I ask first.[2]

FLORINDA: Prithee be not so wild.

HELLENA: Now you have provided your self with a Man, you take no Care for poor me — Prithee tell me, what dost thou see about me that is unfit for Love — have not I a world of Youth? a Humour gay? a Beauty passable? a Vigour desirable? well shap'd? clean limb'd? sweet breath'd? and Sense enough to know how all these ought to be employ'd to the best Advantage: yes, I do and will. Therefore lay aside your Hopes of my Fortune, by my being a Devotee, and tell me how you came acquainted with this *Belvile*; for I perceive you knew him before he came to *Naples*.

FLORINDA: Yes, I knew him at the Siege of *Pampelona*, he was then a Colonel of *French* Horse, who when the Town was ransack'd, nobly treated my Brother and my self, preserving us from all Insolencies; and I must own, (besides great Obligations) I have I know not what, that pleads kindly for him about my Heart, and will suffer no other to enter — But see my Brother.

(*Enter* DON PEDRO, STEPHANO, *with a Masquing Habit,*[3] *and* CALLIS.)

PEDRO: Good morrow, Sister. Pray, when saw you your Lover Don *Vincentio*?

FLORINDA: I know not, Sir — *Callis*, when was he here? for I consider it so little, I know not when it was.

PEDRO: I have a Command from my Father here to tell you, you ought not to despise him, a Man of so vast a Fortune, and such a Passion for you — *Stephano*, my things — (*Puts on his Masquing Habit.*)

FLORINDA: A Passion for me! 'tis more than e'er I saw, or had a desire should be known — I hate *Vincentio*, and I would not have a Man so dear to me as my Brother follow the ill Customs of our Country, and make a Slave of his Sister — And Sir, my Father's Will, I'm sure, you may divert.

---

1 Englishman. 2 even if I have to do the asking. 3 masquerade costume.

PEDRO: I know not how dear I am to you, but I wish only to be rank'd in your Esteem, equal with the *English* Colonel *Belvile* — Why do you frown and blush? Is there any Guilt belongs to the Name of that Cavalier?

FLORINDA: I'll not deny I value *Belvile*: when I was expos'd to such Dangers as the licens'd Lust of common Soldiers threatned, when Rage and Conquest flew thro the City — then *Belvile*, this Criminal for my sake, threw himself into all Dangers to save my Honour, and will you not allow him my Esteem?

PEDRO: Yes, pay him what you will in Honour — but you must consider Don *Vincentio's* Fortune, and the Jointure[4] he'll make you.

FLORINDA: Let him consider my Youth, Beauty and Fortune; which ought not to be thrown away on his Age and Jointure.

PEDRO: 'Tis true, he's not so young and fine a Gentleman as that *Belvile* — but what Jewels will that Cavalier present you with? those of his Eyes and Heart?

HELLENA: And are not those better than any Don *Vincentio* has brought from the *Indies*?

PEDRO: Why how now! Has your Nunnery-breeding taught you to understand the Value of Hearts and Eyes?

HELLENA: Better than to believe *Vincentio* deserves Value from any woman — He may perhaps encrease her Bags, but not her Family.

PEDRO: This is fine — Go up to your Devotion, you are not design'd for the Conversation of Lovers.

HELLENA: *(Aside.)* Nor Saints yet a while I hope — Is't not enough you make a Nun of me, but you must cast my Sister away too, exposing her to a worse Confinement than a religious Life?

PEDRO: The Girl's mad — Is it a Confinement to be carry'd into the Country, to an antient Villa belonging to the Family of the *Vincentio's* these five hundred Years, and have no other Prospect than that pleasing one of seeing all her own that meets her Eyes — a fine Air, large Fields and Gardens, where she may walk and gather Flowers?

HELLENA: When? By Moon-Light? For I'm sure she dares not encounter with the heat of the Sun; that were a Task only for Don *Vincentio* and his *Indian* Breeding, who loves it in the Dog-days[5] — And if these be her daily Divertisements, what are those of the Night? to lie in a wide Moth-eaten Bed-Chamber with Furniture in Fashion in the Reign of King *Sancho* the First;[6] the Bed that which his Forefathers liv'd and dy'd in.

PEDRO: Very well.

HELLENA: This Apartment (new furbisht and fitted out for the young Wife) he (out of Freedom) makes his Dressing-room; and being a frugal and a jealous Coxcomb, instead of a Valet to uncase his feeble Carcase, he desires you to do that Office — Signs of Favour, I'll assure you, and such as you must not hope for, unless your Woman be out of the way.

PEDRO: Have you done yet?

---

4 estate settled on a wife that she possesses after her husband's death. 5 the hottest days of summer, so called because Sirius, the Dog Star, is overhead. 6 king of Spain in the tenth century.

HELLENA: That Honour being past, the Giant stretches it self, yawns and sighs a Belch or two as loud as a Musket, throws himself into Bed, and expects you in his foul Sheets, and e'er you can get your self undrest, calls you with a Snore or two — And are not these fine Blessings to a young Lady?

PEDRO: Have you done yet?

HELLENA: And this man you must kiss, nay, you must kiss none but him too — and nuzle thro his Beard to find his Lips — and this you must submit to for threescore Years, and all for a Jointure.

PEDRO: For all your Character of Don *Vincentio*, she is as like to marry him as she was before.

HELLENA: Marry Don *Vincentio*! hang me, such a Wedlock would be worse than Adultery with another Man: I had rather see her in the *Hostel de Dieu*,[7] to waste her Youth there in Vows, and be a Handmaid to Lazers[8] and Cripples, than to lose it in such a Marriage.

PEDRO: You have consider'd, Sister, that *Belvile* has no Fortune to bring you to, is banisht his Country, despis'd at home, and pity'd abroad.

HELLENA: What then? the Vice-Roy's Son is better than that Old Sir Fifty. Don *Vincentio*! Don *Indian*! he thinks he's trading to *Gambo*[9] still, and wou'd barter himself (that Bell and Bawble) for your Youth and Fortune.

PEDRO: *Callis*, take her hence, and lock her up all this Carnival, and at Lent she shall begin her everlasting Penance in a Monastery.

HELLENA: I care not, I had rather be a Nun, than be oblig'd to marry as you wou'd have me, if I were design'd for't.

PEDRO: Do not fear the Blessing of that Choice — you shall be a Nun.

HELLENA: *(Aside.)* Shall I so? you may chance to be mistaken in my way of Devotion — A Nun! yes I am like to make a fine Nun! I have an excellent Humour for a Grate: No, I'll have a Saint of my own to pray to shortly, if I like any that dares venture on me.

PEDRO: *Callis*, make it your Business to watch this wild Cat. As for you, *Florinda*, I've only try'd you all this while, and urg'd my Father's Will; but mine is, that you would love *Antonio*, he is brave and young, and all that can compleat the Happiness of a gallant Maid — This Absence of my Father will give us opportunity to free you from *Vincentio*, by marrying here, which you must do to morrow.

FLORINDA: To morrow!

PEDRO: To morrow, or 'twill be too late — 'tis not my Friendship to *Antonio*, which makes me urge this, but Love to thee, and Hatred to *Vincentio* — therefore resolve upon't to morrow.

FLORINDA: Sir, I shall strive to do, as shall become your Sister.

PEDRO: I'll both believe and trust you — Adieu.

(Exit PEDRO *and* STEPHANO.*)*

HELLENA: As becomes his Sister! — That is, to be as resolved your way, as he is his — *(*HELLENA *goes to* CALLIS.*)*

7 hospital for the poor operated by a religious order. 8 beggars afflicted with an infectious disease such as leprosy. 9 a British colony in western Africa.

FLORINDA: I ne'er till now perceiv'd my Ruin near,
    I've no Defence against *Antonio's* Love,
    For he has all the Advantages of Nature,
    The moving Arguments of Youth and Fortune.

HELLENA: But hark you, *Callis*, you will not be so cruel to lock me up indeed:
    will you?

CALLIS: I must obey the Commands I hate — besides, do you consider what a
150   Life you are going to lead?

HELLENA: Yes, *Callis*, that of a Nun: and till then I'll be indebted a World of
    Prayers to you, if you let me now see, what I never did, the Divertisements
    of a Carnival.

CALLIS: What, go in Masquerade? 'twill be a fine farewell to the World I take
    it — pray what wou'd you do there?

HELLENA: That which all the World does, as I am told, be as mad as the rest, and
    take all innocent Freedom — Sister, you'll go too, will you not? come
    prithee be not sad — We'll out-wit twenty Brothers, if you'll be ruled by me
    — Come put off this dull Humour with your Clothes, and assume one as
160   gay, and as fantastick as the Dress my Cousin *Valeria* and I have provided,
    and let's ramble.

FLORINDA: *Callis*, will you give us leave to go?

CALLIS: *(Aside.)* I have a youthful Itch of going myself — Madam, if I thought
    your Brother might not know it, and I might wait on you, for by my troth
    I'll not trust young Girls alone.

FLORINDA: Thou see'st my Brother's gone already, and thou shalt attend and
    watch us.

(Enter STEPHANO.*)*

STEPHANO: Madam, the Habits are come, and your Cousin Valeria is drest,
    and stays for you.

170 FLORINDA: 'Tis well — I'll write a Note, and if I chance to see *Belvile*, and want
    an opportunity to speak to him, that shall let him know what I've resolv'd
    in favour of him.

HELLENA: Come, let's in and dress us. *(Exeunt.)*

SCENE 2. *(A Long Street.)*

(Enter BELVILE, *melancholy,* BLUNT *and* FREDERICK.*)*

FREDERICK: Why, what the Devil ails the Colonel, in a time when all the
    World is gay, to look like mere Lent thus? Hadst thou been long enough in
    Naples to have been in love, I should have sworn some such Judgment
    had befall'n thee.

BELVILE: No, I have made no new Amours since I came to Naples.

FREDERICK: You have left none behind you in Paris.

BELVILE: Neither.

FREDERICK: I can't divine the Cause then; unless the old Cause, the want of
    Money.

10 BLUNT: And another old Cause, the want of a Wench — Wou'd not that revive you?

BELVILE: You're mistaken, *Ned*.

BLUNT: Nay, 'Sheartlikins,[1] then thou art past Cure.

FREDERICK: I have found it out; thou hast renew'd thy Acquaintance with the Lady that cost thee so many Sighs at the Siege of *Pampelona* — pox on't, what d've call her — her Brother's a noble *Spaniard* — Nephew to the dead General — *Florinda* — ay, *Florinda* — And will nothing serve thy turn but that damn'd virtuous Woman, whom on my Conscience thou lov'st in spite too, because thou seest little or no possibility of gaining her?

20 BELVILE: Thou art mistaken, I have Interest enough in that lovely Virgin's Heart, to make me proud and vain, were it not abated by the Severity of a Brother, who perceiving my Happiness —

FREDERICK: Has civilly forbid thee the House?

BELVILE: 'Tis so, to make way for a powerful Rival, the Vice-Roy's Son, who has the advantage of me, in being a Man of Fortune, a *Spaniard*, and her Brother's Friend; which gives him liberty to make his Court, whilst I have recourse only to Letters, and distant Looks from her Window, which are as soft and kind as those which Heav'n sends down on Penitents.

BLUNT: Hey day! 'Sheartlikins, Simile! by this Light the Man is quite spoil'd — *Frederick*, what the Devil are we made of, that we cannot be thus con-
30 cern'd for a Wench?— 'Sheartlikins, our *Cupids* are like the Cooks of the Camp, they can roast or boil a Woman, but they have none of the fine Tricks to set 'em off, no Hogoes[2] to make the Sauce pleasant, and the Stomach sharp.

FREDERICK: I dare swear I have had a hundred as young, kind and handsome as this *Florinda*; and Dogs eat me, if they were not as troublesome to me i'th' Morning as they were welcome o'er night.

BLUNT: And yet, I warrant, he wou'd not touch another Woman, if he might have her for nothing.

BELVILE: That's thy Joy, a cheap Whore.

40 BLUNT: Why, 'dsheartlikins, I love a frank Soul — When did you ever hear of an honest Woman that took a Man's Money? I warrant 'em good ones — But, Gentlemen, you may be free, you have been kept so poor with Parliaments and Protectors, that the little Stock you have is not worth preserving — but I thank my Stars, I have more Grace than to forfeit my Estate by Cavaliering.[3]

BELVILE: Methinks only following the Court should be sufficient to entitle 'em to that.

BLUNT: 'Sheartlikins, they know I follow it to do it no good, unless they pick a hole in my Coat for lending you Money now and then; which is a greater
50 Crime to my Conscience, Gentlemen, than to the Common-wealth.

(*Enter* WILLMORE.)

WILLMORE: Ha! dear *Belvile*! noble Colonel!

BELVILE: *Willmore*! welcome ashore, my dear Rover! — what happy Wind blew us this good Fortune?

---

1 by God's heart (a mild oath). 2 relishes. 3 during the English Civil War, many Royalist ("Cavalier") estates were confiscated by order of the Puritan government of Oliver Cromwell, Lord Protector of England.

WILLMORE: Let me salute you my dear *Fred*, and then command me — How is't honest Lad?

FREDERICK: Faith, Sir, the old Complement, infinitely the better to see my dear mad *Willmore* again — Prithee why camest thou ashore? and where's the Prince?[4]

WILLMORE: He's well, and reigns still Lord of the watery Element — I must aboard again within a Day or two, and my Business ashore was only to enjoy my self a little this Carnival.

BELVILE: Pray know our new Friend, Sir, he's but bashful, a raw Traveller, but honest, stout, and one of us. (*Embraces* BLUNT.)

WILLMORE: That you esteem him, gives him an Interest here.

BLUNT: Your Servant, Sir.

WILLMORE: But well — Faith I'm glad to meet you again in a warm Climate, where the kind Sun has its god-like Power still over the Wine and Woman. — Love and Mirth are my Business in *Naples*; and if I mistake not the Place, here's an excellent Market for Chapmen[5] of my Humour.

BELVILE: See here be those kind Merchants of Love you look for.

(*Enter several Men in masquing Habits, some playing on Musick, others dancing after; Women drest like Curtezans, with Papers pinn'd to their Breasts, and Baskets of Flowers in their Hands.*)

BLUNT: 'Sheartlikins, what have we here!

FREDERICK: Now the Game begins.

WILLMORE: Fine pretty Creatures! may a stranger have leave to look and love?— What's here — *Roses for every Month!* (*Reads the Paper.*)

BLUNT: Roses for every Month! what means that?

BELVILE: They are, or wou'd have you think they're Curtezans, who here in *Naples* are to be hir'd by the Month.

WILLMORE: Kind and obliging to inform us — Pray where do these Roses grow? I would fain plant some of 'em in a Bed of mine.

WOMAN: Beware such Roses, Sir.

WILLMORE: A Pox of fear: I'll be bak'd with thee between a pair of Sheets, and that's thy proper Still,[6] so I might but strow such Roses over me and under me — Fair one, wou'd you wou'd give me leave to gather at your Bush this idle Month, I wou'd go near to make some Body smell of it all the Year after.

BELVILE: And thou hast need of such a Remedy, for thou stinkest of Tar and Rope-ends, like a Dock or Pesthouse.

(*The Woman puts her self into the Hands of a Man, and they Exit.*)

WILLMORE: Nay, nay, you shall not leave me so.

BELVILE: By all means use no Violence here.

WILLMORE: Death! just as I was going to be damnably in love, to have her led off! I could pluck that Rose out of his Hand, and even kiss the Bed, the Bush it grew in.

FREDERICK: No Friend to Love like a long Voyage at Sea.

BLUNT: Except a Nunnery, *Fred*.

4 Prince Charles, leader of the Royalist forces, who became Charles II in 1660. 5 pedlars, merchants. 6 state (?).

WILLMORE: Death! but will they not be kind, quickly be kind? Thou know'st I'm no tame Sigher, but a rampant Lion of the Forest.

(*Two Men drest all over with Horns*[7] *of several sorts, making Grimaces at one another, with Papers pinn'd on their Backs, advance from the farther end of the Scene.*)

BELVILE: Oh the fantastical Rogues, how they are dress'd! 'tis a Satire against the whole Sex.

WILLMORE: Is this a Fruit that grows in this warm Country?

BELVILE: Yes: 'Tis pretty to see these *Italians* start, swell, and stab at the Word
100   *Cuckold*, and yet stumble at Horns on every Threshold.

WILLMORE: See what's on their Back (*Reads.*) *Flowers for every Night.* — Ah Rogue! And more sweet than Roses of ev'ry Month! This is a Gardiner of *Adam's* own breeding. (*They dance.*)

BELVILE: What think you of those grave People? — is a Wake in *Essex* half so mad or extravagant?

WILLMORE: I like their sober grave way, 'tis a kind of legal authoriz'd Fornication, where the Men are not chid for't, nor the Women despis'd, as amongst our dull *English*; even the Monsieurs[8] want that part of good Manners.

BELVILE: But here in *Italy* a Monsieur is the humblest best-bred Gentleman —
110   Duels are so baffled by Bravoes that an age shews not one, but between a *Frenchman* and a Hang-man, who is as much too hard for him on the Piazza, as they are for a *Dutchman* on the new Bridge — But see another Crew.

(*Enter* FLORINDA, HELLENA, *and* VALERIA, *drest like Gipsies;* CALLIS *and* STEPHANO, LUCETTA, PHILIPPO *and* SANCHO *in Masquerade.*)

HELLENA: Sister, there's your *Englishman*, and with him a handsome proper Fellow — I'll to him, and instead of telling him his Fortune, try my own.

WILLMORE: Gipsies, on my Life — Sure these will prattle if a Man cross their Hands.[9] (*Goes to* HELLENA) — Dear pretty (and I hope) young Devil, will you tell an amorous Stranger what Luck he's like to have?

HELLENA: Have a care how you venture with me, Sir, lest I pick your Pocket,
120   which will more vex your *English* Humour, than an *Italian* Fortune will please you.

WILLMORE: How the Devil cam'st thou to know my Country and Humour?

HELLENA: The first I guess by a certain forward Impudence, which does not displease me at this time; and the Loss of your Money will vex you, because I hope you have but very little to lose.

WILLMORE: Egad Child, thou'rt i'th' right; it is so little, I dare not offer it thee for a Kindness — But cannot you divine what other things of more value I have about me, that I would more willingly part with?

HELLENA: Indeed no, that's the Business of a Witch, and I am but a Gipsy
130   yet — Yet, without looking in your Hand, I have a parlous Guess, 'tis some foolish Heart you mean, an inconstant *English* Heart, as little worth stealing as your Purse.

---

7 horns were the traditional emblem of a cuckold. 8 the French. 9 gives them money.

WILLMORE: Nay, then thou dost deal with the Devil, that's certain — Thou hast guess'd as right as if thou hadst been one of that Number it has languisht for — I find you'll be better acquainted with it; nor can you take it in a better time, for I am come from Sea, Child; and *Venus* not being propitious to me in her own Element,[10] I have a world of Love in store — Wou'd you would be good-natur'd, and take some on't off my Hands.

HELLENA: Why — I could be inclin'd that way — but for a foolish Vow I am going to make — to die a Maid.

WILLMORE: Then thou art damn'd without Redemption; and as I am a good Christian, I ought in charity to divert so wicked a Design — therefore prithee, dear Creature, let me know quickly when and where I shall begin to set a helping hand to so good a Work.

HELLENA: If you should prevail with my tender Heart (as I begin to fear you will, for you have horrible loving Eyes) there will be difficulty in't that you'll hardly undergo for my sake.

WILLMORE: Faith, Child, I have been bred in Dangers, and wear a Sword that has been employ'd in a worse Cause, than for a handsome kind Woman — Name the Danger — let it be any thing but a long Siege, and I'll undertake it.

HELLENA: Can you storm?

WILLMORE: Oh, most furiously.

HELLENA: What think you of a Nunnery-wall? for he that wins me, must gain that first.

WILLMORE: A Nun! Oh how I love thee for't! there's no Sinner like a young Saint — Nay, now there's no denying me: the old Law had no Curse (to a Woman) like dying a Maid; witness *Jephtha's* Daughter.[11]

HELLENA: A very good Text this, if well handled; and I perceive, Father Captain, you would impose no severe Penance on her who was inclin'd to console her self before she took Orders.

WILLMORE: If she be young and handsome.

HELLENA: Ay, there's it — but if she be not —

WILLMORE: By this Hand, Child, I have an implicit Faith, and dare venture on thee with all Faults — besides, 'tis more meritorious to leave the World when thou hast tasted and prov'd the Pleasure on't; then 'twill be a Virtue in thee, which now will be pure Ignorance.

HELLENA: I perceive, good Father Captain, you design only to make me fit for Heaven — but if on the contrary you should quite divert me from it, and bring me back to the World again, I should have a new Man to seek I find; and what a grief that will be — for when I begin, I fancy I shall love like any thing: I never try'd yet.

WILLMORE: Egad, and that's kind — Prithee, dear Creature, give me Credit for a Heart, for faith, I'm a very honest Fellow — Oh, I long to come first to the Banquet of Love; and such a swinging[12] Appetite I bring — Oh, I'm impatient. Thy Lodging, Sweetheart, thy Lodging, or I'm a dead man.

---

10 Venus, the Roman goddess of love, was born from the sea. 11 Jephtha, a judge of Israel, sacrificed his daughter and only child to fulfil a vow made before going into battle (see Judges 11:1–12:7). 12 huge, powerful.

HELLENA: Why must we be either guilty of Fornication or Murder, if we converse with you Men?— And is there no difference between leave to love me, and leave to lie with me?

180 WILLMORE: Faith, Child, they were made to go together.

LUCETTA: Are you sure this is the Man? (*Pointing to* BLUNT.)

SANCHO: When did I mistake your Game?

LUCETTA: This is a stranger, I know by his gazing; if he be brisk he'll venture to follow me; and then, if I understand my Trade, he's mine: he's *English* too, and they say that's a sort of good natur'd loving People, and have generally so kind an opinion of themselves, that a Woman with any Wit may flatter 'em into any sort of Fool she pleases.

BLUNT: 'Tis so — she is taken — I have Beauties which my false Glass at home did not discover.

(*She often passes by* BLUNT *and gazes on him; he struts, and cocks,*[13] *and walks, and gazes on her.*)

190 FLORINDA: This woman watches me so, I shall get no Opportunity to discover my self to him, and so miss the intent of my coming — But as I was saying, Sir — by this Line you should be a Lover. (*Looking in his Hand.*)

BELVILE: I thought how right you guess'd, all Men are in love, or pretend to be so — Come, let me go, I'm weary of this fooling. (*Walks away.*)

FLORINDA: I will not, till you have confess'd whether the Passion that you have vow'd *Florinda* be true or false. (*She holds him, he strives to get from her.*)

BELVILE: *Florinda*! (*Turns quick towards her.*)

FLORINDA: Softly.

BELVILE: Thou hast nam'd one will fix me here for ever.

200 FLORINDA: She'll be disappointed then, who expects you this Night at the Garden-gate, and if you'll fail not — as let me see the other Hand — you will go near to do — she vows to die or make you happy. (*Looks on* CALLIS, *who observes 'em.*)

BELVILE: What canst thou mean?

FLORINDA: That which I say — Farewel. (*Offers to go.*)

BELVILE: Oh charming Sybil,[14] stay, complete that Joy, which, as it is, will turn into Distraction! — Where must I be? at the Garden-gate? I know it — at night you say — I'll sooner forfeit Heaven than disobey.

(*Enter* DON PEDRO *and other Masquers, and pass over the Stage.*)

CALLIS: Madam, your Brother's here.

FLORINDA: Take this to instruct you farther. (*Gives him a Letter, and goes off.*)

210 FREDERICK: Have a care, Sir, what you promise; this may be a Trap laid by her Brother to ruin you.

BELVILE: Do not disturb my Happiness with Doubts.

(*Opens the Letter.*)

WILLMORE: My dear pretty Creature, a Thousand Blessings on thee; still in this Habit, you say, and after Dinner at this Place.

13 stands up jauntily, like a rooster. 14 prophetess.

HELLENA: Yes, if you will swear to keep your Heart, and not bestow it between this time and that.

WILLMORE: By all the little Gods of Love I swear, I'll leave it with you; and if you run away with it, those Deities of Justice will revenge me.

(*Exeunt all the Women except* LUCETTA.)

FREDERICK: Do you know the Hand?

BELVILE: 'Tis *Florinda's*. All Blessings fall upon the virtuous Maid.

FREDERICK: Nay, no Idolatry, a sober Sacrifice I'll allow you.

BELVILE: Oh Friends! the welcom'st News, the softest Letter! — nay, you shall see it; and could you now be serious, I might be made the happiest Man the Sun shines on.

WILLMORE: The Reason of this mighty Joy.

BELVILE: See how kindly she invites me to deliver her from the threaten'd Violence of her Brother — will you not assist me?

WILLMORE: I know not what thou mean'st, but I'll make one at any Mischief where a Woman's concern'd — but she'll be grateful to us for the Favour, will she not?

BELVILE: How mean you?

WILLMORE: How should I mean? Thou know'st there's but one way for a Woman to oblige me.

BELVILE: Don't prophane — the Maid is nicely[15] virtuous.

WILLMORE: Who, pox, then she's fit for nothing but a Husband; let her e'en go, Colonel.

FREDERICK: Peace, she's the Colonel's Mistress, Sir.

WILLMORE: Let her be the Devil; if she be thy Mistress, I'll serve her — name the way.

BELVILE: Read here this Postscript. (*Gives him a letter.*)

WILLMORE: (*Reads.*) *At Ten at night — at the Garden-Gate — of which, if I cannot get the Key, I will contrive a way over the Wall — come attended with a Friend or two.—* Kind heart, if we three cannot weave a String to let her down a Garden-Wall, 'twere pity but the Hangman wove one for us all.

FREDERICK: Let her alone for that: your Woman's Wit, your fair kind Woman, will out-trick a Brother or a Jew, and contrive like a Jesuit in Chains — but see, *Ned Blunt* is stoln out after the Lure of a Damsel. (*Exeunt* BLUNT *and* LUCETTA.)

BELVILE: So he'll scarce find his way home again, unless we get him cry'd by the Bell-man[16] in the Market-place, and 'twou'd sound prettily — a lost *English* Boy of Thirty.

FREDERICK: I hope 'tis some common crafty Sinner, one that will fit him; it may be she'll sell him for *Peru*, the Rogue's sturdy and would work well in a Mine; at least I hope she'll dress him for our Mirth; cheat him of all, then have him well-favour'dly bang'd,[17] and turn'd out naked at Midnight.

WILLMORE: Prithee what Humour is he of, that you wish him so well?

15 scrupulously. 16 town crier. 17 soundly beaten.

BELVILE: Why, of an *English* Elder Brother's Humour, educated in a Nursery, with a Maid to tend him till Fifteen, and lies with his Grand-mother till he's of Age; one that knows no Pleasure beyond riding to the next Fair, or going up to *London* with his right Worshipful Father in Parliament-time; wearing gay Clothes, or making honourable Love to his Lady Mother's Laundry-Maid; gets drunk at a Hunting-Match, and ten to one then gives some Proofs of his Prowess — A pox upon him, he's our Banker, and has all our Cash about him, and if he fail we are all broke.

FREDERICK: Oh let him alone for that matter, he's of a damn'd stingy Quality, that will secure our Stock. I know not in what Danger it were indeed, if the Jilt should pretend she's in love with him, for 'tis a kind believing Coxcomb; otherwise if he part with more than a Piece of Eight[18]— geld him: for which offer he may chance to be beaten, if she be a Whore of the first Rank.

BELVILE: Nay the Rogue will not be easily beaten, he's stout enough; perhaps if they talk beyond his Capacity, he may chance to exercise his Courage upon some of them; else I'm sure they'll find it as difficult to beat as to please him.

WILLMORE: 'Tis a lucky Devil to light upon so kind a Wench!

FREDERICK: Thou hadst a great deal of talk with thy little Gipsy, coud'st thou do no good upon her? for mine was hard-hearted.

WILLMORE: Hang her, she was some damn'd honest Person of Quality, I'm sure, she was so very free and witty. If her Face be but answerable to her Wit and Humour, I would be bound to Constancy this Month to gain her. In the mean time, have you made no kind Acquaintance since you came to Town?— You do not use to be honest[19] so long, Gentlemen.

FREDERICK: Faith, Love has kept us honest: we have been all fir'd with a Beauty newly come to Town, the famous *Paduana*[20] *Angelica Bianca*.

WILLMORE: What, the Mistress of the dead *Spanish* General?

BELVILE: Yes, she's now the only ador'd Beauty of all the Youth in *Naples*, who put on all their Charms to appear lovely in her sight, their Coaches, Liveries, and themselves, all gay, as on a Monarch's Birth-Day, to attract the Eyes of this fair Charmer, while she has the Pleasure to behold all languish for her that see her.

FREDERICK: 'Tis pretty to see with how much Love the Men regard her, and how much Envy the Women.

WILLMORE: What Gallant has she?

BELVILE: None, she's exposed to Sale, and four Days in the Week she's yours — for so much a Month.

WILLMORE: The very Thought of it quenches all manner of Fire in me — yet prithee let's see her.

BELVILE: Let's first to Dinner, and after that we'll pass the Day as you please — but at Night ye must all be at my Devotion.

WILLMORE: I will not fail you. (*Exeunt.*)

---

18 Spanish coin, a dollar. 19 chaste. 20 woman from Padua.

ACT TWO

SCENE 1. (*The Long Street.*)

> (*Enter* BELVILE *and* FREDERICK *in Masquing-Habits, and* WILLMORE *in his own Clothes, with a Vizard*[1] *in his Hand.*)

WILLMORE: But why thus disguis'd and muzzl'd?

BELVILE: Because whatever Extravagances we commit in these Faces, our own may not be oblig'd to answer 'em.

WILLMORE: I should have chang'd my Eternal Buff[2] too: but no matter, my little Gipsy wou'd not have found me out then: for if she should change hers, it is impossible I should know her, unless I should hear her prattle — A Pox on't, I cannot get her out of my Head: Pray Heaven, if ever I do see her again, she prove damnable ugly, that I may fortify my self against her Tongue.

BELVILE: Have a care of Love, for o' my conscience she was not of a Quality to give thee any hopes.

WILLMORE: Pox on 'em, why do they draw a Man in then? She has play'd with my Heart so, that 'twill never lie still till I have met with some kind Wench, that will play the Game out with me — Oh for my Arms full of soft, white, kind — Woman! such as I fancy *Angelica*.

BELVILE: This is her House, if you were but in stock[3] to get admittance; they have not din'd yet; I perceive the Picture is not out.

> (*Enter* BLUNT.)

WILLMORE: I long to see the Shadow of the fair Substance, a Man may gaze on that for nothing.

BLUNT: Colonel, thy Hand — and thine, *Fred.* I have been an Ass, a deluded Fool, a very Coxcomb from my Birth till this Hour, and heartily repent my little Faith.

BELVILE: What the Devil's the matter with thee *Ned*?

BLUNT: Oh, such a Mistress, *Fred.* Such a Girl!

WILLMORE: Ha! where?

FREDERICK: Ay where!

BLUNT: So fond, so amorous, so toying and fine! and all for sheer Love, ye Rogue! Oh how she lookt and kiss'd! and sooth'd my Heart from my Bosom. I cannot think I was awake, and yet methinks I see and feel her Charms still — *Fred.* — Try if she have not left the taste of her balmy Kisses upon my Lips — (*Kisses him.*)

BELVILE: Ha, ha, ha!

WILLMORE: Death Man, where is she?

BLUNT: What a Dog was I to stay in dull *England* so long — How have I laught at the Colonel when he sigh'd for Love! but now the little Archer has reveng'd him, and by his own Dart, I can guess at all his Joys, which then I took for Fancies, mere Dreams and Fables — Well, I'm resolved to sell all in *Essex*, and plant here for ever.

---

1 face-mask attached to a stick. 2 military coat made of tough leather. 3 costume.

BELVILE: What a Blessing 'tis, thou hast a Mistress thou dar'st boast of; for I know
40   thy Humour is rather to have a proclaim'd Clap, than a secret Amour.

WILLMORE: Dost know her Name?

BLUNT: Her Name? No, 'sheartlikins; what care I for Names?   She's fair, young,
brisk and kind, even to ravishment: and what a Pox care I for knowing
her by another Title?

WILLMORE: Didst give her anything?

BLUNT: Give her! — Ha, ha, ha! why, she's a Person of Quality — That's a
good one, give her! 'sheartlikins dost think such Creatures are to be
bought? Or are we provided for such a Purchase? Give her, quoth ye?
Why she presented me with this Bracelet, for the Toy of a Diamond I
50   us'd to wear: No, Gentlemen, *Ned Blunt* is not every Body — She expects
me again to night.

WILLMORE: Egad that's well; we'll all go.

BLUNT: Not a Soul: No, Gentlemen, you are Wits; I am a dull Country Rogue, I.

FREDERICK: Well, Sir, for all your Person of Quality, I shall be very glad to
understand your Purse be secure; 'tis our whole Estate at present, which we
are loth to hazard in one Bottom:[4] come, Sir, unload.

BLUNT: Take the necessary Trifle, useless now to me, that am belov'd by such
a Gentlewoman — 'sheartlikins Money! Here take mine too.

FREDERICK: No, keep that to be cozen'd,[5] that we may laugh.

60   WILLMORE: Cozen'd! — Death! wou'd I cou'd meet with one, that wou'd cozen
me of all the Love I cou'd spare to night.

FREDERICK: Pox 'tis some common Whore upon my Life.

BLUNT: A Whore! yes with such Clothes! such Jewels! such a House! such
Furniture, and so attended! a Whore!

BELVILE: Why yes, Sir, they are Whores, tho they'll neither entertain you with
Drinking, Swearing, or Baudy; are Whores in all those gay Clothes, and
right[6] Jewels; are Whores with great Houses richly furnisht with Velvet
Beds, Store of Plate,[7] handsome Attendance, and fine Coaches, are Whores
and errant[8] ones.

70   WILLMORE: Pox on't, where do these fine Whores live?

BELVILE: Where no Rogue in Office yclep'd[9] Constables dare give 'em laws,
nor the Wine-inspired Bullies of the Town break their Windows; yet they
are Whores, tho this *Essex* Calf believe them Persons of Quality.

BLUNT: 'Sheartlikins, y'are all Fools, there are things about this *Essex* Calf,
that shall take with the Ladies, beyond all your Wits and Parts — This
Shape and Size, Gentlemen, are not to be despis'd; my Waste[10] tolerably
long, with other inviting Signs, that shall be nameless.

WILLMORE: Egad I believe he may have met with some Person of Quality that
may be kind to him.

80   BELVILE: Dost thou perceive any such tempting things about him, should make
a fine Woman, and of Quality, pick him out from all Mankind, to throw
away her Youth and Beauty upon, nay, and her dear Heart too? — no, no,
Angelica has rais'd the Price too high.

---

4 ship (punningly). 5 tricked, cheated. 6 genuine. 7 silver utensils. 8 thorough; through and through.
9 called. 10 waist.

WILLMORE: May she languish for Mankind till she die, and be damn'd for that one Sin alone.

(*Enter two Bravoes, and hang up a great Picture of* ANGELICA's, *against the Balcony, and two little ones at each side of the Door.*)

BELVILE: See there the fair Sign to the Inn, where a Man may lodge that's Fool enough to give her Price. (WILLMORE *gazes on the Picture.*)

BLUNT: 'Sheartlikins, Gentlemen, what's this?

BELVILE: A famous Curtezan that's to be sold.

90 BLUNT: How! to be sold! nay then I have nothing to say to her — sold! what Impudence is practis'd in this Country? — With Order and Decency Whoring's established here by virtue of the Inquisition — Come let's be gone, I'm sure we're no Chapmen for this Commodity.

FREDERICK: Thou art none, I'm sure, unless thou could'st have her in thy Bed at the Price of a Coach in the Street.

WILLMORE: How wondrous fair she is — a Thousand Crowns a Month — by Heaven as many Kingdoms were too little. A plague of this Poverty — of which I ne'er complain, but when it hinders my Approach to Beauty, which Virtue ne'er could purchase. (*Turns from the Picture.*)

100 BLUNT: What's this? — (*Reads*) *A Thousand Crowns a Month!* — 'Sheartlikins, here's a Sum! sure 'tis a mistake. — Hark you, Friend, does she take or give so much by the Month!

FREDERICK: A Thousand Crowns! Why, 'tis a Portion for the *Infanta*.[11]

BLUNT: Hark ye, Friends, won't she trust?

BRAVO: This is a Trade, Sir, that cannot live by Credit.

(*Enter* DON PEDRO *in Masquerade, follow'd by* STEPHANO.)

BELVILE: See, here's more Company, let's walk off a while.

(*Exeunt* ENGLISH.) (PEDRO *Reads.*)

PEDRO: Fetch me a Thousand Crowns, I never wish to buy this Beauty at an easier Rate. (*Passes off.*)

(*Enter* ANGELICA *and* MORETTA *in the Balcony, and draw a Silk Curtain.*)

ANGELICA: Prithee what said those Fellows to thee?

110 BRAVO: Madam the first were Admirers of Beauty only, but no purchasers; they were merry with your Price and Picture, laught at the Sum, and so past off.

ANGELICA: No matter, I'm not displeas'd with their rallying; their Wonder feeds my Vanity, and he that wishes to buy, gives me more Pride, than he that gives my Price can make me Pleasure.

BRAVO: Madam, the last I knew thro all his disguises to be Don *Pedro*, Nephew to the General, and who was with him in *Pampelona*.

ANGELICA: Don *Pedro*! my old Gallant's Nephew! When his Uncle dy'd, he left him a vast Sum of Money; it is he who was so in love with me at *Padua*, and who us'd to make the General so jealous.

120 MORETTA: Is this he that us'd to prance before our Window and take such care

11 dowry for the Princess of Spain.

to shew himself an amorous Ass? if I am not mistaken, he is the likeliest Man to give your Price.

ANGELICA: The Man is brave and generous, but of an Humour so uneasy and inconstant, that the victory over his Heart is as soon lost as won; a Slave that can add little to the Triumph of the Conqueror: but inconstancy's the Sin of all Mankind, therefore I'm resolved that nothing but Gold shall charm my Heart.

MORETTA: I'm glad on't; 'tis only interest that Women of our Profession ought to consider: tho I wonder what has kept you from that general Disease of
130 our Sex so long, I mean that of being in Love.

ANGELICA: A kind, but sullen Star, under which I had the Happiness to be born; yet I have had no time for Love; the bravest and noblest of Mankind have pur- chas'd my Favours at so dear a Rate, as if no Coin but Gold were current with our Trade — But here's Don *Pedro* again, fetch me my Lute — for 'tis for him or Don *Antonio* the Vice-Roy's Son, that I have spread my Nets.

(Enter at one Door DON PEDRO, *and* STEPHANO; DON ANTONIO *and* DIEGO *[his page], at the other Door, with People following him in Masquerade, antickly* [12] *attir'd, some with Musick: they both go up to the Picture.)*

ANTONIO: A thousand Crowns! had not the Painter flatter'd her, I should not think it dear.

PEDRO: Flatter'd her! by Heaven he cannot. I have seen the Original, nor is there one Charm here more than adorns her Face and Eyes; all this soft and
140 sweet, with a certain languishing Air, that no Artist can represent.

ANTONIO: What I heard of her Beauty before had fir'd my Soul, but this con- firmation of it has blown it into a flame.

PEDRO: Ha!

PAGE: Sir, I have known you throw away a Thousand Crowns on a worse Face, and tho y' are near your Marriage, you may venture a little Love here; *Florinda* — will not miss it.

PEDRO: *(Aside.)* Ha! *Florinda!* Sure 'tis *Antonio.*

ANTONIO: *Florinda!* name not those distant Joys, there's not one thought of her will check my Passion here.

150 PEDRO: *(Aside.) Florinda* scorn'd! and all my Hopes defeated of the Possession of *Angelica!* (*A noise of a Lute above.* ANTONIO *gazes up.*) Her Injuries by Heaven he shall not boast of.

(Song to a Lute above.)

SONG

When Damon *first began to love,*
He languisht *in a soft Desire,*
And knew not how the Gods to move,
To lessen or increase his Fire,
For Caelia in her charming Eyes
Wore *all Love's Sweet, and all his Cruelties.*

12 grotesquely.

II

But as beneath a Shade he lay,
160   *Weaving of Flow'rs for Caelia's Hair,*
She chanc'd to lead her Flock that way,
And saw the am'rous Shepherd there.
She gaz'd around upon the Place,
And saw the Grove (resembling Night)
To all the Joys of Love invite,
Whilst guilty Smile and Blushes drest her Face.
At this the bashful youth all Transport grew,
And with kind Force he taught the Virgin how
To yield what all his Sighs cou'd never do.

170   ANTONIO: By Heav'n she's charming fair!

(ANGELICA *throws open the Curtains, and bows to* ANTONIO, *who pulls off his Vizard, and bows and blows up Kisses.* PEDRO *unseen looks in his Face.*)

PEDRO: 'Tis he, the false *Antonio!*
ANTONIO: (*To the* BRAVO.) Friend, where must I pay my offering of Love?
    My Thousand Crowns I mean.
PEDRO: That Offering I have design'd to make
    And yours will come too late.
ANTONIO: Prithee be gone, I shall grow angry else,
    And then thou art not safe.
PEDRO: My Anger may be fatal, Sir, as yours;
    And he that enters here may prove this Truth.
180   ANTONIO: I know not who thou art, but I am sure thou'rt worth my killing, and
    aiming at *Angelica.* (*They draw and fight.*)

(*Enter* WILLMORE *and* BLUNT, *who draw and part 'em.*)

BLUNT: 'Sheartlikins, here's fine doings.
WILLMORE: Tilting for the Wench I'm sure — nay gad, if that wou'd win her, I
    have as good a Sword as the best of ye — Put up — put up, and take another
    time and place, for this is design'd for Lovers only. (*They all put up.*)
PEDRO: We are prevented; dare you meet me to morrow on the *Molo?*[13]
    For I've a Title to a better quarrel,
    That of *Florinda*, in whose credulous Heart
    Thou'st made an Int'rest, and destroy'd my Hopes.
190   ANTONIO: Dare?
    I'll meet thee there as early as the Day.
PEDRO: We will come thus disguis'd, that whosoever chance to get the better,
    he may escape unknown.
ANTONIO: It shall be so. (*Exeunt* PEDRO *and* STEPHANO.)
    Who shou'd this Rival be? unless the *English* Colonel, of whom I've often
    heard Don *Pedro* speak; it must be he, and time he were removed, who
    lays a Claim to all my Happiness.

---

13 mall, promenade.

(WILLMORE *having gaz'd all this while on the Picture, pulls down a little one.*)

WILLMORE: This posture's loose and negligent,
    The sight on't wou'd beget a warm desire
200   In Souls, whom Impotence and Age had chill'd.
    — This must along with me.
BRAVO: What means this rudeness, Sir?— restore the Picture.
ANTONIO: Ha! Rudeness committed to the fair *Angelica!* — Restore the Picture,
    Sir.
WILLMORE: Indeed I will not, Sir.
ANTONIO: By Heav'n but you shall.
WILLMORE: Nay, do not shew your Sword; if you do, by this dear Beauty — I will
    shew mine too.
ANTONIO: What right can you pretend to't?
210 WILLMORE: That of Possession which I will maintain — you perhaps have 1000
    Crowns to give for the Original.
ANTONIO: No matter, Sir, you shall restore the Picture.
ANGELICA: Oh, *Moretta!* what's the matter? (ANGELICA *and* MORETTA *above.*)
ANTONIO: Or leave your Life behind.
WILLMORE: Death! you lye — I will do neither.
ANGELICA: Hold, I command you, if for me you fight.

(*They fight, the* SPANIARDS *join with* ANTONIO, BLUNT *laying on like mad.*)

(*They leave off and bow.*)

WILLMORE: How heavenly fair she is! — ah Plague of her Price.
ANGELICA: You Sir in Buff, you that appear a Soldier, that first began this
    Insolence.
220 WILLMORE: 'Tis true, I did so, if you call it Insolence for a Man to preserve
    himself; I saw your charming Picture, and was wounded: quite thro my
    Soul each pointed Beauty ran; and wanting a Thousand Crowns to procure
    my remedy, I laid this little Picture to my Bosom — which if you cannot
    allow me, I'll resign.
ANGELICA: No, you may keep the Trifle.
ANTONIO: You shall first ask my leave, and this. (*Fight again as before.*)

(*Enter* BELVILE *and* FREDERICK, *who join with the* ENGLISH.)

ANGELICA: Hold; will you ruin me?—*Bisky, Sebastian*, part them. (*The* SPANIARDS
    are beaten off.)
MORETTA: Oh Madam, we're undone, a pox upon that rude Fellow, he's set
    on to ruin us: we shall never see good days, till all these fighting poor Rogues
230   are sent to the Gallies.[14]

(*Enter* BELVILE, BLUNT, FREDERICK *and* WILLMORE, *with his shirt bloody.*)

BLUNT: 'Sheartlikins, beat me at this Sport, and I'll ne'er wear Sword more.

---

14 galleys: large rowing ships powered by slaves and criminals.

BELVILE: The Devil's in thee for a mad Fellow, thou art always one at an unlucky Adventure. — Come, let's be gone whilst we're safe, and remember these are *Spaniards*, a sort of People that know how to revenge an Affront.

FREDERICK: You bleed; I hope you are not wounded. (*To* WILLMORE.)

WILLMORE: Not much: — a plague upon your Dons, if they fight no better they'll ne'er recover *Flanders*.[15] — What the Devil was't to them that I took down the Picture?

BLUNT: Took it! 'Sheartlikins, we'll have the great one too; 'tis ours by Conquest. — Prithee, help me up, and I'll pull it down. —

ANGELICA: Stay, Sir, and e'er you affront me further, let me know how you durst commit this Outrage — To you I speak, Sir, for you appear like a Gentleman.

WILLMORE: To me, Madam? — Gentlemen, your Servant. (BELVILE *stays him.*)

BELVILE: Is the Devil in thee? Do'st know the danger of entring the house of an incens'd Curtezan?

WILLMORE: I thank you for your care — but there are other matters in hand, there are, tho we have no great Temptation. — Death! let me go.

FREDERICK: Yes, to your Lodging, if you will, but not in here. — Damn these gay Harlots — by this Hand I'll have as sound and handsome a Whore for a Patacoone.[16] — Death, Man, she'll murder thee.

WILLMORE: Oh! fear me not, shall I not venture where a Beauty calls? a lovely charming Beauty? for fear of danger! when by Heaven there's none so great as to long for her, whilst I want Money to purchase her.

FREDERICK: Therefore 'tis loss of time, unless you had the thousand Crowns to pay.

WILLMORE: It may be she may give a Favour, at least I shall have the pleasure of saluting her when I enter, and when I depart.

BELVILE: Pox, she'll as soon lie with thee, as kiss thee, and sooner stab than do either — you shall not go.

ANGELICA: Fear not, Sir, all I have to wound with, is my Eyes.

BLUNT: Let him go, 'Sheartlikins, I believe the Gentlewoman means well.

BELVILE: Well, take thy Fortune, we'll expect you in the next Street. — Farewell Fool, — farewell —

WILLMORE: 'Bye Colonel — (*Goes in.*)

FREDERICK: The Rogue's stark mad for a Wench. (*Exeunt.*)

SCENE 2. (*A Fine Chamber.*)

(*Enter* WILLMORE, ANGELICA, *and* MORETTA.)

ANGELICA: Insolent Sir, how durst you pull down my Picture?

WILLMORE: Rather, how durst you set it up, to tempt poor amorous Mortals with so much Excellence? which I find you have but too well consulted by the unmerciful price you set upon't. — Is all this Heaven of Beauty shewn to move Despair in those that cannot buy? and can you think the effects of that Despair shou'd be less extravagant than I have shewn?

---

15 France had recently annexed part of Flanders in the Spanish Netherlands. 16 Spanish coin of little value.

ANGELICA: I sent for you to ask my Pardon, Sir, not to aggravate your Crime. —
   I thought I shou'd have seen you at my Feet imploring it.

WILLMORE: You are deceived, I came to rail at you, and talk such Truths, too,
10   as shall let you see the Vanity of that Pride, which taught you how to set
   such a Price on Sin. For such it is, whilst that which is Love's due is meanly
   barter'd for.

ANGELICA: Ha, ha, ha, alas, good Captain, what pity 'tis your edifying Doctrine
   will do no good upon me — *Moretta*, fetch the Gentleman a Glass, and let
   him survey himself, to see what Charms he has, — (*Aside in a soft tone.*) and
   guess my Business.

MORETTA: He knows himself of old, I believe those Breeches and he have been
   acquainted ever since he was beaten at *Worcester*.[1]

ANGELICA: Nay, do not abuse the poor Creature. —

20   MORETTA: Good Weather-beaten Corporal, will you march off? we have no need
   of your Doctrine, tho you have of our Charity; but at present we have no
   Scraps, we can afford no kindness for God's sake; in fine, Sirrah, the Price
   is too high i'th' Mouth for you, therefore troop,[2] I say.

WILLMORE: Here, good Fore-Woman of the Shop, serve me, and I'll be gone.

MORETTA: Keep it to pay your Laundress, your Linen stinks of the Gun-Room;
   for here's no selling by Retail.

WILLMORE: Thou hast sold plenty of thy stale Ware at a cheap Rate.

MORETTA: Ay, the more silly kind Heart I, but this is an Age wherein Beauty
   is at higher Rates. — In fine, you know the price of this.

30   WILLMORE: I grant you 'tis here set down a thousand Crowns a Month — Baud,
   take your black Lead and sum it up, that I may have a Pistole[3]-worth of
   these vain gay things, and I'll trouble you no more.

MORETTA: Pox on him, he'll fret me to Death: — abominable Fellow, I tell
   thee, we only sell by the whole Piece.

WILLMORE: 'Tis very hard, the whole Cargo or nothing — Faith, Madam, my
   Stock will not reach it, I cannot be your Chapman. — Yet I have Countrymen in Town, Merchants of Love, like me; I'll see if they'l put for a share,
   we cannot lose much by it, and what we have no use for, we'll sell upon the
   Friday's Mart, at — *Who gives more?* I am studying, Madam, how to purchase
40   you, tho at present I am unprovided of Money.

ANGELICA: (*Aside.*) Sure, this from any other Man would anger me — nor shall
   he know the Conquest he has made — Poor angry Man, how I despise this
   railing.

WILLMORE: Yes, I am poor — but I'm a Gentleman,
   And one that scorns this Baseness which you practise.
   Poor as I am, I would not sell my self,
   No, not to gain your charming high-priz'd Person.
   Tho I admire you strangely for your Beauty,
   Yet I contemn your Mind.

---

1 site of the decisive battle in 1651 in which the Royalist forces of Charles II were defeated by the Puritan
army led by Cromwell. 2 march. 3 Spanish coin worth about an English pound.

50   — And yet I wou'd at any rate enjoy you;
At your own rate — but cannot — See here
The only Sum I can command on Earth;
I know not where to eat when this is gone:
Yet such a Slave I am to Love and Beauty,
This last reserve I'll sacrifice to enjoy you.
— Nay, do not frown, I know you are to be bought,
And wou'd be bought by me, by me,
For a mean trifling Sum, if I could pay it down.
Which happy knowledge I will still repeat,
60   And lay it to my Heart, it has a Virtue in't,
And soon will cure those Wounds your Eyes have made.
— And yet — there's something so divinely powerful there —
Nay, I will gaze — to let you see my Strength.

(*Holds her, looks on her, and pauses and sighs.*)

By Heaven, bright Creature — I would not for the World
Thy Fame were half so fair as is thy Face.

(*Turns her away from him.*)

ANGELICA: (*Aside.*) His words go thro me to the very Soul.
     — If you have nothing else to say to me.
WILLMORE: Yes, you shall hear how infamous you are —
     For which I do not hate thee:
70   But that secures my Heart, and all the Flames it feels
Are but so many Lusts,
I know it by their sudden bold intrusion.
The Fire's impatient and betrays, 'tis false —
For had it been the purer Flame of Love,
I should have pin'd and languish'd at your Feet,
Ere found the Impudence to have discover'd it.
I now dare stand your Scorn, and your Denial.
MORETTA: Sure she's bewitcht, that she can stand thus tamely, and hear his saucy
     railing. — Sirrah, will you be gone?
80 ANGELICA: (*To Moretta.*) How dare you take this liberty? — Withdraw. — Pray,
tell me, Sir, are not you guilty of the same mercenary Crime? When a
Lady is proposed to you for a Wife, you never ask how fair, discreet, or
virtuous she is; but what's her Fortune — which if but small, you cry — She
will not do my business — and basely leave her, tho she languish for you. —
Say, is not this as poor?
WILLMORE: It is a barbarous Custom, which I will scorn to defend in our Sex,
and do despise in yours.
ANGELICA: Thou art a brave Fellow! put up thy Gold, and know,
That were thy Fortune large, as is thy Soul,
90   Thou shouldst not buy my Love,
Couldst thou forget those mean Effects of Vanity,
Which set me out to sale; and as a Lover, prize
My yielding Joys.

Canst thou believe they'l be entirely thine,
Without considering they were mercenary?
WILLMORE: I cannot tell, I must bethink me first (*Aside.*) — ha,
Death, I'm going to believe her.
ANGELICA: Prithee, confirm that Faith — or if thou canst not — flatter me a
little, 'twill please me from thy Mouth.
100 WILLMORE: (*Aside.*) Curse on thy charming Tongue! dost thou return
My feign'd Contempt with so much subtilty?
Thou'st found the easiest way into my Heart,
Tho I yet know that all thou say'st is false.

(*Turning from her in a Rage.*)

ANGELICA: By all that's good 'tis real,
I never lov'd before, tho oft a Mistress.
— Shall my first Vows be slighted?
WILLMORE: (*Aside.*) What can she mean?
ANGELICA: (*In an angry tone.*) I find you cannot credit me.
WILLMORE: I know you take me for an errant Ass,
110 An Ass that may be sooth'd into Belief,
And then be us'd at pleasure.
— But, Madam I have been so often cheated
By perjur'd, soft, deluding Hypocrites,
That I've no Faith left for the cozening Sex,
Especially for Women of your Trade.
ANGELICA: The low esteem you have of me, perhaps,
May bring my Heart again:
For I have Pride that yet surmounts my Love.

(*She turns with Pride, he holds her.*)

WILLMORE: Throw off this Pride, this Enemy to Bliss,
120 And shew the Power of Love: 'tis with those Arms
I can be only vanquisht, made a Slave.
ANGELICA: Is all my mighty Expectation vanisht?
— No, I will not hear thee talk, — thou hast a Charm
In every word, that draws my Heart away.
And all the thousand Trophies I design'd,
Thou hast undone — Why art thou soft?
Thy Looks are bravely rough, and meant for War.
Could thou not storm on still?
I then perhaps had been as free as thou.
130 WILLMORE: (*Aside.*) Death! how she throws her Fire about my Soul!
— Take heed, fair Creature, how you raise my Hopes,
Which once assum'd pretend to all Dominion.
There's not a Joy thou hast in store
I shall not then command:
For which I'll pay thee back my Soul, my Life.
Come, let's begin th' account this happy minute.
ANGELICA: And will you pay me then the Price I ask?

WILLMORE: Oh, why dost thou draw me from an awful[4] Worship,
    By shewing thou art no Divinity?
140   Conceal the Fiend, and shew me all the Angel;
    Keep me but ignorant, and I'll be devout,
    And pay my Vows for ever at this Shrine.

(*Kneels, and kisses her Hand.*)

ANGELICA: The Pay I mean is but thy Love for mine.
    — Can you give that?
WILLMORE: Intirely — come, let's withdraw: where I'll renew my Vows, — and
    breathe 'em with such Ardour, thou shalt not doubt my Zeal.
ANGELICA: Thou hast a Power too strong to be resisted.

(*Exeunt* WILLMORE *and* ANGELICA.)

MORETTA: Now my Curse go with you — Is all our Project fallen to this? to love
    the only Enemy to our Trade? Nay, to love such a Shameroon,[5] a very
150   Beggar; nay, a Pirate-Beggar, whose Business is to rifle and be gone, a
    No-Purchase, No-Pay Tatterdemalion, an *English* Piccaroon;[6] a Rogue
    that fights for daily Drink, and takes a Pride in being loyally lousy — Oh,
    I could curse now, if I durst — This is the Fate of most Whores.
        Trophies, which from believing Fops we win,
        Are Spoils to those who cozen us again. (*Exit.*)

ACT THREE

SCENE 1. (*A Street.*)

(*Enter* FLORINDA, VALERIA, HELLENA, *in antick*[1] *different Dresses from what
they were in before,* CALLIS *attending.*)

FLORINDA: I wonder what should make my Brother in so ill a Humour: I hope
    he has not found out our Ramble this Morning.
HELLENA: No, if he had, we should have heard on't at both Ears, and have
    been mew'd up[2] this Afternoon; which I would not for the World should
    have happen'd — Hey ho! I'm sad as a Lover's Lute.
VALERIA: Well, methinks we have learnt this Trade of Gipsies as readily as if we
    had been bred upon the Road to *Loretto:*[3] and yet I did so fumble, when I
    told the Stranger his Fortune, that I was afraid I should have told my own
    and yours by mistake — But methinks *Hellena* has been very serious ever
10   since.
FLORINDA: I would give my Garters she were in love, to be reveng'd upon her,
    for abusing me — How is't, *Hellena?*
HELLENA: Ah! — would I had never seen my mad Monsieur — and yet for all
    your laughing I am not in love — and yet this small Acquaintance, o'my
    Conscience, will never out of my Head.

---

4 awe-inspiring. 5 cheat, imposter. 6 confidence trickster.
1 bizarre. 2 caged, confined. 3 Italian town, site of a famous shrine and so a centre for Gypsies.

VALERIA: Ha, ha, ha — I laugh to think how thou art fitted with a Lover, a Fellow that, I warrant, loves every new Face he sees.

HELLENA: Hum — he has not kept his Word with me here — and may be taken up — that thought is not very pleasant to me — what the Duce should this be now that I feel?

VALERIA: What is't like?

HELLENA: Nay, the Lord knows — but if I should be hanged, I cannot chuse but be angry and afraid, when I think that mad Fellow should be in love with any Body but me — What to think of my self I know not — Would I could meet with some true damn'd Gipsy, that I might know my Fortune.

VALERIA: Know it! why there's nothing so easy; thou wilt love this wandring Inconstant till thou find'st thy self hanged about his Neck, and then be as mad to get free again.

FLORINDA: Yes, *Valeria*; we shall see her bestride his Baggage-horse, and follow him to the Campaign.

HELLENA: So, so; now you are provided for, there's no care taken of poor me — But since you have set my Heart a wishing, I am resolv'd to know for what. I will not die of the Pip,[4] so I will not.

FLORINDA: Art thou mad to talk so? Who will like thee well enough to have thee, that hears what a mad Wench thou art?

HELLENA: Like me! I don't intend every he that likes me shall have me, but he that I like: I shou'd have staid in the Nunnery still, if I had lik'd my Lady Abbess as well as she lik'd me. No, I came thence, not (as my wise Brother imagines) to take an eternal Farewel of the World, but to love and to be belov'd; and I will be belov'd, or I'll get one of your Men, so I will.

VALERIA: Am I put into the Number of Lovers?

HELLENA: You! why Coz, I know thou art too good natur'd to leave us in any Design: Thou wou't venture a Cast, tho thou comest off a Loser, especially with such a Gamester — I observ'd your Man, and your willing Ears incline that way; and if you are not a Lover, 'tis an Art soon learnt — that I find. (*Sighs.*)

FLORINDA: I wonder how you learnt to love so easily, I had a thousand Charms to meet my Eyes and Ears, ere I cou'd yield; and 'twas the knowledge of *Belvile's* Merit, not the surprising Person, took my Soul — Thou art too rash to give a Heart at first sight.

HELLENA: Hang your considering Lover; I ne'er thought beyond the Fancy, that 'twas a very pretty, idle, silly kind of Pleasure to pass one's time with, to write little, soft, nonsensical Billets,[5] and with great difficulty and danger receive Answers; in which I shall have my Beauty prais'd, my Wit admir'd (tho little or none) and have the Vanity and Power to know I am desirable; then I have the more Inclination that way, because I am to be a Nun, and so shall not be suspected to have any such earthly Thoughts about me — But when I walk thus — and sigh thus — they'll think my Mind's upon my Monastery, and cry, how happy 'tis she's so resolv'd! — But not a Word of Man.

---

4 vague minor ailment or fit of bad temper. 5 billet-doux, love letters.

FLORINDA: What a mad Creature's this!

HELLENA: I'll warrant, if my Brother hears either of you sigh, he cries (gravely) — "I fear you have the Indiscretion to be in love, but take heed of the Honour of our House, and your own unspotted Fame;" and so he conjures on till he has laid the soft-wing'd God in your Hearts, or broke the Bird's-nest — But see here comes your Lover: but where's my inconstant? let's step aside, and we may learn something. (*Go aside.*)

(*Enter* BELVILE, FREDERICK *and* BLUNT.)

BELVILE: What means this? the Picture's taken in.

BLUNT: It may be the Wench is good-natur'd, and will be kind *gratis*. Your Friend's a proper handsom Fellow.

BELVILE: I rather think she has cut his Throat and is fled: I am mad he should throw himself into Dangers — Pox on't, I shall want him to night — let's knock and ask for him.

HELLENA: My heart goes a-pit a-pat, for fear 'tis my Man they talk of. (*Knock,* MORETTA *above.*)

MORETTA: What would you have?

BELVILE: Tell the Stranger that enter'd here about two Hours ago, that his Friends stay here for him.

MORETTA: A curse upon him for *Moretta,*[6] would he were at the Devil — but he's coming to you. (*Enter* WILLMORE.)

HELLENA: I, I, 'tis he. Oh how this vexes me.

BELVILE: And how, and how, dear Lad, has Fortune smil'd? Are we to break her Windows, or raise up Altars to her! hah!

WILLMORE: Does not my Fortune sit triumphant on my Brow? dost not see the little wanton God there all gay and smiling? have I not an Air about my Face and Eyes, that distinguish me from the Croud of common Lovers? By Heav'n, *Cupid's* Quiver has not half so many Darts as her Eyes — Oh such a *Bona Roba,*[7] to sleep in her Arms is lying in Fresco,[8] all perfum'd Air about me.

HELLENA: (*Aside.*) Here's fine encouragement for me to fool on.

WILLMORE: Hark ye, where didst thou purchase that rich Canary[9] we drank to-day? Tell me, that I may adore the Spigot, and sacrifice to the Butt: the Juice was divine, into which I must dip my Rosary, and then bless all things that I would have bold or fortunate.

BELVILE: Well, Sir, let's go take a Bottle, and hear the Story of your Success.

FREDERICK: Would not *French* Wine do better?

WILLMORE: Damn the hungry Balderdash;[10] cheerful Sack[11] has a generous Virtue in't, inspiring a successful Confidence, gives Eloquence to the Tongue, and Vigour to the Soul; and has in a few Hours compleated all my Hopes and Wishes. There's nothing left to raise a new Desire in me — Come let's be gay and wanton — and, Gentlemen, study, study what you want, for here are Friends (*Jingles coins.*) — that will supply, Gentlemen, —

6 from Moretta. 7 willing wench. 8 in the fresh air. 9 sweet wine from the Canary Islands. 10 worthless mixture of wines. 11 sherry.

hark! what a charming sound they make — 'tis he and she Gold whilst here, shall beget new Pleasures every moment.

BLUNT: But hark ye, Sir, you are not married, are you?

WILLMORE: All the Honey of Matrimony, but none of the Sting, Friend.

BLUNT: 'Sheartlikins, thou'rt a fortunate Rogue.

WILLMORE: I am so, Sir, let these inform you. — Ha, how sweetly they chime! Pox of Poverty, it makes a Man a Slave, makes Wit and Honour sneak. My Soul grew lean and rusty for want of Credit.

110 BLUNT: 'Sheartlikins, this I like well, it looks like my lucky Bargain! Oh how I long for the Approach of my Squire, that is to conduct me to her House again. Why! here's two provided for.

FREDERICK: By this light y're happy Men.

BLUNT: Fortune is pleased to smile on us, Gentlemen, — to smile on us.

(*Enter* SANCHO, *and pulls* BLUNT *by the Sleeve. They go aside.*)

SANCHO: Sir, my Lady expects you — she has remov'd all that might oppose your Will and Pleasure — and is impatient till you come.

BLUNT: Sir, I'll attend you — Oh the happiest Rogue! I'll take no leave, lest they either dog me, or stay me. (*Exit with* SANCHO.)

BELVILE: But then the little Gipsy is forgot?

120 WILLMORE: A Mischief on thee for putting her into my thoughts; I had quite forgot her else, and this Night's Debauch had drunk her quite down.

HELLENA: Had it so, good Captain? (*Claps him on the Back.*)

WILLMORE: (*Aside.*) Ha! I hope she did not hear.

HELLENA: What, afraid of such a Champion?

WILLMORE: Oh! you're a fine Lady of your word, are you not? to make a Man languish a whole day —

HELLENA: In tedious search of me.

WILLMORE: Egad, Child, thou'rt in the right, hadst thou seen what a melancholy Dog I have been ever since I was a Lover, how I have walkt the Streets like 130 a *Capuchin*,[12] with my Hands in my Sleeves — Faith, Sweetheart, thou wouldst pity me.

HELLENA: Now, if I should be hang'd, I can't be angry with him, he dissembles so heartily — Alas, good Captain, what pains you have taken — Now were I ungrateful not to reward so true a Servant.

WILLMORE: Poor Soul! that's kindly said, I see thou bearest a Conscience — come then for a beginning shew me thy dear Face.

HELLENA: I'm afraid, my small Acquaintance, you have been staying[13] that swinging stomach you boasted of this morning; I remember then my little Collation[14] would have gone down with you, without the Sauce of a hand- 140 some Face — Is your Stomach so queasy now?

WILLMORE: Faith long fasting, Child, spoils a Man's Appetite — yet if you durst treat, I could so lay about me still.

HELLENA: And would you fall to, before a Priest says Grace?

WILLMORE: Oh fie, fie, what an old out-of-fashion'd thing hast thou nam'd?

12 Franciscan friar. 13 appeasing. 14 light meal.

Thou could'st not dash me more out of Countenance, shouldst thou shew me an ugly Face.

(*Whilst he is seemingly courting* HELLENA, *enter* ANGELICA, MORETTA, BISKY, *and* SEBASTIAN, *all in Masquerade:* ANGELICA *sees* WILLMORE *and starts.*)

ANGELICA: Heavens, is't he? and passionately fond to see another Woman?

MORETTA: What cou'd you less expect from such a Swaggerer?

ANGELICA: Expect! as much as I paid him, a Heart intire,
150   Which I had pride enough to think when e'er I gave
    It would have rais'd the Man above the Vulgar,
    Made him all Soul, and that all soft and constant.

HELLENA: You see, Captain, how willing I am to be Friends with you, till Time and Ill-luck make us Lovers; and ask you the Question first, rather than put your Modesty to the blush, by asking me: for alas, I know you Captains are such strict Men, severe Observers of your Vows to Chastity, that 'twill be hard to prevail with your tender Conscience to marry a young willing Maid.

WILLMORE: Do not abuse me, for fear I should take thee at thy word, and marry
160   thee indeed, which I'm sure will be Revenge sufficient.

HELLENA: O' my Conscience, that will be our Destiny, because we are both of one humour; I am as inconstant as you, for I have considered, Captain, that a handsome Woman has a great deal to do whilst her Face is good, for then is our Harvest-time to gather Friends; and should I in these days of my Youth, catch a fit of foolish Constancy, I were undone; 'tis loitering by day-light in our great Journey: therefore declare, I'll allow but one year for Love, one year for Indifference, and one year for Hate — and then — go hang your self — for I profess myself the gay, the kind, and the inconstant — the Devil's in't if this won't please you.

170 WILLMORE: Oh most damnably! — I have a Heart with a hole quite thro it too, no Prison mine to keep a Mistress in.

ANGELICA: (*Aside.*) Perjur'd Man! how I believe thee now!

HELLENA: Well, I see our Business as well as Humours are alike, yours to cozen as many Maids as will trust you, and I as many Men as have Faith — See if I have not as desperate a lying look, as you can have for the heart of you. (*Pulls off her Vizard; he starts.*)
    — How do you like it, Captain?

WILLMORE: Like it! by Heav'n, I never saw so much Beauty. Oh the Charms of those sprightly black Eyes, that strangely fair Face, full of Smiles and
180   Dimples! those soft round melting cherry Lips! and small even white Teeth! not to be exprest, but silently adored! — Oh one Look more, and strike me dumb, or I shall repeat nothing else till I am mad.

(*He seems to court her to pull off her Vizard: she refuses.*)

ANGELICA: I can endure no more — nor is it fit to interrupt him; for if I do, my Jealousy has so destroy'd my Reason, — I shall undo him — Therefore I'll retire. And you *Sebastian* (*To one of her Bravoes.*) follow that Woman, and learn who 'tis; while you *(To the other Bravo.)* tell the Fugitive, I would speak to him instantly. *(Exit.)*

(This while FLORINDA *is talking to* BELVILE, *who stands sullenly.* FREDERICK *courting* VALERIA.*)*

VALERIA: *(To* BELVILE.*)* Prithee, dear Stranger, be not so sullen; for tho you have lost your Love, you see my Friend frankly offers you hers, to play
190   with in the mean time.

BELVILE: Faith, Madam, I am sorry I can't play at her Game.

FREDERICK: *(To* VALERIA.*)* Pray leave your Intercession, and mind your own Affair, they'll better agree apart; he's a model Sigher in Company, but alone no Woman escapes him.

FLORINDA: *(Aside.)* Sure he does but rally[15]— yet if it should be true — I'll tempt him farther — Believe me, noble Stranger, I'm no common Mistress — and for a little proof on't — wear this Jewel[16]— nay, take it, Sir, 'tis right, and Bills of Exchange[17] may sometimes miscarry.

BELVILE: Madam, why am I chose out of all Mankind to be the Object of your
200   Bounty?

VALERIA: There's another civil Question askt.

FREDERICK: *(Aside.)* Pox of's Modesty, it spoils his own Markets, and hinders mine.

FLORINDA: Sir, from my Window I have often seen you; and Women of Quality have so few opportunities for Love, that we ought to lose none.

FREDERICK: *(To* VALERIA.*)* Ay, this is something! here's a Woman! — When shall I be blest with so much kindness from your fair Mouth? *(Aside to* BELVILE.*)* Take the Jewel, Fool.

BELVILE: You tempt me strangely, Madam, every way.

210 FLORINDA: *(Aside.)* So, if I find him false, my whole Repose is gone.

BELVILE: And but for a Vow I've made to a very fine Lady, this Goodness had subdu'd me.

FREDERICK: Pox on't be kind, in pity to me be kind, for I am to thrive here but as you treat her Friend.

HELLENA: Tell me what did you in yonder House, and I'll unmasque.

WILLMORE: Yonder House — oh — I went to — a — to — why, there's a Friend of mine lives there.

HELLENA: What a she, or a he Friend?

WILLMORE: A Man upon my Honour! a Man — A She Friend! no, no, Madam,
220   you have done my Business, I thank you.

HELLENA: And was't your Man Friend, that had more Darts in's Eyes than *Cupid* carries in a whole Budget[18] of Arrows?

WILLMORE: So —

HELLENA: "Ah such a *Bona Roba*: to be in her Arms is lying in *Fresco*, all perfumed Air about me" — Was this your Man Friend too?

WILLMORE: So —

---

15 tease, banter. 16 valuable ornament; here, a locket. 17 money orders. 18 quiver.

HELLENA: That gave you the He, and the She — Gold, that begets young Pleasures.

WILLMORE: Well, well, Madam, then you see there are Ladies in the World, that will not be cruel — there are, Madam, there are —

HELLENA: And there be Men too as fine, wild, inconstant Fellows as your self, there be, Captain, there be, if you go to that now — therefore I'm resolv'd —

WILLMORE: Oh!

HELLENA: To see your Face no more —

WILLMORE: Oh!

HELLENA: Till to morrow.

WILLMORE: Egad you frighted me.

HELLENA: Nor then neither, unless you'l swear never to see that Lady more.

WILLMORE: See her! — why! never to think of Womankind again.

HELLENA: Kneel, and swear. (Kneels, she gives him her hand.)

WILLMORE: I do, never to think — to see — to love — nor lie with any but thy self.

HELLENA: Kiss the Book.

WILLMORE: Oh, most religiously. (Kisses her Hand.)

HELLENA: Now what a wicked Creature am I, to damn a proper Fellow.

CALLIS: (To FLORINDA.) Madam, I'll stay no longer, 'tis e'en dark.

FLORINDA: However, Sir, I'll leave this with you — that when I'm gone, you may repent the opportunity you have lost by your modesty. (Gives him the Jewel, which is her Picture, and Exit. He gazes after her.)

WILLMORE: (To HELLENA.) 'Twill be an Age till to morrow, — and till then I will most impatiently expect you — Adieu, my dear pretty Angel. (Exeunt all the WOMEN.)

BELVILE: Ha! Florinda's Picture! 'twas she her self — what a dull Dog was I? I would have given the World for one minute's discourse with her. —

FREDERICK: This comes of your Modesty, — ah pox on your Vow, 'twas ten to one but we had lost the Jewel by't.

BELVILE: Willmore! the blessed'st Opportunity lost! — Florinda, Friends, Florinda!

WILLMORE: Ah Rogue! such black Eyes, such a Face, such a Mouth, such Teeth, — and so much Wit!

BELVILE: All, all, and a thousand Charms besides.

WILLMORE: Why, dost thou know her?

BELVILE: Know her! ay, ay, and a Pox take me with all my Heart for being Modest.

WILLMORE: But hark ye, Friend of mine, are you my Rival? and have I been only beating the Bush all this while?

BELVILE: I understand thee not — I'm mad — see here — (Shews the Picture.)

WILLMORE: Ha! whose Picture is this? — 'tis a fine Wench.

FREDERICK: The Colonel's Mistress, Sir.

WILLMORE: Oh, oh, here (Gives the Picture back.) — I thought it had been another Prize — come, come, a Bottle will set thee right again.

BELVILE: I am content to try, and by that time 'twill be late enough for our Design.

WILLMORE: Agreed.
Love does all day the Soul's great Empire keep,
But Wine at night lulls the soft God asleep. (Exeunt.)

SCENE 2. (LUCETTA's *House*.)

(*Enter* BLUNT *and* LUCETTA *with a Light*.)

LUCETTA: Now we are safe and free, no fears of the coming home of my old jealous Husband, which made me a little thoughtful when you came in first — but now Love is all the business of my Soul.

BLUNT: I am transported — (*Aside*.) Pox on't, that I had but some fine things to say to her, such as Lovers use — I was a Fool not to learn of *Frederick* a little by Heart before I came — something I must say. — 'Sheartlikins, sweet Soul, I am not us'd to complement, but I'm an honest Gentleman, and thy humble Servant.

LUCETTA: I have nothing to pay for so great a Favour, but such a Love as cannot but be great, since at first sight of that sweet Face and Shape it made me your absolute Captive.

BLUNT: (*Aside*.) Kind heart, how prettily she talks! Egad I'll show her Husband a *Spanish* Trick; send him out of the World, and marry her: she's damnably in love with me, and will ne'er mind Settlements,[1] and so there's that sav'd.

LUCETTA: Well, Sir, I'll go and undress me, and be with you instantly.

BLUNT: Make haste then, for 'dsheartlikins, dear Soul, thou canst not guess at the pain of a longing Lover, when his Joys are drawn within the compass of a few minutes.

LUCETTA: You speak my Sense, and I'll make haste to provide it. (*Exit*.)

BLUNT: 'Tis a rare Girl, and this one night's enjoyment with her will be worth all the days I ever past in *Essex*. — Would she'd go with me into *England*, tho to say truth, there's plenty of Whores there already. — But a pox on 'em they are such mercenary prodigal Whores, that they want such a one as this, that's free and generous, to give 'em good Examples: — Why, what a House she has! how rich and fine!

(*Enter* SANCHO.)

SANCHO: Sir, my Lady has sent me to conduct you to her Chamber.

BLUNT: Sir, I shall be proud to follow — (*Aside*.) Here's one of her Servants too: 'dsheartlikins, by his Garb and Gravity he might be a Justice of Peace in *Essex*, and is but a Pimp here. (*Exeunt*.)

(*The Scene changes to a Chamber with an Alcove-Bed in it, a Table, &c.*
LUCETTA *in Bed. Enter* SANCHO *and* BLUNT, *who takes the Candle of*
SANCHO *at the Door*.)

SANCHO: Sir, my Commission reaches no farther.

BLUNT: Sir, I'll excuse your Complement — what, in Bed, my sweet Mistress?

LUCETTA: You see, I still out-do you in kindness.

BLUNT: And thou shalt see what haste I'll make to quit scores — oh the luck-iest Rogue! (*Undresses himself*.)

LUCETTA: Shou'd you be false or cruel now!

BLUNT: False, 'Sheartlikins, what dost thou take me for a *Jew*? an insensible

---

1 marriage contracts guaranteeing the wife a separate income.

Heathen, — A Pox of thy old jealous Husband: and he were dead, egad,
sweet Soul, it shou'd be none of my fault, if I did not marry thee.

40 LUCETTA: It never shou'd be mine.

BLUNT: Good Soul, I'm the fortunatest Dog!

LUCETTA: Are you not undrest yet?

BLUNT: As much as my Impatience will permit.

(*Goes towards the Bed in his Shirt and Drawers.*)

LUCETTA: Hold, Sir, put out the Light, it may betray us else.

BLUNT: Any thing, I need no other Light but that of thine Eyes! — (*Aside.*)
'sheartlikins, there I think I had it.

(*Puts out the Candle, the Bed descends, he gropes about to find it.*)

— Why — why — where am I got? what, not yet? — where are you sweetest? — ah, the Rogue's silent now — a pretty Love-trick this — how she'll
laugh at me anon! — you need not, my dear Rogue! you need not! I'm

50 all on a fire already — come, come, now call me in for pity — Sure I'm
enchanted! I have been round the Chamber, and can find neither Woman,
nor Bed — I lockt the Door, I'm sure she cannot go that way; or if she
cou'd, the Bed cou'd not — Enough, enough, my pretty Wanton, do not
carry the Jest too far — Ha, betray'd! Dogs! Rogues! Pimps! help! help!
(*Lights on a Trap, and is let down.*)

(*Enter* LUCETTA, PHILIPPO, *and* SANCHO *with a Light.*)

PHILIPPO: Ha, ha, ha, he's dispatcht finely.

LUCETTA: Now, Sir, had I been coy, we had mist of this Booty.

PHILIPPO: Nay when I saw 'twas a substantial Fool, I was mollified; but when you
doat upon a Serenading Coxcomb, upon a Face, fine Clothes, and a Lute,
it makes me rage.

60 LUCETTA: You know I never was guilty of that Folly, my dear *Philippo*, but with
your self — But come let's see what we have got by this.

PHILIPPO: A rich Coat! — Sword and Hat! — these Breeches too — are well
lin'd! — see here a Gold Watch! — a Purse — ha! Gold! — at least two
hundred Pistoles! a bunch of Diamond Rings; and one with the Family
Arms! — A Gold Box! — with a Medal of his King! and his Lady Mother's
Picture! — these were sacred Reliques, believe me! — see, the Wasteband
of his Breeches have a Mine of Gold! — Old Queen *Bess's*. We have a
Quarrel to her ever since *Eighty Eight*,[2] and may therefore justify the Theft;
the Inquisition might have committed it.

70 LUCETTA: See, a Bracelet of bow'd[3] Gold, these his Sister ty'd about his Arm
at parting — but well — for all this, I fear his being a Stranger may make
a noise, and hinder our Trade with them hereafter.

PHILIPPO: That's our security; he is not only a Stranger to us, but to the Country
too — the Common-Shore[4] into which he is descended, thou know'st,
conducts him into another Street, which this Light will hinder him from

---

2 1588, the year in which the Spanish Armada was defeated by England. 3 bent. 4 sewer.

ever finding again — he knows neither your Name, nor the Street where your House is, nay, nor the way to his own Lodgings.

LUCETTA: And art not thou an unmerciful Rogue, not to afford him one Night for all this?— I should not have been such a *Jew.*

80   PHILIPPO: Blame not me, *Lucetta,* to keep as much of thee as I can to my self — come, that thought makes me wanton, — let's to Bed, —*Sancho,* lock up these.

> This is the Fleece which Fools do bear,
> Design'd for witty Men to shear. (*Exeunt.*)

(*The Scene changes, and discovers* BLUNT, *creeping out of a Common Shore, his Face &c., all dirty.*)

BLUNT: Oh Lord! (*Climbing up.*)
I am got out at last, and (which is a Miracle) without a Clue — and now to Damning and Cursing, — but if that would ease me, where shall I begin? with my Fortune, my self, or the Quean[5] that cozen'd me — What a dog was I to believe in Women! Oh Coxcomb — ignorant conceited Coxcomb! to fancy she cou'd be enamour'd with my Person, at the first sight enam-

90   our'd — Oh, I'm a cursed Puppy, 'tis plain, Fool was writ upon my Forehead, she perceiv'd it, — saw the *Essex* Calf there — for what Allurements could there be in this Countenance? which I can indure, because I'm acquainted with it — Oh, dull silly Dog! to be thus sooth'd into a Cozening! Had I been drunk, I might fondly have credited the young Quean! but as I was in my right Wits, to be thus cheated, confirms I am a dull believing *English* Country Fop. — But my Comrades! Death and the Devil, there's the worst of all — then a Ballad will be sung to Morrow on the *Prado,*[6] to a lousy Tune of the enchanted Squire, and the annihilated Damsel — But *Frederick* that Rogue, and the Colonel, will abuse me beyond all Christian patience

100 — had she left me my Clothes, I have a Bill of Exchange at home wou'd have sav'd my Credit — but now all hope is taken from me — Well, I'll home (if I can find the way) with this Consolation, that I am not the first kind believing Coxcomb; but there are, Gallants, many such good Natures amongst ye.

> And tho you've better Arts to hide your Follies,
> 'Adsheartlikins, y'are all as errant Cullies.[7]

SCENE 3. (*The Garden, in the Night.*)

(*Enter* FLORINDA *undress'd,*[1] *with a Key, and a little Box.*)

FLORINDA: Well, thus far I'm in my way to Happiness; I have got my self free from *Callis;* my Brother too, I find by yonder light, is gone into his Cabinet,[2] and thinks not of me: I have by good Fortune got the Key of the Garden Back-door, — I'll open it, to prevent *Belvile's* knocking, — a little noise will now alarm my Brother. Now am I as fearful as a young Thief. (*Unlocks the Door.*) — Hark, — what noise is that?— Oh, 'twas the Wind that plaid amongst the Boughs. — *Belvile* stays long, methinks — it's time — stay —

---

5 slut. 6 promenade. 7 dupes.
1 in undress, dressed informally. 2 study.

for fear of a surprize, I'll hide these Jewels in yonder Jessamin.[3] (*She goes to lay down the Box.*)

(*Enter* WILLMORE *drunk.*)

WILLMORE: What the Devil is become of these Fellows, *Belvile* and *Frederick*?
They promis'd to stay at the next corner for me, but who the Devil knows the corner of a full Moon? — Now — whereabouts am I? — hah — what have we here? a Garden! — a very convenient place to sleep in — hah — what has God sent us here? — a Female — by this light, a Woman; I'm a Dog if it be not a very Wench. —

FLORINDA: He's come! — hah — who's there?

WILLMORE: Sweet Soul, let me salute thy Shoe-string.

FLORINDA: 'Tis not my *Belvile* — good Heavens, I know him not. — Who are you, and from whence come you?

WILLMORE: Prithee — prithee, Child — not so many hard Questions — let it suffice I am here, Child — Come, come kiss me.

FLORINDA: Good Gods! what luck is mine?

WILLMORE: Only good luck, Child, parlous[4] good luck. — Come hither, — 'tis a delicate shining Wench, — by this Hand she's perfum'd, and smells like any Nosegay. — Prithee, dear Soul, let's not play the Fool, and lose time, — precious time — for as Gad shall save me, I'm as honest a Fellow as breathes, tho I am a little disguis'd at present. — Come, I say, — why, thou may'st be free with me, I'll be very secret. I'll not boast who 'twas oblig'd me, not I — for hang me if I know thy Name.

FLORINDA: Heavens! what a filthy beast is this!

WILLMORE: I am so, and thou oughtst the sooner to lie with me for that reason, — for look you, Child, there will be no Sin in't, because 'twas neither design'd nor premeditated; 'tis pure Accident on both sides — that's a certain thing now — Indeed should I make love to you, and you vow Fidelity — and swear and lye till you believ'd and yielded — Thou art therefore (as thou art a good Christian) oblig'd in Conscience to deny me nothing. Now — come, be kind, without any more idle prating.

FLORINDA: Oh, I am ruin'd — wicked Man, unhand me.

WILLMORE: Wicked! Egad, Child, a Judge, were he young and vigorous, and saw those Eyes of thine, would know 'twas they gave the first blow — the first provocation. — Come, prithee let's lose no time, I say — this is a fine convenient place.

FLORINDA: Sir, let me go, I conjure you, or I'll call out.

WILLMORE: Ay, ay, you were best to call Witness to see how finely you treat me — do.

FLORINDA: I'll cry Murder, Rape, or any thing, if you do not instantly let me go.

WILLMORE: A Rape! Come, come, you lye, you Baggage, you lye: What, I'll warrant you would fain have the World believe now that you are not so forward as I. No, not you, — why at this time of Night was your Cobweb-door set open, dear Spider — but to catch Flies? — Hah! Come — or I shall be damnably angry. — Why what a Coil[5] is here. —

3 box perfumed with jasmine. 4 extremely. 5 commotion.

FLORINDA: Sir, can you think —

WILLMORE: That you'd do it for nothing? oh, oh, I find what you'd be at — look here, here's a Pistole for you — here's a work indeed — here — take it, I say. —

FLORINDA: For Heaven's sake, Sir, as you're a Gentleman —

WILLMORE: So — now — she would be wheedling me for more — what, you will not take it then — you're resolv'd you will not. — Come, come, take it, or I'll put it up again; for, look ye, I never give more. — Why, how now, Mistress, are you so high i'th' Mouth, a Pistole won't down with you? — hah — why, what a work's here — in good time — come, no struggling, be gone — But an y'are good at a dumb Wrestle, I'm for ye, — look ye, — I'm for ye. — (*She struggles with him.*)

(*Enter* BELVILE *and* FREDERICK.)

BELVILE: The Door is open, a Pox of this mad Fellow, I'm angry that we've lost him, I durst have sworn he had follow'd us.

FREDERICK: But you were so hasty, Colonel, to be gone.

FLORINDA: Help, help, — Murder! — help — oh, I'm ruin'd.

BELVILE: Ha, sure that's *Florinda's* Voice. (*Comes up to them.*)
— A Man! Villain, let go that Lady.

(*A noise;* WILLMORE *turns and draws;* FREDERICK *interposes.*)

FLORINDA: *Belvile!* Heavens! my Brother too is coming, and 'twill be impossible to escape. — *Belvile,* I conjure you to walk under my Chamber-window, from whence I'll give you some instructions what to do — This rude Man has undone us. (*Exit.*)

WILLMORE: *Belvile!*

(*Enter* PEDRO, STEPHANO, *and other Servants with Lights.*)

PEDRO: I'm betray'd; run, *Stephano,* and see if *Florinda* be safe. (*Exit* STEPHANO.) So whoe'er they be, all is not well, I'll to *Florinda's* Chamber. (*They fight, and* PEDRO's *Party beats 'em out; going out, meets* STEPHANO.)

STEPHANO: You need not, Sir, the poor Lady's fast asleep, and thinks no harm: I wou'd not wake her, Sir, for fear of frightning her with your danger.

PEDRO: I'm glad she's there — Rascals, how came the Garden-Door open?

STEPHANO: That Question comes too late, Sir: some of my Fellow-Servants Masquerading I'll warrant.

PEDRO: Masquerading! a lewd Custom to debauch our Youth — there's something more in this than I imagine. (*Exeunt.*)

SCENE 4. (*Changes to the Street.*)

(*Enter* BELVILE *in a Rage,* FREDERICK *holding him, and* WILLMORE *melancholy.*)

WILLMORE: Why, how the Devil shou'd I know *Florinda?*

BELVILE: Ah plague of your ignorance! if it had not been *Florinda,* must you be a Beast? — a Brute, a senseless Swine?

WILLMORE: Well, Sir, you see I am endu'd with Patience — I can bear — tho egad y're very free with me methinks, — I was in good hopes the Quarrel wou'd have been on my side, for so uncivilly interrupting me.

BELVILE: Peace, Brute, whilst thou'rt safe — oh, I'm distracted.

WILLMORE: Nay, nay, I'm an unlucky Dog, that's certain.

BELVILE: Ah curse upon the Star that rul'd my Birth! or whatsoever other Influence that makes me still so wretched.

WILLMORE: Thou break'st my Heart with these Complaints; there is no Star in fault, no Influence but Sack, the cursed Sack I drank.

FREDERICK: Why, how the Devil came you so drunk?

WILLMORE: Why, how the Devil came you so sober?

BELVILE: A curse upon his thin Skull, he was always before-hand that way.

FREDERICK: Prithee, dear Colonel, forgive him, he's sorry for his fault.

BELVILE: He's always so after he has done a mischief — a plague on all such Brutes.

WILLMORE: By this Light I took her for an errant Harlot.

BELVILE: Damn your debaucht Opinion: tell me, Sot, hadst thou so much sense and light about thee to distinguish her to be a Woman, and could'st not see something about her Face and Person, to strike an awful Reverence into thy Soul?

WILLMORE: Faith no, I consider'd her as mere a Woman as I could wish.

BELVILE: 'Sdeath I have no patience — draw, or I'll kill you.

WILLMORE: Let that alone till to morrow, and if I set not all right again, use your Pleasure.

BELVILE: To morrow, damn it.
The spiteful Light will lead me to no happiness.
To morrow is *Antonio's*, and perhaps
Guides him to my undoing; — oh that I could meet
This Rival, this powerful Fortunate.

WILLMORE: What then?

BELVILE: Let thy own Reason, or my Rage instruct thee.

WILLMORE: I shall be finely inform'd then, no doubt; hear me, Colonel — hear me — shew me the Man and I'll do his Business.[1]

BELVILE: I know him no more than thou, or if I did, I should not need thy aid.

WILLMORE: This you say is *Angelica's* House, I promis'd the kind Baggage to lie with her to Night. (*Offers to go in.*)

(*Enter* ANTONIO *and his* PAGE. ANTONIO *knocks on the Hilt of his Sword.*)

ANTONIO: You paid the thousand Crowns I directed?

PAGE: To the Lady's old Woman, Sir, I did.

WILLMORE: Who the Devil have we here?

BELVILE: I'll now plant my self under *Florinda's* Window, and if I find no comfort there, I'll die. (*Exeunt* BELVILE *and* FREDERICK.)

(*Enter* MORETTA.)

MORETTA: Page!

PAGE: Here's my Lord.

WILLMORE: How is this, a Piccaroon going to board my Frigate! here's one Chase-Gun[2] for you.

---

1 take care of him (i.e., kill him).   2 ship's cannon.

(Drawing his Sword, justles ANTONIO, *who turns and draws. They fight,* ANTONIO *falls.)*

MORETTA: Oh, bless us, we are all undone! *(Runs in, and shuts the Door.)*

50   PAGE: Help, Murder!

*(*BELVILE *returns at the noise of fighting.)*

BELVILE: Ha, the mad Rogue's engag'd in some unlucky Adventure again.

(Enter two or three Masqueraders.)

MASQUERADER: Ha, a Man kill'd!

WILLMORE: How! a Man kill'd! then I'll go home to sleep. *(Puts up, and reels out. Exeunt Masqueraders another way.)*

BELVILE: Who shou'd it be! pray Heaven the Rogue is safe, for all my Quarrel to him. *(As* BELVILE *is groping about, enter an Officer and six Soldiers.)*

SOLDIER: Who's there?

OFFICER: So, here's one dispatcht — secure the Murderer.

BELVILE: Do not mistake my Charity for Murder:
   I came to his Assistance. *(Soldiers seize on* BELVILE.)

60   OFFICER: That shall be tried, Sir. — St. *Jago*,[3] Swords drawn in the Carnival time!
   (Goes to ANTONIO.)

ANTONIO: Thy Hand prithee.

OFFICER: Ha, Don *Antonio!* look well to the Villain there. — How is't, Sir?

ANTONIO: I'm hurt.

BELVILE: Has my Humanity made me a Criminal?

OFFICER: Away with him.

BELVILE: What a curst Chance is this! *(Exeunt Soldiers with* BELVILE.)

ANTONIO: This is the Man that has set upon me twice — *(To the Officer.)* carry him to my Apartment till you have further Orders from me.

(Exit ANTONIO, *led.)*

ACT FOUR

SCENE 1. *(A fine Room.)*

(Discovers BELVILE, *as by Dark alone.)*

BELVILE: When shall I be weary of railing on Fortune, who is resolv'd never to turn with Smiles upon me? — Two such Defeats in one Night — none but the Devil and that mad Rogue could have contriv'd to have plagued me with — I am here a Prisoner — but where? — Heaven knows — and if there be Murder done, I can soon decide the Fate of a Stranger in a Nation without Mercy — Yet this is nothing to the Torture my Soul bows with, when I think of losing my fair, my dear *Florinda*. — Hark — my Door

3 by St. James (especially venerated in Spain).

opens — a Light — a Man — and seems of Quality — arm'd too. — Now shall I die like a Dog without defence.

(*Enter* ANTONIO *in a Night-Gown, with a Light; his Arm in a Scarf, and a Sword under his Arm: He sets the Candle on the Table.*)

10   ANTONIO: Sir, I am come to know what Injuries I have done you, that could provoke you to so mean an Action, as to attack me basely, without allowing time for my Defence.

BELVILE: Sir, for a Man in my Circumstances to plead Innocence, would look like Fear — but view me well, and you will find no marks of a Coward on me, nor any thing that betrays the Brutality you accuse me of.

ANTONIO: In vain, Sir, you impose upon my Sense,
You are not only he who drew on me last Night,
But yesterday before the same House, that of *Angelica.*
Yet there is something in your Face and Mien —

20   BELVILE: I own I fought to day in the defence of a Friend of mine, with whom you (if you're the same) and your Party were first engag'd.
Perhaps you think this Crime enough to kill me,
But if you do, I cannot fear you'll do it basely.

ANTONIO: No, Sir, I'll make you fit for a Defence with this. (*Gives him the Sword.*)

BELVILE: This Gallantry surprizes me — nor know I how to use this Present, Sir, against a Man so brave.

ANTONIO: You shall not need;
For know, I come to snatch you from a Danger
That is decreed against you;
30   Perhaps your Life, or long Imprisonment.
And 'twas with so much Courage you offended,
I cannot see you punisht.

BELVILE: How shall I pay this Generosity?

ANTONIO: It had been safer to have kill'd another,
Than have attempted me.
To shew your Danger, Sir, I'll let you know my Quality;[1]
And 'tis the Vice-Roy's Son whom you have wounded.

BELVILE: The Vice-Roy's Son! (*Aside.*)
Death and Confusion! was this Plague reserved
40   To compleat all the rest? — oblig'd by him!
The Man of all the World I would destroy.

ANTONIO: You seem disorder'd, Sir.

BELVILE: Yes, trust me, Sir, I am, and 'tis with pain
That Man receives such Bounties,
Who wants the pow'r to pay 'em back again.

ANTONIO: To gallant Spirits 'tis indeed uneasy;
— But you may quickly over-pay me, Sir.

BELVILE: Then I am well — (*Aside.*) kind Heaven! but set us even,
That I may fight with him, and keep my Honour safe.

---

1 rank.

50   — Oh, I'm impatient, Sir, to be discounting[2]
       The mighty Debt I owe you; command me quickly —
ANTONIO: I have a Quarrel with a Rival, Sir,
       About the Maid we love.
BELVILE: (*Aside.*) Death, 'tis *Florinda* he means —
       That Thought destroys my Reason, and I shall kill him —
ANTONIO: My Rival, Sir,
       Is one has all the Virtues Man can boast of.
BELVILE: (*Aside.*) Death! who shou'd this be?
ANTONIO: He challeng'd me to meet him on the *Molo*,
60   As soon as Day appear'd; but last Night's quarrel
       Has made my Arm unfit to guide a Sword.
BELVILE: I apprehend you, Sir, you'd have me kill the Man
       That lays a claim to the Maid you speak of.
       — I'll do't — I'll fly to do it.
ANTONIO: Sir, do you know her?
BELVILE: — No, Sir, but 'tis enough she is admired by you.
ANTONIO: Sir, I shall rob you of the Glory on't,
       For you must fight under my Name and Dress.
BELVILE: That Opinion must be strangely obliging that makes
70   You think I can personate the brave *Antonio*,
       Whom I can but strive to imitate.
ANTONIO: You say too much to my Advantage.
       Come, Sir, the Day appears that calls you forth.
       Within, Sir, is the Habit. (*Exit* ANTONIO.)
BELVILE: Fantastick Fortune, thou deceitful Light,
       That cheats the wearied Traveller by Night,
       Tho on a Precipice each step you tread,
       I am resolv'd to follow where you lead. (*Exit.*)

SCENE 2. (*The Molo.*)

(*Enter* FLORINDA *and* CALLIS *in Masques, with* STEPHANO.)

FLORINDA: (*Aside.*) I'm dying with my fears; *Belvile's* not coming,
       As I expected, underneath my Window,
       Makes me believe that all those Fears are true.
       — Canst thou not tell with whom my Brother fights?
STEPHANO: No, Madam, they were both in Masquerade, I was by when they
       challeng'd one another, and they had decided the Quarrel then, but were
       prevented by some Cavaliers; which made 'em put it off till now — but I
       am sure 'tis about you they fight.
FLORINDA: (*Aside.*) Nay, then 'tis with *Belvile*, for what other Lover have I
10   that dares fight for me, except *Antonio*? and he is too much in favour with
       my Brother — If it be he, for whom shall I direct my Prayers to Heaven?
STEPHANO: Madam, I must leave you; for if my Master see me, I shall be hang'd

2 paying back.

for being your Conductor. — I escap'd narrowly for the Excuse I made for
you last night i'th' Garden.

FLORINDA: And I'll reward thee for't — prithee no more. (*Exit* STEPHANO.)

(*Enter* DON PEDRO *in his Masquing Habit.*)

PEDRO: *Antonio's* late to day, the place will fill, and we may be prevented.
(*Walks about.*)

FLORINDA: (*Aside.*) *Antonio!* sure I heard amiss.

PEDRO: But who will not excuse a happy Lover
     When soft fair Arms confine the yielding Neck;
20   And the kind Whisper languishingly breathes,
     "Must you be gone so soon?"
     Sure I had dwelt for ever on her Bosom.
     — But stay, he's here.

(*Enter* BELVILE *drest in* ANTONIO's *Clothes.*)

FLORINDA: (*Aside.*) 'Tis not *Belvile*, half my Fears are vanisht.

PEDRO: *Antonio!* —

BELVILE: (*Aside.*) This must be he.
     You're early, Sir; I do not use to be out-done this way.

PEDRO: The wretched, Sir, are watchful, and 'tis enough
     You have the advantage of me in *Angelica.*

30   BELVILE: (*Aside.*) *Angelica!*
     Or[1] I've mistook my Man! Or else *Antonio*,
     Can he forget his Interest in *Florinda*,
     And fight for common Prize?

PEDRO: Come, Sir, you know our terms —

BELVILE: (*Aside.*) By Heaven, not I.
     — No talking, I am ready, Sir.
     (*Offers to fight.* FLORINDA *runs in.*)

FLORINDA: (*To* BELVILE.) Oh, hold! whoe'er you be, I do conjure you hold.
     If you strike here — I die —

PEDRO: *Florinda!*

40   BELVILE: *Florinda* imploring for my Rival!

PEDRO: Away, this Kindness is unseasonable.

(*Puts her by, they fight; she runs in just as* BELVILE *disarms* PEDRO.)

FLORINDA: Who are you, Sir, that dare deny my Prayers?

BELVILE: Thy Prayers destroy him; if thou wouldst preserve him.
     Do that thou'rt unacquainted with, and curse him. (*She holds him.*)

FLORINDA: By all you hold most dear, by her you love,
     I do conjure you, touch him not.

BELVILE: By her I love?
     See — I obey — and at your Feet resign
     The useless Trophy of my Victory. (*Lays his sword at her Feet.*)

50   PEDRO: *Antonio*, you've done enough to prove you love *Florinda.*

1 either.

BELVILE: Love *Florinda*!

Does Heaven love Adoration, Pray'r, or Penitence?

Love her! here Sir, — your Sword again. (*Snatches up the Sword, and gives it him.*)

Upon this Truth I'll fight my Life away.

PEDRO: No, you've redeem'd my Sister, and my Friendship.

(*He gives him* FLORINDA, *and pulls off his Vizard to shew his Face, and puts it on again.*)

BELVILE: Don *Pedro*!

PEDRO: Can you resign your Claims to other Women,

And give your Heart intirely to *Florinda*?

BELVILE: Intire, as dying Saints' Confessions are.

60   I can delay my happiness no longer.

This minute let me make *Florinda* mine.

PEDRO: This minute let it be — no time so proper,

This Night my Father will arrive from *Rome*,

And possibly may hinder what we purpose.

FLORINDA: Oh Heavens! this Minute?

(*Enter Masqueraders, and pass over.*)

BELVILE: Oh, do not ruin me!

PEDRO: The place begins to fill; and that we may not be observ'd, do you walk off to St. *Peter's* Church, where I will meet you, and conclude your Happiness.

BELVILE: I'll meet you there — (*Aside.*) if there be no more Saints Churches in

70 *Naples.*

FLORINDA: Oh stay, Sir, and recall your hasty Doom:

Alas I have not yet prepar'd my Heart

To entertain so strange a Guest.

PEDRO: Away, this silly Modesty is assum'd too late.

BELVILE: Heaven, Madam! what do you do?

FLORINDA: Do? despise the Man that lays a Tyrant's Claim

To what he ought to conquer by Submission.

BELVILE: You do not know me — move a little this way. (*Draws her aside.*)

FLORINDA: Yes, you may even force me to the Altar,

80   But not the holy Man that offers there

Shall force me to be thine. (PEDRO *talks to* CALLIS *this while.*)

BELVILE: Oh do not lose so blest an opportunity!

See — 'tis your *Belvile* — not *Antonio*,

Whom your mistaken Scorn and Anger ruins. (*Pulls off his Vizard.*)

FLORINDA: *Belvile*!

Where was my Soul it cou'd not meet thy Voice,

And take this knowledge in?

(*As they are talking, enter* WILLMORE *finely drest, and* FREDERICK.)

WILLMORE: No Intelligence! no News of *Belvile* yet — well I am the most unlucky Rascal in Nature — ha! — am I deceiv'd — or is it he — look, *Frederick.* —

90   'tis he — my dear *Belvile*.

(Runs and embraces him. BELVILE's *Vizard falls out on's Hand.)*

BELVILE: Hell and Confusion seize thee!

PEDRO: Ha! *Belvile!* I beg your Pardon, Sir. *(Takes* FLORINDA *from him.)*

BELVILE: Nay, touch her not, she's mine by Conquest, Sir.
     I won her by my Sword.

WILLMORE: Did'st thou so? — and egad, Child, we'll keep her by the Sword.
     (Draws on PEDRO, BELVILE *goes between.)*

BELVILE: Stand off!
     Thou'rt so profanely lewd, so curst by Heaven,
     All Quarrels thou espousest must be fatal.

WILLMORE: Nay, an[2] you be so hot, my Valour's coy,

100   And shall be courted when you want it next. *(Puts up his Sword.)*

BELVILE: *(To* PEDRO.) You know I ought to claim a Victor's Right,
     But you're the Brother to divine *Florinda*,
     To whom I'm such a Slave — to purchase her,
     I durst not hurt the Man she holds so dear.

PEDRO: 'Twas by *Antonio's*, not by *Belvile's* Sword,
     This Question should have been decided, Sir:
     I must confess much to your Bravery's due,
     Both now, and when I met you last in Arms.
     But I am nicely[3] punctual in my word,

110   As Men of Honour ought, and beg your Pardon.
     — For this Mistake another Time shall clear.
     — *(Aside to* FLORINDA, *as they are going out.)* This was
          some Plot between you and *Belvile*:
     But I'll prevent you.

*(*BELVILE *looks after her, and begins to walk up and down in a Rage.)*

WILLMORE: Do not be modest now, and lose the Woman:
     but if we shall fetch her back, so —

BELVILE: Do not speak to me.

WILLMORE: Not speak to you! — Egad, I'll speak to you, and will be answered too.

BELVILE: Will you, Sir?

WILLMORE: I know I've done some mischief, but I'm so dull a Puppy, that I am

120   the Son of a Whore, if I know how, or where — prithee inform my Under-
     standing. —

BELVILE: Leave me I say, and leave me instantly!

WILLMORE: I will not leave you in this humour, nor till I know my Crime.

BELVILE: Death, I'll tell you, Sir —

(Draws and runs at WILLMORE; *he runs out,* BELVILE *after him;* FREDERICK *interposes.)*

(Enter ANGELICA, MORETTA, *and* SEBASTIAN.*)*

ANGELICA: Ha — *Sebastian* — Is not that *Willmore?* haste, haste, and bring him
     back.

2 if. 3 scrupulously.

FREDERICK: (*Aside.*) The Colonel's mad — I never saw him thus before; I'll after 'em, lest he do some mischief, for I am sure *Willmore* will not draw on him. (*Exit.*)

130   ANGELICA: I am all Rage! my first desires defeated
    For one, for ought he knows, that has no
    Other Merit than her Quality, —
    Her being Don *Pedro's* Sister — He loves her:
    I know 'tis so — dull, dull, insensible —
    He will not see me now tho oft invited;
    And broke his Word last night — false perjur'd Man!
    — He that but yesterday fought for my Favours,
    And would have made his Life a Sacrifice
    To've gain'd one Night with me,
140   Must now be hired and courted to my Arms.

MORETTA: I told you what wou'd come on't, but *Moretta's* an old doating Fool — Why did you give him five hundred Crowns, but to set himself out for other Lovers? You shou'd have kept him poor, if you had meant to have had any good from him.

ANGELICA: Oh, name not such mean Trifles. — Had I given him all
    My Youth has earn'd from Sin,
    I had not lost a Thought nor Sigh upon't.
    But I have given him my eternal Rest,
    My whole Repose, my future Joys, my Heart;
150   My Virgin Heart. *Moretta!* oh 'tis gone!

MORETTA: Curse on him, here he comes;
    How fine she has made him too!

(*Enter* WILLMORE *and* SEBASTIAN. ANGELICA *turns and walks away.*)

WILLMORE: How now, turn'd Shadow?
    Fly when I pursue, and follow when I fly!

[*Sings.*]

> Stay gentle Shadow of my Dove,
>   And tell me ere I go,
> Whether the Substance may not prove
>   A fleeting Thing like you.

There's a soft kind Look remaining yet.

(*As she turns she looks on him.*)

160   ANGELICA: Well, Sir, you may be gay; all Happiness, all Joys pursue you still. Fortune's your Slave, and gives you every hour choice of new Hearts and Beauties, till you are cloy'd with the repeated Bliss, which others vainly languish for — But know, false Man, that I shall be reveng'd. (*Turns away in a Rage.*)

WILLMORE: So, 'gad, there are of those faint-hearted Lovers, whom such a sharp Lesson next their Hearts would make as impotent as Fourscore — pox o' this whining — my Bus'ness is to laugh and love — a pox on't; I hate your sullen Lover, a Man shall lose as much time to put you in Humour now, as would serve to gain a new Woman.

ANGELICA: I scorn to cool that Fire I cannot raise,
170   Or do the Drudgery of your virtuous Mistress.

WILLMORE: A virtuous Mistress! Death, what a thing thou hast found out for me! why what the Devil should I do with a virtuous Woman?— a sort of ill-natur'd Creatures, that take a Pride to torment a Lover. Virtue is but an Infirmity in Women, a Disease that renders even the handsome ungrateful; whilst the ill-favour'd, for want of Sollicitations and Address, only fancy themselves so.— I have lain with a Woman of Quality, who has all the while been railing at Whores.

ANGELICA: I will not answer for your Mistress's Virtue,
    Tho she be young enough to know no Guilt:
180   And I could wish you would persuade my Heart,
    'Twas the two hundred thousand Crowns you courted.

WILLMORE: Two hundred thousand Crowns! what Story's this?— what Trick?— what Woman?— ha.

ANGELICA: How strange you make it! have you forgot the Creature you entertain'd on the Piazza last night?

WILLMORE: (Aside.) Ha, my Gipsy worth two hundred thousand Crowns!— oh how I long to be with her — pox, I knew she was of Quality.

ANGELICA: False Man, I see my Ruin in thy Face.
    How many vows you breath'd upon my Bosom,
190   Never to be unjust — have you forgot so soon?

WILLMORE: Faith no, I was just coming to repeat 'em — but here's a Humour indeed — would make a Man a Saint — (Aside.) Wou'd she'd be angry enough to leave me, and command me not to wait on her.

(Enter HELLENA, drest in Man's Clothes.)

HELLENA: (Aside.) This must be Angelica, I know it by her mumping[4] Matron here — Ay, ay, 'tis she: my mad Captain's with her too, for all his swearing — how this unconstant Humour makes me love him:— pray, good grave Gentlewoman, is not this Angelica?

MORETTA: My too young Sir, it is — I hope 'tis one from Don Antonio. (Goes to ANGELICA.)

HELLENA: (Aside.) Well, something I'll do to vex him for this.

200 ANGELICA: I will not speak with him; am I in humour to receive a Lover?

WILLMORE: Not speak with him? why I'll be gone — and wait your idler minutes — Can I shew less Obedience to the thing I love so fondly? (Offers to go.)

ANGELICA: A fine Excuse this — stay —

WILLMORE: And hinder your Advantage: should I repay your Bounties so ungratefully?

ANGELICA: (To HELLENA.) Come hither, Boy, — (To WILLMORE.) that I may let you see
    How much above the Advantages you name
    I prize one Minute's Joy with you.

4 grimacing, sullen.

WILLMORE: Oh, you destroy me with this Endearment. (*Impatient to be gone.*)
210   — Death, how shall I get away? — Madam, 'twill not be fit I should be
seen with you — besides, it will not be convenient — and I've a Friend
— that's dangerously sick.

ANGELICA: I see you're impatient — yet you shall stay.

WILLMORE: (*Aside.*) And miss my Assignation with my Gipsy. (*Walks about
impatiently.*)

HELLENA: Madam, (MORETTA *brings* HELLENA, *who addresses herself to* ANGELICA.)
You'l hardly pardon my Intrusion,
When you shall know my Business;
And I'm too young to tell my Tale with Art:
But there must be a wondrous store of Goodness
220   Where so much Beauty dwells.

ANGELICA: A pretty Advocate, whoever sent thee,
— Prithee proceed — Nay, Sir, you shall not go. (*To* WILLMORE *who is stealing off.*)

WILLMORE: (*Aside.*) Then I shall lose my dear Gipsy for ever.
— Pox on't, she stays me out of spite.

HELLENA: I am related to a Lady, Madam,
Young, rich, and nobly born, but has the fate
To be in love with a young *English* Gentleman.
Strangely she loves him, at first sight she lov'd him,
But did adore him when she heard him speak;
230   For he, she said, had Charms in every word,
That fail'd not to surprize, to wound, and conquer —

WILLMORE: (*Aside.*) Ha, Egad I hope this concerns me.

ANGELICA: 'Tis my false Man, he means — wou'd he were gone. (*Aside.*)
This Praise will raise his Pride and ruin me — (*To* WILLMORE.) Well,
Since you are so impatient to be gone,
I will release you, Sir.

WILLMORE: (*Aside.*) Nay, then I'm sure 'twas me he spoke of, this cannot be the
Effects of Kindness in her.
— No, Madam, I've consider'd better on't,
240   And will not give you cause of Jealousy.

ANGELICA: But, Sir, I've — business, that —

WILLMORE: This shall not do, I know 'tis but to try me.

ANGELICA: Well, to your Story, Boy, — (*Aside.*) tho 'twill undo me.

HELLENA: With this Addition to his other Beauties,
He won her unresisting tender Heart,
He vow'd and sigh'd, and swore he lov'd her dearly;
And she believ'd the cunning Flatterer,
And thought her self the happiest Maid alive:
To day was the appointed time by both,
250   To consummate their Bliss;
The Virgin, Altar, and the Priest were drest,
And whilst she languisht for the expected Bridegroom,
She heard, he paid his broken Vows to you.

WILLMORE: (*Aside.*) So, this is some dear Rogue that's in love with me, and this way lets me know it; or if it be not me, he means some one whose place I may supply.

ANGELICA: Now I perceive
 The cause of thy Impatience to be gone,
 And all the business of this glorious Dress.

260 WILLMORE: Damn the young Prater, I know not what he means.

HELLENA: Madam,
 In your fair Eyes I read too much concern
 To tell my farther Business.

ANGELICA: Prithee, sweet Youth, talk on thou may'st perhaps
 Raise here a Storm that may undo my Passion,
 And then I'll grant thee any thing.

HELLENA: Madam, 'tis to intreat you, (oh unreasonable!)
 You wou'd not see this Stranger;
 For if you do, she vows you are undone,
270 Tho Nature never made a Man so excellent;
 And sure he'ad been a God, but for Inconstancy.

WILLMORE: (Aside.) Ah, Rogue, how finely he's instructed!
 —'Tis plain some Woman that has seen me *en passant.*

ANGELICA: Oh, I shall burst with Jealousy! do you know the Man you speak of?—

HELLENA: Yes, Madam, he us'd to be in Buff and Scarlet.

ANGELICA: (To WILLMORE.) Thou, false as Hell, what canst thou say to this?

WILLMORE: By Heaven —

ANGELICA: Hold, do not damn thy self —

280 HELLENA: Nor hope to be believ'd. (He walks about, they follow.)

ANGELICA: Oh, perjur'd Man!
 Is't thus you pay my generous Passion back?

HELLENA: Why wou'd you, Sir, abuse my Lady's Faith?

ANGELICA: And use me so inhumanly?

HELLENA: A Maid so young, so innocent —

WILLMORE: Ah, young Devil!

ANGELICA: Dost thou not know thy Life is in my Power?

HELLENA: Or think my Lady cannot be reveng'd?

WILLMORE: (Aside.) So, so, the Storm comes finely on.

290 ANGELICA: Now thou art silent, Guilt has struck thee dumb.
 Oh, hadst thou still been so, I'd liv'd in safety. (She turns away and weeps.)

WILLMORE: (Aside to HELLENA.) Sweetheart, the Lady's Name and House —
 quickly: I'm impatient to be with her. — (Looks toward ANGELICA to watch
 her turning; and as she comes towards them, he meets her.)

HELLENA: (Aside.) So now is he for another woman.

WILLMORE: The impudent'st young thing in Nature!
 I cannot persuade him out of his Error, Madam.

ANGELICA: I know he's in the right, — yet thou'st a Tongue
 That wou'd persuade him to deny his Faith. (In Rage walks away.)

WILLMORE: Her Name, her Name, dear Boy — (Said softly to HELLENA.)

300 HELLENA: Have you forgot it, Sir?

WILLMORE: *(Aside.)* Oh, I perceive he's not to know I am a Stranger to his Lady.

— Yes, yes, I do know — but — I have forgot the — (ANGELICA *turns.*)

— By Heaven, such early confidence I never saw.

ANGELICA: Did I not charge you with this Mistress, Sir?

Which you denied, tho I beheld your Perjury.

This little Generosity of thine has render'd back my Heart. *(Walks away.)*

WILLMORE: So, you have made sweet work here, my little mischief;

Look your Lady be kind and good-natur'd now, or

310 I shall have but a cursed Bargain on't. (ANGELICA *turns towards them.*)

— The Rogue's bred up to Mischief,

Art thou so great a Fool to credit him?

ANGELICA: Yes, I do; and you in vain impose upon me.

— Come hither, Boy — Is not this he you speak of?

HELLENA: I think — it is; I cannot swear, but I vow he has just such another lying Lover's look. (HELLENA *looks in his Face, he gazes on her.*)

WILLMORE: *(Aside.)* Hah! do not I know that Face? —

By Heaven, my little Gipsy! what a dull Dog was I?

Had I but lookt that way, I'd known her.

320 Are all my hopes of a new Woman banisht?

— Egad, if I don't fit thee for this, hang me.

— Madam, I have found out the Plot.

HELLENA: *(Aside.)* Oh Lord, what does he say, am I discover'd now?

WILLMORE: Do you see this young Spark here?

HELLENA: *(Aside.)* He'll tell her who I am.

WILLMORE: Who do you think this is?

HELLENA: *(Aside.)* Ay, ay, he does know me. — Nay, dear Captain,

I'm undone if you discover me.

WILLMORE: Nay, nay, no cogging;[5] she shall know what a precious Mistress I

330 have.

HELLENA: Will you be such a Devil!

WILLMORE: Nay, nay, I'll teach you to spoil sport you will not make. — This small Ambassador comes not from a Person of Quality, as you imagine, and he says; but from a very errant Gipsy, the talkingst, pratingst, cantingst little Animal thou ever saw'st.

ANGELICA: What news you tell me! that's the thing I mean.

HELLENA: *(Aside.)* Wou'd I were well off the place. — If ever I go a Captain-hunting again. —

WILLMORE: Mean that thing? that Gipsy thing? thou may'st as well be jealous

340 of thy Monkey, or Parrot as her: a *German* Motion[6] were worth a dozen of her, and a Dream were a better Enjoyment, a Creature of Constitution fitter for Heaven than Man.

HELLENA: *(Aside.)* Tho I'm sure he lyes, yet this vexes me.

ANGELICA: You are mistaken, she's a *Spanish* Woman

Made up of no such dull Materials.

5 wheedling. 6 puppet show.

WILLMORE: Materials! Egad, and she be made of any that will either dispense, or admit of Love, I'll be bound to continence.

HELLENA: *(Aside to him.)* Unreasonable Man, do you think so?

WILLMORE: You may Return, my little Brazen Head,[7] and tell your Lady, that till
350   she be handsome enough to be belov'd, or I dull enough to be religious, there will be small hopes of me.

ANGELICA: Did you not promise then to marry her?

WILLMORE: Not I, by Heaven.

ANGELICA: You cannot undeceive my fears and torments, till you have vow'd you will not marry her.

HELLENA: *(Aside.)* If he swears that, he'll be reveng'd on me indeed for all my Rogueries.

ANGELICA: I know what Arguments you'll bring against me: Fortune and Honour.
360 WILLMORE: Honour! I tell you, I hate it in your Sex; and those that fancy them-selves possest of that Foppery, are the most impertinently troublesome of all Woman-kind, and will transgress nine Commandments to keep one: and to satisfy your Jealousy I swear —

HELLENA: *(Aside to him.)* Oh, no swearing, dear Captain —

WILLMORE: If it were possible I should ever be inclin'd to marry, it should be some kind young Sinner, one that has Generosity enough to give a favour handsomely to one that can ask it discreetly, one that has Wit enough to manage an Intrigue of Love — oh, how civil such a Wench is, to a Man that does her the Honour to marry her.

370 ANGELICA: By Heaven, there's no Faith in any thing he says.

(Enter SEBASTIAN.)

SEBASTIAN: Madam, Don *Antonio* —

ANGELICA: Come hither.

HELLENA: *(Aside.)* Ha, *Antonio*! he may be coming hither, and he'll certainly discover me. I'll therefore retire without a Ceremony. *(Exit HELLENA.)*

ANGELICA: I'll see him, get my Coach ready.

SEBASTIAN: It waits you, Madam.

WILLMORE: This is lucky: what, Madam, now I may be gone and leave you to the enjoyment of my Rival?

ANGELICA: Dull Man, that canst not see how ill, how poor
380   That false dissimulation looks — Be gone,
And never let me see thy cozening Face again,
Lest I relapse and kill thee.

WILLMORE: Yes, you can spare me now, — farewell till you are in a better Humour — I'm glad of this release — *(Aside.)*
Now for my Gipsy:
For tho to worse we change, yet still we find
New Joys, New Charms, in a new Miss that's kind. *(Exit WILLMORE.)*

ANGELICA: He's gone, and in this Ague of My Soul
The shivering Fit returns;

---

7 a fabled gigantic head considered omniscient; according to legend, it told those who consulted it whatever they required to know.

390   Oh with what willing haste he took his leave,
    As if the long'd for Minute were arriv'd,
    Of some blest Assignation.
    In vain I have consulted all my Charms,
    In vain this Beauty priz'd, in vain believ'd
    My eyes cou'd kindle any lasting Fires.
    I had forgot my Name, my Infamy,
    And the Reproach that Honour lays on those
    That dare pretend a sober passion here.
    Nice Reputation, tho it leave behind
400   More Virtues than inhabit where that dwells,
    Yet that once gone, those virtues shine no more.
    — Then since I am not fit to be belov'd,
    I am resolv'd to think on a Revenge
    On him that sooth'd me thus to my undoing. (*Exeunt.*)

SCENE 3. (*A Street.*)

(*Enter* FLORINDA *and* VALERIA *in Habits different from what they have been seen in.*)

FLORINDA: We're happily escap'd, yet I tremble still.

VALERIA: A Lover and fear! why, I am but half a one, and yet I have Courage for any Attempt. Would *Hellena* were here. I wou'd fain have had her as deep in this Mischief as we; she'll fare but ill else, I doubt.

FLORINDA: She pretended a Visit to the *Augustine* Nuns,[1] but I believe some other design carried her out; pray Heavens we light on her.
    — Prithee what didst do with *Callis?*

VALERIA: When I saw no Reason wou'd do good on her, I follow'd her into the Wardrobe, and as she was looking for something in a great Chest, I
10   tumbled her in by the Heels, snatched the Key of the Apartment where you were confin'd, lockt her in, and left her bawling for help.

FLORINDA: 'Tis well you resolve to follow my Fortunes, for thou darest never appear at home again after such an Action.

VALERIA: That's according as the young Stranger and I shall agree — But to our business — I deliver'd your Note to *Belvile* when I got out under pretence of going to Mass. I found him at his Lodging, and believe me it came seasonably; for never was Man in so desperate a Condition. I told him of your Resolution of making your escape to day, if your Brother would be absent long enough to permit you; if not, die rather than be *Antonio's.*

20 FLORINDA: Thou shou'dst have told him I was confin'd to my Chamber upon my Brother's suspicion, that the Business on the *Molo* was a Plot laid between him and I.

VALERIA: I said all this, and told him your Brother was now gone to his Devotion, and he resolves to visit every Church till he find him; and not only undeceive him in that, but caress him so as shall delay his return home.

---

1 order of nuns following the Rule of St. Augustine, which enjoined poverty, prayer, obedience, and chastity.

FLORINDA: Oh Heavens! he's here, and *Belvile* with him too. (*They put on their Vizards.*)

(*Enter* DON PEDRO, BELVILE, WILLMORE; BELVILE *and* DON PEDRO *seeming in serious Discourse.*)

VALERIA: Walk boldly by them; I'll come at a distance, lest he suspect us. (*She walks by them, and looks back on them.*)

WILLMORE: Ha! A Woman! and of an excellent Mien!

PEDRO: She throws a kind look back on you.

30 WILLMORE: Death, 'tis a likely Wench, and that kind look shall not be cast away — I'll follow her.

BELVILE: Prithee do not.

WILLMORE: Do not! By Heavens to the Antipodes, with such an Invitation. (*She goes out, and* WILLMORE *follows her.*)

BELVILE: 'Tis a mad Fellow for a Wench.

(*Enter* FREDERICK.)

FREDERICK: Oh Colonel, such News.

BELVILE: Prithee what?

FREDERICK: News that will make you laugh in spite of Fortune.

BELVILE: What, *Blunt* has had some damn'd Trick put upon him? Cheated, bang'd, or clapt?

40 FREDERICK: Cheated, Sir, rarely cheated of all but his Shirt and Drawers; the unconscionable Whore too turn'd him out before Consummation, so that traversing the Streets at Midnight, the Watch found him in this *Fresco*, and conducted him home: By Heaven 'tis such a slight, and yet I durst as well have been hang'd as laugh at him, or pity him; he beats all that do but ask him a Question, and is in such an Humour —

PEDRO: Who is't has met with this ill usage, Sir?

BELVILE: A Friend of ours, whom you must see for Mirth's sake. (*Aside.*) I'll imploy him to give *Florinda* time for an escape.

PEDRO: Who is he?

50 BELVILE: A young Countryman of ours, one that has been educated at so plentiful a rate he yet ne'er knew the want of Money, and 'twill be a great Jest to see how simply he'll look without it. For my part I'll lend him none, and the Rogue knows not how to put on a borrowing Face, and ask first. I'll let him see how good 'tis to play our parts whilst I play his — Prithee, *Fred*, do go home and keep him in that posture till we come. (*Exeunt.*)

(*Enter* FLORINDA *from the farther end of the Scene, looking behind her.*)

FLORINDA: I am follow'd still — hah — my Brother too advancing this way good Heavens defend me from being seen by him. (*She goes off.*)

(*Enter* WILLMORE, *and after him* VALERIA, *at a little distance.*)

WILLMORE: Ah! There she sails, she looks back as she were willing to be boarded; I'll warrant her Prize. (*He goes out,* VALERIA *following.*)

(*Enter* HELLENA, *just as he goes out, with a Page.*)

60 HELLENA: Hah, is not that my Captain that has a Woman in chase? — 'tis not
Angelica. Boy, follow those People at a distance, and bring me an Account
where they go in. — (Exit Page.) I'll find his Haunts, and plague him every
where. — ha — my Brother!

(BELVILE, WILLMORE, PEDRO cross the Stage: HELLENA runs off.)

(Scene changes to another Street. Enter FLORINDA.)

FLORINDA: What shall I do? My Brother now pursues me.
Will no kind Power protect me from his Tyranny?
— Hah, here's a Door open, I'll venture in, since nothing can be worse
than to fall into his Hands, my Life and Honour are at stake, and my
Necessity has no choice. (She goes in.)

(Enter VALERIA, and HELLENA's PAGE peeping after FLORINDA.)

PAGE: Here she went in, I shall remember this House. (Exit Boy.)

70 VALERIA: This is Belvile's Lodgings; she's gone in as readily as if she knew it —
hah — here's that mad Fellow again; I dare not venture in — I'll watch
my Opportunity. (Goes aside.)

(Enter WILLMORE, gazing about him.)

WILLMORE: I have lost her hereabouts — Pox on't she must not scape me so.
(Goes out.)

(Scene changes to BLUNT's Chamber, discovers him sitting on a Couch in his
Shirt and Drawers, reading.)

BLUNT: So, now my Mind's a little at Peace, since I have resolv'd Revenge — A
Pox on this Taylor tho, for not bringing home the Clothes I bespoke; and a
Pox of all poor Cavaliers, a Man can never keep a spare Suit for 'em; and I shall
have these Rogues come in and find me naked; and then I'm undone; but I'm
resolv'd to arm my self — the Rascals shall not insult over me too much.

(Puts on an old rusty Sword and Buff-Belt.)

80 — Now, how like a Morrice-Dancer[2] I am equipt — a fine Lady-like Whore
to cheat me thus, without affording me a Kindness for my Money, a Pox
light on her, I shall never be reconciled to the Sex more, she has made
me as faithless as a Physician, as uncharitable as a Churchman, and as
ill-natur'd as a Poet. O how I'll use all Women-kind hereafter! what wou'd
I give to have one of 'em within my reach now! any Mortal thing in
Petticoats, kind Fortune, send me; and I'll forgive thy last Night's Malice —
Here's a cursed Book too — a Warning to all young Travellers — that can
instruct me how to prevent such Mischiefs now 'tis too late. Well 'tis a
rare convenient thing to read a little now and then, as well as hawk and

90 hunt. (Sits down again and reads.)

(Enter to him FLORINDA.)

2 morris dances are British folk dances performed by dancers wearing antique and fantastical costumes to
represent legendary characters.

FLORINDA: This House is haunted sure, 'tis well furnisht and no living thing inhabits it — hah — a Man! Heavens how he's attir'd! sure 'tis some Rope-dancer, or Fencing-Master; I tremble now for fear, and yet I must venture now to speak to him — Sir, if I may not interrupt your Meditations — *(He starts up and gazes.)*

BLUNT: Hah — what's here? Are my wishes granted? and is not that a she Creature? 'Adsheartlikins 'tis! what wretched thing art thou — hah!

FLORINDA: Charitable Sir, you've told your self already what I am; a very wretched Maid, forc'd by a strange unlucky Accident, to seek a safety here, and must be ruin'd, if you do not grant it.

100 BLUNT: Ruin'd! Is there any Ruin so inevitable as that which now threatens thee? Dost thou know, miserable Woman, into what Den of Mischiefs thou art fall'n? what a Bliss of Confusion?— hah — dost not see something in my looks that frights thy guilty Soul, and makes thee wish to change that Shape of Woman for any humble Animal, or Devil? for those were safer for thee, and less mischievous.

FLORINDA: Alas, what mean you, Sir? I must confess your Looks have something in 'em makes me fear; but I beseech you, as you seem a Gentleman, pity a harmless Virgin, that takes your House for Sanctuary.

BLUNT: Talk on, talk on, and weep too, till my faith return. Do, flatter me out
110 of my Senses again — a harmless Virgin with a Pox, as much one as t'other, 'adsheartlikins. Why, what the Devil can I not be safe in my House for you? not in my Chamber? nay, even being naked too cannot secure me? This is an Impudence greater than has invaded me yet.— Come, no Resistance. *(Pulls her rudely.)*

FLORINDA: Dare you be so cruel?

BLUNT: Cruel, 'adsheartlikins as a Galley-slave, or a *Spanish* Whore: Cruel, yes, I will kiss and beat thee all over; kiss, and see thee all over; thou shalt lie with me too, not that I care for the Injoyment, but to let you see I have ta'en deliberated Malice to thee, and will be revenged on one Whore for the Sins of another; I will smile and deceive thee, flatter thee, and
120 beat thee, kiss and swear, and lye to thee, imbrace thee and rob thee, as she did me, fawn on thee, and strip thee stark naked, then hang thee out at my Window by the Heels, with a Paper of scurvey Verses fasten'd to thy Breast, in praise of damnable Women — Come, come along.

FLORINDA: Alas, Sir, must I be sacrific'd for the Crimes of the most infamous of my Sex? I never understood the Sins you name.

BLUNT: Do, persuade the Fool you love him, or that one of you can be just or honest; tell me I was not an easy Coxcomb, or any strange impossible Tale: it will be believ'd sooner than thy false Showers or Protestations. A Generation of damn'd Hypocrites, to flatter my very Clothes from my
130 back! dissembling Witches! are these the Returns you make an honest Gentleman that trusts, believes, and loves you?— But if I be not even with you — Come along, or I shall — *(Pulls her again.)*

(Enter FREDERICK.*)*

FREDERICK: Hah, what's here to do?

BLUNT: 'Adsheartlikins, *Fred* I am glad thou art come, to be a Witness of my dire Revenge.

FREDERICK: What's this, a Person of Quality too, who is upon the Ramble to supply the Defects of some grave impotent Husband?

BLUNT: No, this has another Pretence, some very unfortunate Accident brought her hither, to save a Life pursued by I know not who, or why, and forc'd to take Sanctuary here at Fool's Haven. 'Adsheartlikins to me of all Mankind for Protection? Is the Ass to be cajol'd again, think ye? No, young one, no Prayers or Tears shall mitigate my Rage; therefore prepare for both my Pleasure of Enjoyment and Revenge, for I am resolved to make up my Loss here on thy Body: I'll take it out in kindness and in beating.

FREDERICK: Now, Mistress of mine, what do you think of this?

FLORINDA: I think he will not — dares not be so barbarous.

FREDERICK: Have a care, *Blunt*, she fetch'd a deep Sigh; she is inamour'd with thy Shirt and Drawers, she'll strip thee even of that. There are of her Calling such unconscionable Baggages, and such dexterous Thieves, they'll flea[3] a Man, and he shall ne'er miss his Skin, till he feels the Cold. There was a Country-man of ours robb'd of a Row of Teeth whilst he was sleeping, which the Jilt made him buy again when he wak'd — You see, Lady, how little Reason we have to trust you.

BLUNT: 'Dsheartlikins, why, this is most abominable!

FLORINDA: Some such Devils there may be, but by all that's holy I am none such, I entered here to save a Life in danger.

BLUNT: For no goodness, I'll warrant her.

FREDERICK: Faith, Damsel, you had e'en confess the plain Truth, for we are Fellows not to be caught twice in the same Trap: Look on that Wreck, a tight Vessel when he set out of Haven, well trim'd and laden, and see how a Female Piccaroon of this Island of Rogues has shatter'd him, and canst thou hope for any Mercy?

BLUNT: No, no, Gentlewoman, come along, 'adsheartlikins we must be better acquainted — we'll both lie with her, and then let me alone to bang her.

FREDERICK: I am ready to serve you in matters of Revenge; that has a double Pleasure in't.

BLUNT: Well said. You hear, little one, how you are condemn'd by publick Vote to the Bed within; there's no resisting your Destiny, Sweetheart. (*Pulls her.*)

FLORINDA: Stay, Sir, I have seen you with *Belvile*, an *English* Cavalier. For his sake use me kindly; you know him, Sir.

BLUNT: *Belvile*! why, yes, Sweeting, we do know *Belvile*, and wish he were with us now. He's a Cormorant at Whore and Bacon,[4] he'd have a Limb or two of thee, my Virgin Pullet: but 'tis no matter, we'll leave him the Bones to pick.

FLORINDA: Sir, if you have any Esteem for that *Belvile*, I conjure you to treat me with more Gentleness; he'll thank you for the Justice.

FREDERICK: Hark ye, *Blunt*, I doubt we are mistaken in this matter.

3 flay. 4 i.e., he has a ravenous sexual appetite.

FLORINDA: Sir, If you find me not worth *Belvile's* Care, use me as you please; and that you may think I merit better treatment than you threaten — pray take this Present —

(Gives him a Ring: He looks on it.)

BLUNT: Hum — A Diamond! why, 'tis a wonderful Virtue now that lies in this Ring, a mollifying Virtue; 'adsheartlikins there's more persuasive Rhetorick in't, than all her Sex can utter.

FREDERICK: I begin to suspect something; and 'twou'd anger us vilely to be truss'd up for a Rape upon a Maid of Quality, when we only believe we ruffle a Harlot.

BLUNT: Thou art a credulous Fellow, but 'adsheartlikins I have no Faith yet; why, my Saint prattled as parlously as this does, she gave me a Bracelet too, a Devil on her: but I sent my Man to sell it to day for Necessaries, and it prov'd as counterfeit as her Vows of Love.

FREDERICK: However, let it reprieve her till we see *Belvile.*

BLUNT: That's hard, yet I will grant it.

(Enter a Servant.)

SERVANT: Oh, Sir, the Colonel is just come in with his new Friend and a *Spaniard* of Quality, and talks of having you to Dinner with 'em.

BLUNT: 'Dsheartlikins, I'm undone — I would not see 'em for the World: Hark ye, *Fred*, lock up the Wench in your Chamber.

FREDERICK: Fear nothing, Madam, whate'er he threatens, you're safe whilst in my Hands. *(Exeunt* FREDERICK *and* FLORINDA.*)*

BLUNT: And, Sirrah — upon your Life, say — I am not at home — or that I am asleep — or — or anything — away — I'll prevent them coming this way. *(Locks the Door and Exeunt.)*

ACT FIVE

SCENE 1. *(*BLUNT's *Chamber.)*

(After a great knocking as at his Chamber-door, enter BLUNT *softly, crossing the Stage in his Shirt and Drawers, as before.)*

VOICES: *(Calls within.)* Ned! Ned Blunt! Ned Blunt!

BLUNT: The Rogues are up in Arms; 'dsheartlikins, this villainous *Frederick* has betray'd me: they have heard of my blessed Fortune.

VOICES: Ned Blunt, Ned, Ned — *(and knocking within.)*

BELVILE: Why, he's dead, Sir, without dispute dead, he has not been seen to day; let's break open the Door — here — Boy —

BLUNT: Ha, break open the Door! 'dsheartlikins that mad Fellow will be as good as his word.

BELVILE: Boy, bring something to force the Door.

(A great noise within at the Door again.)

10 BLUNT: So, now must I speak in my own Defence; I'll try what Rhetorick will
do — hold — hold, what do you mean, Gentlemen, what do you mean?
BELVILE: Oh Rogue, art alive? prithee open the Door, and convince us.
BLUNT: Yes, I am alive, Gentlemen — but at present a little busy.
BELVILE: (*Within.*) How! *Blunt* grown a man of Business! come, come, open, and
let's see this Miracle.
BLUNT: No, no, no, no, Gentlemen, 'tis no great Business — but — I am —
at — my Devotion, —'dsheartlikins, will you not allow a man time to pray?
BELVILE: (*Within.*) Turn'd religious! a greater Wonder than the first, therefore
open quickly, or we shall unhinge, we shall.
20 BLUNT: (*Aside.*) This won't do — Why, hark ye, Colonel; to tell you the plain
Truth, I am about a necessary Affair of Life. — I have a Wench with me —
you apprehend me? the Devil's in't if they be so uncivil as to disturb me now.
WILLMORE: (*Within.*) How, a Wench! Nay, then we must enter and partake;
no Resistance, — unless it be your Lady of Quality, and then we'll keep
our distance.
BLUNT: So, the Business is out.
WILLMORE: (*Within.*) Come, come, lend more hands to the Door, — now heave
altogether — so, well done, my Boys — (*Breaks open the Door.*)

(*Enter* BELVILE, WILLMORE, FREDERICK, PEDRO, *and* BELVILE's *Page:* BLUNT
looks simply;[1] *they all laugh at him, he lays his hand on his Sword, and comes
up to* WILLMORE.)

BLUNT: Hark ye, Sir, laugh out your laugh quickly, d'ye hear, and be gone, I shall
30 spoil your sport else; 'dsheartlikins, Sir, I shall — the Jest has been carried
on too long, — (*Aside.*) a Plague upon my Taylor —
WILLMORE: 'Sdeath, how the Whore has drest him! Faith, Sir, I'm sorry.
BLUNT: Are you so, Sir? keep't to your self then, Sir, I advise you, d'ye hear? for
I can as little endure your Pity as his Mirth. (*Lays his Hand on's Sword.*)
BELVILE: Indeed, *Willmore*, thou wert a little too rough with *Ned Blunt's* Mistress;
call a Person of Quality Whore, and one so young, so handsome, and so elo-
quent! — ha, ha, ha.
BLUNT: Hark ye, Sir, you know me, and know I can be angry; have a care — for
'dsheartlikins I can fight too — I can, Sir, — do you mark me — no more.
40 BELVILE: Why so peevish, good *Ned*? some Disappointments, I'll warrant —
What! did the jealous Count her Husband return just in the nick?
BLUNT: Or the Devil, Sir, — (*They laugh.*) d'ye laugh? Look ye, settle me a
good sober Countenance, and that quickly too, or you shall know *Ned
Blunt* is not —
BELVILE: Not every Body, we know that.
BLUNT: Not an Ass, to be laught at, Sir.
WILLMORE: Unconscionable Sinner, to bring a Lover so near his Happiness, a
vigorous passionate Lover, and then not only cheat him of his Moveables,
but his Desires too.
50 BELVILE: Ah, Sir, a Mistress is a Trifle with *Blunt*, he'll have a dozen the next time

1 foolishly.

he looks abroad; his Eyes have Charms not to be resisted: There needs no more than to expose that taking Person to the view of the Fair, and he leads 'em all in Triumph.

PEDRO: Sir, tho I'm a stranger to you, I'm ashamed at the rudeness of my Nation; and could you learn who did it, would assist you to make an Example of 'em.

BLUNT: Why, ay, there's one speaks sense now, and handsomely; and let me tell you Gentlemen, I should not have shew'd my self like a Jack-Pudding, [2] thus to have made you Mirth, but that I have revenge within my power; for know, I have got into my possession a Female, who had better have fallen under any Curse, than the Ruin I design her: 'dsheartlikins, she assaulted me here in my own Lodgings, and hast doubtless committed a Rape upon me, had not this Sword defended me.

FREDERICK: I knew not that, but o' my Conscience thou hadst ravisht her, had she not redeem'd her self with a Ring — let's see't, *Blunt.* (BLUNT *shews the Ring.*)

BELVILE: *(Aside.)* Hah! — the Ring I gave *Florinda* when we exchang'd our Vows! — hark ye, *Blunt* — *(Goes to whisper to him.)*

WILLMORE: No whispering, good Colonel, there's a Woman in the case, no whispering.

BELVILE: Hark ye, Fool, be advis'd, and conceal both the Ring and the Story, for your Reputation's sake; don't let people know what despis'd Cullies we *English* are: to be cheated and abus'd by one Whore, and another rather bribe thee than be kind to thee, is an Infamy to our Nation.

WILLMORE: Come, come, where's the Wench? we'll see her, let her be what she will, we'll see her.

PEDRO: Ay, ay, let us see her, I can soon discover whether she be of Quality, or for your Diversion.

BLUNT: She's in *Fred's* Custody.

WILLMORE: Come, come, the Key. (*To* FREDERICK, *who gives him the Key; they are going.*)

BELVILE: *(Aside.)* Death! what shall I do? — stay, Gentlemen — *(Aside.)* yet if I hinder 'em, I shall discover all — hold, let's go one at once [3] — give me the Key.

WILLMORE: Nay, hold there, Colonel, I'll go first.

FREDERICK: Nay, no Dispute, *Ned* and I have the property of her.

WILLMORE: Damn Property — then we'll draw Cuts. (BELVILE *goes to whisper* WILLMORE.)

Nay, no Corruption, good Colonel: come, the longest Sword carries her. — *(They all draw, forgetting* DON PEDRO, *being a* Spaniard, *had the longest.)*

BLUNT: I yield up my Interest to you Gentlemen, and that will be Revenge sufficient.

WILLMORE: *(To* PEDRO.*)* The Wench is yours — *(Aside.)* Pox of his *Toledo,* [4] I had forgot that.

FREDERICK: Come, Sir, I'll conduct you to the Lady.

---

2 clown. 3 one at a time. 4 sword (Toledo in Spain was known for its fine swords).

(Exeunt FREDERICK *and* PEDRO.*)*

BELVILE: *(Aside.)* To hinder him will certainly discover her —
   Dost know, dull Beast, what Mischief thou hast done?
   *(*WILLMORE, *walking up and down out of Humour.)*
WILLMORE: Ay, ay, to trust our Fortune to Lots, a Devil on't, 'twas madness, that's
   the Truth on't.
BELVILE: Oh intolerable Sot!

   (Enter FLORINDA, *running masqu'd,* PEDRO *after her,* WILLMORE *gazing
   round her.)*

FLORINDA: *(Aside.)* Good Heaven, defend me from discovery.
PEDRO: 'Tis but in vain to fly me, you are fallen to my Lot.
BELVILE: *(Aside.)* Sure she is undiscover'd yet, but now I fear there is no way to
100   bring her off.
WILLMORE: *(Aside.)* Why, what a Pox is not this my Woman, the same I follow'd
   but now?

   *(*PEDRO *talking to* FLORINDA, *who walks up and down.)*

PEDRO: As if I did not know ye, and your Business here.
FLORINDA: *(Aside.)* Good Heaven! I fear he does indeed —
PEDRO: Come, pray be kind, I know you meant to be so when you enter'd here,
   for these are proper Gentlemen.
WILLMORE: But, Sir — perhaps the Lady will not be impos'd upon, she'll chuse
   her Man.
PEDRO: I am better bred, than not to leave her Choice free.

   (Enter VALERIA, *and is surpriz'd at the Sight of* DON PEDRO.*)*

110   VALERIA: *(Aside.)* Don *Pedro* here! there's no avoiding him.
FLORINDA: *(Aside.)* *Valeria!* then I'm undone —
VALERIA: Oh! have I found you, Sir — *(To* PEDRO, *running to him.)*
   — The strangest Accident — if I had breath — to tell it.
PEDRO: Speak — is *Florinda* safe? *Hellena* well?
VALERIA: Ay, ay, Sir — *Florinda* — is safe — *(Aside.)* from any fears of you.
PEDRO: Why, where's *Florinda?* — speak.
VALERIA: Ay, where indeed, Sir? I wish I could inform you, — But to hold you
   no longer in doubt —
FLORINDA: *(Aside.)* Oh, what will she say!
120   VALERIA: She's fled away in the Habit of one of her Pages, Sir — but *Callis*
   thinks you may retrieve her yet, if you make haste away; she'll tell you, Sir,
   the rest — *(Aside.)* if you can find her out.
PEDRO: Dishonourable Girl, she has undone my Aim — Sir — you see my
   necessity of leaving you, and I hope you'll pardon it: my Sister, I know,
   will make her flight to you; and if she do, I shall expect she should be render'd back.
BELVILE: I shall consult my Love and Honour, Sir. *(Exit* PEDRO.*)*
FLORINDA: *(To* VALERIA.*)* My dear Preserver, let me imbrace thee.
WILLMORE: What the Devil's all this?

130   BLUNT: Mystery by this Light.

VALERIA: Come, come, make haste and get your selves married quickly, for your Brother will return again.

BELVILE: I am so surpriz'd with Fears and Joys, so amaz'd to find you here in safety, I can scarce persuade my Heart into a Faith of what I see —

WILLMORE: Hark ye, Colonel, is this that Mistress who has cost you so many Sighs, and me so many Quarrels with you?

BELVILE: It is — (To FLORINDA.) Pray give him the Honour of your Hand.

WILLMORE: Thus it must be receiv'd then. (Kneels and kisses her Hand.) And with it give your Pardon too.

140   FLORINDA: The Friend to Belvile may command me anything.

WILLMORE: (Aside.) Death, wou'd I might, 'tis a surprizing Beauty.

BELVILE: Boy, run and fetch a Father instantly. (Exit BOY.)

FREDERICK: So, now do I stand like a Dog, and have not a Syllable to plead my own Cause with: by this Hand, Madam, I was never thorowly confounded before, nor shall I ever more dare look up with Confidence, till you are pleased to pardon me.

FLORINDA: Sir, I'll be reconcil'd to you on one Condition, that you'll follow the Example of your Friend, in marrying a Maid that does not hate you, and whose Fortune (I believe) will not be unwelcome to you.

150   FREDERICK: Madam, had I no Inclinations that way, I shou'd obey your kind Commands.

BELVILE: Who, Fred marry? he has so few Inclinations for Womankind, that had he been possest of Paradise, he might have continu'd there to this Day, if no Crime but Love cou'd have disinherited him.

FREDERICK: Oh, I do not use to boast of my Intrigues.

BELVILE: Boast! why thou do'st nothing but boast; and I dare swear, wer't thou as innocent from the Sin of the Grape, as thou art from the Apple, thou might'st yet claim that right in Eden which our first Parents lost by too much loving.

160   FREDERICK: I wish this Lady would think me so modest a Man.

VALERIA: She shou'd be sorry then, and not like you half so well, and I shou'd be loth to break my Word with you; which was, That if your Friend and mine are agreed, it shou'd be a Match between you and I. (She gives him her Hand.)

FREDERICK: Bear witness, Colonel, 'tis a Bargain. (Kisses her Hand.)

BLUNT: (To FLORINDA.) I have a Pardon to beg too; but 'adsheartlikins I am so out of Countenance, that I am a Dog if I can say any thing to purpose.

FLORINDA: Sir, I heartily forgive you all.

BLUNT: That's nobly said, sweet Lady — Belvile, prithee present her her Ring again, for I find I have not Courage to approach her my self. (Gives him the Ring, he gives it to FLORINDA.)

(Enter BOY.)

170   BOY: Sir, I have brought the Father that you sent for. (Exit BOY.)

BELVILE: 'Tis well, and now my dear Florinda, let's fly to compleat that mighty Joy we have so long wish'd and sigh'd for. — Come, Fred you'll follow?

FREDERICK: Your Example, Sir, 'twas ever my Ambition in War, and must be so in Love.

WILLMORE: And must not I see this juggling[5] Knot ty'd?

BELVILE: No, thou shalt do us better Service, and be our Guard, lest Don Pedro's sudden Return interrupt the Ceremony.

WILLMORE: Content; I'll secure this Pass.

(*Exeunt* BELVILE, FLORINDA, FREDERICK, *and* VALERIA.)

(*Enter* BOY.)

180   BOY: (*To* WILLMORE.) Sir, there's a Lady without wou'd speak to you.

WILLMORE: Conduct her in, I dare not quit my Post.

BOY: (*To* BLUNT.) And, Sir, your Taylor waits you in your Chamber.

BLUNT: Some comfort yet, I shall not dance naked at the Wedding.

(*Exeunt* BLUNT *and* BOY.)

(*Enter again the* BOY, *conducting in* ANGELICA *in her masquing Habit and a Vizard.* WILLMORE *runs to her.*)

WILLMORE: This can be none but my pretty Gipsy — Oh, I see you can follow as well as fly — Come, confess thy self the most malicious Devil in Nature; you think you have done my Bus'ness with *Angelica* —

ANGELICA: Stand off, base Villain — (*She draws a Pistol and holds it to his Breast.*)

WILLMORE: Hah, 'tis not she: who art thou? and what's thy Business?

ANGELICA: One thou hast injur'd, and who comes to kill thee for't.

190   WILLMORE: What the Devil canst thou mean?

ANGELICA: By all my Hopes to kill thee —
   (*Holds still the Pistol to his Breast, he going back, she following still.*)

WILLMORE: Prithee on what Acquaintance? for I know thee not.

ANGELICA: Behold this Face! — so lost to thy Remembrance!
   And then call all thy Sins about thy Soul,
   And let them die with thee. (*Pulls off her Vizard.*)

WILLMORE: *Angelica!*

ANGELICA: Yes, Traitor.
   Does not thy guilty Blood run shivering thro thy Veins?
   Hast thou no Horrour at this Sight, that tells thee,
200   Thou hast not long to boast thy shameful Conquest?

WILLMORE: Faith, no Child, my Blood keeps its old Ebbs and Flows still, and that usual Heat too, that cou'd oblige thee with a Kindness, had I but opportunity.

ANGELICA: Devil! dost wanton with my Pain — have at thy Heart!

WILLMORE: Hold, dear Virago! hold thy Hand a little,
   I am not now at leisure to be kill'd — hold and hear me — (*Aside.*)
   Death, I think she's in earnest.

ANGELICA: (*Aside, turning from him.*) Oh if I take not heed,
   My coward Heart will leave me to his Mercy.

5 cheating (of Florinda's family).

210   — What have you, Sir, to say? — but should I hear thee,
     Thoud'st talk away all that is brave about me: *(Follows him with the Pistol to*
     his Breast.)
     And I have vow'd thy Death, by all that's sacred.

WILLMORE: Why, then there's an end of a proper handsome Fellow, that might
     have liv'd to have done good Service yet: — That's all I can say to't.

ANGELICA: *(Pausingly.)* Yet — I wou'd give thee — time for Penitence.

WILLMORE: Faith, Child, I thank God, I have ever took care to lead a good,
     sober, hopeful Life, and am of a Religion that teaches me to believe, I
     shall depart in Peace.

ANGELICA: So will the Devil: tell me
220   How many poor believing Fools thou hast undone;
     How many Hearts thou hast betray'd to ruin!
     — Yet these are little Mischiefs to the Ills
     Thou'st taught mine to commit: thou'st taught it Love.

WILLMORE: Egad, 'twas shrewdly[6] hurt the while.

ANGELICA: — Love, that has robb'd it of its Unconcern,
     Of all that Pride that taught me how to value it,
     And in its room a mean submissive Passion was convey'd,
     That made me humbly bow, which I ne'er did
     To any thing but Heaven.
230   — Thou, perjur'd Man, didst this, and with thy Oaths,
     Which on thy Knees thou didst devoutly make,
     Soften'd my yielding Heart — And then, I was a Slave —
     Yet still had been content to've worn my Chains,
     Worn 'em with Vanity and Joy for ever,
     Hadst thou not broke those Vows that put them on.
     — 'Twas then I was undone. *(All this while follows him with a Pistol to his*
     Breast.)

WILLMORE: Broke my Vows! why, where hast thou lived?
     Amongst the Gods? For I never heard of mortal Man,
     That has not broke a thousand Vows.

240 ANGELICA: Oh, Impudence!

WILLMORE: *Angelica!* that Beauty has been too long tempting,
     Not to have made a thousand Lovers languish,
     Who in the amorous Favour, no doubt have sworn
     Like me; did they all die in that Faith? still adoring?
     I do not think they did.

ANGELICA: No, faithless Man: had I repaid their Vows, as I did thine, I wou'd
     have kill'd the ungrateful that had abandon'd me.

WILLMORE: This old General has quite spoil'd thee; nothing makes a Woman
     so vain, as being flatter'd; your old Lover ever supplies the Defects of Age,
250   with intolerable Dotage, vast Charge, and that which you call Constancy;
     and attributing all this to your own Merits, you domineer, and throw your
     Favours in's Teeth, upbraiding him still with the Defects of Age, and
     cuckold him as often as he deceives your Expectations. But the gay, young,

6 painfully.

brisk Lover, that brings his equal Fires, and can give you Dart for Dart,
he'll be as nice[7] as you sometimes.

ANGELICA: All this thou'st made me know, for which I hate thee.
Had I remain'd in innocent Security,
I shou'd have thought all Men were born my Slaves;
And worn my Pow'r like Lightning in my Eyes,
260   To have destroy'd at Pleasure when offended.
— But when Love held the Mirror, the undeceiving Glass
Reflected all the Weakness of my Soul, and made me know,
My richest Treasure being lost, my Honour,
All the remaining Spoil cou'd not be worth
The Conqueror's Care or Value.
— Oh how I fell like a long worship'd Idol,
Discovering all the Cheat!
Wou'd not the Incense and rich Sacrifice,
Which blind Devotion offer'd at my Altars,
270   Have fall'n to thee?
Why woud'st thou then destroy my fancy'd Power?

WILLMORE: By Heaven thou art brave, and I admire thee strangely.
I wish I were that dull, that constant thing,
Which thou woud'st have, and Nature never meant me:
I must, like chearful Birds, sing in all Groves,
And perch on every Bough,
Billing the next kind She that flies to meet me;
Yet after all cou'd build my Nest with thee,
Thither repairing when I'd lov'd my round,
280   And still reserve a tributary Flame.
— To gain your Credit, I'll pay you back your Charity,
And be oblig'd for nothing but for Love. (*Offers her a Purse of Gold.*)

ANGELICA: Oh that thou wert in earnest!
So mean a Thought of me,
Wou'd turn my Rage to Scorn, and I shou'd pity thee,
And give thee leave to live;
Which for the publick Safety of our Sex,
And my own private Injuries, I dare not do.
Prepare — (*Follows still, as before.*)
290   — I will no more be tempted with Replies.

WILLMORE: Sure —

ANGELICA: Another Word will damn thee! I've heard thee talk too long. (*She follows him with a Pistol ready to shoot: he retires still amaz'd.*)

(*Enter* DON ANTONIO, *his Arm in a Scarf, and lays hold on the Pistol.*)

ANTONIO: Hah! *Angelica!*

ANGELICA: *Antonio!* What Devil brought thee hither?

ANTONIO: Love and Curiosity, seeing your Coach at Door. Let me disarm you of this unbecoming Instrument of Death. — (*Takes away the Pistol.*)

7 fastidious.

Amongst the Number of your Slaves, was there not one worthy the Honour
to have fought your Quarrel?
— Who are you, Sir, that are so very wretched

300   To merit Death from her?

WILLMORE: One, Sir, that cou'd have made a better End of an amorous Quarrel
without you, than with you.

ANTONIO: Sure 'tis some Rival — hah — the very Man took down her Picture
yesterday — the very same that set on me last night — Blest opportunity — (Offers to shoot him.)

ANGELICA: Hold, you're mistaken, Sir.

ANTONIO: By Heaven the very same!
— Sir, what pretensions have you to this Lady?

WILLMORE: Sir, I don't use to be examin'd, and am ill at all Disputes but this —
(Draws, ANTONIO offers to shoot.)

310   ANGELICA: (To WILLMORE.) Oh, hold! you see he's arm'd with certain Death:
— And you, Antonio, I command you hold,
By all the Passion you've so lately vow'd me.

(Enter DON PEDRO, sees ANTONIO, and stays.)

PEDRO: (Aside.) Hah, Antonio! and Angelica!

ANTONIO: When I refuse Obedience to your Will,
May you destroy me with your mortal Hate.
By all that's Holy I adore you so,
That even my Rival, who has Charms enough
To make him fall a Victim to my Jealousy,
Shall live, nay, and have leave to love on still.

320   PEDRO: (Aside.) What's this I hear?

ANGELICA: (Pointing to WILLMORE.) Ah thus, 'twas thus he talk'd, and I believ'd.
— Antonio, yesterday,
I'd not have sold my Interest in his Heart,
For all the Sword has won and lost in Battle.
— But now to show my utmost of Contempt,
I give thee Life — which if thou would'st preserve,
Live where my Eyes may never see thee more,
Live to undo some one, whose Soul may prove
So bravely constant to revenge my Love.

(Goes out. ANTONIO follows, but PEDRO pulls him back.)

330   PEDRO: Antonio — stay.

ANTONIO: Don Pedro —

PEDRO: What Coward Fear was that prevented thee
From meeting me this Morning on the Molo?

ANTONIO: Meet thee?

PEDRO: Yes me; I was the Man that dar'd thee to't.

ANTONIO: Hast thou so often seen me fight in War,
To find no better Cause to excuse my Absence?
— I sent my Sword and one to do thee Right,
Finding my self uncapable to use a Sword.

340 PEDRO: But 'twas *Florinda's* Quarrel that we fought,
And you to shew how little you esteem'd her,
Sent me your Rival, giving him your Interest.
— But I have found the Cause of this Affront,
And when I meet you fit for the Dispute,
— I'll tell you my Resentment.

ANTONIO: I shall be ready, Sir, e'er long to do you Reason. *(Exit* ANTONIO.*)*

PEDRO: If I cou'd find *Florinda,* now, whilst my Anger's high, I think I shou'd be kind, and give her to *Belvile* in Revenge.

WILLMORE: Faith, Sir, I know not what you wou'd do, but I believe the Priest
350 within has been so kind.

PEDRO: How! my Sister married?

WILLMORE: I hope by this time she is, and bedded too, or he has not my long-ings about him.

PEDRO: Dares he do thus? Does he not fear my Pow'r?

WILLMORE: Faith not at all. If you will go in, and thank him for the Favour he has done your Sister, so; if not, Sir, my Power's greater in this House than yours; I have a damn'd surly Crew here, that will keep you till the next Tide, and then clap you on board my Prize; my Ship lies but a League off the *Molo,* and we shall show your Donship a damn'd *Tramontana* Rover's[8]
360 Trick.

(Enter BELVILE.*)*

BELVILE: This Rogue's in some new Mischief — hah, *Pedro* return'd!

PEDRO: Colonel *Belvile,* I hear you have married my Sister.

BELVILE: You have heard truth then, Sir.

PEDRO: Have I so? then, Sir, I wish you Joy.

BELVILE: How!

PEDRO: By this Embrace I do, and I am glad on't.

BELVILE: Are you in earnest?

PEDRO: By our long Friendship and my Obligations to thee, I am. The sudden Change I'll give you Reasons for anon. Come lead me in to my Sister, that
370 she may know I now approve her Choice. *(Exit* BELVILE *with* PEDRO.*)*

*(*WILLMORE *goes to follow them. Enter* HELLENA *as before in Boy's Clothes, and pulls him back.)*

WILLMORE: Ha! my Gipsy — Now a thousand Blessings on thee for this Kind-ness. Egad, Child, I was e'en in despair of ever seeing thee again; my Friends are all provided for within, each Man his kind Woman.

HELLENA: Hah! I thought they had serv'd me some such Trick.

WILLMORE: And I was e'en resolv'd to go aboard, condemn my self to my lone Cabin, and the Thoughts of thee.

HELLENA: And cou'd you have left me behind? wou'd you have been so ill-natur'd?

WILLMORE: Why, 'twou'd have broke my Heart, Child — but since we are met
380 again, I defy foul Weather to part us.

8 foreign (here, English) pirate's.

HELLENA: And wou'd you be a faithful Friend now, if a Maid shou'd trust you?

WILLMORE: For a Friend I cannot promise: thou art of a Form so excellent, a Face and Humour too good for cold dull Friendship. I am parlously afraid of being in love, Child; and you have not forgot how severely you have us'd me?

HELLENA: That's all one; such Usage you must still look for, to find out all your Haunts, to rail at you to all that love you, till I have made you love only me in your Defence, because no body else will love you.

WILLMORE: But hast thou no better Quality to recommend thy self by?

HELLENA: Faith none, Captain — Why, 'twill be the greater Charity to take me for thy Mistress. I am a lone Child, a kind of Orphan Lover; and why I shou'd die a Maid, and in a Captain's Hands too, I do not understand.

WILLMORE: Egad, I was never claw'd away with Broad-Sides from any Female before. Thou hast one Virtue I adore, good-Nature; I hate a coy demure Mistress, she's as troublesome as a Colt; I'll break none; no, give me a mad Mistress when mew'd, and in flying one I dare trust upon the Wing, that whilst she's kind will come to the Lure.[9]

HELLENA: Nay, as kind as you will, good Captain, whilst it lasts; but let's lose no time.

WILLMORE: My time's as precious to me, as thine can be; therefore, dear Creature, since we are so well agreed, let's retire to my Chamber, and if ever thou wert treated with such savory Love — Come — My Bed's prepar'd for such a Guest, all clean and sweet as thy fair self; I love to steal a Dish and a Bottle with a Friend, and hate long Graces — Come, let's retire and fall to.

HELLENA: 'Tis but getting my Consent, and the Business is soon done; let but old Gaffer[10] Hymen and his Priest say Amen to't, and I dare lay my Mother's Daughter by as proper a Fellow as your Father's Son, without fear or blushing.

WILLMORE: Hold, hold, no Bugg[11] Words, Child. Priest and Hymen: prithee add Hangman to 'em to make up the Consort — No, no, we'll have no Vows but Love, Child, nor Witness but the Lover; the kind Deity injoins naught but love and enjoy. Hymen and Priest wait still upon Portion, and Joynture; Love and Beauty have their own Ceremonies. Marriage is as certain a Bane to Love, as lending Money is to Friendship: I'll neither ask nor give a Vow, tho I could be content to turn Gipsy, and become a Left-hand[12] Bridegroom, to have the Pleasure of working that great Miracle of making a Maid a Mother, if you durst venture; 'tis upse[13] Gipsy that, and if I miss, I'll lose my Labour.

HELLENA: And if you do not lose, what shall I get? A Cradle full of Noise and Mischief, with a Pack of Repentance at my Back? Can you teach me to weave Incle[14] to pass my time with? 'Tis upse Gipsy that too.

WILLMORE: I can teach thee to weave a true Love's Knot better.

HELLENA: So can my Dog.

WILLMORE: Well, I see we are both upon our Guard, and I see there's no way to

---

9 falconer's device for recalling a hawk. 10 grandfather. 11 scary (as in "bogy" and "bugbear").
12 common-law. 13 in the manner of. 14 linen tape.

conquer good Nature, but by yielding — here — give me thy Hand — one Kiss and I am thine —

HELLENA: One Kiss! How like my Page he speaks; I am resolv'd you shall have none, for asking such a sneaking Sum — He that will be satisfied with one Kiss, will never die of that Longing; good Friend single-Kiss, is all your talking come to this? A Kiss, a Caudle![15] farewel, Captain single-Kiss. (*Going out he stays her.*)

WILLMORE: Nay, if we part so, let me die like a Bird upon a Bough, at the Sheriff's Charge. By Heaven, both the *Indies* shall not buy thee from me. I adore thy Humour and will marry thee, and we are so of one Humour, it must be a Bargain — give me thy Hand — (*Kisses her hand.*) And now let the blind ones (Love and Fortune) do their worst.

HELLENA: Why, God-a-mercy, Captain!

WILLMORE: But hark ye — The Bargain is now made; but is it not fit we should know each other's Names? That when we have Reason to curse one another hereafter, and People ask me who 'tis I give to the Devil, I may at least be able to tell what Family you came of.

HELLENA: Good reason, Captain; and where I have cause, (as I doubt not but I shall have plentiful) that I may know at whom to throw my — Blessings — I beseech ye your Name.

WILLMORE: I am call'd *Robert the Constant.*

HELLENA: A very fine Name! pray was it your Faulkner[16] or Butler that christen'd you? Do they not use to whistle when they call you?

WILLMORE: I hope you have a better, that a Man may name without crossing himself, you are so merry with mine.

HELLENA: I am call'd *Hellena the Inconstant.*

(*Enter* PEDRO, BELVILE, FLORINDA, FREDERICK, VALERIA.)

PEDRO: Hah! *Hellena!*

FLORINDA: *Hellena!*

HELLENA: The very same — hah my Brother! now, Captain, shew your Love and Courage; stand to your Arms, and defend me bravely, or I am lost for ever.

PEDRO: What's this I hear? false Girl, how came you hither, and what's your Business? Speak! (*Goes roughly to her.*)

WILLMORE: Hold off, Sir; you have leave to parley only. (*Puts himself between.*)

HELLENA: I had e'en as good tell it, as you guess it. Faith, Brother, my Business is the same with all living Creatures of my Age, to love, and be loved, and here's the Man.

PEDRO: Perfidious Maid, hast thou deceiv'd me too, deceiv'd thy self and Heaven?

HELLENA: 'Tis time enough to make my Peace with that: Be you but kind, let me alone with Heaven.

PEDRO: *Belvile,* I did not expect this false Play from you; was't not enough you'd gain *Florinda* (which I pardon'd), but your lewd Friends too must be inrich'd with the Spoils of a noble Family?

15 warm gruel for invalids. 16 falconer, hawk-keeper.

BELVILE: Faith, Sir, I am as much surpriz'd at this as you can be: Yet, Sir, my Friends are Gentlemen, and ought to be esteem'd for their Misfortunes, since they have the Glory to suffer with the best of Men and Kings; 'tis true, he's a Rover of Fortune, yet a Prince aboard his little wooden World.

PEDRO: What's this to the maintenance of a Woman of her Birth and Quality?

WILLMORE: Faith, Sir, I can boast of nothing but a Sword which does me Right where-e'er I come, and has defended a worse Cause than a Woman's: and since I lov'd her before I either knew her Birth or Name, I must pursue my Resolution, and marry her.

PEDRO: And is all your holy Intent of becoming a Nun debauch'd into a Desire of Man?

HELLENA: Why — I have consider'd the matter, Brother, and find the Three hundred thousand Crowns my Uncle left me (and you cannot keep from me) will be better laid out in Love than in Religion, and turn to as good an Account — let most Voices carry it, for Heaven or the Captain?

(ALL cry.) A Captain! a Captain!

HELLENA: Look ye, Sir, 'tis a clear Case.

PEDRO: Oh I am mad — (Aside.) if I refuse, my Life's in Danger —
— Come — There's one motive induces me — take her — I shall now be free from the fears of her Honour; guard it you now, if you can; I have been a Slave to't long enough. (Gives her to him.)

WILLMORE: Faith, Sir, I am of a Nation, that are of opinion a Woman's Honour is not worth guarding when she has a mind to part with it.

HELLENA: Well said, Captain.

PEDRO: (To VALERIA.) This was your Plot, Mistress, but I hope you have married one that will revenge my Quarrel to you —

VALERIA: There's no altering Destiny, Sir.

PEDRO: Sooner than a Woman's Will; therefore I forgive you all — and wish you may get my Father's Pardon as easily; which I fear.

(Enter BLUNT drest in a Spanish Habit, looking very ridiculously; his MAN adjusting his Band.)

MAN: 'Tis very well, Sir.

BLUNT: Well, Sir, 'dsheartlikins I tell you 'tis damnable ill, Sir — a Spanish Habit, good Lord! cou'd the Devil and my Taylor devise no other Punishment for me, but the Mode of a Nation I abominate?

BELVILE: What's the matter, Ned?

BLUNT: Pray view me round, and judge — (Turns round.)

BELVILE: I must confess thou art a kind of odd Figure.

BLUNT: In a Spanish Habit with a Vengeance! I had rather be in the Inquisition for Judaism, than in this Doublet[17] and Breeches; a Pillory were an easy Collar to this, three Handfuls high; and these Shoes too are worse than the Stocks, with the Sole an Inch shorter than my Foot: In fine, Gentlemen, methinks I look altogether like a Bag of Bays[18] stuff'd full of Fool's Flesh.

---

17 undercoat. 18 spice-bag.

BELVILE: Methinks 'tis well, and makes thee look *en Cavalier*: Come, Sir, settle your Face, and salute our Friends, Lady —

510 BLUNT: Hah! Say'st thou so, my little Rover? *(To* HELLENA.) Lady — (if you be one) give me leave to kiss your Hand, and tell you, 'adsheartlikins, for all I look so, I am your humble Servant — A Pox of my *Spanish* Habit!

WILLMORE: Hark — what's this? *(Musick is heard to Play.)*

(Enter BOY.)

BOY: Sir, as the Custom is, the gay People in Masquerade, who make every Man's House their own, are coming up.

(Enter several Men and Women in masquing Habits, with Musick; they put themselves in order and dance.)

BLUNT: 'Adsheartlikins, wou'd 'twere lawful to pull off their false Faces, that I might see if my Doxy [19] were not amongst 'em.

BELVILE: *(To the Masquers.)* Ladies and Gentlemen, since you are come so *a propos*, you must take a small Collation with us.

520 WILLMORE: *(To* HELLENA.) Whilst we'll to the Good Man within, who stays to give us a Cast of his Office. [20] — Have you no trembling at the near approach?

HELLENA: No more than you have in an Engagement or a Tempest.

WILLMORE: Egad, thou'rt a brave Girl, and I admire thy Love and Courage.
> Lead on, no other Dangers they can dread,
> Who venture in the Storms o' th' Marriage-Bed. *(Exeunt.)*

EPILOGUE

THE banisht Cavaliers! a Roving Blade! [1]
A popish Carnival! a Masquerade!
The Devil's in't if this will please the Nation,
In these our blessed Times of Reformation,
When Conventicling [2] *is so much in Fashion.*
And yet —
That mutinous Tribe less Factions do beget,
Than your continual differing in Wit;
Your Judgment's (as your Passions) a Disease:
10 *Nor Muse or Miss your Appetite can please;*
You're grown as nice as queasy Consciences,
Whose each Convulsion, when the Spirit moves,
Damns every thing that Maggot [3] *disapproves.*
> *With canting Rule you wou'd the Stage refine,*
> *And to dull Method all our Sense confine.*

19 wench. 20 a sample of his work.
1 rake. 2 a conventicle was a chapel attended by Dissenting or nonconforming (i.e., strict and puritanical) Protestants. 3 whim or caprice; here, the inner light that Dissenters claimed as their guide.

With th' Insolence of Common-wealths you rule,
Where each gay Fop, and politick brave Fool
On Monarch Wit impose without controul.
As for the last,[4] who seldom sees a Play,
20 Unless it be the old Black-Fryers[5] way,
Shaking his empty Noddle[6] o'er Bamboo,[7]
He crys — "Good Faith, these Plays will never do.
— Ah, Sir, in my young days, what lofty Wit,
What high-strain'd Scenes of Fighting there were writ:
These are slight airy Toys. But tell me, pray
What has the House of Commons done to day?"
Then shews his Politicks, to let you see
Of State Affairs he'll judge as notably,
As he can do of Wit and Poetry.
30 The younger Sparks, who hither do resort,
Cry —
"Pox o' your gentle things, give us more Sport;
— Damn me, I'm sure 'twill never please the Court."
Such Fops are never pleas'd, unless the Play
Be stuff'd with Fools, as brisk and dull as they.
Such might the Half-Crown spare, and in a Glass
At home behold a more accomplisht Ass.
Where they may set their Cravats, Wigs and Faces,
And practice all their Buffoonry Grimaces;
40 See how this — Huff becomes — this Dammy[8]— stare —
Which they at home may act, because they dare,
But — must with prudent Caution do elsewhere.
Oh that our Nokes, or Tony Lee[9] could show
A Fop but half so much to th' Life as you.

4 i.e., the "politick brave Fool." 5 Blackfriars, a London theatre popular in the early 1600s and destroyed under the Puritans. 6 head. 7 a cane. 8 Damn me. 9 James Nokes and Tony Lee were popular comic actors on the Restoration stage.

Oscar Wilde (1854–1900)

Born into a family of Anglo-Irish privilege, Wilde attended Trinity College, Dublin, where he studied classics and won the Berkeley Gold Medal for Greek. In 1878, he graduated from Oxford with first-class honours and went on to London where he published books of poetry (*Poems* [1881], *The Sphinx* [1894]), verse dramas *Vera* (1881) and *The Duchess of Padua* (1883), articles and reviews in such periodicals as *Pall Mall Gazette*, *The Woman's World*, and *Dramatic Review*, and a volume of essays titled *Intentions* (1891). His well-known novel *The Picture of Dorian Gray* was also published in 1891. In 1882, he toured throughout Canada and the United States, lecturing on topics of aesthetic taste such as "The English Renaissance," "The House Beautiful," and "Decorative Art in America."

Gifted with outrageous intellect and wit, Wilde loved to stir ironies in his listeners and audiences with such quips as his constant fear of "not being misunderstood." He insisted on "art for art's sake," declaring the most important feature of art to be its essential, valuable uselessness. Through such radical aestheticism, even dandyism, Wilde registered himself as a voice of paradox opposed to the stuffy morality of late-Victorian society. His string of successful plays on London's West End stages include *Lady Windermere's Fan* (1892), *A Woman of No Importance* (1893), and *An Ideal Husband* (1895). These society comedies both celebrate and mock the social pretensions of their time through ironic exposures of wealth and class, manners and morality. Wilde's farcical masterpiece *The Importance of Being Earnest* (1895) followed fast, transcending his other plays in terms of quick wit, shrewd satire, and disjunctive comic creativity.

Later in 1895, Wilde was convicted on charges of homosexual indecency and sentenced to two years in jail. Released from the prison in Reading in 1897, he was disgraced, divorced, and bankrupt. He lived abroad the rest of his life in Italy and France, and died in Paris in 1900. Interviewed a few days before his death, he remained paradoxical to the end, recycling a well-known line from his most famous play when he stated: "Some said my life was a lie but I always knew it to be the truth; for like the truth it was rarely pure and never simple."

INTRODUCTION TO *THE IMPORTANCE OF BEING EARNEST*

The Importance of Being Earnest opened at St. James's Theatre in London's West End on February 14, 1895. Cleverly subtitled "A Trivial Comedy for Serious People," Wilde's play was an instant sensation with its exquisite one-liners, crisp satirical inversions, vigorous departures from realist melodrama, and ludicrous dependence on the pun "earnest" in the title. In his *Spectator* review the following week, A. B. Walkley praised Wilde as an "artist in sheer nonsense."

But Wilde's "nonsense" represents a farcical comic strategy that delights in even as it devastatingly mocks Victorian earnestness. Indeed, Victorian society was earnest about *everything*: morals, manners, marriage, money, education, entertainment, personal grooming, social class, and political affiliation. Wilde's play takes jabs at all of these issues through characters that glitter in their cool styling even as they make ridiculously authoritative pronouncements. In doing so, they unconsciously perform the silliness of taking everything so seriously. If *everything* is equally serious then even the ridiculous becomes serious, freeing behaviours from contexts and making them ripe for satirical putdown, as Algernon does near the end of Act 2 when he defies Jack's earnestness:

> What on earth you are so serious about I haven't got the remotest idea. About everything, I should fancy. You have such an absolutely trivial nature.

Both Jack and Algernon, of course, wish to become "Ernest" in order to marry the girl of their respective dreams. The girls, Cecily and Gwendolen, are both independently fixated on marrying a man named Ernest, a Victorian "earnest" man. As Gwendolen rhapsodizes in Act 1:

> My ideal has always been to love someone of the name of Ernest. There is something in that name that inspires absolute confidence. The moment Algernon first mentioned to me that he had a friend called Ernest, I knew I was destined to love you.

Her idealism is a joke. As young Victorian gentlemen, Jack and Algernon are jokes too. Wealthy, sophisticated, leisured, and pointless — they are "Earnest" about everything and nothing. Polite deception is and always was their purpose.

But even their deceptions are as laughably ineffective as they are ironic. Algernon calls himself Ernest but denies Ernest's reputation for wickedness. Cecily replies: "I hope you have not been leading a double life, pretending to be wicked and being really good all the time. That would be hypocrisy." Near the end of the play, Jack realizes that he really is Ernest and confesses: "Gwendolen, it is a terrible thing for a man to find out suddenly that all his life he has been speaking nothing but the truth. Can you forgive me?" And Gwendolen is firm in her irony: "I can, for I feel that you are sure to change." Deception, too, represents reality, if it is "earnest." The play resonates with a philosophical notion, at once whimsical and serious, that asserts and mocks personal performance as personal identity. At the conclusion Jack must inquire, both ridiculously and crucially (but always politely): "Lady Bracknell, I hate to seem inquisitive, but would you kindly inform me who I am?"

In this play about mannered social position, birth, breeding, and identity are explored through comic farce. True identity (a baby forgotten in a handbag, an upper-class English person knowledgeable equally about high tea and social legislation) gets lampooned through the twisted contrivances of the plot. Of course all plots in plays are contrived. *The Importance of Being Earnest* takes special pains to detail its contrivances where all identities and actions are performed as external roles. Herein, Society makes the rules, and people play their socially constructed roles. To protest is to relegate oneself to lower status. As Lady Bracknell patronizingly reproves, "Never speak disrespectfully of Society, Algernon. Only people who can't get into it do that."

Lady Bracknell, of course, represents social order. She is authoritative on all aspects of culture, class, politics, identity, and behaviour, and so stands firmly in the way as comic obstacle to the romantic couples. She also moves through every scene of the play from her nephew's apartment in London to the English country house and garden where "Ernest" is discovered. A local cleric, a prim governess, and a pair of young ladies competing "earnestly" for a man named Ernest — all are regulated by Lady Bracknell's imposing comic presence. As satirical symbol of Victorian authority, and as vital provider of character information, she powers this comedy to its conclusion — a conclusion at once ludicrous and compelling.

THE IMPORTANCE OF BEING EARNEST

THE PERSONS OF THE PLAY

JOHN WORTHING, J.P.
ALGERNON MONCRIEFF
REV. CANON CHASUBLE, D.D.
MERRIMAN, butler
LANE, manservant
LADY BRACKNELL
HON. GWENDOLEN FAIRFAX
CECILY CARDEW
MISS PRISM, governess

THE SCENES OF THE PLAY

ACT I
Algernon Moncrieff's flat in Half-Moon Street, W.

ACT II
The garden at the Manor House, Woolton

ACT III
Drawing-Room at the Manor House, Woolton

TIME
The Present

FIRST ACT

SCENE *Morning-room in Algernon's flat in Half-Moon Street.*[1] *The room is luxuriously and artistically furnished. The sound of a piano is heard in the adjoining room.*

(LANE *is arranging afternoon tea on the table and, after the music has ceased,* ALGERNON *enters.*)

ALGERNON: Did you hear what I was playing, Lane?
LANE: I didn't think it polite to listen, sir.
ALGERNON: I'm sorry for that, for your sake. I don't play accurately — anyone can play accurately — but I play with wonderful expression. As far as the piano is concerned, sentiment is my forte. I keep science for Life.

---

1 street in London's fashionable West End just off Piccadilly near Green Park.

LANE: Yes, sir.

ALGERNON: And, speaking of the science of Life, have you got the cucumber sandwiches cut for Lady Bracknell?

LANE: Yes, sir. (*Hands them on a salver.*)

10 ALGERNON: (*Inspects them, takes two, and sits down on the sofa*) Oh! ... by the way, Lane, I see from your book that on Thursday night, when Lord Shoreman and Mr Worthing were dining with me, eight bottles of champagne are entered as having been consumed.

LANE: Yes, sir; eight bottles and a pint.

ALGERNON: Why is it that at a bachelor's establishment the servants invariably drink the champagne? I ask merely for information.

LANE: I attribute it to the superior quality of the wine, sir. I have often observed that in married households the champagne is rarely of a first-rate brand.

ALGERNON: Good heavens! Is marriage so demoralising as that?

20 LANE: I believe it *is* a very pleasant state, sir. I have had very little experience of it myself up to the present. I have only been married once. That was in consequence of a misunderstanding between myself and a young person.

ALGERNON: (*languidly*) I don't know that I am much interested in your family life, Lane.

LANE: No, sir; it is not a very interesting subject. I never think of it myself.

ALGERNON: Very natural, I am sure. That will do, Lane, thank you.

LANE: Thank you, sir.

(LANE *goes out.*)

ALGERNON: Lane's views on marriage seem somewhat lax. Really, if the lower orders don't set us a good example, what on earth is the use of them? They 30 seem, as a class, to have absolutely no sense of moral responsibility.

(*Enter* LANE.)

LANE: Mr Ernest Worthing.

(*Enter* JACK. LANE *goes out.*)

ALGERNON: How are you, my dear Ernest? What brings you up to town?

JACK: Oh, pleasure, pleasure! What else should bring one anywhere? Eating as usual, I see, Algy!

ALGERNON: (*stiffly*) I believe it is customary in good society to take some slight refreshment at five o'clock. Where have you been since last Thursday?

JACK: (*sitting down on the sofa*) In the country.

ALGERNON: What on earth do you do there?

JACK: (*pulling off his gloves*) When one is in town one amuses oneself. When one 40 is in the country one amuses other people. It is excessively boring.

ALGERNON: And who are the people you amuse?

JACK: (*airily*) Oh, neighbours, neighbours.

ALGERNON: Got nice neighbours in your part of Shropshire?[2]

---

2 Jack's country place is in Hertfordshire north of London, but he attempts to deceive Algernon by insisting on this false location. Shropshire is far to the west on the Welsh border.

JACK: Perfectly horrid! Never speak to one of them.

ALGERNON: How immensely you must amuse them! (*Goes over and takes sandwich.*) By the way, Shropshire is your county, is it not?

JACK: Eh? Shropshire? Yes, of course. Hallo! Why all these cups? Why cucumber sandwiches? Why such reckless extravagance in one so young? Who is coming to tea?

50   ALGERNON: Oh! merely Aunt Augusta and Gwendolen.

JACK: How perfectly delightful!

ALGERNON: Yes, that is all very well; but I am afraid Aunt Augusta won't quite approve of your being here.

JACK: May I ask why?

ALGERNON: My dear fellow, the way you flirt with Gwendolen is perfectly disgraceful. It is almost as bad as the way Gwendolen flirts with you.

JACK: I am in love with Gwendolen. I have come up to town expressly to propose to her.

ALGERNON: I thought you had come up for pleasure?...I call that business.

60   JACK: How utterly unromantic you are!

ALGERNON: I really don't see anything romantic in proposing. It is very romantic to be in love. But there is nothing romantic about a definite proposal. Why, one may be accepted. One usually is, I believe. Then the excitement is all over. The very essence of romance is uncertainty. If ever I get married, I'll certainly try to forget the fact.

JACK: I have no doubt about that, dear Algy. The Divorce Court was specially invented for people whose memories are so curiously constituted.

ALGERNON: Oh! there is no use speculating on that subject. Divorces are made in Heaven — (JACK *puts out his hand to take a sandwich.* ALGERNON *at once*
70   *interferes.*) Please don't touch the cucumber sandwiches. They are ordered specially for Aunt Augusta. (*Takes one and eats it.*)

JACK: Well, you have been eating them all the time.

ALGERNON: That is quite a different matter. She is my aunt. (*Takes plate from below.*) Have some bread and butter. The bread and butter is for Gwendolen. Gwendolen is devoted to bread and butter.

JACK: (*advancing to table and helping himself*) And very good bread and butter it is too.

ALGERNON: Well, my dear fellow, you need not eat as if you were going to eat it all. You behave as if you were married to her already. You are not married
80   to her already, and I don't think you ever will be.

JACK: Why on earth do you say that?

ALGERNON: Well, in the first place, girls never marry the men they flirt with. Girls don't think it right.

JACK: Oh, that is nonsense!

ALGERNON: It isn't. It is a great truth. It accounts for the extraordinary number of bachelors that one sees all over the place. In the second place, I don't give my consent.

JACK: Your consent!

ALGERNON: My dear fellow, Gwendolen is my first cousin. And before I allow you
90   to marry her, you will have to clear up the whole question of Cecily. (*Rings bell.*)

JACK: Cecily! What on earth do you mean? What do you mean, Algy, by Cecily! I don't know any one of the name of Cecily.

(*Enter* LANE.)

ALGERNON: Bring me that cigarette case Mr Worthing left in the smoking-room the last time he dined here.

LANE: Yes, sir.

(LANE *goes out.*)

JACK: Do you mean to say you have had my cigarette case all this time? I wish to goodness you had let me know. I have been writing frantic letters to Scotland Yard about it. I was very nearly offering a large reward.

ALGERNON: Well, I wish you would offer one. I happen to be more than usually hard up.

JACK: There is no good offering a large reward now that the thing is found.

(*Enter* LANE *with the cigarette case on a salver.* ALGERNON *takes it at once.* LANE *goes out.*)

ALGERNON: I think that is rather mean of you, Ernest, I must say. (*Opens case and examines it.*) However, it makes no matter, for, now that I look at the inscription inside, I find that the thing isn't yours after all.

JACK: Of course it's mine. (*Moving to him.*) You have seen me with it a hundred times, and you have no right whatsoever to read what is written inside. It is a very ungentlemanly thing to read a private cigarette case.

ALGERNON: Oh! it is absurd to have a hard and fast rule about what one should read and what one shouldn't. More than half of modern culture depends on what one shouldn't read.

JACK: I am quite aware of the fact, and I don't propose to discuss modern culture. It isn't the sort of thing one should talk of in private. I simply want my cigarette case back.

ALGERNON: Yes; but this isn't your cigarette case. This cigarette case is a present from someone of the name of Cecily, and you said you didn't know anyone of that name.

JACK: Well, if you want to know, Cecily happens to be my aunt.

ALGERNON: Your aunt!

JACK: Yes. Charming old lady she is, too. Lives at Tunbridge Wells. Just give it back to me, Algy.

ALGERNON: (*retreating to back of sofa*) But why does she call herself little Cecily if she is your aunt and lives at Tunbridge Wells? (*Reading.*) "From little Cecily with her fondest love."

JACK: (*moving to sofa and kneeling upon it*) My dear fellow, what on earth is there in that? Some aunts are tall, some aunts are not tall. That is a matter that surely an aunt may be allowed to decide for herself. You seem to think that every aunt should be exactly like your aunt! That is absurd! For Heaven's sake give me back my cigarette case. (*Follows* ALGERNON *round the room.*)

ALGERNON: Yes. But why does your aunt call you her uncle? "From little Cecily, with her fondest love to her dear Uncle Jack." There is no objection, I admit, to an aunt being a small aunt, but why an aunt, no matter what her size may be, should call her own nephew her uncle, I can't quite make out. Besides, your name isn't Jack at all; it is Ernest.

JACK: It isn't Ernest; it's Jack.

ALGERNON: You have always told me it was Ernest. I have introduced you to everyone as Ernest. You answer to the name of Ernest. You look as if your name was Ernest. You are the most earnest-looking person I ever saw in my life. It is perfectly absurd your saying that your name isn't Ernest. It's on your cards. Here is one of them. (*Taking it from case.*) "Mr Ernest Worthing, B.4, The Albany." I'll keep this as a proof that your name is Ernest if ever you attempt to deny it to me, or to Gwendolen, or to anyone else. (*Puts the card in his pocket.*)

JACK: Well, my name is Ernest in town and Jack in the country, and the cigarette case was given to me in the country.

ALGERNON: Yes, but that does not account for the fact that your small Aunt Cecily, who lives at Tunbridge Wells, calls you her dear uncle. Come, old boy, you had much better have the thing out at once.

JACK: My dear Algy, you talk exactly as if you were a dentist. It is very vulgar to talk like a dentist when one isn't a dentist. It produces a false impression.

ALGERNON: Well, that is exactly what dentists always do. Now, go on! Tell me the whole thing. I may mention that I have always suspected you of being a confirmed and secret Bunburyist; and I am quite sure of it now.

JACK: Bunburyist? What on earth do you mean by a Bunburyist?

ALGERNON: I'll reveal to you the meaning of that incomparable expression as soon as you are kind enough to inform me why you are Ernest in town and Jack in the country.

JACK: Well, produce my cigarette case first.

ALGERNON: Here it is. (*Hands cigarette case.*) Now produce your explanation, and pray make it improbable. (*Sits on sofa.*)

JACK: My dear fellow, there is nothing improbable about my explanation at all. In fact it's perfectly ordinary. Old Mr Thomas Cardew, who adopted me when I was a little boy, made me in his will guardian to his granddaughter, Miss Cecily Cardew. Cecily, who addresses me as her uncle from motives of respect that you could not possibly appreciate, lives at my place in the country under the charge of her admirable governess, Miss Prism.

ALGERNON: Where is that place in the country, by the way?

JACK: That is nothing to you, dear boy. You are not going to be invited....I may tell you candidly that the place is not in Shropshire.

ALGERNON: I suspected that, my dear fellow! I have Bunburyed all over Shropshire on two separate occasions. Now, go on. Why are you Ernest in town and Jack in the country?

JACK: My dear Algy, I don't know whether you will be able to understand my real motives. You are hardly serious enough. When one is placed in the position of guardian, one has to adopt a very high moral tone on all subjects. It's one's duty to do so. And as a high moral tone can hardly be said to conduce very much to either one's health or one's happiness, in order to get up to town I have always pretended to have a younger brother of the name of Ernest, who lives in the Albany, and gets into the most dreadful scrapes. That, my dear Algy, is the whole truth pure and simple.

ALGERNON: The truth is rarely pure and never simple. Modern life would be very
tedious if it were either, and modern literature a complete impossibility!

JACK: That wouldn't be at all a bad thing.

ALGERNON: Literary criticism is not your forte, my dear fellow. Don't try it.
You should leave that to people who haven't been at a University. They do
it so well in the daily papers. What you really are is a Bunburyist. I was quite
right in saying you were a Bunburyist. You are one of the most advanced
Bunburyists I know.

JACK: What on earth do you mean?

ALGERNON: You have invented a very useful younger brother called Ernest, in
order that you may be able to come up to town as often as you like. I have
invented an invaluable permanent invalid called Bunbury, in order that I
may be able to go down into the country whenever I choose. Bunbury is perfectly invaluable. If it wasn't for Bunbury's extraordinary bad health, for
instance, I wouldn't be able to dine with you at Willis's[3] tonight, for I have
been really engaged to Aunt Augusta for more than a week.

JACK: I haven't asked you to dine with me anywhere tonight.

ALGERNON: I know. You are absurdly careless about sending out invitations. It is very
foolish of you. Nothing annoys people so much as not receiving invitations.

JACK: You had much better dine with your Aunt Augusta.

ALGERNON: I haven't the smallest intention of doing anything of the kind. To
begin with, I dined there on Monday, and once a week is quite enough to
dine with one's own relations. In the second place, whenever I do dine
there I am always treated as a member of the family, and sent down[4] with
either no woman at all, or two. In the third place, I know perfectly well
whom she will place me next to, tonight. She will place me next Mary
Farquhar, who always flirts with her own husband across the dinner-table.
That is not very pleasant. Indeed, it is not even decent... and that sort of
thing is enormously on the increase. The amount of women in London who
flirt with their own husbands is perfectly scandalous. It looks so bad. It is
simply washing one's clean linen in public. Besides, now that I know you
to be a confirmed Bunburyist I naturally want to talk to you about
Bunburying. I want to tell you the rules.

JACK: I'm not a Bunburyist at all. If Gwendolen accepts me, I am going to kill
my brother, indeed I think I'll kill him in any case. Cecily is a little too
much interested in him. It is rather a bore. So I am going to get rid of
Ernest. And I strongly advise you to do the same with Mr... with your
invalid friend who has the absurd name.

ALGERNON: Nothing will induce me to part with Bunbury, and if you ever get
married, which seems to me extremely problematic, you will be very glad
to know Bunbury. A man who marries without knowing Bunbury has a very
tedious time of it.

JACK: That is nonsense. If I marry a charming girl like Gwendolen, and she is
the only girl I ever saw in my life that I would marry, I certainly won't
want to know Bunbury.

3 fashionable restaurant in King St. near St. James's Theatre.
4 at formal Victorian dinners, guests congregated in a drawing room upstairs before being "sent down" to the
dining room with their partners.

ALGERNON: Then your wife will. You don't seem to realize, that in married life three is company and two is none.

JACK: (*sententiously*) That, my dear young friend, is the theory[5] that the corrupt French Drama has been propounding for the last fifty years.

ALGERNON: Yes; and that the happy English home has proved in half the time.

JACK: For heaven's sake, don't try to be cynical. It's perfectly easy to be cynical.

230 ALGERNON: My dear fellow, it isn't easy to be anything nowadays. There's such a lot of beastly competition about. (*The sound of an electric bell is heard.*) Ah! that must be Aunt Augusta. Only relatives, or creditors, ever ring in that Wagnerian manner.[6] Now, if I get her out of the way for ten minutes, so that you can have an opportunity for proposing to Gwendolen, may I dine with you tonight at Willis's?

JACK: I suppose so, if you want to.

ALGERNON: Yes, but you must be serious about it. I hate people who are not serious about meals. It is so shallow of them.

(*Enter* LANE.)

LANE: Lady Bracknell and Miss Fairfax.

(ALGERNON *goes forward to meet them. Enter* LADY BRACKNELL *and* GWENDOLEN.)

240 LADY BRACKNELL: Good afternoon, dear Algernon, I hope you are behaving very well.

ALGERNON: I'm feeling very well, Aunt Augusta.

LADY BRACKNELL: That's not quite the same thing. In fact the two things rarely go together. (*Sees* JACK *and bows to him with icy coldness.*)

ALGERNON: (*to* GWENDOLEN) Dear me, you are smart![7]

GWENDOLEN: I am always smart! Am I not, Mr Worthing?

JACK: You're quite perfect, Miss Fairfax.

GWENDOLEN: Oh! I hope I am not that. It would leave no room for developments, and I intend to develop in many directions.

(GWENDOLEN *and* JACK *sit down together in the corner.*)

250 LADY BRACKNELL: I'm sorry if we are a little late, Algernon, but I was obliged to call on dear Lady Harbury. I hadn't been there since her poor husband's death. I never saw a woman so altered; she looks quite twenty years younger. And now I'll have a cup of tea, and one of those nice cucumber sandwiches you promised me.

ALGERNON: Certainly, Aunt Augusta. (*Goes over to tea-table.*)

LADY BRACKNELL: Won't you come and sit here, Gwendolen?

GWENDOLEN: Thanks, mamma, I'm quite comfortable where I am.

ALGERNON: (*picking up empty plate in horror*) Good heavens! Lane! Why are there no cucumber sandwiches? I ordered them specially.

260 LANE: (*gravely*) There were no cucumbers in the market this morning, sir. I went down twice.

---

5 this refers to the recurrent theme of marital infidelity. 6 the loud music of the operas of Richard Wagner.
7 well-dressed.

ALGERNON: No cucumbers!

LANE: No, sir. Not even for ready money.

ALGERNON: That will do, Lane, thank you.

LANE: Thank you, sir. (*Goes out.*)

ALGERNON: I am greatly distressed, Aunt Augusta, about there being no cucumbers, not even for ready money.

LADY BRACKNELL: It really makes no matter, Algernon. I had some crumpets[8] with Lady Harbury, who seems to me to be living entirely for pleasure now.

270 ALGERNON: I hear her hair has turned quite gold from grief.

LADY BRACKNELL: It certainly has changed its colour. From what cause I, of course, cannot say. (ALGERNON *crosses and hands tea.*) Thank you, I've quite a treat for you tonight, Algernon. I am going to send you down with Mary Farquhar. She is such a nice woman, and so attentive to her husband. It's delightful to watch them.

ALGERNON: I am afraid, Aunt Augusta, I shall have to give up the pleasure of dining with you tonight after all.

LADY BRACKNELL: (*frowning*) I hope not, Algernon. It would put my table completely out. Your uncle would have to dine upstairs. Fortunately he is accus-
280 tomed to that.

ALGERNON: It is a great bore, and, I need hardly say, a terrible disappointment to me, but the fact is I have just had a telegram to say that my poor friend Bunbury is very ill again. (*Exchanges glances with* JACK.) They seem to think I should be with him.

LADY BRACKNELL: It is very strange. This Mr Bunbury seems to suffer from curiously bad health.

ALGERNON: Yes; poor Bunbury is a dreadful invalid.

LADY BRACKNELL: Well, I must say, Algernon, that I think it is high time that Mr Bunbury made up his mind whether he was going to live or to die.
290 This shilly-shallying with the question is absurd. Nor do I in any way approve of the modern sympathy with invalids. I consider it morbid. Illness of any kind is hardly a thing to be encouraged in others. Health is the primary duty of life. I am always telling that to your poor uncle, but he never seems to take much notice...as far as any improvement in his ailments goes. I should be much obliged if you would ask Mr Bunbury, from me, to be kind enough not to have a relapse on Saturday, for I rely on you to arrange my music for me. It is my last reception, and one wants something that will encourage conversation, particularly at the end of the season when everyone has practically said whatever they had to say, which, in most cases, was
300 probably not much.

ALGERNON: I'll speak to Bunbury, Aunt Augusta, if he is still conscious, and I think I can promise you he'll be all right by Saturday. Of course the music is a great difficulty. You see, if one plays good music, people don't listen, and if one plays bad music people don't talk. But I'll run over the programme I've drawn out, if you will kindly come into the next room for a moment.

LADY BRACKNELL: Thank you, Algernon. It is very thoughtful of you. (*Rising, and following* ALGERNON.) I'm sure the programme will be delightful, after

---

8 soft cake like a waffle, usually toasted.

a few expurgations. French songs I cannot possibly allow. People always seem to think that they are improper, and either look shocked, which is vulgar, or laugh, which is worse. But German sounds a thoroughly respectable language, and indeed, I believe is so. Gwendolen, you will accompany me.

GWENDOLEN: Certainly mamma.

(LADY BRACKNELL and ALGERNON go into the music-room, GWENDOLEN remains behind.)

JACK: Charming day it has been, Miss Fairfax.

GWENDOLEN: Pray don't talk to me about the weather, Mr Worthing. Whenever people talk to me about the weather, I always feel quite certain that they mean something else. And that makes me so nervous.

JACK: I do mean something else.

GWENDOLEN: I thought so. In fact, I am never wrong.

JACK: And I would like to be allowed to take advantage of Lady Bracknell's temporary absence...

GWENDOLEN: I would certainly advise you to do so. Mamma has a way of coming back suddenly into a room that I have often had to speak to her about.

JACK: (nervously) Miss Fairfax, ever since I met you I have admired you more than any girl...I have ever met since...I met you.

GWENDOLEN: Yes, I am quite well aware of the fact. And I often wish that in public, at any rate, you had been more demonstrative. For me you have always had an irresistible fascination. Even before I met you I was far from indifferent to you. (JACK looks at her in amazement.) We live, as I hope you know, Mr Worthing, in an age of ideals. The fact is constantly mentioned in the more expensive monthly magazines, and has reached the provincial pulpits, I am told; and my ideal has always been to love someone of the name of Ernest. There is something in that name that inspires absolute confidence. The moment Algernon first mentioned to me that he had a friend called Ernest, I knew I was destined to love you.

JACK: You really love me, Gwendolen?

GWENDOLEN: Passionately!

JACK: Darling! You don't know how happy you've made me.

GWENDOLEN: My own Ernest!

JACK: But you don't really mean to say that you couldn't love me if my name wasn't Ernest?

GWENDOLEN: But your name is Ernest.

JACK: Yes, I know it is. But supposing it was something else? Do you mean to say you couldn't love me then?

GWENDOLEN: (glibly) Ah! that is clearly a metaphysical speculation, and like most metaphysical speculations has very little reference at all to the actual facts of real life, as we know them.

JACK: Personally, darling, to speak quite candidly, I don't much care about the name of Ernest....I don't think the name suits me at all.

GWENDOLEN: It suits you perfectly. It is a divine name. It has music of its own. It produces vibrations.

JACK: Well, really, Gwendolen, I must say that I think there are lots of other much nicer names. I think Jack, for instance, a charming name.

GWENDOLEN: Jack?...No, there is very little music in the name Jack, if any at all, indeed. It does not thrill. It produces absolutely no vibrations....I have known several Jacks, and they all, without exception, were more than usually plain. Besides, Jack is a notorious domesticity for John! And I pity any woman who is married to a man called John. She would probably never be allowed to know the entrancing pleasure of a single moment's solitude. The only really safe name is Ernest.

360 JACK: Gwendolen, I must get christened at once — I mean we must get married at once. There is no time to be lost.

GWENDOLEN: Married, Mr Worthing?

JACK: (astounded) Well...surely. You know that I love you, and you led me to believe, Miss Fairfax, that you were not absolutely indifferent to me.

GWENDOLEN: I adore you. But you haven't proposed to me yet. Nothing has been said at all about marriage. The subject has not even been touched on.

JACK: Well...may I propose to you now?

GWENDOLEN: I think it would be an admirable opportunity. And to spare you any possible disappointment, Mr Worthing, I think it only fair to tell you 370 quite frankly beforehand that I am fully determined to accept you.

JACK: Gwendolen!

GWENDOLEN: Yes, Mr Worthing, what have you got to say to me?

JACK: You know what I have got to say to you.

GWENDOLEN: Yes, but you don't say it.

JACK: Gwendolen, will you marry me? (Goes on his knees.)

GWENDOLEN: Of course I will, darling. How long you have been about it! I am afraid you have had very little experience in how to propose.

JACK: My own one, I have never loved anyone in the world but you.

GWENDOLEN: Yes, but men often propose for practice. I know my brother 380 Gerald does. All my girl-friends tell me so. What wonderfully blue eyes you have, Ernest! They are quite, quite blue. I hope you will always look at me just like that, especially when there are other people present.

(Enter LADY BRACKNELL.)

LADY BRACKNELL: Mr Worthing! Rise, sir, from this semi-recumbent posture. It is most indecorous.

GWENDOLEN: Mamma! (He tries to rise; she restrains him.) I must beg you to retire. This is no place for you. Besides, Mr Worthing has not quite finished yet.

LADY BRACKNELL: Finished what, may I ask?

GWENDOLEN: I am engaged to Mr Worthing, mamma. (They rise together.)

LADY BRACKNELL: Pardon me, you are not engaged to anyone. When you do 390 become engaged to some one, I, or your father, should his health permit him, will inform you of the fact. An engagement should come on a young girl as a surprise, pleasant or unpleasant, as the case may be. It is hardly a matter that she could be allowed to arrange for herself....And now I have a few questions to put to you, Mr Worthing. While I am making these inquiries, you, Gwendolen, will wait for me below in the carriage.

GWENDOLEN: (reproachfully) Mamma!

LADY BRACKNELL: In the carriage, Gwendolen! (GWENDOLEN goes to the door. She and JACK blow kisses to each other behind LADY BRACKNELL's back. LADY

BRACKNELL *looks vaguely about as if she could not understand what the noise was. Finally turns round.*) Gwendolen, the carriage!

GWENDOLEN: Yes, mamma. (*Goes out, looking back at* JACK.)

LADY BRACKNELL: (*sitting down.*) You can take a seat, Mr Worthing.

(*Looks in her pocket for note-book and pencil.*)

JACK: Thank you, Lady Bracknell, I prefer standing.

LADY BRACKNELL: (*pencil and note-book in hand*) I feel bound to tell you that you are not down on my list of eligible young men, although I have the same list as the dear Duchess of Bolton has. We work together, in fact. However, I am quite ready to enter your name, should your answers be what a really affectionate mother requires. Do you smoke?

JACK: Well, yes, I must admit I smoke.

LADY BRACKNELL: I am glad to hear it. A man should always have an occupation of some kind. There are far too many idle men in London as it is. How old are you?

JACK: Twenty-nine.

LADY BRACKNELL: A very good age to be married at. I have always been of opinion that a man who desires to get married should know either everything or nothing. Which do you know?

JACK: (*after some hesitation*) I know nothing, Lady Bracknell.

LADY BRACKNELL: I am pleased to hear it. I do not approve of anything that tampers with natural ignorance. Ignorance is like a delicate exotic fruit; touch it and the bloom is gone. The whole theory of modern education is radically unsound. Fortunately in England, at any rate, education produces no effect whatsoever. If it did, it would prove a serious danger to the upper classes, and probably lead to acts of violence in Grosvenor Square.[9] What is your income?

JACK: Between seven and eight thousand a year.

LADY BRACKNELL: (*makes a note in her book*) In land, or in investments?

JACK: In investments, chiefly.

LADY BRACKNELL: That is satisfactory. What between the duties expected of one during one's lifetime, and the duties[10] exacted from one after one's death, land has ceased to be either a profit or a pleasure. It gives one position, and prevents one from keeping it up. That's all that can be said about land.

JACK: I have a country house with some land, of course, attached to it, about fifteen hundred acres, I believe; but I don't depend on that for my real income. In fact, as far as I can make out, the poachers are the only people who make anything out of it.

LADY BRACKNELL: A country house! How many bedrooms? Well, that point can be cleared up afterwards. You have a town house, I hope? A girl with a simple, unspoiled nature, like Gwendolen, could hardly be expected to reside in the country.

JACK: Well, I own a house in Belgrave Square, but it is let by the year to Lady Bloxham. Of course, I can get it back whenever I like, at six months' notice.

LADY BRACKNELL: Lady Bloxham? I don't know her.

9 fashionable area in London's Mayfair district. 10 taxes.

JACK: Oh, she goes about very little. She is a lady considerably advanced in years.

LADY BRACKNELL: Ah, nowadays that is no guarantee of respectability of character. What number in Belgrave Square?

JACK: 149.

LADY BRACKNELL: (shaking her head) The unfashionable side. I thought there was something. However, that could easily be altered.

JACK: Do you mean the fashion, or the side?

LADY BRACKNELL: (sternly) Both, if necessary, I presume. What are your
450   politics?

JACK: Well, I am afraid I really have none. I am a Liberal Unionist.

LADY BRACKNELL: Oh, they count as Tories. They dine with us. Or come in the evening, at any rate. Now to minor matters. Are your parents living?

JACK: I have lost both my parents.

LADY BRACKNELL: To lose one parent, Mr Worthing, may be regarded as a misfortune; to lose both looks like carelessness. Who was your father? He was evidently a man of some wealth. Was he born in what the Radical papers call the purple of commerce,[11] or did he rise from the ranks of the aristocracy?

JACK: I am afraid I really don't know. The fact is, Lady Bracknell, I said I had
460   lost my parents. It would be nearer the truth to say that my parents seem to have lost me.... I don't actually know who I am by birth. I was ... well, I was found.

LADY BRACKNELL: Found!

JACK: The late Mr Thomas Cardew, an old gentleman of a very charitable and kindly disposition, found me, and gave me the name of Worthing, because he happened to have a first-class ticket for Worthing in his pocket at the time. Worthing is a place in Sussex. It is a seaside resort.

LADY BRACKNELL: Where did the charitable gentleman who had a first-class ticket for this seaside resort find you?

470   JACK: (gravely) In a hand-bag.

LADY BRACKNELL: A hand-bag?

JACK: (very seriously) Yes, Lady Bracknell. I was in a hand-bag — a somewhat large, black leather hand-bag, with handles to it — an ordinary hand-bag in fact.

LADY BRACKNELL: In what locality did this Mr James, or Thomas, Cardew come across this ordinary hand-bag?

JACK: In the cloak-room at Victoria Station. It was given to him in mistake for his own.

LADY BRACKNELL: The cloak-room at Victoria Station?

480   JACK: Yes. The Brighton line.

LADY BRACKNELL: The line is immaterial. Mr Worthing, I confess I feel somewhat bewildered by what you have just told me. To be born, or at any rate bred, in a hand-bag, whether it had handles or not, seems to me to display a contempt for the ordinary decencies of family life that reminds one of the worst excesses of the French Revolution. And I presume you know what that unfortunate movement led to? As for the particular locality in which the hand-bag was found, a cloak-room at a railway station might serve to

---

11 "born in the purple": of aristocratic birth.

conceal a social indiscretion — has probably, indeed, been used for that purpose before now — but it could hardly be regarded as an assured basis for a recognised position in good society.

JACK: May I ask you then what you would advise me to do? I need hardly say I would do anything in the world to ensure Gwendolen's happiness.

LADY BRACKNELL: I would strongly advise you, Mr Worthing, to try and acquire some relations as soon as possible, and to make a definite effort to produce at any rate one parent, of either sex, before the season is quite over.

JACK: Well, I don't see how I could possibly manage to do that. I can produce the hand-bag at any moment. It is in my dressing-room at home. I really think that should satisfy you, Lady Bracknell.

LADY BRACKNELL: Me, sir! What has it to do with me? You can hardly imagine that I and Lord Bracknell would dream of allowing our only daughter — a girl brought up with the utmost care — to marry into a cloak-room, and form an alliance with a parcel? Good morning, Mr Worthing!

(LADY BRACKNELL *sweeps out in majestic indignation.*)

JACK: Good morning! (ALGERNON, *from the other room, strikes up the Wedding March.* JACK *looks perfectly furious, and goes to the door.*) For goodness' sake don't play that ghastly tune, Algy! How idiotic you are!

(*The music stops and* ALGERNON *enters cheerily.*)

ALGERNON: Didn't it go off all right, old boy? You don't mean to say Gwendolen refused you? I know it is a way she has. She is always refusing people. I think it is most ill-natured of her.

JACK: Oh, Gwendolen is as right as a trivet.[12] As far as she is concerned, we are engaged. Her mother is perfectly unbearable. Never met such a Gorgon. ...I don't really know what a Gorgon is like, but I am quite sure that Lady Bracknell is one. In any case, she is a monster, without being a myth, which is rather unfair....I beg your pardon, Algy, I suppose I shouldn't talk about your own aunt in that way before you.

ALGERNON: My dear boy, I love hearing my relations abused. It is the only thing that makes me put up with them at all. Relations are simply a tedious pack of people, who haven't got the remotest knowledge of how to live, nor the smallest instinct about when to die.

JACK: Oh, that is nonsense!

ALGERNON: It isn't!

JACK: Well, I won't argue about the matter. You always want to argue about things.

ALGERNON: That is exactly what things were originally made for.

JACK: Upon my word, if I thought that, I'd shoot myself.... (*A pause.*) You don't think there is any chance of Gwendolen becoming like her mother in about a hundred and fifty years, do you, Algy?

ALGERNON: All women become like their mothers. That is their tragedy. No man does. That's his.

---

12 three- or four-legged stand for a hot pot or a teapot. The allusion is that it must be level and standing firmly on its legs ("right").

JACK: Is that clever?

ALGERNON: It is perfectly phrased! and quite as true as any observation in civilised life should be.

JACK: I am sick to death of cleverness. Everybody is clever nowadays. You can't go anywhere without meeting clever people. The thing has become an absolute public nuisance. I wish to goodness we had a few fools left.

ALGERNON: We have.

JACK: I should extremely like to meet them. What do they talk about?

ALGERNON: The fools? Oh! about the clever people, of course.

JACK: What fools!

ALGERNON: By the way, did you tell Gwendolen the truth about your being Ernest in town, and Jack in the country?

JACK: (in a very patronizing manner) My dear fellow, the truth isn't quite the sort of thing one tells to a nice, sweet, refined girl. What extraordinary ideas you have about the way to behave to a woman!

ALGERNON: The only way to behave to a woman is to make love to her, if she is pretty, and to someone else, if she is plain.

JACK: Oh, that is nonsense.

ALGERNON: What about your brother? What about the profligate Ernest?

JACK: Oh, before the end of the week I shall have got rid of him. I'll say he died in Paris of apoplexy. Lots of people die of apoplexy, quite suddenly, don't they?

ALGERNON: Yes, but it's hereditary, my dear fellow. It's a sort of thing that runs in families. You had much better say a severe chill.

JACK: You are sure a severe chill isn't hereditary, or anything of that kind?

ALGERNON: Of course it isn't!

JACK: Very well, then. My poor brother Ernest is carried off suddenly, in Paris, by a severe chill. That gets rid of him.

ALGERNON: But I thought you said that . . . Miss Cardew was a little too much interested in your poor brother Ernest? Won't she feel his loss a good deal?

JACK: Oh, that is all right. Cecily is not a silly romantic girl, I am glad to say. She has got a capital appetite, goes on long walks, and pays no attention at all to her lessons.

ALGERNON: I would rather like to see Cecily.

JACK: I will take very good care you never do. She is excessively pretty, and she is only just eighteen.

ALGERNON: Have you told Gwendolen yet that you have an excessively pretty ward who is only just eighteen?

JACK: Oh! one doesn't blurt these things out to people. Cecily and Gwendolen are perfectly certain to be extremely great friends. I'll bet you anything you like that half an hour after they have met, they will be calling each other sister.

ALGERNON: Women only do that when they have called each other a lot of other things first. Now, my dear boy, if we want to get a good table at Willis's, we really must go and dress. Do you know it is nearly seven?

JACK: (irritably) Oh! it always is nearly seven.

ALGERNON: Well, I'm hungry.

JACK: I never knew you when you weren't. . . .

ALGERNON: What shall we do after dinner? Go to a theatre?

JACK: Oh no! I loathe listening.

ALGERNON: Well, let us go to the Club?

JACK: Oh, no! I hate talking.

580 ALGERNON: Well, we might trot round to the Empire[13] at ten?

JACK: Oh, no! I can't bear looking at things. It is so silly.

ALGERNON: Well, what shall we do?

JACK: Nothing!

ALGERNON: It is awfully hard work doing nothing. However, I don't mind hard work where there is no definite object of any kind.

(*Enter* LANE.)

LANE: Miss Fairfax.

(*Enter* GWENDOLEN. LANE *goes out.*)

ALGERNON: Gwendolen, upon my word!

GWENDOLEN: Algy, kindly turn your back. I have something very particular to say to Mr Worthing.

590 ALGERNON: Really, Gwendolen, I don't think I can allow this at all.

GWENDOLEN: Algy, you always adopt a strictly immoral attitude towards life. You are not quite old enough to do that. (ALGERNON *retires to the fireplace.*)

JACK: My own darling!

GWENDOLEN: Ernest, we may never be married. From the expression on mamma's face I fear we never shall. Few parents nowadays pay any regard to what their children say to them. The old-fashioned respect for the young is fast dying out. Whatever influence I ever had over mamma, I lost at the age of three. But although she may prevent us from becoming man and wife, and I may marry someone else, and marry often, nothing that she can possibly do 600 can alter my eternal devotion to you.

JACK: Dear Gwendolen!

GWENDOLEN: The story of your romantic origin, as related to me by mamma, with unpleasing comments, has naturally stirred the deeper fibres of my nature. Your Christian name has an irresistible fascination. The simplicity of your character makes you exquisitely incomprehensible to me. Your town address at the Albany I have. What is your address in the country?

JACK: The Manor House, Woolton, Hertfordshire.

(ALGERNON, *who has been carefully listening, smiles to himself, and writes the address on his shirt-cuff. Then picks up the Railway Guide.*)

GWENDOLEN: There is a good postal service, I suppose? It may be necessary to do something desperate. That of course will require serious consideration. 610 I will communicate with you daily.

JACK: My own one!

GWENDOLEN: How long do you remain in town?

JACK: Till Monday.

GWENDOLEN: Good! Algy, you may turn round now.

13 a music hall in Leicester Square, London, featuring acrobatics and burlesque ballet.

ALGERNON: Thanks, I've turned round already.

GWENDOLEN: You may also ring the bell.

JACK: You will let me see you to your carriage, my own darling?

GWENDOLEN: Certainly.

JACK: (*to* LANE, *who now enters*) I will see Miss Fairfax out.

620 LANE: Yes, sir. (JACK *and* GWENDOLEN *go off.*)

> (LANE *presents several letters on a salver, to* ALGERNON. *It is to be surmised that they are bills, as* ALGERNON, *after looking at the envelopes, tears them up.*)

ALGERNON: A glass of sherry, Lane.

LANE: Yes, sir.

ALGERNON: Tomorrow, Lane, I'm going Bunburying.

LANE: Yes, sir.

ALGERNON: I shall probably not be back till Monday. You can put up my dress clothes, my smoking jacket, and all the Bunbury suits...

LANE: Yes, sir. (*Handing sherry.*)

ALGERNON: I hope tomorrow will be a fine day, Lane.

LANE: It never is, sir.

630 ALGERNON: Lane, you're a perfect pessimist.

LANE: I do my best to give satisfaction, sir.

> (*Enter* JACK. LANE *goes off.*)

JACK: There's a sensible, intellectual girl! the only girl I ever cared for in my life. (ALGERNON *is laughing immoderately.*) What on earth are you so amused at?

ALGERNON: Oh, I'm a little anxious about poor Bunbury, that is all.

JACK: If you don't take care, your friend Bunbury will get you into a serious scrape some day.

ALGERNON: I love scrapes. They are the only things that are never serious.

JACK: Oh, that's nonsense, Algy. You never talk anything but nonsense.

ALGERNON: Nobody ever does.

> (JACK *looks indignantly at him, and leaves the room.* ALGERNON *lights a cigarette, reads his shirt-cuff, and smiles.*)

ACT DROP

SECOND ACT

SCENE *Garden at the Manor House. A flight of grey stone steps leads up to the house. The garden, an old-fashioned one, full of roses. Time of year, July. Basket chairs, and a table covered with books, are set under a large yew-tree.*

> (MISS PRISM *discovered seated at the table.* CECILY *is at the back watering flowers.*)

MISS PRISM: (*calling*) Cecily, Cecily! Surely such a utilitarian occupation as the watering of flowers is rather Moulton's duty than yours? Especially at a moment when intellectual pleasures await you. Your German grammar is on the table. Pray open it at page fifteen. We will repeat yesterday's lesson.

CECILY: *(coming over very slowly)* But I don't like German. It isn't at all a becoming language. I know perfectly well that I look quite plain after my German lesson.

MISS PRISM: Child, you know how anxious your guardian is that you should improve yourself in every way. He laid particular stress on your German, as he was leaving for town yesterday. Indeed, he always lays stress on your German when he is leaving for town.

CECILY: Dear Uncle Jack is so very serious! Sometimes he is so serious that I think he cannot be quite well.

MISS PRISM: *(drawing herself up)* Your guardian enjoys the best of health, and his gravity of demeanour is especially to be commended in one so comparatively young as he is. I know no one who has a higher sense of duty and responsibility.

CECILY: I suppose that is why he often looks a little bored when we three are together.

MISS PRISM: Cecily! I am surprised at you. Mr Worthing has many troubles in his life. Idle merriment and triviality would be out of place in his conversation. You must remember his constant anxiety about that unfortunate young man his brother.

CECILY: I wish Uncle Jack would allow that unfortunate young man, his brother, to come down here sometimes. We might have a good influence over him, Miss Prism. I am sure you certainly would. You know German, and geology, and things of that kind influence a man very much. (CECILY *begins to write in her diary.*)

MISS PRISM: *(shaking her head)* I do not think that even I could produce any effect on a character that according to his own brother's admission is irretrievably weak and vacillating. Indeed I am not sure that I would desire to reclaim him. I am not in favour of this modern mania for turning bad people into good people at a moment's notice. As a man sows so let him reap. You must put away your diary, Cecily. I really don't see why you should keep a diary at all.

CECILY: I keep a diary in order to enter the wonderful secrets of my life. If I didn't write them down, I should probably forget all about them.

MISS PRISM: Memory, my dear Cecily, is the diary that we all carry about with us.

CECILY: Yes, but it usually chronicles the things that have never happened, and couldn't possibly have happened. I believe that Memory is responsible for nearly all the three-volume novels that Mudie[1] sends us.

MISS PRISM: Do not speak slightingly of the three-volume novel, Cecily. I wrote one myself in earlier days.

CECILY: Did you really, Miss Prism? How wonderfully clever you are! I hope it did not end happily? I don't like novels that end happily. They depress me so much.

MISS PRISM: The good ended happily, and the bad unhappily. That is what Fiction means.

---

1 well-known circulating library and bookstore.

CECILY: I suppose so. But it seems very unfair. And was your novel ever published?

50 MISS PRISM: Alas! no. The manuscript unfortunately was abandoned. (CECILY *starts.*) I use the word in the sense of lost or mislaid. To your work, child, these speculations are profitless.

CECILY: (*smiling*) But I see dear Dr Chasuble coming up through the garden.

MISS PRISM: (*rising and advancing*) Dr Chasuble! This is indeed a pleasure.

(*Enter* CANON CHASUBLE.)

CHASUBLE: And how are we this morning? Miss Prism, you are, I trust, well?

CECILY: Miss Prism has just been complaining of a slight headache. I think it would do her so much good to have a short stroll with you in the Park, Dr Chasuble.

MISS PRISM: Cecily, I have not mentioned anything about a headache.

60 CECILY: No, dear Miss Prism, I know that, but I felt instinctively that you had a headache. Indeed I was thinking about that, and not about my German lesson, when the Rector came in.

CHASUBLE: I hope, Cecily, you are not inattentive.

CECILY: Oh, I am afraid I am.

CHASUBLE: That is strange. Were I fortunate enough to be Miss Prism's pupil, I would hang upon her lips. (MISS PRISM *glares.*) I spoke metaphorically.— My metaphor was drawn from bees. Ahem! Mr Worthing, I suppose, has not returned from town yet?

MISS PRISM: We do not expect him till Monday afternoon.

70 CHASUBLE: Ah yes, he usually likes to spend his Sunday in London. He is not one of those whose sole aim is enjoyment, as, by all accounts, that unfortunate young man his brother seems to be. But I must not disturb Egeria[2] and her pupil any longer.

MISS PRISM: Egeria? My name is Laetitia, Doctor.

CHASUBLE: (*bowing*) A classical allusion merely, drawn from the Pagan authors. I shall see you both no doubt at Evensong?

MISS PRISM: I think, dear Doctor, I will have a stroll with you. I find I have a headache after all, and a walk might do it good.

CHASUBLE: With pleasure, Miss Prism, with pleasure. We might go as far as

80 the schools and back.

MISS PRISM: That would be delightful. Cecily, you will read your Political Economy in my absence. The chapter on the Fall of the Rupee[3] you may omit. It is somewhat too sensational. Even these metallic problems have their melodramatic side.

(*Goes down the garden with* DR CHASUBLE.)

CECILY: (*picks up books and throws them back on table*) Horrid Political Economy! Horrid Geography! Horrid, horrid German!

(*Enter* MERRIMAN *with a card on a salver.*)

MERRIMAN: Mr Ernest Worthing has just driven over from the station. He has

---

2 in Roman mythology, a nymph who was the wife and instructor of a Roman king and who was transformed into a fountain at his death. 3 the basic unit of money in India and Pakistan, part of the British Empire in Wilde's time.

brought his luggage with him.

CECILY: *(takes the card and reads it)* "Mr Ernest Worthing, B.4, The Albany, W."
Uncle Jack's brother! Did you tell him Mr Worthing was in town?

MERRIMAN: Yes, Miss. He seemed very much disappointed. I mentioned that you and Miss Prism were in the garden. He said he was anxious to speak to you privately for a moment.

CECILY: Ask Mr Ernest Worthing to come here. I suppose you had better talk to the housekeeper about a room for him.

MERRIMAN: Yes, Miss. (MERRIMAN *goes off.)*

CECILY: I have never met any really wicked person before. I feel rather frightened. I am so afraid he will look just like every one else.

(Enter ALGERNON, *very gay and debonair.)*

He does!

ALGERNON: *(raising his hat)* You are my little cousin Cecily, I'm sure.

CECILY: You are under some strange mistake. I am not little. In fact, I believe I am more than usually tall for my age. (ALGERNON *is rather taken aback.)* But I am your cousin Cecily. You, I see from your card, are Uncle Jack's brother, my cousin Ernest, my wicked cousin Ernest.

ALGERNON: Oh! I am not really wicked at all, cousin Cecily. You mustn't think that I am wicked.

CECILY: If you are not, then you have certainly been deceiving us all in a very inexcusable manner. I hope you have not been leading a double life, pretending to be wicked and being really good all the time. That would be hypocrisy.

ALGERNON: *(looks at her in amazement)* Oh! Of course I have been rather reckless.

CECILY: I am glad to hear it.

ALGERNON: In fact, now you mention the subject, I have been very bad in my own small way.

CECILY: I don't think you should be so proud of that, though I am sure it must have been very pleasant.

ALGERNON: It is much pleasanter being here with you.

CECILY: I can't understand how you are here at all. Uncle Jack won't be back till Monday afternoon.

ALGERNON: That is a great disappointment. I am obliged to go up by the first train on Monday morning. I have a business appointment that I am anxious ... to miss!

CECILY: Couldn't you miss it anywhere but in London?

ALGERNON: No: the appointment is in London.

CECILY: Well, I know, of course, how important it is not to keep a business engagement, if one wants to retain any sense of the beauty of life, but still I think you had better wait till Uncle Jack arrives. I know he wants to speak to you about your emigrating.

ALGERNON: About my what?

CECILY: Your emigrating. He has gone up to buy your outfit.

ALGERNON: I certainly wouldn't let Jack buy my outfit. He has no taste in neckties at all.

CECILY: I don't think you will require neckties. Uncle Jack is sending you to Australia.

ALGERNON: Australia! I'd sooner die.

CECILY: Well, he said at dinner on Wednesday night, that you would have to choose between this world, the next world, and Australia.

ALGERNON: Oh, well! The accounts I have received of Australia and the next world are not particularly encouraging. This world is good enough for me, cousin Cecily.

CECILY: Yes, but are you good enough for it?

ALGERNON: I'm afraid I'm not that. That is why I want you to reform me. You might make that your mission, if you don't mind, cousin Cecily.

CECILY: I'm afraid I've no time, this afternoon.

ALGERNON: Well, would you mind my reforming myself this afternoon?

CECILY: It is rather Quixotic of you. But I think you should try.

ALGERNON: I will. I feel better already.

CECILY: You are looking a little worse.

ALGERNON: That is because I am hungry.

CECILY: How thoughtless of me. I should have remembered that when one is going to lead an entirely new life, one requires regular and wholesome meals. Won't you come in?

ALGERNON: Thank you. Might I have a buttonhole[4] first? I never have any appetite unless I have a buttonhole first.

CECILY: A Maréchal Niel?[5] *(Picks up scissors.)*

ALGERNON: No, I'd sooner have a pink rose.

CECILY: Why? *(Cuts a flower.)*

ALGERNON: Because you are like a pink rose, Cousin Cecily.

CECILY: I don't think it can be right for you to talk to me like that. Miss Prism never says such things to me.

ALGERNON: Then Miss Prism is a short-sighted old lady. (CECILY *puts the rose in his buttonhole.*) You are the prettiest girl I ever saw.

CECILY: Miss Prism says that all good looks are a snare.

ALGERNON: They are a snare that every sensible man would like to be caught in.

CECILY: Oh, I don't think I would care to catch a sensible man. I shouldn't know what to talk to him about.

(They pass into the house. MISS PRISM *and* DR CHASUBLE *return.)*

MISS PRISM: You are too much alone, dear Dr Chasuble. You should get married. A misanthrope I can understand — a woman-thrope, never!

CHASUBLE: *(with a scholar's shudder)* Believe me, I do not deserve so neologistic a phrase. The precept as well as the practice of the Primitive Church was distinctly against matrimony.

MISS PRISM: *(sententiously)* That is obviously the reason why the Primitive Church has not lasted up to the present day. And you do not seem to realize, dear Doctor, that by persistently remaining single, a man converts himself into a permanent public temptation. Men should be more careful; this very celibacy leads weaker vessels astray.

CHASUBLE: But is a man not equally attractive when married?

MISS PRISM: No married man is ever attractive except to his wife.

---

4 flower worn on a jacket lapel. 5 exotic breed of yellow rose.

CHASUBLE: And often, I've been told, not even to her.

180   MISS PRISM: That depends on the intellectual sympathies of the woman. Maturity can always be depended on. Ripeness can be trusted. Young women are green. (DR CHASUBLE *starts.*) I spoke horticulturally. My metaphor was drawn from fruits. But where is Cecily?

CHASUBLE: Perhaps she followed us to the schools.

(*Enter* JACK *slowly from the back of the garden. He is dressed in the deepest mourning, with crape hatband and black gloves.*)

MISS PRISM: Mr Worthing!

DR CHASUBLE: Mr Worthing?

MISS PRISM: This is indeed a surprise. We did not look for you till Monday afternoon.

JACK: (*shakes* MISS PRISM's *hand in a tragic manner*) I have returned sooner than
190   I expected. Dr Chasuble, I hope you are well?

CHASUBLE: Dear Mr Worthing, I trust this garb of woe does not betoken some terrible calamity?

JACK: My brother.

MISS PRISM: More shameful debts and extravagance?

CHASUBLE: Still leading his life of pleasure?

JACK: (*shaking his head*) Dead!

CHASUBLE: Your brother Ernest dead?

JACK: Quite dead.

MISS PRISM: What a lesson for him! I trust he will profit by it.

200   CHASUBLE: Mr Worthing, I offer you my sincere condolence. You have at least the consolation of knowing that you were always the most generous and forgiving of brothers.

JACK: Poor Ernest! He had many faults, but it is a sad, sad blow.

CHASUBLE: Very sad indeed. Were you with him at the end?

JACK: No. He died abroad; in Paris, in fact. I had a telegram last night from the manager of the Grand Hotel.

CHASUBLE: Was the cause of death mentioned?

JACK: A severe chill, it seems.

MISS PRISM: As a man sows, so shall he reap.

210   CHASUBLE: (*raising his hand*) Charity, dear Miss Prism, charity! None of us are perfect. I myself am peculiarly susceptible to draughts. Will the interment take place here?

JACK: No. He seems to have expressed a desire to be buried in Paris.

CHASUBLE: In Paris! (*Shakes his head.*) I fear that hardly points to any very serious state of mind at the last. You would no doubt wish me to make some slight allusion to this tragic domestic affliction next Sunday. (JACK *presses his hand convulsively.*) My sermon on the meaning of the manna in the wilderness can be adapted to almost any occasion, joyful, or, as in the present case, distressing. (*All sigh.*) I have preached it at harvest celebra-
220   tions, christenings, confirmations, on days of humiliation and festal days. The last time I delivered it was in the Cathedral, as a charity sermon on behalf of the Society for the Prevention of Discontent among the Upper Orders. The Bishop, who was present, was much struck by some of the

analogies I drew.

JACK: Ah! that reminds me, you mentioned christenings I think, Dr Chasuble? I suppose you know how to christen all right? (DR CHASUBLE *looks astounded.*) I mean, of course, you are continually christening, aren't you?

MISS PRISM: It is, I regret to say, one of the Rector's most constant duties in this parish. I have often spoken to the poorer classes on the subject. But they don't seem to know what thrift is.

230

CHASUBLE: But is there any particular infant in whom you are interested, Mr Worthing? Your brother was, I believe, unmarried, was he not?

JACK: Oh, yes.

MISS PRISM: *(bitterly)* People who live entirely for pleasure usually are.

JACK: But it is not for any child, dear Doctor. I am very fond of children. No! the fact is, I would like to be christened myself, this afternoon, if you have nothing better to do.

CHASUBLE: But surely, Mr Worthing, you have been christened already?

JACK: I don't remember anything about it.

240

CHASUBLE: But have you any grave doubts on the subject?

JACK: I certainly intend to have. Of course I don't know if the thing would bother you in any way, or if you think I am a little too old now.

CHASUBLE: Not at all. The sprinkling, and, indeed, the immersion of adults is a perfectly canonical practice.

JACK: Immersion!

CHASUBLE: You need have no apprehensions. Sprinkling is all that is necessary, or indeed I think advisable. Our weather is so changeable. At what hour would you wish the ceremony performed?

JACK: Oh, I might trot round about five if that would suit you.

250

CHASUBLE: Perfectly, perfectly! In fact I have two similar ceremonies to perform at that time. A case of twins that occurred recently in one of the outlying cottages on your own estate. Poor Jenkins the carter, a most hard-working man.

JACK: Oh! I don't see much fun in being christened along with other babies. It would be childish. Would half-past five do?

CHASUBLE: Admirably! Admirably! (*Takes out watch.*) And now, dear Mr Worthing, I will not intrude any longer into a house of sorrow. I would merely beg you not to be too much bowed down by grief. What seem to us bitter trials are often blessings in disguise.

MISS PRISM: This seems to me a blessing of an extremely obvious kind.

(*Enter* CECILY *from the house.*)

260

CECILY: Uncle Jack! Oh, I am pleased to see you back. But what horrid clothes you have got on! Do go and change them.

MISS PRISM: Cecily!

CHASUBLE: My child! my child! (CECILY *goes towards* JACK; *he kisses her brow in a melancholy manner.*)

CECILY: What is the matter, Uncle Jack? Do look happy! You look as if you had toothache, and I have got such a surprise for you. Who do you think is in the dining-room? Your brother!

JACK: Who?

CECILY: Your brother Ernest. He arrived about half an hour ago.

JACK: What nonsense! I haven't got a brother.

270 CECILY: Oh, don't say that. However badly he may have behaved to you in the past he is still your brother. You couldn't be so heartless as to disown him. I'll tell him to come out. And you will shake hands with him, won't you, Uncle Jack? (*Runs back into the house.*)

CHASUBLE: These are very joyful tidings.

MISS PRISM: After we had all been resigned to his loss, his sudden return seems to me peculiarly distressing.

JACK: My brother is in the dining-room? I don't know what it all means. I think it is perfectly absurd.

(*Enter* ALGERNON *and* CECILY *hand in hand. They come slowly up to* JACK.)

JACK: Good heavens! (*Motions* ALGERNON *away.*)

280 ALGERNON: Brother John, I have come down from town to tell you that I am very sorry for all the trouble I have given you, and that I intend to lead a better life in the future. (JACK *glares at him and does not take his hand.*)

CECILY: Uncle Jack, you are not going to refuse your own brother's hand?

JACK: Nothing will induce me to take his hand. I think his coming down here disgraceful. He knows perfectly well why.

CECILY: Uncle Jack, do be nice. There is some good in everyone. Ernest has just been telling me about his poor invalid friend Mr Bunbury whom he goes to visit so often. And surely there must be much good in one who is kind to an invalid, and leaves the pleasures of London to sit by a bed of pain.

290 JACK: Oh! he has been talking about Bunbury, has he?

CECILY: Yes, he has told me all about poor Mr Bunbury, and his terrible state of health.

JACK: Bunbury! Well, I won't have him talk to you about Bunbury or about any-thing else. It is enough to drive one perfectly frantic.

ALGERNON: Of course I admit that the faults were all on my side. But I must say that I think that Brother John's coldness to me is peculiarly painful. I expected a more enthusiastic welcome, especially considering it is the first time I have come here.

CECILY: Uncle Jack, if you don't shake hands with Ernest I will never forgive you.

300 JACK: Never forgive me?

CECILY: Never, never, never!

JACK: Well, this is the last time I shall ever do it. (*Shakes hands with* ALGERNON *and glares.*)

CHASUBLE: It's pleasant, is it not, to see so perfect a reconciliation? I think we might leave the two brothers together.

MISS PRISM: Cecily, you will come with us.

CECILY: Certainly, Miss Prism. My little task of reconciliation is over.

CHASUBLE: You have done a beautiful action today, dear child.

MISS PRISM: We must not be premature in our judgments.

CECILY: I feel very happy. (*They all go off except* JACK *and* ALGERNON.)

310 JACK: You young scoundrel, Algy, you must get out of this place as soon as possible. I don't allow any Bunburying here.

(*Enter* MERRIMAN.)

MERRIMAN: I have put Mr Ernest's things in the room next to yours, sir. I suppose that is all right?

JACK: What?

MERRIMAN: Mr Ernest's luggage, sir. I have unpacked it and put it in the room next to your own.

JACK: His luggage?

MERRIMAN: Yes, sir. Three portmanteaus, a dressing-case, two hat-boxes, and a large luncheon-basket.

320 ALGERNON: I am afraid I can't stay more than a week this time.

JACK: Merriman, order the dog-cart[6] at once. Mr Ernest has been suddenly called back to town.

MERRIMAN: Yes, sir. (*Goes back into the house.*)

ALGERNON: What a fearful liar you are, Jack. I have not been called back to town at all.

JACK: Yes, you have.

ALGERNON: I haven't heard anyone call me.

JACK: Your duty as a gentleman calls you back.

ALGERNON: My duty as a gentleman has never interfered with my pleasures in
330 the smallest degree.

JACK: I can quite understand that.

ALGERNON: Well, Cecily is a darling.

JACK: You are not to talk of Miss Cardew like that. I don't like it.

ALGERNON: Well, I don't like your clothes. You look perfectly ridiculous in them. Why on earth don't you go up and change? It is perfectly childish to be in deep mourning for a man who is actually staying for a whole week with you in your house as a guest. I call it grotesque.

JACK: You are certainly not staying with me for a whole week as a guest or anything else. You have got to leave . . . by the four-five train.

340 ALGERNON: I certainly won't leave you so long as you are in mourning. It would be most unfriendly. If I were in mourning you would stay with me, I suppose. I should think it very unkind if you didn't.

JACK: Well, will you go if I change my clothes?

ALGERNON: Yes, if you are not too long. I never saw anybody take so long to dress, and with such little result.

JACK: Well, at any rate, that is better than being always over-dressed as you are.

ALGERNON: If I am occasionally a little over-dressed, I make up for it by being always immensely over-educated.

JACK: Your vanity is ridiculous, your conduct an outrage, and your presence in
350 my garden utterly absurd. However, you have got to catch the four-five, and I hope you will have a pleasant journey back to town. This Bunburying, as you call it, has not been a great success for you.

(*Goes into the house.*)

ALGERNON: I think it has been a great success. I'm in love with Cecily, and that

---

6 small two-wheeled cart with two seats, often including a box for transporting hunting dogs.

is everything.

(*Enter* CECILY *at the back of the garden. She picks up the can and begins to water the flowers.*)

But I must see her before I go, and make arrangements for another Bunbury. Ah, there she is.

CECILY: Oh, I merely came back to water the roses. I thought you were with Uncle Jack.

ALGERNON: He's gone to order the dog-cart for me.

360 CECILY: Oh, is he going to take you for a nice drive?

ALGERNON: He's going to send me away.

CECILY: Then have we got to part?

ALGERNON: I am afraid so. It's a very painful parting.

CECILY: It is always painful to part from people whom one has known for a very brief space of time. The absence of old friends one can endure with equanimity. But even a momentary separation from any one to whom one has just been introduced is almost unbearable.

ALGERNON: Thank you.

(*Enter* MERRIMAN.)

MERRIMAN: The dog-cart is at the door, sir.

(ALGERNON *looks appealingly at* CECILY.)

370 CECILY: It can wait, Merriman . . . for . . . five minutes.

MERRIMAN: Yes, miss.

(*Exit* MERRIMAN.)

ALGERNON: I hope, Cecily, I shall not offend you if I state quite frankly and openly that you seem to me to be in every way the visible personification of absolute perfection.

CECILY: I think your frankness does you great credit, Ernest. If you will allow me, I will copy your remarks into my diary. (*Goes over to table and begins writing in diary.*)

ALGERNON: Do you really keep a diary? I'd give anything to look at it. May I?

CECILY: Oh no. (*Puts her hand over it.*) You see, it is simply a very young girl's record of her own thoughts and impressions, and consequently meant for

380 publication. When it appears in volume form I hope you will order a copy. But pray, Ernest, don't stop. I delight in taking down from dictation. I have reached "absolute perfection." You can go on. I am quite ready for more.

ALGERNON: (*somewhat taken aback*) Ahem! Ahem!

CECILY: Oh, don't cough, Ernest. When one is dictating one should speak fluently and not cough. Besides, I don't know how to spell a cough. (*Writes as* ALGERNON *speaks.*)

ALGERNON: (*speaking very rapidly*) Cecily, ever since I first looked upon your wonderful and incomparable beauty, I have dared to love you wildly, passionately, devotedly, hopelessly.

CECILY: I don't think that you should tell me that you love me wildly, pas-

390 sionately, devotedly, hopelessly. Hopelessly doesn't seem to make much

sense, does it?

ALGERNON: Cecily!

(*Enter* MERRIMAN.)

MERRIMAN: The dog-cart is waiting, sir.

ALGERNON: Tell it to come round next week, at the same hour.

MERRIMAN: (*looks at* CECILY, *who makes no sign*) Yes, sir.

(MERRIMAN *retires.*)

CECILY: Uncle Jack would be very much annoyed if he knew you were staying on till next week, at the same hour.

ALGERNON: Oh, I don't care about Jack. I don't care for anybody in the whole world but you. I love you, Cecily. You will marry me, won't you?

CECILY: You silly boy! Of course. Why, we have been engaged for the last three months.

ALGERNON: For the last three months?

CECILY: Yes, it will be exactly three months on Thursday.

ALGERNON: But how did we become engaged?

CECILY: Well, ever since dear Uncle Jack first confessed to us that he had a younger brother who was very wicked and bad, you of course have formed the chief topic of conversation between myself and Miss Prism. And of course a man who is much talked about is always very attractive. One feels there must be something in him, after all. I daresay it was foolish of me, but I fell in love with you, Ernest.

ALGERNON: Darling! And when was the engagement actually settled?

CECILY: On the 14th of February last. Worn out by your entire ignorance of my existence, I determined to end the matter one way or the other, and after a long struggle with myself I accepted you under this dear old tree here. The next day I bought this little ring in your name, and this is the little bangle with the true lover's knot I promised you always to wear.

ALGERNON: Did I give you this? It's very pretty, isn't it?

CECILY: Yes, you've wonderfully good taste, Ernest. It's the excuse I've always given for your leading such a bad life. And this is the box in which I keep all your dear letters. (*Kneels at table, opens box, and produces letters tied up with blue ribbon.*)

ALGERNON: My letters! But, my own sweet Cecily, I have never written you any letters.

CECILY: You need hardly remind me of that, Ernest. I remember only too well that I was forced to write your letters for you. I wrote always three times a week, and sometimes oftener.

ALGERNON: Oh, do let me read them, Cecily?

CECILY: Oh, I couldn't possibly. They would make you far too conceited. (*Replaces box.*) The three you wrote me after I had broken off the engagement are so beautiful, and so badly spelled, that even now I can hardly read them without crying a little.

ALGERNON: But was our engagement ever broken off?

CECILY: Of course it was. On the 22nd of last March. You can see the entry if you like. (*Shows diary.*) "Today I broke off my engagement with Ernest. I feel it is better to do so. The weather still continues charming."

ALGERNON: But why on earth did you break it off? What had I done? I had done nothing at all. Cecily, I am very much hurt indeed to hear you broke it off. Particularly when the weather was so charming.

CECILY: It would hardly have been a really serious engagement if it hadn't been broken off at least once. But I forgave you before the week was out.

ALGERNON: (*crossing to her, and kneeling*) What a perfect angel you are, Cecily.

440 CECILY: You dear romantic boy. (*He kisses her, she puts her fingers through his hair.*) I hope your hair curls naturally, does it?

ALGERNON: Yes, darling, with a little help from others.

CECILY: I am so glad.

ALGERNON: You'll never break off our engagement again, Cecily?

CECILY: I don't think I could break it off now that I have actually met you. Besides, of course, there is the question of your name.

ALGERNON: Yes, of course. (*Nervously.*)

CECILY: You must not laugh at me, darling, but it had always been a girlish dream of mine to love some one whose name was Ernest. (ALGERNON *rises*, CECILY 450 *also.*) There is something in that name that seems to inspire absolute confidence. I pity any poor married woman whose husband is not called Ernest.

ALGERNON: But, my dear child, do you mean to say you could not love me if I had some other name?

CECILY: But what name?

ALGERNON: Oh, any name you like — Algernon — for instance...

CECILY: But I don't like the name of Algernon.

ALGERNON: Well, my own dear, sweet, loving little darling, I really can't see why you should object to the name of Algernon. It is not at all a bad name. In fact, it is rather an aristocratic name. Half of the chaps who get into the 460 Bankruptcy Court are called Algernon. But seriously, Cecily... (*moving to her*) ... if my name was Algy, couldn't you love me?

CECILY: (*rising*) I might respect you, Ernest, I might admire your character, but I fear that I should not be able to give you my undivided attention.

ALGERNON: Ahem! Cecily! (*Picking up hat.*) Your Rector here is, I suppose, thoroughly experienced in the practice of all the rites and ceremonials of the Church?

CECILY: Oh, yes, Dr Chasuble is a most learned man. He has never written a single book, so you can imagine how much he knows.

ALGERNON: I must see him at once on a most important christening — I mean 470 on most important business.

CECILY: Oh!

ALGERNON: I shan't be away more than half an hour.

CECILY: Considering that we have been engaged since February the 14th, and that I only met you today for the first time, I think it is rather hard that you should leave me for so long a period as half an hour. Couldn't you make it twenty minutes?

ALGERNON: I'll be back in no time. (*Kisses her and rushes down the garden.*)

CECILY: What an impetuous boy he is! I like his hair so much. I must enter his proposal in my diary.

(Enter MERRIMAN.)

480 MERRIMAN: A Miss Fairfax has just called to see Mr Worthing. On very important business, Miss Fairfax states.

CECILY: Isn't Mr Worthing in his library?

MERRIMAN: Mr Worthing went over in the direction of the Rectory some time ago.

CECILY: Pray ask the lady to come out here; Mr Worthing is sure to be back soon. And you can bring tea.

MERRIMAN: Yes, Miss.

(Goes out.)

CECILY: Miss Fairfax! I suppose one of the many good elderly women who are associated with Uncle Jack in some of his philanthropic work in London. I don't quite like women who are interested in philanthropic work. I think 490 it is so forward of them.

(Enter MERRIMAN.)

MERRIMAN: Miss Fairfax.

(Enter GWENDOLEN. Exit MERRIMAN.)

CECILY: *(advancing to meet her)* Pray let me introduce myself to you. My name is Cecily Cardew.

GWENDOLEN: Cecily Cardew? *(Moving to her and shaking hands.)* What a very sweet name! Something tells me that we are going to be great friends. I like you already more than I can say. My first impressions of people are never wrong.

CECILY: How nice of you to like me so much after we have known each other such a comparatively short time. Pray sit down.

GWENDOLEN: *(still standing up)* I may call you Cecily, may I not?

500 CECILY: With pleasure!

GWENDOLEN: And you will always call me Gwendolen, won't you?

CECILY: If you wish.

GWENDOLEN: Then that is all quite settled, is it not?

CECILY: I hope so. *(A pause. They both sit down together.)*

GWENDOLEN: Perhaps this might be a favourable opportunity for my mentioning who I am. My father is Lord Bracknell. You have never heard of papa, I suppose?

CECILY: I don't think so.

GWENDOLEN: Outside the family circle, papa, I am glad to say, is entirely 510 unknown. I think that is quite as it should be. The home seems to me to be the proper sphere for the man. And certainly once a man begins to neglect his domestic duties he becomes painfully effeminate, does he not? And I don't like that. It makes men so very attractive. Cecily, mamma, whose views on education are remarkably strict, has brought me up to be extremely short-sighted; it is part of her system; so do you mind my looking at you through my glasses?

CECILY: Oh! not at all, Gwendolen. I am very fond of being looked at.

GWENDOLEN: *(after examining CECILY carefully through a lorgnette)* You are here on a short visit, I suppose.

520   CECILY: Oh no! I live here.

GWENDOLEN: *(severely)* Really? Your mother, no doubt, or some female relative of advanced years, resides here also?

CECILY: Oh no! I have no mother, nor, in fact, any relations.

GWENDOLEN: Indeed?

CECILY: My dear guardian, with the assistance of Miss Prism, has the arduous task of looking after me.

GWENDOLEN: Your guardian?

CECILY: Yes, I am Mr Worthing's ward.

GWENDOLEN: Oh! It is strange he never mentioned to me that he had a ward.
530   How secretive of him! He grows more interesting hourly. I am not sure, however, that the news inspires me with feelings of unmixed delight. *(Rising and going to her.)* I am very fond of you, Cecily; I have liked you ever since I met you! But I am bound to state that now that I know that you are Mr Worthing's ward, I cannot help expressing a wish you were — well, just a little older than you seem to be — and not quite so very alluring in appearance. In fact, if I may speak candidly —

CECILY: Pray do! I think that whenever one has anything unpleasant to say, one should always be quite candid.

GWENDOLEN: Well, to speak with perfect candour, Cecily, I wish that you were
540   fully forty-two, and more than usually plain for your age. Ernest has a strong upright nature. He is the very soul of truth and honour. Disloyalty would be as impossible to him as deception. But even men of the noblest possible moral character are extremely susceptible to the influence of the physical charms of others. Modern, no less than Ancient History, supplies us with many most painful examples of what I refer to. If it were not so, indeed, History would be quite unreadable.

CECILY: I beg your pardon, Gwendolen, did you say Ernest?

GWENDOLEN: Yes.

CECILY: Oh, but it is not Mr Ernest Worthing who is my guardian. It is his
550   brother — his elder brother.

GWENDOLEN: *(sitting down again)* Ernest never mentioned to me that he had a brother.

CECILY: I am sorry to say they have not been on good terms for a long time.

GWENDOLEN: Ah! that accounts for it. And now that I think of it I have never heard any man mention his brother. The subject seems distasteful to most men. Cecily, you have lifted a load from my mind. I was growing almost anxious. It would have been terrible if any cloud had come across a friendship like ours, would it not? Of course you are quite, quite sure that it is not Mr Ernest Worthing who is your guardian?

560   CECILY: Quite sure. *(A pause.)* In fact, I am going to be his.

GWENDOLEN: *(inquiringly)* I beg your pardon?

CECILY: *(rather shy and confidingly)* Dearest Gwendolen, there is no reason why I should make a secret of it to you. Our little county newspaper is sure to chronicle the fact next week. Mr Ernest Worthing and I are engaged to be married.

GWENDOLEN: *(quite politely, rising)* My darling Cecily, I think there must be some slight error. Mr Ernest Worthing is engaged to me. The announcement will appear in the *Morning Post* on Saturday at the latest.

CECILY: *(very politely, rising)* I am afraid you must be under some misconception. Ernest proposed to me exactly ten minutes ago. *(Shows diary.)*

GWENDOLEN: *(examines diary through her lorgnette carefully)* It is very curious, for he asked me to be his wife yesterday afternoon at 5:30. If you would care to verify the incident, pray do so. *(Produces diary of her own.)* I never travel without my diary. One should always have something sensational to read in the train. I am so sorry, dear Cecily, if it is any disappointment to you, but I am afraid I have the prior claim.

CECILY: It would distress me more than I can tell you, dear Gwendolen, if it caused you any mental or physical anguish, but I feel bound to point out that since Ernest proposed to you he clearly has changed his mind.

GWENDOLEN: *(meditatively)* If the poor fellow has been entrapped into any foolish promise I shall consider it my duty to rescue him at once, and with a firm hand.

CECILY: *(thoughtfully and sadly)* Whatever unfortunate entanglement my dear boy may have got into, I will never reproach him with it after we are married.

GWENDOLEN: Do you allude to me, Miss Cardew, as an entanglement? You are presumptuous. On an occasion of this kind it becomes more than a moral duty to speak one's mind. It becomes a pleasure.

CECILY: Do you suggest, Miss Fairfax, that I entrapped Ernest into an engagement? How dare you? This is no time for wearing the shallow mask of manners. When I see a spade I call it a spade.

GWENDOLEN: *(satirically)* I am glad to say that I have never seen a spade. It is obvious that our social spheres have been widely different.

(Enter MERRIMAN, *followed by the footman. He carries a salver, table cloth, and plate stand.* CECILY *is about to retort. The presence of the servants exercises a restraining influence, under which both girls chafe.)*

MERRIMAN: Shall I lay tea here as usual, Miss?

CECILY: *(sternly, in a calm voice)* Yes, as usual. (MERRIMAN *begins to clear table and lay cloth. A long pause.* CECILY *and* GWENDOLEN *glare at each other.)*

GWENDOLEN: Are there many interesting walks in the vicinity, Miss Cardew?

CECILY: Oh! yes! a great many. From the top of one of the hills quite close one can see five counties.

GWENDOLEN: Five counties! I don't think I should like that; I hate crowds.

CECILY: *(sweetly)* I suppose that is why you live in town? (GWENDOLEN *bites her lip, and beats her foot nervously with her parasol.)*

GWENDOLEN: *(looking around)* Quite a well-kept garden this is, Miss Cardew.

CECILY: So glad you like it, Miss Fairfax.

GWENDOLEN: I had no idea there were any flowers in the country.

CECILY: Oh, flowers are as common here, Miss Fairfax, as people are in London.

GWENDOLEN: Personally I cannot understand how anybody manages to exist in the country, if anybody who is anybody does. The country always bores me to death.

CECILY: Ah! This is what the newspapers call agricultural depression, is it not? I believe the aristocracy are suffering very much from it just at present. It is almost an epidemic amongst them, I have been told. May I offer you some tea, Miss Fairfax?

GWENDOLEN: *(with elaborate politeness)* Thank you. *(Aside.)* Detestable girl! But I require tea!

CECILY: *(sweetly)* Sugar?

GWENDOLEN: *(superciliously)* No, thank you. Sugar is not fashionable any more. *(CECILY looks angrily at her, takes up the tongs and puts four lumps of sugar into the cup.)*

CECILY: *(severely)* Cake or bread and butter?

GWENDOLEN: *(in a bored manner)* Bread and butter, please. Cake is rarely seen at the best houses nowadays.

CECILY: *(cuts a very large slice of cake and puts it on the tray)* Hand that to Miss Fairfax.

(MERRIMAN does so, and goes out with footman. GWENDOLEN drinks the tea and makes a grimace. Puts down cup at once, reaches out her hand to the bread and butter, looks at it, and finds it is cake. Rises in indignation.)

GWENDOLEN: You have filled my tea with lumps of sugar, and though I asked most distinctly for bread and butter, you have given me cake. I am known for the gentleness of my disposition, and the extraordinary sweetness of my nature, but I warn you, Miss Cardew, you may go too far.

CECILY: *(rising)* To save my poor, innocent, trusting boy from the machinations of any other girl there are no lengths to which I would not go.

GWENDOLEN: From the moment I saw you I distrusted you. I felt that you were false and deceitful. I am never deceived in such matters. My first impressions of people are invariably right.

CECILY: It seems to me, Miss Fairfax, that I am trespassing on your valuable time. No doubt you have many other calls of a similar character to make in the neighbourhood.

(Enter JACK.)

GWENDOLEN: *(catching sight of him)* Ernest! My own Ernest!

JACK: Gwendolen! Darling! *(Offers to kiss her.)*

GWENDOLEN: *(drawing back)* A moment! May I ask if you are engaged to be married to this young lady? *(Points to CECILY.)*

JACK: *(laughing)* To dear little Cecily! Of course not! What could have put such an idea into your pretty little head?

GWENDOLEN: Thank you. You may! *(Offers her cheek.)*

CECILY: *(very sweetly)* I knew there must be some misunderstanding, Miss Fairfax. The gentleman whose arm is at present round your waist is my guardian, Mr John Worthing.

GWENDOLEN: I beg your pardon?

CECILY: This is Uncle Jack.

GWENDOLEN: *(receding)* Jack! Oh!

(Enter ALGERNON.)

CECILY: Here is Ernest.

ALGERNON: *(goes straight over to CECILY without noticing anyone else)* My own love!

(Offers to kiss her.)

CECILY: *(drawing back)* A moment, Ernest! May I ask you — are you engaged to be married to this young lady?

ALGERNON: *(looking round)* To what young lady? Good heavens! Gwendolen!

CECILY: Yes! to good heavens, Gwendolen, I mean to Gwendolen.

650 ALGERNON: *(laughing)* Of course not! What could have put such an idea into your pretty little head?

CECILY: Thank you. *(Presenting her cheek to be kissed.)* You may. *(ALGERNON kisses her.)*

GWENDOLEN: I felt there was some slight error, Miss Cardew. The gentleman who is now embracing you is my cousin, Mr Algernon Moncrieff.

CECILY: *(breaking away from ALGERNON)* Algernon Moncrieff! Oh! *(The two girls move towards each other and put their arms round each other's waists as if for protection.)*

CECILY: Are you called Algernon?

ALGERNON: I cannot deny it.

CECILY: Oh!

GWENDOLEN: Is your name really John?

660 JACK: *(standing rather proudly)* I could deny it if I liked. I could deny anything if I liked. But my name certainly is John. It has been John for years.

CECILY: *(to GWENDOLEN)* A gross deception has been practised on both of us.

GWENDOLEN: My poor wounded Cecily!

CECILY: My sweet wronged Gwendolen!

GWENDOLEN: *(slowly and seriously)* You will call me sister, will you not? *(They embrace. JACK and ALGERNON groan and walk up and down.)*

CECILY: *(rather brightly)* There is just one question I would like to be allowed to ask my guardian.

GWENDOLEN: An admirable idea! Mr Worthing, there is just one question I would like to be permitted to put to you. Where is your brother Ernest? We

670 are both engaged to be married to your brother Ernest, so it is a matter of some importance to us to know where your brother Ernest is at present.

JACK: *(slowly and hesitatingly)* Gwendolen — Cecily — it is very painful for me to be forced to speak the truth. It is the first time in my life that I have ever been reduced to such a painful position, and I am really quite inexperienced in doing anything of the kind. However, I will tell you quite frankly that I have no brother Ernest. I have no brother at all. I never had a brother in my life, and I certainly have not the smallest intention of ever having one in the future.

CECILY: *(surprised)* No brother at all?

JACK: *(cheerily)* None!

GWENDOLEN: *(severely)* Had you never a brother of any kind?

JACK: *(pleasantly)* Never. Not even of any kind.

680 GWENDOLEN: I am afraid it is quite clear, Cecily, that neither of us is engaged to be married to anyone.

CECILY: It is not a very pleasant position for a young girl suddenly to find herself in. Is it?

GWENDOLEN: Let us go into the house. They will hardly venture to come after us there.

CECILY: No, men are so cowardly, aren't they?

(They retire into the house with scornful looks.)

690 JACK: This ghastly state of things is what you call Bunburying, I suppose!

ALGERNON: Yes, and a perfectly wonderful Bunbury it is. The most wonderful Bunbury I have ever had in my life.

JACK: Well, you've no right whatsoever to Bunbury here.

ALGERNON: That is absurd. One has a right to Bunbury anywhere one chooses. Every serious Bunburyist knows that.

JACK: Serious Bunburyist? Good heavens!

ALGERNON: Well, one must be serious about something, if one wants to have any amusement in life. I happen to be serious about Bunburying. What on earth you are serious about I haven't got the remotest idea. About every-
700 thing, I should fancy. You have such an absolutely trivial nature.

JACK: Well, the only small satisfaction I have in the whole of this wretched busi-ness is that your friend Bunbury is quite exploded. You won't be able to run down to the country quite so often as you used to do, dear Algy. And a very good thing too.

ALGERNON: Your brother is a little off colour, isn't he, dear Jack? You won't be able to disappear to London quite so frequently as your wicked custom was. And not a bad thing either.

JACK: As for your conduct towards Miss Cardew, I must say that your taking in a sweet, simple, innocent girl like that is quite inexcusable. To say nothing of the fact that she is my ward.

ALGERNON: I can see no possible defence at all for your deceiving a brilliant, clever, thoroughly experienced young lady like Miss Fairfax. To say nothing
710 of the fact that she is my cousin.

JACK: I wanted to be engaged to Gwendolen, that is all. I love her.

ALGERNON: Well, I simply wanted to be engaged to Cecily. I adore her.

JACK: There is certainly no chance of your marrying Miss Cardew.

ALGERNON: I don't think there is much likelihood, Jack, of you and Miss Fairfax being united.

JACK: Well, that is no business of yours.

720 ALGERNON: If it was my business, I wouldn't talk about it. *(Begins to eat muffins.)* It is very vulgar to talk about one's business. Only people like stockbrokers do that, and then merely at dinner parties.

JACK: How can you sit there, calmly eating muffins when we are in this horrible trouble, I can't make out. You seem to me to be perfectly heartless.

ALGERNON: Well, I can't eat muffins in an agitated manner. The butter would probably get on my cuffs. One should always eat muffins quite calmly. It is the only way to eat them.

JACK: I say it's perfectly heartless your eating muffins at all, under the circumstances.

ALGERNON: When I am in trouble, eating is the only thing that consoles me.
730 Indeed, when I am in really great trouble, as any one who knows me inti-mately will tell you, I refuse everything except food and drink. At the present moment I am eating muffins because I am unhappy. Besides, I am particularly fond of muffins. *(Rising.)*

JACK: *(rising)* Well, that is no reason why you should eat them all in that greedy way. (*Takes muffins from* ALGERNON.)

ALGERNON: (*offering tea-cake*) I wish you would have tea-cake instead. I don't like tea-cake.

JACK: Good heavens! I suppose a man may eat his own muffins in his own garden.

740   ALGERNON: But you have just said it was perfectly heartless to eat muffins.

JACK: I said it was perfectly heartless of you, under the circumstances. That is a very different thing.

ALGERNON: That may be. But the muffins are the same. (*He seizes the muffin-dish from* JACK.)

JACK: Algy, I wish to goodness you would go.

ALGERNON: You can't possibly ask me to go without having some dinner. It's absurd. I never go without my dinner. No one ever does, except vegetarians and people like that. Besides I have just made arrangements with Dr Chasuble to be christened at a quarter to six under the name of Ernest.

750   JACK: My dear fellow, the sooner you give up that nonsense the better. I made arrangements this morning with Dr Chasuble to be christened myself at 5.30, and I naturally will take the name of Ernest. Gwendolen would wish it. We cannot both be christened Ernest. It's absurd. Besides, I have a perfect right to be christened if I like. There is no evidence at all that I ever have been christened by anybody. I should think it extremely probable I never was, and so does Dr Chasuble. It is entirely different in your case. You have been christened already.

ALGERNON: Yes, but I have not been christened for years.

JACK: Yes, but you have been christened. That is the important thing.

760   ALGERNON: Quite so. So I know my constitution can stand it. If you are not quite sure about your ever having been christened, I must say I think it rather dangerous your venturing on it now. It might make you very unwell. You can hardly have forgotten that someone very closely connected with you was very nearly carried off this week in Paris by a severe chill.

JACK: Yes, but you said yourself that a severe chill was not hereditary.

ALGERNON: It usen't to be, I know — but I daresay it is now. Science is always making wonderful improvements in things.

JACK: (*picking up the muffin-dish*) Oh, that is nonsense; you are always talking

770   nonsense.

ALGERNON: Jack, you are at the muffins again! I wish you wouldn't. There are only two left. (*Takes them.*) I told you I was particularly fond of muffins.

JACK: But I hate tea-cake.

ALGERNON: Why on earth then do you allow tea-cake to be served up for your guests? What ideas you have of hospitality!

JACK: Algernon! I have already told you to go. I don't want you here. Why don't you go!

ALGERNON: I haven't quite finished my tea yet! and there is still one muffin left. (JACK *groans, and sinks into a chair.* ALGERNON *continues eating.*)

ACT DROP

THIRD ACT

SCENE *Drawing-room at the Manor House*

(GWENDOLEN *and* CECILY *are at the window, looking out into the garden.*)

GWENDOLEN: The fact that they did not follow us at once into the house, as anyone else would have done, seems to me to show that they have some sense of shame left.

CECILY: They have been eating muffins. That looks like repentance.

GWENDOLEN: (*after a pause*) They don't seem to notice us at all. Couldn't you cough?

CECILY: But I haven't got a cough.

GWENDOLEN: They're looking at us. What effrontery!

CECILY: They're approaching. That's very forward of them.

10   GWENDOLEN: Let us preserve a dignified silence.

CECILY: Certainly. It's the only thing to do now.

(*Enter* JACK *followed by* ALGERNON. *They whistle some dreadful popular air from a British Opera.*)

GWENDOLEN: This dignified silence seems to produce an unpleasant effect.

CECILY: A most distasteful one.

GWENDOLEN: But we will not be the first to speak.

CECILY: Certainly not.

GWENDOLEN: Mr Worthing, I have something very particular to ask you. Much depends on your reply.

CECILY: Gwendolen, your common sense is invaluable. Mr Moncrieff, kindly answer me the following question. Why did you pretend to be my guardian's

20   brother?

ALGERNON: In order that I might have an opportunity of meeting you.

CECILY: (*to* GWENDOLEN) That certainly seems a satisfactory explanation, does it not?

GWENDOLEN: Yes, dear, if you can believe him.

CECILY: I don't. But that does not affect the wonderful beauty of his answer.

GWENDOLEN: True. In matters of grave importance, style, not sincerity, is the vital thing. Mr Worthing, what explanation can you offer to me for pretending to have a brother? Was it in order that you might have an opportunity of coming up to town to see me as often as possible?

30   JACK: Can you doubt it, Miss Fairfax?

GWENDOLEN: I have the gravest doubts upon the subject. But I intend to crush them. This is not the moment for German scepticism.[1] (*Moving to* CECILY.) Their explanations appear to be quite satisfactory, especially Mr Worthing's. That seems to me to have the stamp of truth upon it.

CECILY: I am more than content with what Mr Moncrieff said. His voice alone inspires one with absolute credulity.

---

1 scepticism holds that no knowledge is absolute and that doubt is necessary to achieve an approximation of certainty. German theological writings at this time were considered especially sceptical in the English popular mind.

GWENDOLEN: Then you think we should forgive them?

CECILY: Yes. I mean no.

GWENDOLEN: True! I had forgotten. There are principles at stake that one cannot surrender. Which of us should tell them? The task is not a pleasant one.

CECILY: Could we not both speak at the same time?

GWENDOLEN: An excellent idea! I nearly always speak at the same time as other people. Will you take the time from me?

CECILY: Certainly. (GWENDOLEN *beats time with uplifted finger.*)

GWENDOLEN AND CECILY: (*speaking together*) Your Christian names are still an insuperable barrier. That is all!

JACK AND ALGERNON: (*speaking together*) Our Christian names! Is that all? But we are going to be christened this afternoon.

GWENDOLEN: (*to* JACK) For my sake you are prepared to do this terrible thing?

JACK: I am.

CECILY: (*to* ALGERNON) To please me you are ready to face this fearful ordeal?

ALGERNON: I am!

GWENDOLEN: How absurd to talk about the equality of the sexes! Where questions of self-sacrifice are concerned, men are infinitely beyond us.

JACK: We are. (*Clasps hands with* ALGERNON.)

CECILY: They have moments of physical courage of which we women know absolutely nothing.

GWENDOLEN: (*to* JACK) Darling!

ALGERNON: (*to* CECILY) Darling! (*They fall into each other's arms.*)

(*Enter* MERRIMAN. *When he enters he coughs loudly, seeing the situation.*)

MERRIMAN: Ahem! Ahem! Lady Bracknell!

JACK: Good heavens!

(*Enter* LADY BRACKNELL. *The couples separate in alarm. Exit* MERRIMAN.)

LADY BRACKNELL: Gwendolen! What does this mean?

GWENDOLEN: Merely that I am engaged to be married to Mr Worthing, mamma.

LADY BRACKNELL: Come here. Sit down. Sit down immediately. Hesitation of any kind is a sign of mental decay in the young, of physical weakness in the old. (*Turns to* JACK.) Apprised, sir, of my daughter's sudden flight by her trusty maid, whose confidence I purchased by means of a small coin, I followed her at once by a luggage train. Her unhappy father is, I am glad to say, under the impression that she is attending a more than usually lengthy lecture by the University Extension Scheme on the Influence of a permanent income on Thought. I do not propose to undeceive him. Indeed I have never undeceived him on any question. I would consider it wrong. But of course, you will clearly understand that all communication between yourself and my daughter must cease immediately from this moment. On this point, as indeed on all points, I am firm.

JACK: I am engaged to be married to Gwendolen, Lady Bracknell!

LADY BRACKNELL: You are nothing of the kind, sir. And now as regards Algernon! ... Algernon!

80 ALGERNON: Yes, Aunt Augusta.

LADY BRACKNELL: May I ask if it is in this house that your invalid friend Mr Bunbury resides?

ALGERNON: (*stammering*) Oh! No! Bunbury doesn't live here. Bunbury is somewhere else at present. In fact, Bunbury is dead.

LADY BRACKNELL: Dead! When did Mr Bunbury die? His death must have been extremely sudden.

ALGERNON: (*airily*) Oh! I killed Bunbury this afternoon. I mean poor Bunbury died this afternoon.

LADY BRACKNELL: What did he die of?

90 ALGERNON: Bunbury? Oh, he was quite exploded.

LADY BRACKNELL: Exploded! Was he the victim of a revolutionary outrage? I was not aware that Mr Bunbury was interested in social legislation. If so, he is well punished for his morbidity.

ALGERNON: My dear Aunt Augusta, I mean he was found out! The doctors found out that Bunbury could not live, that is what I mean — so Bunbury died.

LADY BRACKNELL: He seems to have had great confidence in the opinion of his physicians. I am glad, however, that he made up his mind at the last to some definite course of action, and acted under proper medical advice. And now that we have finally got rid of this Mr Bunbury, may I ask, Mr

100 Worthing, who is that young person whose hand my nephew Algernon is now holding in what seems to me a peculiarly unnecessary manner?

JACK: That lady is Miss Cecily Cardew, my ward. (LADY BRACKNELL *bows coldly to* CECILY.)

ALGERNON: I am engaged to be married to Cecily, Aunt Augusta.

LADY BRACKNELL: I beg your pardon?

CECILY: Mr Moncrieff and I are engaged to be married, Lady Bracknell.

LADY BRACKNELL: (*with a shiver, crossing to the sofa and sitting down*) I do not know whether there is anything peculiarly exciting in the air of this particular part of Hertfordshire, but the number of engagements that go on seems to me considerably above the proper average that statistics have laid down for our

110 guidance. I think some preliminary inquiry on my part would not be out of place. Mr Worthing, is Miss Cardew at all connected with any of the larger railway stations in London? I merely desire information. Until yesterday I had no idea that there were any families or persons whose origin was a Terminus. (JACK *looks perfectly furious, but restrains himself.*)

JACK: (*in a cold, clear voice*) Miss Cardew is the grand-daughter of the late Mr Thomas Cardew of 149 Belgrave Square, S.W.; Gervase Park, Dorking, Surrey; and the Sporran, Fifeshire, N.B.[2]

LADY BRACKNELL: That sounds not unsatisfactory. Three addresses always inspire confidence, even in tradesmen. But what proof have I of their authenticity?

120 JACK: I have carefully preserved the Court Guides[3] of the period. They are open to your inspection, Lady Bracknell.

LADY BRACKNELL: (*grimly*) I have known strange errors in that publication.

2 North Britain (used commonly in Wilde's day for postal addresses north of the Scottish border).
3 a directory of addresses of the English gentry and nobility.

JACK: Miss Cardew's family solicitors are Messrs Markby, Markby, and Markby.

LADY BRACKNELL: Markby, Markby, and Markby? A firm of the very highest position in their profession. Indeed I am told that one of the Mr Markby's is occasionally to be seen at dinner parties. So far I am satisfied.

JACK: (*very irritably*) How extremely kind of you, Lady Bracknell! I have also in my possession, you will be pleased to hear, certificates of Miss Cardew's birth, baptism, whooping cough, registration, vaccination, confirmation, and the measles; both the German and the English variety.

LADY BRACKNELL: Ah! A life crowded with incident, I see; though perhaps somewhat too exciting for a young girl. I am not myself in favour of premature experiences. (*Rises, looks at her watch.*) Gwendolen! the time approaches for our departure. We have not a moment to lose. As a matter of form, Mr Worthing, I had better ask you if Miss Cardew has any little fortune?

JACK: Oh! about a hundred and thirty thousand pounds in the Funds.[4] That is all. Good-bye, Lady Bracknell. So pleased to have seen you.

LADY BRACKNELL: (*sitting down again*) A moment, Mr Worthing. A hundred and thirty thousand pounds! And in the Funds! Miss Cardew seems to me a most attractive young lady, now that I look at her. Few girls of the present day have any really solid qualities, any of the qualities that last, and improve with time. We live, I regret to say, in an age of surfaces. (*To* CECILY.) Come over here, dear. (CECILY *goes across.*) Pretty child! your dress is sadly simple, and your hair seems almost as Nature might have left it. But we can soon alter all that. A thoroughly experienced French maid produces a really marvellous result in a very brief space of time. I remember recommending one to young Lady Lancing, and after three months her own husband did not know her.

JACK: And after six months nobody knew her.

LADY BRACKNELL: (*glares at* JACK *for a few moments. Then bends, with a practised smile, to* CECILY) Kindly turn round, sweet child. (CECILY *turns completely round.*) No, the side view is what I want. (CECILY *presents her profile.*) Yes, quite as I expected. There are distinct social possibilities in your profile. The two weak points in our age are its want of principle and its want of profile. The chin a little higher, dear. Style largely depends on the way the chin is worn. They are worn very high, just at present. Algernon!

ALGERNON: Yes, Aunt Augusta!

LADY BRACKNELL: There are distinct social possibilities in Miss Cardew's profile.

ALGERNON: Cecily is the sweetest, dearest, prettiest girl in the whole world. And I don't care twopence about social possibilities.

LADY BRACKNELL: Never speak disrespectfully of Society, Algernon. Only people who can't get into it do that. (*To* CECILY.) Dear child, of course you know that Algernon has nothing but his debts to depend upon. But I do not approve of mercenary marriages. When I married Lord Bracknell I had no fortune of any kind. But I never dreamed for a moment of allowing that to stand in my way. Well, I suppose I must give my consent.

ALGERNON: Thank you, Aunt Augusta.

LADY BRACKNELL: Cecily, you may kiss me!

CECILY: (*kisses her*) Thank you, Lady Bracknell.

4 government bonds.

LADY BRACKNELL: You may also address me as Aunt Augusta for the future.

170 CECILY: Thank you, Aunt Augusta.

LADY BRACKNELL: The marriage, I think, had better take place quite soon.

ALGERNON: Thank you, Aunt Augusta.

CECILY: Thank you, Aunt Augusta.

LADY BRACKNELL: To speak frankly, I am not in favour of long engagements. They give people the opportunity of finding out each other's character before marriage, which I think is never advisable.

JACK: I beg your pardon for interrupting you, Lady Bracknell, but this engagement is quite out of the question. I am Miss Cardew's guardian, and she cannot marry without my consent until she comes of age. That consent I

180 absolutely decline to give.

LADY BRACKNELL: Upon what grounds, may I ask? Algernon is an extremely, I may almost say ostentatiously, eligible young man. He has nothing, but he looks everything. What more can one desire?

JACK: It pains me very much to have to speak frankly to you, Lady Bracknell, about your nephew, but the fact is that I do not approve at all of his moral character. I suspect him of being untruthful. (ALGERNON and CECILY look at him in indignant amazement.)

LADY BRACKNELL: Untruthful! My nephew Algernon? Impossible! He is an Oxonian.[5]

JACK: I fear there can be no possible doubt about the matter. This afternoon

190 during my temporary absence in London on an important question of romance, he obtained admission to my house by means of the false pretence of being my brother. Under an assumed name he drank, I've just been informed by my butler, an entire pint bottle of my Perrier-Jouet, Brut, '89; wine I was specially reserving for myself. Continuing his disgraceful deception, he succeeded in the course of the afternoon in alienating the affections of my only ward. He subsequently stayed to tea, and devoured every single muffin. And what makes his conduct all the more heartless is, that he was perfectly well aware from the first that I have no brother, that I never had a brother, and that I don't intend to have a

200 brother, not even of any kind. I distinctly told him so myself yesterday afternoon.

LADY BRACKNELL: Ahem! Mr Worthing, after careful consideration I have decided entirely to overlook my nephew's conduct to you.

JACK: That is very generous of you, Lady Bracknell. My own decision, however, is unalterable. I decline to give my consent.

LADY BRACKNELL: (to CECILY) Come here, sweet child. (CECILY goes over.) How old are you, dear?

CECILY: Well, I am really only eighteen, but I always admit to twenty when I go to evening parties.

210 LADY BRACKNELL: You are perfectly right in making some slight alteration. Indeed, no woman should ever be quite accurate about her age. It looks so calculating.... (In a meditative manner.) Eighteen, but admitting to twenty at evening parties. Well, it will not be very long before you are of age and

5 graduate of Oxford University.

free from the restraints of tutelage. So I don't think your guardian's consent is, after all, a matter of any importance.

JACK: Pray excuse me, Lady Bracknell, for interrupting you again, but it is only fair to tell you that according to the terms of her grandfather's will Miss Cardew does not come legally of age till she is thirty-five.

LADY BRACKNELL: That does not seem to me to be a grave objection. Thirty-five
220   is a very attractive age. London society is full of women of the very highest birth who have, of their own free choice, remained thirty-five for years. Lady Dumbleton is an instance in point. To my own knowledge she has been thirty-five ever since she arrived at the age of forty, which was many years ago now. I see no reason why our dear Cecily should not be even still more attractive at the age you mention than she is at present. There will be a large accumulation of property.

CECILY: Algy, could you wait for me till I was thirty-five?

ALGERNON: Of course I could, Cecily. You know I could.

230   CECILY: Yes, I felt it instinctively, but I couldn't wait all that time. I hate waiting even five minutes for anybody. It always makes me rather cross. I am not punctual myself, I know, but I do like punctuality in others, and waiting, even to be married, is quite out of the question.

ALGERNON: Then what is to be done, Cecily?

CECILY: I don't know, Mr Moncrieff.

LADY BRACKNELL: My dear Mr Worthing, as Miss Cardew states positively that she cannot wait till she is thirty-five — a remark which I am bound to say seems to me to show a somewhat impatient nature — I would beg of you to reconsider your decision.

240   JACK: But my dear Lady Bracknell, the matter is entirely in your own hands. The moment you consent to my marriage with Gwendolen, I will most gladly allow your nephew to form an alliance with my ward.

LADY BRACKNELL: (rising and drawing herself up) You must be quite aware that what you propose is out of the question.

JACK: Then a passionate celibacy is all that any of us can look forward to.

LADY BRACKNELL: That is not the destiny I propose for Gwendolen. Algernon, of course, can choose for himself. (Pulls out her watch.) Come, dear (GWEN-DOLEN rises), we have already missed five, if not six, trains. To miss any more might expose us to comment on the platform.

(Enter DR CHASUBLE.)

250   CHASUBLE: Everything is quite ready for the christenings.

LADY BRACKNELL: The christenings, sir! Is not that somewhat premature?

CHASUBLE: (looking rather puzzled, and pointing to JACK and ALGERNON) Both these gentlemen have expressed a desire for immediate baptism.

LADY BRACKNELL: At their age? The idea is grotesque and irreligious! Algernon, I forbid you to be baptized. I will not hear of such excesses. Lord Bracknell would be highly displeased if he learned that that was the way in which you wasted your time and money.

CHASUBLE: Am I to understand then that there are to be no christenings at all this afternoon?

260   JACK: I don't think that, as things are now, it would be of much practical value
      to either of us, Dr Chasuble.
      CHASUBLE: I am grieved to hear such sentiments from you, Mr Worthing. They
      savour of the heretical views of the Anabaptists,[6] views that I have com
      pletely refuted in four of my unpublished sermons. However, as your present
      mood seems to be one peculiarly secular, I will return to the church at
      once. Indeed, I have just been informed by the pew-opener[7] that for the last
      hour and a half Miss Prism has been waiting for me in the vestry.
      LADY BRACKNELL: (starting) Miss Prism! Did I hear you mention a Miss Prism?
      CHASUBLE: Yes, Lady Bracknell. I am on my way to join her.
270   LADY BRACKNELL: Pray allow me to detain you for a moment. This matter may
      prove to be one of vital importance to Lord Bracknell and myself. Is this Miss
      Prism a female of repellent aspect, remotely connected with education?
      CHASUBLE: (somewhat indignantly) She is the most cultivated of ladies, and
      the very picture of respectability.
      LADY BRACKNELL: It is obviously the same person. May I ask what position she
      holds in your household?
      CHASUBLE: (severely) I am a celibate, madam.
      JACK: (interposing) Miss Prism, Lady Bracknell, has been for the last three years
      Miss Cardew's esteemed governess and valued companion.
280   LADY BRACKNELL: In spite of what I hear of her, I must see her at once. Let
      her be sent for.
      CHASUBLE: (looking off) She approaches; she is nigh.

      (Enter MISS PRISM hurriedly.)

      MISS PRISM: I was told you expected me in the vestry, dear Canon. I have been
      waiting for you there for an hour and three-quarters. (Catches sight of LADY
      BRACKNELL, who has fixed her with a stony glare. MISS PRISM grows pale and
      quails. She looks anxiously round as if desirous to escape.)
      LADY BRACKNELL: (in a severe, judicial voice) Prism! (MISS PRISM bows her head in
      shame.) Come here, Prism! (MISS PRISM approaches in a humble manner.)
      Prism! Where is that baby? (General consternation. The CANON starts back in
      horror. ALGERNON and JACK pretend to be anxious to shield CECILY and GWEN-
      DOLEN from hearing the details of a terrible public scandal.) Twenty-eight years
      ago, Prism, you left Lord Bracknell's house, Number 104, Upper Grosvenor
290   Street, in charge of a perambulator that contained a baby of the male sex.
      You never returned. A few weeks later, through the elaborate investiga-
      tions of the Metropolitan police, the perambulator was discovered at mid-
      night standing by itself in a remote corner of Bayswater. It contained the
      manuscript of a three-volume novel of more than usually revolting senti-
      mentality. (MISS PRISM starts in involuntary indignation.) But the baby was not
      there! (Everyone looks at MISS PRISM.) Prism! Where is that baby? (A pause.)
      MISS PRISM: Lady Bracknell, I admit with shame that I do not know. I only
      wish I did. The plain facts of the case are these. On the morning of the

---

6 Protestant sect that opposed infant baptism and required a second or adult baptism. 7 an usher; pews in
older churches were enclosed boxes of seats that were reserved for particular families.

day you mention, a day that is for ever branded on my memory, I prepared as usual to take the baby out in its perambulator. I had also with me a some what old, but capacious hand-bag in which I intended to place the manuscript of a work of fiction that I had written during my few unoccupied hours. In a moment of mental abstraction, for which I never can forgive myself, I deposited the manuscript in the bassinette, and placed the baby in the hand-bag.

JACK: *(who has been listening attentively)* But where did you deposit the hand-bag?

MISS PRISM: Do not ask me, Mr Worthing.

JACK: Miss Prism, this is a matter of no small importance to me. I insist on knowing where you deposited the hand-bag that contained that infant.

MISS PRISM: I left it in the cloak-room of one of the larger railway stations in London.

JACK: What railway station?

MISS PRISM: *(quite crushed)* Victoria. The Brighton line. *(Sinks into a chair.)*

JACK: I must retire to my room for a moment. Gwendolen, wait here for me.

GWENDOLEN: If you are not too long, I will wait here for you all my life. *(Exit JACK in great excitement.)*

CHASUBLE: What do you think this means, Lady Bracknell?

LADY BRACKNELL: I dare not even suspect, Dr Chasuble. I need hardly tell you that in families of high position strange coincidences are not supposed to occur. They are hardly considered the thing.

(Noises heard overhead as if someone was throwing trunks about. Everyone looks up.)

CECILY: Uncle Jack seems strangely agitated.

CHASUBLE: Your guardian has a very emotional nature.

LADY BRACKNELL: This noise is extremely unpleasant. It sounds as if he was having an argument. I dislike arguments of any kind. They are always vulgar, and often convincing.

CHASUBLE: *(looking up)* It has stopped now. *(The noise is redoubled.)*

LADY BRACKNELL: I wish he would arrive at some conclusion.

GWENDOLEN: This suspense is terrible. I hope it will last.

(Enter JACK with a hand-bag of black leather in his hand.)

JACK: *(rushing over to MISS PRISM)* Is this the hand-bag, Miss Prism? Examine it carefully before you speak. The happiness of more than one life depends on your answer.

MISS PRISM: *(calmly)* It seems to be mine. Yes, here is the injury it received through the upsetting of a Gower Street omnibus in younger and happier days. Here is the stain on the lining caused by the explosion of a temperance beverage, an incident that occurred at Leamington. And here, on the lock, are my initials. I had forgotten that in an extravagant mood I had had them placed there. The bag is undoubtedly mine. I am delighted to have it so unexpectedly restored to me. It has been a great inconvenience being without it all these years.

JACK: *(in a pathetic voice)* Miss Prism, more is restored to you than this hand-bag. I was the baby you placed in it.

MISS PRISM: *(amazed)* You?

JACK: *(embracing her)* Yes . . . mother!

MISS PRISM: *(recoiling in indignant astonishment)* Mr Worthing! I am unmarried!

JACK: Unmarried! I do not deny that is a serious blow. But after all, who has the right to cast a stone against one who has suffered? Cannot repentance wipe out an act of folly? Why should there be one law for men, and another for women? Mother, I forgive you. *(Tries to embrace her again.)*

MISS PRISM: *(still more indignant)* Mr Worthing, there is some error. *(Pointing to* LADY BRACKNELL.*)* There is the lady who can tell you who you really are.

350 JACK: *(after a pause)* Lady Bracknell, I hate to seem inquisitive, but would you kindly inform me who I am?

LADY BRACKNELL: I am afraid that the news I have to give you will not altogether please you. You are the son of my poor sister, Mrs Moncrieff, and consequently Algernon's elder brother.

JACK: Algy's elder brother! Then I have a brother after all. I knew I had a brother! I always said I had a brother! Cecily — how could you have ever doubted that I had a brother? *(Seizes hold of* ALGERNON.*)* Dr Chasuble, my unfortunate brother. Miss Prism, my unfortunate brother. Gwendolen, my unfortunate brother. Algy, you young scoundrel, you will have to treat me with 360 more respect in the future. You have never behaved to me like a brother in all your life.

ALGERNON: Well, not till today, old boy, I admit. I did my best, however, though I was out of practice.

(Shakes hands.)

GWENDOLEN: *(to* JACK*)* My own! But what own are you? What is your Christian name, now that you have become someone else?

JACK: Good heavens! . . . I had quite forgotten that point. Your decision on the subject of my name is irrevocable, I suppose?

GWENDOLEN: I never change, except in my affections.

CECILY: What a noble nature you have, Gwendolen!

370 JACK: Then the question had better be cleared up at once. Aunt Augusta, a moment. At the time when Miss Prism left me in the hand-bag, had I been christened already?

LADY BRACKNELL: Every luxury that money could buy, including christening, had been lavished on you by your fond and doting parents.

JACK: Then I was christened! That is settled. Now, what name was I given? Let me know the worst.

LADY BRACKNELL: Being the eldest son you were naturally christened after your father.

JACK: *(irritably)* Yes, but what was my father's Christian name?

380 LADY BRACKNELL: *(meditatively)* I cannot at the present moment recall what the General's Christian name was. But I have no doubt he had one. He was eccentric, I admit. But only in later years. And that was the result of the Indian climate, and marriage, and indigestion, and other things of that kind.

JACK: Algy! Can't you recollect what our father's Christian name was?

ALGERNON: My dear boy, we were never even on speaking terms. He died before I was a year old.

JACK: His name would appear in the Army Lists of the period, I suppose, Aunt Augusta?

LADY BRACKNELL: The General was essentially a man of peace, except in his domestic life. But I have no doubt his name would appear in any military directory.

JACK: The Army Lists of the last forty years are here. These delightful records should have been my constant study. (*Rushes to bookcase and tears the books out.*) M. Generals... Mallam, Maxbohm, Magley — what ghastly names they have — Markby, Migsby, Mobbs, Moncrieff! Lieutenant 1840, Captain, Lieutenant-Colonel, Colonel, General 1869, Christian names, Ernest John. (*Puts book very quietly down and speaks quite calmly.*) I always told you, Gwendolen, my name was Ernest, didn't I? Well, it is Ernest after all. I mean it naturally is Ernest.

LADY BRACKNELL: Yes, I remember now that the General was called Ernest. I knew I had some particular reason for disliking the name.

GWENDOLEN: Ernest! My own Ernest! I felt from the first that you could have no other name!

JACK: Gwendolen, it is a terrible thing for a man to find out suddenly that all his life he has been speaking nothing but the truth. Can you forgive me?

GWENDOLEN: I can. For I feel that you are sure to change.

JACK: My own one!

CHASUBLE: (*to* MISS PRISM) Laetitia! (*Embraces her.*)

MISS PRISM: (*enthusiastically*) Frederick! At last!

ALGERNON: Cecily! (*Embraces her.*) At last!

JACK: Gwendolen! (*Embraces her.*) At last!

LADY BRACKNELL: My nephew, you seem to be displaying signs of triviality.

JACK: On the contrary, Aunt Augusta, I've now realised for the first time in my life the vital Importance of Being Earnest.

TABLEAU

CURTAIN

Tennessee Williams (1911–1983)

Born in Columbus, Mississippi, Tom Williams moved north to St. Louis with his mother and sister when he was seven years old. Reunited there as a family with his domineering father (who mocked his sensitive son with the nickname "Miss Nancy"), Williams lived through a dysfunctional and emotionally charged childhood. Indeed his childhood anxieties seem reflected in the themes, situations, and characters of his mature drama: a lost Southern gentility asserted by a mother at once conscientious but insistent; an uncompromising father fully capable of both large sympathies and instant violence; an emotionally fragile even somewhat disturbed daughter at once sexually receptive and resistant; and a lost son lashing out in a world of personal uncertainties where no interaction is stable.

After leaving home, Williams worked at a variety of jobs and travelled widely. He enrolled briefly at the University of Missouri and at Washington University, St. Louis, before taking dramatic arts at the University of Iowa where he graduated in 1938 with a B.A. in English and a nickname relating to his strong southern accent: "Tennessee." The following year, he won a Rockefeller Foundation scholarship which sent him to New York and the Dramatic Workshop at the New School for Social Research. His plays dominate American theatre in the middle of the twentieth century, beginning with *The Glass Menagerie* (1945) and including *Summer and Smoke* (1947), *A Streetcar Named Desire* (1947), *Cat on a Hot Tin Roof* (1955), *Suddenly Last Summer* (1958), *Sweet Bird of Youth* (1959), and *The Night of the Iguana* (1961). All of these plays were released as Hollywood films shortly after their initial stage runs.

At once lyrical and metaphorical but also rudely expressionist and naturalistic, Tennessee Williams's plays both psychologize and eroticize the stage through the inner lives and external conflicts of his characters. His dramas are explosively conflictual and interpersonal where characters are individualized through well-voiced emotional dialogue. Theatrical attention to detail in lighting, music, movement, sound effects, and set design work together to create mood and excitement in Williams's drama. The American South figures prominently in literal and figurative terms, with its pervading sense of hot and humid emotional distress, aristocratic idealism, moral decay, gothic insecurity, and complicated personal motivation.

INTRODUCTION TO *CAT ON A HOT TIN ROOF*

Tennessee Williams's early dramatic success continued with *Cat on a Hot Tin Roof* (1955), which won for him his second Pulitzer Prize. This immediate "hit" in the theatre translated well onto the big screen. Metro-Goldwyn-Mayer paid half a million dollars for the film rights, producing a full-length motion picture in 1958 with Elizabeth Taylor, Paul Newman, and Burl Ives in the cast.

Cat on a Hot Tin Roof surpasses the expressionist symbolism and poetic reach of Williams's earlier plays to represent his broadest dramatic sympathy and most fully explored, realist dramatic situation. He enunciates his primary concern in a lengthy interpretive note in Act 2 of the play (see stage direction, p. 659):

The bird that I hope to catch in the net of this play is not the solution of one man's psychological problem. I'm trying to catch the true quality of experience in a group of people, that cloudy, flickering, evanescent — fiercely charged! — interplay of live human beings in the thundercloud of a common crisis.

The "common crisis" of the play involves the true nature of Big Daddy's medical condition on his sixty-fifth birthday, Brick's drunken detachment from the family and especially from his wife, Maggie, and the fraudulent attentions of Mae and Gooper as inheritors of Big Daddy's estate. In one emotionally charged night, convenient "truths" long ago elevated to unchallengeable status are torn down, bashed about, and interrogated by the Pollitt family.

Mendacity, according to Big Daddy "one of them five dollar words that cheap politicians throw back and forth at each other" (see Act 2, ll. 646–47, p. 656), represents the central theme of the play. Everyone at the Pollitt family estate consciously suppresses truth. Their false emotionality, polite pretension, and self-deceit lead to generalized self-delusion, a comfortable, collective, sincere self-delusion that easily replaces painful fact. Thus, through Big Daddy's birthday party, the family tries desperately to celebrate and reinforce his health, despite the fact that everyone, except Big Mama and Big Daddy himself, knows he is dying of cancer. They all cling to the acceptable "truth" that he suffers merely from a spastic colon — a significant metaphorical condition, considering the play's many falsehoods and Big Daddy's own favourite declarative: "Crap!" Mae and Gooper encourage his show of virility through exaggerated affection, all the while planning to benefit from the inheritance which they know to be imminent. Big Mama, too, uninformed but hoping blindly for the best, encourages Big Daddy's forced show of vigour, which manifests itself in vulgar unceremoniousness and private sexual daydreams. Brick, alone, refuses to take part in the family charade, but he is himself living in the falsity of his former glory as football star and life-buddy of Skipper, his dead teammate. The fact that Brick has broken his ankle on the Glorious Hill High School athletic field might seem to indicate his refusal to admit the "hill" which he is now well over as an adult and an alcoholic. Significantly, the immature action responsible for his injury the night before has provided him with a literal crutch, which he does not hesitate to use as a weapon on his wife, whom he blames for his grieving condition toward Skipper.

The situation of Act 1 sets up conflicts to be dramatically explored. In Act 2, Brick and Big Daddy confront each other on topics of truth, lies, communication — family mendacity in general. The two characters probe and evade a shared disgust, a generalized disgust that suppresses truth for psychological purposes as opposed to the calculating mendacity of the active liars in the household. Big Daddy wants to get at the root of Brick's drinking, while Brick wants to further evade his responsibilities as son, heir, and husband. Brick claims to drink out of "DISGUST," but Big Daddy itemizes the disgust with which he has lived his 65 years. In fact, only as Big Daddy probes the issue of Maggie's involvement with Skipper and the homosexual nature of Skipper's devotion and suicide does the truth of Brick's generalized "disgust" become any clearer. Threatened, Brick trades truth for truth, hinting at the extent of Big Daddy's terminal condition, and their discussion falls apart in raging expletives.

And yet their discussion is itself a form of mendacity in the play because real communication is so difficult to accomplish. "Why is it so damn hard for people to talk?" (see Act 2, l. 329 p. 647) asks Big Daddy, and Brick responds noncommittally "Yeah...." Later, Brick declares "Communication is — awful hard between people an'— somehow between you and me, it just don't — happen" (see Act 2, ll. 419–21 p. 649). Their dialogue itself is often dissonant, non-communicative, tentative, unsure, touching on main themes of mortality, mendacity, sexuality, and the social pretension and responsibility from which both seek to escape. Brick and Big Daddy, however, develop prominence and some sympathy within the play, at the same time as they come to a gradual realization of their shared evasions concerning ambition, marriage, and family allegiance — evasions that impede effective communication.

Most communicative and probably most sympathetic, the character of Maggie is developed as central to the conflicts of *Cat on a Hot Tin Roof*. Indeed, the image of nervous instability suggested by the play's title relates most closely to Maggie's character. She wants to reclaim Brick as her husband and gain for both of them their rightful inheritance of the Pollitt estate. Although a childless outsider (and she is often reminded of this), Maggie demonstrates commitment to her husband and to the family in general that clearly exceeds Mae and Gooper's cosy family posturing. She detests the grasping self-interest of her in-laws at the same time as she comforts Big Mama in her confusion and loathing. But Maggie herself is not beyond half-truth in her own startling announcement near the play's conclusion. Clearly Big Daddy's favourite "daughter," Maggie refuses to jump off the "hot tin roof" of her situation until her will has been effected, she and Brick are reconciled, and "Big Daddy's Dream Come True" of a grandchild from their union is assured. Her final assertion of love and life in the face of hypocrisy and death is something not even Brick contradicts, suggesting ambivalent interpretive possibilities.

Tennessee Williams best summarizes the realistic ambivalence throughout *Cat on a Hot Tin Roof* in the conclusion to his interpretive note previously quoted (see Act 2, p. 659):

> Some mystery should be left in the revelation of character in a play, just as a great deal of mystery is always left in the revelation of character in life, even in one's own character to himself. This does not absolve the playwright of his duty to observe and probe as clearly and deeply as he *legitimately* can: but it should steer him away from "pat" conclusions, facile definitions which make a play just a play, not a snare for the truth of human experience.

CAT ON A HOT TIN ROOF

CHARACTERS OF THE PLAY

MARGARET
BRICK
MAE, sometimes called Sister Woman
BIG MAMA
DIXIE, a little girl
BIG DADDY
REVEREND TOOKER
GOOPER, sometimes called Brother Man
DOCTOR BAUGH, pronounced "Baw"
LACEY, a Negro servant
SOOKEY, another
CHILDREN

NOTES FOR THE DESIGNER

The set is the bed-sitting-room of a plantation home in the Mississippi Delta. It is along an upstairs gallery which probably runs around the entire house; it has two pairs of very wide doors opening onto the gallery, showing white balustrades against a fair summer sky that fades into dusk and night during the course of the play, which occupies precisely the time of its performance, excepting, of course, the fifteen minutes of intermission.

Perhaps the style of the room is not what you would expect in the home of the Delta's biggest cotton-planter. It is Victorian with a touch of the Far East. It hasn't changed much since it was occupied by the original owners of the place, Jack Straw and Peter Ochello, a pair of old bachelors who shared this room all their lives together. In other words, the room must evoke some ghosts; it is gently and poetically haunted by a relationship that must have involved a tenderness which was uncommon. This may be irrelevant or unnecessary, but I once saw a reproduction of a faded photograph of the verandah of Robert Louis Stevenson's home on that Samoan Island where he spent his last years, and there was a quality of tender light on weathered wood, such as porch furniture made of bamboo and wicker, exposed to tropical suns and tropical rains, which came to mind when I thought about the set for this play, bringing also to mind the grace and comfort of light, the reassurance it gives, on a late and fair afternoon in summer, the way that no matter what, even dread of death, is gently touched and soothed by it. For the set is the background for a play that deals with human extremities of emotion, and it needs that softness behind it.

The bathroom door, showing only pale-blue tile and silver towel racks, is in one side wall; the hall door in the opposite wall. Two articles of furniture need mention: a big double bed which staging should make a functional part of the set as often as suitable, the surface of which should be slightly raked to make figures on it seen more easily; and against the wall space between the two huge double doors upstage: a monumental monstrosity peculiar to our times, a *huge* console combination of radio-phonograph (hi-fi with three speakers) TV set *and* liquor cabinet, bearing and containing many glasses and bottles, all in one piece, which is a composition of muted silver tones, and the opalescent tones of reflecting glass, a chromatic link, this thing, between the sepia (tawny gold) tones of the interior and the cool (white and blue) tones of the gallery and sky. This piece of furniture (?!), this monument, is a very complete and compact little shrine to virtually all the comforts and illusions behind which we hide from such things as the characters in the play are faced with....

The set should be far less realistic than I have so far implied in this description of it. I think the walls below the ceiling should dissolve mysteriously into air; the set should be roofed by the sky; stars and moon suggested by traces of milky pallor, as if they were observed through a telescope lens out of focus.

Anything else I can think of? Oh, yes, fanlights (transoms shaped like an open glass fan) above all the doors in the set, with panes of blue and amber, and above all, the designer should take as many pains to give the actors room to move about freely (to show their restlessness, their passion for breaking out) as if it were a set for a ballet.

An evening in summer. The action is continuous, with two intermissions.

ACT ONE

At the rise of the curtain someone is taking a shower in the bathroom, the door of which is half open. A pretty young woman, with anxious lines in her face, enters the bedroom and crosses to the bathroom door.

MARGARET: (*shouting above roar of water*) One of those no-neck monsters hit me with a hot buttered biscuit so I have t' change!

(MARGARET'S *voice is both rapid and drawling. In her long speeches she has the vocal tricks of a priest delivering a liturgical chant, the lines are almost sung, always continuing a little beyond her breath so she has to gasp for another. Sometimes she intersperses the lines with a little wordless singing, such as "Da-da-daaaa!"*)

(*Water turns off and* BRICK *calls out to her, but is still unseen. A tone of politely feigned interest, masking indifference, or worse, is characteristic of his speech with* MARGARET.)

BRICK: Wha'd you say, Maggie? Water was on s' loud I couldn't hearya....

MARGARET: Well, I! — just remarked that! — one of th' no-neck monsters messed up m' lovely lace dress so I got t'— cha-a-ange....

(*She opens and kicks shut drawers of the dresser.*)

BRICK: Why d'ya call Gooper's kiddies no-neck monsters?

MARGARET: Because they've got no necks! Isn't that a good enough reason?

BRICK: Don't they have any necks?

MARGARET: None visible. Their fat little heads are set on their fat little bodies without a bit of connection.

BRICK: That's too bad.

MARGARET: Yes, it's too bad because you can't wring their necks if they've got no necks to wring! Isn't that right, honey?

(*She steps out of her dress, stands in a slip of ivory satin and lace.*)

Yep, they're no-neck monsters, all no-neck people are monsters....

(*Children shriek downstairs.*)

Hear them? Hear them screaming? I don't know where their voice boxes are located since they don't have necks. I tell you I got so nervous at that table tonight I thought I would throw back my head and utter a scream you could hear across the Arkansas border an' parts of Louisiana an' Tennessee. I said to your charming sister-in-law, Mae, honey, couldn't you feed those precious little things at a separate table with an oilcloth cover? They make such a mess an' the lace cloth looks *so* pretty! She made enormous eyes at me and said, "Ohhh, noooooo! On Big Daddy's birthday? Why, he would never forgive me!" Well, I want you to know, Big Daddy hadn't been at the table two minutes with those five no-neck monsters slobbering and drooling over their food before he threw down his fork an' shouted, "Fo' God's sake, Gooper, why don't you put them pigs at a trough in th' kitchen?" — Well, I swear, I simply could have di-ieed!

Think of it, Brick, they've got five of them and number six is coming. They've brought the whole bunch down here like animals to display at a county fair. Why, they have those children doin' tricks all the time! "Junior, show Big Daddy how you do this, show Big Daddy how you do that, say your little piece fo' Big Daddy, Sister. Show your dimples, Sugar. Brother, show Big Daddy how you stand on your head!" — It goes on all the time, along with constant little remarks and innuendos about the fact that you and I have not produced any children, are totally childless and therefore totally useless! — Of course it's comical but it's also disgusting since it's so obvious what they're up to!

BRICK: (*without interest*) What are they up to, Maggie?

MARGARET: Why, you know what they're up to!

BRICK: (*appearing*) No, I don't know what they're up to.

(*He stands there in the bathroom doorway drying his hair with a towel and hanging onto the towel rack because one ankle is broken, plastered and bound. He is still slim and firm as a boy. His liquor hasn't started tearing him down outside. He has the additional charm of that cool air of detachment that people have who have given up the struggle. But now and then, when disturbed, something flashes behind it, like lightning in a fair sky, which shows that at some deeper level he is far from peaceful. Perhaps in a stronger light he would show some signs of deliquescence, but the fading, still warm, light from the gallery treats him gently.*)

MARGARET: I'll tell you what they're up to, boy of mine! — They're up to cutting you out of your father's estate, and —

(*She freezes momentarily before her next remark. Her voice drops as if it were somehow a personally embarrassing admission.*)

— Now we know that Big Daddy's dyin' of — *cancer*. . . .

(*There are voices on the lawn below: long-drawn calls across distance.*
MARGARET *raises her lovely bare arms and powders her armpits with a*
light sigh.)

(*She adjusts the angle of a magnifying mirror to straighten an eyelash, then*
rises fretfully saying:)

There's so much light in the room it —
BRICK: (*softly but sharply*) Do we?
MARGARET: Do we what?
BRICK: Know Big Daddy's dyin' of cancer?
MARGARET: Got the report today.
BRICK: Oh . . .
MARGARET: (*letting down bamboo blinds which cast long, gold-fretted shadows over*
50   *the room*) Yep, got th' report just now . . . it didn't surprise me, Baby. . . .

(*Her voice has range, and music; sometimes it drops low as a boy's and you*
have a sudden image of her playing boys' games as a child.)

I recognized the symptoms soon's we got here last spring and I'm willin' to bet
you that Brother Man and his wife were pretty sure of it, too. That more than
likely explains why their usual summer migration to the coolness of the
Great Smokies was passed up this summer in favor of — hustlin' down here
ev'ry whipstitch with their whole screamin' tribe! And why so many allusions
have been made to Rainbow Hill lately. You know what Rainbow Hill is?
Place that's famous for treatin' alcoholics an' dope fiends in the movies!
BRICK: I'm not in the movies.
MARGARET: No, and you don't take dope. Otherwise you're a perfect candidate
60   for Rainbow Hill, Baby, and that's where they aim to ship you — over my dead
body! Yep, over my dead body they'll ship you there, but nothing would
please them better. Then Brother Man could get a-hold of the purse strings
and dole out remittances to us, maybe get power of attorney and sign checks
for us and cut off our credit wherever, whenever he wanted! Son-of-
a-bitch! — How'd you like that, Baby? — Well, you've been doin' just about
ev'rything in your power to bring it about, you've just been doin' ev'rything
you can think of to aid and abet them in this scheme of theirs! Quittin'
work, devoting yourself to the occupation of drinkin'! — Breakin' your ankle
last night on the high school athletic field: doin' what? Jumpin' hurdles?
70   At two or three in the morning? Just fantastic! Got in the paper. *Clarksdale*
Register carried a nice little item about it, human interest story about a
well-known former athlete stagin' a one-man track meet on the Glorious Hill
High School athletic field last night, but was slightly out of condition and
didn't clear the first hurdle! Brother Man Gooper claims he exercised his
influence t' keep it from goin' out over AP or UP or every goddam "P."
    But Brick? You still have one big advantage!

(*During the above swift flood of words,* BRICK *has reclined with contrapuntal*
leisure on the snowy surface of the bed and has rolled over carefully on his side
or belly.)

BRICK: *(wryly)* Did you *say* something, Maggie?

MARGARET: Big Daddy dotes on you, honey. And he can't stand Brother Man and Brother Man's wife, that monster of fertility, Mae. Know how I know? By little expressions that flicker over his face when that woman is holding fo'th on one of her choice topics such as — how she refused twilight sleep! — when the twins were delivered! Because she feels motherhood's an experience that a woman ought to experience fully! — in order to fully appreciate the wonder and beauty of it! HAH! — and how she made Brother Man come in an' stand beside her in the delivery room so he would not miss out on the "wonder and beauty" of it either! — producin' those no-neck monsters. . . .

(A speech of this kind would be antipathetic from almost anybody but MARGARET; she makes it oddly funny, because her eyes constantly twinkle and her voice shakes with laughter which is basically indulgent.)

— Big Daddy shares my attitude toward those two! As for me, well — I give him a laugh now and then and he tolerates me. In fact! — I sometimes suspect that Big Daddy harbors a little unconscious "lech" fo' me. . . .

BRICK: What makes you think that Big Daddy has a lech for you, Maggie?

MARGARET: Way he always drops his eyes down my body when I'm talkin' to him, drops his eyes to my boobs an' licks his old chops! Ha ha!

BRICK: That kind of talk is disgusting.

MARGARET: Did anyone ever tell you that you're an ass-aching Puritan, Brick?

I think it's mighty fine that that ole fellow, on the doorstep of death, still takes in my shape with what I think is deserved appreciation!

And you wanta know something else? Big Daddy didn't know how many little Maes and Goopers had been produced! "How many kids have you got?" he asked at the table, just like Brother Man and his wife were new acquaintances to him! Big Mama said he was jokin', but that ole boy wasn't jokin', Lord no!

And when they infawmed him that they had five already and were turning out number six! — the news seemed to come as a sort of unpleasant surprise . . .

(Children yell below.)

Scream, monsters!

(Turns to BRICK with a sudden, gay, charming smile which fades as she notices that he is not looking at her but into fading gold space with a troubled expression.)

(It is constant rejection that makes her humor "bitchy.")

Yes, you should of been at that supper-table, Baby.

(Whenever she calls him "baby" the word is a soft caress.)

Y'know, Big Daddy, bless his ole sweet soul, he's the dearest ole thing in the world, but he does hunch over his food as if he preferred not to notice anything else. Well, Mae an' Gooper were side by side at the table, direckly across from Big Daddy, watchin' his face like hawks while they jawed an' jabbered about the cuteness an' brillance of th' no-neck monsters!

(She giggles with a hand fluttering at her throat and her breast and her long throat arched.)

(She comes downstage and recreates the scene with voice and gesture.)

And the no-neck monsters were ranged around the table, some in high chairs and some on th' *Books of Knowledge*, all in fancy little paper caps in honor of Big Daddy's birthday, and all through dinner, well, I want you to know that Brother Man an' his partner never once, for one moment, stopped exchanging pokes an' pinches an' kicks an' signs an' signals! — Why, they were like a couple of cardsharps fleecing a sucker. — Even Big Mama, bless her ole sweet soul, she isn't th' quickest an' brightest thing in the world, she finally noticed, at last, an' said to Gooper, "Gooper, what are you an' Mae makin' all these signs at each other about?" — I swear t' goodness, I nearly choked on my chicken!

(MARGARET, back at the dressing table, still doesn't see BRICK. He is watching her with a look that is not quite definable — Amused? shocked? contemptuous? — part of those and part of something else.)

Y'know — your brother Gooper still cherishes the illusion he took a giant step up on the social ladder when he married Miss Mae Flynn of the Memphis Flynns.

But I have a piece of Spanish news for Gooper. The Flynns never had a thing in this world but money and they lost that, they were nothing at all but fairly successful climbers. Of course, Mae Flynn came out in Memphis eight years before I made my debut in Nashville, but I had friends at Ward-Belmont who came from Memphis and they used to come to see me and I used to go to see them for Christmas and spring vacations, and so I know who rates an' who doesn't rate in Memphis society. Why, y'know ole Papa Flynn, he barely escaped doing time in the Federal pen for shady manipulations on th' stock market when his chain stores crashed, and as for Mae having been a cotton carnival queen, as they remind us so often, lest we forget, well, that's one honor that I don't envy her for! — Sit on a brass throne on a tacky float an' ride down Main Street, smilin', bowin', and blowin' kisses to all the trash on the street —

(She picks out a pair of jeweled sandals and rushes to the dressing table.)

Why, year before last, when Susan McPheeters was singled out fo' that honor, y' know what happened to her? Y'know what happened to poor little Susie McPheeters?

BRICK: *(absently)* No. What happened to little Susie McPheeters?

MARGARET: Somebody spit tobacco juice in her face.

BRICK: *(dreamily)* Somebody spit tobacco juice in her face?

MARGARET: That's right, some old drunk leaned out of a window in the Hotel Gayoso and yelled, "Hey, Queen, hey, hey, there, Queenie!" Poor Susie looked up and flashed him a radiant smile and he shot out a squirt of tobacco juice right in poor Susie's face.

BRICK: Well, what d'you know about that.

MARGARET: *(gaily)* What do I know about it? I was there, I saw it!

BRICK: *(absently)* Must have been kind of funny.

MARGARET: Susie didn't think so. Had hysterics. Screamed like a banshee. They had to stop th' parade an' remove her from her throne an' go on with —

(She catches sight of him in the mirror, gasps slightly, wheels about to face him. Count ten.)

— Why are you looking at me like that?

BRICK: *(whistling softly, now)* Like what, Maggie?

MARGARET: *(intensely, fearfully)* The way y' were lookin' at me just now, befo' I caught your eye in the mirror and you started t' whistle! I don't know how t' describe it but it froze my blood! — I've caught you lookin' at me like that so often lately. What are you thinkin' of when you look at me like that?

BRICK: I wasn't conscious of lookin' at you, Maggie.

MARGARET: Well, I was conscious of it! What were you thinkin'?

BRICK: I don't remember thinking of anything, Maggie.

MARGARET: Don't you think I know that — ? Don't you — ? — Think I know that — ?

BRICK: *(coolly)* Know *what*, Maggie?

MARGARET: *(struggling for expression)* That I've gone through this — *hideous!* — *transformation*, become — *hard! Frantic!*

(Then she adds, almost tenderly:)

— *cruel!!*

That's what you've been observing in me lately. How could y' help but observe it? That's all right. I'm not — thin-skinned any more, can't afford t' be thin-skinned any more.

(She is now recovering her power.)

— But Brick? Brick?

BRICK: Did you say something?

MARGARET: I was *goin'* t' say something: that I get — lonely. Very!

BRICK: Ev'rybody gets that...

MARGARET: Living with someone you love can be lonelier — than living entirely *alone!* — if the one that y' love doesn't love you....

(There is a pause. BRICK hobbles downstage and asks, without looking at her:)

BRICK: Would you like to live alone, Maggie?

(Another pause: then — after she has caught a quick, hurt breath:)

MARGARET: *No! — God! — I wouldn't!*

(Another gasping breath. She forcibly controls what must have been an impulse to cry out. We see her deliberately, very forcibly, going all the way back to the world in which you can talk about ordinary matters.)

Did you have a nice shower?

BRICK: Uh-huh.

MARGARET: Was the water cool?

BRICK: No.

MARGARET: But it made y' feel fresh, huh?

BRICK: Fresher. . . .

MARGARET: I know something would make y' feel *much fresher!*

BRICK: What?

MARGARET: An alcohol rub. Or cologne, a rub with cologne!

BRICK: That's good after a workout but I haven't been workin' out, Maggie.

MARGARET: You've kept in good shape, though.

190   BRICK: (*indifferently*) You think so, Maggie?

MARGARET: I always thought drinkin' men lost their looks, but I was plainly
mistaken.

BRICK: (*wryly*) Why, thanks, Maggie.

MARGARET: You're the only drinkin' man I know that it never seems t' put fat on.

BRICK: I'm gettin' softer, Maggie.

MARGARET: Well, sooner or later it's bound to soften you up. It was just beginning to soften up Skipper when —

(*She stops short.*)

I'm sorry. I never could keep my fingers off a sore — I wish you *would* lose your
looks. If you did it would make the martyrdom of Saint Maggie a little more
200   bearable. But no such goddam luck. I actually believe you've gotten better
looking since you've gone on the bottle. Yeah, a person who didn't know you
would think you'd never had a tense nerve in your body or a strained muscle.

(*There are sounds of croquet on the lawn below: the click of mallets, light
voices, near and distant.*)

Of course, you always had that detached quality as if you were playing a
game without much concern over whether you won or lost, and now that
you've lost the game, not lost but just quit playing, you have that rare sort
of charm that usually only happens in very old or hopelessly sick people,
the charm of the defeated. — You look so cool, so cool, so enviably cool.

REVEREND TOOKER: (*off stage right*) Now looka here, boy, lemme show you how
to get outa that!

210   MARGARET: They're playing croquet. The moon has appeared and it's white, just
beginning to turn a little bit yellow. . . .
    You were a wonderful lover. . . .
    Such a wonderful person to go to bed with, and I think mostly because
you were really indifferent to it. Isn't that right? Never had any anxiety
about it, did it naturally, easily, slowly, with absolute confidence and perfect
calm, more like opening a door for a lady or seating her at a table than
giving expression to any longing for her. Your indifference made you wonderful at lovemaking — *strange?* — but true. . . .

REVEREND TOOKER: Oh! That's a beauty.

220   DOCTOR BAUGH: Yeah. I got you boxed.

MARGARET: You know, if I thought you would never, never, *never* make love to
me again — I would go downstairs to the kitchen and pick out the longest
and sharpest knife I could find and stick it straight into my heart, I swear
that I would!

REVEREND TOOKER: Watch out, you're gonna miss it.

DOCTOR BAUGH: You just don't know me, boy!

MARGARET: But one thing I don't have is the charm of the defeated, my hat is still in the ring, and I am determined to win!

(*There is the sound of croquet mallets hitting croquet balls.*)

REVEREND TOOKER: Mmm — You're too slippery for me.

230 MARGARET: — What is the victory of a cat on a hot tin roof? — I wish I knew. . . . Just staying on it, I guess, as long as she can. . . .

DOCTOR BAUGH: Jus' like an eel, boy, jus' like an eel!

(*More croquet sounds.*)

MARGARET: Later tonight I'm going to tell you I love you an' maybe by that time you'll be drunk enough to believe me. Yes, they're playing croquet . . . Big Daddy is dying of cancer. . . .
What were you thinking of when I caught you looking at me like that? Were you thinking of Skipper?

(BRICK *takes up his crutch, rises.*)

Oh, excuse me, forgive me, but laws of silence don't work! No, laws of silence don't work. . . .

(BRICK *crosses to the bar, takes a quick drink, and rubs his head with a towel.*)

240 Laws of silence don't work. . . .
When something is festering in your memory or your imagination, laws of silence don't work, it's just like shutting a door and locking it on a house on fire in hope of forgetting that the house is burning. But not facing a fire doesn't put it out. Silence about a thing just magnifies it. It grows and festers in silence, becomes malignant. . . .

(*He drops his crutch.*)

BRICK: Give me my crutch.

(*He has stopped rubbing his hair dry but still stands hanging onto the towel rack in a white towel-cloth robe.*)

MARGARET: Lean on me.

BRICK: No, just give me my crutch.

MARGARET: Lean on my shoulder.

250 BRICK: *I don't want to lean on your shoulder, I want my crutch!*

(*This is spoken like sudden lightning.*)

Are you going to give me my crutch or do I have to get down on my knees on the floor and —

MARGARET: *Here, here, take it, take it!*

(*She has thrust the crutch at him.*)

BRICK: (*hobbling out*) Thanks . . .

MARGARET: We mustn't scream at each other, the walls in this house have ears. . . .

(He hobbles directly to liquor cabinet to get a new drink.)

— but that's the first time I've heard you raise your voice in a long time, Brick. A crack in the wall?— Of composure?

— I think that's a good sign. . . .

A sign of nerves in a player on the defensive!

(BRICK turns and smiles at her coolly over his fresh drink.)

BRICK: It just hasn't happened yet, Maggie.

MARGARET: What?

BRICK: The click I get in my head when I've had enough of this stuff to make me peaceful. . . .

Will you do me a favor?

MARGARET: Maybe I will. What favor?

BRICK: Just, just keep your voice down!

MARGARET: *(in a hoarse whisper)* I'll do you that favor, I'll speak in a whisper, if not shut up completely, if *you* will do *me* a favor and make that drink your last one till after the party.

BRICK: What party?

MARGARET: Big Daddy's birthday party.

BRICK: Is this Big Daddy's birthday?

MARGARET: You know this is Big Daddy's birthday!

BRICK: No, I don't, I forgot it.

MARGARET: Well, I remembered it for you. . . .

(They are both speaking as breathlessly as a pair of kids after a fight, drawing deep exhausted breaths and looking at each other with faraway eyes, shaking and panting together as if they had broken apart from a violent struggle.)

BRICK: Good for you, Maggie.

MARGARET: You just have to scribble a few lines on this card.

BRICK: You scribble something, Maggie.

MARGARET: It's got to be your handwriting; it's your present, I've given him my present; it's got to be your handwriting!

(The tension between them is building again, the voices becoming shrill once more.)

BRICK: I didn't get him a present.

MARGARET: I got one for you.

BRICK: All right. You write the card, then.

MARGARET: And have him know you didn't remember his birthday?

BRICK: I didn't remember his birthday.

MARGARET: You don't have to prove you didn't!

BRICK: I don't want to fool him about it.

MARGARET: Just write "Love, Brick!" for God's —

BRICK: No.

MARGARET: You've *got* to!

BRICK: I don't have to do anything I don't want to do. You keep forgetting the conditions on which I agreed to stay on living with you.

MARGARET: (*out before she knows it*) I'm not living with you. We occupy the same cage.

BRICK: You've got to remember the conditions agreed on.

SONNY: (*off stage*) Mommy, give it to me. I had it first.

MAE: Hush.

MARGARET: They're impossible conditions!

300 BRICK: Then why don't you — ?

SONNY: I want it, I want it!

MAE: Get away!

MARGARET: HUSH! Who is out there? Is somebody at the door?

(*There are footsteps in hall.*)

MAE: (*outside*) May I enter a moment?

MARGARET: Oh, *you!* Sure. Come in, Mae.

(MAE *enters bearing aloft the bow of a young lady's archery set.*)

MAE: Brick, is this thing yours?

MARGARET: Why, Sister Woman — that's my Diana Trophy. Won it at the intercollegiate archery contest on the Ole Miss[1] campus.

MAE: It's a mighty dangerous thing to leave exposed round a house full of
310 nawmal rid-blooded children attracted t'weapons.

MARGARET: "Nawmal rid-blooded children attracted t'weapons" ought t'be taught to keep their hands off things that don't belong to them.

MAE: Maggie, honey, if you had children of your own you'd know how funny that is. Will you please lock this up and put the key out of reach?

MARGARET: Sister Woman, nobody is plotting the destruction of your kiddies. — Brick and I still have our special archers' license. We're goin' deer-huntin' on Moon Lake as soon as the season starts. I love to run with dogs through chilly woods, run, run leap over obstructions —

(*She goes into the closet carrying the bow.*)

MAE: How's the injured ankle, Brick?

320 BRICK: Doesn't hurt. Just itches.

MAE: Oh, my! Brick — Brick, you should've been downstairs after supper! Kiddies put on a show. Polly played the piano, Buster an' Sonny drums, an' then they turned out the lights an' Dixie an' Trixie puhfawmed a toe dance in fairy costume with *spahkluhs!* Big Daddy just beamed! He just beamed!

MARGARET: (*from the closet with a sharp laugh*) Oh, I bet. It breaks my heart that we missed it!

(*She reenters.*)

But Mae? Why did y'give dawgs' names to all your kiddies?

MAE: *Dogs'* names?

1 University of Mississippi.

330 MARGARET: (*sweetly*) Dixie, Trixie, Buster, Sonny, Polly! — Sounds like four dogs and a parrot...

MAE: Maggie?

(MARGARET *turns with a smile.*)

Why are you so catty?

MARGARET: Cause I'm a cat! But why can't *you* take a joke, Sister Woman?

MAE: Nothin' pleases me more than a joke that's funny. You know the real names of our kiddies. Buster's real name is Robert. Sonny's real name is Saunders. Trixie's real name is Marlene and Dixie's —

(GOOPER *downstairs calls for her.* "Hey, Mae! Sister Woman, intermission is over!"*— She rushes to door, saying:*)

Intermission is over! See ya later!

MARGARET: I wonder what Dixie's real name is?

340 BRICK: Maggie, being catty doesn't help things any...

MARGARET: I know! *WHY!*— Am I so catty?— Cause I'm consumed with envy an' eaten up with longing?— Brick, I'm going to lay out your beautiful Shantung silk suit from Rome and one of your monogrammed silk shirts. I'll put your cuff links in it, those lovely star sapphires I get you to wear so rarely....

BRICK: I can't get trousers on over this plaster cast.

MARGARET: Yes, you can, I'll help you.

BRICK: I'm not going to get dressed, Maggie.

MARGARET: Will you just put on a pair of white silk pajamas?

350 BRICK: Yes, I'll do that, Maggie.

MARGARET: *Thank* you, thank you so *much!*

BRICK: Don't mention it.

MARGARET: *Oh, Brick!* How long does it have t' go on? This punishment? Haven't I done time enough, haven't I served my term, can't I apply for a — pardon?

BRICK: Maggie, you're spoiling my liquor. Lately your voice always sounds like you'd been running upstairs to warn somebody that the house was on fire!

MARGARET: Well, no wonder, no wonder. Y'know what I feel like, Brick? *I feel all the time like a cat on a hot tin roof!*

BRICK: Then jump off the roof, jump off it, cats can jump off roofs and land on 360 their four feet uninjured!

MARGARET: Oh, yes!

BRICK: Do it! — fo' God's sake, do it...

MARGARET: Do what?

BRICK: Take a lover!

MARGARET: I can't see a man but you! Even with my eyes closed, I just see you! Why don't you get ugly, Brick, why don't you please get fat or ugly or something so I could stand it?

(*She rushes to hall door, opens it, listens.*)

The concert is still going on! Bravo, no-necks, bravo!

(*She slams and locks door fiercely.*)

BRICK: What did you lock the door for?

370 MARGARET: To give us a little privacy for a while.

BRICK: You know better, Maggie.

MARGARET: No, I don't know better . . . .

(She rushes to gallery doors, draws the rose-silk drapes across them.)

BRICK: Don't make a fool of yourself.

MARGARET: I don't mind makin' a fool of myself over you!

BRICK: I mind, Maggie. I feel embarrassed for you.

MARGARET: Feel embarrassed! But don't continue my torture. I can't live on and on under these circumstances.

BRICK: You agreed to —

MARGARET: I know but —

380 BRICK: — Accept that condition!

MARGARET: *I CAN'T! CAN'T! CAN'T!*

(She seizes his shoulder.)

BRICK: Let go!

(He breaks away from her and seizes the small boudoir chair and raises it like a lion-tamer facing a big circus cat.)

(Count five. She stares at him with her fist pressed to her mouth, then bursts into shrill, almost hysterical laughter. He remains grave for a moment, then grins and puts the chair down.)

(BIG MAMA calls through closed door.)

BIG MAMA: Son? Son? Son?

BRICK: What is it, Big Mama?

BIG MAMA: *(outside)* Oh, son! We got the most wonderful news about Big Daddy. I just had t' run up an' tell you right this —

(She rattles the knob.)

— What's this door doin', locked, faw? You all think there's robbers in the house?

MARGARET: Big Mama, Brick is dressin', he's not dressed yet.

390 BIG MAMA: That's all right, it won't be the first time I've seen Brick not dressed. Come on, open this door!

(MARGARET, with a grimace, goes to unlock and open the hall door, as BRICK hobbles rapidly to the bathroom and kicks the door shut. BIG MAMA has disappeared from the hall.)

MARGARET: Big Mama?

(BIG MAMA appears through the opposite gallery doors behind MARGARET, huffing and puffing like an old bulldog. She is a short, stout woman; her sixty years and 170 pounds have left her somewhat breathless most of the time; she's always tensed like a boxer, or rather, a Japanese wrestler. Her "family" was maybe a little superior to BIG DADDY's, but not much. She wears a black

or silver lace dress and at least half a million in flashy gems. She is very sincere.)

BIG MAMA: *(loudly, startling* MARGARET*)* Here — I come through Gooper's and Mae's gall'ry door. Where's Brick? *Brick* — Hurry on out of there, son, I just have a second and want to give you the news about Big Daddy. — I hate locked doors in a house. . . .

MARGARET: *(with affected lightness)* I've noticed you do, Big Mama, but people have got to have *some* moments of privacy, don't they?

BIG MAMA: No, ma'am, not in *my* house. *(without pause)* Whacha took off you' dress faw? I thought that little lace dress was so sweet on yuh, honey.

MARGARET: I thought it looked sweet on me, too, but one of m' cute little table-partners used it for a napkin so — !

BIG MAMA: *(picking up stockings on floor)* What?

MARGARET: You know, Big Mama, Mae and Gooper's so touchy about those children — thanks, Big Mama . . .

(BIG MAMA *has thrust the picked-up stockings in* MARGARET*'s hand with a grunt.)*

— that you just don't dare to suggest there's any room for improvement in their —

BIG MAMA: Brick, hurry out! — Shoot, Maggie, you just don't like children.

MARGARET: I do SO like children! Adore them! — well brought up!

BIG MAMA: *(gentle — loving)* Well, why don't you have some and bring them up well, then, instead of all the time pickin' on Gooper's an' Mae's?

GOOPER: *(shouting up the stairs)* Hey, hey, Big Mama, Betsy an' Hugh got to go, waitin' t' tell yuh g'by!

BIG MAMA: Tell 'em to hold their hawses, I'll be right down in a jiffy!

GOOPER: Yes ma'am!

(She turns to the bathroom door and calls out.)

BIG MAMA: Son? Can you hear me in there?

(There is a muffled answer.)

We just got the full report from the laboratory at the Ochsner Clinic, completely negative, son, ev'rything negative, right on down the line! Nothin' a-tall's wrong with him but some little functional thing called a spastic colon. Can you hear me, son?

MARGARET: He can hear you, Big Mama.

BIG MAMA: Then why don't he say something? God Almighty, a piece of news like that should make him shout. It made *me* shout, I can tell you. I shouted and sobbed and fell right down on my knees! — Look!

(She pulls up her skirt.)

See the bruises where I hit my kneecaps? Took both doctors to haul me back on my feet!

(She laughs — she always laughs like hell at herself.)

Big Daddy was furious with me! But ain't that wonderful news?

(*Facing bathroom again, she continues:*)

After all the anxiety we been through to git a report like that on Big Daddy's birthday? Big Daddy tried to hide how much of a load that news took off his mind, but didn't fool *me*. He was mighty close to crying about it *himself!*

(*Goodbyes are shouted downstairs, and she rushes to door.*)

GOOPER: Big Mama!
BIG MAMA: *Hold those people down there, don't let them go!*— Now, git dressed, we're all comin' up to this room fo' Big Daddy's birthday party because of your ankle.— How's his ankle, Maggie?
MARGARET: Well, he broke it, Big Mama.
BIG MAMA: I know he broke it.

(*A phone is ringing in hall. A Negro voice answers: "Mistuh Polly's res'dence."*)

I mean does it hurt him much still.
MARGARET: I'm afraid I can't give you that information, Big Mama. You'll have to ask Brick if it hurts much still or not.
SOOKEY: (*in the hall*) It's Memphis, Mizz Polly, it's Miss Sally in Memphis.
BIG MAMA: Awright, Sookey.

(BIG MAMA *rushes into the hall and is heard shouting on the phone:*)

Hello, Miss Sally. How are you, Miss Sally?— Yes, well, I was just gonna call you about it. *Shoot!* —
MARGARET: Brick, don't!

(BIG MAMA *raises her voice to a bellow.*)

BIG MAMA: *Miss Sally? Don't ever call me from the Gayoso Lobby, too much talk goes on in that hotel lobby, no wonder you can't hear me!* Now listen, Miss Sally. They's nothin' serious wrong with Big Daddy. We got the report just now, they's nothin' wrong but a thing called a — spastic! *SPASTIC!* — colon...

(*She appears at the hall door and calls to* MARGARET.)

— Maggie, come out here and talk to that fool on the phone. I'm shouted breathless!
MARGARET: (*goes out and is heard sweetly at phone*) Miss Sally? This is Brick's wife, Maggie. So nice to hear your voice. Can you hear *mine?* Well, good! — Big Mama just wanted you to know that they've got the report from the Ochsner Clinic and what Big Daddy has is a spastic colon. Yes. Spastic colon, Miss Sally. That's right, spastic colon. G'bye, Miss Sally, hope *I'll see you real soon!*

(*Hangs up a little before Miss Sally was probably ready to terminate the talk. She returns through the hall door.*)

She heard me perfectly. I've discovered with deaf people the thing to do is
460 not shout at them but just enunciate clearly. My rich old Aunt Cornelia was
deaf as the dead but I could make her hear me just by sayin' each word
slowly, distinctly, close to her ear. I read her the *Commercial Appeal* ev'ry
night, read her the classified ads in it, even, she never missed a word of it.
But was she a mean ole thing! Know what I got when she died? Her unex-
pired subscriptions to five magazines and the Book-of-the-Month Club and
a LIBRARY full of ev'ry dull book ever written! All else went to her hellcat
of a sister... meaner than she was, even!

(BIG MAMA *has been straightening things up in the room during this speech.*)

BIG MAMA: (*closing closet door on discarded clothes*) Miss Sally sure is a case! Big
Daddy says she's always got her hand out fo' something. He's not mis-
470 taken. That poor ole thing always has her hand out fo' somethin'. I don't
think Big Daddy gives her as much as he should.
GOOPER: Big Mama! Come on now! Betsy and Hugh can't wait no longer!
BIG MAMA: (*shouting*) I'm comin'!

(*She starts out. At the hall door, turns and jerks a forefinger, first toward the
bathroom door, then toward the liquor cabinet, meaning: "Has Brick been
drinking?"* MARGARET *pretends not to understand, cocks her head and raises
her brows as if the pantomimic performance was completely mystifying to her.*)

(BIG MAMA *rushes back to* MARGARET:)

Shoot! Stop playin' so dumb! — I mean has he been drinkin' that stuff much
yet?
MARGARET: (*with a little laugh*) Oh! I think he had a highball after supper.
BIG MAMA: Don't laugh about it! — Some single men stop drinkin' when they
git married and others start! Brick never touched liquor before he — !
MARGARET: (*crying out*) *THAT'S NOT FAIR!*
480 BIG MAMA: Fair or not fair I want to ask you a question, one question: D'you
make Brick happy in bed?
MARGARET: Why don't you ask if he makes *me* happy in bed?
BIG MAMA: Because I know that —
MARGARET: *It works both ways!*
BIG MAMA: Something's not right! You're childless and my son drinks!
GOOPER: Come on, Big Mama!

(GOOPER *has called her downstairs and she has rushed to the door on the line
above. She turns at the door and points at the bed.*)

— When a marriage goes on the rocks, the rocks are *there*, right *there!*
MARGARET: *That's* —

(BIG MAMA *has swept out of the room and slammed the door.*)

— not — *fair...*

(MARGARET *is alone, completely alone, and she feels it. She draws in,
hunches her shoulders, raises her arms with fists clenched, shuts her eyes tight*

as a child about to be stabbed with a vaccination needle. When she opens her eyes again, what she sees is the long oval mirror and she rushes straight to it, stares into it with a grimace and says: "Who are you?"— Then she crouches a little and answers herself in a different voice which is high, thin, mocking: "I am Maggie the Cat!"— Straightens quickly as bathroom door opens a little and BRICK *calls out to her.)*

490   BRICK: Has Big Mama gone?

MARGARET: She's gone.

(He opens the bathroom door and hobbles out, with his liquor glass now empty, straight to the liquor cabinet. He is whistling softly. MARGARET's *head pivots on her long, slender throat to watch him.)*

(She raises a hand uncertainly to the base of her throat, as if it was difficult for her to swallow, before she speaks:)

You know, our sex life didn't just peter out in the usual way, it was cut off short, long before the natural time for it to, and it's going to revive again, just as sudden as that. I'm confident of it. That's what I'm keeping myself attractive for. For the time when you'll see me again like other men see me. Yes, like other men see me. They still see me, Brick, and they like what they see. Uh-huh. Some of them would give their —

   Look, Brick!

(She stands before the long oval mirror, touches her breast and then her hips with her two hands.)

How high my body stays on me! — Nothing has fallen on me — not a fraction. . . .

(Her voice is soft and trembling: a pleading child's. At this moment as he turns to glance at her — a look which is like a player passing a ball to another player, third down and goal to go — she has to capture the audience in a grip so tight that she can hold it till the first intermission without any lapse of attention.)

500   Other men still want me. My face looks strained, sometimes, but I've kept my figure as well as you've kept yours, and men admire it. I still turn heads on the street. Why, last week in Memphis everywhere that I went men's eyes burned holes in my clothes, at the country club and in restaurants and department stores, there wasn't a man I met or walked by that didn't just eat me up with his eyes and turn around when I passed him and look back at me. Why, at Alice's party for her New York cousins, the best-lookin' man in the crowd — followed me upstairs and tried to force his way in the powder room with me, followed me to the door and tried to force his way in!

BRICK: Why didn't you let him, Maggie?

510   MARGARET: Because I'm not that common, for one thing. Not that I wasn't almost tempted to. You like to know who it was? It was Sonny Boy Maxwell, that's who!

BRICK: Oh, yeah, Sonny Boy Maxwell, he was a good end-runner but had a little injury to his back and had to quit.

MARGARET: He has no injury now and has no wife and still has a lech for me!

BRICK: I see no reason to lock him out of a powder room in that case.

MARGARET: And have someone catch me at it? I'm not that stupid. Oh, I might sometime cheat on you with someone, since you're so insultingly eager to have me do it! — But if I do, you can be damned sure it will be in a place and a time where no one but me and the man could possibly know. Because I'm not going to give you any excuse to divorce me for being unfaithful or anything else. . . .

BRICK: Maggie, I wouldn't divorce you for being unfaithful or anything else. Don't you know that? Hell. I'd be relieved to know that you'd found yourself a lover.

MARGARET: Well, I'm taking no chances. No, I'd rather stay on this hot tin roof.

BRICK: A hot tin roof's 'n uncomfo'table place t' stay on. . . .

(He starts to whistle softly.)

MARGARET: *(through his whistle)* Yeah, but I can stay on it just as long as I have to.

BRICK: You could leave me, Maggie.

(He resumes whistle. She wheels about to glare at him.)

MARGARET: *Don't want to and will not!* Besides if I did, you don't have a cent to pay for it but what you get from Big Daddy and he's dying of cancer!

(For the first time a realization of BIG DADDY'S *doom seems to penetrate to* BRICK'S *consciousness, visibly, and he looks at* MARGARET.*)*

BRICK: Big Mama just said he *wasn't*, that the report was okay.

MARGARET: That's what she thinks because she got the same story that they gave Big Daddy. And was just as taken in by it as he was, poor ole things. . . .

But tonight they're going to tell her the truth about it. When Big Daddy goes to bed, they're going to tell her that he is dying of cancer.

(She slams the dresser drawer.)

— It's malignant and it's terminal.

BRICK: Does Big Daddy know it?

MARGARET: Hell, do they *ever* know it? Nobody says, "You're dying." You have to fool them. They have to fool *themselves*.

BRICK: Why?

MARGARET: *Why?* Because human beings dream of life everlasting, that's the reason! But most of them want it on earth and not in heaven.

(He gives a short, hard laugh at her touch of humor.)

Well. . . . *(She touches up her mascara.)* That's how it is, anyhow. . . . *(She looks about.)* Where did I put down my cigarette? Don't want to burn up the home-place, at least not with Mae and Gooper and their five monsters in it!

(She has found it and sucks at it greedily. Blows out smoke and continues:)

So this is Big Daddy's last birthday. And Mae and Gooper, they know it, oh, *they* know it, all right. They got the first information from the Ochsner

550 Clinic. That's why they rushed down here with their no-neck monsters. Because. Do you know something? Big Daddy's made no will? Big Daddy's never made out any will in his life, and so this campaign's afoot to impress him, forcibly as possible, with the fact that you drink and I've borne no children!

(He continues to stare at her a moment, then mutters something sharp but not audible and hobbles rather rapidly out onto the long gallery in the fading, much faded, gold light.)

MARGARET: *(continuing her liturgical chant)* Y'know, I'm *fond* of Big Daddy, I am genuinely fond of that old man, I really *am*, you know....

BRICK: *(faintly, vaguely)* Yes, I know you are....

MARGARET: I've always sort of admired him in spite of his coarseness, his four-letter words and so forth. Because Big Daddy *is* what he *is*, and he makes no bones about it. He hasn't turned gentleman farmer, he's still a Mississippi redneck,
560 as much of a redneck as he must have been when he was just overseer here on the old Jack Straw and Peter Ochello place. But he got hold of it an' built it into th' biggest an' finest plantation in the Delta. — I've always *liked* Big Daddy....

(She crosses to the proscenium.)

Well, this is Big Daddy's last birthday. I'm sorry about it. But I'm facing the facts. It takes money to take care of a drinker and that's the office that I've been elected to lately.

BRICK: You don't have to take care of me.

MARGARET: Yes, I do. Two people in the same boat have got to take care of each other. At least you want money to buy more Echo Spring when this supply
570 is exhausted, or will you be satisfied with a ten-cent beer?

Mae an' Gooper are plannin' to freeze us out of Big Daddy's estate because you drink and I'm childless. But we can defeat that plan. We're *going* to defeat that plan!

Brick, y'know, I've been so God damn disgustingly poor all my life! — That's the *truth*, Brick!

BRICK: I'm not sayin' it isn't.

MARGARET: Always had to suck up to people I couldn't stand because they had money and I was poor as Job's turkey. You don't know what that's like. Well, I'll tell you, it's like you would feel a thousand miles away from Echo Spring! —
580 And had to get back to it on that broken ankle ... without a crutch!

That's how it feels to be as poor as Job's turkey and have to suck up to relatives that you hated because they had money and all you had was a bunch of hand-me-down clothes and a few old moldly three-per-cent government bonds. My daddy loved his liquor, he fell in love with his liquor the way you've fallen in love with Echo Spring! — And my poor Mama, having to maintain some semblance of social position, to keep appearances up, on an income of one hundred and fifty dollars a month on those old government bonds!

When I came out, the year that I made my debut, I had just two evening
590 dresses! One Mother made me from a pattern in *Vogue*, the other a hand-me-down from a snotty rich cousin I hated!

— The dress that I married you in was my grandmother's weddin' gown.... So that's why I'm like a cat on a hot tin roof!

(BRICK *is still on the gallery. Someone below calls up to him in a warm Negro voice,* "Hiya, Mistuh Brick, how yuh feelin'?" BRICK *raises his liquor glass as if that answered the question.*)

MARGARET: You can be young without money, but you can't be old without it. You've got to be old *with* money because to be old without it is just too awful, you've got to be one or the other, either *young* or *with money*, you can't be old and *without* it. — That's the *truth*, Brick....

(BRICK *whistles softly, vaguely.*)

Well, now I'm dressed, I'm all dressed, there's nothing else for me to do.

(*Forlornly, almost fearfully.*)

I'm dressed, all dressed, nothing else for me to do....

(*She moves about restlessly, aimlessly, and speaks, as if to herself.*)

600 What am I — ? Oh! — my bracelets....

(*She starts working a collection of bracelets over her hands onto her wrists, about six on each, as she talks.*)

I've thought a whole lot about it and now I know when I made my mistake. Yes, I made my mistake when I told you the truth about that thing with Skipper. Never should have confessed it, a fatal error, tellin' you about that thing with Skipper.

BRICK: Maggie, shut up about Skipper. I mean it, Maggie; you got to shut up about Skipper.

MARGARET: You ought to understand that Skipper and I —

BRICK: You don't think I'm serious, Maggie? You're fooled by the fact that I am saying this quiet? Look, Maggie. What you're doing is a dangerous thing to

610 do. You're — you're — you're — foolin' with something that — nobody ought to fool with.

MARGARET: This time I'm going to finish what I have to say to you. Skipper and I made love, if love you could call it, because it made both of us feel a little bit closer to you. You see, you son of a bitch, you asked too much of people, of me, of him, of all the unlucky poor damned sons of bitches that happen to love you, and there was a whole pack of them, yes, there was a pack of them besides me and Skipper, you asked too goddam much of people that loved you, you — superior creature! — you godlike being! —

And so we made love to each other to dream it was you, both of us! Yes,

620 yes, yes! Truth, truth! What's so awful about it? I like it, I think the truth is — yeah! I shouldn't have told you....

BRICK: (*holding his head unnaturally still and uptilted a bit*) It was Skipper that told me about it. Not you, Maggie.

MARGARET: I told you!

BRICK: After he told me!

MARGARET: What does it matter who — ?

DIXIE: I got your mallet, I got your mallet.

TRIXIE: Give it to me, give it to me. IT's mine.

(BRICK *turns suddenly out upon the gallery and calls:*)

BRICK: Little girl! Hey, little girl!

630 LITTLE GIRL: (*at a distance*) What, Uncle Brick?

BRICK: Tell the folks to come up! — Bring everybody upstairs!

TRIXIE: It's mine, it's mine.

MARGARET: I can't stop myself! I'd go on telling you this in front of them all, if I had to!

BRICK: Little girl! Go on, go on, will you? Do what I told you, call them!

DIXIE: Okay.

MARGARET: Because it's got to be told and you, you! — you never let me!

(*She sobs, then controls herself, and continues almost calmly.*)

It was one of those beautiful, ideal things they tell about in the Greek legends, it couldn't be anything else, you being you, and that's what made 640 it so sad, that's what made it so awful, because it was love that never could be carried through to anything satisfying or even talked about plainly.

BRICK: Maggie, you gotta stop this.

MARGARET: Brick, I tell you, you got to believe me, Brick, I *do* understand all about it! I — I think it was —*noble!* Can't you tell I'm sincere when I say I respect it? My only point, the only point that I'm making, is life has got to be allowed to continue even after the *dream* of life is — all — over. . . .

(BRICK *is without his crutch. Leaning on furniture, he crosses to pick it up as she continues as if possessed by a will outside herself:*)

Why I remember when we double-dated at college, Gladys Fitzgerald and I and you and Skipper, it was more like a date between you and Skipper. Gladys and I were just sort of tagging along as if it was necessary to chap-650 erone you! — to make a good public impression —

BRICK: (*turns to face her, half lifting his crutch*) Maggie, you want me to hit you with this crutch? Don't you know I could kill you with this crutch?

MARGARET: Good Lord, man, d' you think I'd care if you did?

BRICK: One man has one great good true thing in his life. One great good thing which is true! — I had friendship with Skipper. — You are naming it dirty!

MARGARET: I'm not naming it dirty! I am naming it clean.

BRICK: Not love with you, Maggie, but friendship with Skipper was that one great true thing, and you are naming it dirty!

MARGARET: Then you haven't been listenin', not understood what I'm saying! 660 I'm naming it so damn clean that it killed poor Skipper! — You two had something that had to be kept on ice, yes, incorruptible, yes! — and death was the only icebox where you could keep it. . . .

BRICK: I married you, Maggie. Why would I marry you, Maggie, if I was — ?

MARGARET: Brick, let me finish! — I know, believe me I know, that it was only Skipper that harbored even any *unconscious* desire for anything not perfectly pure between you two! — Now let me skip a little. You married me early that summer we graduated out of Ole Miss, and we were happy, weren't we, we were blissful, yes, hit heaven together ev'ry time that we loved! But that fall you an' Skipper turned down wonderful offers of jobs in order to keep on bein' football heroes — pro-football heroes. You organized the Dixie Stars that fall, so you could keep on bein' teammates forever! But somethin' was not right with it! — *Me included!* — between you. Skipper began hittin' the bottle... you got a spinal injury — couldn't play the Thanksgivin' game in Chicago, watched it on TV from a traction bed in Toledo. I joined Skipper. The Dixie Stars lost because poor Skipper was drunk. We drank together that night all night in the bar of the Blackstone and when cold day was comin' up over the Lake an' we were comin' out drunk to take a dizzy look at it, I said, "SKIPPER! STOP LOVIN' MY HUSBAND OR TELL HIM HE'S GOT TO LET YOU ADMIT IT TO HIM!" — one way or another!

HE SLAPPED ME HARD ON THE MOUTH! — then turned and ran without stopping once, I am sure, all the way back into his room at the Blackstone....

— When I came to his room that night, with a little scratch like a shy little mouse at his door, he made that pitiful, ineffectual little attempt to prove that what I had said wasn't true....

(BRICK *strikes at her with crutch, a blow that shatters the gemlike lamp on the table.*)

— In this way, I destroyed him, by telling him truth that he and his world which he was born and raised in, yours and his world, had told him could not be told?

— From then on Skipper was nothing at all but a receptacle for liquor and drugs....

—*Who shot cock robin? I with my* —

(*She throws back her head with tight shut eyes.*)

— *merciful arrow!*

(BRICK *strikes at her; misses.*)

Missed me! — Sorry, — I'm not tryin' to whitewash my behavior, Christ, no! Brick, I'm not good. I don't know why people have to pretend to be good, nobody's good. The rich or the well-to-do can afford to respect moral patterns, conventional moral patterns, but I could never afford to, yeah, but — I'm honest! Give me credit for just that, will you *please?*— Born poor, raised poor, expect to die poor unless I manage to get us something out of what Big Daddy leaves when he dies of cancer! But Brick?! — *Skipper is dead! I'm alive!* Maggie the cat is —

(BRICK *hops awkwardly forward and strikes at her again with his crutch.*)

— alive! I am alive, alive! I am...

(*He hurls the crutch at her, across the bed she took refuge behind, and pitches forward on the floor as she completes her speech.*)

— *alive!*

(*A little girl,* DIXIE, *bursts into the room, wearing an Indian war bonnet and firing a cap pistol at* MARGARET *and shouting: "Bang, bang, bang!"*)

(*Laughter downstairs floats through the open hall door.* MARGARET *had crouched gasping to bed at child's entrance. She now rises and says with cool fury:*)

Little girl, your mother or someone should teach you— (*gasping*)— to knock at a door before you come into a room. Otherwise people might think that you — lack — good breeding. . . .

DIXIE: Yanh, yanh, yanh, what is Uncle Brick doin' on th' floor?

BRICK: I tried to kill your Aunt Maggie, but I failed — and I fell. Little girl, give me my crutch so I can get up off th' floor.

MARGARET: Yes, give your uncle his crutch, he's a cripple, honey, he broke his ankle last night jumping hurdles on the high school athletic field!

DIXIE: What were you jumping hurdles for, Uncle Brick?

BRICK: Because I used to jump them, and people like to do what they used to do, even after they've stopped being able to do it. . . .

MARGARET: That's right, that's your answer, now go away, little girl.

(DIXIE *fires cap pistol at* MARGARET *three times.*)

Stop, you stop that, monster! You little no-neck monster!

(*She seizes the cap pistol and hurls it through gallery doors.*)

DIXIE: (*with a precocious instinct for the cruelest thing*) You're *jealous!*— You're just jealous because you can't have babies!

(*She sticks out her tongue at* MARGARET *as she sashays past her with her stomach stuck out, to the gallery.* MARGARET *slams the gallery doors and leans panting against them. There is a pause.* BRICK *has replaced his spilt drink and sits, faraway, on the great four-poster bed.*)

MARGARET: You see?— they gloat over us being childless, even in front of their five little no-neck monsters!

(*Pause. Voices approach on the stairs.*)

Brick?— I've been to a doctor in Memphis, a — a gynecologist. . . .
I've been completely examined, and there is no reason why we can't have a child whenever we want one. And this is my time by the calendar to conceive. Are you listening to me? Are you? Are you LISTENING TO ME!

BRICK: Yes. I hear you, Maggie.

(*His attention returns to her inflamed face.*)

— But how in hell on earth do you imagine — that you're going to have a child by a man that can't stand you?

MARGARET: That's a problem that I will have to work out.

(*She wheels about to face the hall door.*)

MAE: (*off stage left*) Come on, Big Daddy. We're all goin' up to Brick's room.

(From off stage left, voices: REVEREND TOOKER, DOCTOR BAUGH, MAE.*)*

MARGARET: Here they come!

(The lights dim.)

CURTAIN

ACT TWO

There is no lapse of time. MARGARET *and* BRICK *are in the same positions they held at the end of Act 1.*

MARGARET: *(at door)* Here they come!

*(*BIG DADDY *appears first, a tall man with a fierce, anxious look, moving carefully not to betray his weakness even, or especially, to himself.)*

GOOPER: I read in the *Register* that you're getting a new memorial window.

(Some of the people are approaching through the hall, others along the gallery: voices from both directions. GOOPER *and* REVEREND TOOKER *become visible outside gallery doors, and their voices come in clearly.)*

(They pause outside as GOOPER *lights a cigar.)*

REVEREND TOOKER: *(vivaciously)* Oh, but St. Paul's in Grenada has three memorial windows, and the latest one is a Tiffany stained-glass window that cost twenty-five hundred dollars, a picture of Christ the Good Shepherd with a Lamb in His arms.

MARGARET: Big Daddy.

BIG DADDY: Well, Brick.

BRICK: Hello Big Daddy. — Congratulations!

10 BIG DADDY: — Crap. . . .

GOOPER: Who give that window, Preach?

REVEREND TOOKER: Clyde Fletcher's widow. Also presented St. Paul's with a baptismal font.

GOOPER: Y'know what somebody ought t' give your church is a *coolin'* system, Preach.

MAE: *(almost religiously)* — Let's see now, they've had their tyyy-phoid shots, and their tetanus shots, their diphtheria shots and their hepatitis shots and their polio shots, they got *those* shots every month from May through September, and — Gooper? Hey! Gooper! — What all have the kiddies

20 been shot faw?

REVEREND TOOKER: Yes, siree, Bob! And y'know what Gus Hamma's family gave in his memory to the church at Two Rivers? A complete new stone parish-house with a basketball court in the basement and a —

BIG DADDY: *(uttering a loud barking laugh which is far from truly mirthful)* Hey, Preach! What's all this talk about memorials, Preach? Y' think somebody's about t' kick off around here? 'S that it?

(Startled by this interjection, REVEREND TOOKER *decides to laugh at the question almost as loud as he can.)*

(How he would answer the question we'll never know, as he's spared that embarrassment by the voice of GOOPER's *wife,* MAE, *rising high and clear as she appears with "*DOC*" BAUGH, the family doctor, through the hall door.)*

MARGARET: *(overlapping a bit)* Turn on the hi-fi, Brick! Let's have some music t' start off th' party with!

BRICK: You turn it on, Maggie.

(The talk becomes so general that the room sounds like a great aviary of chattering birds. Only BRICK *remains unengaged, leaning upon the liquor cabinet with his faraway smile, an ice cube in a paper napkin with which he now and then rubs his forehead. He doesn't respond to* MARGARET's *command. She bounds forward and stoops over the instrument panel of the console.)*

30 GOOPER: We gave 'em that thing for a third anniversary present, got three speakers in it.

(The room is suddenly blasted by the climax of a Wagnerian opera or a Beethoven symphony.)

BIG DADDY: *Turn that dam thing off!*

(Almost instant silence, almost instantly broken by the shouting charge of BIG MAMA, *entering through hall door like a charging rhino.)*

BIG MAMA: *Wha's my Brick, wha's mah precious baby!!*

BIG DADDY: *Sorry! Turn it back on!*

(Everyone laughs very loud. BIG DADDY *is famous for his jokes at* BIG MAMA's *expense, and nobody laughs louder at these jokes than* BIG MAMA *herself, though sometimes they're pretty cruel and* BIG MAMA *has to pick up or fuss with something to cover the hurt that the loud laugh doesn't quite cover.)*

(On this occasion, a happy occasion because the dread in her heart has also been lifted by the false report on BIG DADDY's *condition, she giggles, grotesquely, coyly, in* BIG DADDY's *direction and bears down upon* BRICK, *all very quick and alive.)*

BIG MAMA: Here he is, here's my precious baby! What's that you've got in your hand? You put that liquor down, son, your hand was made fo' holdin' somethin' better than that!

GOOPER: Look at Brick put it down!

*(*BRICK *has obeyed* BIG MAMA *by draining the glass and handing it to her. Again everyone laughs, some high, some low.)*

BIG MAMA: Oh, you bad boy, you, you're my bad little boy. Give Big Mama a kiss,
40 you bad boy, you! — Look at him shy away, will you? Brick never liked bein' kissed or made a fuss over, I guess because he's always had too much of it!

Son, you turn that thing off!

(BRICK *has switched on the TV set.*)

I can't stand TV, radio was bad enough but TV has gone it one better, I mean — (*plops wheezing in chair*) — one worse, ha ha! Now what'm I sittin' down here faw? I want t' sit next to my sweetheart on the sofa, hold hands with him and love him up a little!

(BIG MAMA *has on a black and white figured chiffon. The large irregular patterns, like the markings of some massive animal, the luster of her great diamonds and many pearls, the brilliants set in the silver frames of her glasses, her riotous voice, booming laugh, have dominated the room since she entered.* BIG DADDY *has been regarding her with a steady grimace of chronic annoyance.*)

BIG MAMA: (*still louder*) Preacher, Preacher, hey, Preach! Give me you' hand an' help me up from this chair!

50   REVEREND TOOKER: None of your tricks, Big Mama!

BIG MAMA: What tricks? You give me you' hand so I can get up an'—

(REVEREND TOOKER *extends her his hand. She grabs it and pulls him into her lap with a shrill laugh that spans an octave in two notes.*)

Ever seen a preacher in a fat lady's lap? Hey, hey, folks! Ever seen a preacher in a fat lady's lap?

(BIG MAMA *is notorious throughout the Delta for this sort of inelegant horseplay.* MARGARET *looks on with indulgent humor, sipping Dubonnet "on the rocks" and watching* BRICK, *but* MAE *and* GOOPER *exchange signs of humorless anxiety over these antics, the sort of behavior which* MAE *thinks may account for their failure to quite get in with the smartest young married set in Memphis, despite all. One of the Negroes,* LACY *or* SOOKEY, *peeks in, cackling. They are waiting for a sign to bring in the cake and champagne. But* BIG DADDY's *not amused. He doesn't understand why, in spite of the infinite mental relief he's received from the doctor's report, he still has these same old fox teeth in his guts. "This spastic condition is something else," he says to himself, but aloud he roars at* BIG MAMA:)

BIG DADDY: BIG MAMA, WILL YOU QUIT HORSIN'? — You're too old an' too fat fo' that sort of crazy kid stuff an' besides a woman with your blood pressure — she had two hundred last spring! — is riskin' a stroke when you mess around like that....

(MAE *blows on a pitch pipe.*)

BIG MAMA: Here comes Big Daddy's birthday!

(NEGROES *in white jackets enter with an enormous birthday cake ablaze with candles and carrying buckets of champagne with satin ribbons about the bottle necks.*)

(MAE *and* GOOPER *strike up song, and everybody, including the* NEGROES *and* CHILDREN, *joins in. Only* BRICK *remains aloof.*)

EVERYONE: Happy birthday to you.
60   Happy birthday to you.
Happy birthday, Big Daddy —

(*Some sing: "Dear, Big Daddy!"*)

Happy birthday to you.

(*Some sing: "How old are you?"*)

(MAE *has come down center and is organizing her children like a chorus. She gives them a barely audible: "One, two, three!" and they are off in the new tune.*)

CHILDREN: Skinamarinka — dinka — dink
Skinamarinka — do
We love you.
Skinamarinka — dinka — dink
Skinamarinka–do.

(*All together, they turn to* BIG DADDY.)

Big Daddy, you!

(*They turn back front, like a musical comedy chorus.*)

We love you in the morning;
We love you in the night.
We love you when we're with you,
And we love you out of sight.
Skinamarinka–dinka–dink
Skinamarinka — do.

(MAE *turns to* BIG MAMA.)

Big Mama, too!

(BIG MAMA *bursts into tears. The* NEGROES *leave.*)

BIG DADDY: Now Ida, what the hell is the matter with you?
MAE: She's just so happy.
BIG MAMA: I'm just so happy, Big Daddy, I have to cry or something.

(*Sudden and loud in the hush:*)

Brick, do you know the wonderful news that Doc Baugh got from the clinic about Big Daddy? Big Daddy's one hundred per cent!
MARGARET: Isn't that wonderful?
BIG MAMA: He's just one hundred per cent. Passed the examination with flying colors. Now that we know there's nothing wrong with Big Daddy but a spastic colon, I can tell you something. I was worried sick, half out of my mind, for fear that Big Daddy might have a thing like —

(MARGARET *cuts through this speech, jumping up and exclaiming shrilly:*)

MARGARET: Brick, honey, aren't you going to give Big Daddy his birthday present?

(*Passing by him, she snatches his liquor glass from him.*)

(*She picks up a fancily wrapped package.*)

Here it is, Big Daddy, this is from Brick!

BIG MAMA: This is the biggest birthday Big Daddy's ever had, a hundred presents and bushels of telegrams from —

MAE: *(at same time)* What is it, Brick?

GOOPER: I bet 500 to 50 that Brick don't *know* what it is.

BIG MAMA: The fun of presents is not knowing what they are till you open the package. Open your present, Big Daddy.

BIG DADDY: Open it you'self. I want to ask Brick somethin! Come here, Brick.

MARGARET: Big Daddy's callin' you, Brick.

(She is opening the package.)

BRICK: Tell Big Daddy I'm crippled.

BIG DADDY: I see you're crippled. I want to know how you got crippled.

MARGARET: *(making diversionary tactics)* Oh, look, oh, look, why, it's a cashmere robe!

(She holds the robe up for all to see.)

MAE: You sound surprised, Maggie.

MARGARET: I never saw one before.

MAE: That's funny. — Hah!

MARGARET: *(turning on her fiercely, with a brilliant smile)* Why is it funny? All my family ever had was family — and luxuries such as cashmere robes still surprise me!

BIG DADDY: *(ominously)* Quiet!

MAE: *(heedless in her fury)* I don't see how you could be so surprised when you bought it yourself at Loewenstein's in Memphis last Saturday. You know how I know?

BIG DADDY: I said, Quiet!

MAE: — I know because the salesgirl that sold it to you waited on me and said, Oh, Mrs. Pollitt, your sister-in-law just bought a cashmere robe for your husband's father!

MARGARET: Sister Woman! Your talents are wasted as a housewife and mother, you really ought to be with the FBI or —

BIG DADDY: QUIET!

(REVEREND TOOKER's reflexes are slower than the others'. He finishes a sentence after the bellow.)

REVEREND TOOKER: *(to DOC BAUGH)* — the Stork and the Reaper are running neck and neck!

(He starts to laugh gaily when he notices the silence and BIG DADDY's glare. His laugh dies falsely.)

BIG DADDY: Preacher, I hope I'm not butting in on more talk about memorial stained-glass windows, am I, Preacher?

(REVEREND TOOKER laughs feebly, then coughs dryly in the embarrassed silence.)

Preacher?

BIG MAMA: Now, Big Daddy, don't you pick on Preacher!

BIG DADDY: *(raising his voice)* You ever hear that expression all hawk and no spit? You bring that expression to mind with that little dry cough of yours, all hawk an' no spit....

(The pause is broken only by a short startled laugh from MARGARET, *the only one there who is conscious of and amused by the grotesque.)*

MAE: *(raising her arms and jangling her bracelets)* I wonder if the mosquitoes are active tonight?

BIG DADDY: What's that, Little Mama? Did you make some remark?

130 MAE: Yes, I said I wondered if the mosquitoes would eat us alive if we went out on the gallery for a while.

BIG DADDY: Well, if they do, I'll have your bones pulverized for fertilizer!

BIG MAMA: *(quickly)* Last week we had an airplane spraying the place and I think it done some good, at least I haven't had a —

BIG DADDY: *(cutting her speech)* Brick, they tell me, if what they tell me is true, that you done some jumping last night on the high school athletic field?

BIG MAMA: Brick, Big Daddy is talking to you, son.

BRICK: *(smiling vaguely over his drink)* What was that, Big Daddy?

BIG DADDY: They said you done some jumping on the high school track field last
140 night.

BRICK: That's what they told me, too.

BIG DADDY: Was it jumping or humping that you were doing out there? What were doing out there at three A.M., layin' a woman on that cinder track?

BIG MAMA: Big Daddy, you are off the sick-list, now, and I'm not going to excuse you for talkin' so —

BIG DADDY: Quiet!

BIG MAMA: — *nasty* in front of Preacher and —

BIG DADDY: QUIET!— I ast you, Brick, if you was cuttin' you'self a piece o' poon-tang last night on that cinder track? I thought maybe you were
150 chasin' poon-tang on that track an' tripped over something in the heat of the chase — 'sthat it?

*(*GOOPER *laughs, loud and false, others nervously following suit.* BIG MAMA *stamps her foot, and purses her lips, crossing to* MAE *and whispering something to her as* BRICK *meets his father's hard, intent, grinning stare with a slow, vague smile that he offers all situations from behind the screen of his liquor.)*

BRICK: No, sir, I don't think so....

MAE: *(at the same time, sweetly)* Reverend Tooker, let's you and I take a stroll on the widow's walk.

(She and the preacher go out on the gallery as BIG DADDY *says:)*

BIG DADDY: Then what the hell were you doing out there at three o'clock in the morning?

BRICK: Jumping the hurdles, Big Daddy, runnin' and jumpin' the hurdles, but those high hurdles have gotten too high for me, now.

BIG DADDY: Cause you was drunk?

160   BRICK: *(his vague smile fading a little)* Sober I wouldn't have tried to jump the *low* ones. . . .

BIG MAMA: *(quickly)* Big Daddy, blow out the candles on your birthday cake!

MARGARET: *(at the same time)* I want to propose a toast to Big Daddy Pollitt on his sixty-fifth birthday, the biggest cotton planter in —

BIG DADDY: *(bellowing with fury and disgust)* I told you to stop it, now stop it, quit this — !

BIG MAMA: *(coming in front of* BIG DADDY *with the cake)* Big Daddy, I will not allow you to talk that way, not even on your birthday, I —

BIG DADDY: I'll talk like I want to on my birthday, Ida, or any other goddam day 170   of the year and anybody here that don't like it knows what they can do!

BIG MAMA: You don't mean that!

BIG DADDY: What makes you think I don't mean it?

(Meanwhile various discreet signals have been exchanged and GOOPER *has also gone out on the gallery.)*

BIG MAMA: I just know you don't mean it.

BIG DADDY: You don't know a goddam thing and you never did!

BIG MAMA: Big Daddy, you don't mean that.

BIG DADDY: Oh, yes, I do, oh, yes, I do, I mean it! I put up with a whole lot of crap around here because I thought I was dying. And you thought I was dying and you started taking over, well, you can stop taking over now, Ida, because I'm not gonna die, you can just stop now this business of taking over 180   because you're not taking over because I'm not dying, I went through the laboratory and the goddam exploratory operation and there's nothing wrong with me but a spastic colon. And I'm not dying of cancer which you thought I was dying of. Ain't that so? Didn't you think that I was dying of cancer, Ida?

(Almost everybody is out on the gallery but the two old people glaring at each other across the blazing cake.)

*(*BIG MAMA's *chest heaves and she presses a fat fist to her mouth.)*

*(*BIG DADDY *continues, hoarsely:)*

Ain't that so, Ida? Didn't you have an idea I was dying of cancer and now you could take control of this place and everything on it? I got that impression, I seemed to get that impression. Your loud voice everywhere, your fat old body butting in here and there!

BIG MAMA: Hush! The Preacher!

190   BIG DADDY: Fuck the goddam preacher!

*(*BIG MAMA *gasps loudly and sits down on the sofa which is almost too small for her.)*

Did you hear what I said? I said fuck the goddam preacher!

(Somebody closes the gallery doors from outside just as there is a burst of fireworks and excited cries from the children.)

BIG MAMA: I never seen you act like this before and I can't think what's got in you!

BIG DADDY: I went through all that laboratory and operation and all just so I would know if you or me was boss here! Well, now it turns out that I am and you ain't — and that's my birthday present — and my cake and champagne! — because for three years now you been gradually taking over. Bossing. Talking. Sashaying your fat old body around the place I made! I made this place! I was overseer on it! I was the overseer on the old Straw and Ochello plantation. I quit school at ten! I quit school at ten years old and went to work like a nigger in the fields. And I rose to be overseer of the Straw and Ochello plantation. And old Straw died and I was Ochello's partner and the place got bigger and bigger and bigger and bigger and bigger! I did all that myself with no goddam help from you, and now you think you're just about to take over. Well, I am just about to tell you that you are not just about to take over, you are not just about to take over a God damn thing. Is that clear to you, Ida? Is that very plain to you, now? Is that understood completely? I been through the laboratory from A to Z. I've had the goddam exploratory operation, and nothing is wrong with me but a spastic colon — made spastic, I guess, by *disgust!* By all the goddam lies and liars that I have had to put up with, and all the goddam hypocrisy that I lived with all these forty years that we been livin' together!

Hey! Ida!! Blow out the candles on the birthday cake! Purse up your lips and draw a deep breath and blow out the goddam candles on the cake!

BIG MAMA: Oh, Big Daddy, oh, oh, oh, Big Daddy!

BIG DADDY: What's the matter with you?

BIG MAMA: *In all these years you never believed that I loved you??*

BIG DADDY: Huh?

BIG MAMA: *And I did, I did so much, I did love you!* — I even loved your hate and your hardness, Big Daddy!

(*She sobs and rushes awkwardly out onto the gallery.*)

BIG DADDY: (*to himself*) *Wouldn't it be funny if that was true. . . .*

(*A pause is followed by a burst of light in the sky from the fireworks.*)

BRICK! HEY, BRICK!

(*He stands over his blazing birthday cake.*)

(*After some moments,* BRICK *hobbles in on his crutch, holding his glass.*)

(MARGARET *follows him with a bright, anxious smile.*)

I didn't call you, Maggie. I called Brick.

MARGARET: I'm just delivering him to you.

(*She kisses* BRICK *on the mouth which he immediately wipes with the back of his hand. She flies girlishly back out.* BRICK *and his father are alone.*)

BIG DADDY: Why did you do that?

BRICK: Do what, Big Daddy?

BIG DADDY: Wipe her kiss off your mouth like she'd spit on you.

BRICK: I don't know. I wasn't conscious of it.

BIG DADDY: That woman of yours has a better shape on her than Gooper's but
somehow or other they got the same look about them.

BRICK: What sort of look is that, Big Daddy?

BIG DADDY: I don't know how to describe it but it's the same look.

BRICK: They don't look peaceful, do they?

BIG DADDY: No, they sure in hell don't.

BRICK: They look nervous as cats?

BIG DADDY: That's right, they look nervous as cats.

BRICK: Nervous as a couple of cats on a hot tin roof?

BIG DADDY: That's right, boy, they look like a couple of cats on a hot tin roof.
It's funny that you and Gooper being so different would pick out the same
type of woman.

BRICK: Both of us married into society, Big Daddy.

BIG DADDY: Crap . . . I wonder what gives them both that look?

BRICK: Well. They're sittin' in the middle of a big piece of land, Big Daddy,
twenty-eight thousand acres is a pretty big piece of land and so they're
squaring off on it, each determined to knock off a bigger piece of it than the
other whenever you let it go.

BIG DADDY: I got a surprise for those women. I'm not gonna let it go for a long
time yet if that's what they're waiting for.

BRICK: That's right, Big Daddy. You just sit tight and let them scratch each
other's eyes out. . . .

BIG DADDY: You bet your life I'm going to sit tight on it and let those sons of
bitches scratch their eyes out, ha ha ha. . . .
     But Gooper's wife's a good breeder, you got to admit she's fertile. Hell,
at supper tonight she had them all at the table and they had to put a
couple of extra leafs in the table to make room for them, she's got five
head of them, now, and another one's comin'.

BRICK: Yep, number six is comin'. . . .

BIG DADDY: Six hell, she'll probably drop a litter next time. Brick, you know, I
swear to God, I don't know the way it happens?

BRICK: The way what happens, Big Daddy?

BIG DADDY: You git you a piece of land, by hook or crook, an' things start
growin' on it, things accumulate on it, and the first thing you know it's completely out of hand, completely out of hand!

BRICK: Well, they say nature hates a vacuum, Big Daddy.

BIG DADDY: That's what they say, but sometimes I think that a vacuum is a
hell of a lot better than some of the stuff that nature replaces it with.
     Is someone out there by that door?

GOOPER: Hey Mae.

BRICK: Yep.

BIG DADDY: Who?

(He has lowered his voice.)

BRICK: Someone int'rested in what we say to each other.

BIG DADDY: Gooper? — *GOOPER!*

(After a discreet pause, MAE *appears in the gallery door.)*

MAE: Did you call Gooper, Big Daddy?

BIG DADDY: Aw, it was you.

MAE: Do you want Gooper, Big Daddy?

BIG DADDY: No, and I don't want you. I want some privacy here, while I'm having a confidential talk with my son Brick. Now it's too hot in here to close them doors, but if I have to close those fuckin' doors in order to have a private talk with my son Brick, just let me know and I'll close 'em. Because I hate eavesdroppers, I don't like any kind of sneakin' an' spyin'.

MAE: Why, Big Daddy —

BIG DADDY: You stood on the wrong side of the moon, it threw your shadow!

MAE: I was just —

BIG DADDY: You was just nothing but *spyin'* an' you *know* it!

MAE: (*begins to sniff and sob*) Oh, Big Daddy, you're so unkind for some reason to those that really love you!

BIG DADDY: Shut up, shut up, shut up! I'm going to move you and Gooper out of that room next to this! It's none of your goddam business what goes on in here at night between Brick an' Maggie. You listen at night like a couple of rutten peekhole spies and go and give a report on what you hear to Big Mama an' she comes to me and says they say such and such and so and so about what they heard goin' on between Brick an' Maggie, and Jesus, it makes me sick. I'm goin' to move you an' Gooper out of that room, I can't stand sneakin' an' spyin', it makes me puke....

(MAE *throws back her head and rolls her eyes heavenward and extends her arms as if invoking God's pity for this unjust martyrdom; then she presses a handkerchief to her nose and flies from the room with a loud swish of skirts.*)

BRICK: (*now at the liquor cabinet*) They listen, do they?

BIG DADDY: Yeah. They listen and give reports to Big Mama on what goes on in here between you and Maggie. They say that —

(*He stops as if embarrassed.*)

— You won't sleep with her, that you sleep on the sofa. Is that true or not true? If you don't like Maggie, get rid of Maggie! — What are you doin' there now?

BRICK: Fresh'nin' up my drink.

BIG DADDY: Son, you know you got a real liquor problem?

BRICK: Yes, sir, yes, I know.

BIG DADDY: Is that why you quit sports-announcing, because of this liquor problem?

BRICK: Yes, sir, yes, sir, I guess so.

(*He smiles vaguely and amiably at his father across his replenished drink.*)

BIG DADDY: Son, don't guess about it, it's too important.

BRICK: (*vaguely*) Yes, sir.

BIG DADDY: And listen to me, don't look at the damn chandelier....

(*Pause.* BIG DADDY's *voice is husky.*)

— Somethin' else we picked up at th' big fire sale in Europe.

(Another pause.)

Life is important. There's nothing else to hold onto. A man that drinks is throwing his life away. Don't do it, hold onto your life, There's nothing else to hold onto. . . .

    Sit down over here so we don't have to raise our voices, the walls have ears in this place.

BRICK: *(hobbling over to sit on the sofa beside him)* All right, Big Daddy.

BIG DADDY: Quit! — how'd that come about? Some disappointment?

BRICK: I don't know. Do you?

BIG DADDY: I'm askin' you, God damn it! How in hell would I know if you don't?

BRICK: I just got out there and found that I had a mouth full of cotton. I was always two or three beats behind what was goin' on on the field and so I —

BIG DADDY: Quit!

BRICK: *(amiably)* Yes, quit.

BIG DADDY: Son?

BRICK: Huh?

BIG DADDY: *(inhales loudly and deeply from his cigar; then bends suddenly a little forward, exhaling loudly and raising a hand to his forehead)* — Whew! — ha ha! — I took in too much smoke, it made me a little lightheaded. . . .

(The mantel clock chimes.)

Why is it so damn hard for people to talk?

BRICK: Yeah. . . .

(The clock goes on sweetly chiming till it has completed the stroke of ten.)

— Nice peaceful-soundin' clock, I like to hear it all night. . . .

(He slides low and comfortable on the sofa; BIG DADDY *sits up straight and rigid with some unspoken anxiety. All his gestures are tense and jerky as he talks. He wheezes and pants and sniffs through his nervous speech, glancing quickly, shyly, from time to time, at his son.)*

BIG DADDY: We got that clock the summer we wint to Europe, me an' Big Mama on that damn Cook's Tour, never had such an awful time in my life, I'm tellin' you, son, those gooks over there, they gouge your eyeballs out in their grand hotels. And Big Mama bought more stuff than you could haul in a couple of boxcars, that's no crap. Everywhere she wint on this whirlwind tour, she bought, bought, bought. Why, half that stuff she bought is still crated up in the cellar, under water last spring!

(He laughs.)

That Europe is nothin' on earth but a great big auction, that's all it is, that bunch of old worn-out places, it's just a big fire-sale, the whole fuckin' thing, an' Big Mama wint wild in it, why, you couldn't hold that woman with a mule's harness! Bought, bought, bought! — lucky I'm a rich man, yes siree, Bob, an' half that stuff is mildewin' in th' basement. It's lucky I'm a rich man, it sure is lucky, well, I'm a rich man, Brick, yep, I'm a mighty rich man.

(His eyes light up for a moment.)

Y'know how much I'm worth? Guess, Brick! Guess how much I'm worth!

(BRICK *smiles vaguely over his drink.*)

Close on ten million in cash an' blue-chip stocks, outside, mind you, of twenty-eight thousand acres of the richest land this side of the valley Nile!

But a man can't buy his life with it, he can't buy back his life with it when his life has been spent, that's one thing not offered in the Europe fire-sale or in the American markets or any markets on earth, a man can't buy his life with it, he can't buy back his life when his life is finished. . . .

That's a sobering thought, a very sobering thought, and that's a thought that I was turning over in my head, over and over and over — until today. . . .

I'm wiser and sadder, Brick, for this experience which I just gone through. They's one thing else that I remember in Europe.

BRICK: What is that, Big Daddy?

BIG DADDY: The hills around Barcelona in the country of Spain and the children running over those bare hills in their bare skins beggin' like starvin' dogs with howls and screeches, and how fat the priests are on the streets of Barcelona, so many of them and so fat and so pleasant, ha ha! — Y'know I could feed that country? I got money enough to feed that goddam country, but the human animal is a selfish beast and I don't reckon the money I passed out there to those howling children in the hills around Barcelona would more than upholster the chairs in this room, I mean pay to put a new cover on this chair!

Hell, I threw them money like you'd scatter feed corn for chickens, I threw money at them just to get rid of them long enough to climb back into th' car and — drive away. . . .

And then in Morocco, them Arabs, why, I remember one day in Marrakech, that old walled Arab city, I set on a broken-down wall to have a cigar, it was fearful hot there and this Arab woman stood in the road and looked at me till I was embarrassed, she stood stock still in the dusty hot road and looked at me till I was embarrassed. But listen to this. She had a naked child with her, a little naked girl with her, barely able to toddle, and after a while she set this child on the ground and give her a push and whispered something to her.

This child come toward me, barely able t' walk, come toddling up to me and —

Jesus, it makes you sick t' remember a thing like this! It stuck out its hand and tried to unbutton my trousers!

That child was not yet five! Can you believe me? Or do you think that I am making this up? I wint back to the hotel and said to Big Mama, Git packed! We're clearing out of this country. . . .

BRICK: Big Daddy, you're on a talkin' jag tonight.

BIG DADDY: *(ignoring this remark)* Yes, sir, that's how it is, the human animal is a beast that dies but the fact that he's dying don't give him pity for others, no, sir, it —

— Did you say something?

BRICK: Yes.

390 BIG DADDY: What?

BRICK: Hand me over that crutch so I can get up.

BIG DADDY: Where you goin'?

BRICK: I'm takin' a little short trip to Echo Spring.

BIG DADDY: To where?

BRICK: Liquor cabinet. . . .

BIG DADDY: Yes, sir, boy —

(He hands BRICK the crutch.)

— the human animal is a beast that dies and if he's got money he buys and buys and buys and I think the reason he buys everything he can buy is that in the back of his mind he has the crazy hope that one of his purchases will be life everlasting! — Which it never can be. . . . The human animal is a beast that —

400

BRICK: *(at the liquor cabinet)* Big Daddy, you sure are shootin' th' breeze here tonight.

(There is a pause and voices are heard outside.)

BIG DADDY: I been quiet here lately, spoke not a word, just sat and stared into space. I had something heavy weighing on my mind but tonight that load was took off me. That's why I'm talking. — The sky looks diff'rent to me. . . .

BRICK: You know what I like to hear most?

BIG DADDY: What?

410 BRICK: Solid quiet. Perfect unbroken quiet.

BIG DADDY: Why?

BRICK: Because it's more peaceful.

BIG DADDY: Man, you'll hear a lot of that in the grave.

(He chuckles agreeably.)

BRICK: Are you through talkin' to me?

BIG DADDY: Why are you so anxious to shut me up?

BRICK: Well, sir, ever so often you say to me, Brick, I want to have a talk with you, but when we talk, it never materializes. Nothing is said. You sit in a chair and gas about this and that and I look like I listen. I try to look like I listen, but I don't listen, not much. Communication is — awful hard between people an'— somehow between you and me, it just don't — happen.

420

BIG DADDY: Have you ever been scared? I mean have you ever felt downright terror of something?

(He gets up.)

Just one moment.

(He looks off as if he were going to tell an important secret.)

BIG DADDY: Brick?

BRICK: What?

BIG DADDY: Son, I thought I had it!

BRICK: Had what? Had what, Big Daddy?

BIG DADDY: Cancer!

430 BRICK: Oh...

BIG DADDY: I thought the old man made out of bones had laid his cold and heavy hand on my shoulder!

BRICK: Well, Big Daddy, you kept a tight mouth about it.

BIG DADDY: A pig squeals. A man keeps a tight mouth about it, in spite of a man not having a pig's advantage.

BRICK: What advantage is that?

BIG DADDY: Ignorance — of mortality — is a comfort. A man don't have that comfort, he's the only living thing that conceives of death, that knows what it is. The others go without knowing which is the way that anything
440 living should go, go without knowing, without any knowledge of it, and yet a pig squeals, but a man sometimes, he can keep a tight mouth about it. Sometimes he —

(There is a deep, smoldering, ferocity in the old man.)

— can keep a tight mouth about it. I wonder if—

BRICK: What, Big Daddy?

BIG DADDY: A whiskey highball would injure this spastic condition?

BRICK: No, sir, it might do it good.

BIG DADDY: *(grins suddenly, wolfishly)* Jesus, I can't tell you! The sky is open! Christ, it's open again! It's open, boy, it's open!

(BRICK looks down at his drink.)

BRICK: You feel better, Big Daddy?

450 BIG DADDY: Better? Hell! I can breathe! — All of my life I been like a doubled up fist. . . .

(He pours a drink.)

— Poundin', smashin', drivin'! — now I'm going to loosen these doubled-up hands and touch things *easy* with them. . . .

(He spreads his hands as if caressing the air.)

You know what I'm contemplating?

BRICK: *(vaguely)* No, sir. What are you contemplating?

BIG DADDY: Ha ha! — *Pleasure!* — pleasure with *women!*

(BRICK's smile fades a little but lingers.)

— Yes, boy. I'll tell you something that you might not guess. I still have desire for women and this is my sixty-fifth birthday.

BRICK: I think that's mighty remarkable, Big Daddy.

460 BIG DADDY: Remarkable?

BRICK: *Admirable*, Big Daddy.

BIG DADDY: You're damn right it is, remarkable and admirable both. I realize now that I never had me enough. I let many chances slip by because of scruples about it, scruples, convention — crap. . . . All that stuff is bull, bull, bull! —

It took the shadow of death to make me see it. Now that shadow's lifted, I'm going to cut loose and have, what is it they call it, have me a — ball!

BRICK: A ball, huh?

BIG DADDY: That's right, a ball, a ball! Hell! — I slept with Big Mama till, let's see, five years ago, till I was sixty and she was fifty-eight, and never even liked her, never did!

(The phone has been ringing down the hall. BIG MAMA *enters, exclaiming:)*

BIG MAMA: Don't you men hear that phone ring? I heard it way out on the gall'ry.

BIG DADDY: There's five rooms off this front gall'ry that you could go through. Why do you go through this one?

*(*BIG MAMA *makes a playful face as she bustles out the hall door.)*

Hunh! — Why, when Big Mama goes out of a room, I can't remember what that woman looks like —

BIG MAMA: Hello.

BIG DADDY: — But when Big Mama comes back into the room, boy, then I see what she looks like, and I wish I didn't!

(Bends over laughing at this joke till it hurts his guts and he straightens with a grimace. The laugh subsides to a chuckle as he puts the liquor glass a little distrustfully down on the table.)

BIG MAMA: Hello, Miss Sally.

*(*BRICK *has risen and hobbled to the gallery doors.)*

BIG DADDY: Hey! Where you goin'?

BRICK: Out for a breather.

BIG DADDY: Not yet you ain't. Stay here till this talk is finished, young fellow.

BRICK: I thought it was finished, Big Daddy.

BIG DADDY: It ain't even begun.

BRICK: My mistake. Excuse me. I just wanted to feel that river breeze.

BIG DADDY: Set back down in that chair.

*(*BIG MAMA's *voice rises, carrying down the hall.)*

BIG MAMA: Miss Sally, you're a case! You're a caution, Miss Sally.

BIG DADDY: Jesus, she's talking to my old maid sister again.

BIG MAMA: Why didn't you give me a chance to explain it to you?

BIG DADDY: Brick, this stuff burns me.

BIG MAMA: Well, goodbye, now, Miss Sally. You come down real soon. Big Daddy's dying to see you.

BIG DADDY: Crap!

BIG MAMA: Yaiss, goodbye, Miss Sally. . . .

(She hangs up and bellows with mirth. BIG DADDY *groans and covers his ears as she approaches.)*

(Bursting in:)

Big Daddy, that was Miss Sally callin' from Memphis again! You know what she done, Big Daddy? She called her doctor in Memphis to git him to tell her what that spastic thing is! Ha-*HAAAA!*— And called back to tell me how relieved she was that — Hey! Let me in!

(BIG DADDY *has been holding the door half closed against her.*)

500 BIG DADDY: Naw I ain't. I told you not to come and go through this room. You just back out and go through those five other rooms.

BIG MAMA: Big Daddy? Big Daddy? Oh, Big Daddy! — You didn't mean those things you said to me, did you?

(*He shuts door firmly against her but she still calls.*)

Sweetheart? Sweetheart? Big Daddy? You didn't mean those awful things you said to me? — I know you didn't. I know you didn't mean those things in your heart. . . .

(*The childlike voice fades with a sob and her heavy footsteps retreat down the hall.* BRICK *has risen once more on his crutches and starts for the gallery again.*)

BIG DADDY: All I ask of that woman is that she leave me alone. But she can't admit to herself that she makes me sick. That comes of having slept with her too many years. Should of quit much sooner but that old woman she
510 never got enough of it — and I was good in bed . . . I never should of wasted so much of it on her. . . . They say you got just so many and each one is numbered. Well, I got a few left in me, a few, and I'm going to pick me a good one to spend 'em on! I'm going to pick me a choice one, I don't care how much she costs, I'll smother her in — minks! Ha ha! I'll strip her naked and smother her in minks and choke her with diamonds! Ha ha! I'll strip her naked and choke her with diamonds and smother her with minks and hump her from hell to breakfast. *Ha aha ha ha ha!*

MAE: (*gaily at door*) Who's that laughin' in there?

GOOPER: Is Big Daddy laughin' in there?

520 BIG DADDY: Crap! — them two — *drips.* . . .

(*He goes over and touches* BRICK'S *shoulder.*)

Yes, son. Brick, boy. — I'm — *happy!* I'm happy, son, I'm happy!

(*He chokes a little and bites his under lip, pressing his head quickly, shyly against his son's head and then, coughing with embarrassment, goes uncertainly back to the table where he set down the glass. He drinks and makes a grimace as it burns his guts.* BRICK *sighs and rises with effort.*)

What makes you so restless? Have you got ants in your britches?

BRICK: Yes, sir . . .

BIG DADDY: Why?

BRICK: — Something — hasn't — happened. . . .

BIG DADDY: Yeah? What is *that!*

BRICK: (*sadly*) — the click. . . .

BIG DADDY: Did you say click?

BRICK: Yes, click.

530 BIG DADDY: What click?

BRICK: A click that I get in my head that makes me peaceful.

BIG DADDY: I sure in hell don't know what you're talking about, but it disturbs me.

BRICK: It's just a mechanical thing.

BIG DADDY: What is a mechanical thing?

BRICK: This click that I get in my head that makes me peaceful. I got to drink till I get it. It's just a mechanical thing, something like a — like a — like a —

BIG DADDY: Like a —

BRICK: Switch clicking off in my head, turning the hot light off and the cool
540   night on and —

(He looks up, smiling sadly.)

— all of a sudden there's — peace!

BIG DADDY: *(whistles long and soft with astonishment; he goes back to* BRICK *and clasps his son's two shoulders)* Jesus! I didn't know it had gotten that bad with you. Why, boy, you're —*alcoholic!*

BRICK: That's the truth, Big Daddy. I'm alcoholic.

BIG DADDY: This shows how I — let things go!

BRICK: I have to hear that little click in my head that makes me peaceful. Usually I hear it sooner than this, sometimes as early as — noon, but —
— Today it's — dilatory. . . .
— I just haven't got the right level of alcohol in my bloodstream yet!

(This last statement is made with energy as he freshens his drink.)

550   BIG DADDY: Uh — huh. Expecting death made me blind. I didn't have no idea that a son of mine was turning into a drunkard under my nose.

BRICK: *(gently)* Well, now you do, Big Daddy, the news has penetrated.

BIG DADDY: UH-huh, yes, now I do, the news has — penetrated. . . .

BRICK: And so if you'll excuse me —

BIG DADDY: No, I won't excuse you.

BRICK: — I'd better sit by myself till I hear that click in my head, it's just a mechanical thing but it don't happen except when I'm alone or talking to no one. . . .

BIG DADDY: You got a long, long time to sit still, boy, and talk to no one, but now
560   you're talkin' to me. At least I'm talking to you. And you set there and listen until I tell you the conversation is over!

BRICK: But this talk is like all the others we've ever had together in our lives! It's nowhere, nowhere! — it's — it's *painful,* Big Daddy. . . .

BIG DADDY: All right, then let it be painful, but don't you move from that chair! — I'm going to remove that crutch. . . .

(He seizes the crutch and tosses it across the room.)

BRICK: I can hop on one foot, and if I fall, I can crawl!

BIG DADDY: If you ain't careful you're gonna crawl off this plantation and then, by Jesus, you'll have to hustle your drinks along Skid Row!

BRICK: That'll come, Big Daddy.

570   BIG DADDY: Naw, it won't. You're my son and I'm going to straighten you out; now that *I'm* straightened out, I'm going to straighten out you!

BRICK: Yeah?

BIG DADDY: Today the report come in from Ochsner Clinic. Y'know what they told me?

(*His face glows with triumph.*)

The only thing that they could detect with all the instruments of science in that great hospital is a little spastic condition of the colon! And nerves torn to pieces by all that worry about it.

(*A little girl bursts into room with a sparkler clutched in each fist, hops and shrieks like a monkey gone mad and rushes back out again as* BIG DADDY *strikes at her.*)

(*Silence. The two men stare at each other. A woman laughs gaily outside.*)

I want you to know I breathed a sigh of relief almost as powerful as the Vicksburg tornado!

(*There is laughter outside, running footsteps, the soft, plushy sound and light of exploding rockets.*)

(BRICK *stares at him soberly for a long moment; then makes a sort of startled sound in his nostrils and springs up on one foot and hops across the room to grab his crutch, swinging on the furniture for support. He gets the crutch and flees as if in horror for the gallery. His father seizes him by the sleeve of his white silk pajamas.*)

580   Stay here, you son of a bitch! — till I say go!

BRICK: I can't.

BIG DADDY: You sure in hell will, God damn it.

BRICK: No, I can't. We talk, you talk, in — circles! We get no where, no where! It's always the same, you say you want to talk to me and don't have a fuckin' thing to say to me!

BIG DADDY: Nothin' to say when I'm tellin' you I'm going to live when I thought I was dying?!

BRICK: Oh — *that!* — Is that what you have to say to me?

BIG DADDY: Why, you son of a bitch! Ain't that, ain't that — *important?!*

590   BRICK: Well, you said that, that's said, and now I —

BIG DADDY: Now you set back down.

BRICK: You're all balled up, you —

BIG DADDY: I ain't balled up!

BRICK: You are, you're all balled up!

BIG DADDY: Don't tell me what I am, you drunken whelp! I'm going to tear this coat sleeve off if you don't set down!

BRICK: Big Daddy —

BIG DADDY: Do what I tell you! I'm the boss here, now! I want you to know I'm back in the driver's seat now!

(BIG MAMA *rushes in, clutching her great heaving bosom.*)

600   BIG MAMA: Big Daddy!

BIG DADDY: What in hell do you want in here, Big Mama?

BIG MAMA: Oh, Big Daddy! Why are you shouting like that? I just cain't *stainnnnnnd* — it. . . .

BIG DADDY: (*raising the back of his hand above his head*) GIT! — outa here.

(*She rushes back out, sobbing.*)

BRICK: (*softly, sadly*) Christ. . . .

BIG DADDY: (*fiercely*) Yeah! Christ! — is right. . . .

(BRICK *breaks loose and hobbles toward the gallery.*)

(BIG DADDY *jerks his crutch from under* BRICK *so he steps with the injured ankle. He utters a hissing cry of anguish, clutches a chair and pulls it over on top of him on the floor.*)

Son of a — tub of — hog fat. . . .

BRICK: Big Daddy! Give me my crutch.

(BIG DADDY *throws the crutch out of reach.*)

Give me that crutch, Big Daddy.

610 BIG DADDY: Why do you drink?

BRICK: Don't know, give me my crutch!

BIG DADDY: You better think why you drink or give up drinking!

BRICK: Will you please give me my crutch so I can get up off this floor?

BIG DADDY: First you answer my question. Why do you drink? Why are you throwing your life away, boy, like somethin' disgusting you picked up on the street?

BRICK: (*getting onto his knees*) Big Daddy, I'm in pain, I stepped on that foot.

BIG DADDY: Good! I'm glad you're not too numb with the liquor in you to feel some pain!

620 BRICK: You — spilled my — drink. . . .

BIG DADDY: I'll make a bargain with you. You tell me why you drink and I'll hand you one. I'll pour you the liquor myself and hand it to you.

BRICK: Why do I drink?

BIG DADDY: Yea! Why?

BRICK: Give me a drink and I'll tell you.

BIG DADDY: Tell me first!

BRICK: I'll tell you in one word.

BIG DADDY: What word?

BRICK: DISGUST!

(*The clock chimes softly, sweetly.* BIG DADDY *gives it a short, outraged glance.*)

630 Now how about that drink?

BIG DADDY: What are you disgusted with? You got to tell me that, first. Otherwise being disgusted don't make no sense!

BRICK: Give me my crutch.

BIG DADDY: You heard me, you got to tell me what I asked you first.

BRICK: I told you, I said to kill my disgust!

BIG DADDY: DISGUST WITH WHAT!

BRICK: You strike a hard bargain.

BIG DADDY: What are you disgusted with?— an' I'll pass you the liquor.

BRICK: I can hop on one foot, and if I fall, I can crawl.

640   BIG DADDY: You want liquor that bad?

BRICK: (*dragging himself up, clinging to bedstead*) Yeah, I want it that bad.

BIG DADDY: If I give you a drink, will you tell me what it is you're disgusted with, Brick?

BRICK: Yes, sir, I will try to.

(*The old man pours him a drink and solemnly passes it to him.*)

(*There is silence as* BRICK *drinks.*)

Have you ever heard the word "mendacity"?

BIG DADDY: Sure. Mendacity is one of them five dollar words that cheap politicians throw back and forth at each other.

BRICK: You know what it means?

BIG DADDY: Don't it mean lying and liars?

650   BRICK: Yes, sir, lying and liars.

BIG DADDY: Has someone been lying to you?

CHILDREN: (*chanting in chorus offstage*)
We want Big Dad-dee!
We want Big Dad-dee!

(GOOPER *appears in the gallery door.*)

GOOPER: Big Daddy, the kiddies are shouting for you out there.

BIG DADDY: (*fiercely*) Keep out, Gooper!

GOOPER: 'Scuse *me!*

(BIG DADDY *slams the doors after* GOOPER.)

BIG DADDY: Who's been lying to you, has Margaret been lying to you, has your wife been lying to you about something, Brick?

BRICK: Not her. That wouldn't matter.

BIG DADDY: Then who's been lying to you, and what about?

660   BRICK: No one single person and no one lie....

BIG DADDY: Then what, what then, for Christ's sake?

BRICK: — The whole, the whole — thing....

BIG DADDY: Why are you rubbing your head? You got a headache?

BRICK: No, I'm tryin' to —

BIG DADDY: — Concentrate, but you can't because your brain's all soaked with liquor, is that the trouble? Wet brain!

(*He snatches the glass from* BRICK's *hand.*)

What do you know about this mendacity thing? Hell! I could write a book on it! Don't you know that? I could write a book on it and still not cover the subject? Well, I could, I could write a goddam book on it and still not cover the subject anywhere near enough!! — Think of all the lies I got to put up with! — Pretenses! Ain't that mendacity? Having to pretend stuff you don't think or feel or have any idea of? Having for instance to act like

I care for Big Mama! — I haven't been able to stand the sight, sound, or smell of that woman for forty years now! — even when I *laid* her! — regular as a piston....

Pretend to love that son of a bitch of a Gooper and his wife Mae and those five same screechers out there like parrots in a jungle? Jesus! Can't stand to look at 'em!

Church! — it bores the bejesus out of me but I go! — I go an' sit there and listen to the fool preacher!

Clubs! — Elks! Masons! Rotary! — *crap!*

(A spasm of pain makes him clutch his belly. He sinks into a chair and his voice is softer and hoarser.)

You I *do* like for some reason, did always have some kind of real feeling for — affection — respect — yes, always....

You and being a success as a planter is all I ever had any devotion to in my whole life! — and that's the truth....

I don't know why, but it is!

I've lived with mendacity! — Why can't *you* live with it? Hell, you *got* to live with it, there's nothing *else* to *live* with except mendacity, is there?

BRICK: Yes, sir. Yes, sir there is something else that you can live with!

BIG DADDY: What?

BRICK: *(lifting his glass)* This! — Liquor....

BIG DADDY: That's not living, that's dodging away from life.

BRICK: I want to dodge away from it.

BIG DADDY: Then why don't you kill yourself, man?

BRICK: I like to drink....

BIG DADDY: Oh, God, I can't talk to you....

BRICK: I'm sorry, Big Daddy.

BIG DADDY: Not as sorry as I am. I'll tell you something. A little while back when I thought my number was up —

(This speech should have torrential pace and fury.)

— before I found out it was just this — spastic — colon. I thought about you. Should I or should I not, if the jig was up, give you this place when I go — since I hate Gooper an' Mae an' know that they hate me, and since all five same monkeys are little Maes an' Goopers. — And I thought, No! — Then I thought, Yes! — I couldn't make up my mind. I hate Gooper and his five same monkeys and that bitch Mae! Why should I turn over twenty-eight thousand acres of the richest land this side of the valley Nile to not my kind? — But why in hell, on the other hand, Brick — should I subsidize a goddam fool on the bottle? — Liked or not liked, well, maybe even — *loved!* — Why should I do that? — Subsidize worthless behavior? Rot? Corruption?

BRICK: *(smiling)* I understand.

BIG DADDY: Well, if you do, you're smarter than I am, God damn it, because I don't understand. And this I will tell you frankly. I didn't make up my mind at all on that question and still to this day I ain't made out no will! — Well, now I don't *have* to. The pressure is gone. I can just wait and see if you pull yourself together or if you don't.

BRICK: That's right, Big Daddy.

BIG DADDY: You sound like you thought I was kidding.

BRICK: (*rising*) No, sir, I know you're not kidding.

BIG DADDY: But you don't care — ?

720   BRICK: (*hobbling toward the gallery door*) No, sir, I don't care. . . .

(*He stands in the gallery doorway as the night sky turns pink and green and gold with successive flashes of light.*)

BIG DADDY: *WAIT!* — Brick. . . .

(*His voice drops. Suddenly there is something shy, almost tender, in his restraining gesture.*)

Don't let's — leave it like this, like them other talks we've had, we've always — talked around things, we've — just talked around things for some fuckin' reason, I don't know what, it's always like something was left not spoken, something avoided because neither of us was honest enough with the — other. . . .

BRICK: I never lied to you, Big Daddy.

BIG DADDY: Did I ever to *you*?

BRICK: No, sir. . . .

730   BIG DADDY: Then there is at least two people that never lied to each other.

BRICK: But we've never *talked* to each other.

BIG DADDY: We can *now*.

BRICK: Big Daddy, there don't seem to be anything much to say.

BIG DADDY: You say that you drink to kill your disgust with lying.

BRICK: You said to give you a reason.

BIG DADDY: Is liquor the only thing that'll kill this disgust?

BRICK: Now. Yes.

BIG DADDY: But not once, huh?

BRICK: Not when I was still young an' believing. A drinking man's someone who

740   wants to forget he isn't still young an' believing.

BIG DADDY: Believing what?

BRICK: Believing. . . .

BIG DADDY: Believing *what*?

BRICK: (*stubbornly evasive*) Believing. . . .

BIG DADDY: I don't know what the hell you mean by believing and I don't think you know what you mean by believing, but if you still got sports in your blood, go back to sports announcing and —

BRICK: Sit in a glass box watching games I can't play? Describing what I can't do while players do it? Sweating out their disgust and confusion in con-

750   tests I'm not fit for? Drinkin' a coke, half bourbon, so I can stand it? That's no goddam good any more, no help — time just outran me, Big Daddy — got there first. . . .

BIG DADDY: I think you're passing the buck.

BRICK: You know many drinkin' men?

BIG DADDY: (*with a slight, charming smile*) I have known a fair number of that species.

BRICK: Could any of them tell you why he drank?

BIG DADDY: Yep, you're passin' the buck to things like time and disgust with "mendacity" and — crap! — if you got to use that kind of language about a thing, it's ninety-proof bull, and I'm not buying any.

BRICK: I had to give you a reason to get a drink!

BIG DADDY: You started drinkin' when your friend Skipper died.

(Silence for five beats. Then BRICK *makes a startled movement, reaching for his crutch.)*

BRICK: What are you suggesting?

BIG DADDY: I'm suggesting nothing.

(The shuffle and clop of BRICK'S *rapid hobble away from his father's steady, grave attention.)*

— But Gooper an' Mae suggested that there was something not right exactly in your —

BRICK: *(stopping short downstage as if backed to a wall)* "Not right"?

BIG DADDY: Not, well, exactly *normal* in your friendship with —

BRICK: They suggested that, too? I thought that was Maggie's suggestion.

*(*BRICK'S *detachment is at last broken through. His heart is accelerated; his forehead sweat-beaded; his breath becomes more rapid and his voice hoarse. The thing they're discussing, timidly and painfully on the side of* BIG DADDY, *fiercely, violently on* BRICK'S *side, is the inadmissible thing that* SKIPPER *died to disavow between them. The fact that if it existed it had to be disavowed to "keep face" in the world they lived in, may be at the heart of the "mendacity" that* BRICK *drinks to kill his disgust with. It may be the root of his collapse. Or maybe it is only a single manifestation of it, not even the most important. The bird that I hope to catch in the net of this play is not the solution of one man's psychological problem. I'm trying to catch the true quality of experience in a group of people, that cloudy, flickering, evanescent — fiercely charged!— interplay of live human beings in the thundercloud of a common crisis. Some mystery should be left in the revelation of character in a play, just as a great deal of mystery is always left in the revelation of character in life, even in one's own character to himself. This does not absolve the playwright of his duty to observe and probe as clearly and deeply as he legitimately can: but it should steer him away from "pat" conclusions, facile definitions which make a play just a play, not a snare for the truth of human experience.)*

(The following scene should be played with great concentration, with most of the power leashed but palpable in what is left unspoken.)

Who else's suggestion is it, is it *yours?* How many others thought that Skipper and I were —

BIG DADDY: *(gently)* Now, hold on, hold on a minute, son. — I knocked around in my time.

BRICK: What's that got to do with —

BIG DADDY: I said "Hold on!" — I bummed, I bummed this country till I was —

BRICK: Whose suggestion, who else's suggestion is it?

BIG DADDY: Slept in hobo jungles and railroad Y's and flophouses in all cities before I —

BRICK: Oh, *you* think so, too, you call me your son and a queer. Oh! Maybe that's why you put Maggie and me in this room that was Jack Straw's and Peter Ochello's, in which that pair of old sisters slept in a double bed where both of 'em died!

BIG DADDY: *Now just don't go throwing rocks at* —

(*Suddenly* REVEREND TOOKER *appears in the gallery doors, his head slightly, playfully, fatuously cocked, with a practised clergyman's smile, sincere as a bird call blown on a hunter's whistle, the living embodiment of the pious, conventional lie.*)

(BIG DADDY *gasps a little at this perfectly timed, but incongruous, apparition.*)

— What're you lookin' for, Preacher?

REVEREND TOOKER: The gentleman's lavatory, ha ha! — heh, heh...

BIG DADDY: (*with strained courtesy*) — Go back out and walk down to the other end of the gallery, Reverend Tooker, and use the bathroom connected with my bedroom, and if you can't find it, ask them where it is!

REVEREND TOOKER: Ah, thanks.

(*He goes out with a deprecatory chuckle.*)

BIG DADDY: It's hard to talk in this place....

BRICK: Son of a — !

BIG DADDY: (*leaving a lot unspoken*) — I seen all things and understood a lot of them, till 1910. Christ, the year that — I had worn my shoes through, hocked my — I hopped off a yellow dog freight car half a mile down the road, slept in a wagon of cotton outside the gin — Jack Straw an' Peter Ochello took me in. Hired me to manage this place which grew into this one. — When Jack Straw died — why, old Peter Ochello quit eatin' like a dog does when its master's dead, and died, too!

BRICK: Christ!

BIG DADDY: I'm just saying I understand such —

BRICK: (*violently*) Skipper is dead. I have not quit eating!

BIG DADDY: No, but you started drinking.

(BRICK *wheels on his crutch and hurls his glass across the room shouting.*)

BRICK: YOU THINK SO, TOO?

(*Footsteps run on the gallery. There are women's calls.*)

(BIG DADDY *goes toward the door.*)

(BRICK *is transformed, as if a quiet mountain blew suddenly up in volcanic flame.*)

BRICK: You think so, too? You think so, too? You think me an' Skipper did, did, did! — sodomy! — together?

BIG DADDY: Hold — !

BRICK: That what you —

BIG DADDY: — ON — a minute!

BRICK: You think we did dirty things between us, Skipper an' —

810   BIG DADDY: Why are you shouting like that? Why are you —
     BRICK: — Me, is that what you think of Skipper, is that —
     BIG DADDY: — so excited? I don't think nothing. I don't know nothing. I'm
        simply telling you what —
     BRICK: You think that Skipper and me were a pair of dirty old men?
     BIG DADDY: Now that's —
     BRICK: Straw? Ochello? A couple of —
     BIG DADDY: Now just —
     BRICK: — fucking sissies? Queers? Is that what you —
     BIG DADDY: Shhh.
820   BRICK: — think?

(He loses his balance and pitches to his knees without noticing the pain. He grabs the bed and drags himself up.)

BIG DADDY: Jesus! — Whew. . . . Grab my hand!
BRICK: Naw, I don't want your hand. . . .
BIG DADDY: Well, I want yours. Git up!

(He draws him up, keeps an arm about him with concern and affection.)

You broken out in a sweat! You're panting like you'd run a race with —
BRICK: *(freeing himself from his father's hold)* Big Daddy, you shock me, Big Daddy, you, you — *shock* me! Talkin' so —

(He turns away from his father.)

— casually! — about a — thing like that. . . .
    — Don't you know how people *feel* about things like that? How, how *disgusted* they are by things like that? Why, at Ole Miss when it was discov-
830 ered a pledge to our fraternity, Skipper's and mine, did a, *attempted* to do a, unnatural thing with —
    We not only dropped him like a hot rock! — We told him to git off the campus, and he did, he got! — All the way to —

(He halts, breathless.)

BIG DADDY: — Where?
BRICK: — North Africa, last I heard!
BIG DADDY: Well, I have come back from further away than that, I have just now returned from the other side of the moon, death's country, son, and I'm not easy to shock by anything here.

(He comes downstage and faces out.)

Always, anyhow, lived with too much space around me to be infected by
840 ideas of other people. One thing you can grow on a big place more important than cotton! — is *tolerance!* — I grown it.

(He returns toward BRICK.)

BRICK: Why can't exceptional friendship, *real, real, deep, deep friendship!* between two men be respected as something clean and decent without being thought of as —

BIG DADDY: It can, it is, for God's sake.

BRICK: —Fairies. . . .

(*In his utterance of this word, we gauge the wide and profound reach of the conventional mores he got from the world that crowned him with early laurel.*)

BIG DADDY: I told Mae an' Gooper —

BRICK: Frig Mae and Gooper, frig all dirty lies and liars! — Skipper and me had a clean, true thing between us! — had a clean friendship, practically all our lives, till Maggie got the idea you're talking about. Normal? No! — It was too rare to be normal, any true thing between two people is too rare to be normal. Oh, once in a while he put his hand on my shoulder or I'd put mine on his, oh, maybe even, when we were touring the country in pro-football an' shared hotel-rooms we'd reach across the space between the two beds and shake hands to say goodnight, yeah, one or two times we —

BIG DADDY: Brick, nobody thinks that that's not normal!

BRICK: Well, they're mistaken, it was! It was a pure an' true thing an' that's not normal.

MAE: (*off stage*) Big Daddy, they're startin' the fireworks.

(*They both stare straight at each other for a long moment. The tension breaks and both turn away as if tired.*)

BIG DADDY: Yeah, it's — hard t' — talk. . . .

BRICK: All right, then, let's — let it go. . . .

BIG DADDY: Why did Skipper crack up? Why have you?

(BRICK *looks back at his father again. He has already decided, without knowing that he has made this decision, that he is going to tell his father that he is dying of cancer. Only this could even the score between them: one inadmissible thing in return for another.*)

BRICK: (*ominously*) All right. You're asking for it, Big Daddy. We're finally going to have that real true talk you wanted. It's too late to stop it, now, we got to carry it through and cover every subject.

(*He hobbles back to the liquor cabinet.*)

Uh-huh.

(*He opens the ice bucket and picks up the silver tongs with slow admiration of their frosty brightness.*)

Maggie declares that Skipper and I went into pro-football after we left Ole Miss because we were scared to grow up . . .

(*He moves downstage with the shuffle and clop of a cripple on a crutch. As* MARGARET *did when her speech became "recitative," he looks out into the house, commanding its attention by his direct, concentrated gaze — a broken, "tragically elegant" figure telling simply as much as he knows of "the Truth":*)

— Wanted to — keep on tossing — those long, long! — high, high! — passes that — couldn't be intercepted except by time, the aerial attack that made us famous! And so we did, we did, we kept it up for one season, that aerial attack, we held it high! — Yeah, but —

— that summer, Maggie, she laid the law down to me, said, Now or never, and so I married Maggie....

BIG DADDY: How was Maggie in bed?

BRICK: (*wryly*) Great! the greatest!

(BIG DADDY *nods as if he thought so.*)

She went on the road that fall with the Dixie Stars. Oh, she made a great show of being the world's best sport. She wore a — wore a — tall bearskin cap! A shako, they call it, a dyed moleskin coat, a moleskin coat dyed red! — Cut up crazy! Rented hotel ballrooms for victory celebrations, wouldn't cancel them when it — turned out — defeat....

MAGGIE THE CAT! Ha ha!

(BIG DADDY *nods.*)

— But Skipper, he had some fever which came back on him which doctors couldn't explain and I got that injury — turned out to be just a shadow on the X-ray plate — and a touch of bursitis....

I lay in a hospital bed, watched our games on TV, saw Maggie on the bench next to Skipper when he was hauled out of a game for stumbles, fumbles! — Burned me up the way she hung on his arm! — Y'know, I think that Maggie had always felt sort of left out because she and me never got any closer together than two people just get in bed, which is not much closer than two cats on a — fence humping....

So! She took this time to work on poor dumb Skipper. He was a less than average student at Ole Miss, you know that, don't you?! — Poured in his mind the dirty, false idea that what we were, him and me, was a frustrated case of that ole pair of sisters that lived in this room, Jack Straw and Peter Ochello! — He, poor Skipper, went to bed with Maggie to prove it wasn't true, and when it didn't work out, he thought it *was* true! — Skipper broke in two like a rotten stick — nobody ever turned so fast to a lush — or died of it so quick....

— Now are you satisfied?

(BIG DADDY *has listened to this story, dividing the grain from the chaff. Now he looks at his son.*)

BIG DADDY: Are *you* satisfied?

BRICK: With what?

BIG DADDY: That half-ass story!

BRICK: What's half-ass about it?

BIG DADDY: Something's left out of that story. What did you leave out?

(*The phone has started ringing in the hall.*)

GOOPER: (*off stage*) Hello.

(*As if it reminded him of something,* BRICK *glances suddenly toward the sound and says:*)

BRICK: Yes! — I left out a long-distance call which I had from Skipper —

GOOPER: Speaking, go ahead.

BRICK: — In which he made a drunken confession to me and on which I hung
up!

GOOPER: No.

BRICK: — Last time we spoke to each other in our lives...

GOOPER: No, sir.

BIG DADDY: You musta said something to him before you hung up.

BRICK: What could I say to him?

BIG DADDY: Anything. Something.

BRICK: Nothing.

BIG DADDY: Just hung up?

BRICK: Just hung up.

BIG DADDY: Uh-huh. Anyhow now! — we have tracked down the lie with
which you're disgusted and which you are drinking to kill your disgust
with, Brick. You been passing the buck. This disgust with mendacity is
disgust with yourself.

You! — dug the grave of your friend and kicked him in it! — before
you'd face truth with him!

BRICK: *His* truth, not *mine!*

BIG DADDY: His truth, okay! But you wouldn't face it with him!

BRICK: Who *can* face truth? Can *you?*

BIG DADDY: Now don't start passin' the rotten buck again, boy!

BRICK: *How about these birthday congratulations, these many, many happy returns
of the day, when ev'rybody knows there won't be any except you!*

(GOOPER, *who has answered the hall phone, lets out a high, shrill laugh; the
voice becomes audible saying:* "No, no, you got it all wrong! Upside down!
Are you crazy?")

(BRICK *suddenly catches his breath as he realized that he has made a shocking
disclosure. He hobbles a few paces, then freezes, and without looking at his
father's shocked face, says:*)

Let's, let's — go out, now, and — watch the fireworks. Come on, Big Daddy.

(BIG DADDY *moves suddenly forward and grabs hold of the boy's crutch like it
was a weapon for which they were fighting for possession.*)

BIG DADDY: Oh, no, no! No one's going out! What did you start to say?

BRICK: I don't remember.

BIG DADDY: "Many happy returns when they know there won't be any"?

BRICK: Aw, hell, Big Daddy, forget it. Come on out on the gallery and look at
the fireworks they're shooting off for your birthday....

BIG DADDY: First you finish that remark you were makin' before you cut off.
"Many happy returns when they know there won't be any"? — Ain't that
what you just said?

BRICK: Look, now. I can get around without that crutch if I have to but it
would be a lot easier on the furniture an' glassware if I didn' have to go
swinging along like Tarzan of th'—

BIG DADDY: FINISH! WHAT YOU WAS SAYIN'!

(An eerie green glow shows in sky behind him.)

BRICK: *(sucking the ice in his glass, speech becoming thick)* Leave th' place to
Gooper and Mae an' their five little same little monkeys. All I want is —
BIG DADDY: "LEAVE TH' PLACE," did you say?
BRICK: *(vaguely)* All twenty-eight acres of the richest land this side
of the valley Nile.
950 BIG DADDY: Who said I was "leaving the place" to Gooper or anybody? This is
my sixty-fifth birthday! I got fifteen years or twenty years left in me! I'll
outlive *you!* I'll bury you an' have to pay for your coffin!
BRICK: Sure. Many happy returns. Now let's go watch the fireworks, come on,
let's —
BIG DADDY: Lying, have they been lying? About the report from th' — clinic?
Did they, did they — find something? — *Cancer.* Maybe?
BRICK: Mendacity is a system that we live in. Liquor is one way out an' death's
the other. . . .

(He takes the crutch from BIG DADDY'S *loose grip and swings out on the
gallery leaving the doors open.)*

(A song, "Pick a Bale of Cotton," is heard.)

MAE: *(appearing in door)* Oh, Big Daddy, the field hands are singin' fo' you!
960 BRICK: I'm sorry, Big Daddy. My head don't work any more and it's hard for me
to understand how anybody could care if he lived or died or was dying or
cared about anything but whether or not there was liquor left in the bottle
and so I said what I said without thinking. In some ways I'm no better than
the others, in some ways worse because I'm less alive. Maybe it's being alive
that makes them lie, and being almost *not* alive makes me sort of accidentally truthful — I don't know but — anyway — we've been friends . . .
— And being friends is telling each other the truth. . . .

(There is a pause.)

You told *me!* I told *you!*
BIG DADDY: *(slowly and passionately)* CHRIST — DAMN —
970 GOOPER: *(off stage)* Let her go!

(Fireworks off stage right.)

BIG DADDY: — ALL — LYING SONS OF — LYING BITCHES!

*(He straightens at last and crosses to the inside door. At the door he turns and
looks back as if he had some desperate question he couldn't put into words.
Then he nods reflectively and says in a hoarse voice:)*

Yes, all liars, all liars, all lying dying liars!

(This is said slowly, slowly, with a fierce revulsion. He goes on out.)

— Lying! Dying! Liars!

*(*BRICK *remains motionless as the lights dim out and the curtain falls.)*

CURTAIN

ACT THREE

There is no lapse of time. BIG DADDY *is seen leaving as at the end of Act 2.*

BIG DADDY: ALL LYIN'— DYIN'! — LIARS! LIARS! — LIARS!

(MARGARET *enters.*)

MARGARET: Brick, what in the name of God was goin' on in this room?

(DIXIE *and* TRIXIE *enter through the doors and circle around* MARGARET *shouting.* MAE *enters from the lower gallery window.*)

MAE: Dixie, Trixie, you quit that!

(GOOPER *enters through the doors.*)

Gooper, will y' please get these kiddies to bed right now!
GOOPER: Mae, you seen Big Mama?
MAE: Not yet.

(GOOPER *and kids exit through the doors.* REVEREND TOOKER *enters through the windows.*)

REVEREND TOOKER: Those kiddies are so full of vitality. I think I'll have to be starting back to town.
MAE: Not yet, Preacher. You know we regard you as a member of this family, one of our closest an' dearest, so you just got t' be with us when Doc Baugh gives Big Mama th' actual truth about th' report from the clinic.
MARGARET: Where do you think you're going?
BRICK: Out for some air.
MARGARET: Why'd Big Daddy shout "Liars"?
MAE: Has Big Daddy gone to bed, Brick?
GOOPER: (*entering*) Now where is that old lady?
REVEREND TOOKER: I'll look for her.

(*He exits to the gallery.*)

MAE: Cain'tcha find her, Gooper?
GOOPER: She's avoidin' this talk.
MAE: I think she senses somethin'.
MARGARET: (*going out on the gallery to* BRICK) Brick, they're goin' to tell Big Mama the truth about Big Daddy and she's goin' to need you.
DOCTOR BAUGH: This is going to be painful.
MAE: Painful things caint always be avoided.
REVEREND TOOKER: I see Big Mama.
GOOPER: Hey, Big Mama, come here.
MAE: Hush, Gooper, don't holler.
BIG MAMA: (*entering*) Too much smell of burnt fireworks makes me feel a little bit sick at my stomach. — Where is Big Daddy?
MAE: That's what I want to know, where has Big Daddy gone?
BIG MAMA: He must have turned in, I reckon he went to baid...
GOOPER: Well, then, now we can talk.

BIG MAMA: What *is* this talk, *what* talk?

(MARGARET *appears on the gallery, talking to* DOCTOR BAUGH.)

MARGARET: (*musically*) My family freed their slaves ten years before abolition. My great-great-grandfather gave his slaves their freedom five years before the War between the States started!

MAE: Oh, for God's sake! Maggie's climbed back up in her family tree!

MARGARET: (*sweetly*) What, Mae?

(*The pace must be very quick: great Southern animation.*)

BIG MAMA: (*addressing them all*) I think Big Daddy was just worn out. He loves his family, he loves to have them around him, but it's a strain on his nerves. He wasn't himself tonight, Big Daddy wasn't himself, I could tell he was all worked up.

REVEREND TOOKER: I think he's remarkable.

BIG MAMA: Yaiss! Just remarkable. Did you all notice the food he ate at that table? Did you all notice the supper he put away? Why he ate like a hawss!

GOOPER: I hope he doesn't regret it.

BIG MAMA: What? Why that man — ate a huge piece of cawn bread with molasses on it! Helped himself twice to hoppin' John.[1]

MARGARET: Big Daddy loves hoppin' John. — We had a real country dinner.

BIG MAMA: (*overlapping* MARGARET) Yaiss, he simply adores it! an' candied yams? Son? That man put away enough food at that table to stuff a *field* hand!

GOOPER: (*with grim relish*) I hope he don't have to pay for it later on . . .

BIG MAMA: (*fiercely*) What's *that*, Gooper?

MAE: Gooper says he hopes Big Daddy doesn't suffer tonight.

BIG MAMA: Oh, shoot, Gooper says, Gooper says! Why should Big Daddy suffer for satisfying a normal appetite? There's nothin' wrong with that man but nerves, he's sound as a dollar! And now he knows he is an' that's why he ate such a supper. He had a big load off his mind, knowin' he wasn't doomed t' — what he thought he was doomed to . . .

MARGARET: (*sadly and sweetly*) Bless his old sweet soul . . .

BIG MAMA: (*vaguely*) Yais, bless his heart, where's Brick?

MAE: Outside.

GOOPER: — Drinkin' . . .

BIG MAMA: I know he's drinkin'. Cain't I see he's drinkin' without you continually tellin' me that boy's drinkin'?

MARGARET: Good for you, Big Mama!

(*She applauds.*)

BIG MAMA: Other people *drink* and *have* drunk an' will *drink*, as long as they make that stuff an' put it in bottles.

MARGARET: That's the truth. I never trusted a man that didn't drink.

BIG MAMA: *Brick? Brick!*

MARGARET: He's still on the gall'ry. I'll go bring him in so we can talk.

BIG MAMA: (*worriedly*) I don't know what this mysterious family conference is about.

---

1 popular Southern dish of rice, pork, and black-eyed peas.

(Awkward silence. BIG MAMA *looks from face to face, then belches slightly and mutters, "Excuse me. . . ." She opens an ornamental fan suspended about her throat. A black lace fan to go with her black lace gown, and fans her wilting corsage, sniffing nervously and looking from face to face in the uncomfortable silence as* MARGARET *calls "Brick?" and* BRICK *sings to the moon on the gallery.)*

MARGARET: Brick, they're gonna tell Big Mama the truth an' she's gonna need you.

BIG MAMA: I don't know what's wrong here, you all have such long faces! Open that door on the hall and let some air circulate through here, will you please, Gooper?

MAE: I think we'd better leave that door closed, Big Mama, till after the talk.

80   MARGARET: Brick!

BIG MAMA: Reveren' Tooker, will *you* please open that door?

REVEREND TOOKER: I sure will, Big Mama.

MAE: I just didn't think we ought t' take any chance of Big Daddy hearin' a word of this discussion.

BIG MAMA: I *swan!* Nothing's going to be said in Big Daddy's house that he caint hear if he want to!

GOOPER: Well, Big Mama, it's —

*(*MAE *gives him a quick, hard poke to shut him up. He glares at her fiercely as she circles before him like a burlesque ballerina, raising her skinny bare arms over her head, jangling her bracelets, exclaiming:)*

MAE: A breeze! A breeze!

REVEREND TOOKER: I think this house is the coolest house in the Delta. — Did
90   you all know that Halsey Banks's widow put air-conditioning units in the church and rectory at Friar's Point in memory of Halsey?

(General conversation has resumed; everybody is chatting so that the stage sounds like a bird cage.)

GOOPER: Too bad nobody cools your church off for you. I bet you sweat in that pulpit these hot Sundays, Reverend Tooker.

REVEREND TOOKER: Yes, my vestments are drenched. Last Sunday the gold in my chasuble faded into the purple.

GOOPER: Reveren', you musta been preachin' hell's fire last Sunday.

MAE: *(at the same time to* DOCTOR BAUGH*)* You reckon those vitamin B12 injections are what they're cracked up t' be, Doc Baugh?

DOCTOR BAUGH: Well, if you want to be stuck with something I guess they're
100   as good to be stuck with as anything else.

BIG MAMA: *(at the gallery door)* Maggie, Maggie, aren't you comin' with Brick?

MAE: *(suddenly and loudly, creating a silence)* I have a strange feeling, I have a peculiar feeling!

BIG MAMA: *(turning from the gallery)* What feeling?

MAE: That Brick said somethin' he shouldn't of said t' Big Daddy.

BIG MAMA: Now what on earth could Brick of said t' Big Daddy that he shouldn't say?

GOOPER: Big Mama, there's somethin'—

MAE: NOW, WAIT!

> (*She rushes up to* BIG MAMA *and gives her a quick hug and kiss.* BIG MAMA *pushes her impatiently off.*)

110   DOCTOR BAUGH: In my day they had what they call the Keeley cure for heavy drinkers.

BIG MAMA: Shoot!

DOCTOR BAUGH: But now I understand they just take some kind of tablets.

GOOPER: They call them "Annie Bust"[2] tablets.

BIG MAMA: *Brick* don't need to take *nothin'*.

> (BRICK *and* MARGARET *appear in gallery doors,* BIG MAMA *unaware of his presence behind her.*)

That boy is just broken up over Skipper's death. You know how poor Skipper died. They gave him a big, big dose of that sodium amytal stuff at his home and then they called the ambulance and give him another big, big dose of it at the hospital and that and all of the alcohol in his system

120   fo' months an' months just proved too much for his heart . . . I'm scared of needles! I'm more scared of a needle than the knife . . . I think more people have been needled out of this world than —

> (*She stops short and wheels about.*)

Oh — here's Brick! My precious baby —

> (*She turns upon* BRICK *with short, fat arms extended, at the same time uttering a loud, short sob, which is both comic and touching.* BRICK *smiles and bows slightly, making a burlesque gesture of gallantry for* MARGARET *to pass before him into the room. Then he hobbles on his crutch directly to the liquor cabinet and there is absolute silence, with everybody looking at* BRICK *as everybody has always looked at* BRICK *when he spoke or moved or appeared. One by one he drops ice cubes in his glass, then suddenly, but not quickly, looks back over his shoulder with a wry, charming smile, and says:*)

BRICK: I'm sorry! Anyone else?

BIG MAMA: (*sadly*) No, son. I *wish* you wouldn't!

BRICK: I wish I didn't have to, Big Mama, but I'm still waiting for that click in my head which makes it all smooth out!

BIG MAMA: Ow, Brick, you — BREAK MY HEART!

MARGARET: (*at same time*) Brick, go sit with Big Mama!

130   BIG MAMA: I just cain't staiiiiii-nnnnnnnd-it . . .

> (*She sobs.*)

MAE: Now that we're all assembled —

GOOPER: We kin talk . . .

BIG MAMA: Breaks my heart . . .

MARGARET: Sit with Big Mama, Brick, and hold her hand.

---

2 Antabuse: trade name for disulphiram, a pharmaceutical used for treating chronic alcoholism.

(BIG MAMA *sniffs very loudly three times, almost like three drumbeats in the pocket of silence.*)

BRICK: You do that, Maggie. I'm a restless cripple. I got to stay on my crutch.

(BRICK *hobbles to the gallery door; leans there as if waiting.*)

(MAE *sits beside* BIG MAMA, *while* GOOPER *moves in front and sits on the end of the couch, facing her.* REVEREND TOOKER *moves nervously into the space between them; on the other side,* DOCTOR BAUGH *stands looking at nothing in particular and lights a cigar.* MARGARET *turns away.*)

BIG MAMA: Why're you all *surroundin'* me — like this? Why're you all starin' at me like this an' makin' signs at each other?

(REVEREND TOOKER *steps back startled.*)

MAE: Calm yourself, Big Mama.

BIG MAMA: Calm you'self, *you'self*, Sister Woman. How could I calm myself with everyone starin' at me as if big drops of blood had broken out on m'face? What's this all about, annh! What?

(GOOPER *coughs and takes a center position.*)

GOOPER: Now, Doc Baugh.

MAE: Doc Baugh?

GOOPER: Big Mama wants to know the complete truth about the report we got from the Ochsner Clinic.

MAE: (*eagerly*)— on Big Daddy's condition!

GOOPER: Yais, on Big Daddy's condition, we got to face it.

DOCTOR BAUGH: Well . . .

BIG MAMA: (*terrified, rising*) Is there? Something? Something that I? Don't — know?

(*In these few words, this startled, very soft, question,* BIG MAMA *reviews the history of her forty-five years with* BIG DADDY, *her great, almost embarrassingly true-hearted and simple-minded devotion to* BIG DADDY, *who must have had something* BRICK *has, who made himself loved so much by the "simple expedient" of not loving enough to disturb his charming detachment, also once coupled, like* BRICK, *with virile beauty.*)

(BIG MAMA *has a dignity at this moment; she almost stops being fat.*)

DOCTOR BAUGH: (*after a pause, uncomfortably*) Yes?—Well—

BIG MAMA: I!!!— want to —*knowwwwww* . . .

(*Immediately she thrusts her fist to her mouth as if to deny that statement. Then for some curious reason, she snatches the withered corsage from her breast and hurls it on the floor and steps on it with her short, fat feet.*)

Somebody must be lyin'! — I want to know!

MAE: Sit down, Big Mama, sit down on this sofa.

MARGARET: Brick, go sit with Big Mama.

BIG MAMA: *What is it, what is it?*

DOCTOR BAUGH: I never have seen a more thorough examination than Big
    Daddy Pollitt was given in all my experience with the Ochsner Clinic.

GOOPER: It's one of the best in the country.

160   MAE: It's THE best in the country — bar *none!*

> (*For some reason she gives* GOOPER *a violent poke as she goes past him. He slaps at her hand without removing his eyes from his mother's face.*)

DOCTOR BAUGH: Of course they were ninety-nine and nine-tenths per cent sure
    before they even started.

BIG MAMA: Sure of what, sure of what, sure of — *what?* — *what?*

> (*She catches her breath in a startled sob.* MAE *kisses her quickly. She thrusts* MAE *fiercely away from her, staring at the* DOCTOR.)

MAE: Mommy, be a brave girl!

BRICK: (*in the doorway, softly*) "By the light, by the light, Of the sil-ve-ry
    mo-oo-n..."

GOOPER: Shut up! — Brick.

BRICK: Sorry...

> (*He wanders out on the gallery.*)

DOCTOR BAUGH: But now, you see, Big Mama, they cut a piece off this growth,
170   a specimen of the tissue and —

BIG MAMA: Growth? You told Big Daddy —

DOCTOR BAUGH: Now wait.

BIG MAMA: (*fiercely*) You told me and Big Daddy there wasn't a thing wrong with
    him but —

MAE: Big Mama, they always —

GOOPER: Let Doc Baugh talk, will yuh?

BIG MAMA: — little spastic condition of —

> (*Her breath gives out in a sob.*)

DOCTOR BAUGH: Yes, that's what we told Big Daddy. But we had this bit of
    tissue run through the laboratory and I'm sorry to say the test was positive
180   on it. It's — well — malignant...

> (*Pause.*)

BIG MAMA: — Cancer?! Cancer?!

> (DOCTOR BAUGH *nods gravely.* BIG MAMA *gives a long gasping cry.*)

MAE AND GOOPER: Now, now, now, Big Mama, you had to know...

BIG MAMA: WHY DIDN'T THEY CUT IT OUT OF HIM? HANH? HANH?

DOCTOR BAUGH: Involved too much, Big Mama, too many organs affected.

MAE: Big Mama, the liver's affected and so's the kidneys, both! It's gone way past
    what they call a —

GOOPER: A surgical risk.

MAE: — Uh-huh...

> (BIG MAMA *draws a breath like a dying gasp.*)

REVEREND TOOKER: Tch, tch, tch, tch, tch!

190 DOCTOR BAUGH: Yes it's gone past the knife.

MAE: *That's why he's turned yellow, Mommy!*

BIG MAMA: *Git away from me, git away from me, Mae!*

(She rises abruptly.)

I want Brick! Where's Brick? Where is my only son?

MAE: Mama! Did she say "*only* son"?

GOOPER: What does that make *me*?

MAE: A sober responsible man with five precious children! —*Six!*

BIG MAMA: I want Brick to tell me! Brick! Brick!

MARGARET: *(rising from her reflections in a corner)* Brick was so upset he went back out.

200 BIG MAMA: *Brick!*

MARGARET: Mama, let *me* tell you!

BIG MAMA: No, no, leave me alone, you're not my blood!

GOOPER: *Mama, I'm your son!* Listen to *me!*

MAE: Gooper's your son, he's your first-born!

BIG MAMA: Gooper never liked Daddy.

MAE: *(as if terribly shocked) That's not TRUE!*

(There is a pause. The minister coughs and rises.)

REVEREND TOOKER: *(to* MAE*)* I think I'd better slip away at this point.

(Discreetly)

Good night, good night, everybody, and God bless you all . . . on this place . . .

(He slips out.)

*(*MAE *coughs and points at* BIG MAMA.*)*

210 DOCTOR BAUGH: Well, Big Mama . . .

(He sighs.)

BIG MAMA: It's all a mistake, I know it's just a bad dream.

DOCTOR BAUGH: We're gonna keep Big Daddy as comfortable as we can.

BIG MAMA: Yes, it's just a bad dream, that's all it is, it's just an awful dream.

GOOPER: In my opinion Big Daddy is having some pain but won't admit that he has it.

BIG MAMA: Just a dream, a bad dream.

DOCTOR BAUGH: That's what lots of them do, they think if they don't admit they're having the pain they can sort of escape the fact of it.

GOOPER: *(with relish)* Yes, they get sly about it, they get real sly about it.

220 MAE: Gooper and I think —

GOOPER: Shut up, Mae! Big Mama, I think — Big Daddy ought to be started on morphine.

BIG MAMA: Nobody's going to give Big Daddy morphine.

DOCTOR BAUGH: Now, Big Mama, when that pain strikes it's going to strike mighty hard and Big Daddy's going to need the needle to bear it.

BIG MAMA: I tell you, nobody's going to give him morphine.

MAE: Big Mama, you don't want to see Big Daddy suffer, you know you —

(GOOPER, *standing beside her, gives her a savage poke.*)

DOCTOR BAUGH: (*placing a package on the table*) I'm leaving this stuff here, so if there's a sudden attack you all won't have to send out for it.

230   MAE: I know how to give a hypo.

BIG MAMA: Nobody's gonna give Big Daddy morphine.

GOOPER: Mae took a course in nursing during the war.

MARGARET: Somehow I don't think Big Daddy would want Mae to give him a hypo.

MAE: You think he'd want *you* to do it?

DOCTOR BAUGH: Well . . .

(DOCTOR BAUGH *rises.*)

GOOPER: Doctor Baugh is goin'.

DOCTOR BAUGH: Yes, I got to be goin'. Well, keep your chin up, Big Mama.

GOOPER: (*with jocularity*) She's gonna keep *both* chins up, aren't you, Big Mama?

(BIG MAMA *sobs.*)

240   Now stop that, Big Mama.

GOOPER: (*at the door with* DOCTOR BAUGH) Well, Doc, we sure do appreciate all you done. I'm telling you, we're surely obligated to you for —

(DOCTOR BAUGH *has gone out without a glance at him.*)

— I guess that doctor has got a lot on his mind but it wouldn't hurt him to act a little more human . . .

(BIG MAMA *sobs.*)

Now be a brave girl, Mommy.

BIG MAMA: It's not true, I know that it's just not true!

GOOPER: Mama, those tests are infallible!

BIG MAMA: Why are you so determined to see your father daid?

MAE: Big Mama!

250   MARGARET: (*gently*) I know what Big Mama means.

MAE: (*fiercely*) Oh, do you?

MARGARET: (*quietly and very sadly*) Yes, I think I do.

MAE: For a newcomer in the family you sure do show a lot of understanding.

MARGARET: Understanding is needed on this place.

MAE: I guess you must have needed a lot of it in your family, Maggie, with your father's liquor problem and now you've got Brick with his!

MARGARET: Brick does not have a liquor problem at all. Brick is devoted to Big Daddy. This thing is a terrible strain on him.

BIG MAMA: Brick is Big Daddy's boy, but he drinks too much and it worries

260   me and Big Daddy, and, Margaret, you've got to co-operate with us, you've got to co-operate with Big Daddy and me in getting Brick straightened out. Because it will break Big Daddy's heart if Brick don't pull himself together and take hold of things.

MAE: Take hold of *what* things, Big Mama?

BIG MAMA: The place.

(*There is a quick violent look between* MAE *and* GOOPER.)

GOOPER: Big Mama, you've had a shock.

MAE: Yais, we've all had a shock, but . . .

270   GOOPER: Let's be realistic —

MAE: — Big Daddy would never, would *never*, be foolish enough to —

GOOPER: — put this place in irresponsible hands!

BIG MAMA: Big Daddy ain't going to leave the place in anybody's hand; Big
Daddy is *not* going to die. I want you to get that in your heads, all of you!

MAE: Mommy, Mommy, Big Mama, we're just as hopeful an' optimistic as you
are about Big Daddy's prospects, we have faith in *prayer*— but nevertheless
there are certain matters that have to be discussed an' dealt with, because
otherwise —

GOOPER: Eventualities have to be considered and now's the time . . . Mae, will
you please get my briefcase out of our room?

MAE: Yes, honey.

(*She rises and goes out through the hall door.*)

280   GOOPER: (*standing over* BIG MAMA) Now, Big Mom. What you said just now
was not at all true and you know it. I've always loved Big Daddy in my
own quiet way. I never made a show of it, and I know that Big Daddy has
always been fond of me in a quiet way, too, and he never made a show of
it neither.

(MAE *returns with* GOOPER's *briefcase.*)

MAE: Here's your briefcase, Gooper, honey.

GOOPER: (*handing the briefcase back to her*) Thank you . . . Of cou'se, my relationship with Big Daddy is different from Brick's.

MAE: You're eight years older'n Brick an' always had t' carry a bigger load of th'
responsibilities than Brick ever had t' carry. He never carried a thing in his
290   life but a football or a highball.

GOOPER: Mae, will y' let me talk, please?

MAE: Yes, honey.

GOOPER: Now, a twenty-eight-thousand-acre plantation's a mighty big thing
t' run.

MAE: Almost singlehanded.

(MARGARET *has gone out onto the gallery and can be heard calling softly to*
BRICK.)

BIG MAMA: You never had to run this place! What are you talking about? As if
Big Daddy was dead and in his grave, you had to run it? Why, you just
helped him out with a few business details and had your law practice at the
same time in Memphis!

300   MAE: Oh, Mommy, Mommy, Big Mommy! Let's be fair!

MARGARET: Brick!

MAE: Why, Gooper has given himself body and soul to keeping this place up for the past five years since Big Daddy's health started failing.

MARGARET: Brick!

MAE: Gooper won't say it, Gooper never thought of it as a duty, he just did it And what did Brick do? Brick kept living in his past glory at college! Still a football player at twenty-seven!

MARGARET: (*returning alone*) Who are you talking about now? Brick? A football player? He isn't a football player and you know it. Brick is a sports announcer on T.V. and one of the best-known ones in the country!

MAE: I'm talking about what he was.

MARGARET: Well, I wish you would just stop talking about my husband.

GOOPER: I've got a right to discuss my brother with other members of MY OWN family, which don't include *you*. Why don't you go out there and drink with Brick?

MARGARET: I've never seen such malice toward a brother.

GOOPER: How about his for me? Why, he can't stand to be in the same room with me!

MARGARET: This is a deliberate campaign of vilification for the most disgusting and sordid reason on earth, and I know what it is! It's *avarice, avarice, greed, greed!*

BIG MAMA: *Oh, I'll scream! I will scream in a moment unless this stops!*

(GOOPER *has stalked up to* MARGARET *with clenched fists at his sides as if he would strike her.* MAE *distorts her face again into a hideous grimace behind* MARGARET'*s back.*)

BIG MAMA: (*sobs*) Margaret. Child. Come here. Sit next to Big Mama.

MARGARET: Precious Mommy. I'm sorry, I'm sorry, I — !

(*She bends her long graceful neck to press her forehead to* BIG MAMA'S *bulging shoulder under its black chiffon.*)

MAE: How beautiful, how touching, this display of devotion! Do you know why she's childless? She's childless because that big beautiful athlete husband of hers won't go to bed with her!

GOOPER: You jest won't let me do this in a nice way, will yah? Aw right — I don't give a goddam if Big Daddy likes me or don't like me or did or never did or will or will never! I'm just appealing to a sense of common decency and fair play. I'll tell you the truth. I've resented Big Daddy's partiality to Brick ever since Brick was born, and the way I've been treated like I was just barely good enough to spit on and sometimes not even good enough for that. Big Daddy is dying of cancer, and it's spread all through him and it's attacked all his vital organs including the kidneys and right now he is sinking into uremia, and you all know what uremia is, it's poisoning of the whole system due to the failure of the body to eliminate its poisons.

MARGARET: (*to herself, downstage, hissingly*) Poisons, poisons! Venomous thoughts and words! In hearts and minds! — That's poisons!

GOOPER: (*overlapping her*) I am asking for a square deal, and, by God, I expect to get one. But if I don't get one, if there's any peculiar shenanigans going on around here behind my back, well, I'm not a corporation lawyer for nothing, I know how to protect my own interests.

(BRICK *enters from the gallery with a tranquil, blurred smile, carrying an empty glass with him.*)

BRICK: Storm coming up.

GOOPER: Oh! A late arrival!

MAE: Behold the conquering hero comes!

GOOPER: The fabulous Brick Pollitt! Remember him?—Who could forget him!

MAE: He looks like he's been injured in a game!

350   GOOPER: Yep, I'm afraid you'll have to warm the bench at the Sugar Bowl this year, Brick!

(MAE *laughs shrilly.*)

Or was it the Rose Bowl that he made that famous run in?—

(*Thunder.*)

MAE: The punch bowl, honey. It was in the punch bowl, the cut-glass punch bowl!

GOOPER: Oh, that's right, I'm getting the bowls mixed up!

MARGARET: Why don't you stop venting your malice and envy on a sick boy?

BIG MAMA: *Now you two hush, I mean it, hush, all of you, hush!*

DAISY, SOOKEY: Storm! Storm comin'! Storm! Storm!

LACEY: Brightie, close them shutters.

360   GOOPER: Lacey, put the top up on my Cadillac, will yuh?

LACEY: Yes, suh, Mistah Pollitt!

GOOPER: (*at the same time*) Big Mama, you know it's necessary for me t' go back to Memphis in th' mornin' t' represent the Parker estate in a lawsuit.

(MAE *sits on the bed and arranges papers she has taken from the briefcase.*)

BIG MAMA: Is it, Gooper?

MAE: Yaiss.

GOOPER: That's why I'm forced to — to bring up a problem that —

MAE: Somethin' that's too important t' be put off!

GOOPER: If Brick was sober, he ought to be in on this.

MARGARET: Brick is present; we're present.

370   GOOPER: Well, good. I will now give you this outline my partner, Tom Bullitt, an' me have drawn up — a sort of dummy — trusteeship.

MARGARET: Oh, that's it! You'll be in charge an' dole out remittances, will you?

GOOPER: This we did as soon as we got the report on Big Daddy from th' Ochsner Laboratories. We did this thing, I mean we drew up this dummy outline with the advice and assistance of the Chairman of the Boa'd of Directors of th' Southern Plantahs Bank and Trust Company in Memphis, C. C. Bellowes, a man who handles estates for all th' prominent fam'lies in West Tennessee and th' Delta.

BIG MAMA: Gooper?

380   GOOPER: *(crouching in front of* BIG MAMA*)* Now this is not — not final, or anything like it. This is just a preliminary outline. But it does provide a basis —
a design — a — possible, feasible —*plan!*

MARGARET: Yes, I'll bet it's a plan.

(Thunder)

MAE: It's a plan to protect the biggest estate in the Delta from irresponsibility
an' —

BIG MAMA: Now you listen to me, all of you, you listen here! They's not goin'
to be any more catty talk in my house! And Gooper, you put that away
before I grab it out of your hand and tear it right up! I don't know what the
hell's in it, and I don't want to know what the hell's in it. I'm talkin' in Big

390   Daddy's language now; I'm his *wife*, not his *widow*, I'm still his *wife!* And
I'm talkin' to you in his language an' —

GOOPER: Big Mama, what I have here is —

MAE: *(at the same time)* Gooper explained that it's just a plan . . .

BIG MAMA: I don't care what you got there. Just put it back where it came
from, an' don't let me see it again, not even the outside of the envelope of
it! Is that understood? Basis! Plan! Preliminary! Design! I say — what is it
Big Daddy always says when he's disgusted?

BRICK: *(from the bar)* Big Daddy says "crap" when he's disgusted.

BIG MAMA: *(rising)* That's right — CRAP! I say CRAP too, like Big Daddy!

(Thunder)

400   MAE: Coarse language doesn't seem called for in this —

GOOPER: Somethin' in me is *deeply outraged* by hearin' you talk like this.

BIG MAMA: *Nobody's goin' to take nothin'!* — till Big Daddy lets go of it — maybe,
just possibly, not — not even then! No, not even then!

(Thunder)

MAE: Sookey, hurry up an' git that po'ch furniture covahed; want th' paint to
come off?

GOOPER: Lacey, put mah car away!

LACEY: Caint, Mistah Pollitt, you got the keys!

GOOPER: Naw, you got 'em, man. Where th' keys to th' car, honey?

MAE: You got 'em in your pocket!

410   BRICK: "You can always hear me singin' this song, Show me the way to go
home."

(Thunder distantly)

BIG MAMA: Brick! Come here, Brick, I need you. Tonight Brick looks like he
used to look when he was a little boy, just like he did when he played wild
games and used to come home when I hollered myself hoarse for him, all
sweaty and pink cheeked and sleepy, with his — red curls shining . . .

*(*BRICK *draws aside as he does from all physical contact and continues the song
in a whisper, opening the ice bucket and dropping in the ice cubes one by one
as if he were mixing some important chemical formula.)*

(Distant thunder.)

Time goes by so fast. Nothin' can outrun it. Death commences too early —
almost before you're half acquainted with life — you meet the other...
Oh, you know we just got to love each other an' stay together, all of us, just
as close as we can, especially now that such a *black* thing has come and
moved into this place without invitation.

(Awkwardly embracing BRICK, *she presses her head to his shoulder.)*

(A dog howls off stage.)

Oh, Brick, son of Big Daddy, Big Daddy does so love you. Y'know what
would be his fondest dream come true? If before he passed on, if Big Daddy
has to pass on...

(A dog howls.)

...you give him a child of yours, a grandson as much like his son as his son
is like Big Daddy...

MARGARET: I know that's Big Daddy's dream.

BIG MAMA: That's his dream.

MAE: Such a pity that Maggie and Brick can't oblige.

BIG DADDY: *(off down stage right on the gallery)* Looks like the wind was takin' liberties with this place.

SERVANT: *(off stage)* Yes, sir, Mr. Pollitt.

MARGARET: *(crossing to the right door)* Big Daddy's on the gall'ry.

*(*BIG MAMA *has turned toward the hall door at the sound of* BIG DADDY'*s voice
on the gallery.)*

BIG MAMA: I can't stay here. He'll see somethin' in my eyes.

*(*BIG DADDY *enters the room from up stage right.)*

BIG DADDY: Can I come in?

(He puts his cigar in an ash tray.)

MARGARET: Did the storm wake you up, Big Daddy?

BIG DADDY: Which stawm are you talkin' about — th' one outside or th' hul-
laballoo in here?

*(*GOOPER *squeezes past* BIG DADDY.*)*

GOOPER: 'Scuse me.

*(*MAE *tries to squeeze past* BIG DADDY *to join* GOOPER, *but* BIG DADDY *puts
his arm firmly around her.)*

BIG DADDY: I heard some mighty loud talk. Sounded like somethin' important was bein' discussed. What was the powwow about?

MAE: *(flustered)* Why — nothin', Big Daddy...

BIG DADDY: *(crossing to extreme left center, taking* MAE *with him)* What is that
pregnant-lookin' envelope you're puttin' back in your briefcase, Gooper?

GOOPER: (*at the foot of the bed, caught, as he stuffs papers into envelope*) That? Nothin', suh — nothin' much of anythin' at all . . .

BIG DADDY: Nothin'? It looks like a whole lot of nothin'!

(*He turns up stage to the group.*)

You all know th' story about th' young married couple —

GOOPER: Yes, sir!

BIG DADDY: Hello, Brick —

450 BRICK: Hello, Big Daddy.

(*The group is arranged in a semicircle above* BIG DADDY, MARGARET *at the extreme right, then* MAE *and* GOOPER, *then* BIG MAMA, *with* BRICK *at the left.*)

BIG DADDY: Young married couple took Junior out to th' zoo one Sunday, inspected all of God's creatures in their cages, with satisfaction.

GOOPER: Satisfaction.

BIG DADDY: (*crossing to up stage center, facing front*) This afternoon was a warm afternoon in spring an' that ole elephant had somethin' else on his mind which was bigger'n peanuts. You know this story, Brick?

(*Gooper nods.*)

BRICK: No, sir, I don't know it.

BIG DADDY: Y'see, in th' cage adjoinin' they was a young female elephant in heat!

BIG MAMA: (*at* BIG DADDY's *shoulder*) Oh, Big Daddy!

460 BIG DADDY: What's the matter, preacher's gone, ain't he? All right. That female elephant in the next cage was permeatin' the atmosphere about her with a powerful and excitin' odor of female fertility! Huh! Ain't that a nice way to put it, Brick?

BRICK: Yes, sir, nothin' wrong with it.

BIG DADDY: Brick says th's nothin' wrong with it!

BIG MAMA: Oh, Big Daddy!

BIG DADDY: (*crossing to down stage center*) So this ole bull elephant still had a couple of fornications left in him. He reared back his trunk an' got a whiff of that elephant lady next door! — began to paw at the dirt in his cage

470 an' butt his head against the separatin' partition and, first thing y'know, there was a conspicuous change in his *profile* — very *conspicuous*! Ain't I tellin' this story in decent language, Brick?

BRICK: Yes, sir, too fuckin' decent!

BIG DADDY: So, the little boy pointed at it and said, "What's that?" His mama said, "Oh, that's — nothin'!" — His papa said, "She's spoiled!"

(BIG DADDY *crosses to* BRICK *at left.*)

You didn't laugh at that story, Brick.

(BIG MAMA *crosses to down stage right crying.* MARGARET *goes to her.* MAE *and* GOOPER *hold up stage right center.*)

BRICK: No, sir, I didn't laugh at that story.

BIG DADDY: What is the smell in this room? Don't you notice it, Brick? Don't you notice a powerful and obnoxious odor of mendacity in this room?

BRICK: Yes, sir, I think I do, sir.

480   GOOPER: Mae, Mae . . .

BIG DADDY: There is nothing more powerful. Is there, Brick?

BRICK: No, sir. No, sir, there isn't, an' nothin' more obnoxious.

BIG DADDY: Brick agrees with me. The odor of mendacity is a powerful and obnoxious odor an' the stawm hasn't blown it away from this room yet. You notice it, Gooper?

GOOPER: What, sir?

BIG DADDY: How about you, Sister Woman? You notice the unpleasant odor of mendacity in this room?

MAE: Why, Big Daddy, I don't even know what that is.

490   BIG DADDY: You can smell it. Hell it smells like death!

(BIG MAMA *sobs.* BIG DADDY *looks toward her.*)

What's wrong with that fat woman over there, loaded with diamonds? Hey, what's-you-name, what's the matter with you?

MARGARET: (*crossing toward* BIG DADDY) She had a slight dizzy spell, Big Daddy.

BIG DADDY: You better watch that, Big Mama. A stroke is a bad way to go.

MARGARET: (*crossing to* BIG DADDY *at center*) Oh, Brick, Big Daddy has on your birthday present to him, Brick, he has on your cashmere robe, the softest material I have ever felt.

BIG DADDY: Yeah, this is my soft birthday, Maggie . . . Not my gold or my silver birthday, but my soft birthday, everything's got to be soft for Big Daddy on

500   this soft birthday.

(MAGGIE *kneels before* BIG DADDY *at center.*)

MARGARET: Big Daddy's got on his Chinese slippers that I gave him, Brick. Big Daddy, I haven't given you my big present yet, but now I will, now's the time for me to present it to you! I have an announcement to make!

MAE: What? What kind of announcement?

GOOPER: A sports announcement, Maggie?

MARGARET: Announcement of life beginning! A child is coming, sired by Brick, and out of Maggie the Cat! I have Brick's child in my body, an' that's my birthday present to Big Daddy on this birthday!

(BIG DADDY *looks at* BRICK *who crosses behind* BIG DADDY *to down stage portal, left.*)

BIG DADDY: Get up, girl, get up off your knees, girl.

(BIG DADDY *helps* MARGARET *to rise. He crosses above her, to her right, bites off the end of a fresh cigar, taken from his bathrobe pocket, as he studies* MARGARET.)

510   *Uh-huh, this girl has life in her body, that's no lie!*

BIG MAMA: BIG DADDY'S DREAM COME TRUE!

BRICK: JESUS!

BIG DADDY: (*crossing right below wicker stand*) Gooper, I want my lawyer in the mornin'.

BRICK: Where are you goin', Big Daddy?

BIG DADDY: Son, I'm goin' up on the roof, to the belvedere on th' roof to look over my kingdom before I give up my kingdom — twenty-eight thousand acres of th' richest land this side of the valley Nile!

(*He exits through right doors, and down right on the gallery.*)

BIG MAMA: (*following*) Sweetheart, sweetheart, sweetheart — can I come with you?

(*She exits down stage right.*)

(MARGARET *is down stage center in the mirror area.* MAE *has joined* GOOPER *and she gives him a fierce poke, making a low hissing sound and a grimace of fury.*)

GOOPER: (*pushing her aside*) Brick, could you possibly spare me one small shot of that liquor?

BRICK: Why, help yourself, Gooper boy.

GOOPER: I will.

MAE: (*shrilly*) Of course we know that this is — a lie.

GOOPER: *Be still, Mae.*

MAE: I won't be still! I know she's made this up!

GOOPER: Goddam it, I said shut up!

MARGARET: Gracious! I didn't know that my little announcement was going to provoke such a storm!

MAE: *That* woman isn't *pregnant!*

GOOPER: Who said she was?

MAE: *She* did.

GOOPER: The doctor didn't. Doc Baugh didn't.

MARGARET: I haven't gone to Doc Baugh.

GOOPER: Then who'd you go to, Maggie?

MARGARET: One of the best gynecologists in the South.

GOOPER: Uh huh, uh huh! — I see . . .

(*He takes out a pencil and notebook.*)

— May we have his name, please?

MARGARET: No, you may not, Mister Prosecuting Attorney!

MAE: He doesn't have any name, he doesn't exist!

MARGARET: Oh, he exists all right, and so does my child, Brick's baby!

MAE: You can't conceive a child by a man that won't sleep with you unless you think you're —

(BRICK *has turned on the phonograph. A scat song[3] cuts* MAE's *speech.*)

GOOPER: *Turn that off!*

3 improvised jazz singing in wordless but expressive syllables.

MAE: We know it's a lie because we hear you in here; he won't sleep with you, we hear you! So don't imagine you're going to put a trick over on us, to fool a dying man with a —

(*A long drawn cry of agony and rage fills the house.* MARGARET *turns the phonograph down to a whisper. The cry is repeated.*)

MAE: Did you hear that, Gooper, did you hear that?
550   GOOPER: Sounds like the pain has struck.
MAE: Go see, Gooper!
GOOPER: Come along and leave these lovebirds together in their nest!

(*He goes out first.* MAE *follows but turns at the door, contorting her face and hissing at* MARGARET.)

MAE: *Liar!*

(*She slams the door.*)

(MARGARET *exhales with relief and moves a little unsteadily to catch hold of* BRICK's *arm.*)

MARGARET: Thank you for — keeping still . . .
BRICK: O.K., Maggie.
MARGARET: It was gallant of you to save my face!

(*He now pours down three shots in quick succession and stands waiting, silent. All at once he turns with a smile and says:*)

BRICK: *There!*
MARGARET: What?
BRICK: The *click* . . .

(*His gratitude seems almost infinite as he hobbles out on the gallery with a drink. We hear his crutch as he swings out of sight. Then, at some distance, he begins singing to himself a peaceful song.* MARGARET *holds the big pillow forlornly as if it were her only companion, for a few moments, then throws it on the bed. She rushes to the liquor cabinet, gathers all the bottles in her arms, turns about undecidedly, then runs out of the room with them, leaving the door ajar on the dim yellow hall.* BRICK *is heard hobbling back along the gallery, singing his peaceful song. He comes back in, sees the pillow on the bed, laughs lightly, sadly, picks it up. He has it under his arm as* MARGARET *returns to the room.* MARGARET *softly shuts the door and leans against it, smiling softly at* BRICK.)

560   MARGARET: Brick, I used to think that you were stronger than me and I didn't want to be overpowered by you. But now, since you've taken to liquor — you know what? — I guess it's bad, but now I'm stronger than you and I can love you more truly! Don't move that pillow. I'll move it right back if you do! — Brick?

(*She turns out all the lamps but a single rose-silk-shaded one by the bed.*)

I really have been to a doctor and I know what to do and — Brick? — this is my time by the calendar to conceive?

BRICK: Yes, I understand, Maggie. But how are you going to conceive a child by a man in love with his liquor?

MARGARET: By locking his liquor up and making him satisfy my desire before
570   I unlock it!

BRICK: Is that what you've done, Maggie?

MARGARET: Look and see. That cabinet's mighty empty compared to before!

BRICK: Well, I'll be a son of a —

(He reaches for his crutch but she beats him to it and rushes out on the gallery, hurls the crutch over the rail and comes back in, panting.)

MARGARET: And so tonight we're going to make the lie true, and when that's done, I'll bring the liquor back here and we'll get drunk together, here, tonight, in this place that death has come into... — What do you say?

BRICK: I don't say anything. I guess there's nothing to say.

MARGARET: Oh, you weak people, you weak, beautiful people! — who give up with such grace. What you want is someone to —

(She turns out the rose-silk lamp.)

580   — take hold of you. — Gently, gently with love hand your life back to you, like somethin' gold you let go of. I *do* love you, Brick, I *do*!

BRICK: *(smiling with charming sadness)* Wouldn't it be funny if that was true?

THE END

Sharon Pollock   (b. 1936)

Originally from Fredericton, Pollock attended the University of New Brunswick before moving on to an acting career in Western Canada. She settled in Calgary, acting in CBC radio dramas as well as with the Prairie Players who evolved into Theatre Calgary. Her earlier published plays involve history as well as personal and political conflict including *Walsh* (1973), about Chief Sitting Bull and the Mountie officer ordered (against his better judgement) to send the Sioux back to the United States to stand trial for the action with General Custer at Little Big Horn, and *The Komagata Maru Incident* (1978), about a boatload of East Indian immigrants in 1914 refused entry at Vancouver even though they were entitled to enter Canada as British citizens. Other work includes *One Tiger to a Hill*, *Generations*, and *Blood Relations*, all published in *Blood Relations and Other Plays* (1981). In *Saucy Jack* (1994) Pollock reinvestigates the notorious unsolved murders of Jack the Ripper. *Moving Pictures*, about Canadian-born silent movie actress/writer/director Nell Shipman, opened in Calgary at Theatre Junction in March 2000.

Pollock's work has been produced across Canada as well as in Australia, India, Japan, Great Britain, and the United States. She is a two-time winner of the Governor General's Award for Drama: *Blood Relations* in 1982 and *Doc* in 1986. In 1987 she won the Canada Australia Literary Award and in 1999 was recipient of the Harry and Martha Cohen Award for her contributions to theatre in Calgary. She has worked as artistic director at Theatre Calgary and Theatre New Brunswick, associate director of the Stratford Festival in Ontario, and as head of the Banff Playwrights' Colony.

INTRODUCTION TO *BLOOD RELATIONS*

Blood Relations is based on the notorious 1892 case of Lizzie Borden, a young woman accused, tried, and acquitted of axe-murdering her parents in their home in Fall River, Massachusetts. Originally titled *My Name is Lisbeth*, the play was first produced as a conventional retrospective narrative with no doubt whatsoever about Lizzie's guilt. But Pollock revised the play fully, introducing a provocative double time frame, complicating motivational issues, and powerfully retitling the drama. As a result *Blood Relations* investigates the case through emotional and psychological reenactment, as Lizzie and her actress friend from Boston replay the key events of ten years before, leading up to the actual double murder.

Set in the house in Fall River in 1902, Lizzie and the Actress enter into a make-believe "dream thesis" of ten years earlier not so much to solve the unsolved case but to explore the complex associations of social, familial, economic, and psychological factors that influence character and behaviour. The Actress takes on Lizzie's role in a play-within-a-play, performing both as the psychologically divided character of Lizzie and as audience guide into the concerns, frustrations, and mentality of Lizzie herself. Lizzie coaches the Actress at first while playing the role of Bridget, Borden family maid in 1892 and perhaps witness/accomplice. The "present" of 1902 allows for deep consideration of the "past" in 1892, including lines spoken in the play by the Defense which are taken from actual transcripts of the trial.

In Lizzie, the audience witnesses a cultured, intelligent, unmarried daughter of 34 years of age, trapped in a position of domestic privilege while at the same time in the process of being cheated out of her inheritance by her stepmother's brother. Frustrated about her position and aware of her predicament, Lizzie lashes out verbally, especially towards her stepmother. But she is powerless in this traditional household and cannot effectively change her circumstances. As a young "lady" in 1892 Lizzie is expected to be quiet and modest and polite. And yet, even though untrained in the world of business and finance, she "impolitely" demands her fair share of the family estate. In so doing, she mirrors the role of women generally in the 1890s, demanding independence, equality, and self-determination.

The puritanical Victorian atmosphere of the 1892 household suffocates Lizzie who, as the rebellious daughter, imagines better circumstances at the same time as she tries to assert herself. Her family, including Emma, her well-behaved older sister, just as constantly and politely interferes with her hopes and dreams. Lizzie's family wishes to see her married off to a local man who is widowed with three small children. Lizzie herself still wishes to accomplish something "different" in the world, even if only the raising of pigeons in a shed in the back yard. The birds symbolize her caged repression which Lizzie protests against as she pleads with her father for meaningful work: "Why can't I do something? . . . Eh? I mean . . . I could . . . I could go into your office . . . I could . . . learn how to keep books?" In response, her father gently patronizes her. As Pollock notes in an early stage direction, *She has the qualities he would like in a son but deplores in a daughter.* Pushed to the limit of his patience, Mr. Borden angrily kills Lizzie's beloved pigeons with a hatchet, and the weapon itself takes centre stage as a powerful and suggestive symbol at the end of the first act.

Pollock presents Lizzie most sympathetically, but any audience that focuses only on guilt and innocence becomes complicit with the staid assumptions of Lizzie's own day. The role-play within the play undercuts Lizzie's given "position" as daughter to perform Lizzie's complicated "action" as self-willed person. And her "action" represents the central fascination of the play. To the constantly implicit, and often explicit, question "Did she? or didn't she?" Lizzie presents the formal verdict: "Acquitted" — disrupting conventional assumptions about moral dilemmas, normal behaviour, and social expectations. As the Actress admits early in the play: "Did Lizzie Borden take an ax?. . . If you didn't I should be disappointed . . . and if you did I should be horrified." Audience reaction at the conclusion might be quite different from either possibility.

BLOOD RELATIONS

CHARACTERS

MISS LIZZIE, *who will play* BRIDGET, *the Irish maid.*
THE ACTRESS, *who will play* LIZZIE BORDEN.
HARRY, *Mrs. Borden's brother.*
EMMA, *Lizzie's older sister.*
ANDREW, *Lizzie's father.*
ABIGAIL, *Lizzie's step-mother*
DR. PATRICK, *the Irish doctor; sometimes* THE DEFENSE.

SETTING

The time proper is late Sunday afternoon and evening, late fall, in Fall River, 1902; the year of the "dream thesis," if one might call it that, is 1892.

The playing areas include (a) within the Borden house: the dining room from which there is an exit to the kitchen; the parlour; a flight of stairs leading to the second floor; and (b) in the Borden yard: the walk outside the house; the area in which the birds are kept.

PRODUCTION NOTE: Action must be free-flowing. There can be no division of the script into scenes by blackout, movement of furniture, or sets. There may be freezes of some characters while other scenes are being played. There is no necessity to "get people off" and "on" again for, with the exception of The Actress and Miss Lizzie (and Emma in the final scene), all characters are imaginary, and all action in reality would be taking place between Miss Lizzie and The Actress in the dining room and parlour of her home.

The Defense may actually be seen, may be a shadow, or a figure behind a scrim.

While Miss Lizzie exits and enters with her Bridget business, she is a presence, often observing unobtrusively when as Bridget she takes no part in the action.

ACT ONE

(Lights up on the figure of a woman standing centre stage. It is a somewhat formal pose. A pause. She speaks:)

"Since what I am about to say must be but that
Which contradicts my accusation, and
The testimony on my part no other
But what comes from myself, it shall scarce boot me
To say 'Not Guilty.'
But, if Powers Divine
Behold our human action as they do,

I doubt not then but innocence shall make
False accusation blush and tyranny
10   Tremble at . . . at . . . "

(*She wriggles the fingers of an outstretched hand searching for the word.*)

"Aaaat" . . . Bollocks!!

(*She raises her script, takes a bite of chocolate.*)

"Tremble at Patience," patience patience! . . . [1]

(MISS LIZZIE *enters from the kitchen with tea service.* THE ACTRESS' *attention drifts to* MISS LIZZIE. THE ACTRESS *watches* MISS LIZZIE *sit in the parlour and proceed to pour two cups of tea.* THE ACTRESS *sucks her teeth a bit to clear the chocolate as she speaks:*)

THE ACTRESS: Which . . . is proper, Lizzie?

MISS LIZZIE: Proper?

THE ACTRESS: To pour first the cream, and add the tea — or first tea and add cream. One is proper. Is the way you do the proper way, the way it's done in circles where it counts?

MISS LIZZIE: Sugar?

THE ACTRESS: Well, is it?

20   MISS LIZZIE: I don't know, sugar?

THE ACTRESS: Mmmn. (MISS LIZZIE *adds sugar.*) I suppose if we had Mrs. Beeton's *Book of Etiquette*, we could look it up.

MISS LIZZIE: I do have it, shall I get it?

THE ACTRESS: No. . . . You could ask your sister, she might know.

MISS LIZZIE: Do you want this tea or not?

THE ACTRESS: I hate tea.

MISS LIZZIE: You drink it every Sunday.

THE ACTRESS: I drink it because you like to serve it.

MISS LIZZIE: Pppu.

30   THE ACTRESS: It's true. You've no idea how I suffer from this toast and tea ritual. I really do. The tea upsets my stomach and the toast makes me fat because I eat so much of it.

MISS LIZZIE: Practice some restraint then.

THE ACTRESS: Mmmm . . . Why don't we ask your sister which is proper?

MISS LIZZIE: You ask her.

THE ACTRESS: How can I? She doesn't speak to me. I don't think she even sees me. She gives no indication of it. (*She looks up the stairs.*) What do you suppose she does up there every Sunday afternoon?

MISS LIZZIE: She sulks.

40   THE ACTRESS: And reads the Bible I suppose, and Mrs. Beeton's *Book of Etiquette*. Oh Lizzie. . . . What a long day. The absolutely longest day. . . . When does that come anyway, the longest day?

MISS LIZZIE: June.

1 the Actress is rehearsing Hermione's speech before the court in Shakespeare's *The Winter's Tale* (3.2.22–32).

THE ACTRESS: Ah yes, June. (*She looks at* MISS LIZZIE.) June?

MISS LIZZIE: June.

THE ACTRESS: Mmmmmm. . . .

MISS LIZZIE: I know what you're thinking.

THE ACTRESS: Of course you do. . . . I'm thinking . . . shall I pour the sherry — or will you.

50   MISS LIZZIE: No.

THE ACTRESS: I'm thinking . . . June . . . in Fall River.

MISS LIZZIE: No.

THE ACTRESS: August in Fall River? (*She smiles. Pause.*)

MISS LIZZIE: We could have met in Boston.

THE ACTRESS: I prefer it here.

MISS LIZZIE: You don't find it . . . a trifle boring?

THE ACTRESS: Au contraire.

(MISS LIZZIE *gives a small laugh at the affectation.*)

THE ACTRESS: What?

MISS LIZZIE: I find it a trifle boring . . . I know what you're doing. You're soaking
60   up the ambience.

THE ACTRESS: Nonsense, Lizzie. I come to see you.

MISS LIZZIE: Why?

THE ACTRESS: Because . . . of us. (*Pause.*)

MISS LIZZIE: You were a late arrival last night. Later than usual.

THE ACTRESS: Don't be silly.

MISS LIZZIE: I wonder why.

THE ACTRESS: The show was late, late starting, late coming down.

MISS LIZZIE: And?

THE ACTRESS: And — then we all went out for drinks.

70   MISS LIZZIE: We?

THE ACTRESS: The other members of the cast.

MISS LIZZIE: Oh yes.

THE ACTRESS: And then I caught a cab . . . all the way from Boston. . . . Do you
know what it cost?

MISS LIZZIE: I should. I paid the bill, remember?

THE ACTRESS: (*Laughs.*) Of course. What a jumble all my thoughts are. There're
too many words running round inside my head today. It's terrible.

MISS LIZZIE: It sounds it.

(*Pause.*)

THE ACTRESS: . . . You know . . . you do this thing . . . you stare at me . . . You look
80   directly at my eyes. I think . . . you think . . . that if I'm lying . . . it will come
up, like lemons on a slot machine. (*She makes a gesture at her eyes.*) Tick.
Tick . . . (*Pause.*) In the alley, behind the theatre the other day, there were
some kids. You know what they were doing?

MISS LIZZIE: How could I?

THE ACTRESS: They were playing skip rope, and you know what they were
singing? (*She sings, and claps her hands arhythmically to:*)

"Lizzie Borden took an ax,
Gave her mother forty whacks,
When the job was nicely done,
She gave her father forty-one."

90

MISS LIZZIE: Did you stop them?

THE ACTRESS: No.

MISS LIZZIE: Did you tell them I was acquitted?

THE ACTRESS: No.

MISS LIZZIE: What did you do?

THE ACTRESS: I shut the window.

MISS LIZZIE: A noble gesture on my behalf.

THE ACTRESS: We were doing lines — the noise they make is dreadful. Sometimes they play ball, ka-thunk, ka-thunk, ka-thunk against the wall. Once

100   I saw them with a cat and —

MISS LIZZIE: And you didn't stop them?

THE ACTRESS: That time I stopped them.

(THE ACTRESS *crosses to table where there is a gramophone. She prepares to
play a record. She stops.*)

THE ACTRESS: Should I?

MISS LIZZIE: Why not?

THE ACTRESS: Your sister, the noise upsets her.

MISS LIZZIE: And she upsets me. On numerous occasions.

THE ACTRESS: You're incorrigible, Lizzie.

(THE ACTRESS *holds out her arms to* MISS LIZZIE. *They dance the latest "in"
dance, a Scott Joplin composition. It requires some concentration, but they
chat while dancing rather formally in contrast to the music.*)

THE ACTRESS: . . . Do you think your jawline's heavy?

MISS LIZZIE: Why do you ask?

110   THE ACTRESS: They said you had jowls.

MISS LIZZIE: Did they.

THE ACTRESS: The reports of the day said you were definitely jowly.

MISS LIZZIE: That was ten years ago.

THE ACTRESS: Imagine. You were only thirty-four.

MISS LIZZIE: Yes.

THE ACTRESS: It happened here, this house.

MISS LIZZIE: You're leading.

THE ACTRESS: I know.

MISS LIZZIE: . . . I don't think I'm jowly. Then or now. Do you?

120   THE ACTRESS: Lizzie? Lizzie.

MISS LIZZIE: What?

THE ACTRESS: . . . did you?

MISS LIZZIE: Did I what?

(*Pause.*)

THE ACTRESS: You never tell *me* anything. (*She turns off the music.*)

MISS LIZZIE: I tell you everything.

THE ACTRESS: No you don't!

MISS LIZZIE: Oh yes, I tell you the most personal things about myself, my thoughts, my dreams, my —

THE ACTRESS: But never that one thing. . . . (*She lights a cigarette.*)

130   MISS LIZZIE: And don't smoke those — they stink.

(THE ACTRESS *ignores her, inhales, exhales a volume of smoke in* MISS LIZZIE'S *direction.*)

MISS LIZZIE: Do you suppose . . . people buy you drinks . . . or cast you even . . . because you have a "liaison" with Lizzie Borden? Do you suppose they do that?

THE ACTRESS: They cast me because I'm good at what I do.

MISS LIZZIE: They never pry? They never ask? What's she really like? Is she really jowly? Did she? Didn't she?

THE ACTRESS: What could I tell them? You never tell me anything.

MISS LIZZIE: I tell you everything.

THE ACTRESS: But that! (*Pause.*) You think everybody talks about you — they 140   don't.

MISS LIZZIE: Here they do.

THE ACTRESS: You think they talk about you.

MISS LIZZIE: But never to me.

THE ACTRESS: Well . . . you give them lots to talk about.

MISS LIZZIE: You know you're right, your mind is a jumble.

THE ACTRESS: I told you so.

(*Pause.*)

MISS LIZZIE: You remind me of my sister.

THE ACTRESS: Oh God, in what way?

MISS LIZZIE: Day in, day out, ten years now, sometimes at breakfast as she rolls 150   little crumbs of bread in little balls, sometimes at noon, or late at night . . . "Did you, Lizzie?" "Lizzie, did you?"

THE ACTRESS: Ten years, day in, day out?

MISS LIZZIE: Oh yes. She sits there where Papa used to sit and I sit there, where I have always sat. She looks at me and at her plate, then at me, and at her plate, then at me and then she says "Did you Lizzie?" "Lizzie, did you?"

THE ACTRESS: (*A nasal imitation of* EMMA'S *voice.*) "Did-you-Lizzie — Lizzie-did-you." (*Laughs.*)

MISS LIZZIE: Did I what?

THE ACTRESS: (*Continues her imitation of* EMMA.) "You know."

160   MISS LIZZIE: Well, what do you think?

THE ACTRESS: "Oh, I believe you didn't, in fact I know you didn't, what a thought! After all, you were acquitted."

MISS LIZZIE: Yes, I was.

THE ACTRESS: "But sometimes when I'm on the street . . . or shopping . . . or at the church even, I catch somebody's eye, they look away . . . and I think to myself 'Did-you-Lizzie — Lizzie-did-you.' "

MISS LIZZIE: (*Laughs.*) Ah, poor Emma.

THE ACTRESS: (*Dropping her* EMMA *imitation.*) Well, did you?

MISS LIZZIE: Is it important?

170 THE ACTRESS: Yes.

MISS LIZZIE: Why?

THE ACTRESS: I have ... a compulsion to know the truth.

MISS LIZZIE: The truth?

THE ACTRESS: Yes.

MISS LIZZIE: ... Sometimes I think you look like me, and you're not jowly.

THE ACTRESS: No.

MISS LIZZIE: You look like me, or how I think I look, or how I ought to look ...
sometimes you think like me ... do you feel that?

THE ACTRESS: Sometimes.

180 MISS LIZZIE: (*Triumphant.*) You shouldn't have to ask then. You should know.
"Did I, didn't I." You tell me.

THE ACTRESS: I'll tell you what I think. ... I think ... that you're aware there is
a certain fascination in the ambiguity. ... You always paint the background
but leave the rest to my imagination. Did Lizzie Borden take an ax? ... If you
didn't I should be disappointed ... and if you did I should be horrified.

MISS LIZZIE: And which is worse?

THE ACTRESS: To have murdered one's parents, or to be a pretentious small-town
spinster? I don't know.

MISS LIZZIE: Why're you so cruel to me?

190 THE ACTRESS: I'm teasing, Lizzie, I'm only teasing. Come on, paint the background again.

MISS LIZZIE: Why?

THE ACTRESS: Perhaps you'll give something away.

MISS LIZZIE: Which you'll dine out on.

THE ACTRESS: Of course. (*Laughs.*) Come on, Lizzie. Come on.

MISS LIZZIE: A game.

THE ACTRESS: What?

MISS LIZZIE: A game? ... And you'll play me.

THE ACTRESS: Oh —

200 MISS LIZZIE: It's your stock in trade, my love.

THE ACTRESS: Alright. ... A game!

MISS LIZZIE: Let me think ... Bridget ... Brrridget. We had a maid then. And her
name was Bridget. Oh, she was a great one for stories, stood like this, very
straight back, and her hair ... and there she was in the courtroom in her new
dress on the stand. "Do you swear to tell the truth, the whole truth, and
nothing but the truth, so help you God?" (*Imitates Irish accent.*)
"I do sir," she said.
"Would you give the court your name."
"Bridget O'Sullivan, sir."

(*Very faint echo of the voice of* THE DEFENSE *under* MISS LIZZIE's *next line.*)

210 "And occupation."
"I'm like what you'd call a maid, sir. I do a bit of everything, cleanin' and
cookin'."

(*The actual voice of* THE DEFENSE *is heard alone; he may also be seen.*)

THE DEFENSE: You've been in Fall River how long?

MISS LIZZIE: (*Who continues as* BRIDGET, *while* THE ACTRESS [*who will play* LIZZIE] *observes.*) Well now, about five years sir, ever since I came over. I worked up on the hill for a while but it didn't — well, you could say, suit me, too lah-de-dah — so I —

THE DEFENSE: Your employer in June of 1892 was?

BRIDGET: Yes sir. Mr. Borden, sir. Well, more rightly, Mrs. Borden for she was the one who —

220   THE DEFENSE: Your impression of the household?

BRIDGET: Well . . . the man of the house, Mr. Borden, was a bit of a . . . tightwad, and Mrs. B. could nag you into the grave, still she helped with the dishes and things which not everyone does when they hire a maid. (HARRY *appears on the stairs; approaches* BRIDGET *stealthily. She is unaware of him.*) Then there was the daughters, Miss Emma and Lizzie, and that day, Mr. Wingate, Mrs. B.'s brother who'd stayed for the night and was — (*He grabs her ass with both hands. She screams.*)

BRIDGET: Get off with you!

HARRY: Come on, Bridget, give me a kiss!

BRIDGET: I'll give you a good poke in the nose if you don't keep your hands to yourself.

230   HARRY: Ohhh-hh-hh Bridget!

BRIDGET: Get away you old sod!

HARRY: Haven't you missed me?

BRIDGET: I have not! I was pinched black and blue last time — and I'll be sufferin' the same before I see the end of you this time.

HARRY: (*Tilts his ass at her.*) You want to see my end?

BRIDGET: You're a dirty old man.

HARRY: If Mr. Borden hears that, you'll be out on the street. (*Grabs her.*) Where's my kiss!

BRIDGET: (*Dumps glass of water on his head.*) There! (HARRY *splutters.*) Would you
240   like another? You silly thing you — and leave me towels alone!

HARRY: You've soaked my shirt.

BRIDGET: Shut up and pour yourself a cup of coffee.

HARRY: You got no sense of fun, Bridget.

BRIDGET: Well now, if you tried actin' like the gentleman farmer you're supposed to be, Mr. Wingate —

HARRY: I'm tellin' you you can't take a joke.

BRIDGET: If Mr. Borden sees you jokin', it's not his maid he'll be throwin' out on the street, but his brother-in-law, and that's the truth.

HARRY: What's between you and me's between you and me, eh?

BRIDGET: There ain't nothin' between you and me.

HARRY: . . . Finest cup of coffee in Fall River.

250   BRIDGET: There's no gettin' on the good side of me now, it's too late for that.

HARRY: . . . Bridget? . . . You know what tickles my fancy?

BRIDGET: No and I don't want to hear.

HARRY: It's your Irish temper.

BRIDGET: It is, is it? . . . Can I ask you something?

HARRY: Ooohhh — anything.

BRIDGET: (*Innocently.*) Does Miss Lizzie know you're here?...I say does Miss Lizzie —

260 HARRY: Why do you bring her up?

BRIDGET: She don't then, eh? (*Teasing.*) It's a surprise visit?

HARRY: No surprise to her father.

BRIDGET: Oh?

HARRY: We got business.

BRIDGET: I'd of thought the last bit of business was enough.

HARRY: It's not for —   [*you to say*]

BRIDGET: You don't learn a thing, from me or Lizzie, do you?

HARRY: Listen here —

BRIDGET: You mean you've forgotten how mad she was when you got her father
270   to sign the rent from the mill house over to your sister? Oh my.

HARRY: She's his wife, isn't she?

BRIDGET: (*Lightly.*) Second wife.

HARRY: She's still got her rights.

BRIDGET: Who am I to say who's got a right? But I can tell you this — Miss Lizzie
    don't see it that way.

HARRY: It don't matter how Miss Lizzie sees it.

BRIDGET: Oh it matters enough — she had you thrown out last time, didn't
    she? By jasus that was a laugh!

HARRY: You mind your tongue.

280 BRIDGET: And after you left, you know what happened?

HARRY: Get away.

BRIDGET: She and sister Emma got her father's rent money from the other mill
    house to make it all even-steven — and now, here you are back again? What
    kind of business you up to this time? (*Whispers in his ear.*) Mind Lizzie doesn't
    catch you.

HARRY: Get away!

BRIDGET: (*Laughs.*) Ohhhh — would you like some more coffee, sir? It's the
    finest coffee in all Fall River! (*She pours it.*) Thank you sir. You're welcome,
    sir. (*She exits to the kitchen.*)

290 HARRY: There'll be no trouble this time!! Do you hear me!

BRIDGET: (*Off.*) Yes sir.

HARRY: There'll be no trouble. (*Sees a basket of crusts.*) What the hell's this? I
    said is this for breakfast!

BRIDGET: (*Entering.*) Is what for — oh no — Mr. Borden's not economizin' to
    that degree yet, it's the crusts for Miss Lizzie's birds.

HARRY: What birds?

BRIDGET: Some kind of pet pigeons she's raisin' out in the shed. Miss Lizzie
    loves her pigeons.

HARRY: Miss Lizzie loves kittens and cats and horses and dogs. What Miss
300   Lizzie doesn't love is people.

BRIDGET: *Some* people. (*She looks past* HARRY *to* THE ACTRESS/LIZZIE. HARRY
    turns to follow BRIDGET'S *gaze.* BRIDGET *speaks, encouraging an invitation for*
    THE ACTRESS *to join her.*) Good mornin' Lizzie.

THE ACTRESS: (*She is a trifle tentative in the role of* LIZZIE.) Is the coffee on?

BRIDGET: Yes ma'am.

LIZZIE: I'll have some then.

BRIDGET: Yes ma'am. (*She makes no move to get it, but watches as* LIZZIE *stares at* HARRY.)

HARRY: Well ... I think ... maybe I'll ... just split a bit of that kindling out back. (*He exits.* LIZZIE *turns to* BRIDGET.)

LIZZIE: Silly ass.

310   BRIDGET: Oh Lizzie. (*She laughs. She enjoys* THE ACTRESS/LIZZIE's *comments as she guides her into her role by "painting the background."*)

LIZZIE: Well, he is. He's a silly ass.

BRIDGET: Can you remember him last time with your Papa? Oh, I can still hear him: "Now Andrew, I've spent my life raisin' horses and I'm gonna tell you somethin'— a *woman* is just like a *horse!* You keep her on a tight rein, or she'll take the bit in her teeth and next thing you know, road, destination, and purpose is all behind you, and you'll be damn lucky if she don't pitch you right in a sewer ditch!"

LIZZIE: Stupid bugger.

BRIDGET: Oh Lizzie, what language! What would your father say if he heard you?

320   LIZZIE: Well ... I've never used a word I didn't hear from him first.

BRIDGET: Do you think he'd be congratulatin' you?

LIZZIE: Possibly. (BRIDGET *gives a subtle shake of her head.*) Not.

BRIDGET: Possibly not is right.... And what if Mrs. B. should hear you?

LIZZIE: I hope and pray that she does.... Do you know what I think, Bridget? I think there's nothing wrong with Mrs. B.... that losing 80 pounds and tripling her intellect wouldn't cure.

BRIDGET: (*Loving it.*) You ought to be ashamed.

LIZZIE: It's the truth, isn't it?

BRIDGET: Still, what a way to talk of your mother.

330   LIZZIE: Step-mother.

BRIDGET: Still you don't mean it, do you?

LIZZIE: Don't I? (*Louder.*) She's a *silly ass* too!

BRIDGET: Shhhh.

LIZZIE: It's alright, she's deaf as a picket fence when she wants to be.... What's he here for?

BRIDGET: Never said.

LIZZIE: He's come to worm more money out of Papa I bet.

BRIDGET: Lizzie.

LIZZIE: What.

340   BRIDGET: Your sister, Lizzie. (BRIDGET *indicates* EMMA, LIZZIE *turns to see her on the stairs.*)

EMMA: You want to be quiet, Lizzie, a body can't sleep for the racket upstairs.

LIZZIE: Oh?

EMMA: You've been makin' too much noise.

LIZZIE: It must have been Bridget, she dropped a pot, didn't you, Bridget.

EMMA: A number of pots from the sound of it.

BRIDGET: I'm all thumbs this mornin', ma'am.

EMMA: You know it didn't sound like pots.

LIZZIE: Oh.

EMMA: Sounded more like voices.

350   LIZZIE: Oh?

EMMA: Sounded like your voice, Lizzie.

LIZZIE: Maybe you dreamt it.

EMMA: I wish I had, for someone was using words no lady would use.

LIZZIE: When Bridget dropped the pot, she did say "pshaw!" didn't you, Bridget.

BRIDGET: Pshaw! That's what I said.

EMMA: That's not what I heard.

(BRIDGET *will withdraw.*)

LIZZIE: Pshaw?

EMMA: If mother heard you, you know what she'd say.

LIZZIE: She's not my mother or yours.

360   EMMA: Well she married our father twenty-seven years ago, if that doesn't make her our mother —

LIZZIE: It doesn't.

EMMA: Don't talk like that.

LIZZIE: I'll talk as I like.

EMMA: We're not going to fight, Lizzie. We're going to be quiet and have our breakfast!

LIZZIE: Is that what we're going to do?

EMMA: Yes.

LIZZIE: Oh.

370   EMMA: At least — that's what I'm going to do.

LIZZIE: Bridget, Emma wants her breakfast!

EMMA: I could have yelled myself.

LIZZIE: You could, but you never do.

(BRIDGET *serves* EMMA, EMMA *is reluctant to argue in front of* BRIDGET.)

EMMA: Thank you, Bridget.

LIZZIE: Did you know Harry Wingate's back for a visit?... He must have snuck in late last night so I wouldn't hear him. Did you?

(EMMA *shakes her head.* LIZZIE *studies her.*)

LIZZIE: Did you know he was coming?

EMMA: No.

LIZZIE: No?

380   EMMA: But I do know he wouldn't be here unless Papa asked him.

LIZZIE: That's not the point. You know what happened last time he was here. Papa was signing property over to her.

EMMA: Oh Lizzie.

LIZZIE: Oh Lizzie nothing. It's bad enough Papa's worth thousands of dollars, and here we are, stuck in this tiny bit of a house on Second Street, when we should be up on the hill — and that's her doing. Or hers and Harry's.

EMMA: Shush.

LIZZIE: I won't shush. They cater to Papa's worst instincts.

EMMA: They'll hear you.

390   LIZZIE: I don't care if they do. It's true, isn't it? Papa tends to be miserly, he probably has the first penny he ever earned — or more likely *she* has it.

EMMA: You talk rubbish.

LIZZIE: Papa *can* be very warm-hearted and generous *but he needs encouragement.*

EMMA: If Papa didn't save his money, Papa wouldn't have any money.

LIZZIE: And neither will we if he keeps signing things over to her.

EMMA: I'm not going to listen.

LIZZIE: Well try thinking.

EMMA: Stop it.

LIZZIE: (*Not a threat, a simple statement of fact.*) Someday Papa will die —

400 EMMA: Don't say that.

LIZZIE: Someday Papa will die. And I don't intend to spend the rest of my life licking Harry Wingate's boots, or toadying to his sister.

MRS. BORDEN: (*From the stairs.*) What's that?

LIZZIE: Nothing.

MRS. BORDEN: (*Making her way downstairs.*) Eh?

LIZZIE: I said, nothing!

BRIDGET: (*Holds out basket of crusts.* LIZZIE *looks at it.*) For your birds, Miss Lizzie.

LIZZIE: (*She takes the basket.*) You want to know what I think? I think she's a fat

410 cow and I hate her. (*She exits.*)

EMMA: . . . Morning, Mother.

MRS. BORDEN: Morning Emma.

EMMA: . . . Did you have a good sleep?

(BRIDGET *will serve breakfast.*)

MRS. BORDEN: So so. . . . It's the heat you know. It never cools off proper at night. It's too hot for a good sleep.

EMMA: . . . Is Papa up?

MRS. BORDEN: He'll be down in a minute . . . sooo. . . . What's wrong with Lizzie this morning?

EMMA: Nothing.

420 MRS. BORDEN: . . . Has Harry come down?

EMMA: I'm not sure.

MRS. BORDEN: Bridget. Has Harry come down?

BRIDGET: Yes ma'am.

MRS. BORDEN: And?

BRIDGET: And he's gone out back for a bit.

MRS. BORDEN: Lizzie see him?

BRIDGET: Yes ma'am. (*Beats it back to the kitchen.*)

(EMMA *concentrates on her plate.*)

MRS. BORDEN: . . . You should have said so. . . . She have words with him?

EMMA: Lizzie has more manners than that.

430 MRS. BORDEN: She's incapable of disciplining herself like a lady and we all know it.

EMMA: Well she doesn't make a habit of picking fights with people.

MRS. BORDEN: That's just it. She does.

EMMA: Well — she may —

MRS. BORDEN: And you can't deny that.

EMMA: *(Louder.)* Well this morning she may have been a bit upset because no one told her he was coming and when she came down he was here. But that's all there was to it.

MRS. BORDEN: If your father wants my brother in for a stay, he's to ask Lizzie's permission I suppose.

EMMA: No.

MRS. BORDEN: You know, Emma —

EMMA: She didn't argue with him or anything like that.

MRS. BORDEN: You spoiled her. You may have had the best of intentions, but you spoiled her.

(MISS LIZZIE/BRIDGET is speaking to ACTRESS/LIZZIE.)

MISS LIZZIE/BRIDGET: I was thirty-four years old, and I still daydreamed.... I did ... I daydreamed ... I dreamt that my name was Lisbeth ... and I lived up on the hill in a corner house ... and my hair wasn't red. I hate red hair. When I was little, everyone teased me.... When I was little, we never stayed in this house for the summer, we'd go to the farm.... I remember ... my knees were always covered with scabs, god knows how I got them, but you know what I'd do? I'd sit in the field, and haul up my skirts, and my petticoat and my bloomers and roll down my stockings and I'd *pick* the scabs on my knees! And Emma would catch me! You know what she'd say? "Nice little girls don't have scabs on their knees!"

(They laugh)

LIZZIE: Poor Emma.

MISS LIZZIE/BRIDGET: I dreamt ... someday I'm going to live ... in a corner house on the hill.... I'll have parties, grand parties. I'll be ... witty, not biting, but witty. Everyone will be witty. Everyone who is *anyone* will want to come to my parties ... and if ... I can't ... live in a corner house on the hill ... I'll live on the farm, all by myself on the farm! There was a barn there, with barn cats and barn kittens and two horses and barn swallows that lived in the eaves.... The birds I kept here were pigeons, not swallows.... They were grey, a dull grey ... but ... when the sun struck their feathers, I'd see blue, a steel blue with a sheen, and when they'd move in the sun they were bright blue and maroon and over it all, an odd sparkle as if you'd ... grated a new silver dollar and the gratings caught in their feathers.... Most of the time they were dull ... and stupid perhaps ... but they weren't really. They were ... hiding I think.... They knew me.... They liked me. ... The truth ... is ...

ACTRESS/LIZZIE: The truth is ... thirty-four is too old to daydream....

MRS. BORDEN: The truth is she's spoilt rotten. (MR. BORDEN *will come down stairs and take his place at the table.* MRS. BORDEN *continues for his benefit.* MR. BORDEN *ignores her. He has learned the fine art of tuning her out. He is not intimidated or henpecked.*) And we're paying the piper for that. In most of the places I've been the people who pay the piper call the tune. Of course I haven't had the advantage of a trip to Europe with a bunch of lady friends like our Lizzie had three years ago, all expenses paid by her father.

EMMA: Morning Papa.

MR. BORDEN: Mornin'.

MRS. BORDEN: I haven't had the benefit of that experience.... Did you know Lizzie's seen Harry?

MR. BORDEN: Has she.

MRS. BORDEN: You should have met him down town. You should never have asked him to stay over.

MR. BORDEN: Why not?

MRS. BORDEN: You know as well as I do why not. I don't want a repeat of last time. She didn't speak civil for months.

MR. BORDEN: There's no reason for Harry to pay for a room when we've got a spare one.... Where's Lizzie?

EMMA: Out back feeding the birds.

MR. BORDEN: She's always out at those birds.

EMMA: Yes Papa.

MR. BORDEN: And tell her to get a new lock for the shed. There's been someone in it again.

EMMA: Alright.

MR. BORDEN: It's those little hellions from next door. We had no trouble with them playin' in that shed before, they always played in their own yard before.

EMMA: ... Papa?

MR. BORDEN: It's those damn birds, that's what brings them into the yard.

EMMA: ... About Harry ...

MR. BORDEN: What about Harry?

EMMA: Well ... I was just wondering why ... [he's here]

MR. BORDEN: You never mind Harry — did you speak to Lizzie about Johnny MacLeod?

EMMA: I ah —

MR. BORDEN: Eh?

EMMA: I said I tried to —

MR. BORDEN: What do you mean, you tried to.

EMMA: Well, I was working my way round to it but —

MR. BORDEN: What's so difficult about telling Lizzie Johnny MacLeod wants to call?

EMMA: Then why don't you tell her? I'm always the one that has to go running to Lizzie telling her this and telling her that, and taking the abuse for it!

MRS. BORDEN: We all know why that is, she can wrap her father round her little finger, always has, always could. If everything else fails, she throws a tantrum and her father buys her off, trip to Europe, rent to the mill house, it's all the same.

EMMA: Papa, what's Harry here for?

MR. BORDEN: None of your business.

MRS. BORDEN: And don't you go runnin' to Lizzie stirring things up.

EMMA: You know I've never done that!

MR. BORDEN: What she means —

EMMA: (*With anger but little fatigue.*) I'm tired, do you hear? Tired! (*She gets up from the table and leaves for upstairs.*)

MR. BORDEN: Emma!

EMMA: You ask Harry here, you know there'll be trouble, and when I try to find out what's going on, so once again good old Emma can stand between you and Lizzie, all you've got to say is "none of your business"! Well then, it's *your* business, you look after it, because I'm not! (*She exits.*)

MRS. BORDEN: ... She's right.

MR. BORDEN: That's enough. I've had enough. I don't want to hear from you too.

530 MRS. BORDEN: I'm only saying she's right. You have to talk straight and plain to Lizzie and tell her things she don't want to hear.

MR. BORDEN: About the farm?

MRS. BORDEN: About Johnny MacLeod! Keep your mouth shut about the farm and she won't know the difference.

MR. BORDEN: Alright.

MRS. BORDEN: Speak to her about Johnny MacLeod.

MR. BORDEN: Alright!

MRS. BORDEN: You know what they're sayin' in town. About her and that doctor.

(MISS LIZZIE/BRIDGET *is speaking to* THE ACTRESS/LIZZIE.)

540 MISS LIZZIE/BRIDGET: They're saying if you live on Second Street and you need a housecall, and you don't mind the Irish, call Dr. Patrick. Dr. Patrick is very prompt with his Second Street house calls.

ACTRESS/LIZZIE: Do they really say that?

MISS LIZZIE/BRIDGET: No they don't. I'm telling a lie. But he is very prompt with a Second Street call, do you know why that is?

ACTRESS/LIZZIE: Why?

MISS LIZZIE/BRIDGET: Well — he's hoping to see someone who lives on Second Street — someone who's yanking up her skirt and showing her ankle — so she can take a decent-sized step — and forgetting everything she was ever
550 taught in Miss Cornelia's School for Girls, and talking to the Irish as if she never heard of the Pope! Oh yes, he's very prompt getting to Second Street ... getting away is something else....

DR. PATRICK: Good morning, Miss Borden!

LIZZIE: I haven't decided ... if it is ... or it isn't ...

DR. PATRICK: No, you've got it all wrong. The proper phrase is "good morning, Dr. Patrick", and then you smile, discreetly of course, and lower the eyes just a titch, twirl the parasol —

LIZZIE: The parasol?

DR. PATRICK: The parasol, but not too fast; and then you murmur in a voice that
560 was ever sweet and low, "And how are you doin' this morning, Dr. Patrick?" Your education's been sadly neglected, Miss Borden.

LIZZIE: You're forgetting something. You're married — and Irish besides — I'm supposed to ignore you.

DR. PATRICK: No.

LIZZIE: Yes. Don't you realize Papa and Emma have fits every time we engage in "illicit conversation". They're having fits right now.

DR. PATRICK: Well, does Mrs. Borden approve?

LIZZIE: Ahhh. She's the real reason I keep stopping and talking. Mrs. Borden is easily shocked. I'm hoping she dies from the shock.

570 DR. PATRICK: (*Laughs.*) Why don't you ... run away from home, Lizzie?

LIZZIE: Why don't you "run away" with me?

DR. PATRICK: Where'll we go?

LIZZIE: Boston.

DR. PATRICK: Boston?

LIZZIE: For a start.

DR. PATRICK: And when will we go?

LIZZIE: Tonight.

DR. PATRICK: But you don't really mean it, you're havin' me on.

LIZZIE: I do mean it.

580   DR. PATRICK: How can you joke — and look so serious?

LIZZIE: It's a gift.

DR. PATRICK: (*Laughs.*) Oh Lizzie —

LIZZIE: Look!

DR. PATRICK: What is it?

LIZZIE: It's those little beggars next door. Hey! Hey get away! Get away there!
. . . They break into the shed to get at my birds and Papa gets angry.

DR. PATRICK: It's a natural thing.

LIZZIE: Well, Papa doesn't like it.

DR. PATRICK: They just want to look at them.

590   LIZZIE: Papa says what's his is his own — you need a formal invitation to get into
our yard. . . . (*Pause.*) How's your wife?

DR. PATRICK: My wife.

LIZZIE: Shouldn't I ask that? I thought nice polite ladies always inquired after
the wives of their friends or acquaintances or . . . whatever.

(HARRY *observes them.*)

DR. PATRICK: You've met my wife, my wife is always the same.

LIZZIE: How boring for you.

DR. PATRICK: Uh-huh.

LIZZIE: And for her —

DR. PATRICK: Yes indeed.

600   LIZZIE: And for me.

DR. PATRICK: Do you know what they say, Lizzie? They say if you live on Second
Street, and you need a house call, and you don't mind the Irish, call Dr.
Patrick. Dr. Patrick is very prompt with his Second Street house calls.

LIZZIE: I'll tell you what I've heard them say — Second Street is a nice place to
visit, but you wouldn't want to live there. I certainly don't.

HARRY: Lizzie.

LIZZIE: Well, look who's here. Have you had the pleasure of meeting my uncle,
Mr. Wingate.

DR. PATRICK: No, Miss Borden, that pleasure has never been mine.

610   LIZZIE: That's exactly how I feel.

DR. PATRICK: Mr. Wingate, sir.

HARRY: Dr. . . . Patrick is it?

DR. PATRICK: Yes it is, sir.

HARRY: Who's sick? (*In other words, "What the hell are you doing here?"*)

LIZZIE: No one. He just dropped by for a visit; you see Dr. Patrick and I are
very old, very dear friends, isn't that so?

(HARRY *stares at* DR. PATRICK.)

DR. PATRICK: Well . . . (LIZZIE *jabs him in the ribs.*) Ouch! . . . It's her sense of
humour, sir . . . a rare trait in a woman

HARRY: You best get in, Lizzie, it's gettin' on for lunch.

620   LIZZIE: Don't be silly, we just had breakfast.

HARRY: You best get in!

LIZZIE: . . . Would you give me your arm, Dr. Patrick? (*She moves away with* DR.
PATRICK, *ignoring* HARRY.)

DR. PATRICK: Now see what you've done?

LIZZIE: What?

DR. PATRICK: You've broken two of my ribs and ruined my reputation all in
one blow.

LIZZIE: It's impossible to ruin an Irishman's reputation.

DR. PATRICK: (*Smiles.*) . . . I'll be seeing you, Lizzie. . . .

MISS LIZZIE/BRIDGET: They're sayin' it's time you were married.

LIZZIE: What time is that?

630   MISS LIZZIE/BRIDGET: You need a place of your own.

LIZZIE: How would getting married get me that?

MISS LIZZIE/BRIDGET: Though I don't know what man would put up with your
moods!

LIZZIE: What about me putting up with his!

MISS LIZZIE/BRIDGET: Oh Lizzie!

LIZZIE: What's the matter, don't men have moods?

HARRY: I'm tellin' you, as God is my witness, she's out in the walk talkin' to that
Irish doctor, and he's fallin' all over her.

MRS. BORDEN: What's the matter with you? For her own sake you should speak

640   to her.

MR. BORDEN: I will.

HARRY: The talk around town can't be doin' you any good.

MRS. BORDEN: Harry's right.

HARRY: Yes sir.

MRS. BORDEN: He's tellin' you what you should know.

HARRY: If a man can't manage his own daughter, how the hell can he manage
a business — that's what people say, and it don't matter a damn whether
there's any sense in it or not.

MR. BORDEN: I know that.

650   MRS. BORDEN: Knowin' is one thing, doin' something about it is another.
What're you goin' to do about it?

MR. BORDEN: God damn it! I said I was goin' to speak to her and I am!

MRS. BORDEN: Well speak good and plain this time!

MR. BORDEN: Jesus christ woman!

MRS. BORDEN: Your "speakin' to Lizzie" is a ritual around here.

MR. BORDEN: Abbie —

MRS. BORDEN: She talks, you listen, and nothin' changes!

MR. BORDEN: That's enough!

MRS. BORDEN: Emma isn't the only one that's fed to the teeth!

660   MR. BORDEN: Shut up!

MRS. BORDEN: You're gettin' old, Andrew! You're gettin' old! *(She exits.)*

(An air of embarrassment from MR. BORDEN *at having words in front of* HARRY. MR. BORDEN *fumbles with his pipe.)*

HARRY: *(Offers his pouch of tobacco.)* Here ... have some of mine.

MR. BORDEN: Don't mind if I do.... Nice mix.

HARRY: It is.

MR. BORDEN: ... I used to think ... by my seventies ... I'd be bouncin' a grandson on my knee....

HARRY: Not too late for that.

MR. BORDEN: Nope ... never had any boys ... and girls ... don't seem to have the same sense of family.... You know it's all well and good to talk about
670   speakin' plain to Lizzie, but the truth of the matter is, if Lizzie puts her mind to a thing, she does it, and if she don't, she don't.

HARRY: It's up to you to see she does.

MR. BORDEN: It's like Abigail says, knowin' is one thing, doin' is another.... You're lucky you never brought any children into the world, Harry, you don't have to deal with them.

HARRY: Now that's no way to be talkin'.

MR. BORDEN: There's Emma ... Emma's a good girl ... when Abbie and I get on, there'll always be Emma.... Well! You're not sittin' here to listen to me and my girls, are you, you didn't come here for that. Business, eh, Harry?

*(*HARRY *whips out a sheet of figures.)*

680 MISS LIZZIE/BRIDGET: I can remember distinctly ... that moment I was undressing for bed, and I looked at my knees — and there were no scabs! At last! I thought I'm the nice little girl Emma wants me to be! ... But it wasn't that at all. I was just growing up. I didn't fall down so often.... *(She smiles.)* Do you suppose ... do you suppose there's a formula, a magic formula for being "a woman"? Do you suppose every girl baby receives it at birth, it's the last thing that happens just before birth, the magic formula is stamped indelibly on the brain — Ka Thud!! *(Her mood of amusement changes.)* ... and ... through some terrible oversight ... perhaps the death of my mother ... I didn't get that Ka Thud!! I was born ... defective.... *(She looks at* THE ACTRESS.*)*

690 LIZZIE: *(Low.)* No.

MISS LIZZIE/BRIDGET: Not defective?

LIZZIE: Just ... born.

THE DEFENSE: Gentlemen of the Jury!! I ask you to look at the defendant, Miss Lizzie Borden. I ask you to recall the nature of the crime of which she is accused. I ask you — do you believe Miss Lizzie Borden, the youngest daughter of a scion of our community, a recipient of the fullest amenities our society can bestow upon its most fortunate members, do you believe Miss Lizzie Borden capable of wielding the murder weapon — thirty-two blows, gentlemen, thirty-two blows — fracturing Abigail Borden's skull, leaving her
700   bloody and broken body in an upstairs bedroom, then, Miss Borden, with no hint of frenzy, hysteria, or trace of blood upon her person, engages in casual conversation with the maid, Bridget O'Sullivan, while awaiting her

father's return home, upon which, after sending Bridget to her attic room, Miss Borden deals thirteen blows to the head of her father, and minutes later — in a state utterly compatible with that of a loving daughter upon discovery of murder most foul — Miss Borden calls for aid! Is this the aid we give her? Accusation of the most heinous and infamous of crimes? Do you believe Miss Lizzie Borden capable of these acts? I can tell you I do not!! I can tell you these acts of violence are acts of madness!! Gentlemen! If this gentlewoman is capable of such an act — I say to you — look to your daughters — if this gentlewoman is capable of such an act, which of us can lie abed at night, hear a step upon the stairs, a rustle in the hall, a creak outside the door.... Which of you can plump your pillow, nudge your wife, close your eyes, and sleep? Gentlemen, Lizzie Borden is not mad. Gentlemen, Lizzie Borden is not guilty.

MR. BORDEN: Lizzie?

LIZZIE: Papa...have you and Harry got business?

HARRY: 'lo Lizzie. I'll ah...finish up later. (*He exits with the figures.* LIZZIE *watches him go.*)

MR. BORDEN: Lizzie?

LIZZIE: What?

MR. BORDEN: Could you sit down a minute?

LIZZIE: If it's about Dr. Patrick again, I —

MR. BORDEN: It isn't.

LIZZIE: Good.

MR. BORDEN: But we could start there.

LIZZIE: Oh Papa.

MR. BORDEN: Sit down Lizzie.

LIZZIE: But I've heard it all before, another chat for a wayward girl.

MR. BORDEN: (*Gently.*) Bite your tongue, Lizzie.

(*She smiles at him, there is affection between them. She has the qualities he would like in a son but deplores in a daughter.*)

MR. BORDEN: Now...first off...I want you to know that I...understand about you and the doctor.

LIZZIE: What do you understand?

MR. BORDEN: I understand...that it's a natural thing.

LIZZIE: What is?

MR. BORDEN: I'm saying there's nothing unnatural about an attraction between a man and a woman. That's a natural thing.

LIZZIE: I find Dr. Patrick...amusing and entertaining...if that's what you mean...is that what you mean?

MR. BORDEN: This attraction...points something up — you're a woman of thirty-four years —

LIZZIE: I know that.

MR. BORDEN: Just listen to me, Lizzie.... I'm choosing my words, and I want you to listen. Now...in most circumstances...a woman of your age would be married, eh? have children, be running her own house, that's the natural thing, eh? (*Pause.*) Eh, Lizzie?

LIZZIE: I don't know.

MR. BORDEN: Of course you know.

LIZZIE: You're saying I'm unnatural... am I supposed to agree, is that what you want?

MR. BORDEN: No, I'm not saying that! I'm saying the opposite to that! ... I'm saying the feelings you have towards Dr. Patrick —

LIZZIE: What feelings?

MR. BORDEN: What's... what's happening there, I can understand, but what you have to understand is that he's a married man, and there's nothing for you there.

LIZZIE: If he weren't married, Papa, I wouldn't be bothered talking to him! ... It's just a game, Papa, it's a game.

MR. BORDEN: A game.

LIZZIE: You have no idea how boring it is looking eligible, interested, and alluring, when I feel none of the three. So I play games. And it's a blessed relief to talk to a married man.

MR. BORDEN: What're his feelings for you?

LIZZIE: I don't know, I don't care. Can I go now?

MR. BORDEN: I'm not finished yet! ... You know Mr. MacLeod, Johnny MacLeod?

LIZZIE: I know his three little monsters.

MR. BORDEN: He's trying to raise three boys with no mother!

LIZZIE: That's not my problem! I'm going.

MR. BORDEN: Lizzie!

LIZZIE: What!

MR. BORDEN: Mr. MacLeod's asked to come over next Tuesday.

LIZZIE: I'll be out that night.

MR. BORDEN: No you won't!

LIZZIE: Yes I will! ... Whose idea was this?

MR. BORDEN: No one's.

LIZZIE: That's a lie. She wants to get rid of me.

MR. BORDEN: I want what's best for you!

LIZZIE: No you don't! 'Cause you don't care what I want!

MR. BORDEN: You don't know what you want!

LIZZIE: But I know what you want! You want me living my life by the Farmers' Almanac; having everyone over for Christmas dinner; waiting up for my husband; and *serving at socials!*

MR. BORDEN: It's good enough for your mother!

LIZZIE: She is *not* my *mother!*

MR. BORDEN: ... John MacLeod is looking for a wife.

LIZZIE: No, god damn it, he isn't!

MR. BORDEN: Lizzie!

LIZZIE: He's looking for a housekeeper and it isn't going to be me!

MR. BORDEN: You've a filthy mouth!

LIZZIE: Is that why you hate me?

MR. BORDEN: You don't make sense.

LIZZIE: Why is it when I pretend things I don't feel, that's when you like me?

MR. BORDEN: You talk foolish.

LIZZIE: I'm supposed to be a mirror. I'm supposed to reflect what you want to see, but everyone wants something different. If no one looks in the mirror, I'm not even there, I don't exist!

MR. BORDEN: Lizzie, you talk foolish!

LIZZIE: No, I don't, that isn't true.

MR. BORDEN: About Mr. MacLeod —

LIZZIE: You can't make me get married!

800 MR. BORDEN: Lizzie, do you want to spend the rest of your life in this house?

LIZZIE: No...No...I want out of it, but I won't get married to do it.

MRS. BORDEN: *(On her way through to the kitchen.)* You've never been asked.

LIZZIE: Oh listen to her! I must be some sort of failure, then, eh? You had no son and a daughter that failed! What does that make you, Papa!

MR. BORDEN: I want you to think about Johnny MacLeod!

LIZZIE: To hell with him!!!

(MR. BORDEN *appears defeated. After a moment,* LIZZIE *goes to him, she holds his hand, strokes his hair.)*

LIZZIE: Papa?...Papa, I love you, I try to be what you want, really I do try, I try ...but...I don't want to get married. I wouldn't be a good mother, I —

MR. BORDEN: How do you know —

810 LIZZIE: I know it!...I want out of all this...I hate this house, I hate...I want out. Try to understand how I feel...Why can't I do something?...Eh? I mean...I could...I could go into your office...I could...learn how to keep books?

MR. BORDEN: Lizzie.

LIZZIE: Why can't I do something like that?

MR. BORDEN: For god's sake, talk sensible.

LIZZIE: Alright then! Why can't we move up on the hill to a house where we aren't in each other's laps!

MRS. BORDEN: *(Returning from kitchen.)* Why don't you move out!

820 LIZZIE: Give me the money and I'll go!

MRS. BORDEN: Money.

LIZZIE: And give me enough that I won't ever have to come back!

MRS. BORDEN: She always gets round to money!

LIZZIE: You drive me to it!

MRS. BORDEN: She's crazy!

LIZZIE: You drive me to it!

MRS. BORDEN: She should be locked up!

LIZZIE: *(Begins to smash the plates in the dining room.)* There!! There!!

MR. BORDEN: Lizzie!

830 MRS. BORDEN: Stop her!

LIZZIE: There!

(MR. BORDEN *attempts to restrain her.)*

MRS. BORDEN: For god's sake, Andrew!

LIZZIE: Lock me up! Lock me up!

MR. BORDEN: Stop it! Lizzie!

(She collapses against him, crying.)

LIZZIE: Oh, Papa, I can't stand it.

MR. BORDEN: There, there, come on now, it's alright, listen to me, Lizzie, it's alright.

MRS. BORDEN: You may as well get down on your knees.

LIZZIE: Look at her. She's jealous of me. She can't stand it whenever you're nice to me.

840   MR. BORDEN: There now.

MRS. BORDEN: Ask her about Dr. Patrick.

MR. BORDEN: I'll handle this my way.

LIZZIE: He's an entertaining person, there're very few around!

MRS. BORDEN: Fall River ain't Paris and ain't that a shame for our Lizzie!

LIZZIE: One trip three years ago and you're still harping on it; it's true, Papa, an elephant never forgets!

MR. BORDEN: Show some respect!

LIZZIE: She's a fat cow and I hate her!

(MR. BORDEN *slaps* LIZZIE. *There is a pause as he regains control of himself.*)

MR. BORDEN: Now...now...you'll see Mr. MacLeod Tuesday night.

850   LIZZIE: No.

MR. BORDEN: God damn it!! I said you'll see Johnny MacLeod Tuesday night!!

LIZZIE: No.

MR. BORDEN: Get the hell upstairs to your room!

LIZZIE: No.

MR. BORDEN: I'm telling you to go upstairs to your room!!

LIZZIE: I'll go when I'm ready.

MR. BORDEN: I said, Go!

(*He grabs her arm to move her forcibly, she hits his arm away.*)

LIZZIE: No!...There's something you don't understand, Papa. You can't make me do one thing that I don't want to do. I'm going to keep on doing just
860   what I want just when I want — like always!

MR. BORDEN: (*Shoves her to the floor to gain a clear exit from the room. He stops on the stairs, looks back to her on the floor.*)...I'm...(*He continues off.*)

MRS. BORDEN: (*Without animosity.*) You know, Lizzie, your father keeps you. You know you got nothing but what he gives you. And that's a fact of life. You got to come to deal with facts. I did.

LIZZIE: And married Papa.

MRS. BORDEN: And married your father. You never made it easy for me. I took on a man with two little ones, and Emma was your mother.

LIZZIE: You got stuck so I should too, is that it?

MRS. BORDEN: What?

870   LIZZIE: The reason I should marry Johnny MacLeod.

MRS. BORDEN: I just know, this time, in the end, you'll do what your Papa says, you'll see.

LIZZIE: No, I won't. I have a right. A right that frees me from all that.

MRS. BORDEN: No, Lizzie, you got no rights.

LIZZIE: I've a legal right to one-third because I am his flesh and blood.

MRS. BORDEN: What you don't understand is your father's not dead yet, your father's got many good years ahead of him, and when his time comes, well, we'll see what his will says then....Your father's no fool, Lizzie....Only a fool would leave money to you. (*She exits.*)

(After a moment, BRIDGET *enters from the kitchen.)*

880   BRIDGET: Ah Lizzie... you outdid yourself that time. *(She is comforting* LIZZIE.*)*
        ... Yes you did... an elephant never forgets!

LIZZIE. Oh Bridget.

BRIDGET: Come on now.

LIZZIE: I can't help it.

BRIDGET: Sure you can... sure you can... stop your cryin' and come and sit
        down... you want me to tell you a story?

LIZZIE: No.

BRIDGET: Sure, a story. I'll tell you a story. Come on now... now... before I
        worked here I worked up on the hill and the lady of the house... are you
890   listenin'? Well, she swore by her cook, finest cook in creation, yes, always
        bowin' and scrapin' and smilin' and givin' up her day off if company arrived.
        Oh the lady of the house she loved that cook — and I'll tell you her name!
        It was Mary! Now listen! Do you know what Mary was doin'? (LIZZIE *shakes*
        her head.) Before eatin' the master'd serve drinks in the parlour — and out
        in the kitchen, Mary'd be spittin' in the soup!

LIZZIE: What?

BRIDGET: She'd spit in the soup! And she'd smile when they served it!

LIZZIE: No.

BRIDGET: Yes. I've seen her cut up hair for an omelette.

900   LIZZIE: You're lying.

BRIDGET: Cross me heart.... They thought it was pepper!

LIZZIE: Oh, Bridget!

BRIDGET: These two eyes have seen her season up mutton stew when it's off and
        gone bad.

LIZZIE: Gone bad?

BRIDGET: Oh and they et it, every bit, and the next day they was hit with...
        stomach flu! so cook called it. By jasus Lizzie, I daren't tell you what she
        served up in their food, for fear you'd be sick!

LIZZIE: That's funny.... *(A fact —* LIZZIE *does not appear amused.)*

910   BRIDGET: *(Starts to clear up the dishes.)* Yes, well, I'm tellin' you I kept on the good
        side of cook.

*(*LIZZIE *watches her for a moment.)*

LIZZIE: ... Do you... like me?

BRIDGET: Sure I do... You should try bein' more like cook, Lizzie. Smile and get
        round them. You can do it.

LIZZIE: It's not... *fair* that I have to.

BRIDGET: There ain't nothin' fair in this world.

LIZZIE: Well then... well then, I don't want to!

BRIDGET: You dream, Lizzie... you dream dreams... Work. Be sensible. What
        could you do?

920   LIZZIE: I could ...

MISS LIZZIE/BRIDGET: No.

LIZZIE: I could ...

MISS LIZZIE/BRIDGET: No.

LIZZIE: I could...

MISS LIZZIE/BRIDGET: No!

LIZZIE: I...dream.

MISS LIZZIE/BRIDGET: You dream...of a carousel...you see a carousel...you see lights that go on and go off...you see yourself on a carousel horse, a red-painted horse with its head in the air, and green staring eyes, and a white flowing mane, it looks wild!...It goes up and comes down, and the carousel whirls round with the music and lights, on and off...and you watch ...watch yourself on the horse. You're wearing a mask, a white mask like the mane of the horse, it looks like your face except that it's rigid and white... and it changes! With each flick of the lights, the expression, it changes, but always so rigid and hard, like the flesh of the horse that is red that you ride. You ride with no hands! No hands on this petrified horse, its head flung in the air, its wide staring eyes like those of a doe run down by the dogs!...And each time you go round, your hands rise a fraction nearer the mask...and the music and the carousel and the horse...they all three slow down, and they stop....You can reach out and touch...you...you on the horse...with your hands so at the eyes....You look into the eyes! (*A sound from* LIZZIE, *she is horrified and frightened. She covers her eyes.*) There are none! None! Just black holes in a white mask....(*Pause.*) Only a dream....The eyes of your birds...are round...and bright...a light shines from inside...they ...can see into your heart...they're pretty...they love you....

MR. BORDEN: I want this settled, Harry, I want it settled while Lizzie's out back.

(MISS LIZZIE/BRIDGET *draws* LIZZIE's *attention to the* MR. BORDEN/HARRY *scene.* LIZZIE *listens, will move closer.*)

HARRY: You know I'm for that.

MR. BORDEN: I want it all done but the signin' of the papers tomorrow, that's if I decide to —

HARRY: You can't lose, Andrew. That farm's just lyin' fallow.

MR. BORDEN: Well, let's see what you got.

HARRY: (*Gets out his papers.*) Look at this...I'll run horse auctions and a buggy rental — now I'll pay no rent for the house or pasturage but you get twenty percent, eh? That figure there —

MR. BORDEN: Mmmn.

HARRY: From my horse auctions last year, it'll go up on the farm and you'll get twenty percent off the top....My buggy rental won't do so well... that's that figure there, approximate...but it all adds up, eh? Adds up for you.

MR. BORDEN: It's a good deal, Harry, but...

HARRY: Now I know why you're worried — but the farm will still be in the family, 'cause aren't I family? and whenever you or the girls want to come over for a visit, why I'll send a buggy from the rental, no need for you to have the expense of a horse, eh?

MR. BORDEN: It looks good on paper.

HARRY: There's...ah...something else, it's a bit awkward but I got to mention it; I'll be severin' a lot of my present connections, and what I figure I've a right to, is some kind of guarantee....

MR. BORDEN: You mean a renewable lease for the farm?

HARRY: Well — what I'm wondering is... No offense, but you're an older man, Andrew... now if something should happen to you, where would the farm stand in regards to your will? That's what I'm wondering

MR. BORDEN: I've not made a will.

HARRY: You know best — but I wouldn't want to be in a position where Lizzie would be havin' anything to do with that farm. The less she knows now the better, but she's bound to find out — I don't feel I'm steppin' out of line by bringin' this up.

(LIZZIE *is within earshot. She is staring at* HARRY *and* MR. BORDEN. *They do not see her.*)

MR. BORDEN: No.

HARRY: If you mind you come right out and say so.

MR. BORDEN: That's alright.

HARRY: Now... if you... put the farm — in Abbie's name, what do you think?

MR. BORDEN: I don't know, Harry.

HARRY: I don't want to push.

MR. BORDEN: ...I should make a will...I want the girls looked after, it don't seem like they'll marry...and Abbie, she's younger than me, I know Emma will see to her, still...money-wise I got to consider these things...it makes a difference no men in the family.

HARRY: You know you can count on me for whatever.

MR. BORDEN: If...If I changed title to the farm, Abbie'd have to come down to the bank, I wouldn't want Lizzie to know.

HARRY: You can send a note for her when you get to the bank; she can say it's a note from a friend, and come down and meet you. Simple as that.

MR. BORDEN: I'll give it some thought.

HARRY: You see, Abbie owns the farm, it's no difference to you, but it gives me protection.

MR. BORDEN: Who's there?

HARRY: It's Lizzie.

MR. BORDEN: What do you want?...Did you lock the shed?...Is the shed locked? (LIZZIE *makes a slow motion which* MR. BORDEN *takes for assent.*) Well you make sure it stays locked! I don't want any more of those god damned. ...I...ah...I think we about covered everything, Harry, we'll...ah... we'll let it go till tomorrow.

HARRY: Good enough...well...I'll just finish choppin' that kindlin', give a shout when it's lunchtime. (*He exits.*)

(LIZZIE *and* MR. BORDEN *stare at each other for a moment.*)

LIZZIE: (*Very low.*) What are you doing with the farm?

(MR. BORDEN *slowly picks up the papers, places them in his pocket.*)

LIZZIE: Papa!...Papa. I want you to show me what you put in your pocket.

MR. BORDEN: It's none of your business.

LIZZIE: The farm is my business.

MR. BORDEN: It's nothing.

LIZZIE: Show me!

1010 MR. BORDEN: I said it's nothing!

(LIZZIE *makes a quick move towards her father to seize the paper from his pocket. Even more quickly and smartly he slaps her face. It is all very quick and clean. A pause as they stand frozen.*)

HARRY: (*Off.*) Andrew, there's a bunch of kids broken into the shed!

MR. BORDEN: Jesus christ.

LIZZIE: (*Whispers.*) What about the farm.

MR. BORDEN: You! You and those god damn birds! I've told you! I've told you time and again!

LIZZIE: What about the farm!

MR. BORDEN: Jesus christ... You never listen! Never!

HARRY: (*Enters carrying the hand hatchet.*) Andrew!!

1020 MR. BORDEN: (*Grabs the hand hatchet from* HARRY, *turns to* LIZZIE.) There'll be no more of your god damn birds in this yard!!

LIZZIE: No!

(MR. BORDEN *raises the hatchet and smashes it into the table as* LIZZIE *screams.*)

LIZZIE: No Papa!! Nooo!!

(*The hatchet is embedded in the table.* MR. BORDEN *and* HARRY *assume a soft freeze as* ACTRESS/LIZZIE *whirls to see* MISS LIZZIE/BRIDGET *observing the scene.*)

LIZZIE: Nooo!

MISS LIZZIE: I loved them.

BLACKOUT

ACT TWO

(*Lights come up on* THE ACTRESS/LIZZIE *sitting at the dining-room table. She is very still, her hands clasped in her lap.* MISS LIZZIE/BRIDGET *is near her. She too is very still. A pause.*)

ACTRESS/LIZZIE: (*Very low.*) Talk to me.

MISS LIZZIE/BRIDGET: I remember...

ACTRESS/LIZZIE: (*Very low.*) No.

MISS LIZZIE/BRIDGET: On the farm, Papa's farm, Harry's farm, when I was little and thought it was my farm and I loved it, we had some puppies, the farm dog had puppies, brown soft little puppies with brown ey... (*She does not complete the word "eyes".*) And one of the puppies got sick. I didn't know it was sick, it seemed like the others, but the mother, she knew. It would lie at the back of the box, she would lie in front of it while she nursed all the others. They ignored it, that puppy didn't exist for the others.... I think inside it was different, and the mother thought the difference she sensed was a sickness... and after a while... anyone could tell it was sick. It had nothing to eat!... And Papa took it and drowned it. That's what you do on a farm with things that are different.

ACTRESS/LIZZIE: Am I different?

MISS LIZZIE/BRIDGET: You kill them.

(ACTRESS/LIZZIE *looks at* MISS LIZZIE/BRIDGET. MISS LIZZIE/BRIDGET *looks towards the top of the stairs.* BRIDGET *gets up and exits to the kitchen.* EMMA *appears at the top of the stairs. She is dressed for travel and carries a small suitcase and her gloves. She stares down at* LIZZIE *still sitting at the table. After several moments* LIZZIE *becomes aware of that gaze and turns to look at* EMMA. EMMA *then descends the stairs. She puts down her suitcase. She is not overjoyed at seeing* LIZZIE, *having hoped to get away before* LIZZIE *arose, nevertheless she begins with an excess of enthusiasm to cover the implications of her departure.*)

EMMA: Well! You're up early... Bridget down?... did you put the coffee on? (*She puts her gloves on the table.*) My goodness, Lizzie, cat got your tongue? (*She exits to the kitchen.* LIZZIE *picks up the gloves.* EMMA *returns.*) Bridget's down, she's in the kitchen.... Well... looks like a real scorcher today, doesn't it?...

LIZZIE: What's the bag for?

EMMA: I... decided I might go for a little trip, a day or two, get away from the heat.... The girls've rented a place out beach way and I thought... with the weather and all...

LIZZIE: How can you do that?

EMMA: Do what?... Anyway, I thought I might stay with them a few days.... Why don't you come with me?

LIZZIE: No.

EMMA: Just for a few days, come with me.

LIZZIE: No.

EMMA: You know you like the water.

LIZZIE: I said no!

EMMA: Oh, Lizzie.

(*Pause.*)

LIZZIE: I don't see how you can leave me like this.

EMMA: I asked you to come with me.

LIZZIE: You know I can't do that.

EMMA: Why not?

LIZZIE: Someone has to *do* something, you just run away from things.

(*Pause.*)

EMMA: ... Lizzie... I'm sorry about the — [*birds*]

LIZZIE: No!

EMMA: Papa was angry.

LIZZIE: I don't want to talk about it.

EMMA: He's sorry now.

LIZZIE: Nobody *listens* to me, can't you hear me? I said *don't* talk about it. I don't want to talk about it. Stop talking about it!!

(BRIDGET *enters with the coffee.*)

EMMA: Thank you, Bridget.

(BRIDGET *withdraws.*)

EMMA: Well! . . . I certainly can use this this morning. . . . Your coffee's there.
LIZZIE: I don't want it.
EMMA: You're going to ruin those gloves.
LIZZIE: I don't care.
EMMA: Since they're not yours.

(LIZZIE *bangs the gloves down on the table. A pause. Then* EMMA *picks them up and smooths them out.*)

LIZZIE: Why are you leaving me?
EMMA: I feel like a visit with the girls. Is there something wrong with that?
LIZZIE: How can you go now?
EMMA: I don't know what you're getting at.
LIZZIE: I heard them. I heard them talking yesterday. Do you know what they're saying?
EMMA: How could I?
LIZZIE: "How could I?" What do you mean "How could I?" Did you know?
EMMA: No, Lizzie, I did not.
LIZZIE: *Did-not-what.*
EMMA: Know.
LIZZIE: But you know now. How do you know now?
EMMA: I've put two and two together and I'm going over to the girls for a visit!
LIZZIE: Please Emma!
EMMA: It's too hot.
LIZZIE: I need you, don't go.
EMMA: I've been talking about this trip.
LIZZIE: That's a lie.
EMMA: They're expecting me.
LIZZIE: You're lying to me!
EMMA: I'm going to the girls' place. You can come if you want, you can stay if you want. I planned this trip and I'm taking it!
LIZZIE: Stop lying!
EMMA: If I want to tell a little white lie to avoid an altercation in this house, I'll do so. Other people have been doing it for years!
LIZZIE: You don't understand, you don't understand anything.
EMMA: Oh, I understand enough.
LIZZIE: You don't! Let me explain it to you. You listen carefully, you listen. . . . Harry's getting the farm, can you understand that? Harry is here and he's moving on the farm and he's going to be there, on the farm, living on the farm. *Our farm.* Do you understand that? . . . Do you understand that!
EMMA: Yes.
LIZZIE: Harry's going to be on the farm. That's the first thing. . . . No . . . no it isn't. . . . The first thing . . . was the mill house, that was the first thing! And *now* the farm. You see there's a pattern, Emma, you can see that, can't you?

EMMA: I don't —

LIZZIE: You can see it! The mill house, then the farm, and the next thing is the
papers for the farm — do you know what he's doing, Papa's doing? He's
signing the farm over to her. It will never be ours, we will never have it, not
ever. It's ours by rights, don't you feel that?

EMMA: The farm — has always meant a great deal to me, yes.

LIZZIE: Then what are you doing about it! You can't leave me now . . . but that's
not all. Papa's going to make a will, and you can see the pattern, can't
you, and if the pattern keeps on, what do you suppose his will will say.
What do you suppose, answer me!

EMMA: I don't know.

LIZZIE: Say it!

EMMA: He'll see we're looked after.

LIZZIE: I don't want to be looked after! What's the matter with you? Do you really
want to spend the rest of your life with that cow, listening to her drone on
and on for years! That's just what they think you'll do. Papa'll leave you a
monthly allowance, just like he'll leave me, just enough to keep us all
living together. We'll be worth millions on paper, and be stuck in this
house and by and by Papa will die and Harry will move in and you will wait
on that cow while she gets fatter and fatter and I — will — sit in my room.

EMMA: Lizzie.

LIZZIE: We have to do something, you can see that. We have to do something!

EMMA: There's nothing we can do.

LIZZIE: Don't say that!

EMMA: Alright, then, what can we do?

LIZZIE: I . . . I . . . don't know. But we have to do something, you have to help me,
you can't go away and leave me alone, you can't do that.

EMMA: Then —

LIZZIE: You know what I thought? I thought you could talk to him, really talk
to him, make him understand that we're people. *Individual people,* and we
have to live separate lives, and his will should make it possible for us to do
that. And the farm can't go to Harry.

EMMA: You know it's no use.

LIZZIE: I can't talk to him anymore. Everytime I talk to him I make everything
worse. I hate him, no. No I don't. I hate her.

(EMMA *looks at her brooch watch.*)

LIZZIE: Don't look at the time.

EMMA: I'll miss my connections.

LIZZIE: No!

EMMA: (*Puts on her gloves.*) Lizzie. There's certain things we have to face. One
of them is, we can't change a thing.

LIZZIE: I won't let you go!

EMMA: I'll be back on the weekend.

LIZZIE: He killed my birds! He took the ax and he killed them! Emma, I ran out
and held them in my hands, I felt their hearts throbbing and pumping and
the blood gushed out of their necks, it was all over my hands, don't you care
about that?

EMMA: I . . . I . . . have a train to catch.

LIZZIE: He didn't care how much he hurt me and you don't care either. Nobody cares.

EMMA: I . . . have to go now.

LIZZIE: That's right. Go away. I don't even like you, Emma. Go away! (EMMA *leaves*, LIZZIE *runs after her calling.*) I'm sorry for all the things I told you! Things I really felt! You pretended to me, and I don't like you!! Go away!! (LIZZIE *runs to the window and looks out after* EMMA's *departing figure. After a moment she slowly turns back into the room.* MISS LIZZIE/BRIDGET *is there.*)

LIZZIE: I want to die . . . I want to die, but something inside won't let me . . . inside something says *no.* (*She shuts her eyes.*) I can do anything.

DEFENSE: Miss Borden.

(*Both* LIZZIES *turn.*)

DEFENSE: Could you describe the sequence of events upon your father's arrival home?

LIZZIE: (*With no animation.*) Papa came in . . . we exchanged a few words . . . Bridget and I spoke of the yard goods sale down town, whether she would buy some. She went up to her room. . . .

DEFENSE: And then?

LIZZIE: I went out back . . . through the yard . . . I picked up several pears from the ground beneath the trees . . . I went into the shed . . . I stood looking out the window and ate the pears . . .

DEFENSE: How many?

LIZZIE: Four.

DEFENSE: It wasn't warm, stifling in the shed?

LIZZIE: No, it was cool.

DEFENSE: What were you doing, apart from eating the pears?

LIZZIE: I suppose I was thinking. I just stood there, looking out the window, thinking, and eating the pears I'd picked up.

DEFENSE: You're fond of pears?

LIZZIE: Otherwise, I wouldn't eat them.

DEFENSE: Go on.

LIZZIE: I returned to the house. I found — Papa. I called for Bridget.

(MRS. BORDEN *descends the stairs.* LIZZIE *and* BRIDGET *turn to look at her.* MRS. BORDEN *is only aware of* LIZZIE's *stare. Pause.*)

MRS. BORDEN: . . . What're you staring at? . . . I said what're you staring at?

LIZZIE: (*Continuing to stare at* MRS. BORDEN.) Bridget.

BRIDGET: Yes ma'am.

(*Pause.*)

MRS. BORDEN: Just coffee and a biscuit this morning, Bridget, it's too hot for a decent breakfast.

BRIDGET: Yes ma'am.

(*She exits for the biscuit and coffee.* LIZZIE *continues to stare at* MRS. BORDEN.)

MRS. BORDEN: ... Tell Bridget I'll have it in the parlour.

LIZZIE: (*Is making an effort to be pleasant, to be "good."* MRS. BORDEN *is more aware of this as unusual behaviour from* LIZZIE *than were she to be rude, biting, or threatening.* LIZZIE, *at the same time, feels caught in a dimension other than the one in which the people around her are operating. For* LIZZIE, *a bell-jar effect. Simple acts seem filled with significance.* LIZZIE *is trying to fulfill other people's expectations of "normal."*)

LIZZIE: It's not me, is it?

MRS. BORDEN: What?

LIZZIE: You're not moving into the parlour because of me, are you?

MRS. BORDEN: What?

LIZZIE: I'd hate to think I'd driven you out of your own dining room.

MRS. BORDEN: No.

LIZZIE: Oh good, because I'd hate to think that was so.

MRS. BORDEN: It's cooler in the parlour.

180 LIZZIE: You know, you're right.

MRS. BORDEN: Eh?

LIZZIE: It is cooler....

(BRIDGET *enters with the coffee and biscuit.*)

LIZZIE: I will, Bridget.

(*She takes the coffee and biscuit, gives it to* MRS. BORDEN. LIZZIE *watches her eat and drink.* MRS. BORDEN *eats the biscuit delicately.* LIZZIE's *attention is caught by it.*)

LIZZIE: Do you like that biscuit?

MRS. BORDEN: It could be lighter.

LIZZIE: You're right.

(MR. BORDEN *enters, makes his way into the kitchen,* LIZZIE *watches him pass.*)

LIZZIE: You know, Papa doesn't look well, Papa doesn't look well at all. Papa looks sick.

MRS. BORDEN: He had a bad night.

190 LIZZIE: Oh?

MRS. BORDEN: Too hot.

LIZZIE: But it's cooler in here, isn't it ... (*Not trusting her own evaluation of the degree of heat.*) Isn't it?

MRS. BORDEN: Yes, yes, it's cooler in here.

(MR. BORDEN *enters with his coffee.* LIZZIE *goes to him.*)

LIZZIE: Papa? You should go in the parlour. It's much cooler in there, really it is.

(*He goes into the parlour.* LIZZIE *remains in the dining room. She sits at the table, folds her hands in her lap.* MR. BORDEN *begins to read the paper.*)

MRS. BORDEN: ... I think I'll have Bridget do the windows today ... they need doing ... get them out of the way first thing.... Anything in the paper, Andrew?

MR. BORDEN: *(As he continues to read.)* Nope.

200 MRS. BORDEN: There never is . . . I don't know why we buy it.

MR. BORDEN: *(Reading.)* Yup.

MRS. BORDEN: You going out this morning?

MR. BORDEN: Business.

MRS. BORDEN: . . . Harry must be having a bit of a sleep-in.

MR. BORDEN: Yup.

MRS. BORDEN: He's always up by — (HARRY *starts down the stairs.*) Well, speak of the devil — coffee and biscuits?

210 HARRY: Sounds good to me.

(MRS. BORDEN *starts off to get it.* LIZZIE *looks at her, catching her eye.* MRS. BORDEN *stops abruptly.*)

LIZZIE: *(Her voice seems too loud.)* Emma's gone over to visit at the girls' place. (MR. BORDEN *lowers his paper to look at her.* HARRY *looks at her. Suddenly aware of the loudness of her voice, she continues softly, too softly.*) . . . Till the weekend.

MR. BORDEN: She didn't say she was going, when'd she decide that?

(LIZZIE *looks down at her hands, doesn't answer. A pause. Then* MRS. BORDEN *continues out to the kitchen.*)

HARRY: Will you be ah . . . going down town today?

MR. BORDEN: This mornin'. I got . . . business at the bank.

(*A look between them. They are very aware of* LIZZIE'S *presence in the dining room.*)

HARRY: This mornin' eh? Well now . . . that works out just fine for me. I can . . . I got a bill to settle in town myself.

(LIZZIE *turns her head to look at them.*)

HARRY: I'll be on my way after that.

220 MR. BORDEN: Abbie'll be disappointed you're not stayin' for lunch.

HARRY: 'Nother time.

MR. BORDEN: *(Aware of* LIZZIE'S *gaze.)* I . . . I don't know where she is with that coffee. I'll —

HARRY: Never you mind, you sit right there, I'll get it. *(He exits.)*

(LIZZIE *and* MR. BORDEN *look at each other. The bell-jar effect is lessened.*)

LIZZIE: *(Softly.)* Good mornin' Papa.

MR. BORDEN: Mornin' Lizzie.

LIZZIE: Did you have a good sleep?

MR. BORDEN: Not bad.

LIZZIE: Papa?

230 MR. BORDEN: Yes Lizzie.

LIZZIE: You're a very strong-minded person, Papa, do you think I'm like you?

MR. BORDEN: In some ways . . . perhaps.

LIZZIE: I must be like someone.

MR. BORDEN: You resemble your mother.

LIZZIE: I look like my mother?

MR. BORDEN: A bit like your mother.

LIZZIE: But my mother's dead.

MR. BORDEN: Lizzie —

LIZZIE: I remember you told me she died because she was sick ... I was born
and she died.... Did you love her?

MR. BORDEN: I married her.

LIZZIE: Can't you say if you loved her?

MR. BORDEN: Of course I did, Lizzie.

LIZZIE: Did you hate me for killing her?

MR. BORDEN: You don't think of it that way, it was just something that happened.

LIZZIE: Perhaps she just got tired and died. She didn't want to go on, and the
chance came up and she took it. I could understand that.... Perhaps she
was like a bird, she could see all the blue sky and she wanted to fly away but
she couldn't. She was caught, Papa, she was caught in a horrible snare,
and she saw a way out and she took it.... Perhaps it was a very brave thing
to do, Papa, perhaps it was the only way, and she hated to leave us because
she loved us so much, but she couldn't breathe all caught in the snare....
(*Long pause.*) Some people have very small wrists, have you noticed? Mine
aren't ...

(*There is a murmur from the kitchen, then muted laughter.* MR. BORDEN *looks
towards it.*)

LIZZIE: Papa! ... I'm a very strong person.

MRS. BORDEN: (*Off, laughing.*) You're tellin' tales out of school, Harry!

HARRY: (*Off.*) God's truth. You should have seen the buggy when they brought
it back.

MRS. BORDEN: (*Off.*) You've got to tell Andrew. (*Pokes her head in.*) Andrew,
come on out here, Harry's got a story. (*Off.*) Now you'll have to start at the
beginning again. Oh my goodness.

(MR. BORDEN *starts for the kitchen. He stops, and looks back at* LIZZIE.)

LIZZIE: Is there anything you want to tell me, Papa?

MRS. BORDEN: (*Off.*) Andrew!

LIZZIE: (*Softly, an echo.*) Andrew.

MR. BORDEN: What is it, Lizzie?

LIZZIE: If I promised to be a good girl forever and ever, would anything change?

MR. BORDEN: I don't know what you're talking about.

LIZZIE: I would be lying ... Papa! ... Don't do any business today. Don't go out.
Stay home.

MR. BORDEN: What for?

LIZZIE: Everyone's leaving. Going away. Everyone's left.

MRS. BORDEN: (*Off.*) Andrew!

LIZZIE: (*Softly, an echo.*) Andrew.

MR. BORDEN: What is it?

LIZZIE: I'm calling you.

(MR. BORDEN *looks at her for a moment, then leaves for the kitchen.* DR.
PATRICK *is heard whistling very softly.* LIZZIE *listens.*)

LIZZIE: Listen . . . can you hear it . . . can you?

MISS LIZZIE/BRIDGET: I can hear it. . . . It's stopped.

(DR. PATRICK *can't be seen. Only his voice is heard.*)

DR. PATRICK: (*Very low.*) Lizzie?

LIZZIE: (*Realization.*) I could hear it before [you]. (*Pause.*) It sounded so sad I
280   wanted to cry.

MISS LIZZIE/BRIDGET: You mustn't cry.

LIZZIE: I mustn't cry.

DR. PATRICK: I bet you know this one. (*He whistles an Irish jig.*)

LIZZIE: I know that! (*She begins to dance.* DR. PATRICK *enters. He claps in time to
the dance.* LIZZIE *finishes the jig.*)

(DR. PATRICK *applauds.*)

DR. PATRICK: Bravo! Bravo!!

LIZZIE: You didn't know I could do that, did you?

DR. PATRICK: You're a woman of many talents, Miss Borden.

LIZZIE: You're not making fun of me?

DR. PATRICK: I would never do that.

290 LIZZIE: I can do anything I want.

DR. PATRICK: I'm sure you can.

LIZZIE: If I wanted to die — I could even do that, couldn't I?

DR. PATRICK: Well now, I don't think so.

LIZZIE: Yes, I could!

DR. PATRICK: Lizzie —

LIZZIE: You wouldn't know — you can't see into my heart.

DR. PATRICK: I think I can.

LIZZIE: Well you can't.

DR. PATRICK: . . . It's only a game.

300 LIZZIE: I never play games.

DR. PATRICK: Sure you do.

LIZZIE: I hate games.

DR. PATRICK: You're playin' one now.

LIZZIE: You don't even know me!

DR. PATRICK: Come on Lizzie, we don't want to fight. I know what we'll do . . . we'll
start all over. . . . Shut your eyes, Lizzie. (*She does so.*) Good mornin' Miss
Borden. . . . Good mornin' Miss Borden. . . .

LIZZIE: . . . I haven't decided. . . . (*She slowly opens her eyes.*) . . . if it is or it isn't.

DR. PATRICK: Much better . . . and now . . . would you take my arm, Miss Borden?
310   How about a wee promenade?

LIZZIE: There's nowhere to go.

DR. PATRICK: That isn't so. . . . What about Boston? . . . Do you think it's too far
for a stroll? . . . I know what we'll do, we'll walk 'round to the side and
you'll show me your birds. (*They walk.*) . . . I waited last night but you never
showed up . . . there I was, travellin' bag and all, and you never appeared
. . . . I know what went wrong! We forgot to agree on an hour! Next time,
Lizzie, you must set the hour. . . . Is this where they're kept?

(LIZZIE *nods, she opens the cage and looks in it.*)

DR. PATRICK: It's empty. *(He laughs.)* And you say you never play games?

LIZZIE: They're gone.

320 DR. PATRICK: You've been havin' me on again, yes you have.

LIZZIE: They've run away.

DR. PATRICK: Did they really exist?

LIZZIE: I had blood on my hands.

DR. PATRICK: What do you say?

LIZZIE: You can't see it now, I washed it off, see?

DR. PATRICK: *(Takes her hands.)* Ah Lizzie....

LIZZIE: Would you...help someone die?

DR. PATRICK: Why do you ask that?

330 LIZZIE: Some people are better off dead. I might be better off dead.

DR. PATRICK: You're a precious and unique person, Lizzie, and you shouldn't think things like that.

LIZZIE: Precious and unique?

DR. PATRICK: All life is precious and unique.

LIZZIE: I am precious and unique?...I *am* precious and unique. You said that.

DR. PATRICK: Oh, I believe it.

LIZZIE: And I am. I know it. People mix things up on you, you have to be careful. I am a person of worth.

DR. PATRICK: Sure you are.

340 LIZZIE: Not like that fat cow in there.

DR. PATRICK: Her life too is —

LIZZIE: No!

DR. PATRICK: Liz —

LIZZIE: Do you know her!

DR. PATRICK: That doesn't matter.

LIZZIE: Yes it does, it does matter.

DR. PATRICK: You can't be —

LIZZIE: You're a doctor, isn't that right?

DR. PATRICK: Right enough there.

350 LIZZIE: So, tell me, tell me, if a dreadful accident occurred...and two people were dying...but you could only save one.... Which would you save?

DR. PATRICK: You can't ask questions like that.

LIZZIE: Yes I can, come on, it's a game. How does a doctor determine? If one were old and the other were young — would you save the younger one first?

DR. PATRICK: Lizzie.

LIZZIE: You said you liked games! If one were a bad person and the other was good, was trying to be good, would you save the one who was good and let the bad person die?

DR. PATRICK: I don't know.

360 LIZZIE: Listen! If you could go back in time...what would you do if you met a person who was evil and wicked?

DR. PATRICK: Who?

LIZZIE: I don't know, Attila the Hun!

DR. PATRICK: *(Laughs.)* Oh my.

LIZZIE: Listen, if you met Attila the Hun, and you were in a position to kill him, would you do it?

DR. PATRICK: I don't know.

LIZZIE: Think of the suffering he caused, the unhappiness.

DR. PATRICK: Yes, but I'm a doctor, not an assassin.

370 LIZZIE: I think you're a coward.

(*Pause.*)

DR. PATRICK: What I do is try to save lives . . .

LIZZIE: But you put poison out for the slugs in your garden.

DR. PATRICK: You got something mixed up.

LIZZIE: I've never been clearer. Everything's clear. I've lived all of my life for this one moment of absolute clarity! If war were declared, would you serve?

DR. PATRICK: I would fight in a war.

LIZZIE: You wouldn't fight, you would kill — you'd take a gun and shoot people, people who'd done nothing to you, people who were trying to be good, you'd kill them! And you say you wouldn't kill Attila the Hun, or that
380 that stupid cow's life is precious — My *life is precious!!*

DR. PATRICK: To you.

LIZZIE: Yes to me, are you stupid!?

DR. PATRICK: And hers is to her.

LIZZIE: I don't care about her! (*Pause.*) I'm glad you're not my doctor, you can't make decisions, can you? You are a coward.

(DR. PATRICK *starts off.*)

LIZZIE: You're afraid of your wife . . . you can *only* play games. . . . If I really wanted to go to Boston, you wouldn't come with me because you're a coward! *I'm not a coward!!*

(LIZZIE *turns to watch* MRS. BORDEN *sit with needlework. After a moment* MRS. BORDEN *looks at* LIZZIE, *aware of her scrutiny.*)

LIZZIE: . . . Where's Papa?

390 MRS. BORDEN: Out.

LIZZIE: And Mr. Wingate?

MRS. BORDEN: He's out too.

LIZZIE: So what are you going to do . . . Mrs. Borden?

MRS. BORDEN: I'm going to finish this up.

LIZZIE: You do that. . . . (*Pause.*) Where's Bridget?

MRS. BORDEN: Out back washing windows. . . . You got clean clothes to go upstairs, they're in the kitchen.

(*Pause.*)

LIZZIE: Did you know Papa killed my birds with the ax? He chopped off their heads. (MRS. BORDEN *is uneasy.*) . . . It's alright. At first I felt bad, but I feel
400 better now. I feel much better now. . . . I am a woman of decision, Mrs. Borden. When I decide to do things, I do them, yes, I do. (*Smiles.*) How many times has Papa said — when Lizzie puts her mind to a thing, she does it — and I do. . . . It's always me who puts the slug poison out because they eat all the flowers and you don't like that, do you? They're bad things, they must die. You see, not all life is precious, is it?

MRS. BORDEN: (*After a moment makes an attempt casually to gather together her things, to go upstairs. She does not want to be in the room with* LIZZIE.)

LIZZIE: Where're you going?

MRS. BORDEN: Upstairs . . . . (*An excuse.*) The spare room needs changing

(*A knock at the back door. . . . A second knock.*)

LIZZIE: Someone's at the door. . . . (*A third knock.*) I'll get it.

(*She exits to the kitchen.* MRS. BORDEN *waits.* LIZZIE *returns. She's a bit out of breath. She carries a pile of clean clothes which she puts on the table. She looks at* MRS. BORDEN.)

LIZZIE: Did you want something?

410 MRS. BORDEN: Who was it? — the door?

LIZZIE: Oh yes. I forgot. I had to step out back for a moment and — it's a note. A message for you.

MRS. BORDEN: Oh.

LIZZIE: Shall I open it?

MRS. BORDEN: That's alright. (*She holds out her hand.*)

LIZZIE: Looks like Papa's handwriting. . . . (*She passes over the note.*) Aren't you going to open it?

MRS. BORDEN: I'll read it upstairs.

LIZZIE: Mrs. Borden! . . . Would you mind . . . putting my clothes in my room? (*She
420 gets some clothes from the table,* MRS. BORDEN *takes them, something she would never normally do. Before she can move away,* LIZZIE *grabs her arm.*) Just a minute . . . I would like you to look into my eyes. What's the matter? Nothing's wrong. It's an experiment. . . . Look right into them. Tell me . . . what do you see . . . can you see anything?

MRS. BORDEN: . . . Myself.

LIZZIE: Yes. When a person dies, retained on her eye is the image of the last thing she saw. Isn't that interesting? (*Pause.*)

(MRS. BORDEN *slowly starts upstairs.* LIZZIE *picks up remaining clothes on table. The hand hatchet is concealed beneath them. She follows* MRS. BORDEN *up the stairs.*)

LIZZIE: Do you know something? If I were to kill someone, I would come up behind them very slowly and quietly. They would never even hear me, they would never turn around. (MRS. BORDEN *stops on the stairs. She
430 turns around to look at* LIZZIE *who is behind her.*) They would be too frightened to turn around even if they heard me. They would be so afraid they'd see what they feared. (MRS. BORDEN *makes a move which might be an effort to go past* LIZZIE *back down the stairs.* LIZZIE *stops her.*) Careful. Don't fall. (MRS. BORDEN *turns and slowly continues up the stairs with* LIZZIE *behind her.*) And then, I would strike them down. With them not turning around, they would retain no image of me on their eye. It would be better that way.

(LIZZIE *and* MRS. BORDEN *disappear at the top of the stairs. The stage is empty for a moment.* BRIDGET *enters. She carries the pail for washing the windows.*

She sets the pail down, wipes her forehead. She stands for a moment looking towards the stairs as if she might have heard a sound. She picks up the pail and exits to the kitchen. LIZZIE *appears on the stairs. She is carrying the pile of clothes she carried upstairs. The hand hatchet is concealed under the clothes.* LIZZIE *descends the stairs, she seems calm, self-possessed. She places the clothes on the table. She pauses, then she slowly turns to look at* MRS. BORDEN's *chair at the table. After a moment she moves to it, pauses a moment, then sits down in it. She sits there at ease, relaxed, thinking.* BRIDGET *enters from the kitchen, she sees* LIZZIE, *she stops, she takes in* LIZZIE *sitting in* MRS. BORDEN's *chair.* BRIDGET *glances towards the stairs, back to* LIZZIE. LIZZIE *looks, for the first time, at* BRIDGET.)

LIZZIE: We must hurry before Papa gets home.

BRIDGET: Lizzie?

440　LIZZIE: I have it all figured out, but you have to help me, Bridget, you have to help me.

BRIDGET: What have you done?

LIZZIE: He would never leave me the farm, not with her on his back, but now *(She gets up from the chair)* I will have the farm, and I will have the money, yes, to do what I please! And you too Bridget, I'll give you some of my money but you've got to help me. *(She moves towards* BRIDGET *who backs away a step.)* Don't be afraid, it's me, it's Lizzie, you like me!

BRIDGET: What have you done! *(Pause.* BRIDGET *moves towards the stairs.)*

LIZZIE: Don't go up there!

450　BRIDGET: You killed her!

LIZZIE: Someone broke in and they killed her.

BRIDGET: They'll know!

LIZZIE: Not if you help me.

BRIDGET: I can't, Miss Lizzie, I can't!

LIZZIE: *(Grabs* BRIDGET's *arm.)* Do you want them to hang me! Is that what you want! Oh Bridget, look! Look! *(She falls to her knees.)* I'm begging for my life, I'm begging. Deny me, and they will kill me. Help me, Bridget, please help me.

BRIDGET: But . . . what . . . could we do?

460　LIZZIE: *(Up off her knees.)* Oh I have it all figured out. I'll go down town as quick as I can and you leave the doors open and go back outside and work on the windows.

BRIDGET: I've finished them, Lizzie.

LIZZIE: Then do them again! Remember last year when the burglar broke in? Today someone broke in and she caught them.

BRIDGET: They'll never believe us.

LIZZIE: Have coffee with Lucy next door, stay with her till Papa gets home and he'll find her, and then each of us swears she was fine when we left, she was alright when we left! — it's going to work, Bridget, I know it!

470　BRIDGET: Your papa will guess.

LIZZIE: *(Getting ready to leave for down town.)* If he found me here he might guess, but he won't.

BRIDGET: Your papa will know!

LIZZIE: Papa loves me, if he has another story to believe, he'll believe it. He'd want to believe it, he'd have to believe it.

BRIDGET: Your papa will know.

LIZZIE: Why aren't you happy? I'm happy. We both should be happy! (LIZZIE *embraces* BRIDGET. LIZZIE *steps back a pace.*) Now — how do I look?

(MR. BORDEN *enters.* BRIDGET *sees him.* LIZZIE *slowly turns to see what* BRIDGET *is looking at.*)

LIZZIE: Papa?

480 MR. BORDEN: What is it? Where's Mrs. Borden?

BRIDGET: I . . . don't know . . . sir . . . I . . . just came in, sir.

MR. BORDEN: Did she leave the house?

BRIDGET: Well, sir . . .

LIZZIE: She went out. Someone delivered a message and she left.

(LIZZIE *takes off her hat and looks at her father.*)

LIZZIE: . . . You're home early, Papa.

MR. BORDEN: I wanted to see Abbie. She's gone out, has she? Which way did she go? (LIZZIE *shrugs, he continues, more thinking aloud.*) Well . . . I . . . I . . . best wait for her here. I don't want to miss her again.

LIZZIE: Help Papa off with his coat, Bridget. . . . I hear there's a sale of dress
490 goods on down-town. Why don't you go buy yourself a yard?

BRIDGET: Oh . . . I don't know, ma'am.

LIZZIE: You don't want any?

BRIDGET: I don't know.

LIZZIE: Then . . . why don't you go upstairs and lie down. Have a rest before lunch.

BRIDGET: I don't think I should.

LIZZIE: Nonsense.

BRIDGET: Lizzie, I —

LIZZIE: You go up and lie down. I'll look after things here.

(LIZZIE *smiles at* BRIDGET. BRIDGET *starts up the stairs, suddenly stops. She looks back at* LIZZIE.)

LIZZIE: It's alright . . . go on . . . it's alright. (BRIDGET *continues up the stairs. For the last bit of interchange,* MR. BORDEN *has lowered the paper he's reading.* LIZZIE *looks at him.*) Hello Papa. You look so tired. . . . I make you unhappy. . . . I don't like to make you unhappy. I love you.

MR. BORDEN: (*Smiles and takes her hand.*) I'm just getting old, Lizzie.

500 LIZZIE: You've got on my ring. . . . Do you remember when I gave you that? . . . When I left Miss Cornelia's — it was in a little blue velvet box, you hid it behind your back, and you said, "guess which hand, Lizzie!" And I guessed. And you gave it to me and you said, "it's real gold, Lizzie, it's for you because you are very precious to me." Do you remember, Papa? (MR. BORDEN *nods.*) And I took it out of the little blue velvet box, and I took your hand,
510 and I put my ring on your finger and I said "thank you, Papa, I love you." . . . You've never taken it off . . . see how it bites into the flesh of your finger. (*She presses his hand to her face.*) I forgive you, Papa, I forgive you for killing

my birds.... You look so tired, why don't you lie down and rest, put your feet up, I'll undo your shoes for you. (*She kneels and undoes his shoes.*)

MR. BORDEN: You're a good girl.

LIZZIE: I could never stand to have you hate me, Papa. Never. I would do anything rather than have you hate me.

MR. BORDEN: I don't hate you, Lizzie.

520   LIZZIE: I would not want you to find out anything that would make you hate me. Because I love you.

MR. BORDEN: And I love you, Lizzie, you'll always be precious to me.

LIZZIE: (*Looks at him, and then smiles.*) Was I — when I had scabs on my knees?

MR. BORDEN: (*Laughs.*) Oh yes. Even then.

LIZZIE: (*Laughs.*) Oh Papa!... Kiss me! (*He kisses her on the forehead.*) Thank you, Papa.

MR. BORDEN: Why're you crying?

LIZZIE: Because I'm so happy. Now... put your feet up and get to sleep... that's right... shut your eyes... go to sleep... go to sleep....

(*She starts to hum, continues humming as* MR. BORDEN *falls asleep.* MISS LIZZIE/BRIDGET *appears on the stairs unobtrusively.* LIZZIE *still humming, moves to the table, slips her hand under the clothes, withdraws the hatchet. She approaches her father with the hatchet behind her back. She stops humming. A pause, then she slowly raises the hatchet very high to strike him. Just as the hatchet is about to start its descent, there is a blackout. Children's voices are heard singing:*)

530   "Lizzie Borden took an ax,
Gave her mother forty whacks,
When the job was nicely done,
She gave her father forty-one!
Forty-one!
Forty-one!"

(*The singing increases in volume and in distortion as it nears the end of the verse till the last words are very loud but discernible, just. Silence. Then the sound of slow measured heavy breathing which is growing into a wordless sound of hysteria. Light returns to the stage, dim light from late in the day.* THE ACTRESS *stands with the hatchet raised in the same position in which we saw her before the blackout, but the couch is empty. Her eyes are shut. The sound comes from her.* MISS LIZZIE *is at the foot of the stairs. She moves to* THE ACTRESS, *reaches up to take the hatchet from her. When* MISS LIZZIE's *hand touches* THE ACTRESS's, THE ACTRESS *releases the hatchet and whirls around to face* MISS LIZZIE *who is left holding the hatchet.* THE ACTRESS *backs away from* MISS LIZZIE. *There is a flickering of light at the top of the stairs.*)

EMMA: (*From upstairs.*) Lizzie! Lizzie! You're making too much noise!

(EMMA *descends the stairs carrying an oil lamp.* THE ACTRESS *backs away from* LIZZIE, *turns and runs into the kitchen.* MISS LIZZIE *turns to see* EMMA. *The hand hatchet is behind* MISS LIZZIE's *back concealed from* EMMA. EMMA *pauses for a moment.*)

EMMA: Where is she?

MISS LIZZIE: Who?

EMMA: *(A pause then* EMMA *moves to the window and glances out.)* It's raining.

MISS LIZZIE: I know.

540 EMMA: *(Puts the lamp down, sits, lowers her voice.)* Lizzie.

MISS LIZZIE: Yes?

EMMA: I want to speak to you, Lizzie.

MISS LIZZIE: Yes Emma.

EMMA: That . . . actress who's come up from Boston.

MISS LIZZIE: What about her?

EMMA: People talk.

MISS LIZZIE: You needn't listen.

EMMA: In your position you should do nothing to *inspire talk.*

MISS LIZZIE: People need so little in the way of inspiration. And Miss Cornelia's
550   classes didn't cover "Etiquette for Acquitted Persons."

EMMA: Common sense should tell you what you ought or ought not do.

MISS LIZZIE: Common sense is repugnant to me. I prefer uncommon sense.

EMMA: I forbid her in this house, Lizzie!

    (Pause.)

MISS LIZZIE: Do you?

EMMA: *(Backing down, softly.)* It's . . . disgraceful.

MISS LIZZIE: I see.

    *(*MISS LIZZIE *turns away from* EMMA *a few steps.)*

EMMA: I simply cannot —

MISS LIZZIE: You could always leave.

EMMA: Leave?

560 MISS LIZZIE: Move. Away. Why don't you?

EMMA: I —

MISS LIZZIE: You could never, could you?

EMMA: If I only —

MISS LIZZIE: Knew.

EMMA: Lizzie, did you?

MISS LIZZIE: Oh Emma, do you intend asking me that question from now till
    death us do part?

EMMA: It's just —

MISS LIZZIE: For if you do, I may well take something sharp to you.

570 EMMA: Why do you joke like that!

MISS LIZZIE: *(Turning back to* EMMA *who sees the hatchet for the first time.* EMMA's
    reaction is not any verbal or untoward movement. She freezes as MISS LIZZIE
    advances on her.) Did you never stop and think that if I did, then you were
    guilty too?

EMMA: What?

    *(*THE ACTRESS *will enter unobtrusively on the periphery. We are virtually
    unaware of her entrance until she speaks and moves forward.)*

MISS LIZZIE: It was you who brought me up, like a mother to me. Almost like a mother. Did you ever stop and think that I was like a puppet, your puppet. My head your hand, yes, your hand working my mouth, me saying all the things you felt like saying, me doing all the things you felt like doing, me spewing forth, me hitting out, and you, you — !

THE ACTRESS: (*Quietly.*) Lizzie.

(MISS LIZZIE *is immediately in control of herself.*)

580 EMMA: (*Whispers.*) I wasn't even here that day.

MISS LIZZIE: I can swear to that.

EMMA: Do you want to drive me mad?

MISS LIZZIE: Oh yes.

EMMA: You didn't . . . did you?

MISS LIZZIE: Poor . . . Emma.

THE ACTRESS: Lizzie. (*She takes the hatchet from* MISS LIZZIE.) Lizzie you did.

MISS LIZZIE: I didn't. (THE ACTRESS *looks to the hatchet — then to the audience.*) You did.

BLACKOUT

Ken Mitchell (b. 1940)

Born in Saskatchewan, Ken Mitchell teaches Canadian literature and creative writing at the University of Regina. A poet, playwright, actor, novelist, and short story writer, Mitchell helped found the Saskatchewan Writers' Guild in 1969. His many publications include a collection of stories, *Everybody Gets Something Here* (1977), and the novels *Wandering Rafferty* (1972), *The Meadowlark Connection* (1975), and *The Con Man* (1979). A keen sense of irony and the spoken word informs Mitchell's various plays including *The Medicine Line* (1976), *Davin: The Politician* (1979), *The Great Cultural Revolution* (1980), and *Gone the Burning Sun* (1985), a one-man show based on the life of Dr. Norman Bethune, to whom Mitchell is distantly related, which successfully toured China in 1987 with Mitchell involved in the production.

The Shipbuilder won the University of Regina's national play-writing competition in 1978 and was subsequently published in *Canadian Theatre Review* (1979). Successive revisions since have resulted in radio adaptations of the play for the CBC, the BBC, Finnish National Radio, and Swedish National Radio. The current version was first published in 1990.

INTRODUCTION TO *THE SHIPBUILDER*

Extremist, independent, obsessive, incapable of compromise even to the point of madness — such is the nature of the central figure of Ken Mitchell's play. *The Shipbuilder* focusses on a single misconceived figure and his unswervable desire to build an ocean-going vessel capable of floating him out of Depression-era Saskatchewan, across the seas, and back to his original home in Finland. Based on a true story — the ship now rests at the Sukanen Ship Pioneer Village and Museum, thirteen kilometres south of Moose Jaw — Jaanus Karkulainen's struggle to achieve his dream suggests much about inflexible determination, pioneer spirit, and a complete refusal to alter one's personal vision in order to accommodate the judgement and opinions of others.

The language of the play is direct and succinct with no time wasted on social niceties. Expressionist staging suggests hard work and a threatening atmosphere through the dominant construction of the ship's hull onstage and powerful hammering percussion throughout. A chorus of opinion and commentary remains onstage, as does the curious figure of Anna-Marie, who doubles as Karkulainen's estranged daughter. These choric figures provide important contextual and background information to suggest that Karkulainen's struggle goes beyond the simple confusions of a crackpot. Indeed the central figure reveals a powerful tension of individual and social definition.

Karkulainen refuses to assimilate in order to satisfy his neighbours or his family. He is tolerated at best, at worst detested by Sholer, Cannon, and others, although they paradoxically thrive on his activity as well. As Anna-Marie observes, in the opening lines of Act 2, "He knew the mockers would come, that they needed his dream as much or more than he needed it himself." Such mocking relates to social and cultural anxiety, anxiety that reveals itself within the play in terms of ethnic divisions, stereotypes, and name-calling. The ridiculous prairie shipbuilder may be obsessed but he is not petty; he is at times nasty but never mean-spirited. In fact his impossible task of building a ship and dragging it across the prairie to the shallow South Saskatchewan River resembles the impossible task of subsistence itself during the dust-bowl 1930s in southern Saskatchewan.

Karkulainen conveys a sense of misconceived heroism in his single-mindedness, a single-mindedness signified by his walking every step west to Saskatchewan, his eccentric but self-sufficient inventions, his cryptic promise to Anna-Marie, his personal defiance of all criticism, even his vaguely confused Old Testament imprecation, "Egyptians!" His violent self-confidence seems always about to erupt, as suggested by his angry refusal of contradiction, his constant hammering of metal which often doubles as thunder, and by his insistent, repeated assertion, "I am Jaanus Karkulainen!"

In a preface to his collection of plays titled *Rebels in Time*, Ken Mitchell admits to a fascination with rebels and anti-heroes. Traditionally, all rebellious heroes are misunderstood by their lesser critics, who crave the comfort and non-involvement of relaxation and anonymity. But heroes and anti-heroes never give up or give in. Karkulainen, part obsessive madman and part cultural visionary, can only see his job at hand and its crucial importance in his own mind as a dream to be accomplished. Everyone, of course, has impossible dreams; the hero actualizes them by refusing to compromise. Crazy or brilliant, obsessive or determined, the heroic visionary can make a ship sail across the dry prairie with its endless and unremitting landscape like the sea, can keep a promise to himself that perhaps only very few can really understand. As Larry Bender, Karkulainen's only sympathizer within the play, enthusiastically states:

> Johnny's dream is real. It's made of wood and iron. It creaks and moves. You kin touch it! Okay, you say he ain't gonna make it — and sometimes I say it too — just to myself — but what if he *does*?

> *(2.2 106–09)*

Early in the play, Karkulainen himself defies his brother's scoffing disbelief of "A thousand miles? Walking?" with strongly centred determination: "The plains are easy to walk, Jukka. Endless. Like the sea. Out here, a man could do — anything (1.3. 69–70)." To accomplish "anything" suggests the extent of Karkulainen's heroic commitment.

His brother condemns him for his *sisu*, his pride, but Karkulainen stays true to his dream. Such commitment suggests an attempt to establish an authentic sense of self to overcome a hostile physical and social environment. At times deadly serious, at other times curiously humorous, Karkulainen represents both relentless striving and paradoxical accomplishment. Perhaps the final paradox resides outside the play in the fact that the actual setting for Karkulainen's venture now lies under the deep water of Lake Diefenbaker behind the Gardiner Dam. But his impossible project works to force his critics to re-examine their own dreams and prejudices. Any sensitive reader or audience of *The Shipbuilder* might feel forced to undertake a similar personal re-examination.

THE SHIPBUILDER

CHARACTERS

JAANUS KARKULAINEN, the shipbuilder
LARRY BENDER, a local farmer
JUKKA CROOK, Karkulainen's younger brother
BETSY CROOK, Jukka's wife
MIKE SHOLER, a businessman
JIMMY CANNON, a town idler
ANNA-MARIE, a young woman
A PERCUSSIONIST
CHORUS

TIME: The Thirties

PLACE: The Great Plains

THE CHORUS *and* ANNA-MARIE *remain on stage throughout the play.*

ACT ONE

SCENE 1

Darkness. PERCUSSIONIST *introduces the distant mutter of thunder. A brilliant flash of lightning, a loud thunderbolt.*

JAANUS KARKULAINEN *appears silhouetted, alone on the empty prairie. He is powerfully built, about 40, wearing rough clothing. He carries a seaman's chest and a canvas satchel full of tools.*

Lights up on a young woman, with a "chorus" downstage.

ANNA-MARIE: He walked. And he walked. A thousand miles he came — striding across the plains. Seeking the dream of his youth.

As sound of thunder fades, lights come up on BETSY CROOK, *working. She hums a Protestant hymn.* BETSY *is a gruff but well-intentioned woman. She does not see* KARKULAINEN *approach.*

JAANUS: Water.
BETSY: Aaa!
JAANUS: Karkulainen.
BETSY: What?
JAANUS: Water! Need water.
BETSY: Water's there — at the pump.
JAANUS: *Kweenka sinala menay.*

10 BETSY: Don't you come no closer now. We don't feed tramps! My husband's in
    the house! Yuki! He has a gun!

JAANUS: Karkulainen. Water. Food.

BETSY: [*Running off*]. Yukiiiiiii!

SCENE 2

> JAANUS *crosses the stage. From the chest, he assembles a small working forge.
> He begins to hammer a piece of metal as lights come fully up. It is a hot day.*

> LARRY BENDER *approaches. He is a farmer, poorly dressed.*

BENDER: Howdy, mister.

> JAANUS *continues to work — four beats.*

BENDER: Hi there! Nice day!

> JAANUS *looks up. He gestures.*

JAANUS: Sun.

BENDER: Huh?

JAANUS: Too much sun.

BENDER: Don't say.

JAANUS: Need rain.

BENDER: [*Pause*]. You farmin' here or what?

> JAANUS *strikes the anvil with his hammer. Pause.*

20 BENDER: My farm's the next section over. Mile away. Name's Bender?

> *Two beats.*

BENDER: Not usetuh havin' neighbours.

JAANUS: No?

BENDER: Person hasta be crazy to live here, on the flats. At least you got a
    little ravine.

JAANUS: Ya.

BENDER: All I got's alkali flats. But — hadda start somewhere. Was all I could
    afford.

JAANUS: Ya. Was cheap.

BENDER: [*Pause.*] Whutchuh workin' on there?

JAANUS: You tell me.

30 BENDER: Blade for a hand plow.

JAANUS: Ya! I am Karkulainen.

BENDER: Howzat?

JAANUS: Kar...ku...lai...nen. Jaanus Karkulainen.

BENDER: Pleased tuh meetchuh. Where you from?

JAANUS: Minnesota.

BENDER: Zatso? Thought yuh might be Finn. [*Pause.*] Lotta Finlanders live
    round here.

JAANUS: Minnesota too.

BENDER: Honest people, Finlanders. Mostly. Whatsis thing, anyway?

BENDER *examines a metal device, all springs and gears.*

40 JAANUS: Clock.

BENDER: Clock?

JAANUS: Ya. Machine — to measure time.

BENDER: Jeeze — sounds complicated. You a perfessional clockmaker er somethin'?

JAANUS: No. Just needed clock.

BENDER: Jeeze. Yuh gotta shack built yet?

JAANUS: Jaanus doesn't need shack.

BENDER: No — not till winter, I giss. Y'are plannin' to farm, arnchuh?

JAANUS: Ya. Next week I start to plow. First quarter.

50 BENDER: First quarter?

JAANUS: [*Pointing.*] Moon. Needs rain, though.

BENDER: Jeeze — Finlanders sure talk funny.

JAANUS: *Funny?*

BENDER: Well — not funny. Kinda — weird, know what I mean?

JAANUS: No.

BENDER: Well — they're all kinda — bolshie, ain't they?

JAANUS: Bolshevik!

BENDER: Take it easy! At's what I heard! At the Finnish hall.

JAANUS: Never Bolshevik!

60 BENDER: Okay! Well — how about the sauna baths?

JAANUS: Sauna?

BENDER: Yuh gotta admit that's sorta funny. First thing a Finn builds — a sauna.

JAANUS: Ya. Me too.

BENDER: Yeah?

JAANUS: There. Beside my creek.

BENDER: That pile of rocks?

JAANUS: Inside. You come tonight. Try it.

BENDER: Oh — I dunno.

JAANUS: Good for muscle.

70 BENDER: Yeah. Gotta take yer cloes off?

JAANUS: [*Smiles.*] You don't remove your clothes, Bender?

BENDER: Oh, once in a while. You know.

Pause. JAANUS *chuckles. Hammering goes on.*

BENDER: Anyways, me and my missus bin wonderin' who was gonna claim this
land. Lotta bush. Heavy work.

JAANUS: Jaanus was made for heavy work.

BENDER *has begun helping* JAANUS, *holding the metal, handing him material.*

JAANUS: You were born here?

BENDER: Me? Naw. Ontario. My brother got the farm. I hadda move west, try
for homestead.

JAANUS: But it's hard?

80 BENDER: Hard for my family. You got any family, uh, Jaanus?

JAANUS: No, not many farms in old country.

BENDER: Not farms. Family! Y'know — wife — kids —

JAANUS: Jaanus was sailor.

BENDER: Oh yeah — back in Finland, yuh mean?

JAANUS: Finland. Russia. Many boats. I sail. Work in shipyards.

BENDER: That where yuh learned tuh make clocks?

JAANUS: Everyting. There I learn the secrets of steel. And on ships — wood and rope.

BENDER: Well — you'll always get work here. And you'll need plenty cash.
90   Can't get it farmin'. Ain't like the old country.

JAANUS: Nothing is ever same as before. Nothing.

BENDER: Driest land I ever seen. And what the weather and the hoppers don't get — the bank does. Merna's ready to call it quits.

JAANUS: You have debts.

BENDER: Don't everybody? How else would yuh buy stuff?

JAANUS: Hmm.

BENDER: Bin here eight years. Still tryin' tuh git my house built. Two kids. Never enough time. You know?

JAANUS: Ya.

100   BENDER: Good to have a neighbour though. How you feel about neighbours?

JAANUS: Jaanus works alone.

BENDER: Oh yeah?

JAANUS: But you ask for help — I give it.

BENDER: Sure. And I kin help you. Co-operate, like.

JAANUS: We try. But no collective!

BENDER: Jeese. How'd you end up in this province?

JAANUS: My brother Jukka. He picked the land.

BENDER: Yuki? Yuki Crook, that farms near town? But you said your name's — !

JAANUS: Me — born Karkulainen, I die Karkulainen.

110   BENDER: Imagine that. Yuki's brother. No other family?

JAANUS: [*Pause.*] Your wife. She helps you farm?

BENDER: Merna? Yeah — she tries. Oh! She sent somethin' over for yuh — I'll just git it from my wagon —

BENDER *goes off left.*

BENDER: [*Off.*] She was doin' her bakin' this morning!

BENDER *returns with a loaf of bread wrapped in cloth.*

BENDER: Hope yuh like homemade bread.

JAANUS: Bread —

BENDER: Made from our own wheat. Torval Skully's got a little mill.

JAANUS *unwraps the loaf with reverence.*

JAANUS: Finn needs two things. Water. Bread. I came here, find good water in my creek. Was very lucky. Now — bread.

JAANUS *rips the loaf in half, lifts it to his nose.*

120   JAANUS: Come — we make coffee.

BENDER: You got coffee? At four bits a pound? Whew! Long time since I had coffee.

JAANUS: Come. Inside my home.

JAANUS *steps toward a ramp upstage right.*

BENDER: Home?
JAANUS: Here. Inside.

JAANUS *lifts a trap door.*

BENDER: Where that stovepipe is?
JAANUS: Is not stovepipe! Is peeriscope!
BENDER: Oh.
JAANUS: I show you — come.

JAANUS *disappears through the trap.* BENDER *turns to audience. Percussion.*

BENDER: Well, Johnny'd dug this hole in the hillside above his creek. And on
130   top was this thing with mirrors — a peeriscope. Said he copied it from an
       underwater ship.
ANNA-MARIE: He could see for miles in all directions. A mariner who sailed
       below the ground.

The periscope turns, as though scanning the prairie.

BENDER: Didden have a single window in his house, but wasn't nobody sneakin'
       up on him with that thing. Oh, Johnny built a slew of such contraptions.
ANNA-MARIE: [*With* CHORUS.] He made all his own equipment. Wagons, tools,
       harness, buildings. He pulled the stones from the fields to build his barns
       and granaries.
BENDER: And we worked together, like a co-op. No contracts. Never need
       money. See, Johnny hated to use money. And you know, my farm began
140   producing!

Lights dim as scene ends.

ANNA-MARIE: They did the labor of four men, Jaanus and Bender, working to
       the rhythm of the sun and moon.
BENDER: And I gotta say — he loved to work. Summer and winter. Loved it. But
       he'd stand for an hour —
ANNA-MARIE: Watching the sun go down —
BENDER: Not movin'—
CHORUS: Not moving, not moving, not moving.

JAANUS *picks up his hammer, works in percussion rhythm.*

SCENE 3

JUKKA *and* BETSY CROOK *approach.*

BETSY: Well, if he'd only *said* something! 'Stead of grunting like an animal!
       You never even told me he was coming!
JUKKA: I didn't think he was serious. So I didn't want to trouble you. But when
       I met Bender in town —

BETSY: My God, whatever must he think? And I took him for a tramp! How could I know he's your brother?

JAANUS's hammering intensifies.

JUKKA: He's a strange man, Betsy. Perhaps he's only testing us.
BETSY: Sure didn't look the family type.
JUKKA: I hope he isn't brooding.
10   BETSY: Oh! There.

They stop a few feet from JAANUS. *He still hammers.*

JUKKA: Jianni! It's me. Jukka.

Another beat.

BETSY: You be careful, now.
JUKKA: Jaanus!
BETSY: Don't you go near till he puts that hammer down!
JUKKA: Betsy — please!
BETSY: Lookin' like the very devil!
JUKKA: Shhh! Do you want to offend him?
BETSY: Offend him! What about me?

Hammering stops abruptly.

BETSY: Oh.

JAANUS removes a metal bar from his mouth.

20   JAANUS: *Kweenka sinala voight, Jukka?* (How are you, Jukka?)
JUKKA: Relieved. Ah — *hyvin, hyvin! Entas itse. Oliko matka hyva.* (Fine, fine, And you? You had a good journey?)
JAANUS: [*Pause.*] *Passin perille.* (I got here.)
BETSY: Ahem. Somebody gonna translate for me?
JUKKA: Ah — Jaanus — my wife, Betsy.

JAANUS goes back to work, snubbing her.

JUKKA: Jaanus!
JAANUS: She refused your house, Jukka.
JUKKA: But — Betsy's not at fault! How could she know it was you?
JAANUS: I told you I was coming here.
30   JUKKA: Well, I advised you to stay in Minnesota. Better land!
JAANUS: I said I'd come in spring to plant.
JUKKA: Yes — yes, I suppose you did. Well — !
BETSY: Didn't you bring your family, Jaanus?
JAANUS: In Suomi, the dirtiest tinker would have been welcomed!
JUKKA: This isn't Finland! And you — looking like that, you scare people. You frightened my wife out of her wits.
JAANUS: [*Bowing formally.*] I am sorry I make you lose your wits — Mrs. Crook.
BETSY: [*Flustered.*] Well, that's awright, I guess. Just don't want you thinkin' we're inhospitable.

40   JUKKA: So, Jianni! It's been a long time. Welcome to Canada. Colder than Suomi!

JAANUS: But there are Finns here?

JUKKA: No — we're all Canadians now!

BETSY: Yuki got his papers last year!

JAANUS: And you have a square mile of farm now, I hear.

JUKKA: Betsy's father's land. He died seven years ago.

JAANUS: So, you've had good fortune, Jukka.

BETSY: Yuki says you have a little girl, is that right?

JAANUS: No. I am alone.

BETSY: Oh. Well, tomorrow's Sunday, y'know. Maybe you'd like to go to church?

50   JUKKA: In Ferguson.

BETSY: With us.

JAANUS: No, thanks.

JUKKA: Jianni, here we all go to church.

BETSY: And it's okay if you're Lutheran. We got a pastor who takes anybody!

JUKKA: It's not religion, it's what people do!

JAANUS: I've no time for such stupidity!

BETSY: Well! On the day you come before God Almighty — !

   JAANUS *strikes the anvil.* BETSY *shrieks.*

JAANUS: Is God found only in your puny church?

JUKKA: Betsy, go and wait at the car. I'll discuss this business with Jianni —

60   BETSY: The minute I laid eyes on him, I knew the devil was in him!

JUKKA: I said, wait by the road!

   BETSY *goes off. Long pause.*

JUKKA: All that *see'su*. Will you ever change?

JAANUS: I have changed. Have you?

JUKKA: You think of nothing but work.

JAANUS: I work to make food, not money.

JUKKA: Hm. Well, how did you get here? Train?

JAANUS: On foot.

JUKKA: A thousand miles? Walking?

JAANUS: The plains are easy to walk, Jukka. Endless. Like the sea. Out here, a

70   man could do — anything.

JUKKA: [*Uneasily.*] Well, yes — there are opportunities. But it's not like the
   old country. More social responsibility. You're expected to set an example.

JAANUS: [*Smiles.*] Like you?

JUKKA: Here, farmers aren't peasants. The Finns respect me.

JAANUS: Of course.

JUKKA: Jaanus — where is your family?

JAANUS: Family?

JUKKA: Your wife — Charlotte? And the child.

JAANUS: I do not speak of the Egyptian woman. The girl will come when I

80   am ready.

JUKKA: I see. Jianni, if there's trouble — you can talk to us. Or the preacher —
   he's a good man —

JAANUS: Send him your wife!

JAANUS *goes back to work, banging.*

JUKKA: You know, you haven't changed at all. What's that you're making?
JAANUS: Gear.
JUKKA: For what?
JAANUS: Sewing machine. Need warm clothing here.
JUKKA: But you'll look ridiculous! People will laugh. Don't you have money?
JAANUS: Money for horses, not for clothes.
90   JUKKA: Jianni — I'll give you trunks of clothes! In good shape. Betsy can alter them —
JAANUS: No!
JUKKA: [*Laughs.*] All right — no clothing! Fine! Do you have seed? Or horses? Tools?
JAANUS: I plant by hand. This week.
JUKKA: Too early. It's still April! There's frost every night.
JAANUS: Full moon. Barley. I cast by hand.
JUKKA: It will never germinate! And if it does, how will you harvest? You certainly can't do that by hand! You'll have to run to me for help!
100 JAANUS: Jaanus never runs for help. You know that, Jukka.
JUKKA: We'll see. Nobody harvests without a thresher.
JAANUS: Do you have a thresher?
JUKKA: No. It belongs to Sholer, the lumber dealer. A 42-inch Rumely! He hires a big threshing crew every fall. That's the only way.
JAANUS: Why don't we build our own?
JUKKA: [*Laughs.*] What an idea! They're huge machines! Made in factories in the east. You can't just throw a bunch of bolts together —
JAANUS: I design. You help me build. Bender will join us. We start our own *ossus liike*!
110 JUKKA: A co-op? You talk like a fool.
JAANUS: Is up to you. I offered.
BETSY: [*Off.*] Yukiiii!

JUKKA *begins to leave, hesitates.*

JUKKA: So your wife — will not be coming?
JAANUS: No more talk!
JUKKA: Jianni — you need your family. You need — love —

JAANUS *pushes* JUKKA *out of his way, snarling.*

JAANUS: *Hut!*
BETSY: [*Off.*] Yukiiiii!
JAANUS: Needs? Needs?! Karkulainen needs nothing! He is a Finn!

JAANUS *slams the metal bar back between his jaws. He hammers the anvil in a cold fury.*

SCENE 4

BETSY: Well, I didden know what to think. What would anybody think? Home-made clothes. Eyes on fire. I ask yuh! Sure, the Bible says be nice to beggars and harlots and the like...

CHORUS: . . . but he'd have vexed the Lord himself!

BETSY: And I was always proud a Yuki. You'd hardly even know he's Finnish! Never hung around the Finnish hall, makin' drunken speeches and carryin' on like others I could name. He worked hard at fittin' in — till Jaanus came along!

CHORUS: Well — talk about a cross to bear.

10 BETSY: Oh, we thought about selling out, but that was the Dirty Thirties, and nobody had any cash at all, so we hadda stay and tough it out.

CHORUS: Be nice to him . . .

BETSY: . . . the preacher said. Nice to him! With that big sledge hammer flyin' through the air! And lookin' like the devil. I mean . . .

CHORUS: . . . the devil! That's right, the devil!

BETSY: Oh, and that piece of iron bar he always clamped between his teeth. Know what that was? A ground!

CHORUS: That's what he called it — an electric ground.

BETSY: Had a theory that he stirred up so much 'lectricity bangin' on that
20 anvil, he had to ground himself on a chunk of steel — else he'd blow his own brains out! I ask yuh! Oh, we tried — really did — but you . . .

CHORUS: . . . could see the writing on the wall . . .

PERCUSSIONIST *develops musical bridge.*

SCENE 5

JAANUS *and* BENDER *work on a rope and block pulley, moving it back and forth across the stage.*

JAANUS: No, Bender. Never Bolshevik. Anarchist! But I went to see Lenin. The great Lenin. In 1917 I left my village forever — with a hundred others. To ride on Lenin's train — Helsinki to Petrograd. I joined the tide of revolution. Anarchist. No class, no wealth, no oppression. We'd build on the rubble of the czar's palace!

BENDER: Excitin' times, eh?

JAANUS: I served on anarchist battleship Pavlovsk. We seized a rich estate and built our soviet.

BENDER: Go on!

10 JAANUS: It was all a fraud. A joke. The soviets were full of secret police. New secret police. Stalin's police. So I come in 1920 to United States of America. Statue of Liberty, you know. A man can build with his own hands. I work in Boston shipyards and there [*Pause.*] — I meet a woman. Her name — doesn't matter. But her eyes were same as — as a girl I knew in Suomi. Same eyes. Same hair. I say, Jaanus, don't do this. But I fall in love with her.

BENDER: Big mistake, huh?

JAANUS: Larry Bender, is not good for sailor to work near the ships. Not if he's married. I know this. We move to Minnesota — buy a farm. Small farm — good for growing family. The immigrant's dream. But land is poor. Rocky.
20 Like Finland. The old story. Some are lucky.

Pause. JAANUS *shakes his head.*

BENDER: And some are not.

JAANUS: They spend their lives as slaves, working for other men. And maybe — [*Sighs.*] — maybe Jaanus makes mistake.

BENDER: Oh?

JAANUS: [*Pause.*] No, not same eyes. She is city girl, from Boston. She is bored on this farm. Tiny shack. We never have enough money. So I work at home at night, building.

BENDER: Building what?

JAANUS: Anything. For money. Tools. Gadgets. I knit coats. Mittens! Made a wheat-puffing machine.

BENDER: A what?

JAANUS: Machine for puff wheat. Big ting like a cannon. You shoot — out puffs wheat. For my daughter to eat puff wheat at breakfast. All the time, "Daddy, want puff wheat!" [*He chuckles.*] So I made one. And *veulu*, too. Old country violin —

BENDER: You made a violin?

JAANUS: So my girl could learn to play. Wife says I'm crazy — wasting time! One day when I am in the fields picking rock, butter churn falls and crushes it. Wife throws it in the fire. So — was like that. [*Pause.*] Then she started talking Egyptian. Not a word could I understand. So I — beat her. You know?

BENDER: Geeze —

JAANUS: I was sick with myself. But — still Egyptian. Hard to live in small house, Larry Bender, once you've sailed the endless seas. I think we make a new start, so I wrote to Jukka, my younger brother.

BENDER: Sure — head for the last frontier. What I thought too.

JAANUS: But all the time, she tries to make my child Egyptian. One night I am out cutting wood. Come back, door is locked. [*Pause.*] So — I start to walk. I walk. And I walk. A thousand miles I come. Striding across the plains. I feel I'm giant, only ting between earth and sky, like a walking lightning rod! Sometimes I feel electricity *crackling* through my body.

Percussion effect, echoing opening scene.

SCENE 6

MIKE SHOLER *is in his lumberyard office. A businessman of German parentage, he is careful to avoid a "kraut" image. Well-dressed, officious.* BENDER *is in winter clothing.*

SHOLER: Well, Bender — what can I do for you?

BENDER: Need some stuff.

SHOLER: We aim to please!

BENDER: Seven hundred and fifty feet of spruce two-by-sixes. Thousand board feet of clapboard siding. Eight squares a cedar shingles.

SHOLER: [*Writing.*] Is this cash, or you want it charged to next fall's crop?

BENDER: Cash.

SHOLER: [*Impressed.*] Figure to do some building, eh?

BENDER: Gonna finish my house by Christmas.

10 SHOLER: Must've got a fair crop this year.

BENDER: Not bad. Average 12 bushels. Be better next year.

SHOLER: [*Whistles.*] Still — that's better than most. Five, ten.

BENDER: I planted early. Like Johnny did.

SHOLER: Johnny? Yuki's brother? The hermit?

BENDER: Oh, he ain't as weird as he looks — perty good farmer.

SHOLER: Yeah, I heard you fellows started a threshing crew. You think Ferguson's big enough for two outfits, Bender?

BENDER: Couldn't hardly call us an outfit. We built a small machine for our own crops. Then we went over to Lucky Lake and cropped for cash over there.

20 SHOLER: Yuh mean to tell me that thing works?

BENDER: Best thresher I ever worked on! Easy to move — never breaks down. Small harvester makes good sense.

SHOLER: Naa. Machines are getting bigger! Efficiency! You'll never compete.

BENDER: We're not trying to compete, Sholer. We got all the work we can handle. When's this stuff gonna be ready?

SHOLER: It's in the yard. Just load it up.

BENDER: I'll pick it up later, awright? Gotta buy some Christmas presents at the store! This year — my kids get treated!

BENDER *goes out.*

SHOLER: Well — Merry Christmas for you!

SHOLER *slams his order book.*

SCENE 7

In JUKKA's *farmhouse,* BETSY *is cleaning a cream separator.* JUKKA *works on leather harness. They hear a sound, off.*

BETSY: Somebody comin'— with a team.

JUKKA: Jaanus?

BETSY: Nope — Larry Bender.

JUKKA: Jaanus sent him! Trouble over threshing....

BETSY: Now, don't get worked up. We'll see.

BENDER *knocks, enters in winter clothing.*

BETSY: C'mon in, Larry.

BENDER: Mrs. Crook. Yuki.

BETSY: How's that new baby of yours?

BENDER: Perty good. How're all you?

10 BETSY: Aw, Yuki's gettin' the migraine again.

JUKKA: So how can I help you, Bender?

BENDER: Well — it's Jaanus.

JUKKA: I knew it!

BETSY: Now — Yuki —

JUKKA: What's he up to now?

BENDER: Uh, Yuki, think I kin talk to yuh in, uh, confidentially?

BETSY: Hmph. Well, I kin take a hint. Calves need to be fed.

BETSY *goes out with a pail of milk.*

JUKKA: If you came to involve me in another of his crackpot schemes, you can save your breath.

20   BENDER: He's gone.

JUKKA: Gone? Where?

BENDER: Dunno. Went over today tuh borrow his auger and — he's gone! So were his horses. The best team.

JUKKA: Perhaps to the city — for supplies.

BENDER: This was sittin' on the table — awready open.

BENDER *takes a letter from his pocket.* JUKKA *takes it, puts on his glasses.*

JUKKA: From Minnesota...

BENDER: Yeah.

JUKKA: The government. It says — his wife is dead!

BENDER: Better read this part.

30   JUKKA: "...the child will be removed to a foster home — provisions of the Orphan's Act..."

BENDER: I think he's gone to do something.

JUKKA: To the States? With horses? There's three feet of snow!

BENDER: That won't stop Johnny. He walked it before.

JUKKA: Yes — he's crazy enough!

BENDER: To get his kid? It's no crazier'n wearin' out his knees in church!

JUKKA: *Si-su!*

BENDER: What?

JUKKA: Finnish word. "Pride." No one can tell that man anything. You be

40   careful, Larry. He'll turn on you.

BENDER: I just wanna know who's gonna tend the rest of his horses. The cattle...

JUKKA: Oh, I — have my own responsibilities —

BENDER: Then I giss it's gonna be me.

BETSY: [*Re-enters.*] Yer private talk over yet?

BENDER: Just goin'.

BETSY: Not without a bite to eat, yuh don't.

BENDER: Don't bother.

BETSY: Cuppa coffee, anyhow.

50   BENDER: I hafta be gettin' home. Supper's waitin'. It's awready dark —

BENDER *leaves.*

BETSY: So, what was all that about?

JUKKA: Jaanus.

BETSY: Don't tell me he 'lectrocuted himself!

JUKKA: His wife died. He's gone back.

BETSY: Oh no!

JUKKA: I knew there'd be trouble if he came! All that *sisu!*

SCENE 8

ANNA-MARIE *appears, childlike.*

ANNA-MARIE: When he left, Mama lived in terror, afraid of the day he'd return.

CHORUS: Now you behave, or your father will get you. Get you. Get you. Get you.

ANNA-MARIE: The day he stormed into my foster home he was wrapped in furs like an animal. His beard covered with ice as though he'd burst out of the ice of Superior.

Light up on JAANUS, *downstage.*

JAANUS: I come for my child!

ANNA-MARIE: He carried me kicking and screaming to his wagon, and drove off with me hidden beneath a horse-hide in the back. Terrified.

PERCUSSION: *a banging gavel.* JUDGE *appears upstage.*

10   JUDGE: Jaanus Karkulainen, alias Johnny Crook. You've been charged with abducting a ward of the state. You've been tried and found guilty. Do you have anything to say? [*Pause. Gavel bangs.*] Thirty days in the county jail. The child will return to its home.

PERCUSSION: *blows of the gavel. Chain on chain.*

ANNA-MARIE: But he came again in the night, breaking the window in a rage. We ran all night through the woods.

JUDGE: Jaanus Karkulainen, alias Johnny Crook. Two days after your release and deportation, you crossed the Canadian border again, and returned to Minneapolis to again abduct the said child, Karen Crook, alias, Karkulainen. I sentence you to 60 days, followed by deportation from the United States

20   of America. The child will be placed in the state reformatory in St. Paul.

PERCUSSION: *gavel and chains.*

ANNA-MARIE: There was steel mesh on the windows, for my protection, they said. But even so — a few weeks later —

PERCUSSION: *scraping on mesh. Lighting on* JAANUS.

JAANUS: Come. I take you home.

ANNA-MARIE: [*Shakes her head.*] No — I can't.

PERCUSSION: *judge's gavel.*

JUDGE: Johnny Crook, the evidence shows you crossed the border a third time with obvious criminal intent. On the night of May sixth, you broke into the child's institution, terrorized the inmates and staff, and destroyed property as you tried to kidnap the child. You attacked the police and had to be subdued by force. [*Pause.*] How do you plead to these charges, Johnny

30   Crook?

JAANUS: I am Jaanus Karkulainen.

JUDGE: I now sentence you to a year in Minnesota State Prison . . .

CHORUS: . . . with three months hard labor.

JUDGE: Deportation to follow.

PERCUSSION: *steel clang and chains. Musical bridge.*

SCENE 9

Lights come up on JAANUS *by his anvil. He tinkers with a wooden water clock.*

BENDER: [*Off.*] Johnny! [*He runs on.*] Johnny — yer back!

JAANUS: I am Jaanus Karkulainen.

BENDER: Hey, it's good tuh see yuh again! Where yuh bin all this time?

JAANUS: Prison.

BENDER: In jail? What for? [*Pause.*] Did you find — the kid?

JAANUS: I have no kid.

BENDER: But — the letter —

JAANUS: She's Egyptian!

BENDER: Oh. [*Pause.*] Well, better forget all that. You come over and have
10   some supper.

JAANUS: I am working.

BENDER: C'mon. We had a baby while you were gone. Four of 'em now! You bin
        away quite a while.

JAANUS: You looked after my animals.

BENDER: Yeah —

JAANUS: Nineteen months, four days. I'll pay you back.

BENDER: Hey — come on! You don't owe me for none of that.

        JAANUS *turns a valve. The water clock begins to tock.*

JAANUS: I made a clock there. To catch time.

BENDER: Well, it's time for supper! C'mon, I'll show yuh my new sawna bath!
20   JAANUS: I have to work.

BENDER: We gotta talk about our co-op. Jesus, man, you just dropped off the face
        of the earth! We could make money threshin' this fall! Giss you could
        use some cash, eh?

JAANUS: Don't need money. Need time.

        BENDER *regards the clock, tocking.*

BENDER: Well — too bad we couldn't swap! Grain sellin' fer two-bits a bushel.
        We're crazy to stick at it —

JAANUS: I owe you for my horses. I make it up. Next year, we grow tons of
        wheat. But now — I work.

BENDER: On what?

30   JAANUS: Plans. For my journey.

BENDER: Journey? Where — ?

JAANUS: To the sea.

BENDER: What? To Montreal?

JAANUS: No. I build a ship.

        JAANUS *hands* BENDER *one end of a cord, and paces across the stage.*

BENDER: A boat?

JAANUS: This long!

BENDER: Jeee-zuz! A steamship! But *why*?

JAANUS: Have you stood by the sea? Mystery. Deeper than God.

BENDER: [*Nervous.*] Uh-huh. Uh-huh. But — why yuh goin?

40 JAANUS: I made a promise.

BENDER: And how — do yuh — get to the sea?

JAANUS: First I build. Then I move ship it overland.

BENDER: How?

JAANUS: Horses.

BENDER: God. Wouldn't it be easier to just — buy a ticket? On a steamship.

JAANUS: I should never have forgot my promise.

BENDER: Tractor could move it better'n horses.

JAANUS: Two years to build a steam tractor.

BENDER: Well — if yuh need a hand with anything — I don't know much about

50 ship building, but I done plenty a haulin' and liftin'.

JAANUS: One ting if you help.

BENDER: Yeah — sure.

JAANUS: We don't talk about this in town.

BENDER: How come?

JAANUS: They will laugh.

BENDER: Yuki?

JAANUS: All Egyptians.

BENDER: Well — awright. So when do we start?

JAANUS: Tonight.

BENDER *laughs.* JAANUS *laughs.*

60 JAANUS: But first, we have coffee, ya?

JAANUS *opens the trap door.*

BENDER: Uh — how long yuh reckon it'll take?

JAANUS: Not long. In six years — finished!

JAANUS *disappears inside.*

BENDER: Six years? What? Hey — whuddaya mean — six years!

Percussion.

SCENE 10

JAANUS *proceeds to build the skeleton of the ship. It is huge, advancing toward the audience.*

SHOLER *and his stooge,* JIMMY CANNON, *are laughing in the beer parlor.*

SHOLER: Aaa, quit pulling my leg!

CANNON: Mike — I swear. Down at the railway siding! Seven rolls of steel cable. At least five tons of iron plate, half-inch thick. Rivets. Bolts. Whole boxcar full of heavy timber!

SHOLER: Pull the other one. It's shorter.

CANNON: I tell yuh, I seen it, Mike.

SHOLER: With no name on it? Nothing to say whose it is?

CANNON: Nope. But who comes drivin' up in a wagon, lookin' dumb as ever — our old pal Bender. He looks around — chrise, stuff piled everywhere!

10   SHOLER: The plot thickens.

CANNON: He sez, I come tuh pick up some stuff for Johnny Crook.

SHOLER: Well, I be damned. He didn't know?

CANNON: Not by the look on his face! Help yourself, I sez, there she is! He nearly fell over. Bugger me, he sez!

They laugh.

SHOLER: Charlie, bring us a couple of brew!

CANNON: He hadda go over Comstock's, try and git a bigger wagon!

SHOLER: "Bugger me!"

They laugh. BENDER *enters, very glum.*

CANNON: Well, if it ain't our old pal Binder!

SHOLER: How's life out in the desert, Bender?

20   BENDER: Could use some wet.

SHOLER: Amen to that.

BENDER: Gimme a Boh,[1] Charlie.

SHOLER: Here, on me!

BENDER: S'okay. I can only stay a minnit.

SHOLER: Ha, listen to him! Come on, Bender, what was the last time you sucked down a mouthful of barley suds?

BENDER: Too long, that's for sure.

CANNON: Siddown!

SHOLER: Listen, what's the crazy hermit up to this time? Bigger thresher?

30   BENDER: What are you talkin' about?

SHOLER: The stuff, Bender — at the freight shed! What's he going to build with it?

BENDER: Giss you'll have to ask him. He don't keep me informed on his plans.

SHOLER: Seems like that Finn hasn't heard there's a depression on. Where's he gettin' the money?

BENDER: Money? What money?

CANNON: That cable there's the best there is.

SHOLER: Maybe you guys make more at threshing than you let on. That it, Bender?

40   CANNON: Bet he's got pisspots fulla money!

SHOLER: And everybody else in the district's broke. Goin' on relief! Is that fair?

CANNON: I heard he was a Red.

BENDER: Yeah?

SHOLER: Is that right, Bender? Is he a Red?

---

1 Bohemian, a lager beer made by Sicks' Bohemian Brewery Ltd., Prince Albert, Saskatchewan, and Lethbridge, Alberta.

BENDER *laughs.*

SHOLER: So how come he doesn't share the wealth?

CANNON: Hey, izzat right he lives in a cave, Binder? And eats gophers?

BENDER: Yup. Grasshoppers too.

CANNON: Uggh!

50 BENDER: Not bad with a few grains a salt.

SHOLER: Least he could is buy his stuff local. Or pay you to haul it. But no —
he just hoards his money! Time for you to wise up, Larry.

CANNON: Share the work, that's his religion!

BENDER *stands and belches.*

SHOLER: They hoard it up so they can bring another gang over on the next boat.
Immigrants! Mark my words. The D.P.s[2] are takin' over the country.

BENDER: Your old man was a D.P., Sholer.

SHOLER: Well, so what? I was born here! I belong here! Folks are asking me to
run for the Conservatives.

CANNON: They don't give a damn if he's German! Right, Mike?

60 SHOLER: I'm not German! My father was Austrian! And a land-owner, not
some bog Irish peasant — !

CANNON: Hey!

BENDER: I gotta go.

SHOLER: Bender. What's he building? What's the secret of his success?

BENDER: Ask him yourself.

CANNON: Fackin' squarehead!

SHOLER: The man's a hermit! Never comes to town. Doesn't drink! Can't tell
me that's normal!

BENDER: What is it you wanna know, Sholer?

70 SHOLER: I wanta know what he's doin' with all this building material! When half
the district's on relief!

BENDER: I got work to do. Thanks for the barley.

BENDER *goes out.*

CANNON: I know! A church! He's gonna build one a them with the great big
domes! A Bolshevik Orthodox Church!

SHOLER: Aaa, shut up and drink your beer!

SCENE 11

JAANUS *builds the ship.* JUKKA *enters. Both are in winter clothing.*

JUKKA: *Kweenka sinala menay,* Jaanus.

JAANUS: [*Pause.*] Jukka.

JUKKA: They say in town you're building.

JAANUS: Ya.

JUKKA: It looks like a — ship.

JAANUS: Good eyes, Jukka.

2 displaced persons.

JUKKA: This is madness, Jaanus! It will take forever!

JAANUS: No — only five years more.

JUKKA: Oh — a mere five years! Practically finished.

10 JAANUS: Ya — goes fast in winter. Iron likes the cold.

JUKKA *reads the name on the boat.*

JUKKA: [*Apprehensively.*] You name it Anna-Marie.

JAANUS: [*Emphatically.*] Anna-Marie.

JUKKA: Jaanus, let go of the past. Nothing can change those events.

JAANUS: I call her Anna-Marie.

JUKKA: Very well. And you'll build the thing yourself?

JAANUS: Bender helps.

JUKKA: Oh? You pay him?

JAANUS: No.

JUKKA: How can you be so callous? The man is on relief — hand to mouth! He
20   should be taking care of his family. Not building your crazy "ship"!

JAANUS: I give him flour. Feed his horses.

JUKKA: You grow so much feed you can give it away? When others are begging?

JAANUS: You need grain, Jukka? My granaries are full.

JUKKA: No wonder they hate you in town. If you heard the talk —

JAANUS: Talk?

JUKKA: Yes! Talk!

JAANUS: The world is full of "talk," Jukka. Babble. Me, I grow wheat. Build in
        winter. No time for talk. The beer hall's filled with talk. And the church.
        Too much *talk*, Jukka.

30 JUKKA: Well — my talk is nearly done.

JAANUS: Good.

JUKKA: Answer one question. You expect this thing to sail?

JAANUS: Stupid question, Jukka.

JUKKA: But there's no water! Look! Your own creek has dried up! Or is it true,
        you're expecting a flood?

JAANUS: You said — one question.

JUKKA: There is no — water! Anywhere!

JAANUS: Eighty per cent of earth surface is water, Jukka. A Finn would know.

JUKKA: You are a lunatic!

40 JAANUS: Look!

JAANUS *unrolls a 20-foot canvas map of North America and the North
Atlantic.*

JAANUS: Here is my farm. When Anna-Marie is built, I move her across the
        prairie. Overland — to Saskatchewan River. With horses. Two, maybe
        three years.

JUKKA: You'll haul it over — land?

Music intensifies. JAANUS *walks along the map.*

JAANUS: Then down river to Lake Winnipeg. Across lake to Nelson River.
        Nelson River to Hudson Bay. Hudson Bay — Hudson Strait. Atlantic Ocean.
        Iceland. To Suomi.

JUKKA: Finland!

JAANUS: The land of our youth.

Lights to black. Percussion.

ACT TWO

SCENE 1

JAANUS completes the structure of his ship with BENDER. He establishes a percussion-enhanced rhythm. Lights up on ANNA-MARIE and BETSY CROOK, in different areas.

ANNA-MARIE: He knew the mockers would come, that they needed his dream as much or more than he needed it himself.

BETSY: Well, the sight of it was blasphemy! Wasting God's good time on a boat that'd never float. And all the loafers goin' out tuh gawk. Just to make fun!

CHORUS: He's out of his mind, you know. Thinks he's building a Noah's ark!

ANNA-MARIE: But he knew — as he laboured in the winds and blowing dust — that one day the ship would sail across the prairie sea.

BETSY: The whole thing kinda got to Yuki — wouldn't go to town no more. Even the Finns were scared of Jaanus.

ANNA-MARIE: The ship of iron, the reddened forge, but most of all — the thunder of —

BETSY: The endless racket of his hammer —

CHORUS: Night and day — week in, week out.

BETSY: At night, you could hear him all the way to our place. He never stopped!

ANNA-MARIE: Except at midnight on Saturday.

Music and JAANUS's hammer cease abruptly.

ANNA-MARIE: And there would be silence for 24 hours — no more — no less. You could set a clock by him.

CHORUS: He was doing it to spite us all.

BETSY: It was like he was mocking God.

Sound of laughter from CHORUS.

CANNON enters, drunk and singing, "Row, Row Your Boat." He halts, stunned.

CANNON: Well, I be punched, bored, and bloody centred! [*He comes closer, calls.*] Mick, come and see this! [*Closer.*] Holy shit. Must be a hunnerd feet long. It *is* a fackin' ark!

SHOLER: [*Entering.*] Like I toljuh — he's a nut!

CANNON: Yuh don't think maybe it's an ark?

SHOLER: Quit talkin' like an idiot.

CANNON: Bible Bill[3] says it's gonna rain 40 days and 40 nights.

---

3 William "Bible Bill" Aberhart (1878–1943): radio evangelist and, later, premier of Alberta from 1935 to 1943.

SHOLER: Aaa — that's just a radio show. Lotta holy-roller bull-shit. No, this guy's up to somethin' funny, and I'm gonna find out what it is —

30 CANNON: "Row, row, row your boat, gently down the streammmmm — !"

SHOLER: Cripes, keep it quiet, can't you?

BENDER *appears.*

BENDER: What can I do for you guys?

CANNON: Hey, Binder, how 'bout taking us out for a little cruise?

BENDER: Take you on a cruise to Battleford, get your fackin' brain examined.

SHOLER: Relax, Bender. We only come out to inspect the, uh, situation.

BENDER: Yeah? Well, what's so dam' funny?

SHOLER: Funny? You don't see nothing funny about a man building a ship in the middle of a goddamn desert? Maybe I'm too — humorous, eh?

CANNON: Yaa, quit bein' such a puke, Binder.

40 BENDER: Okay, Sholer. It's funny. What else?

CANNON: What'sa story on the ark, Binder? 'Sere gonna be a mighty flood, gonna come and drown all us sinners?

BENDER: Well, yuh never know. Happened before.

SHOLER: I hear he's quit farming, is that right?

BENDER: Ask him. He'll be here in a minute.

SHOLER: Bender, are you trying to annoy me? I've got a responsibility here.

CANNON: Yeah — he's the MLA now, 'member?

SHOLER: So just gimme the story on the ark —

BENDER: It ain't an ark!

50 SHOLER: Don't quibble. Where's he planning to sail this? Across Torval Skully's slough?

CANNON: "Merrily, merrily, merrily, life is but a dreammmmmm!"

CANNON *laughs.* JAANUS *suddenly appears on the ship. He carries his hammer.*

JAANUS: Egyptians!

CANNON: There he is!

BENDER: It's awright, Jaanus. They're leavin'.

CANNON: Jeeze, he even looks kinda like Noah, don't he, Mike? Bloody square-head. Hey, Noah, where's your wife? She out roundin' up the elephants?

SHOLER: Cannon! I'm tryna sort this out. Don't pay him any mind, Crook. He's been tipping the whiskey bottle . . .

60 JAANUS: You want to talk to me, mister?

SHOLER: The name's Mike Sholer. I run the lumberyard?

JAANUS: And the thresher.

SHOLER: [*A tight smile.*] Yes. And the threshing outfit. But there's lots of room for both of us! I never complain about legitimate competition. There's plenty a little farmers need help with their crops . . .

BENDER: Get to the point, will yuh, Sholer?

SHOLER: I came about your, uh — construction.

JAANUS: Oh?

SHOLER: Some folks in our community, are, well, growin' a little concerned,
70 wanta know why you're buildin' this — ship. They got a right to know!

JAANUS: Have they?

SHOLER: And I thought if I could help, you know, explain it to them —

JAANUS: You've not heard? I expect a big flood!

CANNON: Well, bugger me with a wire brush!

BENDER: Johnny! [*To* SHOLER.] He's gonna sail it down the river and take it back to Finland.

SHOLER: He's moving this to the ocean?

CANNON: That's the dumbest thing I ever heard!

BENDER: What do you know about it, Cannon?

80 CANNON: It's crazier than the fackin' ark!

BENDER: Aaa, you bin suckin' Sholer's ass so long yer brains're fulla shit!

CANNON: C'mere you dumb plow jockey, I'll kick yer teeth so far down — !

SHOLER: Bender, this is none of your affair — so just back away like a good boy —

JAANUS: Egyptians!

He leaps to the ground, grabs a suspended iron hook.

BENDER: Johnny, don't — !

CANNON: Look out!

SHOLER: Hey!

JAANUS *lifts* SHOLER *onto the hook suspended from a pulley mounted on the ship.* JAANUS *hoists him aloft.*

CANNON: What're you doin'?

90 SHOLER: Put me down!

BENDER: Stand back, Cannon.

SHOLER: Let me down, you son of a bitch! Jump him, Cannon! Bust his brains in!

JAANUS *works, whistling* "Row, Row Your Boat."

SHOLER: Do something, Bender! Get me down! I'll have the law on both of you!

BENDER: That won't cut much ice, Sholer. You came here lookin' fer trouble. So start apologizin'— maybe he'll let you down.

CANNON: Don't worry, Mike, I'll drive to town and get help!

SHOLER: Don't leave, Jimmy! Fer crissake!

CANNON: Now don't panic, Mike. I won't be long —

CANNON *runs off.* SHOLER *continues to swing.*

100 SHOLER: Listen, Crook — I'm sorry — about this. Cannon's such a loudmouth. I promise he won't bother you again — all right? Crook?

JAANUS: Karkulainen.

SHOLER: I'm sorry —

JAANUS: Karkulainen.

SHOLER: Carolinaa . . .

JAANUS *lowers him to the ground.* SHOLER *runs off, whimpering.*

BENDER: Those dam' Egyptians, eh?

BENDER *and* JAANUS *laugh.*

SCENE 2

> BETSY *assembles a cream separator.* JUKKA *faces the audience. He wears work clothes. Lights up on* ANNA-MARIE.

JUKKA: No one could have stopped him. So why did everyone look at me? As though I was responsible... You'd think the Finns would understand! Jaanus was my elder brother!

CHORUS: Well, somebody's got to do somethin! And you're on the local council! He's started assaulting people now — and with no provocation!

> JUKKA *shakes his head.*

JUKKA: I should have foreseen it all when he first spoke of Anna-Marie.

BETSY: And just who was this Anna-Marie?

CHORUS: Anna-Marie. Anna-Marie.

JUKKA: A girl in Finland, in our home town. The daughter of a wealthy
10   merchant.

BETSY: Oh? And how'd he meet her while he's workin' as a sailor?

JUKKA: Well — she was a little odd herself.

BETSY: Odd?

JUKKA: Something of a mystic. A poet.

CHORUS: A mystic. A poet. She was touched!

BETSY: Good Lord. There's no end to it!

JUKKA: [*Laughs.*] And she flirted with all the young men! Once she danced alone in the town square.

BETSY: No!

20   JUKKA: She and Jianni were seen together. There was a public scandal. The town was outraged.

CHORUS: I heard he put her in the family way! And they wouldn't get married!

BETSY: Oh!

JUKKA: Jianni was thrown in jail. And there he became — political. I helped arrange for him to leave, he had to get out of town. He asked me to look out for her. Me! I was only 17!

BETSY: Did she have the child?

JUKKA: Who knows? Her parents sent her to the country. There was nothing I could do, see? We didn't talk about her then.

30   CHORUS: Or him either. All in bad taste. He went with Lenin to Russia, you know.

> BETSY *adjusts the separator, lights a lantern.* JUKKA *enters the farm house with a pail of milk, which he pours into the separator bowl.*

BETSY: So what're we gonna do now?

JUKKA: I'll write to Minnesota, and see if we can find where the daughter lives.

BETSY: I suppose she's changed her name.

JUKKA: Or disappeared forever.

BETSY: Larry agreed to come tonight?

JUKKA: Yes. But he's under Jianni's influence.

BETSY: I suppose he didn't have a choice. Needed the handouts for his family. You think he'll help?

40 JUKKA: He might refuse.
BETSY: You got to make him see the sense!
BENDER: [*Off.*] Haloo. Anybody home?
JUKKA: Come in!
BENDER: Evening, Yuki. Mrs. Crook.
BETSY: How them kids a yours doin'?
BENDER: Not too bad.
JUKKA: Have you eaten?
BENDER: Supper's waitin' at home. You wanted to see me about somethin'?
JUKKA: About Jaanus.
50 BENDER: Yeah, I figgered that much. Well?
JUKKA: Sit down, sit down. Take off your coat.

   JUKKA *sits him down.* BETSY *begins separating the milk.*

JUKKA: You're still working on his ship?
BENDER: Issat why you called me over here?
JUKKA: I want to know! How is he?
BENDER: Well, we're nearly done the hull and the decks. Move it all to the
   river and then we'll start on the boiler.
JUKKA: How does he intend to move it?
BENDER: Horses. We got the winch and tackle all set. Harness for eight horses.
JUKKA: You're going along with this madness?
60 BENDER: Have to. He's gonna need some help.
JUKKA: That's true, Larry! He does need help. Desperately. And you could
   give it. He'll listen to you.
BENDER: Dunno about that.
JUKKA: You could persuade him to give it up, Bender. He can't do it alone!
BENDER: He ain't alone, Yuki.
JUKKA: Look. Sholer says there's a freight car full of oak timber at the siding.
   What did he order that for?
BENDER: Why the hell doncha ask Sholer?
JUKKA: They're for the cabins, aren't they? He orders quarter-cut oak — shipped
70   all the way from Kentucky — for "cabins" on a make-believe boat!
BENDER: [*Rising.*] I ain't the one to discuss this —
JUKKA: You know that — folly will never sail!
BENDER: That's what some folks say —
JUKKA: Larry, how deep is the keel, below water?
BENDER: Sixteen feet — more or less.
JUKKA: And you're launching *that* in the river? The South Saskatchewan
   River?
BENDER: [*Pause.*] Lissen, I gotta go — Merna's waitin'—
JUKKA: Wait! I — we, have — a favor — to ask of you. If you have time —
80   could you go to — Battleford?
BENDER: Battleford!
JUKKA: With Jaanus. I'll pay your expenses.
BENDER: What? To the nut-house? Nuthin' doin'!
JUKKA: There are good doctors there. Jaanus could be — examined.
BENDER: Forget it!

JUKKA: It'll only be a day or two. They could help him at Battleford.

BENDER: They might, if they had the time.

JUKKA: Time, of course they have time! It's a public institution.

BENDER: Get serious, Yuki. The looney-bin? It's chock-a-block with basket cases. Stuffin' them in the broom closets. Bloody Depression's drove half a Saskatchewan right round the bend! There's no room there for Johnny — who's only building a ship — and not hurtin' anybody else. You oughta be shamed a yourself.

JUKKA: Well, I'm not. You live out on the flat. You don't have to listen to people. He's a freak!

BETSY *has finished with the separator.*

BETSY: It's Yuki who has to suffer.

JUKKA: And now he's threatening people!

BENDER: Sholer got what he deserved.

JUKKA: This — lunacy must end! For his sake!

BENDER: That's enough! It's not up to you, or Sholer, or anybody else to decide what's good and what ain't. The guy's a genius! Okay, he's *weird*, but he isn't nuts! Christ, don't you understand what Johnny's doing?

JUKKA: It's just a dream. A fantasy.

BENDER: Well, what the hell is wrong with that? We all got dreams! That's what I bin livin' on fer 15 years. A dream of having my own place, make it go. Or you — bein' a big shot in town. No different — 'cept Johnny's dream is real. It's made of wood and iron. It creaks and moves. You kin touch it! Okay, you say he ain't gonna make it — and sometimes I say it too — just to myself — but what if he *does*? *What if he makes it to the river?* And then on down to Hudson Bay? Can you be so goddamn sure he won't? I bet they all told John A. Macdonald he was crazy to build a railroad across 4,000 miles a wasted hell — but he did her, didn't he? And when Columbus set off across the Atlantic, I bet they laughed their heads off! That's how it is with some guys — they just go ahead and bloody do it! Well — I like that. [*Pause.*] So I'm stickin' by him!

JUKKA: Then you're as big a fool as he is.

BETSY: And you with a family to support!

BENDER: Will you shut up about my family?

Stunned silence. Everyone is embarrassed.

BENDER: I — I gotta be on my way.

BETSY: Here, take some a this cream with you. And we got some extra eggs!

BENDER: I couldn't.

BETSY: You take it! And if you can't use 'em, give some to him! They say in town he's took to eatin' gophers. I won't have people thinkin' we let him starve!

BENDER: All right. I'll pass them on.

JUKKA: Don't forget — I'll pay any expense.

BENDER: I gotta go now. So long.

BENDER *goes out with cream.*

SCENE 3

In the darkness, the sound of furious action: winches, pulleys, the horses whinnying and snorting. Music is intense. JAANUS *can be heard shouting at full volume.*

JAANUS: Aaa-hup! Aaaa-hup! Aaa-hup!

A sharp crack from a broken timber, the scream of a frightened horse. As the lights come up, we see JAANUS *at the prow of the ship, driving the horses.*

JAANUS *leaps off the ship to soothe the horses.*

JAANUS: [*Off.*] Easy, friends. Calm down, Lady. *Alla hataille.* I fix it, Yur-ye. Take it easy — rest, my friends.

JAANUS *pulls harness back to the base of the boat, and connects it. If there is a winch, he can turn it with a ratchet sound.*

JAANUS: We're ready again. Easy now.

BENDER *enters with the cream, looking anxious.*

BENDER: Hi Jaanus. How's she comin'? Looks like yuh made good distance.
JAANUS: Very good. Fifteen yards.
BENDER: Fifteen years?
JAANUS: Yards. From that mark.
BENDER: Cripes. Seems like 15 years.
10 JAANUS: Two more years. We reach the river.
BENDER: Yeah. [*Gestures off.*] If the horses last.
JAANUS: Is hard on horses. But — they're strong.
BENDER: Hmm. [*Gestures again.*] See Prince up and died.
JAANUS: Last night.
BENDER: Bloody hard on the horses.
JAANUS: Prince was old.
BENDER: Gonna bury him?
JAANUS: No. I butcher him tonight.
BENDER: Butcher? What for?
20 JAANUS: I need the blood.
BENDER: Blood?
JAANUS: To paint the keel. Protects from salt water. And I'll eat the flesh.
BENDER: Uggh. Horse meat?
JAANUS: [*Laughs.*] Long way to go before you know hunger, Bender. True hunger.
BENDER: Well, I got a treat for you tonight. Look.

BENDER *holds out cream and eggs.*

JAANUS: Keep it for yourself.
BENDER: Don't need it. Got it from a neighbour.
JAANUS: No thanks.
30 BENDER: Yuh gotta keep your strength up! Still a long way to go.
JAANUS: Don't worry. I am good for 20 more years.

BENDER: Oh — sure! I can see that, but —

JAANUS: Something troubles you, Bender?

BENDER: Well, no, but — I bin thinkin' about the haul and — well, whadda we do when we hit Skully's Ravine?

JAANUS: Ravine?

BENDER: Yeah. How we gonna cross that coulee? Must be 50 yards across. I just don't see —

JAANUS: We roll her on logs.

40 BENDER: Oh yeah?

JAANUS: Down one side. Up the other. Extra winches to help the horses.

BENDER: Yeah, that'd work. But uh, Jaanus? There's another thing. Yuki sez —

JAANUS: [*Ominous.*] You were talking to Jukka again?

BENDER: Well, yeah — we did have a chat. Nothing important. But he sez —

JAANUS: Jukka says, Jukka says! You work for Jukka?

BENDER: No, I don't work for Yuki.

JAANUS: Damn right!

BENDER: And I don't work for you, Johnny. Just because I bin breakin' my back gettin' this ship to the goddamn river — a river it don't even belong in — neglecting my own work — don't give you the right to boss me! I'm my own man — so don't forget.

50

JAANUS: I am sorry, Bender. [*Pause.*] And why doesn't Anna-Marie belong in river?

BENDER: You ever checked the river's depth?

JAANUS: No — map shows big river . . .

BENDER: Oh, it's big, but ain't deep. It's a prairie river. Maybe 12 feet —

JAANUS: [*Stunned.*] Twelve feet?

BENDER: At the deepest. In spring flood. Yuh never — checked?

JAANUS: But it's a mile across!

60 BENDER: Good God, we done all this work for nothin'?

JAANUS: No — there will be a way! There must.

JAANUS *is disturbed for the first time. He strides around, banging on objects with his hammer.*

BENDER: One thing I did think of — Johnny —

JAANUS: Why didn't I measure it? Even a chart!

BENDER: Would be to build a couple big rafts —

JAANUS: Rafts?

BENDER: Yeah. You know. Timber rafts.

JAANUS: By God.

BENDER: You think?

JAANUS: Ya! Will work! One for the ship. One for horses. We float them down to Hudson Bay! Is better!

70

BENDER: Might take more time.

JAANUS: Bah! Only six months. That's all. We build them at the river, ya?

BENDER: Sure. If we make it there. But you bin workin' awful hard. What'sa last time you saw a doctor?

JAANUS: [*Smiling.*] Jukka is concerned for my health?

BENDER: Well — natcherly. He's your brother.

JAANUS: Tell Jukka I will outlive him 10 years. In Finland, I will father children.

BENDER: Awright.

JAANUS: And now, Bender. We go on?

80   BENDER: You bet. Could break for lunch, though.

JAANUS: No. Three more yards.

BENDER: Let's go!

JAANUS: Aaa-hup! Come on, Yurye! Now Lady! Aaa-hup!

The men and horses struggle to move the boat forward. Music builds to a climax. The boat moves — even a few inches.

SCENE 4

ANNA-MARIE *appears in a light.*

ANNA-MARIE: He frightened the people with the noise and the dying horses. The farmers cursed as they plowed their barren fields to the pulse of Karkulainen's hammer.

JAANUS *appears upstage at his anvil. He wears a ragged home-made coat and on the chest of his overalls is pinned a silver alarm clock.*

ANNA-MARIE: The Niskalas lived near the river. He went one day to borrow a knife. He needed to butcher his final horse. The father was away in town. The mother shrieked from behind a door, but the little girl gave him the knife.

JAANUS *stands erect. He holds a gleaming knife.*

ANNA-MARIE: On his chest was pinned a clock, a silver clock, like a medal. Then he left, refusing even a cup of water — but the girl followed him to the stranded ship, her Mama's screams echoing up and down the waterless
10   valley. She went to help him on his journey.

SCENE 5

Lights up on a town meeting, with SHOLER *facing the group. There is much excitement.*

CHORUS: But we knew somethin' was going on. He had his eyes on little girls! Threatenin' people with butcher knives! We saw the writing on the wall!

SHOLER: I'm glad to see we have so many public-minded citizens — prepared to help us solve this problem in our community.

CHORUS: What's it about? About the hermit? He had a knife? No, it's the ark. So what do we do? We have to act.

SHOLER: Yuki, you want to speak to this?

JUKKA: You're the chairman, Mr. Sholer. It's got nothing to do with me.

CHORUS: Mighta known it'd be a Finn. Watch, they'll try and protect him!

10   SHOLER: The important thing is we act together — democratically.

CHORUS: As long as it's anonymous. We don't want the Mounties involved, causing a big public stink.

SHOLER: We can solve this among ourselves. He needs protection — for his sake!

BETSY: Maybe we should bring his daughter?

CHORUS: What kinda help is she gonna be? He's become a public menace!

SHOLER: I guess you heard what he did to me, only a couple of years ago. I was lucky he didn't kill me! I only wanted to talk to him!

CHORUS: To bring him to his senses. Man like that should be put away.

BETSY: Maybe we're being a little hasty. I mean, nobody's really been injured. He hasn't committed any crime.

CHORUS: So why did he ask for that knife, eh? Or interfere with the Niskala girl! And now he's eating grasshoppers!

SHOLER: So nobody'll object if we take along a couple of two-by-fours.

CHORUS: For protection! He's dangerous. That awful hammer. Now be careful!

BETSY: Maybe if we asked the preacher along —

SHOLER: This isn't preacher's work, Missus. Nobody likes it — but it has to be done. I warned you all about him. Nobody'd listen — till it was too late.

CHORUS: Damn squarehead. Rotten bohunk. Drivin' us nuts with that hammering. And what caused the drought, anyhow? Just like a Finn. A German. A bohunk.

CANNON: Let's go!

The crowd sweeps out, leaving BETSY. *She follows slowly.*

SCENE 6

JAANUS *works on the boiler near his ship, wearing the home-made coat. Light on* ANNA-MARIE, *watching from above.*

JAANUS: Anna-Marie.

JAANUS *hammers in great sonorous gongs.* BENDER *runs in.*

BENDER: Johnny! They're coming, Johnny!

JAANUS: They?

BENDER: Sholer and the others. From town. Passed my place a little while ago.

JAANUS: Look — a double seam of rivets.

BENDER: Johnny — there's gonna be trouble.

JAANUS: Is my best cold seam ever.

BENDER: Yeah — looks great. Jaanus, maybe we better go over to Skully's farm.

JAANUS: For what?

BENDER: Just somethin' to do. We could call the Mounties from there —

JAANUS: Bender, don't worry about these people. They're only men.

BENDER: Yeah but, they're gonna — !

JAANUS: You trust this hammer. He protects us.

JAANUS *strikes the boiler again.*

BENDER: Jaanus — I don't think we can do it —

CHORUS: [*Off.*] Over there! Behind the ship!

BENDER: There they are.

JAANUS: Egyptians.

BENDER: Just let me talk to them, awright?

SHOLER: Spread out now. Jimmy, you there?

20   CANNON: Right here.

SHOLER: And all you others?

CHORUS: All set.

BENDER: Jaanus, I gotta know. *Why do you have to go by ship?*

JAANUS: I made a promise.

BENDER: But who to?

SHOLER: All right, Bender. Stand aside.

JAANUS: To Anna-Marie. I made a vow.

SHOLER: Nobody's got a quarrel with you.

BENDER: But how do yuh know she's there? She might be dead for all you

30   know!

     JAANUS *looks to* ANNA-MARIE.

JAANUS: It wouldn't matter. Still a promise.

BENDER: Good God.

SHOLER: Bender! Take a walk.

BENDER: Gimme a dam' minute, can't yuh?

SHOLER: We only wanta talk to him.

BENDER: What about?

SHOLER: Battleford.

BENDER: You need a legal paper for that.

SHOLER: Yuki's agreed to it.

40   BENDER: Not enough. I done some checkin' on it, Sholer. You need the daugh-

    ter's say-so first.

SHOLER: Yuki! Read that letter you got!

     JUKKA *steps forward, reads a letter.*

JUKKA AND ANNA-MARIE: I know he is a very unhappy man, and must be seri-

    ously disturbed to be doing this impossible thing. I agree to his committal

    to Battleford.

     JAANUS *stares at her, transfixed. Everyone stares at him.*

SHOLER: Get ready. We'll have to rush him.

BENDER: I'm not gonna let you do this!

JUKKA: Bender — don't be a fool. It's over.

BENDER: Jaanus. We'll get to Finland, okay? We'll go and see Anna-Marie.

50   Look up your old home-town — all that. But — let's just go to Regina,

    and we can buy a steamship ticket. You got lots of money. You don't have

    to move the ship to the ocean!

JAANUS: No. I must go. I am a Finn.

SHOLER: Ready, men?

CHORUS: Yeah, ready.

SHOLER: Let's go!

BENDER: Jaanus. Gimme the hammer.

JAANUS: Egyptian!

SHOLER: Now!

     Everyone rushes to the centre. JAANUS *raises his hammer to strike.* BENDER
    seizes his arm.

60 JAANUS: *I am Jaanus Karkulainen!*

> *Tableau of violence. Reverberating gong from* PERCUSSIONIST. *Lights fade. Spot on* ANNA-MARIE, *isolated.*

ANNA-MARIE: They took him to Battleford in chains. But even behind the locked doors, his eyes retained a gaze that spanned oceans and continents and centuries. Atop the great ship's cabin lay the carcass of his final horse, a flame of stink and blue flies. But his course holds true as ever and I hear his hammer in my blood.

> *Light comes up on* JAANUS *at the prow of the ship.*

PERCUSSION: *ship's horn.*

ANNA-MARIE: He still pursues his endless dream, standing on the bridge of his ship, his heart rounding the last outcrop of the last fjord going to Suomi, and the image of a girl standing on a village dock —

JAANUS: Anna-Marie.

70 ANNA-MARIE: — waiting still.

> *Light fades to black.*

Judith Thompson (b. 1954)

Born in Montreal, Judith Thompson grew up in Kingston, Ontario, where she graduated from Queen's University in 1976. She enrolled in the three-year program for actors at the National Theatre School, graduating in 1979 and working for a year as a professional actor. But she had already begun scripting the character monologues for Theresa, a complicated, somewhat mentally challenged girl with a large capacity for social survival within degrading circumstances. This character helped shape Thompson's breakthrough play *The Crackwalker* which was produced by Theatre Passe Muraille at the Backspace in Toronto in 1980. Other critical successes followed, including *White Biting Dog* (1984), *I Am Yours* (1987), and *Lion in the Streets* (1990) which won the Floyd S. Chalmers Canadian Play Award in 1991. *Perfect Pie* premiered in Toronto in January 2000. Thompson is a two-time winner of the Governor General's Award for Drama: for *White Biting Dog* (1984), and for her first collection of plays, *The Other Side of the Dark* (1989).

Like *Sled*, first produced by Tarragon Theatre in Toronto (1997), all of Thompson's plays involve brutality and tenderness, reality and fantasy, humiliation and triumph, evoking actions that constantly breathe and bristle with human distress. Theatrical extremes of vivid fantasy and deep suffering dominate but also empower her work, as in the character Cape Race from *White Biting Dog* who must find a way to save himself by saving his dying father. In a series of short scenes, *I Am Yours* probes the deep capacity for human evil linked to the innocence of childbirth. With an uncanny capacity for forgiveness, Isobel's ghost haunts and comments upon *Lion in the Streets*. In *Perfect Pie*, two long-estranged friends recover a terrible memory from their past. Thompson's work, which also includes the award-winning radio plays *Tornado* (1987) and *White Sand* (1991), has enjoyed international acclaim. But beyond her many awards, Judith Thompson has gained a reputation for powerful voice both within the theatre and on the page.

Introduction to *Sled*

Big, bleak, visceral, powerful, and cold—*Sled* suggests itself in terms large enough to cover the vastness of the North, the capacity for evil, even the capacity for human memory itself. In this play, sordid violence meets Canadian consciousness with the life-and-death force of high tragedy. Almost every character searches out a past that cannot be reclaimed but which influences the present in complicated and surprising twists that destabilize relationships, families, and neighbourhoods. And, as always, the truth is stranger than fiction. The character Evangeline notes it herself, laughing incredulously at her situation with Kevin near the end of Act 2: "It's - it's - it's - it's like something out of Charles Dickens. *Little Dorrit*." Dickens's novels are full of comic twists. *Sled*, however, contains the thumping inevitability of tragic fate.

Haunted by violence, coincidence, sexuality, and fear, *Sled* expresses itself like something out of a horrible dream, a nightmare. And yet the storyline moves with the swiftly irrational uncaring of crime. The willful murder of lounge singer Annie Delaney passes as a hunting accident but is meant as vengeance. The killer, Kevin, clearly a repeat violent offender of some sort, finds his way home to the neighbourhood from which he was abducted as a child. There, he victimizes his newfound half-sister, Evangeline, herself an acquaintance of his initial murder victim. Evangeline begins a relationship with Jack, a hypermacho Toronto cop nicknamed "Diablo" and husband of the murdered singer. Joe, a friendly older neighbour living in the past, knows and sympathizes with all the local secrets and truths. As he puts it himself early in the play: "instead of those urgent things, I keep seeing: what has already happened."

The past itself operates curiously within the play. Annie haunts present circumstances through song, voice, and flashback as well as through the significant evidence of her long red dress. But everyone's present is haunted in a sense. Annie dreams of her Irish ancestry in Gaelic. Evangeline wants to know about her biological father, a native Cree. Kevin, fair-haired and fair-skinned, spouts Norse like a homicidal battle cry, but he also wishes to reconnect emotionally with his family — inasmuch as emotional connection is possible for him. Joe, almost nostalgically, recalls his own immigrant indignities in childhood poverty along with the shocking death of his own father and his mother's subsequent resentment. Jack, recklessly angry about most things, wishes off his own French Canadian heritage with disgusted expletives. All the characters need to reconnect — painfully, even somewhat dangerously — with personal and cultural pasts.

By its very title, *Sled* connects itself constantly and unsentimentally to the Canadian North. It's more dangerous and more various out there than one might think. And it's dangerous inside too; dangerous but beautiful. To reconnect is to take terrible risks. As original director Duncan MacIntosh put it in his foreword to the Playwrights Canada Press edition of the play (1997): "*Sled*'s size, like Canada's, is overwhelming. Its horrors are the same too: implicit, only their tiny heads are seen before they strike. Omnipresent. Its redemption possible only from the hearts of the characters who inhabit it" (p. 14). Yearning for her lost brother early in the play, Evangeline declares, "But don't you think he'd want to come and find his real sister? And mother? I mean everyone wants to know their real family." Joe's response, "I don't know about that," suggests deep caution and understanding. Haunted lovingly by her brother's murder victim, Evangeline bears a child she names Annie Northstar. At the end of the play, Evangeline carries her dead brother through the cold wilderness illuminated by the Northen Lights. A snowy owl hoots in the long night. It is very Canadian, very scary, but also curiously hopeful — like great tragedy.

SLED

PLAYWRIGHT'S PRODUCTION NOTES

The play should run no longer than 2 hours and 15 minutes (not counting the intermissions). The audience should be out no later than 10:50 pm, given an 8:00 pm curtain. The key to a good pace, other than in the playing, is in the transitions between scenes which should, in almost every case, be instantaneous — the last word of one scene immediately followed by the first word of the next. The designer, of course, can facilitate the speedy transitions.

CHARACTERS

ANNIE DELANEY
JACK
JOE
EVANGELINE
KEVIN
VOLKER, MIKE, JASON, M.C.
MOTHER, MARSHA, CARMELLA

SETTING: The present, Toronto; a lodge in Northern Ontario and its snowmobile trails; a wilderness farther north.

ACT ONE

SCENE 1

(*White birches, snow, a great snowy owl, and a trail, with a hill, running around behind or through the audience.* ANNIE *appears walking fast and hard, out of breath through deep snow and birches. The music is mounting, ominous like a heart beating harder and faster but moving towards a dark euphoria;* ANNIE, *walks the trail around or through the audience and climbs the hill. At the top of the hill, she looks down over the scene. The music for "Oh heavenly time of day" plays. She sings:*)

ANNIE: Oh heavenly time of day
    the snow and the quiet
    the birch
    white pine
    so high and so high
    Shall I sink in the snow and just lie there for hours
    alone there for hours
    til dark night

erases me?
Oh heavenly time of day

(*ANNIE breathes in the air. There is the sound of a wolf howling. She sings.*)

ANNIE: lie on the white snow and
stare at the dark sky
the sky full of stars
who are people who died
maybe people I know
hello Maeve O'Hara
my mother's mother's
mother's mother's
motherrrr....hello!

(*A wolf howls. She makes her way down the hill.*)

SCENE 2

(*A residential street, with mostly red brick houses with high pointed roofs, some three-storey, but most, two-storey workers' houses. The houses, however, look as though they are in the middle of a forest. The birches remain.*)

JOE: "*America Bella! Si abbandonare a me!*" That's what she used to say whenever things were — fallin' apart. My mother. I don't think she ever said the word "Canada." It was always "America." "*America bella.*" This here used to be a cow path. The whole of what you see now, of Clinton Street, wasn't nothin' but a cow path. My mother an' father and the nine of us kids we were livin' south of College, that was about 1918, my dad workin' at the slaughterhouse at Clinton and Bloor. It's still there to this day, they won't move it; we'd come up here to the pastures and we'd watch as the cows walked down the cow path to the slaughterhouse, to become ground meat. Led always by the great black bull. Course we'd never see the meat, nor the milk, never saw milk till I went in the Air Force. But I loved sittin' on the fence and watchin' all these cows walkin' down. And all the Italian ladies, they would chase after these cows, to catch the manure they dropped on the way. For their gardens. And my mother, Carmella? She would be the first. She would always be first.

SCENE 3

(*The Lounge Dining Room at Pickerel and Jack Lake Lodge. A warm fire crackles in the fireplace. There is a trophy on the wall, a deer with antlers. VOLKER, the proprietor, has a German accent.*)

VOLKER: Good evening everybody. My name is Volker, and this is my lovely wife Marsha. Welcome to Pickerel and Jack Lake Lodge: The snowmobiling mecca of North America. Marsha and me hope you are really enjoying your stay and that you have seen the 500 kilometres of snowmobile trails out there, and have wind-burned faces, but now it's time to warm up, yes? So we have brought for your entertainment tonight a great honour, a beautiful diva, the sexy singer of Toronto nightclubs, the very interesting and I think such a good singer, the great Annie Delaney. Let's give her a warm hand, yes?

(ANNIE DELANEY *steps out of the shadows in a beautiful red dress with long red velvet gloves and performs a simple transformation or act of magic, as she sings:*)

10 ANNIE: Oh heavenly time of day … the fog and the quiet …
the mist
no sun
I move out of my dream and into this day as the fog
it clears so slowly away to
reveal…
to reveal…
to reveal…

(KEVIN *enters, interrupting. An awkward silence. He sits down.*)

VOLKER: Isn't she fantastic?

ANNIE: I saw a fox this morning. On the green trail. The long one? Early this
20 morning. I was walking along, thinking: there's still snow here. it's all melting down there, in the city. Mud rivers running everywhere. But here: snow, spruce, evergreens. I was walking toward a heart-stopping stand of birch, and I saw a fox. A red fox. We looked at each other, for a moment. A wonder. At dawn; a secret time of day.

My son, Jason, was born at dawn; that time of day gives me hope. Whereas, the hour *before* dawn? In the winter? The job that degraded day after day, that picked at my being. It was dark when I rose and I walked down the empty cold street and I am nauseous just before dawn I wake up, with dread. My heart beating very fast. I know I will die just
30 before dawn.

(*She sings one again:* "Thursday in November.")

Thursday in November
at that duskish time of day
Walking west on Bloor Street. Past Italian groceries, Korean fruit
and flowers, Hungarian deli … I feel a sharp pain in my knee a red
dog, no, a fox, has bitten me …

(*spoken*)It's a fox.

(*sung*)At Bloor and Bathurst my downtown
in the rushing
A red fox
40 Is here and
has bitten my knee and it stands and it stares back at me.
And we all
go down on our — knees on the spit covered
sidewalk and say

Oh heavenly time of day
ohhh heavenly time of day
A fox on the street
the geese in the V twisting this way and that
The lights through the dark clouds the blues and the
50   indigos, breathe in the chatter, the down to the
subway and buses to homes
See the fox on the street
grab a paper, a Mars bar, a *People*, and rest your head
Let the thoughts drift like I did on Pickerel Lake.
Just drift
Oh Heavenly time of day
Gives me some hope
And I do, believe that I'll stay
For a while
60   With this fox
On this street
A red coat
For a while
with its dusk
With its eyes

SCENE 4

(Lodge dining room lounge: MIKE HEAD *and* KEVIN DORNER *are eating dinner at one table.* ANNIE *sits down and immediately* JACK *praises her.)*

JACK: Beautiful. That was beautiful. Never heard that one before. It's something.

*(*ANNIE *rests for a moment.)*

ANNIE: How's the dinner? Are you enjoying it?
JACK: Beautiful roast of beef.

(He offers her a bite, she turns her head away.)

ANNIE: What did you mean "something."
JACK: What?
ANNIE: You said "It's something." My song. As if it was deranged.
JACK: I liked it. It was good.
ANNIE: But…?
10   JACK: You're not gonna get a fox on Bloor Street.
ANNIE: Well. I saw a fox in Trinity Bellwoods Park once. Early in the morning.
JACK: You did?
ANNIE: Yes. I did. I told you about that —
JACK: Shit. Shit I forgot to cancel the paper. What a fucking idiot I am.
ANNIE: Shhhh, don't worry, Joe will do it.
JACK: Joe?
ANNIE: Old Joe from across the street.

JACK: Oh yeah, Joe. Ace.

ANNIE: He'll pick them up for us. He knows we're going away. He's my pal.

20 JACK: Why does he sit there watchin everybody all day? Doesn't he have anything better to do?

ANNIE: Give him a break, he worked like a dog for fifty years, he's earned his rest. Besides, it's great for us: He never misses a thing on that street.

(He touches her knee under the table. She enjoys it.)

ANNIE: Jack.

(He takes her hand.)

JACK: So I never asked you, what'd you do Thursday, did you swim?

ANNIE: Seventy-three lengths.

JACK: You're amazing. But you like that, don't you, just thinkin' your thoughts.

ANNIE: Actually I don't think at all. I just don't have a thought in all that green water.

30 JACK: You are looking incredibly beautiful tonight.

ANNIE: To your eyes only.

JACK: You're the most beautiful woman in this room.

ANNIE: You look very handsome yourself. That jacket does look nice on you.

JACK: It better for thirteen hundred bucks. Hey. That was very wonderful last night. Last night you were all…

ANNIE: Shhhh.

JACK: I did pretty good with the hand last night, eh? You had, how many, four fireworks last night, didn't you? You are so unpredictable. My quiet woman.

(He touches her. She looks at his fingers on her arm.)

40 ANNIE: Jack? How long do someone's fingerprints … last? Say, in a house?

JACK: Ten years. Give or take. Less they're wiped off.

ANNIE: So if I don't clean, if I don't polish, my mother and father; their fingerprints will stay with us for ten more years after they …

JACK: *(nods)* Annie. I won't talk about hockey. If you don't talk about death. Deal?

ANNIE: "Behold I shall tell you a mystery. We shall not all sleep but we shall all be changed." I wish I believed that. For even a minute.

JACK: Hey. Look at the fire. You love fires.

(At the other table, KEVIN, and MIKE are getting rowdy).

KEVIN: Sunday roast beef dinner, eh? Just like my old lady used to make.

50 MIKE: Right. Sunday my old lady would open a box of potato flakes. Throw some boiling water on 'em. There's Sunday dinner. I'm not fucking kidding.

KEVIN: Look at that waitress. Fuck, man, looks like she swallowed the Skydome.

MIKE: This beef is fine, man.

KEVIN: But where's the Yorkshire pudding? I want my fuckin' Yorkshire pudding.

MIKE: Yeah. Yorkshire fucking pudding.

(On the other side of the room:)

ANNIE: Is it working, Jack? This weekend? You think things are going to be alright? With us?

60   JACK: It's working. I haven't seen you like this in months. Maybe it's the nature, the snow, whatever. You're actually, I don't know, happy.

ANNIE: Yes. I am, aren't I.

JACK: Yes. You are.

KEVIN: HEY. WAITRESS.

MARSHA: Were you born in a barn? Or was it a sewer?

KEVIN: Sewer. That's good, that's good. You're Big Marsha aren't ya? Didn't you used to work at The Keg in Huntsville?

MARSHA: Yes I worked at The Keg. I think I tossed you out a couple of times, did I not? What can I get for you boys?

70   KEVIN: I was just wondering … um, like … did I fuck you?

MARSHA: That's not funny. I don't think that's funny at all. You're out of here.

(MARSHA leaves their table.)

KEVIN: I'm sorry.

MIKE: We didn't mean nothin'.

MARSHA: Everything okay here, folks?

ANNIE: Yes, thank you, wonderful.

JACK: My compliments to the chef. The roast is excellent.

MARSHA: Well thank you. I made the roast myself tonight. Chef was off sick, he's got some kinda kidney trouble. So Volker says, "Marsha you're doin' the roast beef". And I don't cook, eh, generally, so I said, "Volker I can't

80   cook a roast of beef." Volker hands me some garlic and some paprika and says, "Rub it on, Marsha, like lotion on a baby's bottom." So there you are, it's not so bad.

ANNIE: Looks very good.

MARSHA: It's very good, I know. Hey. I meant to tell you, I like your singing. It's unusual. Different.

ANNIE: Thank you.

KEVIN: Waitress. Excuse me, not to bother you or anything, but like, we were wondering. Like where's our Yorkshire pudding. It says on the menu "Yorkshire pudding." Pardon my French.

90   MARSHA: That is Yorkshire pudding.

MIKE: Where? Am I like, buh-lind?

MARSHA: On your plate. There.

(KEVIN points to the Yorkshire pudding.)

KEVIN: THAT? You are tellin' me that THAT is Yorkshire pudding?

MIKE: No fuckin' way.

MARSHA: Yes, that is Yorkshire pudding. I made it myself.

KEVIN: Looks like my grandmother's tit, man.

MARSHA: That is it.

(MARSHA exits. They laugh hysterically. JACK and ANNIE exchange a look. Annie is pleading with him silently not to do anything.)

KEVIN: Look at those two, they are pissed.

MIKE: Excuse me, miss? No, you, big guy's woman.

100 ANNIE: Are you talking to me?

MIKE: Like, how did you get so tall and skinny anyways? Did you, like, eat the
CN Tower?

*(Note: If the actress does not fit this physical description, replace the lines with
"How'd you get so homely lookin' anyways? Did you, like, eat Yonge Street?"*

They laugh even harder. JACK stands up, furious.)

KEVIN: And that guy over there, he ate Exhibition Stadium, man.

(They laugh some more, knocking over some plates etc. JACK walks over.)

JACK: Before we go any further, I would like you both to go down on your
knees and apologize, to my wife, NOW.

ANNIE: It doesn't matter, Jack. Let's go.

JACK: You are going to get an apology. Do it boys. Do it now.

(Silence.)

KEVIN: It's a free country, sir, I believe. And I would like to keep eatin' my
supper.

110 MIKE: I'm really enjoying these green beans. Deliciooooso.

JACK: You are going to apologize to my wife and to every other diner in this
establishment, or I will make you sorry.

MIKE: What the fuck? Is this, like, a Sylvester Stallone movie or something?

KEVIN: He's a cop, man. I see it in the white of his fuckin' eyes. He's one of
those, that shoves ya up against the car and bangs your head over and
over.

JACK: *Diablo.*

KEVIN: What?

JACK: Just do what I told you to do.

120 ANNIE: Jack.

JACK: Everything's gonna be just fine. Annie. Just stay where you are.

(There is a long pause. KEVIN and MIKE laugh and start eating again.)

KEVIN: So as I was saying, Mike, I wouldn't fuck that wife of his if you paid
me a fuckin' million, like fuckin' the railroad tracks, right? She likely
smells down there, anyways, right? Like a fuckin' can of sardines.

(MIKE is laughing like a kid, snorting.

JACK slams MIKE's head into the table, knocking him out.)

JACK: I have had just about enough out of you, you piece of fucking trash —
you fucking apologize NOW.

*(JACK drags KEVIN to his table, forces him to his knees and into a bow. KEVIN
goes for his hunting knife strapped to his belt but JACK pins KEVIN's arm behind
him, pressing hard.)*

JACK: Now learn some goddamned respect.

SCENE 5

(JOE *sits, rocks on the porch.*)

JOE: I used to have the satellite. Because I enjoyed the television quite a bit. Because I was a TV salesman at Eaton's for forty-three years. That was my profession. So I enjoyed my television. But since Essie got sick, I can't watch it no more. I turn it on, and I just can't watch it. Because I got to watch the street. That is what I am here for. Now that my kids are grown and gone. To watch the street. Trouble is, a kind of strange thing is happening to me. I'll sit here, sippin' on my coffee, and instead of watchin' out for how things are, right now, like if little Claire and Joshua two doors up come home from school on time, or if too many people seem to be livin' in the house on the corner, instead of those urgent things, I keep seeing: what has already happened.

10

SCENE 6

(*Hotel room.* MUSIC: *sexy like Santana.*[1] *Presumably coming from radio.*

JACK *and* ANNIE. *They start at some distance from each other and move slowly together dancing in response to the music.*)

SCENE 7

(KEVIN *and* MIKE *in enclosed shack getting ready to go out sledding.* KEVIN *loads his gun.*)

KEVIN: Fuckin' cocksucker. I'll kill that cocksucker.

MIKE: Forget it, man, you know what cops are like.

KEVIN: Nobody does that to me. NOBODY.

MIKE: Well somebody did. A fuckin' psycho cop did. And it could have been a hell of a lot worse, we coulda been dead, he'd get away with it. Now let's get over it and go man. Let's go do what we're here for, we fuckin' risked our necks gettin' this sled, let's shoot us a moose!

KEVIN: MOOSE!

MIKE: Whoooo!

(*They whoop and bark like dogs as they run out.*)

SCENE 8

(ANNIE *and* JACK's *room. He is asleep. She is lying next to him, looking out the window. An owl hoots. She sees the owl and the owl sees her.*)

ANNIE: Ohhh.

(*She turns, excited.*)

ANNIE: Jack? Are you awake? It's an owl, a great snowy owl. I'm going to go for a walk. I'm gonna go and walk until dawn. Wait for the light. Sweet dreams.

1 Latin Rock band, led by guitarist Carlos Santana.

SCENE 9

(It is a dark night lit only by a mass of stars. A night bird sings ominously. We are looking at a snowmobile trail in Northern Ontario. A green or pink neon sign in handwriting overhead says: "Pickerel and Jack Lake Lodge: Snowmobiling Mecca of North America!" And then in small letters, underneath, in a different colour of neon, it says: "50 km. of Pristine X-country ski trails!" The cross-country ski trail is zig-zagging through a stand of birches. ANNIE walks by the sign and heads down a steep hill. It is very steep. She edges down it, grabbing onto trees occasionally, slipping.)

ANNIE: All alone, in the woods, in the dark. In the middle of Northern Ontario by myself at night. I've never swam across Lake Ontario. I've never run across the 401. I've never driven across the frozen ice. But I am here.

(She sings briefly in Gaelic. A shimmering, strange music. She sees a vision in the distance.)

ANNIE: I see her again. The girl. On the ship. A dark, battered, dying ship. In Gaelic, my blood tongue, say: *Long an bhais* [pronounced: Long on vache] Big holes in the mast. The crashing of fifty foot waves. Maeve. The raining. Maeve O'Hara, born in Connemara,[2] December 6, 1791. Praying. Standing on the mast of the ship. Praying to our Lord Jesus Christ. And everybody else down under, is dead. Of fever. Babies and mothers and fathers and families, all dead, piled together. They threw them overboard, one by one, wrapped up in sheets, until there was nobody left to throw them. Only Maeve, to say prayers for the dead. And she looks out to sea. For land, or whales, or fairies of the sea. In Gaelic, say: *Si na farraige.* And a cold wind comes up, cold and strong and she hangs on, she doesn't fall but her hair, her hair stands straight up. I know this is true. I know this girl is my great-great-grandmother. I know this girl is me.

(She hears the sound of breaking branches. The shadow of a moose appears. They stare at one another for a moment.

She reaches up to touch the moose.)

ANNIE: Oh. God. What is it? It couldn't be. Oh my God it is. A moose. I don't believe this. Hello. You are so big. Hey I'm not going to hurt you. Wait!

(The moose runs. A snowmobile approaches. ANNIE stands, terrified in the moonlight.)

ANNIE: Oh my God. This is all I need.

(The snowmobile's light beams on her. There are birches between her and the snowmobile. There is a stand of birches blocking their view of her.)

KEVIN: Hey hey shut off shut off. I see somethin' through those trees.

(He shuts it off.)

2 a county in northwest Ireland.

ANNIE: Hello. Hello.

(*KEVIN motions* MIKE *to stay back.* MIKE *keeps his sunglasses and headphones on. He is drunk.* KEVIN *moves in.*)

KEVIN: Well look at that. We got ourselves a she moose.

MIKE: Moose. Fuck.

ANNIE: Hey, fellows! It's not a moose. It's me from the lodge. The singer. Hey. Can you hear me!

MIKE: Shoot her, man, before she takes off.

30   KEVIN: Right cornered she is.

MIKE: Fuckin' shoot it.

ANNIE: No! No! Please answer me, guys. Hello! I'm here, through the bushes. What, are you wearing headphones? Take off your headphones.

KEVIN: Let's cut open her belly, and if there's a calf there, we pull out the calf.

MIKE: Where is she man, I can't fuckin see her.

(*ANNIE gasps and goes into shock.*)

ANNIE: This is not funny. Will you answer me please. Please. PULL OUT YOUR HEADPHONES.

KEVIN: Let's pull out the calf. Just shoot her, cut her open, and pull out the calf. Take it to a vet, leave it on the steps, whatever.

40   MIKE: Did you shoot it?

KEVIN: Just pull the calf right out. Alright.

(*KEVIN moves through the brush until he has quite a clear view of* ANNIE.)

ANNIE: My husband will kill you.

KEVIN: I want the antlers.

ANNIE: I'm sorry about the thing at the lodge, my husband went too far. He will apologize to you.

KEVIN: We split the meat. Shove it in the freezer, that's supper all winter. Moose and chips, moose and fries, moose and rice, moose and Yorkshire pudding.

ANNIE: Please.

MIKE: Why isn't she movin', man? What's wrong with her?

50   KEVIN: She's froze; in the light of the sled. She's froze.

MIKE: I can't fuckin' see her!

KEVIN: *Ek skal skjota ther huortu I gegnum* [This is Norse and pronounced: Yeg skal skeeota tear hertu ee gagnum]. Let's shoot her man. Right through the heart.

(*Two shots. Blackout.*)

SCENE 10

(*EVANGELINE comes out on her porch and looks around with great expectation. She is looking for another neighbour's tame pigeons. She sees them, flying in circles. She follows them with her eyes. They make quite a racket.*)

EVANGELINE: Morning Joe.

JOE: Morning.

EVANGELINE: See the pigeons?

JOE: Where? Oh yeah. A whole flock of 'em.

EVANGELINE: Have you noticed they do this every day at this time? Fly around in a circle, from here to the Loblaws over to the Food City, and down to Fiesta Farms and back.

JOE: Now that you mention it. I do see 'em flying around every day. I didn't think nothing of it. Don't care for pigeons.

10   EVANGELINE: They belong to a guy over on Grace. 'Parently he races them, down in the States every spring. They're in training.

JOE: Training?

EVANGELINE: For the races.

JOE: Well well.

EVANGELINE: How's Essie today, Joe?

JOE: I tried to cut her toenails for her and I couldn't. They're too hard. And yellow. Don't know what that means. I'm gonna have to give the doctor a call. Get that mobile foot clinic over here.

EVANGELINE: I could come do them later Joe. Before I go to work.

20   JOE: It's a nasty job, Ev.

EVANGELINE: Agh.

(EVANGELINE looks at ANNIE and JACK's house. The house looks ominous to her.)

EVANGELINE: Ooooh. That house give me the shivers today. Looks empty.

JOE: Workin' holiday for Annie up north. Singin' in a lodge up there. She's a lounge singer. The two of them went for the weekend.

EVANGELINE: You know I don't think I've ever seen him.

JOE: Long hours. He's a police detective. 14 Division.

EVANGELINE: So they're way up north.

JOE: Don't tell nobody though. 'Specially that nosey check-out, over at Fiesta Farms.

30   EVANGELINE: Hah. She's always askin' me when I'm getting married. Next time, I'm gonna just tell her "It's none of your business, you potato-faced grocery girl." HAH. That'd be funny.

JOE: I'd like to see that.

EVANGELINE: Joe.

JOE: Yeah.

EVANGELINE: Will you think I'm crazy?

JOE: No.

EVANGELINE: I heard footsteps last night. And the night before that. On the street. Real clear, like it was summer. And I thought I heard someone

40   climbing the steps and coming up on the porch. When I looked out the window, I didn't see anyone.

JOE: Maybe you should get a dog. Although they do shed something terrible. Our Dory she was a piece of work; she would get up on the couch soon as we went up to bed. One night my stomach was bad, I come down for a Brio, I'm half asleep and I think I see my mother sittin on our couch. I go "now what are you doin' comin' back from the dead and sittin' on my couch in my parlour when you never let me so much as touch that precious couch of yours" and Dory she kinda whimpers and jumps off. Ha. Oh, I felt a fool.

50 EVANGELINE: Joe? Do you think, maybe, I mean, don't you think, there is some possibility that it might be him?

JOE: Who?

EVANGELINE: You know. Kevin. My brother. Joe? Do you think?

JOE: Oh dear.

EVANGELINE: Well, it's possible.

JOE: I don't see how, Evangeline. It's been 20 years.

EVANGELINE: But maybe he — found out somehow, about who he was. That he belongs right here. On Clinton Street. Like maybe she got sick and she wanted to just tell him the truth, people do that, you know, they get
60 tired of keepin' somethin' buried.

JOE: Even if he did know the truth, Ev, what makes you think he's gonna come back here? This is not home to him no more, not since he was took. He was only four years old, remember. He's got a life there, wherever that woman stole him to, could be Australia for all we know, he likely has a job, a girlfriend —

EVANGELINE: But don't you think he'd want to come and find his real sister? And mother? I mean everyone wants to know their real family.

JOE: I don't know about that.

EVANGELINE: He'll be real disappointed when I tell him Mama's dead.

70 JOE: Evangeline, dear. Please don't count on him comin'.

EVANGELINE: I heard those footsteps. Joe? I know I did. Are you sure you didn't hear nothing?

JOE: Well…

EVANGELINE: You did? You did Joe? You heard them too?

JOE: More than likely it's just some drunkard comin' home from the Tasty's Tavern.

EVANGELINE: I'm going to stay awake all night tonight, and watch out the window. Then I'll be sure not to miss him.

JOE: Evy, there's no point in you losing a good night's sleep.

80 EVANGELINE: He's gonna want to know everything about Mama, about our life before he was took. I gotta be ready. Tell me, Joe. Tell me about like, how she used to keep the house so nice. Before. Before she got sick.

JOE: She made apple crisp. That's the mother you should remember.

EVANGELINE: She made apple crisp? With brown sugar on top? With what kind of apple, Joe?

JOE: I'm not so sure about that…

EVANGELINE: But what kind do you think … like … MacIntosh?

JOE: Yes, that's what it was. It was MacIntosh.

90 EVANGELINE: Oh. MacIntosh!

SCENE 11

(*Trail at night.* ANNIE, *in her red dress, lies in the snow before a towering tree. Sound of an owl hooting.* ANNIE *slowly wakes up looks up at the owl.*)

ANNIE: This is very strange. This is very strange. My heart is not beating, the blood is pouring, gushing out of me — In my Gaelic, *Vee a mer egg foil vache* [this is the phonetic spelling] I am dying. I will be buried. Deep, unmoving inside a box under the ground, eyes never moving my tongue curling up mouldy inside my mouth these hands folded, living only in dreams, and thoughts, and hurried conversations in front of Steven's Milk, with dogs pulling at the leash and kids dancing round, "Did you hear who died?" or at the skating rink, flirting, buying hot dogs, "Did you hear?" less and less, and less, present only in my recycled clothes, hanging at the Goodwill, in the hairs I have left in the brushes all over the house, in my fingerprints which will fade in ten years, she disappeared; they the neighbours they will go on for years Valerie Pratt rushing her three children out the door at two minutes to nine, every day, for years and years to come, Joe will sit on his porch the Sikh men will deliver flyers to our door every Sunday and the kids will play road hockey and I will have left so little; I wish to leave more on this earth, more than I have, (*big raspy breath*) oh let me go back, to lie naked in the wet cement, to spray paint my name in blue all over my city, (*another big breath*) to French kiss the men lying in doorways and stinking of urine, to run from rooftop to steeple, to stand on a speeding train and r-r-r-rave (*breathing becomes more difficult and shallower*). I have made such a faint impression in the world a bird alighting on a branch (*breath*) I want to go back and resume my life and just be be be (*breath*) with my son, my husband, just walk, breathe just breathe again in the leaves in the snow, walk (*breath*) and the snow can cover my footprints the blue light of the snow dropping bare feet on burning sand (*breath*) the August humidity wrapping around me, diving into murky lakes with weeds the rough of my husband's cheek (*breath*) the smell of his neck in the summer, the breath of my child, with a cold, (*breath*) the smell of his head his head in the night oh! let me resume —

(*Final breath.*
She lies, still.
The owl hoots.)

SCENE 12

(JACK *in the hotel room.*)

JACK: Annie? You in the bath? You enjoy your bath, I won't bother you. I know how you love your long bath. I was thinking about what you were talking about, my temper. Like my ... anger. The local punks callin' me "*Diablo.*" What I did to those kids tonight and that thing with Pochinshky on Eglinton. I was thinking — I have to tell you something I haven't told you yet.

Remember, we ran into that — Jemma? The legal secretary from Brantford, blonde with the moussed hair — in February. Remember? At Yorkdale Mall? And remember how uncomfortable you said you felt? The way she looked at you? You said you thought there was something ...

I used to ... get very pissed at Jemma. Sometimes I think it was because she was blonde. And she was so big breasted. I, like, I wanted to own her. I would leave you at home reading in your nightgown, tellin' you I had to work all night and I would drive to Brantford to see Jemma, to have sex with her four, five times every which way. I did things to her that … and then I would drive home and slide into bed next to you and we would talk that sweet night talk and you were so trusting — I was an animal. I was out of control. I still don't get it. I don't get why it happened. I didn't tell you before because I was afraid you wouldn't forgive me; maybe you won't forgive me, maybe you'll get outta the bath and say you want a separation, I wouldn't blame you. But I love you so much I wanted to tell you the whole truth. I was good as golden right up till I was nine. You know? The perfect kid. I would give my dad the paper, ask him if he wanted a beer, go get it for him, help my Mama with the table, change my baby sister. Sundays, I would put on the little suit, and we'd go to church. My sister and I would get under a blanket on the couch and watch cartoons all morning. I'd talk French with my gramma, sing songs with her; I played every sport goin', hockey, baseball, soccer, everything. I slept with my football. And then this kid, at school, he started to pick on me. Take off my hat, in the winter, throw it around. Say I was cheating in ball hockey. I never cheated. But he was a grade older, bigger, and said I couldn't play ball hockey. And I would sit there, on the side, and hope to be asked.

It was around then, I got — angry at home. I put holes in the walls with my fists. I wouldn't talk French wouldn't eat French, if my mother put tortière and sugar pie on the table I would throw 'em on the floor, "You stupid bitch, I want a hamburger and a fuckin' popcicle not this frog shit, not this...." I never kissed a woman till you, Annie. I would turn away. I would say, I'm not one for kissing. Because kissing meant … I don't know. Being there. Goin' inside like an underwater cave with someone, swimmin' in, hand in hand, and you're under the water, inside the cave, with this person, and so much so much could go wrong. You're not the first woman I slept with, as you know, and maybe not the last, as you also know, but you are the first, and the last woman I will ever kiss.

Annie?

SCENE 13

(*EVANGELINE's house. She is in a slip, about to get dressed for her job at Fran's. The ghost of her mother stands behind her.*)

MOTHER: Evangeline. My lovely girl.

EVANGELINE: Oh Mama, I am so lonely. I am missing you so much.

MOTHER: I'm all around you, Vange.

EVANGELINE: I've been waitin' so long for Kevy I've forgotten how to make friends.

MOTHER: I can see him coming, like a storm, my love.

EVANGELINE: My Kevin? My brother? Is coming back?

MOTHER: Oh. My lovely child. Just…

(*MOTHER is trying to warn her.*)

SCENE 14

(The two snowmobilers walk through the brush towards ANNIE's *fallen body. They do not see her yet.)*

MIKE: Wait'll my dad sees all this moose meat in his freezer. He's always after me sayin' I never bring home nothin' he will go freaky when he sees a pair of antlers sittin' on his kitchen table.

KEVIN: Hey. I'm getting the antlers. I'm the one that...

*(*MIKE *sees* ANNIE *lying in the snow.)*

MIKE: Oh my God. Oh my fucking God.

KEVIN: The lady from the lodge.

*(*MIKE *vomits and throws down the earphones.)*

MIKE: I told you we shouldn't wear these fucking things. Fuck. I'm blind in one eye, man, I didn't fuckin' see her through all them trees. What's your fuckin' excuse? Eh? Eh? Why didn't you see her?

10   KEVIN: I did see her. And so did you, Mike.

MIKE: What? What do you mean you did see her? What are you talking about?

KEVIN: Mike.

MIKE: What do you mean "Mike." WHAT THE HELL?

KEVIN: We were gettin' back at the cop, right?

MIKE: You are saying you knew it was her? You saw it was a lady, man? Why didn't you tell me?

KEVIN: I thought you were jokin' around, man. I thought you could see.

MIKE: No!

20   KEVIN: We messed him up good, man.

MIKE: I don't give a fuck about that, Kevin.

KEVIN: You know and I know we followed her here. Mike.

MIKE: I'm tellin' you I didn't see her. I can't see without my glasses, man. I thought she was an animal.

KEVIN: We only meant to scare her, Mike. We didn't mean to kill her.

MIKE: But we did kill her. We shot her. YOU shot her.

KEVIN: We shot her. Right through the heart.

MIKE: *(pushes* KEVIN *to ground)* Why didn't you say nothin', asshole. Why didn't you fuckin' say nothin'? You want to end up in fucking Millhaven?[3]

30   Do you know what that fuckin' place is like? It's a rat's fuckin asshole, man, it's worse than any fuckin' hell in any fuckin' bible. I heard stories, man, see what happened to Kendal? Kendal got knifed in three days man, the place is a fuckin' hellhole. I'll kill you man, I'll fuckin' kill you if we get sent down. *(*MIKE *unpins* KEVIN)

KEVIN: Mike.

MIKE: What?

KEVIN: Do you feel it?

MIKE: What?

3 maximum security prison, Kingston, Ontario.

KEVIN: The rush.

MIKE: That's the devil, Kevin. That's the devil, shakin' your hand.

SCENE 15

(*JACK walks along the trail, pointing the flashlight in various directions.*)

JACK: (*passing close by* ANNIE) Annie? Annie? Annie?

SCENE 16

(*EVANGELINE is getting into her waitress uniform.*)

EVANGELINE: I like working the graveyard shift at Fran's. Because it's quiet. And people who come in, mostly just want to think. They have scrambled eggs and toast with butter, ice cream and chocolate sauce, macaroni and cheese. And always coffee. They always have their coffee. With cream. With sugar. They are very much alone. I can see it in their eyes. Looking down. Smoking. Lately I been thinkin' about things. Last things. Many people say they don't believe in God or life after death or heaven or hell but I have seen God. I have seen God in the deep brown eyes of the smoking people who ask for rice pudding at three forty-five in the morning. The Indians, teasing me, "Hey Apple," whatever that means, watching me.

And I have seen hell in their raw dirty hands. The boy prostitutes from Grosvenor Street. Talking. Together. Lookin' around the room, never resting. Smoking. Joking around with me. Want fries. Jesus Christ. In their voices. The way their voices sing. In the way their hair falls over their eyes. Sons of God. I touch their shoulders, sometimes. And in those times, I know … I know … that … I have seen…

(*KEVIN starts taking ANNIE's dress off.*)

I hope Patty's working tonight she always has the best stories. She's got this great big family out in Etobicoke, like six brothers and sisters and fourteen cousins and her mother and father and they have these big, funny dinners. And the way she tells it, she keeps saying everything is "so fabulous" and "so hideous" and she is just so funny.

And every time after she tells me a story I think it's that much more possible that when I get home…

SCENE 17

(*Night trail with* KEVIN *beside* ANNIE's *body.* MIKE *is watching in shock as* KEVIN *takes dress off the body.*)

MIKE: I don't fuckin' know you man.

(*MIKE picks up his gun and exits.* KEVIN *finishes and stuffs the dress into his jacket.*

Sound of owl. JACK *walks into clearing.*)

JACK: (*off, shouting*) Annie?

(*KEVIN hears him, takes off, and hides.*)

JACK: Annie. Oh my God.

(He walks over to her. He kneels, he shakes her. He tries to give her the kiss of life, sees she is dead. He sees the bullet holes. He puts his coat over her. He picks her up.)

JACK: Annie!

SCENE 18

JOE: I was there. At the table, in the kitchen. Sittin' on the boarder's knee. About to eat my pepper and egg. When I saw my father killed by his own brother. Shot through the heart. With the gun from the garden. They'd had to dig up my mother's climbing yellow roses to get it, it was hid, ya see, under the roses. They had dug it up from the ground to scare some Irish fellows that were botherin' them at all hours, askin' for whores and for whisky. My uncle, he was sittin' at one head of the table, across from my father, and he was cleaning the gun. My mother, she says "get the *pistola* offa my table." My father he tells her, "be quiet" and he and my uncle they are joking around about this and that and boom. My father falls back. Blood. Spraying out of him. Over the walls. Over me. Her face. She falls to her knees. And she cries: *"America Bella, se abbandonare ah meeeeeeeeee!"* I still hear her sometimes, just outta nowhere, I'll be bringing home a bag of groceries from Fiesta Farms, or walkin' to the bus up on Dupont...

SCENE 19

(On the trail. Dawn. MIKE is sitting, drinking. We hear the sound of KEVIN's snowmobile and we see the beams of its headlights. KEVIN enters, the headlights lighting his way.)

KEVIN: Beautiful night. Clear.

MIKE: Kev?

KEVIN: Yeah, Mike.

MIKE: What was that ... shit you said ... before you ... shot her? That fuckin... "Ek skal" ... what was that?

(KEVIN laughs.)

KEVIN: English teacher back home. Fag. Used to buy me cigarettes, CD's, down jackets, whatever I fuckin' wanted. Knew all these, like, ancient languages. Said I woulda been Norse, like a thousand years ago. Took me hunting. Deer. Taught me how to say *"Ek skal skjota ther huorti geognum,"* "Let's shoot her man, right through the heart." You like that?

MIKE: I'm turning myself in.

KEVIN: What?

MIKE: To the O.P.P.[4] First for the stolen sled. And then for the manslaughter.

KEVIN: WHAT?

MIKE: You can't stop me, man.

4 Ontario Provincial Police.

KEVIN: I'll fuckin' stop you, Mike.

MIKE: Kev, look. It was an accident. These things happen all the time up here. My uncle, he got shot in the Kap[5] — I'm gettin' married for Christ sake, Kevin. I don't want this on my conscience. Kev. Come with me. If we own up we get manslaughter at the worst. That's nothin'.

KEVIN: You're not gettin' out of these woods, Mike. I got things goin' on, things — waitin' on me —

MIKE: Don't play asshole with me, Kev. I can beat your ass.

KEVIN: Oh yeah?

(MIKE *moves to* KEVIN *who then points his rifle at* MIKE.)

KEVIN: I couldn't take the green paint, man. In the jail. All the jail's a kind of green to make you sick to your stomach, never seen another green like that to make you feel less than a piece of shit crawlin' with maggots, they'll put me in with the Jamaicans again man, cause they hate me, the cops already hate me; living with that green, a kind of green that gets into your mouth, turns all your food rancid, I'm not livin' in the green again, not because of your fuckin' conscience.

(KEVIN *shoots him.* MIKE *is felled. As he dies,* KEVIN *talks to him.*

During the following speech, the Northern Lights appear in the sky, lighting up KEVIN *and darkening him, flashing across his face and body.*)

KEVIN: Mike, I'm gonna tell you about the greatest sled of my life. My ride through the Northwest Territories. It was this friendship thing I was hired on: promotional. I replaced the guy who owned the Bombardier[6] dealership I was workin' in Thunder Bay, you know Pierre, he was sick, right, he knew I was keen and he seen how I handle a sled, so he sends me on this fuckin' ride. First off, everything you have heard about the toughness of pullin' off a ride in the interior of NWT is totally true. On the other hand, it happens to be the most beautiful place on this earth. From the Bering Strait to the tundra there it's like nothing you've ever seen, Mike. And all that wind, and snow and nothin' like nothin' for miles and miles and no trees and you are, well, very much alone. But you're not, Michael, you're not really alone, right? Cause come nightfall, you'll be sittin' there, and … Mike? (*pulling out his hunting knife*) have you ever seen…?

the lights?

You know, (*drawing his knife across* MIKE's *throat*) the Northern Lights?

(*Northern Lights on* KEVIN, *as* MIKE *dies.*)

ACT TWO

SCENE 1

(*The North. Under music.* KEVIN *is running, breathless, away from the scene of his crime, on the trail. A light and music change.* KEVIN, *with his bag, is in*

5 Kapuskasing area of northern Ontario.
6 maker of the original Ski-Doo snowmobile.

Toronto, walking up Clinton Street, searching for his house. The ghost of his mother appears, full of sadness, for she senses what horror is to come.)

MOTHER: Kevin. Oh Kevin. I remember the day you were born. My water broke on the Bathurst streetcar, goin' down Bathurst to Queen, and there I was, stretched over the back seat; my waters gushing out of me, pouring out, like a fast stream, over everybody's boots and shopping bags. Well when the car stopped at Queen I somehow got off, crossed the street, everyone staring, staring at me and into Galaxy Donuts. The front of my dress is soaked and I'm there with the donuts. The chocolate sprinkle, the sugared, the iced, and smell of coffee overpowering and BOOM I pass out and the next thing I know you're crowning and the nurse said she said she said "would you like to feel your baby's head?" and I reached down and then I pushed and I pushed and whoooooooo there you were, Kevin, all wet and blue and bloody and they put you on my tummy and oh my goodness you had such a wise little face. I have never forgotten your wise little face. Kevin? Ohhhhhh Kevin. Please — *(disappearing)*

(KEVIN walks up the street and stops in front of her house. He stares at the house. He looks at the next house. EVANGELINE calls out.)

EVANGELINE: Um Excuse me? Hello?

(He turns.)

EVANGELINE: Are you looking for somebody in particular? I uh — know the neighbourhood pretty well.

KEVIN: Yeah. Yeah I am.

(He searches in his bag for a notebook with the particulars written on it. He finds it and reads her name.)

KEVIN: I'm lookin' for a — uh — a woman called Evangeline Melnyk? The street number got blurred, right? But the name, I can read. Is there anyone of that name who lives around here? Or did? With her mother, name of — Crystal — ? But, then, the mother, I was told she passed away sometime last year, so this Evangeline, she would be livin' alone now. If she was still here.

(She is in shock so he doesn't see a response in her face.)

KEVIN: It must be other side of Bloor then. Okay, *thanks* for your *help*, have a good day!

(He heads down the road. She lets him go till he is almost out of sight.)

EVANGELINE: Kevin?

(He turns, slowly. They look at one another. They know. During JOE's speech, they slowly make their way inside.)

SCENE 2

(JOE is at the grocery store. We see the fruit and vegetable stand. He calls in to the owner, and then walks home.)

JOE: *Grazie, Vincente! Ciao!* (*he starts his walk home*) I don't read Italian and I don't write Italian. But I can speak it. Pretty well. I grew up speakin' it. To my mother. To the fella who ran this store. To a couple of neighbours. To everyone else, I spoke English. You have to bury all that. Once you're here. In Canada. My father, Carlo, he arrived at Union Station in 1909, all by himself. He gets off the train and he leaves the station and he walks up Yonge Street. What else is he gonna do? He sees a man selling bananas, he goes up to him he says "*Paesano*, can you tell me where I might get a room, and a job." The guy sellin' bananas he's Calabrese, and he tells him he can work on the railroad for 7 cents an hour, or sell bananas, then he asks my father if he has a gun, a *pistola*, and my father says "Yeah," and then the guy says to him "Bury your gun." Like, in the garden. He tells him if the cops catch you with a gun, you're on the next boat back.

I speak Italian when I get together with my brothers and sisters, you know, a mix of Italian and Canadian, I speak it to old Annunciata, down the street. But to tell you the truth, I'm always behind, translating, back into English in my head. So I guess I don't really speak it. My children, they don't speak it at all.

SCENE 3

(*In the sitting room.*)

KEVIN: Until a few months ago, I thought I'd never been to Toronto. I thought I was born in North Bay and I thought Diane was my true mother.
EVANGELINE: Kevin. Oh Kevin.
KEVIN: So she's in hospital with cancer last year and she calls me to her bedside and she tells me that she's not my mother at all. She says she had been my babysitter and she had stole me away from my home in Toronto when I was four years old. At first I thought she was delirious, right? With the morphine, eh? I didn't think nothin' of it.
EVANGELINE: It's true. She stole you away from us Kevin. We nearly died of it, the whole city was lookin' for you, flowers on our porch every day, hundreds and hundreds of cards, the police, the whole city —

(KEVIN *goes into his backpack and pulls out a wind-up music box from home.*)

KEVIN: (*winding the music box*) Then I had to be in T.O. on business. And ... I found the name and address she gave me, right? So I thought I'd check it out.

(*He gives it to her. It plays.*)

EVANGELINE: Oh Kevin. I've been waiting for you for so long.
KEVIN: I'd forgotten about you. And my real mother. Everything. Because I was so young ... when she ... fuck. This is fucking...

(*An awkward silence.*)

EVANGELINE: And Diane, did she — Was she — ?

(He sees EVANGELINE *is wondering if he was ill-treated. He was, so he can't answer.)*

20 KEVIN: Huh? Yeah … What are the — uh — balloons and that for?

(He is starting to get edgy, looking through the curtain out into the street, nervous that cops might have followed him.)

EVANGELINE: Just — your birthday.
KEVIN: It's not — Oh yeah?
EVANGELINE: March 27th. Didn't — ?
KEVIN: No. She didn't.
EVANGELINE: You're twenty-four, right?
KEVIN: Yeah. Today. I guess.
EVANGELINE: I always wished you Happy Birthday. Every year.
KEVIN: Cool.
EVANGELINE: You're shaking. Kevin? What's the matter?
30 KEVIN: Crashed. Snowmobile. White snow, dark, and —
EVANGELINE: What, a moose? A deer? Kev? You crashed into a moose?

SCENE 4

*(*JOE *is working in his garden. Sound of a car driving up to the back. Door slamming.* JACK *walks along the side path to the front of the house, with luggage. He ignores* JOE *and carries the luggage up the front steps.)*

JOE: Jack. How was your holiday? Still got snow up there?

*(*JACK *just stares.)*

JOE: Everything okay? Jack?

*(*JACK *appears frozen. He tries to get his keys.)*

JOE: I got your papers, if you want 'em. You forgot to cancel. I know what that's like, I'm forgetful too. Where's Annie?

(Sound of robins.)

JOE: Oh listen to that. First robin. First robin of the year.
JACK: There uh … there was …

(Silence.)

JACK: I didn't know how to give her the kiss. If I'd known how to give her the kiss, she would be alive today.
JOE: Oh my God.
10 JACK: They go into the woods. For deer meat. They're jittery, they been drinking, they been there for days, nights, seen nothing. They see a shape. They shoot. Guy told me it happens a lot up there. People get shot. Mistaken for deer, usually. Should never go walking at night. I told Volker he should have put up a sign. It's very dangerous in the woods up there. Annie thought, people think it's like a … conservation area so

they are safe. They think because they are in the woods, in their own country, and there is a warm fire back at the lodge, they are safe. They're not safe.

(JOE *nods.*)

JACK: There was ... the poacher, he has something of hers, her dress, her red.... I am going to find him, if I have to spend the rest of my life doing it, Joe. I am going to find him and I am going to tear him apart.

JOE: *Si abbandonare ah me.*

JACK: What?

JOE: I said if there's anything we can do, please, just let us know. I mean that, Jack.

JACK: Yeah uh thanks. I don't exactly ...

(*Silence.* JACK *goes into the house.*)

JOE: (*an echo of* CARMELLA) *Si abbandonare ah me.*

SCENE 5

(EVANGELINE'*s house:* KEVIN *crouched on the floor of his room stares at* ANNIE'*s dress hanging there. In his underwear, he sits on a diagonal from the dress in the corner, shivering. He puts on the dress.* EVANGELINE *is calling to him while she makes dinner:*)

EVANGELINE: You know what, guess what? I was thinkin' we could start like a business?

(ANNIE'*s ghost appears. She is a little wonky, as this is her first visit back to her home and neighbourhood since her death. She moves slowly. She stares at her home with longing, and she turns and sees* EVANGELINE. *She sees the horror* EVANGELINE *faces, and she reaches for her to give her the strength on her journey.*)

Cause like I know the ladies at the bank of Montreal up at Christie and Dupont really well, they're really really nice to me, especially Gloria. (EVANGELINE *becomes aware of* ANNIE'*s presence and stops talking for a moment.*) I think if we saved up my tips from Fran's, and you start workin soon, we could save up and then go and ask 'em for a loan and then just start up our own business. I was thinking maybe a bed and breakfast. After all we have the house, it's paid for. It's got the six bedrooms. Alls it needs is well, quite a bit of work, but we could do a lot of it ourselves, hire some students, and ...

(EVANGELINE *looks directly at* ANNIE'*s ghost, and she knows something has happened. She is deeply shaken.*

In his room, KEVIN *is putting on* ANNIE'*s dress. It is very clingy, sexy. He looks in the mirror, terrified.*

EVANGELINE *walks almost in a trance outside to* JOE, *who is standing on his porch.*)

EVANGELINE: What happened? Did something happen? To Annie Delaney?

JOE: A poacher. In the woods. Shootin' after deer. A terrible accident.

(She stands, leaning against the porch, in shock.

ANNIE's *ghost appears as* KEVIN's *reflection in the mirror.)*

SCENE 6

*(*JACK's *place. He makes some calls.)*

JACK: Yeah, Hello, is this The Bay credit office? I'm calling about my payment? Just to let you know that my cheque is in the mail, I put it in Friday. Yes, okay.

(He lays out some clothes for ANNIE *in her coffin. He lays out a red dress and shoes in the image of her body on the floor.*

Meanwhile, KEVIN *has heard from* EVANGELINE *about* ANNIE. *He looks out his window at* JACK's *house. He initially thinks of leaving, but decides he would like to stay. In the danger.)*

JACK: Yeah, can I have the number of the Bank of Montreal on Dupont and Christie. Hello. Yeah is Gloria there. Gloria. It's Jack Prevost. Fine fine how are you. Yeah. I was phoning about locking money in that high yielding account because my wife she she is in the morgue, on a cold in a cold her body is on / her heart isn't beating / a slab they are cutting / the coroner / her blood isn't running/ is cutting to see the insides how the insides she isn't even thinking her quiet thoughts her quiet quiet —

(He drops the phone.)

SCENE 7

JOE: *(to audience)* I ran; when he was shot and I ran out the door and for blocks and blocks all the way over to Yonge Street, where I found myself by the movie theatre, with the celluloid they used to throw out, after the show, I picked it up, rolls and rolls of it, put it in my pocket and I held it to the sun, so I could watch it burst into flames, it always calmed me, doin' that, I sat on the curb and held it and I watched as the fire flamed and then travelled around and around and into my pocket and fwoof I was fire, burning, red, my father, blood, spraying hot, hot and like it was like it — snowed, and white, holy white surrounded me, and it was white and it was quiet and there was only the smell of sweet bread. And then I passed out. In and out, in a cloud of white flour. Because the baker next door, he had seen me, on fire, from his window, where he was pounding dough, and he had run with a giant bag of flour and emptied it over me, over the fire, and surrounded me with his sweet-smelling arms.

SCENE 8

*(*EVANGELINE *with a candle lit for* ANNIE. *She prays and cries.* KEVIN *watches her silently.)*

KEVIN: I know what you're goin' through. I lost people too. Blurry snowfall, can't see too well. I'm walkin' towards this figure I seen, on the ice, on the lake, hearing the wind, the figure don't move. I get closer and I see it's a man. It's a frozen man. His hand, like, out. Stretched. He doesn't look human any more I'm tellin' you. And I'm just starin' at him and then I hear, like a breath. And his, one of his eyes, like was lookin'. At me. He's alive. And I look over into the bush and I see his sled crashed, and I walked up real close and I breathed my hot breath onto his face, to try to … he breathed in some air one more time and then his eye went dead like the other one and he was just froze. He was the frozen man.

EVANGELINE: When someone's dead they're dead forever. So long…

(KEVIN goes to her and comforts her.)

KEVIN: Hey now, don't cry. Don't cry.

(His actions become sexual. EVANGELINE breaks away.)

EVANGELINE: What are you doing? Kevin, what are you doing?
KEVIN: Givin' you some brotherly love.
EVANGELINE: It's not right.
KEVIN: Uncut nine inches, babe.

(EVANGELINE throws him across the room. She is very strong.)

EVANGELINE: You are my brother. And you're in shock. That's all. You're not right because of your crash. So I will forgive you this once. But you must never ever ever do this again. You musn't ever.
KEVIN: Harsh me out why don't ya.
EVANGELINE: We're brother and sister.

(KEVIN approaches her.)

EVANGELINE: No!

(She slaps him. KEVIN moves away from her and sits down, crying.)

EVANGELINE: It's not right. It's not right for you to talk to me like that.
KEVIN: Not right, not right. Nothing's been right since she took me away from you, my whole life, nothing. I should just go and fuckin' die. That's what I'm gonna do, I'm gonna fuckin' walk right down Bathurst Street into the lake and I'll be outta your way and bother you no more.

(KEVIN puts on his coat and goes to leave. She tries to stop him.)

EVANGELINE: Kevin please.

(He goes to leave again.)

EVANGELINE: Kevin.

(He comes back in. He undoes his jeans and rubs himself against her breasts until he ejaculates. [Whether this is seen or not is optional.] He then holds her tightly. She is confused. KEVIN moves away.)

KEVIN: Anyways, don't worry about it. It's not like we have the same father.

(She looks at him amazed.)

KEVIN: Well, look at your hair. Look at your hair, and then look at my hair. Oh, by the way, I been lookin' over our accounts? And we gotta get you makin' some cash.

SCENE 9

(The North. ANNIE *walks very close to* EVANGELINE, *and gives her solace with a touch or a look. The following speech is in reaction to what has happened.)*

ANNIE: I am a silent woman. That is what they say about me. When they have to say something about me. Oh, Annie, she's … quiet. When she's not on stage, singing her quirky songs or telling her strange stories she is … quiet. Jack, he really liked my silences. That's why he married me.

When I was a child, I would lie in my bed and hear the voices of my parents fighting, underneath me, night after night. All their words like a claw in my chest; I would go for days without talking, days and nights and days and there was only one place I found peace and that was … under my dear grandmother's skirts. A kind of chapel, there. Blossom was her name, her real name was Catherine but they called her Blossom. It was dark and fragrant under there, 4711 I think, lemonish scent, and I loved to look at her veiny legs. Beautiful blue worms. Tea and toast. Sweet wine. Falling asleep, together. She lived with us, she spent her time looking out the window, and doing watercolours of birds, and my mother was always exasperated with her. "Mother, will you just get OUT of my kitchen?" "Mother, do you need to go to the toilet?" When she fell and broke her hip, she was moved to a home for the aged. It smelled of Phisohex[7] and creamed corn. The look on her face, when we left her there, on a cold autumn morning, sitting on her designated bed. She held onto her coat her brown coat and the look of … there is no word; I stood there, treachery, looking at the floor. A few weeks later, my grandmother walked out of the home with a razor blade she had stolen from one of the old men and into the Rosedale ravine and she cut her wrists and she walked and walked through the brown and yellow leaves and she turned in circles and then bowed, deeply, I think.

*(*ANNIE *grabs the curtain behind her, or an imaginary dress and wraps herself in it.)*

Ahhhhhhh! Ohhh there she is. Waiting for me. Huge. With her big skirt……
This silence is perfect.
This is silence exquisite.
This is …

SCENE 10

*(*EVANGELINE *in a nightie, remembering. Her mother's ghost is there, and speaks, slightly drunkenly.)*

MOTHER: Oh babe you woulda loved Nathan. He was a dreamer, like you, always … tellin' me his funny stories in that deep sexy voice, wearing that tall black hat, with his black glossy hair, long: Him and me we made

7 antibacterial soap.

this seafood soup with the, the shrimp and the whitefish and after we lay in the backyard under the lilac tree…

(*EVANGELINE walks over to JOE's porch and checks to find him rocking in his chair.*)

JOE: Everything okay?

EVANGELINE: I couldn't sleep.

JOE: Nope. Me neither.

EVANGELINE: Joe. Do you mind if I ask you something?

JOE: Go right ahead.

EVANGELINE: Did you know my father?

JOE: Sure, I knew Bert, when he was around. Worked up at the TTC.[8] Nice fella. Till he took to the bottle. But that's not his fault, really.

EVANGELINE: And Bert was my father. My real and natural father.

(*JOE is silent.*)

EVANGELINE: Joe? Do you know anything that I don't know?

(*Silence.*)

EVANGELINE: Joe? I always knew I looked well not like my mother and father but I figured I must be some you know, genetic throwback to like an Indian or Spanish great grandmother, somethin' like that; my mother when she was drinking she used to say something about … a man named Nathan?

(*Silence.*)

EVANGELINE: Joe?

JOE: There was a guy. Used to come around. Before she married Bert.

(*Silence.*)

EVANGELINE: Did she have me before she married Bert? Joe, please, just tell me the truth.

JOE: Bert, he didn't seem to mind. I always figured she had told you.

EVANGELINE: No.

JOE: I don't think she told the guy neither.

EVANGELINE: His name was Nathan?

JOE: Yes, yes I think it was. He was a nice enough fellow. Tall, with the long hair, an Indian fellow I believe. You know, Canadian Indian.

EVANGELINE: Indian? Oh my goodness. Indian?

JOE: He said … somethin' about he was teaching book writing at George Brown.[9] He had a couple of books you could buy in the bookstores. And your Mom she was going for the cooking, to become a chef. She brought him home one night. I could hear the two of them laughing from two blocks away. Your mom told me they stayed up all night cooking and laughing. Oh he brought out the woman's laugh. She stopped laughing when she married Bert.

8 Toronto Transit Commission. 9 George Brown College, Toronto.

EVANGELINE: Nathan was my father.

40 JOE: I think that's what your mom told Essie.

EVANGELINE: (*touching her hair*) And you say he was Indian? Joe?

(*They sit in silence.*)

SCENE 11

JOE: After he was killed, my mother became nervous. She was nervous of me. Second son. Because she blamed me. Second son. For the shooting. She thought my playing with the pepper and egg distracted my uncle, caused him to shoot off the gun. And kill my father. Second son. The way she looked at me when he fell … it is a look — I wish I had never…

SCENE 12

(*EVANGELINE and KEVIN walking down the street. She wears spiked high heels that he has given her.*)

KEVIN: Beautiful. Remember: smile, talk nice.

EVANGELINE: I don't know what to say.

KEVIN: Don't say nothin'. I'll say.

EVANGELINE: Only for a couple weeks, right? Just till we get up the money for the roof.

KEVIN: You're wobbling.

EVANGELINE: I am not.

KEVIN: Don't fucking wobble. If you wobble you won't get the fucking job.

EVANGELINE: Well maybe I don't want the job, you bad-breath pimp.

10 Whoremonger. (*as KEVIN walks away*) I'm sorry. I'm sorry okay, your breath is fine, I didn't mean it.

KEVIN: You're tryin' to make me feel bad, aren't you?

EVANGELINE: No.

KEVIN: Don't try to make me feel bad, Evangeline, I'm just tryin' to keep us alive here. Okay? Let me tell you something: There is only one thing in this world I ever ever did that I feel bad about and that is —

(*JOE appears on his porch.*)

EVANGELINE: (*cutting him off*) Kevin. C'mere, I want you to meet somebody.

(*They move to JOE's porch.*)

JOE: Hello. Good morning.

EVANGELINE: Joe? I would like you to meet my brother Kevin. Again.

20 JOE: Kevin. It's a huge pleasure. And a very big surprise. Ev told me this morning on the phone and I almost fell to the floor! I remember you very well indeed. You would climb up our stairs and you would stand in front of the door and say "Open." "Open." Curly blonde hair. Essie would say "That kid is too cute for words." She'd laugh.

KEVIN: A long time ago.

JOE: "Even the fox must sleep," that's what Essie would say when we seen you sleepin' on the porch.

KEVIN: Oh yeah?

JOE: Well you've made your sister very happy.

30 KEVIN: That's nice.

JOE: Gonna stay for a while? Get some work?

(*JACK enters onto his porch for a breath of air.*)

KEVIN: I'll stay for a while.

JOE: It's good to have you back.

KEVIN: Even the fox must sleep.

(*JOE waves to JACK. When KEVIN sees him we hear the sound of the bullet that killed ANNIE.*)

KEVIN: C'mon, we gotta go.

(*EVANGELINE and KEVIN leave.*)

JOE: Bye now.

(*JOE watches EVANGELINE wobble up the road. This reminds him of the past. JOE's mother, CARMELLA, comes up the road with a shoe in her hand and a broom.*)

CARMELLA: Joe.

JOE: Mama!

CARMELLA: I told you not to go climbing fences and playing rough. We can't
40 afford another pair of shoes. What are you trying to do?

JOE: Ya can't get me a pair of shoes?

CARMELLA: We can't afford nothing. We can't afford a loaf of bread for the ten of us, Joe. You know that. You do this on purpose, to make me cry, don't you, you bad, bad…

(*She hits him with her broom.*)

JOE: Ask the priest, Mama. The priest always helps us.

CARMELLA: I canno go that priest again, Joey. I canno do that.

JOE: Mama. Please. What am I going to wear?

(*She is silent.*)

JOE: Mama.

(*CARMELLA takes off her Depression-era widow shoes and presents them.*)

50 CARMELLA: You will wear my shoes to school.

JOE: But Mama, I can't. I can't wear your shoes.

CARMELLA: If you want shoes so bad, you wear my shoes. Put them on.

JOE: No.

CARMELLA: Put them on.

JOE: NO.

(CARMELLA *hits him hard. He cries and slowly puts the shoes on. He is totally humiliated. They are way too big. He walks, with difficulty, across the stage. His mother is very upset for him, but cannot show it.*)

SCENE 13

(JACK *dusts the house for fingerprints. They come up very clear. He spots* ANNIE's, *and puts his hand on her prints. If the theatre is unable to do this just drop it.*)

SCENE 14

(*Funeral music.*)

JACK: Thank you all very much for coming. Annie and I used to place bets who'd get a bigger turnout at their funeral. It's clear she's the winner. Annie, I'll pay you later. Ummm, Annie, she was afraid of getting old. And now she never will be getting old. (*Long pause.*) I don't know if you heard this already or not. Anyway, I wanted to play it.

(ANNIE, *the ghost, appears. Song: "My mother and father."*)

ANNIE: my father and mother
    are getting old
    I and my brother
    were sad when they sold
10   our old house
    with its sagging porch
    and kitchen mouse
    and view of the forks
    of the Credit River
    we were puppies biting at their heels
    now they are old
    don't finish their meals

    They were big bright so perfect
    now they are old
20   not as happy somehow
    not as quick
    not as clean
    can't sleep very long
    they get up before dawn
    sit in the dark
    Watch the dew
    on the grass
    My mother and father are old
    When I say good-bye after Thanksgiving dinner
30   They have tears in their eyes
    so do I.
    for something lost
    Something lost. And gone.

Am I saying good-bye to ghosts
(*spoken*) oh no.
(*sung*) my mother and father
Are getting old.

SCENE 15

(*JOE's house.*)

JOE: My older sister, Annabella, married young, seventeen, very young, to get away from my mother. Niko, her husband, he was older, in his forties, but he was good to her. The problem was that he couldn't see. He couldn't see. And it was the Depression. Who had money for glasses? And when she was crying in pain with her menstrual cramps, eh? Niko goes to get her medicine. And he thinks he's gettin' like a Alka-Seltzer and he puts the tablet in water and he gives it to her. It was athlete's foot medicine. It killed her in two days. I'm playin' ball in the schoolyard, I refused to go see her in hospital. I didn't like hospitals. Her body looked so stiff. In the coffin. The ring on her finger. Her face ... with the terrible makeup ... her lips and fingernails inky blue.

God forgive me, Annabella.

(*seeing a ball land on his lawn*) GET THAT BALL OFFA MY LAWN. I'M GOING TO CUT IT INTO LITTLE BITS NEXT TIME THAT BALL LANDS ON MY LAWN, YOU HEAR ME? DO YOU HEAR WHAT I'M SAYING?

SCENE 16

(*ZANZIBAR strip club. EVANGELINE as a Mother Superior. JACK walks in mid-dance and stands at the back, electrified by her. She directs most of her dance to him. She throws her garter to him. Back stage: KEVIN is in the dressing room, waiting, watching and notices that she is dancing for JACK. He is enraged. She comes in and covers herself with a bathrobe.*)

M.C.: Let's have a big hand, gents for Sister Fantasia, our Lady of Perpetual Love!

(*EVANGELINE gives KEVIN six twenties.*)

KEVIN: Seen you flashin' that cop out there. I told you to stay away from him, Evangeline.
EVANGELINE: Are you coming home tonight?
KEVIN: If I see you lookin' at him again you know what I'm gonna do.
EVANGELINE: Shall I thaw the chicken? Make some chicken curry?
KEVIN: And another thing. You're not bringing home cash. You gotta show more pussy, I tole ya. Flash a little candy floss.
EVANGELINE: Go to hell.
KEVIN: The house is fallin' down, Evy, we need the money. If we don't start workin' on it, we may have to leave it.
EVANGELINE: (*after a silence, loud*) Ha! Ha! Ha! Ha! Ha! Ha!
KEVIN: What's so funny?

EVANGELINE: This. It's — it's — it's — it's like something out of Charles Dickens. *Little Dorrit*.

KEVIN: What?

EVANGELINE: You know, you comin' back here, forcing me into a life of ... ill-repute ... but you know what? To tell you the truth I love it. I love fancy dancing. EXOTIC DANCING. Takin' my clothes off. I love the griminess of the place and the men's hungry faces I love watching them jack off to the sight of my swaying hips. I'm Lucifer, I'm bringing them light, and I just think it's so funny that you think you're this bad dude and I'm this poor little —

M.C.: And coming up in a few minutes, the pure and lovely Fantasia, guys, she is just getting herself ready for you as we speak...

KEVIN: Are you makin' fun of me?

(She looks at him, kisses him. Aroused, he pursues it.)

M.C. And now ... the temperature rises, the temperature soars. What's happening? Are we moving closer to the sun? Oh no, my friends, we have a furnace here. A furnace named FANTASIA. Gentlemen, please will you put your filthy hands together for Fantasia.

KEVIN: Now you get out there. And remember, your brother loves you.

(She leaves. KEVIN watches her dance towards JACK and shouts.)

KEVIN: ALWAYS!!

ACT THREE

SCENE 1

(JACK, in his dressing gown, remembers. He enters his and ANNIE's living room. She is reading on the couch.)

JACK: I got us a movie.

ANNIE: Oh. What did you get?

JACK: A special movie. You know. Romantic.

ANNIE: Oh.

JACK: I think you'll like this one. The girl ... is very good.

ANNIE: Ohhhkay. If you say so.

JACK: Listen, if you don't want me to put it on, just say so. I just thought something ... erotic might be fun. Help me forget the shitty day I had.

ANNIE: No, no, it's okay. Actually I'm kind of interested.

(JACK puts in the videotape. The porno type of music starts up. They watch. ANNIE is amused at first. JACK is also amused but the amusement turns to arousal.)

JACK: Look at that one. The blonde.

ANNIE: You like her?

JACK: I just think she's good. She's a good actress. I don't know. She really seems to be liking ... all the guys at once. I don't think she's acting. Do you know what I mean?

ANNIE: Hmm.

(They both become aroused. JACK begins to kiss her. They begin to make love in an almost violent way. JACK cannot keep his eyes off the screen, and both times he looks at it he is more violent with her.

Suddenly, ANNIE gets up and covers herself.)

JACK: What's wrong, you okay?

ANNIE: I just ... I just don't feel so well.

JACK: Yeah? What is it.

(The porno music blares.)

JACK: Is it the movie?

ANNIE: No, no, I think I'm getting sick, that's all. I had a headache before.

JACK: Are you sure it's not the movie?

ANNIE: Yeah.

JACK: Okay. Do you want me to get you something? An Alka Seltzer?

(ANNIE shakes her head. He turns back to the movie.)

ANNIE: Would you mind, turning down the volume?

(He turns down the volume but still looks at the screen.)

ANNIE: Would you ... take it out, please? Take it out of the machine. Take it out of the machine.

(He does so. He puts it down on the table.)

JACK: I thought you were enjoying it.

(Silence.)

ANNIE: All those men, crowding around her...

JACK: You shoulda said something. How come you didn't say nothing?

ANNIE: Their faces: dogs.

JACK: Oh come on. You were enjoying it at first. I know you were.

ANNIE: Crowding her.

JACK: But honey, it was what she wanted. She was the one that asked them all...

ANNIE: No.

JACK: Annie.

ANNIE: No.

JACK: Would you relax? It's just a movie. A sexy movie. Sex between consenting adults. What's the big deal?

(ANNIE is silent. She is deeply distressed, JACK doesn't know what to do.)

JACK: There was no violence, I made sure of that. I just thought, something different...

(ANNIE begins an activity she always begins when she goes into one of her silences.)

JACK: Please. Don't go into one of your silences. This is not a good time for me.

ANNIE: I'm going to go — for a walk.

JACK: A walk? At this time of night?

ANNIE: I need a walk. When I return I want it to be out of our house.

JACK: I'll put it out with the garbage tomorrow.

ANNIE: Tonight. Take it out of our house tonight. I'm not coming back till it's out of the house. I'll walk the streets all night if I have to.

JACK: Oh for God's sake.

ANNIE: Out of our house!

50 JACK: Alright. You go for your walk and I will take the movie out of the house. I'll take it right out of the neighbourhood. Will that make you happy?

(ANNIE *slams the door.*)

ANNIE: OUT OF MY HOUSE!

JACK: I want to make you happy, Annie.

SCENE 2

(*The North.* KEVIN *is in the dark. In the woods. In the spot where he killed* MIKE. MIKE *is frozen there, like a statue.* KEVIN *has driven all the way up north. He approaches* MIKE'S *frozen body.*)

KEVIN: Two and a half hours, 120 all the way, Mike. You shoulda seen these bozo's from Quebec playin' chicken with me I pushed em off the road man, they're still waitin' for a tow.

(KEVIN *covers* MIKE'S *body with evergreen boughs as he speaks.*)

KEVIN: I can't believe they didn't find ya, Mike, fuckin' search party probably walked right by you I'm sittin' there down in Toronto thinkin' I gotta bury Mike. He's my best friend in the whole world and I will not have his body torn apart by wolves. Goodnight Michael, I'll be thinkin' about you.

(*He covers him up.* ANNIE *appears behind him, in the same position as she was when he shot her. He faces her.*

He runs away from ANNIE.)

SCENE 3

(JOE *and* EVANGELINE *on* JOE'S *porch.*)

EVANGELINE: Tell me more about my father?

JOE: Well, like I said, he was funny.

EVANGELINE: Funny? How? How was he funny?

JOE: Like TV. Very funny. Make ya laugh out loud kind of funny.

EVANGELINE: Did he talk much about … his people?

JOE: He never said. Well, once he said somethin' about he could never do the sun dance. He didn't have the patience. And he said his mother lived out at some reserve in Manitoba. He'd go out to see her once in a while. I think he said he was of the Cree nation. I think.

10 EVANGELINE: Cree. So that's why I've always felt so — apart from ... Cree? Will I ever know him, Joe?

JOE: You may. You may not.

EVANGELINE: I just feel things are going in a certain way. And there's nothin' I can do to stop them. Like I'm in a sled, right? In a runaway sled goin down a mountain of ice, faster and faster and if I tip over I will break my neck and bones for sure but if I keep going, what's at the bottom, what's at the bottom Joe is the lake. I'll crack through the foot-thick ice in a moment and down into the frigid waters, stopping my heart and my breath...

20 JOE: I know the feeling.

EVANGELINE: My very life is shaken, Joe. If you know what I mean.

JOE: Yeah. I know what you mean.

SCENE 4

(*EVANGELINE's house. KEVIN goes into the bedroom and looks out the window. She wakes.*)

KEVIN: Hold me, baby. Please hold me.

(*She moves to the window and puts her arms around him.*)

KEVIN: I missed you so much. I missed you so fuckin' much.

EVANGELINE: Hardly seen ya in the last few weeks, Kevin. I was gettin' worried.

KEVIN: That cop from across the street — has he been around?

EVANGELINE: Haven't noticed, really.

KEVIN: Just hold me.

EVANGELINE: Steer escaped from the slaughterhouse today. Ran right up the street.

KEVIN: Yeah? Fuck. What ... happened?

10 EVANGELINE: They shot it through the head and dragged it back down the street. Blood all over the street.

(*KEVIN opens the window.*)

KEVIN: Fucking — dogs.

EVANGELINE: You know what he was sayin'? The guy that runs the video store?

KEVIN: What?

EVANGELINE: That the earth is gonna get hit by a comet. Like, soon.

KEVIN: How does he know?

EVANGELINE: The scientists, the astronomers have said, soon. What will we do when that happens? What will we do, Kev?

20 KEVIN: We fill up a needle. And we shoot ourselves into deep dark space.

EVANGELINE: So we won't feel the quaking. The fires.

KEVIN: We don't feel sweet nothin'. Just like that steer. He's not afraid any more. He's not anything.

SCENE 5

(JACK's house. He sitting in the dark, in his dressing gown. He walks over to a table where ANNIE is sitting, doing some translating.)

ANNIE: *(Gaelic) Ghiomar ag fail bhais den ocras in Eirinn.* [Pronounced: Vee a mer egg foil vagh den ocras in Airinn.] We — were — getting death — of the hunger — in Ireland. I want to go to Ireland. To Connemara, to look at the graves.

JACK: Why? What for?

ANNIE: I want to know —

JACK: Who you are.

ANNIE: Yes.

JACK: You and about three hundred thousand American tourists a year.

10   ANNIE: Jack, I want to hear my natural language.

JACK: They hate you over there. They have no interest in you whatsoever. They don't see you as family, they see you as American.

ANNIE: I don't believe it. If I were to meet a Delaney I know it would be … a very beautiful … it would help me, Jack.

JACK: I have absolutely no desire ever to visit France, or even Quebec. Just because my name is Prevost? And my grandfather grew up in Rimouski? I have nothing to do with those people. *Oh tabernaque, je me souviens je suis très* fuckin' *triste* and pissed off that Wolfe *il triumph de Montcalm* on the fuckin' Plains of Abraham and *je suis triste vive le Quebec libre vive le*

20   *Quebec libre* that was my ancestors, on both sides, two generations ago, but that is not me do you ever see me watch the French station? No! No! I am this now, THIS.

ANNIE: I am going to Ireland. In the spring.

JACK: And leave me alone?

ANNIE: I need to go.

JACK: And if I ask you not to?

(ANNIE is silent.)

JACK: If I ask you not to?

ANNIE: And why would you do that, Jack?

JACK: Because … I would worry about you, over there all by yourself. The

30   IRA is everywhere —

ANNIE: The IRA? Why are you LYING Jack you are a LIAR you are not worried about me being shot by the IRISH REPUBLICAN ARMY you are worried about me doing something that has nothing to do with you; the way you were with your girlfriend Jemma; *(she prods and hits him)* you gonna hit me too? Throw me up against the wall and then fuck me up the ass and piss on me the way you did with her?

JACK: *(breathless)* Annie.

ANNIE: You are just like the pathetic husband in the story of the selkie, the half-woman half-seal, terrified his beautiful wife he he stole from the sea

40   would find her seal skin, her true skin because he knows if she finds it then nothing, not children, not love, not any amount of pleading, will keep her from the sea. YOU WANT TO KEEP ME FROM THE SEA.

(She collapses.)

JACK: *(in the present)* Annie, you didn't know about Jemma then, I hadn't told you, this isn't fair, this isn't…

(ANNIE weeps.)

ANNIE: But of course I knew, I knew in — here.

(She pounds her gut.)

50 JACK: I even said I'd go, I said if you feel that strongly about it, let's just … wait till my holidays in August, and we'll go together. What about that? Do one of those walking tour things you like.

ANNIE: No.

JACK: Why not for God's sake? Hey it's quite a sacrifice for me even goin' there, you know I like Trinidad and Tobago, or St. Lucia, I love to lie in the sun I HATE the rain. I mean, Annie, Ireland is just like fuckin' New Brunswick. And who wants to go there?

(ANNIE glares at him.)

ANNIE: You don't understand at all, do you?

(He looks at her.)

JACK: I'm trying to, Annie. I'm really really trying to. I just thought if we went together, maybe —

ANNIE: I need to go alone. And you will have to accept that.

JACK: How long have you been sleeping with him?

ANNIE: WHO?

60 JACK: Whoever it is you are meeting there, Annie. This is classic —

(She laughs.)

JACK: A lot of things are making sense now.

ANNIE: What are you talking about?

JACK: Your coldness. In the last few months.

ANNIE: What?

JACK: Like making love to a fucking corpse.

ANNIE: Go to hell. And fucking burn there.

JACK: You don't make a sound, you don't move. I don't remember the last time you gave me a back massage.

(ANNIE turns away.)

JACK: What is his name? Annie? Who is it? Do you do for him what you
70 haven't done for me in five years?

ANNIE: Jack. First of all, I swear on my life there is nobody else. And secondly, I am your wife not your concubine. NOT your concubine! If I am like a — corpse —

JACK: Worse than a corpse because you lie there and you send out these waves, these waves of like, hatred.

ANNIE: And that hasn't stopped you, has it? Maybe you like that, maybe you like — fucking a dead woman.

JACK: Get the fuck out of here. Go to fucking Ireland and suck your boyfriend's dick dry.

80   ANNIE: Aghhhhhhhh! (*She attacks, they struggle.*)

JACK: Please don't lie to me. If you have any respect for me.

ANNIE: There is no one else. But I have been cold. I've been feeling — very — cold. I feel as though I may never get warm again.

JACK: And may I ask why?

ANNIE: I don't … know. I don't know.

JACK: Okay. Can I take a guess? You've ah … fallen out of — love with me. After twenty years. It's okay, I mean it happens. And I'm not exactly any great catch. You always much preferred the company of your son to my company, the two of you ignore me when he's here, home from college,

90   maybe you're longing for his Daddy, your one night stand from where was it? The El Mocambo?[10] I would just like to know for certain, okay? And once I know, I would appreciate the chance to to to…

ANNIE: Jack, Jack, it's it's listen. It's just sometimes I'm not sure who you are. I hear these rumours about you being a brutal cop, being called *Diablo* by the local kids and —

JACK: So you're saying I'm like a stranger. Like someone you might brush past on the subway. Twenty years wiped out, like that.

ANNIE: I'm going to work on it, I promise, I don't know, maybe if we go away, north to the country —

100   JACK: My brothers said this would happen. They said you were too good for me, too educated, too — swish. I'm a cop from Mississauga with a grade twelve education. They would go "What the hell is she doin' with you?"

ANNIE: No Jack, it's not any of that, believe me, our differences, I love, they kept things electric for so long.

JACK: So what's happened? WHAT has happened?

ANNIE: I have been having this dream. For the last year or so. And I am having it more and more. In the dream, you are walking towards me with an aluminum bucket in your hand. And in that bucket is a rattlesnake. (*makes rattle sound*) And I'm saying "Please, Jack, please don't come

110   closer," (*makes rattle sound*) and you are humming to yourself and you keep approaching … you have this rattlesnake in this bucket and I think the dream it is something to do with I don't know, with me sensing or my body sensing that you have…

JACK: Secrets.

(*ANNIE nods. JACK is silent. He does some cleaning.*)

JACK: Well we all have secrets. Don't we? (*exiting*)

SCENE 6

(*Zanzibar. Music: EVANGELINE does a table dance for JACK. Their eyes meet. They have connected in a way that transcends the grotty environment. She gives him a bracelet.*)

---

10 Toronto nightclub on Spadina Avenue.

SCENE 7

(JOE's *porch*.)

JOE: I risked my life for this country! That's the thing. I was a belly gunner. In a Lancaster. Seventeen missions. It's cold, man, on your belly, you better believe it at 20,000 feet. They were always shooting at us, I shit my pants twice. It's the coldest I ever was in the belly there. Most belly gunners didn't last three missions. Because the Messhershmitt, they wiped us out. And the Night Fighters. I remember this one. We're moving along. And there's a Messhershmitt coming that way, and the other way. Well soon enough the pilot's dead, the second dicky's dead, he was a boy of nineteen on his second mission, and the nose gunner's dead (*taking a moment to recover from the memory*). When the war was over I come back to Toronto. And Eatons, they got signs up everywhere "We want vets." "Vets please apply." Well I went down to apply, with a few of my buddies, other vets. We filled out the application. And under religion, I put Catholic. Because I was. Well all the other vets I knew, they were Protestant. They all got the job, right off. They were called the next day. I didn't get any calls, nothing. I said to one, "I wonder how come I never got called." He looked at me, he says, "You didn't say you were Catholic?" "Well, yes," I says. He says "You'll never get a job if you're Catholic. Not in Toronto. Not in Ontario." So I went to an Anglican priest and I told him my predicament. I told him I wanted to change religions and he was very accommodating. He made me an Anglican. So I went back down, and I filled out the form again. And this time where it said "Religion" I wrote down Anglican. And I got the job the next day. But to tell you the truth, although I was an Anglican, I was still a Catholic. You always are.

SCENE 8

(A *piano bar at night with cocktails*.)

JACK: How did you think up a dance like that? 'Cause that is really exotic.

EVANGELINE: Oh. I don't know. I just got bored with the same old thing.

JACK: So you came up with this?

EVANGELINE: You think it's okay?

JACK: It's ... enchanting.

EVANGELINE: It's a kind of a ...

JACK: What?

EVANGELINE: Nothing.

JACK: No, what were you going to say?

EVANGELINE: Prayer. In a way. You think I'm crazy.

JACK: No, I don't. I think that's cool. I pray too. By driving fast. Seriously. In a chase. Chasin' some guy who's just robbed a bank, or knocked down a kid, hit and run. It's like a prayer.

EVANGELINE: Because the other kind of prayer, on your knees and putting your palms together? And repeating words you learned in Sunday school? Those don't work.

JACK: I know, I used to try it. Please GOD make my brother get run over by a truck so my dad and I can get Swiss Chalet Christmas dinner. Please GOD let the guy not have a gun on him, please GOD let my wife have a heartbeat. It never —

EVANGELINE: You okay? You're trembling, aren't you? Here, let me —

(*She puts her jacket on him.*)

JACK: They should turn the goddamn heat up in here. What are they trying to do, freeze us out?

(*She is silent.*)

JACK: So how do you like the boss, is he okay? I heard this one he doesn't treat the girls so well.
EVANGELINE: No.
JACK: Well … do you … like working there?

(*EVANGELINE laughs.*)

EVANGELINE: You're asking me if I like working there?
JACK: Isn't there … isn't there … anything else that you wanted to do? With your life?

(*She turns to him. There is so much to say that there is not much point in saying anything.*)

JACK: So why do you stay there?
EVANGELINE: You don't understand.

(*EVANGELINE smiles.*)

EVANGELINE: I've seen you. You live in my neighbourhood.
JACK: Where do you live.
EVANGELINE: Clinton just south of Dupont.
JACK: Oh. That's close to me. I'm closer to Follis.
EVANGELINE: You're a policeman.
JACK: Is that bad?
EVANGELINE: Your wife. Annie Delaney. The singer.
JACK: Yeah.
EVANGELINE: "As a hart yearns for channels of water, so my soul yearns for thee."
JACK: Oh you've heard Annie's — (*EVANGELINE nods.*) It's hard at night. (*ANNIE's ghost enters.*) Sometimes I just get up, go out, for a walk. Sit in some all-night donut place. Keep away the thoughts.
EVANGELINE: I know what that's like.
JACK: At work, and at the bar, I can almost forget, you know, distracted. But as soon as I get home.
EVANGELINE: Yeah.
JACK: Get into bed. That bed. It's like … I swear to God I've seen her. In the house.
EVANGELINE: I've seen my mother.
JACK: Yeah?

EVANGELINE: You loved her. Annie Delaney.

(*Silence.* EVANGELINE *nods, smiles.*)

JACK: Annie would have liked you. She would have liked you a lot.

EVANGELINE: I said "Hi" to her a few times on the sidewalk. We even talked about the weather. Our gardens. You think so?

JACK: Yeah.

(EVANGELINE *caresses his face.*)

EVANGELINE: I like those lines from the ends of your eyes.

60 JACK: You do? I hate them. Reminds me I'm getting old. Hey. Am I too old for you?

(EVANGELINE *is embarrassed.*)

JACK: Because I would like to, I don't know. Hang out with you. Go to the Botanical Gardens, you ever been to the Botanical Gardens?

(EVANGELINE *shakes her head.*)

JACK: Oh you'll love the Botanical Gardens.

(EVANGELINE *kisses him. He kisses her back.*)

JACK: Do you mind if I tell you, I find you very beautiful?

EVANGELINE: Me?

JACK: And mysterious. A forest. In winter.

EVANGELINE: No.

JACK: Would you like to dance?

(*He touches her, caresses her.*

The ghost ANNIE *sings. They dance to* ANNIE'S *music. They dance politely, and then more and more sensually.*)

SCENE 9

(*Song: "Morning in bright fall."*)

ANNIE: A morning in bright fall
In Caledon Hills

Maple leaves my bouquet
I had chills

Oh my day (*pause*)
from my lips to my knees
Love (*small pause*)
You were stung by a bumblebee
the ringing of bells
10 Your cheek swelled
as you said (*pause*)

Till death us do part
Clear eyes and clean consciences
Oh when did this start
This painful infection (*pause*)

Of our strong our red heart?

Oh when did this start?
Are, (*tiny pause*) we so far apart? (*pause*)

20 That morning in bright fall
Maple leaves — my bouquet
You were my prince
And now what you say
Makes me sad (*pause*)
Makes me fear

You said you were the sun dear
And I was the sky
But are you the gun dear
I carry inside?
Waiting to fire
30 To kill your tall bride

Oh when did this start
Are we so far apart
Are we so far apart?

SCENE 10

(*Dawn breaks.* JACK *and* EVANGELINE *are on Clinton Street, looking at the stars.*)

JACK: You see that there? That's the North Star.

EVANGELINE: *Keeweetinok Atchak.* In Cree. I'm half Cree.

JACK: Yeah?

EVANGELINE: That star stays still. The other stars, they swirl around but that one stays just still.

JACK: You know it.

EVANGELINE: I studied the stars. The stars and some Cree. Songs, a few phrases. I got books from the library.

JACK: Wow. I like that, I like it that you studied the stars, and the Cree,
10 that's elegant.

EVANGELINE: Your eyes — like a sea of glass.

(*She laughs, and kisses him. From inside,* KEVIN *sees, and, drunk, wanders out.*)

KEVIN: What the hell are you doing, Evangeline?

(*They start and turn.*)

EVANGELINE: You'd better go.

JACK: Who are you? Are you the brother?

KEVIN: Who the fuck are you?

EVANGELINE: Kev, please.

JACK: Jack, pleased to meet you. I'm just walking Evangeline home.

KEVIN: You come near her again and I'll kill you. Now get the fuck off my property.

20 JACK: Is this your house?

EVANGELINE: Kevy please don't talk to my friend that way. He's been very nice to me.

KEVIN: Get offa my property. Fuckin' now.

JACK: Evangeline is an adult, Kevin. And what she does is none of your business.

KEVIN: Evy, get inside.

EVANGELINE: I can do what I want to do, Kev. You can't stop me anymore.

KEVIN: I said GET INSIDE.

JACK: Hey you don't —

> (KEVIN *hits her.* JACK *hits him. They fight.* KEVIN *is trying to escape* JACK *and the fight moves inside, and towards* KEVIN'*s bedroom.* EVANGELINE *tries to stop them, crying "Please." "Stop it." and "Don't." They are there, squaring off, when* JACK *sees the red dress hanging in* KEVIN'*s room. He looks back at* KEVIN, *and back again at the dress. He touches the dress. They freeze.*)

JACK: Annie!

> (*He turns to* KEVIN. KEVIN *laughs.*)

30 KEVIN: We thought she was an animal, man.

EVANGELINE: Kevin?

KEVIN: We couldn't see through the branches. In the dark. It happens.

> (JACK *attacks* KEVIN *hard.*)

EVANGELINE: No. Stop it. Stop it you two. I'll call the cops. Stop it. You're hurting him.

> (*They are fighting,* JACK *is about to kill* KEVIN *by strangling him.* EVANGELINE *grabs the gun.*)

EVANGELINE: Stop it or I'll shoot. I swear to God I'll shoot.

> (EVANGELINE *has a moment of terrible indecision, but then her need for her brother, for family, wins out and she kills* JACK. *The sound of the bullet is naturalistic this time, to avoid comic melodrama. He falls to the ground.* MUSIC *should come in right away.*
>
> KEVIN *gets up, takes the gun, then steals the money out of* JACK'*s pockets and takes off.*
>
> EVANGELINE *has blood all over her hands. She is in shock. She puts on the red dress. She sings a Cree song of lamentation over* JACK'*s body [see music for* "Evangeline's Lament" *at end of play].*
>
> *She walks outside.* JOE *sees her.*)

EVANGELINE: Help me.

JOE: What happened? What happened child?

> (EVANGELINE *staggers down Clinton Street.*)

SCENE 11

> (*Night.* KEVIN *appears out of* JOE'*s front door, rifling through* ESSIE'*s purse and throwing it away.* JOE *is on the porch.*)

JOE: Who's that? Who's there?

KEVIN: Cover your face. Cover your face or I fuckin' kill you.

JOE: My wife is not well. Please don't hurt her. You can have anything you want.

KEVIN: Shut the fuck up, Joe.

JOE: Kevin. What are you doing here? Where's Evangeline?

KEVIN: Where's your wallet? Where is your fuckin' wallet, old man.

JOE: It's okay. Now calm down Kevin, you're welcome to anything you want. It's right here, in my jacket.

10   KEVIN: Okay, now what's your PIN number? Tell me the wrong one, I come back and shoot your fuckin' head off.

JOE: Okay. It's — uh ... 6?

KEVIN: NOW. NOW!

JOE: 6 ... 5, no 4 ... no, 5, 7, 9. Yes, that's it.

KEVIN: 6579.

JOE: Kevin? It's not too late to give yourself up.

KEVIN: Are you tellin' me what to fuckin do? YOU, who sat on your fuckin' porch and watched as I was dragged away from my home only four years old? You sat and you rocked and you didn't do nothing. You didn't do

20   nothing.

JOE: Kevin.

KEVIN: I remember the sound of the chair. The sound of the rocking. I remember it, man. I have nightmares.

JOE: I thought she was takin' you down to Christie Pits, to play on the big airplane. You loved that big airplane.

KEVIN: Bullshit.

JOE: It's God's truth.

KEVIN: Bullshit.

(*KEVIN goes to leave.*)

JOE: Kevin. May God forgive you.

30   KEVIN: Fuck that.

(*KEVIN leaves.*)

SCENE 12

(*Night. Bloor Street. Fruit and vegetable stand. Streetlight shines on it. EVANGELINE is standing still among the fruit and vegetables. We can see Honest Ed's neon signs flashing across the street.*)

EVANGELINE: (*whispers*) Hail Oh Hail Annie full of Grace we are soaked we are soaked in our neighbour's blood my brother and I the Law the Law is with thee. Come to me, I wait here, behind the apples and avocados and oranges sweet, I will wait for you to guide me are you here? Are you —

(*ANNIE appears.*)

EVANGELINE: Annie. Hey. Have you come to smote me down? I wouldn't blame you. I am murder see my hands? *Geen-sa. Ni nipbo* [I have killed somebody. I am death] Soaked in blood His blood —

ANNIE: Evangeline, walk.

EVANGELINE: Walk?

(*ANNIE swings around and points north.*)

10   ANNIE: *Keeweetinok Atchak.* The North Star to the northern star walk you'll reach the dark forest where the air is clear you lie on the moss you will have your baby on moss not a grimy jail floor; clean your baby with clear water not infected jail water you go, and walk and disappear. It happens in Canada all the time, a disappearing woman, nobody minds. Just walk. Disappear.

EVANGELINE: Oh. Annie. Will you ever sing to me again?

(*ANNIE disappears.*)

EVANGELINE: You know my baby? I'm callin' her after you, Annie.

(*EVANGELINE fills her bag with oranges and apples.* KEVIN, *meanwhile, is all over the neighbourhood looking for her.*)

KEVIN: We gotta take off, babe, cause they're comin' after us. There's buses every hour we can be outta here in twenty minutes.

(*She starts to walk up the street.*)

20   EVANGELINE: We are walking.

KEVIN: Walking? (*pausing and watching her walk*) Walking.

(*They walk together into the horizon, up Yonge Street. We see* JOE's *rocking chair, a yellow police ribbon around* EVANGELINE's *house. About halfway through the speech we see* KEVIN *and* EVANGELINE, *in the woods, in a sled or on a stump. He seems to be sleeping, in a sleeping bag beside her. She is heavily pregnant.*)

EVANGELINE: *Tansi niskneeksqueem* [hello my daughter] dear my darling daughter.

Happy eighth birthday Annie Northstar. *Kisageetin ooma* that means I love you, baby, in Cree; the language of your blood I hope this finds you happy and strong. My dear friend Patty is giving you this letter. Patty is your mother now and I know she is tellin' you funny stories and bringing home rice pudding from Fran's for ya, and taking real good care of you. I wanted more than life itself to keep you, love, but I had to send you

30   down to Patty to keep you safe, because I am doomed to walk, forever. And that's no way for you to live. Your feet would get tired. I want you to have school, and friends, and gymnastic classes and all of that. I do not know what lies ahead, on my travels. I know one thing only, and that is that you will see me, in the North Star, because, the North Star, in Cree: "*kewe tinok atchak,*" is always there in the sky, Annie, and guides us.

Nell, whatever people may tell you about your father, I want you to know that what you are is a long summer evening, Nell, Clinton Street, kids playing outside our window my friend Joe cutting his roses, talking with the neighbours, and we lined up barefoot for soft ice cream and

40   Kevin he got a vanilla with hot chocolate dip and I got the warm butter-

scotch and we brought them inside and we sat in the dark and we licked them faster and as the ice cream melted his face melted too, melted along with the ice cream we had no fans, Nell our house was so hot, and the laughing boy was there underneath, that boy who said park and I saw him again and he was gentle and sweet and your father, my love, was not the man but the sweet heavenly child.

Kisageetin ooma, I love you so, *kisageetin ooma.*

SCENE 13

EVANGELINE: Oh I wish I could be near you, Annie, while you read this, touching the lights in your soft hair, wish it were possible but I know that it isn't, for the bone in the air it has broke I am doomed to walk till I cannot walk more till I fall on my knees to the ground till I fall on my —

Kisageetin ooma, I love you so, *kisageetin ooma kisageetin ooma kisageetin ooma*

daughter

Kev? Kev, come on, wake up.

KEVIN: Leave me alone. I gotta sleep.

EVANGELINE: Kevin it's time. We have to walk.

KEVIN: Fuckin' cold, fuckin' wolves, howlin' in my ear —

EVANGELINE: You're going to be fine. Come on.

(They walk together for a while along the trail. They struggle.)

KEVIN: My foot is killin' me, Ev. I can't fuckin' walk no more. Don't make me, don't —

(He falls.)

EVANGELINE: No resting, Kevin. If we rest we fall into the fires! We burn. Forever. Now come on. You can do it. Come on. Stand. Up. Now. One foot in front of the other. Come on.

(She tries to make him walk, like a puppet.)

KEVIN: Have some mercy, woman. Mer-cy. Can't you see I'm dyin' here? I'm goin' blind. Left eye is worse. Everything's startin' to look shimmery. Just the way it happened with the right one.

(He buckles.)

EVANGELINE: Keeeevin!!

KEVIN: And the cold. Ev. I can't take the cold no more, I never felt such cold. This fuckin' country. How come you don't feel the cold?

EVANGELINE: Come on.

KEVIN: Take me home. I want to go home.

EVANGELINE: We have no home! You know that.

KEVIN: Then I'll go to fucking Millhaven. At least there's television there. Regular food.

EVANGELINE: Kevin. Kevin look at me.

30 KEVIN: (*he laughs*) What are you going to do, have the baby out here? In the bush? And then keep walkin' with her? What do you do when it's time to put her in school?

EVANGELINE: I have plans for Annie, Kevin. Annie will be just fine. Now can you please try to walk?

(EVANGELINE *decides to carry him. She lifts him over her shoulder. She sings to him, a Cree lullaby [see music for "Evangeline Carries Kevin" at end of play]. She lifts him onto her back and they climb the hill where* ANNIE *was killed.* KEVIN *wakes, a final burst of energy before dying. He hears wolves.*

The Northern Lights light up the sky.)

KEVIN: Wha's that sound? 'Vangeline, it's the wolves. Oh yes. There they are. In the blizzard, can you see them?

EVANGELINE: Oh, no, my little brother. No! It's something else. Something kind. Yes. *Cheepyuk Neemeetowuk.* They've finally come for us. Oh. Dancing spirits. Yes. They're every bit as lovely as you said, Kev.

(*His breathing has become shallow, quick, as breathing often does before death. The Northern Lights surround them.* ANNIE *sings:*)

40 ANNIE: Oh heavenly time of day…
the fog and the quiet.
The mist, no sun. I move out of my dream and into
this day as
the fog it clears so slowly away to reveal … to reveal…

(*The snowy owl hoots.*)

THE END

Evangeline's Lament for Jack

Evangeline Carries Kevin

INTERVIEW
with Judith Thompson

Q. *Please describe the process by which* Sled *came about.*

A. Sled came about with a few images: the snowy woods, a woman being killed in the snow, alone, from me having stood alone on snowy trails thinking "no one knows where I am, I could be killed by an animal and no one would know"— the idea of a SILENT WOMAN. One of the Australian aboriginal gods has no mouth because she is silent, and so many women I know are virtually silent. Also the image of the red dress includes sexuality, the woman as artist, even our own Maple Leaf flag.

Q. *Can you describe the particularly "Canadian" quality of* Sled? *How does this quality go beyond setting?*

A. The proximity of the wilderness suggests itself. One day we can be face to face with a bear, and the next, on the sixty-second floor of the Bank of Montreal tower. Another strong image is from talking with my neighbour, Carl, about his youth on this street, when it was a cow path. He would tell me how he never had milk till he went into the army, how his dad was shot dead in front of him and his mother had to support nine children with almost no money, how he had to wear his mother's shoes to school. Personal history is history, and Carl's dad came from Italy and that is what Canada is now — diverse. We are far, far from the Loyalist enclave we were. In Annie and Jack, there is a mixing of class, and of course Evangeline, her name borrowed from the story of Evangeline, walking from Acadian Nova Scotia down to Louisiana, after being expelled. In Sled, Evangeline actually being a Cree Woman, is adopted into a white household — the situation in a sense, of the First Nations, with residential schools and pressure to assimilate, and only in the last forty years or so turning back to their language, their roots, and their empowerment. In fact, they carry OUR sins on their back the way that Evangeline carries her half brother Kevin, an evil, pure evil, white man, on her back at the end of the play.

Q. *How would you describe the relationship between character and action in the play?*

A. Character and action — I suppose, yes, all the characters can be defined by their action, or lack of it. I don't know how to answer that one, because in this play fate is a road they are destined to take, perhaps destined by their ancestors, by their programming

Q. *Can you expand on Annie and Evangeline as characters in relation to each other? to men? to social environment?*

A. Evangeline is defined by the act of waiting — waiting for her kidnapped brother to return. She is not even aware of her Cree blood until she is in her twenties.

Annie says "I am a silent woman," and lives through most of the play as a ghost and a memory. She feels most alive while singing her unique poemsongs and at that moment in the play, a memory-scene, in which she is repelled by the violent pornography that Jack is playing and demands that it be thrown out of the house.

Q. *In The Poetics, Aristotle speaks of an emotional pleasure in tragedy that stems from pity and fear, and he links it especially to violence done between friends, associates, and family members. Can you link these observations on tragedy to Sled?*

A. Emotional pleasure? Hmmmmm. . . . Certainly Annie's shooting is terrifying, but what I am in a way showing is that women begin the journey to themselves in a state of being destroyed by the culture. Then there is the operatic moment near the end when Evangeline shoots her lover to protect her brother. She has to make a choice, and she makes the choice she is programmed to make: blood is thicker than water. She waited for him all her life; she cannot accept that he is evil and that her lover will probably betray her.

Q. *Sled involves people getting back to their roots and recovering their heritage. How does this theme operate in the play?*

A. That is who we are. I realized that as an Irish Canadian I knew NOTHING about my heritage. Did my great, great, greats come in the famine? Were they Catholic or Protestant or what? My own ancestral language was almost wiped out by the English, and now I witness the near eradication of many First Nations languages. The question is, do we keep the roots alive, or become something new together? Canada is still very much becoming. We will only know in five hundred years who we really are. Certainly the Queen of England has nothing to do with that. Yet she is still featured on our currency. Why are we fearful of looking to the future? of turning away from the racist colony we once were? It is incredible to me that with the threat of Quebec separation, we STILL have the Queen on the currency, knowing how it must anger the Quebecois, who were basically invaded by the English.

Q. *Sled also involves revenge. Can you expand on the nature of vengeance as action? Energy? Motivation?*

A. I think entire lives are governed by vengeance. Because only in vengeance do we gain back lost power. Humiliation results in vengeance. Otherwise, the one who is humiliated will eventually die in some way. The IRA is vengeance, and independence. All political movements are a blend of the two. WOMEN must be vengeful in a sense, to regain power. And yet, vengeance is sinful from a Christian perspective — does it have to be violent? Is that all we know?

Q. *What about the character of Kevin and his vengeance/violence in the play? Is he programmed to be evil or a victim himself of his environment?*

A. Kevin is radical evil in human form — yes, his kidnapping had something to do with that. But generally, the only explanation for Kevin is that he is a walking reflection of the evil in our culture. He is the ruthless stare of the S.S. who has a gun to the back of your head; he is what is amoral and predatory in all of us. And the worst part is that in some ways this makes him exciting, attractive. After they have killed Annie, Kevin speaks of a "rush" and his friend replies, "that's the devil, shakin' your hand." Evangeline loves him because he is her brother. When she must choose between his life and Jack's life, she chooses to save her brother.

Q. *What does drama and theatre teach to people?*

A. It gives us a look at the subterranean movements in our lives. The subtext of every conversation, how every moment we make a choice, and we perform our very selves, and our culture. It gives us the language of the unconscious, and it celebrates the music of the human voice by itself and in dialogue.

Q. *How would you relate drama to other forms of expression such as fiction and poetry?*

A. Drama is voice and body used to convey the real play which is the underneathness, the subtext. Fiction and poetry, it seems to me, are the text.

Q. *Why is theatre the medium in which you work?*

A.   I work in the theatre because I love the human voice. I see and revel in the hidden emotion, the suppressed thought. I want us all to see the lies we tell ourselves about ourselves, and I live for the stunning electricity of live performance.

Q.   *What, finally, would you want students to understand about* Sled? *about theatre in general?*

A.   *Sled* is a long, operatic dream about the forming of Canada and of the self. And that is what theatre is: a dream of the self.

SHORT FICTION

INTRODUCTION

The daily lives of most people are full of stories, sometimes written down but, more often, not. People imagine, develop plans for a successful day, relate accounts (sometimes true and sometimes embroidered) about what they have done, or gossip about other people. They personalize, modify, and extend stories they have heard or read; retell and sometimes add variations to jokes and anecdotes; read newspaper stories; listen to country and western ballads; watch movies, television programs, and commercials (which are often mini-dramas). They receive some of their religious and political messages in the form of stories included in sermons and election speeches.

The processes of creating, transmitting, and receiving stories are among the most basic human activities. "One wants to tell a story, like Scheherazade," novelist Carlos Fuentes wrote, "in order not to die. It's one of the oldest urges of mankind. It's a way of stalling death." Like eating, sleeping, and breathing, it is a necessary human activity, and like breathing, so natural that we are often unaware that it is occurring. In *Tellers and Listeners: The Narrative Imagination*, the noted British critic Barbara Hardy has written:

> Nature, not art, makes us all story-tellers. Daily and nightly we devise fictions and chronicles, calling some of them daydreams or dreams, some of them nightmares, some of them truths, records, reports, and plans. Some of them we call, or refuse to call lies. Narrative imagination is a common human possession, differentiating us ... from the animals.

The creation of all stories involves the selection and structuring of details that assist the storytellers in achieving their intended purposes. While in the types of stories described by Hardy these activities may be casual and haphazard, in those written as short stories and novels they are usually very deliberate and precise. Authors include only those characters, events, objects, and details that they consider to be necessary for their stories, and they arrange them in artistically satisfying and meaningful patterns. As an example, we know that in their day-to-day lives people spend much time on routine activities such as obtaining, preparing, and eating food. Although some people have transformed them into highly entertaining events, authors describe these only when they are important to their stories in some way: to development of plot and conflict, perhaps, or to portray character.

Some stories make few demands on their readers, offering light entertainment. Others require attentive readers, not only because their characters and themes are more complex and involved, but also because their authors frequently imply, rather than explain, elements of character and theme. Authors may, for example, leave the significance of actions, dialogue, and objects for readers to discover. They may create narrators who are not reliable reporters or interpreters. Moreover, they may present events in other than chronological order or may not supply clear links or bridges between sections of a story.

Readers easily recognize the basic elements of most stories — characters, actions, and settings — and the basic organizing pattern, which is the introduction, development, and resolution of one or more conflicts. An understanding of the varied and complex ways in which both these elements and the pattern of conflict are used by authors, along with an awareness of the significance of such techniques as narrative point of view, symbolism, and irony will bring to readers fuller, richer comprehension of the stories they encounter. Careful attention to these elements is especially important in the reading of short stories, in which authors must achieve their purposes within a limited space, generally a few thousand words. Like lyric poets, to whom they have been frequently compared, they cannot waste words and must make each word contribute to their stories' total effect and meaning.

PLOT AND CONFLICT

Key to many stories are the incidents they contain; readers want to know what happens next and how a story ends. Authors select and organize events and then add details that contribute to the **plot** and lead toward a satisfying conclusion. The plot of a story provides more than factual information about who did what and when; it helps readers understand why these events occurred.

In most short stories, the plot begins with an **exposition** and then is organized around the introduction, development, and **resolution** of one or more **conflicts**. The exposition provides necessary background about characters, settings, and events. Those stories told or narrated in the same order in which the events occurred, or chronological order, usually introduce the conflict near the beginning. The events that follow form the **rising action**, or sequence of actions, leading to the **climax** or turning point, which is the most significant moment in the story. The **dénouement**, or final outcome or consequence of events, and the resolution of the conflict usually follow quickly. "The Naked Man," "Rappaccini's Daughter," and "Bliss" present events in chronological order, helping to reveal both the relationships between actions and the nature of the characters' responses to them.

Many writers use **flashbacks**, interrupting the chronological presentation of events to introduce earlier actions that clarify the immediate present of the narrative. For example, during a Christmas vacation in Mexico, Sarah and Edward, the childless couple in "The Resplendent Quetzal," think about their courtship and unhappy married life in Toronto. By presenting these thoughts, which neither communicates to the other, the author clarifies the significance of their actions during an excursion to some Aztec ruins. While she sits in a bar, the central character in "Too Much to Explain" has several brief, but painful memories of the past while she is trying to extricate herself from a destructive relationship. Other writers use **foreshadowing**, providing clues which hint at significant events that occur later in the story. In "A Rose for Emily," the reasons for the title character's purchase of arsenic are not explained. Only at the conclusion are her motivations and the ironic significance of the notation on the package, "For rats," made clear.

Most readers demand more than an exciting plot to stimulate their imaginations or develop their understanding of themselves and the world around them. This is particularly the case in many modern short stories, where the plot is minimal, there are few, if any, physical actions, and the events may initially appear to be almost trivial. Interest in the motivations of characters and their responses frequently leads to a rereading of such stories. Do they develop during the course of a plot? Do they gain clearer understandings of themselves and their situations? What are the causes of the changes or insights, or the failure to achieve them?

When they change, the central characters, or **protagonists**, often do so as a result of conflicts with one or more of three kinds of opposing characters or forces, often referred to as **antagonists**. First, individuals may be in conflict with themselves. In "Rappacini's Daughter," Giovanni must wrestle with his conflicting opinions about Beatrice, attitudes that reveal more about different sides of his own nature than they do about the young woman. In contrast, the narrator's mother in "Borders" is in conflict with the immigration officials who demand that she declare herself either a Canadian or an American citizen. Her struggle symbolizes that between Native peoples and colonial powers that will not allow the subjects to define themselves in their own terms.

Second, characters find themselves in conflict with those around them — quite often brothers and sisters, parents and children, husbands and wives. Because family conflicts are among the most intense and intimate that most people experience, the frequency with which these occur in stories is not surprising. Often, in quarrelling with those closest to them, individuals are trying to define themselves and to define their positions in the relationships. In "The Naked Man," the members of a family are reunited when the son returns from a year-long trip to Australia. From the parents' surprise over his call from the airport, to the mother's anxiety to get to her hair appointment, to the welcome-home party at which the young man considers himself an outsider, the lack of family cohesiveness becomes increasingly apparent. The reclusive heroine of "A Rose for Emily," the last member of a once-proud and wealthy Southern family, asserts her own status by defying the townspeople, refusing to pay taxes, and flaunting her Northern lover before them. In both "Squatter" and "The Motor Car," young immigrants to Canada find themselves in conflict with the cultures of their new country.

Third, conflict may place the central characters in opposition to natural or supernatural forces. In "The Open Boat," four men attempt to survive a violent storm, while in "The Lamp at Noon," a husband and wife are virtually helpless in the face of drought and dust storms that are destroying their farm. In both stories, characters respond differently to the struggle with nature. While they have little chance of success against the elements, those who display courage and determination, like the Oiler in "The Open Boat," achieve a kind of moral victory.

Most stories present conflicts of more than one type and usually examine the interrelationships between them. In "The Conversion of the Jews," for example, Ozzie seeks to define himself while attempting to deal with the conflicting expectations of his mother, the rabbi, and his peers. The narrator of "Bartleby, the Scrivener," while attempting to understand the motives behind Bartleby's behaviour, is also wrestling with his own opposing attitudes and with the dehumanizing effect of life in New York.

Not all stories conclude with conflicts resolved. In some, the characters confront forces or realities they cannot alter, as is the case in "A Clean, Well-Lighted Place." In others, their own inner flaws do not permit resolution. The narrator of "Why I Live at the P.O." believes she has triumphed over her family by leaving home. Although she does not appear to realize it, it is she who has created many of the situations that have made conditions intolerable at the house, and, in her account of events, she unconsciously reveals that her anger and hostility, the sources of much of the conflict, remain.

CHARACTER AND CHARACTERIZATION

Short stories generally focus on one or two major **characters**. These are almost always **rounded**; that is, they possess the complexities, contradictions, and depths of personality associated with actual human beings. They are distinguished from **flat characters**, whose personalities are presented briefly and in little depth. They may also be **dynamic**, changing during the course of a story. The change may be positive, as it is for Fido in "Inside Passage." At first suspicious and resentful of her cabin mate, Fido reveals her own insecurities and vulnerabilities. However, she is able both to understand and accept the other woman's weakness and to control her own vulnerability sufficiently to declare her new-found love. Character change may also be negative, as in the case of Giovanni in "Rappaccini's Daughter." At first he is merely a naïve young man in a strange city. But the uncertainties he develops about Beatrice are based on his own self-centred concerns, and he must bear a great deal of responsibility for the disastrous outcome of the events.

In some modern short stories, characters are **static**, undergoing no development. Lack of change may be a result of the brevity of a story; there simply may not be the space to portray development. It may also be a reflection of the characters' inability to grow or to develop, or it may represent a thematic and philosophical position that views people as subject to outside forces that they can neither understand nor control. In "A Clean, Well-Lighted Place," for example, the older waiter, who is sympathetic to the old man who frequents the café, does not change as a result of his knowledge of the meaninglessness of life, a condition he cannot change. He merely accepts what is.

At the conclusion of many short stories, one or more of the major characters may experience what James Joyce called an "**epiphany**," a moment of revelation that brings understanding of a character's situation in life. In "Araby," the boy, while standing in the darkness, perceives the truth of his motivations for coming to the bazaar and the nature of his feelings for his friend's older sister. Annie, the narrator of "Fogbound in Avalon," finally realizes that returning to her home town has not helped her to overcome the unhappiness of her adult life.

In presenting characters confronting the conflicts in their lives, authors seldom engage in direct character analysis. Instead, they employ a variety of devices, especially **dialogue** and **action**, that reveal character implicitly. The conversation of the two waiters in "A Clean, Well-Lighted Place" consists of short, often abrupt phrases and sentences that seem very similar in style;

however, the younger man asks a number of questions that reveal his lack of understanding of either his fellow worker or their customer. His partner gives simple answers without elaboration; these are the facts he accepts without questioning or resistance. In "The Naked Man," Dennis's and his parents' attitudes toward his Studebaker car indicate his new and somewhat awkward relationship in his family.

In these stories, the contrasting actions of people in the same situations reveal character. "Bartleby, the Scrivener" and "The Boat" also use this method, and there are many other examples. In the former story, the work patterns of Turkey and Nippers, two copyists for a New York lawyer, represent contrasts that the cautious narrator is able to keep in balance. While each exhibits some extreme behaviours, the fact that their personalities complement each other allows the lawyer to maintain the calmness of his daily routine. However, the arrival of the title character upsets both his routine and peace of mind. The lives of the mother and father in "The Boat" have been tied to the sea since their youth, but each views the attachment and their children's attitude to the sea differently. The father seems to have sacrificed his love of literature to the necessity of fishing; the mother, who has never read a book since high school, sees making a living on the water the natural and honourable thing to do. Not surprisingly, the father is more sympathetic to his daughters' desires to leave; the mother sees their departures as almost a desertion.

Characters' thoughts and statements about themselves and other people also cast light on their own personalities. Their analyses and judgements should not necessarily be taken at face value. Rather, the reasons for them should be analyzed to discover what there is about particular characters that makes them view themselves and other people the way they do. For example, the narrator of "Why I Live at the P.O.," in expressing her negative opinion of her sister, reveals her own insecurity and resentment. In "Bartleby, the Scrivener," the narrator's satisfaction with his occupation and his position in New York legal circles may help to explain why he reacts to Bartleby as he does.

Physical objects, such as possessions or clothing, can reveal character. The items belonging to the dead priest in "Araby" reveal a great deal about both him and the young narrator. The two women sharing a cabin in "Inland Passage" dress differently, a reflection of how they are coping with the events of their pasts. By wearing her best silk dress to travel into the United States to visit her daughter, the mother of the narrator in "Borders" is indicating elements of her character that will become more evident in her confrontation with the officials.

Finally, authors' descriptions of the physical appearance of individuals assist in the delineation of character. Melville carefully describes not only the clothing, but also the faces of the three scriveners in "Bartleby." While Turkey and Nippers are obvious, simple contrasts in looks and behaviour, Bartleby, considered in relation to them, is far more ambiguous. Hawthorne makes careful use of physical description in "Rappaccini's Daughter." Rappaccini's "sickly and sallow hue," his "stooping posture," and his fixity of gaze are all intended to symbolize the negative effects of his intense, almost total preoccupation with his scientific pursuits.

SETTING

Settings of stories, the locations and times in which the actions occur, can be specific social or cultural contexts, such as a character's home, neighbourhood, or place of work; larger, more generalized geographical regions, such as the Canadian Prairies, or the coastline of eastern Florida; specific times of the day or of the year; and historical periods. Even weather conditions may be an important part of setting. In addition to assisting readers in visualizing events, settings provide contexts for the actions and contribute to the delineation of character, the creation of mood, and the development of theme. Settings are frequently symbolic, representing internal emotional states of characters. Readers who interpret settings rather than simply read them literally, who question why authors have selected particular times and places for their stories, will gain fuller understanding of the works they encounter.

In Sinclair Ross's "The Lamp at Noon," set on a Saskatchewan farm during the drought of the 1930s, the use made of buildings, landscape, and weather contributes to the development of the theme. Although the summer season and the time of day should bring both brightness and hope, a three-day dust storm has obscured the sun and blown away the precious topsoil needed to grow crops. The dust settling over everything in the dimly lit kitchen symbolizes the hopelessness the farm wife experiences. In "When Twilight Falls on the Stump Lots," the semi-cleared land midway between forest and farm underscores the implicit clash between the natural and human worlds.

A major setting in many stories is the home of the central character, a place that should represent security, stability, and nurturance. Frequently, characters leave homes that do not possess these qualities. In "The Motor Car," Calvin departs from Barbados because his life there seems unfulfilling compared with the lives of the Canadian tourists who visit the island. He believes that Toronto will be everything for him that his home is not. In "The Naked Man," Dennis expects to return to a place that is emotionally, as well as physically, the same as when he left it. However, not only is his prized car missing, he is displaced from his own bedroom by a stranger, and his parents seem to resent his return as an intrusion into the new routines of their lives. The decaying condition of the House of Usher, which is described in detail by Poe's narrator, parallels the psychological state of the man for whom it is home. Introverted and melancholy, his withdrawal from the larger world leads to his destruction, just as the instability of the house leads to its collapsing in on itself.

Even though the characters in many stories have dwellings to which they can return, these places do not always offer them security. In "The Resplendent Quetzal," the fact that Sarah and Edward spend Christmas, a time associated with home and family, on vacation in Mexico implies much about their lives back in Canada. Unlike his younger colleague, the older waiter in "A Clean, Well-Lighted Place" is not anxious to return to his lodgings, preferring to stay until dawn in a bar where he can better endure his life.

POINT OF VIEW

The narrator of a story, the person reporting on the characters, actions, and settings of a story, is as important as these elements themselves. While authors write their stories, they do not tell them directly; they create **narrators**, through whose voices the stories are related. By the choice of narrative **point of view**, the perspective from which a story is told, an author influences its interpretation. Third-person narrators are not characters in the stories they tell. They may be objective, reporting only the observable facts of the story without direct comment; omniscient, delving into the minds of several or all of the characters; or limited, delving only into the mind of the central character. First-person narrators are present in the stories they tell, either as observers or minor participants, or as major characters. It is interesting, after reading a story, to speculate how its meaning might have been altered had the author selected a different point of view or narrator.

Each type of narrator provides specific advantages to an author. Immediately observable in objective third-person narrators is their detachment from the scenes they recount. During most of Hemingway's "A Clean, Well-Lighted Place," the narrator describes, without comment, the bar and café, the actions of the old man, and the conversations between the two waiters. Only at the conclusion of the story does the narrator present the thoughts of the older waiter. This shift from objective to limited third-person narration casts light on the "facts" of the earlier part of the narration. Knowing the attitude of the waiter, readers can perceive that the apparently objective reporting earlier in the story consisted of elements carefully selected to reveal the characters' attitudes toward life.

Choosing a third-person omniscient narrator who reports on the emotions and thoughts of several characters allows an author to develop comparisons between individuals and to portray more fully the nature of the relationships between them. Atwood's "The Resplendent Quetzal" consists of five sections. In the first four, the narrator reports alternately on the thoughts of Sarah and her husband, Edward, each of whom is in a different part of the Aztec ruins they are touring. Even in the concluding section, when Edward returns to his wife, the narrator presents the thoughts first of one and then the other. The abruptly shifting point of view indicates the nature of the couple's relationship.

Although able to enter into the mind of only one character, a limited third-person narrator is able to explore that character fully, often exposing the character's failure to perceive the nature of the situations in which she finds herself, as is the case in "Bliss," or presenting aspects of the character not understood by those around her, as in "The Story of an Hour." In the latter story, other people attribute the heroine's death to her shock of joy on discovering that her husband, presumed dead, is still alive. The narrator, in presenting the woman's thoughts as she sits alone after receiving the news of her husband's supposed death, provides readers with information that explains the true cause of her death.

Because they are characters in the stories they report on, first-person narrators usually have access to less information than do third-person narrators. The words of first-person narrators raise such questions as: "How reliably does the narrator interpret events, his or her own character, and the characters of other people?" The observer narrator, a representative of the townspeople in "A Rose for Emily," recounts incidents he has heard of or seen from a distance. Using such phrases as "we believed," "we said," and "we were sure," he also presents hypotheses about the recluse. Only after her death, when he, along with other townsmen, has entered her bedroom, does he make a discovery that provides an explanation of the elderly woman's life and casts light on the accuracy of her neighbours' suppositions about it. Through the use of this type of narrator, Faulkner creates a story that is as much about the townspeople who interpret and judge Emily Grierson as it is about her life itself.

First-person narrators who are the main characters in a story are also limited by the extent of the knowledge they possess. Moreover, qualities of their personalities may cause them to ignore, overlook, or misinterpret the significance of the actions in which they are involved and the characters with whom they interact as in the case in "Why I Live at the P.O." Other narrators may be more aware of themselves, and their narratives may present their consciousness of character change, as in "Bartleby, the Scrivener," in which the narrator seems to be as interested in explaining how the young man influenced him as he is in analyzing Bartleby himself. For the mature narrators of "What I Learned from Caesar" and "The Boat," their remembrance of their boyhood relationships with their fathers provides them with fuller understanding of important aspects of their childhood and adolescence.

SYMBOLISM

Through an author's careful employment of **symbols** — objects, characters, or actions that stand for something beyond themselves — specific elements of many stories assume greater significance. Universal symbols, often called **archetypes,** are interpreted in much the same way in many different cultures. The use of the cycles of day and night and of the seasons to present the phases of human life is a familiar example. Cultural symbols hold special meanings for a specific group. For example, the cross embodies a number of complex spiritual beliefs for Christians. **Contextual symbols** are given or take on meaning only within the stories that contain them.

When employing universal or cultural symbols, authors usually assume their readers' general knowledge of the relationship between the literal objects, events, and characters and their symbolic meanings. Readers use this knowledge to interpret the symbols and hence to understand the stories they read more fully. For example, early in "Rappaccini's Daughter," Giovanni looks at the enclosed garden outside his window. Considering the garden in relation to the biblical Garden of Eden, readers may come to a fuller understanding of the theme of the fall from innocence and of the author's view of the character of the young man.

In "The Resplendent Quetzal," a cultural symbol takes on contextual meanings unique to the story. A sacred bird, whose feathers symbolize the souls of unborn babies to the Aztecs, it is the only bird Sarah decides she wishes to see. Edward, who "felt he was allowed to see birds only when they wanted him to," does not think there are any in the area they are visiting. He is correct: neither one sees a quetzal. An understanding of what the bird symbolizes for each of them illuminates aspects of their characters. Atwood also draws on the fact that male quetzals play an important role in the hatching and raising of offspring, staying close to and assisting their mates during the entire process.

In "Borders" and "The Loons," the titles introduce the major contextual symbols, which acquire additional meanings each time they appear. In the former story, the international boundary between Canada and the United States, the "border," comes to represent divisions, not only between countries, but also between cultures and even between members of a family. In "The Loons," the calls of the shy, elusive birds were "plaintive, and yet with a quality of chilling mockery...[and] belonged to a world separated by aeons from our neat world of summer cottages and the lighted lamps of home." To the teenage narrator of the story, they stand for Piquette, a young, lonely Métis woman whom she had tried unsuccessfully to befriend.

IRONY

Irony, one of the most frequently used techniques in stories, is of three types. Verbal irony is created when there is a difference between the apparent and actual meanings of a speaker's words. In "Rappaccini's Daughter," Baglioni offers Giovanni a cure for the sickness affecting him, heartily announcing, "Be of good cheer, son of my friend! It is not yet too late for the rescue." However, to himself he admits his true motivation: "We will thwart Rappaccini yet!" In dramatic irony, readers have clearer perceptions of situations than do the characters involved in them. In "Araby," the narrator is so involved in his emotions about Mangin's sister that he does not see how his thoughts and actions are indications of infatuation and sexual arousal, emotions that Joyce makes clear to the reader. Again, "Rappaccini's Daughter" provides an example. Giovanni offers Beatrice what he believes will be an antidote and thinks that, once cured of her toxic qualities, the two will live happily together. What results is not what he expected.

In some stories, the situational irony is of cosmic dimensions, as characters struggle against natural or supernatural forces that frequently defeat them. In "The Open Boat," the Oiler, who has been presented as the strongest and most courageous of the four men in the lifeboat, is the only person to die. Merit is of no importance in a harsh and impersonal universe, one that may have no guiding powers, as the Correspondent has vaguely realized during the ordeal.

Katherine Mansfield's "Bliss" contains all three types of irony. Harry practises verbal irony when speaking of Miss Fulton, a dinner guest, in terms that conceal his true attitude about her. The situational irony is introduced in the title, "Bliss," which refers to the emotion Bertha experiences for the first time. Because of it, she is "waiting for something...divine to happen...that she knew must happen... infallibly." However, the events of the evening result in her feeling far from blissful. Bertha perceives the blossoming pear tree as a visual embodiment of her emotion and believes that Miss Fulton does as well. She is correct, but does not realize the cause of the other woman's feelings. On first reading, an attentive reader may notice in "Bliss" several instances of dramatic irony that subtly foreshadow the story's conclusion. These hints provide an undercurrent that contrasts Bertha's perceptions and anticipations with the realities of her situation.

INTERPRETATION AND PERSONAL RESPONSE

Because of differences in gender, age, cultural backgrounds, and personal experiences, readers respond individually to short stories. Their interpretation begins with the words of the works themselves, for as creations of other individuals, these are influenced by their authors' gender, age, cultural and literary background, and personal experience. Full, informed response to a work requires that readers initially relinquish freedom of response, giving consideration to the contexts out of which a story emerged and the technical aspects of language used in writing it. Careful, analytical attention to a story will lead to speculation on an author's purpose in writing. Based on such inquiry, readers can engage in more informed evaluation of a work, considering how clearly and artistically the author has communicated and judging the validity of the work's theme. Then, having responded to it on its own terms, they can respond to it personally, relating it to their own lives, identifying with or reacting against the characters, accepting or rejecting the author's attitudes toward or interpretation of life, or modifying their own views in the light of those presented. In making informed personal responses, readers achieve a new freedom, one that helps them to enjoy stories more fully and to make the creating, telling, and reading of stories an integral part of their lives.

Nathaniel Hawthorne (1804–1864)

A native of Salem, Massachusetts, where an ancestor was a judge in the seventeenth-century witch trials, Nathaniel Hawthorne set many of his short stories
and *The Scarlet Letter*, his best-known novel, in colonial New England. He was
more than a creator of historical fiction, however, describing himself as a writer
who delved into "the depths of our common human nature." "Rappaccini's
Daughter," for example, is set in sixteenth-century Italy, but does not deal with
Renaissance history. Instead, it presents a common plot structure and theme: a
young man's journey from country to city, symbolic of his coming of age.
Hawthorne uses the garden as his central setting, introducing into the story the
idea of a moral fall from innocence to experience. In addition to presenting
Giovanni's ambiguous response to adult sexuality, as seen in the youth's shifting reactions to Beatrice and the garden, Hawthorne examines the profound
effect that professional jealousies between the older authority figures, Baglioni
and Rappaccini, have on the lives of Giovanni and Beatrice.

RAPPACCINI'S DAUGHTER
From the Writings of Aubépine[1]

A young man, named Giovanni Guasconti, came, very long ago, from the
more southern region of Italy, to pursue his studies at the University of Padua.
Giovanni, who had but a scanty supply of gold ducats in his pocket, took
lodgings in a high and gloomy chamber of an old edifice, which looked not
unworthy to have been the palace of a Paduan noble, and which, in fact,
exhibited over its entrance the armorial bearings of a family long since extinct.
The young stranger, who was not unstudied in the great poem of his country,[2]
recollected that one of the ancestors of this family, and perhaps an occupant
of this very mansion, had been pictured by Dante as a partaker of the immortal agonies of his Inferno. These reminiscences and associations, together
with the tendency to heart-break natural to a young man for the first time out
of his native sphere, caused Giovanni to sigh heavily, as he looked around
the desolate and ill-furnished apartment.

"Holy Virgin, Signor," cried old dame Lisabetta, who, won by the youth's
remarkable beauty of person, was kindly endeavoring to give the chamber a habitable air, "what a sigh was that to come out of a young man's heart! Do you find
this old mansion gloomy? For the love of heaven, then, put your head out of
the window, and you will see as bright sunshine as you have in Naples."

Guasconti mechanically did as the old woman advised, but could not
quite agree with her that the Paduan sunshine was as cheerful as that of southern Italy. Such as it was, however, it fell upon a garden beneath the window,
and expended its fostering influences on a variety of plants, which seemed to
have been cultivated with exceeding care.

1 French for Hawthorn (tree). 2 *The Divine Comedy*, by Dante Alighieri. In this early-fourteenth-century
Italian poem, the narrator is guided in a dream vision through Hell and Purgatory by the classical Roman
poet Virgil, and through Heaven by a young maiden, Beatrice.

"Does this garden belong to the house?" asked Giovanni.

5   "Heaven forbid, Signor! — unless it were fruitful of better pot-herbs than any that grow there now," answered old Lisabetta. "No; that garden is cultivated by the own hands of Signor Giacomo Rappaccini, the famous Doctor, who, I warrant him, has been heard of as far as Naples. It is said that he distils these plants into medicines that are as potent as a charm. Oftentimes you may see the Signor Doctor at work, and perchance the Signora his daughter, too, gathering the strange flowers that grow in the garden."

The old woman had now done what she could for the aspect of the chamber, and, commending the young man to the protection of the saints, took her departure.

Giovanni still found no better occupation than to look down into the garden beneath his window. From its appearance, he judged it to be one of those botanic gardens, which were of earlier date in Padua than elsewhere in Italy, or in the world. Or, not improbably, it might once have been the pleasure-place of an opulent family; for there was the ruin of a marble fountain in the centre, sculptured with rare art, but so wofully shattered that it was impossible to trace the original design from the chaos of remaining fragments. The water, however, continued to gush and sparkle into the sunbeams as cheerfully as ever. A little gurgling sound ascended to the young man's window, and made him feel as if the fountain were an immortal spirit, that sung its song unceasingly, and without heeding the vicissitudes around it; while one century embodied it in marble, and another scattered the perishable garniture on the soil. All about the pool into which the water subsided, grew various plants, that seemed to require a plentiful supply of moisture for the nourishment of gigantic leaves, and, in some instances, flowers gorgeously magnificent. There was one shrub in particular, set in a marble vase in the midst of the pool, that bore a profusion of purple blossoms, each of which had the lustre and richness of a gem; and the whole together made a show so resplendent that it seemed enough to illuminate the garden, even had there been no sunshine. Every portion of the soil was peopled with plants and herbs, which, if less beautiful, still bore tokens of assiduous care; as if all had their individual virtues, known to the scientific mind that fostered them. Some were placed in urns, rich with old carving, and others in common garden-pots; some crept serpent-like along the ground, or climbed on high, using whatever means of ascent was offered them. One plant had wreathed itself round a statue of Vertumnus,[3] which was thus quite veiled and shrouded in a drapery of hanging foliage, so happily arranged that it might have served a sculptor for a study.

While Giovanni stood at the window, he heard a rustling behind a screen of leaves, and became aware that a person was at work in the garden. His figure soon emerged into view, and showed itself to be that of no common laborer, but a tall, emaciated, sallow, and sickly-looking man, dressed in a scholar's garb of black. He was beyond the middle term of life, with grey hair, a thin grey beard, and a face singularly marked with intellect and cultivation, but which could never, even in his more youthful days, have expressed much warmth of heart.

3 the Roman god of vegetation who seduced Pomona, goddess of fruits.

Nothing could exceed the intentness with which this scientific gardener examined every shrub which grew in his path; it seemed as if he was looking into their inmost nature, making observations in regard to their creative essence, and discovering why one leaf grew in this shape, and another in that, and wherefore such and such flowers differed among themselves in hue and perfume. Nevertheless, in spite of this deep intelligence on his part, there was no approach to intimacy between himself and these vegetable existences. On the contrary, he avoided their actual touch, or the direct inhaling of their odors, with a caution that impressed Giovanni most disagreeably; for the man's demeanor was that of one walking among malignant influences, such as savage beasts, or deadly snakes, or evil spirits, which, should he allow them one moment of license, would wreak upon him some terrible fatality. It was strangely frightful to the young man's imagination, to see this air of insecurity in a person cultivating a garden, that most simple and innocent of human toils, and which had been alike the joy and labor of the unfallen parents of the race. Was this garden, then, the Eden of the present world?—and this man, with such a perception of harm in what his own hands caused to grow, was he the Adam?

10　　The distrustful gardener, while plucking away the dead leaves or pruning the too luxuriant growth of the shrubs, defended his hands with a pair of thick gloves. Nor were these his only armor. When, in his walk through the garden, he came to the magnificent plant that hung its purple gems beside the marble fountain, he placed a kind of mask over his mouth and nostrils, as if all this beauty did but conceal a deadlier malice. But finding his task still too dangerous, he drew back, removed the mask, and called loudly, but in the infirm voice of a person affected with inward disease:

"Beatrice!—Beatrice!"

"Here am I, my father! What would you?" cried a rich and youthful voice from the window of the opposite house; a voice as rich as a tropical sunset, and which made Giovanni, though he knew not why, think of deep hues of purple or crimson, and of perfumes heavily delectable.—"Are you in the garden?"

"Yes, Beatrice," answered the gardener, "and I need your help."

Soon there emerged from under a sculptured portal the figure of a young girl, arrayed with as much richness of taste as the most splendid of the flowers, beautiful as the day, and with a bloom so deep and vivid that one shade more would have been too much. She looked redundant with life, health, and energy; all of which attributes were bound down and compressed, as it were, and girdled tensely, in their luxuriance, by her virgin zone.[4] Yet Giovanni's fancy must have grown morbid, while he looked down into the garden; for the impression which the fair stranger made upon him was as if here were another flower, the human sister of those vegetable ones, as beautiful as they—more beautiful than the richest of them—but still to be touched only with a glove, nor to be approached without a mask. As Beatrice came down the garden path, it was observable that she handled and inhaled the odor of several of the plants, which her father had most sedulously avoided.

15　　"Here, Beatrice," said the latter,—"see how many needful offices require to be done to our chief treasure. Yet, shattered as I am, my life might pay the

4 outer girdle-type garment worn on a woman's lower hips.

penalty of approaching it so closely as circumstances demand. Henceforth, I fear, this plant must be consigned to your sole charge."

"And gladly will I undertake it," cried again the rich tones of the young lady, as she bent towards the magnificent plant, and opened her arms as if to embrace it. "Yes, my sister, my splendor, it shall be Beatrice's task to nurse and serve thee; and thou shalt reward her with thy kisses and perfumed breath, which to her is as the breath of life!"

Then, with all the tenderness in her manner that was so strikingly expressed in her words, she busied herself with such attentions as the plant seemed to require; and Giovanni, at his lofty window, rubbed his eyes, and almost doubted whether it were a girl tending her favorite flower, or one sister performing the duties of affection to another. The scene soon terminated. Whether Doctor Rappaccini had finished his labors in the garden, or that his watchful eye had caught the stranger's face, he now took his daughter's arm and retired. Night was already closing in; oppressive exhalations seemed to proceed from the plants, and steal upward past the open window; and Giovanni, closing the lattice, went to his couch, and dreamed of a rich flower and beautiful girl. Flower and maiden were different and yet the same, and fraught with some strange peril in either shape.

But there is an influence in the light of morning that tends to rectify whatever errors of fancy, or even of judgment, we may have incurred during the sun's decline, or among the shadows of the night, or in the less wholesome glow of moonshine. Giovanni's first movement on starting from sleep, was to throw open the window, and gaze down into the garden which his dreams had made so fertile of mysteries. He was surprised, and a little ashamed, to find how real and matter-of-fact an affair it proved to be, in the first rays of the sun, which gilded the dew-drops that hung upon leaf and blossom, and, while giving a brighter beauty to each rare flower, brought everything within the limits of ordinary experience. The young man rejoiced, that, in the heart of the barren city, he had the privilege of overlooking this spot of lovely and luxuriant vegetation. It would serve, he said to himself, as a symbolic language, to keep him in communion with Nature. Neither the sickly and thought-worn Doctor Giacomo Rappaccini, it is true, nor his brilliant daughter, were now visible; so that Giovanni could not determine how much of the singularity which he attributed to both, was due to their own qualities, and how much to his wonder-working fancy. But he was inclined to take a most rational view of the whole matter.

In the course of the day, he paid his respects to Signor Pietro Baglioni, professor of medicine in the University, a physician of eminent repute, to whom Giovanni had brought a letter of introduction. The Professor was an elderly personage, apparently of genial nature, and habits that might almost be called jovial; he kept the young man to dinner, and made himself very agreeable by the freedom and liveliness of his conversation, especially when warmed by a flask or two of Tuscan wine. Giovanni, conceiving that men of science, inhabitants of the same city, must needs be on familiar terms with one another, took an opportunity to mention the name of Doctor Rappaccini. But the Professor did not respond with so much cordiality as he had anticipated.

"Ill would it become a teacher of the divine art of medicine," said Professor Pietro Baglioni, in answer to a question of Giovanni, "to withhold due and

20

well-considered praise of a physician so eminently skilled as Rappaccini. But, on the other hand, I should answer it but scantily to my conscience, were I to permit a worthy youth like yourself, Signor Giovanni, the son of an ancient friend, to imbibe erroneous ideas respecting a man who might hereafter chance to hold your life and death in his hands. The truth is, our worshipful Doctor Rappaccini has as much science as any member of the faculty — with perhaps one single exception — in Padua, or all Italy. But there are certain grave objections to his professional character."

"And what are they?" asked the young man.

"Has my friend Giovanni any disease of body or heart, that he is so inquisitive about physicians?" said the Professor, with a smile. "But as for Rappaccini, it is said of him — and I, who know the man well, can answer for its truth — that he cares infinitely more for science than for mankind. His patients are interesting to him only as subjects for some new experiment. He would sacrifice human life, his own among the rest, or whatever else was dearest to him, for the sake of adding so much as a grain of mustard-seed to the great heap of his accumulated knowledge."

"Methinks he is an awful man, indeed," remarked Guasconti, mentally recalling the cold and purely intellectual aspect of Rappaccini. "And yet, worshipful Professor, is it not a noble spirit? Are there many men capable of so spiritual a love of science?"

"God forbid," answered the Professor, somewhat testily — "at least, unless they take sounder views of the healing art than those adopted by Rappaccini. It is his theory, that all medicinal virtues are comprised within those substances which we term vegetable poisons. These he cultivates with his own hands, and is said even to have produced new varieties of poison, more horribly deleterious than Nature, without the assistance of this learned person, would ever have plagued the world withal. That the Signor Doctor does less mischief than might be expected, with such dangerous substances, is undeniable. Now and then, it must be owned, he has effected — or seemed to effect — a marvellous cure. But, to tell you my private mind, Signor Giovanni, he should receive little credit for such instances of success — they being probably the work of chance — but should be held strictly accountable for his failures, which may justly be considered his own work."

25   The youth might have taken Baglioni's opinions with many grains of allowance, had he known that there was a professional warfare of long continuance between him and Doctor Rappaccini, in which the latter was generally thought to have gained the advantage. If the reader be inclined to judge for himself, we refer him to certain black-letter tracts on both sides, preserved in the medical department of the University of Padua.

"I know not, most learned Professor," returned Giovanni, after musing on what had been said of Rappaccini's exclusive zeal for science — "I know not how dearly this physician may love his art; but surely there is one object more dear to him. He has a daughter."

"Aha!" cried the Professor with a laugh. "So now our friend Giovanni's secret is out. You have heard of this daughter, whom all the young men in Padua are wild about, though not half a dozen have ever had the good hap to see her face. I know little of the Signora Beatrice, save that Rappaccini is said to have instructed her deeply in his science, and that, young and beautiful as fame reports her, she is already qualified to fill a professor's chair. Perchance her father destines her for mine! Other absurd rumors there be, not worth talking about, or listening to. So now, Signor Giovanni, drink off your glass of Lacryma."[5]

Guasconti returned to his lodgings somewhat heated with the wine he had quaffed, and which caused his brain to swim with strange fantasies in reference to Doctor Rappaccini and the beautiful Beatrice. On his way, happening to pass by a florist's, he bought a fresh bouquet of flowers.

Ascending to his chamber, he seated himself near the window, but within the shadow thrown by the depth of the wall, so that he could look down into the garden with little risk of being discovered. All beneath his eye was a solitude. The strange plants were basking in the sunshine, and now and then nodding gently to one another, as if in acknowledgment of sympathy and kindred. In the midst, by the shattered fountain, grew the magnificent shrub, with its purple gems clustering all over it; they glowed in the air, and gleamed back again out of the depths of the pool, which thus seemed to overflow with colored radiance from the rich reflection that was steeped in it. At first, as we have said, the garden was a solitude. Soon, however, — as Giovanni had half-hoped, half-feared, would be the case, — a figure appeared beneath the antique sculptured portal, and came down between the rows of plants, inhaling their various perfumes, as if she were one of those beings of old classic fable, that lived upon sweet odors. On again beholding Beatrice, the young man was even startled to perceive how much her beauty exceeded his recollection of it; so brilliant, so vivid was its character, that she glowed amid the sunlight, and, as Giovanni whispered to himself, positively illuminated the more shadowy intervals of the garden path. Her face being now more revealed than on the former occasion, he was struck by its expression of simplicity and sweetness; qualities that had not entered into his idea of her character, and which made him ask anew, what manner of mortal she might be. Nor did he fail again to observe, or imagine, an analogy between the beautiful girl and the gorgeous shrub that hung its gem-like flowers over the fountain; a resemblance which Beatrice seemed to have indulged a fantastic humor in heightening, both by the arrangement of her dress and the selection of its hues.

30   Approaching the shrub, she threw open her arms, as with a passionate ardor, and drew its branches into an intimate embrace; so intimate, that her features were hidden in its leafy bosom, and her glistening ringlets all intermingled with the flowers.

"Give me thy breath, my sister," exclaimed Beatrice; "for I am faint with common air! And give me this flower of thine, which I separate with gentlest fingers from the stem, and place it close beside my heart."

With these words, the beautiful daughter of Rappaccini plucked one of the richest blossoms of the shrub, and was about to fasten it in her bosom. But now, unless Giovanni's draughts of wine had bewildered his senses, a singular incident occurred. A small orange-colored reptile, of the lizard or chameleon species, chanced to be creeping along the path, just at the feet of Beatrice. It appeared to Giovanni — but, at the distance from which he gazed, he could

5 strong, sweet red wine named after the tears of Christ.

scarcely have seen anything so minute — it appeared to him, however, that a drop or two of moisture from the broken stem of the flower descended upon the lizard's head. For an instant, the reptile contorted itself violently, and then lay motionless in the sunshine. Beatrice observed this remarkable phenomenon, and crossed herself, sadly, but without surprise; nor did she therefore hesitate to arrange the fatal flower in her bosom. There it blushed, and almost glimmered with the dazzling effect of a precious stone, adding to her dress and aspect the one appropriate charm, which nothing else in the world could have supplied. But Giovanni, out of the shadow of his window, bent forward and shrank back, and murmured and trembled.

"Am I awake? Have I my senses?" said he to himself. "What is this being?— beautiful, shall I call her?— or inexpressibly terrible?"

Beatrice now strayed carelessly through the garden, approaching closer beneath Giovanni's window, so that he was compelled to thrust his head quite out of its concealment in order to gratify the intense and painful curiosity which she excited. At this moment, there came a beautiful insect over the garden wall; it had perhaps wandered through the city and found no flowers nor verdure among those antique haunts of men, until the heavy perfumes of Doctor Rappaccini's shrubs had lured it from afar. Without alighting on the flowers, this winged brightness seemed to be attracted by Beatrice, and lingered in the air and fluttered about her head. Now, here it could not be but that Giovanni Guasconti's eyes deceived him. Be that as it might, he fancied that while Beatrice was gazing at the insect with childish delight, it grew faint and fell at her feet;— its bright wings shivered; it was dead — from no cause that he could discern, unless it were the atmosphere of her breath. Again Beatrice crossed herself and sighed heavily, as she bent over the dead insect.

35   An impulsive movement of Giovanni drew her eyes to the window. There she beheld the beautiful head of the young man — rather a Grecian than an Italian head, with fair, regular features, and a glistening of gold among his ringlets — gazing down upon her like a being that hovered in mid-air. Scarcely knowing what he did, Giovanni threw down the bouquet which he had hitherto held in his hand.

"Signora," said he, "there are pure and healthful flowers. Wear them for the sake of Giovanni Guasconti!"

"Thanks, Signor," replied Beatrice, with her rich voice, that came forth as it were like a gush of music; and with a mirthful expression half childish and half woman-like. "I accept your gift, and would fain recompense it with this precious purple flower; but if I toss it into the air, it will not reach you. So Signor Guasconti must even content himself with my thanks."

She lifted the bouquet from the ground, and then as if inwardly ashamed at having stepped aside from her maidenly reserve to respond to a stranger's greeting, passed swiftly homeward through the garden. But, few as the moments were, it seemed to Giovanni when she was on the point of vanishing beneath the sculptured portal, that his beautiful bouquet was already beginning to wither in her grasp. It was an idle thought; there could be no possibility of distinguishing a faded flower from a fresh one at so great a distance.

For many days after this incident, the young man avoided the window that looked into Doctor Rappaccini's garden, as if something ugly and monstrous would have blasted his eye-sight, had he been betrayed into a glance. He felt conscious of having put himself, to a certain extent, within the influence of an unintelligible power, by the communication which he had opened with Beatrice. The wisest course would have been, if his heart were in any real danger, to quit his lodgings and Padua itself, at once; the next wiser, to have accustomed himself, as far as possible, to the familiar and day-light view of Beatrice; thus bringing her rigidly and systematically within the limits of ordinary experience. Least of all, while avoiding her sight, ought Giovanni to have remained so near this extraordinary being, that the proximity and possibility even of intercourse, should give a kind of substance and reality to the wild vagaries which his imagination ran riot continually in producing. Guasconti had not a deep heart — or at all events, its depths were not sounded now — but he had a quick fancy, and an ardent southern temperament, which rose every instant to a higher fever-pitch. Whether or no Beatrice possessed those terrible attributes — that fatal breath — the affinity with those so beautiful and deadly flowers — which were indicated by what Giovanni had witnessed, she had at least instilled a fierce and subtle poison into his system. It was not love, although her rich beauty was a madness to him; nor horror, even while he fancied her spirit to be imbued with the same baneful essence that seemed to pervade her physical frame; but a wild offspring of both love and horror that had each parent in it, and burned like one and shivered like the other. Giovanni knew not what to dread; still less did he know what to hope; yet hope and dread kept a continual warfare in his breast, alternately vanquishing one another and starting up afresh to renew the contest. Blessed are all simple emotions, be they dark or bright! It is the lurid intermixture of the two that produces the illuminating blaze of the infernal regions.

40   Sometimes he endeavored to assuage the fever of his spirit by a rapid walk through the streets of Padua, or beyond its gates; his footsteps kept time with the throbbings of his brain, so that the walk was apt to accelerate itself to a race. One day, he found himself arrested; his arm was seized by a portly personage who had turned back on recognizing the young man, and expended much breath in overtaking him.

"Signor Giovanni! — stay, my young friend!" cried he. "Have you forgotten me? That might well be the case, if I were as much altered as yourself."

It was Baglioni, whom Giovanni had avoided, ever since their first meeting, from a doubt that the Professor's sagacity would look too deeply into his secrets. Endeavoring to recover himself, he stared forth wildly from his inner world into the outer one, and spoke like a man in a dream:

"Yes; I am Giovanni Guasconti. You are Professor Pietro Baglioni. Now let me pass!"

"Not yet — not yet, Signor Giovanni Guasconti," said the Professor, smiling, but at the same time scrutinizing the youth with an earnest glance. — "What; did I grow up side by side with your father, and shall his son pass me like a stranger, in these old streets of Padua? Stand still, Signor Giovanni; for we must have a word or two, before we part."

45   "Speedily, then, most worshipful Professor, speedily!" said Giovanni, with feverish impatience. "Does not your worship see that I am in haste?"

Now, while he was speaking, there came a man in black along the street, stooping and moving feebly, like a person in inferior health. His face was all overspread with a most sickly and sallow hue, but yet so pervaded with an expression of piercing and active intellect, that an observer might easily have overlooked the merely physical attributes, and have seen only this wonderful energy. As he passed, this person exchanged a cold and distant salutation with Baglioni, but fixed his eyes upon Giovanni with an intentness that seemed to bring out whatever was within him worthy of notice. Nevertheless, there was a peculiar quietness in the look, as if taking merely a speculative, not a human, interest in the young man.

"It is Doctor Rappaccini!" whispered the Professor, when the stranger had passed. — "Has he ever seen your face before?"

"Not that I know," answered Giovanni, starting at the name.

"He *has* seen you! — he must have seen you!" said Baglioni, hastily. "For some purpose or other, this man of science is making a study of you. I know that look of his! It is the same that coldly illuminates his face, as he bends over a bird, a mouse, or a butterfly, which, in pursuance of some experiment, he has killed by the perfume of a flower; — a look as deep as Nature itself, but without Nature's warmth of love. Signor Giovanni, I will stake my life upon it, you are the subject of one of Rappaccini's experiments!"

50 "Will you make a fool of me?" cried Giovanni, passionately. "*That*, Signor Professor, were an untoward experiment."

"Patience, patience!" replied the imperturbable Professor. — "I tell thee, my poor Giovanni, that Rappaccini has a scientific interest in thee. Thou hast fallen into fearful hands! And the Signora Beatrice? What part does she act in this mystery?"

But Guasconti, finding Baglioni's pertinacity intolerable, here broke away, and was gone before the Professor could again seize his arm. He looked after the young man intently, and shook his head.

"This must not be," said Baglioni to himself. "The youth is the son of my old friend, and shall not come to any harm from which the arcana of medical science can preserve him. Besides, it is too insufferable an impertinence in Rappaccini, thus to snatch the lad out of my own hands, as I may say, and make use of him for his infernal experiments. This daughter of his! It shall be looked to. Perchance, most learned Rappaccini, I may foil you where you little dream of it!"

Meanwhile, Giovanni had pursued a circuitous route, and at length found himself at the door of his lodgings. As he crossed the threshold, he was met by old Lisabetta, who smirked and smiled, and was evidently desirous to attract his attention; vainly, however, as the ebullition of his feelings had momentarily subsided into a cold and dull vacuity. He turned his eyes full upon the withered face that was puckering itself into a smile, but seemed to behold it not. The old dame, therefore, laid her grasp upon his cloak.

55 "Signor! — Signor!" whispered she, still with a smile over the whole breadth of her visage, so that it looked not unlike a grotesque carving in wood, darkened by centuries — "Listen, Signor! There is a private entrance into the garden!"

"What do you say?" exclaimed Giovanni, turning quickly about, as if an inanimate thing should start into feverish life. — "A private entrance into Doctor Rappaccini's garden!"

"Hush! hush! — not so loud!" whispered Lisabetta, putting her hand over his mouth. "Yes; into the worshipful Doctor's garden, where you may see all his fine shrubbery. Many a young man in Padua would give gold to be admitted among those flowers."

Giovanni put a piece of gold into her hand.

"Show me the way," said he.

60   A surmise, probably excited by his conversation with Baglioni, crossed his mind, that this interposition of old Lisabetta might perchance be connected with the intrigue, whatever were its nature, in which the Professor seemed to suppose that Doctor Rappaccini was involving him. But such a suspicion, though it disturbed Giovanni, was inadequate to restrain him. The instant that he was aware of the possibility of approaching Beatrice, it seemed an absolute necessity of his existence to do so. It mattered not whether she were angel or demon; he was irrevocably within her sphere, and must obey the law that whirled him onward, in ever lessening circles, towards a result which he did not attempt to foreshadow. And yet, strange to say, there came across him a sudden doubt, whether this intense interest on his part were not delusory — whether it were really of so deep and positive a nature as to justify him in now thrusting himself into an incalculable position — whether it were not merely the fantasy of a young man's brain, only slightly, or not at all, connected with his heart!

He paused — hesitated — turned half about — but again went on. His withered guide led him along several obscure passages, and finally undid a door, through which, as it was opened, there came the sight and sound of rustling leaves, with the broken sunshine glimmering among them. Giovanni stepped forth, and forcing himself through the entanglement of a shrub that wreathed its tendrils over the hidden entrance, he stood beneath his own window, in the open area of Doctor Rappaccini's garden.

How often is it the case, that, when impossibilities have come to pass, and dreams have condensed their misty substance into tangible realities, we find ourselves calm, and even coldly self-possessed, amid circumstances which it would have been a delirium of joy or agony to anticipate! Fate delights to thwart us thus. Passion will choose his own time to rush upon the scene, and lingers sluggishly behind, when an appropriate adjustment of events would seem to summon his appearance. So was it now with Giovanni. Day after day, his pulses had throbbed with feverish blood, at the improbable idea of an interview with Beatrice, and of standing with her, face to face, in this very garden, basking in the Oriental sunshine of her beauty, and snatching from her full gaze the mystery which he deemed the riddle of his own existence. But now there was a singular and untimely equanimity within his breast. He threw a glance around the garden to discover if Beatrice or her father were present, and perceiving that he was alone, began a critical observation of the plants.

The aspect of one and all of them dissatisfied him; their gorgeousness seemed fierce, passionate, and even unnatural. There was hardly an individual shrub which a wanderer, straying by himself through a forest, would not have been startled to find growing wild, as if an unearthly face had glared at him out of the thicket. Several, also, would have shocked a delicate instinct by an appearance of artificialness, indicating that there had been such commixture, and, as it were, adultery of various vegetable species, that the production was no longer of God's making, but the monstrous offspring of man's depraved fancy, glowing with only an evil mockery of beauty. They were probably the result of experiment, which, in one or two cases, had succeeded in mingling plants individually lovely into a compound possessing the questionable and ominous character that distinguished the whole growth of the garden. In fine, Giovanni recognized but two or three plants in the collection, and those of a kind that he well knew to be poisonous. While busy with these contemplations, he heard the rustling of a silken garment, and turning, beheld Beatrice emerging from beneath the sculptured portal.

Giovanni had not considered with himself what should be his deportment; whether he should apologize for his intrusion into the garden, or assume that he was there with the privity, at least, if not by the desire, of Doctor Rappaccini or his daughter. But Beatrice's manner placed him at his ease, though leaving him still in doubt by what agency he had gained admittance. She came lightly along the path, and met him near the broken fountain. There was surprise in her face, but brightened by a simple and kind expression of pleasure.

65 "You are a connoisseur in flowers, Signor," said Beatrice with a smile, alluding to the bouquet which he had flung her from the window. "It is no marvel, therefore, if the sight of my father's rare collection has tempted you to take a nearer view. If he were here, he could tell you many strange and interesting facts as to the nature and habits of these shrubs, for he has spent a lifetime in such studies, and this garden is his world."

"And yourself, lady" — observed Giovanni — "if fame says true — you, likewise, are deeply skilled in the virtues indicated by these rich blossoms, and these spicy perfumes. Would you deign to be my instructress, I should prove an apter scholar than if taught by Signor Rappaccini himself."

"Are there such idle rumors?" asked Beatrice, with the music of a pleasant laugh. "Do people say that I am skilled in my father's science of plants? What a jest is there! No; though I have grown up among these flowers, I know no more of them than their hues and perfume; and sometimes, methinks I would fain rid myself of even that small knowledge. There are many flowers here, and those not the least brilliant, that shock and offend me, when they meet my eye. But, pray, Signor, do not believe these stories about my science. Believe nothing of me save what you see with your own eyes."

"And must I believe all that I have seen with my own eyes?" asked Giovanni pointedly, while the recollection of former scenes made him shrink. "No, Signora, you demand too little of me. Bid me believe nothing, save what comes from your own lips."

It would appear that Beatrice understood him. There came a deep flush to her cheek; but she looked full into Giovanni's eyes, and responded to his gaze of uneasy suspicion with a queen-like haughtiness.

70 "I do so bid you, Signor!" she replied. "Forget whatever you may have fancied in regard to me. If true to the outward senses, still it may be false in its

essence. But the words of Beatrice Rappaccini's lips are true from the depths of the heart outward. Those you may believe!"

A fervor glowed in her whole aspect, and beamed upon Giovanni's consciousness like the light of truth itself. But while she spoke, there was a fragrance in the atmosphere around her, rich and delightful, though evanescent, yet which the young man, from an indefinable reluctance, scarcely dared to draw into his lungs. It might be the odor of the flowers. Could it be Beatrice's breath, which thus embalmed her words with a strange richness, as if by steeping them in her heart? A faintness passed like a shadow over Giovanni, and flitted away; he seemed to gaze through the beautiful girl's eyes into her transparent soul, and felt no more doubt or fear.

The tinge of passion that had colored Beatrice's manner vanished; she became gay, and appeared to derive a pure delight from her communion with the youth, not unlike what the maiden of a lonely island might have felt, conversing with a voyager from the civilized world.[6] Evidently her experience of life had been confined within the limits of that garden. She talked now about matters as simple as the daylight or summer-clouds, and now asked questions in reference to the city, or Giovanni's distant home, his friends, his mother, and his sisters; questions indicating such seclusion, and such lack of familiarity with modes and forms, that Giovanni responded as if to an infant. Her spirit gushed out before him like a fresh rill, that was just catching its first glimpse of the sunlight, and wondering at the reflections of earth and sky which were flung into its bosom. There came thoughts, too, from a deep source, and fantasies of a gem-like brilliancy, as if diamonds and rubies sparkled upward among the bubbles of the fountain. Ever and anon, there gleamed across the young man's mind a sense of wonder, that he should be walking side by side with the being who had so wrought upon his imagination — whom he had idealized in such hues of terror — in whom he had positively witnessed such manifestations of dreadful attributes — that he should be conversing with Beatrice like a brother, and should find her so human and so maiden-like. But such reflections were only momentary; the effect of her character was too real, not to make itself familiar at once.

In this free intercourse, they had strayed through the garden, and now, after many turns among its avenues, were come to the shattered fountain, beside which grew the magnificent shrub with its treasury of glowing blossoms. A fragrance was diffused from it, which Giovanni recognized as identical with that which he had attributed to Beatrice's breath, but incomparably more powerful. As her eyes fell upon it, Giovanni beheld her press her hand to her bosom, as if her heart were throbbing suddenly and painfully.

"For the first time in my life," murmured she, addressing the shrub, "I had forgotten thee!"

"I remember, Signora," said Giovanni, "that you once promised to reward me with one of these living gems for the bouquet, which I had the happy boldness to fling to your feet. Permit me now to pluck it as a memorial of this interview."

75

6 implicit reference to the meeting of Miranda and Ferdinand in William Shakespeare's *The Tempest* (see page 478).

He made a step towards the shrub, with extended hand. But Beatrice darted forward, uttering a shriek that went through his heart like a dagger. She caught his hand, and drew it back with the whole force of her slender figure. Giovanni felt her touch thrilling through his fibres.

"Touch it not!" exclaimed she, in a voice of agony. "Not for thy life! It is fatal!"

Then, hiding her face, she fled from him, and vanished beneath the sculptured portal. As Giovanni followed her with his eyes, he beheld the emaciated figure and pale intelligence of Doctor Rappaccini, who had been watching the scene, he knew not how long, within the shadow of the entrance.

No sooner was Guasconti alone in his chamber, than the image of Beatrice came back to his passionate musings, invested with all the witchery that had been gathering around it ever since his first glimpse of her, and now likewise imbued with a tender warmth of girlish womanhood. She was human: her nature was endowed with all gentle and feminine qualities; she was worthiest to be worshipped; she was capable, surely, on her part, of the height and heroism of love. Those tokens, which he had hitherto considered as proofs of a frightful peculiarity in her physical and moral system, were now either forgotten, or, by the subtle sophistry of passion, transmuted into a golden crown of enchantment, rendering Beatrice the more admirable, by so much as she was the more unique. Whatever had looked ugly, was now beautiful; or, if incapable of such a change, it stole away and hid itself among those shapeless half-ideas, which throng the dim region beyond the daylight of our perfect consciousness. Thus did he spend the night, nor fell asleep, until the dawn had begun to awake the slumbering flowers in Doctor Rappaccini's garden, whither Giovanni's dreams doubtless led him. Up rose the sun in his due season, and flinging his beams upon the young man's eyelids, awoke him to a sense of pain. When thoroughly aroused, he became sensible of a burning and tingling agony in his hand — in his right hand — the very hand which Beatrice had grasped in her own, when he was on the point of plucking one of the gem-like flowers. On the back of that hand there was now a purple print, like that of four small fingers, and the likeness of a slender thumb upon his wrist.

Oh, how stubbornly does love — or even that cunning semblance of love which flourishes in the imagination, but strikes no depth of root into the heart — how stubbornly does it hold its faith, until the moment come, when it is doomed to vanish into thin mist! Giovanni wrapt a handkerchief about his hand, and wondered what evil thing had stung him, and soon forgot his pain in a reverie of Beatrice.

After the first interview, a second was in the inevitable course of what we call fate. A third; a fourth; and a meeting with Beatrice in the garden was no longer an incident in Giovanni's daily life, but the whole space in which he might be said to live; for the anticipation and memory of that ecstatic hour made up the remainder. Nor was it otherwise with the daughter of Rappaccini. She watched for the youth's appearance, and flew to his side with confidence as unreserved as if they had been playmates from early infancy — as if they were such playmates still. If, by any unwonted chance, he failed to come at the appointed moment, she stood beneath the window, and sent up the rich sweetness of her tones to float around him in his chamber, and echo and reverberate throughout his heart — "Giovanni! Giovanni! Why tarriest thou? Come down!" — And down he hastened into that Eden of poisonous flowers.

But, with all this intimate familiarity, there was still a reserve in Beatrice's demeanor, so rigidly and invariably sustained, that the idea of infringing it scarcely occurred to his imagination. By all appreciable signs, they loved; they had looked love, with eyes that conveyed the holy secret from the depths of one soul into the depths of the other, as if it were too sacred to be whispered by the way; they had even spoken love, in those gushes of passion when their spirits darted forth in articulated breath, like tongues of long-hidden flame; and yet there had been no seal of lips, no clasp of hands, nor any slightest caress, such as love claims and hallows. He had never touched one of the gleaming ringlets of her hair; her garment — so marked was the physical barrier between them — had never been waved against him by a breeze. On the few occasions when Giovanni had seemed tempted to overstep the limit, Beatrice grew so sad, so stern, and withal wore such a look of desolate separation, shuddering at itself, that not a spoken word was requisite to repel him. At such times, he was startled at the horrible suspicions that rose, monster-like, out of the caverns of his heart, and stared him in the face; his love grew thin and faint as the morning-mist; his doubts alone had substance. But when Beatrice's face brightened again, after the momentary shadow, she was transformed at once from the mysterious, questionable being, whom he had watched with so much awe and horror; she was now the beautiful and unsophisticated girl, whom he felt that his spirit knew with a certainty beyond all other knowledge.

A considerable time had now passed since Giovanni's last meeting with Baglioni. One morning, however, he was disagreeably surprised by a visit from the Professor, whom he had scarcely thought of for whole weeks, and would willingly have forgotten still longer. Given up, as he had long been, to a pervading excitement, he could tolerate no companions, except upon condition of their perfect sympathy with his present state of feeling. Such sympathy was not to be expected from Professor Baglioni.

The visitor chatted carelessly, for a few moments, about the gossip of the city and the University, and then took up another topic.

85   "I have been reading an old classic author lately," said he, "and met with a story that strangely interested me. Possibly you may remember it. It is of an Indian prince, who sent a beautiful woman as a present to Alexander the Great. She was as lovely as the dawn, and gorgeous as the sunset; but what especially distinguished her was a certain rich perfume in her breath — richer than a garden of Persian roses. Alexander, as was natural to a youthful conqueror, fell in love at first sight with this magnificent stranger. But a certain sage physician, happening to be present, discovered a terrible secret in regard to her."

"And what was that?" asked Giovanni, turning his eyes downward to avoid those of the Professor.

"That this lovely woman," continued Baglioni, with emphasis, "had been nourished with poisons from her birth upward, until her whole nature was so imbued with them, that she herself had become the deadliest poison in existence. Poison was her element of life. With that rich perfume of her breath, she blasted the very air. Her love would have been poison! — her embrace death! Is not this a marvelous tale?"

"A childish fable," answered Giovanni, nervously starting from his chair. "I marvel how your worship finds time to read such nonsense, among your graver studies."

"By the bye," said the Professor, looking uneasily about him, "what singular fragrance is this in your apartment? Is it the perfume of your gloves? It is faint, but delicious, and yet, after all, by no means agreeable. Were I to breathe it long, methinks it would make me ill. It is like the breath of a flower — but I see no flowers in the chamber."

90   "Nor are there any," replied Giovanni, who had turned pale as the Professor spoke; "nor, I think, is there any fragrance, except in your worship's imagination. Odors, being a sort of element combined of the sensual and the spiritual, are apt to deceive us in this manner. The recollection of a perfume — the bare idea of it — may easily be mistaken for a present reality."

"Aye; but my sober imagination does not often play such tricks," said Baglioni; "and were I to fancy any kind of odor, it would be that of some vile apothecary drug, wherewith my fingers are likely enough to be imbued. Our worshipful friend Rappaccini, as I have heard, tinctures his medicaments with odors richer than those of Araby.[7] Doubtless, likewise, the fair and learned Signora Beatrice would minister to her patients with draughts as sweet as a maiden's breath. But woe to him that sips them!"

Giovanni's face evinced many contending emotions. The tone in which the Professor alluded to the pure and lovely daughter of Rappaccini was a torture to his soul; and yet, the intimation of a view of her character, opposite to his own, gave instantaneous distinctness to a thousand dim suspicions, which now grinned at him like so many demons. But he strove hard to quell them, and to respond to Baglioni with a true lover's perfect faith.

"Signor Professor," said he, "you were my father's friend — perchance, too, it is your purpose to act a friendly part towards his son. I would fain feel nothing towards you, save respect and deference. But I pray you to observe, Signor, that there is one subject on which we must not speak. You know not the Signora Beatrice. You cannot, therefore, estimate the wrong — the blasphemy, I may even say — that is offered to her character by a light or injurious word."

"Giovanni! — my poor Giovanni!" answered the Professor, with a calm expression of pity, "I know this wretched girl far better than yourself. You shall hear the truth in respect to the poisoner Rappaccini, and his poisonous daughter. Yes; poisonous as she is beautiful! Listen; for even should you do violence to my grey hairs, it shall not silence me. That old fable of the Indian woman has become a truth, by the deep and deadly science of Rappaccini, and in the person of the lovely Beatrice!"

95   Giovanni groaned and hid his face.

"Her father," continued Baglioni, "was not restrained by natural affection from offering up his child, in this horrible manner, as the victim of his insane zeal for science. For — let us do him justice — he is as true a man of science as ever distilled his own heart in an alembic. What, then, will be your fate? Beyond a doubt, you are selected as the material of some new experiment. Perhaps the

---

7 the Middle East, a source of perfumes and spices popular in Europe.

result is to be death — perhaps a fate more awful still! Rappaccini, with what he calls the interest of science before his eyes, will hesitate at nothing."

"It is a dream!" muttered Giovanni to himself, "surely it is a dream!"

"But," resumed the Professor, "be of good cheer, son of my friend! It is not yet too late for the rescue. Possibly, we may even succeed in bringing back this miserable child within the limits of ordinary nature, from which her father's madness has estranged her. Behold this little silver vase! It was wrought by the hands of the renowned Benvenuto Cellini,[8] and is well worthy to be a love-gift to the fairest dame in Italy. But its contents are invaluable. One little sip of this antidote would have rendered the most virulent poisons of the Borgias innocuous. Doubt not that it will be as efficacious against those of Rappaccini. Bestow the vase, and the precious liquid within it, on your Beatrice, and hopefully await the result."

Baglioni laid a small, exquisitely wrought silver phial on the table, and withdrew, leaving what he had said to produce its effect upon the young man's mind.

100   "We will thwart Rappaccini yet!" thought he, chuckling to himself, as he descended the stairs. "But, let us confess the truth of him, he is a wonderful man! — a wonderful man indeed! A vile empiric, however, in his practice, and therefore not to be tolerated by those who respect the good old rules of the medical profession!"

Throughout Giovanni's whole acquaintance with Beatrice, he had occasionally, as we have said, been haunted by dark surmises as to her character. Yet, so thoroughly had she made herself felt by him as a simple, natural, most affectionate and guileless creature, that the image now held up by Professor Baglioni, looked as strange and incredible, as if it were not in accordance with his own original conception. True, there were ugly recollections connected with his first glimpses of the beautiful girl; he could not quite forget the bouquet that withered in her grasp, and the insect that perished amid the sunny air, by no ostensible agency, save the fragrance of her breath. These incidents, however, dissolving in the pure light of her character, had no longer the efficacy of facts, but were acknowledged as mistaken fantasies, by whatever testimony of the senses they might appear to be substantiated. There is something truer and more real, than what we can see with the eyes, and touch with the finger. On such better evidence, had Giovanni founded his confidence in Beatrice, though rather by the necessary force of her high attributes, than by any deep and generous faith, on his part. But, now, his spirit was incapable of sustaining itself at the height to which the early enthusiasm of passion had exalted it; he fell down, grovelling among earthly doubts, and defiled therewith the pure whiteness of Beatrice's image. Not that he gave her up; he did but distrust. He resolved to institute some decisive test that should satisfy him, once for all, whether there were those dreadful peculiarities in her physical nature, which could not be supposed to exist without some corresponding monstrosity of soul. His eyes, gazing down afar, might have deceived him as to the lizard, the insect, and the flowers. But if he could witness, at the distance of a few paces, the sudden blight of one fresh and healthful flower in Beatrice's

8 sixteenth-century Italian sculptor and goldsmith.

hand, there would be room for no further question. With this idea, he hastened to the florist's, and purchased a bouquet that was still gemmed with the morning dew-drops.

It was now the customary hour of his daily interview with Beatrice. Before descending into the garden, Giovanni failed not to look at his figure in the mirror; a vanity to be expected in a beautiful young man, yet, as displaying itself at that troubled and feverish moment, the token of a certain shallowness of feeling and insincerity of character. He did gaze, however, and said to himself, that his features had never before possessed so rich a grace, nor his eyes such vivacity, nor his cheeks so warm a hue of superabundant life.

"At least," thought he, "her poison has not yet insinuated itself into my system. I am no flower to perish in her grasp!"

With that thought, he turned his eyes on the bouquet, which he had never once laid aside from his hand. A thrill of indefinable horror shot through his frame, on perceiving that those dewy flowers were already beginning to droop; they wore the aspect of things that had been fresh and lovely, yesterday. Giovanni grew white as marble, and stood motionless before the mirror, staring at his own reflection there, as at the likeness of something frightful. He remembered Baglioni's remark about the fragrance that seemed to pervade the chamber. It must have been the poison in his breath! Then he shuddered — shuddered at himself! Recovering from his stupor, he began to watch, with curious eye, a spider that was busily at work, hanging its web from the antique cornice of the apartment, crossing and re-crossing the artful system of inter-woven lines, as vigorous and active a spider as ever dangled from an old ceiling. Giovanni bent towards the insect, and emitted a deep, long breath. The spider suddenly ceased its toil; the web vibrated with a tremor originating in the body of the small artizan. Again Giovanni sent forth a breath, deeper, longer, and imbued with a venomous feeling out of his heart; he knew not whether he were wicked or only desperate. The spider made a convulsive gripe with his limbs, and hung dead across the window.

"Accursed! Accursed!" muttered Giovanni, addressing himself. "Hast thou grown so poisonous, that this deadly insect perishes by thy breath?"

At that moment, a rich, sweet voice came floating up from the garden:—

"Giovanni! Giovanni! It is past the hour! Why tarriest thou! Come down!"

"Yes," muttered Giovanni again. "She is the only being whom my breath may not slay! Would that it might!"

He rushed down, and in an instant, was standing before the bright and loving eyes of Beatrice. A moment ago, his wrath and despair had been so fierce that he could have desired nothing so much as to wither her by a glance. But, with her actual presence, there came influences which had too real an exis-tence to be at once shaken off; recollections of the delicate and benign power of her feminine nature, which had so often enveloped him in a religious calm; recollections of many a holy and passionate outgush of her heart, when the pure fountain had been unsealed from its depths, and made visible in its trans-parency to his mental eye; recollections which, had Giovanni known how to estimate them, would have assured him that all this ugly mystery was but an earthly illusion, and that, whatever mist of evil might seem to have gathered over her, the real Beatrice was a heavenly angel. Incapable as he was of such high faith, still her presence had not utterly lost its magic. Giovanni's rage was quelled into an aspect of sullen insensibility. Beatrice, with a quick spiritual sense, immediately felt that there was a gulf of blackness between them, which neither he nor she could pass. They walked on together, sad and silent, and came thus to the marble fountain, and to its pool of water on the ground, in the midst of which grew the shrub that bore gem-like blossoms. Giovanni was affrighted at the eager enjoyment — the appetite, as it were — with which he found himself inhaling the fragrance of the flowers.

110 "Beatrice," asked he abruptly, "whence came this shrub?"

"My father created it," answered she, with simplicity.

"Created it! created it!" repeated Giovanni. "What mean you, Beatrice?"

"He is a man fearfully acquainted with the secrets of nature," replied Beatrice; "and, at the hour when I first drew breath, this plant sprang from the soil, the offspring of his science, of his intellect, while I was but his earthly child. Approach it not!" continued she, observing with terror that Giovanni was drawing nearer to the shrub. "It has qualities that you little dream of. But I, dearest Giovanni, — I grew up and blossomed with the plant, and was nourished with its breath. It was my sister, and I loved it with a human affection: for — alas! hast thou not suspected it? there was an awful doom."

Here Giovanni frowned so darkly upon her that Beatrice paused and trembled. But her faith in his tenderness reassured her, and made her blush that she had doubted for an instant.

115 "There was an awful doom," she continued, — "the effect of my father's fatal love of science — which estranged me from all society of my kind. Until Heaven sent thee, dearest Giovanni, Oh! how lonely was thy poor Beatrice!"

"Was it a hard doom?" asked Giovanni, fixing his eyes upon her.

"Only of late have I known how hard it was," answered she tenderly. "Oh, yes; but my heart was torpid, and therefore quiet."

Giovanni's rage broke forth from his sullen gloom like a lightning-flash out of a dark cloud.

"Accursed one!" cried he, with venomous scorn and anger. "And finding thy solitude wearisome, thou hast severed me, likewise, from all the warmth of life, and enticed me into thy region of unspeakable horror!"

120 "Giovanni!" exclaimed Beatrice, turning her large bright eyes upon his face. The force of his words had not found its way into her mind; she was merely thunder-struck.

"Yes, poisonous thing!" repeated Giovanni, beside himself with passion. "Thou hast done it! Thou hast blasted me! Thou hast filled my veins with poison! Thou hast made me as hateful, as ugly, as loathsome and deadly a creature as thyself, — a world's wonder of hideous monstrosity! Now — if our breath be happily as fatal to ourselves as to all others — let us join our lips in one kiss of unutterable hatred, and so die!"

"What has befallen me?" murmured Beatrice, with a low moan out of her heart. "Holy Virgin pity me, a poor heart-broken child!"

"Thou! Dost thou pray?" cried Giovanni, still with the same fiendish scorn. "Thy very prayers, as they come from thy lips, taint the atmosphere with death. Yes, yes; let us pray! Let us to church, and dip our fingers in the holy water at the portal! They that come after us will perish as by a pestilence. Let us sign crosses in the air! It will be scattering curses abroad in the likeness of holy symbols!"

"Giovanni," said Beatrice calmly, for her grief was beyond passion, "why dost thou join thyself with me thus in those terrible words? I, it is true, am the horrible thing thou namest me. But thou! — what hast thou to do, save with one other shudder at my hideous misery, to go forth out of the garden and mingle with thy race, and forget that there ever crawled on earth such a monster as poor Beatrice?"

125 "Dost thou pretend ignorance?" asked Giovanni, scowling upon her. "Behold! This power have I gained from the pure daughter of Rappaccini!"

There was a swarm of summer-insects flitting through the air, in search of the food promised by the flower-odors of the fatal garden. They circled round Giovanni's head, and were evidently attracted towards him by the same influence which had drawn them, for an instant, within the sphere of several of the shrubs. He sent forth a breath among them, and smiled bitterly at Beatrice, as at least a score of the insects fell dead upon the ground.

"I see it! I see it!" shrieked Beatrice. "It is my father's fatal science! No, no, Giovanni; it was not I! Never, never! I dreamed only to love thee, and be with thee a little time, and so to let thee pass away, leaving but thine image in mine heart. For, Giovanni — believe it — though my body be nourished with poison, my spirit is God's creature, and craves love as its daily food. But my father! — he has united us in this fearful sympathy. Yes; spurn me! — tread upon me! — kill me! Oh, what is death, after such words as thine? But it was not I! Not for a world of bliss would I have done it!"

Giovanni's passion had exhausted itself in its outburst from his lips. There now came across him a sense, mournful, and not without tenderness, of the intimate and peculiar relationship between Beatrice and himself. They stood, as it were, in an utter solitude, which would be made none the less solitary by the densest throng of human life. Ought not, then, the desert of humanity around them to press this insulated pair closer together? If they should be cruel to one another, who was there to be kind to them? Besides, thought Giovanni, might there not still be a hope of his returning within the limits of ordinary nature, and leading Beatrice — the redeemed Beatrice — by the hand? Oh, weak, and selfish, and unworthy spirit, that could dream of an earthly union and earthly happiness as possible, after such deep love had been so bitterly wronged as was Beatrice's love by Giovanni's blighting words! No, no; there could be no such hope. She must pass heavily, with that broken heart, across the borders of Time — she must bathe her hurts in some fount of Paradise, and forget her grief in the light of immortality — and *there* be well!

But Giovanni did not know it.

130 "Dear Beatrice," said he, approaching her, while she shrank away, as always at his approach, but now with a different impulse — "dearest Beatrice, our fate is not yet so desperate. Behold! There is a medicine, potent, as a wise physician has assured me, and almost divine in its efficacy. It is composed of ingredients the most opposite to those by which thy awful father has brought this calamity upon thee and me. It is distilled of blessed herbs. Shall we not quaff it together, and thus be purified from evil?"

"Give it me!" said Beatrice, extending her hand to receive the little silver phial which Giovanni took from his bosom. She added, with a peculiar emphasis: "I will drink — but do thou await the result."

She put Baglioni's antidote to her lips; and, at the same moment, the figure of Rappaccini emerged from the portal, and came slowly towards the marble fountain. As he drew near, the pale man of science seemed to gaze with a triumphant expression at the beautiful youth and maiden, as might an artist who should spend his life in achieving a picture or a group of statuary, and finally be satisfied with his success. He paused — his bent form grew erect with conscious power, he spread out his hands over them, in the attitude of a father imploring a blessing upon his children. But those were the same hands that had thrown poison into the stream of their lives! Giovanni trembled. Beatrice shuddered nervously, and pressed her hand upon her heart.

"My daughter," said Rappaccini, "thou art no longer lonely in the world! Pluck one of those precious gems from thy sister shrub, and bid thy bridegroom wear it in his bosom. It will not harm him now! My science, and the sympathy between thee and him, have so wrought within his system, that he now stands apart from common men, as thou dost, daughter of my pride and triumph, from ordinary women. Pass on, then, through the world, most dear to one another, and dreadful to all besides!"

"My father," said Beatrice, feebly — and still, as she spoke, she kept her hand upon her heart — "wherefore didst thou inflict this miserable doom upon thy child?"

"Miserable!" exclaimed Rappaccini. "What mean you, foolish girl? Dost thou deem it misery to be endowed with marvellous gifts, against which no power nor strength could avail an enemy? Misery, to be able to quell the mightiest with a breath? Misery, to be as terrible as thou art beautiful? Wouldst thou, then, have preferred the condition of a weak woman, exposed to all evil, and capable of none?"

"I would fain have been loved, not feared," murmured Beatrice, sinking down upon the ground. — "But now it matters not; I am going, father, where the evil, which thou hast striven to mingle with my being, will pass away like a dream — like the fragrance of these poisonous flowers, which will no longer taint my breath among the flowers of Eden. Farewell, Giovanni! Thy words of hatred are like lead within my heart — but they, too, will fall away as I ascend. Oh, was there not, from the first, more poison in thy nature than in mine?"

To Beatrice — so radically had her earthly part been wrought upon by Rappaccini's skill — as poison had been life, so the powerful antidote was death. And thus the poor victim of man's ingenuity and of thwarted nature, and of the fatality that attends all such efforts of perverted wisdom, perished there, at the feet of her father and Giovanni. Just at that moment, Professor Pietro Baglioni looked forth from the window, and called loudly, in a tone of triumph mixed with horror, to the thunder-stricken man of science:

"Rappaccini! Rappaccini! And is *this* the upshot of your experiment?"

(1844)

Edgar Allan Poe   (1809–1849)

Born in Boston and raised by foster parents in Richmond, Virginia, Edgar Allan Poe struggled all his adult life to earn a living as a professional author, serving as a magazine editor and writing poetry, short stories, and reviews. A controversial figure before and after his death, he is remembered as a poet whose works influenced late-nineteenth- and early-twentieth-century French, British, and American poets, and as one of the first major writers of the short story. He developed a theory of the short story as a brief prose piece, capable of being read in no more than an hour, in which all details are selected and arranged to create a unified effect. Poe applied this theory skillfully in his story "The Fall of the House of Usher." The narrator's response to the setting, the Usher twins, and the events communicates a sense of increasing horror. Not only does he witness Roderick Usher's increasing madness, he seems drawn into the unnatural atmosphere and barely escapes with his sanity and his life.

THE FALL OF THE HOUSE OF USHER

Son coeur est un luth suspendu;
Sitôt qu'on le touché il résonne.
— De Béranger.[1]

During the whole of a dull, dark, and soundless day in the autumn of the year, when the clouds hung oppressively low in the heavens, I had been passing alone, on horseback, through a singularly dreary tract of country; and at length found myself, as the shades of the evening drew on, within view of the melancholy House of Usher. I know not how it was — but, with the first glimpse of the building, a sense of insufferable gloom pervaded my spirit. I say insufferable; for the feeling was unrelieved by any of that half-pleasurable, because poetic, sentiment, with which the mind usually receives even the sternest natural images of the desolate or terrible. I looked upon the scene before me — upon the mere house, and the simple landscape features of the domain — upon the bleak walls — upon the vacant eye-like windows — upon a few rank sedges — and upon a few white trunks of decayed trees — with an utter depression of soul which I can compare to no earthly sensation more properly than to the after-dream of the reveller upon opium — the bitter lapse into everyday life — the hideous dropping off of the veil. There was an iciness, a sinking, a sickening of the heart — an unredeemed dreariness of thought which no goading of the imagination could torture into aught of the sublime. What was it — I paused to think — what was it that so unnerved me in the contemplation of the House of Usher? It was a mystery all insoluble; nor could I grapple with the shadowy fancies that crowded upon me as I pondered. I was forced to fall back upon the unsatisfactory conclusion, that while, beyond

---

1   "His heart is a tightly stringed lute; as soon as one touches it, it resonates" — based on eighteenth-century French poet Pierre-Jean de Béranger's "Le Rufus."

doubt, there are combinations of very simple natural objects which have the power of thus affecting us, still the analysis of this power lies among considerations beyond our depth. It was possible, I reflected, that a mere different arrangement of the particulars of the scene, of the details of the picture, would be sufficient to modify, or perhaps to annihilate its capacity for sorrowful impression; and, acting upon this idea, I reined my horse to the precipitous brink of a black and lurid tarn that lay in unruffled lustre by the dwelling, and gazed down — but with a shudder even more thrilling than before — upon the remodelled and inverted images of the gray sedge, and the ghastly tree-stems, and the vacant and eye-like windows.

Nevertheless, in this mansion of gloom I now proposed to myself a sojourn of some weeks. Its proprietor, Roderick Usher, had been one of my boon companions in boyhood; but many years had elapsed since our last meeting. A letter, however, had lately reached me in a distant part of the country — a letter from him — which, in its wildly importunate nature, had admitted of no other than a personal reply. The MS. gave evidence of nervous agitation. The writer spoke of acute bodily illness — of a mental disorder which oppressed him — and of an earnest desire to see me, as his best, and indeed his only personal friend, with a view of attempting, by the cheerfulness of my society, some alleviation of his malady. It was the manner in which all this, and much more, was said — it was the apparent *heart* that went with his request — which allowed me no room for hesitation; and I accordingly obeyed forthwith what I still considered a very singular summons.

Although, as boys, we had been even intimate associates, yet I really knew little of my friend. His reserve had been always excessive and habitual. I was aware, however, that his very ancient family had been noted, time out of mind, for a peculiar sensibility of temperament, displaying itself, through long ages, in many works of exalted art, and manifested, of late, in repeated deeds of munificent yet unobtrusive charity, as well as in a passionate devotion to the intricacies, perhaps even more than to the orthodox and easily recognisable beauties, of musical science. I had learned, too, the very remarkable fact, that the stem of the Usher race, all time-honoured as it was, had put forth, at no period, any enduring branch; in other words, that the entire family lay in the direct line of descent, and had always, with very trifling and very temporary variation, so lain. It was this deficiency, I considered, while running over in thought the perfect keeping of the character of the premises with the accredited character of the people, and while speculating upon the possible influence which the one, in the long lapse of centuries, might have exercised upon the other — it was this deficiency, perhaps, of collateral issue, and the consequent undeviating transmission, from sire to son, of the patrimony with the name, which had, at length, so identified the two as to merge the original title of the estate in the quaint and equivocal appellation of the "House of Usher" — an appellation which seemed to include, in the minds of the peasantry who used it, both the family and the family mansion.

I have said that the sole effect of my somewhat childish experiment — that of looking down within the tarn — had been to deepen the first singular impression. There can be no doubt that the consciousness of the rapid increase of my superstition — for why should I not so term it? — served mainly to accelerate the increase itself. Such, I have long known, is the paradoxical law of all sentiments having terror as a basis. And it might have been for this reason only, that, when I again uplifted my eyes to the house itself, from its image in the pool, there grew in my mind a strange fancy — a fancy so ridiculous, indeed, that I but mention it to show the vivid force of the sensations which oppressed me. I had so worked upon my imagination as really to believe that about the whole mansion and domain there hung an atmosphere peculiar to themselves and their immediate vicinity — an atmosphere which had no affinity with the air of heaven, but which had reeked up from the decayed trees, and the gray wall, and the silent tarn — a pestilent and mystic vapour, dull, sluggish, faintly discernible, and leaden-hued.

Shaking off from my spirit what *must* have been a dream, I scanned more narrowly the real aspect of the building. Its principal feature seemed to be that of an excessive antiquity. The discoloration of ages had been great. Minute fungi overspread the whole exterior, hanging in a fine tangled web-work from the eaves. Yet all this was apart from any extraordinary dilapidation. No portion of the masonry had fallen; and there appeared to be a wild inconsistency between its still perfect adaptation of parts, and the crumbling condition of the individual stones. In this there was much that reminded me of the specious totality of old wood-work which has rotted for long years in some neglected vault, with no disturbance from the breath of the external air. Beyond this indication of extensive decay, however, the fabric gave little token of instability. Perhaps the eye of a scrutinizing observer might have discovered a barely perceptible fissure, which, extending from the roof of the building in front, made its way down the wall in a zigzag direction, until it became lost in the sullen waters of the tarn.

5   Noticing these things, I rode over a short causeway to the house. A servant in waiting took my horse, and I entered the Gothic archway of the hall. A valet, of stealthy step, thence conducted me, in silence, through many dark and intricate passages in my progress to the *studio* of his master. Much that I encountered on the way contributed, I know not how, to heighten the vague sentiments of which I have already spoken. While the objects around me — while the carvings of the ceilings, the sombre tapestries of the walls, the ebon blackness of the floors, and the phantasmagoric armorial trophies which rattled as I strode, were but matters to which, or to such as which, I had been accustomed from my infancy — while I hesitated not to acknowledge how familiar was all this — I still wondered to find how unfamiliar were the fancies which ordinary images were stirring up. On one of the staircases, I met the physician of the family. His countenance, I thought, wore a mingled expression of low cunning and perplexity. He accosted me with trepidation and passed on. The valet now threw open a door and ushered me into the presence of his master.

The room in which I found myself was very large and lofty. The windows were long, narrow, and pointed, and at so vast a distance from the black oaken floor as to be altogether inaccessible from within. Feeble gleams of encrimsoned light made their way through the trellised panes, and served to render sufficiently distinct the more prominent objects around; the eye, however, struggled in vain to reach the remoter angles of the chamber, or the recesses of the vaulted and fretted ceiling. Dark draperies hung upon the walls. The general furniture was profuse, comfortless, antique, and tattered. Many books and musical instruments lay scattered about, but failed to give any vitality to the scene. I felt that I breathed an atmosphere of sorrow. An air of stern, deep, and irredeemable gloom hung over and pervaded all.

Upon my entrance, Usher arose from a sofa on which he had been lying at full length, and greeted me with a vivacious warmth which had much in it, I at first thought, of an overdone cordiality — of the constrained effort of the *ennuyé* man of the world. A glance, however, at his countenance, convinced me of his perfect sincerity. We sat down; and for some moments, while he spoke not, I gazed upon him with a feeling half of pity, half of awe. Surely, man had never before so terribly altered, in so brief a period, as had Roderick Usher! It was with difficulty that I could bring myself to admit the identity of the wan being before me with the companion of my early boyhood. Yet the character of his face had been at all time remarkable. A cadaverousness of complexion; an eye large, liquid, and luminous beyond comparison; lips some-what thin and very pallid, but of a surpassingly beautiful curve; a nose of a delicate Hebrew model, but with a breadth of nostril unusual in similar for-mations; a finely moulded chin, speaking, in its want of prominence, of a want of moral energy; hair of a more than web-like softness and tenuity; these fea-tures, with an inordinate expansion above the regions of the temple, made up altogether a countenance not easily to be forgotten. And now in the mere exaggeration of the prevailing character of these features, and of the expres-sion they were wont to convey, lay so much of change that I doubted to whom I spoke. The now ghastly pallor of the skin, and the now miraculous lustre of the eye, above all things startled and even awed me. The silken hair, took, had been suffered to grow all unheeded, and as, in its wild gossamer texture, it floated rather than fell about the fact, I could not, even with effort, connect its Arabesque expression with any idea of simple humanity.

In the manner of my friend I was at once struck with an incoherence — an inconsistency; and I soon found this to arise from a series of feeble and futile struggles to overcome an habitual trepidancy — an excessive nervous agi-tation. For something of this nature I had indeed been prepared, no less by his letter, than by reminiscences of certain boyish traits, and by conclusions deduced from his peculiar physical conformation and temperament. His action was alternately vivacious and sullen. His voice varied rapidly from a tremulous indecision (when the animal spirits seemed utterly in abeyance) to that species of energetic concision — that abrupt, weighty, unhurried, and hollow-sound-ing enunciation — that leaden, self-balanced and perfectly modulated guttural utterance, which may be observed in the lost drunkard, or the irreclaimable eater of opium, during the periods of his most intense excitement.

It was thus that he spoke of the object of my visit, of his earnest desire to see me, and of the solace he expected me to afford him. He entered, at some length, into what he conceived to be the nature of his malady. It was, he said, a constitutional and a family evil, and one for which he despaired to find a remedy — a mere nervous affection, he immediately added, which would undoubtedly soon pass off. It displayed itself in a host of unnatural sensations. Some of these, as he detailed them, interested and bewildered me; although, perhaps, the terms, and the general manner of the narration had their weight.

He suffered much from a morbid acuteness of the senses; the most insipid food was alone endurable; he could wear only garments of certain texture; the odours of all flowers were oppressive; his eyes were tortured by even a faint light; and there were but peculiar sounds, and these from stringed instruments, which did not inspire him with horror.

10 To an anomalous species of terror I found him a bounden slave. "I shall perish," said he, "I *must* perish in this deplorable folly. Thus, thus, and not otherwise, shall I be lost. I dread the events of the future, not in themselves, but in their results. I shudder at the thought of any, even the most trivial, incident, which may operate upon this intolerable agitation of soul. I have, indeed, no abhorrence of danger, except in its absolute effect — in terror. In this unnerved — in this pitiable condition — I feel that the period will sooner or later arrive when I must abandon life and reason together, in some struggle with the grim phantasm, Fear."

I learned, moreover, at intervals, and through broken and equivocal hints, another singular feature of his mental condition. He was enchained by certain superstitious impressions in regard to the dwelling which he tenanted, and whence, for many years, he had never ventured forth — in regard to an influence whose supposititious force was conveyed in terms too shadowy here to be re-stated — an influence which some peculiarities in the mere form and substance of his family mansion, had, by dint of long sufferance, he said, obtained over his spirit — an effect which the *physique* of the gray walls and turrets, and of the dim tarn into which they all looked down, had, at length, brought about upon the *morale* of his existence.

He admitted, however, although with hesitation, that much of the peculiar gloom which thus afflicted him could be traced to a more natural and far more palpable origin — to the severe and long-continued illness — indeed to the evidently approaching dissolution — of a tenderly beloved sister — his sole companion for long years — his last and only relative on earth. "Her decease," he said, with a bitterness which I can never forget, "would leave him (him the hopeless and the frail) the last of the ancient race of the Ushers." While he spoke, the lady Madeline (for so was she called) passed slowly through a remote portion of the apartment, and, without having noticed my presence, disappeared. I regarded her with an utter astonishment not unmingled with dread — and yet I found it impossible to account for such feelings. A sensation of stupor oppressed me, as my eyes followed her retreating steps. When a door, at length, closed upon her, my glance sought instinctively and eagerly the countenance of the brother — but he had buried his face in his hands, and I could only perceive that a far more than ordinary wanness had overspread the emaciated fingers through which trickled many passionate tears.

The disease of the lady Madeline had long baffled the skill of her physicians. A settled apathy, a gradual wasting away of the person, and frequent although transient affections of a partially cataleptical character, were the unusual diagnosis. Hitherto she had steadily borne up against the pressure of her malady, and had not betaken herself finally to bed; but, on the closing in of the evening of my arrival at the house, she succumbed (as her brother told me at night with inexpressible agitation) to the prostrating power of the destroyer; and I learned that the glimpse I had obtained of her person would thus probably be the last I should obtain — that the lady, at least while living, would be seen by me no more.

For several days ensuing, her name was unmentioned by either Usher or myself: and during this period I was busied in earnest endeavours to alleviate the melancholy of my friend. We painted and read together; or I listened, as if in a dream, to the wild improvisations of his speaking guitar. And thus, as a closer and still closer intimacy admitted me more unreservedly into the recesses of his spirit, the more bitterly did I perceive the futility of all attempt at cheering a mind from which darkness, as if an inherent positive quality, poured forth upon all objects of the moral and physical universe, in one unceasing radiation of gloom.

15   I shall ever bear about me a memory of the many solemn hours I thus spent alone with the master of the House of Usher. Yet I should fail in any attempt to convey an idea of the exact character of the studies, or of the occupations, in which he involved me, or led me the way. An excited and highly distempered ideality threw a sulphureous lustre over all. His long improvised dirges will ring forever in my ears. Among other things, I hold painfully in mind a certain singular perversion and amplification of the wild air of the last waltz of Von Weber.[2] From the paintings over which his elaborate fancy brooded, and which grew, touch by touch, into vaguenesses at which I shuddered the more thrillingly, because I shuddered knowing not why; — from these paintings (vivid as their images now are before me) I would in vain endeavour to educe more than a small portion which should lie within the compass of merely written words. By the utter simplicity, by the nakedness of his designs, he arrested and overawed attention. If ever mortal painted an idea, that mortal was Roderick Usher. For me at least — in the circumstances then surrounding me — there arose out of the pure abstractions which the hypochondriac contrived to throw upon his canvas, an intensity of intolerable awe, no shadow of which felt I ever yet in the contemplation of the certainly glowing yet too concrete reveries of Fuseli.[3]

One of the phantasmagoric conceptions of my friend, partaking not so rigidly of the spirit of abstraction, may be shadowed forth, although feebly, in words. A small picture presented the interior of an immensely long and rectangular vault or tunnel, with low walls, smooth, white, and without interruption or device. Certain accessory points of the design served well to convey the idea that this excavation lay at an exceeding depth below the surface of the earth. No outlet was observed in any portion of its vast extent, and no torch, or other artificial source of light was discernible; yet a flood of intense rays rolled throughout, and bathed the whole in a ghastly and inappropriate splendour.

I have just spoken of that morbid condition of the auditory nerve which rendered all music intolerable to the sufferer, with the exception of certain effects of stringed instruments. It was, perhaps, the narrow limits to which he thus confined himself upon the guitar, which gave birth, in great measure, to the fantastic character of his performances. But the fervid *facility* of his *impromptus* could not be so accounted for. They must have been, and were, in

2   Composed by Karl Gottlieb Reissiger in honour of Karl Maria Von Weber, nineteenth-century German composer of operas.   3   late eighteenth- early nineteenth-century Swiss painter interested in psychological horror and the supernatural.

the notes, as well as in the words of his wild fantasias (for he not unfrequently accompanied himself with rhymed verbal improvisations), the result of that intense mental collectedness and concentration to which I have previously alluded as observable only in particular moments of the highest artificial excitement. The words of one of these rhapsodies I have easily remembered. I was, perhaps, the more forcibly impressed with it, as he gave it, because, in the under or mystic current of its meaning, I fancied that I perceived, and for the first time, a full consciousness on the part of Usher, of the tottering of his lofty reason upon her throne. The verses, which were entitled "The Haunted Palace," ran very nearly, if not accurately, thus:

I.

In the greenest of our valleys,
    By good angels tenanted,
Once a fair and stately palace —
    Radiant palace — reared its head.
In the monarch Thought's dominion —
    It stood there!
Never seraph spread a pinion
    Over fabric half so fair.

II.

Banners yellow, glorious, golden,
    On its roof did float and flow;
(This — all this — was in the olden
    Time long ago)
And every gentle air that dallied,
    In that sweet day,
Along the ramparts plumed and pallid,
    A winged odour went away.

III.

20 Wanderers in that happy valley
        Through two luminous windows saw
    Spirits moving musically
        To a lute's well-tuned law,
    Round about a throne, where sitting
        (Porphyrogene!)[4]
    In state his glory well befitting,
        The ruler of the realm was seen.

IV.

And all with pearl and ruby glowing
    Was the fair palace door,
Through which came flowing, flowing, flowing
    And sparkling evermore,
A troop of Echoes whose sweet duty
    Was but to sing,

4 of royal birth.

In voices of surpassing beauty,
    The wit and wisdom of their king.

V.

But evil things, in robes of sorrow,
    Assailed the monarch's high estate;
(Ah, let us mourn, for never morrow
    Shall dawn upon him, desolate!)
And, round about his home, the glory
    That blushed and bloomed
Is but a dim-remembered story
    Of the old time entombed.

VI.

And travellers now within that valley,
    Through the red-litten windows, see
Vast forms that move fantastically
    To a discordant melody;
While, like a rapid ghastly river,
    Through the pale door,
A hideous throng rush out forever,
    And laugh — but smile no more.

I well remember that suggestions arising from this ballad, led us into a train of thought wherein there became manifest an opinion of Usher's which I mention not so much on account of its novelty, (for other men have thought thus,) as on account of the pertinacity with which he maintained it. This opinion, in its general form, was that of the sentience of all vegetable things. But, in his disordered fancy, the idea had assumed a more daring character, and trespassed, under certain conditions, upon the kingdom of inorganization. I lack words to express the full extent, or the earnest *abandon* of his persuasion. The belief, however, was connected (as I have previously hinted) with the gray stones of the home of his forefathers. The conditions of the sentience had been here, he imagined, fulfilled in the method of collocation of these stones — in the order of their arrangement, as well as in that of the many *fungi* which overspread them, and of the decayed trees which stood around — above all, in the long undisturbed endurance of this arrangement, and in its reduplication in the still waters of the tarn. Its evidence — the evidence of the sentience — was to be seen, he said (and I here started as he spoke,) in the gradual yet certain condensation of an atmosphere of their own about the waters and the walls. The result was discoverable, he added, in that silent, yet importunate and terrible influence which for centuries had moulded the destinies of his family, and which made *him* what I now saw him — what he was. Such opinions need no comment, and I will make none.

Our books[5] — the books which, for years, had formed no small portion of the mental existence of the invalid — were, as might be supposed, in strict keeping with this character of phantasm. We pored together over such works

25

5   these obscure books deal with supernatural occurrences, death, and damnation.

as the Ververt et Chartreuse of Gresset; the Belphegor of Machiavelli; the Heaven and Hell of Swedenborg; the Subterranean Voyage of Nicholas Klimm by Holberg; the Chiromancy of Robert Flud, of Jean D'Indaginé, and of De la Chambre; the Journey into the Blue Distance of Tieck; and the City of the Sun of Campanella. One favourite volume was a small octavo edition of the *Directorium Inquisitorum,* by the Dominican Eymeric de Gironne; and there were passages in Pomponius Mela, about the old African Satyrs and Ægipans, over which Usher would sit dreaming for hours. His chief delight, however, was found in the perusal of an exceedingly rare and curious book in quarto Gothic — the manual of a forgotten church — the *Vigiliae Mortuorum secundum Chorum Ecclesiae Maguntinæ.*

I could not help thinking of the wild ritual of this work, and of its probable influence upon the hypochondriac, when, one evening, having informed me abruptly that the lady Madeline was no more, he stated his intention of preserving her corpse for a fortnight, (previously to its final interment,) in one of the numerous vaults within the main walls of the building. The worldly reason, however, assigned for this singular proceeding, was one which I did not feel at liberty to dispute. The brother had been led to his resolution (so he told me) by consideration of the unusual character of the malady of the deceased, of certain obtrusive and eager inquiries on the part of her medical men, and of the remote and exposed situation of the burial-ground of the family. I will not deny that when I called to mind the sinister countenance of the person whom I met upon the staircase, on the day of my arrival at the house, I had no desire to oppose what I regarded as at best but a harmless, and by no means an unnatural, precaution.

At the request of Usher, I personally aided him in the arrangements for the temporary entombment. The body having been encoffined, we two alone bore it to its rest. The vault in which we placed it (and which had been so long unopened that our torches, half smothered in its oppressive atmosphere, gave us little opportunity for investigation) was small, damp, and entirely without means of admission for light; lying, at great depth, immediately beneath that portion of the building in which was my own sleeping apartment. It had been used, apparently, in remote feudal times, for the worst purposes of a donjon-keep, and, in later days, as a place of deposit for powder, or some other highly combustible substance, as a portion of its floor, and the whole interior of a long archway through which we reached it, were carefully sheathed with copper. The door, of massive iron, had been, also, similarly protected. Its immense weight caused an unusually sharp grating sound, as it moved upon its hinges.

Having deposited our mournful burden upon tressels within this region of horror, we partially turned aside the yet unscrewed lid of the coffin, and looked upon the face of the tenant. A striking similitude between the brother and sister now first arrested my attention; and Usher, divining, perhaps, my thoughts, murmured out some few words from which I learned that the deceased and himself had been twins, and that sympathies of a scarcely intelligible nature had always existed between them. Our glances, however, rested not long upon the dead — for we could not regard her unawed. The disease which had thus entombed the lady in the maturity of youth, had left, as usual in all maladies of a strictly cataleptical character, the mockery of a faint blush upon the bosom and the face, and that suspiciously lingering smile upon the lip which is so terrible in death. We replaced and screwed down the lid, and, having secured the door of iron, made our way, with toil, into the scarcely less gloomy apartments of the upper portion of the house.

And now, some days of bitter grief having elapsed, an observable change came over the features of the mental disorder of my friend. His ordinary manner had vanished. His ordinary occupations were neglected or forgotten. He roamed from chamber to chamber with hurried, unequal, and objectless step. The pallor of his countenance had assumed, if possible, a more ghastly hue — but the luminousness of his eye had utterly gone out. The once occasional huskiness of his tone was heard no more; and a tremulous quaver, as if of extreme terror, habitually characterized his utterance. There were times, indeed, when I thought his unceasingly agitated mind was labouring with some oppressive secret, to divulge which he struggled for the necessary courage. At times, again, I was obliged to resolve all into the mere inexplicable vagaries of madness, for I beheld him gazing upon vacancy for long hours, in an attitude of the profoundest attention, as if listening to some imaginary sound. It was no wonder that his condition terrified — that it infected me. I felt creeping upon me, by slow yet certain degrees, the wild influences of his own fantastic yet impressive superstitions.

30   It was, especially, upon retiring to bed late in the night of the seventh or eighth day after the placing of the lady Madeline within the donjon, that I experienced the full power of such feelings. Sleep came not near my couch — while the hours waned and waned away. I struggled to reason off the nervousness which had dominion over me. I endeavoured to believe that much, if not all of what I felt, was due to the bewildering influence of the gloomy furniture of the room — of the dark and tattered draperies, which, tortured into motion by the breath of a rising tempest, swayed fitfully to and fro upon the walls, and rustled uneasily about the decorations of the bed. But my efforts were fruitless. An irrepressible tremour gradually pervaded my frame; and, at length, there sat upon my very heart an incubus of utterly causeless alarm. Shaking this off with a gasp and a struggle, I uplifted myself upon the pillows, and, peering earnestly within the intense darkness of the chamber, hearkened — I know not why, except that an instinctive spirit prompted me — to certain low and indefinite sounds which came, through the pauses of the storm, at long intervals, I knew not whence. Overpowered by an intense sentiment of horror, unaccountable yet unendurable, I threw on my clothes with haste (for I felt that I should sleep no more during the night), and endeavoured to arouse myself from the pitiable condition into which I had fallen, by pacing rapidly to and fro through the apartment.

I had taken but few turns in this manner, when a light step on an adjoining staircase arrested my attention. I presently recognised it as that of Usher. In an instant afterward he rapped, with a gentle touch, at my door, and entered, bearing a lamp. His countenance was, as usual, cadaverously wan — but, moreover, there was a species of mad hilarity in his eyes — an evidently restrained *hysteria* in his whole demeanour. His air appalled me — but anything was preferable to the solitude which I had so long endured, and I even welcomed his presence as a relief.

"And you have not seen it?" he said abruptly, after having stared about him for some moments in silence — "you have not then seen it? — but, stay! you shall." Thus speaking, and having carefully shaded his lamp, he hurried to one of the casements, and threw it freely open to the storm.

The impetuous fury of the entering gust nearly lifted us from our feet. It was, indeed, a tempestuous yet sternly beautiful night, and one wildly singular in its terror and its beauty. A whirlwind had apparently collected its force in our vicinity; for there were frequent and violent alterations in the direction of the wind; and the exceeding density of the clouds (which hung so low as to press upon the turrets of the house) did not prevent our perceiving the life-like velocity with which they flew careering from all points against each other, without passing away into the distance. I say that even their exceeding density did not prevent our perceiving this — yet we had no glimpse of the moon or stars — nor was there any flashing forth of the lightning. But the under surfaces of the huge masses of agitated vapour, as well as all terrestrial objects immediately around us, were glowing in the unnatural light of a faintly luminous and distinctly visible gaseous exhalation which hung about and enshrouded the mansion.

"You must not — you shall not behold this!" said I, shudderingly, to Usher, as I led him, with a gentle violence, from the window to a seat. "These appearances, which bewilder you, are merely electrical phenomena not uncommon — or it may be that they have their ghastly origin in the rank miasma of the tarn. Let us close this casement; — the air is chilling and dangerous to your frame. Here is one of your favourite romances. I will read, and you shall listen; — and so we will pass away this terrible night together."

35   The antique volume which I had taken up was the "Mad Trist" of Sir Launcelot Canning;[6] but I had called it a favourite of Usher's more in sad jest than in earnest; for, in trust, there is little in its uncouth and unimaginative prolixity which could have had interest for the lofty and spiritual ideality of my friend. It was, however, the only book immediately at hand; and I indulged a vague hope that the excitement which now agitated the hypochondriac, might find relief (for the history of mental disorder is full of similar anomalies) even in the extremeness of the folly which I should read. Could I have judged, indeed, by the wild overstrained air of vivacity with which he hearkened, or apparently hearkened, to the words of the tale, I might well have congratulated myself upon the success of my design.

I had arrived at that well-known portion of the story where Ethelred, the hero of the Trist, having sought in vain for peaceable admission into the dwelling of the hermit, proceeds to make good an entrance by force. Here, it will be remembered, the words of the narrative runs thus:

"And Ethelred, who was by nature of a doughty heart, and who was now mighty withal, on account of the powerfulness of the wine which he had drunken, waited no longer to hold parley with the hermit, who, in sooth, was of an obstinate and maliceful turn, but, feeling the rain upon his shoulders, and fearing the rising of the tempest, uplifted his mace outright, and, with blows, made quickly room in the plankings of the door for his gauntleted hand; and now pulling therewith sturdily, he so cracked, and ripped, and tore all asunder, that the noise of the dry and hollow-sounding wood alarmed and reverberated throughout the forest."

At the termination of this sentence I started, and for a moment, paused; for it appeared to me (although I at once concluded that my excited fancy had

6   the author and book are imaginary; Poe wrote the descriptions to fit this story.

deceived me) — it appeared to me that, from some very remote portion of the mansion, there came, indistinctly, to my ears, what might have been, in its exact similarity of character, the echo (but a stifled and full one certainly) of the very cracking and ripping sound which Sir Launcelot had so particularly described. It was, beyond doubt, the coincidence alone which had arrested my attention; for, amid the rattling of the sashes of the casements, and the ordinary commingled noises of the still increasing storm, the sound, in itself, had nothing, surely, which should have interested or disturbed me. I continued the story:

"But the good champion Ethelred, now entering within the door, was sore enraged and amazed to perceive no signal of the maliceful hermit; but, in the stead thereof, a dragon of a scaly and prodigious demeanour, and of a fiery tongue, which sate in guard before a palace of gold, with a floor of silver; and upon the wall there hung a shield of shining brass with this legend enwritten —

40
> Who entereth herein, a conqueror hath bin;
> Who slayeth the dragon, the shield he shall win;

And Ethelred uplifted his mace, and struck upon the head of the dragon, which fell before him, and gave up his pesty breath, with a shriek so horrid and harsh, and withal so piercing, that Ethelred had fain to close his ears with his hands against the dreadful noise of it, the like whereof was never before heard."

Here again I paused abruptly, and now with a feeling of wild amazement — for there could be no doubt whatever that, in this instance, I did actually hear (although from what direction it proceeded I found it impossible to say) a low and apparently distant, but harsh, protracted, and most unusual screaming or grating sound — the exact counterpart of what my fancy had already conjured up for the dragon's unnatural shriek as described by the romancer.

Oppressed, as I certainly was, upon the occurrence of the second and most extraordinary coincidence, by a thousand conflicting sensations, in which wonder and extreme terror were predominant, I still retained sufficient presence of mind to avoid exciting, by any observation, the sensitive nervousness of my companion. I was by no means certain that he had noticed the sounds in question; although, assuredly, a strange alteration had, during the last few minutes, taken place in his demeanour. From a position fronting my own, he had gradually brought round his chair, so as to sit with his face to the door of the chamber; and thus I could but partially perceive his features, although I saw that his lips trembled as if he were murmuring inaudibly. His head had dropped upon his breast — yet I knew that he was not asleep, from the wide and rigid opening of the eye as I caught a glance of it in profile. The motion of his body, too, was at variance with this idea — for he rocked from side to side with a gentle yet constant and uniform sway. Having rapidly taken notice of all this, I resumed the narrative of Sir Launcelot, which thus proceeded:

"And now, the champion, having escaped from the terrible fury of the dragon, bethinking himself of the brazen shield, and of the breaking up of the enchantment which was upon it, removed the carcass from out of the way before him, and approached valorously over the silver pavement of the castle to where the shield was upon the wall; which in sooth tarried not for his full coming, but fell down at his feet upon the silver floor, with a mighty great and terrible ringing sound."

No sooner had these syllables passed my lips, than — as if a shield of brass had indeed, at the moment, fallen heavily upon a floor of silver — I became aware of a distinct, hollow, metallic, and clangorous, yet apparently muffled reverberation. Completely unnerved, I leaped to my feet; but the measured rocking movement of Usher was undisturbed. I rushed to the chair in which he sat. His eyes were bent fixedly before him, and throughout his whole countenance there reigned a stony rigidity. But, as I placed my hand upon his shoulder, there came a strong shudder over his whole person; a sickly smile quivered about his lips; and I saw that he spoke in a low, hurried, and gibbering murmur, as if unconscious of my presence. Bending closely over him, I at length drank in the hideous import of his words.

45   "Not hear it? — yes, I hear it, and *have* heard it. Long — long — long — many minutes, many hours, many days, have I heard it — yet I dared not — oh, pity me, miserable wretch that I am! — I dared not — I *dared* not speak! *We have put her living in the tomb!* Said I not that my senses were acute? I *now* tell you that I heard her first feeble movements in the hollow coffin. I heard them, many, many days ago — yet I dared not — *I dared not speak!* And now — to-night — Ethelred — ha! ha! — the breaking of the hermit's door, and the death-cry of the dragon, and the clangour of the shield! — say, rather, the rending of her coffin, and the grating of the iron hinges of her prison, and her struggles within the coppered archway of the vault! Oh whither shall I fly? Will she not be here anon? Is she not hurrying to upbraid me for my haste? Have I not heard her footstep on the stair? Do I not distinguish that heavy and horrible beating of her heart? MADMAN!" here he sprang furiously to his feet, and shrieked out his syllables, as if in the effort he were giving up his soul — "MADMAN! I TELL YOU THAT SHE NOW STANDS WITHOUT THE DOOR!"

As if in the superhuman energy of his utterance there had been found the potency of a spell — the huge antique panels to which the speaker pointed, threw slowly back, upon the instant, their ponderous and ebony jaws. It was the work of the rushing gust — but then without those doors there DID stand the lofty and enshrouded figure of the lady Madeline of Usher. There was blood upon her white robes, and the evidence of some bitter struggle upon every portion of her emaciated frame. For a moment she remained trembling and reeling to and fro upon the threshold, then, with a low moaning cry, fell heavily inward upon the person of her brother, and in her violent and now final death-agonies, bore him to the floor a corpse, and a victim to the terrors he had anticipated.

From that chamber, and from that mansion, I fled aghast. The storm was still abroad in all its wrath as I found myself crossing the old causeway. Suddenly there shot along the path a wild light, and I turned to see whence a gleam so unusual could have issued; for the vast house and its shadows were alone behind me. The radiance was that of the full, setting, and blood-red moon which now shone vividly through that once barely discernible fissure of which I have before spoken as extending from the roof of the building, in a zigzag direction, to the base. While I gazed, this fissure rapidly widened — there came a fierce breath of the whirlwind — the entire orb of the satellite burst at once upon my sight — my brain reeled as I saw the mighty walls rushing asunder — there was a long tumultuous shouting sound like the voice of a thousand waters — and the deep and dank tarn at my feet closed sullenly and silently over the fragments of the "HOUSE OF USHER."

(1839)

Herman Melville　(1819–1891)

Born in New York City, Herman Melville spent many years as a sailor, including a cruise on a whaling ship, before becoming a writer. His most famous book, *Moby-Dick*, combined factual details about whaling with a symbolic examination about the nature of reality, particularly the conflict between good and evil. It is narrated by Ishmael, a quiet, thoughtful crew member, and presents the monomaniacal quest of Captain Ahab to slay a great white whale. Although "Bartleby, the Scrivener," written shortly after the novel, is much shorter and is set in a large city, it bears many similarities to *Moby-Dick*. The unnamed narrator is fascinated by a character who is much different from him, as Ishmael was fascinated by Ahab. The realistic and mundane details of a law office are given symbolic meanings, particularly the blank wall at which Bartleby stares. The lonely scrivener represents the condition of many human beings, orphans and "isolatoes," as Melville termed them, in a world where the significance of life, if there is any, cannot usually be understood. The short story also satirizes nineteenth-century Americans' preoccupation with the acquisition of wealth.

BARTLEBY, THE SCRIVENER
A Story of Wall-Street

I am a rather elderly man. The nature of my avocations for the last thirty years has brought me into more than ordinary contact with what would seem an interesting and somewhat singular set of men, of whom as yet nothing that I know of has ever been written:— I mean the law-copyists or scriveners. I have known very many of them, professionally and privately, and if I pleased, could relate divers histories, at which good-natured gentlemen might smile, and sentimental souls might weep. But I waive the biographies of all other scriveners for a few passages in the life of Bartleby, who was a scrivener the strangest I ever saw or heard of. While of other law-copyists I might write the complete life, of Bartleby nothing of that sort can be done. I believe that no materials exist for a full and satisfactory biography of this man. It is an irreparable loss to literature. Bartleby was one of those beings of whom nothing is ascertainable, except from the original sources, and in his case those are very small. What my own astonished eyes saw of Bartleby, *that* is all I know of him, except, indeed, one vague report which will appear in the sequel.

Ere introducing the scrivener, as he first appeared to me, it is fit I make some mention of myself, my *employés*, my business, my chambers, and general surroundings; because some such description is indispensable to an adequate understanding of the chief character about to be presented.

Imprimis: I am a man who, from his youth upwards, has been filled with a profound conviction that the easiest way of life is the best. Hence, though I belong to a profession proverbially energetic and nervous, even to turbulence, at times, yet nothing of that sort have I ever suffered to invade my peace. I am one of those unambitious lawyers who never addresses a jury, or in any way draws down public applause; but in the cool tranquillity of a snug retreat, do a snug business among rich men's bonds and mortgages and title-deeds. All who know me, consider me an eminently *safe* man. The late John Jacob Astor,[1] a personage little given to poetic enthusiasm, had no hesitation in pronouncing my first grand point to be prudence; my next, method. I do not speak it in vanity, but simply record the fact, that I was not unemployed in my profession by the late John Jacob Astor; a name which, I admit, I love to repeat, for it hath a rounded and orbicular sound to it, and rings like unto bullion. I will freely add, that I was not insensible to the late John Jacob Astor's good opinion.

Some time prior to the period at which this little history begins, my avocations had been largely increased. The good old office, now extinct in the State of New-York, of a Master in Chancery,[2] had been conferred upon me. It was not a very arduous office, but very pleasantly remunerative. I seldom lose my temper; much more seldom indulge in dangerous indignation at wrongs and outrages; but I must be permitted to be rash here and declare, that I consider the sudden and violent abrogation of the office of Master in Chancery, by the new Constitution, as a — premature act; inasmuch as I had counted upon a life-lease of the profits, whereas I only received those of a few short years. But this is by the way.

5   My chambers were up stairs at No. — Wall-street.[3] At one end they looked upon the white wall of the interior of a spacious sky-light shaft, penetrating the building from top to bottom. This view might have been considered rather tame than otherwise, deficient in what landscape painters call "life." But if so, the view from the other end of my chambers offered, at least, a contrast, if nothing more. In that direction my windows commanded an unobstructed view of a lofty brick wall, black by age and everlasting shade; which wall required no spy-glass to bring out its lurking beauties, but for the benefit of all near-sighted spectators, was pushed up to within ten feet of my window panes. Owing to the great height of the surrounding buildings, and my chambers being on the second floor, the interval between this wall and mine not a little resembled a huge square cistern.

At the period just preceding the advent of Bartleby, I had two persons as copyists in my employment, and a promising lad as an office-boy. First, Turkey; second, Nippers; third, Ginger Nut. These may seem names, the like of which are not usually found in the Directory. In truth they were nicknames, mutually conferred upon each other by my three clerks, and were deemed expressive of their respective persons or characters. Turkey was a short, pursy Englishman of about my own age, that is, somewhere not far from sixty. In the morning, one might say, his face was of a fine florid hue, but after twelve o'clock, meridian — his dinner hour — it blazed like a grate full of Christmas coals; and continued blazing — but, as it were, with a gradual wane — till 6 o'clock, P.M. or thereabouts, after which I saw no more of the proprietor of the face, which gaining its meridian with the sun, seemed to set with it, to rise, culminate, and decline the following day, with the like regularity and undiminished glory.

1 at the time of his death in 1848, Astor was the richest man in the United States. 2 officer of the court whose duties included taking testimonies, administering oaths, and acknowledging deeds. 3 located in New York City, the financial centre of the United States.

There are many singular coincidences I have known in the course of my life, not the least among which was the fact, that exactly when Turkey displayed his fullest beams from his red and radiant countenance, just then, too, at that critical moment, began the daily period when I considered his business capacities as seriously disturbed for the remainder of the twenty-four hours. Not that he was absolutely idle, or averse to business then; far from it. The difficulty was, he was apt to be altogether too energetic. There was a strange, inflamed, flurried, flighty recklessness of activity about him. He would be incautious in dipping his pen into his inkstand. All his blots upon my documents, were dropped there after twelve o'clock, meridian. Indeed, not only would he be reckless and sadly given to making blots in the afternoon, but some days he went further, and was rather noisy. At such times, too, his face flamed with augmented blazonry, as if cannel coal had been heaped on anthracite. He made an unpleasant racket with his chair; spilled his sandbox; in mending his pens, impatiently split them all to pieces, and threw them on the floor in a sudden passion; stood up and leaned over his table, boxing his papers about in a most indecorous manner, very sad to behold in an elderly man like him. Nevertheless, as he was in many ways a most valuable person to me, and all the time before twelve o'clock, meridian, was the quickest, steadiest creature too, accomplishing a great deal of work in a style not easy to be matched — for these reasons, I was willing to overlook his eccentricities, though indeed, occasionally, I remonstrated with him. I did this very gently, however, because, though the civilest, nay, the blandest and most reverential of men in the morning, yet in the afternoon he was disposed, upon provocation, to be slightly rash with his tongue, in fact, insolent. Now, valuing his morning services as I did, and resolved not to lose them; yet, at the same time made uncomfortable by his inflamed ways after twelve o'clock; and being a man of peace, unwilling by my admonitions to call forth unseemly retorts from him; I took upon me, one Saturday noon (he was always worse on Saturdays), to hint to him, very kindly, that perhaps now that he was growing old, it might be well to abridge his labors; in short, he need not come to my chambers after twelve o'clock, but, dinner over, had best go home to his lodgings and rest himself till tea-time. But no; he insisted upon his afternoon devotions. His countenance became intolerably fervid, as he oratorically assured me — gesticulating with a long ruler at the other end of the room — that if his services in the morning were useful, how indispensable, then, in the afternoon?

"With submission, sir," said Turkey on this occasion, "I consider myself your right-hand man. In the morning I but marshal and deploy my columns; but in the afternoon I put myself at their head, and gallantly charge the foe, thus!" — and he made a violent thrust with the ruler.

"But the blots, Turkey," intimated I.

"True, — but, with submission, sir, behold these hairs! I am getting old. Surely, sir, a blot or two of a warm afternoon is not to be severely urged against gray hairs. Old age — even if it blot the page — is honorable. With submission, sir, we *both* are getting old."

This appeal to my fellow-feeling was hardly to be resisted. At all events, I saw that go he would not. So I made up my mind to let him stay, resolving, nevertheless, to see to it, that during the afternoon he had to do with my less important papers.

Nippers, the second on my list, was a whiskered, sallow, and, upon the whole, rather piratical-looking young man of about five and twenty. I always deemed him the victim of two evil powers — ambition and indigestion. The ambition was evinced by a certain impatience of the duties of a mere copyist, an unwarrantable usurpation of strictly professional affairs, such as the original drawing up of legal documents. The indigestion seemed betokened in an occasional nervous testiness and grinning irritability, causing the teeth to audibly grind together over mistakes committed in copying; unnecessary maledictions, hissed, rather than spoken, in the heat of business; and especially by a continual discontent with the height of the table where he worked. Though of a very ingenious mechanical turn, Nippers could never get this table to suit him. He put chips under it, blocks of various sorts, bits of pasteboard, and at last went so far as to attempt an exquisite adjustment by final pieces of folded blotting-paper. But no invention would answer. If, for the sake of easing his back, he brought the table lid at a sharp angle well up towards his chin, and wrote there like a man using the steep roof of a Dutch house for his desk: — then he declared that it stopped the circulation in his arms. If now he lowered the table to his waistbands, and stooped over it in writing, then there was a sore aching in his back. In short, the truth of the matter was, Nippers knew not what he wanted. Or, if he wanted any thing, it was to be rid of a scrivener's table altogether. Among the manifestations of his diseased ambition was a fondness he had for receiving visits from certain ambiguous-looking fellows in seedy coats, whom he called his clients. Indeed I was aware that not only was he, at times, considerable of a ward-politician,[4] but he occasionally did a little business at the Justices' courts, and was not unknown on the steps of the Tombs.[5] I have good reason to believe, however, that one individual who called upon him at my chambers, and who, with a grand air, he insisted was his client, was no other than a dun, and the alleged title-deed, a bill. But with all his failings, and the annoyances he caused me, Nippers, like his compatriot Turkey, was a very useful man to me; wrote a neat, swift hand; and, when he chose, was not deficient in a gentlemanly sort of deportment. Added to this, he always dressed in a gentlemanly sort of way; and so, incidentally, reflected credit upon my chambers. Whereas with respect to Turkey, I had much ado to keep him from being a reproach to me. His clothes were apt to look oily and smell of eating-houses. He wore his pantaloons very loose and baggy in summer. His coats were execrable; his hat not to be handled. But while the hat was a thing of indifference to me, inasmuch as his natural civility and deference, as a dependent Englishman, always led him to doff it the moment he entered the room, yet his coat was another matter. Concerning his coats, I reasoned with him; but with no effect. The truth was, I suppose, that a man with so small an income, could not afford to sport such a lustrous face and a lustrous coat at one and the same time. As Nippers once observed, Turkey's money went chiefly for red ink. One winter day I presented Turkey with a highly-respectable looking coat of my own, a padded gray coat, of a most comfortable warmth, and which buttoned straight up from the knee to the neck. I thought Turkey would appreciate the favor, and abate his rashness and

4 similar to an alderman or town-councillor. 5 New York City prison.

obstreperousness of afternoons. But no. I verily believe that buttoning himself up in so downy and blanket-like a coat had a pernicious effect upon him; upon the same principle that too much oats are bad for horses. In fact, precisely as a rash, restive horse is said to feel his oats, so Turkey felt his coat. It made him insolent. He was a man whom prosperity harmed.

Though concerning the self-indulgent habits of Turkey I had my own private surmises, yet touching Nippers I was well persuaded that whatever might be his faults in other respects, he was, at least, a temperate young man. But indeed, nature herself seemed to have been his vintner, and at his birth charged him so thoroughly with an irritable, brandy-like disposition, that all subsequent potations were needless. When I consider how, amid the stillness of my chambers, Nippers would sometimes impatiently rise from his seat, and stooping over his table, spread his arms wide apart, seize the whole desk, and move it, and jerk it, with a grim, grinding motion on the floor, as if the table were a perverse voluntary agent, intent on thwarting and vexing him; I plainly perceive that for Nippers, brandy and water were altogether superfluous.

It was fortunate for me that, owing to its peculiar cause — indigestion — the irritability and consequent nervousness of Nippers, were mainly observable in the morning, while in the afternoon he was comparatively mild. So that Turkey's paroxysms only coming on about twelve o'clock, I never had to do with their eccentricities at one time. Their fits relieved each other like guards. When Nippers' was on, Turkey's was off; and *vice versa*. This was a good natural arrangement under the circumstances.

Ginger Nut, the third on my list, was a lad some twelve years old. His father was a carman,[6] ambitious of seeing his son on the bench instead of a cart, before he died. So he sent him to my office as student at law, errand boy, and cleaner and sweeper, at the rate of one dollar a week. He had a little desk to himself, but he did not use it much. Upon inspection, the drawer exhibited a great array of the shells of various sorts of nuts. Indeed, to this quick-witted youth the whole noble science of the law was contained in a nut-shell. Not the least among the employments of Ginger Nut, as well as one which he discharged with the most alacrity, was his duty as cake and apple purveyor for Turkey and Nippers. Copying law papers being proverbially a dry, husky sort of business, my two scriveners were fain to moisten their mouths very often with Spitzenbergs[7] to be had at the numerous stalls nigh the Custom House and Post Office. Also, they sent Ginger Nut very frequently for that peculiar cake — small, flat, round, and very spicy — after which he had been named by them. Of a cold morning when business was but dull, Turkey would gobble up scores of these cakes, as if they were mere wafers — indeed they sell them at the rate of six or eight for a penny — the scrape of his pen blending with the crunching of the crisp particles in his mouth. Of all the fiery afternoon blunders and flurried rashnesses of Turkey, was his once moistening a ginger-cake between his lips, and clapping it on to a mortgage for a seal. I came within an ace of dismissing him then. But he mollified me by making an oriental bow, and saying — "With submission, sir, it was generous of me to find you in stationery on my own account."

6 driver of a cart. 7 variety of apple.

15   Now my original business — that of a conveyancer[8] and title hunter, and drawer-up of recondite documents of all sorts — was considerably increased by receiving the master's office. There was now great work for scriveners. Not only must I push the clerks already with me, but I must have additional help. In answer to my advertisement, a motionless young man one morning, stood upon my office threshold, the door being open, for it was summer. I can see that figure now — pallidly neat, pitiably respectable, incurably forlorn! It was Bartleby.

     After a few words touching his qualifications, I engaged him, glad to have among my corps of copyists a man of so singularly sedate an aspect, which I thought might operate beneficially upon the flighty temper of Turkey, and the fiery one of Nippers.

     I should have stated before that ground glass folding-doors divided my premises into two parts, one of which was occupied by my scriveners, the other by myself. According to my humor I threw open these doors, or closed them. I resolved to assign Bartleby a corner by the folding-doors, but on my side of them, so as to have this quiet man within easy call, in case any trifling thing was to be done. I placed his desk close up to a small side-window in that part of the room, a window which originally had afforded a lateral view of certain grimy back-yards and bricks, but which, owing to subsequent erections, commanded at present no view at all, though it gave some light. Within three feet of the panes was a wall, and the light came down from far above, between two lofty buildings, as from a very small opening in a dome. Still further to a satisfactory arrangement, I procured a high green folding screen, which might entirely isolate Bartleby from my sight, though not remove him from my voice. And thus, in a manner, privacy and society were conjoined.

     At first Bartleby did an extraordinary quantity of writing. As if long famishing for something to copy, he seemed to gorge himself on my documents. There was no pause for digestion. He ran a day and night line, copying by sun-light and by candle-light. I should have been quite delighted with his application, had he been cheerfully industrious. But he wrote on silently, palely, mechanically.

     It is, of course, an indispensable part of a scrivener's business to verify the accuracy of his copy, word by word. Where there are two or more scriveners in an office, they assist each other in this examination, one reading from the copy, the other holding the original. It is a very dull, wearisome, and lethargic affair. I can readily imagine that to some sanguine temperaments it would be altogether intolerable. For example, I cannot credit that the mettlesome poet Byron[9] would have contentedly sat down with Bartleby to examine a law document of, say five hundred pages, closely written in a crimpy hand.

20   Now and then, in the haste of business, it had been my habit to assist in comparing some brief document myself, calling Turkey or Nippers for this purpose. One object I had in placing Bartleby so handy to me behind the screen, was to avail myself of his services on such trivial occasions. It was on the third day, I think, of his being with me, and before any necessity had arisen for having his own writing examined, that, being much hurried to complete a

---

8 person who prepares documents for property transfers.   9 an English poet of the early nineteenth century, Byron (see pages 138–139) was known for his flamboyant temperament.

small affair I had in hand, I abruptly called to Bartleby. In my haste and natural expectancy of instant compliance, I sat with my head bent over the original on my desk, and my right hand sideways, and somewhat nervously extended with the copy, so that immediately upon emerging from his retreat, Bartleby might snatch it and proceed to business without the least delay.

In this very attitude did I sit when I called to him, rapidly stating what it was I wanted him to do — namely, to examine a small paper with me. Imagine my surprise, nay, my consternation, when without moving from his privacy, Bartleby in a singularly mild, firm voice, replied, "I would prefer not to."

I sat awhile in perfect silence, rallying my stunned faculties. Immediately it occurred to me that my ears had deceived me, or Bartleby had entirely misunderstood my meaning. I repeated my request in the clearest tone I could assume. But in quite as clear a one came the previous reply, "I would prefer not to."

"Prefer not to," echoed I, rising in high excitement, and crossing the room with a stride. "What do you mean? Are you moon-struck? I want you to help me compare this sheet here — take it," and I thrust it towards him.

"I would prefer not to," said he.

25   I looked at him steadfastly. His face was leanly composed; his gray eye dimly calm. Not a wrinkle of agitation rippled him. Had there been the least uneasiness, anger, impatience or impertinence in his manner; in other words, had there been any thing ordinarily human about him, doubtless I should have violently dismissed him from the premises. But as it was, I should have as soon thought of turning my pale plaster-of-paris bust of Cicero out of doors. I stood gazing at him awhile, as he went on with his own writing, and then reseated myself at my desk. This is very strange, thought I. What had one best do? But my business hurried me. I concluded to forget the matter for the present, reserving it for my future leisure. So calling Nippers from the other room, the paper was speedily examined.

A few days after this, Bartleby concluded four lengthy documents, being quadruplicates of a week's testimony taken before me in my High Court of Chancery. It became necessary to examine them. It was an important suit, and great accuracy was imperative. Having all things arranged I called Turkey, Nippers and Ginger Nut from the next room, meaning to place the four copies in the hands of my four clerks, while I should read from the original. Accordingly Turkey, Nippers and Ginger Nut had taken their seats in a row, each with his document in hand, when I called to Bartleby to join this interesting group.

"Bartleby! quick, I am waiting."

I heard a slow scrape of his chair legs on the uncarpeted floor, and soon he appeared standing at the entrance of his hermitage.

"What is wanted?" said he mildly.

30   "The copies, the copies," said I hurriedly. "We are going to examine them. There" — and I held towards him the fourth quadruplicate.

"I would prefer not to," he said, and gently disappeared behind the screen.

For a few moments I was turned into a pillar of salt,[10] standing at the head of my seated column of clerks. Recovering myself, I advanced towards the screen, and demanded the reason for such extraordinary conduct.

10 in Genesis 19, Lot's wife was turned into a pillar of salt for disobeying God's orders not to look at the evil city of Sodom, which He was destroying.

"Why do you refuse?"

"I would prefer not to."

35   With any other man I should have flown outright into a dreadful passion, scorned all further words, and thrust him ignominiously from my presence. But there was something about Bartleby that not only strangely disarmed me, but in a wonderful manner touched and disconcerted me. I began to reason with him.

"These are your own copies we are about to examine. It is labor saving to you, because one examination will answer for your four papers. It is common usage. Every copyist is bound to help examine his copy. Is it not so? Will you not speak? Answer!"

"I prefer not to," he replied in a flute-like tone. It seemed to me that while I had been addressing him, he carefully revolved every statement that I made; fully comprehended the meaning; could not gainsay the irresistible conclusion; but, at the same time, some paramount consideration prevailed with him to reply as he did.

"You are decided, then, not to comply with my request — a request made according to common usage and common sense?"

He briefly gave me to understand that on that point my judgment was sound. Yes: his decision was irreversible.

40   It is not seldom the case that when a man is browbeaten in some unprecedented and violently unreasonable way, he begins to stagger in his own plainest faith. He begins, as it were, vaguely to surmise that, wonderful as it may be, all the justice and all the reason is on the other side. Accordingly, if any distinterested persons are present, he turns to them for some reinforcement for his own faltering mind.

"Turkey," said I, "what do you think of this? Am I not right?"

"With submission, sir," said Turkey, with his blandest tone, "I think that you are."

"Nippers," said I, "what do you think of it?"

"I think I should kick him out of the office."

45   (The reader of nice perceptions will here perceive that, it being morning, Turkey's answer is couched in polite and tranquil terms, but Nippers replies in ill-tempered ones. Or, to repeat a previous sentence, Nippers's ugly mood was on duty, and Turkey's off.)

"Ginger Nut," said I, willing to enlist the smallest suffrage in my behalf, "what do you think of it?"

"I think, sir, he's a little luny," replied Ginger Nut, with a grin.

"You hear what they say," said I, turning towards the screen, "come forth and do your duty."

But he vouchsafed no reply. I pondered a moment in sore perplexity. But once more business hurried me. I determined again to postpone the consideration of this dilemma to my future leisure. With a little trouble we made out to examine the papers without Bartleby, though at every page or two, Turkey deferentially dropped his opinion that this proceeding was quite out of the common; while Nippers, twitching in his chair with a dyspeptic nervousness, ground out between his set teeth occasional hissing maledictions against the stubborn oaf behind the screen. And for his (Nippers's) part, this was the first and the last time he would do another man's business without pay.

50   Meanwhile Bartleby sat in his hermitage, oblivious to every thing but his own peculiar business there.

Some days passed, the scrivener being employed upon another lengthy work. His late remarkable conduct led me to regard his ways narrowly. I observed that he never went to dinner; indeed that he never went any where. As yet I had never of my personal knowledge known him to be outside of my office. He was a perpetual sentry in the corner. At about eleven o'clock though, in the morning, I noticed that Ginger Nut would advance toward the opening in Bartleby's screen, as if silently beckoned thither by a gesture invisible to me where I sat. The boy would then leave the office jingling a few pence, and reappear with a handful of ginger-nuts which he delivered in the hermitage, receiving two of the cakes for his trouble.

He lives, then, on ginger-nuts, thought I; never eats a dinner, properly speaking; he must be a vegetarian then; but no; he never eats even vegetables, he eats nothing but ginger-nuts. My mind then ran on in reveries concerning the probable effects upon the human constitution of living entirely on ginger-nuts. Ginger-nuts are so called because they contain ginger as one of their peculiar constituents, and the final flavoring one. Now what was ginger? A hot, spicy thing. Was Bartleby hot and spicy? Not at all. Ginger, then, had no effect upon Bartleby. Probably he preferred it should have none.

Nothing so aggravates an earnest person as a passive resistance. If the individual so resisted be of a not inhumane temper, and the resisting one perfectly harmless in his passivity; then, in the better moods of the former, he will endeavor charitably to construe to his imagination what proves impossible to be solved by his judgment. Even so, for the most part, I regarded Bartleby and his ways. Poor fellow! thought I, he means no mischief; it is plain he intends no insolence; his aspect sufficiently evinces that his eccentricities are involuntary. He is useful to me. I can get along with him. If I turn him away, the chances are he will fall in with some less indulgent employer, and then he will be rudely treated, and perhaps driven forth miserably to starve. Yes. Here I can cheaply purchase a delicious self-approval. To befriend Bartleby; to humor him in his strange wilfulness, will cost me little or nothing, while I lay up in my soul what will eventually prove a sweet morsel for my conscience. But this mood was not invariable with me. The passiveness of Bartleby sometimes irritated me. I felt strangely goaded on to encounter him in new opposition, to elicit some angry spark from him answerable to my own. But indeed I might as well have essayed to strike fire with my knuckles against a bit of Windsor soap.[11] But one afternoon the evil impulse in me mastered me, and the following little scene ensued:

"Bartleby," said I, "when those papers are all copied, I will compare them with you."

55   "I would prefer not to."

"How? Surely you do not mean to persist in that mulish vagary?"

No answer.

I threw open the folding-doors near by, and turning upon Turkey and Nippers, exclaimed:

11 brown-coloured, scented soap.

"Bartleby a second time says, he won't examine his papers. What do you think of it, Turkey?"

60 It was afternoon, be it remembered. Turkey sat glowing like a brass boiler, his bald head steaming, his hands reeling among his blotted papers.

"Think of it?" roared Turkey; "I think I'll just step behind his screen, and black his eyes for him!"

So saying, Turkey rose to his feet and threw his arms into a pugilistic position. He was hurrying away to make good his promise, when I detained him, alarmed at the effect of incautiously rousing Turkey's combativeness after dinner.

"Sit down, Turkey," said I, "and hear what Nippers has to say. What do you think of it, Nippers? Would I not be justified in immediately dismissing Bartleby?"

"Excuse me, that is for you to decide, sir. I think his conduct quite unusual, and indeed unjust, as regards Turkey and myself. But it may only be a passing whim."

65 "Ah," exclaimed I, "you have strangely changed your mind then — you speak very gently of him now."

"All beer," cried Turkey; "gentleness is effects of beer — Nippers and I dined together to-day. You see how gentle I am, sir. Shall I go and black his eyes?"

"You refer to Bartleby, I suppose. No, not to-day, Turkey," I replied; "pray, put up your fists."

I closed the doors, and again advanced towards Bartleby. I felt additional incentives tempting me to my fate. I burned to be rebelled against again. I remembered that Bartleby never left the office.

"Bartleby," said I, "Ginger Nut is away; just step round to the Post Office, won't you? (it was but a three minutes walk,) and see if there is any thing for me."

70 "I would prefer not to."

"You *will* not?"

"I *prefer* not."

I staggered to my desk, and sat there in a deep study. My blind inveteracy returned. Was there any other thing in which I could procure myself to be ignominiously repulsed by this lean, penniless wight? — my hired clerk? What added thing is there, perfectly reasonable, that he will be sure to refuse to do?

"Bartleby!"

75 No answer.

"Bartleby," in a louder tone.

No answer.

"Bartleby," I roared.

Like a very ghost, agreeably to the laws of magical invocation, at the third summons, he appeared at the entrance of his hermitage.

80 "Go to the next room, and tell Nippers to come to me."

"I prefer not to," he respectfully and slowly said, and mildly disappeared.

"Very good, Bartleby," said I, in a quiet sort of serenely severe self-possessed tone, intimating the unalterable purpose of some terrible retribution very close at hand. At the moment I half intended something of the kind. But upon the whole, as it was drawing towards my dinner-hour, I thought it best to put on my hat and walk home for the day, suffering much from perplexity and distress of mind.

Shall I acknowledge it? The conclusion of this whole business was, that it soon became a fixed fact of my chambers, that a pale young scrivener, by the name of Bartleby, had a desk there; that he copied for me at the usual rate of four cents a folio (one hundred words); but he was permanently exempt from examining the work done by him, that duty being transferred to Turkey and Nippers, out of compliment doubtless to their superior acuteness; moreover, said Bartleby was never on any account to be dispatched on the most trivial errand of any sort; and that even if entreated to take upon him such a matter, it was generally understood that he would prefer not to — in other words, that he would refuse point-blank.

As days passed on, I became considerably reconciled to Bartleby. His steadiness, his freedom from all dissipation, his incessant industry (except when he chose to throw himself into a standing revery behind his screen), his great stillness, his unalterableness of demeanor under all circumstances, made him a valuable acquisition. One prime thing was this, — *he was always there;* — first in the morning, continually through the day, and the last at night. I had a singular confidence in his honesty. I felt my most precious papers perfectly safe in his hands. Sometimes to be sure I could not, for the very soul of me, avoid falling into sudden spasmodic passions with him. For it was exceeding difficult to bear in mind all the time those strange peculiarities, privileges, and unheard of exemptions, forming the tacit stipulations on Bartleby's part under which he remained in my office. Now and then, in the eagerness of dispatching pressing business, I would inadvertently summon Bartleby, in a short, rapid tone, to put his finger, say, on the incipient tie of a bit of red tape with which I was about compressing some papers. Of course, from behind the screen the usual answer, "I prefer not to," was sure to come; and then, how could a human creature with the common infirmities of our nature, refrain from bitterly exclaiming upon such perverseness — such unreasonableness. However, every added repulse of this sort which I received only tended to lessen the probability of my repeating the inadvertence.

85   Here it must be said, that according to the custom of most legal gentlemen occupying chambers in densely populated law buildings, there were several keys to my door. One was kept by a woman residing in the attic, which person weekly scrubbed and daily swept and dusted my apartments. Another was kept by Turkey for convenience sake. The third I sometimes carried in my own pocket. The fourth I knew not who had.

Now, one Sunday morning I happened to go to Trinity Church, to hear a celebrated preacher, and finding myself rather early on the ground, I thought I would walk round to my chambers for a while. Luckily I had my key with me; but upon applying it to the lock, I found it resisted by something inserted from the inside. Quite surprised, I called out; when to my consternation a key was turned from within; and thrusting his lean visage at me, and holding the door ajar, the apparition of Bartleby appeared, in his shirt sleeves, and otherwise in a strangely tattered dishabille, saying quietly that he was sorry, but he was deeply engaged just then, and — preferred not admitting me at present.

In a brief word or two, he moreover added, that perhaps I had better walk round the block two or three times, and by that time he would probably have concluded his affairs.

Now, the utterly unsurmised appearance of Bartleby, tenanting my law-chambers of a Sunday morning, with his cadaverously gentlemanly *nonchalance*, yet withal firm and self-possessed, had such a strange effect upon me, that incontinently I slunk away from my own door, and did as desired. But not without sundry twinges of impotent rebellion against the mild effrontery of this unaccountable scrivener. Indeed, it was his wonderful mildness chiefly, which not only disarmed me, but unmanned me, as it were. For I consider that one, for the time, is a sort of unmanned when he tranquilly permits his hired clerk to dictate to him, and order him away from his own premises. Furthermore, I was full of uneasiness as to what Bartleby could possibly be doing in my office in his shirt sleeves, and in an otherwise dismantled condition of a Sunday morning. Was any thing amiss going on? Nay, that was out of the question. It was not to be thought of for a moment that Bartleby was an immoral person. But what could he be doing there? — copying? Nay again, whatever might be his eccentricities, Bartleby was an eminently decorous person. He would be the last man to sit down to his desk in any state approaching to nudity. Besides, it was Sunday; and there was something about Bartleby that forbade the sup-position that he would by any secular occupation violate the proprieties of the day.

Nevertheless, my mind was not pacified; and full of a restless curiosity, at last I returned to the door. Without hindrance I inserted my key, opened it, and entered. Bartleby was not to be seen. I looked round anxiously, peeped behind his screen; but it was very plain that he was gone. Upon more closely examining the place, I surmised that for an indefinite period Bartleby must have ate, dressed, and slept in my office, and that too without plate, mirror, or bed. The cushioned seat of a ricketty old sofa in one corner bore the faint impress of a lean, reclining form. Rolled away under his desk, I found a blanket; under the empty grate, a blacking box and brush; on a chair, a tin basin, with soap and a ragged towel; in a newspaper a few crumbs of ginger-nuts and a morsel of cheese. Yes, thought I, it is evident enough that Bartleby has been making his home here, keeping bachelor's hall all by himself. Immediately then the thought came sweeping across me, What miserable friendlessness and loneli-ness are here revealed! His poverty is great; but his solitude, how horrible! Think of it. Of a Sunday, Wall-street is deserted as Petra;[12] and every night of every day it is an emptiness. This building too, which of week-days hums with industry and life, at nightfall echoes with sheer vacancy, and all through Sunday is forlorn. And here Bartleby makes his home; sole spectator of a soli-tude which he has seen all populous — a sort of innocent and transformed Marius[13] brooding among the ruins of Carthage![14]

For the first time in my life a feeling of overpowering stinging melan-choly seized me. Before, I had never experienced aught but a not-unpleasing sadness. The bond of a common humanity now drew me irresistibly to gloom.

12 destroyed and abandoned city in north Africa. 13 Roman military commander who fled to Africa in the first century B.C. 14 north African city destroyed by the Romans in the second century B.C.

A fraternal melancholy! For both I and Bartleby were sons of Adam. I remembered the bright silks and sparkling faces I had seen that day, in gala trim, swan-like sailing down the Mississippi of Broadway; and I contrasted them with the pallid copyist, and thought to myself, Ah, happiness courts the light, so we deem the world is gay; but misery hides aloof, so we deem that misery there is none. These sad fancyings — chimeras, doubtless, of a sick and silly brain — led on to other and more special thoughts, concerning the eccentricities of Bartleby. Presentiments of strange discoveries hovered round me. The scrivener's pale form appeared to me laid out, among uncaring strangers, in its shivering winding sheet.

90 Suddenly I was attracted by Bartleby's closed desk, the key in open sight left in the lock.

I mean no mischief, seek the gratification of no heartless curiosity, thought I; besides, the desk is mine, and its contents too, so I will make bold to look within. Every thing was methodically arranged, the papers smoothly placed. The pigeon holes were deep, and removing the files of documents, I groped into their recesses. Presently I felt something there, and dragged it out. It was an old bandanna handkerchief, heavy and knotted. I opened it, and saw it was a savings' bank.

I now recalled all the quiet mysteries which I had noted in the man. I remembered that he never spoke but to answer; that though at intervals he had considerable time to himself, yet I had never seen him reading — no, not even a newspaper; that for long periods he would stand looking out, at his pale window behind the screen, upon the dead brick wall; I was quite sure he never visited any refectory or eating house; while his pale face clearly indicated that he never drank beer like Turkey, or tea and coffee even, like other men; that he never went any where in particular that I could learn; never went out for a walk, unless indeed that was the case at present; that he had declined telling who he was, or whence he came, or whether he had any relatives in the world; that though so thin and pale, he never complained of ill health. And more than all, I remembered a certain unconscious air of pallid — how shall I call it? — of pallid haughtiness, say, or rather an austere reserve about him, which had positively awed me into my tame compliance with his eccentricities, when I had feared to ask him to do the slightest incidental thing for me, even though I might know, from his long-continued motionlessness, that behind his screen he must be standing in one of those dead-wall reveries of his.

Revolving all these things, and coupling them with the recently discovered fact that he made my office his constant abiding place and home, and not forgetful of his morbid moodiness; revolving all these things, a prudential feeling began to steal over me. My first emotions had been those of pure melancholy and sincerest pity; but just in proportion as the forlornness of Bartleby grew and grew to my imagination, did that same melancholy merge into fear, that pity into repulsion. So true it is, and so terrible too, that up to a certain point the thought or sight of misery enlists our best affections; but, in certain special cases, beyond that point it does not. They err who would assert that invariably this is owing to the inherent selfishness of the human heart. It rather proceeds from a certain hopelessness of remedying excessive and organic ill. To a sensitive being, pity is not seldom pain. And when at last it is perceived that such pity cannot lead to effectual succor, common sense bids the soul be rid of it. What I saw that morning persuaded me that the scrivener was the victim of innate and incurable disorder. I might give alms to his body; but his body did not pain him; it was his soul that suffered, and his soul I could not reach.

I did not accomplish the purpose of going to Trinity Church that morning. Somehow, the things I had seen disqualified me for the time from church-going. I walked homeward, thinking what I would do with Bartleby. Finally, I resolved upon this; — I would put certain calm questions to him the next morning, touching his history, &c., and if he declined to answer them openly and unreservedly (and I supposed he would prefer not), then to give him a twenty dollar bill over and above whatever I might owe him, and tell him his services were no longer required; but that if in any other way I could assist him, I would be happy to do so, especially if he desired to return to his native place, wherever that might be, I would willingly help to defray the expenses. Moreover, if, after reaching home, he found himself at any time in want of aid, a letter from him would be sure of a reply.

95   The next morning came.

"Bartleby," said I, gently calling to him behind his screen.

No reply.

"Bartleby," said I, in a still gentler tone, "come here; I am not going to ask you to do any thing you would prefer not to do — I simply wish to speak to you."

Upon this he noiselessly slid into view.

100   "Will you tell me, Bartleby, where you were born?"

"I would prefer not to."

"Will you tell me *any thing* about yourself?"

"I would prefer not to."

"But what reasonable objection can you have to speak to me? I feel friendly towards you."

105   He did not look at me while I spoke, but kept his glance fixed upon my bust of Cicero,[15] which as I then sat, was directly behind me, some six inches above my head.

"What is your answer, Bartleby?" said I, after waiting a considerable time for a reply, during which his countenance remained immovable, only there was the faintest conceivable tremor of the white attenuated mouth.

"At present I prefer to give no answer," he said, and retired into his hermitage.

It was rather weak in me I confess, but his manner on this occasion nettled me. Not only did there seem to lurk in it a certain calm disdain, but his perverseness seemed ungrateful, considering the undeniable good usage and indulgence he had received from me.

Again I sat ruminating what I should do. Mortified as I was at his behavior, and resolved as I had been to dismiss him when I entered my office, nevertheless I strangely felt something superstitious knocking at my heart, and forbidding me to carry out my purpose, and denouncing me for a villain if I dared to breathe one bitter word against this forlornest of mankind. At last,

15 renowned Roman orator of the first century B.C.

familiarly drawing my chair behind his screen, I sat down and said: "Bartleby, never mind then about revealing your history; but let me entreat you as a friend, to comply as far as may be with the usages of this office. Say now you will help to examine papers to-morrow or next day: in short, say now that in a day or two you will begin to be a little reasonable:— say so, Bartleby."

"At present I would prefer not to be a little reasonable," was his mildly cadaverous reply.

Just then the folding-doors opened, and Nippers approached. He seemed suffering from an unusually bad night's rest, induced by severer indigestion than common. He overheard those final words of Bartleby.

"*Prefer not*, eh?" gritted Nippers — "I'd *prefer* him, if I were you, sir," addressing me — "I'd *prefer* him; I'd give him preferences, the stubborn mule! What is it, sir, pray, that he *prefers* not to do now?"

Bartleby moved not a limb.

"Mr. Nippers," said I, "I'd prefer that you would withdraw for the present."

Somehow, of late I had got into the way of involuntarily using this word "prefer" upon all sorts of not exactly suitable occasions. And I trembled to think that my contact with the scrivener had already and seriously affected me in a mental way. And what further and deeper aberration might it not yet produce? This apprehension had not been without efficacy in determining me to summary measures.

As Nippers, looking very sour and sulky, was departing, Turkey blandly and deferentially approached.

"With submission, sir," said he, "yesterday I was thinking about Bartleby here, and I think that if he would but prefer to take a quart of good ale every day, it would do much towards mending him, and enabling him to assist in examining his papers."

"So you have got the word too," said I, slightly excited.

"With submission, what word, sir," asked Turkey, respectfully crowding himself into the contracted space behind the screen, and by so doing, making me jostle the scrivener. "What word, sir?"

"I would prefer to be left alone here," said Bartleby, as if offended at being mobbed in his privacy.

"*That's* the word, Turkey," said I — "*that's* it."

"Oh, *prefer*? oh yes — queer word. I never use it myself. But, sir, as I was saying, if he would but prefer —"

"Turkey," interrupted I, "you will please withdraw."

"Oh certainly, sir, if you prefer that I should."

As he opened the folding-doors to retire, Nippers at his desk caught a glimpse of me, and asked whether I would prefer to have a certain paper copied on blue paper or white. He did not in the least roguishly accent the word prefer. It was plain that it involuntarily rolled from his tongue. I thought to myself, surely I must get rid of a demented man, who already has in some degree turned the tongues, if not the heads of myself and clerks. But I thought it prudent not to break the dismission at once.

The next day I noticed that Bartleby did nothing but stand at his window in his dead-wall revery. Upon asking him why he did not write, he said that he had decided upon doing no more writing.

"Why, how now? what next?" exclaimed I, "do no more writing?"

"No more."

"And what is the reason?"

130 "Do you not see the reason for yourself," he indifferently replied.

I looked steadfastly at him, and perceived that his eyes looked dull and glazed. Instantly it occurred to me, that his unexampled diligence in copying by his dim window for the first few weeks of his stay with me might have temporarily impaired his vision.

I was touched. I said something in condolence with him. I hinted that of course he did wisely in abstaining from writing for a while; and urged him to embrace that opportunity of taking wholesome exercise in the open air. This, however, he did not do. A few days after this, my other clerks being absent, and being in a great hurry to dispatch certain letters by the mail, I thought that, having nothing else earthly to do, Bartleby would surely be less inflexible than usual, and carry these letters to the post-office. But he blankly declined. So, much to my inconvenience, I went myself.

Still added days went by. Whether Bartleby's eyes improved or not, I could not say. To all appearance, I thought they did. But when I asked him if they did, he vouchsafed no answer. At all events, he would do no copying. At last, in reply to my urgings, he informed me that he had permanently given up copying.

"What!" exclaimed I; "suppose your eyes should get entirely well — better than ever before — would you not copy then?"

135 "I have given up copying," he answered, and slid aside.

He remained as ever, a fixture in my chamber. Nay — if that were possible — he became still more of a fixture than before. What was to be done? He would do nothing in the office: why should he stay there? In plain fact, he had now become a millstone to me, not only useless as a necklace, but afflictive to bear. Yet I was sorry for him. I speak less than truth when I say that, on his own account, he occasioned me uneasiness. If he would but have named a single relative or friend, I would instantly have written, and urged their taking the poor fellow away to some convenient retreat. But he seemed alone, absolutely alone in the universe. A bit of wreck in the mid Atlantic. At length, necessities connected with my business tyrannized over all other considerations. Decently as I could, I told Bartleby that in six days' time he must unconditionally leave the office. I warned him to take measures, in the interval, for procuring some other abode. I offered to assist him in this endeavor, if he himself would but take the first step towards a removal. "And when you finally quit me, Bartleby," added I, "I shall see that you go not away entirely unprovided. Six days from this hour, remember."

At the expiration of that period, I peeped behind the screen, and lo! Bartleby was there.

I buttoned up my coat, balanced myself; advanced slowly towards him, touched his shoulder, and said, "The time has come; you must quit this place; I am sorry for you; here is money, but you must go."

"I would prefer not," he replied, with his back still towards me.

140 "You *must*."

He remained silent.

Now I had an unbounded confidence in this man's common honesty. He had frequently restored to me sixpences and shillings carelessly dropped upon the floor, for I am apt to be very reckless in such shirt-button affairs. The proceeding then which followed will not be deemed extraordinary.

"Bartleby," said I, "I owe you twelve dollars on account; here are thirty-two; the odd twenty are yours. — Will you take it?" and I handed the bills towards him.

But he made no motion.

"I will leave them here then," putting them under a weight on the table. Then taking my hat and cane and going to the door I tranquilly turned and added — "After you have removed your things from these offices, Bartleby, you will of course lock the door — since every one is now gone for the day but you — and if you please, slip your key underneath the mat, so that I may have it in the morning. I shall not see you again; so good-bye to you. If hereafter in your new place of abode I can be of any service to you, do not fail to advise me by letter. Good-bye, Bartleby, and fare you well."

But he answered not a word; like the last column of some ruined temple, he remained standing mute and solitary in the middle of the otherwise deserted room.

As I walked home in a pensive mood, my vanity got the better of my pity. I could not but highly plume myself on my masterly management in getting rid of Bartleby. Masterly I call it, and such it must appear to any dispassionate thinker. The beauty of my procedure seemed to consist in its perfect quietness. There was no vulgar bullying, no bravado of any sort, no choleric hectoring, and striding to and fro across the apartment, jerking out vehement commands for Bartleby to bundle himself off with his beggarly traps. Nothing of the kind. Without loudly bidding Bartleby depart — as an inferior genius might have done — I *assumed* the ground that depart he must; and upon that assumption built all I had to say. The more I thought over my procedure, the more I was charmed with it. Nevertheless, next morning, upon awakening, I had my doubts, — I had somehow slept off the fumes of vanity. One of the coolest and wisest hours a man has, is just after he wakes in the morning. My procedure seemed as sagacious as ever, — but only in theory. How it would prove in practice — there was the rub. It was truly a beautiful thought to have assumed Bartleby's departure; but, after all, that assumption was simply my own, and none of Bartleby's. The great point was, not whether I had assumed that he would quit me, but whether he would prefer so to do. He was more a man of preferences than assumptions.

After breakfast, I walked down town, arguing the probabilities *pro* and *con*. One moment I thought it would prove a miserable failure, and Bartleby would be found all alive at my office as usual; the next moment it seemed certain that I should find his chair empty. And so I kept veering about. At the corner of Broadway and Canal-street, I saw quite an excited group of people standing in earnest conversation.

"I'll take odds he doesn't," said a voice as I passed.

"Doesn't go? — done!" said I, "put up your money."

I was instinctively putting my hand in my pocket to produce my own, when I remembered that this was an election day. The words I had overheard bore no reference to Bartleby, but to the success or non-success of some candidate for the mayoralty. In my intent frame of mind, I had, as it were, imagined that all Broadway shared in my excitement, and were debating the same question with me. I passed on, very thankful that the uproar of the street screened my momentary absent mindedness.

As I had intended, I was earlier than usual at my office door. I stood listening for a moment. All was still. He must be gone. I tried the knob. The door was locked. Yes, my procedure had worked to a charm; he indeed must be vanished. Yet a certain melancholy mixed with this: I was almost sorry for my brilliant success. I was fumbling under the door mat for the key, which Bartleby was to have left there for me, when accidentally my knee knocked against a panel, producing a summoning sound, and in response a voice came to me from within — "Not yet; I am occupied."

It was Bartleby.

I was thunderstruck. For an instant I stood like the man who, pipe in mouth, was killed one cloudless afternoon long ago in Virginia, by summer lightning; at his own warm open window he was killed, and remained leaning out there upon the dreamy afternoon, till some one touched him, when he fell.

155 "Not gone!" I murmured at last. But again obeying that wondrous ascendancy which the inscrutable scrivener had over me, and from which ascendancy, for all my chafing, I could not completely escape, I slowly went down stairs and out into the street, and while walking round the block, considered what I should next do in this unheard-of perplexity. Turn the man out by an actual thrusting I could not; to drive him away by calling him hard names would not do; calling in the police was an unpleasant idea; and yet, permit him to enjoy his cadaverous triumph over me, — this too I could not think of. What was to be done? or, if nothing could be done, was there any thing further that I could *assume* in the matter? Yes, as before I had prospectively assumed that Bartleby would depart, so now I might retrospectively assume that departed he was. In the legitimate carrying out of this assumption, I might enter my office in a great hurry, and pretending not to see Bartleby at all, walk straight against him as if he were air. Such a proceeding would in a singular degree have the appearance of a home-thrust. It was hardly possible that Bartleby could withstand such an application of the doctrine of assumptions. But upon second thoughts the success of the plan seemed rather dubious. I resolved to argue the matter over with him again.

"Bartleby," said I, entering the office, with a quietly severe expression, "I am seriously displeased. I am pained, Bartleby. I had thought better of you. I had imagined you of such a gentlemanly organization, that in any delicate dilemma a slight hint would suffice — in short, an assumption. But it appears I am deceived. Why," I added, unaffectedly starting, "you have not even touched that money yet," pointing to it, just where I had left it the evening previous.

He answered nothing.

"Will you, or will you not, quit me?" I now demanded in a sudden passion, advancing close to him.

"I would prefer *not* to quit you," he replied, gently emphasizing the *not*.

160 "What earthly right have you to stay here? Do you pay any rent? Do you pay my taxes? Or is this property yours?"

He answered nothing.

"Are you ready to go on and write now? Are your eyes recovered? Could you copy a small paper for me this morning? or help examine a few lines? or step round to the post-office? In a word, will you do any thing at all, to give a coloring to your refusal to depart the premises?"

He silently retired into his hermitage.

I was now in such a state of nervous resentment that I thought it but prudent to check myself at present from further demonstrations. Bartleby and I were alone. I remembered the tragedy of the unfortunate Adams and the still more unfortunate Colt[16] in the solitary office of the latter; and how poor Colt, being dreadfully incensed by Adams, and imprudently permitting himself to get wildly excited, was at unawares hurried into his fatal act — an act which certainly no man could possibly deplore more than the actor himself. Often it had occurred to me in my ponderings upon the subject, that had that altercation taken place in the public street, or at a private residence, it would not have terminated as it did. It was the circumstance of being alone in a solitary office, up stairs, of a building entirely unhallowed by humanizing domestic associations — an uncarpeted office, doubtless, of a dusty, haggard sort of appearance; — this it must have been, which greatly helped to enhance the irritable desperation of the hapless Colt.

165   But when this old Adam[17] of resentment rose in me and tempted me concerning Bartleby, I grappled him and threw him. How? Why, simply by recalling the divine injunction: "A new commandment give I unto you, that ye love one another." Yes, this it was that saved me. Aside from higher considerations, charity often operates as a vastly wise and prudent principle — a great safeguard to its possessor. Men have committed murder for jealousy's sake, and anger's sake, and hatred's sake, and selfishness' sake, and spiritual pride's sake; but no man that ever I heard of, ever committed a diabolical murder for sweet charity's sake. Mere self-interest, then, if no better motive can be enlisted, should, especially with high-tempered men, prompt all beings to charity and philanthropy. At any rate, upon the occasion in question, I strove to drown my exasperated feelings towards the scrivener by benevolently construing his conduct. Poor fellow, poor fellow! thought I, he don't mean any thing; and besides, he has seen hard times, and ought to be indulged.

I endeavored also immediately to occupy myself, and at the same time to comfort my despondency. I tried to fancy that in the course of the morning, at such time as might prove agreeable to him, Bartleby, of his own free accord, would emerge from his hermitage, and take up some decided line of march in the direction of the door. But no. Half-past twelve o'clock came; Turkey began to glow in the face, overturn his inkstand, and become generally obstreperous; Nippers abated down into quietude and courtesy; Ginger Nut munched his noon apple; and Bartleby remained standing at his window in one of his profoundest dead-wall reveries. Will it be credited? Ought I to acknowledge it? That afternoon I left the office without saying one further word to him.

16 Samuel Adams was killed in 1841 in a fight with John Colt, a brother of the manufacturer of guns.
17 reference to the biblical first man, whose temperament was believed to have been passed on to all the human race.

Some days now passed, during which, at leisure intervals I looked a little into "Edwards on the Will,"[18] and "Priestley on Necessity."[19] Under the circumstances, those books induced a salutary feeling. Gradually I slid into the persuasion that these troubles of mine touching the scrivener, had been all predestinated from eternity, and Bartleby was billeted upon me for some mysterious purpose of an all-wise Providence, which it was not for a mere mortal like me to fathom. Yes, Bartleby, stay there behind your screen, thought I; I shall persecute you no more; you are harmless and noiseless as any of these old chairs; in short, I never feel so private as when I know you are here. At last I see it, I feel it; I penetrate to the predestinated purpose of my life. I am content. Others may have loftier parts to enact; but my mission in this world, Bartleby, is to furnish you with office-room for such period as you may see fit to remain.

I believe that this wise and blessed frame of mind would have continued with me, had it not been for the unsolicited and uncharitable remarks obtruded upon me by my professional friends who visited the rooms. But thus it often is, that the constant friction of illiberal minds wears out at last the best resolves of the more generous. Though to be sure, when I reflected upon it, it was not strange that people entering my office should be struck by the peculiar aspect of the unaccountable Bartleby, and so be tempted to throw out some sinister observations concerning him. Sometimes an attorney having business with me, and calling at my office, and finding no one but the scrivener there, would undertake to obtain some sort of precise information from him touching my whereabouts; but without heeding his idle talk, Bartleby would remain standing immovable in the middle of the room. So after contemplating him in that position for a time, the attorney would depart, no wiser than he came.

Also, when a Reference[20] was going on, and the room full of lawyers and witnesses and business was driving fast; some deeply occupied legal gentleman present, seeing Bartleby wholly unemployed, would request him to run round to his (the legal gentleman's) office and fetch some papers for him. Thereupon, Bartleby would tranquilly decline, and yet remain idle as before. Then the lawyer would give a great stare, and turn to me. And what could I say? At last I was made aware that all through the circle of my professional acquaintance, a whisper of wonder was running round, having reference to the strange creature I kept at my office. This worried me very much. And as the idea came upon me of his possibly turning out a long-lived man, and keep occupying my chambers, and denying my authority; and perplexing my visitors; and scandalizing my professional reputation; and casting a general gloom over the premises; keeping soul and body together to the last upon his savings (for doubtless he spent but half a dime a day), and in the end perhaps outlive me, and claim possession of my office by right of his perpetual occupancy: as all these dark anticipations crowded upon me more and more, and my friends continually intruded their relentless remarks upon the apparition in my room;

18 eighteenth-century American philosopher who believed that human beings' will was controlled by God.
19 eighteenth-century English philosopher who believed that, to prevent revolution, rulers should act in the interests of those they govern. 20 legal hearing in which two parties submit their differences to an arbitrator.

a great change was wrought in me. I resolved to gather all my faculties together, and for ever rid me of this intolerable incubus.

170 Ere revolving any complicated project, however, adapted to this end, I first simply suggested to Bartleby the propriety of his permanent departure. In a calm and serious tone, I commended the idea to his careful and mature consideration. But having taken three days to meditate upon it, he apprised me that his original determination remained the same; in short, that he still preferred to abide with me.

What shall I do? I now said to myself, buttoning up my coat to the last button. What shall I do? what ought I to do? what does conscience say I *should* do with this man, or rather ghost? Rid myself of him, I must; go, he shall. But how? You will not thrust him, the poor, pale, passive mortal, — you will not thrust such a helpless creature out of your door? you will not dishonor yourself by such cruelty? No, I will not, I cannot do that. Rather would I let him live and die here, and then mason up his remains in the wall. What then will you do? For all your coaxing, he will not budge. Bribes he leaves under your own paperweight on your table; in short, it is quite plain that he prefers to cling to you.

Then something severe, something unusual must be done. What! surely you will not have him collared by a constable, and commit his innocent pallor to the common jail? And upon what ground could you procure such a thing to be done? — a vagrant, is he? What! he a vagrant, a wanderer, who refuses to budge? It is because he will *not* be a vagrant, then, that you seek to count him *as* a vagrant. That is too absurd. No visible means of support: there I have him. Wrong again: for undubitably he *does* support himself, and that is the only unanswerable proof that any man can show of his possessing the means so to do. No more then. Since he will not quit me, I must quit him. I will change my offices; I will move elsewhere; and give him fair notice, that if I find him on my new premises I will then proceed against him as a common trespasser.

Acting accordingly, next day I thus addressed him: "I find these chambers too far from the City Hall; the air is unwholesome. In a word, I propose to remove my offices next week, and shall no longer require your services. I tell you this now, in order that you may seek another place."

He made no reply, and nothing more was said.

175 On the appointed day I engaged carts and men, proceeded to my chambers, and having but little furniture, every thing was removed in a few hours. Throughout, the scrivener remained standing behind the screen, which I directed to be removed the last thing. It was withdrawn; and being folded up like a huge folio, left him the motionless occupant of a naked room. I stood in the entry watching him a moment, while something from within me upbraided me.

I re-entered, with my hand in my pocket — and — and my heart in my mouth.

"Good-bye, Bartleby; I am going — good-bye, and God some way bless you; and take that," slipping something in his hand. But it dropped upon the floor, and then, — strange to say — I tore myself from him whom I had so longed to be rid of.

Established in my new quarters, for a day or two I kept the door locked, and started at every footfall in the passages. When I returned to my rooms after any little absence, I would pause at the threshold for an instant, and attentively listen, ere applying my key. But these fears were needless. Bartleby never came nigh me.

I thought all was going well, when a perturbed looking stranger visited me, inquiring whether I was the person who had recently occupied rooms at No.—— Wall-street.

180 Full of forebodings, I replied that I was.

"Then sir," said the stranger, who proved a lawyer, "you are responsible for the man you left there. He refuses to do any copying; he refuses to do any thing; he says he prefers not to; and he refuses to quit the premises."

"I am very sorry, sir" said I, with assumed tranquillity, but an inward tremor, "but, really, the man you allude to is nothing to me — he is no relation or apprentice of mine, that you should hold me responsible for him."

"In mercy's name, who is he?"

"I certainly cannot inform you. I know nothing about him. Formerly I employed him as a copyist; but he has done nothing for me now for some time past."

185 "I shall settle him then,—— good morning, sir."

Several days passed, and I heard nothing more; and though I often felt a charitable prompting to call at the place and see poor Bartleby, yet a certain squeamishness of I know not what withheld me.

All is over with him, by this time, thought I at last, when through another week no further intelligence reached me. But coming to my room the day after, I found several persons waiting at my door in a high state of nervous excitement.

"That's the man — here he comes," cried the foremost one, whom I recognized as the lawyer who had previously called upon me alone.

"You must take him away, sir, at once," cried a portly person among them, advancing upon me, and whom I knew to be the landlord of No.—— Wall-street. "These gentlemen, my tenants, cannot stand it any longer; Mr. B——" pointing to the lawyer, "has turned him out of his room, and he now persists in haunting the building generally, sitting upon the banisters of the stairs by day, and sleeping in the entry by night. Every body is concerned; clients are leaving the offices; some fears are entertained of a mob; something you must do, and that without delay."

190 Aghast at this torrent, I fell back before it, and would fain have locked myself in my new quarters. In vain I persisted that Bartleby was nothing to me — no more than to any one else. In vain:—— I was the last person known to have any thing to do with him, and they held me to the terrible account. Fearful then of being exposed in the papers (as one person present obscurely threatened) I considered the matter, and at length said, that if the lawyer would give me a confidential interview with the scrivener, in his (the lawyer's) own room, I would that afternoon strive my best to rid them of the nuisance they complained of.

Going up stairs to my old haunt, there was Bartleby silently sitting upon the banister at the landing.

"What are you doing here, Bartleby?" said I.

"Sitting upon the banister," he mildly replied.

I motioned him into the lawyer's room, who then left us.

195   "Bartleby," said I, "are you aware that you are the cause of great tribulation to me, by persisting in occupying the entry after being dismissed from the office?"

No answer.

"Now one of two things must take place. Either you must do something, or something must be done to you. Now what sort of business would you like to engage in? Would you like to re-engage in copying for some one?"

"No; I would prefer not to make any change."

"Would you like a clerkship in a dry-goods store?"

200   "There is too much confinement about that. No, I would not like a clerkship; but I am not particular."

"Too much confinement," I cried, "why you keep yourself confined all the time!"

"I would prefer not to take a clerkship," he rejoined, as if to settle that little item at once.

"How would a bar-tender's business suit you? There is no trying of the eyesight in that."

"I would not like it at all; though, as I said before, I am not particular."

205   His unwonted wordiness inspirited me. I returned to the charge.

"Well then, would you like to travel through the country collecting bills for the merchants? That would improve your health."

"No, I would prefer to be something else."

"How then would going as a companion to Europe, to entertain some young gentleman with your conversation, — how would that suit you?"

"Not at all. It does not strike me that there is any thing definite about that. I like to be stationary. But I am not particular."

210   "Stationary you shall be then," I cried, now losing all patience, and for the first time in all my exasperating connection with him fairly flying into a passion. "If you do not go away from these premises before night, I shall feel bound — indeed I *am* bound — to — to — to quit the premises myself!" I rather absurdly concluded, knowing not with what possible threat to try to frighten his immobility into compliance. Despairing of all further efforts, I was precipitately leaving him, when a final thought occurred to me — one which had not been wholly unindulged before.

"Bartleby," said I, in the kindest tone I could assume under such exciting circumstances, "will you go home with me now — not to my office, but my dwelling — and remain there till we can conclude upon some convenient arrangement for you at our leisure? Come, let us start now, right away."

"No: at present I would prefer not to make any change at all."

I answered nothing; but effectually dodging every one by the suddenness and rapidity of my flight, rushed from the building, ran up Wall-street towards Broadway, and jumping into the first omnibus was soon removed from pursuit. As soon as tranquillity returned I distinctly perceived that I had now done all that I possibly could, both in respect to the demands of the landlord and his tenants, and with regard to my own desire and sense of duty, to benefit Bartleby, and shield him from rude persecution. I now strove to be entirely care-free and quiescent; and my conscience justified me in the attempt; though indeed it was not so successful as I could have wished. So fearful was I of being again hunted out by the incensed landlord and his exasperated tenants, that, surrendering my business to Nippers, for a few days I drove about the upper part of the town and through the suburbs, in my rockaway;[21] crossed over to Jersey City and Hoboken, and paid fugitive visits to Manhattanville and Astoria. In fact I almost lived in my rockaway for the time.

When again I entered my office, lo, a note from the landlord lay upon the desk. I opened it with trembling hands. It informed me that the writer had sent to the police, and had Bartleby removed to the Tombs as a vagrant. Moreover, since I knew more about him than any one else, he wished me to appear at that place, and make a suitable statement of the facts. These tidings had a conflicting effect upon me. At first I was indignant; but at last almost approved. The landlord's energetic, summary disposition, had led him to adopt a procedure which I do not think I would have decided upon myself; and yet as a last resort, under such peculiar circumstances, it seemed the only plan.

215 　 As I afterwards learned, the poor scrivener, when told that he must be conducted to the Tombs, offered not the slightest obstacle, but in his pale unmoving way, silently acquiesced.

Some of the compassionate and curious bystanders joined the party; and headed by one of the constables arm in arm with Bartleby, the silent procession filed its way through all the noise, and heat, and joy of the roaring thoroughfares at noon.

The same day I received the note I went to the Tombs, or to speak more properly, the Halls of Justice. Seeking the right officer, I stated the purpose of my call, and was informed that the individual I described was indeed within. I then assured the functionary that Bartleby was a perfectly honest man, and greatly to be compassionated, however unaccountably eccentric. I narrated all I knew, and closed by suggesting the idea of letting him remain in as indulgent confinement as possible till something less harsh might be done — though indeed I hardly knew what. At all events, if nothing else could be decided upon, the alms-house must receive him. I then begged to have an interview.

Being under no disgraceful charge, and quite serene and harmless in all his ways, they had permitted him freely to wander about the prison, and especially in the inclosed grass-platted yards thereof. And so I found him there, standing all alone in the quietest of the yards, his face towards a high wall, while all around, from the narrow slits of the jail windows, I thought I saw peering out upon him the eyes of murderers and thieves.

"Bartleby!"

220 　 "I know you," he said, without looking round, — "and I want nothing to say to you."

"It was not I that brought you here, Bartleby," said I, keenly pained at his implied suspicion. "And to you, this should not be so vile a place. Nothing reproachful attaches to you by being here. And see, it is not so sad a place as one might think. Look, there is the sky, and here is the grass."

"I know where I am," he replied, but would say nothing more, and so I left him.

As I entered the corridor again, a broad meat-like man, in an apron, accosted me, and jerking his thumb over his shoulder said — "Is that your friend?"

21 luxury carriage.

"Yes."

225 "Does he want to starve? If he does, let him live on the prison fare, that's all."

"Who are you?" asked I, not knowing what to make of such an unofficially speaking person in such a place.

"I am the grub-man. Such gentlemen as have friends here, hire me to provide them with something good to eat."

"Is this so?" said I, turning to the turnkey.

He said it was.

230 "Well then," said I, slipping some silver into the grub-man's hands (for so they called him). "I want you to give particular attention to my friend there; let him have the best dinner you can get. And you must be as polite to him as possible."

"Introduce me, will you?" said the grub-man, looking at me with an expression which seemed to say he was all impatience for an opportunity to give a specimen of his breeding.

Thinking it would prove of benefit to the scrivener, I acquiesced; and asking the grub-man his name, went up with him to Bartleby.

"Bartleby, this is Mr. Cutlets; you will find him very useful to you."

"Your sarvant, sir, your sarvant," said the grub-man, making a low salutation behind his apron. "Hope you find it pleasant here, sir; nice grounds — cool apartments, sir — hope you'll stay with us some time — try to make it agreeable. May Mrs. Cutlets and I have the pleasure of your company to dinner, sir, in Mrs. Cutlet's private room?"

235 "I prefer not to dine to-day," said Bartleby, turning away. "It would disagree with me; I am unused to dinners." So saying he slowly moved to the other side of the inclosure, and took up a position fronting the dead-wall.

"How's this?" said the grub-man, addressing me with a stare of astonishment. "He's odd, aint he?"

"I think he is a little deranged," said I, sadly.

"Deranged? deranged is it? Well now, upon my word, I thought that friend of yourn was a gentleman forger; they are always pale and genteel-like, them forgers. I can't help pity 'em — can't help it, sir. Did you know Monroe Edwards?" he added touchingly, and paused. Then, laying his hand pityingly on my shoulder, sighed, "he died of consumption at Sing-Sing.[22] So you weren't acquainted with Monroe?"

"No, I was never socially acquainted with any forgers. But I cannot stop longer. Look to my friend yonder. You will not lose by it. I will see you again."

240 Some few days after this, I again obtained admission to the Tombs, and went through the corridors in quest of Bartleby; but without finding him.

"I saw him coming from his cell not long ago," said a turnkey, "may be he's gone to loiter in the yards."

So I went in that direction.

"Are you looking for the silent man?" said another turnkey passing me. "Yonder he lies — sleeping in the yard there. 'Tis not twenty minutes since I saw him lie down."

22 state prison north of New York City.

The yard was entirely quiet. It was not accessible to the common prisoners. The surrounding walls, of amazing thickness, kept off all sounds behind them. The Egyptian character of the masonry weighed upon me with its gloom. But a soft imprisoned turf grew under foot. The heart of the eternal pyramids, it seemed, wherein, by some strange magic, through the clefts, grass-seed, dropped by birds, had sprung.

245 Strangely huddled at the base of the wall, his knees drawn up, and lying on his side, his head touching the cold stones, I saw the wasted Bartleby. But nothing stirred. I paused; then went close up to him; stooped over, and saw that his dim eyes were open; otherwise he seemed profoundly sleeping. Something prompted me to touch him. I felt his hand, when a tingling shiver ran up my arm and down my spine to my feet.

The round face of the grub-man peered upon me now. "His dinner is ready. Won't he dine to-day, either? Or does he live without dining?"

"Lives without dining," said I, and closed the eyes.

"Eh! — He's asleep, aint he?"

"With kings and counsellors,"[23] murmured I.

*****

250 There would seem little need for proceeding further in this history. Imagination will readily supply the meagre recital of poor Bartleby's interment. But ere parting with the reader, let me say, that if this little narrative has sufficiently interested him, to awaken curiosity as to who Bartleby was, and what manner of life he led prior to the present narrator's making his acquaintance, I can only reply, that in such curiosity I fully share, but am wholly unable to gratify it. Yet here I hardly know whether I should divulge one little item of rumor, which came to my ear a few months after the scrivener's decease. Upon what basis it rested, I could never ascertain; and hence, how true it is I cannot now tell. But inasmuch as this vague report has not been without a certain strange suggestive interest to me, however sad, it may prove the same with some others; and so I will briefly mention it. The report was this: that Bartleby had been a subordinate clerk in the Dead Letter Office at Washington, from which he had been suddenly removed by a change in the administration. When I think over this rumor, hardly can I express the emotions which seize me. Dead letters! does it not sound like dead men? Conceive a man by nature and misfortune prone to a pallid hopelessness, can any business seem more fitted to heighten it than that of continually handling these dead letters, and assorting them for the flames? For by the cart-load they are annually burned. Sometimes from out the folded paper the pale clerk takes a ring: — the finger it was meant for, perhaps, moulders in the grave; a bank-note sent in swiftest charity: — he whom it would relieve, nor eats nor hungers any more; pardon for those who died despairing; hope for those who died unhoping; good tidings for those who died stifled by unrelieved calamities. On errands of life, these letters speed to death.

Ah Bartleby! Ah humanity!

(1853)

---

23 see Job 3:14. A reference to death as a condition of tranquillity.

Kate Chopin (1851–1904)

Kate Chopin, who received a traditional Catholic upbringing and moved in the society circles of her native city, St. Louis, Missouri, began a career as an author after the death of her husband. She stated that she strove to present "human existence in its subtle, complex, true meaning, stripped of the veil with which ethical and conventional standards have draped it." Her novel *The Awakening* (1899), now considered a classic, is the story of a young mother's escape from her socially imposed roles; it was condemned as immoral and was mostly ignored until the 1960s, as were such stories as "A Shameful Affair" and "The Storm." "The Story of an Hour," which is praised for its conciseness and its presentation of "daring" themes, focuses on the surface and the secret life of the central character. Chopin's use of the limited third-person narrator and the surprise ending enables readers to understand the conventional attitudes of the other characters and Mrs. Mallard's own, unspoken views.

THE STORY OF AN HOUR

Knowing that Mrs. Mallard was afflicted with a heart trouble, great care was taken to break to her as gently as possible the news of her husband's death.

It was her sister Josephine who told her, in broken sentences; veiled hints that revealed in half concealing. Her husband's friend Richards was there, too, near her. It was he who had been in the newspaper office when intelligence of the railroad disaster was received, with Brently Mallard's name leading the list of "killed." He had only taken the time to assure himself of its truth by a second telegram, and had hastened to forestall any less careful, less tender friend in bearing the sad message.

She did not hear the story as many women have heard the same, with a paralyzed inability to accept its significance. She wept at once, with sudden, wild abandonment, in her sister's arms. When the storm of grief had spent itself she went away to her room alone. She would have no one follow her.

There stood, facing the open window, a comfortable, roomy armchair. Into this she sank, pressed down by a physical exhaustion that haunted her body and seemed to reach into her soul.

5   She could see in the open square before her house the tops of trees that were all aquiver with the new spring life. The delicious breath of rain was in the air. In the street below a peddler was crying his wares. The notes of a distant song which some one was singing reached her faintly, and countless sparrows were twittering in the eaves.

There were patches of blue sky showing here and there through the clouds that had met and piled one above the other in the west facing her window.

She sat with her head thrown back upon the cushion of the chair, quite motionless, except when a sob came up into her throat and shook her, as a child who has cried itself to sleep continues to sob in its dreams.

She was young, with a fair, calm face, whose lines bespoke repression and even a certain strength. But now there was a dull stare in her eyes, whose gaze was fixed away off yonder on one of those patches of blue sky. It was not a glance of reflection, but rather indicated a suspension of intelligent thought.

There was something coming to her and she was waiting for it, fearfully. What was it? She did not know; it was too subtle and elusive to name. But she felt it, creeping out of the sky, reaching toward her through the sounds, the scents, the color that filled the air.

10   Now her bosom rose and fell tumultuously. She was beginning to recognize this thing that was approaching to possess her, and she was striving to beat it back with her will — as powerless as her two white slender hands would have been.

When she abandoned herself a little whispered word escaped her slightly parted lips. She said it over and over under her breath: "free, free, free!" The vacant stare and the look of terror that had followed it went from her eyes. They stayed keen and bright. Her pulses beat fast, and the coursing blood warmed and relaxed every inch of her body.

She did not stop to ask if it were or were not a monstrous joy that held her. A clear and exalted perception enabled her to dismiss the suggestion as trivial.

She knew that she would weep again when she saw the kind, tender hands folded in death; the face that had never looked save with love upon her, fixed and gray and dead. But she saw beyond that bitter moment a long procession of years to come that would belong to her absolutely. And she opened and spread her arms out to them in welcome.

There would be no one to live for her during those coming years; she would live for herself. There would be no powerful will bending hers in that blind persistence with which men and women believe they have a right to impose a private will upon a fellow-creature. A kind intention or a cruel intention made the act seem no less a crime as she looked upon it in that brief moment of illumination.

15   And yet she had loved him — sometimes. Often she had not. What did it matter! What could love, the unsolved mystery, count for in face of this possession of self-assertion which she suddenly recognized as the strongest impulse of her being!

"Free! Body and soul free!" she kept whispering.

Josephine was kneeling before the closed door with her lips to the keyhole, imploring for admission. "Louise, open the door! I beg; open the door — you will make yourself ill. What are you doing, Louise? For heaven's sake open the door."

"Go away. I am not making myself ill." No; she was drinking in a very elixir of life through that open window.

Her fancy was running riot along those days ahead of her. Spring days, and summer days, and all sorts of days that would be her own. She breathed a quick prayer that life might be long. It was only yesterday she had thought with a shudder that life might be long.

20   She arose at length and opened the door to her sister's importunities. There was a feverish triumph in her eyes, and she carried herself unwittingly like a goddess of Victory. She clasped her sister's waist, and together they descended the stairs. Richards stood waiting for them at the bottom.

Some one was opening the front door with a latchkey. It was Brently Mallard who entered, a little travel-stained, composedly carrying his grip-sack and umbrella. He had been far from the scene of accident, and did not even know there had been one. He stood amazed at Josephine's piercing cry; at Richards' quick motion to screen him from the view of his wife.

But Richards was too late.

When the doctors came they said she had died of heart disease — of joy that kills.

(1894)

Joseph Conrad (1857–1924)

Born in the Ukraine of Polish parents, Joseph Conrad worked at sea for twenty years before settling in England. There he began writing novels and short stories, all in his third language, English, which he did not learn until he was an adult. His novels, such as *Lord Jim* and *Nostromo*, are dominated by a concern with the complexities of character and motivation, and focus on the degeneration and corruption of the human spirit. Like *Heart of Darkness* (1902), his best-known short novel, the story "An Outpost of Progress" presents a bleak view of civilization in its portrayal of the two white administrators of an isolated African trading post. Without the support of their own familiar world, Kayerts and Carlier are defeated by their own weaknesses.

AN OUTPOST OF PROGRESS

I

There were two white men in charge of the trading station. Kayerts, the chief, was short and fat; Carlier, the assistant, was tall, with a large head and a very broad trunk perched upon a long pair of thin legs. The third man on the staff was a Sierra Leone nigger, who maintained that his name was Henry Price. However, for some reason or other, the natives down the river had given him the name of Makola, and it stuck to him through all his wanderings about the country. He spoke English and French with a warbling accent, wrote a beautiful hand, understood bookkeeping, and cherished in his innermost heart the worship of evil spirits. His wife was a negress from Loanda, very large and very noisy. Three children rolled about in sunshine before the door of his low, shed-like dwelling. Makola, taciturn and impenetrable, despised the two white men. He had charge of a small clay storehouse with a dried-grass roof, and pretended to keep a correct account of beads, cotton cloth, red kerchiefs, brass wire, and other trade goods it contained. Besides the storehouse and Makola's hut, there was only one large building in the cleared ground of the station. It was built neatly of reeds, with a verandah on all the four sides. There were three rooms in it. The one in the middle was the living-room, and had two rough tables and a few stools in it. The other two were the bedrooms for the white men. Each had a bedstead and a mosquito net for all furniture. The plank floor was littered with the belongings of the white men; open half-empty boxes, town wearing apparel, old boots; all the things dirty, and all the things broken, that accumulate mysteriously round untidy men. There was also another dwelling-place some distance away from the buildings. In it, under a tall cross much out of the perpendicular, slept the man who had seen the beginning of all this; who had planned and had watched the construction of this outpost of progress. He had been, at home, an unsuccessful painter who, weary of pursuing fame on an empty stomach, had gone out there through high protections. He had been the first chief of that station. Makola had watched the energetic artist die of fever in the just finished house with his usual kind of "I told you so" indifference. Then, for a time, he dwelt alone with his family, his account books, and the Evil Spirit that rules the lands under the equator. He got on very well with his god. Perhaps he had propitiated him by a promise of more white men to play with, by and by. At any rate the director of the Great Trading Company, coming up in a steamer that resembled an enormous sardine box with a flat-roofed shed erected on it, found the station in good order, and Makola as usual quietly diligent. The director had the cross put up over the first agent's grave, and appointed Kayerts to the post. Carlier was told off as second in charge. The director was a man ruthless and efficient, who at times, but very imperceptibly, indulged in grim humour. He made a speech to Kayerts and Carlier, pointing out to them the promising aspect of their station. The nearest trading-post was about three hundred miles away. It was an exceptional opportunity for them to distinguish themselves and to earn percentages on the trade. This appointment was a favour done to beginners. Kayerts was moved almost to tears by his director's kindness. He would, he said, by doing his best, try to justify the flattering confidence, &c., &c. Kayerts had been in the Administration of the Telegraphs, and knew how to express himself correctly. Carlier, an ex-non-commissioned officer of cavalry in an army guaranteed from harm by several European Powers, was less impressed. If there were commissions to get, so much the better; and, trailing a sulky glance over the river, the forests, the impenetrable bush that seemed to cut off the station from the rest of the world, he muttered between his teeth, "We shall see, very soon."

Next day, some bales of cotton goods and a few cases of provisions having been thrown on shore, the sardine-box steamer went off, not to return for another six months. On the deck the director touched his cap to the two agents, who stood on the bank waving their hats, and turning to an old servant of the Company on his passage to headquarters, said, "Look at those two imbeciles. They must be mad at home to send me such specimens. I told those fellows to plant a vegetable garden, build new storehouses and fences, and construct a landing-stage. I bet nothing will be done! They won't know how to begin. I always thought the station on this river useless, and they just fit the station!"

"They will form themselves there," said the old stager with a quiet smile.

"At any rate, I am rid of them for six months," retorted the director.

The two men watched the steamer round the bend, then, ascending arm in arm the slope of the bank, returned to the station. They had been in this vast and dark country only a very short time, and as yet always in the midst of other white men, under the eye and guidance of their superiors. And now, dull as they were to the subtle influences of surroundings, they felt themselves very much alone, when suddenly left unassisted to face the wilderness; a wilderness rendered more strange, more incomprehensible by the mysterious glimpses of the vigorous life it contained. They were two perfectly insignificant and incapable individuals, whose existence is only rendered possible through the high organization of civilized crowds. Few men realize that their life, the very essence of their character, their capabilities and their audacities, are only the expression of their belief in the safety of their surroundings. The courage, the composure, the confidence; the emotions and principles; every great and every insignificant thought belongs not to the individual but to the crowd: to the crowd that believes blindly in the irresistible force of its institutions and of its morals, in the power of its police and of its opinion. But the contact with pure unmitigated savagery, with primitive nature and primitive man, brings sudden and profound trouble into the heart. To the sentiment of being alone of one's kind, to the clear perception of the loneliness of one's thoughts, of one's sensations — to the negation of the habitual, which is safe, there is added the affirmation of the unusual, which is dangerous; a suggestion of things vague, uncontrollable, and repulsive, whose discomposing intrusion excites the imagination and tries the civilized nerves of the foolish and the wise alike.

Kayerts and Carlier walked arm in arm, drawing close to one another as children do in the dark; and they had the same, not altogether unpleasant, sense of danger which one half suspects to be imaginary. They chatted persistently in familiar tones. "Our station is prettily situated," said one. The other assented with enthusiasm, enlarging volubly on the beauties of the situation. Then they passed near the grave. "Poor devil!" said Kayerts. "He died of fever, didn't he?" muttered Carlier, stopping short. "Why," retorted Kayerts, with indignation, "I've been told that the fellow exposed himself recklessly to the sun. The climate here, everybody says, is not at all worse than at home, as long as you keep out of the sun. Do you hear that, Carlier? I am chief here, and my orders are that you should not expose yourself to the sun!" He assumed his superiority jocularly, but his meaning was serious. The idea that he would, perhaps, have to bury Carlier and remain alone, gave him an inward shiver. He felt suddenly that this Carlier was more precious to him here, in the centre of Africa, than a brother could be anywhere else. Carlier, entering into the spirit of the thing, made a military salute and answered in a brisk tone, "Your orders shall be attended to, chief!" Then he burst out laughing, slapped Kayerts on the back and shouted, "We shall let life run easily here! Just sit still and gather in the ivory those savages will bring. This country has its good points, after all!" They both laughed loudly while Carlier thought: That poor Kayerts; he is so fat and unhealthy. It would be awful if I had to bury him here. He is a man I respect.... Before they reached the verandah of their house they called one another "my dear fellow."

The first day they were very active, pottering about with hammers and nails and red calico, to put up curtains, make their house habitable and pretty; resolved to settle down comfortably to their new life. For them an impossible task. To grapple effectually with even purely material problems requires more serenity of mind and more lofty courage than people generally imagine. No two beings could have been more unfitted for such a struggle. Society, not from any tenderness, but because of its strange needs, had taken care of those two men, forbidding them all independent thought, all initiative, all departure from routine; and forbidding it under pain of death. They could only live on condition of being machines. And now, released from the fostering care of men with pens behind the ears, or of men with gold lace on the sleeves, they were like those lifelong prisoners who, liberated after many years, do not know what use to make of their freedom. They did not know what use to make of their faculties, being both, through want of practice, incapable of independent thought.

At the end of two months Kayerts often would say, "If it was not for my Melie, you wouldn't catch me here." Melie was his daughter. He had thrown up his post in the Administration of the Telegraphs, though he had been for seventeen years perfectly happy there, to earn a dowry for his girl. His wife was dead, and the child was being brought up by his sisters. He regretted the streets, the pavements, the cafés, his friends of many years; all the things he used to see, day after day; all the thoughts suggested by familiar things — the thoughts effortless, monotonous, and soothing of a Government clerk; he regretted all the gossip, the small enmities, the mild venom, and the little jokes of Government offices. "If I had had a decent brother-in-law," Carlier would remark, "a fellow with a heart, I would not be here." He had left the army and had made himself so obnoxious to his family by his laziness and impudence, that an exasperated brother-in-law had made superhuman efforts to procure him an appointment in the Company as a second-class agent. Having not a penny in the world he was compelled to accept this means of livelihood as soon as it became quite clear to him that there was nothing more to squeeze out of his relations. He, like Kayerts, regretted his old life. He regretted the clink of sabre and spurs on a fine afternoon, the barrack-room witticisms, the girls of garrison towns; but, besides, he had also a sense of grievance. He was evidently a much ill-used man. This made him moody, at times. But the two men got on well together in the fellowship of their stupidity and laziness. Together they did nothing, absolutely nothing, and enjoyed the sense of idleness for which they were paid. And in time they came to feel something resembling affection for one another.

They lived like blind men in a large room, aware only of what came in contact with them (and of that only imperfectly), but unable to see the general aspect of things. The river, the forest, all the great land throbbing with life, were like a great emptiness. Even the brilliant sunshine disclosed nothing intelligible. Things appeared and disappeared before their eyes in an unconnected and aimless kind of way. The river seemed to come from nowhere and flow nowhither. It flowed through a void. Out of that void, at times, came canoes, and men with spears in their hands would suddenly crowd the yard of the station. They were naked, glossy black, ornamented with snowy shells and glistening brass wire, perfect of limb. They made an uncouth babbling noise when they spoke, moved in a stately manner, and sent quick, wild glances out of their startled, never-resting eyes. Those warriors would squat in long rows, four or more deep, before the verandah, while their chiefs bargained for hours with Makola over an elephant tusk. Kayerts sat on his chair and looked down on the proceedings, understanding nothing. He stared at them with his round blue eyes, called out to Carlier, "Here, look! look at that fellow there — and that other one, to the left. Did you ever see such a face? Oh, the funny brute!"

Carlier, smoking native tobacco in a short wooden pipe, would swagger up twirling his moustaches, and surveying the warriors with haughty indulgence, would say —

"Fine animals. Brought any bone? Yes? It's not any too soon. Look at the muscles of that fellow — third from the end. I wouldn't care to get a punch on the nose from him. Fine arms, but legs no good below the knee. Couldn't make cavalry men of them." And after glancing down complacently at his own shanks, he always concluded: "Pah! Don't they stink! You, Makola! Take that herd over to the fetish" (the storehouse was in every station called the fetish, perhaps because of the spirit of civilization it contained) "and give them up some of the rubbish you keep there. I'd rather see it full of bone than full of rags."

Kayerts approved.

"Yes, yes! Go and finish that palaver over there, Mr. Makola. I will come round when you are ready, to weigh the tusk. We must be careful." Then turning to his companion: "This is the tribe that lives down the river; they are rather aromatic. I remember, they had been once before here. D'ye hear that row? What a fellow has got to put up with in this dog of a country! My head is split."

Such profitable visits were rare. For days the two pioneers of trade and progress would look on their empty courtyard in the vibrating brilliance of vertical sunshine. Below the high bank, the silent river flowed on glittering and steady. On the sands in the middle of the stream, hippos and alligators sunned themselves side by side. And stretching away in all directions, surrounding the insignificant cleared spot of the trading post, immense forests, hiding fateful complications of fantastic life, lay in the eloquent silence of mute greatness. The two men understood nothing, cared for nothing but for the passage of days that separated them from the steamer's return. Their predecessor had left some torn books. They took up these wrecks of novels, and, as they had never read anything of the kind before, they were surprised and amused. Then during long days there were interminable and silly discussions about plots and personages. In the centre of Africa they made acquaintance of Richelieu and of d'Artagnan, of Hawk's Eye and of Father Goriot, and of many other people.[1] All these imaginary personages became subjects for gossip as if they had been living friends. They discounted their virtues, suspected their motives, decried their successes; were scandalized at their duplicity or were doubtful about their courage. The accounts of crimes filled them with indignation, while tender or pathetic passages moved them deeply. Carlier cleared his throat and said in a soldierly voice, "What nonsense!" Kayerts, his round eyes suffused with tears, his fat cheeks quivering, rubbed his bald head, and declared, "This is a splendid book. I had no idea there were such clever fellows in the world." They also found some old copies of a home paper. That print discussed what it was pleased to call "Our Colonial Expansion" in high-flown language. It spoke much of the rights and duties of civilization, of the sacredness of the civilizing work, and extolled the merits of those who went about bringing light, and faith and commerce to the dark places of the earth. Carlier and Kayerts read, wondered, and began to think better of themselves. Carlier said one evening, waving his hand about, "In a hundred years, there will be perhaps a town here. Quays, and warehouses, and barracks, and — and — billiard-rooms. Civilization, my boy, and virtue — and all. And then, chaps will read that two good fellows, Kayerts and Carlier, were the first civilized men to live in this very spot!" Kayerts nodded, "Yes, it is a consolation to think of that." They seemed to forget their dead predecessor; but, early one day, Carlier went out and replanted the cross firmly. "It used to make me squint whenever I walked that way," he explained to Kayerts over the morning coffee. "It made me squint,

1 heroes in popular adventure novels by Alexandre Dumas, James Fenimore Cooper, and Honoré de Balzac, respectively.

leaning over so much. So I just planted it upright. And solid, I promise you! I suspended myself with both hands to the cross-piece. Not a move. Oh, I did that properly."

15   At times Gobila came to see them. Gobila was the chief of the neighbouring villages. He was a gray-headed savage, thin and black, with a white cloth round his loins and a mangy panther skin hanging over his back. He came up with long strides of his skeleton legs, swinging a staff as tall as himself, and, entering the common room of the station, would squat on his heels to the left of the door. There he sat, watching Kayerts, and now and then making a speech which the other did not understand. Kayerts, without interrupting his occupation, would from time to time say in a friendly manner: "How goes it, you old image?" and they would smile at one another. The two whites had a liking for that old and incomprehensible creature, and called him Father Gobila. Gobila's manner was paternal, and he seemed really to love all white men. They all appeared to him very young, indistinguishably alike (except for stature), and he knew that they were all brothers, and also immortal. The death of the artist, who was the first white man whom he knew intimately, did not disturb this belief, because he was firmly convinced that the white stranger had pretended to die and got himself buried for some mysterious purpose of his own, into which it was useless to inquire. Perhaps it was his way of going home to his own country? At any rate, these were his brothers, and he transferred his absurd affection to them. They returned it in a way. Carlier slapped him on the back, and recklessly struck off matches for his amusement. Kayerts was always ready to let him have a sniff at the ammonia bottle. In short, they behaved just like that other white creature that had hidden itself in a hole in the ground. Gobila considered them attentively. Perhaps they were the same being with the other — or one of them was. He couldn't decide — clear up that mystery; but he remained always very friendly. In consequence of that friendship the women of Gobila's village walked in single file through the reedy grass, bringing every morning to the station, fowls, and sweet potatoes, and palm wine, and sometimes a goat. The Company never provisions the stations fully, and the agents required those local supplies to live. They had them through the good-will of Gobila, and lived well. Now and then one of them had a bout of fever, and the other nursed him with gentle devotion. They did not think much of it. It left them weaker, and their appearance changed for the worse. Carlier was hollow-eyed and irritable. Kayerts showed a drawn, flabby face above the rotundity of his stomach, which gave him a weird aspect. But being constantly together, they did not notice the change that took place gradually in their appearance, and also in their dispositions.

Five months passed in that way.

Then, one morning, as Kayerts and Carlier, lounging in their chairs under the verandah, talked about the approaching visit of the steamer, a knot of armed men came out of the forest and advanced towards the station. They were strangers to that part of the country. They were tall, slight, draped classically from neck to heel in blue fringed cloths, and carried percussion muskets over their bare right shoulders. Makola showed signs of excitement, and ran out of the storehouse (where he spent all his days) to meet these visitors. They came into the courtyard and looked about them with steady, scornful glances. Their leader, a powerful and determined-looking negro with bloodshot eyes, stood in front of the verandah and made a long speech. He gesticulated much, and ceased very suddenly.

There was something in his intonation, in the sounds of the long sentences he used, that startled the two whites. It was like a reminiscence of something not exactly familiar, and yet resembling the speech of civilized men. It sounded like one of those impossible languages which sometimes we hear in our dreams.

"What lingo is that?" said the amazed Carlier. "In the first moment I fancied the fellow was going to speak French. Anyway, it is a different kind of gibberish to what we ever heard."

20 "Yes," replied Kayerts. "Hey, Makola, what does he say? Where do they come from? Who are they?

But Makola, who seemed to be standing on hot bricks, answered hurriedly, "I don't know. They come from very far. Perhaps Mrs. Price will understand. They are perhaps bad men."

The leader, after waiting for a while, said something sharply to Makola, who shook his head. Then the man, after looking round, noticed Makola's hut and walked over there. The next moment Mrs. Makola was heard speaking with great volubility. The other strangers — they were six in all — strolled about with an air of ease, put their heads through the door of the storeroom, congregated round the grave, pointed understandingly at the cross, and generally made themselves at home.

"I don't like those chaps — and, I say, Kayerts, they must be from the coast; they've got firearms," observed the sagacious Carlier.

Kayerts also did not like those chaps. They both, for the first time, became aware that they lived in conditions where the unusual may be dangerous, and that there was no power on earth outside of themselves to stand between them and the unusual. They became uneasy, went in and loaded their revolvers. Kayerts said, "We must order Makola to tell them to go away before dark."

25 The strangers left in the afternoon, after eating a meal prepared for them by Mrs. Makola. The immense woman was excited, and talked much with the visitors. She rattled away shrilly, pointing here and there at the forests and at the river. Makola sat apart and watched. At times he got up and whispered to his wife. He accompanied the strangers across the ravine at the back of the station-ground, and returned slowly looking very thoughtful. When questioned by the white men he was very strange, seemed not to understand, seemed to have forgotten French — seemed to have forgotten how to speak altogether. Kayerts and Carlier agreed that the nigger had had too much palm wine.

There was some talk about keeping a watch in turn, but in the evening everything seemed so quiet and peaceful that they retired as usual. All night they were disturbed by a lot of drumming in the villages. A deep, rapid roll near by would be followed by another far off — then all ceased. Soon short appeals would rattle out here and there, then all mingle together, increase, become vigorous and sustained, would spread out over the forest, roll through the night, unbroken and ceaseless, near and far, as if the whole land had been one immense drum booming out steadily an appeal to heaven. And through the deep and tremendous noise sudden yells that resembled snatches of songs from a madhouse darted shrill and high in discordant jets of sound which seemed to rush far above the earth and drive all peace from under the stars.

Carlier and Kayerts slept badly. They both thought they had heard shots fired during the night — but they could not agree as to the direction. In the morning Makola was gone somewhere. He returned about noon with one of yesterday's strangers, and eluded all Kayerts' attempts to close with him: had become deaf apparently. Kayerts wondered. Carlier, who had been fishing off the bank, came back and remarked while he showed his catch, "The niggers seem to be in a deuce of a stir; I wonder what's up. I saw about fifteen canoes cross the river during the two hours I was there fishing." Kayerts, worried, said, "Isn't this Makola very queer to-day?" Carlier advised, "Keep all our men together in case of some trouble."

II

There were ten station men who had been left by the Director. Those fellows, having engaged themselves to the Company for six months (without having any idea of a month in particular and only a very faint notion of time in general), had been serving the cause of progress for upwards of two years. Belonging to a tribe from a very distant part of the land of darkness and sorrow, they did not run away, naturally supposing that as wandering strangers they would be killed by the inhabitants of the country; in which they were right. They lived in straw huts on the slope of a ravine overgrown with reedy grass, just behind the station buildings. They were not happy, regretting the festive incantations, the sorceries, the human sacrifices of their own land; where they also had parents, brothers, sisters, admired chiefs, respected magicians, loved friends, and other ties supposed generally to be human. Besides, the rice rations served out by the Company did not agree with them, being a food unknown to their land, and to which they could not get used. Consequently they were unhealthy and miserable. Had they been of any other tribe they would have made up their minds to die — for nothing is easier to certain savages than suicide — and so have escaped from the puzzling difficulties of existence. But belonging, as they did, to a warlike tribe with filed teeth, they had more grit, and went on stupidly living through disease and sorrow. They did very little work, and had lost their splendid physique. Carlier and Kayerts doctored them assiduously without being able to bring them back into condition again. They were mustered every morning and told off to different tasks — grass-cutting, fence-building, tree-felling, &c., &c., which no power on earth could induce them to execute efficiently. The two whites had practically very little control over them.

In the afternoon Makola came over to the big house and found Kayerts watching three heavy columns of smoke rising above the forests. "What is that?" asked Kayerts. "Some villages burn," answered Makola, who seemed to have regained his wits. Then he said abruptly: "We have got very little ivory; bad six months' trading. Do you like get a little more ivory?"

"Yes," said Kayerts, eagerly. He thought of percentages which were low.

"Those men who came yesterday are traders from Loanda who have got more ivory than they can carry home. Shall I buy? I know their camp."

"Certainly," said Kayerts. "What are those traders?"

"Bad fellows," said Makola, indifferently. "They fight with people, and catch women and children. They are bad men, and got guns. There is a great disturbance in the country. Do you want ivory?"

"Yes," said Kayerts. Makola said nothing for a while. Then: "Those workmen of ours are no good at all," he muttered, looking round. "Station in very bad order, sir. Director will growl. Better get a fine lot of ivory, then he say nothing."

"I can't help it; the men won't work," said Kayerts. "When will you get that ivory?"

"Very soon," said Makola. "Perhaps to-night. You leave it to me, and keep indoors, sir. I think you had better give some palm wine to our men to make a dance this evening. Enjoy themselves. Work better to-morrow. There's plenty palm wine — gone a little sour."

Kayerts said yes, and Makola, with his own hands, carried big calabashes to the door of his hut. They stood there till the evening, and Mrs. Makola looked into every one. The men got them at sunset. When Kayerts and Carlier retired, a big bonfire was flaring before the men's huts. They could hear their shouts and drumming. Some men from Gobila's village had joined the station hands, and the entertainment was a great success.

In the middle of the night, Carlier waking suddenly, heard a man shout loudly; then a shot was fired. Only one. Carlier ran out and met Kayerts on the verandah. They were both startled. As they went across the yard to call Makola, they saw shadows moving in the night. One of them cried, "Don't shoot! It's me, Price." Then Makola appeared close to them. "Go back, go back, please," he urged, "you spoil all." "There are strange men about," said Carlier. "Never mind; I know," said Makola. Then he whispered, "All right. Bring ivory. Say nothing! I know my business." The two white men reluctantly went back to the house, but did not sleep. They heard footsteps, whispers, some groans. It seemed as if a lot of men came in, dumped heavy things on the ground, squabbled a long time, then went away. They lay on their hard beds and thought: "This Makola is invaluable." In the morning Carlier came out, very sleepy, and pulled at the cord of the big bell. The station hands mustered every morning to the sound of the bell. That morning nobody came. Kayerts turned out also, yawning. Across the yard they saw Makola come out of his hut, a tin basin of soapy water in his hand. Makola, a civilized nigger, was very neat in his person. He threw the soapsuds skilfully over a wretched little yellow cur he had, then turning his face to the agent's house, he shouted from the distance, "All the men gone last night!"

They heard him plainly, but in their surprise they both yelled out together: "What!" Then they stared at one another. "We are in a proper fix now," growled Carlier. "It's incredible!" muttered Kayerts. "I will go to the huts and see," said Carlier, striding off. Makola coming up found Kayerts standing alone.

"I can hardly believe it," said Kayerts, tearfully. "We took care of them as if they had been our children."

"They went with the coast people," said Makola after a moment of hesitation.

"What do I care with whom they went — the ungrateful brutes!" exclaimed the other. Then with sudden suspicion, and looking hard at Makola, he added: "What do you know about it?"

Makola moved his shoulders, looking down on the ground. "What do I know? I think only. Will you come and look at the ivory I've got there? It is a fine lot. You never saw such."

He moved towards the store. Kayerts followed him mechanically, thinking about the incredible desertion of the men. On the ground before the door of the fetish lay six splendid tusks.

45 "What did you give for it?" asked Kayerts, after surveying the lot with satisfaction.

"No regular trade," said Makola. "They brought the ivory and gave it to me. I told them to take what they most wanted in the station. It is a beautiful lot. No station can show such tusks. Those traders wanted carriers badly, and our men were no good here. No trade, no entry in books; all correct."

Kayerts nearly burst with indignation. "Why!" he shouted, "I believe you have sold our men for these tusks!" Makola stood impassive and silent. "I — I — will — I," stuttered Kayerts. "You fiend!" he yelled out.

"I did the best for you and the Company," said Makola, imperturbably. "Why you shout so much? Look at this tusk."

"I dismiss you! I will report you — I won't look at the tusk. I forbid you to touch them. I order you to throw them into the river. You — you!"

50 "You very red, Mr. Kayerts. If you are so irritable in the sun, you will get fever and die — like the first chief!" pronounced Makola impressively.

They stood still, contemplating one another with intense eyes, as if they had been looking with effort across immense distances. Kayerts shivered. Makola had meant no more than he said, but his words seemed to Kayerts full of ominous menace! He turned sharply and went away to the house. Makola retired into the bosom of his family; and the tusks, left lying before the store, looked very large and valuable in the sunshine.

Carlier came back on the verandah. "They're all gone, hey?" asked Kayerts from the far end of the common room in a muffled voice. "You did not find anybody?"

"Oh, yes," said Carlier, "I found one of Gobila's people lying dead before the huts — shot through the body. We heard that shot last night."

Kayerts came out quickly. He found his companion staring grimly over the yard at the tusks, away by the store. They both sat in silence for a while. Then Kayerts related his conversation with Makola. Carlier said nothing. At the midday meal they ate very little. They hardly exchanged a word that day. A great silence seemed to lie heavily over the station and press on their lips. Makola did not open the store; he spent the day playing with his children. He lay full-length on a mat outside his door, and the youngsters sat on his chest and clambered all over him. It was a touching picture. Mrs. Makola was busy cooking all day as usual. The white men made a somewhat better meal in the evening. Afterwards, Carlier smoking his pipe strolled over to the store; he stood for a long time over the tusks, touched one or two with his foot, even tried to lift the largest one by its small end. He came back to his chief, who had not stirred from the verandah, threw himself in the chair and said —

55   "I can see it! They were pounced upon while they slept heavily after drinking all that palm wine you've allowed Makola to give them. A put-up job! See? The worst is, some of Gobila's people went there, and got carried off too, no doubt. The least drunk woke up, and got shot for his sobriety. This is a funny country. What will you do now?"

"We can't touch it, of course," said Kayerts.

"Of course not," assented Carlier.

"Slavery is an awful thing," stammered out Kayerts in an unsteady voice.

"Frightful — the sufferings," grunted Carlier with conviction.

60   They believed their words. Everybody shows a respectful deference to certain sounds that he and his fellows can make. But about feelings people really know nothing. We talk with indignation or enthusiasm; we talk about oppression, cruelty, crime, devotion, self-sacrifice, virtue, and we know nothing real beyond the words. Nobody knows what suffering or sacrifice mean — except, perhaps the victims of the mysterious purpose of these illusions.

Next morning they saw Makola very busy setting up in the yard the big scales used for weighing ivory. By and by Carlier said: "What's that filthy scoundrel up to?" and lounged out into the yard. Kayerts followed. They stood watching. Makola took no notice. When the balance was swung true, he tried to lift a tusk into the scale. It was too heavy. He looked up helplessly without a word, and for a minute they stood round that balance as mute and still as three statues. Suddenly Carlier said: "Catch hold of the other end, Makola — you beast!" and together they swung the tusk up. Kayerts trembled in every limb. He muttered, "I say! O! I say!" and putting his hand in his pocket found there a dirty bit of paper and the stump of a pencil. He turned his back on the others, as if about to do something tricky, and noted stealthily the weights which Carlier shouted out to him with unnecessary loudness. When all was over Makola whispered to himself: "The sun's very strong here for the tusks." Carlier said to Kayerts in a careless tone: "I say, chief, I might just as well give him a lift with this lot into the store."

As they were going back to the house Kayerts observed with a sigh: "It had to be done." And Carlier said: "It's deplorable, but, the men being Company's men the ivory is Company's ivory. We must look after it." "I will report to the Director, of course," said Kayerts. "Of course; let him decide," approved Carlier.

At midday they made a hearty meal. Kayerts sighed from time to time. Whenever they mentioned Makola's name they always added to it an opprobrious epithet. It eased their conscience. Makola gave himself a half-holiday, and bathed his children in the river. No one from Gobila's villages came near the station that day. No one came the next day, and the next, nor for a whole week. Gobila's people might have been dead and buried for any sign of life they gave. But they were only mourning for those they had lost by the witchcraft of white men, who had brought wicked people into their country. The wicked people were gone, but fear remained. Fear always remains. A man may destroy everything within himself, love and hate and belief, and even doubt; but as long as he clings to life he cannot destroy fear: the fear, subtle, indestructible, and terrible, that pervades his being; that tinges his thoughts; that lurks in his heart; that watches on his lips the struggle of his last breath. In his fear, the mild old Gobila offered extra human sacrifices to all the Evil Spirits that had taken possession of his white friends. His heart was heavy. Some warriors spoke about burning and killing, but the cautious old savage dissuaded them. Who could foresee the woe those mysterious creatures, if irritated, might bring? They should be left alone. Perhaps in time they would disappear into the earth as the first one had disappeared. His people must keep away from them, and hope for the best.

Kayerts and Carlier did not disappear, but remained above on this earth, that, somehow, they fancied had become bigger and very empty. It was not the absolute and dumb solitude of the post that impressed them so much as an inarticulate feeling that something from within them was gone, something that worked for their safety, and had kept the wilderness from interfering with their hearts. The images of home; the memory of people like them, of men that thought and felt as they used to think and feel, receded into distances made indistinct by the glare of unclouded sunshine. And out of the great silence of the surrounding wilderness, its very hopelessness and savagery seemed to approach them nearer, to draw them gently, to look upon them, to envelop them with a solicitude irresistible, familiar, and disgusting.

65   Days lengthened into weeks, then into months. Gobila's people drummed and yelled to every new moon, as of yore, but kept away from the station. Makola and Carlier tried once in a canoe to open communications, but were received with a shower of arrows, and had to fly back to the station for dear life. That attempt set the country up and down the river into an uproar that could be very distinctly heard for days. The steamer was late. At first they spoke of delay jauntily, then anxiously, then gloomily. The matter was becoming serious. Stores were running short. Carlier cast his lines off the bank, but the river was low, and the fish kept out in the stream. They dared not stroll far away from the station to shoot. Moreover, there was no game in the impenetrable forest. Once Carlier shot a hippo in the river. They had no boat to secure it, and it sank. When it floated up it drifted away, and Gobila's people secured the carcase. It was the occasion for a national holiday, but Carlier had a fit of rage over it and talked about the necessity of exterminating all the niggers before the country could be made habitable. Kayerts mooned about silently; spent hours looking at the portrait of his Melie. It represented a little girl with long bleached tresses and a rather sour face. His legs were much swollen, and he could hardly walk. Carlier, undermined by fever, could not swagger any more, but kept tottering about, still with a devil-may-care air, as became a man who remembered his crack regiment. He had become hoarse, sarcastic, and inclined to say unpleasant things. He called it "being frank with you." They had long ago reckoned their percentages on trade, including in them that last deal of "this infamous Makola." They had also concluded not to say anything about it. Kayerts hesitated at first — was afraid of the Director.

"He has seen worse things done on the quiet," maintained Carlier, with a hoarse laugh. "Trust him! He won't thank you if you blab. He is no better than you or me. Who will talk if we hold our tongues? There is nobody here."

That was the root of the trouble! There was nobody there; and being left there alone with their weakness, they became daily more like a pair of accomplices than like a couple of devoted friends. They had heard nothing from home for eight months. Every evening they said, "To-morrow we shall see the steamer." But one of the Company's steamers had been wrecked, and the Director was busy with the other, relieving very distant and important stations on the main river. He thought that the useless station, and the useless men, could wait. Meantime Kayerts and Carlier lived on rice boiled without salt, and cursed the Company, all Africa, and the day they were born. One must have lived on such diet to discover what ghastly trouble the necessity of swallowing one's food may become. There was literally nothing else in the station but rice and coffee; they drank the coffee without sugar. The last fifteen lumps Kayerts had solemnly locked away in his box, together with a half-bottle of Cognâc, "in case of sickness," he explained. Carlier approved. "When one is sick," he said, "any little extra like that is cheering."

They waited. Rank grass began to sprout over the courtyard. The bell never rang now. Days passed, silent, exasperating, and slow. When the two men spoke, they snarled; and their silences were bitter, as if tinged by the bitterness of their thoughts.

One day after a lunch of boiled rice, Carlier put down his cup untasted, and said: "Hang it all! Let's have a decent cup of coffee for once. Bring out that sugar, Kayerts!"

70 "For the sick," muttered Kayerts, without looking up.

"For the sick," mocked Carlier. "Bosh! ... Well! I am sick."

"You are no more sick than I am, and I go without," said Kayerts in a peaceful tone.

"Come! out with that sugar, you stingy old slave-dealer."

Kayerts looked up quickly. Carlier was smiling with marked insolence. And suddenly it seemed to Kayerts that he had never seen that man before. Who was he? He knew nothing about him. What was he capable of? There was a surprising flash of violent emotion within him, as if in the presence of something undreamt-of, dangerous, and final. But he managed to pronounce with composure —

75 "That joke is in very bad taste. Don't repeat it."

"Joke!" said Carlier, hitching himself forward on his seat. "I am hungry — I am sick — I don't joke! I hate hypocrites. You are a hypocrite. You are a slave-dealer. I am a slave-dealer. There's nothing but slave-dealers in this cursed country. I mean to have sugar in my coffee to-day, anyhow!"

"I forbid you to speak to me in that way," said Kayerts with a fair show of resolution.

"You! — What?" shouted Carlier, jumping up.

Kayerts stood up also. "I am your chief," he began, trying to master the shakiness of his voice.

80 "What?" yelled the other. "Who's chief? There's no chief here. There's nothing here: there's nothing but you and I. Fetch the sugar — you potbellied ass."

"Hold your tongue. Go out of this room," screamed Kayerts. "I dismiss you — you scoundrel!"

Carlier swung a stool. All at once he looked dangerously in earnest. "You flabby, good-for-nothing civilian — take that!" he howled.

Kayerts dropped under the table, and the stool struck the grass inner wall of the room. Then, as Carlier was trying to upset the table, Kayerts in desperation made a blind rush, head low, like a cornered pig would do, and over-turning his friend, bolted along the verandah, and into his room. He locked the door, snatched his revolver, and stood panting. In less than a minute, Carlier was kicking at the door furiously, howling, "If you don't bring out that sugar, I will shoot you at sight, like a dog. Now then — one — two — three. You won't? I will show you who's the master."

Kayerts thought the door would fall in, and scrambled through the square hole that served for a window in his room. There was then the whole breadth of the house between them. But the other was apparently not strong enough to break in the door, and Kayerts heard him running round. Then he also began to run laboriously on his swollen legs. He ran as quickly as he could, grasping the revolver, and unable yet to understand what was happening to him. He saw in succession Makola's house, the store, the river, the ravine, and the low bushes; and he saw all those things again as he ran for the second time round the house. Then again they flashed past him. That morning he could not have walked a yard without a groan.

85   And now he ran. He ran fast enough to keep out of sight of the other man.

Then as, weak and desperate, he thought, "Before I finish the next round I shall die," he heard the other man stumble heavily, then stop. He stopped also. He had the back and Carlier the front of the house, as before. He heard him drop into a chair cursing, and suddenly his own legs gave way, and he slid down into a sitting posture with his back to the wall. His mouth was as dry as a cinder, and his face was wet with perspiration — and tears. What was it all about? He thought it must be a horrible illusion; he thought he was dreaming; he thought he was going mad! After a while he collected his senses. What did they quarrel about? That sugar! How absurd! He would give it to him — didn't want it himself. And he began scrambling to his feet with a sudden feeling of security. But before he had fairly stood upright, a common-sense reflection occurred to him and drove him back into despair. He thought: If I give way now to that brute of a soldier, he will begin this horror again to-morrow — and the day after — every day — raise other pretensions, trample on me, torture me, make me his slave — and I will be lost! Lost! The steamer may not come for days — may never come. He shook so that he had to sit down on the floor again. He shivered forlornly. He felt he could not, would not move any more. He was completely distracted by the sudden perception that the position was without issue — that death and life had in a moment become equally difficult and terrible.

All at once he heard the other push his chair back; and he leaped to his feet with extreme facility. He listened and got confused. Must run again! Right or left? He heard footsteps. He darted to the left, grasping his revolver, and at the very same instant, as it seemed to him, they came into violent collision. Both shouted with surprise. A loud explosion took place between them; a roar of red fire, thick smoke; and Kayerts, deafened and blinded, rushed back thinking: I am hit — it's all over. He expected the other to come round — to gloat over his agony. He caught hold of an upright of the roof — "All over!" Then he heard a crashing fall on the other side of the house, as if somebody had tumbled headlong over a chair — then silence. Nothing more happened. He did not die. Only his shoulder felt as if it had been badly wrenched, and he had lost his revolver. He was disarmed and helpless! He waited for his fate. The other man made no sound. It was a stratagem. He was stalking him now! Along what side? Perhaps he was taking aim this very minute!

After a few moments of an agony frightful and absurd, he decided to go and meet his doom. He was prepared for every surrender. He turned the corner, steadying himself with one hand on the wall; made a few paces, and nearly swooned. He had seen on the floor, protruding past the other corner, a pair of turned-up feet. A pair of white naked feet in red slippers. He felt deadly sick, and stood for a time in profound darkness. Then Makola appeared before him, saying quietly: "Come along, Mr. Kayerts. He is dead." He burst into tears of gratitude; a loud, sobbing fit of crying. After a time he found himself sitting in a chair and looking at Carlier, who lay stretched on his back. Makola was kneeling over the body.

"Is this your revolver?" asked Makola, getting up.

90 "Yes," said Kayerts; then he added very quickly, "He ran after me to shoot me — you saw!"

"Yes, I saw," said Makola. "There is only one revolver; where's his?"

"Don't know," whispered Kayerts in a voice that had become suddenly very faint.

"I will go and look for it," said the other, gently. He made the round along the verandah, while Kayerts sat still and looked at the corpse. Makola came back empty-handed, stood in deep thought, then stepped quietly into the dead man's room, and came out directly with a revolver, which he held up before Kayerts. Kayerts shut his eyes. Everything was going round. He found life more terrible and difficult than death. He had shot an unarmed man.

After meditating for a while, Makola said softly, pointing at the dead man who lay there with his right eye blown out —

95 "He died of fever." Kayerts looked at him with a stony stare. "Yes," repeated Makola, thoughtfully, stepping over the corpse, "I think he died of fever. Bury him to-morrow."

And he went away slowly to his expectant wife, leaving the two white men alone on the verandah.

Night came, and Kayerts sat unmoving on his chair. He sat quiet as if he had taken a dose of opium. The violence of the emotions he had passed through produced a feeling of exhausted serenity. He had plumbed in one short afternoon the depths of horror and despair, and now found repose in the conviction that life had no more secrets for him: neither had death! He sat by the corpse thinking; thinking very actively, thinking very new thoughts. He seemed to have broken loose from himself altogether. His old thoughts, convictions, likes and dislikes, things he respected and things he abhorred, appeared in their true light at last! Appeared contemptible and childish, false and ridiculous. He revelled in his new wisdom while he sat by the man he had killed. He argued with himself about all things under heaven with that kind of wrong-headed lucidity which may be observed in some lunatics. Incidentally he reflected that the fellow dead there had been a noxious beast anyway; that men died every day in thousands; perhaps in hundreds of thousands — who could tell? — and that in the number, that one death could not possibly make any difference; couldn't have any importance, at least to a thinking creature.

He, Kayerts, was a thinking creature. He had been all his life, till that moment, a believer in a lot of nonsense like the rest of mankind — who are fools; but now he thought! He knew! He was at peace; he was familiar with the highest wisdom! Then he tried to imagine himself dead, and Carlier sitting in his chair watching him; and his attempt met with such unexpected success, that in a very few moments he became not at all sure who was dead and who was alive. This extraordinary achievement of his fancy startled him, however, and by a clever and timely effort of mind he saved himself just in time from becoming Carlier. His heart thumped, and he felt hot all over at the thought of that danger. Carlier! What a beastly thing! To compose his now disturbed nerves — and no wonder! — he tried to whistle a little. Then, suddenly, he fell asleep, or thought he had slept; but at any rate there was a fog, and somebody had whistled in the fog.

He stood up. The day had come, and a heavy mist had descended upon the land: the mist penetrating, enveloping, and silent; the morning mist of tropical lands; the mist that clings and kills; the mist white and deadly, immaculate and poisonous. He stood up, saw the body, and threw his arms above his head with a cry like that of a man who, waking from a trance, finds himself immured forever in a tomb. "*Help! . . . My God!*"

A shriek inhuman, vibrating and sudden, pierced like a sharp dart the white shroud of that land of sorrow. Three short, impatient screeches followed, and then, for a time, the fog-wreaths rolled on, undisturbed, through a formidable silence. Then many more shrieks, rapid and piercing, like the yells of some exasperated and ruthless creature, rent the air. Progress was calling to Kayerts from the river. Progress and civilization and all the virtues. Society was calling to its accomplished child to come, to be taken care of, to be instructed, to be judged, to be condemned; it called him to return to that rubbish heap from which he had wandered away, so that justice could be done.

Kayerts heard and understood. He stumbled out of the verandah, leaving the other man quite alone for the first time since they had been thrown there together. He groped his way through the fog, calling in his ignorance upon the invisible heaven to undo its work. Makola flitted by in the mist, shouting as he ran —

"Steamer! Steamer! They can't see. They whistle for the station. I go ring the bell. Go down to the landing, sir. I ring."

He disappeared. Kayerts stood still. He looked upwards; the fog rolled low over his head. He looked round like a man who has lost his way; and he saw a dark smudge, a cross-shaped stain, upon the shifting purity of the mist. As he began to stumble towards it, the station bell rang in a tumultuous peal its answer to the impatient clamour of the steamer.

The Managing Director of the Great Civilizing Company (since we know that civilization follows trade) landed first, and incontinently lost sight of the steamer. The fog down by the river was exceedingly dense; above, at the station, the bell rang unceasing and brazen.

The Director shouted loudly to the steamer:

"There is nobody down to meet us; there may be something wrong, though they are ringing. You had better come, too!"

And he began to toil up the steep bank. The captain and the engine-driver of the boat followed behind. As they scrambled up the fog thinned, and they could see their Director a good way ahead. Suddenly they saw him start forward, calling to them over his shoulder:—"Run! Run to the house! I've found one of them. Run, look for the other!"

He had found one of them! And even he, the man of varied and startling experience, was somewhat discomposed by the manner of this finding. He stood and fumbled in his pockets (for a knife) while he faced Kayerts, who was hanging by a leather strap from the cross. He had evidently climbed the grave, which was high and narrow, and after tying the end of the strap to the arm, had swung himself off. His toes were only a couple of inches above the ground; his arms hung stiffly down; he seemed to be standing rigidly at attention, but with one purple cheek playfully posed on the shoulder. And, irreverently, he was putting out a swollen tongue at his Managing Director.

(1897)

Charlotte Perkins Gilman (1860–1935)

Although "The Yellow Wallpaper" has recently been praised as a major feminist short story, it was virtually unknown until the early 1960s, and its author, a native of Hartford, Connecticut, was remembered chiefly as an important theorist in the women's movement during the early decades of this century. In such book-length tracts as *Women and Economics* (1898) and short stories as "If I Were a Man" and "The Widow's Might," she studied the nature of women's lives and their relationships with men. "The Yellow Wallpaper," one of her first short stories, was based on the extreme mental depression she suffered in part as the result of psychiatric treatments prescribed after the birth of her daughter. It was written, she later stated, "not...to drive people crazy, but to save people from being driven crazy...." Often compared to Edgar Allan Poe's tales that examine the narrator's descent into madness, the story, with its depiction of the prison-like room and its grotesquely designed wallpaper, is often interpreted as a presentation of the destructive effects on women of the repressive patriarchal society of the nineteenth century.

THE YELLOW WALLPAPER

It is very seldom that mere ordinary people like John and myself secure ancestral halls for the summer.

A colonial mansion, a hereditary estate, I would say a haunted house and reach the height of romantic felicity — but that would be asking too much of fate!

Still I will proudly declare that there is something queer about it.

Else, why should it be let so cheaply? And why have stood so long untenanted?

5   John laughs at me, of course, but one expects that.

John is practical in the extreme. He has no patience with faith, an intense horror of superstition, and he scoffs openly at any talk of things not to be felt and seen and put down in figures.

John is a physician, and *perhaps* — (I would not say it to a living soul, of course, but this is dead paper and a great relief to my mind) — *perhaps* that is one reason I do not get well faster.

You see, he does not believe I am sick! And what can one do?

If a physician of high standing, and one's own husband, assures friends and relatives that there is really nothing the matter with one but temporary nervous depression — a slight hysterical tendency — what is one to do?

10   My brother is also a physician, and also of high standing, and he says the same thing.

So I take phosphates or phosphites — whichever it is — and tonics, and air and exercise, and journeys, and am absolutely forbidden to "work" until I am well again.

Personally, I disagree with their ideas.

Personally, I believe that congenial work, with excitement and change, would do me good.

But what is one to do?

15   I did write for a while in spite of them; but it *does* exhaust me a good deal — having to be so sly about it, or else meet with heavy opposition.

I sometimes fancy that in my condition, if I had less opposition and more society and stimulus — but John says the very worst thing I can do is to think about my condition, and I confess it always makes me feel bad.

So I will let it alone and talk about the house.

The most beautiful place! It is quite alone, standing well back from the road, quite three miles from the village. It makes me think of English places that you read about, for there are hedges and walls and gates that lock, and lots of separate little houses for the gardeners and people.

There is a *delicious* garden! I never saw such a garden — large and shady, full of box-bordered paths, and lined with long grape-covered arbors with seats under them.

20   There were greenhouses, but they are all broken now.

There was some legal trouble, I believe, something about the heirs and co-heirs; anyhow, the place has been empty for years.

That spoils my ghostliness, I am afraid, but I don't care — there is something strange about the house — I can feel it.

I even said so to John one moonlight evening, but he said what I felt was a draught, and shut the window.

I get unreasonably angry with John sometimes. I'm sure I never used to be so sensitive. I think it is due to this nervous condition.

25   But John says if I feel so I shall neglect proper self-control; so I take pains to control myself — before him, at least, and that makes me very tired.

I don't like our room a bit. I wanted one downstairs that opened onto the piazza and had roses all over the window, and such pretty old-fashioned chintz hangings! But John would not hear of it.

He said there was only one window and not room for two beds, and no near room for him if he took another.

He is very careful and loving, and hardly lets me stir without special direction.

I have a schedule prescription for each hour in the day; he takes all care from me, and so I feel basely ungrateful not to value it more.

30   He said he came here solely on my account, that I was to have perfect rest and all the air I could get. "Your exercise depends on your strength, my dear," said he, "and your food somewhat on your appetite; but air you can absorb all the time." So we took the nursery at the top of the house.

It is a big, airy room, the whole floor nearly, with windows that look all ways, and air and sunshine galore. It was nursery first, and then playroom and gymnasium, I should judge, for the windows are barred for little children, and there are rings and things in the walls.

The paint and paper look as if a boys' school had used it. It is stripped off — the paper — in great patches all around the head of my bed, about as far as I can reach, and in a great place on the other side of the room low down. I never saw a worse paper in my life. One of those sprawling, flamboyant patterns committing every artistic sin.

It is dull enough to confuse the eye in following, pronounced enough constantly to irritate and provoke study, and when you follow the lame uncertain curves for a little distance they suddenly commit suicide — plunge off at out-rageous angles, destroy themselves in unheard-of contradictions.

The color is repellent, almost revolting: a smouldering unclean yellow, strangely faded by the slow-turning sunlight. It is a dull yet lurid orange in some places, a sickly sulphur tint in others.

No wonder the children hated it! I should hate it myself if I had to live in this room long.

There comes John, and I must put this away — he hates to have me write a word.

We have been here two weeks, and I haven't felt like writing before, since that first day.

I am sitting by the window now, up in this atrocious nursery, and there is nothing to hinder my writing as much as I please, save lack of strength.

John is away all day, and even some nights when his cases are serious.

I am glad my case is not serious!

But these nervous troubles are dreadfully depressing.

John does not know how much I really suffer. He knows there is no reason to suffer, and that satisfies him.

Of course it is only nervousness. It does weigh on me so not to do my duty in any way!

I meant to be such a help to John, such a real rest and comfort, and here I am a comparative burden already!

Nobody would believe what an effort it is to do what little I am able — to dress and entertain, and order things.

It is fortunate Mary is so good with the baby. Such a dear baby!

And yet I *cannot* be with him, it makes me so nervous.

I suppose John never was nervous in his life. He laughs at me so about this wallpaper!

At first he meant to repaper the room, but afterward he said that I was letting it get the better of me, and that nothing was worse for a nervous patient than to give way to such fancies.

He said that after the wallpaper was changed it would be the heavy bed-stead, and then the barred windows, and then that gate at the head of the stairs, and so on.

"You know the place is doing you good," he said, "and really, dear, I don't care to renovate the house just for a three months' rental."

"Then do let us go downstairs," I said. "There are such pretty rooms there."

Then he took me in his arms and called me a blessed little goose, and said he would go down cellar, if I wished, and have it whitewashed into the bargain.

But he is right enough about the beds and windows and things.

It is as airy and comfortable a room as anyone need wish, and, of course, I would not be so silly as to make him uncomfortable just for a whim.

I'm really getting quite fond of the big room, all but that horrid paper.

Out of one window I can see the garden — those mysterious deep-shaded arbors, the riotous old-fashioned flowers, and bushes and gnarly trees.

Out of another I get a lovely view of the bay and a little private wharf belonging to the estate. There is a beautiful shaded lane that runs down there from the house. I always fancy I see people walking in these numerous paths and arbors, but John has cautioned me not to give way to fancy in the least. He says that with my imaginative power and habit of story-making, a nervous weakness like mine is sure to lead to all manner of excited fancies, and that I ought to use my will and good sense to check the tendency. So I try.

I think sometimes that if I were only well enough to write a little it would relieve the press of ideas and rest me.

60 But I find I get pretty tired when I try.

It is so discouraging not to have any advice and companionship about my work. When I get really well, John says we will ask Cousin Henry and Julia down for a long visit; but he says he would as soon put fireworks in my pillow-case as to let me have those stimulating people about now.

I wish I could get well faster.

But I must not think about that. This paper looks to me as if it *knew* what a vicious influence it had!

There is a recurrent spot where the pattern lolls like a broken neck and two bulbous eyes stare at you upside down.

65 I get positively angry with the impertinence of it and the everlastingness. Up and down and sideways they crawl, and those absurd unblinking eyes are everywhere. There is one place where two breadths didn't match, and the eyes go all up and down the line, one a little higher than the other.

I never saw so much expression in an inanimate thing before, and we all know how much expression they have! I used to lie awake as a child and get more entertainment and terror out of blank walls and plain furniture than most children could find in a toy-store.

I remember what a kindly wink the knobs of our big old bureau used to have, and there was one chair that always seemed like a strong friend.

I used to feel that if any of the other things looked too fierce I could always hop into that chair and be safe.

The furniture in this room is no worse than inharmonious, however, for we had to bring it all from downstairs. I suppose when this was used as a play-room they had to take the nursery things out, and no wonder! I never saw such ravages as the children have made here.

70 The wallpaper, as I said before, is torn off in spots, and it sticketh closer than a brother — they must have had perseverance as well as hatred.

Then the floor is scratched and gouged and splintered, the plaster itself is dug out here and there, and this great heavy bed, which is all we found in the room, looks as if it had been through the wars.

But I don't mind it a bit — only the paper.

There comes John's sister. Such a dear girl as she is, and so careful of me! I must not let her find me writing.

She is a perfect and enthusiastic housekeeper, and hopes for no better profession. I verily believe she thinks it is the writing which made me sick!

75 But I can write when she is out, and see her a long way off from these windows.

There is one that commands the road, a lovely shaded winding road, and one that just looks off over the country. A lovely country, too, full of great elms and velvet meadows.

This wallpaper has a kind of sub-pattern in a different shade, a particularly irritating one, for you can only see it in certain lights, and not clearly then.

But in the places where it isn't faded and where the sun is just so — I can see a strange, provoking, formless sort of figure that seems to skulk about behind that silly and conspicuous front design.

There's sister on the stairs!

80 Well, the Fourth of July[1] is over! The people are all gone, and I am tired out. John thought it might do me good to see a little company, so we just had Mother and Nellie and the children down for a week.

Of course I didn't do a thing. Jennie sees to everything now.

But it tired me all the same.

John says if I don't pick up faster he shall send me to Weir Mitchell[2] in the fall.

But I don't want to go there at all. I had a friend who was in his hands once, and she says he is just like John and my brother, only more so!

85 Besides, it is such an undertaking to go so far.

I don't feel as if it was worthwhile to turn my hand over for anything, and I'm getting dreadfully fretful and querulous.

I cry at nothing, and cry most of the time.

Of course I don't when John is here, or anybody else, but when I am alone.

And I am alone a good deal just now. John is kept in town very often by serious cases, and Jennie is good and lets me alone when I want her to.

90 So I walk a little in the garden or down that lovely lane, sit on the porch under the roses, and lie down up here a good deal.

I'm getting really fond of the room in spite of the wallpaper. Perhaps *because* of the wallpaper.

It dwells in my mind so!

I lie here on this great immovable bed — it is nailed down, I believe — and follow that pattern about by the hour. It is as good as gymnastics, I assure you. I start, we'll say, at the bottom, down in the corner over there where it has not been touched, and I determine for the thousandth time that I *will* follow that pointless pattern to some sort of a conclusion.

I know a little of the principle of design, and I know this thing was not arranged on any laws of radiation, or alternation, or repetition, or symmetry, or anything else that I ever heard of.

95 It is repeated, of course, by the breadths, but not otherwise.

Looked at in one way, each breadth stands alone; the bloated curves and flourishes — a kind of "debased Romanesque"[3] with delirium tremens — go waddling up and down in isolated columns of fatuity.

---

1 American Independence Day. 2 Gilman's own physician, Silas Weir Mitchell, popularized the "rest cure" for people suffering from nervous disorders. 3 style of architecture prevalent from the ninth to the twelfth century in Europe, when the Gothic style began to replace it. It is characterized by thick walls and plain, rounded arches supported by columns.

But, on the other hand, they connect diagonally, and the sprawling out-lines run off in great slanting waves of optic horror, like a lot of wallowing sea-weeds in full chase.

The whole thing goes horizontally, too, at least it seems so, and I exhaust myself trying to distinguish the order of its going in that direction.

They have used a horizontal breadth for a frieze, and that adds wonderfully to the confusion.

100 There is one end of the room where it is almost intact, and there, when the crosslights fade and the low sun shines directly upon it, I can almost fancy radiation after all — the interminable grotesque seems to form around a common center and rush off in headlong plunges of equal distraction.

It makes me tired to follow it. I will take a nap, I guess.

I don't know why I should write this.

I don't want to.

I don't feel able.

105 And I know John would think it absurd. But I *must* say what I feel and think in some way — it is such a relief!

But the effort is getting to be greater than the relief.

Half the time now I am awfully lazy, and lie down ever so much. John says I mustn't lose my strength, and has me take cod liver oil and lots of tonics and things, to say nothing of ale and wine and rare meat.

Dear John! He loves me very dearly, and hates to have me sick. I tried to have a real earnest reasonable talk with him the other day, and tell him how I wish he would let me go and make a visit to Cousin Henry and Julia.

But he said I wasn't able to go, nor able to stand it after I got there; and I did not make out a very good case for myself, for I was crying before I had finished.

110 It is getting to be a great effort for me to think straight. Just this nervous weakness, I suppose.

And dear John gathered me up in his arms, and just carried me upstairs and laid me on the bed, and sat by me and read to me till it tired my head.

He said I was his darling and his comfort and all he had, and that I must take care of myself for his sake, and keep well.

He says no one but myself can help me out of it, that I must use my will and self-control and not let any silly fancies run away with me.

There's one comfort — the baby is well and happy, and does not have to occupy this nursery with the horrid wallpaper.

115 If we had not used it, that blessed child would have! What a fortunate escape! Why, I wouldn't have a child of mine, an impressionable little thing, live in such a room for worlds.

I never thought of it before, but it is lucky that John kept me here after all; I can stand it so much easier than a baby, you see.

Of course I never mention it to them any more — I am too wise — but I keep watch for it all the same.

There are things in that wallpaper that nobody knows about but me, or ever will.

Behind that outside pattern the dim shapes get clearer every day.

120 It is always the same shape, only very numerous.

And it is like a woman stooping down and creeping about behind that pattern. I don't like it a bit. I wonder — I begin to think — I wish John would take me away from here!

It is so hard to talk with John about my case, because he is so wise, and because he loves me so.

But I tried it last night.

It was moonlight. The moon shines in all around just as the sun does.

125 I hate to see it sometimes, it creeps so slowly, and always comes in by one window or another.

John was asleep and I hated to waken him, so I kept still and watched the moonlight on that undulating wallpaper till I felt creepy.

The faint figure behind seemed to shake the pattern, just as if she wanted to get out.

I got up softly and went to feel and see if the paper *did* move, and when I came back John was awake.

"What is it, little girl?" he said. "Don't go walking about like that — you'll get cold."

130 I thought it was a good time to talk, so I told him that I really was not gaining here, and that I wished he would take me away.

"Why, darling!" said he. "Our lease will be up in three weeks, and I can't see how to leave before.

"The repairs are not done at home, and I cannot possibly leave town just now. Of course, if you were in any danger, I could and would, but you really are better, dear, whether you can see it or not. I am a doctor, dear, and I know. You are gaining flesh and color, you appetite is better, I feel really much easier about you."

"I don't weigh a bit more," said I, "nor as much; and my appetite may be better in the evening when you are here but it is worse in the morning when you are away!"

"Bless her little heart!" said he with a big hug. "She shall be as sick as she pleases! But now let's improve the shining hours by going to sleep, and talk about it in the morning!"

135 "And you won't go away?" I asked gloomily.

"Why, how can I, dear? It is only three weeks more and then we will take a nice little trip of a few days while Jennie is getting the house ready. Really, dear, you are better!"

"Better in body perhaps —" I began, and stopped short, for he sat up straight and looked at me with such a stern, reproachful look that I could not say another word.

"My darling," said he, "I beg of you, for my sake and for our child's sake, as well as for your own, that you will never for one instant let that idea enter your mind! There is nothing so dangerous, so fascinating, to a temperament like yours. It is a false and foolish fancy. Can you not trust me as a physician when I tell you so?"

So of course I said no more on that score, and we went to sleep before long. He thought I was asleep first, but I wasn't, and lay there for hours trying to decide whether that front pattern and the back pattern really did move together or separately.

140 On a pattern like this, by daylight, there is a lack of sequence, a defiance of law, that is a constant irritant to a normal mind.

The color is hideous enough, and unreliable enough, and infuriating enough, but the pattern is torturing.

You think you have mastered it, but just as you get well under way in following, it turns a back-somersault and there you are. It slaps you in the face, knocks you down, and tramples upon you. It is like a bad dream.

The outside pattern is a florid arabesque,[4] reminding one of a fungus. If you can imagine a toadstool in joints, an interminable string of toadstools, budding and sprouting in endless convolutions — why, that is something like it.

That is, sometimes!

145 There is one marked peculiarity about this paper, a thing nobody seems to notice but myself, and that is that it changes as the light changes.

When the sun shoots in through the east window — I always watch for that first long, straight ray — it changes so quickly that I never can quite believe it.

That is why I watch it always.

By moonlight — the moon shines in all night when there is a moon — I wouldn't know it was the same paper.

At night in any kind of light, in twilight, candlelight, lamplight, and worst of all by moonlight, it becomes bars! The outside pattern, I mean, and the woman behind it is as plain as can be.

150 I didn't realize for a long time what the thing was that showed behind, that dim sub-pattern, but now I am quite sure it is a woman.

By daylight she is subdued, quiet. I fancy it is the pattern that keeps her so still. It is so puzzling. It keeps me quiet by the hour.

I lie down ever so much now. John says it is good for me, and to sleep all I can.

Indeed he started the habit by making me lie down for an hour after each meal.

It is a very bad habit, I am convinced, for you see, I don't sleep.

155 And that cultivates deceit, for I don't tell them I'm awake — oh, no!

The fact is I am getting a little afraid of John.

He seems very queer sometimes, and even Jennie has an inexplicable look.

It strikes me occasionally, just as a scientific hypothesis, that perhaps it is the paper!

I have watched John when he did not know I was looking, and come into the room suddenly on the most innocent excuses, and I've caught him several times *looking at the paper*! And Jennie too. I caught Jennie with her hand on it once.

160 She didn't know I was in the room, and when I asked her in a quiet, a very quiet voice, with the most restrained manner possible, what she was doing with the paper, she turned around as if she had been caught stealing, and looked quite angry — asked me why I should frighten her so!

4 interwoven pattern of flowers and designs.

Then she said that the paper stained everything it touched, that she had found yellow smooches on all my clothes and John's and she wished we would be more careful!

Did not that sound innocent? But I know she was studying that pattern, and I am determined that nobody shall find it out but myself!

Life is very much more exciting now than it used to be. You see, I have something more to expect, to look forward to, to watch. I really do eat better, and am more quiet than I was.

John is so pleased to see me improve! He laughed a little the other day, and said I seemed to be flourishing in spite of my wallpaper.

165 I turned it off with a laugh. I had no intention of telling him it was *because* of the wallpaper — he would make fun of me. He might even want to take me away.

I don't want to leave now until I have found it out. There is a week more, and I think that will be enough.

I'm feeling so much better!

I don't sleep much at night, for it is so interesting to watch developments; but I sleep a good deal during the daytime.

In the daytime it is tiresome and perplexing.

170 There are always new shoots on the fungus, and new shades of yellow all over it. I cannot keep count of them, though I have tried conscientiously.

It is the strangest yellow, that wallpaper! It makes me think of all the yellow things I ever saw — not beautiful ones like buttercups, but old, foul, bad yellow things.

But there is something else about that paper — the smell! I noticed it the moment we came into the room, but with so much air and sun it was not bad. Now we have had a week of fog and rain, and whether the windows are open or not, the smell is here.

It creeps all over the house.

I find it hovering in the dining-room, skulking in the parlor, hiding in the hall, lying in wait for me on the stairs.

175 It gets into my hair.

Even when I go to ride, if I turn my head suddenly and surprise it — there is that smell!

Such a peculiar odor, too! I have spent hours in trying to analyze it, to find what it smelled like.

It is not bad — at first — and very gentle, but quite the subtlest, most enduring odor I ever met.

In this damp weather it is awful. I wake up in the night and find it hanging over me.

180 It used to disturb me at first. I thought seriously of burning the house — to reach the smell.

But now I am used to it. The only thing I can think of that it is like is the *color* of the paper! A yellow smell.

There is a very funny mark on this wall, low down, near the mopboard. A streak that runs round the room. It goes behind every piece of furniture, except the bed, a long, straight, even *smooch*, as if it had been rubbed over and over.

I wonder how it was done and who did it, and what they did it for. Round and round and round — round and round and round — it makes me dizzy!

I really have discovered something at last.

185 Through watching so much at night, when it changes so, I have finally found out.

The front pattern *does* move — and no wonder! The woman behind shakes it!

Sometimes I think there are a great many women behind, and sometimes only one, and she crawls around fast, and her crawling shakes it all over.

Then in the very bright spots she keeps still, and in the very shady spots she just takes hold of the bars and shakes them hard.

And she is all the time trying to climb through. But nobody could climb through that pattern — it strangles so; I think that is why it has so many heads.

190 They get through, and then the pattern strangles them off and turns them upside down, and makes their eyes white!

If those heads were covered or taken off it would not be half so bad.

I think that woman gets out in the daytime!

And I'll tell you why — privately — I've seen her!

I can see her out of every one of my windows!

195 It is the same woman, I know, for she is always creeping, and most women do not creep by daylight.

I see her in that long shaded lane, creeping up and down. I see her in those dark grape arbors, creeping all around the garden.

I see her on that long road under the trees, creeping along, and when a carriage comes she hides under the blackberry vines.

I don't blame her a bit. It must be very humiliating to be caught creeping by daylight!

I always lock the door when I creep by daylight. I can't do it at night, for I know John would suspect something at once.

200 And John is so queer now that I don't want to irritate him. I wish he would take another room! Besides, I don't want anybody to get that woman out at night but myself.

I often wonder if I could see her out of all the windows at once.

But, turn as fast as I can, I can only see out of one at one time.

And though I always see her, she *may* be able to creep faster than I can turn! I have watched her sometimes away off in the open country, creeping as fast as a cloud shadow in a wind.

If only that top pattern could be gotten off from the under one! I mean to try it, little by little.

205 I have found out another funny thing, but I shan't tell it this time! It does not do to trust people too much.

There are only two more days to get this paper off, and I believe John is beginning to notice. I don't like the look in his eyes.

And I heard him ask Jennie a lot of professional questions about me. She had a very good report to give.

She said I slept a good deal in the daytime.

John knows I don't sleep very well at night, for all I'm so quiet!

210 He asked me all sorts of questions, too, and pretended to be very loving and kind.

As if I couldn't see through him!

Still, I don't wonder he acts so, sleeping under this paper for three months.

It only interests me, but I feel sure John and Jennie are affected by it.

Hurrah! This is the last day, but it is enough. John is to stay in town over night, and won't be out until this evening.

215 Jennie wanted to sleep with me — the sly thing; but I told her I should undoubtedly rest better for a night all alone.

That was clever, for really I wasn't alone a bit! As soon as it was moonlight and that poor thing began to crawl and shake the pattern, I got up and ran to help her.

I pulled and she shook. I shook and she pulled, and before morning we had peeled off yards of that paper.

A strip about as high as my head and half around the room.

And then when the sun came and that awful pattern began to laugh at me, I declared I would finish it today!

220 We go away tomorrow, and they are moving all my furniture down again to leave things as they were before.

Jennie looked at the wall in amazement, but I told her merrily that I did it out of pure spite at the vicious thing.

She laughed and said she wouldn't mind doing it herself, but I must not get tired.

How she betrayed herself that time!

But I am here, and no person touches this paper but Me — not *alive*!

225 She tried to get me out of the room — it was too patent! But I said it was so quiet and empty and clean now that I believed I would lie down again and sleep all I could, and not to wake me even for dinner — I would call when I woke.

So now she is gone, and the servants are gone, and the things are gone, and there is nothing left but that great bedstead nailed down, with the canvas mattress we found on it.

We shall sleep downstairs tonight, and take the boat home tomorrow.

I quite enjoy the room, now it is bare again.

How those children did tear about here!

230 This bedstead is fairly gnawed!

But I must get to work.

I have locked the door and thrown the key down into the front path.

I don't want to go out, and I don't want to have anybody come in, till John comes.

I want to astonish him.

235 I've got a rope up here that even Jennie did not find. If that woman does get out, and tries to get away, I can tie her!

But I forgot I could not reach far without anything to stand on!

This bed will *not* move!

I tried to lift and push it until I was lame, and then I got so angry I bit off a little piece at one corner — but it hurt my teeth.

Then I peeled off all the paper I could reach standing on the floor. It sticks horribly and the pattern just enjoys it! All those strangled heads and bulbous eyes and waddling fungus growths just shriek with derision!

240   I am getting angry enough to do something desperate. To jump out of the window would be admirable exercise, but the bars are too strong even to try.

Besides I wouldn't do it. Of course not. I know well enough that a step like that is improper and might be misconstrued.

I don't like to *look* out of the windows even — there are so many of those creeping women, and they creep so fast.

I wonder if they all come out of that wallpaper as I did?

But I am securely fastened now by my well-hidden rope — you don't get *me* out in the road there!

245   I suppose I shall have to get back behind the pattern when it comes night, and that is hard!

It is so pleasant to be out in this great room and creep around as I please!

I don't want to go outside. I won't, even if Jennie asks me to.

For outside you have to creep on the ground, and everything is green instead of yellow.

But here I can creep smoothly on the floor, and my shoulder just fits in that long smooch around the wall, so I cannot lose my way.

250   Why, there's John at the door!

It is no use, young man, you can't open it!

How he does call and pound!

Now he's crying to Jennie for an axe.

It would be a shame to break down that beautiful door!

255   "John, dear!" said I in the gentlest voice. "The key is down by the front steps, under a plantain leaf!"

That silenced him for a few moments.

Then he said, very quietly indeed, "Open the door, my darling!"

"I can't," said I. "The key is down by the front door under a plantain leaf!" And then I said it again, several times, very gently and slowly, and said it so often that he had to go and see, and he got it of course, and came in. He stopped short by the door.

"What is the matter?" he cried. "For God's sake, what are you doing!"

260   I kept on creeping just the same, but I looked at him over my shoulder.

"I've got out at last," said I, "in spite of you and Jane. And I've pulled off most of the paper, so you can't put me back!"

Now why should that man have fainted? But he did, and right across my path by the wall, so that I had to creep over him every time!

(1892)

Sir Charles G. D. Roberts (1860–1943)

Along with fellow Canadian Ernest Thompson Seton, Roberts is considered one of the foremost writers of realistic animal stories. Among his best-known works are the novel *Red Fox* (1905) and several collections of short animal stories, including *The Kindred of the Wild* (1902), from which "When Twilight Falls on the Stump Lots" is taken. He was a careful observer of the habits of wild creatures; however, he went far beyond presenting accurate descriptions of his animal characters. "Having got one's facts right," he once commented, "enough of them to generalize from safely, — the exciting adventure lies in the effort to 'get under the skins' ... to discern their motives, to understand and chart their simple mental processes." In "When Twilight Falls," the animals are given human characteristics through the use of such terms as "rapturously," "ecstatic," and "coveted." The story is structured around a series of contrasts such as life and death, children and parents, civilization and nature, human beings and animals. The main setting, a semi-cleared rural area, is the place in which the opposites clash. Although human beings are not directly present, they have profound impact on the lives of the central characters. (See also the introduction to Roberts's poetry, page 218.)

WHEN TWILIGHT FALLS ON THE STUMP LOTS

The wet, chill first of the spring, its blackness made tender by the lilac wash of the afterglow, lay upon the high, open stretches of the stump lots. The winter-whitened stumps, the sparse patches of juniper and bay just budding, the rough-mossed hillocks, the harsh boulders here and there up-thrusting from the soil, the swampy hollows wherein a coarse grass began to show green, all seemed anointed, as it were, to an ecstasy of peace by the chrism of that paradisal colour. Against the lucid immensity of the April sky the thin tops of five or six soaring ram-pikes aspired like violet flames. Along the skirts of the stump lots a fir wood reared a ragged-crested wall of black against the red amber of the horizon.

Late that afternoon, beside a juniper thicket not far from the centre of the stump lots, a young black and white cow had given birth to her first calf. The little animal had been licked assiduously by the mother's caressing tongue till its colour began to show a rich dark red. Now it had struggled to its feet, and, with its disproportionately long, thick legs braced wide apart, was beginning to nurse. Its blunt wet muzzle and thick lips tugged eagerly, but somewhat blunderingly as yet, at the unaccustomed teats; and its tail lifted, twitching with delight, as the first warm streams of mother milk went down its throat. It was a pathetically awkward, unlovely little figure, not yet advanced to that youngling winsomeness which is the heritage, to some degree and at some period, of the infancy of all the kindreds that breathe upon the earth. But to the young mother's eyes it was the most beautiful of things. With her head twisted far around, she nosed and licked its heaving flanks as it nursed; and between deep, ecstatic breathings she uttered in her throat low murmurs, unspeakably tender, of encouragement and caress. The delicate but pervading flood of sunset colour had the effect of blending the ruddy-hued calf into the tones of the landscape; but the cow's insistent blotches of black and white stood out sharply, refusing to harmonise. The drench of violet light was of no avail to soften their staring contrasts. They made her vividly conspicuous across the whole breadth of the stump lots, to eyes that watched her from the forest coverts.

The eyes that watched her — long, fixedly, hungrily — were small and red. They belonged to a lank she-bear, whose gaunt flanks and rusty coat proclaimed a season of famine in the wilderness. She could not see the calf, which was hidden by a hillock and some juniper scrub; but its presence was very legibly conveyed to her by the mother's solicitous watchfulness. After a motionless scrutiny from behind the screen of fir branches, the lean bear stole noiselessly forth from the shadows into the great wash of violet light. Step by step, and very slowly, with the patience that endures because confident of its object, she crept toward that oasis of mothering joy in the vast emptiness of the stump lots. Now crouching, now crawling, turning to this side and to that, taking advantage of every hollow, every thicket, every hillock, every aggressive stump, her craft succeeded in eluding even the wild and menacing watchfulness of the young mother's eyes.

The spring had been a trying one for the lank she-bear. Her den, in a dry tract of hemlock wood some furlongs back from the stump lots, was a snug little cave under the uprooted base of a lone pine, which had somehow grown up among the alien hemlocks only to draw down upon itself at last, by its superior height, the fury of a passing hurricane. The winter had contributed but scanty snowfall to cover the bear in her sleep; and the March thaws, unseasonably early and ardent, had called her forth to activity weeks too soon. Then frosts had come with belated severity, sealing away the budding tubers, which are the bear's chief dependence for spring diet; and worst of all, a long stretch of intervale meadow by the neighbouring river, which had once been rich in ground-nuts, had been ploughed up the previous spring and subjected to the producing of oats and corn. When she was feeling the pinch of meagre rations, and when the fat which a liberal autumn of blueberries had laid up about her ribs was getting as shrunken as the last snow in the thickets, she gave birth to two hairless and hungry little cubs. They were very blind, and ridiculously small to be born of so big a mother; and having so much growth to make during the next few months, their appetites were immeasurable. They tumbled, and squealed, and tugged at their mother's teats, and grew astonishingly, and made huge haste to cover their bodies with fur of a soft and silken black; and all this vitality of theirs made a strenuous demand upon their mother's milk. There were no more bee-trees left in the neighbourhood. The long wanderings which she was forced to take in her search for roots and tubers were in themselves a drain upon her nursing powers. At last, reluctant though she was to attract the hostile notice of the settlement, she found herself forced to hunt on the borders of the sheep pastures. Before all else in life was it important to her that these two tumbling little ones in the den should not go hungry. Their eyes were open now — small and dark and whimsical, their ears quaintly large and inquiring for their roguish little faces. Had she not been driven by the unkind season to so much hunting and foraging, she would have passed near all her time rapturously in the den under the pine root, fondling those two soft miracles of her world.

5   With the killing of three lambs — at widely scattered points, so as to mislead retaliation — things grew a little easier for the harassed bear; and presently she grew bolder in tampering with the creatures under man's protection. With one swift, secret blow of her mighty paw she struck down a young ewe which had strayed within reach of her hiding-place. Dragging her prey deep into the wood, she fared well upon it for some days, and was happy with her growing cubs. It was just when she had begun to feel the fasting which came upon the exhaustion of this store that, in a hungry hour, she sighed the conspicuous markings of the black-and-white cow.

It is altogether unusual for the black bear of the eastern woods to attack any quarry so large as a cow, unless under the spur of fierce hunger or fierce rage. The she-bear was powerful beyond her fellows. She had the strongest possible incentive to bold hunting, and she had lately grown confident beyond her wont. Nevertheless, when she began her careful stalking of this big game which she coveted, she had no definite intention of forcing a battle with the cow. She had observed that cows, accustomed to the protection of man, would at times leave their calves asleep and stray off some distance in their pasturing. She had even seen calves left all by themselves in a field, from morning till night, and had wondered at such negligence in their mothers. Now she had a confident idea that sooner or later the calf would lie down to sleep, and the young mother roam a little wide in search of the scant young grass. Very softly, very self-effacingly, she crept nearer step by step, following up the wind, till at last, undiscovered, she was crouching behind a thick patch of juniper, on the slope of a little hollow not ten paces distant from the cow and the calf.

By this time the tender violet light was fading to a grayness over hillock and hollow; and with the deepening of the twilight the faint breeze, which had been breathing from the northward, shifted suddenly and came in slow, warm pulsations out of the south. At the same time the calf, having nursed sufficiently, and feeling his baby legs tired of the weight they had not yet learned to carry, laid himself down. On this the cow shifted her position. She turned half round, and lifted her head high. As she did so a scent of peril was borne in upon her fine nostrils. She recognised it instantly. With a snort of anger she sniffed again; then stamped a challenge with her fore hoofs, and levelled the lance-points of her horns toward the menace. The next moment her eyes, made keen by the fear of love, detected the black outline of the bear's head through the coarse screen of the juniper. Without a second's hesitation, she flung up her tail, gave a short bellow, and charged.

The moment she saw herself detected, the bear rose upon her hindquarters; nevertheless she was in a measure surprised by the sudden blind fury of the attack. Nimbly she swerved to avoid it, aiming at the same time a stroke with her mighty forearm, which, if it had found its mark, would have smashed her adversary's neck. But as she struck out, in the act of shifting her position, a depression of the ground threw her off her balance. The next instant one sharp horn caught her slantingly in the flank, ripping its way upward and inward, while the mad impact threw her upon her back.

Grappling, she had her assailant's head and shoulders in a trap, and her gigantic claws cut through the flesh and sinew like knives; but at the desperate disadvantage of her position she could inflict no disabling blow. The cow, on the other hand, though mutilated and streaming with blood, kept pounding with her whole massive weight, and with short tremendous shocks crushing the breath from her foe's ribs.

10   Presently, wrenching herself free, the cow drew off for another battering charge; and as she did so the bear hurled herself violently down the slope, and gained her feet behind a dense thicket of bay shrub. The cow, with one eye blinded and the other obscured by blood, glared around for her in vain, then, in a panic of mother terror, plunged back to her calf.

Snatching at the respite, the bear crouched down, craving that invisibility which is the most faithful shield of the furtive kindred. Painfully, and leaving a drenched red trail behind her, she crept off from the disastrous neighbourhood. Soon the deepening twilight sheltered her. But she could not make haste; and she knew that death was close upon her.

Once within the woods, she struggled straight toward the den that held her young. She hungered to die licking them. But destiny is as implacable as iron to the wilderness people, and even this was denied her. Just a half score of paces from the lair in the pine root, her hour descended upon her. There was a sudden redder and fuller gush upon the trail; the last light of longing faded out of her eyes; and she lay down upon her side.

The merry little cubs within the den were beginning to expect her, and getting restless. As the night wore on, and no mother came, they ceased to be merry. By morning they were shivering with hunger and desolate fear. But the doom of the ancient wood was less harsh than its wont, and spared them some days of starving anguish; for about noon a pair of foxes discovered the dead mother, astutely estimated the situation, and then, with the boldness of good appetite, made their way into the unguarded den.

As for the red calf, its fortune was ordinary. Its mother, for all her wounds, was able to nurse and cherish it through the night; and with morning came a searcher from the farm and took it, with the bleeding mother, safely back to the settlement. There it was tended and fattened, and within a few weeks found its way to the cool marble slabs of a city market.

(1902)

Stephen Crane (1871–1900)

Before his death from tuberculosis at age 28, New Jersey–born Stephen Crane had published short stories, poetry, and a novel, *The Red Badge of Courage* (1896). One of a group of authors now known as naturalists, who rejected traditional social and religious beliefs as invalid, Crane examined the courage of individuals living in a world in which victory or defeat in struggles was a matter of chance. "The Open Boat," which was highly praised by both Joseph Conrad and Ernest Hemingway, is based on personal experience. Travelling to Cuba as a newspaper correspondent, Crane had been one of three survivors of a shipwreck off the Atlantic coast of Florida. In a newspaper account published a few days after his rescue, Crane focussed on the events leading to the sinking of the vessel, giving only a few sentences in the final paragraph to the time spent in the lifeboat and the rescue. Subtitled "A Tale Intended to Be after the Fact," "The Open Boat" explores the four men's 30 hours in the three-metre dinghy, examining their growing camaraderie and the correspondent's developing awareness of the impersonality of nature.

THE OPEN BOAT

A Tale Intended to Be after the Fact. Being the Experience of Four Men from the Sunk Steamer 'Commodore'

I

None of them knew the colour of the sky. Their eyes glanced level, and were fastened upon the waves that swept toward them. These waves were of the hue of slate, save for the tops, which were of foaming white, and all of the men knew the colours of the sea. The horizon narrowed and widened, and dipped and rose, and at all times its edge was jagged with waves that seemed thrust up in points like rocks.

Many a man ought to have a bath-tub larger than the boat which here rode upon the sea. These waves were most wrongfully and barbarously abrupt and tall, and each froth-top was a problem in small boat navigation.

The cook squatted in the bottom and looked with both eyes at the six inches of gunwale which separated him from the ocean. His sleeves were rolled over his fat forearms, and the two flaps of his unbuttoned vest dangled as he bent to bail out the boat. Often he said: "Gawd! That was a narrow clip." As he remarked it he invariably gazed eastward over the broken sea.

The oiler, steering with one of the two oars in the boat, sometimes raised himself suddenly to keep clear of water that swirled in over the stern. It was a thin little oar and it seemed often ready to snap.

5   The correspondent, pulling at the other oar, watched the waves and wondered why he was there.

The injured captain, lying in the bow, was at this time buried in that profound dejection and indifference which comes, temporarily at least, to even the bravest and most enduring when, willy nilly, the firm fails, the army loses, the ship goes down. The mind of the master of a vessel is rooted deep in the timbers of her, though he commanded for a day or a decade, and this captain had on him the stern impression of a scene in the greys of dawn of seven turned faces, and later a stump of a top-mast with a white ball on it that slashed to and fro at the waves, went low and lower, and down. Thereafter there was something strange in his voice. Although steady, it was deep with mourning, and of a quality beyond oration or tears.

"Keep 'er a little more south, Billie," said he.

"'A little more south,' sir," said the oiler in the stern.

A seat in this boat was not unlike a seat upon a bucking broncho, and, by the same token, a broncho is not much smaller. The craft pranced and reared, and plunged like an animal. As each wave came, and she rose for it, she seemed like a horse making at a fence outrageously high. The manner of her scramble over these walls of water is a mystic thing, and, moreover, at the top of them were ordinarily these problems in white water, the foam racing down from the summit of each wave, requiring a new leap, and a leap from the air. Then, after scornfully bumping a crest, she would slide, and race, and splash down a long incline, and arrive bobbing and nodding in front of the next menace.

A singular disadvantage of the sea lies in the fact that after successfully surmounting one wave you discover that there is another behind it just as important and just as nervously anxious to do something effective in the way of swamping boats. In a ten-foot dingey one can get an idea of the resources of the sea in the line of waves that is not probable to the average experience, which is never at sea in a dingey. As each salty wall of water approached, it shut all else from the view of the men in the boat, and it was not difficult to imagine that this particular wave was the final outburst of the ocean, the last effort of the grim water. There was a terrible grace in the move of the waves, and they came in silence, save for the snarling of the crests.

In the wan light, the faces of the men must have been grey. Their eyes must have glinted in strange ways as they gazed steadily astern. Viewed from a balcony, the whole thing would doubtlessly have been weirdly picturesque. But the men in the boat had no time to see it, and if they had had leisure there were other things to occupy their minds. The sun swung steadily up the sky, and they knew it was broad day because the colour of the sea changed from slate to emerald-green, streaked with amber lights, and the foam was like tumbling snow. The process of the breaking day was unknown to them. They were aware only of this effect upon the colour of the waves that rolled toward them.

In disjointed sentences the cook and the correspondent argued as to the difference between a life-saving station and a house of refuge. The cook had said: "There's a house of refuge just north of the Mosquito Inlet Light,[1] and as soon as they see us, they'll come off in their boat and pick us up."

"As soon as who see us?" said the correspondent.

"The crew," said the cook.

1 located on the Atlantic coast of northern Florida.

15 "Houses of refuge don't have crews," said the correspondent. "As I understand them, they are only places where clothes and grub are stored for the benefit of shipwrecked people. They don't carry crews."

"Oh, yes, they do," said the cook.

"No, they don't," said the correspondent.

"Well, we're not there yet, anyhow," said the oiler, in the stern.

"Well," said the cook, "perhaps it's not a house of refuge that I'm thinking of as being near Mosquito Inlet Light. Perhaps it's a life-saving station."

20 "We're not there yet," said the oiler, in the stern.

II

As the boat bounced from the top of each wave, the wind tore through the hair of the hatless men, and as the craft plopped her stern down again the spray slashed past them. The crest of each of these waves was a hill, from the top of which the men surveyed, for a moment, a broad tumultuous expanse, shining and wind-riven. It was probably splendid. It was probably glorious, this play of the free sea, wild with lights of emerald and white and amber.

"Bully good thing it's an on-shore wind," said the cook. "If not, where would we be? Wouldn't have a show."

"That's right," said the correspondent.

The busy oiler nodded his assent.

25 Then the captain, in the bow, chuckled in a way that expressed humour, contempt, tragedy, all in one. "Do you think we've got much of a show now, boys?" said he.

Whereupon the three were silent, save for a trifle of hemming and hawing. To express any particular optimism at this time they felt to be childish and stupid, but they all doubtless possessed this sense of the situation in their mind. A young man thinks doggedly at such times. On the other hand, the ethics of their condition was decidedly against any open suggestion of hopelessness. So they were silent.

"Oh, well," said the captain, soothing his children, "we'll get ashore all right."

But there was that in his tone which made them think, so the oiler quoth: "Yes! If this wind holds!"

The cook was bailing: "Yes! If we don't catch hell in the surf."

30 Canton flannel gulls flew near and far. Sometimes they sat down on the sea, near patches of brown seaweed that rolled over the waves with a movement like carpets on a line in a gale. The birds sat comfortably in groups, and they were envied by some in the dingey, for the wrath of the sea was no more to them than it was to a covey of prairie chickens a thousand miles inland. Often they came very close and stared at the men with black bead-like eyes. At these times they were uncanny and sinister in their unblinking scrutiny, and the men hooted angrily at them, telling them to be gone. One came, and evidently decided to alight on the top of the captain's head. The bird flew parallel to the boat and did not circle, but made short sidelong jumps in the air in

chicken-fashion. His black eyes were wistfully fixed upon the captain's head. "Ugly brute," said the oiler to the bird. "You look as if you were made with a jack-knife." The cook and the correspondent swore darkly at the creature. The captain naturally wished to knock it away with the end of the heavy painter; but he did not dare do it, because anything resembling an emphatic gesture would have capsized this freighted boat, and so with his open hand, the captain gently and carefully waved the gull away. After it had been discouraged from the pursuit the captain breathed easier on account of his hair, and others breathed easier because the bird struck their minds at this time as being somehow grewsome and ominous.

In the meantime the oiler and the correspondent rowed. And also they rowed.

They sat together in the same seat, and each rowed an oar. Then the oiler took both oars; then the correspondent took both oars; then the oiler; then the correspondent. They rowed and they rowed. The very ticklish part of the business was when the time came for the reclining one in the stern to take his turn at the oars. By the very last star of truth, it is easier to steal eggs from under a hen than it was to change seats in the dingey. First the man in the stern slid his hand along the thwart and moved with care, as if he were of Sèvres.[2] Then the man in the rowing seat slid his hand along the other thwart. It was all done with the most extraordinary care. As the two sidled past each other, the whole party kept watchful eyes on the coming wave, and the captain cried: "Look out now! Steady there!"

The brown mats of sea-weed that appeared from time to time were like islands, bits of earth. They were travelling, apparently, neither one way nor the other. They were, to all intents, stationary. They informed the men in the boat that it was making progress slowly toward the land.

The captain, rearing cautiously in the bow, after the dingey soared on a great swell, said that he had seen the lighthouse at Mosquito Inlet. Presently the cook remarked that he had seen it. The correspondent was at the oars then, and for some reason he too wished to look at the lighthouse, but his back was toward the far shore and the waves were important, and for some time he could not seize an opportunity to turn his head. But at last there came a wave more gentle than the others, and when at the crest of it he swiftly scoured the western horizon.

35   "See it?" said the captain.

"No," said the correspondent slowly, "I didn't see anything."

"Look again," said the captain. He pointed. "It's exactly in that direction."

At the top of another wave, the correspondent did as he was bid, and this time his eyes chanced on a small still thing on the edge of the swaying horizon. It was precisely like the point of a pin. It took an anxious eye to find a lighthouse so tiny.

"Think we'll make it, captain?"

40   "If this wind holds and the boat don't swamp, we can't do much else," said the captain.

2 beautiful, delicate porcelain made in the commune of the same name on the Seine River in northern France.

The little boat, lifted by each towering sea, and splashed viciously by the crests, made progress that in the absence of seaweed was not apparent to those in her. She seemed just a wee thing wallowing, miraculously top-up, at the mercy of five oceans. Occasionally, a great spread of water, like white flames, swarmed into her.

"Bail her, cook," said the captain serenely.

"All right, captain," said the cheerful cook.

III

It would be difficult to describe the subtle brotherhood of men that was here established on the seas. No one said that it was so. No one mentioned it. But it dwelt in the boat, and each man felt it warm him. They were a captain, an oiler, a cook, and a correspondent, and they were friends, friends in a more curiously iron-bound degree than may be common. The hurt captain, lying against the water-jar in the bow, spoke always in a low voice and calmly, but he could never command a more ready and swiftly obedient crew than the motley three of the dingey. It was more than a mere recognition of what was best for the common safety. There was surely in it a quality that was personal and heart-felt. And after this devotion to the commander of the boat there was this comradeship that the correspondent, for instance, who had been taught to be cynical of men, knew even at the time was the best experience of his life. But no one said that it was so. No one mentioned it.

45   "I wish we had a sail," remarked the captain. "We might try my overcoat on the end of an oar and give you two boys a chance to rest." So the cook and the correspondent held the mast and spread wide the overcoat. The oiler steered, and the little boat made good way with her new rig. Sometimes the oiler had to scull sharply to keep a sea from breaking into the boat, but otherwise sailing was a success.

Meanwhile the lighthouse had been growing slowly larger. It had now almost assumed colour, and appeared like a little grey shadow on the sky. The man at the oars could not be prevented from turning his head rather often to try for a glimpse of this little grey shadow.

At last, from the top of each wave the men in the tossing boat could see land. Even as the lighthouse was an upright shadow on the sky, this land seemed but a long black shadow on the sea. It certainly was thinner than paper. "We must be about opposite New Smyrna,"[3] said the cook, who had coasted this shore often in schooners. "Captain, by the way, I believe they abandoned that life-saving station there about a year ago."

"Did they?" said the captain.

The wind slowly died away. The cook and the correspondent were not now obliged to slave in order to hold high the oar. But the waves continued their old impetuous swooping at the dingey, and the little craft, no longer under way, struggled woundily over them. The oiler or the correspondent took the oars again.

3 located 25 kilometres south of Daytona Beach.

50   Shipwrecks are à *propos* of nothing. If men could only train for them and have them occur when the men had reached pink condition, there would be less drowning at sea. Of the four in the dingey none had slept any time worth mentioning for two days and two nights previous to embarking in the dingey, and in the excitement of clambering about the deck of a foundering ship they had also forgotten to eat heartily.

    For these reasons, and for others, neither the oiler nor the correspondent was fond of rowing at this time. The correspondent wondered ingenuously how in the name of all that was sane could there be people who thought it amusing to row a boat. It was not an amusement; it was a diabolical punishment, and even a genius of mental aberrations could never conclude that it was anything but a horror to the muscles and a crime against the back. He mentioned to the boat in general how the amusement of rowing struck him, and the weary-faced oiler smiled in full sympathy. Previously to the foundering, by the way, the oiler had worked double-watch in the engine-room of the ship.

    "Take her easy, now, boys," said the captain. "Don't spend yourselves. If we have to run a surf you'll need all your strength, because we'll sure have to swim for it. Take your time."

    Slowly the land arose from the sea. From a black line it became a line of black and a line of white, trees and sand. Finally, the captain said that he could make out a house on the shore. "That's the house of refuge, sure," said the cook. "They'll see us before long, and come out after us."

    The distant lighthouse reared high. "The keeper ought to be able to make us out now, if he's looking through a glass," said the captain. "He'll notify the life-saving people."

55   "None of those other boats could have got ashore to give word of the wreck," said the oiler, in a low voice. "Else the lifeboat would be out hunting us."

    Slowly and beautifully the land loomed out of the sea. The wind came again. It had veered from the north-east to the south-east. Finally, a new sound struck the ears of the men in the boat. It was the low thunder of the surf on the shore. "We'll never be able to make the lighthouse now," said the captain. "Swing her head a little more north, Billie," said he.

    "'A little more north,' sir," said the oiler.

    Whereupon the little boat turned her nose once more down the wind, and all but the oarsman watched the shore grow. Under the influence of this expansion doubt and direful apprehension was leaving the minds of the men. The management of the boat was still most absorbing, but it could not prevent a quiet cheerfulness. In an hour, perhaps, they would be ashore.

    Their backbones had become thoroughly used to balancing in the boat, and they now rode this wild colt of a dingey like circus men. The correspondent thought that he had been drenched to the skin, but happening to feel in the top pocket of his coat, he found therein eight cigars. Four of them were soaked with sea-water; four were perfectly scatheless. After a search, somebody produced three dry matches, and thereupon the four waifs rode impudently in their little boat, and with an assurance of an impending rescue shining in their eyes, puffed at the big cigars and judged well and ill of all men. Everybody took a drink of water.

IV

60 "Cook," remarked the captain, "there don't seem to be any signs of life about your house of refuge."

"No," replied the cook. "Funny they don't see us!"

A broad stretch of lowly coast lay before the eyes of the men. It was of dunes topped with dark vegetation. The roar of the surf was plain, and sometimes they could see the white lip of a wave as it spun up the beach. A tiny house was blocked out black upon the sky. Southward, the slim lighthouse lifted its little grey length.

Tide, wind, and waves were swinging the dingey northward. "Funny they don't see us," said the men.

The surf's roar was here dulled, but its tone was, nevertheless, thunderous and mighty. As the boat swam over the great rollers, the men sat listening to this roar. "We'll swamp sure," said everybody.

65 It is fair to say here that there was not a life-saving station within twenty miles in either direction, but the men did not know this fact, and in consequence they made dark and opprobrious remarks concerning the eyesight of the nation's life-savers. Four scowling men sat in the dingey and surpassed records in the invention of epithets.

"Funny they don't see us."

The light-heartedness of a former time had completely failed. To their sharpened minds it was easy to conjure pictures of all kinds of incompetency and blindness and, indeed, cowardice. There was the shore of the populous land, and it was bitter and bitter to them that from it came no sign.

"Well," said the captain, ultimately, "I suppose we'll have to make a try for ourselves. If we stay out here too long, we'll none of us have strength left to swim after the boat swamps."

And so the oiler, who was at the oars, turned the boat straight for the shore. There was a sudden tightening of muscles. There was some thinking.

70 "If we don't all get ashore —" said the captain. "If we don't all get ashore, I suppose you fellows know where to send news of my finish?"

They then briefly exchanged some addresses and admonitions. As for the reflections of the men, there was a great deal of rage in them. Perchance they might be formulated thus: "If I am going to be drowned — if I am going to be drowned — if I am going to be drowned, why, in the name of the seven mad gods who rule the sea, was I allowed to come thus far and contemplate sand and trees? Was I brought here merely to have my nose dragged away as I was about to nibble the sacred cheese of life? It is preposterous. If this old ninny-woman, Fate, cannot do better than this, she should be deprived of the management of men's fortunes. She is an old hen who knows not her intention. If she has decided to drown me, why did she not do it in the beginning and save me all this trouble? The whole affair is absurd. . . . But no, she cannot mean to drown me. She dare not drown me. She cannot drown me. Not after all this work." Afterward the man might have had an impulse to shake his fist at the clouds: "Just you drown me, now, and then hear what I call you!"

The billows that came at this time were more formidable. They seemed always just about to break and roll over the little boat in a turmoil of foam.

There was a preparatory and long growl in the speech of them. No mind unused to the sea would have concluded that the dingey could ascend these sheer heights in time. The shore was still afar. The oiler was a wily surfman. "Boys," he said swiftly, "she won't live three minutes more, and we're too far out to swim. Shall I take her to sea again, captain?"

"Yes! Go ahead!" said the captain.

This oiler, by a series of quick miracles, and fast and steady oarsmanship, turned the boat in the middle of the surf and took her safely to sea again.

There was a considerable silence as the boat bumped over the furrowed sea to deeper water. Then somebody in gloom spoke. "Well, anyhow, they must have seen us from the shore by now."

The gulls went in slanting flight up the wind toward the grey desolate east. A squall, marked by dingy clouds, and clouds brick-red, like smoke from a burning building, appeared from the south-east.

"What do you think of those life-saving people? Ain't they peaches?"

"Funny they haven't seen us."

"Maybe they think we're out here for sport! Maybe they think we're fishin'. Maybe they think we're damned fools."

It was a long afternoon. A changed tide tried to force them southward, but wind and wave said northward. Far ahead, where coast-line, sea, and sky formed their mighty angle, there were little dots which seemed to indicate a city on the shore.

"St. Augustine?"[4]

The captain shook his head. "Too near Mosquito Inlet."

And the oiler rowed, and then the correspondent rowed. Then the oiler rowed. It was a weary business. The human back can become the seat of more aches and pains than are registered in books for the composite anatomy of a regiment. It is a limited area, but it can become the theatre of innumerable muscular conflicts, tangles, wrenches, knots, and other comforts.

"Did you ever like to row, Billie?" asked the correspondent.

"No," said the oiler. "Hang it."

When one exchanged the rowing-seat for a place in the bottom of the boat, he suffered a bodily depression that caused him to be careless of everything save an obligation to wiggle one finger. There was cold sea-water swashing to and fro in the boat, and he lay in it. His head, pillowed on a thwart, was within an inch of the swirl of a wave crest, and sometimes a particularly obstreperous sea came in-board and drenched him once more. But these matters did not annoy him. It is almost certain that if the boat had capsized he would have tumbled comfortably out upon the ocean as if he felt sure that it was a great soft mattress.

"Look! There's a man on the shore!"

"Where?"

"There! See 'im? See 'im?"

"Yes, sure! He's walking along."

"Now he's stopped. Look! He's facing us!"

"He's waving at us!"

4 city on the Atlantic coast of northern Florida.

"So he is! By thunder!"

"Ah, now we're all right! Now we're all right! There'll be a boat out here for us in half-an-hour."

95 "He's going on. He's running. He's going up to that house there."

The remote beach seemed lower than the sea, and it required a searching glance to discern the little black figure. The captain saw a floating stick and they rowed to it. A bath-towel was by some weird chance in the boat, and, tying this on the stick, the captain waved it. The oarsman did not dare turn his head, so he was obliged to ask questions.

"What's he doing now?"

"He's standing still again. He's looking, I think. . . . There he goes again. Towards the house. . . . Now he's stopped again."

"Is he waving at us?"

100 "No, not now! he was, though."

"Look! There comes another man!"

"He's running."

"Look at him go, would you."

"Why, he's on a bicycle. Now he's met the other man. They're both waving at us. Look!"

105 "There comes something up the beach."

"What the devil is that thing?"

"Why, it looks like a boat."

"Why, certainly it's a boat."

"No, it's on wheels."

110 "Yes, so it is. Well, that must be the life-boat. They drag them along shore on a wagon."

"That's the life-boat, sure."

"No, by —, it's — it's an omnibus."

"I tell you it's a life-boat."

"It is not! It's an omnibus. I can see it plain. See? One of these big hotel omnibuses."

115 "By thunder, you're right. It's an omnibus, sure as fate. What do you suppose they are doing with an omnibus? Maybe they are going around collecting the life-crew, hey?"

"That's it, likely. Look! There's a fellow waving a little black flag. He's standing on the steps of the omnibus. There come those other two fellows. Now they're all talking together. Look at the fellow with the flag. Maybe he ain't waving it."

"That ain't a flag, is it? That's his coat. Why certainly, that's his coat."

"So it is. It's his coat. He's taken it off and is waving it around his head. But would you look at him swing it."

"Oh, say, there isn't any life-saving station there. That's just a winter resort hotel omnibus that has brought over some of the boarders to see us drown."

120 "What's that idiot with the coat mean? What's he signaling, anyhow?"

"It looks as if he were trying to tell us to go north. There must be a life-saving station up there."

"No! He thinks we're fishing. Just giving us a merry hand. See? Ah, there, Willie."

"Well, I wish I could make something out of those signals. What do you suppose he means?"

"He don't mean anything. He's just playing."

125 "Well, if he'd just signal us to try the surf again, or to go to sea and wait, or go north, or go south, or go to hell — there would be some reason in it. But look at him. He just stands there and keeps his coat revolving like a wheel. The ass!"

"There come more people."

"Now there's quite a mob. Look! Isn't that a boat?"

"Where? Oh, I see where you mean. No, that's no boat."

"That fellow is still waving his coat."

130 "He must think we like to see him do that. Why don't he quit it? It don't mean anything."

"I don't know. I think he is trying to make us go north. It must be that there's a life-saving station there somewhere."

"Say, he ain't tired yet. Look at 'im wave."

"Wonder how long he can keep that up. He's been revolving his coat ever since he caught sight of us. He's an idiot. Why aren't they getting men to bring a boat out? A fishing boat — one of those big yawls — could come out here all right. Why don't he do something?"

"Oh, it's all right, now."

135 "They'll have a boat out here for us in less than no time, now that they've seen us."

A faint yellow tone came into the sky over the low land. The shadows on the sea slowly deepened. The wind bore coldness with it, and the men began to shiver.

"Holy smoke!" said one, allowing his voice to express his impious mood, "if we keep on monkeying out here! If we've got to flounder out here all night!"

"Oh, we'll never have to stay here all night! Don't you worry. They've seen us now, and it won't be long before they'll come chasing out after us."

The shore grew dusky. The man waving a coat blended gradually into this gloom, and it swallowed in the same manner the omnibus and the group of people. The spray, when it dashed uproariously over the side, made the voyagers shrink and swear like men who were being branded.

140 "I'd like to catch the chump who waved the coat. I feel like soaking him one, just for luck."

"Why? What did he do?"

"Oh, nothing, but then he seemed so damned cheerful."

In the meantime the oiler rowed, and then the correspondent rowed, and then the oiler rowed. Grey-faced and bowed forward, they mechanically, turn by turn, plied the leaden oars. The form of the lighthouse had vanished from the southern horizon, but finally a pale star appeared, just lifting from the sea. The streaked saffron in the west passed before the all-merging darkness, and the sea to the east was black. The land had vanished, and was expressed only by the low and drear thunder of the surf.

"If I am going to be drowned — if I am going to be drowned — if I am going to be drowned, why, in the name of the seven mad gods who rule the sea, was I allowed to come thus far and contemplate sand and trees? Was I brought here merely to have my nose dragged away as I was about to nibble the sacred cheese of life?"

145 The patient captain, drooped over the water-jar, was sometimes obliged to speak to the oarsman.

"Keep her head up! Keep her head up!"

"'Keep her head up,' sir." The voices were weary and low.

This was surely a quiet evening. All save the oarsman lay heavily and listlessly in the boat's bottom. As for him, his eyes were just capable of noting the tall black waves that swept forward in a most sinister silence, save for an occasional subdued growl of a crest.

The cook's head was on a thwart, and he looked without interest at the water under his nose. He was deep in other scenes. Finally he spoke. "Billie," he murmured, dreamfully, "what kind of pie do you like best?"

V

150 "Pie," said the oiler and the correspondent, agitatedly. "Don't talk about those things, blast you!"

"Well," said the cook, "I was just thinking about ham sandwiches, and —"

A night on the sea in an open boat is a long night. As darkness settled finally, the shine of the light, lifting from the sea in the south, changed to full gold. On the northern horizon a new light appeared, a small bluish gleam on the edge of the waters. These two lights were the furniture of the world. Otherwise there was nothing but waves.

Two men huddled in the stern, and distances were so magnificent in the dingey that the rower was enabled to keep his feet partly warmed by thrusting them under his companions. Their legs indeed extended far under the rowing-seat until they touched the feet of the captain forward. Sometimes, despite the efforts of the tired oarsman, a wave came piling into the boat, an icy wave of the night, and the chilling water soaked them anew. They would twist their bodies for a moment and groan, and sleep the dead sleep once more, while the water in the boat gurgled about them as the craft rocked.

The plan of the oiler and the correspondent was for one to row until he lost the ability, and then arouse the other from his sea-water couch in the bottom of the boat.

155 The oiler plied the oars until his head drooped forward, and the overpowering sleep blinded him. And he rowed yet afterward. Then he touched a man in the bottom of the boat, and called his name. "Will you spell me for a little while?" he said, meekly.

"Sure, Billie," said the correspondent, awakening and dragging himself to a sitting position. They exchanged places carefully, and the oiler, cuddling down in the sea-water at the cook's side, seemed to go to sleep instantly.

The particular violence of the sea had ceased. The waves came without snarling. The obligation of the man at the oars was to keep the boat headed so that the tilt of the rollers would not capsize her, and to preserve her from filling when the crests rushed past. The black waves were silent and hard to be seen in the darkness. Often one was almost upon the boat before the oarsman was aware.

In a low voice the correspondent addressed the captain. He was not sure that the captain was awake, although this iron man seemed to be always awake. "Captain, shall I keep her making for that light north, sir?"

The same steady voice answered him. "Yes. Keep it about two points off the port bow."

160   The cook had tied a life-belt around himself in order to get even the warmth which this clumsy cork contrivance could donate, and he seemed almost stove-like when a rower, whose teeth invariably chattered wildly as soon as he ceased his labour, dropped down to sleep.

The correspondent, as he rowed, looked down at the two men sleeping under-foot. The cook's arm was around the oiler's shoulders, and, with their fragmentary clothing and haggard faces, they were the babes of the sea, a grotesque rendering of the old babes in the wood.[5]

Later he must have grown stupid at his work, for suddenly there was a growling of water, and a crest came with a roar and a swash into the boat, and it was a wonder that it did not set the cook afloat in his life-belt. The cook continued to sleep, but the oiler sat up, blinking his eyes and shaking with the new cold.

"Oh, I'm awful sorry, Billie," said the correspondent contritely.

"That's all right, old boy," said the oiler, and lay down again and was asleep.

165   Presently it seemed that even the captain dozed, and the correspondent thought that he was the one man afloat on all the oceans. The wind had a voice as it came over the waves, and it was sadder than the end.

There was a long, loud swishing astern of the boat, and a gleaming trail of phosphorescence, like blue flame, was furrowed on the black waters. It might have been made by a monstrous knife.

Then there came a stillness, while the correspondent breathed with the open mouth and looked at the sea.

Suddenly there was another swish and another long flash of bluish light, and this time it was alongside the boat, and might almost have been reached with an oar. The correspondent saw an enormous fin speed like a shadow through the water, hurling the crystalline spray and leaving the long glowing trail.

The correspondent looked over his shoulder at the captain. His face was hidden, and he seemed to be asleep. He looked at the babes of the sea. They certainly were asleep. So, being bereft of sympathy, he leaned a little way to one side and swore softly into the sea.

170   But the thing did not then leave the vicinity of the boat. Ahead or astern, on one side or the other, at intervals long or short, fled the long sparkling streak, and there was to be heard the whiroo of the dark fin. The speed and power of the thing was greatly to be admired. It cut the water like a gigantic and keen projectile.

---

5 popular nineteenth-century children's story about children who become lost and die in a forest.

The presence of this biding thing did not affect the man with the same horror that it would if he had been a picnicker. He simply looked at the sea dully and swore in an undertone.

Nevertheless, it is true that he did not wish to be alone. He wished one of his companions to awaken by chance and keep him company with it. But the captain hung motionless over the water-jar, and the oiler and the cook in the bottom of the boat were plunged in slumber.

VI

"If I am going to be drowned — if I am going to be drowned — if I am going to be drowned, why, in the name of the seven mad gods who rule the sea, was I allowed to come thus far and contemplate sand and trees?"

During this dismal night, it may be remarked that a man would conclude that it was really the intention of the seven mad gods to drown him, despite the abominable injustice of it. For it was certainly an abominable injustice to drown a man who had worked so hard, so hard. The man felt it would be a crime most unnatural. Other people had drowned at sea since galleys swarmed with painted sails, but still —

175   When it occurs to a man that nature does not regard him as important, and that she feels she would not maim the universe by disposing of him, he at first wishes to throw bricks at the temple, and he hates deeply the fact that there are no bricks and no temples. Any visible expression of nature would surely be pelleted with his jeers.

Then, if there be no tangible thing to hoot he feels, perhaps, the desire to confront a personification and indulge in pleas, bowed to one knee, and with hands supplicant, saying: "Yes, but I love myself."

A high cold star on a winter's night is the word he feels that she says to him. Thereafter he knows the pathos of his situation.

The men in the dingey had not discussed these matters, but each had, no doubt, reflected upon them in silence and according to his mind. There was seldom any expression upon their faces save the general one of complete weariness. Speech was devoted to the business of the boat.

To chime the notes of his emotion, a verse mysteriously entered the correspondent's head. He had even forgotten that he had forgotten this verse, but it suddenly was in his mind.

> A soldier of the Legion lay dying in Algiers,
> There was lack of woman's nursing, there was dearth of woman's tears;
> But a comrade stood beside him, and he took that comrade's hand,
> And he said: "I shall never see my own, my native land."[6]

180   In his childhood, the correspondent had been made acquainted with the fact that a soldier of the Legion lay dying in Algiers, but he had never regarded the fact as important. Myriads of his school-fellows had informed him of the soldier's plight, but the dinning had naturally ended by making him perfectly indifferent. He had never considered it his affair that a soldier of the Legion

6 these are the opening lines, somewhat inexactly quoted, from "Bingen on the Rhine" by Caroline Norton (1808–1877).

lay dying in Algiers, nor had it appeared to him as a matter for sorrow. It was less to him than the breaking of a pencil's point.

Now, however, it quaintly came to him as a human, living thing. It was no longer merely a picture of a few throes in the breast of a poet, meanwhile drinking tea and warming his feet at the grate, it was an actuality — stern, mournful, and fine.

The correspondent plainly saw the soldier. He lay on the sand with his feet out straight and still. While his pale left hand was upon his chest in an attempt to thwart the going of his life, the blood came between his fingers. In the far Algerian distance, a city of low square forms was set against a sky that was faint with the last sunset hues. The correspondent, plying the oars and dreaming of the slow and slower movements of the lips of the soldier, was moved by a profound and perfectly impersonal comprehension. He was sorry for the soldier of the Legion who lay dying in Algiers.

The thing which had followed the boat and waited, had evidently grown bored at the delay. There was no longer to be heard the slash of the cut-water, and there was no longer the flame of the long trail. The light in the north still glimmered, but it was apparently no nearer to the boat. Sometimes the boom of the surf rang in the correspondent's ears, and he turned the craft seaward then and rowed harder. Southward, some one had evidently built a watch-fire on the beach. It was too low and too far to be seen, but it made a shimmering, roseate reflection upon the bluff back of it, and this could be discerned from the boat. The wind came stronger, and sometimes a wave suddenly raged out like a mountain-cat, and there was to be seen the sheen and sparkle of a broken crest.

The captain, in the bow, moved on his water-jar and sat erect. "Pretty long night," he observed to the correspondent. He looked at the shore. "Those life-saving people take their time."

185 "Did you see that shark playing around?"

"Yes, I saw him. He was a big fellow, all right."

"Wish I had known you were awake."

Later the correspondent spoke into the bottom of the boat.

"Billie!" There was a slow and gradual disentanglement. "Billie, will you spell me?"

190 "Sure," said the oiler.

As soon as the correspondent touched the cold comfortable sea-water in the bottom of the boat, and had huddled close to the cook's life-belt he was deep in sleep, despite the fact that his teeth played all the popular airs. This sleep was so good to him that it was but a moment before he heard a voice call his name in a tone that demonstrated the last stages of exhaustion. "Will you spell me?"

"Sure, Billie."

The light in the north had mysteriously vanished, but the correspondent took his course from the wide-awake captain.

Later in the night they took the boat farther out to sea, and the captain directed the cook to take one oar at the stern and keep the boat facing the seas. He was to call out if he should hear the thunder of the surf. This plan enabled the oiler and the correspondent to get respite together. "We'll give those boys a chance to get into shape again," said the captain. They curled down and, after a few preliminary chatterings and trembles, slept once more the dead sleep. Neither knew they had bequeathed to the cook the company of another shark, or perhaps the same shark.

195   As the boat caroused on the waves, spray occasionally bumped over the side and gave them a fresh soaking, but this had no power to break their repose. The ominous slash of the wind and the water affected them as it would have affected mummies.

"Boys," said the cook, with the notes of every reluctance in his voice, "she's drifted in pretty close. I guess one of you had better take her to sea again." The correspondent, aroused, heard the crash of the toppled crests.

As he was rowing, the captain gave him some whisky-and-water, and this steadied the chills out of him. "If I ever get ashore and anybody shows me even a photograph of an oar —"

At last there was a short conversation.

"Billie. . . . Billie, will you spell me?"

200   "Sure," said the oiler.

VII

When the correspondent again opened his eyes, the sea and the sky were each of the grey hue of the dawning. Later, carmine and gold was painted upon the waters. The morning appeared finally, in its splendour, with a sky of pure blue, and the sunlight flamed on the tips of the waves.

On the distant dunes were set many little black cottages, and a tall white windmill reared above them. No man, nor dog, nor bicycle appeared on the beach. The cottages might have formed a deserted village.

The voyagers scanned the shore. A conference was held in the boat. "Well," said the captain, "if no help is coming we might better try a run through the surf right away. If we stay out here much longer we will be too weak to do anything for ourselves at all." The others silently acquiesced in this reasoning. The boat was headed for the beach. The correspondent wondered if none ever ascended the tall wind-tower, and if then they never looked seaward. This tower was a giant, standing with its back to the plight of the ants. It represented in a degree, to the correspondent, the serenity of nature amid the struggles of the individual — nature in the wind, and nature in the vision of men. She did not seem cruel to him then, nor beneficent, nor treacherous, nor wise. But she was indifferent, flatly indifferent. It is, perhaps, plausible that a man in this situation, impressed with the unconcern of the universe, should see the innumerable flaws of his life, and have them taste wickedly in his mind and wish for another chance. A distinction between right and wrong seems absurdly clear to him, then, in this new ignorance of the grave-edge, and he understands that if he were given another opportunity he would mend his conduct and his words, and be better and brighter during an introduction or at a tea.

"Now, boys," said the captain, "she is going to swamp, sure. All we can do is to work her in as far as possible, and then when she swamps, pile out and scramble for the beach. Keep cool now, and don't jump until she swamps sure."

205   The oiler took the oars. Over his shoulders he scanned the surf. "Captain," he said, "I think I'd better bring her about, and keep her head-on to the seas and back her in."

"All right, Billie," said the captain. "Back her in." The oiler swung the boat then and, seated in the stern, the cook and the correspondent were obliged to look over their shoulders to contemplate the lonely and indifferent shore.

The monstrous in-shore rollers heaved the boat high until the men were again enabled to see the white sheets of water scudding up the slanted beach. "We won't get in very close," said the captain. Each time a man could wrest his attention from the rollers, he turned his glance toward the shore, and in the expression of the eyes during this contemplation there was a singular quality. The correspondent, observing the others, knew that they were not afraid, but the full meaning of their glances was shrouded.

As for himself, he was too tired to grapple fundamentally with the fact. He tried to coerce his mind into thinking of it, but the mind was dominated at this time by the muscles, and the muscles said they did not care. It merely occurred to him that if he should drown it would be a shame.

There were no hurried words, no pallor, no plain agitation. The men simply looked at the shore. "Now, remember to get well clear of the boat when you jump," said the captain.

210 Seaward the crest of a roller suddenly fell with a thunderous crash, and the long white comber came roaring down upon the boat.

"Steady now," said the captain. The men were silent. They turned their eyes from the shore to the comber and waited. The boat slid up the incline, leaped at the furious top, bounced over it, and swung down the long back of the wave. Some water had been shipped and the cook bailed it out.

But the next crest crashed also. The tumbling boiling flood of white water caught the boat and whirled it almost perpendicular. Water swarmed in from all sides. The correspondent had his hands on the gunwale at this time, and when the water entered at that place he swiftly withdrew his fingers, as if he objected to wetting them.

The little boat, drunken with this weight of water, reeled and snuggled deeper into the sea.

"Bail her out, cook! Bail her out," said the captain.

215 "All right, captain," said the cook.

"Now, boys, the next one will do for us, sure," said the oiler. "Mind to jump clear of the boat."

The third wave moved forward, huge, furious, implacable. It fairly swallowed the dingey, and almost simultaneously the men tumbled into the sea. A piece of lifebelt had lain in the bottom of the boat, and as the correspondent went overboard he held this to his chest with his left hand.

The January water was icy, and he reflected immediately that it was colder than he had expected to find it off the coast of Florida. This appeared to his dazed mind as a fact important enough to be noted at the time. The coldness of the water was sad; it was tragic. This fact was somehow so mixed and confused with his opinion of his own situation that it seemed almost a proper reason for tears. The water was cold.

When he came to the surface he was conscious of little but the noisy water. Afterward he saw his companions in the sea. The oiler was ahead in the race. He was swimming strongly and rapidly. Off to the correspondent's left, the cook's great white and corked back bulged out of the water, and in the rear the captain was hanging with his one good hand to the keel of the overturned dingey.

220   There is a certain immovable quality to a shore, and the correspondent wondered at it amid the confusion of the sea.

It seemed also very attractive, but the correspondent knew that it was a long journey, and he paddled leisurely. The piece of life-preserver lay under him, and sometimes he whirled down the incline of a wave as if he were on a hand-sled.

But finally he arrived at a place in the sea where travel was beset with difficulty. He did not pause swimming to inquire what manner of current had caught him, but there his progress ceased. The shore was set before him like a bit of scenery on a stage, and he looked at it and understood with his eyes each detail of it.

As the cook passed, much farther to the left, the captain was calling to him, "Turn over on your back, cook! Turn over on your back and use the oar."

"All right, sir." The cook turned on his back, and, paddling with an oar, went ahead as if he were a canoe.

225   Presently the boat also passed to the left of the correspondent with the captain clinging with one hand to the keel. He would have appeared like a man raising himself to look over a board fence, if it were not for the extraordinary gymnastics of the boat. The correspondent marvelled that the captain could still hold to it.

They passed on, nearer to shore — the oiler, the cook, the captain — and following them went the water-jar, bouncing gaily over the seas.

The correspondent remained in the grip of this strange new enemy — a current. The shore, with its white slope of sand and its green bluff, topped with little silent cottages, was spread like a picture before him. It was very near to him then, but he was impressed as one who in a gallery looks at a scene from Brittany[7] or Holland.

He thought: "Am I going to drown? Can it be possible? Can it be possible? Can it be possible?" Perhaps an individual must consider his own death to be the final phenomenon of nature.

But later a wave perhaps whirled him out of this small deadly current, for he found suddenly that he could again make progress toward the shore. Later still, he was aware that the captain, clinging with one hand to the keel of the dingey, had his face turned away from the shore and toward him, and was calling his name. "Come to the boat! Come to the boat!"

230   In his struggle to reach the captain and the boat, he reflected that when one gets properly wearied, drowning must really be a comfortable arrangement, a cessation of hostilities accompanied by a large degree of relief, and he was glad of it, for the main thing in his mind for some moments had been horror of the temporary agony. He did not wish to be hurt.

Presently he saw a man running along the shore. He was undressing with most remarkable speed. Coat, trousers, shirt, everything flew magically off him.

"Come to the boat," called the captain.

7 rural region in northwestern France.

"All right, captain." As the correspondent paddled, he saw the captain let himself down to the bottom and leave the boat. Then the correspondent performed his one little marvel of the voyage. A large wave caught him and flung him with ease and supreme speed completely over the boat and far beyond it. It struck him even then as an event in gymnastics, and a true miracle of the sea. An overturned boat in the surf is not a plaything to a swimming man.

The correspondent arrived in water that reached only to his waist, but his condition did not enable him to stand for more than a moment. Each wave knocked him into a heap, and the under-tow pulled at him.

Then he saw the man who had been running and undressing, and undressing and running, come bounding into the water. He dragged ashore the cook, and then waded towards the captain, but the captain waved him away, and sent him to the correspondent. He was naked, naked as a tree in winter, but a halo was about his head, and he shone like a saint. He gave a strong pull, and a long drag, and a bully heave at the correspondent's hand. The correspondent, schooled in the minor formulæ, said: "Thanks, old man." But suddenly the man cried: "What's that?" He pointed a swift finger. The correspondent said: "Go."

In the shallows, face downward, lay the oiler. His forehead touched sand that was periodically, between each wave, clear of the sea.

The correspondent did not know all that transpired afterward. When he achieved safe ground he fell, striking the sand with each particular part of his body. It was as if he had dropped from a roof, but the thud was grateful to him.

It seems that instantly the beach was populated with men with blankets, clothes, and flasks, and women with coffee-pots and all the remedies sacred to their minds. The welcome of the land to the men from the sea was warm and generous, but a still and dripping shape was carried slowly up the beach, and the land's welcome for it could only be the different and sinister hospitality of the grave.

When it came night, the white waves paced to and fro in the moonlight, and the wind brought the sound of the great sea's voice to the men on shore, and they felt that they could then be interpreters.

(1897)

James Joyce (1882–1941)

Although Dublin-born, James Joyce lived most of his adult life in Europe, including twenty years in Paris, where he wrote most of his books about Dublin and its people: *Dubliners,* a collection of short stories; and three novels, *A Portait of the Artist as a Young Man, Ulysses,* and *Finnegans Wake.* The first three of these were filled with minutely depicted presentations of scenes and characters of Dublin. In *Dubliners,* from which "Araby" is taken, the details are given symbolic meanings that transform specific aspects of late-nineteenth-century Irish life into the universal. Many of the characters experience what Joyce called an "epiphany," a moment of insight in which they understand the nature of their lives. At the edge of adolescence, the young narrator experiences a profound conflict between his emerging sexuality and his strict religious upbringing. From the opening sentence's reference to a "blind" street to the concluding one's references to the darkness of the bazaar, Joyce carefully selects and arranges details to emphasize the boy's movement from innocence and ignorance to insight.

ARABY[1]

North Richmond Street, being blind,[2] was a quiet street except at the hour when the Christian Brothers' School set the boys free. An uninhabited house of two storeys stood at the blind end, detached from its neighbours in a square ground. The other houses of the street, conscious of decent lives within them, gazed at one another with brown imperturbable faces.

The former tenant of our house, a priest, had died in the back drawing-room. Air, musty from having been long enclosed, hung in all the rooms, and the waste room behind the kitchen was littered with old useless papers. Among these I found a few paper-covered books, the pages of which were curled and damp: *The Abbot,*[3] by Walter Scott, *The Devout Communicant*[4] and *The Memoirs of Vidocq.*[5] I liked the last best because its leaves were yellow. The wild garden behind the house contained a central apple-tree and a few straggling bushes under one of which I found the late tenant's rusty bicycle-pump. He had been a very charitable priest; in his will he had left all his money to institutions and the furniture of his house to his sister.

When the short days of winter came dusk fell before we had well eaten our dinners. When we met in the street the houses had grown sombre. The space of sky above us was the colour of ever-changing violet and towards it the lamps of the street lifted their feeble lanterns. The cold air stung us and we played till our bodies glowed. Our shouts echoed in the silent street. The career of our play brought us through the dark muddy lanes behind the houses where we ran the gantlet of the rough tribes from the cottages, to the back doors

---

1 Dublin charity bazaar with a name evoking the romance and mystery of Arabia. 2 dead-end street.
3 in Sir Walter Scott's 1820 novel set in the sixteenth century, a young man loyally serves Mary Queen of Scots. 4 nineteenth-century religious tract. 5 François Vidocq was an early-nineteenth-century French thief turned detective.

of the dark dripping gardens where odours arose from the ashpits, to the dark odorous stables where a coachman smoothed and combed the horse or shook music from the buckled harness. When we returned to the street light from the kitchen windows had filled the areas. If my uncle was seen turning the corner we hid in the shadow until we had seen him safely housed. Or if Mangan's sister came out on the doorstep to call her brother in to his tea we watched her from our shadow peer up and down the street. We waited to see whether she would remain or go in and, if she remained, we left our shadow and walked up to Mangan's steps resignedly. She was waiting for us, her figure defined by the light from the half-opened door. Her brother always teased her before he obeyed and I stood by the railings looking at her. Her dress swung as she moved her body and the soft rope of her hair tossed from side to side.

Every morning I lay on the floor in the front parlour watching her door. The blind was pulled down to within an inch of the sash so that I could not be seen. When she came out on the doorstep my heart leaped. I ran to the hall, seized my books and followed her. I kept her brown figure always in my eye and, when we came near the point at which our ways diverged, I quickened my pace and passed her. This happened morning after morning. I had never spoken to her, except for a few casual words, and yet her name was like a summons to all my foolish blood.

5   Her image accompanied me even in places the most hostile to romance. On Saturday evenings when my aunt went marketing I had to go to carry some of the parcels. We walked through the flaring streets, jostled by drunken men and bargaining women, amid the curses of labourers, the shrill litanies of shop-boys who stood on guard by the barrels of pigs' cheeks, the nasal chant-ing of street-singers, who sang a *come-all-you* about O'Donovan Rossa,[6] or a ballad about the troubles in our native land. These noises converged in a single sensation of life for me: I imagined that I bore my chalice safely through a throng of foes. Her name sprang to my lips at moments in strange prayers and praises which I myself did not understand. My eyes were often full of tears (I could not tell why) and at times a flood from my heart seemed to pour itself out into my bosom. I thought little of the future. I did not know whether I would ever speak to her or not or, if I spoke to her, how I could tell her of my confused adoration. But my body was like a harp and her words and gestures were like fingers running upon the wires.

One evening I went into the back drawing-room in which the priest had died. It was a dark rainy evening and there was no sound in the house. Through one of the broken panes I heard the rain impinge upon the earth, the fine incessant needles of water playing in the sodden beds. Some distant lamp or lighted window gleamed below me. I was thankful that I could see so little. All my senses seemed to desire to veil themselves and, feeling that I was about to slip from them, I pressed the palms of my hands together until they trembled, murmuring: *O love! O love!* many times.

At last she spoke to me. When she addressed the first words to me I was so confused that I did not know what to answer. She asked me was I going to

6 popular street ballad about a nineteenth-century Irish revolutionary.

Araby. I forget whether I answered yes or no. It would be a splendid bazaar, she said; she would love to go.

— And why can't you? I asked.

While she spoke she turned a silver bracelet round and round her wrist. She could not go, she said, because there would be a retreat that week in her convent. Her brother and two other boys were fighting for their caps and I was alone at the railings. She held one of the spikes, bowing her head towards me. The light from the lamp opposite our door caught the white curve of her neck, lit up her hair that rested there and, falling, lit up the hand upon the railing. It fell over one side of her dress and caught the white border of a petticoat, just visible as she stood at ease.

10   — It's well for you, she said.

— If I go, I said, I will bring you something.

What innumerable follies laid waste my waking and sleeping thoughts after that evening! I wished to annihilate the tedious intervening days. I chafed against the work of school. At night in my bedroom and by day in the classroom her image came between me and the page I strove to read. The syllables of the word *Araby* were called to me through the silence in which my soul luxuriated and cast an Eastern enchantment over me. I asked for leave to go to the bazaar on Saturday night. My aunt was surprised and hoped it was not some Freemason[7] affair. I answered few questions in class. I watched my master's face pass from amiability to sternness; he hoped I was not beginning to idle. I could not call my wandering thoughts together. I had hardly any patience with the serious work of life which, now that it stood between me and my desire, seemed to me child's play, ugly monotonous child's play.

On Saturday morning I reminded my uncle that I wished to go to the bazaar in the evening. He was fussing at the hallstand, looking for the hat-brush, and answered me curtly:

— Yes, boy, I know.

15   As he was in the hall I could not go into the front parlour and lie at the window. I left the house in bad humour and walked slowly towards the school. The air was pitilessly raw and already my heart misgave me.

When I came home to dinner my uncle had not yet been home. Still it was early. I sat staring at the clock for some time and, when its ticking began to irritate me, I left the room. I mounted the staircase and gained the upper part of the house. The high cold empty gloomy rooms liberated me and I went from room to room singing. From the front window I saw my companions playing below in the street. Their cries reached me weakened and indistinct and, leaning my forehead against the cool glass, I looked over at the dark house where she lived. I may have stood there for an hour, seeing nothing but the brown-clad figure cast by my imagination, touched discreetly by the lamplight at the curved neck, at the hand upon the railings and at the border below the dress.

When I came downstairs again I found Mrs Mercer sitting at the fire. She was an old garrulous woman, a pawnbroker's widow, who collected used stamps for some pious purpose. I had to endure the gossip of the tea-table.

7 the Protestant Masons were considered enemies of Irish Roman Catholics.

The meal was prolonged beyond an hour and still my uncle did not come. Mrs Mercer stood up to go: she was sorry she couldn't wait any longer, but it was after eight o'clock and she did not like to be out late, as the night air was bad for her. When she had gone I began to walk up and down the room, clenching my fists. My aunt said:

— I'm afraid you may put off your bazaar for this night of Our Lord.

At nine o'clock I heard my uncle's latchkey in the halldoor. I heard him talking to himself and heard the hallstand rocking when it had received the weight of his overcoat. I could interpret these signs. When he was midway through his dinner I asked him to give me the money to go to the bazaar. He had forgotten.

20 — The people are in bed and after their first sleep now, he said.

I did not smile. My aunt said to him energetically:

— Can't you give him the money and let him go? You've kept him late enough as it is.

My uncle said he was very sorry he had forgotten. He said he believed in the old saying: *All work and no play makes Jack a dull boy*. He asked where I was going and, when I had told him a second time he asked me did I know *The Arab's Farewell to his Steed*.[8] When I left the kitchen he was about to recite the opening lines of the piece to my aunt.

I held a florin[9] tightly in my hand as I strode down Buckingham Street towards the station. The sight of the streets thronged with buyers and glaring with gas recalled to me the purpose of my journey. I took my seat in a third-class carriage of a deserted train. After an intolerable delay the train moved out of the station slowly. It crept onward among ruinous houses and over the twinkling river. At Westland Row Station a crowd of people pressed to the carriage doors; but the porters moved them back, saying that it was a special train for the bazaar. I remained alone in the bare carriage. In a few minutes the train drew up beside an improvised wooden platform. I passed out on to the road and saw by the lighted dial of a clock that it was ten minutes to ten. In front of me was a large building which displayed the magical name.

25 I could not find any sixpenny entrance and, fearing that the bazaar would be closed, I passed in quickly through a turnstile, handing a shilling to a weary-looking man. I found myself in a big hall girdled at half its height by a gallery. Nearly all the stalls were closed and the greater part of the hall was in darkness. I recognized a silence like that which pervades a church after a service. I walked into the centre of the bazaar timidly. A few people were gathered about the stalls which were still open. Before a curtain, over which the words *Café Chantant* were written in coloured lamps, two men were counting money on a salver. I listened to the fall of the coins.

Remembering with difficulty why I had come I went over to one of the stalls and examined porcelain vases and flowered tea-sets. At the door of the stall a young lady was talking and laughing with two young gentlemen. I remarked their English accents and listened vaguely to their conversation.

— Oh, I never said such a thing!

8 sentimental nineteenth-century poem about a man who, disconsolate at selling his horse, reclaims it.
9 two-shilling coin worth about 50 cents at that time.

— O, but you did!

— O, but I didn't!

30   — Didn't she say that?

— Yes. I heard her.

— O, there's a . . . fib!

Observing me the young lady came over and asked me did I wish to buy anything. The tone of her voice was not encouraging; she seemed to have spoken to me out of a sense of duty. I looked humbly at the great jars that stood like eastern guards at either side of the dark entrance to the stall and murmured:

— No, thank you.

35   The young lady changed the position of one of the vases and went back to the two young men. They began to talk of the same subject. Once or twice the young lady glanced at me over her shoulder.

I lingered before her stall, though I knew my stay was useless, to make my interest in her wares seem the more real. Then I turned away slowly and walked down the middle of the bazaar. I allowed the two pennies to fall against the sixpence in my pocket. I heard a voice call from one end of the gallery that the light was out. The upper part of the hall was now completely dark.

Gazing up into the darkness I saw myself as a creature driven and derided by vanity; and my eyes burned with anguish and anger.

(1914)

Katherine Mansfield (1888–1923)

Born in Wellington, New Zealand, Katherine Mansfield (the pseudonym of Kathleen Beauchamp) moved to London when she was twenty and shortly after began her career as a writer. Critics have compared her works to those of Russian author Anton Chekhov, whose ironic view of life and whose technical innovations, particularly the use of small details to reveal character, she greatly admired. In her collections of short stories, three of which—*In a German Pension*, *Bliss*, and *The Garden Party*—were published during her life, she examined the nature of childhood and the troubled relationships between men and women. The description of the heroine's activities in the early pages of "Bliss" reveals the happiness Bertha feels as she prepares for a dinner party, while later details indicate her changing emotions. Events of the narrative and her emotions and feelings subtly foreshadow the story's conclusion.

BLISS

Although Bertha Young was thirty she still had moments like this when she wanted to run instead of walk, to take dancing steps on and off the pavement, to bowl a hoop, to throw something up in the air and catch it again, or to stand still and laugh at — nothing — at nothing, simply.

What can you do if you are thirty and, turning the corner of your own street, you are overcome, suddenly, by a feeling of bliss — absolute bliss! — as though you'd suddenly swallowed a bright piece of that late afternoon sun and it burned in your bosom, sending out a little shower of sparks into every particle, into every finger and toe?...

Oh, is there no way you can express it without being "drunk and disorderly"? How idiotic civilization is! Why be given a body if you have to keep it shut up in a case like a rare, rare fiddle?

"No, that about the fiddle is not quite what I mean," she thought, running up the steps and feeling in her bag for the key — she's forgotten it, as usual — and rattling the letter-box. "It's not what I mean, because — Thank you, Mary" — she went into the hall. "Is nurse back?"

5   "Yes, M'm."

"And has the fruit come?"

"Yes, M'm. Everything's come."

"Bring the fruit up to the dining-room, will you? I'll arrange it before I go upstairs."

It was dusky in the dining-room and quite chilly. But all the same Bertha threw off her coat; she could not bear the tight clasp of it another moment, and the cold air fell on her arms.

10   But in her bosom there was still that bright glowing place — that shower of little sparks coming from it. It was almost unbearable. She hardly dared to breathe for fear of fanning it higher, and yet she breathed deeply, deeply. She hardly dared to look into the cold mirror — but she did look, and it gave her back a woman, radiant, with smiling, trembling lips, with big, dark eyes and an air of listening,

waiting for something…divine to happen…that she knew must happen… infallibly.

Mary brought in the fruit on a tray and with it a glass bowl, and a blue dish, very lovely, with a strange sheen on it as though it had been dipped in milk.

"Shall I turn on the light, M'm?"

"No, thank you. I can see quite well."

There were tangerines and apples stained with strawberry pink. Some yellow pears, smooth as silk, some white grapes covered with a silver bloom and a big cluster of purple ones. These last she had bought to tone in with the new dining-room carpet. Yes, that did sound rather far-fetched and absurd, but it was really why she had bought them. She had thought in the shop: "I must have some purple ones to bring the carpet up to the table." And it had seemed quite sense at the time.

15 When she had finished with them and had made two pyramids of these bright round shapes, she stood away from the table to get the effect — and it really was most curious. For the dark table seemed to melt into the dusky light and the glass dish and the blue bowl to float in the air. This, of course in her present mood, was so incredibly beautiful....She began to laugh.

"No, no. I'm getting hysterical." And she seized her bag and coat and ran upstairs to the nursery.

Nurse sat at a low table giving Little B her supper after her bath. The baby had on a white flannel gown and a blue woollen jacket, and her dark, fine hair was brushed up into a funny little peak. She looked up when she saw her mother and began to jump.

"Now, my lovey, eat it up like a good girl," said Nurse, setting her lips in a way that Bertha knew, and that meant she had come into the nursery at another wrong moment.

"Has she been good, Nanny?"

20 "She's been a little sweet all the afternoon," whispered Nanny. "We went to the park and I sat down on a chair and took her out of the pram and a big dog came along and put his head on my knee and she clutched its ear, tugged it. Oh, you should have seen her."

Bertha wanted to ask if it wasn't rather dangerous to let her clutch at a strange dog's ear. But she did not dare to. She stood watching them, her hands by her side, like the poor little girl in front of the rich little girl with the doll.

The baby looked up at her again, stared, and then smiled so charmingly that Bertha couldn't help crying:

"Oh, Nanny, do let me finish giving her her supper while you put the bath things away."

"Well, M'm, she oughtn't to be changed hands while she's eating," said Nanny, still whispering. "It unsettles her; it's very likely to upset her."

25 How absurd it was. Why have a baby if it has to be kept — not in a case like a rare, rare fiddle — but in another woman's arms?

"Oh, I must!" said she.

Very offended, Nanny handed her over.

"Now, don't excite her after her supper. You know you do, M'm. And I have such a time with her after!"

Thank heaven! Nanny went out of the room with the bath towels.

30 "Now I've got you to myself, my little precious," said Bertha, as the baby leaned against her.

She ate delightfully, holding up her lips for the spoon and then waving her hands. Sometimes she wouldn't let the spoon go; and sometimes, just as Bertha had filled it, she waved it away to the four winds.

When the soup was finished Bertha turned round to the fire.

"You're nice — you're very nice!" said she, kissing her warm baby. "I'm fond of you. I like you."

And, indeed, she loved Little B so much — her neck as she bent forward, her exquisite toes as they shone transparent in the firelight — that all her feeling of bliss came back again, and again she didn't know how to express it — what to do with it.

35 "You're wanted on the telephone," said Nanny, coming back in triumph and seizing *her* Little B.

Down she flew. It was Harry.

"Oh, is that you, Ber? Look here. I'll be late. I'll take a taxi and come along as quickly as I can, but get dinner put back ten minutes — will you? All right?"

"Yes, perfectly. Oh, Harry!"

"Yes?"

40 What had she to say? She'd nothing to say. She only wanted to get in touch with him for a moment. She couldn't absurdly cry: "Hasn't it been a divine day!"

"What is it?" rapped out the little voice.

"Nothing. *Entendu*,"[1] said Bertha, and hung up the receiver, thinking how more than idiotic civilization was.

They had people coming to dinner. The Norman Knights — a very sound couple — he was about to start a theatre, and she was awfully keen on interior decoration, a young man, Eddie Warren, who had just published a little book of poems and whom everybody was asking to dine, and a "find" of Bertha's called Pearl Fulton. What Miss Fulton did, Bertha didn't know. They had met at the club and Bertha had fallen in love with her, as she always did fall in love with beautiful women who had something strange about them.

The provoking thing was that, though they had been about together and met a number of times and really talked, Bertha couldn't yet make her out. Up to a certain point Miss Fulton was rarely, wonderfully frank, but the certain point was there, and beyond that she would not go.

45 Was there anything beyond it? Harry said "No." Voted her dullish, and "cold like all blond women, with a touch, perhaps, of anaemia of the brain." But Bertha wouldn't agree with him; not yet, at any rate.

"No, the way she has of sitting with her head a little on one side, and smiling, has something behind it, Harry, and I must find out what that something is."

"Most likely it's a good stomach," answered Harry.

He made a point of catching Bertha's heels with replies of that kind . . . "liver frozen, my dear girl," or "pure flatulence," or "kidney disease," . . . and so on. For some strange reason Bertha liked this, and almost admired it in him very much.

She went into the drawing-room and lighted the fire; then, picking up the cushions, one by one, that Mary had disposed so carefully, she threw them back

[1] understood, agreed.

on to the chairs and the couches. That made all the difference; the room came alive at once. As she was about to throw the last one she surprised herself by suddenly hugging it to her, passionately, passionately. But it did not put out the fire in her bosom. Oh, on the contrary!

50 The windows of the drawing-room opened on to a balcony overlooking the garden. At the far end, against the wall, there was a tall, slender pear tree in fullest, richest bloom; it stood perfect, as though becalmed against the jade-green sky. Bertha couldn't help feeling, even from this distance, that it had not a single bud or a faded petal. Down below, in the garden beds, the red and yellow tulips, heavy with flowers, seemed to lean upon the dusk. A grey cat, dragging its belly, crept across the lawn, and a black one, its shadow, trailed after. The sight of them, so intent and so quick, gave Bertha a curious shiver.

"What creepy things cats are!" she stammered, and she turned away from the window and began walking up and down....

How strong the jonquils smelled in the warm room. Too strong? Oh, no. And yet, as though overcome, she flung down on a couch and pressed her hands to her eyes.

"I'm too happy — too happy!" she murmured.

And she seemed to see on her eyelids the lovely pear tree with its wide open blossoms as a symbol of her own life.

55 Really — really — she had everything. She was young. Harry and she were as much in love as ever, and they got on together splendidly and were really good pals. She had an adorable baby. They didn't have to worry about money. They had this absolutely satisfactory house and garden. And friends — modern, thrilling friends, writers and painters and poets or people keen on social questions — just the kind of friends they wanted. And then there were books, and there was music, and she had found a wonderful little dressmaker, and they were going abroad in the summer, and their new cook made the most superb omelettes....

"I'm absurd! Absurd!" She sat up; but she felt quite dizzy, quite drunk. It must have been the spring.

Yes, it was the spring. Now she was so tired she could not drag herself upstairs to dress.

A white dress, a string of jade beads, green shoes and stockings. It wasn't intentional. She had thought of this scheme hours before she stood at the drawing-room window.

Her petals rustled softly into the hall, and she kissed Mrs. Norman Knight, who was taking off the most amusing orange coat with a procession of black monkeys round the hem and up the fronts.

60 "... Why! Why! Why is the middle-class so stodgy — so utterly without a sense of humour! My dear, it's only by a fluke that I am here at all — Norman being the protective fluke. For my darling monkeys so upset the train that it rose to a man and simply ate me with its eyes. Didn't laugh — wasn't amused — that I should have loved. No, just stared — and bored me through and through."

"But the cream of it was," said Norman, pressing a large tortoiseshell-rimmed monocle into his eye, "you don't mind me telling this, Face, do you?" (In their home and among their friends they called each other Face and Mug.) "The cream of it was when she, being full fed, turned to the woman beside her and said: 'Haven't you ever seen a monkey before?'"

"Oh, yes!" Mrs. Norman Knight joined in the laughter. "Wasn't that too absolutely creamy?"

And a funnier thing still was that now her coat was off she did look like a very intelligent monkey — who had even made that yellow silk dress out of scraped banana skins. And her amber ear-rings; they were like little dangling nuts.

"This is a sad, sad fall!" said Mug, pausing in front of Little B's perambulator. "When the perambulator comes into the hall —" and he waved the rest of the quotation away.

65 The bell rang. It was lean, pale Eddie Warren (as usual) in a state of acute distress.

"It *is* the right house, *isn't* it?" he pleaded.

"Oh, I think so — I hope so," said Bertha brightly.

"I have had such a *dreadful* experience with a taxi-man; he was *most* sinister. I couldn't get him to *stop*. The *more* I knocked and called the *faster* he went. And *in* the moonlight this *bizarre* figure with the *flattened* head *crouching* over the *lit-tle* wheel...."

He shuddered, taking off an immense white silk scarf. Bertha noticed that his socks were white, too — most charming.

70 "But how dreadful!" she cried.

"Yes, it really was," said Eddie, following her into the drawing-room. "I saw myself *driving* through Eternity in a *timeless* taxi."

He knew the Norman Knights. In fact, he was going to write a play for N.K. when the theatre scheme came off.

"Well, Warren, how's the play?" said Norman Knight, dropping his monocle and giving his eye a moment in which to rise to the surface before it was screwed down again.

And Mrs. Norman Knight: "Oh, Mr. Warren, what happy socks?"

75 "I *am* so glad you like them," said he, staring at his feet. "They seem to have got so *much* whiter since the moon rose." And he turned his lean sorrowful young face to Bertha. "There *is* a moon, you know."

She wanted to cry: "I am sure there is — often — often!"

He really was a most attractive person. But so was Face, crouched before the fire in her banana skins, and so was Mug, smoking a cigarette and saying as he flicked the ash: "Why doth the bridegroom tarry?"

"There he is, now."

Bang went the front door open and shut. Harry shouted: "Hullo, you people. Down in five minutes." And they heard him swarm up the stairs. Bertha couldn't help smiling; she knew how he loved doing things at high pressure. What, after all, did an extra five minutes matter? But he would pretend to himself that they mattered beyond measure. And then he would make a great point of coming into the drawing-room, extravagantly cool and collected.

80 Harry had such a zest for life. Oh, how she appreciated it in him. And his passion for fighting — for seeking in everything that came up against him another test of his power and of his courage — that, too, she understood. Even when it made him just occasionally, to other people, who didn't know him well, a little ridiculous perhaps.... For there were moments when he rushed into battle where no battle was.... She talked and laughed and positively forgot until he had come in (just as she had imagined) that Pearl Fulton had not turned up.

"I wonder if Miss Fulton has forgotten?"

"I expect so," said Harry. "Is she on the 'phone?"

"Ah! There's a taxi, now." And Bertha smiled with that little air of proprietorship that she always assumed while her women finds were new and mysterious. "She lives in taxis."

"She'll run to fat if she does," said Harry coolly, ringing the bell for dinner. "Frightful danger for blond women."

85   "Harry — don't," warned Bertha, laughing up at him.

Came another tiny moment, while they waited, laughing and talking, just a trifle too much at their ease, a trifle too unaware. And then Miss Fulton, all in silver, with a silver fillet binding her pale blond hair, came in smiling, her head a little on one side.

"Am I late?"

"No, not at all," said Bertha. "Come along." And she took her arm and they moved into the dining-room.

What was there in the touch of that cool arm that could fan — fan — start blazing — blazing — the fire of bliss that Bertha did not know what to do with?

90   Miss Fulton did not look at her; but then she seldom did look at people directly. Her heavy eyelids lay upon her eyes and the strange half smile came and went upon her lips as though she lived by listening rather than seeing. But Bertha knew, suddenly, as if the longest, most intimate look had passed between them — as if they had said to each other: "You, too?" — that Pearl Fulton, stirring the beautiful red soup in the grey plate, was feeling just what she was feeling.

And the others? Face and Mug, Eddie and Harry, their spoons rising and falling — dabbing their lips with their napkins, crumbling bread, fiddling with the forks and glasses and talking.

"I met her at the Alpha shore — the weirdest little person. She'd not only cut off her hair, but she seemed to have taken a dreadfully good snip off her legs and arms and her neck and her poor little nose as well."

"Isn't she very *liée*[2] with Michael Oat?"

"The man who wrote *Love in False Teeth*?"

95   "He wants to write a play for me. One act. One man. Decides to commit suicide. Gives all the reasons why he should and why he shouldn't. And just as he has made up his mind either to do it or not to do it — curtain. Not half a bad idea."

"What's he going to call it —'Stomach Trouble'?"

"I *think* I've come across the *same* idea in a lit-tle French review, *quite* unknown in England."

No, they didn't share it. They were dears — dears — and she loved having them there, at her table, and giving them delicious food and wine. In fact, she longed to tell them how delightful they were, and what a decorative group they made, how they seemed to set one another off and how they reminded her of a play by Tchekof![3]

Harry was enjoying his dinner. It was part of his — well, not his nature, exactly, and certainly not his pose — his — something or other — to talk about food and to glory in his "shameless passion for the white flesh of the lobster" and "the green of pistachio ices — green and cold like the eyelids of Egyptian dancers."

100   When he looked up at her and said: "Bertha, this is a very admirable *soufflée*!" she almost could have wept with child-like pleasure.

2 attached (involved). 3 Anton Chekhov, nineteenth-century Russian writer of ironic dramas and short stories.

Oh, why did she feel so tender towards the whole world tonight? Everything was good — was right. All that happened seemed to fill again her brimming cup of bliss.

And still, in the back of her mind, there was the pear tree. It would be silver now, in the light of poor dear Eddie's moon, silver as Miss Fulton, who sat there turning a tangerine in her slender fingers that were so pale a light seemed to come from them.

What she simply couldn't make out — what was miraculous — was how she should have guessed Miss Fulton's mood so exactly and so instantly. For she never doubted for a moment that she was right, and yet what had she to go on? Less than nothing.

"I believe this does happen very, very rarely between women. Never between men," thought Bertha. "But while I am making the coffee in the drawing-room perhaps she will 'give a sign.'"

105   What she meant by that she did not know, and what would happen after that she could not imagine.

While she thought like this she saw herself talking and laughing. She had to talk because of her desire to laugh.

"I must laugh or die."

But when she noticed Face's funny little habit of tucking something down the front of her bodice — as if she kept a tiny, secret hoard of nuts there, too — Bertha had to dig her nails into her hands — so as not to laugh too much.

It was over at last. And: "Come and see my new coffee machine," said Bertha.

110   "We only have a new coffee machine once a fortnight," said Harry. Face took her arm this time; Miss Fulton bent her head and followed after.

The fire had died down in the drawing-room to a red, flickering "nest of baby phoenixes," said Face.

"Don't turn up the light for a moment. It is so lovely." And down she crouched by the fire again. She was always cold... "without her little red flannel jacket, of course," thought Bertha.

At that moment Miss Fulton "gave the sign."

"Have you a garden?" said the cool, sleepy voice.

115   This was so exquisite on her part that all Bertha could do was to obey. She crossed the room, pulled the curtains apart, and opened those long windows.

"There!" she breathed.

And the two women stood side by side looking at the slender, flowering tree. Although it was so still it seemed, like the flame of a candle, to stretch up, to point, to quiver in the bright air, to grow taller and taller as they gazed — almost to touch the rim of the round, silver moon.

How long did they stand there? Both, as it were, caught in that circle of unearthly light, understanding each other perfectly, creatures of another world, and wondering what they were to do in this one with all this blissful treasure that burned in their bosoms and dropped, in silver flowers, from their hair and hands?

For ever — for a moment? And did Miss Fulton murmur: "Yes. Just *that*." Or did Bertha dream it?

120   Then the light was snapped on and Face made the coffee and Harry said: "My dear Mrs. Knight, don't ask me about my baby. I never see her. I shan't feel the slightest interest in her until she has a lover," and Mug took his eye out of the conservatory for a moment and then put it under glass again and Eddie Warren drank his coffee and set down the cup with a face of anguish as though he had drunk and seen the spider.

"What I want to do is to give the young men a show. I believe London is simply teeming with first-chop, unwritten plays. What I want to say to 'em is: 'Here's the theatre. Fire ahead.'"

"You know, my dear, I am going to decorate a room for the Jacob Nathans. Oh, I am so tempted to do a fried-fish scheme, with the backs of the chairs shaped like frying pans and lovely chip potatoes embroidered all over the curtains."

"The trouble with our young writing men is that they are still too romantic. You can't put out to sea without being seasick and wanting a basin. Well, why won't they have the courage of those basins?"

"A *dreadful* poem about a *girl* who was *violated* by a beggar *without* a nose in a lit-tle wood...."

125   Miss Fulton sank into the lowest, deepest chair and Harry handed round the cigarettes.

From the way he stood in front of her shaking the silver box and saying abruptly: "Egyptian? Turkish? Virginian? They're all mixed up," Bertha realized that she not only bored him; he really disliked her. And she decided from the way Miss Fulton said: "No, thank you, I won't smoke," that she felt it, too, and was hurt.

"Oh, Harry, don't dislike her. You are quite wrong about her. She's wonderful, wonderful. And, besides, how can you feel so differently about some one who means so much to me. I shall try to tell you when we are in bed tonight what has been happening. What she and I have shared."

At those last words something strange and almost terrifying darted into Bertha's mind. And this something blind and smiling whispered to her: "Soon these people will go. The house will be quiet — quiet. The lights will be out. And you and he will be alone together in the dark room — the warm bed...."

She jumped up from her chair and ran over to the piano.

130   "What a pity some one does not play!" she cried. "What a pity somebody does not play."

For the first time in her life Bertha Young desired her husband.

Oh, she'd loved him — she'd been in love with him, of course, in every other way, but just not in that way. And, equally, of course, she'd understood that he was different. They'd discussed it so often. It had worried her dreadfully at first to find that she was so cold, but after a time it had not seemed to matter. They were so frank with each other — such good pals. That was the best of being modern.

But now — ardently! ardently! The word ached in her ardent body! Was this what that feeling of bliss had been leading up to? But then — then —

"My dear," said Mrs. Norman Knight, "you know our shame. We are the victims of time and train. We live in Hampstead. It's been so nice."

135   "I'll come with you into the hall," said Bertha. "I love having you. But you must not miss the last train. That's so awful, isn't it?"

"Have a whisky, Knight, before you go?" called Harry.

"No, thanks, old chap."

Bertha squeezed his hand for that as she shook it.

"Good night, good-bye," she cried from the top step, feeling that this self of hers was taking leave of them for ever.

When she got back into the drawing-room the others were on the move.

"... Then you can come part of the way in my taxi."

"I shall be *so* thankful *not* to have to face *another* drive *alone* after my *dreadful* experience."

"You can get a taxi at the rank just at the end of the street. You won't have to walk more than a few yards."

"That's comfort. I'll go and put on my coat."

Miss Fulton moved towards the hall and Bertha was following when Harry almost pushed past.

"Let me help you."

Bertha knew that he was repenting his rudeness — she let him go. What a boy he was in some ways — so impulsive — so — simple.

And Eddie and she were left by the fire.

"I *wonder* if you have seen Bilks' *new* poem called *Table d'Hôte*," said Eddie softly. "It's *so* wonderful. In the last Anthology. Have you got a copy? I'd *so* like to *show* it to you. It begins with an *incredibly* beautiful line: 'Why Must it Always be Tomato Soup?'"

"Yes," said Bertha. And she moved noiselessly to a table opposite the drawing-room door and Eddie glided noiselessly after her. She picked up the little book and gave it to him; they had not made a sound.

While he looked it up she turned her head towards the hall. And she saw. . . Harry with Miss Fulton's coat in his arms and Miss Fulton with her back turned to him and her head bent. He tossed the coat away, put his hands on her shoulders and turned her violently to him. His lips said: "I adore you," and Miss Fulton laid her moonbeam fingers on his cheeks and smiled her sleepy smile. Harry's nostrils quivered; his lips curled back in a hideous grin while he whispered: "Tomorrow," and with her eyelids Miss Fulton said "Yes."

"Here it is," said Eddie. "'Why Must it Always be Tomato Soup?' It's so *deeply* true, don't you feel? Tomato soup is so *dreadfully* eternal."

"If you prefer," said Harry's voice, very loud, from the hall, "I can 'phone you a cab to come to the door."

"Oh, no. It's not necessary," said Miss Fulton, and she came up to Bertha and gave her the slender fingers to hold.

"Good-bye. Thank you so much."

"Good-bye," said Bertha.

Miss Fulton held her hand a moment longer.

"Your lovely pear tree!" she murmured.

And then she was gone, with Eddie following, like the black cat following the grey cat.

"I'll shut up shop," said Harry, extravagantly cool and collected.

"Your lovely pear tree — pear tree — pear tree!"

Bertha simply ran over to the long windows.

"Oh, what is going to happen now?" she cried.

But the pear tree was as lovely as ever and as full of flower and as still.

(1918)

William Faulkner (1897–1962)

In his 1950 acceptance speech for the Nobel Prize for literature, William Faulkner defined his subject matter as "the human heart in conflict with itself, which alone can make good writing because only that is worth writing about." Universal in their themes, most of his novels and short stories are set in Yoknapatawpha County, a fictionalized version of West Lafayette County, Mississippi, where he was born and lived most of his life. A major focus in many of his works is the central characters' awareness of the degeneration of their families from a once glorious past and their sense of imprisonment in memories of that past. In such novels as *Absalom, Absalom!* and *The Reivers*, Faulkner is as interested in attempts by the characters to understand the past as he is in that past itself. "A Rose for Emily," which begins after the death of the title character, presents an unnamed townsman's account and interpretation of details of Emily Grierson's life, many of which occurred before his birth, and the discovery he and the villagers make about her when they break into one of the rooms of her home after her funeral. With new knowledge, the narrator finally understands the recluse's character and her actions.

A ROSE FOR EMILY

I

When Miss Emily Grierson died, our whole town went to her funeral: the men through a sort of respectful affection for a fallen monument, the women mostly out of curiosity to see the inside of her house, which no one save an old man-servant — a combined gardener and cook — had seen in at least ten years.

It was a big, squarish frame house that had once been white, decorated with cupolas and spires and scrolled balconies in the heavily lightsome style of the seventies, set on what had once been our most select street. But garages and cotton gins had encroached and obliterated even the august names of that neighborhood; only Miss Emily's house was left, lifting its stubborn and coquettish decay above the cotton wagons and the gasoline pumps — an eyesore among eyesores. And now Miss Emily had gone to join the representatives of those august names where they lay in the cedar-bemused cemetery among the ranked and anonymous graves of Union and Confederate soldiers[1] who fell at the battle of Jefferson.[2]

Alive, Miss Emily had been a tradition, a duty, and a care; a sort of hereditary obligation upon the town, dating from that day in 1894 when Colonel Sartoris, the mayor — he who fathered the edict that no Negro woman should appear on the streets without an apron — remitted her taxes, the dispensation dating from the death of her father on into perpetuity. Not that Miss Emily

---

1 soldiers who fought for the North and South, respectively, during the American Civil War.
2 Civil War battle fought in Mississippi; Jefferson is Faulkner's fictional name for Oxford, Mississippi.

would have accepted charity. Colonel Sartoris invented an involved tale to the effect that Miss Emily's father had loaned money to the town, which the town, as a matter of business, preferred this way of repaying. Only a man of Colonel Sartoris' generation and thought could have invented it, and only a woman could have believed it.

When the next generation, with its more modern ideas, became mayors and aldermen, this arrangement created some little dissatisfaction. On the first of the year they mailed her a tax notice. February came, and there was no reply. They wrote her a formal letter, asking her to call at the sheriff's office at her convenience. A week later the mayor wrote her himself, offering to call or to send his car for her, and received in reply a note on paper of an archaic shape, in a thin, flowing calligraphy in faded ink, to the effect that she no longer went out at all. The tax notice was also enclosed, without comment.

5   They called a special meeting of the Board of Aldermen. A deputation waited upon her, knocked at the door through which no visitor had passed since she ceased giving china-painting lessons eight or ten years earlier. They were admitted by the old Negro into a dim hall from which a stairway mounted into still more shadow. It smelled of dust and disuse — a close, dank smell. The Negro led them into the parlor. It was furnished in heavy, leather-covered furniture. When the Negro opened the blinds of one window, they could see that the leather was cracked; and when they sat down, a faint dust rose sluggishly about their thighs, spinning with slow motes in the single sun-ray. On a tarnished gilt easel before the fireplace stood a crayon portrait of Miss Emily's father.

They rose when she entered — a small, fat woman in black, with a thin gold chain descending to her waist and vanishing into her belt, leaning on an ebony cane with a tarnished gold head. Her skeleton was small and spare; perhaps that was why what would have been merely plumpness in another was obesity in her. She looked bloated, like a body long submerged in motionless water, and of that pallid hue. Her eyes, lost in the fatty ridges of her face, looked like two small pieces of coal pressed into a lump of dough as they moved from one face to another while the visitors stated their errand.

She did not ask them to sit. She just stood in the door and listened quietly until the spokesman came to a stumbling halt. Then they could hear the invisible watch ticking at the end of the gold chain.

Her voice was dry and cold. "I have no taxes in Jefferson. Colonel Sartoris explained it to me. Perhaps one of you can gain access to the city records and satisfy yourselves."

"But we have. We are the city authorities, Miss Emily. Didn't you get a notice from the sheriff, signed by him?"

10   "I received a paper, yes," Miss Emily said. "Perhaps he considers himself the sheriff...I have no taxes in Jefferson."

"But there is nothing on the books to show that, you see. We must go by the —"

"See Colonel Sartoris. I have no taxes in Jefferson."

"But, Miss Emily —"

"See Colonel Sartoris." (Colonel Sartoris had been dead almost ten years.) "I have no taxes in Jefferson. Tobe!" The Negro appeared. "Show these gentlemen out."

II

15   So she vanquished them, horse and foot, just as she had vanquished their fathers thirty years before about the smell. That was two years after her father's death and a short time after her sweetheart — the one we believed would marry her — had deserted her. After her father's death she went out very little; after her sweetheart went away, people hardly saw her at all. A few of the ladies had the temerity to call, but were not received, and the only sign of life about the place was the Negro man — a young man then — going in and out with a market basket.

"Just as if a man — any man — could keep a kitchen properly," the ladies said; so they were not surprised when the smell developed. It was another link between the gross, teeming world and the high and mighty Griersons.

A neighbor, a woman, complained to the mayor, Judge Stevens, eighty years old.

"But what will you have me do about it, madam?" he said.

"Why, send her word to stop it," the woman said. "Isn't there a law?"

20   "I'm sure that won't be necessary," Judge Stevens said. "It's probably just a snake or a rat that nigger of hers killed in the yard. I'll speak to him about it."

The next day he received two more complaints, one from a man who came in diffident deprecation. "We really must do something about it, Judge. I'd be the last one in the world to bother Miss Emily, but we've got to do something." That night the Board of Aldermen met — three graybeards and one younger man, a member of the rising generation.

"It's simple enough," he said. "Send her word to have her place cleaned up. Give her a certain time to do it in, and if she don't . . ."

"Dammit, sir," Judge Stevens said, "will you accuse a lady to her face of smelling bad?"

So the next night, after midnight, four men crossed Miss Emily's lawn and slunk about the house like burglars, sniffing along the base of the brick-work and at the cellar openings while one of them performed a regular sowing motion with his hand out of a sack slung from his shoulder. They broke open the cellar door and sprinkled lime there, and in all the outbuildings. As they recrossed the lawn, a window that had been dark was lighted and Miss Emily sat in it, the light behind her, and her upright torso motionless as that of an idol. They crept quietly across the lawn and into the shadow of the locusts that lined the street. After a week or two the smell went away.

25   That was when people had begun to feel really sorry for her. People in our town, remembering how old lady Wyatt, her great-aunt, had gone com-pletely crazy at last, believed that the Griersons held themselves a little too high for what they really were. None of the young men were quite good enough for Miss Emily and such. We had long thought of them as a tableau, Miss Emily a slender figure in white in the background, her father a spraddled silhouette in the foreground, his back to her and clutching a horsewhip, the two of them framed by the back-flung front door. So when she got to be thirty and was still single, we were not pleased exactly, but vindicated; even with insanity in the family she wouldn't have turned down all of her chances if they had really materialized.

When her father died, it got about that the house was all that was left to her; and in a way, people were glad. At last they could pity Miss Emily. Being left alone, and a pauper, she had become humanized. Now she too would know the old thrill and the old despair of a penny more or less.

The day after his death all the ladies prepared to call at the house and offer condolence and aid, as is our custom. Miss Emily met them at the door, dressed as usual and with no trace of grief on her face. She told them that her father was not dead. She did that for three days, with the ministers calling on her, and the doctors, trying to persuade her to let them dispose of the body. Just as they were about to resort to law and force, she broke down, and they buried her father quickly.

We did not say she was crazy then. We believed she had to do that. We remembered all the young men her father had driven away, and we knew that with nothing left, she would have to cling to that which had robbed her, as people will.

III

She was sick for a long time. When we saw her again, her hair was cut short, making her look like a girl, with a vague resemblance to those angels in colored church windows — sort of tragic and serene.

30   The town had just let the contracts for paving the sidewalks, and in the summer after her father's death they began the work. The construction company came with niggers and mules and machinery, and a foreman named Homer Barron, a Yankee — a big, dark, ready man, with a big voice and eyes lighter than his face. The little boys would follow in groups to hear him cuss the niggers, and the niggers singing in time to the rise and fall of picks. Pretty soon he knew everybody in town. Whenever you heard a lot of laughing anywhere about the square, Homer Barron would be in the center of the group. Presently we began to see him and Miss Emily on Sunday afternoons driving in the yellow-wheeled buggy and the matched team of bays from the livery stable.

At first we were glad that Miss Emily would have an interest, because the ladies all said, "Of course a Grierson would not think seriously of a Northerner, a day laborer." But there were still others, older people, who said that even grief could not cause a real lady to forget *noblesse oblige*[3] — without calling it *noblesse oblige*. They just said, "Poor Emily. Her kinsfolk should come to her." She had some kin in Alabama; but years ago her father had fallen out with them over the estate of old lady Wyatt, the crazy woman, and there was no communication between the two families. They had not even been represented at the funeral.

And as soon as the old people said, "Poor Emily," the whispering began. "Do you suppose it's really so?" they said to one another. "Of course it is. What else could . . ." This behind their hands; rustling of craned silk and satin behind jalousies closed upon the sun of Sunday afternoon as the thin, swift clop-clop-clop of the matched team passed: "Poor Emily."

---

3 the responsibility of privileged, high-born people to be honourable.

She carried her head high enough — even when we believed that she was fallen. It was as if she demanded more than ever the recognition of her dignity as the last Grierson; as if it had wanted that touch of earthiness to reaffirm her imperviousness. Like when she bought the rat poison, the arsenic. That was over a year after they had begun to say "Poor Emily," and while the two female cousins were visiting her.

"I want some poison," she said to the druggist. She was over thirty then, still a slight woman, though thinner than usual, with cold, haughty black eyes in a face the flesh of which was strained across the temples and about the eye-sockets as you imagine a lighthouse-keeper's face ought to look. "I want some poison," she said.

"Yes, Miss Emily. What kind? For rats and such? I'd recom —"

"I want the best you have. I don't care what kind."

The druggist named several. "They'll kill anything up to an elephant. But what you want is —"

"Arsenic," Miss Emily said. "Is that a good one?"

"Is . . . arsenic? Yes, ma'am. But what you want —"

"I want arsenic."

The druggist looked down at her. She looked back at him, erect, her face like a strained flag. "Why, of course," the druggist said. "If that's what you want. But the law requires you to tell what you are going to use it for."

Miss Emily just stared at him, her head tilted back in order to look him eye for eye, until he looked away and went and got the arsenic and wrapped it up. The Negro delivery boy brought her the package; the druggist didn't come back. When she opened the package at home there was written on the box, under the skull and bones: "For rats."

IV

So the next day we all said, "She will kill herself"; and we said it would be the best thing. When she had first begun to be seen with Homer Barron, we had said, "She will marry him." Then we said, "She will persuade him yet," because Homer himself had remarked — he liked men, and it was known that he drank with the younger men in the Elks' Club — that he was not a marrying man. Later we said, "Poor Emily" behind the jalousies as they passed on Sunday afternoon in the glittering buggy, Miss Emily with her head high and Homer Barron with his hat cocked and a cigar in his teeth, reins and whip in a yellow glove.

Then some of the ladies began to say that it was a disgrace to the town and a bad example to the young people. The men did not want to interfere, but at last the ladies forced the Baptist minister — Miss Emily's people were Episcopal[4] — to call upon her. He would never divulge what happened during that interview, but he refused to go back again. The next Sunday they again drove about the streets, and the following day the minister's wife wrote to Miss Emily's relations in Alabama.

So she had blood-kin under her roof again and we sat back to watch developments. At first nothing happened. Then we were sure that they were

---

4 the Anglican Church in the United States.

to be married. We learned that Miss Emily had been to the jeweler's and ordered a man's toilet set in silver, with the letters H.B. on each piece. Two days later we learned that she had bought a complete outfit of men's clothing, including a nightshirt, and we said, "They are married." We were really glad. We were glad because the two female cousins were even more Grierson than Miss Emily had ever been.

So we were not surprised when Homer Barron — the streets had been finished some time since — was gone. We were a little disappointed that there was not a public blowing-off, but we believed that he had gone on to prepare for Miss Emily's coming, or to give her a chance to get rid of the cousins. (By that time it was a cabal, and we were all Miss Emily's allies to help circumvent the cousins.) Sure enough, after another week they departed. And, as we had expected all along, within three days Homer Barron was back in town. A neighbor saw the Negro man admit him at the kitchen door at dusk one evening.

And that was the last we saw of Homer Barron. And of Miss Emily for some time. The Negro man went in and out with the market basket, but the front door remained closed. Now and then we would see her at a window for a moment, as the men did that night when they sprinkled the lime, but for almost six months she did not appear on the streets. Then we knew that this was to be expected too; as if that quality of her father which had thwarted her woman's life so many times had been too virulent and too furious to die.

When we next saw Miss Emily, she had grown fat and her hair was turning gray. During the next few years it grew grayer and grayer until it attained an even pepper-and-salt iron-gray, when it ceased turning. Up to the day of her death at seventy-four it was still that vigorous iron-gray, like the hair of an active man.

From that time on her front door remained closed, save for a period of six or seven years, when she was about forty, during which she gave lessons in china-painting. She fitted up a studio in one of the downstairs rooms, where the daughters and granddaughters of Colonel Sartoris' contemporaries were sent to her with the same regularity and in the same spirit that they were sent to church on Sundays with a twenty-five-cent piece for the collection plate. Meanwhile her taxes had been remitted.

50   Then the newer generation became the backbone and the spirit of the town, and the painting pupils grew up and fell away and did not send their children to her with boxes of color and tedious brushes and pictures cut from the ladies' magazines. The front door closed upon the last one and remained closed for good. When the town got free postal delivery, Miss Emily alone refused to let them fasten the metal numbers above her door and attach a mailbox to it. She would not listen to them.

Daily, monthly, yearly we watched the Negro grow grayer and more stooped, going in and out with the market basket. Each December we sent her a tax notice, which would be returned by the post office a week later, unclaimed. Now and then we would see her in one of the downstairs windows — she had evidently shut up the top floor of the house — like the carven torso of an idol in a niche, looking or not looking at us, we could never tell which. Thus she passed from generation to generation — dear, inescapable, impervious, tranquil, and perverse.

And so she died. Fell ill in the house filled with dust and shadows, with only a doddering Negro man to wait on her. We did not even know she was sick;

we had long since given up trying to get any information from the Negro. He talked to no one, probably not even to her, for his voice had grown harsh and rusty, as if from disuse.

She died in one of the downstairs rooms, in a heavy walnut bed with a curtain, her gray head propped on a pillow yellow and moldy with age and lack of sunlight.

V

The Negro met the first of the ladies at the front door and let them in, with their hushed, sibilant voices and their quick, curious glances, and then he disappeared. He walked right through the house and out the back and was not seen again.

The two female cousins came at once. They held the funeral on the second day, with the town coming to look at Miss Emily beneath a mass of bought flowers, with the crayon face of her father musing profoundly above the bier and the ladies sibilant and macabre; and the very old men — some in their brushed Confederate uniforms — on the porch and the lawn, talking of Miss Emily as if she had been a contemporary of theirs, believing that they had danced with her and courted her perhaps, confusing time with its mathematical progression, as the old do, to whom all the past is not a diminishing road but, instead, a huge meadow which no winter ever quite touches, divided from them now by the narrow bottle-neck of the most recent decade of years.

Already we knew that there was one room in that region above stairs which no one had seen in forty years, and which would have to be forced. They waited until Miss Emily was decently in the ground before they opened it.

The violence of breaking down the door seemed to fill this room with pervading dust. A thin, acrid pall as of the tomb seemed to lie everywhere upon this room decked and furnished as for a bridal: upon the valance curtains of faded rose color, upon the rose-shaded lights, upon the dressing table, upon the delicate array of crystal and the man's toilet things backed with tarnished silver, silver so tarnished that the monogram was obscured. Among them lay a collar and tie, as if they had just been removed, which, lifted, left upon the surface a pale crescent in the dust. Upon a chair hung the suit, carefully folded; beneath it the two mute shoes and the discarded socks.

The man himself lay in the bed.

For a long while we just stood there, looking down at the profound and fleshless grin. The body had apparently once lain in the attitude of an embrace, but now the long sleep that outlasts love, that conquers even the grimace of love, had cuckolded him. What was left of him, rotted beneath what was left of the nightshirt, had become inextricable from the bed in which he lay; and upon him and upon the pillow beside him lay that even coating of the patient and biding dust.

Then we noticed that in the second pillow was the indentation of a head. One of us lifted something from it, and leaning forward, that faint and invisible dust dry and acrid in the nostrils, we saw a long strand of iron-gray hair.

(1930)

Ernest Hemingway   (1899–1961)

Like Stephen Crane, whose short stories he admired, Ernest Hemingway, a native of Oak Park, Illinois, began his writing career as a newspaper correspondent. The short sentences, crisp description of settings and actions, and relative lack of authorial comment that are distinguishing features of his mature style no doubt reflect his background in journalism. Hemingway's experiences in Italy during World War I, where he was injured while serving as an ambulance driver, and in Paris during the 1920s, where he was a member of the so-called Lost Generation (individuals who no longer believed in absolute moral or religious values), contributed to the development of his major theme: the need of the individual to live with control and dignity in a violent world devoid of spiritual meaning. Most fully developed in *The Sun Also Rises* (1926) and *A Farewell to Arms* (1929), two of his finest novels, these ideas are also expressed in "A Clean, Well-Lighted Place." The prose, which at first appears simply reportorial, implicitly develops the themes and symbols of the story.

A CLEAN, WELL-LIGHTED PLACE

It was late and every one had left the café except an old man who sat in the shadow the leaves of the tree made against the electric light. In the day time the street was dusty, but at night the dew settled the dust and the old man liked to sit late because he was deaf and now at night it was quiet and he felt the difference. The two waiters inside the café knew that the old man was a little drunk, and while he was a good client they knew that if he became too drunk he would leave without paying, so they kept watch on him.

"Last week he tried to commit suicide," one waiter said.

"Why?"

"He was in despair."

5   "What about?"

"Nothing."

"How do you know it was nothing?"

"He has plenty of money."

They sat together at a table that was close against the wall near the door of the café and looked at the terrace where the tables were all empty except where the old man sat in the shadow of the leaves of the tree that moved slightly in the wind. A girl and a soldier went by in the street. The street light shone on the brass number on his collar. The girl wore no head covering and hurried beside him.

10   "The guard will pick him up," one waiter said.

"What does it matter if he gets what he's after?"

"He had better get off the street now. The guard will get him. They went by five minutes ago."

The old man sitting in the shadow rapped on his saucer with his glass. The younger waiter went over to him.

"What do you want?"

15   The old man looked at him. "Another brandy," he said.

"You'll be drunk," the waiter said. The old man looked at him. The waiter went away.

"He'll stay all night," he said to his colleague. "I'm sleepy now. I never get into bed before three o'clock. He should have killed himself last week."

The waiter took the brandy bottle and another saucer from the counter inside the café and marched out to the old man's table. He put down the saucer and poured the glass full of brandy.

"You should have killed yourself last week," he said to the deaf man. The old man motioned with his finger. "A little more," he said. The waiter poured on into the glass so that the brandy slopped over and ran down the stem into the top saucer of the pile. "Thank you," the old man said. The waiter took the bottle back inside the café. He sat down at the table with his colleague again.

20   "He's drunk now," he said.

"He's drunk every night."

"What did he want to kill himself for?"

"How should I know."

"How did he do it?"

25   "He hung himself with a rope."

"Who cut him down?"

"His niece."

"Why did she do it?"

"Fear for his soul."

30   "How much money has he got?"

"He's got plenty."

"He must be eighty years old."

"Anyway I should say he was eighty."

"I wish he would go home. I never get to bed before three o'clock. What kind of hour is that to go to bed?"

35   "He stays up because he likes it."

"He's lonely. I'm not lonely. I have a wife waiting in bed for me."

"He had a wife once too."

"A wife would be no good to him now."

"You can't tell. He might be better with a wife."

40   "His niece looks after him. You said she cut him down."

"I know."

"I wouldn't want to be that old. An old man is a nasty thing."

"Not always. This old man is clean. He drinks without spilling. Even now, drunk. Look at him."

"I don't want to look at him. I wish he would go home. He has no regard for those who must work."

45   The old man looked from his glass across the square, then over at the waiters.

"Another brandy," he said, pointing to his glass. The waiter who was in a hurry came over.

"Finished," he said, speaking with that omission of syntax stupid people employ when talking to drunken people or foreigners. "No more tonight. Close now."

"Another," said the old man.

"No. Finished." The waiter wiped the edge of the table with a towel and shook his head.

The old man stood up, slowly counted the saucers, took a leather coin purse from his pocket and paid for the drinks, leaving half a peseta tip.

The waiter watched him go down the street, a very old man walking unsteadily but with dignity.

"Why didn't you let him stay and drink?" the unhurried waiter asked. They were putting up the shutters. "It is not half-past two."

"I want to go home to bed."

"What is an hour?"

"More to me than to him."

"An hour is the same."

"You talk like an old man yourself. He can buy a bottle and drink at home."

"It's not the same."

"No, it is not," agreed the waiter with a wife. He did not wish to be unjust. He was only in a hurry.

"And you? You have no fear of going home before your usual hour?"

"Are you trying to insult me?"

"No, hombre, only to make a joke."

"No," the waiter who was in a hurry said, rising from pulling down the metal shutters. "I have confidence. I am all confidence."

"You have youth, confidence, and a job," the older waiter said. "You have everything."

"And what do you lack?"

"Everything but work."

"You have everything I have."

"No. I have never had confidence and I am not young."

"Come on. Stop talking nonsense and lock up."

"I am with those who like to stay late at the café," the older waiter said. "With all those who do not want to go to bed. With all those who need a light for the night."

"I want to go home and into bed."

"We are of two different kinds," the older waiter said. He was now dressed to go home. "It is not only a question of youth and confidence although those things are very beautiful. Each night I am reluctant to close up because there may be some one who needs the café."

"Hombre, there are bodegas open all night long."

"You do not understand. This is a clean and pleasant café. It is well lighted. The light is very good and also, now, there are shadows of the leaves."

"Good night," said the younger waiter.

"Good night," the other said. Turning off the electric light he continued the conversation with himself. It is the light of course but it is necessary that the place be clean and pleasant. You do not want music. Certainly you do not want music. Nor can you stand before a bar with dignity although that is all that is provided for these hours. What did he fear? It was not fear or dread. It was a nothing that he knew too well. It was all a nothing and a man was nothing too. It was only that and light was all it needed and a certain cleanness and order. Some lived in it and never felt it but he knew it all was nada y pues nada y nada y pues nada.[1] Our nada who art in nada, nada be thy name thy kingdom nada thy will be nada in nada as it is in nada. Give us this nada our daily nada and nada us our nada as we nada our nadas and nada us not into nada but deliver us from nada; pues nada. Hail nothing full of nothing, nothing is with thee. He smiled and stood before a bar with a shining steam pressure coffee machine.

"What's yours?" asked the barman.

"Nada."

"Otro loco mas,"[2] said the barman and turned away.

80   "A little cup," said the waiter.

The barman poured it for him.

"The light is very bright and pleasant but the bar is unpolished," the waiter said.

The barman looked at him but did not answer. It was too late at night for conversation.

"You want another copita?"[3]

85   "No, thank you," said the waiter and went out. He disliked bars and bodegas. A clean, well-lighted café was a very different thing. Now, without thinking further, he would go home to his room. He would lie in the bed and finally, with daylight, he would go to sleep. After all, he said to himself, it is probably only insomnia. Many must have it.

(1933)

---

1 nothing, and therefore nothing. 2 another crazy one. 3 small cup.

Sinclair Ross (1908–1996)

Born on a farm near Prince Albert, Saskatchewan, Sinclair Ross, in his novel *As For Me and My House* (1941) and his first collection of short stories, *The Lamp at Noon* (1968), portrays life on the Canadian prairies during the "Dust Bowl" era of the 1930s. In addition to depicting the hardship and isolation, courage, and loneliness of his characters, Ross emphasizes the power of the land, which, as Margaret Laurence noted, appears "almost as a chief protagonist." In "The Lamp at Noon," the contrasting reactions of a husband and wife to a three-day dust storm that all but destroys their farm are presented in part by Ross's careful selection of physical symbols: the storm, the barren landscape, the barn to which the husband retreats, and the kitchen feebly illuminated by the lamp.

THE LAMP AT NOON

A little before noon she lit the lamp. Demented wind fled keening past the house: a wail through the eaves that died every minute or two. Three days now without respite it had held. The dust was thickening to an impenetrable fog.

She lit the lamp, then for a long time stood at the window motionless. In dim, fitful outline the stable and oat granary still were visible; beyond, obscuring fields and landmarks, the lower of dust clouds made the farmyard seem an isolated acre, poised aloft above a sombre void. At each blast of wind it shook, as if to topple and spin hurtling with the dust-reel into space.

From the window she went to the door, opening it a little, and peering toward the stable again. He was not coming yet. As she watched there was a sudden rift overhead, and for a moment through the tattered clouds the sun raced like a wizened orange. It shed a soft, diffused light, dim and yellow as if it were the light from the lamp reaching out through the open door.

She closed the door, and going to the stove tried the potatoes with a fork. Her eyes all the while were fixed and wide with a curious immobility. It was the window. Standing at it, she had let her forehead press against the pane until the eyes were strained apart and rigid. Wide like that they had looked out to the deepening ruin of the storm. Now she could not close them.

5 The baby started to cry. He was lying in a homemade crib over which she had arranged a tent of muslin. Careful not to disturb the folds of it, she knelt and tried to still him, whispering huskily in a singsong voice that he must hush and go to sleep again. She would have liked to rock him, to feel the comfort of his little body in her arms, but a fear had obsessed her that in the dust-filled air he might contract pneumonia. There was dust sifting everywhere. Her own throat was parched with it. The table had been set less than ten minutes, and already a film was gathering on the dishes. The little cry continued, and with wincing, frightened lips she glanced around as if to find a corner where the air was less oppressive. But while the lips winced the eyes maintained their wide, immobile stare. "Sleep," she whispered again. "It's too soon for you to be hungry. Daddy's coming for his dinner."

He seemed a long time. Even the clock, still a few minutes off noon, could not dispel a foreboding sense that he was longer than he should be. She went to the door again — and then recoiled slowly to stand white and breathless in the middle of the room. She mustn't. He would only despise her if she ran to the stable looking for him. There was too much grim endurance in his nature ever to let him understand the fear and weakness of a woman. She must stay quiet and wait. Nothing was wrong. At noon he would come — and perhaps after dinner stay with her awhile.

Yesterday, and again at breakfast this morning, they had quarrelled bitterly. She wanted him now, the assurance of his strength and nearness, but he would stand aloof, wary, remembering the words she had flung at him in her anger, unable to understand it was only the dust and wind that had driven her.

Tense, she fixed her eyes upon the clock, listening. There were two winds: the wind in flight, and the wind that pursued. The one sought refuge in the eaves, whimpering, in fear; the other assailed it there, and shook the eaves apart to make it flee again. Once as she listened this first wind sprang inside the room, distraught like a bird that has felt the graze of talons on its wing; while furious the other wind shook the walls, and thudded tumbleweeds against the window till its quarry glanced away again in fright. But only to return — to return and quake among the feeble eaves, as if in all this dust-mad wilderness it knew no other sanctuary.

Then Paul came. At his step she hurried to the stove, intent upon the pots and frying pan. "The worst wind yet," he ventured, hanging up his cap and smock. "I had to light the lantern in the tool shed, too."

10   They looked at each other, then away. She wanted to go to him, to feel his arms supporting her, to cry a little just that he might soothe her, but because his presence made the menace of the wind seem less, she gripped herself and thought, "I'm in the right. I won't give in. For his sake, too, I won't."

He washed, hurriedly, so that a few dark welts of dust remained to indent upon his face a haggard strength. It was all she could see as she wiped the dishes and set the food before him: the strength, the grimness, the young Paul growing old and hard, buckled against a desert even grimmer than his will. "Hungry?" she asked, touched to a twinge of pity she had not intended. "There's dust in everything. It keeps coming faster than I can clean it up."

He nodded. "Tonight, though, you'll see it go down. This is the third day."

She looked at him in silence a moment, and then as if to herself muttered broodingly, "Until the next time. Until it starts again."

There was a dark resentment in her voice now that boded another quarrel. He waited, his eyes on her dubiously as she mashed a potato with her fork. The lamp between them threw strong lights and shadows on their faces. Dust and drought, earth that betrayed alike his labour and his faith, to him the struggle had given sternness, an impassive courage. Beneath the whip of sand his youth had been effaced. Youth, zest, exuberance — there remained only a harsh and clenched virility that yet became him, that seemed at the cost of more engaging qualities to be fulfilment of his inmost and essential nature. Whereas to her the same debts and poverty had brought a plaintive indignation, a nervous dread of what was still to come. The eyes were hollowed, the lips pinched dry and colourless. It was the face of a woman that had aged without maturing, that had loved the little vanities of life, and lost them wistfully.

15 "I'm afraid, Paul," she said suddenly. "I can't stand it any longer. He cries all the time. You will go, Paul — say you will. We aren't living here — not really living   "

The pleading in her voice now, after its shrill bitterness yesterday, made him think that this was only another way to persuade him. He answered evenly, "I told you this morning, Ellen; we keep on right where we are. At least I do. It's yourself you're thinking about, not the baby."

This morning such an accusation would have stung her to rage; now, her voice swift and panting, she pressed on, "Listen, Paul — I'm thinking of all of us — you, too. Look at the sky — what's happening. Are you blind? Thistles and tumbleweeds — it's a desert. You won't have a straw this fall. You won't be able to feed a cow or a chicken. Please, Paul, say we'll go away —"

"Go where?" His voice as he answered was still remote and even, inflexibly in unison with the narrowed eyes and the great hunch of muscle-knotted shoulder. "Even as a desert it's better than sweeping out your father's store and running his errands. That's all I've got ahead of me if I do what you want."

"And here —" she faltered. "What's ahead of you here? At least we'll get enough to eat and wear when you're sweeping out his store. Look at it — look at it, you fool. Desert — the lamp lit at noon —"

20 "You'll see it come back. There's good wheat in it yet."

"But in the meantime — year after year — can't you understand, Paul? We'll never get them back —"

He put down his knife and fork and leaned toward her across the table. "I can't go, Ellen. Living off your people — charity — stop and think of it. This is where I belong. I can't do anything else."

"Charity!" she repeated him, letting her voice rise in derision. "And this — you call this independence! Borrowed money you can't even pay the interest on, seed from the government — grocery bills — doctor bills —"

"We'll have crops again," he persisted. "Good crops — the land will come back. It's worth waiting for."

25 "And while we're waiting, Paul!" It was not anger now, but a kind of sob. "Think of me — and him. It's not fair. We have our lives, too, to live."

"And you think that going home to your family — taking your husband with you —"

"I don't care — anything would be better than this. Look at the air he's breathing. He cries all the time. For his sake, Paul. What's ahead of him here, even if you do get crops?"

He clenched his lips a minute, then, with his eyes hard and contemptuous, struck back, "As much as in town, growing up a pauper. You're the one who wants to go, it's not for his sake. You think that in town you'd have a better time — not so much work — more clothes —"

"Maybe —" She dropped her head defencelessly. "I'm young still. I like pretty things."

30 There was silence now — a deep fastness of it enclosed by rushing wind and creaking walls. It seemed the yellow lamplight cast a hush upon them. Through the haze of dusty air the walls receded, dimmed, and came again. At last she

raised her head and said listlessly, "Go on — your dinner's getting cold. Don't sit and stare at me. I've said it all."

The spent quietness in her voice was even harder to endure than her anger. It reproached him, against his will insisted that he see and understand her lot. To justify himself he tried, "I was a poor man when you married me. You said you didn't mind. Farming's never been easy, and never will be."

"I wouldn't mind the work or the skimping if there was something to look forward to. It's the hopelessness — going on — watching the land blow away."

"The land's all right," he repeated. "The dry years won't last forever."

"But it's not just dry years, Paul!" The little sob in her voice gave way suddenly to a ring of exasperation. "Will you never see? It's the land itself — the soil. You've plowed and harrowed it until there's not a root or fibre left to hold it down. That's why the soil drifts — that's why in a year or two there'll be nothing left but the bare clay. If in the first place you farmers had taken care of your land — if you hadn't been so greedy for wheat every year —"

35 She had taught school before she married him, and of late in her anger there had been a kind of disdain, an attitude almost of condescension, as if she no longer looked upon the farmers as her equals. He sat still, his eyes fixed on the yellow lamp flame, and seeming to know how her words had hurt him, she went on softly, "I want to help you, Paul. That's why I won't sit quiet while you go on wasting your life. You're only thirty — you owe it to yourself as well as me."

He sat staring at the lamp without answering, his mouth sullen. It seemed indifference now, as if he were ignoring her, and stung to anger again she cried, "Do you ever think what my life is? Two rooms to live in — once a month to town, and nothing to spend when I get there. I'm still young — I wasn't brought up this way."

"You're a farmer's wife now. It doesn't matter what you used to be, or how you were brought up. You get enough to eat and wear. Just now that's all I can do. I'm not to blame that we've been dried out five years."

"Enough to eat!" she laughed back shrilly. "Enough salt pork — enough potatoes and eggs. And look —" Springing to the middle of the room she thrust out a foot for him to see the scuffed old slipper. "When they're completely gone I suppose you'll tell me I can go barefoot — that I'm a farmer's wife — that it's not your fault we're dried out —"

"And what about these?" He pushed his chair away from the table now to let her see what he was wearing. "Cowhide — hard as boards — but my feet are so calloused I don't feel them any more."

40 Then he stood up, ashamed of having tried to match her hardships with his own. But frightened now as he reached for his smock she pressed close to him. "Don't go yet. I brood and worry when I'm left alone. Please, Paul — you can't work on the land anyway."

"And keep on like this? You start before I'm through the door. Week in and week out — I've troubles enough of my own."

"Paul — please stay —" The eyes were glazed now, distended a little as if with the intensity of her dread and pleading. "We won't quarrel any more. Hear it! I can't work — I just stand still and listen —"

The eyes frightened him, but responding to a kind of instinct that he must withstand her, that it was his self-respect and manhood against the fretful weakness of a woman, he answered unfeelingly, "In here safe and quiet — you don't know how well off you are. If you were out in it — fighting it — swallowing it —"

"Sometimes, Paul, I wish I was. I'm so caged — if I could only break away and run. See I stand like this all day. I can't relax. My throat's so tight it aches —"

With a jerk he freed his smock from her clutch. "If I stay we'll only keep on all afternoon. Wait till tomorrow — we'll talk things over when the wind goes down."

Then without meeting her eyes again he swung outside, and doubled low against the buffets of the wind, fought his way slowly toward the stable. There was a deep hollow calm within, a vast darkness engulfed beneath the tides of moaning wind. He stood breathless a moment, hushed almost to a stupor by the sudden extinction of the storm and the stillness that enfolded him. It was a long, far-reaching stillness. The first dim stalls and rafters led the way into cavern-like obscurity, into vaults and recesses that extended far beyond the stable walls. Nor in these first quiet moments did he forbid the illusion, the sense of release from a harsh, familiar world into one of peace and darkness. The contentious mood that his stand against Ellen had roused him to, his tenacity and clenched despair before the ravages of wind, it was ebbing now, losing itself in the cover of darkness. Ellen and the wheat seemed remote, unimportant. At a whinny from the bay mare, Bess, he went forward and into her stall. She seemed grateful for his presence, and thrust her nose deep between his arm and body. They stood a long time motionless, comforting and assuring each other.

For soon again the first deep sense of quiet and peace was shrunken to the battered shelter of the stable. Instead of release or escape from the assaulting wind, the walls were but a feeble stand against it. They creaked and sawed as if the fingers of a giant hand were tightening to collapse them; the empty loft sustained a pipelike cry that rose and fell but never ended. He saw the dust-black sky again, and his fields blown smooth with drifted soil.

But always, even while listening to the storm outside, he could feel the tense and apprehensive stillness of the stable. There was not a hoof that clumped or shifted, not a rub of halter against manger. And yet, though it had been a strange stable, he would have known, despite the darkness, that every stall was filled. They, too, were all listening.

From Bess he went to the big grey gelding, Prince. Prince was twenty years old, with rib-grooved sides, and high, protruding hipbones. Paul ran his hand over the ribs, and felt a sudden shame, a sting of fear that Ellen might be right in what she said. For wasn't it true — nine years a farmer now on his own land, and still he couldn't even feed his horses? What, then, could he hope to do for his wife and son?

There was much he planned. And so vivid was the future of his planning, so real and constant, that often the actual present was but half felt, but half endured. Its difficulties were lessened by a confidence in what lay beyond them. A new house — land for the boy — land and still more land — or education, whatever he might want.

But all the time was he only a blind and stubborn fool? Was Ellen right? Was he trampling on her life, and throwing away his own? The five years since he married her, were they to go on repeating themselves, five, ten, twenty, until all the brave future he looked forward to was but a stark and futile past?

She looked forward to no future. She had no faith or dream with which to make the dust and poverty less real. He understood suddenly. He saw her face again as only a few minutes ago it had begged him not to leave her. The darkness round him now was as a slate on which her lonely terror limned itself. He went from Prince to the other horses, combing their manes and forelocks with his fingers, but always it was her face before him, its staring eyes and twisted suffering. "See Paul — I stand like this all day. I just stand still — My throat's so tight it aches —"

And always the wind, the creak of walls, the wild lipless wailing through the loft. Until at last as he stood there, staring into the livid face before him, it seemed that this scream of wind was a cry from her parched and frantic lips. He knew it couldn't be, he knew that she was safe within the house, but still the wind persisted as a woman's cry. The cry of a woman with eyes like those that watched him through the dark. Eyes that were mad now — lips that even as they cried still pleaded, "See, Paul — I stand like this all day. I just stand still — so caged! If I could only run!"

He saw her running, pulled and driven headlong by the wind, but when at last he returned to the house, compelled by his anxiety, she was walking quietly back and forth with the baby in her arms. Careful, despite his concern, not to reveal a fear or weakness that she might think capitulation to her wishes, he watched a moment through the window, and then went off to the tool shed to mend harness. All afternoon he stitched and riveted. It was easier with the lantern lit and his hands occupied. There was a wind whining high past the tool shed too, but it was only wind. He remembered the arguments with which Ellen had tried to persuade him away from the farm, and one by one he defeated them. There would be rain again — next year or the next. Maybe in his ignorance he had farmed his land the wrong way, seeding wheat every year, working the soil till it was lifeless dust — but he would do better now. He would plant clover and alfalfa, breed cattle, acre by acre and year by year restore to his land its fibre and fertility. That was something to work for, a way to prove himself. It was ruthless wind, blackening the sky with his earth, but it was not his master. Out of his land it had made a wilderness. He now, out of the wilderness, would make a farm and home again.

Tonight he must talk with Ellen. Patiently, when the wind was down, and they were both quiet again. It was she who had told him to grow fibrous crops, who had called him an ignorant fool because he kept on with summer fallow and wheat. Now she might be gratified to find him acknowledging her wisdom. Perhaps she would begin to feel the power and steadfastness of the land, to take a pride in it, to understand that he was not a fool, but working for her future and their son's.

And already the wind was slackening. At four o'clock he could sense a lull. At five, straining his eyes from the tool shed doorway, he could make out a neighbour's buildings half a mile away. It was over — three days of blight and havoc like a scourge — three days so bitter and so long that for a moment he stood still, unseeing, his senses idle with a numbness of relief.

But only for a moment. Suddenly he emerged from the numbness; suddenly the fields before him struck his eyes to comprehension. They lay black, naked. Beaten and mounded smooth with dust as if a sea in gentle swell had turned to stone. And though he had tried to prepare himself for such a scene, though he had known since yesterday that not a blade would last the storm, still now, before the utter waste confronting him, he sickened and stood cold. Suddenly like the fields he was naked. Everything that had sheathed him a little from the realities of existence: vision and purpose, faith in the land, in the future, in himself—it was all rent now, stripped away. "Desert," he heard her voice begin to sob. "Desert, you fool — the lamp lit at noon!"

In the stable again, measuring out their feed to the horses, he wondered what he would say to her tonight. For so deep were his instincts of loyalty to the land that still, even with the images of his betrayal stark upon his mind, his concern was how to withstand her, how to go on again and justify himself. It had not occurred to him yet that he might or should abandon the land. He had lived with it too long. Rather was his impulse still to defend it — as a man defends against the scorn of strangers even his most worthless kin.

He fed his horses, then waited. She too would be waiting, ready to cry at him, "Look now — that crop that was to feed and clothe us! And you'll still keep on! You'll still say 'Next year — there'll be rain next year'!"

But she was gone when he reached the house. The door was open, the lamp blown out, the crib empty. The dishes from their meal at noon were still on the table. She had perhaps begun to sweep, for the broom was lying in the middle of the floor. He tried to call, but a terror clamped upon his throat. In the wan, returning light it seemed that even the deserted kitchen was straining to whisper what it had seen. The tatters of the storm still whimpered through the eaves, and in their moaning told the desolation of the miles they had traversed. On tiptoe at last he crossed to the adjoining room; then at the threshold, without even a glance inside to satisfy himself that she was really gone, he wheeled again and plunged outside.

He ran a long time — distraught and headlong as a few hours ago he had seemed to watch her run — around the farmyard, a little distance into the pasture, back again blindly to the house to see whether she had returned — and then at a stumble down the road for help.

They joined him in the search, rode away for others, spread calling across the fields in the direction she might have been carried by the wind — but nearly two hours later it was himself who came upon her. Crouched down against a drift of sand as if for shelter, her hair in matted strands around her neck and face, the child clasped tightly in her arms.

The child was quite cold. It had been her arms, perhaps, too frantic to protect him, or the smother of dust upon his throat and lungs. "Hold him," she said as he knelt beside her. "So — with his face away from the wind. Hold him until I tidy my hair."

Her eyes were still wide in an immobile stare, but with her lips she smiled at him. For a long time he knelt transfixed, trying to speak to her, touching fearfully with his fingertips the dustgrimed cheeks and eyelids of the child. At last she said, "I'll take him again. Such clumsy hands — you don't know how to hold a baby yet. See how his head falls forward on your arm."

65   Yet it all seemed familiar — a confirmation of what he had known since noon. He gave her the child, then, gathering them up in his arms, struggled to his feet, and turned toward home.

It was evening now. Across the fields a few spent clouds of dust still shook and fled. Beyond, as if through smoke, the sunset smouldered like a distant fire.

He walked with a long dull stride, his eyes before him, heedless of her weight. Once he glanced down and with her eyes she still was smiling. "Such strong arms, Paul — and I was so tired just carrying him. . . ."

He tried to answer, but it seemed that now the dusk was drawn apart in breathless waiting, a finger on its lips until they passed. "You were right, Paul. . . ." Her voice came whispering, as if she too could feel the hush. "You said tonight we'd see the storm go down. So still now, and a red sky — it means tomorrow will be fine."

(1938)

Eudora Welty (1909–2001)

Like fellow Mississippian William Faulkner, whose works she admired, Eudora Welty set most of her short stories in and around the city where she was born and lived most of her life, Jackson. Family and a sense of place are most important for her characters, for a place of one's own provides "a base of reference," and enables "individuals to put out roots." "Why I Live at the P.O.," which takes place on July 4, American Independence Day, traditionally a time of family reunions, focusses on the developing hostility the narrator feels toward her family and her own declaration of independence from them. Ironically, in its portrayal of the disintegrating interrelationships, the story provides a negative example of Welty's belief that "communication and hope of it are conditions of life itself."

WHY I LIVE AT THE P.O.

I was getting along fine with Mama, Papa-Daddy and Uncle Rondo until my sister Stella-Rondo just separated from her husband and came back home again. Mr. Whitaker! Of course I went with Mr. Whitaker first, when he first appeared here in China Grove,[1] taking "Pose Yourself" photos, and Stella-Rondo broke us up. Told him I was one-sided. Bigger on one side than the other, which is a deliberate, calculated falsehood: I'm the same. Stella-Rondo is exactly twelve months to the day younger than I am and for that reason she's spoiled.

She's always had anything in the world she wanted and then she'd throw it away. Papa-Daddy gave her this gorgeous Add-a-Pearl necklace when she was eight years old and she threw it away playing baseball when she was nine, with only two pearls.

So as soon as she got married and moved away from home the first thing she did was separate! From Mr. Whitaker! This photographer with the popeyes she said she trusted. Came home from one of those towns up in Illinois and to our complete surprise brought this child of two.

Mama said she like to made her drop dead for a second. "Here you had this marvelous blonde child and never so much as wrote your mother a word about it," says Mama. "I'm thoroughly ashamed of you." But of course she wasn't.

Stella-Rondo just calmly takes off this *hat*, I wish you could see it. She says, "Why, Mama, Shirley-T.'s adopted, I can prove it."

"How?" says Mama, but all I says was, "H'm!" There I was over the hot stove, trying to stretch two chickens over five people and a completely unexpected child into the bargain, without one moment's notice.

"What do you mean—'H'm!'?" says Stella-Rondo, and Mama says, "I heard that, Sister."

I said that oh, I didn't mean a thing, only that whoever Shirley-T. was, she was the spit-image of Papa-Daddy if he'd cut off his beard, which of course he'd never do in the world. Papa-Daddy's Mama's papa and sulks.

---

1 town in central Mississippi.

Stella-Rondo got furious! She said, "Sister, I don't need to tell you you got a lot of nerve and always did have and I'll thank you to make no future reference to my adopted child whatsoever."

10   "Very well," I said. "Very well, very well. Of course I noticed at once she looks like Mr. Whitaker's side too. That frown. She looks like a cross between Mr. Whitaker and Papa-Daddy."

"Well, all I can say is she isn't."

"She looks exactly like Shirley Temple[2] to me," says Mama, but Shirley-T. just ran away from her.

So the first thing Stella-Rondo did at the table was turn Papa-Daddy against me.

"Papa-Daddy," she says. He was trying to cut up his meat. "Papa-Daddy!" I was taken completely by surprise. Papa-Daddy is about a million years old and's got this long-long beard. "Papa-Daddy, Sister says she fails to understand why you don't cut off your beard."

15   So Papa-Daddy l-a-y-s down his knife and fork! He's real rich. Mama says he is, he says he isn't. So he says, "Have I heard correctly? You don't understand why I don't cut off my beard?"

"Why," I says, "Papa-Daddy, of course I understand, I did not say any such of a thing, the idea!"

He says, "Hussy!"

I says, "Papa-Daddy, you know I wouldn't any more want you to cut off your beard than the man in the moon. It was the farthest thing from my mind! Stella-Rondo sat there and made that up while she was eating breast of chicken."

But he says, "So the postmistress fails to understand why I don't cut off my beard. Which job I got you through my influence with the government. 'Bird's nest'— is that what you call it?"

20   Not that it isn't the next to smallest P.O. in the entire state of Mississippi.

I says, "Oh, Papa-Daddy," I says, "I didn't say any such of a thing, I never dreamed it was a bird's nest, I have always been grateful though this is the next to smallest P.O. in the state of Mississippi, and I do not enjoy being referred to as a hussy by my own grandfather."

But Stella-Rondo says, "Yes, you did say it too. Anybody in the world could of heard you, that had ears."

"Stop right there," says Mama, looking at me.

So I pulled my napkin straight back through the napkin ring and left the table.

25   As soon as I was out of the room Mama says, "Call her back, or she'll starve to death," but Papa-Daddy says, "This is the beard I started growing on the Coast when I was fifteen years old." He would of gone on till nightfall if Shirley-T. hadn't lost the Milky Way she ate in Cairo.[3]

So Papa-Daddy says, "I am going out and lie in the hammock, and you can all sit here and remember my words: I'll never cut off my beard as long as I live, even one inch, and I don't appreciate it in you at all." Passed right by me in the hall and went straight out and got in the hammock.

2 American child movie star of the 1930s. 3 town in southern Illinois.

It would be a holiday. I wasn't five minutes before Uncle Rondo suddenly appeared in the hall in one of Stella-Rondo's flesh-colored kimonos, all cut on the bias, like something Mr. Whitaker probably thought was gorgeous.

"Uncle Rondo!" I says. "I didn't know who that was! Where are you going?"

"Sister," he says, "get out of my way, I'm poisoned."

30   "If you're poisoned stay away from Papa-Daddy," I says. "Keep out of the hammock. Papa-Daddy will certainly beat you on the head if you come within forty miles of him. He thinks I deliberately said he ought to cut off his beard after he got me the P.O., and I've told him and told him and told him, and he acts like he just don't hear me. Papa-Daddy must of gone stone deaf."

"He picked a fine day to do it then," says Uncle Rondo, and before you could say "Jack Robinson" flew out in the yard.

What he'd really done, he'd drunk another bottle of that prescription. He does it every single Fourth of July as sure as shooting, and it's horribly expensive. Then he falls over in the hammock and snores. So he insisted on zigzagging right on out to the hammock, looking like a half-wit.

Papa-Daddy woke up with this horrible yell and right there without moving an inch he tried to turn Uncle Rondo against me. I heard every word he said. Oh, he told Uncle Rondo I didn't learn to read till I was eight years old and he didn't see how in the world I ever got the mail put up at the P.O., much less read it all, and he said if Uncle Rondo could only fathom the lengths he had gone to to get me that job! And he said on the other hand he thought Stella-Rondo had a brilliant mind and deserved credit for getting out of town. All the time he was just lying there swinging as pretty as you please and looping out his beard, and poor Uncle Rondo was *pleading* with him to slow down the hammock, it was making him as dizzy as a witch to watch it. But that's what Papa-Daddy likes about a hammock. So Uncle Rondo was too dizzy to get turned against me for the time being. He's Mama's only brother and is a good case of a one-track mind. Ask anybody. A certified pharmacist.

Just then I heard Stella-Rondo raising the upstairs window. While she was married she got this peculiar idea that it's cooler with the windows shut and locked. So she has to raise the window before she can make a soul hear her outdoors.

35   So she raises the window and says, "*Oh!*" You would have thought she was mortally wounded.

Uncle Rondo and Papa-Daddy didn't even look up, but kept right on with what they were doing. I had to laugh.

I flew up the stairs and threw the door open! I says, "What in the wide world's the matter, Stella-Rondo? You mortally wounded?"

"No," she says, "I am not mortally wounded but I wish you would do me the favor of looking out that window there and telling me what you see."

So I shade my eyes and look out the window.

40   "I see the front yard," I says.

"Don't you see any human beings?" she says.

"I see Uncle Rondo trying to run Papa-Daddy out of the hammock," I says. "Nothing more. Naturally, it's so suffocating-hot in the house, with all the windows shut and locked, everybody who cares to stay in their right mind will have to go out and get in the hammock before the Fourth of July is over."

"Don't you notice anything different about Uncle Rondo?" asks Stella-Rondo.

"Why, no, except he's got on some terrible-looking flesh-colored contraption I wouldn't be found dead in, is all I can see," I says.

45 "Never mind, you won't be found dead in it, because it happens to be part of my trousseau, and Mr. Whitaker took several dozen photographs of me in it," says Stella-Rondo. "What on earth could Uncle Rondo *mean* by wearing part of my trousseau out in the broad open daylight without saying so much as 'Kiss my foot,' *knowing* I only got home this morning after my separation and hung my negligee up on the bathroom door, just as nervous as I could be?"

"I'm sure I don't know, and what do you expect me to do about it?" I says. "Jump out the window?"

"No, I expect nothing of the kind. I simply declare that Uncle Rondo looks like a fool in it, that's all," she says. "It makes me sick to my stomach."

"Well, he looks as good as he can," I says. "As good as anybody in reason could." I stood up for Uncle Rondo, please remember. And I said to Stella-Rondo, "I think I would do well not to criticize so freely if I were you and came home with a two-year-old child I had never said a word about, and no explanation whatever about my separation."

"I asked you the instant I entered this house not to refer one more time to my adopted child, and you gave me your word of honor you would not," was all Stella-Rondo would say, and started pulling out every one of her eyebrows with some cheap Kress tweezers.

50 So I merely slammed the door behind me and went down and made some green-tomato pickle. Somebody had to do it. Of course Mama had turned both the niggers loose; she always said no earthly power could hold one anyway on the Fourth of July, so she wouldn't even try. It turned out that Jaypan fell in the lake and came within a very narrow limit of drowning.

So Mama trots in. Lifts up the lid and says, "H'm! Not very good for your Uncle Rondo in his precarious condition, I must say. Or poor little adopted Shirley-T. Shame on you!"

That made me tired. I says, "Well, Stella-Rondo had better thank her lucky stars it was her instead of me came trotting in with that very peculiar-looking child. Now if it had been me that trotted in from Illinois and brought a peculiar-looking child of two, I shudder to think of the reception I'd of got, much less controlled the diet of an entire family."

"But you must remember, Sister, that you were never married to Mr. Whitaker in the first place and didn't go up to Illinois to live," says Mama, shaking a spoon in my face. "If you had I would of been just as overjoyed to see you and your little adopted girl as I was to see Stella-Rondo, when you wound up with your separation and came on back home."

"You would not," I says.

55 "Don't contradict me, I would," says Mama.

But I said she couldn't convince me though she talked till she was blue in the face. Then I said, "Besides, you know as well as I do that that child is not adopted."

"She most certainly is adopted," says Mama, stiff as a poker.

I says, "Why, Mama, Stella-Rondo had her just as sure as anything in this world, and just too stuck up to admit it."

"Why, Sister," said Mama. "Here I thought we were going to have a pleasant Fourth of July, and you start right out not believing a word your own baby sister tells you!"

60 "Just like Cousin Annie Flo. Went to her grave denying the facts of life," I remind Mama.

"I told you if you ever mentioned Annie Flo's name I'd slap your face," says Mama, and slaps my face.

"All right, you wait and see," I says.

"I," says Mama, "I prefer to take my children's word for anything when it's humanly possible." You ought to see Mama, she weighs two hundred pounds and has real tiny feet.

Just then something perfectly horrible occurred to me.

65 "Mama," I says, "can that child talk?" I simply had to whisper! "Mama, I wonder if that child can be — you know — in any way? Do you realize," I says, "that she hasn't spoken one single, solitary word to a human being up to this minute? This is the way she looks," I says, and I looked like this.

Well, Mama and I just stood there and stared at each other. It was horrible!

"I remember well that Joe Whitaker frequently drank like a fish," says Mama. "I believed to my soul he drank *chemicals*." And without another word she marches to the foot of the stairs and calls Stella-Rondo.

"Stella-Rondo? O-o-o-o-o! Stella-Rondo!"

"What?" says Stella-Rondo from upstairs. Not even the grace to get up off the bed.

70 "Can that child of yours talk?" asks Mama.

Stella-Rondo says, "Can she what?"

"Talk! Talk!" says Mama. "Burdyburdyburdyburdy!"

So Stella-Rondo yells back, "Who says she can't talk?"

"Sister says so," says Mama.

75 "You didn't have to tell me, I know whose word of honor don't mean a thing in this house," says Stella-Rondo.

And in a minute the loudest Yankee voice I ever heard in my life yells out, "OE'm Pop-OE the Sailor-r-r-r Ma-a-an!" and then somebody jumps up and down in the upstairs hall. In another second the house would of fallen down.

"Not only talks, she can tap-dance!" calls Stella-Rondo. "Which is more than some people I won't name can do."

"Why, the little precious darling thing!" Mama says, so surprised. "Just as smart as she can be!" Starts talking baby talk right there. Then she turns on me. "Sister, you ought to be thoroughly ashamed! Run upstairs this instant and apologize to Stella-Rondo and Shirley-T."

"Apologize for what?" I says. "I merely wondered if the child was normal, that's all. Now that she's proved she is, why, I have nothing further to say."

80 But Mama just turned on her heel and flew out, furious. She ran right upstairs and hugged the baby. She believed it was adopted. Stella-Rondo hadn't done a thing but turn her against me from upstairs while I stood there

helpless over the hot stove. So that made Mama, Papa-Daddy and the baby all on Stella-Rondo's side.

Next, Uncle Rondo.

I must say that Uncle Rondo has been marvelous to me at various times in the past and I was completely unprepared to be made to jump out of my skin, the way it turned out. Once Stella-Rondo did something perfectly horrible to him — broke a chain letter from Flanders Field[4] — and he took the radio back he had given her and gave it to me. Stella-Rondo was furious! For six months we all had to call her Stella instead of Stella-Rondo, or she wouldn't answer. I always thought Uncle Rondo had all the brains of the entire family. Another time he sent me to Mammoth Cave,[5] with all expenses paid.

But this would be the day he was drinking that prescription, the Fourth of July.

So at supper Stella-Rondo speaks up and says she thinks Uncle Rondo ought to try to eat a little something. So finally Uncle Rondo said he would try a little cold biscuits and ketchup, but that was all. So *she* brought it to him.

85 "Do you think it wise to disport with ketchup in Stella-Rondo's flesh-colored kimono?" I says. Trying to be considerate! If Stella-Rondo couldn't watch out for her trousseau, somebody had to.

"Any objections?" asks Uncle Rondo, just about to pour out all the ketchup.

"Don't mind what she says, Uncle Rondo," says Stella-Rondo. "Sister has been devoting this solid afternoon to sneering out my bedroom window at the way you look."

"What's that?" says Uncle Rondo. Uncle Rondo has got the most terrible temper in the world. Anything is liable to make him tear the house down if it comes at the wrong time.

So Stella-Rondo says, "Sister says, 'Uncle Rondo certainly does look like a fool in that pink kimono!'"

90 Do you remember who it was really said that?

Uncle Rondo spills out all the ketchup and jumps out of his chair and tears off the kimono and throws it down on the dirty floor and puts his foot on it. It had to be sent all the way to Jackson to the cleaners and re-pleated.

"So that's your opinion of your Uncle Rondo, is it?" he says. "I look like a fool, do I? Well, that's the last straw. A whole day in this house with nothing to do, and then to hear you come out with a remark like that behind my back!"

"I didn't say any such of a thing, Uncle Rondo," I says, "and I'm not saying who did, either. Why, I think you look all right. Just try to take care of yourself and not talk and eat at the same time," I says. "I think you better go lie down."

"Lie down my foot," says Uncle Rondo. I ought to of known by that he was fixing to do something perfectly horrible.

95 So he didn't do anything that night in the precarious state he was in — just played Casino with Mama and Stella-Rondo and Shirley-T. and gave Shirley-T. a nickel with a head on both sides. It tickled her nearly to death, and she

---

4 in Belgium, site of graves of World War I soldiers. 5 popular tourist attraction in Kentucky.

called him "Papa." But at 6:30 A.M. the next morning, he threw a whole five-cent package of some unsold one-inch firecrackers from the store as hard as he could into my bedroom and they every one went off. Not one bad one in the string. Anybody else, there'd be one that wouldn't go off.

Well, I'm just terribly susceptible to noise of any kind, the doctor has always told me I was the most sensitive person he had ever seen in his whole life, and I was simply prostrated. I couldn't eat! People tell me they heard it as far as the cemetery, and old Aunt Jep Patterson, that had been holding her own so good, thought it was Judgment Day and she was going to meet her whole family. It's usually so quiet here.

And I'll tell you it didn't take me any longer than a minute to make up my mind what to do. There I was with the whole entire house on Stella-Rondo's side and turned against me. If I have anything at all I have pride.

So I just decided I'd go straight down to the P.O. There's plenty of room there in the back, I says to myself.

Well! I made no bones about letting the family catch on to what I was up to. I didn't try to conceal it.

100   The first thing they knew, I marched in where they were all playing Old Maid and pulled the electric oscillating fan out by the plug, and everything got real hot. Next I snatched the pillow I'd done the needlepoint on right off the davenport from behind Papa-Daddy. He went "Ugh!" I beat Stella-Rondo up the stairs and finally found my charm bracelet in her bureau drawer under a picture of Nelson Eddy.[6]

"So that's the way the land lies," says Uncle Rondo. There he was, piecing on the ham. "Well, Sister, I'll be glad to donate my army cot if you got any place to set it up, providing you'll leave right this minute and let me get some peace." Uncle Rondo was in France.

"Thank you kindly for the cot and 'peace' is hardly the word I would select if I had to resort to firecrackers at 6:30 A.M. in a young girl's bedroom," I says back to him. "And as to where I intend to go, you seem to forget my position as postmistress of China Grove, Mississippi," I says. "I've always got the P.O."

Well, that made them all sit up and take notice.

I went out front and started digging up some four-o'clocks to plant around the P.O.

105   "Ah-ah-ah!" says Mama, raising the window. "Those happen to be my four-o'clocks. Everything planted in that star is mine. I've never known you to make anything grow in your life."

"Very well," I says. "But I take the fern. Even you, Mama, can't stand there and deny that I'm the one watered that fern. And I happen to know where I can send in a box top and get a packet of one thousand mixed seeds, no two the same kind, free."

"Oh, where?" Mama wants to know.

But I says, "Too late. You 'tend to your house, and I'll 'tend to mine. You hear things like that all the time if you know how to listen to the radio. Perfectly marvelous offers. Get anything you want free."

6 popular American singer on radio programs of the 1930s.

So I hope to tell you I marched in and got that radio, and they could of all bit a nail in two, especially Stella-Rondo, that it used to belong to, and she well knew she couldn't get it back, I'd sue for it like a shot. And I very politely took the sewing-machine motor I helped pay the most on to give Mama for Christmas back in 1929, and a good big calendar, with the first-aid remedies on it. The thermometer and the Hawaiian ukulele certainly were rightfully mine, and I stood on the step-ladder and got all my watermelon-rind preserves and every fruit and vegetable I'd put up, every jar. Then I began to pull the tacks out of the bluebird wall vases on the archway to the dining room.

110   "Who told you you could have those, Miss Priss?" says Mama, fanning as hard as she could.

"I bought 'em and I'll keep track of 'em," I says. "I'll tack 'em up one on each side the post-office window, and you can see 'em when you come to ask me for your mail, if you're so dead to see 'em."

"Not I! I'll never darken the door to that post office again if I live to be a hundred," Mama says. "Ungrateful child! After all the money we spent on you at the Normal."[7]

"Me either," says Stella-Rondo. "You can just let my mail lie there and *rot*, for all I care. I'll never come and relieve you of a single, solitary piece."

"I should worry," I says. "And who you think's going to sit down and write you all those big fat letters and postcards, by the way? Mr. Whitaker? Just because he was the only man ever dropped down in China Grove and you got him — unfairly — is he going to sit down and write you a lengthy correspondence after you come home giving no rhyme nor reason whatsoever for your separation and no explanation for the presence of that child? I may not have your brilliant mind, but I fail to see it."

115   So Mama says, "Sister, I've told you a thousand times that Stella-Rondo simply got homesick, and this child is far too big to be hers," and she says, "Now, why don't you all just sit down and play Casino?"

Then Shirley-T. sticks out her tongue at me in this perfectly horrible way. She has no more manners than the man in the moon. I told her she was going to cross her eyes like that some day and they'd stick.

"It's too late to stop me now," I says. "You should have tried that yesterday. I'm going to the P.O. and the only way you can possibly see me is to visit me there."

So Papa-Daddy says, "You'll never catch me setting foot in that post office, even if I should take a notion into my head to write a letter some place." He says, "I won't have you reachin' out of that little old window with a pair of shears and cuttin' off any beard of mine. I'm too smart for you!"

"We all are," says Stella-Rondo.

120   But I said, "If you're so smart, where's Mr. Whitaker?"

So then Uncle Rondo says, "I'll thank you from now on to stop reading all the orders I get on postcards and telling everybody in China Grove what you think is the matter with them," but I says, "I draw my own conclusions and will continue in the future to draw them." I says, "If people want to write their

7 teachers' college.

inmost secrets on penny postcards, there's nothing in the wide world you can do about it, Uncle Rondo."

"And if you think we'll ever *write* another postcard you're sadly mistaken," says Mama.

"Cutting off your nose to spite your face then," I says. "But if you're all determined to have no more to do with the U.S. mail, think of this: What will Stella-Rondo do now, if she wants to tell Mr. Whitaker to come after her?"

"Wah!" says Stella-Rondo. I knew she'd cry. She had a conniption fit right there in the kitchen.

125 "It will be interesting to see how long she holds out," I says. "And now — I am leaving."

"Good-bye," says Uncle Rondo.

"Oh, I declare," says Mama, "to think that a family of mine should quarrel on the Fourth of July, or the day after, over Stella-Rondo leaving old Mr. Whitaker and having the sweetest little adopted child! It looks like we'd all be glad!"

"Wah!" says Stella-Rondo, and has a fresh conniption fit.

"*He* left *her* — you mark my words," I says. "That's Mr. Whitaker. I know Mr. Whitaker. After all, I knew him first. I said from the beginning he'd up and leave her. I foretold every single thing that's happened."

130 "Where did he go?" asks Mama.

"Probably to the North Pole, if he knows what's good for him," I says.

But Stella-Rondo just bawled and wouldn't say another word. She flew to her room and slammed the door.

"Now look what you've gone and done, Sister," says Mama. "You go apologize."

"I haven't got time, I'm leaving," I says.

135 "Well, what are you waiting around for?" asks Uncle Rondo.

So I just picked up the kitchen clock and marched off, without saying "Kiss my foot" or anything, and never did tell Stella-Rondo goodbye.

There was a nigger girl going along on a little wagon right in front.

"Nigger girl," I says, "come help me haul these things down the hill, I'm going to live in the post office."

Took her nine trips in her express wagon. Uncle Rondo came out on the porch and threw her a nickel.

140 And that's the last I've laid eyes on any of my family or my family laid eyes on me for five solid days and nights. Stella-Rondo may be telling the most horrible tales in the world about Mr. Whitaker, but I haven't heard them. As I tell everybody, I draw my own conclusions.

But oh, I like it here. It's ideal, as I've been saying. You see, I've got everything cater-cornered, the way I like it. Hear the radio? All the war news. Radio, sewing machine, book ends, ironing board and that great big piano lamp — peace, that's what I like. Butter-bean vines planted all along the front where the strings are.

Of course, there's not much mail. My family are naturally the main people in China Grove, and if they prefer to vanish from the face of the earth, for all the mail they get or the mail they write, why, I'm not going to open my mouth.

Some of the folks here in town are taking up for me and some turned against me. I know which is which. There are always people who will quit buying stamps just to get on the right side of Papa-Daddy.

But here I am, and here I'll stay. I want the world to know I'm happy.

And if Stella-Rondo should come to me this minute, on bended knees, and *attempt* to explain the incidents of her life with Mr. Whitaker, I'd simply put my fingers in both my ears and refuse to listen.

(1941)

Mavis Gallant   (b. 1922)

Montreal-born novelist and short story writer Mavis Gallant has acknowledged the influence of James Joyce and Katherine Mansfield on both the style and themes of her short stories. Unlike most of her works, such as the stories in *The Other Paris*, which are set in Europe and often deal with rootless Canadian and American expatriates, "My Heart Is Broken" takes place in a remote construction camp in the Canadian bush. However, like her other stories, it deals with lonely individuals who feel alienated from the life around them. In the account of the short meeting between an older and a younger woman, Gallant's careful depiction of setting and presentation of the two people's emotionally intense dialogue reveals a great deal about their characters, their past lives, and their possible futures.

MY HEART IS BROKEN

"When that Jean Harlow[1] died," Mrs. Thompson said to Jeannie, "I was on the 83 streetcar with a big, heavy paper parcel in my arms. I hadn't been married for very long, and when I used to visit my mother she'd give me a lot of canned stuff and preserves. I was standing up in the streetcar because nobody'd given me a seat. All the men were unemployed in those days, and they just sat down wherever they happened to be. You wouldn't remember what Montreal was like then. *You* weren't even on earth. To resume what I was saying to you, one of these men sitting down had an American paper — the *Daily News*, I guess it was — and I was sort of leaning over him, and I saw in big print 'JEAN HARLOW DEAD.' You can believe me or not, just as you want to, but that was the most terrible shock I ever had in my life. I never got over it."

Jeannie had nothing to say to that. She lay flat on her back across the bed, with her head toward Mrs. Thompson and her heels just touching the crate that did as a bedside table. Balanced on her flat stomach was an open bottle of coral-pink Cutex nail polish. She held her hands up over her head and with some difficulty applied the brush to the nails of her right hand. Her legs were brown and thin. She wore nothing but shorts and one of her husband's shirts. Her feet were bare.

Mrs. Thompson was the wife of the paymaster in a road-construction camp in northern Quebec. Jeannie's husband was an engineer working on the same project. The road was being pushed through country where nothing had existed until now except rocks and lakes and muskeg. The camp was established between a wild lake and the line of raw dirt that was the road. There were no towns between the camp and the railway spur, sixty miles distant.

Mrs. Thompson, a good deal older than Jeannie, had become her best friend. She was a nice, plain, fat, consoling sort of person, with varicosed legs,

---

1 American movie star and sex symbol of the 1930s.

shoes unlaced and slit for comfort, blue flannel dressing gown worn at all hours, pudding-bowl haircut, and coarse gray hair. She might have been Jeannie's own mother, or her Auntie Pearl. She rocked her fat self in the rocking chair and went on with what she had to say: "What I was starting off to tell you is you remind me of her, of Jean Harlow. You've got the same teeny mouth, Jeannie, and I think your hair was a whole lot prettier before you started fooling around with it. That peroxide's no good. It splits the ends. I know you're going to tell me it isn't peroxide but something more modern, but the result is the same."

5   Vern's shirt was spotted with coral-pink that had dropped off the brush. Vern wouldn't mind; at least, he wouldn't say that he minded. If he hadn't objected to anything Jeannie did until now, he wouldn't start off by complaining about a shirt. The campsite outside the uncurtained window was silent and dark. The waning moon would not appear until dawn. A passage of thought made Mrs. Thompson say, "Winter soon."

Jeannie moved sharply and caught the bottle of polish before it spilled. Mrs. Thompson was crazy; it wasn't even September.

"Pretty soon," Mrs. Thompson admitted. "Pretty soon. That's a long season up here, but I'm one person doesn't complain. I've been up here or around here every winter of my married life, except for that one winter Pops was occupying Germany."

"I've been up here seventy-two days," said Jeannie, in her soft voice. "Tomorrow makes seventy-three."

"Is that right?" said Mrs. Thompson, jerking the rocker forward, suddenly snappish. "Is that a fact? Well, who asked you to come up here? Who asked you to come and start counting days like you was in some kind of jail? When you got married to Vern, you must of known where he'd be taking you. He told you, didn't he, that he liked road jobs, construction jobs, and that? Did he tell you, or didn't he?"

10   "Oh, he told me," said Jeannie.

"You know what, Jeannie?" said Mrs. Thompson. "If you'd of just listened to me, none of this would have happened. I told you that first day, the day you arrived here in your high-heeled shoes, I said, 'I know this cabin doesn't look much, but all the married men have the same sort of place.' You remember I said that? I said, 'You just get some curtains up and some carpets down and it'll be home.' I took you over and showed you my place, and you said you'd never seen anything so lovely."

"I meant it," said Jeannie. "Your cabin is just lovely. I don't know why, but I never managed to make this place look like yours."

Mrs. Thompson said, "That's plain enough." She looked at the cold grease spattered behind the stove, and the rag of towel over by the sink. "It's partly the experience," she said kindly. She and her husband knew exactly what to take with them when they went on a job, they had been doing it for so many years. They brought boxes for artificial flowers, a brass door knocker, a portable bar decorated with sea shells, a cardboard fireplace that looked real, and an electric fire that sent waves of light rippling over the ceiling and walls. A concealed gramophone played the records they loved and cherished — the good old tunes. They had comic records that dated back to the year 1, and sad soprano records about shipwrecks and broken promises and babies' graves. The first time Jeannie heard one of the funny records, she was scared to death. She was paying a formal call, sitting straight in her chair, with her skirt pulled around her knees. Vern and Pops Thompson were talking about the Army.

"I wish to God I was back," said old Pops.

"Don't I?" said Vern. He was fifteen years older than Jeannie and had been through a lot.

At first there were only scratching and whispering noises, and then a mosquito orchestra started to play, and a dwarf's voice came into the room. "Little Johnnie Green, little Sallie Brown," squealed the dwarf, higher and faster than any human ever could. "Spooning in the park with the grass all around."

"Where is he?" Jeannie cried, while the Thompsons screamed with laughter and Vern smiled. The dwarf sang on: "And each little bird in the treetop high / Sang 'Oh you kid!' and winked his eye."

It was a record that had belonged to Pops Thompson's mother. He had been laughing at it all his life. The Thompsons loved living up north and didn't miss cities or company. Their cabin smelled of cocoa and toast. Over their beds were oval photographs of each other as children, and they had some Teddy bears and about a dozen dolls.

Jeannie capped the bottle of polish, taking care not to press it against her wet nails. She sat up with a single movement and set the bottle down on the bedside crate. Then she turned to face Mrs. Thompson. She sat cross-legged, with her hands outspread before her. Her face was serene.

"Not an ounce of fat on you," said Mrs. Thompson. "You know something? I'm sorry you're going. I really am. Tomorrow you'll be gone. You know that, don't you? You've been counting days, but you won't have to any more. I guess Vern'll take you back to Montreal. What do you think?"

Jeannie dropped her gaze, and began smoothing wrinkles on the bedspread. She muttered something Mrs. Thompson could not understand.

"Tomorrow you'll be gone," Mrs. Thompson continued. "I know it for a fact. Vern is at this moment getting his pay, and borrowing a jeep from Mr. Sherman, and a Polack driver to take you to the train. He sure is loyal to *you*. You know what I heard Mr. Sherman say? He said to Vern, 'If you want to send her off, Vern, you can always stay,' and Vern said, 'I can't very well do that, Mr. Sherman.' And Mr. Sherman said, 'This is the second time you've had to leave a job on account of her, isn't it?,' and then Mr. Sherman said, 'In my opinion, no man by his own self can rape a girl, so there were either two men or else she's invented the whole story.' Then he said, 'Vern, you're either a saint or a damn fool.' That was all I heard. I came straight over here, Jeannie, because I thought you might be needing me." Mrs. Thompson waited to hear she was needed. She stopped rocking and sat with her feet flat and wide apart. She struck her knees with her open palms and cried, "I *told* you to keep away from the men. I told you it would make trouble, all that being cute and dancing around. I said to you, I remember saying it, I said nothing makes trouble faster in a place like this than a grown woman behaving like a little girl. Don't you remember?"

"I only went out for a walk," said Jeannie. "Nobody'll believe me, but that's all. I went down the road for a walk."

"In high heels?" said Mrs. Thompson. "With a purse on your arm, and a hat on your head? You don't go taking a walk in the bush that way. There's no place to walk *to*. Where'd you think you were going? I could smell Evening in Paris a quarter mile away."

25   "There's no place to go," said Jeannie, "but what else is there to do? I just felt like dressing up and going out."

"You could have cleaned up your home a bit," said Mrs. Thompson. "There was always that to do. Just look at that sink. That basket of ironing's been under the bed since July. I know it gets boring around here, but you had the best of it. You had the summer. In winter it gets dark around three o'clock. Then the wives have a right to go crazy. I knew one used to sleep the clock around. When her Nembutal[2] ran out, she took about a hundred aspirin. I knew another learned to distill her own liquor, just to kill time. Sometimes the men get so's they don't like the life, and that's death for the wives. But here you had a nice summer, and Vern liked the life."

"He likes it better than anything," said Jeannie. "He liked the Army, but this was his favorite life after that."

"There," said Mrs. Thompson, "you had every reason to be happy. What'd you do if he sent you off alone, now, like Mr. Sherman advised? You'd be alone and you'd have to work. Women don't know when they're well off. Here you've got a good, sensible husband working for you and you don't appreciate it. You have to go and do a terrible thing."

"I only went for a walk," said Jeannie. "That's all I did."

30   "It's possible," said Mrs. Thompson, "but it's a terrible thing. It's about the worst thing that's ever happened around here. I don't know why you let it happen. A woman can always defend what's precious, even if she's attacked. I hope you remembered to think about bacteria."

"What d'you mean?"

"I mean Javel,[3] or something."

Jeannie looked uncomprehending and then shook her head.

"I wonder what it must be like," said Mrs. Thompson after a time, looking at the dark window. "I mean, think of Berlin and them Russians and all. Think of some disgusting fellow you don't know. Never said hello to, even. Some girls ask for it, though. You can't always blame the man. The man loses his job, his wife if he's got one, everything, all because of a silly girl."

35   Jeannie frowned, absently. She pressed her nails together, testing the polish. She licked her lips and said, "I was more beaten up, Mrs. Thompson. It wasn't exactly what you think. It was only afterwards I thought to myself, Why, I was raped and everything."

Mrs. Thompson gasped, hearing the word from Jeannie. She said, "Have you got any marks?"

"On my arms. That's why I'm wearing this shirt. The first thing I did was change my clothes."

---

2 brand of sleeping pill. 3 bleach solution.

Mrs. Thompson thought this over, and went on to another thing: "Do you ever think about your mother?"

"Sure."

40 "Do you pray? If this goes on at nineteen —"

"I'm twenty."

"— what'll you be by the time you're thirty? You've already got a terrible, terrible memory to haunt you all your life."

"I already can't remember it," said Jeannie. "Afterwards I started walking back to camp, but I was walking the wrong way. I met Mr. Sherman. The back of his car was full of coffee, flour, all that. I guess he'd been picking up supplies. He said, 'Well, get in.' He didn't ask any questions at first. I couldn't talk anyway."

"Shock," said Mrs. Thompson wisely.

45 "You know, I'd have to see it happening to know what happened. All I remember is that first we were only talking..."

"You and Mr. Sherman?"

"No, no, before. When I was taking my walk."

"Don't say who it was," said Mrs. Thompson. "We don't any of us need to know."

"We were just talking, and he got sore all of a sudden and grabbed my arm."

50 "Don't say the name!" Mrs. Thompson cried.

"Like when I was little, there was this Lana Turner movie. She had two twins. She was just there and then a nurse brought her in the two twins. I hadn't been married or anything, and I didn't know anything, and I used to think if I just kept on seeing the movie I'd know how she got the two twins, you know, and I went, oh, I must have seen it six times, the movie, but in the end I never knew any more. They just brought her the two twins."

Mrs. Thompson sat quite still, trying to make sense of this. "Taking advantage of a woman is a criminal offense," she observed. "I heard Mr. Sherman say another thing, Jeannie. He said, 'If your wife wants to press a charge and talk to some lawyer, let me tell you,' he said, 'you'll never work again anywhere,' he said. Vern said, 'I know that, Mr. Sherman.' And Mr. Sherman said, 'Let me tell you, if any reporters or any investigators start coming around here, they'll get their...they'll never...' Oh, he was mad. And Vern said, 'I came over to tell you I was quitting, Mr. Sherman.' " Mrs. Thompson had been acting this with spirit, using a quiet voice when she spoke for Vern and a blustering tone for Mr. Sherman. In her own voice, she said, "If you're wondering how I came to hear all this, I was strolling by Mr. Sherman's office window — his bungalow, that is. I had Maureen out in her pram." Maureen was the Thompsons' youngest doll.

Jeannie might not have been listening. She started to tell something else: "You know, where we were before, on Vern's last job, we weren't in a camp. He was away a lot, and he left me in Amos, in a hotel. I liked it. Amos isn't all that big, but it's better than here. There was this German in the hotel. He was selling cars. He'd drive me around if I wanted to go to a movie or anything. Vern didn't like him, so we left. It wasn't anybody's fault."

"So he's given up two jobs," said Mrs. Thompson. "One because he couldn't leave you alone, and now this one. Two jobs, and you haven't been married five months. Why should another man be thrown out of work? We don't need to know a thing. I'll be sorry if it was Jimmy Quinn," she went on slowly. "I like that boy. Don't say the name, dear. There's Evans. Susini. Palmer. But it might have been anybody, because you had them all on the boil. So it might have been Jimmy Quinn — let's say — and it could have been anyone else, too. Well, now let's hope they can get their minds back on the job."

55   "I thought they all liked me," said Jeannie sadly. "I get along with people. Vern never fights with me."

"Vern never fights with anyone. But he ought to have thrashed *you*."

"If he . . . you know. I won't say the name. If he'd liked me, I wouldn't have minded. If he'd been friendly. I really mean that. I wouldn't have gone wandering up the road, making all this fuss."

"Jeannie," said Mrs. Thompson, "you don't even know what you're saying."

"He could at least have liked me," said Jeannie. "He wasn't even friendly. It's the first time in my life somebody hasn't liked me. My heart is broken, Mrs. Thompson. My heart is just broken."

60   She has to cry, Mrs. Thompson thought. She has to have it out. She rocked slowly, tapping her foot, trying to remember how she'd felt about things when she was twenty, wondering if her heart had ever been broken, too.

(1961)

Margaret Laurence (1926–1987)

Margaret Laurence's best-known novels and short stories are set in Manawaka, a fictionalized version of her home town of Neepawa, Manitoba. However, her first novel, *This Side Jordan* (1960), grew out of her experiences living in Africa during the 1950s and reflects her life-long concern with the repression of Native peoples. Later, in such novels as *The Stone Angel* (1964) and *A Jest of God* (1966), she depicted the social conflicts of the largely Scots-Presbyterian Manitoba community and the struggles of the women who grew up in it. "The Loons" is from *A Bird in the House* (1970), a collection of stories in which the portrayal of the maturation of Vanessa MacLeod is what Laurence called "fictionalized biography." In this story, the narrator examines the nature of her relationship to a Métis friend after the young woman's death.

THE LOONS

Just below Manawaka, where the Wachakwa River ran brown and noisy over the pebbles, the scrub oak and grey-green willow and chokecherry bushes grew in a dense thicket. In a clearing at the centre of the thicket stood the Tonnerre family's shack. The basis of this dwelling was a small square cabin made of poplar poles and chinked with mud, which had been built by Jules Tonnerre some fifty years before, when he came back from Batoche[1] with a bullet in his thigh, the year that Riel was hung and the voices of the Metis entered their long silence.[2] Jules had only intended to stay the winter in the Wachakwa Valley, but the family was still there in the thirties, when I was a child. As the Tonnerres had increased, their settlement had been added to, until the clearing at the foot of the town hill was a chaos of lean-tos, wooden packing cases, warped lumber, discarded car tyres, ramshackle chicken coops, tangled strands of barbed wire and rusty tin cans.

The Tonnerres were French halfbreeds, and among themselves they spoke a *patois* that was neither Cree nor French. Their English was broken and full of obscenities. They did not belong among the Cree of the Galloping Mountain reservation, further north, and they did not belong among the Scots-Irish and Ukrainians of Manawaka, either. They were, as my Grandmother MacLeod would have put it, neither flesh, fowl, or good salt herring. When their men were not working at odd jobs or as section hands on the C.P.R., they lived on relief. In the summers, one of the Tonnerre youngsters, with a face that seemed totally unfamiliar with laughter, would knock at the doors of the town's brick houses and offer for sale a lard-pail full of bruised wild strawberries, and if he got as much as a quarter he would grab the coin and run before the customer had time to change her mind. Sometimes old Jules, or his son Lazarus, would get mixed up in a Saturday-night brawl, and would hit out at whoever was nearest, or howl drunkenly among the offended shoppers on

---

1 near Prince Albert, Saskatchewan; in 1855, the site of a major battle in the Northwest Rebellion.
2 Louis Riel was the leader of the Métis people, who were of mixed white and Native blood.

Main Street, and then the Mountie would put them for the night in the barred cell underneath the Court House, and the next morning they would be quiet again.

Piquette Tonnerre, the daughter of Lazarus, was in my class at school. She was older than I, but she had failed several grades, perhaps because her attendance had always been sporadic and her interest in schoolwork negligible. Part of the reason she had missed a lot of school was that she had had tuberculosis of the bone, and had once spent many months in hospital. I knew this because my father was the doctor who had looked after her. Her sickness was almost the only thing I knew about her, however. Otherwise, she existed for me only as a vaguely embarrassing presence, with her hoarse voice and her clumsy limping walk and her grimy cotton dresses that were always miles too long. I was neither friendly nor unfriendly towards her. She dwelt and moved somewhere within my scope of vision, but I did not actually notice her very much until that peculiar summer when I was eleven.

"I don't know what to do about that kid," my father said at dinner one evening. "Piquette Tonnerre, I mean. The damn bone's flared up again. I've had her in hospital for quite a while now, and it's under control all right, but I hate like the dickens to send her home again."

5 "Couldn't you explain to her mother that she has to rest a lot?" my mother said.

"The mother's not there," my father replied. "She took off a few years back. Can't say I blame her. Piquette cooks for them, and she says Lazarus would never do anything for himself as long as she's there. Anyway, I don't think she'd take much care of herself, once she got back. She's only thirteen, after all. Beth, I was thinking — what about taking her up to Diamond Lake with us this summer? A couple of months rest would give that bone a much better chance."

My mother looked stunned.

"But Ewen — what about Roddie and Vanessa?"

"She's not contagious," my father said. "And it would be company for Vanessa."

10 "Oh dear," my mother said in distress, "I'll bet anything she has nits in her hair."

"For Pete's sake," my father said crossly, "do you think Matron would let her stay in the hospital for all this time like that? Don't be silly, Beth."

Grandmother MacLeod, her delicately featured face as rigid as a cameo, now brought her mauve-veined hands together as though she were about to begin a prayer.

"Ewen, if that half-breed youngster comes along to Diamond Lake, I'm not going," she announced. "I'll go to Morag's for the summer."

I had trouble in stifling my urge to laugh, for my mother brightened visibly and quickly tried to hide it. If it came to a choice between Grandmother MacLeod and Piquette, Piquette would win hands down, nits or not.

15 "It might be quite nice for you, at that," she mused. "You haven't seen Morag for over a year, and you might enjoy being in the city for a while. Well, Ewen dear, you do what you think best. If you think it would do Piquette some good, then we'll be glad to have her, as long as she behaves herself."

So it happened that several weeks later, when we all piled into my father's old Nash, surrounded by suitcases and boxes of provisions and toys for my ten-month-old brother, Piquette was with us and Grandmother MacLeod, miraculously, was not. My father would only be staying at the cottage for a couple of weeks, for he had to get back to his practice, but the rest of us would stay at Diamond Lake until the end of August.

Our cottage was not named, as many were, "Dew Drop Inn" or "Bide-a-Wee," or "Bonnie Doon." The sign on the roadway bore in austere letters only our name, MacLeod. It was not a large cottage, but it was on the lakefront. You could look out the windows and see, through the filigree of the spruce trees, the water glistening greenly as the sun caught it. All around the cottage were ferns, and sharp-branched raspberry bushes, and moss that had grown over fallen tree trunks. If you looked carefully among the weeds and grass, you could find wild strawberry plants which were in white flower now and in another month would bear fruit, the fragrant globes hanging like miniature scarlet lanterns on the thin hairy stems. The two grey squirrels were still there, gossiping at us from the tall spruce beside the cottage, and by the end of the summer they would again be tame enough to take pieces of crust from my hands. The broad moose antlers that hung above the back door were a little more bleached and fissured after the winter, but otherwise everything was the same. I raced joyfully around my kingdom, greeting all the places I had not seen for a year. My brother, Roderick, who had not been born when we were here last summer, sat on the car rug in the sunshine and examined a brown spruce cone, meticulously turning it round and round in his small and curious hands. My mother and father toted the luggage from car to cottage, exclaiming over how well the place had wintered, no broken windows, thank goodness, no apparent damage from storm-felled branches or snow.

Only after I had finished looking around did I notice Piquette. She was sitting on the swing, her lame leg held stiffly out, and her other foot scuffing the ground as she swung slowly back and forth. Her long hair hung black and straight around her shoulders, and her broad coarse-featured face bore no expression — it was blank, as though she no longer dwelt within her own skull, as though she had gone elsewhere. I approached her very hesitantly.

"Want to come and play?"

Piquette looked at me with a sudden flash of scorn.

"I ain't a kid," she said.

Wounded, I stamped angrily away, swearing I would not speak to her for the rest of the summer. In the days that followed, however, Piquette began to interest me, and I began to want to interest her. My reasons did not appear bizarre to me. Unlikely as it may seem, I had only just realised that the Tonnerre family, whom I had always heard called half-breeds, were actually Indians, or as near as made no difference. My acquaintance with Indians was not extensive. I did not remember ever having seen a real Indian, and my new awareness that Piquette sprang from the people of Big Bear and Poundmaker,[3] of Tecumseh,[4] of the Iroquois who had eaten Father Brebeuf's heart[5] — all this

20

3 nineteenth-century Cree chiefs who supported Louis Riel. 4 Shawnee chief, allied with the British in the War of 1812. 5 Jesuit missionary killed by Iroquois in 1649.

gave her an instant attraction in my eyes. I was a devoted reader of Pauline Johnson[6] at this age, and sometimes would orate aloud and in an exalted voice, *West Wind, blow from your prairie nest; Blow from the mountains, blow from the west*— and so on. It seemed to me that Piquette must be in some way a daughter of the forest, a kind of junior prophetess of the wilds, who might impart to me, if I took the right approach, some of the secrets which she undoubtedly knew — where the whippoorwill made her nest, how the coyote reared her young, or whatever it was that it said in Hiawatha.

I set about gaining Piquette's trust. She was not allowed to go swimming, with her bad leg, but I managed to lure her down to the beach — or rather, she came because there was nothing else to do. The water was always icy, for the lake was fed by springs, but I swam like a dog, thrashing my arms and legs around at such speed and with such an output of energy that I never grew cold. Finally, when I had had enough, I came out and sat beside Piquette on the sand. When she saw me approaching, her hand squashed flat the sand castle she had been building, and she looked at me sullenly, without speaking.

"Do you like this place?" I asked, after a while, intending to lead on from there into the question of forest lore.

Piquette shrugged. "It's okay. Good as anywhere."

"I love it," I said. "We come here every summer."

"So what?" Her voice was distant, and I glanced at her uncertainly, wondering what I could have said wrong.

"Do you want to come for a walk?" I asked her. "We wouldn't need to go far. If you walk just around the point there, you come to a bay where great big reeds grow in the water, and all kinds of fish hang around there. Want to? Come on."

She shook her head.

"Your dad said I ain't supposed to do no more walking than I got to."

I tried another line.

"I bet you know a lot about the woods and all that, eh?" I began respectfully.

Piquette looked at me from her large dark unsmiling eyes.

"I don't know what in hell you're talkin' about," she replied. "You nuts or somethin'? If you mean where my old man, and me, and all them live, you better shut up, by Jesus, you hear?"

I was startled and my feelings were hurt, but I had a kind of dogged perseverance. I ignored her rebuff.

"You know something, Piquette? There's loons here, on this lake. You can see their nests just up the shore there, behind those logs. At night, you can hear them even from the cottage, but it's better to listen from the beach. My dad says we should listen and try to remember how they sound, because in a few years when more cottages are built at Diamond Lake and more people come in, the loons will go away."

Piquette was picking up stones and snail shells and then dropping them again.

"Who gives a good goddamn?" she said.

6 early-twentieth-century Native writer.

It became increasingly obvious that, as an Indian, Piquette was a dead loss. That evening I went out by myself, scrambling through the bushes that overhung the steep path, my feet slipping on the fallen spruce needles that covered the ground. When I reached the shore, I walked along the firm damp sand to the small pier that my father had built, and sat down there. I heard someone else crashing through the undergrowth and the bracken, and for a moment I thought Piquette had changed her mind, but it turned out to be my father. He sat beside me on the pier and we waited, without speaking.

At night the lake was like black glass with a streak of amber which was the path of the moon. All around, the spruce trees grew tall and close-set, branches blackly sharp against the sky, which was lightened by a cold flickering of stars. Then the loons began their calling. They rose like phantom birds from the nests on the shore, and flew out onto the dark still surface of the water.

No one can ever describe that ululating sound, the crying of the loons, and no one who has heard it can ever forget it. Plaintive, and yet with a quality of chilling mockery, those voices belonged to a world separated by aeons from our neat world of summer cottages and the lighted lamps of home.

"They must have sounded just like that," my father remarked, "before any person ever set foot here."

Then he laughed. "You could say the same, of course, about sparrows, or chipmunks, but somehow it only strikes you that way with the loons."

"I know," I said.

Neither of us suspected that this would be the last time we would ever sit here together on the shore, listening. We stayed for perhaps half an hour, and then we went back to the cottage. My mother was reading beside the fireplace. Piquette was looking at the burning birch log, and not doing anything.

"You should have come along," I said, although in fact I was glad she had not.

"Not me," Piquette said. "You wouldn' catch me walkin' way down there jus' for a bunch of squawkin' birds."

Piquette and I remained ill at ease with one another. I felt I had somehow failed my father, but I did not know what was the matter, nor why she would not or could not respond when I suggested exploring the woods or playing house. I thought it was probably her slow and difficult walking that held her back. She stayed most of the time in the cottage with my mother, helping her with the dishes or with Roddie, but hardly ever talking. Then the Duncans arrived at their cottage, and I spent my days with Mavis, who was my best friend. I could not reach Piquette at all, and I soon lost interest in trying. But all that summer she remained as both a reproach and a mystery to me.

That winter my father died of pneumonia, after less than a week's illness. For some time I saw nothing around me, being completely immersed in my own pain and my mother's. When I looked outward once more, I scarcely noticed that Piquette Tonnerre was no longer at school. I do not remember seeing her at all until four years later, one Saturday night when Mavis and I were having Cokes in the Regal Café. The jukebox was booming like tuneful thunder, and beside it, leaning lightly on its chrome and its rainbow glass, was a girl.

Piquette must have been seventeen then, although she looked about twenty. I stared at her, astounded that anyone could have changed so much. Her face, so stolid and expressionless before, was animated now with a gaiety that was almost violent. She laughed and talked very loudly with the boys around her. Her lipstick was bright carmine, and her hair was cut short and frizzily permed. She had not been pretty as a child, and she was not pretty now, for her features were still heavy and blunt. But her dark and slightly slanted eyes were beautiful, and her skin-tight skirt and orange sweater displayed to enviable advantage a soft and slender body.

She saw me, and walked over. She teetered a little, but it was not due to her once-tubercular leg, for her limp was almost gone.

"Hi, Vanessa." Her voice still had the same hoarseness. "Long time no see, eh?"

"Hi," I said. "Where've you been keeping yourself, Piquette?"

"Oh, I been around," she said. "I been away almost two years now. Been all over the place — Winnipeg, Regina, Saskatoon. Jesus, what I could tell you! I come back this summer, but I ain't stayin'. You kids goin' to the dance?"

55 "No," I said abruptly, for this was a sore point with me. I was fifteen, and thought I was old enough to go to the Saturday-night dances at the Flamingo. My mother, however, thought otherwise.

"Y'oughta come," Piquette said. "I never miss one. It's just about the on'y thing in this jerkwater town that's any fun. Boy, you couldn' catch me stayin' here. I don' give a shit about this place. It stinks."

She sat down beside me, and I caught the harsh over-sweetness of her perfume.

"Listen, you wanna know something, Vanessa?" she confided, her voice only slightly blurred. "Your dad was the only person in Manawaka that ever done anything good to me."

I nodded speechlessly. I was certain she was speaking the truth. I knew a little more than I had that summer at Diamond Lake, but I could not reach her now any more than I had then. I was ashamed, ashamed of my own timidity, the frightened tendency to look the other way. Yet I felt no real warmth towards her — I only felt that I ought to, because of that distant summer and because my father had hoped she would be company for me, or perhaps that I would be for her, but it had not happened that way. At this moment, meeting her again, I had to admit that she repelled and embarrassed me, and I could not help despising the self-pity in her voice. I wished she would go away. I did not want to see her. I did not know what to say to her. It seemed that we had nothing to say to one another.

60 "I'll tell you something else," Piquette went on. "All the old bitches an' biddies in this town will sure be surprised. I'm gettin' married this fall — my boyfriend, he's an English fella, works in the stockyards in the city there, a very tall guy, got blond wavy hair. Gee, is he ever handsome. Got this real classy name. Alvin Gerald Cummings — some handle, eh? They call him Al."

For the merest instant, then, I saw her. I really did see her, for the first and only time in all the years we had both lived in the same town. Her defiant face, momentarily, became unguarded and unmasked, and in her eyes there was a terrifying hope.

"Gee, Piquette —" I burst out awkwardly, "that's swell. That's really wonderful. Congratulations — good luck — I hope you'll be happy —"

As I mouthed the conventional phrases, I could only guess how great her need must have been, that she had been forced to seek the very things she so bitterly rejected.

When I was eighteen, I left Manawaka and went away to college. At the end of my first year, I came back home for the summer. I spent the first few days in talking non-stop with my mother, as we exchanged all the news that somehow had not found its way into letters — what had happened in my life and what had happened here in Manawaka while I was away. My mother searched her memory for events that concerned people I knew.

65 "Did I ever write you about Piquette Tonnerre, Vanessa?" she asked one morning.

"No, I don't think so," I replied. "Last I heard of her, she was going to marry some guy in the city. Is she still there?"

My mother looked perturbed, and it was a moment before she spoke, as though she did not know how to express what she had to tell and wished she did not need to try.

"She's dead," she said at last. Then, as I stared at her, "Oh, Vanessa, when it happened, I couldn't help thinking of her as she was that summer — so sullen and gauche and badly dressed. I couldn't help wondering if we could have done something more at that time — but what could we do? She used to be around in the cottage there with me all day, and honestly, it was all I could do to get a word out of her. She didn't even talk to your father very much, although I think she liked him, in her way."

"What happened?" I asked.

70 "Either her husband left her, or she left him," my mother said. "I don't know which. Anyway, she came back here with two youngsters, both only babies — they must have been born very close together. She kept house, I guess, for Lazarus and her brothers, down in the valley there, in the old Tonnerre place. I used to see her on the street sometimes, but she never spoke to me. She'd put on an awful lot of weight, and she looked a mess, to tell you the truth, a real slattern, dressed any old how. She was up in court a couple of times — drunk and disorderly, of course. One Saturday night last winter, during the coldest weather, Piquette was alone in the shack with the children. The Tonnerres made home brew all the time, so I've heard, and Lazarus said later she'd been drinking most of the day when he and the boys went out that evening. They had an old woodstove there — you know the kind, with exposed pipes. The shack caught fire. Piquette didn't get out, and neither did the children."

I did not say anything. As so often with Piquette, there did not seem to be anything to say. There was a kind of silence around the image in my mind of the fire and the snow, and I wished I could put from my memory the look that I had seen once in Piquette's eyes.

I went up to Diamond Lake for a few days that summer, with Mavis and her family. The MacLeod cottage had been sold after my father's death, and I did not even go to look at it, not wanting to witness my long-ago kingdom possessed now by strangers. But one evening I went down to the shore by myself.

The small pier which my father had built was gone, and in its place there was a large and solid pier built by the government, for Galloping Mountain was now a national park, and Diamond Lake had been re-named Lake Wapakata, for it was felt that an Indian name would have a greater appeal to tourists. The one store had become several dozen, and the settlement had all the attributes of a flourishing resort — hotels, a dance-hall, cafés with neon signs, the penetrating odours of potato chips and hot dogs.

I sat on the government pier and looked out across the water. At night the lake at least was the same as it had always been, darkly shining and bearing within its black glass the streak of amber that was the path of the moon. There was no wind that evening, and everything was quiet all around me. It seemed too quiet, and then I realized that the loons were no longer here. I listened for some time, to make sure, but never once did I hear that long-drawn call, half mocking and half plaintive, spearing through the stillness across the lake.

75   I did not know what had happened to the birds. Perhaps they had gone away to some far place of belonging. Perhaps they had been unable to find such a place, and had simply died out, having ceased to care any longer whether they lived or not.

I remembered how Piquette had scorned to come along, when my father and I sat there and listened to the lake birds. It seemed to me now that in some unconscious and totally unrecognised way, Piquette might have been the only one, after all, who had heard the crying of the loons.

(1966)

Alice Munro   (b. 1931)

Born in Wingham, Ontario, Alice Munro began writing short stories in high school but did not publish her first collection, *Dance of the Happy Shades*, winner of the Governor General's Award for fiction, until 1968. Like the American writer Eudora Welty, whose work she admires, Munro is essentially a regional writer, portraying girls and women from small-town western Ontario confronting the various stages of their lives and the nature of their relationships with other people. She has been praised for her precise depiction of the events and settings that are used to reveal aspects of the personalities of her characters. In "Wild Swans," from *Who Do You Think You Are?*, another winner of the Governor General's Award, a girl's first trip alone from her small southwestern Ontario town to the metropolis of Toronto is presented as a transition period in her coming of age. Rose's ambiguous response to the actions of the man next to her will have a lasting effect on her attitudes toward sexuality.

WILD SWANS

Flo said to watch out for White Slavers. She said this was how they operated: an old woman, a motherly or grandmotherly sort, made friends while riding beside you on a bus or train. She offered you candy, which was drugged. Pretty soon you began to droop and mumble, were in no condition to speak for yourself. Oh, Help, the woman said, my daughter (granddaughter) is sick, please somebody help me get her off so that she can recover in the fresh air. Up stepped a polite gentleman, pretending to be a stranger, offering assistance. Together, at the next stop, they hustled you off the train or bus, and that was the last the ordinary world ever saw of you. They kept you a prisoner in the White Slave place (to which you had been transported drugged and bound so you wouldn't even know where you were), until such time as you were thoroughly degraded and in despair, your insides torn up by drunken men and invested with vile disease, your mind destroyed by drugs, your hair and teeth fallen out. It took about three years, for you to get to this state. You wouldn't want to go home, then, maybe couldn't remember home, or find your way if you did. So they let you out on the streets.

Flo took ten dollars and put it in a little cloth bag which she sewed to the strap of Rose's slip. Another thing likely to happen was that Rose would get her purse stolen.

Watch out, Flo said as well, for people dressed up as ministers. There were the worst. That disguise was commonly adopted by White Slavers, as well as those after your money.

Rose said she didn't see how she could tell which ones were disguised.

Flo had worked in Toronto once. She had worked as a waitress in a coffee shop in Union Station. That was how she knew all she knew. She never saw sunlight, in those days, except on her days off. But she saw plenty else. She saw a man cut another man's stomach with a knife, just pull out his shirt and do a tidy cut, as if it was a watermelon not a stomach. The stomach's owner just saw looking down surprised, with no time to protest. Flo implied that that was nothing, in Toronto. She saw two bad women (that was what Flo called whores, running the two words together, like badminton) get into a fight, and a man laughed at them, other men stopped and laughed and egged them on, and they had their fists full of each other's hair. At last the police came and took them away, still howling and yelping.

She saw a child die of a fit, too. Its face was black as ink.

"Well I'm not scared," said Rose provokingly. "There's the police, anyway."

"Oh, them! They'd be the first ones to diddle you!"

She did not believe anything Flo said on the subject of sex. Consider the undertaker.

A little bald man, very neatly dressed, would come into the store sometimes and speak to Flo with a placating expression.

"I only wanted a bag of candy. And maybe a few packages of gum. And one or two chocolate bars. Could you go to the trouble of wrapping them?"

Flo in her mock-deferential tone would assure him that she could. She wrapped them in heavy-duty white paper, so there were something like presents. He took his time with the selection, humming and chatting, then dawdling for a while. He might ask how Flo was feeling. And how Rose was, if she was there.

"You look pale. Young girls need fresh air." To Flo he would say, "You work too hard. You've worked hard all your life."

"No rest for the wicked," Flo would say agreeably.

When he went out she hurried to the window. There it was — the old black hearse with its purple curtains.

"He'll be after them today!" Flo would say as the hearse rolled away at a gentle pace, almost a funeral pace. The little man had been an undertaker, but he was retired now. The hearse was retired too. His sons had taken over the undertaking and bought a new one. He drove the old hearse all over the country, looking for women. So Flo said. Rose could not believe it. Flo said he gave them the gum and the candy. Rose said he probably ate them himself. Flo said he had been seen, he had been heard. In mild weather he drove with the windows down, singing, to himself or to somebody out of sight in the back.

> Her brow is like the snowdrift
> Her throat is like the swan

Flo imitated him singing. Gently overtaking some woman walking on a back road, or resting at a country crossroads. All compliments and courtesy and chocolate bars, offering a ride. Of course every women who reported being asked said she had turned him down. He never pestered anybody, drove politely on. He called in at houses, and if the husband was home he seemed to like just as well as anything to sit and chat. Wives said that was all he ever did anyway but Flo did not believe it.

"Some women are taken in," she said. "A number." She liked to speculate on what the hearse was like inside. Plush. Plush on the walls and the roof and the floor. Soft purple, the color of the curtains, the color of dark lilacs.

All nonsense, Rose thought. Who could believe it, of a man that age?

Rose was going to Toronto on the train for the first time by herself. She had been once before, but that was with Flo, long before her father died. They took along their own sandwiches and bought milk from the vendor on the train. It was sour. Sour chocolate milk. Rose kept taking tiny sips, unwilling to admit that something so much desired could fail her. Flo sniffed it, then hunted up and down the train until she found the old man in his red jacket, with no teeth and the tray hanging around his neck. She invited him to sample chocolate milk. She invited people nearby to smell it. He let her have some ginger ale for nothing. It was slightly warm.

"I let him know," Flo said looking around after he had left. "You have to let them know."

A woman agreed with her but most people looked out the window. Rose drank the warm ginger ale. Either that, or the scene with the vendor, or the conversation Flo and the agreeing woman now got into about where they came from, why there were going to Toronto, and Rose's morning constipation which was why she was lacking color, or the small amount of chocolate milk she had got inside her, caused her to throw up in the train toilet. All day long she was afraid people in Toronto could smell vomit on her coat.

This time Flo started the trip off by saying, "Keep an eye on her, she's never been away from home before!" to the conductor, then looking around and laughing, to show that was jokingly meant. Then she had to get off. It seemed the conductor had no more need for jokes than Rose had, and no intention of keeping an eye on anybody. He never spoke to Rose except to ask for her ticket. She had a window seat, and was soon extraordinarily happy. She felt Flo receding, West Hanratty flying away from her, her own wearying self discarded as easily as everything else. She loved the towns less and less known. A woman was standing at her back door in her nightgown, not caring if everybody on the train saw her. They were traveling south, out of the snow belt, into an earlier spring, a tenderer sort of landscape. People could grow peach trees in their backyards.

25   Rose collected in her mind the things she had to look for in Toronto. First, things for Flo. Special stockings for her varicose veins. A special kind of cement for sticking handles on pots. And a full set of dominoes.

For herself Rose wanted to buy hair-remover to put on her arms and legs, and if possible an arrangement of inflatable cushions, supposed to reduce your hips and thighs. She thought they probably had hair-remover in the drug-store in Hanratty, but the woman in there was a friend of Flo's and told every-thing. She told Flo who bought hair dye and slimming medicine and French safes.[1] As for the cushion business, you could send away for it but there was sure to be a comment at the Post Office, and Flo knew people there as well. She also hoped to buy some bangles, and an angora sweater. She had great hopes of silver bangles and powder-blue angora. She thought they could transform her, make her calm and slender and take the frizz out of her hair, dry her underarms and turn her complexion to pearl.

The money for these things, as well as the money for the trip, came from a prize Rose had won, for writing an essay called "Art and Science in the World

1   condoms.

of Tomorrow." To her surprise, Flo asked if she could read it, and while she was reading it, she remarked that they must have thought they had to give Rose the prize for swallowing the dictionary. Then she said shyly, "It's very interesting."

She would have to spend the night at Cela McKinney's. Cela McKinney was her father's cousin. She had married a hotel manager and thought she had gone up in the world. But the hotel manager came home one day and sat down on the dining room floor between two chairs and said, "I am never going to leave this house again." Nothing unusual had happened, he had just decided not to go out of the house again, and he didn't, until he died. That had made Cela McKinney odd and nervous. She locked her doors at eight o'clock. She was also very stingy. Supper was usually oatmeal porridge, with raisins. Her house was dark and narrow and smelled like a bank.

The train was filling up. A Brantford a man asked if she would mind if he sat down beside her.

30 "It's cooler out than you'd think," he said. He offered her part of his newspaper. She said no thanks.

Then lest he think her rude she said it really was cooler. She went on looking out the window at the spring morning. There was no snow left, down here. The trees and bushes seemed to have a paler bark than they did at home. Even the sunlight looked different. It was as different from home, here, as the coast of the Mediterranean would be, or the valleys of California.

"Filthy windows, you'd think they'd take more care," the man said. "Do you travel much by train?"

She said no.

35 Water was lying in the fields. He nodded at it and said there was a lot this year.

"Heavy snows."

She noticed his saying *snows*, a poetic-sounding word. Anyone at home would have said *snow*.

"I had an unusual experience the other day. I was driving out in the country. In fact I was on my way to see one of my parishioners, a lady with a heart condition —"

She looked quickly at his collar. He was wearing an ordinary shirt and tie and a dark blue suit.

40 "Oh, yes," he said. "I'm a United Church minister. But I don't always wear my uniform. I wear it for preaching in. I'm off duty today."

"Well as I said I was driving through the country and I saw some Canada geese down on a pond, and I took another look, and there were some swans down with them. A whole great flock of swans. What a lovely sight they were. They would be on their spring migration, I expect, heading up north. What a spectacle. I never saw anything like it."

Rose was unable to think appreciatively of the wild swans because she was afraid he was going to lead the conversation from them to Nature in general and then to God, the way a minister would feel obliged to do. But he did not, he stopped with the swans.

"A very fine sight. You would have enjoyed them."

He was between fifty and sixty years old, Rose thought. He was short, and energetic-looking, with a square ruddy face and bright waves of gray hair combed straight up from his forehead. When she realized he was not going to mention God she felt she ought to show her gratitude.

45   She said they must have been lovely.

"It wasn't even a regular pond, it was just some water lying in a field. It was just by luck the water was lying there and I had to drive by there. And they came down and I came driving by at the right time. Just by luck. They come in at the east end of Lake Erie, I think. But I never was lucky enough to see them before."

She turned by degrees to the window, and he returned to his paper. She remained slightly smiling, so as not to seem rude, not to seem to be rejecting conversation altogether. The morning really was cool, and she had taken down her coat off the hook where she put it when she first got on the train, she had spread it over herself, like a lap robe. She had set her purse on the floor when the minister sat down, to give him room. He took the sections of the paper apart, shaking and rustling them in a leisurely, rather showy, way. He seemed to her the sort of person who does everything in a showy way. A ministerial way. He brushed aside the sections he didn't want at the moment. A corner of newspaper touched her leg, just at the edge of her coat.

She thought for some time that it was the paper. Then she said to herself, what if it is a hand? That was the kind of thing she could imagine. She would sometimes look at men's hands, at the fuzz on their forearms, their concentrating profiles. She would think about everything they could do. Even the stupid ones. For instance the driver-salesman who brought the bread to Flo's store. The ripeness and confidence of manner, the settled mixture of ease and alertness, with which he handled the bread truck. A fold of mature belly over the belt did not displease her. Another time she had her eye on the French teacher at school. Not a Frenchman at all, really, his name was McLaren, but Rose thought teaching French had rubbed off on him, made him look like one. Quick and sallow; sharp shoulders; hooked nose and sad eyes. She saw him lapping and coiling his way through slow pleasures, a perfect autocrat of indulgences. She had a considerable longing to be somebody's object. Pounded, pleasured, reduced, exhausted.

But what if it was a hand? What if it really was a hand? She shifted slightly, moved as much as she could towards the window. Her imagination seemed to have created this reality, a reality she was not prepared for at all. She found it alarming. She was concentrating on that leg, that bit of skin with the stocking over it. She could not bring herself to look. Was there a pressure, or was there not? She shifted again. Her legs had been, and remained, tightly closed. It was. It was a hand. It was a hand's pressure.

50   Please don't. That was what she tried to say. She shaped the words in her mind, tried them out, then couldn't get them past her lips. Why was that? The embarrassment, was it, the fear that people might hear? People were all around them, the seats were full.

It was not only that.

She did manage to look at him, not raising her head but turning it cautiously. He had tilted his seat back and closed his eyes. There was his dark blue suit sleeve, disappearing under the newspaper. He had arranged the paper so that it overlapped Rose's coat. His hand was underneath, simply resting, as if flung out in sleep.

Now, Rose could have shifted the newspaper and removed her coat. If he was not asleep, he would have been obliged to draw back his hand. If he was asleep, if he did not draw it back, she could have whispered, *Excuse me*, and set his hand firmly on his own knee. This solution, so obvious and foolproof, did not occur to her. And she would have to wonder, why not? The minister's hand was not, or not yet, at all welcome to her. It made her feel uncomfortable, resentful, slightly disgusted, trapped and wary. But she could not take charge of it, to reject it. She could not insist that it was there, when he seemed to be insisting that it was not. How could she declare him responsible, when he lay there so harmless and trusting, resting himself before his busy day, with such a pleased and healthy face? A man older than her father would be, if he were living, a man used to deference, an appreciator of Nature, delighter in wild swans. If she did say *Please don't* she was sure he would ignore her, as if over-looking some silliness or impoliteness on her part. She knew that as soon as she said it she would hope he had not heard.

But there was more to it than that. Curiosity. More constant, more impe-rious, than any lust. A lust in itself, that will make you draw back and wait, wait too long, risk almost anything, just to see what will happen. *To see what will happen.*

The hand began, over the next several miles, the most delicate, the most timid, pressures and investigations. Not asleep. Or if he was, his hand wasn't. She did feel disgust. She felt a faint, wandering nausea. She thought of flesh: lumps of flesh, pink snouts, fat tongues, blunt fingers, all on their way trotting and creeping and lolling and rubbing, looking for their comfort. She thought of cats in heat rubbing themselves along the top of board fences, yowling with their miserable complaint. It was pitiful, infantile, this itching and shoving and squeezing. Spongy tissues, inflamed membranes, tormented nerve-ends, shame-ful smells; humiliation.

All that was starting. His hand, that she wouldn't ever have wanted to hold, that she wouldn't have squeezed back, his stubborn patient hand was able, after all, to get the ferns to rustle and the streams to flow, to waken a sly luxuriance.

Nevertheless, she would rather not. She would still rather not. Please remove this, she said out the window. Stop it, please, she said to the stumps and barns. The hand moved up her leg past the top of her stocking to her bare skin, had moved higher, under her suspender, reached her underpants and the lower part of her belly. Her legs were still crossed, pinched together. While her legs stayed crossed she could lay claim to innocence, she had not admitted anything. She could still believe that she would stop this in a minute. Nothing was going to happen, nothing more. Her legs were never going to open.

But they were. They were. As the train crossed the Niagara Escarpment above Dundas, as they looked down at the preglacial valley, the silver-wooded rubble of little hills, as they came sliding down to the shores of Lake Ontario, she would make this slow, and silent, and definite, declaration, perhaps dis-appointing as much as satisfying the hand's owner. He would not lift his eyelids, his face would not alter, his fingers would not hesitate, but would go powerfully and discreetly to work. Invasion, and welcome, and sunlight flashing far and wide on the lake water; miles of bare orchards stirring round Burlington.

This was disgrace, this was beggary. But what harm in that, we say to ourselves at such moments, what harm in anything, the worse the better, as we ride the cold wave of greed, of greedy assent. A stranger's hand, or root vegetables or humble kitchen tools that people tell jokes about; the world is tumbling with innocent-seeming objects ready to declare themselves, slippery and obliging. She was careful of her breathing. She could not believe this. Victim and accomplice she was borne past Glassco's Jams and Marmalades, past the big pulsating pipes of oil refineries. They glided into suburbs where bedsheets, and towels used to wipe up intimate stains flapped leeringly on the clotheslines, where even the children seemed to be frolicking lewdly in the schoolyards, and the very truckdrivers stopped at the railway crossings must be thrusting their thumbs gleefully into curled hands. Such cunning antics now, such popular visions. The gates and towers of the Exhibition Grounds came to view the painted domes and pillars floated marvellously against her eyelids' rosy sky. Then flew apart in celebration. You could have had such a flock of birds, wild swans, even, wakened under one big dome together, exploding from it, taking to the sky.

60   She bit the edge of her tongue. Very soon the conductor passed through the train, to stir the travelers, warn them back to life.

In the darkness under the station the United Church minister, refreshed, opened his eyes and got his paper folded together, then asked if she would like some help with her coat. His gallantry was self-satisfied, dismissive. No, said Rose, with a sore tongue. He hurried out of the train ahead of her. She did not seem him in the station. She never saw him again in her life. But he remained on call, so to speak, for year and years, ready to slip into place at a critical moment, without even any regard, later on, for husband or lovers. What recommended him? She could never understand it. His simplicity, his arrogance, his perversely appealing lack of handsomeness, even of ordinary grown-up masculinity? When he stood up she saw that he was shorter even than she had thought, that his face was pink and shiny, that there was something crude and pushy and childish about him.

Was he a minister, really, or was that only what he said? Flo had mentioned people who were not ministers, dressed up as if they were. Not real ministers dressed as if they were not. Or, stranger still, men who were not real ministers pretending to be real but dressed as if they were not. But that she had come as close as she had, to what could happen, was an unwelcome thing. Rose walked through Union Station feeling the little bag with the ten dollars rubbing at her, knew she would feel it all day long, rubbing its reminder against her skin.

She couldn't stop getting Flo's messages, even with that. She remembered, because she was in Union Station, that there was a girl named Mavis working here, in the Gift Shop, when Flo was working in the coffee shop. Mavis had warts on her eyelids that looked like they were going to turn into sties but they didn't, they went away. Maybe she had them removed, Flo didn't ask. She was very good looking, without them. There was a movie star in those days she looked a lot like. The movie star's name was Frances Farmer.[2]

Frances Farmer. Rose had never heard of her.

2   an American actress popular in the 1930s and early 1940s.

65   That was the name. And Mavis went and bought herself a big hat that dipped over one eye and a dress entirely made of lace. She went off for the weekend to Georgian Bay, to a resort up there. She booked herself in under the name of Florence Farmer. To give everybody the idea she was really the other one, Frances Farmer, but calling herself Florence because she was on holidays and didn't want to be recognized. She had a little cigarette holder that was black and mother-of-pearl. She could have been arrested, Flo said. For the *nerve*.

Rose almost went over to the Gift Shop, to see if Mavis was still there and if she could recognize her. She thought it would be an especially fine thing, to manage a transformation like that. To dare it; to get away with it, to enter on preposterous adventures in your own, but newly named, skin.

(1978)

Jane Rule (b. 1931)

Born in Plainfield, New Jersey, Jane Rule taught creative writing for several years at the University of British Columbia, before moving to her present home on Galiano Island, British Columbia. Beginning with her first novel, *Desert of the Heart*, published in 1964, Rule has explored the complex nature of lesbian relationships. In novels, short stories, and critical essays, she examines not only the social pressures on such partnerships, but also the insecurities, vulnerabilities, and joys of the women involved. Her works have been praised for the sensitivity and compassion with which individuals are portrayed. Lesbianism is seen as a natural part of life, as are the relationships between other characters, often marginalized, that she creates. In "Inland Passage," a boat journey from Vancouver, through the narrow waterways between the British Columbia mainland and offshore islands, symbolizes the careful navigation two women who have recently lost loved ones must execute in the beginning stages of their new relationship. In the cramped quarters of their cabin, both Troy and Fido must "get [their] bearings" as individuals and potential partners.

INLAND PASSAGE

"The other lady . . ." the ship's steward began.

"We're not together," a quiet but determined female voice explained from the corridor, one hand thrust through the doorway insisting that he take her independent tip for the bag he had just deposited on the lower bunk.

There was not room for Troy McFadden to step into the cabin until the steward had left.

"It's awfully small," Fidelity Munroe, the first occupant of the cabin, confirmed, shrinking down into her oversized duffle coat.

5   "It will do if we take turns," Troy McFadden decided. "I'll let you settle first, shall I?"

"I just need a place to put my bag."

The upper bunk was bolted against the cabin ceiling to leave headroom for anyone wanting to sit on the narrow upholstered bench below.

"Under my bunk," Troy McFadden suggested.

There was no other place. The single chair in the cabin was shoved in under the small, square table, and the floor of the minute closet was taken up with life jackets. The bathroom whose door Troy McFadden opened to inspect, had a coverless toilet, sink and triangle of a shower. The one hook on the back of the door might make dressing there possible. When she stepped back into the cabin, she bumped into Fidelity Munroe, crouching down to stow her bag.

10   "I'm sorry," Fidelity said, standing up, "But I can get out now."

"Let's both get out."

They sidled along the narrow corridor, giving room to other passengers in search of their staterooms.

Glancing into one open door, Troy McFadden said, "At least we have a window."

"Deck?" Fidelity suggested.

15   "Oh, yes."

Neither had taken off her coat. They had to shoulder the heavy door together before they could step out into the moist sea air. Their way was blocked to the raised prow of the ship where they might otherwise have watched the cars, campers, and trucks being loaded. They turned instead and walked to the stern of the ferry to find rows of wet, white empty benches facing blankly out to sea.

"You can't even see the Gulf Islands this morning," Troy McFadden observed.

"Are you from around here?"

"Yes, from North Vancouver. We should introduce ourselves, shouldn't we?"

20   "I'm Fidelity Munroe. Everyone calls me Fido."

"I'm Troy McFadden, and nearly everyone calls me Mrs. McFadden."

They looked at each other uncertainly, and then both women laughed.

"Are you going all the way to Prince Rupert?" Fidelity asked.

"And back, just for the ride."

25   "So am I. Are we going to see a thing?"

"It doesn't look like it," Troy McFadden admitted. "I'm told you rarely do on this trip. You sail into mist and maybe get an occasional glimpse of forest or the near shore or an island. Mostly you seem to be going nowhere."

"Then why...?"

"For that reason, I suppose," Troy McFadden answered, gathering her fur collar more closely around her ears.

"I was told it rarely gets rough," Fidelity Munroe offered.

30   "We're in open sea only two hours each way. All the rest is inland passage."

"You've been before then."

"No," Troy McFadden said. "I've heard about it for years."

"So have I, but I live in Toronto. There you hear it's beautiful."

"*Mrs.* Munroe?"

35   "Only technically," Fidelity answered.

"I don't think I can call you Fido."

"It's no more ridiculous than Fidelity once you get used to it."

"Does your mother call you Fido?"

"My mother hasn't spoken to me for years," Fidelity Munroe answered.

40   Two other passengers, a couple in their agile seventies, joined them on the deck.

"Well..." Troy McFadden said, in no one's direction, "I think I'll get my bearings."

She turned away, a woman who did not look as if she ever lost her bearings.

You're not really old enough to be my mother, Fidelity wanted to call after her, *Why take offense?* But it wasn't just that remark. Troy McFadden would be as daunted as Fidelity by such sudden intimacy, the risk of its smells as much as its other disclosures. She would be saying to herself, *I'm too old for this. Why on earth didn't I spend the extra thirty dollars?* Or she was on her way to the purser to see if she might be moved, if not into a single cabin then into one with someone less... more...

Fidelity looked down at Gail's much too large duffle coat, her own jeans and hiking boots. Well, there wasn't room for the boots in her suitcase, and, ridiculous as they might look for walking the few yards of deck, they might be very useful for exploring the places the ship docked.

Up yours, Mrs. McFadden, with your fur collar and your expensive, sensible shoes and matching bag. Take up the whole damned cabin!

All Fidelity needed for this mist-bound mistake of a cruise was a book out of her suitcase. She could sleep in the lounge along with the kids and the Indians, leave the staterooms (what a term!) to the geriatrics and Mrs. McFadden.

Fidelity wrenched the door open with her own strength, stomped back along the corridor like one of the invading troops, and unlocked and opened the cabin door in one gesture. There sat Troy McFadden, in surprised tears.

"I'm sorry..." Fidelity began, but she could not make her body retreat. Instead she wedged herself around the door and closed it behind her. Then she sat down beside Troy McFadden, took her hand, and stared quietly at their unlikely pairs of feet. A shadow passed across the window. Fidelity looked up to meet the eyes of another pasenger glancing in. She reached up with her free hand and pulled the small curtain across the window.

"I simply can't impose..." Troy finally brought herself to say.

"Look," Fidelity said, turning to her companion, "I may cry most of the way myself... it doesn't matter."

"I just can't make myself... walk into those public rooms... alone."

"How long have you been alone?" Fidelity asked.

"My husband died nearly two years ago... there's no excuse."

"Somebody said to me the other day, 'Shame's the last stage of grief.' 'What a rotten arrangement then,' I said. 'To be ashamed for the rest of my life.'"

"You've lost your husband?"

Fidelity shook her head, "Years ago. I divorced him."

"You hardly look old enough..."

"I know, but I am. I'm forty-one. I've got two grown daughters."

"I have two sons," Troy said. "One offered to pay for this trip just to get me out of town for a few days. The other thought I should lend him the money instead."

"And you'd rather have?"

"It's so humiliating," Troy said.

"To be alone?"

"To be afraid."

The ship's horn sounded.

"We're about to sail," Troy said. "I didn't even have the courage to get off the ship, and here I am, making you sit in the dark..."

"Shall we go out and get our bearings together?"

"Let me put my face back on," Troy said.

Only then did Fidelity let go of her hand so that she could take her matching handbag into the tiny bathroom and smoothe courage back into her quite handsome and appealing face.

Fidelity pulled her bag out from under the bunk, opened it and got out her own sensible shoes. If she was going to offer this woman any sort of reassurance, she must make what gestures she could to be a bird of her feather.

The prow of the ship had been lowered and secured, and the reverse engines had ceased their vibrating by the time the two women joined the bundled passengers on deck to see, to everyone's amazement, the sun breaking through, an ache to the eyes on the shining water.

Troy McFadden reached for her sunglasses. Fidelity Munroe had forgotten hers.

"This is your captain," said an intimate male voice from a not very loud speaker just above their heads. "We are sailing into a fair day."

The shoreline they had left remained hidden in clouds crowded up against the Vancouver mountains, but the long wooded line of Galiano Island and beyond it to the west the mountains of Vancouver Island lay in a clarity of light.

75   "I'm hungry," Fidelity announced. "I didn't get up in time to have breakfast."

"I couldn't eat," Troy confessed.

When she hesitated at the entrance to the cafeteria, Fidelity took her arm firmly and directed her into the short line that had formed.

"Look at that!" Fidelity said with pleasure. "Sausages, ham, bacon, pancakes. How much can we have?"

"As much as you want," answered the young woman behind the counter.

80   "Oh, am I ever going to pig out on this trip!"

Troy took a bran muffin, apple juice and a cup of tea.

"It isn't fair," she said as they unloaded their contrasting trays at a window table. "My husband could eat like that, too, and never gain a pound."

Fidelity, having taken off her coat, revealed just how light-bodied she was.

"My kids call me bird bones. They have their father to thank for being human size. People think I'm their little brother."

85   "Once children tower over you, being their mother is an odd business," Troy mused.

"That beautiful white hair must help," Fidelity said.

"I've had it since I was twenty-five. When the boys were little, people thought I was their grandmother."

"I suppose only famous people are mistaken for themselves in public," Fidelity said, around a mouthful of sausage; so she checked herself and chewed instead of elaborating on that observation.

"Which is horrible in its way, too, I suppose," Troy said.

90   Fidelity swallowed. "I don't know. I've sometimes thought I'd like it: Mighty Mouse[1] fantasies."

She saw Troy try to smile and for a second lose the trembling control of her face. She hadn't touched her food.

"Drink your juice," Fidelity said, in the no-nonsense, cheerful voice of motherhood.

Troy's dutiful hand shook as she raised the glass to her lips, but she took a sip. She returned the glass to the table without accident and took up the much less dangerous bran muffin.

"I would like to be invisible," Troy said, a rueful apology in her voice.

95   "Well, we really are, aren't we?" Fidelity asked. "Except to a few people."

"Have you traveled alone a lot?"

1 cartoon character who uses super powers in his battles with cats.

"No," Fidelity said, "just about never. I had the girls, and they're still only semi-independent. And I had a friend, Gail. She and I took trips together. She died last year."

"I'm so sorry."

"Me, too. It's a bit like being a widow, I guess, except, nobody expects it to be. Maybe that helps."

100   "Did you live with Gail?"

"No, but we thought maybe we might...someday."

Troy sighed.

"So here we both are at someday," Fidelity said. "Day one of someday and not a bad day at that."

They both looked out at the coast, ridge after ridge of tall trees, behind which were sudden glimpses of high peaks of snow-capped mountains.

105   Back on the deck other people had also ventured, dressed and hatted against the wind, armed with binoculars for sighting of eagles and killer whales, for inspecting the crews of fishing boats, tugs, and pleasure craft.

"I never could use those things," Fidelity confessed. "It's not just my eyes. I feel like that woman in the Colville[2] painting."

"Do you like his work?" Troy asked.

"I admire it," Fidelity said. "There's something a bit sinister about it: all those figures seem prisoners of normality. That woman at the shore, about to get into the car..."

"With the children, yes," Troy said. "They seem so vulnerable."

110   "Here's Jonathan Seagull!" a woman called to her binocular-blinded husband, "Right here on the rail."

"I loathed that book," Troy murmured to Fidelity.

Fidelity chuckled. "In the first place, I'm no friend to seagulls."

Finally chilled, the two women went back inside. At the door to the largest lounge, again Troy hesitated.

"Take my arm," Fidelity said, wishing it and she were more substantial.

115   They walked the full length of that lounge and on into the smaller space of the gift shop where Troy was distracted from her nerves by postcards, travel books, toys and souvenirs.

Fidelity quickly picked up half a dozen postcards.

"I'd get home before they would," Troy said.

"I probably will, too, but everybody likes mail."

From the gift shop, they found their way to the forward lounge where tv sets would later offer a movie, on into the children's playroom, a glassed-in area heavily padded where several toddlers tumbled and stumbled about.

120   "It's like an aquarium," Fidelity said.

"There aren't many children aboard."

"One of the blessings of traveling in October," Fidelity said. "Oh, I don't feel about kids the way I do about seagulls, but they aren't a holiday."

"No," Troy agreed. "I suppose I really just think I miss mine."

Beyond the playroom they found the bar with only three tables of prelunch drinkers. Troy looked in, shook her head firmly and retreated.

2 twentieth-century Canadian artist whose paintings depict everyday events and scenes.

125 "Not a drinker?" Fidelity asked.

"I have a bottle of scotch in my case," Troy said. "I don't think I could ever...alone..."

"Mrs. McFadden," Fidelity said, taking her arm, "I'm going to make a hard point. You're not alone. You're with me, and we're both old enough to be grandmothers, and we're approaching the turn of the 21st not the 20th century, and I think we both could use a drink."

Troy McFadden allowed herself to be steered into the bar and settled at a table, but, when the waiter came, she only looked at her hands.

"Sherry," Fidelity decided. "Two sherries," and burst out laughing.

130 Troy looked over at her, puzzled.

"Sherry is my idea of what you would order. I've never tasted it in my life."

"You're quite right," Troy said. "Am I such a cliché?"

"Not a cliché, an ideal. I don't know, maybe they're the same thing when it comes down to it. You have style. I really admire that. If I ever got it together enough to have shoes and matching handbag, I'd lose one of the shoes."

"Is that really your coat?" Troy asked.

135 Fidelity looked down at herself. "No, it belonged to Gail. It's my Linus blanket."[3]

"I've been sleeping in my husband's old pajamas. I had to buy a night-gown to come on this trip," Troy confided. "I think it's marvelous the way you do what you want."

Fidelity bit her lip and screwed her face tight for a moment. Then she said, "But I don't want to cry any more than you do."

The waiter put their sherries before them, and Fidelity put a crumpled ten dollar bill on the table.

"Oh, you should let me," Troy said, reaching for her purse.

140 "Next round," Fidelity said.

Troy handled her glass more confidently than she had at breakfast, and, after her first sip, she said with relief, "Dry."

"This is your captain," the intimate male voice asserted again. "A pod of killer whales is approaching to starboard."

Fidelity and Troy looked out the window and waited. No more than a hundred yards away, a killer whale broke the water, then another, then another, their black backs arching, their bellies unbelievably white.

"They don't look real," Fidelity exclaimed.

145 Then one surfaced right alongside the ferry, and both women caught their breath.

"This trip is beginning to feel less like somebody else's day dream," Fidelity said. "Just look at that!"

For some moments after the whales had passed, the women continued to watch the water, newly interested in its possibilities for surprise. As if as a special reward for their attention, an enormous bird dropped out of the sky straight into the sea, then lifted off the water with a strain of great wings, a flash of fish in its talons.

---

3 security blanket clutched by a character in Charles Schultz's cartoon "Peanuts."

"What on earth was that?" Fidelity cried.

"A bald eagle catching a salmon," Troy replied.

150 The ship had slowed to navigate a quite narrow passage between the mainland and a small island, its northern crescent shore fingered with docks, reached by flights of steps going back up into the trees where the glint of windows and an occasional line of roof could be seen.

"Do people live there all year long?" Fidelity asked.

"Not many. They're summer places mostly."

"How do people get there?"

"Private boats or small planes."

155 "Ain't the rich wealthy?" Fidelity sighed.

Troy frowned.

"Did I make a personal remark by mistake?"

"Geoff and I had a place when the boys were growing up. We didn't *have* money, but he earned a good deal...law. He hadn't got around to thinking about...retiring. I'm just awfully grateful the boys had finished their education. It scares me to think what it might have been like if it had happened earlier. You just don't think...we didn't anyway. Oh, now that I've sold the house, I'm perfectly comfortable. When you're just one person..."

"Well, on this trip with the food all paid for, I'm going to eat like an army," Fidelity said. "Let's have lunch."

160 Though the ship wasn't crowded, there were more people in the cafeteria than there had been for breakfast.

"Let's not sit near the Jonathan Seagulls," Fidelity said, leading the way through the tables to a quiet corner where they could do more watching than being watched. Troy had chosen a seafood salad that Fidelity considered a first course to which she added a plate of lamb chops, rice and green beans.

"I really don't believe you could eat like that all the time," Troy said.

"Would if I could."

Fidelity tried not to let greed entirely overtake her, yet she needed to eat quickly not to leave Troy with nothing to do.

165 "See those two over there?" Fidelity said, nodding to a nondescript pair of middle-aged women. "One's a lady cop. The other's her prisoner."

"How did you figure that out?"

"Saw the handcuffs. That's why they're sitting side by side."

"They're both right handed," Troy observed critically.

"On their ankles."

170 "What's she done?"

"Blown up a mortgage company," Fidelity said.

"She ought to get a medal."

"A fellow anarchist, are you?"

"Only armchair," Troy admitted modestly.

175 "Mrs. McFadden, you're a fun lady. I'm glad we got assigned to the same shoe box."

"Do call me Troy."

"Only if you call me Fido."

"Will you promise not to bark?"

"No," Fidelity said and growled convincingly at a lamb chop but quietly enough not to attract attention.

"Fido, would it both antisocial and selfish of me to take a rest after lunch?"

"Of course not," Fidelity said. "I'll just come up and snag a book."

"Then later you could have a rest."

"I'm not good at them," Fidelity said. "I twitch and have horrible dreams if I sleep during the day. But, look, I do have to know a few intimate things about you, like do you play bridge or Scrabble or poker because I don't, but I could probably scout out some people who do..."

"I loathe games," Troy said. "In any case, please don't feel responsible for me. I do feel much better, thanks to you."

A tall, aging fat man nodded to Troy as they left the cafeteria and said, "Lovely day."

"Don't panic," Fidelity said out of the side of her mouth. "I bite too, that is, unless you're in the market for a shipboard romance."

"How about you?" Troy asked wryly.

"I'm not his type."

"Well, he certainly isn't mine!"

Fidelity went into the cabin first, struggled to get her case out from under the bunk and found her book, Alice Walker's[4] collection of essays.

"Is she good?" Troy asked, looking at the cover.

"I think she's terrific, but I have odd tastes."

"Odd?"

"I'm a closet feminist."

"But isn't that perfectly respectable by now?" Troy asked.

"Nothing about me is perfectly respectable."

"You're perfectly dear," Troy said and gave Fidelity a quick, hard hug before she went into the cabin.

Fidelity paused for a moment outside the closed door to enjoy that affectionate praise before she headed off to find a window seat in the lounge where she could alternately read and watch the passing scene. An occasional deserted Indian village was now the only sign of habitation on the shores of this northern wilderness.

The book lay instead neglected in her lap, and the scenery became a transparency through which Fidelity looked at her inner landscape, a place of ruins.

A man whose wife had died of the same cancer that had killed Gail said to Fidelity, "I don't even want to take someone out to dinner without requiring her to have a thorough physical examination first."

The brutality of that remark shocked Fidelity because it located in her her own denied bitterness, that someone as lovely and funny and strong as Gail could be not only physically altered out of recognition but so horribly transformed humanly until she seemed to have nothing left but anger, guilt, and fear, burdens she tried to shift, as she couldn't her pain, onto Fidelity's shoulders,

---

4 feminist African American writer (see page 1096).

until Fidelity found herself praying for Gail's death instead of her life. Surely she had loved before she grew to dread the sight of Gail, the daily confrontations with her appalled and appalling fear. It was a face looking into hell Fidelity knew did not exist, and yet her love had failed before it. Even now it was her love she mourned rather than Gail, for without it she could not go back to the goodness between them, believe in it and go on.

She felt herself withdraw from her daughters as if her love for them might also corrupt and then fail them. In the way of adolescents they both noticed and didn't, excused her grief and then became impatient with it. They were anyway perched at the edge of their own lives, ready to be free of her.

"Go," she encouraged them, and they did.

"I guess I only think I miss them," Troy said. Otherwise this convention of parent abandonment would be intolerable, a cruel and unusual punishment for all those years of intimate attention and care.

205 And here she was, temporarily paired with another woman as fragile and shamed by self-pity as she was. At least they wouldn't be bleeding all over the other passengers. If they indulged in pitying each other, well, what was the harm in it?

Fidelity shifted uncomfortably. The possibility of harm was all around her.

"Why did you marry me then?" she had demanded of her hostile husband.

"I felt *sorry* for you," he said.

"That's a lie!"

210 "It's the honest truth."

So pity, even from someone else, is the seed of contempt.

Review resolutions for this trip: be cheerful, eat, indulge in Mighty Mouse fantasies, and enjoy the scenery.

An island came into focus, a large bird perched in a tree, another eagle no doubt, and she would not think of the fish except in its surprised moment of flight.

"This is your captain speaking..."

215 Fidelity plugged her ears and also shut her eyes, for even if she missed something more amazing than whales, she wanted to see or not see for herself.

"Here you are," Troy said. "What on earth are you doing?"

"Do you think he's going to do that all through the trip?" Fidelity demanded.

"Probably not after dark."

"Pray for an early sunset."

220 It came, as they stood watching it on deck, brilliantly red with promise, leaving the sky christened with stars.

"Tell me about these boys of yours," Fidelity said as they sat over a pre-dinner drink in the crowded bar. "We've spent a whole day together without even taking out our pictures. That's almost unnatural."

"In this den of iniquity," Troy said, glancing around, "I'm afraid people will think we're exchanging dirty post-cards."

"Why oh why did I leave mine at home?"

Fidelity was surprised that Troy's sons were not better looking than they were, and she suspected Troy was surprised at how much better looking her daughters were than she had any right to expect. It's curious how really rare a handsome couple is. Beauty is either too vain for competition or indifferent to itself. Troy would have chosen a husband for his character. Fidelity had fallen for narcissistic good looks, for which her daughters were her only and lovely reward.

"Ralph's like his father," Troy said, taking back the picture of her older son, "conservative with some attractive independence of mind. So many of our friends had trouble with first children and blame it on their own inexperience. Geoff used to say, 'I guess the more we knew, the worse we did.'"

"What's the matter with Colin?" Fidelity asked.

"I've never thought there was anything the matter with him," Troy said, "except perhaps the world. Geoff didn't like his friends or his work (Colin's an actor). It was the only hard thing between Geoff and me, but it was very hard."

The face Fidelity studied was less substantial and livelier than Ralph's, though it was easy enough to tell that they were brothers.

"We ought to pair at least two of them off, don't you think?" Fidelity suggested flippantly. "Let's see. Is it better to put the conservative, responsible ones together, and let the scallywags go off and have fun, or should each kite have a tail?"

"Colin won't marry," Troy said. "He's homosexual."

Fidelity looked up from the pictures to read Troy's face. Her dark blue eyes held a question rather than a challenge.

"How lucky for him that you're his mother," Fidelity said. "Did you realize that I am, too?"

"I wondered when you spoke about your friend Gail," Troy said.

"Sometimes I envy people his age," Fidelity said. "There's so much less guilt, so much more acceptance."

"In some quarters," Troy said. "Geoff let it kill him."

"How awful!"

"That isn't true," Troy said. "It's the first time I've ever said it out loud, and it simply isn't true. But I've been so afraid Colin thought so, so angry, yes, *angry*. I always thought Geoff would finally come round. He was basically a fair-minded man. Then he had a heart attack and died. If he'd had any warning, if he'd had time . . ."

Fidelity shook her head. She did not want to say how easily that might have been worse. Why did people persist in the fantasy that facing death brought out the best in people when so often it did just the opposite?

"How does Colin feel about his father?"

"He always speaks of him very lovingly, remembering all the things he did with the boys when they were growing up. He never mentions those last, awful months when Geoff was remembering the same things but only so that he didn't have to blame himself."

"Maybe Colin's learning to let them go," Fidelity suggested.

"So why can't I?" Troy asked.

There was Fidelity's own question in Troy's mouth. *It's because they're dead*, she thought. *How do you go about forgiving the dead for dying?* Then, because she had no answer, she simply took Troy's hand.

"Is that why your mother doesn't speak to you?" Troy asked.

"That and a thousand other things," Fidelity said. "It used to get to me, but, as my girls have grown up, I think we're all better off for not trying to please someone who won't be pleased. Probably it hasn't anything to do with me, just luck, that I like my kids, and they like me pretty well most of the time."

"Did they know about you and Gail?"

"Did and didn't. We've never actually talked about it. I would have, but Gail was dead set against it. I didn't realize just how much that had to do with her own hang-ups. Once she was gone, there didn't seem to be much point, for them."

"But for you?"

"Would you like another drink?" Fidelity asked as she signaled the waiter and, at Troy's nod, ordered two. "For myself, I'd like to tell the whole damned world, but I'm still enough of my mother's child to hear her say, 'Another one of your awful self-indulgences' and to think maybe she has a point."

"It doesn't seem to me self-indulgent to be yourself," Troy said.

Fidelity laughed suddenly. "Why that's exactly what it is! Why does everything to do with the *self* have such a bad press: self-pity, self-consciousness, self-indulgence, self-satisfaction, practices of selfish people, people being themselves?"

"The way we are," Troy said.

"Yes, and I haven't felt as good about myself in months."

"Nor I," Troy said, smiling.

"Are we going to watch the movie tonight, or are we going to go on telling each other the story of our lives?"

"We have only three days," Troy said. "And this one is nearly over."

"I suppose we'd better eat before the cafeteria closes."

They lingered long over coffee after dinner until they were alone in the room, and they were still there when the movie goers came back for a late night snack. Troy yawned and looked at her watch.

"Have we put off the evil hour as long as we can?" Fidelity asked.

"You're going to try to talk me out of the lower bunk."

"I may be little, but I'm very agile," Fidelity claimed.

The top bunk had been made up, leaving only a narrow corridor in which to stand or kneel, as they had to to get at their cases. Troy took her nightgown and robe and went into the bathroom. Fidelity changed into her flannel tent and climbed from the chair to the upper bunk, too close to the ceiling for sitting. She lay on her side, her head propped up on her elbow.

It occurred to her that this cabin was the perfect setting for the horrible first night of a honeymoon and she was about to tell Troy so as she came out of the bathroom but she looked both so modest and so lovely that an easy joke seemed instead tactless.

"I didn't have the courage for a shower," Troy confessed. "Really, you know, we're too old for this."

265   "I think that's beginning to be part of the fun."

When they had both settled and turned out their lights, Fidelity said, "Good night, Troy."

"Good night, dear Fido."

Fidelity did not expect to sleep at once, her head full of images and revelations, but the gentle motion of the ship lulled her, and she felt herself letting go and dropping away. When she woke, it was morning, and she could hear the shower running.

"You did it!" Fidelity shouted as Troy emerged fully dressed in a plum and navy pant suit, her night things over her arm.

270   "I don't wholeheartedly recommend it as an experience, but I do feel better for it."

Fidelity followed Troy's example. It seemed to her the moment she turned on the water, the ship's movement became more pronounced, and she had to hang onto a bar which might have been meant for a towel rack to keep her balance, leaving only one hand for the soaping. By the time she was through, the floor was awash, and she had to sit on the coverless toilet to pull on her grey and patchily soggy trousers and fresh wool shirt.

"We're into open water," Troy said, looking out their window.

"Two hours, you said?"

"Yes."

275   "I think I'm going to be better off on deck," Fidelity admitted, her normally pleasurable hunger pangs suddenly unresponsive to the suggestion of sausages and eggs. "Don't let me keep you from breakfast."

"What makes you think I'm such an old sea dog myself?"

Once they were out in the sun and air of a lovely morning, the motion of the open sea was exciting. They braced themselves against the railing and plunged with the ship, crossing from the northern tip of Vancouver Island to the mainland.

A crewman informed them that the ship would be putting in at Bella Bella to drop off supplies and pick up passengers.

"Will there be time to go ashore?" Fidelity asked.

280   "You can see everything there is to see from here," the crewman answered.

"No stores?"

"Just the Indian store . . . for the Indians," he said, as he turned to climb to the upper deck.

"A real, lived-in Indian village!" Fidelity said. "Do you want to go ashore?"

"It doesn't sound to me as if we'd be very welcome," Troy said.

285   "Why not?"

"You're not aware that we're not very popular with the Indians?"

Fidelity sighed. She resented, as she always did, having to take on the sins and clichés of her race, nation, sex, and yet she was less willing to defy welcome at an Indian village than she was at the ship's bar.

They were able to see the whole of the place from the deck, irregular rows of raw wood houses climbing up a hill stripped of trees. There were more dogs than people on the dock. Several family groups, cheaply but more formally dressed than most of the other passengers, boarded.

"It's depressing," Fidelity said.

290   "I wish we knew how to expect something else and make it happen."

"I'm glad nobody else was living on the moon," Fidelity said, turning sadly away.

The Indian families were in the cafeteria where Troy and Fidelity went for their belated breakfast. The older members of the group were talking softly among themselves in their own language. The younger ones were chatting with the crew in a friendly enough fashion. They were all on their way to a great wedding in Prince Rupert that night and would be back on board ship when it sailed south again at midnight.

"Do you work?" Troy suddenly asked Fidelity as she put a large piece of ham in her mouth.

Fidelity nodded as she chewed.

295   "What do you do?"

"I'm a film editor," Fidelity said.

"Something as amazing as that, and you haven't even bothered to tell me?"

"It's nothing amazing," Fidelity said. "You sit in a dark room all by yourself, day after day, trying to make a creditable half hour or hour and a half out of hundreds of hours of film."

"You don't like it at all?"

300   "Oh, well enough," Fidelity said. "Sometimes it's interesting. Once I did a film on Haida carving that was shot up here in the Queen Charlottes, one of the reasons I've wanted to see this part of the country."

"How did you decide to be a film editor?"

"I didn't really. I went to art school. I was going to be a great painter. Mighty Mouse fantasy number ten. I got married instead. He didn't work; so I had to. It was a job, and after a while I got pretty good at it."

"Did he take care of the children?"

"My mother did," Fidelity said, "until they were in school. They've had to be pretty independent."

305   "Oh, Fido, you've done so much more with your life than I have."

"Got divorced and earned a living because I had to. Not exactly things to brag about."

"But it's ongoing, something of your own to do."

"I suppose so," Fidelity admitted, "but you know, after Gail died, I looked around me and realized that, aside from my kids, I didn't really have any friends. I worked alone. I lived alone. I sometimes think now I should quit, do something entirely different. I can't risk that until the girls are really independent, not just playing house with Mother's off-stage help. Who knows? One of them might turn up on my doorstep as I did on my mother's."

"I'd love a job," Troy said, "but I'd never have the courage..."

310   "Of course you would," Fidelity said.

"Are you volunteering to take me by the hand as you did yesterday and say to the interviewer, 'This is my friend, Mrs. McFadden. She can't go into strange places by herself?'"

"Sure," Fidelity said. "I'll tell you what, let's go into business together."

"What kind of business?"

"Well, we could run a selling gallery and lose our shirts."

315   "Or a bookstore and lose our shirts... I don't really have a shirt to lose."

"Let's be more practical. How about a gay bar?"

"Oh, Fido," Troy said, laughing and shaking her head.

The ship now had entered a narrow inland passage, moving slowly and carefully past small islands. The captain, though he still occasionally pointed out a deserted cannery, village or mine site, obviously had to pay more attention to the task of bringing his ship out of this narrow reach in a nearly silent wilderness into the noise and clutter of the town of Prince Rupert.

A bus waited to take those passengers who had signed up for a tour of the place, and Troy and Fidelity were among them. Their driver and guide was a young man fresh from Liverpool, and he looked on his duty as bizarre, for what was there really to see in Prince Rupert but one ridge of rather expensive houses overlooking the harbor and a small neighborhood of variously tasteless houses sold to fishermen in seasons when they made too much money so that they could live behind pretentious front doors on unemployment all the grey winter long. The only real stop was a small museum of Indian artifacts and old tools. The present Indian population was large and poor and hostile.

320   "It's like being in Greece," Fidelity said, studying a small collection of beautifully patterned baskets. "Only here it's been over for less than a hundred years."

They ate delicious seafood at an otherwise unremarkable hotel and then skipped an opportunity to shop at a mall left open in the evening for the tour's benefit, business being what it was in winter. Instead they took a taxi back to the ship.

"I think it's time to open my bottle of scotch," Troy suggested.

They got ice from a vending machine and went back to their cabin, where Fidelity turned the chair so that she could put her feet up on the bunk and Troy could sit at the far end with her feet tucked under her.

"Cozy," Troy decided.

325   "I wish I liked scotch," Fidelity said, making a face.

By the time the steward came to make up the bunks, returning and new passengers were boarding the ship. Troy and Fidelity out on deck watched the Indians being seen off by a large group of friends and relatives who must also have been to the wedding. Fidelity imagined them in an earlier time getting into great canoes to paddle south instead of settling down to a few hours' sleep on the lounge floor. She might as well imagine herself and Troy on a sailing ship bringing drink and disease.

A noisy group of Australians came on deck.

"You call this a ship?" they said to each other. "You call those cabins?"

They had traveled across the States and had come back across Canada, and they were not happily prepared to spend two nights in cabins even less comfortable than Fidelity's and Troy's.

330 "Maybe the scenery will cheer them up," Fidelity suggested as they went back to their cabin.

"They sound to me as if they've already had more scenery than they can take."

True enough. The Australians paced the decks like prisoners looking at the shore only to evaluate their means of escape, no leaping whale or plummeting eagle compensation for this coastal ferry which had been described in their brochures as a "cruise ship." How different they were from the stoically settled Indians who had quietly left the ship at Bella Bella shortly after dawn.

Fidelity and Troy stayed on deck for the open water crossing to Port Hardy on Vancouver Island, went in only long enough to get warm, then back out into the brilliant sun and sea wind to take delight in every shape of island, contour of hill, the play of light on the water, the least event of sea life until even their cloud of complaining gulls seemed part of the festival of their last day.

"Imagine preferring something like The Love Boat,"[5] Troy said.

335 "Gail and I were always the ferry, barge, and freighter types," Fidelity said.

Film clips moved through her mind, Gail sipping ouso in a café in Athens, Gail hailing a cab in London, Gail . . . a face she had begun to believe stricken from her memory was there in its many moods at her bidding.

"What is it?" Troy asked.

"Some much better reruns in my head," Fidelity said, smiling. "I guess it takes having fun to remember how often I have."

"What time is your plane tomorrow?" Troy asked.

340 The question hit Fidelity like a blow.

"Noon," she managed to say before she excused herself and left Troy for the first time since she had pledged herself to Troy's need.

Back in their cabin, sitting on the bunk that was also Troy's bed, Fidelity was saying to herself, "You're such an idiot, such an idiot, such an idiot!"

Two and a half days playing Mighty Mouse better than she ever had in her life, and suddenly she was dissolving into a maudlin fool, into tears of a sort she hadn't shed since her delayed adolescence.

"I can't want her. I just can't," Fidelity chanted.

345 It was worse than coming down with a toothache, breaking out in boils, this stupid, sweet desire which she simply had to hide from a woman getting better and better at reading her face unless she wanted to wreck the last hours of this lovely trip.

Troy shoved open the cabin door.

"Did I say something . . . ?"

Fidelity shook her head, "No, just my turn, I guess."

5 television series in which passengers on a cruise ship often discover romance.

"You don't want to miss your last dinner, do you?"

350 "Of course not," Fidelity said, trying to summon up an appetite she could indulge in.

They were shy of each other over dinner, made conversation in a way they hadn't needed to from the first few minutes of their meeting. The strain of it made Fidelity both long for sleep and dread the intimacy of their cabin where their new polite reserve would be unbearable.

"Shall we have an early night?" Troy suggested. "We have to be up awfully early to disembark."

As they knelt together, getting out their night things, Troy said, mocking their awkward position, "I'd say a prayer of thanks if I thought there was anybody up there to pray to."

Fidelity *was* praying for whatever help there was against her every instinct.

355 "I'm going to find it awfully hard to say good-bye to you, Fido."

Fidelity had to turn then to Troy's lovely, vulnerable face.

"I just can't . . ." Fidelity began.

Then, unable to understand that it could happen, Fidelity was embracing Troy, and they moved into love-making as trustingly as they had talked.

At six in the morning, when Troy's travel alarm went off, she said, "I don't think I can move."

360 Fidelity, unable to feel the arm that lay under Troy, whispered, "We're much too old for this."

"I was afraid you thought I was," Troy said as she slowly and painfully untangled herself, "and now I'm going to prove it."

"Do you know what I almost said to you the first night?" Fidelity asked, loving the sight of Troy's naked body in the light of the desk lamp she'd just turned on. "I almost said, 'what a great setting for the first horrible night of a honeymoon.'"

"Why didn't you?"

"You were so lovely, coming out of the bathroom," Fidelity explained, knowing it wasn't an explanation.

365 "You were wrong," Troy said, defying her painful stiffness to lean down to kiss Fidelity.

"Young lovers would skip breakfast," Fidelity said.

"But you're starved."

Fidelity nodded, having no easy time getting out of bed herself.

It occurred to her to disturb the virgin neatness of her own upper bunk only because it would have been the first thing to occur to Gail, a bed ravager of obsessive proportions. If it didn't trouble Troy, it would not trouble Fidelity.

370 As they sat eating, the sun rose over the Vancouver mountains, catching the windows of the apartment blocks on the north shore.

"I live over there," Troy said.

"Troy?"

"Will you invite me to visit you in Toronto?"

"Come with me."

375 "I have to see Colin . . . and Ralph. I could be there in a week."

"I was wrong about those two over there," Fidelity said. "They sit side by side because they're lovers."

"And you thought so in the first place," Troy said.

Fidelity nodded.

"This is your captain speaking..."

380   Because he was giving them instructions about how to disembark, Fidelity did listen but only with one ear, for she had to keep her own set of instructions clearly in her head. She, of course, had to see her children, too.

(1985)

Elizabeth McGrath   (b. 1932)

A native of St. John's, Newfoundland, short story writer and English professor Elizabeth McGrath grew up in St. John's, St. Mary's, Harbour Grace, and Montreal. She studied and taught at several Canadian universities before returning to Newfoundland to teach at Memorial University. In "Fogbound in Avalon," which first appeared in *The New Yorker* magazine, the narrator attempts, after the breakup of her marriage, to find focus in her life by returning to her home town and renewing old friendships. The fog that shrouds the airport and the rough landing it causes are physical foreshadowings of the psychological difficulties that the narrator will face.

FOGBOUND IN AVALON [1]

Neither Laurel nor I will ever be certifiable, I imagine, though, having put in, between us, going on a hundred years in this world, we have inevitably had a brush or two with the darker side of things. So this will not be a story of alienation. And to put your mind at rest, right from the beginning, we have never been in love with each other, in spite of having been reared in the most repressive of girls' schools from the ages of five to eighteen.

Laurel and I, middle-aged, neurotic, still thin, still suffering, still fascinated by the world and ourselves in it, are friends. We were born on this rock, Newfoundland, and are fixed in the cracks of it, through and beyond the sparse topsoil, in a way that makes us neither want to nor be able to free ourselves, ever. Laurel, except for holidays in Europe and the Caribbean and occasional forays into New York, has been here all her life. I, Anne-Marie, onetime academic — Presentation Convent, Collège Sophie-Barat, Memorial, Oxford — am another kettle of fish.

For about twenty years we circled each other, meeting once a year when I came back from wherever I had been, tentative, polite, mildly admiring of each other, gradually spilling a bean here and a bean there until so many beans had been spilled that there was no going back from it. And we found ourselves, not unhappily, in that giggling communion characteristic of the passionate friendships of thirteen and a half. What we don't know about each other now you could put in your eye. What is more, what she and I don't know about the others on this rock isn't worth knowing. When we put our heads together, and we frequently do, we can pool enough of everyone's tatty little secrets to blackmail all the professions, including the oldest, the civil service, the clergy, and every House of Assembly back to 1855.

Just about everybody here is related by blood, marriage, or sheer tom-foolery to everybody else, and we all know our cousins to the third and fourth degree. At the rate we reproduce, emigrate, wander the world, and keep in

---

1 the most southeasterly peninsula of Newfoundland. In Celtic mythology, the blessed island of Avalon was believed to be the final resting place of King Arthur.

touch, there is no secret service that can approach us. What may be called ESP elsewhere can be nailed down here by genealogy, and we are all expert. Yesterday morning Laurel was telling me that when they were five she and her twin brother took the diapers off the minister's daughter to get a look at what was so carefully concealed. In the afternoon I called her and said, "Hey, remember Daphne Green?" "Remember her?" said Laurel. "She's the one Leonard and I took the diapers off. What in God's name made you ask about her?" "I've been hearing little baby voices all day," I said, "whispering to me *'Daphne Green, Daphne Green.'*"

5   The truth is, I'd been warming a bench at Canada Manpower most of the afternoon with one of the other rock-born overeducated, bilingual unemployed and Daphne's name came up, the way names do, because I'd asked who his wife was. All you need in this town to get a reputation for extraordinary powers is a large acquaintance, a few elementary research skills, and coincidence. Laurel, of course, being a thoroughgoing romantic, wants to believe in the spookies and so she does. I don't, but I like to cater to her. My own reluctant rationalism is one of the things that keep me from going mad, but I do break out from time to time.

Fern, Laurel's husband — surgeon, reliable backbencher, utterly devoted to her (christened, unfortunately, Ferdinand, because his mother was a great reader of the lesser works of Lord Beaconsfield)[2] — is the only one of us who can pass muster as a healthy, well-integrated, well-adjusted dealer with life. If he weren't there to remind us unremittingly of health, sanity, hard work, and the old-fashioned values of the Church of England in Canada, I don't know where we'd be. He and Laurel have lived amid her storms and his calms for twenty years, and their daughters, both at college on the mainland, are beautiful and bright and loving and a credit to them. Actually, all our children are pretty good.

Though the men on this island are great talkers — never shutting up, as the rest of the country has cause to know — they don't talk much about themselves to women. If they do talk to each other of how they feel, they certainly don't let on about it. As a charter member of the Status of Women Council I should, I suppose, hack away at that, but I don't and won't. I am concerned with what people do. What they think in the inner recesses of their own beings is their own damned business. Unless they are moved to tell me, I will never know, and it is better not to ask. It wasn't very long ago that my children's father, Con O'Neill, told me what was in his head, at my request. It took him four and a half days, at the end of which I prevailed upon him to buy me four plane tickets from Vancouver to St. John's. I then resigned from the only really good job I have ever had and launched myself back to the rock, the Public Service Commission, Canada Manpower, the vagaries of Memorial University, and a dilapidated three-story frame dwelling fifty yards from where I had been born forty-two years before.

*****

2 Benjamin Disraeli, nineteenth-century British prime minister and novelist. Ferdinand is the hero of his novel *Henrietta Temple* (1837).

Not five hours out of Vancouver, coincidence and further disaster overtook me in the person of Hugh Forbes, run into at Halifax Airport as I shepherded three dazed and baffled kids off one flight and onto another. Hugh, asking loudly, "Jesus, Annie, what have you got there, a traveling circus?" Hugh, whom I hadn't seen since the winter I was twenty-one, changed almost beyond recall but merging into himself, Cape Shore[3] voice and all, as we talked on the two-seat side of the DC-9 and the kids slept, across the aisle, on the three-seat side.

I had braced myself for what had appeared to be only the first of many awkward but insignificant encounters with my past. After the usual stylized exchanges, I realized I had miscalculated.

10 "Going home on holiday, Annie?" asked Hugh.

"Not exactly," I said.

The feeling of being at a disadvantage with Hugh was familiar. Even the setting was eerily appropriate — Hugh and I, side by side in some vehicle, each wondering who would be the first to break the silence. I plunged in. "As a matter of fact, I am right this moment *leaving* home. I'm a bit punchy, so don't expect me to make too much sense."

"Annie, I don't remember your ever making too much sense. But I think I get the message. You blew it."

Lack of directness had never been one of Hugh's failings. I must have looked stricken, for he was immediately contrite and slightly embarrassed.

15 "Annie, I'm sorry. I didn't mean to be quite so blunt."

"It's all right," I said, making a face at him. "I find it reassuring that you haven't changed all that much."

He still looked embarrassed.

"Perhaps I'd better go sit somewhere else." He started to unbuckle his seat belt. "You'd probably rather not be bothered with me right now."

"Hugh, no," I said. "I'd like to talk. Please."

20 I looked at him. He seemed solid and friendly and, in spite of being annoyed with himself for his blunder, amused and curious. So I gave him fifteen minutes of the story of my life.

He listened without interrupting. As I talked, I watched his hands rebuckling the seat belt, unbuttoning his jacket, adjusting the tray, reaching for coffee from the stewardess, scratching his head, using a handkerchief, twisting his ring. Guilt and nostalgia flooded over me.

"Your hands," I said, "your arms, they're all right!"

He turned his palms upward, flexed his fingers, stretched his arms. "Yes," he said. "Good enough."

"How did you do it?"

25 "On hate, mostly."

There was a long silence. Nineteen fifty-nine had been the year of the last St. John's polio epidemic. Hugh, home from McGill, engineer's iron ring on his finger, job offer in his pocket, had found himself one August morning, after a weekend of pain and fever, flat on his back in the Fever Hospital with both arms immovable.

---

3 residents of the area between Placentia and Cape St. Mary's speak with a distinctive, almost Irish, accent.

"September," he said quietly, looking at me with a face devoid of expression. "All September I spent two hours a day watching my girl Annie making a public spectacle of herself on bloody television. I told myself that I was going to get my hands and arms back, if only to wring your neck. I hated and Ma prayed. It worked like a charm. By Christmas I was going to dances. My arms were in slings, but the fingers were good. By spring I had the slings off. After eighteen months I was able to work. After two years I was ready to pick a fight with Con O'Neill and break his jaw. After that I packed my bags and lit out for Ontario, all cured."

"None of it had anything to do with Con," I said.

"As I perceived it, it had a great deal to do with Con. And apart from everything else I was disgusted with your whole carry on."

30 "I was afraid of you," I said. "You scared me to death. All I could see was you beating around while I minded youngsters and forgot how to read and write."

"It wouldn't have been like that."

"Don't tell me," I said. "Anyway, what about my neck?"

"What?" He was momentarily puzzled.

"Do you want to wring it?"

35 "Hell, no, girl. I never wring ladies' necks when they're down and out. I kiss them instead. Better for everybody."

He leaned across and kissed me. The tears stung in my eyes.

"Oh my God, Annie, you're not still at that!"

"I always get tears in my eyes when in the grip of strong feeling," I said in my lecture-room voice.

He looked at me in amazed disbelief, then looked again and exploded into laughter. I could feel the hot blush climbing to my hairline.

40 "Dear Lord above! Every time I'd put my arm around you, you'd start to bawl. I thought you were afraid for your virtue. Well, I'm damned."

I blinked, sniffed, and smiled at him. "Well, now you know," I said. "Better late than never."

Hugh smiled back. "Thanks, Annie."

Sweetest Mother, I thought, I love him. "Hugh," I said quietly, "I think we scuttled the ship."

"Yes," he said. "We sure as hell did."

45 He turned to look out the window, then adjusted his seat to the horizontal and closed his eyes.

"My son Gerald," he said. "My wife Clare."

Again there was silence. He readjusted his seat to the vertical and turned back to face me. "Gerald died one night when he was six months old. Crib death, they called it; no explanation, no one's guilt, they said. Still, Clare took to the bottle and after three years of it I took to the girls. And there we are. But we're still married and we're going to stay married. Make no mistake."

I said nothing. Hugh's forthrightness had left me stunned.

"One thing more, Annie. If you and I are going to be friends, you will never refer to any of it again. But I want you to keep it in mind."

50 He pointed a thumb across the aisle at the sleeping children. "What about them? Were you good at it?"

"Yes," I said, clutching at a subject I could at least talk about. "Like falling off a log. It's in the blood."

He looked at me speculatively. "I should have stuffed you full of babies and stuck you down with Mom on Cape St. Mary's.[4] She'd have learned you the five sorrowful mysteries[5] all right."

"I learned," I said.

"I don't know. Seems to me you could still use some toughening up."

55   He took my hand, called the stewardess, ordered a bottle of champagne, and told her we had just got engaged.

"Forbes," she said, "if you get engaged on my flight one more time, I will personally drown you in champagne."

The landing was the worst I have ever had, even in Torbay fog.[6] Passengers I recognized as old hands showed in the rigid set of their shoulders what I myself felt — too much airspeed, the runway overshot, and a violent touchdown with too many rebounds off the tarmac. I was trying to remember if the runway ended at a cliff, a hill, or the woods, when we came to a shuddering stop. There was absolute quiet and then the captain's voice: "Ladies and gentlemen, as you may have noticed, we have just landed at St. John's."

A ripple of laughter ran through the aircraft and an audible communal sigh of relief. Hugh stood up, collected his briefcase and raincoat, and touched my shoulder with his free hand. "That time, Annie, it almost ended happily ever after." He smiled bleakly. "I'll call you."

I watched him as he headed up the aisle, and then I busied myself with the children. My sister Catherine met me in the crowded terminal. We went to Mother's, put the still groggy children to bed, took care of half a bottle of Captain Morgan,[7] and turned in ourselves. The next morning I was going to have to turf my tenants out of my house on St. Columb's Street and start job hunting.

*****

60   What happens when you bolt after sixteen years, four universities, three kids, the whole of Eng. Lit. read together, Paris, Florence, London, Oxford, Toronto, Lisbon, Washington, Vancouver, and hundreds of friends held in common? What I did was stash my books in Vancouver and go back home. I went because I wanted to do nothing else. I didn't want to face another city, another group of strangers. My ears hungered for the accents of the island. I wanted the smells and sights and sounds of St. John's Harbor, my father's grave, my mother's tenacious grip on life, old people I had known when they were young, middle-aged people I had known when they were children. I wanted my house on St. Columb's Street, groceries from Belbin's, gas from Fred and Eric Adams, vitamins from Stowe's Pharmacy, understanding from Laurel and Fern, and the children of my friends for my children. I wanted to terrify myself climbing up Barter's Hill in the sleet, to drive to Corner Brook and back in a night and a day, seeing if I could still evade the Mounties and not kill myself, to lie

4 the most southwesterly tip of the Avalon Peninsula. 5 grief of the Virgin Mary for the sufferings of Christ. 6 Torbay Airport, St. John's, is noted for its dense fogs. 7 brand of rum.

on the grass listening to the blessed silence in St. Mary's, and to breathe on
the embers of old friendships and see if the flames would light my way out of
the dark.

In spite of the encounter with Hugh, I was in good shape when I arrived.
"Am I not the very picture of the wronged wife?" I said to Fern, and he laughed
and hugged me and we all had a drink to celebrate. Five months later I had lost
twenty-five pounds I could ill afford losing, my temper was unreliable, and I was
still unemployed, but my children were happy and my house was looking less
like a slum.

St. Columb's Street used to be solidly middle-class, occupied by people
associated with the ships and stores of the port. My own house once belonged
to a ship's chandler.[8] Some of the others were built by captains and shipown-
ers who lived here because of the incomparable view of the town and the
harbor — every ship that comes and goes can be seen from my kitchen window.
Now many of the bigger houses have become "multiple-family dwellings," the
pretty, decrepit terraces are occupied by the poor, and some foreign entrepre-
neur has put up a yellow brick apartment house directly opposite me. The
roadway is potholed, the sidewalks crumbling and cracked. Rough-looking
teen-agers skylark and catcall outside the corner stores, speaking a dialect
that suggests a lengthy inheritance of infected adenoids and bad teeth.

But at the top of the street is the hospital where I was born: farther down
is St. Columb's Church, which my grandmother's grandfather helped build; and
beside it is St. Columb's Convent, which houses an elderly nun who taught me
to read and write and made me, over six years, memorize the whole of Butler's
Catechism and MacLaren and Campbell's *Grammar*.[9] These are the things I
think about on the days when I struggle with the idea that I do not really
belong here. And, try as I may, I cannot see myself old, with my grandchildren
visiting, in this house on St. Columb's Street. It makes me unbearably, unut-
terably, sad. The Heritage Foundation is interested in us now and determined
to improve us. I am afraid I may have to move, along with the other poor,
since I cannot afford to be improved any further. Sooner or later someone
with the money to repair the roof flashings and the rotting window frames
and the exterior paint and the leaking laundry room will make me an offer and
I will have to accept it.

The house — my house for the moment — is a narrow, plain three-story
with bow windows and a peaked roof. It must have been intended for a large
family with no servants, for the kitchen is the biggest room and there is only
one bathroom and no back stairs. Built the year that I was born, it just misses
being good, even of its kind. I suppose the ship's chandler ran out of money, too.
The house has that look. The exterior walls and the floors are sound and
strong and draftproof; the fireplaces are pleasant thirties neoclassical; the
doors are paneled and the windows big and generously framed. But the walls
are surfaced with painted or papered fiberboard instead of plaster, and the
wainscoting and the additions made over the years are ill-conceived and
cheap, running to plywood and wood-grained Arborite and acoustic tile.

8 merchant who sells supplies and equipment to ships. 9 standard religious and grammar texts in
Newfoundland Catholic schools of the 1940s and 1950s.

65   How I acquired the house at all is an earnest of the emotional myopia with which I am afflicted. My marriage to Con had gone through one of its intermittent crises following a move from Toronto to Vancouver. Con suggested that since we hadn't much capital, certainly not enough to buy a house in expensive Vancouver, it would be sensible to invest in a house in an older part of St. John's, live in it for a summer, and then rent it. Our children would then have a base of operations, a home that would exist in their minds wherever they happened to be in actuality. To me the proposal made perfect sense. I had never seen myself as an emigrant, merely a traveler. The idea of a home on the island appealed to me and I liked the implicit promise that we would eventually all return. When the break came, the house was there, with boxes of old toys and baby clothes in the attic, discarded prams and pushchairs in the cellar, clothes hooks with the children's names on them in the bathroom, and odds and ends of furniture from my own childhood home in the bedrooms and living room.

By then responsibility for the house, for keeping it insured and tenanted, had gradually devolved on me. I was mildly mystified but not displeased. I saw the process as being one with the independence I was gaining as the children grew older and I settled, once again, into a fulltime job at the university. The years during which I had been, uncomfortably and resentfully, a financial dependent faded away and I assumed, along with the house on St. Columb's Street, responsibility for paying almost everything to do with myself and the children, except keeping the Vancouver roof over our heads. Food, clothing, dentistry, toys, Christmas, birthdays came out of my income from my job. We had been setting the stage for years. When the curtain went up, I said my lines and made my moves. We all did, even the children. "We knew it was a matter of time," my daughter said. "We just didn't know when. We thought it wouldn't be so soon." Nor did I.

*****

My first morning in St. John's, Laurel met me at Mother's and came with me to look at the house. All my tenants had been university students, so I assumed that not much housekeeping had been done. They had rented rooms to one another in a complex set of permutations that I had never tried to keep track of as long as they paid the rent punctually. Time and the salt air had worked their will on the exterior paint of the house, but it had been fairly shabby to begin with. When I opened the door, Laurel went rigid with shock. An effluvium of Victorian dimensions asssaulted us. The hall was crammed with old boots and dust-laden cartons of empty beer bottles. The windows were opaque with dirt, and where the panes had been broken, on either side of the door, pieces of plastic had been stretched over them and secured with bits of rough lath nailed into the moldings. The walls and floors had not been washed since I had left. The carpets were stained and felted with dog hair. Filthy and half furnished, without curtains or pictures, with its paint scabby, its wallpaper peeling, and its plastic tile discolored, the house was tawdry. "You cannot propose to live in this," Laurel said flatly. But I could and I did.

The children, when I moved them in, wept over their shattered fantasies. I attacked what I could with bucket and mop, Glass Wax and cloth, crowbar and paintbrush. The children, after their initial distress, channeled their energies and their disappointment into working with me. They took apart the broken fences and cut them into kindling. They lugged out sheets of wallboard and plywood and eight-foot two-by-fours as my crowbar did its work. They carried mattresses and bedsteads down from the attic and up from the cellar. I had not realized how strong ten- and twelve-year-olds can be when they have a job they want to do. When a semblance of normality had been achieved, they just quit and concentrated once again on their private concerns — school, games, hobbies, squabbling, television, and eating.

They were puzzled by my evident lack of pleasure in just being alive, in having a house to live in and enough to eat and wear and them to love me. I overheard one saying, "Why is she unhappy?" and another answering, "Life gave her a raw deal." I felt ashamed of not being happier and tried to smile more, but they asked me why I had that funny look on my face. I opted for the truth, which they found odd but uninteresting.

The process of recovering the house was alternately uplifting and depressing. "I refuse to lie here and watch you seesaw," said my mother, but did it nonetheless. When I had got one room fit for human habitation I persuaded her to stop for lunch on her way back from a visit to her doctor. "This is perfectly respectable," she said, on looking around my sitting room. "I fail to see what you are making such a fuss about." At that point, I found myself wanting not even to think about another tin of paint. I let the brushes dry and the children revert to their usual slovenly practices. I began, in spite of myself, to think of what it was going to mean to be on my own with no one to bitch at, no one to protect the kids from my habitual anxieties, no one to lean on, no one to sleep with, and, above all, no one to tell me, perhaps for the rest of my life, that I was essential to his breathing and being. Hugh? It was two months before Hugh turned up.

I was hammering palings into the front fence when a Land-Rover stopped at the curb and Hugh got out. I wanted to put my arms around him, but he had a very don't-touch-me look about him, so I just said it was good to see him and held on to my hammer for security. He said that he had just swung by to see how I was getting on and that I should write or call if there was anything he could do to help. I replied dryly that there were more accessible sources of help than his sweet self but that I would be glad to see him any time he got tired of doing whatever it was he did. He gave me his card, said he'd be back to share a dinner the following weekend, got into his Land-Rover, saluted, and drove off. I looked at the card and put it in my pocket. It had a Toronto address, and I thought how for seven years we had probably lived no more than fifteen blocks from each other in Don Mills.[10]

I threw down the hammer and went into the house to make tea. I drank it too fast, burned my tongue, and fired the mug viciously against the fireplace, smashing it and splattering tea over the newly scrubbed hearthrug. The mug had had a motto painted on the side. Later, I fitted the bits together, and read, "A house is made of bricks and stone but a home is made of love alone." I put the pieces on the hearth and bashed them to powder with the poker.

10 district in the City of North York, Ontario.

Hugh then appeared out of nowhere every two or three weeks, only to disappear into nowhere again. It seemed he did something with fish and oil and airplanes for the federal government. That made for a connection with Fern and Laurel. Sometimes he arrived on my doorstep monumentally plastered,[11] mirthful and bawdy, two quintals[12] and a fathom of black-hearted, cod-fed bayman.[13] Sometimes, rarely, he was sober and subtle, all civil servant and about as friendly as a cobra. I would hear his acquired Toronto accent overpowering the dental *t*'s and fog-soft vowels of the Cape Shore, and it served to remind me of what I would have preferred to forget.

I didn't ask questions of Hugh. He was there or he wasn't. He was sober or he wasn't. He loved me or he didn't. When he was drunk, I told him how beautiful he was and how I adored him. When he was sober, we talked politics and oil and mutual friends; I was careful not to show temper, and we tacitly avoided discussing how we felt. Either way, I was put into a state of elevation that sometimes lasted for days. The rest of my life the cats could have. But what was there to do? Making things happen was not my line. I watched, I listened, I cared. Nothing else was possible for me. I was through with moral imperatives: I care, therefore I am. I think, therefore I will make mistakes.

75   Though jobless, I was neither idle nor solitary. There was, if anything, too much to do, too many obligations, hordes of visiting children, and endless chores. I was ruthless about protecting my privacy, however, and my three hours of peace after the children were in bed and before midnight had overtaken me. I did not, except on very rare occasions, turn on television or stereo or take to drink. Except for smoking, I tried to do myself as little physical and spiritual harm as possible. Sometimes I even went to mass at St. Columb's, just in case. But I did, all the same, spend many days and nights in domestic squalor and intellectual tedium. I would go as much as six or eight weeks without balancing my checkbook, reading nothing but old copies of the *Atlantic* and the *Saturday Review*, washing the children's clothes in the bathwater and hanging them to dry on the bannister rails because I couldn't be bothered calling the repairman to fix the washer and dryer. I was sick to death of being bullied by ambition, concepts of efficiency, the demands of an academic conscience, fear at being out of work or even my own convenience.

Laurel held Hugh responsible for my otherwise unaccountable behaviour. I was a veteran of unrequited love, though, and surely familiar with its symptoms. I diagnosed, rather, some unease of the soul. Muddled and grubby, I read third-rate fiction and fourth-rate biography, thought fifth-rate thoughts, and felt sixth-rate emotions. And I was not at home on St. Columb's Street. I was instead, like a bird on a bush, waiting for whatever would happen next so that I would know what to do.

I talked a lot to Laurel. We were on the phone for at least thirty minutes a day. She visited me only rarely, for both the house and the neighborhood were in a world she did not care to inhabit and they made her uneasy. More frequently I visited her, early in the morning after I left the children off at school. I entered her world more easily than she did mine. We would sit in her ordered

---

11 drunk. 12 in Newfoundland, a measure of 112 pounds, or about 50.8 kilograms, usually of dried and salted cod fish. 13 a rural or outport person.

living room (oh, the relief of it!), me in jeans and sweater, with untidy hair, she combed and brushed and tidily made up but in an ugly green fuzzy dressing gown, hands shaking from insomnia and cigarettes and not following the diet required by her mild diabetes. We would ask each other if we were, as people told us, eccentric or simply mad as hares. We considered our acquaintances and determined that by and large they were even more appalling than ourselves, apart from the few saints who were out of our league and therefore irrelevant to the discussion. We concluded that we did not want to be other than who we were. What we were was another question. We spent a scandalous amount of time talking it out. I talked about my past, my emotions, unemployment, the current state of my house, my mind, or my bank account. She talked about her depression, the causes of which had never emerged. I talked about my rages, the causes of which had been only too evident. We compared childhoods, holiday trips, attitudes, fantasies. I suggested that she got depressed because of hunger, perversity, boredom, and the indulgence of an excess of sensibility. She suggested that my malaise could be cured by Hugh. I told her that it was just as likely to be cured by the Atlantic Loto, the riding of Placentia-St. Mary's, or the Henrietta Harvey Professorship.[14] Even as I said it, I thought it was probably not true. But if I had lived my life as Hugh said I should have done, I should now be like Laurel and be hankering after the kind of life I had had and botched.

Laurel knows that everyone assumes that she is lazy and self-indulgent and ought to have a job to do. But I am aware of how scared she is and how her mind and energy are drained by fear, so that she stays in bed for days and weeks at a time. Her concern for Fern makes her come awake long enough to straighten the house and get the meals, and she always seems to deal with any emergencies, including the most trivial social ones. Her usual waking time, though, is between three and eight in the morning, when she reads, makes notes, writes letters and poems in her head that never see the light of day, thinks of killing herself, and tries to stop the shakes by force of will. Her will power is irresistible, and sooner or later anyone who has much to do with her will be made to dance to her tune. Though she has had virtually every psychogenic symptom known to medicine, she succeeds always in looking as healthy as a chestnut in blossom.

Once Laurel actually did swallow sleeping pills and then, in her wayward fashion, followed them with a tin of anchovies and was sick all over the kitchen. She cleaned up while Fern continued to sleep the sleep of the just. As she tells it, he had one of his rare fits of furious exasperation when she refused to get up and prepare his breakfast. There is no questioning that in Laurel's life the farcical element continually intrudes.

All the same, her headlong emotionalism may be one of the things that make Laurel a superb political wife. She and Fern attract a variegated tribe of friends, because he is true blue and she is beautiful and amusing and enormously sympathetic. Some of her enthusiasms have led to dinner parties that could bring the government down, and Fern has learned to keep a covert eye on their guest list. Because Laurel takes everyone at face value, she is the repository of a multitude of confidences, which frequently inspire her to quixotic

14 distinguished professorship in the English Department of Memorial University of Newfoundland.

action. One Saturday, early on, she dropped in at my house without calling first and encountered Hugh. Hugh will inflict his adventures on anyone he can pin down, but even when well oiled[15] he tends to keep himself to himself. Laurel got more out of him in ten minutes than I had done in as many weeks.

After she had left, he turned to me indignantly and said, "Why do I tell Laurel all that stuff? I must be cracked."

"People do," I said, and shrugged. "They spend five minutes with her or get her when they've dialed a wrong number and she has their life stories, just like that."

"I suppose she knows enough of both of us now to write the book."

"No," I said. "But she has eyes in her head. And she loves me. She may try to help things along. I can't stop her, you know."

85   He made a particularly vulgar comment.

*****

When Laurel gets upset and concerned about someone, she has the gall of a robber's horse. Last February, I had an especially trying couple of weeks, with frozen water pipes, an ill-functioning furnace, kids home from school with the flu, and three job interviews at which I had been told I was overqualified. I was tense and miserable and jumpy. I had been expecting Hugh and looking forward to seeing him, but he hadn't turned up. Laurel called to say that she and Fern had met Hugh at a government function the previous night and that he had been in great form. One of the crosses I was having to bear was being unable to prevent Laurel from reporting on Hugh's whereabouts. I heard her out and then I ventilated for an hour and used some fairly extravagant language, including a reference to slitting my wrists Roman style[16] so that I wouldn't leave too much mess behind.

That evening Hugh was at my door. I had temporarily dismissed him from my mind and had been attempting to concentrate on sick, crotchety children and on the dirt and snow and oil handprints left by furnace men and plumbers. I needed a bath and was red-eyed and sleepless from nights of keeping coal fires going in the bedroom grates and was in no mood for dealing with Hugh's usual attitude of detached amusement at my ridiculous plight.

"Come in," I said. "If you can get in." A gust of icy wind accompanied him — and more snow. "Don't bother taking off your boots. The mess is past the point where I even care about it."

"You're all right, though?" he asked, looking at me warily.

90   "Sure," I said. "Dandy." I jammed my coal-blackened hands into the pockets of my jeans and leaned against the newel post.

"You look done in," he said.

"Beat to a rag. Want some coffee?"

"No thanks. I just took a notion to stop by. I've got a meeting to get back to. You're sure you're all right?"

15 drunk. 16 Roman suicides often slit their wrists while bathing.

"Perfectly fine." I tried what I hoped was a cheerful grin. "I'm cold, I'm tired, I'm unemployed, and the house is falling down. Don't expect Pollyanna[17] in this climate."

95 "Kids O.K.?"

~~"Sick as pigs," I said. "And crooked as sin."~~

"Anything I can do? You've only to ask."

"I know," I said, "I know. But there isn't anything, truly. I just need some sleep and a change in the weather."

"Don't overdo it, Annie." He put his hand under my chin and made me look at him. "Anything on your mind? You're sure you're all right?"

100 This sort of solicitude was unheard of from Hugh, who would normally only inquire about my state of being if he found me with my head under my arm like the ghost of Anne Boleyn.[18] I had a sudden shattering glimmer of understanding.

"Have you seen Fern lately?" I hazarded.

"Not this trip," he replied blandly. "Too busy." He looked at his watch. "I'd better get back. Take care, Annie."

"Sure," I said. "Pray for a thaw."

As soon as I'd closed the door on Hugh, I called Laurel.

105 "What did you tell him, Laurel?" I said. "That I was about to hang myself in my garters because he done me wrong?"

"An-nie, you puz-zle me," she said in her most nervous and distinct Bishop Spencer College[19] accents.

"And you are a damned liar," I said.

"You know I ne-ver tell an untruth, An-nie."

"Laurel," I said, "I can tell when you're lying within five syllables. I'll see you in the morning if I don't die of shame first." I hung up.

110 After another night of sleeplessness, half a bottle of Irish whiskey, and a packet of lethal American cigarettes from our all-night pizza parlor, I went to Laurel's to tell her to get off my case. It wasn't easy. In twenty years we had never had a serious difference. With the help of a couple of pints of Strongbow,[20] I managed to enlighten her on the enormity of what she had done. By lunchtime, when Fern got home, I was wandering the house barefoot, hugging the cider mug and humming a dirty song that I'd learned from Hugh when I was a freshman. Fern patted me on the head, said it must be great to have nothing to do, and went back to the hospital to see someone whose legs were in traction. Laurel took her telling-off better than I dealt it out, and promised never to interfere again.

Then she asked me how my life was going and how I thought it would all work out. I turned the question back to her, and she said she should never have thrown up the pills. I said that perhaps she and Hugh would be killed in a car crash when they wickedly, and in heedless contravention of all the ground rules of friendship, slipped off to Clarenville for a weekend, leaving me and Fern, given a decent interval of mourning, to console each other. Her eyes widened and she laughed with delight.

---

17 optimistic heroine in early-twentieth-century children's novels written by Eleanor Porter. 18 the second wife of Henry VIII of England, she was beheaded in 1536. 19 Protestant high school in St. John's, generally attended by students of wealthier families. 20 brand of alcoholic cider.

"An-nie, you are naugh-ty," she said. "How per-fect!" And I knew I had not been all that far from the truth.

"It won't work," I said. "It's a horrible cliché."

"No, no," she said, and laughed again. "I can't wait to tell Fern."

What actually did occur was one night in early spring, having read myself into a stupor, fully clothed in my bed, along with dirty ashtrays, my accounts and calculator, carbons of job applications, the phone, an alarm clock, unanswered letters, unsent Christmas cards, *The Oxford Book of Oxford*, unread, *The Pauper's Cook Book*, and an illustrated essay on the paintings of Edvard Munch,[21] I fell asleep smoking a cigarette and woke at dawn to find that I had burned a hole through two carbons, a book bill from Blackwell's, and my only pair of sheets.

For some minutes I stared at the burn without moving, then I headed for the bathroom. My hands were shaking and my eyes were large and dark and frightened. My impulse was to wrap myself in a blanket, crawl back into bed, and go to sleep — deeply, deeply to sleep — when one of the children knocked at the door and asked the time. I snapped to attention, cleaned out the sink, called the others, and went downstairs. I made an unusually big breakfast and insisted that it be eaten. After I had taken the children to school, I returned home, washed the dishes, then gathered up all the loose papers I could find — the year's small collection of books and the 1669 Donne[22] I had brought in my pocket from Vancouver. I put them in the ashcan, and carried it out to the sidewalk. I washed my hair, had a bath, and dressed in a silk shirt and a suit. I called my mother's cleaning woman and arranged for three days of her time. As I left the house again, the phone rang, and while I stood in the doorway, not answering it, I saw that the ashmen had been and gone. I got into the car and drove slowly down St. Columb's Street.

The fog was coming in through the Narrows, but the sun was still shining and the town and the harbor were brilliant with color and beautiful beyond the reaches of fantasy. My throat hurt and I could hardly see. I thought about my grandmother's grandfather leaning out over the unfinished walls of St. Columb's, watching the arrival of the White Fleet.[23] I thought about Sister Columba in her convent and about the day I was born in the hospital at the top of the street. I thought about Hugh and Laurel and Fern and the Heritage Foundation. My heart was breaking, for I knew inescapably that I had already, once again, set out on my travels.

(1980)

---

21 early-twentieth-century Norwegian expressionist artist whose paintings explored the depths of human feelings. 22 early and therefore valuable edition of the works of English poet John Donne (see pages 42–48). 23 the white-painted boats of the Portuguese fishing fleet would sail into St. John's harbour for supplies or to escape bad weather.

Philip Roth (b. 1933)

Philip Roth, a native of Newark, New Jersey, achieved international attention in 1959 with the publication of his first book, *Goodbye, Columbus*, a collection of short stories. In many of these stories, as in such later novels as *Portnoy's Complaint* and *The Ghost Writer*, Roth explores the attempts by Jewish boys and men to reconcile individual desires with the conflicting forces of contemporary American society and their religious heritage. "The Conversion of the Jews," from his first book, focuses on the religious earnestness and inner rebelliousness of Ozzie Freedman. As he confronts his mother and the rabbi, Ozzie seeks answers to questions that deeply puzzle him; he also looks to achieve a kind of heroism in the eyes of his fellow students. The title may have been taken from a line in Andrew Marvell's seventeenth-century poem "To His Coy Mistress" (see page 64), referring to an event many people believed would not occur until the end of time.

THE CONVERSION OF THE JEWS

"You're a real one for opening your mouth in the first place," Itzie said. "What do you open your mouth all the time for?"

"I didn't bring it up, Itz, I didn't," Ozzie said.

"What do you care about Jesus Christ for anyway?"

"I didn't bring up Jesus Christ. He did. I didn't even know what he was talking about. Jesus is historical, he kept saying. Jesus is historical." Ozzie mimicked the monumental voice of Rabbi Binder.

5   "Jesus was a person that lived like you and me," Ozzie continued. "That's what Binder said —"

"Yeah?... So what! What do I give two cents whether he lived or not. And what do you gotta open your mouth!" Itzie Lieberman favored closed-mouthedness, especially when it came to Ozzie Freedman's questions. Mrs. Freedman had to see Rabbi Binder twice before about Ozzie's questions and this Wednesday at four-thirty would be the third time. Itzie preferred to keep *his* mother in the kitchen; he settled for behind-the-back subtleties such as gestures, faces, snarls and other less delicate barnyard noises.

"He was a real person, Jesus, but he wasn't like God, and we don't believe he is God." Slowly, Ozzie was explaining Rabbi Binder's position to Itzie, who had been absent from Hebrew School the previous afternoon.

"The Catholics," Itzie said helpfully, "they believe in Jesus Christ, that he's God." Itzie Lieberman used "the Catholics" in its broadest sense — to include the Protestants.

Ozzie received Itzie's remark with a tiny head bob, as though it were a footnote, and went on. "His mother was Mary, and his father probably was Joseph," Ozzie said. "But the New Testament says his real father was God."

10   "His *real* father?"

"Yeah," Ozzie said, "that's the big thing, his father's supposed to be God."

"Bull."

"That's what Rabbi Binder says, that it's impossible —"

"Sure it's impossible. That stuff's all bull. To have a baby you gotta get laid," Itzie theologized. "Mary hadda get laid."

15 "That's what Binder says: 'The only way a woman can have a baby is to have intercourse with a man.'"

"He said *that*, Ozz?" For a moment it appeared that Itzie had put the theological question aside. "He said that, intercourse?" A little curled smile shaped itself in the lower half of Itzie's face like a pink mustache. "What you guys do, Ozz, you laugh or something?"

"I raised my hand."

"Yeah? Whatja say?"

"That's when I asked the question."

20 Itzie's face lit up. "Whatja ask about — intercourse?"

"No, I asked the question about God, how if He could create the heaven and earth in six days — the light especially, that's what always gets me, that He could make the light. Making fish and animals, that's pretty good —"

"That's damn good." Itzie's appreciation was honest but unimaginative: it was as though God had just pitched a one-hitter.[1]

"But making light . . . I mean when you think about it, it's really something," Ozzie said. "Anyway, I asked Binder if He could make all that in six days, and He could *pick* the six days He wanted right out of nowhere, why couldn't He let a woman have a baby without having intercourse."

"You said intercourse, Ozz, to Binder?"

25 "Yeah."

"Right in class?"

"Yeah."

Itzie smacked the side of his head.

"I mean, no kidding around," Ozzie said, "that'd really be nothing. After all that other stuff, that'd practically be nothing."

30 Itzie considered a moment. "What'd Binder say?"

"He started all over again explaining how Jesus was historical and how he lived like you and me but he wasn't God. So I said I under*stood* that. What I wanted to know was different."

What Ozzie wanted to know was always different. The first time he had wanted to know how Rabbi Binder could call the Jews "The Chosen People" if the Declaration of Independence claimed all men to be created equal. Rabbi Binder tried to distinguish for him between political equality and spiritual legitimacy, but what Ozzie wanted to know, he insisted vehemently, was different. That was the first time his mother had to come.

Then there was the plane crash. Fifty-eight people had been killed in a plane crash at La Guardia. In studying a casualty list in the newspaper his mother had discovered among the list of those dead eight Jewish names (his grandmother had nine but she counted Miller as a Jewish name); because of the eight she said the plane crash was "a tragedy." During free-discussion time on Wednesday Ozzie had brought to Rabbi Binder's attention this matter of "some of his relations" always picking out the Jewish names. Rabbi Binder had begun to explain cultural unity and some other things when Ozzie stood up at his seat

---

1 baseball game in which the pitcher yields only one base hit.

and said that what he wanted to know was different. Rabbi Binder insisted that he sit down and it was then that Ozzie shouted that he wished all fifty-eight were Jews. That was the second time his mother came.

"And he kept explaining about Jesus being historical, and so I kept asking him. No kidding, Itz, he was trying to make me look stupid."

"So what he finally do?"

35

"Finally he starts screaming that I was deliberately simple-minded and a wise guy, and that my mother had to come, and this was the last time. And that I'd never get bar-mitzvahed if he could help it. Then, Itz, then he starts talking in that voice like a statue, real slow and deep, and he says that I better think over what I said about the Lord. He told me to go to his office and think it over." Ozzie leaned his body towards Itzie. "Itz, I thought it over for a solid hour, and now I'm convinced God could do it."

*****

Ozzie had planned to confess his latest transgression to his mother as soon as she came home from work. But it was a Friday night in November and already dark, and when Mrs. Freedman came through the door she tossed off her coat, kissed Ozzie quickly on the face, and went to the kitchen table to light the three yellow candles, two for the Sabbath[2] and one for Ozzie's father.

When his mother lit the candles she would move her two arms slowly towards her, dragging them through the air, as though persuading people whose minds were half made up. And her eyes would get glassy with tears. Even when his father was alive Ozzie remembered that her eyes had gotten glassy, so it didn't have anything to do with his dying. It had something to do with lighting the candles.

As she touched the flaming match to the unlit wick of a Sabbath candle, the phone rang, and Ozzie, standing only a foot from it, plucked it off the receiver and held it muffled to his chest. When his mother lit candles Ozzie felt there should be no noise; even breathing, if you could manage it, should be softened. Ozzie pressed the phone to his breast and watched his mother dragging whatever she was dragging, and he felt his own eyes get glassy. His mother was a round, tired, gray-haired penguin of a woman whose gray skin had begun to feel the tug of gravity and the weight of her own history. Even when she was dressed up she didn't look like a chosen person. But when she lit candles she looked like something better; like a woman who knew momentarily that God could do anything.

40

After a few mysterious minutes she was finished. Ozzie hung up the phone and walked to the kitchen table where she was beginning to lay the two places for the four-course Sabbath meal. He told her that she would have to see Rabbi Binder next Wednesday at four-thirty, and then he told her why. For the first time in their life together she hit Ozzie across the face with her hand.

All through the chopped liver and chicken soup part of the dinner Ozzie cried; he didn't have any appetite for the rest.

*****

2 celebration of the Jewish Sabbath begins at sundown Friday.

On Wednesday, in the largest of the three basement classrooms of the synagogue, Rabbi Marvin Binder, a tall, handsome, broad-shouldered man of thirty with thick strong-fibered black hair, removed his watch from his pocket and saw that it was four o'clock. At the rear of the room Yakov Blotnik, the seventy-one-year-old custodian, slowly polished the large window, mumbling to himself, unaware that it was four o'clock or six o'clock, Monday or Wednesday. To most of the students Yakov Blotnik's mumbling, along with his brown curly beard, scythe nose, and two heel-trailing black cats, made him an object of wonder, a foreigner, a relic, towards whom they were alternately fearful and disrespectful. To Ozzie the mumbling had always seemed a monotonous, curious prayer; what made it curious was that old Blotnik had been mumbling so steadily for so many years, Ozzie suspected he had memorized the prayers and forgotten all about God.

"It is now free-discussion time," Rabbi Binder said. "Feel free to talk about any Jewish matter at all — religion, family, politics, sports —"

There was silence. It was a gusty, clouded November afternoon and it did not seem as though there ever was or could be a thing called baseball. So nobody this week said a word about that hero from the past, Hank Greenberg[3] — which limited free discussion considerably.

45   And the soul-battering Ozzie Freedman had just received from Rabbi Binder had imposed its limitation. When it was Ozzie's turn to read aloud from the Hebrew book the rabbi had asked him petulantly why he didn't read more rapidly. He was showing no progress. Ozzie said he could read faster but that if he did he was sure not to understand what he was reading. Nevertheless, at the rabbi's repeated suggestion Ozzie tried, and showed a great talent, but in the midst of a long passage he stopped short and said he didn't understand a word he was reading, and started in again at a drag-footed pace. Then came the soul-battering.

Consequently when free-discussion time rolled around none of the students felt too free. The rabbi's invitation was answered only by the mumbling of feeble old Blotnik.

"Isn't there anything at all you would like to discuss?" Rabbi Binder asked again, looking at his watch. "No questions or comments?"

There was a small grumble from the third row. The rabbi requested that Ozzie rise and give the rest of the class the advantage of his thought.

Ozzie rose. "I forget it now," he said, and sat down in his place.

50   Rabbi Binder advanced a seat towards Ozzie and poised himself on the edge of the desk. It was Itzie's desk and the rabbi's frame only a dagger's-length away from his face snapped him to sitting attention.

"Stand up again, Oscar," Rabbi Binder said calmly, "and try to assemble your thoughts."

Ozzie stood up. All his classmates turned in their seats and watched as he gave an unconvincing scratch to his forehead.

"I can't assemble any," he announced, and plunked himself down.

"Stand up!" Rabbi Binder advanced from Itzie's desk to the one directly in front of Ozzie; when the rabbinical back was turned Itzie gave it five-fingers

3 all-star player for the Detroit Tigers baseball team in the 1930s and 1940s.

off the tip of his nose, causing a small titter in the room. Rabbi Binder was too absorbed in squelching Ozzie's nonsense once and for all to bother with titters. "Stand up, Oscar. What's your question about?"

55 Ozzie pulled a word out of the air. It was the handiest word. "Religion."

"Oh, now you remember?"

"Yes."

"What is it?"

Trapped, Ozzie blurted the first thing that came to him. "Why can't He make anything he wants to make!"

60 As Rabbi Binder prepared an answer, a final answer, Itzie, ten feet behind him, raised one finger on his left hand, gestured it meaningfully towards the rabbi's back, and brought the house down.

Binder twisted quickly to see what had happened and in the midst of the commotion Ozzie shouted into the rabbi's back what he couldn't have shouted to his face. It was a loud, toneless sound that had the timbre of something stored inside for about six days.

"You don't know! You don't know anything about God!"

The rabbi spun back towards Ozzie. "What?"

"You don't know — you don't —"

65 "Apologize, Oscar, apologize!" It was a threat.

"You don't —"

Rabbi Binder's hand flicked out at Ozzie's cheek. Perhaps it had only meant to clamp the boy's mouth shut, but Ozzie ducked and the palm caught him squarely on the nose.

The blood came in a short, red spurt on to Ozzie's shirt front.

The next moment was all confusion. Ozzie screamed, "You bastard, you bastard!" and broke for the classroom door. Rabbi Binder lurched a step backwards, as though his own blood had started flowing violently in the opposite direction, then gave a clumsy lurch forward and bolted out the door after Ozzie. The class followed after the rabbi's huge blue-suited back, and before old Blotnik could turn from his window, the room was empty and everyone was headed full speed up the three flights leading to the roof.

*****

70 If one should compare the light of day to the life of man: sunrise to birth; sunset — the dropping down over the edge — to death; then as Ozzie Freedman wiggled through the trapdoor of the synagogue roof, his feet kicking backwards bronco-style at Rabbi Binder's outstretched arms — at that moment the day was fifty years old. As a rule, fifty or fifty-five reflects accurately the age of late afternoons in November, for it is in that month, during those hours, that one's awareness of light seems no longer a matter of seeing, but of hearing: light begins clicking away. In fact, as Ozzie locked shut the trapdoor in the rabbi's face, the sharp click of the bolt into the lock might momentarily have been mistaken for the sound of the heavier gray that had just throbbed through the sky.

With all his weight Ozzie kneeled on the locked door; any instant he was certain that Rabbi Binder's shoulder would fling it open, splintering the wood into shrapnel and catapulting his body into the sky. But the door did not move and below him he heard only the rumble of feet, first loud then dim, like thunder rolling away.

A question shot through his brain. "Can this be *me*?" For a thirteen-year-old who had just labeled his religious leader a bastard, twice, it was not an improper question. Louder and louder the question came to him — "Is it me?" "Is it me?" — until he discovered himself no longer kneeling, but racing crazily towards the edge of the roof, his eyes crying, his throat screaming, and his arms flying everywhichway as though not his own!

"Is it me? Is it me ME ME ME! It has to be me — but is it!"

It is the question a thief must ask himself the night he jimmies open his first window, and it is said to be the question with which bridegrooms quiz themselves before the altar.

75   In the few wild seconds it took Ozzie's body to propel him to the edge of the roof, his self-examination began to grow fuzzy. Gazing down at the street, he became confused as to the problem beneath the question: was it, is-it-me-who-called-Binder-a-bastard? or, is-it-me-prancing-around-on-the-roof? However, the scene below settled all, for there is an instant in any action when whether it is you or somebody else is academic. The thief crams the money in his pockets and scoots out the window. The bridegroom signs the hotel register for two. And the boy on the roof finds a streetful of people gaping at him, necks stretched backwards, faces up, as though he were the ceiling of the Hayden Planetarium. Suddenly you know it's you.

"Oscar! Oscar Freedman!" A voice rose from the center of the crowd, a voice that, could it have been seen, would have looked like the writing on scroll. "Oscar Freedman, get down from there. Immediately!" Rabbi Binder was pointing one arm stiffly up at him; and at the end of that arm, one finger aimed menacingly. It was the attitude of a dictator, but one — the eyes confessed all — whose personal valet had spit neatly in his face.

Ozzie didn't answer. Only for a blink's length did he look towards Rabbi Binder. Instead his eyes began to fit together the world beneath him, to sort out people from places, friends from enemies, participants from spectators. In little jagged starlike clusters his friends stood around Rabbi Binder, who was still pointing. The topmost point on a star compounded not of angels but of five adolescent boys was Itzie. What a world it was, with those stars below, Rabbi Binder below ... Ozzie, who a moment earlier hadn't been able to control his own body, started to feel the meaning of the word control: he felt Peace and he felt Power.

"Oscar Freedman, I'll give you three to come down."

Few dictators give their subjects three to do anything; but, as always, Rabbi Binder only looked dictatorial.

80   "Are you ready, Oscar?"

Ozzie nodded his head yes, although he had no intention in the world — the lower one or the celestial one he'd just entered — of coming down even if Rabbi Binder should give him a million.

"All right then," said Rabbi Binder. He ran a hand through his black Samson hair as though it were the gesture prescribed for uttering the first digit. Then, with his other hand cutting a circle out of the small piece of sky around him, he spoke. "One!"

There was no thunder. On the contrary, at that moment, as though "one" was the cue for which he had been waiting, the world's least thunderous person appeared on the synagogue steps. He did not so much come out of the synagogue door as lean out, onto the darkening air. He clutched at the doorknob with one hand and looked up at the roof.

"Oy!"

85   Yakov Blotnik's old mind hobbled slowly, as if on crutches, and though he couldn't decide precisely what the boy was doing on the roof, he knew it wasn't good — that is, it wasn't-good-for-the-Jews. For Yakov Blotnik life had fractionated itself simply: things were either good-for-the-Jews or no-good-for-the-Jews.

He smacked his free hand to his in-sucked cheek, gently. "Oy, Gut!"[4] And then quickly as he was able, he jacked down his head and surveyed the street. There was Rabbi Binder (like a man at an auction with only three dollars in his pocket, he had just delivered a shaky "Two!"); there were the students, and that was all. So far it-wasn't-so-bad-for-the-Jews. But the boy had to come down immediately, before anybody saw. The problem: how to get the boy off the roof?

Anybody who has ever had a cat on the roof knows how to get him down. You call the fire department. Or first you call the operator and you ask her for the fire department. And the next thing there is great jamming of brakes and clanging of bells and shouting of instructions. And then the cat is off the roof. You do the same thing to get a boy off the roof.

That is, you do the same thing if you are Yakov Blotnik and you once had a cat on the roof.

*****

When the engines, all four of them, arrived, Rabbi Binder had four times given Ozzie the count of three. The big hook-and-ladder swung around the corner and one of the firemen leaped from it, plunging headlong towards the yellow fire hydrant in front of the synagogue. With a huge wrench he began to unscrew the top nozzle. Rabbi Binder raced over to him and pulled at his shoulder.

90   "There's no fire . . ."

The fireman mumbled back over his shoulder and, heatedly, continued working at the nozzle.

"But there's no fire, there's no fire . . ." Binder shouted. When the fireman mumbled again, the rabbi grasped his face with both his hands and pointed it up at the roof.

To Ozzie it looked as though Rabbi Binder was trying to tug the fireman's head out of his body, like a cork from a bottle. He had to giggle at the picture they made: it was a family portrait — rabbi in black skullcap, fireman in red fire hat, and the little yellow hydrant squatting beside like a kid brother, bareheaded. From the edge of the roof Ozzie waved at the portrait, a one-handed, flapping, mocking wave; in doing it his right foot slipped from under him. Rabbi Binder covered his eyes with his hands.

4 Yiddish expression signifying dismay.

Firemen work fast. Before Ozzie had even regained his balance, a big, round, yellowed net was being held on the synagogue lawn. The firemen who held it looked up at Ozzie with stern, feelingless faces.

95 One of the firemen turned his head towards Rabbi Binder. "What, is the kid nuts or something?"

Rabbi Binder unpeeled his hands from his eyes, slowly, painfully, as if they were tape. Then he checked: nothing on the sidewalk, no dents in the net.

"Is he gonna jump, or what?" the fireman shouted.

In a voice not at all like a statue, Rabbi Binder finally answered, "Yes, yes, I think so . . . He's been threatening to . . ."

Threatening to? Why, the reason he was on the roof, Ozzie remembered, was to get away: he hadn't even thought about jumping. He had just run to get away, and the truth was that he hadn't really headed for the roof as much as he'd been chased there.

100 "What's his name, the kid?"

"Freedman," Rabbi Binder answered. "Oscar Freedman."

The fireman looked up at Ozzie. "What is it with you, Oscar? You gonna jump, or what?"

Ozzie did not answer. Frankly, the question had just arisen.

"Look, Oscar, if you're gonna jump, jump — and if you're not gonna jump, don't jump. But don't waste our time, willya?"

105 Ozzie looked at the fireman and then at Rabbi Binder. He wanted to see Rabbi Binder cover his eyes one more time.

"I'm going to jump."

And then he scampered around the edge of the roof to the corner, where there was no net below, and he flapped his arms at his sides, swishing the air and smacking his palms to his trousers on the downbeat. He began screaming like some kind of engine, "Wheeeee . . . wheeeeee," and leaning way out over the edge with the upper half of his body. The firemen whipped around to cover the ground with the net. Rabbi Binder mumbled a few words to somebody and covered his eyes. Everything happened quickly, jerkily, as in a silent movie. The crowd, which had arrived with the fire engines, gave out a long, Fourth-of-July fireworks oooh-aahhh. In the excitement no one had paid the crowd much heed, except, of course, Yakov Blotnik, who swung from the door now counting heads. "Fier und tsvansik . . . finf und tsvansik.[5] Oy, Gut!" It wasn't like this with the cat.

Rabbi Binder peeked through his fingers, checked the sidewalk and net. Empty. But there was Ozzie racing to the other corner. The firemen raced with him but were unable to keep up. Whenever Ozzie wanted to he might jump and splatter himself upon the sidewalk, and by the time the firemen scooted to the spot all they could do with their net would be to cover the mess.

"Wheeeee . . . wheeeeee . . ."

110 "Hey, Oscar," the winded fireman yelled, "What the hell is this, a game or something?"

"Wheeeee . . . wheeeee . . ."

"Hey, Oscar —"

5 Twenty-four . . . twenty-five.

But he was off now to the other corner, flapping his wings fiercely. Rabbi Binder couldn't take it any longer — the fire engines from nowhere, the screaming suicidal boy, the net. He fell to his knees, exhausted, and with his hands curled together in front of his chest like a little dome, he pleaded, "Oscar, stop it, Oscar. Don't jump, Oscar. Please come down ... Please don't jump."

And further back in the crowd a single voice, a single young voice, shouted a lone word to the boy on the roof.

115 "Jump!"

It was Itzie. Ozzie momentarily stopped flapping.

"Go ahead, Ozz — jump!" Itzie broke off his point of the star and courageously, with the inspiration not of a wise-guy but of a disciple, stood alone. "Jump, Ozz, jump!"

Still on his knees, his hands still curled, Rabbi Binder twisted his body back. He looked at Itzie, then, agonizingly, back to Ozzie.

"OSCAR, DON'T JUMP! PLEASE, DON'T JUMP ... PLEASE, PLEASE ..."

120 "Jump! This time it wasn't Itzie but another point of the star. By the time Mrs. Freedman arrived to keep her four-thirty appointment with Rabbi Binder, the whole little upside down heaven was shouting and pleading for Ozzie to jump, and Rabbi Binder no longer was pleading with him not to jump, but was crying into the dome of his hands.

*****

Understandably Mrs. Freedman couldn't figure out what her son was doing on the roof. So she asked.

"Ozzie, my Ozzie, what are you doing? My Ozzie, what is it?"

Ozzie stopped wheeeeeing and slowed his arms down to a cruising flap, the kind birds use in soft winds, but he did not answer. He stood against the low, clouded, darkening sky — light clicked down swiftly now, as on a small gear — flapping softly and gazing down at the small bundle of a woman who was his mother.

"What are you doing, Ozzie?" She turned towards the kneeling Rabbi Binder and rushed so close that only a paper-thickness of dust lay between her stomach and his shoulders.

125 "What is my baby doing?"

Rabbi Binder gaped up at her but he too was mute. All that moved was the dome of his hands; it shook back and forth like a weak pulse.

"Rabbi, get him down! He'll kill himself. Get him down, my only baby ..."

"I can't," Rabbi Binder said, "I can't ..." and he turned his handsome head towards the crowd of boys behind him. "It's them. Listen to them."

And for the first time Mrs. Freedman saw the crowd of boys, and she heard what they were yelling.

130 "He's doing it for them. He won't listen to me. It's them." Rabbi Binder spoke like one in a trance.

"For them?"

"Yes."

"Why for them?"

"They want him to ..."

135   Mrs. Freedman raised her two arms upward as though she were conducting the sky. "For them he's doing it!" And then in a gesture older than pyramids, older than prophets and floods, her arms came slapping down to her
sides. "A martyr I have. Look!" She tilted her head to the roof. Ozzie was still
flapping softly. "My martyr."

       "Oscar, come down, *please*," Rabbi Binder groaned.

       In a startling even voice Mrs. Freedman called to the boy on the roof.
"Ozzie, come down, Ozzie. Don't be a martyr, my baby."

       As though it were a litany, Rabbi Binder repeated her words. "Don't be a
martyr, my baby. Don't be a martyr."

       "Gawhead, Ozz — *be* a Martin!" It was Itzie. "Be a Martin, be a Martin,"
and all the voices joined in singing for Martindom, whatever *it* was. "Be a
Martin, be a Martin . . ."

*****

140   Somehow when you're on a roof the darker it gets the less you can hear. All
Ozzie knew was that two groups wanted two new things: his friends were spir-
ited and musical about what they wanted; his mother and the rabbi were
eventoned, chanting, about what they didn't want. The rabbi's voice was
without tears now and so was his mother's.

       The big net stared up at Ozzie like a sightless eye. The big, clouded sky
pushed down. From beneath it looked like a gray corrugated board. Suddenly,
looking up into that unsympathetic sky, Ozzie realized all the strangeness of what
these people, his friends, were asking: they wanted him to jump, to kill himself;
they were singing about it now — it made them happy. And there was an even
greater strangeness: Rabbi Binder was on his knees, trembling. If there was a question to be asked now it was not "Is it me?" but rather "Is it us? . . . Is it us?"

       Being on the roof, it turned out, was a serious thing. If he jumped would
the singing become dancing? Would it? What would jumping stop? Yearningly,
Ozzie wished he could rip open the sky, plunge his hands through, and pull out
the sun; and on the sun, like a coin, would be stamped JUMP or DON'T JUMP.

       Ozzie's knees rocked and sagged a little under him as though they were
setting him for a dive. His arms tightened, stiffened, froze, from shoulders to fingernails. He felt as if each part of his body were going to vote as to whether he
should kill himself or not — and each part as though it were independent of *him*.

       The light took an unexpected click down and the new darkness, like a gag,
hushed the friends singing for this and the mother and rabbi chanting for that.

145   Ozzie stopped counting votes, and in a curiously high voice, like one who
wasn't prepared for speech, he spoke.

       "Mamma?"

       "Yes, Oscar."

       "Mamma, get down on your knees, like Rabbi Binder."

       "Oscar —"

150   "Get down on your knees," he said, "or I'll jump."

       Ozzie heard a whimper, then a quick rustling, and when he looked down
where his mother had stood he saw the top of a head and beneath that a circle
of dress. She was kneeling beside Rabbi Binder.

He spoke again. "Everybody kneel." There was the sound of everybody kneeling.

Ozzie looked around. With one hand he pointed towards the synagogue entrance. "Make *him* kneel."

There was a noise, not of kneeling, but of body-and-cloth stretching. Ozzie could hear Rabbi Binder saying in a gruff whisper, "... or he'll *kill* himself," and when next he looked there was Yakov Blotnik off the doorknob and for the first time in his life upon his knees in the Gentile[6] posture of prayer.

155   As for the firemen — it is not as difficult as one might imagine to hold a net taut while you are kneeling.

Ozzie looked around again; and then he called to Rabbi Binder.

"Rabbi?"

"Yes, Oscar."

"Rabbi Binder, do you believe in God?"

160   "Yes."

"Do you believe God can do Anything?" Ozzie leaned his head out into the darkness. "Anything?"

"Oscar, I think —"

"Tell me you believe God can do Anything."

There was a second's hesitation. Then: "God can do Anything."

165   "Tell me you believe God can make a child without intercourse."

"He can."

"Tell me!"

"God," Rabbi Binder admitted, "can make a child without intercourse."

"Mamma, you tell me."

170   "God can make a child without intercourse," his mother said.

"Make *him* tell me." There was no doubt who *him* was.

In a few moments Ozzie heard an old comical voice say something to the increasing darkness about God.

Next, Ozzie made everybody say it. And then he made them all say they believed in Jesus Christ — first one at a time, then all together.

When the catechizing was through it was the beginning of evening. From the street it sounded as if the boy on the roof might have sighed.

175   "Ozzie?" A woman's voice dared to speak. "You'll come down now?"

There was no answer, but the woman waited, and when a voice finally did speak it was thin and crying, and exhausted as that of an old man who has just finished pulling the bells.

"Mamma, don't you see — you shouldn't hit me. He shouldn't hit me. You shouldn't hit me about God, Mamma. You should never hit anybody about God —"

"Ozzie, please come down now."

"Promise me, promise me you'll never hit anybody about God."

180   He had asked only his mother, but for some reason everyone kneeling in the street promised he would never hit anybody about God.

6 non-Jewish people; generally refers to Christians.

Once again there was silence.

"I can come down now, Mamma," the boy on the roof finally said. He turned his head both ways as though checking the traffic lights. "Now I can come down..."

And he did, right into the center of the yellow net that glowed in the evening's edge like an overgrown halo.

(1959)

Austin C. Clarke (b. 1934)

Barbadian-born novelist and short story writer Austin Clarke, who moved to Toronto in 1955, has chronicled the lives of his compatriots both in the Caribbean and in Canada, the latter often referred to as "that cold, ungodly place" by his characters. His acclaimed Toronto trilogy, *The Meeting Point*, *Storm of Fortune*, and *The Bigger Light*, portrays the tensions that exist among poor men and women who have travelled to Toronto in search of better lives and found low-paying jobs and racial prejudice. "The Motor Car" uses the familiar initiation journey structure, tracing the move of a young man from a small town to a big city. The result of Calvin's search for happiness, which involves an attempt to deny his past and to find materialistic well-being through ownership of an automobile, symbolizes the lot of the immigrant in modern Canadian society. The story exemplifies the author's sensitive understanding of his characters, the gentle humour with which he depicts their situations, and his accurate reproduction of the dialect and rhythms of Barbadian speech.

THE MOTOR CAR

That Canadian thing you see lying down there in that bed is Calvin woman, I mean *was* Calvin woman. Calvin wash motor cars back in Barbados till his back hurt and his belly burn, and when the pain stop in the body it start up fresh in his mind. Good thing Calvin was a God-faring man, cause if not he would have let go some real bad curse words that would have blow way the garage itself. But instead o' talking to the customers bout the hard work, instead o' talking to the boss bout the slave work he was making Calvin do in 1968 in these modern days, Calvin talk to God. Calvin didn' know if God did really hear him, cause the more he talk to God every morning before he went to work on his old Raleigh green three-speed bicycle, and after work when his head hit that pillow, the more the work did get harder. One day Calvin take in with a bout o' bad-feels, and the moment he come outta the fit or the trance, or the *hellucinations* as his boss call it, right that very second Calvin swear blind to God that he leffing Barbados. One time. For good. First chance. Is only the governorship or the governor-generalship that could get Calvin to stay in Barbados. That is the kind o' swearing he put pon God. And it ain't really clear, even at this time, if God really understand the kind o' message that Calvin put to him. But Calvin didn't care. Calvin decide already. Calvin start to work hard, more harder than he ever work in his life, from the very day after he decide that he pulling outta Barbados. And is to Canada he coming. Now the problems start falling pon top o' Calvin head like rainwater. First problem: he can't get a Canadian visa. He seeing Canadian tourisses morning noon and night all bout his island, walking bout like if they own the blasted place, and if you don't look out they getting on as if they want to own Calvin too. Calvin hit a low point o' studyation. The work done now and he pack already, two big big imitation leather valises; and he manage to buy the ticket too, although there is a regulation down there in the island that say a black man can't buy a ticket pon *Air Canada* saving he have a job and a roof to come to in Canada, or he have family here, or some kind o' support, cause Trudeau[1] get vex vex as hell bout supporting the boys when they come up here and can't find proper ployment. Calvin walking bout Bridgetown the capital all day telling people he pulling out next week for Canada. Next week come and he still walking bout Bridgetown. He ain't pull out in trute, yuh: he ain't like he pulling out at all, man; that is what the boys was beginning to think. They start laughing at Calvin behind his back, and Calvin grinning and telling them, "Gorblummuh, you laugh! *laugh*! he who laugh last, laugh…" And for purpose, he won't finish the saying at all, he only ordering a next round o' steam for his friends, and his mind focus-on pon a new shining motto-car that he going buy up in Canada before he even living there a year. He done make up his mind that he going work at two car-wash places, and if the Lord hear his prayers, and treat he nice, he going hustle a next job on top o' them two, too. Well, the more the boys laugh, the more Calvin decide with a piece o' real bad-mind that he going buy a brand-new Chevvy, perhaps even a custom-build *Galaxie*. And then, all of a sudden, one night when the fellas drink three free-round o' rum offa Calvin, Calvin really start to laugh. He push he hand inside his pocket, and he pull out a thing that look real important and official, and all he say is, "I taking off at nine in the morning." Calvin then throw a new-brand twenty dollar bill pon Marcus rum shop counter, and the fellas gone wild, be-Christ, cause is now real drinking going begin. Calvin stand up like a man. Every one that his best friend Willy fire, Calvin fire one, too. Willy, who didn' lick he mouth too much gainst Calvin going way, when he reach the fifth straight *Mount Gay*, Calvin was right there with him. Is rum for rum. Drink for drink. They start eating raw salt fish, and Calvin iamming the cod fish as if he catch it himself off the banks o' Newfoundland in the same Canada that he heading out to. The fellas eat off all o' Marcus bad half-rotten salt fish, and then start-on pon a tin o' corn beef and raw onions and you would have think that Calvin was pon a real religious fast during the time he was worrying bout the Canadian visa. "I going tell you fellas something," Willy say, for no conceivable reason at all, cause they just then telling Calvin that he ain' going see no good cricket when he get up in that cold ungodly place call Canada. "I going tell you fellas something now," Willy say, after he clear his throat for effect, and to make the fellas stop drinking and eating and listen to him. "Godblummuh! Calvin is the most luckiest one o' we, yuh! Calvin lucky-lucky-lucky as shite!" He say the last two "lucky" like if they was one word. Anyhow, he went on, "Calvin is a king to we!" Now, nobody ain' know what the arse Willy trying to say, cause Willy is a man who does try to talk big and talk a lot o' shite in the bargain. But this time, solemn occasion as it be, the fellas decide to give Willy a listen. "We lis'ning, man, so talk yuh talk. We lis'ning." Willy take a long pull pon the rum bottle, and he stuff bout a half-pound o' corn beef inside his mouth, with the biscuits flying bout the place like big drops o' spit. "You see that salt fish that we just put way? Well, it make up in Canada. Tha's where Calvin here going. Now understand this when I say it. I only say that to say this. Comprehend? The salt fish that we does

---

1 Pierre Elliott Trudeau, prime minister of Canada from 1968 to 1979 and 1980 to 1984.

get down here, send-down by Canada, is the same quality o' salt fish that they uses to send down here to feed we when we was slaves. It smell stink. You could tell when a woman cooking salt fish. We even invent a term to go long with this kind o' salt fish and this kind o' stinkingness. We does say to a person who uses *profine* words, 'Yuh mouth smell like a fucking salt-fish barrel,' Unnerstand? I going to lay a bet pon any one o' you bitches in here now, drinking this rum. I going wager five dollars gainst a quarter that the brand o' salt fish Calvin going get to buy and eat up in that place call Canada is a better quality o' salt fish. It rass-hole bound to be, cause that is where it produce. And if you ever study Marx, you would understand the kind o' social-ism I talking bout." Nobody ain' answer Willy for a time, all they do is laugh. "Laugh! laugh!" Willy say with scorn, "cause godblindme!..." And then Calvin say, like if he didn' really want to say the words at-all, "Be-Jesus Christ, when you see me leff this blasted backwards place, call Barbados, that is the last time I eating salt fish. I eating steaks!"

Well, they poured Calvin on pon the *Air Canada*, next morning, nine sharp, drunk as a flying-fish. Good thing Calvin mother did pack the fry dolphin steak, a bottle o' Cod Liver Oil, in case the bowels do a thing and give trouble in that cold ungodly climate, as she call Canada; and she pack some Phensic for headache, just in case; she pack some miraculous bush, for medi-cine, "cause they ain' have doctor no place under the sun who know the good-ness in this mirac'lous bush-tea as we does, so you tek it along with you, son; you going up in that strange savage place, and you far from me, and I ain' near enough no more to run to you and rub your face with a lime and some Limacol, and tie it up with oil-leaves and candle-grease..."; and she put in half dozen limes and two bottle o' Limacol; man, is a good-good thing that Calvin mother had the presence o' mind to pack these things for Calvin whilst Calvin was walking bout Broadstreet in Bridgetown like if he was one o' them Canadian tourisses. Calvin mother do a real good job, and when she done pack the things, and she inspect the clothes that Calvin carrying way, she tie-up the two valises with a strong piece o' string, although they had brand-new locks pon them. "Good!" is the last thing she say to Calvin, as she was holding over the kitchen door, whilst Willy was revving up the hired car and blowing the horn — which, of course, Calvin pay for, the hired car I mean — plus dropping a ten dollar bill inside Willy hand for old times sake. "Go long in the name o' the Lord, and make yuh fortune, son." A tear or two drop outta she eye, too; but she was glad-glad in she heart that she boy-child was leffing Barbados. "Too much foreigners and tourisses and crooks living here with we, now, son. Canada more brighter than here." Calvin get vex-vex when he see the water in his mother eye, and he was embarrass as hell, cause he always use to brag how nothing he do, or don't do, could make his mother belly burn she. Good thing Willy had the car motor revving, cause Calvin get in such a state over the tears and heart-break on the part of his mother that he almost forget that deep-down he is a christian-minded man and say a bad word, whiching as he did know full-well, God would be vex as hell with him for. The motto-car was making good time moving like hell going up the airport road, and every-body Calvin know, and everybody that he barely know in the twenty-nine years he born and living in Barbados, he hold half of his body out through the car window, and yell out, "Boy, I going this morning! Canada, in your arse!" All the people who see and hear, wave back and grin their teet', if they could hear from the distance and through the speed; and some o' them say, "Bless." If everybody in Barbados, down Broadstreet, at the airport didn' know that Calvin pulling out for Canada at quarter-to-nine that morning, by nine o'clock the whole world did know. Friend or no friend, every time he see a face, or a hand, he saying, "Well, I won't be see you for a while, man, I going up." And they did all know what he meant, cause it was a time when all the young boys and young girls was pulling outta the island and going to Amer'ca, Britain, although Britain begin to tighten up things for the fellas because o' Powell; and some o' them start running up in Canada. And they was more *Air Canada* planes all bout Seawell Airport in Barbados in them days that you would have think that Barbados did own *Air Canada*. But is the other way round. Anyhow, drunk as Calvin was when he step pon that plane, and the white lady smile at him and say, "Good morning, sir" — first time in Calvin life white woman ever call him that, that way — well, Calvin know long time that he make the right move. Canada nice, he say in his heart; and he end it up with "Praise God." Canada now gone straight to Calvin head, long time and with a kind o' power, that when the airplane start up Calvin imagine that he own the whole blasted plane along with the white ladies who tell him, "Good morning, sir"; he feel that the plane is the big motto-car he intend to own one year after he land pon Canadian soil. The plane making time fast fast, and Calvin drink rum after rum till he went fast asleep and didn' even know he was in Toronto. The white lady come close to him, and tap him soft soft pon his new tropical suit and say, "Sir?", like if she asking some important question, when all she want is to wake up Calvin outta the white man plane. Well, Calvin wake up. He stretch like how he uses to stretch when he wake up in his mother bed. He yawn so hard that the white lady move back a step or two, after she see the pink inside his mouth and the black and blue gums running round them white pearly teets. Calvin eyes red red as a cheery from lack o' sleep and too much rum drinking, and the body tired like how it uses to get tired and wrap-up like a old motto-car fender. But is Canada, old man, and in a jiffy, before the white lady get to the front o' the plane to put down the last glass, Calvin looking out through the window. "Toronto in your arse!" he went to say to himself, but it come out too loud, as if he was saying it to Willy and the boys who didn' think he was really going to come through. "Toronto in your arse, man!" The plane touch down, and the first man outta the plane is, well, no need to tell you who it was. Calfuckingvin! And he pass through the customs like if he was born in Toronto. The white man didn' even ask him a question. Something like it was wrong, cause Calvin did know as far away as in Barbados that the Immigration and Customs men in Toronto is the roughest in the world, when they see a black face in front o' them. But this white gentleman must have been down in the islands recently, cause all he tell Calvin was, "Don't tell me! Don't tell me! You're a Bajun!" For years after, Calvin wondering how the hell this white man know so much bout black people. Before the first week come and gone, Calvin take up pen and paper and send off a little thing to Willy and the boys: ... *and I am going to tell you something, this place is the greatest place for a working man to live. I hear some things about this place, but*

I isn't a man to complain, because while I know I am a man, and I won't take no shit from no Canadian, white, black or red, I still have another piece of knowledge which says that I didn't born here. So I controls myself to suit, and make the white man money. The car only a couple of months off. I see one already that I got my eyes on. And if God willing, by the next two months, DV, I sitting down in the drivers seat. The car I got my eyes on is a red one, with white tires. The steering wheel as you know is on the left hand side, and we drives on the right hand side of the road up here, not like back in Barbados where you drive on the left hand. Next week, I taking out my licents. I not found a church I like yet, mainly because I see some strange things happening up here in churches. You don't know, man, Willy, but black people can't or don't go in the same church as white people. God must be have two colours then. One for black people and one for white people. And a next thing. There is some fellas up here from the islands who talking a lot of shite about Black Power, and I hear that one of them is a Barbadian. But I am one man who don't want to hear no shit about Black Power. I am here working for a living and a motor car and if my mother herself come in my way and be an obstacle against me getting them two things, a living and a motor car, I would kill her by Christ... Calvin was going to write more: about the room he was renting for twenty dollars a week, which a white fellow tell him was pure robbery, because he was paying ten dollars for a more larger room on the ground floor in the same house; and he didn' write Willy bout the car-wash job he got the next day down Spadina Avenue, working for a dollar a hour, and when the first three hours pass he felt he been working for three days, the work was so hard; he didn' tell Willy that a certain kind of white people in Canada didn' sit too close to him on the street car, that they didn' speak to him on the street... lots o' things he didn' worry to tell Willy, cause he did want Willy to think that he was really a king to the boys back home, a champion for emigrading to Canada. Willy send back a post card with a mauby[2] woman on the colour side selling mauby, and on the writing side, in his scribbly handwriting, "As man!" But be-Christ, Calvin didn' care what they do, he was here for two purpose; one, living, and number two, motto-car. If they touch my motto-car, now, well, that would be something else... and Calvin work hard, man, Calvin work more harder than when he was washing-off cars back in Barbados. The money was good too. Sal'ry and tips. From the two car-wash jobs he uses to clear a hundred dollars a week, and that is two hundred back home, and not even Dipper does make that kind o' money, and he is the fucking prime minister! The third job, Calvin land like a dream; nightwatchman with a big big important company which put him in big big important uniform and thing, big leather belt like what he uses to envy the officers in the Volunteer Force back home wearing pon a Queen Birthday parade on the Garrison Savannah,[3] shoes the company people even provide, and the only thing that was missing, according to what Calvin figure out some months afterwards, was that the holster at his side, join-on to the leather belt, didn' have in no blasted gun. He tell it to a next Barbadian he make friends with, and the Bajan just laugh and say, "They think you going rass-hole shoot yourself, boy!" But Calvin did already become Canadified enough to know that the only people he see in them uniforms with guns in the leather

2 West Indian herbal beverage. 3 race track in Barbados.

holster was certain white people, and he know he wasn' Canadified so much that he did turn white overnight. "Once it don't stop me from getting that *Galaxie*!" Work work work, a occasional postcard to Willy, cause envelopes was costing too much all of a sudden, and postage stamps was going up too, no pleasure for Calvin: he went down by the *Tropics Club* where they play calypsoes and dance, one time, and he never went back cause the ugly Grenadian fellow at the door ask him for "Three dollars to come in!", and he curse the fellow and leff. But the bank account was mounting and climbing like a woman belly when she in the family-way. Quick-quick so, Calvin have a thousand dollars pon the bank. Fellas who get to know Calvin and who Calvin won't sociate with because "sociating does cost money, boy!", them fellas so who here donkey years, still borrowing money to help pay their rent, fellas gambling like hell, throwing dice every Fridee night right into Mondee morning early, missing work and getting fired from work, fellas playing poker and betting, "Forty dollars more for these two fours, in your rass, sah! I *raise*!", them brand o' Trinidadian, Bajan, Jamaician, Grenadian and thing, them so can't understand at-all how Calvin just land and he get rich so fast. "I bet all-yuh Calvin selling pussy!" one fella say. A next bad-minded fella say, "He peddling his arse to white boys down Yonge Street," and a third fella who did just bet fifty dollars 'pon a pair o' deuces, and get broke at the poker game, say quick-quick before the words fall-out o' the other fella mouth, "I going peddle mine too, then! Bread is bread." Calvin start slacking up on the first car wash work, and he humming as he shine the white people car, he skinning his teet in the shine and he smiling, and the white people thinking he smiling because he like the work and them, cause his hands never tarried whilst he was car-dreaming, they drop a little dollar bill pon Calvin as a tip, and a regular twenty-five cent piece, and Calvin pinching pon the groceries, eating a lotta pigs feet and chicken necks and salt fish . . . "I gotta write Willy and tell him bout the brand o' salt fish in this place. Willy was right!" . . . Calvin won't spend thirty cents pon a beer with a sinner, only time he even reading is when he clean out a car in the car wash and it happen to have a used paper inside it, or a throw-away paperback book. But Calvin decide long time that he didn' come here for eddication. He come for a living and a motto-car. A new one, too! And he intend to get both. And by the look o' things, be-Christ, both almost in his hand. Only now waiting to see the right model o' motor car, with the right colour inside it, and the right mileage and thing. The motto-car must have the right colour o' tires, right colour o' gear shift and in the handle too. And it have to have-in radio; and he see a fella in the car wash with a thing inside his Cadillac, and Calvin gone crazy over Cadillacs until he walk down by Bay Street and price the price of a old one. He bawl for murder. "Better stick to the *Galaxie*, boy!" he tell himself; and he do that. But he really like the thing inside the white man Cadillac and he ask the man one morning what it was, and the man tell Calvin. Now Calvin *must* have red *Galaxie*, with not more than 20,000 miles on the register, black upholstery, red gear shift, radio, AM *and FM and a tellyfone* . . . Them last three things is what the man had inside his Cadillac. Calvin working even on a Sundee, bank holidays ain' touching Calvin, and the Old Queen back home who send a occasional letter asking Calvin to remember the house rent and the Poor Box in the Nazarene Church where he was a testifying brother, preaching and thing, and also to remember "who birthed him", well, Calvin tell the Old Queen, his own-own mother; *Things hard up here, mother. Don't let nobody fool you that because a man emigrade it mean that he elevate. That isn't true. But I am sending this Canadian money order for five dollars, which is ten dollars back home, and I hope that next week I would find myself a nice job, and then I am going to send you a little something more. Your loving son, Calvin. P.S. Pray for me.* Calvin start thinking that maybe the Old Queen had a bad mind for him; he start one long stewpsing, and the fellas at work even had to ask him if he sick or something, he even stop laughing and chumming around with the Canadians at work; he refuse to play Frisbee and throw the ball in the other fellas mittens, he even stop begging the German fella for a lift home after work. Calvin start getting ingrown like a toenail: pressure in Calvin arse. The studyation take a hold o' him and one weekend it capsize him in bed, Fridee night, Sardah morning and Sardah night, Sundee and right into Mondee morning half hour before he is to leff for work. Landlady couldn' even come in and change the filthy linens and bed sheets. But Calvin make sure he went to work that Mondee. "Can't lose that money now, boy!" Willy was the next joker at this time o' hardship and studyation. Willy send a letter registered and thing, in a real pretty envelope with the colours o' the Union Jack, to Calvin: . . . *and if it isn't asking too much, Calvin, I wonder if you can see your way in sending me down a piece of change. I am thinking about emigrading too, because Barbados is at a standstill for people like me, people who don't have no high school education, no big kind of skills and no kiss-me-arse godfather in big jobs in the civil service. My kind of man in Barbados is loss. I hope I am not imposing when I ask you if you could see your way in lending me the passage money, one way, and I am going to open a new bank account with it and take a picture of it and show it to the Canadian immigration people down here, because another fellow promise to do the same thing for me with the return part of the passage money. The Canadian high commission place in Trinidad giving the fellows a hard time. But we smarter than any number of Canadian immigration people they send down here. So I asking this favour for old times sake, because not that I hard on you, but I don't want to remind you of the time when you had the accident with the motor car that didn't belongst to you, and you was in hospital, and you know who help you out, so . . .* Calvin get in a bad bad mood straightaway, thinking that everybody back home think he is a millionaire, everybody back there getting on like crabs, willing to pull him down the moment he come up for breath. "Be-Christ, not me!" and in that frame o' mind Calvin take up a piece o' stationery he borrow from a Jamaican fellow who had a job in the General Hospital, and a envelope to match, with the hospital name on both, and he ask a next fellow who had a typewriter to write this letter back to Willy: *Dear Willy, I have been laid up in this hospital for two months now. I am getting a friend who is in the hospital too, but who is not confine to bed and who can barely walk around, to post this letter to you for me. Things really bad, man . . .* because all my friends back home think I is a arse or something, they see me emigrade to this place and they think that I get rich overnight, or that I don't work hard as hell for my money, but that ain't true. Willy didn' answer back immediately, but a month and a half later, two days before Calvin decide he see the right automobile, a card drop through the door where Calvin living, address to Calvin: *What are you doing up there, then?*

Canadians buying out all the island. You standing for that? Send down a couple of dollars and let me invest it in a piece of beach land for you, Brother. Power to the people! Salaam and love. Willy X. Calvin get so blasted vex, so damn vex, cause he sure now that Willy gone mad too, like everybody else he been reading bout in the States and in England; black people gone mad, Calvin say; and he get more vex when he think that it was the landlady, Mistress Silvermann who take up the post card from the linoleum and hand it to him, and he swear blind that she hand it to him after she done read the thing: and now she must be frighten like hell for Calvin, cause Calvin getting letters from these political extremists, and birds of a feather does flock together, she thinking now that Calvin perhaps is some kind o' political maniac, crying Black Power! all this damn foolishness bout Power to the People, and signing his name Willy X, when everybody in Barbados know that that damn fool's name is really William Fortesque: Calvin get shame-shame-shame that the landlady thinking different bout him, because sometimes she does be in the house alone all night with Calvin, and she must be even thinking bout giving him notice, which would be a damn bad thing to happen right now, cause the motto-car just two days off, the room he renting now is a nice one, the rent come down like the temperature in May when he talk plain to Mistress Silvermann bout how he paying twice as much as other tenants, but what really get Calvin really vex-vex-vex as hell is that a little Canadian thing in the room over his head come downstairs one night in a mini-dress and thing, bubbies jumping bout inside her bosom, free and thing and looking juicy, and giggling all the time and calling sheself a women liberation, all her skin at the door, and the legs nice and fat just as Calvin like his meats, and Calvin already gone thinking that this thing is the right woman to drive-bout in his new automobile with, this Canadian thing coming downstairs every night for the past month, and out of the blue asking him, "You'll like a coffee?" When she say so the first time, coffee was as far from Calvin mind as lending Willy twenty-five cents for the downpayment for the house spot pon the beach back home. Now, be-Christ, Willy X, or whatever the hell that bastard calling himself nowadays, is going to stay right there down in Barbados and mash up Calvin life so! Just so? Simple so? Oh God, no, man! But the landlady couldn' read English, she did only uses to pretend she is a genius; the Canadian girl is who tell Calvin not to worry; one night when they was drinking the regular coffee in the communal kitchen, the Canadian girl say, "Missis Silvermann is only a D.P.[4] She can't read English." Calvin take courage. The bank book walking bout with him, inside his trousers all the time, he counting the digits going to work, coming from work, in the back seat alone, pon the street car, while waiting for the subway early on a morning at the Ossington Station, and then he make a plan. He plan it down to a T. Every penny organize for the proper thing, every nickel with its own work to do: the bottle of wine that the Canadian girl gave him the name to; the new suit from Eaton's that he see in the display window one night when he get hold of the girl and he get bold bold as hell and decide to take she for a lover's walk down Yonge Street; the new shoes, brown-brown till they look red to match the car; and the shirt and tie — every-blasted-thing matching-up like if he is a new bride

4 displaced person; derogatory term for a post–World War II European refugee or immigrant.

stepping down the aisle to the wedding march. And he even have a surprise up his sleeve for the thing, too. He isn' no longer a stingy man, cause he see his goal; and his goal is like gold. The car delivery arrange for three o'clock, Sardah; no work; the ice box in his room have in a beer or two, plus the wine; and he have a extra piece o' change in his pocket... "I going have to remember to change the money from this pocket," he tell himself, as if he was talking to somebody else in the room with him, "to the next pocket in the new suit" ...and he have Chinese food now on his mind because the Canadian thing mention a nice Chinese restaurant down in Chinatown near Elizabeth Street. Calvin nervous as arse all Fridee night; all Fridee night the thing in Calvin room (here of late she behaving as if she live in Calvin room!), and Calvin is a man with ambitions: one night she tantalize Calvin head so much that he start talking bout high-rise apartment; perhaps, if she behave sheself he might even put a little gold thing pon her pretty little pink finger...the girl start asking Calvin if he want *some*; not in them exact words, but that is what she did mean; and Calvin turn shame-shame and nearly blush, only thing, as you know black people can't show really if they blushing or if they mad as shite with a white person, and Calvin turn like a virgin on the night before she getting hang in church and in marriage, and he saying all the time because his mind pon the mileage in the motto-car, "Want some o' what?" And the girl laugh, and she throw back she head and show she gold fillings and she pink tongue and the little speck o' dirt under she neck; and she laugh and say to sheself, "This one is a real gentleman, not like what my girlfriend say to expect from West Indian men, at all...." And you know something? She start one big confessing: "...and do you know what, Calvin? Would you like to hear something that I been thinking..." Calvin thinking bout motto-car and this blasted white woman humbugging him bout sex! Calvin get vex, he play he get vex bout something different from the woman and she sex, and he send she flying back upstairs to she own room. He get in bed too, but he ain' sleeping, he wide awake in the dark like a thief, and he eyes open wide-wide-wide like a owl eyes, and in that darkness in that little little room that only have one small window way up by the ceiling and facing the clothes-lines and the dingy sheets that the landlady does spend all week washing, Calvin see the whole o' Toronto standing up and watching him drive by in his new motto-car — with the Canadian thing beside o' him in the front seat! — dream turn into different dream that Fridee night, because he was free to dream as much as he like since Sardah wasn' no work. Sardah is car day. He have everything plan. Go for the motto-car, pick it up, drive it home, pick up the Canadian thing, go for a spin down Bloor as far as Yonge, swing back up by Harbord, turn left at Spadina, take in College Street, and every West Indian in Toronto bound to see him in new car, before he get back home. Park she in front o' the house, *let everybody see me getting outta she, come in, have a little bite, change, change into the new suit, give the Canadian thing the surprise, and whilst she dressing, I sit down in the car*... "And I hope she take a long time dressing so I would have to press the car-horn, press the horn just a little, a soft little thing, and call she outside, to see me in the..." Morning break nice. It was a nice morning round the middle o' September, fall time in the air, everybody stretching and holding up their head cause the weather nice.

Even the cops have a smile on their fissiogomy.[5] Calvin get up at five, take a quick look at the alarm clock, curse the clock for being so damn slow, went back to sleep, had a dream in which he see Willy as the garage mechanic at the car-place taking too long over the *Galaxie*; he curse Willy in the dream and nearly didn' get up in time, then turn round and curse Willy for coming into his dream; he left without tea, travelling with the Canadian thing half-sleep beside him, and gone fast pon the subway at Ossington down Danforth for the machine. The salesman-man smile and shake Calvin hand strong, and give Calvin the history of the bird although Calvin did already hear the bird history before. The salesman-man come outta the office still smiling, holding the motto-car keys between the index finger and the big thumb, and he drop them in Calvin hand. Calvin make a shiver. A shiver o' pride and ownership. "*Galaxie in your arse!*" He say that in his mind, and he thinking o' Willy and the boys back in Marcus rum shop. He get in the car. He shuffle bout a bit in the leather seat. He straighten he trouser seams. He touch the leather. He start up the motor. Listen to the motor. It ticking over like a fucking charm. He put the thing in gear. And he make a little thing through the car park, and he would have gone straight back up Danforth if the Canadian thing didn' wave she handbag to remind Calvin that she come with he, cause Calvin did forget she standing up there looking at a white convertible Cadillac, which she say is the car for Calvin, that there is lots o' "Negro-men driving cars, even in Nova Scotia where I come from," that Calvin should have buy one o' them. "You start spending my blasted money already, woman! This is *mine!*" He didn' tell she out loud in words what he was really thinking bout she, but he was thinking so, though. The Canadian gash get in the motto-car, cause driving in a *Galaxie* more better than walking behind a Cadillac, and she sit down so comfortable that it look like if she own the car and she was giving Calvin a chance to try she out, and that it wasn' Calvin own-own money that pay-down pon the car. Calvin didn't like that at all: he want she to sit down in the front seat like if *he* own the motto-car. But Calvin gone up Danforth with new motto-car and white woman beside o' him, like if he going to a funeral: "got to break she in gently, man"; and the Canadian thing not too please that Calvin didn' listen to her advice as a woman should advise a man, and buy the Cadillac, but she still please and proud that Calvin get the *Galaxie*. She sitting in it like if she belong there by birth. And Calvin don't really mind, cause he have the car, and it driving like oil pon a tar road back home. He make a thing along Danforth as far as Bloor, turn pon Yonge and gone as far as Harbord ... the itinerry ain' exactly as he first think it out, but it would do ... make a thing along Harbord and meet up with Spadina, and continue according to plan. And in all this time so, not one blasted West Indian or black person in sight to look at Calvin new car and make a thing with his head, or laugh, or wave. When he make a right pon College at the corner o' Spadina, a woman with a bag mark HONEST ED'S start walking through the green light, drop a tomato, and she bend down to pick it up, and Calvin now, whether he looking for the woman tomato or he looking the wrong way, nearly run-over she. Blam! Brakes on, and the Canadian thing nearly break she

5 physiognomy, or face.

blasted neck 'gainst the windshield. Calvin rattle bad like a snake. Police come. Police look inside the car, see Calvin, turn he eyes pon the Canadian thing who get frighten as hell, and he say, "Okay, move along now, buster!" Calvin shaking till he get the Galaxie in front o' the landlady rooming house, and he ain' remember nothing bout what he plan to do when he bring home the prize of a motto-car; the police upset him and he trembling bad. "Give me a drink o' water," he say to the Canadian thing. She rubbing she neck all the time like if it really break in truth, and she get out, and she didn' even look back at the new car, whiching as you would understand is what Calvin expect any man who just have a new motto-car, to do: yuh have to walk out of the door, close the door soft-soft because it ain' the same thing as getting out of a taxi, make sure the door close, and when you know it close, open it again to show yuhself that it close proper, and then really close it a next time; then walk off, look at the car, turn yuh head right and left like if you escaping from a light jab to the head, rub yuh hand over the chrome, walk round to the door where the passenger does sit down, open that door too, close it, and open it, and then, lock it. Then yuh does have to forget something inside the car, so yuh could have a chance to open the doors a next time and play with the car, hoping in the meantime that somebody who never see you before with a car, see you now with this new one and would say something like, "My! How much horsepower?", because according to Calvin, a "Car in some ways is like a woman, yuh does have to care she!" Calvin do all these things, and he didn't forget to walk to the back o' the Galaxie, stoop down and play he looking at the tires, give them a little kick with his shoes to see if they got in enough air, look under the car to see what the muffler look like, and things like that, although he know full-well that he don't know one blasted thing bout motto-cars except to wash them off, or that yuh does drive them. He do the same thing when he walk round to the front o' the car. The Canadian thing gone inside the house long time; and Calvin remember the glass o' water and he walking up the front steps. Not one blasted person on the whole street look out at Calvin new motto-car. Then the landlady, Mistress Silvermann walk out, "Don't forget Mr. Kingston, today your rent is due." Calvin tell her in his mind something bad, and she look at the car as she reach the sidewalk, without looking back, she say, "Do you know the owner of this car, Mr. Kingston? Tell him to move it please...I don't want cars blocking my driveway..." Well, Calvin gone mad now. He walk in the house, and he catch the Canadian thing sitting down in his room, with the glass o' water in she hand, as if she dreaming, just sitting and looking at the air. He drink the water, but it was like drinking miraculous bush-tea the Old Queen uses to make when the bowels was giving trouble back in Barbados. Calvin think bout the Old Queen, put the Old Queen outta his head, and start dressing. He noticed that something was wrong with his dresser: perhaps the landlady was looking for she rent; perhaps the Canadian thing was... "That's why she didn' come back outside with the water! Anyhow..." He put on his clothes, the new suit, shoes and tie and shirt new and matching the Galaxie outside shining in the sun, and meantime the Canadian thing gone upstairs. Calvin finish dress, take up a old kerchief... "Gotta have a shammy-cloth, gotta buy one Mondee!"... and he gone outside polishing the motto-car. Back inside, he gone up to the Canadian thing room, knock soft, the door open, and out from behind his back he take a thing, and say in a sweet loving voice, "I buy this for you." Ohhhhhhhh! Myyyyyyyyyyyyyyyyy! "You shouldn't realllllllyyyyyyy!" But all the time she did know it was dress Calvin buy for she for the occasion, cause when she went inside for the water, she start searching all the man things, and she had a nice peep at the dress. She even know it cost twenty-nine dollars without tax: and she wonder if Calvin really love she so much. Well, they dress-off and they coming out like husband and wife going to church. The *Galaxie* smiling so, like if the *Galaxie* itself in love with the two o' them, too. The dress nearly red like the car, everybody in red, and looking nice. Calvin steal a peep at the Canadian thing and she look good-good-good, like something to eat! He inspect the tires a next time, though he just done looking at them, but what the hell it is his motto-car; and then he check the gas tank and the tank say, "Let's go for a long one, man!", and Calvin get in, fix the seams in the new trousers, adjust the tie, look at the knot in the mirror, fix the mirror two times, and then ask the Canadian thing if she comfortable. "I'm fine, thank you!" Calvin rev-up the thing, she turn over nice, and he ready to go. "You not nervous?" She smile. A dimple and a gold filling show when she smile. Nice. She ain' nervous. "Don't mind what happen just now by Spadina, eh?" She smile nice again. She ain' mind what happen by Spadina. Darling come to she lips with the smile. Calvin happy as hell now. He think he might treat this Canadian thing nice, and do the right thing with a gold ring even. "I take those things in my stride usually, but now it seems like an omen," she say, just as they turn into Bloor. Calvin ain' thinking bout omen, cause the only omen he know bout is that he pray for a *Galaxie* and he get a *Galaxie*! And the horses under the bonnet roaring like hell. Well, they drive and drive like if they was two explorers exploring Toronto: through Rosedale where the Canadian thing say she would *just love* to own a house; and in his mind, Calvin promise she she going get one in Rosedale; through the Bridle Path where she say the cheapest house cost a million dollars; through Don Mills where they see the big tall Foresters' Building, all up there by IBM; "You should get a job at IBM, dear" ("Doing wha'? Cleaning out the closets?")... this Canadian thing like she is the wrong kind o' woman for me, Calvin thinking: I hads better get a black woman!); all this she talk as they driving back on the Don Valley Parkway. The highway nice. The motto-car open a new whole life to Calvin, and he love Canada even better. Damn good thing he left Barbados! The *Galaxie* like a horse, prancing pon the white man road. Night fall long time as they travelling, and Calvin experimenting with the dip-lights and the high beam. It nice to play with. The FM radio thing ain' working good, cause Calvin never play one o' them radios before, and he forget to practise pon it when he was visiting the car in the lot after he pay-down something pon it, so that the salesman would keep it for him. So he working the AM thing overtime. A nice tune come on. Before the tune come on, he thinking again that the Canadian thing maybe the right woman for him: she nice, she tidy and she quiet. And he raise-up liking quiet women; his mother tell him never married a woman who ain' quiet, and like church. The tune is a calypso, man. "It's a nice calypso," Calvin say. "Sparrow, in you arse!" he shout, and he beg the Canadian pardon, he excited because it is the first time he hear a calypso on the radio. He start liking Canada bad bad again. "Look at me, though! New car! A *Galaxie*, and you beside me..." The Canadian thing start working up she behind beside o' Calvin; she start saying she been going down in the islands for years now, that she have more calypso records than any white woman in Toronto, and she wish she had the money to take them outta storage and play one or two for Calvin. She start singing the tune, and Calvin vex as hell, cause he don't like no woman who does sing calypso, his Old Queen didn' even let him sing calypso when he was a boy in Barbados. And he was a *man*! Besides, the calypso that the Canadian thing singing now is a thing bout "...*three white women travelling through Africa!*", and something bout "*Uh never had a white meat, yet!*", and this nice woman, the simple-looking Canadian girl know all the words, and she enjoying sheself too, and Calvin thinking that Sparrow watching him from through the AM radio thing, and laughing at him, and he vex as shite, cause the calypso mean that certain white women like black men to lash them, and... "Don't sing that!" he order the thing, as if he talking to his wife; and the Canadian thing tell him, in a sharp voice, that she isn' his damn wife, so "Don't you be uppity with me, buster!" Well, who tell she she could talk-back to a Bajan man like Calvin? Calvin slam on the brakes. The motto-car cry out, *screeennnnchhhhh*! The Canadian thing head hit the windshield, bram! and she neck like it break this time, in truth. The motto-car half-way in the middle o' the highway. Traffics whizzing by, and the wind from them like it want to smash-up Calvin new *Galaxie*. Calvin vex as shite but he can't do nothing cause he trembling like hell: the woman in the front seat turning white-white-white like a piece o' paper, and the blood gone outta she face; Calvin ain' see no dimples in she face; and she ain' moving, she ain' talking, not a muscle ain' shiver. Traffics whizzing by and one come so damn close that Calvin close he eyes, and pray. "Look my blasted crosses! And my *Galaxie* ain' a fucking day old yet!" He try to start-up the motor and the motor only coughing like it have consumption. The woman like she sleeping or dead or something. The calypso still blaring over the AM radio, and Calvin so jittery he can't find the right button to turn the blasted thing off. And sudden so, one of the traffics flying by is a police. Calvin hear, *weeeeeeeeeeeeeeeeeeennnnnnnnnnnnnnnnnnnnnnnn*! Sirens! A police car in the rear-view mirror. Calvin stop shaking sudden-sudden. He start thinking. White woman deading in his new motto-car, the car new, and he is a stranger in Canada. He jump out, and lift-up the hood, and he back his new jacket, and he touching this and touching that, playing he is a mechanic. The police stop. He face red as a beet. "What's holding you up, boy!" Calvin hear the "boy," and he get vex, but he can't say nothing, cause they is two against his one, and he remember that he black. But he ain' no damn fool. He talk fast and sweet, and soft, and he impress the police: "...and officer I *just-now-now-now* give this lady a lift as I pass she on the highway, she say she feeling bad, and I was taking she to the hospital, cause as a West Indian I learn how to be a good samaritan, and..." The police ask for the licents, and when he see that the ownership papers say that Calvin only had the car this morning, he smile, and say, "Help me with her in the cruiser. You *are* a good samaritan, fellow. Wish our coloured people were more like you West Indians..." They lift the Canadian thing with she neck half-popped outta the *Galaxie*, and into the cruiser, and

Calvin even had a tear in his eye too. But the police take she way, and the sireen start-up again, weeeeeeennnnnnn...Calvin manage to get the *Galaxie* outta the middle o' the road, the traffics still flying by, but now the new motto-car safe at the side o' the road. He put back on his jacket, and he shrug the jacket in shape and in fit pon his shoulders, he turn off the AM radio thing with the calypso, another calypso it was playing now, and fix the seams in his trousers, look back on the highway in the rear view mirror, start-up the *Galaxie*. He driving slow slow on the highway and the traffics blowing their horn to tell him get the fuck outta the road, nigger, but all the time he smiling and holding his hand outta the window and waving them on. He hold over outta habit to say something to the Canadian thing beside him, forgetting that she ain' there no more, and he still say, "This *Galaxie* is car for so! And godblummuh, look what a close shave I had!" He see the Canadian thing handbag open on the seat beside o' him, and he run his hand through it, searching. It had in five single dollar bills. He snap the handbag shut, leaving the money, touch the automatic window-winder, and throw the blasted handbag out on the Don Valley Parkway road.

(1971)

Alistair MacLeod (b. 1936)

A professor of English and creative writing at the University of Windsor, MacLeod was born in North Battleford, Saskatchewan, but spent his later childhood and teenage years on Nova Scotia's Cape Breton Island, home of his coal miner father. He has published two collections of short stories, *The Lost Salt Gift of Blood* (1976), and *As Birds Bring Forth The Sun* (1986), and a novel, *No Great Mischief* (1999). Most of his stories are set on Cape Breton Island and examine the harsh landscape and the hard lives of coal miners and fishermen as they are remembered by the narrators who have frequently moved away from their childhood homes. "The Boat," MacLeod's first published story, is such a recollection, as a professor in a midwestern American University recalls his childhood and the drowning of his fisherman father. The story incorporates a series of opposites, including the attitudes of the mother and father and the father's life as a fisherman and his unfulfilled desire of attending university. MacLeod's treatment of the perils of being at sea in a small boat provides an interesting contrast to Crane's in "The Open Boat."

THE BOAT

There are times even now, when I awake at four o'clock in the morning with the terrible fear that I have overslept; when I imagine that my father is waiting for me in the room below the darkened stairs or that the shorebound men are tossing pebbles against my window while blowing their hands and stomping their feet impatiently on the frozen steadfast earth. There are times when I am half out of bed and fumbling for socks and mumbling for words before I realize that I am foolishly alone, that no one waits at the base of the stairs and no boat rides restlessly in the waters by the pier.

At such times only the grey corpses on the overflowing ashtray beside my bed bear witness to the extinction of the latest spark and silently await the crushing out of the most recent of their fellows. And then because I am afraid to be alone with death, I dress rapidly, make a great to-do about clearing my throat, turn on both faucets in the sink and proceed to make loud splashing ineffectual noises. Later I go out and walk the mile to the all-night restaurant.

In the winter it is a very cold walk and there are often tears in my eyes when I arrive. The waitress usually gives a sympathetic little shiver and says, "Boy, it must be really cold out there; you got tears in your eyes."

"Yes," I say, "it sure is; it really is."

5   And then the three or four of us who are always in such places at such times make uninteresting little protective chit-chat until the dawn reluctantly arrives. Then I swallow the coffee which is always bitter and leave with a great busy rush because by that time I have to worry about being late and whether I have a clean shirt and whether my car will start and about all the other countless things one must worry about when he teaches at a great Midwestern university. And I know then that that day will go by as have all the days of the past ten years, for the call and the voices and the shapes and

the boat were not really there in the early morning's darkness and I have all kinds of comforting reality to prove it. They are only shadows and echoes, the animals a child's hands make on the wall by lamplight, and the voices from the rain barrel; the cuttings from an old movie made in the black and white of long ago.

I first became conscious of the boat in the same way and at almost the same time that I became aware of the people it supported. My earliest recollection of my father is a view from the floor of gigantic rubber boots and then of being suddenly elevated and having my face pressed against the stubble of his cheek, and of how it tasted of salt and of how he smelled of salt from his red-soled rubber boots to the shaggy whiteness of his hair.

When I was very small, he took me for my first ride in the boat. I rode the half-mile from our house to the wharf on his shoulders and I remember the sound of his rubber boots galumphing along the gravel beach, the tune of the indecent little song he used to sing, and the odour of the salt.

The floor of the boat was permeated with the same odour and in its constancy I was not aware of change. In the harbour we made our little circle and returned. He tied the boat by its painter, fastened the stern to its permanent anchor and lifted me high over his head to the solidity of the wharf. Then he climbed up the little iron ladder that led to the wharf's cap, placed me once more upon his shoulders and galumphed off again.

When we returned to the house everyone made a great fuss over my precocious excursion and asked, "How did you like the boat?" "Were you afraid in the boat?" "Did you cry in the boat?" They repeated "the boat" at the end of all their questions and I knew it must be very important to everyone.

10

My earliest recollection of my mother is of being alone with her in the mornings while my father was away in the boat. She seemed to be always repairing clothes that were "torn in the boat," preparing food "to be eaten in the boat" or looking for "the boat" through our kitchen window which faced upon the sea. When my father returned about noon, she would ask, "Well, how did things go in the boat today?" It was the first question I remember asking: "Well, how did things go in the boat today?" "Well, how did things go in the boat today?"

The boat in our lives was registered at Port Hawkesbury. She was what Nova Scotians called a Cape Island boat and was designed for the small inshore fishermen who sought the lobsters of the spring and mackerel of summer and later the cod and haddock and hake. She was thirty-two feet long and nine wide, and was powered by an engine from a Chevrolet truck. She had a marine clutch and a high speed reverse gear and was painted light green with the name *Jenny Lynn* stencilled in black letters on her bow and painted on an oblong plate across her stern. Jenny Lynn had my mother's maiden name and the boat was called after her as another link in the chain of tradition. Most of the boats that berthed at the wharf bore the names of some female member of their owner's household.

I say this now as if I knew it all then. All at once, all about the boat dimensions and engines, and as if on the day of my first childish voyage I noticed the difference between a stencilled name and a painted name. But of course it was not that way at all, for I learned it all very slowly and there was not time enough.

I learned first about our house which was one of about fifty which marched around the horseshoe of our harbour and the wharf which was its heart. Some of them were so close to the water that during a storm the sea spray splashed against their windows while others were built farther along the beach as was the case with ours. The houses and their people, like those of the neighbouring towns and villages, were the result of Ireland's discontent and Scotland's Highland Clearances and America's War of Independence. Impulsive emotional Catholic Celts who could not bear to live with England and shrewd determined Protestant Puritans who, in the years after 1776,[1] could not bear to live without.

The most important room in our house was one of those oblong old-fashioned kitchens heated by a wood- and coal-burning stove. Behind the stove was a box of kindlings and beside it a coal scuttle. A heavy wooden table with leaves that expanded or reduced its dimensions stood in the middle of the floor. There were five wooden home-made chairs which had been chipped and hacked by a variety of knives. Against the east wall, opposite the stove, there was a couch which sagged in the middle and had a cushion for a pillow, and above it a shelf which contained matches, tobacco, pencils, odd fishhooks, bits of twine, and a tin can filled with bills and receipts. The south wall was dominated by a window which faced the sea and on the north there was a five-foot board which bore a variety of clothes hooks and the burdens of each. Beneath the board there was jumble of odd footwear, mostly of rubber. There was also, on this wall, a barometer, a map of the marine area and a shelf which held a tiny radio. The kitchen was shared by all of us and was a buffer zone between the immaculate order of ten other rooms and the disruptive chaos of the single room that was my father's.

15   My mother ran her house as her brothers ran their boats. Everything was clean and spotless and in order. She was tall and dark and powerfully energetic. In later years she reminded me of the women of Thomas Hardy, particularly Eustacia Vye,[2] in a physical way. She fed and clothed a family of seven children, making all of the meals and most of the clothes. She grew miraculous gardens and magnificent flowers and raised broods of hens and ducks. She would walk miles on berry-picking expeditions and hoist her skirts to dig for clams when the tide was low. She was fourteen years younger than my father, whom she had married when she was twenty-six and had been a local beauty for a period of ten years. My mother was of the sea as were all of her people, and her horizons were the very literal ones she scanned with her dark and fearless eyes.

Between the kitchen clothes rack and barometer, a door opened into my father's bedroom. It was a room of disorder and disarray. It was as if this wind which so often clamoured about the house succeeded in entering this single

1   after the American Declaration of Independence many British colonists moved to Nova Scotia.
2   the passionate and unhappy heroine of British novelist Thomas Hardy's *The Return of the Native* (1878) drowns.

room and after whipping it into turmoil stole quietly away to renew its knowing laughter from without.

My father's bed was against the south wall. It always looked rumpled and unmade because he lay on top of it more than he slept within any folds it might have had. Beside it, there was a little brown table. An archaic goose-necked reading light, a battered table radio, a mound of wooden matches, one or two packages of tobacco, a deck of cigarette papers and an overflowing ashtray cluttered its surface. The brown larvae of tobacco shreds and the grey flecks of ash covered both the table and the floor beneath it. The once-varnished surface of the table was disfigured by numerous black scars and gashes inflicted by the neglected burning cigarettes of many years. They had tumbled from the ashtray unnoticed and branded their statements permanently and quietly into the wood until the odour of their burning caused the snuffing out of their lives. At the bed's foot there was a single window which looked upon the sea.

Against the adjacent wall there was a battered bureau and beside it there was a closet which held his single ill-fitting serge suit, the two or three white shirts that strangled him and the square black shoes that pinched. When he took off his more friendly clothes, the heavy woollen sweaters, mitts and socks which my mother knitted for him and the woollen and doeskin shirts, he dumped them unceremoniously on a single chair. If a visitor entered the room while he was lying on the bed, he would be told to throw the clothes on the floor and take their place upon the chair.

Magazines and books covered the battered bureau and competed with the clothes for domination of the chair. They furthered overburdened the heroic little table and lay on top of the radio. They filled a baffling and unknowable cave beneath the bed, and in the corner by the bureau they spilled from the walls and grew up from the floor.

20   The magazines were the most conventional: *Time, Newsweek, Life, , Maclean's, Family Herald, Reader's Digest*. They were the result of various cut-rate subscriptions or the gift subscriptions associated with Christmas, "the two whole years for only $3.50."

The books were more varied. There were a few hard-cover magnificents and bygone Book-of-the-Month wonders and some were Christmas or birthday gifts. The majority of them, however, were used paperbacks which came from those second-hand bookstores which advertise in the backs of magazines: "Miscellaneous Used Paperbacks 10¢ Each." At first he sent for them himself, although my mother resented the expense, but in later years they came more and more often from my sisters who had moved to the cities. Especially at first they were very weird and varied. Mickey Spillane and Ernest Haycox vied with Dostoyevsky and Faulkner, and the Penguin Poets edition of Gerard Manley Hopkins[3] arrived in the same box as a little book on sex technique called *Getting the Most Out of Love*. The former had been assiduously annotated by a very fine hand using a very blue-inked fountain pen while the latter had been studied by some with very large

---

3 Spillane and Haycox were writers of popular detective novels and westerns respectively; nineteenth-century Russian novelist Fyodor Dostoyevsky wrote *Crime and Punishment* and *The Brothers Karamazov*; Faulkner, twentieth-century American author, wrote novels about the American South (see page 950); Hopkins, nineteenth century English poet (see page 213).

thumbs, the prints of which were still visible in the margins. At the slight-est provocation it would open almost automatically to particularly graphic and well-smudged pages.

When he was not in the boat, my father spent most of his time lying on the bed in his socks, the top two buttons of his trousers undone, his discarded shirt on the ever-ready chair and the sleeves of the woollen Stanfield underwear, which he wore both summer and winter, drawn half way up to his elbows. The pillows propped up the whiteness of his head and the goose-necked lamp illuminated the pages in his hands. The cigarettes smoked and smouldered on the ashtray and on the table and the radio played constantly, sometimes low and sometimes loud. At midnight and at one, two, three and four, one could some-times hear the radio, his occasional cough, the rustling thud of a completed book being tossed to the corner heap, or the movement necessitated by his sitting on the edge of the bed to roll the thousandth cigarette. He seemed never to sleep, only to doze, and the light shone constantly from his window to the sea.

My mother despised the room and all it stood for and she had stopped sleeping in it after I was born. She despised disorder in rooms and in houses and in hours and in lives, and she had not read a book since high school. There she had read *Ivanhoe*[4] and considered it a colossal waste of time. Still the room remained, like a solid rock of opposition in the sparkling waters of a clear deep harbour, opening off the kitchen where we really lived our lives, with its door always open and its contents visible to all.

The daughters of the room and of the house were very beautiful. They were tall and willowy like my mother and had her fine facial features set off the reddish copper-coloured hair that had apparently once been my father's before it turned to white. All of them were very clever in school and helped my mother a great deal about the house. When they were young they sang and were very happy and very nice to me because I was the youngest and the family's only boy.

My father never approved of their playing about the wharf like the other children, and they went there only when my mother sent them on an errand. At such times they almost always overstayed, playing screaming games of tag or hide-and-seek in and about the fishing shanties, the piled traps and tubs of trawl, shouting down to the perch that swam languidly about the wharf's algae-covered piles, or jumping in and out of the boats that tugged gently at their lines. My mother was never uneasy about them at such times, and when her husband criticized her she would say, "Nothing will happen to them there," or "They could be doing worse things in worse places."

By about the ninth or tenth grade my sisters one by one discovered my father's bedroom and then the change would begin. Each would go into the room one morning when he was out. She would go with the ideal hope of imposing order or with the more practical objective of emptying the ashtray, and later she would be found spellbound by the volume in her hand. My mother's reaction was always abrupt, bordering on the angry. "Take your nose out of that trash and come and do your work," she would say, and once I saw

---

4 Sir Walter Scott's 1819 novel of adventure is set in the early middle ages and was a standard English high school text in the first half of the twentieth century.

her slap my youngest sister so hard that the print of her hand was scarletly emblazoned upon her daughter's cheek while the broken-spined paperback fluttered uselessly to the floor.

Thereafter my mother would launch a campaign against what she had discovered but could not understand. At times although she was not overly religious she would bring in God to bolster her arguments, saying, "In the next world God will see to those who waste their lives reading useless books when they should be about their work." Or without theological aid, "I would like to know how books help anyone to live a life." If my father were in, she would repeat the remarks louder than necessary, and her voice would carry into his room where he lay upon his bed. His usual reaction was to turn up the volume of the radio, although that action in itself betrayed the success of the initial thrust.

Shortly after my sisters began to read the books, they grew restless and lost interest in darning socks and baking bread, and all of them eventually went to work as summer waitresses in the Sea Food Restaurant. The restaurant was run by a big American concern from Boston and catered to the tourists that flooded the area during July and August. My mother despised the whole operation. She said the restaurant was not run by "our people," and "our people" did not eat there, and that it was run by outsiders for outsiders.

"Who are these people anyway?" she would ask, tossing back her dark hair, "and what do they, though they go about with their cameras for a hundred years, know about the way it is here, and what do they care about me and mine, and why should I care about them?"

She was angry that my sisters should even conceive of working in such a place and more angry when my father made no move to prevent it, and she was worried about herself and about her family and about her life. Sometimes she would say softly to her sisters, "I don't know what's the matter with my girls. It seems none of them are interested in any of the right things." And sometimes there would be bitter savage arguments. One afternoon I was coming in with three mackerel I'd been given at the wharf when I heard her say, "Well I hope you'll be satisfied when they come home knocked up and you'll have had your way."

It was the most savage thing I'd ever heard my mother say. Not just the words but the way she said them, and I stood there in the porch afraid to breathe for what seemed like the years from ten to fifteen, feeling the damp moist mackerel with their silver glassy eyes growing clammy against my leg.

Through the angle in the screen door I saw my father who had been walking into his room wheel around on one of his rubber-booted heels and look at her with his blue eyes flashing like clearest ice beneath the snow that was his hair. His usually ruddy face was drawn and grey, reflecting the exhaustion of a man of sixty-five who had been working in those rubber boots for eleven hours on an August day, and for a fleeting moment I wondered what I would do if he killed my mother while I stood there in the porch with those three foolish mackerel in my hand. Then he turned and went into his room and the radio blared forth the next day's weather forecast and I retreated under the noise and returned again, stamping my feet and slamming the door too loudly to signal my approach. My mother was busy at the stove when I came in, and did not raise her head when I threw the mackerel in a pan. As I looked into my father's room, I said, "Well, how did things go in the boat today?" and he replied, "Oh not too badly, all things considered." He was lying on his back and lighting the first cigarette and the radio was talking about the Virginia coast.

All of my sisters made good money on tips. They bought my father an electric razor which he tried to use for a while and they took out even more magazine subscriptions. They bought my mother a great many clothes of the type she was very fond of, the wide-brimmed hats and the brocaded dresses, but she locked them all in trunks and refused to wear any of them.

On one August day my sisters prevailed upon my father to take some of their restaurant customers for an afternoon ride in the boat. The tourists with their expensive clothes and cameras and sun glasses awkwardly backed down the iron ladder at the wharf's side to where my father waited below, holding the rocking *Jenny Lynn* in snug against the wharf with one hand on the iron ladder and steadying his descending passengers with the other. They tried to look both prim and wind-blown like the girls in the Pepsi-Cola ads and did the best they could, sitting on the thwarts where the newspapers were spread to cover the splattered blood and fish entrails, crowding to one side so that they were in danger of capsizing the boat, taking the inevitable pictures or merely trailing their fingers through the water of their dreams.

35   All of them liked my father very much and, after he'd brought them back from their circles in the harbour, they invited him to their rented cabins which were located high on a hill overlooking the village to which they were so alien. He proceeded to get very drunk up there with the beautiful view and the strange company and the abundant liquor, and late in the afternoon he began to sing.

I was just approaching the wharf to deliver my mother's summons when he began, and the familiar yet unfamiliar voice that rolled down from the cabins made me feel as I had never felt before in my young life or perhaps as I had always felt without really knowing it, and I was ashamed yet proud, young yet old and saved yet forever lost, and there was nothing I could do to control my legs which trembled nor my eyes which wept for what they could not tell.

The tourists were equipped with tape recorders and my father sang for more than three hours. His voice boomed down the hill and bounced off the surface of the harbour, which was an unearthly blue on that hot August day, and was then reflected to the wharf and the fishing shanties where it was absorbed amidst the men who were baiting their lines for the next day's haul.

He sang all the old sea chanties which had come across from the old world and by which men like him had pulled ropes for generations, and he sang the East Coast sea songs which celebrated the sealing vessels of Northumberland Strait and the long liners of the Grand Banks, and of Anticosti, Sable Island, Grand Manan, Boston Harbor, Nantucket and Block Island. Gradually he shifted to the seemingly unending Gaelic drinking songs with their twenty or more verses and inevitable refrains, and the men in the shanties smiled at the coarseness of some of the verses and at the thought that the singer's immediate audience did not know what they were applauding nor recording to take back to staid old Boston. Later as the sun was setting he switched to the laments and the wild and haunting Gaelic war songs of those spattered Highland ancestors he had never seen, and when his voice ceased, the savage melancholy of three hundred years seemed to hang over the peaceful harbour and the quiet boats and the men leaning in the doorways of their shanties with their cigarettes glowing in the dusk and the women looking to the sea from their open windows with their children in their arms.

When he came home he threw the money he had earned on the kitchen table as he did with all his earnings but my mother refused to touch it and the next day he went with the rest of the men to bait his trawl in the shanties. The tourists came to the door that evening and my mother met them there and told them that her husband was not in although he was lying on the bed only a few feet away with the radio playing and the cigarette upon his lips. She stood in the doorway until they reluctantly went away.

40   In the winter they sent him a picture which had been taken on the day of the singing. On the back it said, "To Our Ernest Hemingway" and the "Our" was underlined. There was also an accompanying letter telling how much they had enjoyed themselves, how popular the tape was proving and explaining who Ernest Hemingway was. In a way it almost did look like one of those unshaven, taken-in-Cuba pictures of Hemingway. He looked both massive and incongruous in the setting. His bulky fisherman's clothes were too big for the green and white lawn chair in which he sat, and his rubber boots seemed to take up all of the well-clipped grass square. The beach umbrella jarred with his sunburned face and because he had already been singing for some time, his lips which chapped in the winds of spring and burned in the water glare of summer had already cracked in several places, producing tiny flecks of blood at their corners and on the whiteness of his teeth. The bracelets of brass chain which he wore to protect his wrists from chafing seemed abnormally large and his broad leather belt had been slackened and his heavy shirt and underwear were open at the throat revealing an uncultivated wilderness of white chest hair bordering on the semicontrolled stubble of his neck and chin. His blue eyes had looked directly into the camera and his hair was whiter than the two tiny clouds which hung over his left shoulder. The sea was behind him and its immense blue flatness stretched out to touch the arching blueness of the sky. It seemed very far away from him or else he was so much in the foreground that he seemed too big for it.

Each year another of my sisters would read the books and work in the restaurant. Sometimes they would stay out quite late on the hot summer nights and when they came up the stairs my mother would ask them many long and involved questions which they resented and tried to avoid. Before ascending the stairs they would go into my father's room and those of us who waited above could hear them throwing his clothes off the chair before sitting on it or the squeak of the bed as they sat on its edge. Sometimes they would talk to him a long time, the murmur of their voices blending with the music of the radio into a mysterious vapour-like sound which floated softly up the stairs.

I say this again as if it all happened at once and as if all my sisters were of identical ages and like so many lemmings going into another sea and, again, it was of course not that way at all. Yet go they did, to Boston, to Montreal, to New York with the young men they met during the summers and later married in those far-away cities. The young men were very articulate and handsome and wore fine clothes and drove expensive cars and my sisters, as I said, were very tall and beautiful with their copper-coloured hair and were tired of darning socks and baking bread.

One by one they went. My mother had each of her daughters for fifteen years, then lost them for two and finally forever. None married a fisherman. My mother never accepted any of the young men, for in her eyes they seemed always a combination of the lazy, the effeminate, the dishonest and the unknown. They never seemed to do any physical work and she could not comprehend their luxurious vacations and she did not know whence they came nor who they were. And in the end she did not really care, for they were not of her people and they were not of her sea.

I say this now with a sense of wonder at my own stupidity in thinking I was somehow free and would go on doing well in school and playing and helping in the boat and passing into my early teens while streaks of grey began to appear in my mother's dark hair and my father's rubber boots dragged sometimes on the pebbles of the beach as he trudged home from the wharf. And there were but three of us in the house that had at one time been so loud.

Then during the winter that I was fifteen he seemed to grow old and ill all at once. Most of January he lay upon the bed, smoking and reading and listening to the radio while the wind howled about the house and the needle-like snow blistered off the ice-covered harbour and the doors flew out of people's hands if they did not cling to them like death.

In February when the men began overhauling their lobster traps he still did not move, and my mother and I began to knit lobster trap headings in the evenings. The twine was as always very sharp and harsh, and blisters formed upon our thumbs and little paths of blood snaked quietly down between our fingers while the seals that had drifted down from distant Labrador wept and moaned like human children on the ice-floes of the Gulf.

In the daytime my mother's brother who had been my father's partner as long as I could remember also came to work upon the gear. He was a year older than my mother and was tall and dark and the father of twelve children.

By March we were very far behind and although I began to work very hard in the evenings I knew it was not hard enough and that there were but eight weeks left before the opening of the season on May first. And I knew that my mother worried and that my uncle was uneasy and that all of our very lives depended on the boat being ready with her gear and two men, by the date of May the first. And I knew then that *David Copperfield* and *The Tempest*[5] and all those friends I had dearly come to love must really go forever. So I bade them all good-bye.

45

---

5   published in 1849-50, *David Copperfield*, the semi-autobiographical novel by Charles Dickens, traces the hero's life from his poor and unhappy childhood to his success as an author. For Shakespeare's play *The Tempest*, see pages 439–94.

The night after my first full day at home and after my mother had gone upstairs he called me into his room where I sat upon the chair beside his bed. "You will go back tomorrow," he said simply.

50   I refused then, saying I had made my decision and was satisfied.

"That is no way to make a decision," he said, "and if you are satisfied I am not. It is best that you go back." I was almost angry then and told him as all children do that I wished he would leave me alone and stop telling me what to do.

He looked at me a long time then, lying there on the same bed on which he had fathered me those sixteen years before, fathered me his only son, out of who knew what emotions when he was already fifty-six and his hair had turned to snow. Then he swung his legs over the edge of the squeaking bed and sat facing me and looked into my own dark eyes with his crystal blue and placed his hand upon my knee. "I am not telling you to do anything," he said softly, "only asking you."

The next morning I returned to school. As I left, my mother followed me to the porch and said, "I never thought a son of mine would choose useless books over the parents that gave him life."

In the weeks that followed he got up rather miraculously and the gear was ready and the *Jenny Lynn* was freshly painted by the last two weeks of April when the ice began to break up and the lonely screaming gulls returned to haunt the silver herring as they flashed within the sea.

55   On the first day of May the boats raced out as they had always done, laden down almost to the gunwales with their heavy cargoes of traps. They were almost like living things as they plunged through the waters of the spring and manoeuvred between the still floating icebergs of crystal white emerald green on their way to the traditional grounds that they sought out every May. And those of us who sat that day in the high school on the hill, discussing the water imagery of Tennyson, watched them as they passed back and forth beneath us until by afternoon the piles of traps which had been stacked upon the wharf were no longer visible but were spread about the bottom of the sea. And the *Jenny Lynn* went too, all day, with my uncle tall and dark, like a latter-day Tashtego[6] standing at the tiller with his legs wide apart and guiding her deftly between the floating pans of ice and my father in the stern standing in the same way with his hands upon the ropes that lashed to the cargo to the deck. And at night my mother asked, "Well, how did things go in the boat today?"

And the spring wore on and the summer came and school ended in the third week of June and the lobster season on July first and I wished that the two things I loved so dearly did not exclude each other in a manner that was so blunt and too clear.

At the conclusion of the lobster season my uncle said he had been offered a berth on a deep sea dragger and had decided to accept. We all knew that he was leaving the *Jenny Lynn* forever and that before the next lobster season he would buy a boat of his own. He was expecting another child and would be supporting fifteen people by the next spring and could not chance my father against the family that he loved.

6   a Native American harpooner in American novelist Herman Melville's 1851 novel *Moby-Dick*.

I joined my father then for the trawling season, and he made no protest and my mother was quite happy. Through the summer we baited the tubs of trawl in the afternoon and set them at sunset and revisited them in the darkness of the early morning. The men would come tramping by our house at four A.M. and we would join them and walk with them to the wharf and be on our way before the sun rose out of the ocean where it seemed to spend the night. If I was not up they would toss pebbles to my window and I would be very embarrassed and tumble downstairs to where my father lay fully clothed atop his bed, reading his book and listening to his radio and smoking his cigarette. When I appeared he would swing off his bed and put on his boots and be instantly ready and then we would take the lunches my mother had prepared the night before and walk off toward the sea. He would make no attempt to wake me himself.

It was in many ways a good summer. There were few storms and we were out almost every day and we lost a minimum of gear and seemed to land a maximum of fish and I tanned dark and brown after the manner of my uncles.

My father did not tan — he never tanned — because of his reddish complexion, and the salt water irritated his skin as it had for sixty years. He burned and reburned over and over again and his lips still cracked so that they bled when he smiled, and his arms, especially the left, still broke out into the oozing saltwater boils as they had ever since as a child I had first watched him soaking and bathing them in a variety of ineffectual solutions. The chafe-preventing bracelets of brass linked chain that all the men wore about their wrists in early spring were his the full season and he shaved but painfully and only once a week.

And I saw then, that summer, many things that I had seen all my life as if for the first time and I thought that perhaps my father had never been intended for a fisherman either physically or mentally. At least not in the manner of my uncles; he had never really loved it. And I remembered that, one evening in his room when we were talking about *David Copperfield*, he had said that he had always wanted to go to the university and I had dismissed it then in the way one dismisses his father's saying he would like to be a tight-rope walker, and we had gone on to talk about the Peggottys and how they loved the sea.[7]

And I thought then to myself that there were many things wrong with all of us and all our lives and I wondered why my father, who was himself an only son, had not married before he was forty and then I wondered why he had. I even thought that perhaps he had had to marry my mother and checked the dates on the flyleaf of the Bible where I learned that my oldest sister had been born a prosaic eleven months after the marriage, and I felt myself then very dirty and debased for my lack of faith and for what I had thought and done.

And then there came into my heart a very great love for my father and I thought it was very much braver to spend a life doing what you really do not want rather than selfishly following forever your own dreams and inclinations. And I knew then that I could never leave him alone to suffer the iron-tipped harpoons which my mother would forever hurl into his soul because he

7   characters in *David Copperfield*.

was a failure as a husband and a father who had retained none of his own. And I felt that I had been very small in a little secret place within me and that even the completion of high school was for me a silly shallow selfish dream.

So I told him one night very resolutely and very powerfully that I would remain with him as long as he lived and we would fish the sea together. And he made no protest but only smiled through the cigarette smoke that wreathed his bed and replied, "I hope you will remember what you've said."

The room was now so filled with books as to be almost Dickensian, but he would not allow my mother to move or change them and he continued to read them, sometimes two or three a night. They came with great regularity now, and there were more hard covers, sent by my sisters who had gone so long ago and now seemed so distant and so prosperous, and sent also pictures of small red-haired grandchildren with baseball bats and dolls which he placed upon his bureau and which my mother gazed at wistfully when she thought no one would see. Red-haired grandchildren with baseball bats and dolls who would never know the sea in hatred or in love.

And so we fished through the heat of August and into the cooler days of September when the water was so clear we could almost see the bottom and the white mists rose like delicate ghosts in the early morning dawn. And one day my mother said to me, "You have given added years to his life."

And we fished on into October when it began to roughen and we could no longer risk night sets but took our gear out each morning and returned at the first sign of the squalls; and on into November when we lost three tubs of trawl and the clear blue water turned to a sullen grey and the trochoidal[8] waves rolled rough and high and washed across our bows and decks as we ran within their troughs. We wore heavy sweaters now and the awkward rubber slickers and the heavy woollen mitts which soaked and froze into masses of ice that hung from our wrists like the limbs of gigantic monsters until we thawed them against the exhaust pipe's heat. And almost every day we would leave for home before noon, driven by the blasts of the northwest wind, coating our eyebrows with ice and freezing our eyelids closed as we leaned into a visibility that was hardly there, charting our course from the compass and the sea, running with the waves and between them but never confronting their towering might.

And I stood at the tiller now, on these homeward lunges, stood in the place and in the manner of my uncle, turning to look at my father and to shout over the roar of the engine and the slop of the sea to where he stood in the stern, drenched and dripping with the snow and the salt and the spray and his bushy eyebrows caked in ice. But on November twenty-first, when it seemed we might be making the final run of the season, I turned and he was not there and I knew even in that instant that he would never be again.

On November twenty-first the waves of the grey Atlantic are very very high and the waters are very cold and there are no signposts on the surface of the sea. You cannot tell where you have been five minutes before and in the squalls of snow you cannot see. And it takes longer than you would believe to

8 rolling in circles.

check a boat that has been running before a gale and turn her ever so carefully in a wide and stupid circle, with timbers creaking and straining, back into the face of the storm. And you know it is useless and that your voice does not carry the length of the boat and that even if you knew the original spot, the relentless waves would carry such a burden perhaps a mile or so by the time you could return. And you know also, the final irony, that your father like your uncles and all the men that form your past, cannot swim a stroke.

The lobster beds off the Cape Breton coast are still very rich and now, from May to July, their offerings are packed in crates of ice, and thundered by the gigantic transport trucks, day and night, through New Glasgow, Amherst, Saint John and Bangor and Portland and into Boston where they are tossed still living into boiling pots of water, their final home.

And though the prices are higher and the competition tighter, the grounds to which the *Jenny Lynn* once went remain untouched and unfished as they have for the last ten years. For if there are no signposts on the sea in storm there are certain ones in calm and the lobster bottoms were distributed in calm before any of us can remember and the grounds my father fished were those his father fished before him and there were others before and before and before. Twice the big boats have come from forty and fifty miles, lured by the promise of the grounds, and strewn the bottom with their traps and twice they have returned to find their buoys cut adrift and their gear lost and destroyed. Twice the Fisheries Officer and the Mounted Police have come and asked many long and involved questions and twice they have received no answers from the men leaning in the doors of their shanties and the women standing at their windows with their children in their arms. Twice they have gone away saying: "There are no legal boundaries in the Marine area"; "No one can own the sea"; "Those grounds don't wait for anyone."

But the men and the women, with my mother dark among them, do not care for what they say, for to them the grounds are sacred and they think they wait for me.

It is not an easy thing to know that your mother lives alone on an inadequate insurance policy and that she is too proud to accept any other aid. And that she looks through her lonely window onto the ice of winter and the hot flat calm of summer and the rolling waves of fall. And that she lies awake in the early morning's darkness when the rubber boots of the men scrunch upon the gravel as they pass beside her house on their way down to the wharf. And she knows that the footsteps never stop, because no man goes from her house, and she alone of all the Lynns has neither son nor son-in-law that walks toward the boat that will take him to the sea. And it is not an easy thing to know that your mother looks upon the sea with love and on you with bitterness because the one has been so constant and the other so untrue.

But neither is it easy to know that your father was found on November twenty-eighth, ten miles to the north and wedged between two boulders at the base of the rock-strewn cliffs where he had been hurled and slammed so many many times. His hands were shredded ribbons as were his feet which had lost their boots to the suction of the sea, and his shoulders came apart in our hands when we tried to move him from the rocks. And the fish had eaten his testicles and the gulls had pecked out his eyes and the white-green stubble of his whiskers had continued to grow in death, like the grass on graves, upon the purple, bloated mass that was his face. There was not much left of my father, physically, as he lay there with the brass chains on his wrists and the seaweed in his hair.

(1968)

INTERVIEW
with Alistair MacLeod

Q. *It has been said that authors draw on the depths of their lives and on the literature that has become important in their lives. Do you agree with this statement and does it apply to your own writing?*

A. I think because I write in the first person, a lot of people think these stories are autobiographical. If you read a whole bunch of them, one is disabused of that notion. But none of them are; none of the events happened to me. But they sound autobiographical. I think that's a result of the technique; because obviously you want the reader to believe that such and such is true.

Q. *But readers do get a tremendous sense of the land and the people of Cape Breton Island; in that sense it could be said that the stories do come from you because you lived there so long.*

A. Well, I think that all authors come from some place; I am knowledgeable concerning that area of the country.

Q. *How about literature? Your characters talk a lot about literature in "The Boat" — Hemingway, Dickens, Haycox, Spillane. Literature seems to be very important to them.*

A. In "The Boat," literature isn't important to the mother, who once read *Ivanhoe* and decides never to do that again. But it is important to some of the characters; it's a kind of link to the larger world. In other cases, literature reinforces the kind of life that you lead. Sometimes it shows there are other ways of leading life than the way you are; and then sometimes it re-emphasizes the life you are leading. You see that the struggles you're going through aren't uniquely yours, or you're not the first person to deal with choice or loss or whatever.

Q. *How did you decide to become a writer? Was there a specific "moment of calling" or "epiphany?"*

A. No, I don't think so. I always liked to read. I think I was like someone with athletic or singing ability, who never took it seriously. In 1963, I went away to the United States to do a Ph.D. One of the things you do in studying for a

Ph.D. is read a lot of literature, study and analyze it. So I began to think then, that instead of analyzing other people's stories, perhaps I could write my own. The other thing was that when I was away from my particular Canadian landscape, I began to think of it more carefully. If you're in something all the time, you just say this is the way it is. When you move away, you look back and notice that this was going on or that was going on. It's kind of like being a certain age and looking back on your childhood and realizing that there were more things going on than you recognized when you were in the midst of it all. I find that when I go to Europe I think of Canada in a different way. Maybe I make comparisons, or maybe I just become more thoughtful. As I said earlier, if you're just in the midst of your own kitchen all the time, you think of it as the world, and you don't think of it being interrelated to so many other things.

Q. *How did "The Boat" evolve?*

A. I wanted to write a story about choice, how sometimes choices are foisted upon you and sometimes you make your own. I was interested in the idea of the spider web, of all the things that go forward from a single action. I also wanted to write a story in which there were essentially no villains; I liked everybody in that story. I like to do that with all my work. I think that very often there are people who have good ideas as far as the individual's life is concerned, but these may not always be the best ideas for others. I thought about particular occupations, those that are hereditary occupations. And I thought about doing what you want to do yourself; or doing what your father wants you to do, what your mother wants you to do, and so on. So I was interested in those kinds of issues. I was also interested in the gender and age of the people, because I thought it was important. Because fishing was then a man's job, I thought it was important that the narrator was born when the father was fifty-six and he was an only son and the last of his parents' children. All of this has a bearing, I hope, on the story. If his father were twenty when the boy was born, it would be very different, or if the boy were one of eleven sons it would be different instead of being the only son born into the relative old age of his parents.

Q. *There are a lot of dichotomies in the story: the boy versus sisters, Cape Breton contrasted to away, father and mother, land and sea, life and death. Is there any sense that these could be resolved? As I reread the stories in* Island *over the last couple of weeks, I felt that the tensions were stronger than the possibilities of resolution in the lives of the characters.*

A. There's a section in "The Boat" where the boy goes back to school and he thinks, "Well, maybe I could just stay studying the water imagery in Tennyson and fishing at the same time." But that's an impossible thing to do given his circumstances. The father is an example of someone like that. He fishes all his life and he doesn't like it, or he thinks he's not very good at it.

Maybe he should have been a literature professor. I think I was interested in looking at our parents' lives. When you're children, you just think, well, your parents are always there. You don't think of your parents as having been fourteen or fifteen because you come into their lives when they are adults. That's all you know of them. He has the chance to think, maybe his father wasn't always this way. Maybe his mother wasn't always that way. But maybe she was — I see her as being more consistent than the father, or more stable in some ways — whether that's good or bad — in her belief. I see her as someone who really knows how to lead a life.

Q. *She's a real pragmatist.*

A. Yes, she is. She does know how to live a life. But it may not be the life for everyone. She thinks of her children who want to lead a life different from hers as frivolous, or disloyal, or silly; but they're not.

Q. *You talked about water imagery in Tennyson. But there's a big difference between the Lady of Shalott floating down the river in a boat, and the fishing boat as a fragile thing and a vital link with the sea, a place so filled with danger.*

A. Young people at university or college, just study what's given them. And if they come from a certain background and they encounter this kind of water — Tennyson's water — they may say this is not the way I see it. But nonetheless, if you're going to pass the exam, this is what you study. I was interested in the irony of that.

Q. *You also refer to Shakespeare's* The Tempest. *And it seems there's a greater affinity to that work in "The Boat": the drowned sailor, the death by water in* The Tempest, *and the father-son relationship.*

A. I think that when you go to university, you are presented with this material and you say, oh, this is interesting, or not interesting or so on. But I think a lot of it does stick with you and becomes a part of your repertorie, your internal makeup, and then you apply it or don't apply it.

Q. *Did you write "The Boat" when you were still in Indiana?*

A. Yes, I was interested in some person who was a long way from where he came from — different landscape, different kind of people. I thought it was an interesting tension. One of the things I was interested in in that character was that he goes away and is successful. But it's not easy. If he'd stayed home — it wouldn't be easy either. It wasn't easy for the father. You pay a price for everything you do, no matter what the choice may be.

Q. *You mentioned how, when you were in Indiana, or Windsor, or Europe, you looked back and thought about where you had come from. There's a children's writer who uses the term "rememory" about her writing, and a lot of what the characters do are as much about remembering as about what they remember. I got a sense in reading "The Boat" that a lot was about remembering the past as a way of keeping it alive, as a way of understanding yourself.*

A. I was interested in that type of character. He's not particularly stupid. I just think that memory is with us a long time — with some people for a long time, certainly for him. And, in the end, he's never going to get over the fact that his mother thinks of him as not doing what she would want him to do, in fact none of her family — they've all gone into the larger world and she says: "None of my family want to do the right things." I think of her as someone — who tried to do her very best, and she feels a failure. But she's not. It's just that what she wants is not necessarily what others want. And I think that that kind of tension occurs when a new world comes into an older world. And no matter what way you go you're going to suffer some kind of pain. Given the way that story was set up — as I said before, if there were eleven sons in that family, maybe three would be happy in the boat and the other eight would be neurosurgeons or something like that. But that's not the kind of family they are, and that's not what's given them. They are unique in their own way.

Q. *The mothers and grandmothers are very strong in your stories.*

A. I think that they have a kind of certainty. And at certain stages in history, in that kind of landscape, women who stayed in the home were in control of their homes. When men went out they had to change their accent, change their language, had to learn new skills to stay alive. There would be a different kind of pressure on them. Maybe they wouldn't work as hard as the women, but they would be under a different kind of pressure. The man would go forth to do his work, not necessarily fishing, but in industry of some kind, at seven-thirty in the morning. He would go forth to a different kind of work than his wife and mother. One way of looking at that is in terms of tradition: women would be able to keep traditions longer than men because they would be in control of their own domains. If you go forth as a man, you would be more buffeted by the modern world.

Q. *Is that, perhaps, why the mother is so disgusted with the father when he sings for the tourists.*

A. She thinks of those summer people as frivolous. She's not given to artistic expression very much. And she sees them as tampering with her life in the same way that she sees the seafood restaurant as being not a great economic opportunity for her daughters, but as being a seductive force which will lead them away from what she has tried to teach them. And in those suspicions she is probably right.

Q. *I noticed in your stories a tremendous amount of love and respect for the people who stayed on Cape Breton Island and a more ambiguous attitude to those who moved away.*

A. I think people who stay there live a certain kind of life. You can live it well. People who go away, who become college professors or whatever, live different lives. Again, it's just people wanting different things, needing different things. I try to be as tolerant as I can. People who move inland to Toronto or Lincoln, Nebraska have different landscapes. Perhaps they have more security. Everything has a price.

Q. *What was there about the short story form that particularly appealed to you?*

A. One of the things I liked was that you could be intense with it. I think of it in track terms like a 100-metre dash; you just go as fast as you can. When you're dealing with a novel, you're more in a marathon mode; you have to conserve your energy. I like the intensity very much. It's good to be as intense as you can for twenty pages. Gradually, the short stories I was writing became forty pages; I just needed more space to say what I wanted to say. One of the limitations of the short story is that you can only have two or three characters, and your issues have to be very clear, only one or two of them. It's a different form — it's like comparing a lyric poem to a long narrative poem. You have just so much space to do what you want to do.

Margaret Atwood   (b. 1939)

Ottawa-born poet, novelist, short story writer, and critic Margaret Atwood is one of Canada's best-known authors, both at home and abroad. Such novels as *Surfacing* (1972) and *Cat's Eye* (1988) have been praised for their portrayal of introspective, contemporary women examining their pasts and their relationships as they search for new directions in their lives. In "The Resplendent Quetzal," the growing alienation between a childless husband and wife is revealed during a vacation tour of Mexico. Their separate reactions to a visit to ancient ruins emphasize the lovelessness of their relationship, which began to disintegrate when their baby died at birth. (See also the introduction to Margaret Atwood's poetry, page 373.)

THE RESPLENDENT QUETZAL

Sarah was sitting near the edge of the sacrificial well. She had imagined something smaller, more like a wishing well, but this was huge, and the water at the bottom wasn't clear at all. It was mud-brown; a few clumps of reeds were growing over to one side, and the trees at the top dangled their roots, or were they vines, down the limestone walls into the water. Sarah thought there might be some point to being a sacrificial victim if the well were nicer, but you would never get her to jump into a muddy hole like that. They were probably pushed, or knocked on the head and thrown in. According to the guidebook the water was deep but it looked more like a swamp to her.

Beside her a group of tourists were being rounded up by the guide, who obviously wanted to get the whole thing over with so he could cram them back onto their pink-and-purple-striped *turismo* bus and relax. These were Mexican tourists, and Sarah found it reassuring that other people besides Canadians and Americans wore big hats and sunglasses and took pictures of everything. She wished she and Edward could make these excursions at a less crowded time of year, if they had to make them at all, but because of Edward's teaching job they were limited to school holidays. Christmas was the worst. It would be the same even if he had a different job and they had children, though; but they didn't have any.

The guide shooed his charges back along the gravel path as if they were chickens, which was what they sounded like. He himself lingered beside Sarah, finishing his cigarette, one foot on a stone block, like a conquistador.[1] He was a small dark man with several gold teeth, which glinted when he smiled. He was smiling at Sarah now, sideways, and she smiled back serenely. She liked it when these men smiled at her or even when they made those juicy sucking noises with their mouths as they walked behind her on the street; so long as they didn't touch. Edward pretended not to hear them. Perhaps they did it so much because she was blonde: blondes were rare here.

---

1 Spanish invader of Mexico and Peru.

She didn't think of herself as beautiful, exactly; the word she had chosen for herself some time ago was "comely." Comely to look upon. You would never use that word for a thin woman.

The guide tossed his cigarette butt into the sacrificial well and turned to follow his flock. Sarah forgot about him immediately. She'd felt something crawling up her leg, but when she looked nothing was there. She tucked the full skirt of her cotton dress in under her thighs and clamped it between her knees. This was the kind of place you could get flea bites, places with dirt on the ground, where people sat. Parks and bus terminals. But she didn't care, her feet were tired and the sun was hot. She would rather sit in the shade and get bitten than rush around trying to see everything, which was what Edward wanted to do. Luckily the bites didn't swell up on her the way they did on Edward.

5   Edward was back along the path, out of sight among the bushes, peering around with his new Leitz binoculars. He didn't like sitting down, it made him restless. On these trips it was difficult for Sarah to sit by herself and just think. Her own binoculars, which were Edward's old ones, dangled around her neck; they weighed a ton. She took them off and put them into her purse.

His passion for birds had been one of the first things Edward had confided to her. Shyly, as if it had been some precious gift, he'd shown her the lined notebook he'd started keeping when he was nine, with its awkward, boyish printing — ROBIN, BLUE JAY, KINGFISHER — and the day and the year recorded beside each name. She'd pretended to be touched and interested, and in fact she had been. She herself didn't have compulsions of this kind; whereas Edward plunged totally into things, as if they were oceans. For a while it was stamps; then he took up playing the flute and nearly drove her crazy with the practising. Now it was pre-Columbian[2] ruins, and he was determined to climb up every heap of old stones he could get his hands on. A capacity for dedication, she guessed you would call it. At first Edward's obsessions had fascinated her, since she didn't understand them, but now they merely made her tired. Sooner or later he'd dropped them all anyway, just as he began to get really good or really knowledgeable; all but the birds. That had remained constant. She herself, she thought, had once been one of his obsessions.

It wouldn't be so bad if he didn't insist on dragging her into everything. Or rather, he had once insisted; he no longer did. And she had encouraged him, she'd let him think she shared or at least indulged his interests. She was becoming less indulgent as she grew older. The waste of energy bothered her, because it was a waste, he stuck with anything, and what use was his encyclopaedic knowledge of birds? It would be different if they had enough money, but they were always running short. If only he would take all that energy and do something productive with it, in his job, for instance. He could be a principal if he wanted to, she kept telling him that. But he wasn't interested, he was content to poke along doing the same thing year after year. His Grade Six children adored him, the boys especially. Perhaps it was because they sensed he was a lot like them.

2 before Columbus arrived in the New World in 1492.

He'd started asking her to go birding, as he called it, shortly after they'd met, and of course she had gone. It would have been an error to refuse. She hadn't complained, then, about her sore feet or standing in the rain under the dripping bushes trying to keep track of some nondescript sparrow, while Edward thumbed through his Peterson's *Field Guide* as if it were the Bible or the bird were the Holy Grail.[3] She'd even become quite good at it. Edward was nearsighted, and she was quicker at spotting movement than he was. With his usual generosity he acknowledged this, and she'd fallen into the habit of using it when she wanted to get rid of him for a while. Just now, for instance.

"There's something over there." She'd pointed across the well to the tangle of greenery on the other side.

10 "Where?" Edward had squinted eagerly and raised his binoculars. He looked a little like a bird himself, she thought, with his long nose and stilt legs.

"That thing there, sitting in that thing, the one with the tufts. The sort of bean tree. It's got orange on it."

Edward focused. "An oriole?"

"I can't tell from here. Oh, it just flew." She pointed over their heads while Edward swept the sky in vain.

"I think it lit back there, behind us."

15 That was enough to send him off. She had to do this with enough real birds to keep him believing, however.

Edward sat down on the root of a tree and lit a cigarette. He had gone down the first side-path he'd come to; it smelled of piss, and he could see by the decomposing Kleenexes further along that this was one of the places people went when they couldn't make it back to the washroom behind the ticket counter.

He took off his glasses, then his hat, and wiped the sweat off his forehead. His face was red, he could feel it. Blushing, Sarah called it. She persisted in attributing it to shyness and boyish embarrassment; she hadn't yet deduced that it was simple rage. For someone so devious she was often incredibly stupid.

She didn't know, for instance, that he'd found out about her little trick with the birds at least three years ago. She'd pointed to a dead tree and said she saw a bird in it, but he himself had inspected that same tree only seconds earlier and there was nothing in it at all. And she was very careless: she described oriole-coloured birds behaving like kingbirds, woodpeckers where there would never be any woodpeckers, mute jays, neckless herons. She must have decided he was a total idiot and any slipshod invention would do.

But why not, since he appeared to fall for it every time? And why did he do it, why did he chase off after her imaginary birds, pretending he believed her? It was partly that although he knew what she was doing to him, he had no idea why. It couldn't be simple malice, she had enough outlets for that. He didn't want to know the real reason, which loomed in his mind as something formless, threatening and final. Her lie about the birds was one of the

3 sacred cup used by Christ at the Last Supper.

many lies that propped things up. He was afraid to confront her, that would be the end, all the pretences would come crashing down and they would be left standing in the rubble, staring at each other. There would be nothing left to say and Edward wasn't ready for that.

She would deny everything anyway. "What do you mean? Of course I saw it. It flew right over there. Why would I make up such a thing?" With her level gaze, blonde and stolid and immoveable as a rock.

Edward had a sudden image of himself, crashing out of the undergrowth like King Kong, picking Sarah up and hurling her over the edge, down into the sacrificial well. Anything to shatter that imperturbable expression, bland and pale and plump and smug, like a Flemish Madonna's.[4] Self-righteous, that's what it was. Nothing was ever her fault. She hadn't been like that when he'd met her. But it wouldn't work: as she fell she would glance at him, not with fear but with maternal irritation, as if he'd spilled chocolate milk on a white tablecloth. And she'd pull her skirt down. She was concerned for appearances, always.

Though there would be something inappropriate about throwing Sarah into the sacrificial well, just as she was, with all her clothes on. He remembered snatches from the several books he'd read before they came down. (And that was another thing: Sarah didn't believe in reading up on places beforehand. "Don't you want to understand what you're looking at?" he'd asked her. "I'll see the same thing in any case, won't I?" she said. "I mean, knowing all those facts doesn't change the actual statue or whatever." Edward found this attitude infuriating; and now that they were here, she resisted his attempts to explain things to her by her usual passive method of pretending not to hear.

("That's a Chac-Mool,[5] see that? That round thing on the stomach held the bowl where they put the hearts, and the butterfly on the head means the soul flying up to the sun."

("Could you get out the suntan lotion, Edward? I think it's in the tote bag, in the left-hand pocket."

And he would hand her the suntan lotion, defeated once again.)

No, she wouldn't be a fit sacrifice, with or without lotion. They only threw people in — or perhaps they jumped in, of their own free will — for the water god, to make it rain and ensure fertility. The drowned were messengers, sent to carry requests to the god. Sarah would have to be purified first, in the stone sweat-house beside the well. Then, naked, she would kneel before him, one arm across her breast in the attitude of submission. He added some ornaments: a gold necklace with a jade medallion, a gold circlet adorned with feathers. Her hair, which she usually wore in a braid coiled at the back of her head, would be hanging down. He thought of her body, which he made slimmer and more taut, with an abstract desire which was as unrelated as he could make it to Sarah herself. This was the only kind of desire he could feel for her any more: he had to dress her up before he could make love to her at all. He thought about their earlier days, before they'd married.

4 painting of the Virgin Mary in the style of sixteenth-century artists from Flanders, in Belgium.
5 Mayan and Toltec statues of the rain god.

It was almost as if he'd had an affair with another woman, she had been so different. He'd treated her body then as something holy, a white-and-gold chalice, to be touched with care and tenderness. And she had liked this; even though she was two years older than he was and much more experienced she hadn't minded his awkwardness and reverence, she hadn't laughed at him. Why had she changed?

Sometimes he thought it was the baby, which had died at birth. At the time he'd urged her to have another right away, and she'd said yes, but nothing had happened. It wasn't something they talked about. "Well, that's that," she said in the hospital afterwards. A perfect child, the doctor said; a freak accident, one of those things that happen. She'd never gone back to university either and she wouldn't get a job. She sat at home, tidying the apartment, looking over his shoulder, towards the door, out the window, as if she was waiting for something.

Sarah bowed her head before him. He, in the feathered costume and long-nosed, toothed mask of the high priest, sprinkled her with blood drawn with thorns from his own tongue and penis. Now he was supposed to give her the message to take to the god. But he couldn't think of anything he wanted to ask for.

And at the same time he thought: what a terrific idea for a Grade Six special project! He'd have them build scale models of the temples, he'd show the slides he'd taken, he'd bring in canned tortillas and tamales for a Mexican lunch, he'd have them make little Chac-Mools out of papier-mâché . . . and the ball game where the captain of the losing team had his head cut off, that would appeal to them, they were bloodthirsty at that age. He could see himself up there in front of them, pouring out his own enthusiasm, gesturing, posturing, acting it out for them, and their response. Yet afterwards he knew he would be depressed. What were his special projects anyway but a substitute for television, something to keep them entertained? They liked him because he danced for them, a funny puppet, inexhaustible and a little absurd. No wonder Sarah despised him.

30   Edward stepped on the remains of his cigarette. He put his hat back on, a wide-brimmed white hat Sarah had bought for him at the market. He had wanted one with a narrower brim, so he could look up through his binoculars without the hat getting in his way; but she'd told him he would look like an American golfer. It was always there, that gentle, patronizing mockery.

He would wait long enough to be plausible; then he would go back.

*****

Sarah was speculating about how she would be doing this whole trip if Edward had conveniently died. It wasn't that she wished him dead, but she couldn't imagine any other way for him to disappear. He was omnipresent, he pervaded her life like a kind of smell; it was hard for her to think or act except in reference to him. So she found it harmless and pleasant to walk herself through the same itinerary they were following now, but with Edward removed, cut neatly out of the picture. Not that she would be here at all if it wasn't for him. She would prefer to lie in a deck chair in, say, Acapulco, and drink cooling drinks. She threw in a few dark young men in bathing suits, but took them out: that would be too complicated and not relaxing. She had often thought about cheating on Edward — somehow it would serve him right, though she wasn't sure what for — but she had never actually done it. She didn't know anyone suitable, any more.

Suppose she was here, then, with no Edward. She would stay at a better hotel, for one thing. One that had a plug in the sink; they had not yet stayed in a hotel with a plug. Of course that would cost more money, but she thought of herself as having more money if Edward were dead: she would have all of his salary instead of just part of it. She knew there wouldn't be any salary if he really were dead, but it spoiled the fantasy to remember this. And she would travel on planes, if possible, or first-class buses, instead of the noisy, crowded second-class ones he insisted on taking. He said you saw more of the local colour that way and there was no point going to another country if you spent all your time with other tourists. In theory she agreed with this, but the buses gave her headaches and she could do without the closeup tour of squalor, the miserable thatched or tin-roofed huts, the turkeys and tethered pigs.

He applied the same logic to restaurants. There was a perfectly nice one in the village where they were staying, she'd seen it from the bus and it didn't look that expensive; but no, they had to eat in a seedy linoleum-tiled hutch, with plastic-covered tablecloths. They were the only customers in the place. Behind them four adolescent boys were playing dominoes and drinking beer, with a lot of annoying laughter, and some smaller children watched television, a program that Sarah realized was a re-run of *The Cisco Kid*, with dubbed voices.

On the bar beside the television set there was a crèche, with three painted plaster Wise Men, one on an elephant, the others on camels. The first Wise Man was missing his head. Inside the stable a stunted Joseph and Mary adored an enormous Christ Child which was more than half as big as the elephant. Sarah wondered how the Mary could possibly have squeezed out this colossus; it made her uncomfortable to think about it. Beside the crèche was a Santa Claus haloed with flashing lights, and beside that a radio in the shape of Fred Flintstone, which was playing American popular songs, all of them ancient.

"*Oh someone help me, help me, plee-ee-ee-eeze . . .*"

"Isn't that Paul Anka?"[6] Sarah asked.

But this wasn't the sort of thing Edward could be expected to know. He launched into a defence of the food, the best he'd had in Mexico, he said. Sarah refused to give him the consolation of her agreement. She found the restaurant even more depressing than it should have been, especially the crèche. It was painful, like a cripple trying to walk, one of the last spastic gestures of a religion no one, surely, could believe in much longer.

Another group of tourists was coming up the path behind her, Americans

6 popular Ottawa-born singer of the 1950s.

by the sound of them. The guide was Mexican, though. He scrambled up onto the altar, preparing to give his spiel.

"Don't go too near the edge, now."

"Who me, I'm afraid of heights. What d'you see down there?"

"Water, what am I supposed to see?"

The guide clapped his hands for attention. Sarah only half-listened: she didn't really want to know anything more about it.

"Before, people said they threw nothing but virgins in here," the guide began. "How they could tell that, I do not know. It is always hard to tell." He waited for the expected laughter, which came. "But this is not true. Soon, I will tell you how we have found this out. Here we have the altar to the rain god Tlaloc . . ."

Two women sat down near Sarah. They were both wearing cotton slacks, high-heeled sandals and wide-brimmed straw hats.

"You go up the big one?"

"Not on your life. I made Alf go up, I took a picture of him at the top."

"What beats me is why they built all those things in the first place."

"It was their religion, that's what he said."

"Well, at least it would keep people busy."

"Solve the unemployment problem." They both laughed.

"How many more of these ruins is he gonna make us walk around?"

"Beats me. I'm about ruined out. I'd rather go back and sit on the bus."

"I'd rather go shopping. Not that there's much to buy."

Sarah, listening, suddenly felt indignant. Did they have no respect? The sentiments weren't that far from her own of a moment ago, but to hear them from these women, one of whom had a handbag decorated with tasteless straw flowers, made her want to defend the well.

"Nature is very definitely calling," said the woman with the handbag. "I couldn't get in before, there was such a lineup."

"Take a Kleenex," the other woman said. "There's no paper. Not only that, you just about have to wade in. There's water all over the floor."

"Maybe I'll just duck into the bushes," the first woman said.

Edward stood up and massaged his left leg, which had gone to sleep. It was time to go back. If he stayed away too long, Sarah would be querulous, despite the fact that it was she herself who had sent him off on this fool's expedition.

He started to walk back along the path. But then there was a flash of orange, at the corner of his eye. Edward swivelled and raised his binoculars. They were there when you least expected it. It was an oriole, partly hidden behind the leaves; he could see the breast, bright orange, and the dark barred wing. He wanted it to be a hooded oriole, he had not yet seen one. He talked to it silently, begging it to come out into the open. It was strange the way birds were completely magic for him the first time only, when he had never seen them before. But there were hundreds of kinds he would never see; no matter how many he saw there would always be one more. Perhaps this was why he kept looking. The bird was hopping further away from him, into the foliage. *Come back*, he called to it wordlessly, but it was gone.

Edward was suddenly happy. Maybe Sarah hadn't been lying to him after all, maybe she had really seen this bird. Even if she hadn't, it had come anyway, in answer to his need for it. Edward felt he was allowed to see birds only when they wanted him to, as if they had something to tell him, a secret, a message. The Aztecs thought hummingbirds were the souls of dead warriors, but why not all birds, why just warriors? Or perhaps they were the souls of the unborn, as some believed. "A jewel, a precious feather," they called an unborn baby, according to *The Daily Life of the Aztecs. Quetzal*, that was *feather*.

"This is the bird I want to see," Sarah said when they were looking through *The Birds of Mexico* before coming down.

"The Resplendent Quetzal," Edward said. It was a green-and-red bird with spectacular iridescent-blue tail plumes. He explained to her that Quetzal Bird meant Feather Bird. "I don't think we're likely to see it," he said. He looked up the habitat. "*Cloud forests.* I don't think we'll be in any cloud forests."

"Well, that's the one I want," Sarah said. "That's the only one I want."

Sarah was always very determined about what she wanted and what she didn't want. If there wasn't anything on a restaurant menu that appealed to her, she would refuse to order anything; or she would permit him to order for her and then pick around the edges, as she had last night. It was no use telling her that this was the best meal they'd had since coming. She never lost her temper or her self-possession, but she was stubborn. Who but Sarah, for instance, would have insisted on bringing a collapsible umbrella to Mexico in the dry season? He'd argued and argued, pointing out its uselessness and the extra weight, but she'd brought it anyway. And then yesterday afternoon it had rained, a real cloudburst. Everyone else had run for shelter, huddling against walls and inside the temple doorways, but Sarah had put up her umbrella and stood under it, smugly. This had infuriated him. Even when she was wrong, she always managed, somehow, to be right. If only just once she would admit... what? That she could make mistakes. This was what really disturbed him: her assumption of infallibility.

And he knew that when the baby had died she had blamed it on him. He still didn't know why. Perhaps it was because he'd gone out for cigarettes, not expecting it to be born so soon. He wasn't there when she was told; she'd had to take the news alone.

"It was nobody's fault," he told her repeatedly. "Not the doctor's, not yours. The cord was twisted."

"I know," she said, and she had never accused him; nevertheless he could feel the reproach, hanging around her like a fog. As if there was anything he could have done.

"I wanted it as much as you did," he told her. And this was true. He hadn't thought of marrying Sarah at all, he'd never mentioned it because it had never occurred to him she would agree, until she told him she was pregnant. Up until that time, she had been the one in control; he was sure he was just an amusement for her. But the marriage hadn't been her suggestion, it had been his. He'd dropped out of Theology, he'd taken his public-school teaching certificate that summer in order to support them. Every evening he had massaged her belly, feeling the child move, touching it through her skin. To him it was a sacred thing, and he included her in his worship. In the sixth month, when she had taken to lying on her back, she had begun to snore, and he would lie awake at night listening to these gentle snores, white and silver they seemed to him, almost songs, mysterious talismans. Unfortunately Sarah had retained this habit, but he no longer felt the same way about it.

70 When the child had died, he was the one who had cried, not Sarah. She had never cried. She got up and walked around almost immediately, she wanted to get out of the hospital as quickly as possible. The baby clothes she'd been buying disappeared from the apartment; he never found out what she'd done with them, he'd been afraid to ask.

Since that time he'd come to wonder why they were still married. It was illogical. If they'd married because of the child and there was no child, and there continued to be no child, why didn't they separate? But he wasn't sure he wanted this. Maybe he was still hoping something would happen, there would be another child. But there was no use demanding it. They came when they wanted to, not when you wanted them to. They came when you least expected it. A jewel, a precious feather.

"Now I will tell you," said the guide. "The archaeologists have dived down into the well. They have dredged up more than fifty skeletons, and they have found that some of them were not virgins at all but men. Also, most of them were children. So as you can see, that is the end of the popular legend." He made an odd little movement from the top of the altar, almost like a bow, but there was no applause. "They do not do these things to be cruel," he continued. "They believe these people will take a message to the rain god, and live forever in his paradise at the bottom of the well."

The woman with the handbag got up. "Some paradise," she said to her friend. "I'm starting back. You coming?"

In fact the whole group was moving off now, in the scattered way they had. Sarah waited until they had gone. Then she opened her purse and took out the plaster Christ Child she had stolen from the crèche the night before. It was inconceivable to her that she had done such a thing, but there it was, she really had.

75 She hadn't planned it beforehand. She'd been standing beside the crèche while Edward was paying the bill, he'd had to go into the kitchen to do it as they were very slow about bringing it to the table. No one was watching her: the domino-playing boys were absorbed in their game and the children were riveted to the television. She'd just suddenly reached out her hand, past the Wise Men and through the door of the stable, picked the child up and put it into her purse.

She turned it over in her hands. Separated from the dwarfish Virgin and Joseph, it didn't look quite so absurd. Its diaper was cast as part of it, more like a tunic, it had glass eyes and a sort of pageboy haircut, quite long for a newborn. A perfect child, except for the chip out of the back, luckily where it would not be noticed. Someone must have dropped it on the floor.

You could never be too careful. All the time she was pregnant, she'd taken meticulous care of herself, counting out the vitamin pills prescribed by the doctor and eating only what the books recommended. She had drunk four glasses of milk a day, even though she hated milk. She had done the exercises and gone to the classes. No one would be able to say she had not done the right things. Yet she had been disturbed by the thought that the child would be born with something wrong, it would be a mongoloid or a cripple, or a hydrocephalic with a huge liquid head like the ones she'd seen taking the sun in their wheelchairs on the lawn of the hospital one day. But the child had been perfect.

She would never take that risk, go through all that work again. Let Edward strain his pelvis till he was blue in the face; "trying again," he called it. She took the pill every day, without telling him. She wasn't going to try again. It was too much for anyone to expect of her.

What had she done wrong? She hadn't done anything wrong, that was the trouble. There was nothing and no one to blame, except, obscurely, Edward; and he couldn't be blamed for the child's death, just for not being there. Increasingly since that time he had simply absented himself. When she no longer had the child inside her he had lost interest, he had deserted her. This, she realized, was what she resented most about him. He had left her alone with the corpse, a corpse for which there was no explanation.

80   "*Lost*," people called it. They spoke of her as having lost the child, as though it was wandering around looking for her, crying plaintively, as though she had neglected it or misplaced it somewhere. But where? What limbo had it gone to, what watery paradise? Sometimes she felt as if there had been some mistake, the child had not been born yet. She could still feel it moving, ever so slightly, holding on to her from the inside.

Sarah placed the baby on the rock beside her. She stood up, smoothing out the wrinkles in her skirt. She was sure there would be more flea bites when she got back to the hotel. She picked up the child and walked slowly towards the well, until she was standing at the very brink.

Edward, coming back up the path, saw Sarah at the well's edge, her arms raised above her head. My God, he thought, she's going to jump. He wanted to shout to her, tell her to stop, but he was afraid to startle her. He could run up behind her, grab her . . . but she would hear him. So he waited, paralyzed, while Sarah stood immobile. He expected her to hurtle downwards, and then what would he do? But she merely drew back her right arm and threw something into the well. Then she turned, half stumbling, towards the rock where he had left her and crouched down.

"Sarah," he said. She had her hands over her face; she didn't lift them. He kneeled so he was level with her. "What is it? Are you sick?"

She shook her head. She seemed to be crying, behind her hands, soundlessly and without moving. Edward was dismayed. The ordinary Sarah, with all her perversity, was something he could cope with, he'd invented ways of coping. But he was unprepared for this. She had always been the one in control.

85   "Come on," he said, trying to disguise his desperation, "you need some

lunch, you'll feel better." He realized as he said this how fatuous it must sound, but for once there was no patronizing smile, no indulgent answer.

"This isn't like you," Edward said, pleading, as if that was a final argument which would snap her out of it, bring back the old calm Sarah.

Sarah took her hands away from her face, and as she did so Edward felt cold fear. Surely what he would see would be the face of someone else, someone entirely different, a woman he had never seen before in his life. Or there would be no face at all. But (and this was almost worse) it was only Sarah, looking much as she always did.

She took a Kleenex out of her purse and wiped her nose. It is like me, she thought. She stood up and smoothed her skirt once more, then collected her purse and her collapsible umbrella.

"I'd like an orange," she said. "They have them, across from the ticket office. I saw them when we came in. Did you find your bird?"

(1977)

Thomas King (b. 1943)

Thomas King, who is of Greek, German, and Cherokee ancestry, has taught at the University of Lethbridge and the University of Minnesota, where he was director of the Native Studies program. His fiction, in which, he says, comedy is used to present often tragic themes, is set in southern Alberta. "I am," he comments, "this Native writer who's out there in the middle, not of nowhere." This quality is found in many of his characters. *Medicine River*, a novel created out of the related stories of several people, focuses on a half-Blackfoot photographer who returns to his home town for his mother's funeral and discovers his own identity. In *Green Grass, Running Water*, five Native people engage in a similar quest. "Borders," from King's collection *One Good Story, That One*, presents the theme of Native people's situation in the modern world in the comic encounter between the narrator's proud mother and Canadian and American immigration officials. The invisible border dividing the two countries symbolizes the many divisions in the story among individuals and between cultures.

BORDERS

When I was twelve, maybe thirteen, my mother announced that we were going to go to Salt Lake City to visit my sister who had left the reserve, moved across the line, and found a job. Laetitia had not left home with my mother's blessing, but over time my mother had come to be proud of the fact that Laetitia had done all of this on her own.

"She did real good," my mother would say.

Then there were the fine points to Laetitia's going. She had not, as my mother liked to tell Mrs. Manyfingers, gone floating after some man like a balloon on a string. She hadn't snuck out of the house, either, and gone to Vancouver or Edmonton or Toronto to chase rainbows down alleys. And she hadn't been pregnant.

"She did real good."

5   I was seven or eight when Laetitia left home. She was seventeen. Our father was from Rocky Boy on the American side.

"Dad's American," Laetitia told my mother, "so I can go and come as I please."

"Send us a postcard."

Laetitia packed her things, and we headed for the border. Just outside of Milk River,[1] Laetitia told us to watch for the water tower.

"Over the next rise. It's the first thing you see."

10   "We got a water tower on the reserve," my mother said. "There's a big one in Lethbridge, too."

"You'll be able to see the tops of the flagpoles, too. That's where the border is."

---

1 river originating in northern Montana that flows north into Alberta before flowing south to the Missouri River.

When we got to Coutts, my mother stopped at the convenience store and bought her and Laetitia a cup of coffee. I got an Orange Crush.

"This is real lousy coffee."

"You're just angry because I want to see the world."

"It's the water. From here on down, they got lousy water."

"I can catch the bus from Sweetgrass. You don't have to lift a finger."

"You're going to have to buy your water in bottles if you want good coffee."

There was an old wooden building about a block away, with a tall sign in the yard that said "Museum." Most of the roof had been blown away. Mom told me to go and see when the place was open. There were boards over the windows and doors. You could tell that the place was closed, and I told Mom so, but she said to go and check anyway. Mom and Laetitia stayed by the car. Neither one of them moved. I sat down on the steps of the museum and watched them, and I don't know that they ever said anything to each other. Finally, Laetitia got her bag out of the trunk and gave Mom a hug.

I wandered back to the car. The wind had come up, and it blew Laetitia's hair across her face. Mom reached out and pulled the strands out of Laetitia's eyes, and Laetitia let her.

"You can still see the mountain from here," my mother told Laetitia in Blackfoot.

"Lots of mountains in Salt Lake," Laetitia told her in English.

"The place is closed," I said. "Just like I told you."

Laetitia tucked her hair into her jacket and dragged her bag down the road to the brick building with the American flag flapping on a pole. When she got to where the guards were waiting, she turned, put the bag down, and waved to us. We waved back. Then my mother turned the car around, and we came home.

We got postcards from Laetitia regular, and, if she wasn't spreading jelly on the truth, she was happy. She found a good job and rented an apartment with a pool.

"And she can't even swim," my mother told Mrs. Manyfingers.

Most of the postcards said we should come down and see the city, but whenever I mentioned this, my mother would stiffen up.

So I was surprised when she bought two new tires for the car and put on her blue dress with the green and yellow flowers. I had to dress up, too, for my mother did not want us crossing the border looking like Americans. We made sandwiches and put them in a big box with pop and potato chips and some apples and bananas and a big jar of water.

"But we can stop at one of those restaurants, too, right?"

"We maybe should take some blankets in case you get sleepy."

"But we can stop at one of those restaurants, too, right?"

The border was actually two towns, though neither one was big enough to amount to anything. Coutts was on the Canadian side and consisted of the convenience store and gas station, the museum that was closed and boarded up, and a motel. Sweetgrass was on the American side, but all you could see was an overpass that arched across the highway and disappeared into the prairies. Just hearing the names of these towns, you would expect that Sweetgrass, which is a nice name and sounds like it is related to other places such as

Medicine Hat and Moose Jaw and Kicking Horse Pass, would be on the Canadian side, and that Coutts, which sounds abrupt and rude, would be on the American side. But this was not the case.

Between the two borders was a duty-free shop where you could buy cigarettes and liquor and flags. Stuff like that.

We left the reserve in the morning and drove until we got to Coutts.

"Last time we stopped here," my mother said, "you had an Orange Crush. You remember that?"

"Sure," I said. "That was when Laetitia took off."

"You want another Orange Crush?"

"That means we're not going to stop at a restaurant, right?"

My mother got a coffee at the convenience store, and we stood around and watched the prairies move in the sunlight. Then we climbed back in the car. My mother straightened the dress across her thighs, leaned against the wheel, and drove all the way to the border in first gear, slowly, as if she were trying to see through a bad storm or riding high on black ice.

The border guard was an old guy. As he walked to the car, he swayed from side to side, his feet set wide apart, the holster on his hip pitching up and down. He leaned into the window, looked into the back seat, and looked at my mother and me.

"Morning, ma'am."

"Good morning."

"Where you heading?"

"Salt Lake City."

"Purpose of your visit?"

"Visit my daughter."

"Citizenship?"

"Blackfoot,"[2] my mother told him.

"Ma'am?"

"Blackfoot," my mother repeated.

"Canadian?"

"Blackfoot."

It would have been easier if my mother had just said "Canadian" and had been done with it, but I could see she wasn't going to do that. The guard wasn't angry or anything. He smiled and looked towards the building. Then he turned back and nodded.

"Morning, ma'am."

"Good morning."

"Any firearms or tobacco?"

"No."

"Citizenship?"

"Blackfoot."

He told us to sit in the car and wait, and we did. In about five minutes, another guard came out with the first man. They were talking as they came, both men swaying back and forth like two cowboys headed for a bar or a gunfight.

2 the Blackfoot Nation has reserves in both Alberta and Montana.

60   "Morning, ma'am."

"Good morning."

"Cecil tells me you and the boy are Blackfoot."

"That's right."

"Now, I know that we got Blackfeet on the American side and the Canadians got Blackfeet on their side. Just so we can keep our records straight, what side do you come from?"

65   I knew exactly what my mother was going to say, and I could have told them if they had asked me.

"Canadian side or American side?" asked the guard.

"Blackfoot side," she said.

It didn't take them long to lose their sense of humor, I can tell you that. The one guard stopped smiling altogether and told us to park our car at the side of the building and come in.

We sat on a wood bench for about an hour before anyone came over to talk to us. This time it was a woman. She had a gun, too.

70   "Hi," she said. "I'm Inspector Pratt. I understand there is a little misunderstanding."

"I'm going to visit my daughter in Salt Lake City," my mother told her. "We don't have any guns or beer."

"It's a legal technicality, that's all."

"My daughter's Blackfoot, too."

The woman opened a briefcase and took out a couple of forms and began to write on one of them. "Everyone who crosses our border has to declare their citizenship. Even Americans. It helps us keep track of the visitors we get from the various countries."

75   She went on like that for maybe fifteen minutes, and a lot of the stuff she told us was interesting.

"I can understand how you feel about having to tell us your citizenship, and here's what I'll do. You tell me, and I won't put it down on the form. No-one will know but you and me."

Her gun was silver. There were several chips in the wood handle and the name "Stella" was scratched into the metal butt.

We were in the border office for about four hours, and we talked to almost everyone there. One of the men bought me a Coke. My mother brought a couple of sandwiches in from the car. I offered part of mine to Stella, but she said she wasn't hungry.

I told Stella that we were Blackfoot and Canadian, but she said that that didn't count because I was a minor. In the end, she told us that if my mother didn't declare her citizenship, we would have to go back to where we came from. Then we got back in the car and drove to the Canadian border, which was only about a hundred yards away.

80   I was disappointed. I hadn't seen Laetitia for a long time, and I had never been to Salt Lake City. When she was still at home, Laetitia would go on and on about Salt Lake City. She had never been there, but her boyfriend Lester Tallbull had spent a year in Salt Lake at a technical school.

"It's a great place," Lester would say. "Nothing but blondes in the whole state."

Whenever he said that, Laetitia would slug him on his shoulder hard enough to make him flinch. He had some brochures on Salt Lake and some maps, and every so often the two of them would spread them out on the table.

"That's the temple. It's right downtown. You got to have a pass to get in."

"Charlotte says anyone can go in and look around."

85 "When was Charlotte in Salt Lake? Just when the hell was Charlotte in Salt Lake?"

"Last year."

"This is Liberty Park. It's got a zoo. There's good skiing in the mountains."

"Got all the skiing we can use," my mother would say. "People come from all over the world to ski at Banff. Cardston's got a temple, if you like those kinds of things."

"Oh, this one is real big," Lester would say. "They got armed guards and everything."

90 "Not what Charlotte says."

"What does she know?"

Lester and Laetitia broke up, but I guess the idea of Salt Lake stuck in her mind.

The Canadian border guard was a young woman, and she seemed happy to see us. "Hi," she said. "You folks sure have a great day for a trip. Where are you coming from?"

"Standoff."

95 "Is that in Montana?"

"No."

"Where are you going?"

"Standoff."

The woman's name was Carol and I don't guess she was any older than Laetitia. "Wow, you both Canadians?"

100 "Blackfoot."

"Really? I have a friend I went to school with who is Blackfoot. Do you know Mike Harley?"

"No."

"He went to school in Lethbridge, but he's really from Browning."[3]

It was a nice conversation and there were no cars behind us, so there was no rush.

105 "You're not bringing any liquor back, are you?"

"No."

"Any cigarettes or plants or stuff like that?"

"No."

"Citizenship?"

110 "Blackfoot."

"I know," said the woman, "and I'd be proud of being Blackfoot if I were Blackfoot. But you have to be American or Canadian."

---

3 town in northern Montana that is the American headquarters of the Blackfoot Nation.

When Laetitia and Lester broke up, Lester took his brochures and maps with him, so Laetitia wrote to someone in Salt Lake City, and, about a month later, she got a big envelope of stuff. We sat at the table and opened up all the brochures, and Laetitia read each one out loud.

"Salt Lake City is the gateway to some of the world's most magnificent skiing.

"Salt Lake City is the home of one of the newest professional basketball franchises, the Utah Jazz.

115   "The Great Salt Lake is one of the natural wonders of the world."

It was kind of exciting seeing all those color brochures on the table and listening to Laetitia read all about how Salt Lake City was one of the best places in the entire world.

"That Salt Lake City place sounds too good to be true," my mother told her.

"It has everything."

"We got everything right here."

120   "It's boring here."

"People in Salt Lake City are probably sending away for brochures of Calgary and Lethbridge and Pincher Creek right now."

In the end, my mother would say that maybe Laetitia should go to Salt Lake City, and Laetitia would say that maybe she would.

We parked the car to the side of the building and Carol led us into a small room on the second floor. I found a confortable spot on the couch and flipped through some back issues of *Saturday Night* and *Alberta Report*.

When I woke up, my mother was just coming out of another office. She didn't say a word to me. I followed her down the stairs and out to the car. I thought we were going home, but she turned the car around and drove back towards the American border, which made me think we were going to visit Laetitia in Salt Lake City after all. Instead she pulled into the parking lot of the duty-free store and stopped.

125   "We going to see Laetitia?"

"No."

"We going home?"

Pride is a good thing to have, you know. Laetitia had a lot of pride, and so did my mother. I figured that someday I'd have it, too.

"So where are we going?"

130   Most of that day, we wandered around the duty-free store, which wasn't very large. The manager had a name tag with a tiny American flag on one side and a tiny Canadian flag on the other. His name was Mel. Towards evening, he began suggesting that we should be on our way. I told him we had nowhere to go, that neither the Americans nor the Canadians would let us in. He laughed at that and told us that we should buy something or leave.

The car was not very comfortable, but we did have all that food and it was April, so even if it did snow as it sometimes does on the prairies, we wouldn't freeze. The next morning my mother drove to the American border.

It was a different guard this time, but the questions were the same. We didn't spend as much time in the office as we had the day before. By noon, we were back at the Canadian border. By two we were back in the duty-free shop parking lot.

The second night in the car was not as much fun as the first, but my mother seemed in good spirits, and, all in all, it was as much an adventure as an inconvenience. There wasn't much food left and that was a problem, but we had lots of water as there was a faucet at the side of the duty-free shop.

One Sunday, Laetitia and I were watching television. Mom was over at Mrs. Manyfingers's. Right in the middle of the program, Laetitia turned off the set and said she was going to Salt Lake City, that life around here was too boring. I had wanted to see the rest of the program and really didn't care if Laetitia went to Salt Lake City or not. When Mom got home, I told her what Laetitia had said.

135   What surprised me was how angry Laetitia got when she found out that I had told Mom.

"You got a big mouth."

"That's what you said."

"What I said is none of your business."

"I didn't say anything."

140   "Well, I'm going for sure, now."

That weekend, Laetitia packed her bags, and we drove her to the border.

Mel turned out to be friendly. When he closed up for the night and found us still parked in the lot, he came over and asked us if our car was broken down or something. My mother thanked him for his concern and told him that we were fine, that things would get straightened out in the morning.

"You're kidding," said Mel. "You'd think they could handle the simple things."

"We got some apples and a banana," I said, "but we're all out of ham sandwiches."

145   "You know, you read about these things, but you just don't believe it. You just don't believe it."

"Hamburgers would be even better because they got more stuff for energy."

My mother slept in the back seat. I slept in the front because I was smaller and could lie under the steering wheel. Late that night, I heard my mother open the car door. I found her sitting on her blanket leaning against the bumper of the car.

"You see all those stars," she said. "When I was a little girl, my grandmother used to take me and my sisters out on the prairies and tell us stories about all the stars."

"Do you think Mel is going to bring us any hamburgers?"

150   "Every one of those stars has a story. You see that bunch of stars over there that look like a fish?"

"He didn't say no."

"Coyote⁴ went fishing, one day. That's how it all started." We sat out under the stars that night, and my mother told me all sorts of stories. She was

---

4 trickster figure in the mythology of several Native peoples of the northern plains.

serious about it, too. She'd tell them slow, repeating parts as she went, as if she expected me to remember each one.

Early the next morning, the television vans began to arrive, and guys in suits and women in dresses came trotting over to us, dragging microphones and cameras and lights behind them. One of the vans had a table set up with orange juice and sandwiches and fruit. It was for the crew, but when I told them we hadn't eaten for a while, a really skinny blonde woman told us we could eat as much as we wanted.

They mostly talked to my mother. Every so often one of the reporters would come over and ask me questions about how it felt to be an Indian without a country. I told them we had a nice house on the reserve and that my cousins had a couple of horses we rode when we went fishing. Some of the television people went over to the American border, and then they went to the Canadian border.

155   Around noon, a good-looking guy in a dark blue suit and an orange tie with little ducks on it drove up in a fancy car. He talked to my mother for a while, and, after they were done talking, my mother called me over, and we got into our car. Just as my mother started the engine, Mel came over and gave us a bag of peanut brittle and told us that justice was a damn hard thing to get, but that we shouldn't give up.

I would have preferred lemon drops, but it was nice of Mel anyway.

"Where are we going now?"

"Going to visit Laetitia."

The guard who came out to our car was all smiles. The television lights were so bright they hurt my eyes, and, if you tried to look through the windshield in certain directions, you couldn't see a thing.

160   "Morning, ma'am."

"Good morning."

"Where you heading?"

"Salt Lake City."

"Purpose of your visit?"

165   "Visit my daughter."

"Any tobacco, liquor, or firearms?"

"Don't smoke."

"Any plants or fruit?"

"Not any more."

170   "Citizenship?"

"Blackfoot."

The guard rocked back on his heels and jammed his thumbs into his gun belt. "Thank you," he said, his fingers patting the butt of the revolver. "Have a pleasant trip."

My mother rolled the car forward, and the television people had to scramble out of the way. They ran alongside the car as we pulled away from the border, and, when they couldn't run any farther, they stood in the middle of the highway and waved and waved and waved.

We got to Salt Lake City the next day. Laetitia was happy to see us, and, that first night, she took us out to a restaurant that made really good soups. The list of pies took up a whole page. I had cherry. Mom had chocolate. Laetitia said that she saw us on television the night before and, during the meal, she had us tell her the story over and over again.

175   Laetitia took us everywhere. We went to a fancy ski resort. We went to the temple. We got to go shopping in a couple of large malls, but they weren't as large as the one in Edmonton, and Mom said so.

After a week or so, I got bored and wasn't at all sad when my mother said we should be heading back home. Laetitia wanted us to stay longer, but Mom said no, that she had things to do back home and that, next time, Laetitia should come up and visit. Laetitia said she was thinking about moving back, and Mom told her to do as she pleased, and Laetitia said that she would.

On the way home, we stopped at the duty-free shop, and my mother gave Mel a green hat that said "Salt Lake" across the front. Mel was a funny guy. He took the hat and blew his nose and told my mother that she was an inspiration to us all. He gave us some more peanut brittle and came out into the parking lot and waved at us all the way to the Canadian border.

It was almost evening when we left Coutts. I watched the border through the rear window until all you could see were the tops of the flagpoles and the blue water tower, and then they rolled over a hill and disappeared.

(1993)

Alice Walker   (b. 1944)

Born in Eatonton in rural Georgia, where her parents were poor sharecrop-
pers, Alice Walker published her first book—a collection of poems entitled
Once—in 1968, shortly after graduating from Sarah Lawrence College in New
York. Active in Mississippi during the civil rights movement of the 1960s, she has
published several books: poetry, short stories, essays, and four novels, of which
the best known, *The Color Purple* (1982), was made into a motion picture. In all
her writing, Walker celebrates the lives of African-American women and their heritage. "Everyday Use" contrasts characters' attitudes toward an old quilt to
reveal the differences between, on the one hand, the narrator and her daughter Maggie, both of whom live simple lives close to the land, and, on the other,
Dee, who has developed a superficial sophistication. In her essay "In Search
of Our Mothers' Gardens," Walker writes of quilts, now often preserved in
museums, as creations of people who possessed "powerful imagination and
deep spiritual feeling."

EVERYDAY USE

FOR YOUR GRANDMAMA

I will wait for her in the yard that Maggie and I made so clean and wavy yesterday afternoon. A yard like this is more comfortable than most people know.
It is not just a yard. It is like an extended living room. When the hard clay is
swept clean as a floor and the fine sand around the edges lined with tiny,
irregular grooves, anyone can come and sit and look up into the elm tree and
wait for the breezes that never come inside the house.

Maggie will be nervous until her sister goes: she will stand hopelessly in
corners, homely and ashamed of the burn scars down her arms and legs, eying
her sister with a mixture of envy and awe. She thinks her sister has held life
always in the palm of one hand, that "no" is a word the world never learned to
say to her.

You've no doubt seen those TV shows where the child who has "made it" is confronted, as a surprise, by her own mother and father, tottering in weakly from
backstage. (A pleasant surprise, of course: What would they do if parent
and child came on the show only to curse out and insult each other?) On TV
mother and child embrace and smile into each other's faces. Sometimes the
mother and father weep, the child wraps them in her arms and leans across the
table to tell how she would not have made it without their help. I have seen
these programs.

Sometimes I dream a dream in which Dee and I are suddenly brought
together on a TV program of this sort. Out of a dark and soft-seated limousine
I am ushered into a bright room filled with many people. There I meet a
smiling, gray, sporty man like Johnny Carson who shakes my hand and tells me
what a fine girl I have. Then we are on the stage and Dee is embracing me with

tears in her eyes. She pins on my dress a large orchid, even though she has told me once that she thinks orchids are tacky flowers.

5   In real life I am a large, big-boned woman with rough, man-working hands. In the winter I wear flannel nightgowns to bed and overalls during the day. I can kill and clean a hog as mercilessly as a man. My fat keeps me hot in zero weather. I can work outside all day, breaking ice to get water for washing; I can eat pork liver cooked over the open fire minutes after it comes steaming from the hog. One winter I knocked a bull calf straight in the brain between the eyes with a sledge hammer and had the meat hung up to chill before nightfall. But of course all this does not show on television. I am the way my daughter would want me to be: a hundred pounds lighter, my skin like an uncooked barley pancake. My hair glistens in the hot bright lights. Johnny Carson has much to do to keep up with my quick and witty tongue.

But that is a mistake. I know even before I wake up. Who ever knew a Johnson with a quick tongue? Who can even imagine me looking a strange white man in the eye? It seems to me I have talked to them always with one foot raised in flight, with my head turned in whichever way is farthest from them. Dee, though. She would always look anyone in the eye. Hesitation was no part of her nature.

"How do I look, Mama?" Maggie says, showing just enough of her thin body enveloped in pink skirt and red blouse for me to know she's there, almost hidden by the door.

"Come out into the yard," I say.

Have you ever seen a lame animal, perhaps a dog run over by some care-less person rich enough to own a car, sidle up to someone who is ignorant enough to be kind to him? That is the way my Maggie walks. She has been like this, chin on chest, eyes on ground, feet in shuffle, ever since the fire that burned the other house to the ground.

10   Dee is lighter than Maggie, with nicer hair and a fuller figure. She's a woman now, though sometimes I forget. How long ago was it that the other house burned? Ten, twelve years? Sometimes I can still hear the flames and feel Maggie's arms sticking to me, her hair smoking and her dress falling off her in little black papery flakes. Her eyes seemed stretched open, blazed open by the flames reflected in them. And Dee. I see her standing off under the sweet gum tree she used to dig gum out of; a look of concentration on her face as she watched the last dingy gray board of the house fall in toward the red-hot brick chimney. Why don't you do a dance around the ashes? I'd wanted to ask her. She had hated the house that much.

I used to think she hated Maggie, too. But that was before we raised the money, the church and me, to send her to Augusta[1] to school. She used to read to us without pity; forcing words, lies, other folks' habits, whole lives upon us two, sitting trapped and ignorant underneath her voice. She washed us in a river of make-believe, burned us with a lot of knowledge we didn't necessarily need to know. Pressed us to her with the serious way she read, to shove us away at just the moment, like dimwits, we seemed about to understand.

1 city in Georgia southeast of Atlanta.

Dee wanted nice things. A yellow organdy dress to wear to her graduation from high school; black pumps to match a green suit she'd made from an old suit somebody gave me. She was determined to stare down any disaster in her efforts. Her eyelids would not flicker for minutes at a time. Often I fought off the temptation to shake her. At sixteen she had a style of her own; and knew what style was.

I never had an education myself. After second grade the school was closed down. Don't ask me why: in 1927 colored asked fewer questions than they do now. Sometimes Maggie reads to me. She stumbles along good-naturedly but can't see well. She knows she is not bright. Like good looks and money, quickness passed her by. She will marry John Thomas (who has mossy teeth in an earnest face) and then I'll be free to sit here and I guess just sing church songs to myself. Although I never was a good singer. Never could carry a tune. I was always better at a man's job. I used to love to milk till I was hooked in the side in '49. Cows are soothing and slow and don't bother you, unless you try to milk them the wrong way.

I have deliberately turned my back on the house. It is three rooms, just like the one that burned, except the roof is tin; they don't make shingle roofs any more. There are no real windows, just some holes cut in the sides, like portholes in a ship, but not round and not square, with rawhide holding the shutters up on the outside. This house is in a pasture, too, like the other one. No doubt when Dee sees it she will want to tear it down. She wrote me once that no matter where we "choose" to live, she will manage to come see us. But she will never bring her friends. Maggie and I thought about this and Maggie asked me, "Mama, when did Dee ever *have* any friends?"

15   She had a few. Furtive boys in pink shirts hanging about on washday after school. Nervous girls who never laughed. Impressed with her they worshiped the well-turned phrase, the cute shape, the scalding humor that erupted like bubbles in lye. She read to them.

When she was courting Jimmy T she didn't have much time to pay to us, but turned all her faultfinding power on him. He *flew* to marry a cheap city girl from a family of ignorant flashy people. She hardly had time to recompose herself.

When she comes I will meet — but there they are!

Maggie attempts to make a dash for the house, in her shuffling way, but I stay her with my hand. "Come back here," I say. And she stops and tries to dig a well in the sand with her toe.

It is hard to see them clearly through the strong sun. But even the first glimpse of leg out of the car tells me it is Dee. Her feet were always neat-looking, as if God himself had shaped them with a certain style. From the other side of the car comes a short, stocky man. Hair is all over his head a foot long and hanging from his chin like a kinky mule tail. I hear Maggie suck in her breath. "Uhnnnh," is what it sounds like. Like when you see the wriggling end of a snake just in front of your foot on the road. "Uhnnnh."

20   Dee next. A dress down to the ground, in this hot weather. A dress so loud it hurts my eyes. There are yellows and oranges enough to throw back the

light of the sun. I feel my whole face warming from the heat waves it throws out. Earrings gold, too, and hanging down to her shoulders. Bracelets dangling and making noises when she moves her arm up to shake the folds of the dress out of her armpits. The dress is loose and flows, and as she walks closer, I like it. I hear Maggie go "Uhnnnh" again. It is her sister's hair. It stands straight up like the wool on a sheep. It is black as night and around the edges are two long pigtails that rope about like small lizards disappearing behind her ears.

"Wa-su-zo-Tean-o!"[2] she says, coming on in that gliding way the dress makes her move. The short stocky fellow with the hair to his navel is all grinning and he follows up with "Asalamalakim,[3] my mother and sister!" He moves to hug Maggie but she falls back, right up against the back of my chair. I feel her trembling there and when I look up I see the perspiration falling off her chin.

"Don't get up," says Dee. Since I am stout it takes something of a push. You can see me trying to move a second or two before I make it. She turns, showing white heels through her sandals, and goes back to the car. Out she peeks next with a Polaroid. She stoops down quickly and lines up picture after picture of me sitting there in front of the house with Maggie cowering behind me. She never takes a shot without making sure the house is included. When a cow comes nibbling around the edge of the yard she snaps it and me and Maggie *and* the house. Then she puts the Polaroid in the back seat of the car, and comes up and kisses me on the forehead.

Meanwhile Asalamalakim is going through motions with Maggie's hand. Maggie's hand is as limp as a fish, and probably as cold, despite the sweat, and she keeps trying to pull it back. It looks like Asalamalakim wants to shake hands but wants to do it fancy. Or maybe he don't know how people shake hands. Anyhow, he soon gives up on Maggie.

"Well," I say. "Dee."

25   "No, Mama," she says. "Not 'Dee,' Wangero Leewanika Kemanjo!"

"What happened to 'Dee'?" I wanted to know.

"She's dead," Wangero said. "I couldn't bear it any longer, being named after the people who oppress me."

"You know as well as me you was named after your aunt Dicie," I said. Dicie is my sister. She named Dee. We called her "Big Dee" after Dee was born.

"But who was *she* named after?" asked Wangero.

30   "I guess after Grandma Dee," I said.

"And who was she named after?" asked Wangero.

"Her mother," I said, and saw Wangero was getting tired. "That's about as far back as I can trace it," I said. Though, in fact, I probably could have carried it back beyond the Civil War through the branches.

"Well," said Asalamalakim, "There you are."

"Uhnnnh," I heard Maggie say.

35   "There I was not," I said, "before 'Dicie' cropped up in our family, so why should I try to trace it that far back?"

---

2 Islamic greeting popular among some African Americans in the 1960s. 3 Islamic greeting also popular during the 1960s.

He just stood there grinning, looking down on me like somebody inspecting a Model A car. Every once in a while he and Wangero sent eye signals over my head.

"How do you pronounce this name?" I asked.

"You don't have to call me by it if you don't want to," said Wangero.

"Why shouldn't I?" I asked. "If that's what you want us to call you, we'll call you."

"I know it might sound awkward at first," said Wangero.

"I'll get used to it," I said. "Ream it out again."

Well, soon we got the name out of the way. Asalamalakim had a name twice as long and three times as hard. After I tripped over it two or three times he told me to just call him Hakim-a-barber. I wanted to ask him was he a barber, but I didn't really think he was, so I didn't ask.

"You must belong to those beef-cattle peoples down the road," I said. They said "Asalamalakim" when they met you, too, but they didn't shake hands. Always too busy: feeding the cattle, fixing the fences, putting up salk-lick shelters, throwing down hay. When the white folks poisoned some of the herd the men stayed up all night with rifles in their hands. I walked a mile and a half just to see the sight.

Hakim-a-barber said, "I accept some of their doctrines, but farming and raising cattle is not my style." (They didn't tell me, and I didn't ask, whether Wangero (Dee) had really gone and married him.)

We sat down to eat and right away he said he didn't eat collards and pork was unclean. Wangero, though, went on through the chitlins and corn bread, the greens and everything else. She talked a blue streak over the sweet potatoes. Everything delighted her. Even the fact that we still used the benches her daddy made for the table when we couldn't afford to buy chairs.

"Oh, Mama!" she cried. Then turned to Hakim-a-barber. "I never knew how lovely these benches are. You can feel the rump prints," she said, running her hands underneath her and along the bench. Then she gave a sigh and her hand closed over Grandma Dee's butter dish. "That's it!" she said. "I knew there was something I wanted to ask you if I could have." She jumped up from the table and went over in the corner where the churn stood, the milk in it clabber by now. She looked at the churn and looked at it.

"This churn top is what I need," she said. "Didn't Uncle Buddy whittle it out of a tree you all used to have?"

"Yes," I said.

"Uh huh," she said happily. "And I want the dasher, too."

"Uncle Buddy whittle that, too?" asked the barber.

Dee (Wangero) looked up at me.

"Aunt Dee's first husband whittled the dash," said Maggie so low you almost couldn't hear her. "His name was Henry, but they called him Stash."

"Maggie's brain is like an elephant's," Wangero said, laughing. "I can use the churn top as a centrepiece for the alcove table," she said, sliding a plate over the churn, "and I'll think of something artistic to do with the dasher."

When she finished wrapping the dasher the handle stuck out. I took it for a moment in my hands. You didn't even have to look to see where hands pushing the dasher up and down to make butter had left a kind of sink in the wood. In fact, there were a lot of small sinks; you could see where thumbs and fingers had sunk into the wood. It was beautiful light yellow wood, from a tree that grew in the yard where Big Dee and Stash had lived.

55   After dinner Dee (Wangero) went to the trunk at the foot of my bed and started rifling through it. Maggie hung back in the kitchen over the dishpan. Out came Wangero with two quilts. They had been pieced by Grandma Dee and then Big Dee and me had hung them on the quilt frames on the front porch and quilted them. One was in the Lone Star pattern. The other was Walk Around the Mountain. In both of them were scraps of dresses Grandma Dee had worn fifty and more years ago. Bits and pieces of Grandpa Jarrell's Paisley shirts. And one teeny faded blue piece, about the size of a penny matchbox, that was from Great Grandpa Ezra's uniform that he wore in the Civil War.

    "Mama," Wangero said sweet as a bird. "Can I have these old quilts?"

    I heard something fall in the kitchen, and a minute later the kitchen door slammed.

    "Why don't you take one or two of the others?" I asked. "These old things was just done by me and Big Dee from some tops your grandma pieced before she died."

    "No," said Wangero. "I don't want those. They are stitched around the borders by machine."

60   "That'll make them last better," I said.

    "That's not the point," said Wangero. "These are all pieces of dresses Grandma used to wear. She did all this stitching by hand. Imagine!" She held the quilts securely in her arms, stroking them.

    "Some of the pieces, like those lavender ones, come from old clothes her mother handed down to her," I said, moving up to touch the quilts. Dee (Wangero) moved back just enough so that I couldn't reach the quilts. They already belonged to her.

    "Imagine!" she breathed again, clutching them closely to her bosom.

    "The truth is," I said, "I promised to give them quilts to Maggie, for when she marries John Thomas."

65   She gasped like a bee had stung her.

    "Maggie can't appreciate these quilts!" she said. "She'd probably be backward enough to put them to everyday use."

    "I reckon she would," I said. "God knows I been saving 'em for long enough with nobody using 'em. I hope she will!" I didn't want to bring up how I had offered Dee (Wangero) a quilt when she went away to college. Then she had told me they were old-fashioned, out of style.

    "But they're *priceless!*" she was saying now, furiously; for she has a temper. "Maggie would put them on the bed and in five years they'd be in rags. Less than that!"

    "She can always make some more," I said. "Maggie knows how to quilt."

70   Dee (Wangero) looked at me with hatred. "You just will not understand. The point is these quilts, *these* quilts!"

    "Well," I said, stumped. "What would *you* do with them?"

    "Hang them," she said. As if that was the only thing you *could* do with quilts.

Maggie by now was standing in the door. I could almost hear the sound her feet made as they scraped over each other.

"She can have them, Mama," she said, like somebody used to never winning anything, or having anything reserved for her. "I can 'member Grandma Dee without the quilts."

75   I looked at her hard. She had filled her bottom lip with checkerberry snuff and it gave her face a kind of dopey, hangdog look. It was Grandma Dee and Big Dee who taught her how to quilt herself. She stood there with her scarred hands hidden in the folds of her skirt. She looked at her sister with something like fear but she wasn't mad at her. This was Maggie's portion. This was the way she knew God to work.

When I looked at her like that something hit me in the top of my head and ran down to the soles of my feet. Just like when I'm in church and the spirit of God touches me and I get happy and shout. I did something I never had done before: hugged Maggie to me, then dragged her on into the room, snatched the quilts out of Miss Wangero's hands and dumped them into Maggie's lap. Maggie just sat there on my bed with her mouth open.

"Take one or two of the others," I said to Dee.

But she turned without a word and went out to Hakim-a-barber.

"You just don't understand," she said, as Maggie and I came out to the car.

80   "What don't I understand," I wanted to know.

"Your heritage," she said. And then she turned to Maggie, kissed her, and said, "You ought to try to make something of yourself, too, Maggie. It's really a new day for us. But from the way you and Mama still live you'd never know it."

She put on some sunglasses that hid everything above the tip of her nose and her chin.

Maggie smiled; maybe at the sunglasses. But a real smile, not scared. After we watched the car dust settle I asked Maggie to bring me a dip of snuff. And then the two of us sat there just enjoying, until it was time to go in the house and go to bed.

(1973)

Greg Hollingshead (b. 1947)

A professor of eighteenth-century literature and creative writing at the University of Alberta, Greg Hollingshead was born in Toronto and studied at the universities of Toronto and London. In three collections of short stories and a novel, *Spin Dry*, Hollingshead examines the mystery and absurdity that lurk beneath the surface of apparently "ordinary" modern life. A student of the eighteenth-century philosopher George Berkeley, he considers writing "an ongoing perception of process and discovery. For me, narrative is philosophy as we actually live it, day by day, all our lives. Each event in a story conveys an understanding of those that precede it. Each raises and addresses the question 'Why?'" "The Naked Man" is from Hollingshead's most recent collection, *The Roaring Girl* (1995), winner of the Governor General's Award for fiction. Like "Rappaccini's Daughter" and "The Motor Car," its central character is a young man who has left his family home. Unlike Giovanni and Calvin, however, Dennis returns. The ambiguous feelings both he and his family experience are, in part, reflected in their attitudes toward his Studebaker, an ornate, chromium-decorated car popular in the 1950s.

THE NAKED MAN

By the time I was eighteen it was getting hard to live at home. Instead of moving out I bought a Studebaker. I loved the Studebaker, but it made no difference, so I left it with my parents and went to Australia. My parents had a double garage with so much junk in it there was hardly room for the family Chev. By stacking the junk higher up the walls I made room for a Studebaker too. This was fine with my parents, but I was uneasy for my car.

When I called home there was always some problem about it. Even just sitting in the garage. Of course, it made parking the Chev tighter, and I heard about that. A few times I hung up with the impression there had been some scraping. My father had talked me into leaving the keys for safety reasons. The first definite thing that happened was they lost the keys.

"Tell me again why you need them," I said to my father.

"Safety reasons," he replied.

5   Reluctantly I explained about the spare key under the front fender. He listened dubiously.

Another time I called he told me the Studebaker was leaking oil.

"It always did," I said. "It's not a leak. It's just a little drip."

"That car of yours is making a terrible mess out there," my mother said when she came on.

"So put a piece of carpeting under it," I said.

10   "A *what?*"

The next time I called they had got in a mechanic to see about the leak.

"He says you need a new clutch," my father told me. "He says you should have arranged to have it started at least every two weeks."

"What'd he say about the leak?"

"There's nothing he can do about the leak. The leak is the least of your worries. Do you realize what this car of yours is costing me?"

15   I told them to just leave the car alone.

After a while it stopped coming up. Sometimes this was how things would happen. Their lives had moved on. As a kind of joke I would say, "So how's my car?" and in a resigned voice my father would say, "Well, it's still there," or, "You realize your mother won't park in the garage any more, don't you."

When I got back from Australia it was six in the morning about a year later, and I had no money at all. But my parents lived twenty minutes from the airport, so I waited until seven and called home.

"Hello —" My father's voice was damaged and incredulous with sleep.

"Hi, Dad, it's Dennis."

20   There was a pause. "Dennis — ?"

"Your son, Dennis,"

"It's Dennis!" my mother cried in the background. She grabbed the phone. "Dennis, you sound so close! Where are you?"

An hour later the Chev pulled up at the Arrivals door with my father clinging to the wheel like a shipwreck victim. His hair fanned straight out at the side, and he was still breathing hard from sleep. I threw my bags in the back seat and got in beside him.

"So how was Australia?" he said. "Are they ahead of us or behind? It was dawn there too?"

25   "Australia was great. It's hard to know where to start —"

"Feed it out slowly, over time." And he told me how with the way interest rates were going it looked like we'd lose the house.

As we turned into the driveway I asked, "So how's the car?"

"It runs, doesn't it? It's not as if I could afford a new one."

My mother was at the foot of the driveway with her coat on, waiting impatiently for the Chev. She had an eight-thirty hair appointment and made us get out immediately.

30   We walked to the house. As soon as we were inside, my father called a cab. "Think I'll slide over to the track," he said, standing in the middle of the kitchen eating a bowl of cornflakes. "Now that I'm up."

As soon as he left I flopped down on the living-room chesterfield and passed out.

I woke up badly disoriented. I was on a different chesterfield, and for a long time I thought I was still in Australia, but I couldn't figure out which city. The only thing worse than waking up from sleeping too long at the wrong time is waking up in a different place from where you fell asleep.

It was my parents' main-floor guest room. When I tried to get up my body was completely without tonus. I fell back on the bed. "Hey Denny." It was my younger sister Sophie, passing the door. She shot me the six-gun salute.

"Sophie!" my mother called from the kitchen. "Why don't you give Dennis a tour of the house?"

35   "No time!" Sophie shouted from the bathroom. "Nothing ever changes!" She was washing her face.

I stepped out the French doors to the garage to take a look at my car. It was not there.

I checked the driveway and the other side of the house. From the darkness of the garage I watched Sophie's ride for work stop out front and pick her up. I waved, but she didn't see me. When I turned on the garage light I saw that I had tracked oil from the puddle where the Studebaker had been.

My mother was in the living room with her hair done, sitting next to a beautiful young woman I had never seen before. I said my name and we shook hands.

"You know Lori," my mother said.

"I never saw Lori before in my life."

"Get off it," my mother said.

Lori worked nearby with disturbed children.

"Lori's staying in the spare room downstairs," my mother explained.

"I didn't know there was a spare room downstairs," I said. There was only my room.

"Well, there isn't now," my mother said.

At that moment a naked man walked past the doorway down the hall between the main-floor bedrooms. A door closed.

"Excuse me," I said quietly, my heart going. "I think there's someone else in the house."

My mother was listing the people she had invited to a party we were having that night. She paused, looking at me. "*I know,*" she said. "It can be kind of a Welcome Home Dennis party."

"What was it before?" I asked with a smile at Lori, who smiled back.

"A naked man just walked past the door," I said more loudly, pointing.

My mother was continuing with her list. "Susan and Ed, and Effie, and the Rauches (the Cy and Doris Rauches, that is), and Aunt B.J., and Wade of course, and the Chatterjees —"

"Who's Wade?" I asked.

"Lori's friend. And Dave Arkett, and Tony and his wife, and —"

I asked if there was a bed I could use.

"Of course there's a bed you can use," my mother said irritably. "Why do you have to put an edge on everything?" There was Dave's old room upstairs, she said. And could I please clear my bags out of the front hall. She didn't want our guests tripping over them.

Dave's bed was a double. I turned back the covers and checked around until I came up with two shades of pubic hair. I dropped these down behind the headboard and brushed away absently at the sheet. I sat on the edge of the mattress and rubbed my shanks. After a while I went to take a shower, but there was somebody in there.

I returned to the living room in Dave's dressing gown. Lori and my mother looked at me expectantly.

"I was going to take a shower, but there's somebody in there," I said.

"I thought you told us you were going to bed," my mother said.

"Can't I shower first?"

"Not if somebody's in there."

"It's not Sophie," I said. "Sophie went to work."

"Nonsense."

"I think she did, Mrs. Weatherall," Lori put in softly. "I heard the door."

65 "Well, I'm sure I don't know who it could be in that case," my mother said with impatience, refusing to be held accountable for strangers in the house.

"By the way," I said. "I've been meaning to ask. Where's my car?"

"What car?"

"The one I left in the garage."

"There's no car in the garage."

70 "That's what I'm saying. What did you do with it?"

"Why are you asking me? I haven't been able to park in my own garage for a year. You'll have to talk to your father."

"Well, I guess the bathroom's free now," I said, but it wasn't.

Instead of returning to the living room, I went on to the kitchen where I made myself a toasted bacon and tomato sandwich. I ate this standing in the middle of the kitchen like my father, I noticed, and then I went to bed.

When I came downstairs again it was dark. Lori was sitting in the same place in the living room, only now she was alone, smoking a cigarette and wearing a sequined gown with a generous neckline.

75 "Hi," I said.

"Hi."

"I guess I should change."

"You don't have to."

"I look like a bum."

80 "You look very nice."

My father entered from the kitchen with a couple of bowls of chips and dip. To Lori he said, "If that dress had slits you could call it a strange sequins of vents."

To me he said, "Help out a little."

In the kitchen my mother was mixing nuts in a bowl. She gave my father and me a look that said, *They'll be here any minute.*

"Right," my father said and rubbed his hands together while glancing around in vague anticipation.

85 She shot us another look that said, *You don't think you're greeting our guests dressed like that, do you?*

My father looked down at himself with his hands at his sides, spread and turned outward in a gesture that said, *What's wrong with the way I'm dressed?*

My mother made no reply.

My father grew silent as if musing. Finally he rubbed his jaw and murmured, "Maybe I'll shave."

An hour later my father had a bar set up on a card table in a corner of the dining room, telling women who ordered their drinks on the rocks, "I only have ice for you," and describing their Bristol Creams as rhapsodies in goo.

90 When he noticed me watching him, my father told me to take over. "Wade's shirking his responsibilities on all fronts," he said from the corner of his mouth.

"Which one's Wade?"

"The shifty one."

As soon as I was behind the bar, people started talking to me. Most of them when they heard I was a Weatherall thought I was my younger brother Dave, at that time in Hawaii. A few thought I was my dead brother Joe.

From behind the bar I could see Lori sitting completely alone in her place on the chesterfield, drinking soda water. As I poured my mother her usual Silent Sam, a cloud of Pepsi, no ice — I asked what was wrong with Lori.

95   "It's Wade," my mother said, scarcely moving her lips. "He's ignored the poor kid all night. She's completely heartbroken."

"Which one is he?"

"Downstairs. Playing table tennis with Gwen Dermott."

"Who's Gwen Dermott?"

"You tell me. She tagged along with the Freibergs."

100   When the men had been drinking long enough to approach Lori and engage her in conversation, she talked and smiled but always sooner or later looked sadly into the distance as she took a long drag on her cigarette, and the men moved soberly away. A few minutes later, during a crush at the bar, as Lou Destaffo stepped in beside me to pour his own drink, I caught a glimpse of sequins in the hall.

"Thanks for taking over, Lou."

I was knocking on the main-floor guest-room door.

"Come in?"

Lori's voice was high and soft with expectation. When she saw who it was, her head pitched back onto the coats. She must have been lying on fifty coats, her body slightly arched. When I approached, she moved over a little to make room. I imagined her rolling down between the bed and wall and becoming lodged there. I took off my shoes and sat alongside her with my heels dug into the edge of the bed.

105   "Look," I said. "I'm really sorry about Wade."

"No, I'm the one who should be sorry."

"You don't have to be sorry."

There was a muffled crash at the door, and my mother rushed in with a cup and saucer. I could see it dripping across the floor. "Coffee!" she cried. "It's all right!" The cup and saucer clattered down on the bedside table and my mother dashed from the room.

"You must like him a lot," I said.

110   The front door slammed, hard. The blow of it shook the house.

"He's all right."

Suddenly there came a violent hammering on the window behind us. I twisted around to see. Nothing. More hammering. A fist! A flash of wild face at the window, mad-eyed and snarling. It fell away. Reappeared. Fell away. Reappeared. Heathcliff[1] on a trampoline. More hammering. For a better look, I turned off the bedside lamp. Immediately the frequency and violence of the hammering increased. At any moment a fist would smash through.

"You'd better turn the light back on," Lori said. "I think he's jealous."

As I switched on the lamp there was a knock at the door. It opened, and my father beckoned. When I went to the door he put an arm around my shoulder and walked me forcibly into the TV room and closed the door behind us.

---

1 the passionate and destructive central character in Emily Brontë's *Wuthering Heights*.

115 "Where's my car?" I said.

"Listen, Dennis. We've got a kid out here who's pretty much in love." My father looked away. The cartilage in his jaw danced. "Don't spoil it."

I shrugged out of his arm and went back to Lori. I asked her why she put up with it.

"Up with what?"

My mother rushed in holding an ashtray way out in front of her. "Ow by iddoo ums?" she cried breathlessly to no one. Keeping her face averted as if Lori and I were physically making love, she snatched up the unused ashtray from the bedside table and banged the other down in its place. She rushed away. Like a spun plate the ashtray took a long time to settle. *Wrowr wrowr wrowr wrowr*— I was stopping it with my hand when the window hammering resumed. And then my mother was back for the cup and saucer. "All right?" she cried on her way out, spilling coffee again. Immediately then, both my parents were at the door.

120 "Dennis!"

"No! Go away!"

But already they were inside the room, with people from the party peering over their shoulders like idle villagers. I sprang forward and tried to push everybody out, but once I got them into the hall my mother slipped past me into the guest room and locked the door.

"You're on the bar," my father said. His lips were thin and he was holding my arm in a vice grip.

My mother of course would not let me back into the guest room.

125 "My shoes are in there," I said.

"Socks are fine," my father said.

I returned to the bar, where people were helping themselves.

I was carrying more mix up from the basement when my father drew me aside, "Better come with me. We've got a major crisis on our hands out here."

Wade had disappeared.

130 "You check the driveway," my father said.

The driveway was all cars. It was a cold night, and I was wearing my father's galoshes without shoes. I didn't know what I was looking for.

When I got back to the house my father came around the corner. "Is it there?" he asked.

"Is what there?"

"His car."

135 "How would I know his car?"

"He's using the Studebaker."

"Who said you could lend out my car?" I cried.

"Relax," my father said. "We couldn't all use the Chev." He was looking over his shoulder into the darkness. "The river!" he cried suddenly and headed off at a jog across the lawn.

"Dad! The river's frozen!"

140 He stopped and walked back with his hands in his blazer pockets. "Let's go inside," he said. "It's cold out here."

In the kitchen my mother was waiting by the oven for a tray of hors d'oeuvres.

"Where's Lori?" I asked her.

"Where's that big platter? I want you to help me serve."

"Did you leave Lori alone?"

145 "Here it is. Never you mind about Lori. Lori's just fine." She handed me the platter. "Here. Arrange them nicely."

I passed around the platter, and then I started to drink. Eventually I went to bed. Some time in the night I staggered naked to the bathroom to throw up. The party was over. I slumped on the edge of the bed with my head in my hands, wondering if I was going to throw up again. But I must have thought I was sleeping in my old room and taken a wrong turn from the bathroom. I heard a stir behind me. I was practically sitting on my mother.

"Wade —" my father said.

"George, it's not Wade," my mother whispered. "I think it's Dave, I mean —"

"Dave, go back to your room."

150 "Dennis?" my mother said.

When I came downstairs the next day Lori was at her usual place. She was wearing jeans and a pale blue cashmere sweater. A cigarette was going in the ashtray alongside her hand.

"Is Wade still asleep?" I asked.

Lori shook her head. "Thanks for being so nice last night. Wade can be such a pain."

"Is he around? I never got a chance to meet him."

155 "I know. I think you'd really like each other, too. He was hoping he'd see you this morning, but he got a call first thing about his car."

"The Studebaker?"

"That's right. He lent it to somebody he didn't know all that well."

"Somebody who drove it drunk and stoned with a suspended licence and no insurance and the car's a write-off?"

"I think he might have still had his licence," Lori said.

(1995)

Lee Maracle (b. 1950)

Maracle, who is of Cree, Metis, and Coast Salish decent, grew up in Vancouver and studied at Simon Fraser University. Her works, all written from a Native and feminist perspective, include *Bobbi Lee: Indian Rebel* (1990), an autobiography; and *Sundogs* (1992), a novel. Maracle has stated that in her stories "all my characters live with both a condition and themselves." Frequently, the condition involves existing in a society in which the majority culture stereotypically defines minorities. However, as she explains, her central characters, frequently Native women, journey from the outside world to enact a "transformation of the internal." In "Too Much to Explain," the central character must deal with her painful memories of past tragedies and a deteriorating relationship. She ends her relationship near Vancouver's aptly named False Creek, an inlet of the sea surrounded by expensive condominiums.

TOO MUCH TO EXPLAIN

She sat on the upper level of the lounge, her chair up against the wall. She didn't want anyone behind her tonight. The table she leaned on was small and dark. There weren't many people in the room; it was, after all, a Tuesday night in October. He was late. It twisted her insides that he didn't have the decency to be on time. Just once, just once, you would think the bastard would be on time, she thought with more venom than was called for. She tapped her cigarette rapidly at the ashtray and scolded herself for smoking so much. She closed her eyes hard to shut out the hum that plagued her ears. The sound of the tapping did little to cancel the hum and closing her eyes did less. She knew both gestures were futile, even absurd, but she made them anyway.

He entered the room with grace and dignity, took a quick look around the room from the doorway before he recognized her tucked up in a corner. *He's probably sizing up the women*, and the humming grew sharp. She resisted putting her hands over her ears. He nodded in her direction, smiled and stroke over to the table.

From the door he had noted that she was thinner than when they first began seeing each other. Still, even thin she was lovelier than the other women he knew. He grinned at his own foolishness. It was not that she was so much lovelier but that he loved her; he liked the way his heart clouded his vision. She had been tense and inattentive lately. He wondered if this outing would suffer the same fate as the last two at Joe Kapp's. He tried to stop thinking about the harangues that had marred the last two occasions. Her smile quelled his momentary cynicism. He was embarrassed by his private recollection and his own suggestion that there might be a pattern developing here.

He stroked her hand lightly and pecked her cheek, then swung easily into the chair. She was nearly finished her margarita. His automatic display of affection did nothing for her. She feared that this exhibition was conducted more for everyone else's benefit — the way the lead wolf in a pack might covetously snuggle his females before younger hopefuls. She resented what might have been a perverse show of male possession. Her hand fidgeted slightly under his caress. A piece of her wanted to scream at him, but she knew that would not be rational. Rational people do not scream. The waiter came up just behind him and asked what they would like to order.

"Two margaritas," and he winked at her. She interpreted the wink and his sickening overconfidence as arrogance, mentally adding this to the list of his crimes. *Gawd, what am I doing? Don't blow this*, and she felt colour come involuntarily to her cheeks. The floor floated towards her as the humiliation she felt filled her face. She argued with herself. *He's taking me for granted ... Gawd, what a stupid catch-all phase that explains nothing and everything that goes wrong between people. The waiter probably thinks I'm one of those ridiculous women lapel-roses that can't speak for myself.* She ignored the fact that she was still toying with a margarita she had ordered earlier.

5   The waiter rested his eyes on her momentarily, awaiting confirmation. She felt his gaze but ceded nothing. Seeing that she was not going to look up, he shrugged and left.

When she looked at the floor her lover was not sure whether she was bored or angry. Then he flushed. He had answered for her again. The realization brought a knot of anxiety to his gut. He sighed annoyance and looked off into space, waiting for the barrel-load of condemnation that would assault his character, but it didn't come. He relaxed slightly, not bothering to reflect on his own internal need to eat up life's mundane and trivial decisions with his own decisiveness.

The pianist in the corner was plunking out a sad tune, "Moody River";[1] the sound was all the more melancholy in the absence of song and band. Just an old Black man, pecking at an even older piano. Pictures of her childhood home, the river and her solitary vigil next to it swam through her head. Her face wore a wistful smile when it turned to look at the piano player. Then her expression changed as she craned her neck to see.

"Dammit, the pole is blocking my view."

"Would you like to move?" he asked, trying to accommodate her. The question jarred her. A veil of darkness filmed her eyes.

10   "Why?"

Oh Christ, instant replay. When will I learn? Every time she invites me out like this, she gives me a hard time, but he didn't say that.

"Well, so you can see the piano player." He lit a cigarette. He rarely smoked and this little display of anxiety annoyed her.

"What do I want to look at some old man for?" She was rigid now, her words came out clipped into neat little pieces and were fed to him through tight lips. He sighed heavily, and even that she interpreted as male condescension in the face of a typical female airhead. The ringing hum in her ears gained volume as a steady stream of accusations whirled about insanely in her mind. Small bits of reason argued with the multitude of doubts until she finally regained her control.

He stared at the margarita in front of him and let his frustration drift

1   a 1961 hit song about a man mourning the drowning of his lover.

around the dimly lit bar while his fingers played with the salty ice ring on the glass. Fatigue crept up on him like a faithless companion. He had been through this before with other women. He was beginning to think that this affair was going nowhere. Age and passion kept him rooted to his chair. He felt weighed down by an anchor of his own making.

15 "How did your day go?" She carefully laminated the remark with layers of creamy sweetness. Surprised relief overtook him. *He knows I'm pissed, why doesn't he say something ... stop that ... Gawd*, and she recognized the voice that dominated her thoughts. She fought to still the voice, to stop the incessant humming. *Think of the river*. It swelled to a torrent and gave way to a memory she had thought dead. The flooding banks and the ranting of her mother returned to haunt her and she wanted to faint.

"Another day of make-work. If the new plans aren't ready soon, I think I'll lose my mind." Her glazed look did not escape him, despite her fawning attempt to disguise it. He ignored it. *What the hell am I supposed to do?* he asked himself. The question was in fact an old justification for doing nothing.

"Don't mock me." It slipped out too fast. *Oh Gawd, there it is, it's out, he'll guess.* Her fingers grabbed the napkin and tried to wring the thought out of her mind by twisting the paper into a white snake of anxiety. Far from surmising any hint of her mental turmoil, he was confused by her response. Neither confusion nor any of his other emotions had ever prompted him to self-examination or indecision before, and he didn't bother thinking about it now. The waiter rescued her with another useless interruption.

It looked like they would be harassed all night by the waiter's bored attentiveness. Her lover considered leaving but didn't want to ask. *No sense inviting trouble*, he told himself, and let the notion pass.

"I wasn't mocking you," he said with exaggerated warmth. The pianist had stopped to change songs, so his words echoed loudly across the emptiness, despite his effort to utter them softly. He reached for her hand. She feared that noncompliance with his overture would call attention to her near admission, but his hands inspired a feeling of revulsion that she could not let go of and so she dropped her hands to her lap. She concentrated on them guiltily.

20 "OK, what is it this time: my disgusting sexism, my appalling arrogance, or are you just generally dissatisfied with the meaninglessness of our relationship?" He laced the question with threat. His voice lied about the concern for his character that his question implied. The noise in her ears rose an octave. The pitch of it deafened her. It blocked out the reality of the bar. The roar of the river on top of the ringing in her ears distorted everything.

The table became a watery, seductive maw, the glass a slender woman staggering and begging to be let go. The weaving woman-glass swayed frantically in the clutches of her own liquid indecision, its every movement an accusatory cry to her for decisiveness. She threw the glass at the table. The margarita bled the content of her memory across the table and it leaked onto the floor. She jumped up babbling about stress, weakly trying to submerge her behaviour in neurotic nonsense. He signalled the waiter, relieved that he had not seen her throw the glass, and was sorry that his remark had been so harsh.

She stood aside while the waiter finished mopping up the drink with his rag. Her body hung limp against the wall. She knew she couldn't keep this façade up much longer. She wanted the floor to swallow her. She prayed that the river of her maddened mind would drown her. Anger abated, he looked at her more seriously now than he could remember doing. Her thinness took on dimensions of anorexic vulnerability. Her strangeness seemed less excusable.

"Is school getting to you?" he asked. She clasped her hands together with too much vigour. That voice, that "Nancy nursey" voice, drove her to the edge. She struggled to collect herself. She fought to rest her nameless agitation on something plausible.

"Don't patronize me. Who do you think you are? You just sit there like you are the only person in the world who can handle life. You don't think I can deal with anything, do you?" The words jerked out too fast between clenched teeth. Her eyes narrowed to slits. She would have said more but the stupid waiter was back again like a phantom, cajoling them to have another drink.

25 "A double daisy for me," she hissed.

"Huh?" The rude bugger didn't have the sense to say "pardon me." She didn't answer. She turned to face the wall and tugged at her cheek with tensed fingers.

"Two double margaritas," her lover said politely. The waiter sensed the tension and left quickly. She wanted to start in on him again, but scenes of the river broke her concentration. Instead of the usual hazy images of the past, the pictures took on a dangerous lucid clarity. *Maybe if I just let it happen ... maybe if I just lose myself in the lousy nightmare of it all instead of trying to stomp it out with rattling nonsense ...*

He was near the breaking point. *I'm just a gawdamn nail-pounder, not a fucking therapist. What the fuck do I know about her feminist anxieties*, and he closed his eyes. This was more than he could deal with. *Fuck yourself* was what he wanted to say, but he continued sitting there for reasons he could not adequately explain to himself.

The blood drained from her fingers and her hands shook from the loss. Weakly, she stood up and numbly walked to the bathroom. He paid the bill. When she returned they left.

30 The sound of the traffic failed to reach her and he had to hold her trembling body against him at the curb to prevent her from stepping out among the cars. He let her lead him into the blackness when the traffic cleared. The world was getting farther away from her. She needed to hear the water, it floated around in her head like a torrent of frustrated feminine rage, liquid unpredictability. They walked wordlessly forward and the hill rolled up behind their scurrying legs.

False Creek lurched into view at the bottom, a poorly lit facsimile of cultivated wild wood and trail. Over the hill of manicured lawn and untended brush the creek stretched out purple-black against a neon skyline. No other lovers were out. The night was cool and the city's citizenry were already asleep in anticipation of the morrow's work.

They climbed down the man-made stone embankment. At the bottom, she sat with knees up, her shins folded in her thin, shivering arms. She hugged herself, waiting for the ringing to subside so the pictures she had long suppressed could return. She forced herself, in the comfort of the night's quiet affection, to watch it all.

He wrapped her in his jacket and waited helplessly. He had no idea what was going to happen but his sense of chivalry and his knowledge of the city would not allow him to desert her. He resigned himself to a night of cold anticipation.

From the riverbank she saw her mother struggling with her husband, screaming at him to give her her papers ... silly little bits of brown bags and napkins that she had scribbled on. He had caught her scribbling poems again. Her six-year-old body watched him through her woman's mind, and the clarity of the moving picture in her mind surprised her. At the end of her memory's eye, her mother disappeared over the roar of the river and her drunken father staggered uselessly after her, calling her name as though she were deserting him and not perishing under the hands of his drunken rage.

35   "They said I was crazy, a bona fide nutcase." Her chuckle came out a murmur. It was the kind of chuckle women let out when they suddenly discover that the mysteries surrounding unplugging a toilet are pathetically simple and wonderment is unwarranted. Her lover lived quite outside her range of subtle emotional variance and so thought the chuckle evidence of the truth of the findings of whoever "they" were, rather than recognizing it as the "I'll be" chortle of realization. He didn't want to hear it. *Christ, what am I supposed to do with this?* He didn't move or answer her aloud. There must be more, and he waited for it. He stared at the lights reflected against the water and thought about how they, too, made a crazy dance pattern against its smooth surface. He rested his face against her neck, trying to search his mind for some hope.

"I spent most of my childhood yo-yoing between lonely foster homes and a mental ward ... Shit." She began to rock back and forth. Her memories rolled into the smooth lap of False Creek as the wall of fear and veil of confusion lifted. She couldn't leave the brutal trap her father had set for her. The little girl, traumatized by the scene, had jumped inside the same trap, running a marathon of imprisoning relationships because she had not wanted to remember. Now the trap sunk.

"The little girl just had no words." He couldn't accept that she was crazy, but this last remark wanted some point of reference to make it rational. If he accepted her insanity he would have to declare insane the hysteria of his mother, the violence of his sister and her breakdown and his own maddened binges of the past. He would have to condemn them all because he just wasn't cut out for looking inside at the why of himself or anyone else. He resigned himself to a crazy destiny, half wishing that he had been born snuggled up against the distant mountains of his ancestors a half millennium earlier.

"You don't have a monopoly on craziness," he said dully. She laughed at his flat sense of self, at the hopelessly two-dimensional perception that he clung to, and she wondered if the man who defined neurosis wasn't just a little like her lover. Without feeling the least bit guilty about the unfairness of leaving him like this, she handed him his jacket and left without saying goodbye.

He followed her up the hill and she left him there in a tangle of confused babbling while she climbed into a cab and drove out of his life. It was all too much to explain. How does one begin to unravel the accumulation of thousands of years of entrapment to a man bent on repairing the rents she occasionally made in the machinery of the trap.

40   "I just don't feel desperate anymore," was all she could come up with. As the cab sped away she could hear him holler in self-defence, "You really are crazy."

(1990)

Guy Vanderhaeghe (b. 1951)

Born in Esterhazy, Saskatchewan, Guy Vanderhaeghe has twice won the Governor General's Award for fiction, for *Man Descending* (1982), a collection of short stories, and for *The Englishman's Boy* (1996), a novel. Influenced by the works of Margaret Laurence and Sinclair Ross, most of the short stories in *Man Descending* are about men and boys working on the Prairies. "What I Learned from Caesar" is an adult's reminiscence of his late childhood in a small Saskatchewan town during the Depression. The thirteen-year-old boy seeks a way of keeping faith in his Belgium-born father, who is suffering a mental breakdown, and finds it in the writings of Julius Caesar.

WHAT I LEARNED FROM CAESAR

The oldest story is the story of flight, the search for greener pastures. But the pastures we flee, no matter how brown and blighted — these travel with us; they can't be escaped.

My father was an immigrant. You would think this no penalty in a nation of immigrants, but even his carefully nurtured, precisely colloquial English didn't spare him much pain. Nor did his marriage to a woman of British stock (as we called it then, before the vicious-sounding acronym Wasp came into use). That marriage should have paid him a dividend of respectability, but it only served to make her suspect in marrying him.

My father was a lonely man, a stranger who made matters worse by pretending he wasn't. It's true that he was familiar enough with his adopted terrain, more familiar than most because he was a salesman. Yet he was never really of it, no matter how much he might wish otherwise. I only began to understand what had happened to him when I, in my turn, left for greener pastures, heading east. I didn't go so far, not nearly so far as he had. But I also learned that there is a price to be paid. Mine was a trivial one, a feeling of mild unease. At odd moments I betrayed myself and my beginnings; I knew that I lacked the genuine ring of a local. And I had never even left my own country.

Occasionally I return to the small Saskatchewan town near the Manitoba border where I grew up. To the unpractised eye of an easterner the countryside around that town might appear undifferentiated and monotonous, part and parcel of that great swath of prairie that vacationers drive through, pitying its inhabitants and deploring is restrooms, intent only on leaving it all behind as quickly as possible. But it is just here that the prairie verges on parkland, breaking into rolling swells of land, and here, too, that it becomes a little greener and easier on the eye. There is still more sky than any country is entitled to, and it teases the traveller into believing he can never escape it or find shelter under it. But if your attention wanders from that hypnotic expanse of blue and the high clouds drifting in it, the land becomes more comfortable as prospects shorten, and the mind rests easier on attenuated distances. There is cropland: fields of rye, oats, barley, and wheat; flat, glassy sloughs shining like mirrors in the sun; a solitary clump of trembling popular; a bluff that gently climbs to nudge the sky.

When I was a boy it was a good deal bleaker. The topsoil had blown off the fields and into the ditches to form black dunes; the crops were withered and burnt; there were no sloughs because they had all dried up. The whole place had a thirsty look. That was during the thirties when we were dealt a doubly cruel hand of drought and economic depression. It was not a time or place that was kindly to my father. He had come out of the urban sprawl of industrial Belgium some twenty-odd years before, and it was only then, I think, that he was beginning to come to terms with a land that must have seemed forbidding after his own tiny country, so well tamed and marked by man. And then this land played him the trick of becoming something more than forbidding; it became fierce, and fierce in every way.

5   It was in the summer of 1931, the summer that I thought was merely marking time before I would pass into high school, that he lost his territory. For as long as I could remember I had been a salesman's son, and then it ended. The company he worked for began to feel the pinch of the Depression and moved to merge its territories. He was let go. So one morning he unexpectedly pulled up at the front door and began to haul his sample cases out of the Ford.

"It's finished," he said to my mother as he flung the cases on to the lawn. "I got the boot. I offered to stay on — strictly commission. He wouldn't hear of it. Said he couldn't see fit to starve two men where there was only a living for one. I'd have starved that other sonofabitch out. He'd have had to hump his back and suck the hind tit when I was through with him." He paused, took off his fedora and nervously ran his index finger around the sweat-band. Clearing his throat, he said, "His parting words were, 'Good luck, Dutchie!' I should have spit in his eye. Jesus H. Christ himself wouldn't dare call me Dutchie. The bastard."

Offence compounded offence. He thought he was indistinguishable, that the accent wasn't there. Maybe his first successes as a salesman owed something to his naivety. Maybe in good times, when there was more than enough to go around, people applauded his performance by buying from him. He was a counterfeit North American who paid them the most obvious of compliments, imitation. Yet hard times make people less generous. Jobs were scarce, business was poor. In a climate like that, perceptions change, and perhaps he ceased to be merely amusing and became, instead, a dangerous parody. Maybe that district manager, faced with a choice, could only think of George Vander Elst as Dutchie. Then again, it might have been that my father just wasn't a good enough salesman. Who can judge at this distance?

But for the first time my father felt as if he had been exposed. He had never allowed himself to remember that he was a foreigner, or if he had, he persuaded himself he had been wanted. After all, he was a northern European, a Belgian. They had been on the preferred list.

He had left all that behind him. I don't even know the name of the town or the city where he was born or grew up. He always avoided my questions about his early life as if they dealt with a distasteful and criminal past that was best forgotten. Never, not even once, did I hear him speak Flemish. There were never any of the lapses you might expect. No pet names in his native language for my mother or myself; no words of endearment which would have had the comfort of childhood use. Not even when driven to one of his frequent rages did he curse in the mother tongue. If he ever prayed, I'm sure it was in English. If a man forgets the cradle language in the transports of prayer, love, and rage — well, it's forgotten.

10   The language he did speak was, in a sense, letter-perfect, fluent, glib. It was the language of wheeler-dealers, and of the heady twenties, of salesmen, high-rollers, and persuaders. He spoke of people as live-wires, go-getters, self-made men. Hyphenated words to describe the hyphenated life of the seller, a life of fits and starts, comings and goings. My father often proudly spoke of himself as a self-made man, but this description was not the most accurate. He was a remade man. The only two pictures of him which I have in my possession are proof of this.

The first is a sepia-toned photograph taken, as nearly as I can guess, just prior to his departure from Belgium. In this picture he is wearing an ill-fitting suit, round-toed, clumsy boots, and a cloth cap. The second was taken by a street photographer in Winnipeg. My father is walking down the street, a snap-brim fedora slanting rakishly over one eye. His suit is what must have been considered stylish then — a three-piece pin-stripe — and he is carrying an overcoat, casually over one arm. He is exactly what he admired most, a "snappy dresser," or since he always had trouble with his p's, a "snabby dresser." The clothes, though they mark a great change, aren't really that important. Something else tells the story.

In the first photograph my father stands rigidly with his arms folded across his chest, unsmiling. Yet I can see that he is a young man who is hesitant and afraid; not of the camera, but of what this picture-taking means. There is a reason why he is having his photograph taken. He must leave something of himself behind with his family so he will not be forgotten, and carry something away with him so that he can remember. That is what makes this picture touching; it is a portrait of a solitary, an exile.

In the second picture his face is blunter, fleshier: nothing surprising in that, he is older. But suddenly you realize he is posing for the camera — not in the formal, European manner of the first photograph but in a manner far more unnatural. You see, he is pretending to be entirely natural and unguarded; yet he betrays himself. The slight smile, the squared shoulder, the overcoat draped over the arm, all are calculated bits of a composition. He has seen the camera from a block away. My father wanted to be caught in exactly this negligent, unassuming pose, sure that it would capture for all time his prosperity, his success, his adaptability. Like most men, he wanted to leave a record. And this was it. And if he had coached himself in such small matters, what would he ever leave to chance?

That was why he was so ashamed when he came home that summer. There was the particular shame of having lost his job, a harder thing for a man than it might be today. There was the shame of knowing that sooner or later we would have to go on relief, because being a lavish spender he had no savings. But there was also the shame of a man who suddenly discovers that all his lies were transparent, and everything he thought so safely hidden had always been in plain view. He had been living one of those dreams. The kind of dream in which you are walking down the street, meeting friends and neighbours, smiling and nodding, and when you arrive at home and pass a mirror you see for the first time you are stark naked. He was sure that behind his back he had always been Dutchie. For a man with so much pride a crueller epithet would have been kinder; to be hated gives a man some kind of status. It was the condescension implicit in that diminutive, its mock playfulness, that made him appear so undignified in his own eyes.

15   And for the first time in my life I was ashamed of him. He didn't have the grace to bear an injustice, imagined or otherwise, quietly. At first he merely brooded, and then like some man with a repulsive sore, he sought pity by showing it. I'm sure he knew that he could only offend, but he was under a compulsion to justify himself. He began with my mother by explaining, where there was no need for explanation, that he had had his job taken from him for no good reason. However, there proved to be little satisfaction in preaching to the converted, so he carried his tale to everyone he knew. At first his references to his plight were tentative and oblique. The responses were polite but equally tentative and equally oblique. This wasn't what he had hoped for. He believed that the sympathy didn't measure up to the occasion. So his story was told and retold, and each time it was enlarged and embellished until the injustice was magnified beyond comprehension. He made a damn fool of himself. This was the first sign, although my mother and I chose not to recognize it.

In time everyone learned my father had lost his job for no good reason. And it wasn't long before the kids of the fathers he had told his story to were following me down the street chanting, "No good reason. No good reason." That's how I learned my family was a topical joke that the town was enjoying with zest. I suppose my father found out too, because it was about that time he stopped going out of the house. He couldn't fight back and neither could I. You never can.

After a while I didn't leave the house unless I had to. I spent my days sitting in our screened verandah reading old copies of *Saturday Evening Post*[1] and *Maclean's*. I was content to do anything that helped me forget the heat and the monotony, the shame and the fear, of that longest of summers. I was thirteen then and in a hurry to grow up, to press time into yielding the bounty I was sure it had in keeping for me. So I was killing time minute by minute with those magazines. I was to enter high school that fall and that seemed a prelude to adulthood and independence. My father's misfortunes couldn't fool me into believing that maturity didn't mean the strength to plunder at will. So when I found an old Latin grammar of my mother's I began to read that too. After all, Latin was the arcane language of the professions, of lawyers and doctors, those divinities owed immediate and unquestioning respect. I decided I would become either one, because respect could never be stolen from them as it had been from my father.

That August was the hottest I can remember. The dry heat made my nose bleed at night, and I often woke to find my pillow stiff with blood. The leaves

1 this popular American weekly magazine during the first half of the 20th century frequently pictured scenes of happy families on its cover.

of the elm tree in the front yard hung straight down on their stems; flies buzzed heavily, their bodies tip-tapping lazily against the screens, and people passing the house moved so languidly they seemed to be walking in water. My father, who had always been careful about his appearance, began to come down for breakfast barefoot, wearing only a vest undershirt and an old pair of pants. He rarely spoke, but carefully picked his way through his meal as if it were a dangerous obstacle course, only pausing to rub his nose thoughtfully. I noticed that he had begun to smell.

One morning he looked up at me, laid his fork carefully down beside his plate and said, "I'll summons him."

"Who?"

"Who do you think?" he said scornfully. "The bastard who fired me. He had no business calling me Dutchie. That's slander."

"You can't summons him."

"I can," he said emphatically. "I'm a citizen. I've got rights. I'll go to law. He spoiled my good name."

"That's not slander."

"It is."

"No, it isn't."

"I'll sue the bastard," he said vaguely, looking around to appeal to my mother, who had left the room. He got up from the table and went to the doorway. "Edith," he called, "tell your son I've got the right to summons that bastard."

Her voice came back faint and timid. "I don't know, George."

He looked back at me. "You're in the same boat, sonny. And taking sides with them don't save you. When we drown we all drown together."

"I'm not taking sides," I said indignantly. "Nobody's taking sides. It's facts. Can't you see …," but I didn't get a chance to finish. He left, walked out on me. I could hear his steps on the stairway, tired, heavy steps. There was so much I wanted to say. I wanted to make it plain that being on his side meant saving him from making a fool of himself again. I wanted him to know he could never win that way. I wanted him to win, not lose. He was my father. But he went up those steps, one at a time, and I heard his foot fall distinctly, every time. Beaten before he started, he crawled back into bed. My mother went up to him several times that day, to see if he was sick, to attempt to gouge him out of that room, but she couldn't. It was only later that afternoon, when I was reading in the verandah, that he suddenly appeared again, wearing only a pair of undershorts. His body shone dully with sweat, his skin looked grey and soiled.

"They're watching us," he said, staring past me at an empty car parked in the bright street.

Frightened, I closed my book and asked who was watching us.

"The relief people," he said tiredly. "They think I've got money hidden somewhere. They're watching me, trying to catch me with it. The joke's on them. I got no money." He made a quick, furtive gesture that drew attention to his almost naked body, as if it were proof of his poverty.

"Nobody is watching us. That car's empty."

"Don't take sides with them," he said, staring through the screen. I thought someone from one of the houses across the street might see him like that, practically naked.

"The neighbours'll see," I said, turning my head to avoid looking at him.

"See what?" he asked, surprised.

"You standing like that. Naked almost."

"There's nothing they can do. A man's home is his castle. That's what the English say, isn't it?"

40 And he went away laughing.

Going down the hallway, drawing close to his door that always stood ajar, what did I hope? To see him dressed, his trousers rolled up to mid-calf to avoid smudging his cuffs, whistling under his breath, shining his shoes? Everything as it was before? Yes. I hoped that. If I had been younger then and still believed that frogs were turned into princes with a kiss,[2] I might even have believed it could happen. But I didn't believe. I only hoped. Every time I approached his door (and that was many times a day, too many), I felt the queasy excitement of hope.

It was always the same. I would look in and see him lying on the tufted pink bedspread, naked or nearly so, gasping for breath in the heat. And I always thought of a whale stranded on a beach because he was such a big man. He claimed he slept all day because of the heat, but he only pretended to. He could feel me watching him and his eyes would open. He would tell me to go away, or bring him a glass of water; or, because his paranoia was growing more marked, ask me to see if they were still in the street. I would go to the window and tell him, yes, they were. Nothing else satisfied him. If I said they weren't, his jaw would shift from side to side unsteadily and his eyes would prick with tears. Then he imagined more subtle and intricate conspiracies.

I would ask him how he felt.

"Hot," he'd say, "I'm always hot. Can't hardly breathe. Damn country," and turn on his side away from me.

45 My mother was worried about money. There was none left. She asked me what to do. She believed women shouldn't make decisions.

"You'll have to go to the town office and apply for relief," I told her.

"No, no," she'd say, shaking her head. "I couldn't go behind his back. I couldn't do that. He'll go himself when he feels better. He'll snap out of it. It takes a little time."

In the evening my father would finally dress and come downstairs and eat something. When it got dark he'd go out into the yard and sit on the swing he'd hung from a limb of our Manitoba maple years before, when I was a little boy. My mother and I would sit and watch him from the verandah. I felt obligated to sit with her. Every night as he settled himself onto the swing she would say the same thing. "He's too big. It'll never hold him. He'll break his back." But the swing held him up and the darkness hid him from the eyes of his enemies, and I like to think that made him happy, for a time.

He'd light a cigarette before he began to swing, and then we'd watch its glowing tip move back and forth in the darkness like a beacon. He'd flick it away when it was smoked, burning a red arc in the night, showering sparks briefly, like a comet. And then he'd light another and another, and we'd watch them glow and swing in the night.

---

2 in "The Frog Prince," a German folktale, only a princess's kiss can return the hero to his human form.

50   My mother would lean over to me and say confidentially, "He's thinking it all out. It'll come to him, what to do."

I never knew whether she was trying to reassure me or herself. At last my mother would get to her feet and call to him, telling him she was going up to bed. He never answered. I waited a little longer, believing that watching him I kept him safe in the night. But I always gave up before he did and went to bed too.

The second week of September I returned to school. Small differences are keenly felt. For the first time there was no new sweater, or unsharpened pencils, or new fountain pen whose nib hadn't spread under my heavy writing hand. The school was the same school I had gone to for eight years, but that day I climbed the stairs to the second floor that housed the high school. Up there the wind moaned more persistently than I remembered it had below, and intermittently it threw handfuls of dirt and dust from the schoolyard against the windows with a gritty rattle.

Our teacher, Mrs. MacDonald, introduced herself to us, though she needed no introduction since everyone knew who she was — she had taught there for over ten years. We were given our texts and it cheered me a little to see I would have no trouble with Latin after my summer's work. Then we were given a form on which we wrote a lot of useless information. When I came to the space which asked for Racial Origin I paused, and then, out of loyalty to my father, numbly wrote in "Canadian."

After that we were told we could leave. I put my texts away in a locker for the first time — we had had none in public school — but somehow it felt strange going home from school empty-handed. So I stopped at the library door and went in. There was no school librarian and only a few shelves of books, seldom touched. The room smelled of dry paper and heat. I wandered around aimlessly, taking books down, opening them, and putting them back. That is, until I happened on Caesar's *The Gallic Wars*.[3] It was a small, thick book that nestled comfortably in the hand. I opened it and saw that the left-hand pages were printed in Latin and the right-hand pages were a corresponding English translation. I carried it away with me, dreaming of more than proficiency in Latin.

When I got home my mother was standing on the front step, peering anxiously up and down the street.

55   "Have you seen your father?" she asked.

"No," I said. "Why?"

She began to cry. "I told him all the money was gone. I asked him if I could apply for relief. He said he'd go himself and have it out with them. Stand on his rights. He took everything with him. His citizenship papers, baptismal certificate, old passport, bank book, everything. I said, 'Everyone knows you. There's no need.' But he said he needed proof. Of what? He'll cause a scandal. He's been gone for an hour."

We went into the house and sat in the living-room. "I'm a foolish woman," she said. She got up and hugged me awkwardly. "He'll be all right."

3 the military writings of Julius Caesar (100–44 B.C.) were standard reading in high school Latin courses.

We sat a long time listening for his footsteps. At last we heard someone come up the walk. My mother got up and said, "There he is." But there was a knock at the door.

60 I heard them talking at the door. The man said, "Edith, you better come with me. George is in some trouble."

My mother asked what trouble.

"You just better come. He gave the town clerk a poke. The constable and doctor have him now. The doctor wants to talk to you about signing some papers."

"I'm not signing any papers," my mother said.

"You'd better come, Edith."

65 She came into the living-room and said to me, "I'm going to get your father."

I didn't believe her for a minute. She put her coat on and went out.

She didn't bring him home. They took him to an asylum. It was a shameful word then, asylum. But I see it in a different light now. It seems the proper word now, suggesting as it does a refuge, a place to hide.

I'm not sure why all this happened to him. Perhaps there is no reason anyone can put their finger on, although I have my ideas.

But I needed a reason then. I needed a reason that would lend him a little dignity, or rather, lend me a little dignity; for I was ashamed of him out of my own weakness. I needed him to be strong, or at least tragic. I didn't know that most people are neither.

70 When you clutch at straws, anything will do. I read my answer out of Caesar's *The Gallic Wars*, the fat little book I had carried home. In the beginning of Book I he writes, "Of all people the Belgae are the most courageous...." I read on, sharing Caesar's admiration for a people who would not submit but chose to fight and see glory in their wounds. I misread it all, and bent it until I was satisfied. I reasoned the way I had to, for my sake, for my father's. What was he but a man dishonoured by faceless foes? His instincts could not help but prevail, and like his ancestors, in the end, on that one day, what could he do but make the shadows real, and fight to be free of them?

(1982)

Amy Tan (b. 1952)

Born in Oakland, California, Amy Tan visited her ancestral homeland of China when she was 35. This visit, during which she met her sisters from her mother's first marriage, inspired the writing of her first book, *The Joy Luck Club*, a series of interrelated stories about Chinese mothers and their American-born daughters. "Two Kinds" depicts the conflicts, based on cultural differences and expectations, between one of these pairs when the young girl resists her mother's hopes of her achieving musical celebrity. The title, which refers explicitly to the piece the girl plays at the recital, implicitly refers to the many tensions the narrator feels within herself and between herself and her mother.

TWO KINDS

My mother believed you could be anything you wanted to be in America. You could open a restaurant. You could work for the government and get good retirement. You could buy a house with almost no money down. You could become rich. You could become instantly famous.

"Of course you can be prodigy, too," my mother told me when I was nine. "You can be best anything. What does Auntie Lindo know? Her daughter, she is only best tricky."

America was where all my mother's hopes lay. She had come here in 1949 after losing everything in China: her mother and father, her family home, her first husband, and two daughters, twin baby girls. But she never looked back with regret. There were so many ways for things to get better.

*****

We didn't immediately pick the right kind of prodigy. At first my mother thought I could be a Chinese Shirley Temple.[1] We'd watch Shirley's old movies on TV as though they were training films. My mother would poke my arm and say, "*Ni kan*" — You watch. And I would see Shirley tapping her feet, or singing a sailor song, or pursing her lips into a very round O while saying, "Oh my goodness."

5   "*Ni Kan*," said my mother as Shirley's eyes flooded with tears. "You already know how. Don't need talent for crying!"

Soon after my mother got this idea about Shirley Temple, she took me to a beauty training school in the Mission district[2] and put me in the hands of a student who could barely hold the scissors without shaking. Instead of getting big fat curls, I emerged with an uneven mass of crinkly black fuzz. My mother dragged me off to the bathroom and tried to wet down my hair.

"You look like Negro Chinese," she lamented, as if I had done this on purpose.

---

1 popular child actor in motion pictures of the 1930s. 2 fashionable residential district of San Francisco.

The instructor of the beauty training school had to lop off these soggy clumps to make my hair even again. "Peter Pan is very popular these days," the instructor assured my mother. I now had hair the length of a boy's, with straight-across bangs that hung at a slant two inches above my eyebrows. I liked the haircut and it made me actually look forward to my future fame.

In fact, in the beginning, I was just as excited as my mother, maybe even more so. I pictured this prodigy part of me as many different images, trying each one on for size. I was a dainty ballerina girl standing by the curtains, waiting to hear the right music that would send me floating on my tiptoes. I was like the Christ child lifted out of the straw manger, crying with holy indignity. I was Cinderella stepping from her pumpkin carriage with sparkly cartoon music filling the air.

10   In all of my imaginings, I was filled with a sense that I would soon become *perfect*. My mother and father would adore me. I would be beyond reproach. I would never feel the need to sulk for anything.

But sometimes the prodigy in me became impatient. "If you don't hurry up and get me out of here, I'm disappearing for good," it warned. "And then you'll always be nothing."

Every night after dinner, my mother and I would sit at the Formica kitchen table. She would present new tests, taking her examples from stories of amazing children she had read in *Ripley's Believe It or Not*, or *Good Housekeeping*, *Reader's Digest*, and a dozen other magazines she kept in a pile in our bathroom. My mother got these magazines from people whose houses she cleaned. And since she cleaned many houses each week, we had a great assortment. She would look through them all, searching for stories about remarkable children.

The first night she brought out a story about a three-year-old boy who knew the capitals of all the states and even most of the European countries. A teacher was quoted as saying the little boy could also pronounce the names of the foreign cities correctly.

"What's the capital of Finland?" my mother asked me, looking at the magazine story.

15   All I knew was the capital of California, because Sacramento was the name of the street we lived on in Chinatown. "Nairobi!" I guessed, saying the most foreign word I could think of. She checked to see if that was possibly one way to pronounce "Helsinki"[3] before showing me the answer.

The tests got harder — multiplying numbers in my head, finding the queen of hearts in a deck of cards, trying to stand on my head without using my hands, predicting the daily temperatures in Los Angeles, New York, and London.

One night I had to look at a page from the Bible for three minutes and then report everything I could remember. "Now Jehoshaphat[4] had riches and honor in abundance and . . . that's all I remember, Ma," I said.

And after seeing my mother's disappointed face once again, something inside of me began to die. I hated the tests, the raised hopes and failed expectations. Before going to bed that night, I looked in the mirror above the bathroom sink

---

3 Nairobi is the capital city of Kenya; Helsinki, the capital of Finland.   4 king of Judah in the ninth century B.C.

and when I saw only my face staring back — and that it would always be this ordinary face — I began to cry. Such a sad, ugly girl! I made high-pitched noises like a crazed animal, trying to scratch out the face in the mirror.

And then I saw what seemed to be the prodigy side of me — because I had never seen that face before. I looked at my reflection, blinking so I could see more clearly. The girl staring back at me was angry, powerful. This girl and I were the same. I had new thoughts, willful thoughts, or rather thoughts filled with lots of won'ts. I won't let her change me, I promised myself. I won't be what I'm not.

20   So now on nights when my mother presented her tests, I performed listlessly, my head propped on one arm. I pretended to be bored. And I was. I got so bored I started counting the bellows of the foghorns out on the bay while my mother drilled me in other areas. The sound was comforting and reminded me of the cow jumping over the moon. And the next day, I played a game with myself, seeing if my mother would give up on me before eight bellows. After a while I usually counted only one, maybe two bellows at most. At last she was beginning to give up hope.

Two or three months had gone by without any mention of my being a prodigy again. And then one day my mother was watching *The Ed Sullivan Show*[5] on TV. The TV was old and the sound kept shorting out. Every time my mother got halfway up from the sofa to adjust the set, the sound would go back on and Ed would be talking. As soon as she sat down, Ed would go silent again. She got up, the TV broke into loud piano music. She sat down. Silence. Up and down, back and forth, quiet and loud. It was like a stiff embraceless dance between her and the TV set. Finally she stood by the set with her hand on the sound dial.

She seemed entranced by the music, a little frenzied piano piece with this mesmerizing quality, sort of quick passages and then teasing lilting ones before it returned to the quick playful parts.

"*Ni kan,*" my mother said, calling me over with hurried hand gestures, "Look here."

I could see why my mother was fascinated by the music. It was being pounded out by a little Chinese girl, about nine years old, with a Peter Pan haircut. The girl had the sauciness of a Shirley Temple. She was proudly modest like a proper Chinese child. And she also did this fancy sweep of a curtsy, so that the fluffy skirt of her white dress cascaded slowly to the floor like the petals of a large carnation.

25   In spite of these warning signs, I wasn't worried. Our family had no piano and we couldn't afford to buy one, let alone reams of sheet music and piano lessons. So I could be generous in my comments when my mother bad-mouthed the little girl on TV.

"Play note right, but doesn't sound good! No singing sound," complained my mother.

"What are you picking on her for?" I said carelessly. "She's pretty good. Maybe she's not the best, but she's trying hard." I knew almost immediately I would be sorry I said that.

5 popular television variety show of the 1950s and 1960s.

"Just like you," she said. "Not the best. Because you not trying." She gave a little huff as she let go of the sound dial and sat down on the sofa.

The little Chinese girl sat down also to play an encore of "Anitra's Dance" by Grieg.[6] I remember the song, because later on I had to learn how to play it.

30   Three days after watching *The Ed Sullivan Show*, my mother told me what my schedule would be for piano lessons and piano practice. She had talked to Mr. Chong, who lived on the first floor of our apartment building. Mr. Chong was a retired piano teacher and my mother had traded housecleaning services for weekly lessons and a piano for me to practice on every day, two hours a day, from four until six.

When my mother told me this, I felt as though I had been sent to hell. I whined and then kicked my foot a little when I couldn't stand it anymore.

"Why don't you like me the way I am? I'm *not* a genius! I can't play the piano. And even if I could, I wouldn't go on TV if you paid me a million dollars!" I cried.

My mother slapped me. "Who ask you be genius?" she shouted. "Only ask you be your best. For you sake. You think I want you be genius? Hnnh! What for! Who ask you!"

"So ungrateful," I heard her mutter in Chinese. "If she had as much talent as she has temper, she would be famous now."

35   Mr. Chong, whom I secretly nicknamed Old Chong, was very strange, always tapping his fingers to the silent music of an invisible orchestra. He looked ancient in my eyes. He had lost most of the hair on top of his head and he wore thick glasses and had eyes that always looked tired and sleepy. But he must have been younger than I thought, since he lived with his mother and was not yet married.

I met Old Lady Chong once and that was enough. She had this peculiar smell like a baby that had done something in its pants. And her fingers felt like a dead person's, like an old peach I once found in the back of the refrigerator; the skin just slid off the meat when I picked it up.

I soon found out why Old Chong had retired from teaching piano. He was deaf. "Like Beethoven!" he shouted to me. "We're both listening only in our head!" And he would start to conduct his frantic silent sonatas.

Our lessons went like this. He would open the book and point to different things, explaining their purpose. "Key! Treble! Bass! No sharps or flats! So this is C major! Listen now and play after me!"

And then he would play the C scale a few times, a simple chord, and then, as if inspired by an old, unreachable itch, he gradually added more notes and running trills and a pounding bass until the music was really something quite grand.

40   I would play after him, the simple scale, the simple chord, and then I just played some nonsense that sounded like a cat running up and down on top of garbage cans. Old Chong smiled and applauded and then said, "Very good! But now you must learn to keep time!"

So that's how I discovered that Old Chong's eyes were too slow to keep up with the wrong notes I was playing. He went through the motions in half-time.

---

6 nineteenth-century Norwegian composer noted for his nationalistic music.

To help me keep rhythm, he stood behind me, pushing down on my right shoulder for every beat. He balanced pennies on top of my wrists so I would keep them still as I slowly played scales and arpeggios.[7] He had me curve my hand around an apple and keep that shape when playing chords. He marched stiffly to show me how to make each finger dance up and down, staccato like an obedient little soldier.

He taught me all these things, and that was how I also learned I could be lazy and get away with mistakes, lots of mistakes. If I hit the wrong notes because I hadn't practiced enough, I never corrected myself. I just kept playing in rhythm. And Old Chong kept conducting his own private reverie.

So maybe I never really gave myself a fair chance. I did pick up the basics pretty quickly, and I might have become a good pianist at that young age. But I was so determined not to try, not to be anybody different that I learned to play only the most ear-splitting preludes, the most discordant hymns.

Over the next year, I practiced like this, dutifully in my own way. And then one day I heard my mother and her friend Lindo Jong both talking in a loud bragging tone of voice so others could hear. It was after church, and I was leaning against the brick wall wearing a dress with stiff white petticoats. Auntie Lindo's daughter, Waverly, who was about my age, was standing farther down the wall about five feet away. We had grown up together and shared all the closeness of two sisters squabbling over crayons and dolls. In other words, for the most part, we hated each other. I thought she was snotty. Waverly Jong had gained a certain amount of fame as "Chinatown's Littlest Chinese Chess Champion."

45   "She bring home too many trophy," lamented Auntie Lindo that Sunday. "All day she play chess. All day I have no time do nothing but dust off her winnings." She threw a scolding look at Waverly, who pretended not to see her.

"You lucky you don't have this problem," said Auntie Lindo with a sigh to my mother.

And my mother squared her shoulders and bragged: "Our problem worser than yours. If we ask Jing-mei wash dish, she hear nothing but music. It's like you can't stop this natural talent."

And right then, I was determined to put a stop to her foolish pride.

A few weeks later, Old Chong and my mother conspired to have me play in a talent show which would be held in the church hall. By then, my parents had saved up enough to buy me a secondhand piano, a black Wurlitzer spinet with a scarred bench. It was the showpiece of our living room.

50   For the talent show, I was to play a piece called "Pleading Child" from Schumann's *Scenes from Childhood*.[8] It was a simple, moody piece that sounded more difficult than it was. I was supposed to memorize the whole thing, playing the repeat parts twice to make the piece sound longer. But I dawdled over it, playing a few bars and then cheating, looking up to see what notes followed. I never really listened to what I was playing. I daydreamed about being somewhere else, about being someone else.

---

7 playing the notes of a musical chord in succession instead of simultaneously; a standard exercise for piano students. 8 series of short, simple piano pieces by the nineteenth-century German composer Robert Schumann.

The part I liked to practice best was the fancy curtsy: right foot out, touch the rose on the carpet with a pointed foot, sweep to the side, left leg bends, look up and smile.

My parents invited all the couples from the Joy Luck Club to witness my debut. Auntie Lindo and Uncle Tin were there. Waverly and her two older brothers had also come. The first two rows were filled with children both younger and older than I was. The littlest ones got to go first. They recited simple nursery rhymes, squawked out tunes on miniature violins, twirled Hula Hoops, pranced in pink ballet tutus, and when they bowed or curtsied, the audience would sigh in unison, "Awww," and then clap enthusiastically.

When my turn came, I was very confident. I remember my childish excitement. It was as if I knew, without a doubt, that the prodigy side of me really did exist. I had no fear whatsoever, no nervousness. I remember thinking to myself, This is it! This is it! I looked out over the audience, at my mother's blank face, my father's yawn, Auntie Lindo's stiff-lipped smile, Waverly's sulky expression. I had on a white dress layered with sheets of lace, and a pink bow in my Peter Pan haircut. As I sat down I envisioned people jumping to their feet and Ed Sullivan rushing up to introduce me to everyone on TV.

And I started to play. It was so beautiful. I was so caught up in how lovely I looked that at first I didn't worry how I would sound. So it was a surprise to me when I hit the first wrong note and I realized something didn't sound quite right. And then I hit another and another followed that. A chill started at the top of my head and began to trickle down. Yet I couldn't stop playing, as though my hands were bewitched. I kept thinking my fingers would adjust themselves back, like a train switching to the right track. I played this strange jumble through two repeats, the sour notes staying with me all the way to the end.

55   When I stood up, I discovered my legs were shaking. Maybe I had just been nervous and the audience, like Old Chong, had seen me go through the right motions and had not heard anything wrong at all. I swept my right foot out, went down on my knee, looked up and smiled. The room was quiet, except for Old Chong, who was beaming and shouting, "Bravo! Bravo! Well done!" But then I saw my mother's face, her stricken face. The audience clapped weakly, and as I walked back to my chair, with my whole face quivering as I tried not to cry, I heard a little boy whisper loudly to his mother, "That was awful," and the mother whispered back, "Well, she certainly tried."

And now I realized how many people were in the audience, the whole world it seemed. I was aware of eyes burning into my back. I felt the shame of my mother and father as they sat stiffly throughout the rest of the show.

We could have escaped during intermission. Pride and some strange sense of honor must have anchored my parents to their chairs. And so we watched it all: the eighteen-year-old boy with a fake mustache who did a magic show and juggled flaming hoops while riding a unicycle. The breasted girl with white makeup who sang from *Madama Butterfly*[9] and got honorable mention.

9 early twentieth-century opera by Giacomo Puccini about a Japanese woman abandoned by her American husband.

And the eleven-year-old boy who won first prize playing a tricky violin song that sounded like a busy bee.

After the show, the Hsus, the Jongs, and the St. Clairs from the Joy Luck Club came up to my mother and father.

"Lots of talented kids," Auntie Lindo said vaguely, smiling broadly.

60 "That was somethin' else," said my father, and I wondered if he was referring to me in a humorous way, or whether he even remembered what I had done.

Waverly looked at me and shrugged her shoulders. "You aren't a genius like me," she said matter-of-factly. And if I hadn't felt so bad, I would have pulled her braids and punched her stomach.

But my mother's expression was what devastated me: a quiet, blank look that said she had lost everything. I felt the same way, and it seemed as if everybody were now coming up, like gawkers at the scene of an accident, to see what parts were actually missing. When we got on the bus to go home, my father was humming the busy-bee tune and my mother was silent. I kept thinking she wanted to wait until we got home before shouting at me. But when my father unlocked the door to our apartment, my mother walked in and then went to the back, into the bedroom. No accusations. No blame. And in a way, I felt disappointed. I had been waiting for her to start shouting, so I could shout back and cry and blame her for all my misery.

I assumed my talent-show fiasco meant I never had to play the piano again. But two days later, after school, my mother came out of the kitchen and saw me watching TV.

"Four clock," she reminded me as if it were any other day. I was stunned, as though she were asking me to go through the talent-show torture again. I wedged myself more tightly in front of the TV.

65 "Turn off TV," she called from the kitchen five minutes later.

I didn't budge. And then I decided. I didn't have to do what my mother said anymore. I wasn't her slave. This wasn't China. I had listened to her before and look what happened. She was the stupid one.

She came out from the kitchen and stood in the arched entryway of the living room. "Four clock," she said once again, louder.

"I'm not going to play anymore," I said nonchalantly. "Why should I? I'm not a genius."

She walked over and stood in front of the TV. I saw her chest was heaving up and down in an angry way.

70 "No!" I said, and I now felt stronger, as if my true self had finally emerged. So this was what had been inside me all along.

"No! I won't!" I screamed.

She yanked me by the arm, pulled me off the floor, snapped off the TV. She was frighteningly strong, half pulling, half carrying me toward the piano as I kicked the throw rugs under my feet. She lifted me up and onto the hard bench. I was sobbing by now, looking at her bitterly. Her chest was heaving even more and her mouth was open, smiling crazily as if she was pleased I was crying.

"You want me to be someone that I'm not!" I sobbed. "I'll never be the kind of daughter you want me to be!"

"Only two kinds of daughters," she shouted in Chinese. "Those who are obedient and those who follow their own mind! Only one kind of daughter can live in this house. Obedient daughter!"

75 "Then I wish I wasn't your daughter. I wish you weren't my mother," I shouted. As I said these things I got scared. It felt like worms and toads and slimy things crawling out of my chest, but it also felt good, as if this awful side of me had surfaced, at last.

"Too late change this," said my mother shrilly.

And I could sense her anger rising to its breaking point. I wanted to see it spill over. And that's when I remembered the babies she had lost in China, the ones we never talked about. "Then I wish I'd never been born!" I shouted. "I wish I were dead! Like them."

It was as if I had said the magic words. Alakazam! — and her face went blank, her mouth closed, her arms went slack, and she backed out of the room, stunned, as if she were blowing away like a small brown leaf, thin, brittle, lifeless.

*****

It was not the only disappointment my mother felt in me. In the years that followed, I failed her so many times, each time asserting my own will, my right to fall short of expectations. I didn't get straight As. I didn't become class president. I didn't get into Stanford. I dropped out of college.

80 For unlike my mother, I did not believe I could be anything I wanted to be. I could only be me.

And for all those years, we never talked about the disaster at the recital or my terrible accusations afterward at the piano bench. All that remained unchecked, like a betrayal that was now unspeakable. So I never found a way to ask her why she had hoped for something so large that failure was inevitable.

And even worse, I never asked her what frightened me the most: Why had she given up hope?

For after our struggle at the piano, she never mentioned my playing again. The lessons stopped. The lid to the piano was closed, shutting out the dust, my misery, and her dreams.

So she surprised me. A few years ago, she offered to give me the piano, for my thirtieth birthday. I had not played in all those years. I saw the offer as a sign of forgiveness, a tremendous burden removed.

85 "Are you sure?" I asked shyly. "I mean, won't you and Dad miss it?"

"No, this your piano," she said firmly. "Always your piano. You only one can play."

"Well, I probably can't play anymore," I said. "It's been years."

"You pick up fast," said my mother, as if she knew this was certain. "You have natural talent. You could been genius if you want to."

"No I couldn't."

90 "You just not trying," said my mother. And she was neither angry nor sad. She said it as if to announce a fact that could never be disproved. "Take it," she said.

But I didn't at first. It was enough that she had offered it to me. And after that, every time I saw it in my parents' living room, standing in front of the bay windows, it made me feel proud, as if it were a shiny trophy I had won back.

Last week I sent a tuner over to my parents' apartment and had the piano reconditioned, for purely sentimental reasons. My mother had died a few months before and I had been getting things in order for my father, a little bit at a time. I put the jewelry in special silk pouches. The sweaters she had knitted in yellow, pink, bright orange — all the colors I hated — I put those in moth-proof boxes. I found some old Chinese silk dresses, the kind with the little slits up the sides. I rubbed the old silk against my skin, then wrapped them in tissue and decided to take them home with me.

After I had the piano tuned, I opened the lid and touched the keys. It sounded even richer than I remembered. Really, it was a very good piano. Inside the bench were the same exercise notes with handwritten scales, the same secondhand music books with their covers held together with yellow tape.

I opened up the Schumann book to the dark little piece I had played at the recital. It was on the left-hand side of the page, "Pleading Child." It looked more difficult than I remembered. I played a few bars, surprised at how easily the notes came back to me.

95 And for the first time, or so it seemed, I noticed the piece on the right-hand side. It was called "Perfectly Contented." I tried to play this one as well. It had a lighter melody but the same flowing rhythm and turned out to be quite easy. "Pleading Child" was shorter but slower; "Perfectly Contented" was longer, but faster. And after I played them both a few times, I realized they were two halves of the same song.

(1989)

Rohinton Mistry (b. 1952)

Born and raised in Bombay, India, Mistry is a Parsi, a religious minority much favored by the British when they ruled in India. Mistry came to Canada in 1975 and began writing while attending the University of Toronto. *Tales from Firozsha Baag* (1987), his first book, is a collection of short stories about the frequently contentious interrelationships among the residents of a Bombay housing complex. His two novels, *Such a Long Journey* (1991), winner of the Governor General's Medal, and *A Fine Balance* (1995), are set in India during the country-wide political crises of the 1970s. "Squatter," the story of a Firozsha Baag resident's unfortunate immigration to Canada, plays on the pun of the title, which not only indicates his physical difficulties, but also his status as a new Canadian. The squatter's problems in an alien environment can be compared to those of Giovanni in Hawthorne's "Rappaccini's Daughter" and Calvin in Clarke's "The Motor Car." In addition to portraying the difficulties faced by immigrants, Mistry also examines the role of the storyteller, an old man who frequently recounts tales to an admiring audience of boys gathered outside his Bombay apartment.

SQUATTER

Whenever Nariman Hansotia returned in the evening from the Cawasji Framji Memorial Library in a good mood the signs were plainly evident.

First, he parked his 1932 Mercedes-Benz (he called it the apple of his eye) outside A Block, directly in front of his ground-floor veranda window, and beeped the horn three long times. It annoyed Rustomji who also had a ground-floor flat in A Block. Ever since he had defied Nariman in the matter of painting the exterior of the building, Rustomji was convinced that nothing the old coot did was untainted by the thought of vengeance and harassment, his retirement pastime.

But the beeping was merely Nariman's signal to let Hirabai inside know that though he was back he would not step indoors for a while. Then he raised the hood, whistling "Rose Marie,"[1] and leaned his tall frame over the engine. He checked the oil, wiped here and there with a rag, tightened the radiator cap, and lowered the hood. Finally, he polished the Mercedes star and let the whistling modulate into the march from *The Bridge on The River Kwai*.[2] The boys playing in the compound knew that Nariman was ready now to tell a story. They started to gather round.

"*Sahibji*,[3] Nariman Uncle," someone said tentatively and Nariman nodded, careful not to lose his whistle, his bulbous nose flaring slightly. The pursed lips had temporarily raised and reshaped his Clark Gable[4] moustache. More boys walked up. One called out, "How about a story, Nariman Uncle?" at which point Nariman's eyes began to twinkle, and he imparted increased energy to the polishing. The cry was taken up by others, "Yes, yes, Nariman Uncle, a story!"

---

1 title song from a 1954 Hollywood musical that depicted a romance between a Mountie and a French-Canadian girl. 2 1957 movie about a British colonel who, with his men, is imprisoned by the Japanese during World War II. 3 Sir, an expression of respect. 4 American movie star of the 1940s and 1950s.

He swung into a final verse of the march. Then the lips relinquished the whistle, the Clark Gable moustache descended. The rag was put away, and he began.

"You boys know the great cricketers: Contractor, Polly Umrigar, and recently, the young chap, Farokh Engineer. Cricket *aficionados*, that's what you all are." Nariman liked to use new words, especially big ones, in the stories he told, believing it was his duty to expose young minds to as shimmering and varied a vocabulary as possible; if they could not spend their days at the Cawasji Framji Memorial Library then he, at least, could carry bits of the library out to them.

The boys nodded; the names of the cricketers were familiar.

"But does any one know about Savukshaw, the greatest of them all?" They shook their heads in unison.

"This, then, is the story about Savukshaw, how he saved the Indian team from a humiliating defeat when they were touring in England." Nariman sat on the steps of A Block. The few diehards who had continued with their games could not resist any longer when they saw the gathering circle, and ran up to listen. They asked their neighbours in whispers what the story was about, and were told: Savukshaw the greatest cricketer. The whispering died down and Nariman began.

"The Indian team was to play the indomitable MCC as part of its tour of England. Contractor was our captain. Now the MCC being the strongest team they had to face, Contractor was almost certain of defeat. To add to Contractor's troubles, one of his star batsmen, Nadkarni, had caught influenza early in the tour, and would definitely not be well enough to play against the MCC. By the way, does anyone know what those letters stand for? You, Kersi, you wanted to be a cricketer once."

Kersi shook his head. None of the boys knew, even though they had heard the MCC mentioned in radio commentaries, because the full name was hardly ever used.

Then Jehangir Bulsara spoke up, or Bulsara Bookworm, as the boys called him. The name given by Pesi *paadmaroo*[5] had stuck even though it was now more than four years since Pesi had been sent away to boarding-school, and over two years since the death of Dr. Mody. Jehangir was still unliked by the boys in the Baag, though they had come to accept his aloofness and respect his knowledge and intellect. They were not surprised that he knew the answer to Nariman's question: "Marylebone Cricket Club."

"Absolutely correct," said Nariman, and continued with the story. "The MCC won the toss and elected to bat. They scored four hundred and ninety-seven runs in the first inning before our spinners could get them out. Early in the second day's play our team was dismissed for one hundred and nine runs, and the extra who had taken Nadkarni's place was injured by a vicious bumper that opened a gash on his forehead." Nariman indicated the spot and the length of the gash on his furrowed brow. "Contractor's worst fears were coming true. The MCC waived their own second inning and gave the Indian team a follow-on, wanting to inflict an inning's defeat. And this time he had to use the second extra. The second extra was as a certain Savukshaw."

5 lotus-boy, a mocking nickname.

The younger boys listened attentively; some of them, like the two sons of the chartered accountant in B Block, had only recently been deemed old enough by their parents to come out and play in the compound, and had not received any exposure to Nariman's stories. But the others like Jehangir, Kersi, and Viraf were familiar with Nariman's technique.

Once, Jehangir had overheard them discussing Nariman's stories, and he could not help expressing his opinion: that unpredictability was the brush he used to paint his tales with, and ambiguity the palette he mixed his colours in. The others looked at him with admiration. Then Viraf asked what exactly he meant by that. Jehangir said that Nariman sometimes told a funny incident in a very serious way, or expressed a significant matter in a light and playful manner. And these were only two rough divisions, in between were lots of subtle gradations of tone and texture. Which, then, was the funny story and which the serious? Their opinions were divided, but ultimately, said Jehangir, it was up to the listener to decide.

15   "So," continued Nariman, "Contractor first sent out his two regular openers, convinced that it was all hopeless. But after five wickets were lost for just another thirty-eight runs, out came Savukshaw the extra. Nothing mattered any more."

The street lights outside the compound came on, illuminating the iron gate where the watchman stood. It was a load off the watchman's mind when Nariman told a story. It meant an early end to the hectic vigil during which he had to ensure that none of the children ran out on the main road, or tried to jump over the wall. For although keeping out riff-raff was his duty, keeping in the boys was as important if he wanted to retain the job.

"The first ball Savukshaw faced was wide outside the off stump. He just lifted his bat and ignored it. But with what style! What panache! As if to say, come on, you blighters, play some polished cricket. The next ball was also wide, but not as much as the first. It missed the off stump narrowly. Again Savukshaw lifted his bat, boredom written all over him. Everyone was now watching closely. The bowler was annoyed by Savukshaw's arrogance, and the third delivery was a vicious fast pitch, right down on the middle stump.

"Savukshaw was ready, quick as lightning. No one even saw the stroke of his bat, but the ball went like a bullet towards the square leg.

"Fielding at square leg was giant fellow, about six feet seven, weighing two hundred and fifty pounds, a veritable Brobdingnagian,[6] with arms like branches and hands like a pair of huge *sapaat*,[7] the kind the Dr Mody used to wear, you remember what big feet Dr Mody had." Jehangir was the only one who did; he nodded. "Just to see him standing there was scary. Not one ball had got past him, and he had taken some great catches. Savukshaw purposely aimed his shot right at him. But he was as quick as Savukshaw, and stuck out his huge *sapaat* of a hand to stop the ball. What do you think happened then, boys?"

20   The older boys knew what Nariman wanted to hear at this point. They asked, "What happened, Nariman Uncle, what happened?" Satisfied, Nariman continued.

6 the giant people in Book II of Jonathan Swift's *Gulliver's Travels*. 7 boots.

"A howl is what happened. A howl from the giant fielder, a howl that rang through the entire stadium, that soared like the cry of a banshee right up to the cheapest seats in the furthest, highest corners, a howl that echoed from the scoreboard and into the pavilion, into the kitchen, startling the chap inside who was preparing tea and scones for after the match, who spilled boiling water all over himself and was severely hurt. But not nearly as bad as the giant fielder at square leg. Never at any English stadium was a howl heard like that one, not in the whole history of cricket. And why do you think he was howling, boys?"

The chorus asked, "Why, Nariman Uncle, why?"

"Because of Savukshaw's bullet-like shot, of course. The hand he had reached out to stop it, he now held up for all to see, and *dhur-dhur, dhur-dhur* the blood was gushing like a fountain in an Italian piazza, like a burst water-main from the Vihar-Powai reservoir, dripping onto his shirt and his white pants, and sprinkling the green grass, and only because he was such a giant of a fellow could he suffer so much blood loss and not faint. But even he could not last forever; eventually, he felt dizzy, and was helped off the field. And where do you think the ball was, boys, that Savukshaw had smacked so hard?"

And the chorus rang out again on the now dark steps of A Block: "Where, Nariman Uncle, where?"

"Past the boundary line, of course. Lying near the fence. Rent asunder. Into two perfect leather hemispheres. All the stitches had ripped, and some of the insides had spilled out. So the umpires sent for a new one, and the game resumed. Now none of the fielders dared to touch any ball that Savukshaw hit. Every shot went to the boundary, all the way for four runs. Single-handedly, Savukshaw wiped out the deficit, and had it not been for loss of time due to rain, he would have taken the Indian team to a thumping victory against the MCC. As it was, the match ended in a draw."

Nariman was pleased with the awed faces of the youngest ones around him. Kersi and Viraf were grinning away and whispering something. From one of the flats the smell of frying fish swam out to explore the night air, and tickled Nariman's nostrils. He sniffed appreciatively, aware that it was in his good wife Hirabai's pan that the frying was taking place. This morning, he had seen the pomfret[8] she had purchased at the door, waiting to be cleaned, its mouth open and eyes wide, like the eyes of some of these youngsters. It was time to wind up the story.

"The MCC will not forget the number of new balls they had to produce that day because of Savukshaw's deadly strokes. Their annual ball budget was thrown badly out of balance. Any other bat would have cracked under the strain, but Savukshaw's was seasoned with a special combination of oils, a secret formula given to him by a *sadhu*[9] who had seen him one day playing cricket when he was a small boy. But Savukshaw used to say his real secret was practice, lots of practice, that was the advice he gave to any young lad who wanted to play cricket."

The story was now clearly finished, but none of the boys showed any sign of dispersing. "Tell us about more matches that Savukshaw played in," they said.

8 a popular fish in India.   9 holy man.

"More nothing. This was his greatest match. Anyway, he did not play cricket for long because soon after the match against the MCC he became a champion bicyclist, the fastest human on two wheels. And later, a pole-vaulter — when he glided over on his pole, so graceful, it was like watching a bird in flight. But he gave that up, too, and became a hunter, the mightiest hunter ever known, absolutely fearless, and so skilful, with a gun he could have, from the third floor of A Block, shaved the whisker of a cat in the back-yard of C Block."

30   "Tell us about that," they said, "about Savukshaw the hunter!"

The fat ayah, Jaakaylee, arrived to take the chartered accountant's two children home. But they refused to go without hearing about Savukshaw the hunter. When she scolded them and things became a little hysterical, some other boys tried to resurrect the ghost she had once seen: "Ayah *bhoot*! Ayah *bhoot*!"[10] Nariman raised a finger in warning — that subject was still taboo in Firozsha Baag; none of the adults was in a hurry to relive the wild and rampageous days that Pesi *paadmaroo* had ushered in, once upon a time, with the *bhoot* games.

Jaakaylee sat down, unwilling to return without the children, and whispered to Nariman to make it short. The smell of frying fish which had tickled Nariman's nostrils ventured into and awakened his stomach. But the story of Savukshaw the hunter was one he had wanted to tell for a long time.

"Savukshaw always went hunting alone, he preferred it that way. There are many incidents in the life of Savukshaw the hunter, but the one I am telling you about involves a terrifying situation. Terrifying for us, of course; Savukshaw was never terrified of anything. What happened was, one night he set up camp, started a fire and warmed up his bowl of chicken-*dhansaak*."

The frying fish had precipitated famishment upon Nariman, and the subject of chicken-*dhansaak* suited him well. His own mouth watering, he elaborated: "Mrs. Savukshaw was as famous for her *dhansaak* as Mr. was for hunting. She used to put in tamarind and brinjal, coriander and cumin, cloves and cinnamon, and dozens of other spices no one knows about. Women used to come from miles around to stand outside her window while she cooked it, to enjoy the fragrance and try to penetrate her secret, hoping to identify the ingredients as the aroma floated out, layer by layer, growing more complex and delicious. But always, the delectable fragrance enveloped the women and they just surrendered to the ecstasy, forgetting what they had come for. Mrs. Savukshaw's secret was safe."

35   Jaakaylee motioned to Nariman to hurry up, it was past the children's dinner-time. He continued: "The aroma of savoury spices soon filled the night air in the jungle, and when the *dhansaak* was piping hot he started to eat, his rifle beside him. But as soon as he lifted the first morsel to his lips, a tiger's eyes flashed in the bushes! Not twelve feet from him! He emerged licking his chops! What do you think happened then, boys?"

"What, what, Nariman Uncle?"

Before he could tell them, the door of his flat opened. Hirabai put her head out and said, "*Chaalo ni*,[11] Nariman, it's time. Then if it gets cold you won't like it."

10 ghost. 11 let's go.

That decided the matter. To let Hirabai's fried fish, crisp on the outside, yet tender and juicy inside, marinated in turmeric and cayenne — to let that get cold would be something that *Khoedaiji*[12] above would not easily forgive. "Sorry boys, have to go. Next time about Savukshaw and the tiger."

There were some groans of disappointment. They hoped Nariman's good spirits would extend into the morrow when he returned from the Memorial Library, or the story would get cold.

But a whole week elapsed before Nariman again parked the apple of his eye outside his ground-floor flat and beeped the horn three times. When he had raised the hood, checked the oil, polished the star and swung into the "Colonel Bogie March,"[13] the boys began drifting towards A Block.

Some of them recalled the incomplete story of Savukshaw and the tiger, but they knew better than to remind him. It was never wise to prompt Nariman until he had dropped the first hint himself, or things would turn out badly.

Nariman inspected the faces: the two who stood at the back, always looking superior and wise, were missing. So was the quiet Bulsara boy, the intelligent one. "Call Kersi, Viraf, and Jehangir," he said. "I want them to listen to today's story."

Jehangir was sitting alone on the stone steps of C Block. The others were chatting by the compound gate with the watchman. Someone went to fetch them.

"Sorry to disturb your conference, boys, and your meditation, Jehangir," Nariman said facetiously, "but I thought you would like to hear this story. Especially since some of you are planning to go abroad."

This was not strictly accurate, but Kersi and Viraf did talk a lot about America and Canada. Kersi had started writing to universities there since his final high-school year, and had also send letters of inquiry to the Canadian High Commission in New Delhi and to the U.S. Consulate at Breach Candy.[14] But so far he had not made any progress. He and Viraf replied with as much sarcasm as their unripe years allowed, "Oh yes, next week, just have to pack our bags."

"Riiiight," drawled Nariman. Although he spoke perfect English, this was the one word with which he allowed himself to take liberties, indulging in a broadness of vowel more American than anything else. "But before we go on with today's story, what did you learn about Savukshaw, from last week's story?"

"That he was a very talented man," said someone.

"What else?"

"He was also a very lucky man, to have so many talents," said Viraf.

"Yes, but what else?"

There was silence for a few moments. Then Jehangir said, timidly: "He was a man searching for happiness, by trying all kinds of different things."

"Exactly! And he never found it. He kept looking for new experiences, and though he was very successful at everything he attempted, it did not bring him happiness. Remember this, success alone does not bring happiness.

---

12 God. 13 a marching tune whistled by captured British soldiers in *The Bridge on the River Kwai*. 14 an affluent, fashionable district of Bombay.

Nor does failure have to bring unhappiness. Keep it in mind when you listen to today's story."

A chant started somewhere in the back: "We-want-a-story! We-want-a-story!"

"Riiiight," said Nariman. "Now, everyone remembers Vera and Dolly, daughters of Najamai from C Block." There were whistles and hoots; Viraf nudged Kersi with his elbow, who was smiling wistfully. Nariman held up his hand: "Now now, boys, behave yourselves. Those two girls went abroad for studies many years ago, and never came back. They settled there happily.

"And like them, a fellow called Sarosh also went abroad, to Toronto, but did not find happiness there. This story is about him. You probably don't know him, he does not live in Firozsha Baag, though he is related to someone who does."

"Who? Who?"

"Curiosity killed the cat," said Nariman, running a finger over each branch of his moustache, "and what's important is the tale. So let us continue. This Sarosh began calling himself Sid after living in Toronto for a few months, but in our story he will be Sarosh and nothing but Sarosh, for that is his proper Parsi name. Besides, that was his own stipulation when he entrusted me with the sad but instructive chronicle of his recent life." Nariman polished his glasses with his handkerchief, put them on again, and began.

"At the point where our story commences, Sarosh had been living in Toronto for ten years. We find him depressed and miserable, perched on top of the toilet, crouching on his haunches, feet planted firmly for balance upon the white plastic oval of the toilet seat.

"Daily for a decade had Sarosh suffered this position. Morning after morning, he had no choice but to climb up and simulate the squat of our Indian latrines. If he sat down, no amount of exertion could produce success.

"At first, this inability was not more than mildly incommodious. As time went by, however, the frustrated attempts caused him grave anxiety. And when the failure stretched unbroken over ten years, it began to torment and haunt all his waking hours."

Some of the boys struggled hard to keep straight faces. They suspected that Nariman was not telling just a funny story, because if he intended them to laugh there was always some unmistakable way to let them know. Only the thought of displeasing Nariman and prematurely terminating the story kept their paroxysms of mirth from bursting forth unchecked.

Nariman continued: "You see, ten years was the time Sarosh had set himself to achieve complete adaptation to the new country. But how could he claim adaptation with any honesty if the acceptable catharsis continually failed to favour him? Obtaining his new citizenship had not helped either. He remained dependent on the old way, and this unalterable fact, strengthened afresh every morning of his life in the new country, suffocated him.

"The ten-year time limit was more an accident than anything else. But it hung over him with the awesome presence and sharpness of a guillotine. Careless words, boys, careless words in a moment of lightheartedness, as is so often the case with us all, had led to it.

"Ten years before, Sarosh had returned triumphantly to Bombay after fulfilling the immigration requirements of the Canadian High Commission in

New Delhi. News of his imminent departure spread amongst relatives and friends. A farewell party was organized. In fact, it was given by his relatives in Firozsha Baag. Most of you will be too young to remember it, but it was a very loud party, went on till late in the night. Very lengthy and heated arguments took place, which is not the thing to do at a party. It started like this: Sarosh was told by some what a smart decision he had made, that his whole life would change for the better; others said he was making a mistake, emigration was all wrong, but if he wanted to be unhappy that was his business, they wished him well.

65   "By and by, after substantial amounts of Scotch and soda and rum and Coke had disappeared, a fierce debate started between the two groups. To this day Sarosh does not know what made him raise his glass and announce: 'My dear family, my dear friends, if I do not become completely Canadian in exactly ten years from the time I land there, then I will come back. I promise. So please, no more arguments. Enjoy the party.' His words were greeted with cheers and shouts of hear! hear! They told him never to fear embarrassment; there was no shame if he decided to return to the country of his birth.

"But shortly, his poor worried mother pulled him aside. She led him to the back room and withdrew her worn and aged prayer book from her purse, saying, 'I want you to place your hand upon the *Avesta*[15] and swear that you will keep that promise.'

"He told her not to be silly, that it was just a joke. But she insisted. '*Kassum khà*[16]— on the *Avesta*. One last thing for your mother. Who knows when you will see me again?' and her voice grew tremulous as it always did when she turned deeply emotional. Sarosh complied, and the prayer book was returned to her purse.

"His mother continued: 'It is better to live in want among your family and your friends, who love you and care for you, than to be unhappy surrounded by vacuum cleaners and dishwashers and big shiny motor cars.' She hugged him. Then they joined the celebration in progress.

"And Sarosh's careless words spoken at the party gradually forged themselves into a commitment as much to himself as to his mother and the others. It stayed with him all his years in the new land, reminding him every morning of what must happen at the end of the tenth, as it reminded him now while he descended from his perch."

70   Jehangir wished the titters and chortles around him would settle down, he found them annoying. When Nariman structured his sentences so carefully and chose his words with extreme care as he was doing now, Jehangir found it most pleasurable to listen. Sometimes, he remembered certain words Nariman had used, or combinations of words, and repeated them to himself, enjoying again the beauty of their sounds when he went for his walks to the Hanging Gardens or was sitting alone on the stone steps of C Block. Mumbling to himself did nothing to mitigate the isolation which the other boys in the Baag had dropped around him like a heavy cloak, but he had grown used to all that by now.

15 sacred Zoroastrian (Parsi) text. 16 swear an oath.

Nariman continued: "In his own apartment Sarosh squatted barefoot. Elsewhere, if he had to go with his shoes on, he would carefully cover the seat with toilet paper before climbing up. He learnt to do this after the first time, when his shoes had left telltale footprints on the seat. He had had to clean it with a wet paper towel. Luckily, no one had seen him.

But there was not much he could keep secret about his ways. The world of washrooms is private and at the same time very public. The absence of his feet below the stall door, the smell of faeces, the rustle of paper, glimpses caught through the narrow crack between stall door and jamb — all these added up to only one thing: a foreign presence in the stall, not doing things in the conventional way. And if the one outside could receive the fetor of Sarosh's business wafting through the door, poor unhappy Sarosh too could detect something malodorous in the air: the presence of xenophobia and hostility."

What a feast, thought Jehangir, what a feast of words! This would be the finest story Nariman had ever told, he just knew it.

"But Sarosh did not give up trying. Each morning he seated himself to push and grunt, grunt and push, squirming and writhing unavailingly on the white plastic oval. Exhausted, he then hopped up, expert at balancing now, and completed the movement quite effortlessly.

75 "The long morning hours in the washroom created new difficulties. He was late going to work on several occasions, and one such day, the supervisor called him in: 'Here's your time-sheet for this month. You've been late eleven times. What's the problem?'"

Here, Nariman stopped because his neighbour Rustomji's door creaked open. Rustomji peered out, scowling and muttered, "Saala[17] loafers, sitting all evening outside people's houses, making a nuisance, and being encouraged by grownups at that."

He stood there a moment longer, fingering the greying chest hair that was easily accessible through his sudra,[18] then went inside. The boys immediately took up a soft and low chant: "Rustomji-the-curmudgeon! Rustomji-the-curmudgeon!"

Nariman held up his hand disapprovingly. But secretly, he was pleased that the name was still popular, the name he had given Rustomji when the latter had refused to pay his share for painting the building. "Quiet, quiet!" said he. "Do you want me to continue or not?"

"Yes, yes!" The chanting died away, and Nariman resumed the story.

80 "So Sarosh was told by his supervisor that he was coming late to work too often. What could poor Sarosh say?"

"What, Nariman Uncle?" rose the refrain.

"Nothing, of course. The supervisor, noting his silence, continued: 'If it keeps up, the consequences could be serious as far as your career is concerned.'

"Sarosh decided to speak. He said embarrassedly, 'It's a different kind of problem. I...I don't know how to explain...it's an immigration-related problem.'

"Now this supervisor must have had experience with other immigrants, because right away he told Sarosh, 'No problem. Just contact your Immigrant Aid Society. They should be able to help you. Every ethnic group has one:

17 dirty. 18 woolen shirt.

Vietnamese, Chinese — I'm certain that one exists for Indians. If you need time off to go there, no problem. That can be arranged, no problem. As long as you do something about your lateness, there's no problem.' That's the way they talk over there, nothing is ever a problem.

85 "So Sarosh thanked him and went to his desk. For the umpteenth time he bitterly rued his oversight. Could fate have plotted it, concealing the western toilet behind a shroud of anxieties which had appeared out of nowhere to beset him just before he left India? After all, he had readied himself meticulously for the new life. Even for the great, merciless Canadian cold he had heard so much about. How could he have overlooked preparation for the western toilet with its matutinal demands unless fate had conspired? In Bombay, you know that offices of foreign businesses offer both options in their bathrooms. So do all hotels with three stars or more. By practising in familiar surroundings, Sarosh was convinced he could have mastered a seated evacuation before departure.

"But perhaps there was something in what the supervisor said. Sarosh found a telephone number for the Indian Immigrant Aid Society and made an appointment. That afternoon, he met Mrs. Maha-Lepate at the Society's office.

Kersi and Viraf looked at each other and smiled. Nariman Uncle had a nerve, there was more *lepate* in his own stories than anywhere else.

"Mrs. Maha-Lepate was very understanding, and made Sarosh feel at ease despite the very personal nature of his problem. She said, 'Yes, we get many referrals. There was a man here last month who couldn't eat Wonder Bread — it made him throw up.'

"By the way, boys, Wonder Bread is a Canadian bread which all happy families eat to be happy in the same way; the unhappy families are unhappy in their own fashion by eating other brands." Jehangir was the only one who understood, and murmured, "Tolstoy,"[19] at Nariman's little joke. Nariman noticed it, pleased. He continued.

90 "Mrs. Maha-Lepate told Sarosh about that case: 'Our immigrant specialist, Dr. No-Ilaaz, recommended that the patient eat cake instead. He explained that Wonder Bread caused vomiting because the digestive system was used to Indian bread only, made with Indian flour in the village he came from. However, since his system was unfamiliar with cake, Canadian or otherwise, it did not react but was digested as a newfound food. In this way he got used to Canadian flour first in cake form. Just yesterday we received a report from Dr. No-Ilaaz. The patient successfully ate his first slice of whole-wheat Wonder Bread with no ill effects. The ultimate goal is pure white Wonder Bread.'

"Like a polite Parsi boy, Sarosh said, 'That's very interesting.' The garrulous Mrs. Maha-Lepate was about to continue, and he tried to interject: 'But I —' but Mrs. Maha-Lepate was too quick for him: 'Oh, there are so many interesting cases I could tell you about. Like the woman from Sri Lanka — referred to us because they don't have their own Society — who could not drink the water here. Dr. No-Ilaaz said it was due to the different mineral content. So he started her on Coca-Cola and then began diluting it with water, bit by bit. Six weeks later she took her first sip of unadulterated Canadian water and managed to keep it down.'

---

19 nineteenth-century Russian author of *War and Peace*; the lines about happy and unhappy families parody the opening of his novel *Anna Karenina*.

"Sarosh could not halt Mrs. Maha-Lepate as she launched from one case history into another: 'Right now, Dr. No-Ilaaz is working on a very unusual case. Involves a whole Pakistani family. Ever since immigrating to Canada, none of them can swallow. They choke on their own saliva, and have to spit constantly. But we are confident that Dr. No-Ilaaz will find a remedy. He has never been stumped by any immigrant problems. Besides, we have an information network with other third-world Immigrant Aid Societies. We all seem to share a history of similar maladies, and regularly compare notes. Some of us thought these problems were linked to retention of original citizenship. But this was a false lead.'

"Sarosh, out of his own experience, vigorously nodded agreement. By now he was truly fascinated by Mrs. Maha-Lepate's wealth of information. Reluctantly, he interrupted: 'But will Dr. No-Ilaaz be able to solve my problem?'

" 'I have every confidence that he will,' replied Mrs. Maha-Lepate in great earnest. 'And if he has no remedy for you right away, he will be delighted to start working on one. He loves to take up new projects.'"

95 Nariman halted to blow his nose, and a clear shrill voice travelled the night air of the Firozsha Baag compound from C Block to where the boys had collected around Nariman in A Block: "Jehangoo! O Jehangoo! Eight o'clock! Upstairs now!"

Jehangir stared at his feet in embarrassment. Nariman looked at his watch and said, "Yes, it's eight." But Jehangir did not move, so he continued.

"Mrs. Maha-Lepate was able to arrange an appointment while Sarosh waited, and he went directly to the doctor's office. What he had heard so far sounded quite promising. Then he cautioned himself not to get overly optimistic, that was the worst mistake he could make. But along the way to the doctor's, he could not help thinking what a lovely city Toronto was. It was the same way he had felt when he first saw it ten years ago, before all the joy had dissolved in the acid of his anxieties."

Once again that shrill voice travelled through the clear night: "*Arré*[20] Jehangoo! *Muà*,[21] do I have to come down and drag you upstairs!"

Jehangir's mortification was now complete. Nariman made it easy for him, though: "The first part of the story is over. Second part continues tomorrow. Same time, same place." The boys were surprised, Nariman did not make such commitments. But never before had he told such a long story. They began drifting back to their homes.

100 As Jehangir strode hurriedly to C Block, falsettos and piercing shrieks followed him in the darkness: "*Arré* Jehangoo! *Muà*, Jehangoo! Bulsara Bookworm! Eight o'clock Jehangoo!" Shaking his head, Nariman went indoors to Hirabai.

Next evening the story punctually resumed when Nariman took his place on the topmost step of A Block: "You remember that we left Sarosh on his way to see the Immigrant Aid Society's doctor. Well, Dr. No-Ilaaz listened patiently to Sarosh's concerns, then said, 'As a matter of fact, there is a remedy which is so new even the IAS does not know about it. Not even that Mrs. Maha-Lepate who knows it all,' he added drolly, twirling his stethoscope like a

20 oh. 21 a good-for-nothing.

stunted lasso. He slipped it on around his neck before continuing: 'It involves a minor operation which was developed with financial assistance from the Multicultural Department. A small device, *Crappus Non Interruptus*, or CNI as we call it, is implanted in the bowel. The device is controlled by an external handheld transmitter similar to the ones used for automatic garage door-openers — you may have seen them in hardware stores.'"

Nariman noticed that most of the boys wore puzzled looks and realized he had to make some things clearer. "The Multicultural Department is a Canadian invention. It is supposed to ensure that ethnic cultures are able to flourish, so that Canadian society will consist of a mosaic of cultures — that's their favourite word, mosaic — instead of one uniform mix, like the American melting pot. If you ask me, mosaic and melting pot are both nonsense, and ethnic is a polite way of saying bloody foreigner. But anyway, you understand Multicultural Department? Good. So Sarosh nodded, and Dr. No-Ilaaz went on: 'You can encode the hand-held transmitter with a personal ten-digit code. Then all you do is position yourself on the toilet seat and activate your transmitter. Just like a garage door, your bowel will open without pushing or grunting.'"

There was some snickering in the audience, and Nariman raised his eye-brows, whereupon they covered up their mouths with their hands. "The doctor asked Sarosh if he had any questions. Sarosh thought for a moment, then asked if it required any maintenance.

"Dr. No-Ilaaz replied: 'CNI is semi-permanent and operates on solar energy. Which means you would have to make it a point to get some sun peri-odically, or it would cease and lead to constipation. However, you don't have to strip for a tan. Exposing ten percent of your skin surface once a week during summer will let the device store sufficient energy for year-round operation.'

"Sarosh's next question was: 'Is there any hope that someday the bowels can work on their own, without operating the device?' at which Dr No-Ilaaz grimly shook his head: 'I'm afraid not. You must think very, very carefully before making a decision. Once CNI is implanted, you can never pass a motion in the natural way — neither sitting nor squatting.'

"He stopped to allow Sarosh time to think it over, then continued: 'And you must understand what that means. You will never be able to live a normal life again. You will be permanently different from your family and friends because of this basic internal modification. In fact, in this country or that, it will set you apart from your fellow countrymen. So you must consider the whole thing most carefully.'

"Dr. No-Ilaaz paused, toyed with his stethoscope, shuffled some papers on his desk, then resumed: 'There are other dangers you should know about. Just as a garage door can be accidentally opened by a neighbour's transmitter on the same frequency, CNI can also be activated by someone with similar apparatus.' To ease the tension he attempted to quick laugh and said, 'Very embarrassing, eh, if it happened at the wrong place and time. Mind you, the risk is not so great at present, because the chances of finding yourself within a fifty-foot radius of another transmitter on the same frequency are infinites-imal. But what about the future? What if CNI becomes very popular? Sufficient permutations may not be available for transmitter frequencies and you could be sharing the code with others. Then the risk of accidents becomes greater.'"

Something landed with a loud thud in the yard behind A Block, making Nariman startle. Immediately, a yowling and screeching and caterwauling went up from the stray cats there, and the *kuchrawalli's*[22] dog started barking. Some of the boys went around the side of A Block to peer over the fence into the backyard. But the commotion soon died down of its own accord. The boys returned and, once again, Nariman's voice was the only sound to be heard.

"By now, Sarosh was on the verge of deciding against the operation. Dr. No-Ilaaz observed this and was pleased. He took pride in being able to dissuade his patients from following the very remedies which he first so painstakingly described. True to his name, Dr. No-Ilaaz believed no remedy is the best remedy, rather than prescribing this-mycin and that-mycin for every little ailment. So he continued: 'And what about our sons and daughters? And the quality of their lives? We still don't know about the long-term effects of CNI. Some researchers speculate that it could generate a genetic deficiency, that the off-spring of a CNI parent would also require CNI. On the other hand, they could be perfectly healthy toilet seat-users, without any congenital defects. We just don't know at this stage.'

110 "Sarosh rose from his chair: 'Thank you very much for your time, Dr. No-Ilaaz. But I don't think I want to take such a drastic step. As you suggest, I will think it over carefully.'

"'Good, good,' said Dr. No-Ilaaz, 'I was hoping you would say that. There is one more thing. The operation is extremely expensive, and is not covered by the province's Health Insurance Plan. Many immigrant groups are lobbying to obtain coverage for special immigration-related health problems. If they succeed, then good for you.'

"Sarosh left Dr. No-Ilaaz's office with his mind made up. Time was running out. There had been a time when it was perfectly natural to squat. Now it seemed a grotesquely aberrant thing to do. Wherever he went he was reminded of the ignominy of his way. If he could not be westernized in all respects, he was nothing but a failure in this land — a failure not just in the washrooms of the nation but everywhere. He knew what he must do if he was to be true to himself and to the decade-old commitment. So what do you think Sarosh did next?"

"What, Nariman Uncle?"

"He went to the travel agent specializing in tickets to India. He bought a fully refundable ticket to Bombay for the day when he would complete exactly ten immigrant years — if he succeeded even once before that day dawned, he would cancel the booking.

115 "The travel agent asked sympathetically, 'Trouble at home?' His name was Mr. Rawaana, and he was from Bombay too.

"'No,' said Sarosh, 'trouble in Toronto.'

"'That's a shame,' said Mr. Rawaana. 'I don't want to poke my nose into your business, but in my line of work I meet so many people who are going back to their homeland because of their problems here. Sometimes I forget I'm a travel agent, that my interest is to convince them to travel. Instead, I tell them: don't give up, God is great, stay and try again. It's bad for my profits

22 security guard.

but gives me a different, a spiritual kind of satisfaction when I succeed. And I succeed about half the time. Which means,' he added with a wry laugh, 'I could double my profits if I minded my own business.'

"After the lengthy sessions with Mrs. Maha-Lepate and Dr. No-Ilaaz, Sarosh felt he had listened to enough advice and kind words. Much as he disliked doing it, he had to hurt Mr. Rawaana's feelings and leave his predicament undiscussed: 'I'm sorry, but I'm in a hurry. Will you be able to look after the booking?'

"'Well, okay,' said Mr. Rawaana, a trifle crestfallen; he did not relish the travel business as much as he did counselling immigrants. 'Hope you solve your problem. I will be happy to refund your fare, believe me.'

120 "Sarosh hurried home. With only four weeks to departure, every spare minute, every possible method had to be concentrated on a final attempt at adaptation.

"He tried laxatives, crunching down the tablets with a prayer that these would assist the sitting position. Changing brands did not help, and neither did various types of suppositories. He spent long stretches on the toilet seat each morning. The supervisor continued to reprimand him for tardiness. To make matters worse, Sarosh left his desk every time he felt the slightest urge, hoping: maybe this time.

"The working hours expended in the washroom were noted with unflagging vigilance by the supervisor. More counselling sessions followed. Sarosh refused to extinguish his last hope, and the supervisor punctiliously recorded 'No Improvement' in his daily log. Finally, Sarosh was fired. It would soon have been time to resign in any case, and he could not care less.

"Now whole days went by seated on the toilet, and he stubbornly refused to relieve himself the other way. The doorbell would ring only to be ignored. The telephone went unanswered. Sometimes, he would awake suddenly in the dark hours before dawn and rush to the washroom like a madman."

Without warning, Rustomji flung open his door and stormed: "Ridiculous nonsense this is becoming! Two days in a row, whole Firozsha Baag gathers here! This is not Chaupatty beach, this is not a squatters' colony, this is a building, people want to live here in peace and quiet!" Then just as suddenly, he stamped inside and slammed the door. Right on cue, Nariman continued, before the boys could say anything.

125 "Time for meals was the only time Sarosh allowed himself off the seat. Even in his desperation he remembered that if he did not eat well, he was doomed — the downward pressure on his gut was essential if there was to be any chance of success.

"But the ineluctable day of departure dawned, with grey skies and the scent of rain, while success remained out of sight. At the airport Sarosh checked in and went to the dreary lounge. Out of sheer habit he started towards the washroom. Then he realized the hopelessness of it and returned to the cold, clammy plastic of the lounge seats. Airport seats are the same almost anywhere in the world.

"The boarding announcement was made, and Sarosh was the first to step onto the plane. The skies were darker now. Out of the window he saw a flash of lightning fork through the clouds. For some reason, everything he'd learned years ago in St. Xavier's about sheet lightning and forked lightning went through his mind. He wished it would change to sheet, there was something sinister and unpropitious about forked lightning."

Kersi, absorbedly listening, began cracking his knuckles quite unconsciously. His childhood habit still persisted. Jehangir frowned at the disturbance, and Viraf nudged Kersi to stop it.

"Sarosh fastened his seat-belt and attempted to turn his thoughts towards the long journey home: to the questions he would be expected to answer, the sympathy and criticism that would be thrust upon him. But what remained uppermost in his mind was the present moment — him in the plane, dark skies lowering, lightning on the horizon — irrevocably spelling out: defeat.

130 "But wait. Something else was happening now. A tiny rumble. Inside him. Or was it his imagination? Was it really thunder outside which, in his present disoriented state, he was internalizing? No, there it was again. He had to go.

"He reached the washroom, and almost immediately the sign flashed to 'Please return to seat and fasten seat-belts.' Sarosh debated whether to squat and finish the business quickly, abandoning the perfunctory seated attempt. But the plane started to move and that decided him; it would be difficult now to balance while squatting.

"He pushed. The plane continued to move. He pushed again, trembling with the effort. The seat-belt sign flashed quicker and brighter now. The plane moved faster and faster. And Sarosh pushed hard, harder than he had ever pushed before, harder than in all his ten years of trying in the new land. And the memories of Bombay, the immigration interview in New Delhi, the farewell party, his mother's tattered prayer book, all these, of their own accord, emerged from beyond the region of the ten years to push with him and give him new-found strength."

Nariman paused and cleared his throat. Dusk was falling, and the frequency of B.E.S.T. buses plying the main road outside Firozsha Baag had dropped. Bats began to fly madly from one end of the compound to the other, silent shadows engaged in endless laps over the buildings.

"With a thunderous clap the rain started to fall. Sarosh felt a splash under him. Could it really be? He glanced down to make certain. Yes, it was. He had succeeded!

135 "But was it already too late? The plane waited at its assigned position on the runway, jet engines at full thrust. Rain was falling in torrents and takeoff could be delayed. Perhaps even now they would allow him to cancel his flight, to disembark. He lurched out of the constricting cubicle.

"A stewardess hurried towards him: 'Excuse me, sir, but you must return to your seat immediately and fasten your belt.'

"'You don't understand!' Sarosh shouted excitedly. 'I must get off the plane! Everything is all right. I don't have to go anymore...'

"'That's impossible, sir!' said the stewardess, aghast. 'No one can leave now. Takeoff procedures are in progress!' The wild look in his sleepless eyes, and the dark rings around them scared her. She beckoned for help.

"Sarosh continued to argue, and a steward and the chief stewardess hurried over: 'What seems to be the problem, sir? You *must* resume your seat. We are authorized, if necessary, to forcibly restrain you, sir.'

140 "The plane began to move again, and suddenly Sarosh felt all the urgency leaving him. His feverish mind, the product of nightmarish days and tortuous nights, was filled again with the calm which had fled a decade ago, and he spoke softly now: 'That…that will not be necessary…it's okay, I understand.' He readily returned to his seat.

"As the aircraft sped down the runway, Sarosh's first reaction was one of joy. The process of adaptation was complete. But later, he could not help wondering if success came before or after the ten-year limit had expired. And since he had already passed through the customs and security check, was he really an immigrant in every sense of the word at the moment of achievement?

"But such questions were merely academic. Or were they? He could not decide. If he returned, what would it be like? Ten years ago, the immigration officer who had stamped his passport had said, 'Welcome to Canada.' It was one of Sarosh's dearest memories, and thinking of it, he fell asleep.

"The plane was flying about the rainclouds. Sunshine streamed into the cabin. A few raindrops were still clinging miraculously to the windows, reminders of what was happening below. They sparkled as the sunlight caught them."

Some of the boys made as if to leave, thinking the story was finally over. Clearly, they had not found this one as interesting as the others Nariman had told. What dolts, thought Jehangir, they cannot recognize a masterpiece when they hear one. Nariman motioned with his hand for silence.

145 "But our story does not end there. There was a welcome-home party for Sarosh a few days after he arrived in Bombay. It was not in Firozsha Baag this time because his relatives in the Baag had a serious sickness in the house. But I was invited to it anyway. Sarosh's family and friends were considerate enough to wait till the jet lag had worked its way out of his system. They wanted him to really enjoy this one.

"Drinks began to flow freely again in his honour: Scotch and soda, rum and Coke, brandy. Sarosh noticed that during his absence all the brand names had changed — the labels were different and unfamiliar. Even for the mixes. Instead of Coke there was Thums-Up, and he remembered reading in the papers about Coca-Cola being kicked out by the Indian Government for refusing to reveal their secret formula.

"People slapped him on the back and shook his hand vigorously, over and over, right through the evening. They said: 'Telling the truth, you made the right decision, look how happy your mother is to live to see this day;' or they asked: 'Well, bossy, what changed your mind?' Sarosh smiled and nodded his way through it all, passing around Canadian currency at the insistence of some of the curious ones who, egged on by his mother, also pestered him to display his Canadian passport and citizenship card. She had been badgering him since his arrival to tell her the real reason: '*Saachoo kahé*, what brought you back?' and was hoping that tonight, among his friends, he might raise his glass and reveal something. But she remained disappointed.

"Weeks went by and Sarosh found himself desperately searching for his old place in the pattern of life he had vacated ten years ago. Friends who had organized the welcome-home party gradually disappeared. He went walking in the evenings along Marine Drive, by the sea-wall, where the old crowd used to congregate. But the people who sat on the parapet while waves crashed behind their backs were strangers. The tetrapods were still there, staunchly protecting the reclaimed land from the fury of the sea. He had watched as a kid when cranes had lowered these cement and concrete hulks of respectable grey into the water. They were grimy black now, and from their angularities rose the distinct stench of human excrement. The old pattern was never found by Sarosh; he searched in vain. Patterns of life are selfish and unforgiving.

"Then one day, as I was driving past Marine Drive, I saw someone sitting alone. He looked familiar, so I stopped. For a moment I did not recognize Sarosh, so forlorn and woebegone was his countenance. I parked the apple of my eye and went to him, saying, 'Hullo, Sid, what are you doing here on your lonesome?' And he said, 'No, no! No more Sid, please, that name reminds me of all my troubles.' Then, on the parapet at Marine Drive, he told me his unhappy and wretched tale, with the waves battering away at the tetrapods, and around us the hawkers screaming about coconut-water and sugar-cane juice and *paan*.

150

"When he finished, he said that he had related to me the whole sad saga because he knew how I told stories to boys in the Baag, and he wanted me to tell this one, especially to those who were planning to go abroad. 'Tell them,' said Sarosh, 'that the world can be a bewildering place, and dreams and ambitions are often paths to the most pernicious of traps.' As he spoke, I could see that Sarosh was somewhere far away, perhaps in New Delhi at his immigration interview, seeing himself as he was then, with what he thought was a life of hope and promise stretching endlessly before him. Poor Sarosh. Then he was back beside me on the parapet.

"'I pray you, in your stories,' said Sarosh, his old sense of humour returning as he deepened his voice for his favourite *Othello* lines" — and here, Nariman produced a basso profundo of his own — "'when you shall these unlucky deeds relate, speak of me as I am; nothing extenuate, nor set down aught in malice: tell them that in Toronto once there lived a Parsi boy as best as he could. Set you down this; and say, besides, that for some it was good and for some it was bad, but for me life in the land of milk and honey was just a pain in the posterior.'"[23]

And now, Nariman allowed his low-pitched rumbles to turn into chuckles. The boys broke into cheers and loud applause and cries of "Encore!" and "More!" Finally, Nariman had to silence them by pointing warningly at Rustomji-the-curmudgeon's door.

While Kersi and Viraf were joking and wondering what to make of it all, Jehangir edged forward and told Nariman this was the best story he had ever told. Nariman patted his shoulder and smiled. Jehangir left, wondering if Nariman would have been as popular if Dr. Mody was still alive. Probably, since the two were liked for different reasons: Dr. Mody used to be constantly jovial, whereas Nariman had his periodic story-telling urges.

23 based on the dying words of Othello, Shakespeare's tragic hero who was an African living in Venice.

Now the group of boys who had really enjoyed the Savukshaw story during the previous week spoke up. Capitalizing on Nariman's extraordinarily good mood, they began clamouring for more Savukshaw: "Nariman Uncle, tell the one about Savukshaw the hunter, the one you had started that day."

155   "What hunter? I don't know which one you mean." He refused to be reminded of it, and got up to leave. But there was a loud protest, and the boys started chanting, "We-want-Savukshaw! We-want-Savukshaw!"

Nariman looked fearfully towards Rustomji's door and held up his hands placatingly: "All right, all right! Next time it will be Savukshaw again. Savukshaw the artist. The story of Parsi Picasso."[24]

(1987)

---

24 twentieth-century Spanish artist who introduced and popularized many abstract styles.

Evelyn Lau (b. 1971)

A poet, short story writer, and autobiographer, Lau commented that she began writing for "the love and acceptance that presumably went along with it." Later, she sought to make "people think ... to have a clearer vision of their own emotional lives, their realities." In *Choose Me* (1999), many of the stories deal with middle-class men and women and the sexual tensions and conflicts that exist between what she has called individuals "walking emotional high wires." "Family" is the story of an outsider responding to a middle-class family. Zoe, a visiting poet, has been emotionally and physically attracted to her host, who invites her to live in his house while he and his family are away for the weekend. Alone, she feel apart from normal family life and often questions the reality of her existence. (See also the introduction to Evelyn Lau's poetry, page 425.)

FAMILY

Zoe stood in Douglas's bedroom, the one he shared with his wife. Outside the wood-framed window the afternoon was silver, the sky the shine of the inside of an oyster shell. Snow drifted through the air, and narrow icicles hung from the trees. The houses dwindling down the block were heritage properties, fronted in brick and stained glass; each resembled the house she was inside.

Douglas had invited her in so calmly. After she set down her bags in the hall with its high ceilings and polished floors, he pushed the keys to his home into her hand, two skeleton keys dangling from a loop of twisted wire. Then he motioned her back out onto the porch, where he wrapped his fingers around hers, demonstrating how to work the locks. Their breath showed in front of them, but his hand pulsed with warmth. She learned to shove the keys in smoothly, to jiggle them, to listen for the muffled internal click that signified the lock had been turned.

"Will you remember this?"

He repeated the code to the burglar alarm by the door, half-concealed by the winter coats hanging on the wooden rack.

"Yes. I think I'll remember."

His wife appeared on the landing at the top of the stairs.

5   "Ellen, this is our visiting poet, Zoe. She's been on campus all week working with the students, and I thought it'd be nice for her to stay in a real home before she leaves, especially since we won't be here."

Ellen came down the first flight of stairs, bending to extend her hand; her arm was long, her palm warm.

"Welcome."

Zoe held his wife's hand in her own and swallowed past the catch in her throat. His wife continued to lean down from the landing, bending her body from the waist, one hand holding the railing, the other clasping Zoe's as though to help her up. Douglas kept his eyes fastened on Ellen's face. Their two children were clamouring around her, tugging and demanding; the girl jumped up and down, whining, while the boy pulled down his trousers to reveal buttocks as smooth as cream.

"Jason, I said no. Look, we have a guest. Say hello, Jason, say hello to Zoe."

The boy ignored her, buying his face in his mother's thigh, squirming his bare bum in the air while his sister hid behind them both.

"Zoe will be staying here while we're at the cabin. You've got to be good and say hello."

After a while, just when it seemed he could not be persuaded, Jason lifted his face and grinned winningly. His eyes were like his father's, only clearer, the colour of amber.

"Hello. Hello!" he shouted.

Douglas pressed the keys once more into her palm. She looked at him then in a moment of terror, the weight and light of the house around her suddenly there for her to both protect and invade. He sensed her fear, mistook it for concern about burglar alarms, difficult locks, the house burning down.

"Got it?"

He repeated the code again.

"Is everything all right? Are you happy?"

He had given her the keys, his hands were empty. At the top of the stairs his wife was saying, "No, no, no," to the children. "No, you *can't* bring that. Look, you already have so much."

"I'm happy."

She stood in the doorway and watched him leave with his family. Ellen was weighted with the children's clothes, warm and puffy jackets that were awkward in her arms. Jason and Julie ran ahead, the tops of their heads bright and new in the winter light. Douglas paused before following them; he placed both his hands on Zoe's upper arms and kissed her on the cheek.

"One more."

He kissed her on the other cheek just as she was pulling away.

She looked over his shoulder and caught the blur of Ellen's face. She felt the sudden tension, her body electric with watchfulness. But the moment passed quickly — it was only a kiss, friendly, sociable. Ellen beamed and waved.

"Have a good time!"

"You too!"

She eased the door shut, the house was hers.

Zoe approached their bed as though it were an altar. It was smooth, flat, wide — a square of white in the room. She sat on its edge, where the comforter was folded back in a triangle, and the cotton sheet slid against her body. She could tell by the paraphernalia on the bedside table, the textbooks and manuscripts piled high, which side of the bed was his.

She wondered what Ellen looked like naked, how she approached him in the dark with the light from the window illuminating her body. Ellen had the figure of an adolescent, long and boyishly thin; her breasts would hardly be more than bumps on her chest, bare mouthfuls, and the bones in her hips and pubis would be prominent, traceable. The length of her would look like a white taper candle, if he opened his eyes in the night to watch her sleep.

Their bedroom was full of photographs — lined up on the mantel, jumbled above the chest of drawers, taped to the vanity mirror. The pictures were almost all of Douglas and the children; in the few where Ellen was present, her face was either obscured by her blowing hair or turned to one side, away from the camera. She appeared in the photos as a sort of ghost, rinsed of ego, her features blurred. It was Douglas who took centre stage, which was why Zoe had the impression when she saw them together on the stairs that he was the more attractive of the two. And yet when she looked again, objectively, she realized she was wrong — it was Ellen who was most attractive. Her face was white and well shaped, like a Madonna's, graceful and open. Her teeth glistened when she smiled. But Douglas had something she lacked, a force of personality that was revealed in the photographs, the same photos that revealed Ellen's down-turned, devolving features.

30   Their family life was documented in the photographs. Douglas, Ellen and the children had taken summer holidays by the shore, stood in portals of museums and crumbling European buildings, hiked among shrub and rock and cliff. In one photograph he held his daughter spilling and giggling over his shoulder while he pointed, laughing, at the camera. In another his face was white with joy as he cradled a swaddled newborn in his arms. In a third he was naked to the waist at the beach, his feet buried in wet sand that flowered around his ankles; she saw the arc of his shoulders, the way he was shaped and curved, and the twin lines of his waist that sloped inwards. He was some-place where her own history was not, could never be.

When Zoe opened his wife's closet doors she saw loose, layered clothes in deep jewel colours. The surface of the vanity next to the closet was scattered with drugstore cosmetics and, incongruously, a shiny, unopened bottle of Chanel No. 5[1] which must have been a gift. Her eye pencils were worn down to blurred nubs, her tube of mascara was dusty, she owned only the palest of lip-sticks. This was the sort of woman his wife was, Zoe realized — natural, unself-conscious, without guile.

The house was old enough to be draughty, the heaters thin and metallic and cool to the touch. The walls were papered in a pattern of wide bronze stripes; the floorboards were stained walnut. That night she woke in their bedroom, curled to Douglas's side of the bed, shivering. She tiptoed across the icy floor to the dresser where one of Ellen's nightshirts hung from a knob; its worn cotton, smelling faintly of soap, was soft against her skin when she pulled it over her head. She wondered how Douglas was sleeping in his cabin. Were his arms wrapped around his wife, her stomach, her breasts? He was the warmest man she had ever met — his mouth, his hands, the heat barely con-tained by the skin of his body. To kiss him was like leaning her face over a hot stove, or into a fire. By comparison, she was cold, or he said, cold-blooded.

"Now I know why you came wearing so few clothes, it's because you're cold-blooded."

But she wore few clothes so that when he touched her, it would be that much more. So that when he took her hand from her lap and lifted it to his mouth, or held it between his own hands, the shock of his heat would be greater. It was deliberate. She had been freezing the whole week, at all the places he had taken her when she was lecturing to students. When they had stood in the organic-foods market with their hands in their pockets, the

1 an expensive and popular brand of French perfume.

breath issuing whitely in front of them, watching the butcher in his bloody apron behind the counter. The chopping blade that fit so firmly into his hand it was like an extension of him. Turkeys, pheasants, a dead deer hung by their hind legs in front of the shop, freshly killed. She imagined their bodies still warm, hearts still beating, had to resist the urge to lean forward and stroke her fingertips down the grain of their feathers and fur, towards the belly warm as the belly of a sleeping man. They were so beautiful, content. The turkeys' creamy eyelids tugged down over their eyes, their closed beaks bearing trem-blingly a single drop of blood. They had stood together, side by side, looking at the dead animals strung silently in front of them. To see then his breath steaming beside hers, to know his hands were warm and alive in his pockets, composed of skin and flesh and bone and circulating blood, to see the flicker of his eyelashes, to know he was swallowing and breathing and thinking and wondering, to know that if she leaned into his chest he would hear the pulse of his heart — it was almost more than she could bear.

35   To drive back to the campus at night with the whole of the highway before them, the planes skimming low with their lit wings towards the airport, the singing stream of traffic, the gas stations along the way with their pumps and phone booths and chocolate bars, the dense black tar of the road painted with lines and signals. His hands on the wheel and then his thumb on the fleshy pocket between her own thumb and forefinger, touching just that part of her, and the balletic perfection of the traffic around them, orange and red taillights sliding past, speeding forward, the coordination of motion, the sense of at least being a part of something whole, his hand wrapping around her hand.

    One day they had stood in a church tower with many windows and walked around and around to take in each disparate view. From here the emerald sea shaking in the distance like a mirage, from here the city with its multiple windows gleaming in the golden light. It had taken them fifteen minutes to climb to the top of the tower, the stairs so steep they had had to twist their bodies nearly sideways, so sharply angled that the steps above bit into their shins. And then they had emerged onto the wooden platform with the light flooding in from all directions, and they had stepped from window to window as though they were dancing, and when they stood next to each other the fringe of his scarf touched the shoulder of her sweater.

    Then they had paused in the entrance of the church, overwhelmed by a window of stained glass. They had whispered to each other and he had wanted to touch her, she saw that, the times when he wanted to touch her, the look that came over his face, how it was turned to her beneath the flood of coloured light and how she had seen the thought in his eyes, his eyes that moved back and forth when he was thinking as though he were scanning the lines of a secret text.

The weekend passed slowly. After Zoe had wandered all the rooms in the house, picking up objects here and there, inspecting and then setting them down again, there was nothing more for her to do. So she was grateful when Douglas's associate at the publishing company called to invite her for lunch. He took her to a Wolfgang Puck restaurant with slender cedar chairs, papaya-coloured walls and preternaturally beautiful women whose heels clicked across the granite floor. During lunch she observed this man's gentleness — his patience with the waiters, his smiling consideration of her — and it made her sad. He was someone she could trust, the way she never would be able to trust Douglas. As they ate their scallop salads, she thought of the afternoon in the French restaurant with the brown and yellow tiles on the floor, when Douglas had made her translate the entire menu. She knew only a little French and he had had to correct her and help her along, from the starters to the specials to the entrées to the desserts, all the way down the menu, not letting her stop.

"How will you know what you want if you don't know what there is?"

What he said was true, so she kept translating. The waiters came and he waved them away. The other diners must have thought they were lovers, because of the way they looked at each other. The tables were set close together, there was no privacy; the women around them had wide mouths and espresso-coloured hair, and the nails that tipped their long fingers were manicured. Cellular phones rang at the tables of the men, who wore suit jackets over jeans. They'd ordered a bottle of wine with their meal, and the first glass of it rushed to her head. She could not pick out her own face in the strip of mirror that ran along the wall above the booths, not among so many faces crowded together. Since childhood it had been necessary for Zoe to see her reflection at all times, as if to assure herself of her own existence. When she tried to find herself in the mirror in the restaurant and could not, she drank the wine instead, to calm herself.

"Zoe, everything I've done in my life has been like an experiment. It started when I was a child. The way I looked at the world was different from the children around me. I was very observant, and because of that I felt removed from everything. I began to direct my own life. As a teenager, I experimented with drugs because I wanted to understand what it was like to lose control. And then I made myself fall in love over and over, for the same reason."

She watched him; everything he said made sense to her. He might have been describing her own past. But it was what was familiar in him that was dangerous to her.

He had chosen this restaurant from all the restaurants that lined the busy, taxi-filled street. They had stood on the corner and he had looked in either direction and then he had chosen this place.

"I know where we'll go. Come, follow me."

They crossed the murderous intersection, shiny cars veering in front and behind them. The stores all along the street were glass-fronted, etched with the names of Italian designers and filled with expensive merchandise — leaden suits, transparent dresses, shoes built with as much attention as one would give to the building of houses.

He let the waiter show them to the table where he had begun and ended relationships with other women. Now she was sitting on the plump red banquette where his other women had fitted their hips.

He was still talking. The women at the next table turned and looked at them. Zoe smiled. The women blinked their heavy lashes and after a while turned back to their salads.

"You seem closed to me. I don't know how to get close to you, other than to become so important to you that you fall in love with me."

Zoe let him talk.

50 "You aren't like anyone who is close to me. The people I value don't have centres that are so solid. I can enter them, they're vulnerable to me."

But she still could not pick out her face in the mirror. Could it be that he was mistaken, that she had no centre, only a space?

After lunch he took her to the downtown publishing office where he worked part-time as an editor. Walking against the direction of the wind, they passed a vendor with his wheelbarrow of roses and carnations, and a café with wrought-iron chairs arranged in circles around outdoor tables. The door to his building was covered in stained glass. He pushed it open, and they walked across a cracked marble floor to the elevator. In the elevator she was struck by a desire to kiss him, but he was already thinking about the work that had accumulated while they were eating. She was drunk only in the way that wine can make you drunk at noon. The angles of the building seemed wrong. The surfaces of things — the metal of desks and elevator doors, the cloth-covered partitions, the lenses of a secretary's glasses as she walked past — all seemed exceptionally bright and sharp. She thought her intoxication must be evident to others, yet there was not a flicker of suspicion or concern in any of the faces that tilted at her, with their black pupils and razor-sharp hair-cuts. Meanwhile he had vanished into the maze of offices, and left her on her own. She wandered towards the reception area and sat on the couch that curved like a crescent moon. The receptionists were carrying on conversations about clothes and lovers, in between the ringing phones.

When he was with her at dinner, even when there were others at their table, academics and editors, he watched her constantly. She saw him always at the edge of her vision, a pale, intense man in a tailored coat. While she talked to others around her, drank a glass of wine, placed her order with the waiter, she felt his eyes upon her. When at last she raised her eyes to his, he would not flinch away, he would only slowly turn his head to the side — as if she had been merely an object in the way of his turning gaze, as if all along he had been meaning to look at the edge of the table, or the spoon that lay on his saucer, or at another woman. This was how the nights of the previous week had passed, in restaurants where the windows were frosted over so that the night outside looked like it was walled in fog, with only the faint light of streetlamps to mark the distances. At their table, there were always people who drank too much, and she was one of them. At the end of the evening they would be drinking flaming shooters and daring each other to keep up, and she would, because when she tried to back down, looking to Douglas for help, he would stir sugar into his coffee and look back at her and not say anything. When she swallowed the contents of a shot glass in one throw of the wrist, the sensation was like dropping through a hole that had suddenly opened up in the sidewalk. Tears would rise in her eyes and she would feel separated from herself. But when her vision cleared he would still be there at the table, his face empty of reproach or encour-agement, only mildly curious as to what she would do next. Later, he would tell her what she was like with other people.

"You manipulate them, you draw them along with you. There is something about you that people can't resist."

He would watch her until the early hours of the morning, when empty shooter glasses lined the tabletop and the party disbanded to stumble through the streets with the fog winding above, the thick heels of their shoes sounding on the cement.

In turn she wanted to believe he was the most genuine person she had ever met. In the market in front of the dead animals when his breath steamed out of him and he spread his arms in wonder. In the car when he sang along with the radio and thumped the wheel and then turned and looked at her as they sat stalled in the black, runny streets. The noises he made when he was thinking, his fingers on the PowerBook keyboard, his head cocked to one side.

"*Tinka tinka tinka. Vroom.*"

He was a grown man, but when he was working he sounded like a child shoving toy race cars down a rubber track. So that one afternoon when they were walking down the street, when for an instant the sun broke through the layers of cloud, she had been astonished to see that his hair was peppered with silver. It was as though someone had taken a handful of needles and scattered them through his dark hair.

He would talk to the words that appeared on his computer screen, give the desk a small slap, wheel around in his chair.

"Yes. Done. Now, where would you like to go for lunch? What would you most like to eat in the whole wide world?"

They would smile at each other and she would see him slowly grow back into himself, see the work fade from his eyes, one wave receding and a different one advancing. He would rise from his chair and stand for a moment with his feet pressed together and his hands clasped behind his back, like someone at the edge of a diving board gazing into the pool, puzzling the point of entry, the locus where his body would knife into the water. She would watch him slowly come back to life the way she had begun to feel her own body assume its life, starting at the nucleus where his hands lay hot on her skin.

During the hours when she was alone in the house, Zoe wondered why Douglas had brought her here, when so much could go wrong. Was it enough that she was in his house, even if he could not be there with her? It was possible he had invited her only out of kindness and affection; after all, he had kissed her boldly on both sides of her face while his wife had watched them from the cobblestone path. Perhaps he felt they had nothing to hide. But she felt that to believe that would be to believe the world itself lacking intelligence and motive. Perhaps he only wanted to see what would happen, to observe his own emotions, his capacity for betrayal or loyalty. And to learn about her capacity for transgression. She saw then that he was the sort of man a woman should never love. Yet she walked about his house in a sort of drunkenness, his home where he lived and ate and slept, and she could almost feel the air parting and streaming around her, the pattern of its current, like she was moving in the corridors of space he had created for her with his own movements. She stood by the sink where he shaved and brushed each morning. She saw his black suit hanging in the bedroom closet, his sneakers flung to the bottom of the wardrobe, the book he was reading lying open on the braided mat that covered the bedside table. Sitting on the edge of their white bed, she felt looming inside her the inevitability of betrayal. It rose in her like the tide, leaving her without will. She knew that as soon as she slept with Douglas in his own house, she would feel relief. She craved it like a junkie; she could taste in her mouth the effects of the drug before it was injected. It would be sweet, his caresses on her body, the pain they would inflict upon his wife.

Once during the weekend the telephone rang for Ellen. Zoe answered it in their bedroom.

"Hello?"

"Ellen? It's Diane. How are you?"

"No. No, Ellen is away for the weekend with the family. Could I take a message?"

When she put down the phone, Zoe rose from their bed and looked at her reflection in their vanity mirror. She put her hand on her neck, felt the shape of her throat with her fingers. Her voice when it came out in the cold room was still hers, accompanied by a thin jet of white breath. She was still herself. She was not his wife.

The day the family came home Zoe woke to the sound of church bells filling the air. The sky was blue and the house so icy she wandered the rooms in a daze, her fingers clenched, her lips chapped. In the bathroom mirror her skin appeared exceptionally pale, stretched over a framework of bone, and the backs of her hands were translucent. She went downstairs to the living room and opened the curtains to look out onto the street. The occupants of the neighbouring houses could be seen here and there in their weekend sweats and denims, climbing into cars, conversing on doorsteps, carrying plastic bins of garbage to the curb. She felt far away from the domestic lives locked within houses such as these and had to remind herself that today, at least, she was on the inside looking out. The hours passed, afternoon darkened into winter evening, and still she waited for Douglas and Ellen. When their car pulled up to the front of the house and they came out with the children, hurrying up the path, she went to the door and let them in as though they were her guests.

"Tell me all about it. What did you do while we were gone?"

His wife was upstairs, putting the children to bed. Zoe heard their footsteps back and forth between the rooms — Ellen's long, purposeful strides, the children's patter. Douglas rose from the sofa to shut the living-room door, and before returning to his seat he detoured to Zoe's chair and ruffled her hair with one hand. He laughed, a self-conscious sound that he bit off quickly. She was so nervous that her upper lip was slick with perspiration, but she said it anyway.

"I missed you horribly."

For the moment he said nothing, but he could not look at her, and that in itself seemed a declaration. They were both saved by the sound of his wife's footsteps down the long stairs, the turn of the doorknob, her presence in the room. Ellen chose the other armchair, the one identical to Zoe's, which also faced the sofa where Douglas sat. Zoe knew that at some point he would not be able to refrain from comparing them, and saw to her surprise that his wife knew this also, by the sudden sharpening of her eyes. Still, it was easy to start a conversation with Ellen. Zoe, to hide her panic, was vivacious and charming, and they talked comfortably about books, children, movies, travel. Douglas became superfluous; he sat back in the sofa and watched them, perhaps for the first time aware of who he had brought into his home, of what she was capable. He saw his own wife warm towards the other woman, saw her caution evaporate, her limbs relax and loosen. When he left the room to escape to his office upstairs, it seemed that neither woman would notice or miss him. But Zoe watched his exit with the care of someone who is making a plan.

"I've got a pile of unmarked essays sitting upstairs. I'll be back down in a while to say goodnight."

Ellen glanced up at her husband.

75 "I'm not planning to stay up late, Douglas. An hour at most, then I'm coming upstairs and falling into bed. You two can chat down here if you want."

Douglas and Zoe did not look at each other.

"Well, anyway. Don't worry about making noise, I'll be fast asleep."

Douglas left the room, closing the door behind him. Ellen turned towards Zoe, cradling her drink near her knee, her face lit by the lamp on the sidetable. They continued to talk for a while, and the conversation turned towards her marriage.

"I was looking at some of the photos in the house," Zoe said.

80 "The two of you, and the children — you have such a wonderful family. I couldn't believe how different Douglas looked when he was younger."

"Yes, I was so in love with him when we first got together. He was beautiful."

Her eyes wrinkled with the memory, and a distant pleasure swept over Ellen's face, softening it, making it vulnerable.

"I thought so, too."

"Did you? Well, he's older now. But you saw how he used to have the most beautiful long curls. He was a gorgeous young man, I can't tell you. Sometimes I have to remind myself of the way he used to be."

85 "But could you imagine yourself with anyone else? I mean, is he your great love, you grand passion?"

The moment of consideration was so slight as to not be there. Then his wife was nodding, smiling.

"Yes. Yes, he is. You know, once when we were still going out, he left me for a year. I couldn't eat, I couldn't sleep, I thought I was going to die. I heard through mutual friends that he was living with another woman, and I couldn't bear it. I wanted to have his children. I couldn't imagine my life without him."

They were silent for a while. On the back of her neck Zoe felt the heat of the lamp behind her chair, and a line of perspiration travelled down her temple. The rest of the room was still cold but she was burning up. The bottle of whisky on the occasional table between them was half empty, and she realized that she had been doing most of the drinking. Ellen gazed into her own glass, the thin, slippery line of alcohol left at its bottom.

"Anyway. I really must get to bed, it all starts again tomorrow. I have to be up early to make the children's breakfast and get them ready. I'll wake you if you want."

90 "Please. I don't want to miss my flight."

Ellen unfolded her legs and stood up. The skin around her eyes had crumpled with exhaustion. She smiled at her guest.

"Thank you. I've enjoyed our talk, Zoe. I feel as if I've made a new friend."

"Goodnight."

Zoe was left alone for a few moments in the living room. Upstairs she heard the toilet flush, and footsteps. She imagined Ellen washing her face, sighing at the feel of the wet washcloth against her skin, then her soft entry into the children's rooms to check on their sleep before she went to her own bed. Zoe drew a deep breath, aware of the pounding of her heart and the tingling in her hands and feet. She poured herself another whisky, neat in the glass. She tapped her foot on the floor, stood up, paced the length of the room twice. Then she heard his footfalls on the stairs; the doorknob turned and he walked into the room. He was carrying a fresh bottle of whisky and two glasses, and he was unsteady on his feet.

95 "Let me pour you a *real* drink."

He took the glass from her hand and set it down, wobbling, on the floor. He handed her the two empty glasses and filled the first one to the brim, the neck of the bottle swaying in his hand. He was not so successful in pouring the second drink; whisky splashed over the rim of the glass, ran down her fingers and onto the floor.

"Oh, I'm sorry."

He grabbed at her wrist in apology.

"No, it's fine."

100 Zoe raised her wet glass and drank from it, smiling to show him everything was all right. They were not, she realized, bad people, either of them. They could not do what they were about to do without getting drunk beforehand.

There was nothing that remained to separate them. When Douglas reached for her, when he kissed her, Zoe found that place inside herself that she had been anticipating all weekend. She found the feeling she remembered — radiant, explosive, obliterating her senses. When his arms went around her body, when his mouth closed over hers, it was like the plunger of the needle pushed home. The drug filled the cavity of her chest, flooded upwards to drown the inside of her mouth, saturated her brain.

The house stood around them, holding its breath, listening to them. The furniture itself seemed suddenly attentive, like spies sent out by Ellen to watch while she slept. Douglas lifted her sweater and touched her breasts, he drew her towards the sofa and closed his mouth over her nipple, so that she looked down upon his shorn dark curls, his bent head. The fabric covering the couch was embroidered with silken threads in a pattern of birds and blossoms; he laid her upon the cushions, knelt above her and touched her face. They were very quiet, barely whispering, both listening for his wife and his children, sleeping in their rooms above. His face leaning over hers was lined around the mouth, under the eyes, but his lips were soft. They kissed for so long that she felt herself disappear, and when he at last drew away she shook her head and pulled him closer. Zoe felt secure at last. His weight along the length of her body, his bones, his flesh, the fabric of his clothes against her clothes. She knelt in front of him and reached up beneath his shirt to find his nipples, the folds in his stomach of incipient fat. She felt the shape of his penis, stroked the length of it with her fingertips, its fevered heat, the slight jumping pulse of its response. What she felt then, what she was amazed to feel, was nothing at all, and she almost drew away. When they had stood shoulder to shoulder in front of the slaughtered animals she had felt the blood in both their bodies, an endless circulating river. But what she felt now, touching the most secret part of his body, was that they were dead. That there was nothing inside them.

It was then that they heard movement in the house. His wife, waking to use the bathroom, to check on the children? They grew still in their embrace, their lips on each other's, slightly parted, motionless. His hands were warm on her back under her sweater. He would keep holding on to her, she realized with amazement, he would push this moment as far as it could go. He didn't care if they were discovered, he wouldn't care about the shock and the pain on his wife's face when she turned the doorknob and opened the door and saw them together. Perhaps he needed the pain.

It was Zoe who pushed him away, scrambled off the couch. When Ellen had seen her earlier that evening, she had been wearing a dark lipstick. Now her lips were bare, blurred with kissing. The tube of lipstick was in her purse, upstairs in the spare room. If his wife walked in, there would be nothing she could say or do to conceal what had happened. She ran over to one of the lamps, switched it off, then realized it wouldn't help for Ellen to discover them in a dark room together at two in the morning, either. There was no escape. Douglas was standing in the corner, watching her. He had lit a cigarette and he was listening to his wife's footsteps upstairs. Zoe looked at him, wide-eyed, wrapping her arms around herself. He blinked and drew on his cigarette.

105 It was then that she knew her life was bound up with the lives of others, with actions that invited consequences. She knew this in a way she had not known when her hand had closed over Ellen's husband's penis. At any moment the door would open, Ellen would stand there outlined in lamplight, the gathered, insubstantial darkness of the hall and the staircase behind her, and she would see their eyes, the disarray of their clothing, Zoe's smeared mouth. She would see all this and her mirroring face and eyes would change.

The footsteps paused on the landing, then turned around and went back to the bedroom. There was silence once more. Zoe's arms dropped to her side. Douglas ground his cigarette clumsily into the ashtray; a plume of smoke continued to rise from the burning butt. It seemed to Zoe that there had existed an opportunity for the world to prove to her that goodness would always triumph, but nothing had happened, and she felt lost.

Douglas was the first to make a sound. He coughed, shook his head as though to clear it, came up to her and touched her arm. The shock of his wife's footsteps had sobered them both, so that they no longer looked or moved like people who had been drinking.

"We must go to bed now. You'll go to yours, and I'll go to mine."

"Will everything be all right?"

110 "Yes, of course. She'll be sleeping now. You got up first, I'll follow later."

In the bathroom as Zoe washed her face and dabbed moisturizer on her cheeks, she had the curious sensation that it was to someone else's face she was ministering. The disjuncture between herself and her body seemed complete, irreparable; she did not know how to climb back inside her own skin. The face in the mirror had nothing to do with who she was, or what she had ever thought or done. She thought that all she had to do was take a step to one side, and she would physically leave her own body standing next to her.

When she left the bathroom — his razor and tufted brush on the edge of the sink, the children's jelly-coloured toothbrushes in a plastic mug, his wife's sponges and herbal soaps in a tray by the tub — she saw him standing on the landing. He was waiting for her, faceless in the dark, his shirt a pale shimmer over his body.

"Goodnight."

They kissed, his mouth open and hot on hers. The tenderness of his mouth, at last opened something in her. She felt herself slide back inside her own body, felt herself fit and fill her own outline.

Only once, in the middle of the night, did she wake. Her heart was racing, and when she coughed she thought she tasted blood in the back of her throat. The formless dark increased her panic — the unfamiliar contours of the room, the distant ceiling, the ghostly high shape of the window with its drawn curtains. She thought of the man and his wife, sleeping only footsteps away, and the children who lay in their small beds. For a moment she imagined herself tiptoeing into the parents' room, easing open the door, fitting herself between their heavy, adult forms. They would each curve an arm around her and she would smell the musk of their skin and the cotton of their nightshirts, the comfort of the warm sheets and pillows, and she would sleep.

(1999)

WRITING ESSAYS ABOUT LITERATURE

PUTTING THE JOB IN PERSPECTIVE

Writing well on any academic subject is demanding work, and writing about literature is among the most demanding kinds of academic writing. It helps to remember, however, that confronting the task seriously will improve not only the way you express what you think but your ability to think, as well. Mastering the critical and interpretive essays required in English courses will prepare you to handle other writing jobs with comparative ease. Whether you are committed to specializing in English or interested mainly in doing as well as you can in a required English course before going on to other areas of study, the advice that follows will help you make your choices sensibly and get the most from the work you do.

Writing about literature often starts with a feeling — you either like something or not — or an intuition about how a piece of writing works. In expressing these inklings in writing, you clarify them for yourself, identify the assumptions behind them, and learn how well they are grounded in the work you are considering. In the process, you not only come to understand better how literature works, but you also discover a good deal about how you think. Writing about literature is challenging for the same reasons it is rewarding — because it requires you to confront yourself as well as what you read.

When you explore literature in essays, you will rarely be looking for answers that are absolutely right or wrong. Depending on the approach taken and the questions asked, a wide variety of conclusions can be drawn about an individual work of literature, and because of the personal element in responses, even writers approaching questions in similar ways will often come up with quite different answers. Think of your essays about literature as part of an ongoing search for understanding, a process that begins when an author, poet, or playwright confronts his or her perceptions about the world in writing and that continues as long as somebody is reading and writing about the original creation. Remembering that you are taking part in a continuing dialogue rather than solving a problem with a single, predetermined answer will help you resist obvious conclusions and make your confrontation with a demanding subject less intimidating.

But again, "less intimidating" does not mean easy. The lack of pat answers, though reassuring in some ways, is no excuse for either slack thinking or sloppy writing. On the contrary, because your essays will be judged more by the quality of thought and expression they demonstrate than by how close they come to some established position, care is especially important. Originality is a start, but your original perceptions have to be supported scrupulously with evidence from the work in question; you must impress your audience by convincing it.

PREPARING TO WRITE

An essay about a literary work should say something illuminating about it, and an illumination depends on focus as well as initial brilliance. Thoughtful insights take time to develop, and an essential step in writing about literature involves clarifying for yourself what it is you want to say. Only when you are sure of your message can you decide how best to present it clearly and convincingly to your readers. The work cannot be rushed at this stage, so it is essential to leave yourself adequate time, not only to draft and revise, but to think, to plan, and to criticize your own ideas, as well.

PROCESS IN SUMMARY

Preparing to Write

Step 1:   Prepare for writing assignments in advance by reading all assigned texts in a course as early as possible and by including speculation about potential lines of argument in your notes.

Step 2:   Once you receive a writing assignment, evaluate it carefully to determine special requirements and anticipate problems.

Step 3:   Choose a subject that interests you.

Step 4:   Choose a topic you can handle well in the time available.

Step 5:   If you are confused about any aspect of an assignment or if you anticipate deviating in any way from the directions, check with your instructor.

Step 6:   Review the primary works you are writing about carefully, taking notes and identifying key passages as you read.

Step 7:   Read whatever background material you consider necessary.

Drafting

Step 1:   Begin generating ideas in writing while you still have more time than you need to complete your essay.

Step 2:   Focus your ideas into a manageable thesis and state this thesis clearly in a single sentence.

Step 3:   Prepare a simple, tentative outline. Do not spend a lot of time on this outline because it will probably have to be modified later. Repeat Step 2 if necessary.

Step 4:   Working from your outline and keeping your thesis statement clearly in mind, complete a rough draft of the entire essay without stopping to revise.

(continued)

Revising and Editing

Step 1:   Review your essay to identify any parts that do not relate clearly to your thesis; cut or adapt these as necessary.

Step 2:   Add support at any point where your conclusions seem to need it.

Step 3:   Revise your opening to ensure that the main points of your essay are clear and supply any additional information your reader may need to follow your approach.

Step 4:   When you are satisfied with the content of your essay, continue revising it for clarity and style until you are satisfied that it is the best you can make it or until the deadline requires you to commit yourself to a final version.

Step 5:   When you are rested and free from distractions, proofread your essay carefully, making neat changes on the manuscript where necessary.

Reading with Awareness

The most fundamental preparation for writing about literature is reading. Read the piece you intend to write about, and then reread it. Read not just superficially to get a basic idea of what the piece says, but carefully, with an awareness of implications beneath the surface and of how the way it is written determines the way it affects you. Taking English courses and studying what others write about literature will teach you the kinds of things to look for, but you will need more. Serious reading, like serious writing, takes practice and cannot be rushed: putting off thinking about literature in general until you are required to write about a particular piece is like putting off training for a race until just before you have to run it. Developing the habit of reading seriously will put you far ahead of students who read only when forced to by an assignment, and it will also yield a great deal of satisfaction in itself.

Taking Notes

While reading thoughtfully is essential, it is not enough. You will find that your reading translates more readily into essays if you record your responses. Take notes as you read, perhaps on the text itself if it is your own copy and an inexpensive one. Marking particularly interesting passages will be a great help when you come back later to sort out evidence for an idea you are developing in an essay. When taking notes in class, record not only what your instructor says but the ideas that occur to you as well. If what is said about one work suggests comparison with another, take note of the possibility. Remark contradictions and unanswered questions. Your dissenting opinions, which you might well forget if you neglected to write them down at the time, will often provide the foundation for your most original essays and may in the long run prove to be the most valuable material you record in class.

An excellent practice for bridging the gap between the sketchy notes you write in class and fully developed essays is to extend your notes in a journal. Rather than reviewing class notes only when you are preparing for an exam, take time between classes to review and expand on the ideas your notes record. Consider which of your ideas may yield topics for essays, and test the manageability of these topics by sketching outlines. Elaborate in a paragraph or two on ideas you have had time to record in only a sentence. If you have recorded questions in your notes, attempt to answer them yourself in writing. The best time to develop your notes into something more useful occurs when the ideas they record are still fresh in your mind. While keeping a literary journal is not so different from taking notes, it allows you time to develop your ideas more thoughtfully and provides practice that will help you become more comfortable with critical writing.

Evaluating Assignments

Before attempting a writing assignment, you must first determine exactly what it requires and whether you can carry out any approach you are considering in the time available. The time you invest in evaluating assignments is rarely wasted. However eager you may be to get started, be cautious; enthusiasm is great, but you will win few races by sprinting off in the wrong direction.

Be especially careful when choosing topics from a list, a point at which the work of a few minutes can make the difference between success and failure. While you can assume that your instructor considers all suggested topics suitable for some students in your class, you cannot assume that all the topics will be suitable for all the students. Resist the temptation to commit yourself to the first topic that catches your interest. Evaluate all your options, eliminating the obvious impossibilities first. It will usually be clear that some works and some approaches are too difficult for you to manage. Personal taste is also an important consideration: until you gain more experience as a critic, you will rarely write successful essays about literary works you dislike. Once you have narrowed the choice to a few possibilities, sketch brief outlines to give yourself a better idea of where you might go with each topic. Determine whether you can meet all the requirements in each case. For example, even though you admire a certain poem, you may not be capable of handling a topic that requires you to produce a successful essay about how that poem's metrical patterns reinforce its meaning. While there can be long-term benefits in taking the extra time required to prepare for specialized topics, be sure you can manage the workload. Be wary of ambitious failures.

Once you find an assignment you think you can handle well, consider its wording carefully. Are you sure what all the terms mean? If not, ask your instructor to explain. Is there anything about the approach you are considering that seems at odds with the assignment as stated? Perhaps, for example, an assignment asks you to compare characterization in two stories, only one of which particularly impresses you. It may be permissible to concentrate on the one you like while using the other to illuminate by contrast what you admire in your favourite, but, then again, your instructor may want a more balanced comparison. Find out before you devote a lot of time to a questionable approach. Similarly, even though you plan no deviations from the stated requirements, you may find an assignment ambiguous in some respect. If you are told to compare two poems, for example, does this mean you are obligated to consider all aspects of the two poems? Or will you be permitted to devote most of your comparison to some aspect that seems especially revealing? While the more focused approach may seem more interesting to you, your instructor may have left the comparison general to test your understanding of a variety of elements in the poems. Any number of misunderstandings can occur, and you will be wise to anticipate them while you still have plenty of time to adapt.

Think early. Check early. Doing so can save you time, effort, and disappointment.

Research

In a very limited sense, any essay you write on a literary subject will involve research: you will have to read the works you intend to write about very carefully, probably a number of times, and even with an assignment that does not formally require research, you will often read other works by the same writer and explore his or her personal and historical background.

In a formal research paper, however, you will also be expected to find and evaluate what others have written about your subject. In this case, finding and properly acknowledging your debt to secondary material — writings about literature rather than the literature itself — will be a major part of your job. A detailed explanation of research methods and the format for acknowledging sources is beyond the scope of this chapter, but most college-level writing textbooks cover such material thoroughly. If you plan to take more than a few English courses, *The MLA Handbook for Writers of Research Papers*, which provides an exhaustive guide to the standard format used in English essays, is a good investment. Here it will suffice to provide a few general hints that can save you a lot of time and trouble.

Many students get into difficulty by confusing random sampling with research. They find the call number of a book on their topic, go to the specified shelf in the library, pull out several books on the same general subject, and consider their search complete. The one advantage of this approach — speed — cannot compensate for the problems it will almost certainly create. Books chosen at random rarely provide more than brief, general comment on an essay topic; what relevant comment they do include is often slanted according to their focal concerns. In addition, books stay on library shelves long after what they say has been qualified by later observations, and the material you find in a random selection will certainly not be the most recent available. This is not to say that books are of no value; the point is that books must be chosen carefully and supplemented by reference to up-to-date articles from scholarly journals.

The annotated bibliographies and the periodical indexes available in reference libraries will allow you to find material relevant to your topic quickly, and they will also give you an overview of the kinds of approaches to the work in question that others have found useful. But, as valuable as they are in saving you the trouble of reviewing irrelevant or barely relevant material, these resources will not solve all your problems. Often, they will list far more apparently relevant resources than you have time to consult. How are you to choose? In some cases your instructor will make suggestions, but such advice may still leave you guessing about which comments are most important and influential. One of the easiest ways into ongoing critical debates is to look first at the most recent writings you can find on your topic, taking careful note of the earlier works these cite. When two or three recent sources refer to an older one, it will usually be worth your while to check what it says directly. No method of sampling is a substitute for an exhaustive review of criticism, but methods that allow you to make an informed selection should be sufficient for most of your essays. They will certainly serve you better than random choice.

Seeking out the most pertinent material is not the only challenge in research, however. When you set out to research critical comment, remember that you are in at least as much danger from what you find as from what you miss. Discovering a source that carries on your line of argument so well that it leaves you little to add will take the satisfaction out of your work as well as the challenge, and you will learn little from basing your essay on such a source. Moreover, depending heavily on a source increases the chances of unintentional plagiarism — not making it entirely clear which ideas are really yours and which are borrowed. Thus, finding a published essay that covers much of what you intend to say about a topic is a good reason to consider changing topics or at least modifying your approach.

Much more serious than occasional reliance on secondary sources for ideas is developing a habit of dependency. It is all too easy to drift into a pattern of reviewing criticism before you begin to form your own ideas, thereby allowing others to shape your views. Always keep in mind when dealing with critical opinions that they are just that — opinions. Be impressed if you like, but never be intimidated. Even the best critics are human and therefore fallible. They are influenced by the prevailing critical assumptions of their times and often by specific theoretical affiliations. You have every right to disagree with published critics or, for that matter, with your instructors, provided you state your case clearly and support it conscientiously with references to the text in question. Consider other views carefully and with the respect any honest effort to advance understanding deserves, but then, when writing your essays, think for yourself.

STARTING TO WRITE

In contrast with the many difficulties involved in completing a good critical essay on time, putting off getting started is one of the easiest things you will ever do — easy and risky. It is human nature to put off the more difficult of competing tasks until the straightforward ones are out of the way, but with writing, the difficult jobs are precisely the ones to start first. Start early. Leave yourself time to explore blind alleys and, when you feel you are getting nowhere, to allow your subconscious mind to work on the problem while you are consciously engaged with other concerns. You will almost always find that ten hours invested in a writing project over a week will yield better results than a single ten-hour stretch of writing immediately before the deadline for submission.

Writer's Block

Unfortunately, even when you are well aware of the advantages of an early start, you may be held up by a psychological quirk commonly referred to as "writer's block."

Writer's block usually sets in at the earliest stages of a project, making it impossible to begin writing at all or, at best, to carry on past the first page or two. Because fear of failure is part of the cause, writer's block often strikes when you can least afford it — when you are involved in an especially important project or working under pressure. If you have never experienced writer's block, you may find the idea amusing, but sooner or later it affects most writers, and when it does, it can be both unpleasant and costly. Moreover, the anxiety created by one experience can lead to others, creating a steadily worsening problem. It makes sense, therefore, to prepare for writer's block before it strikes by experimenting with methods of resistance in order to determine which work best for you.

The methods described below are primarily intended to help you generate and shape ideas, but because they also encourage you to start writing early, not just when you have time to complete a project but when you have time to waste, they help eliminate writer's block as well. So, even if you find it fairly easy to think of things to say without writing, writing will usually help, and it will certainly make your work no harder.

Questions

Perhaps the most straightforward way to clarify what you think about a subject is to ask yourself questions about it. In order to avoid writer's block, not to mention loss and confusion, keep a record of your questions and answers in writing.

Beginning with very general questions, such as why you like or dislike something, progress gradually to questions that are more specific, quickly abandoning lines of inquiry that lead away from manageable topics. If you need help devising questions, you will find the lists included in writing textbooks many and varied, and most of them will work adequately up to a point. Watch for that point. At first, any question that forces you to examine your ideas will be better than none, but the further you carry on with a ready-made list, the more likely the questions are to limit your answers. As soon as a suggested line of inquiry begins to get in the way of your developing ideas, abandon it and strike off on your own. Such lists are generally more useful for getting started than for leading you to conclusions.

Be wary also of lists of questions not designed for students of literature. For example, lists are often based on the journalistic standard: Who? What? Where? When? Why? How? While such lists encourage thoroughness in getting at the facts of a situation, an essay about literature is, of course, far more subtle than a news story. Normally, your readers will be familiar with the facts of the works you are discussing and will not require a review. Thus you will be wise to pass quickly over the Who? What? Where? and When? and concentrate on questions concerned with Why? and How? More often than not, you will begin forming a useful argument only when you begin addressing these last two.

Interaction

If asking and answering questions by yourself seems lonely work, you may prefer to involve others. Approaches vary according to circumstances and temperament.

One common method of generating ideas, sometimes called brainstorming, involves gathering a group together, with tape recorder running or one member taking notes, and throwing out ideas. The exchange is kept as informal as possible to avoid inhibiting creativity. This sort of exercise works better in developing advertising slogans than critical essays, and a lot of what results will be useless, but finding and rejecting inappropriate approaches to a subject will often help you progress toward forming better ones. At least such an exchange of ideas will get you started.

If you lack the informed group required for brainstorming, you can sometimes develop ideas and free yourself from writer's block by talking to a single listener. Even if this person knows little about your subject, his or her responses can help you decide where your views lack clarity or need support. Remember, however, that in the end it should be you who judges and refines the ideas: using another person as a sounding board for your own ideas is not the same thing as allowing another person to tell you what to think. For the sake of honesty and your development as a critical thinker, avoid working with someone whose superior knowledge of your subject may make it hard to rely on your own judgement.

Free Writing

One of the most reliable ways of breaking writer's block is called "free writing." Free writing is a way of freeing yourself from worry about imperfections in expression that can inhibit the flow of ideas early in a project. It involves committing yourself to writing for a predetermined period of time. You simply sit down in a place where you will not be interrupted and, keeping your subject in mind, write until the time is up. Resist pausing for reflection or stopping to revise. At best, you will be well into a rough draft by the time you finish. At worst, what you produce will be only vaguely relevant to your subject, but, even if the written result is of little value, you will still have broken your writer's block and moved closer to understanding what you want to say. You can always begin a second session of free writing by reacting to the shortcomings of your first.

FOCUSING

Once you put your early inhibitions behind you and begin accumulating ideas, you will soon find yourself with more than you can hope to bring together in a paper. This is the time to turn your attention from generating ideas to pruning and focusing. Handling the focusing stage of a writing project well can save you a great deal of time later on, but it takes discipline. Piling up ideas becomes so easy once you get started that it is tempting to carry on too long, deluding yourself that you are accomplishing something when in fact you are rambling out of control. While writing anything is better than writing nothing at the start of the writing process, this does not remain true throughout. Avoid the common mistake of trying to substitute quantity for quality.

You can approach the job of focusing from two general directions — working from a thesis or toward one. If you are lucky, you will discover one particularly interesting line of argument early along. Stating your main ideas as a proposition to be proved — a proposition often referred to as a "thesis" and commonly announced near the beginning of an essay in a sentence termed a "thesis statement" — will provide you with a guide as you write, a premise to refer to as you choose which of your secondary ideas to expand, which to subordinate, and which to cut. If no clear thesis has emerged by the time you are ready to start focusing, you can develop one by grouping the most promising ideas and then pruning obvious loose ends. The more loose ends you cut, the more clearly you will see the best potential lines of argument. By the time you have narrowed the possibilities to two or three, you will not only be in a good position to choose the best, but you will also have developed a general idea of how best to support the one you choose.

Be certain, however, that you do not stop before the job is done. Just as it is important to begin focusing before you are overwhelmed with an unmanageable accumulation of ideas, it is also vital to carry on to the desired end — a single, supportable thesis:

> **Not** "Although Andrew Marvell's 'To His Coy Mistress' is manipulative to some extent in taking advantage of flattery, sophistry, and shocking images of mutability, it sometimes reveals a genuine regard for the object of passion and leaves the reader wondering how fully the object of Marvell's affection — or lust — would be capable of appreciating what is going on in the poem."

> **But** "In 'To His Coy Mistress,' Andrew Marvell is addressing a well-educated woman whose intelligence he respects."

> **Or** "Andrew Marvell's most compelling means of seduction in 'To His Coy Mistress' is neither flattery nor shock, but logic."

The first statement above has more than its share of interesting ideas, but it would likely yield either two or three papers tacked loosely together or, worse still, a muddled blend. Parting with ideas can be hard, but attempting to fit more notions into an essay than you can explain and support adequately will be much harder. Saving a few minutes by rushing the focusing stage can cost you many hours later on.

Outlines

Quite a few writing textbooks advise preparing a detailed outline before attempting the first draft, a practice that is usually less effective for critical arguments than expository essays. In essays devoted mainly to reviewing large amounts of factual information, information that is readily gathered and organized in advance of writing, a detailed outline will prove an invaluable tool, one that can greatly speed the process of writing and revision. In more speculative essays, however, the kind of essays commonly written about literature, the difficulty of deciding what you are going to say, and in what order, without a certain amount of groping on paper will often make a detailed outline harder to produce than a draft.

Therefore, using outlines for essays on literature requires flexibility. If planning is one of your strengths, beginning your writing with an outline will definitely speed the work that follows. But if you find preparing outlines more difficult than diving in and writing a draft without one, you will be wise not to spend too much time struggling to follow advice that is more appropriate for some types of writers and for some types of writing than others. Do what works for you.

Tree-Diagramming

If you like working from an outline yet find outlines difficult to organize while you are still generating ideas, try "tree-diagramming," a method that can help you form an outline in something the same way free writing helps you progress toward a first draft. Place a word or phrase representing your central idea in the middle of a large sheet of paper and work outward, connecting related ideas through a series of branches. Though the result of this exercise will rarely resemble a tree, it will provide you with an overview of relationships, revealing both dead ends and useful lines of inquiry quickly. (See Figures 1 and 2.)

WRITING AND REVISING

If you start early and use your time efficiently, you should have developed and focused your ideas several days before your essay is due. At this point, you will have at least a general idea of how your essay will be organized to support your thesis, and you will probably have done some drafting. The next step, completing your first draft, should be fairly straightforward if you resist the temptation to stop and polish style.

Once you have a completed draft that makes sense and includes all your main points, distance yourself from what you have written by leaving it alone

Figure 1 Writer's Block: First Tree Diagram

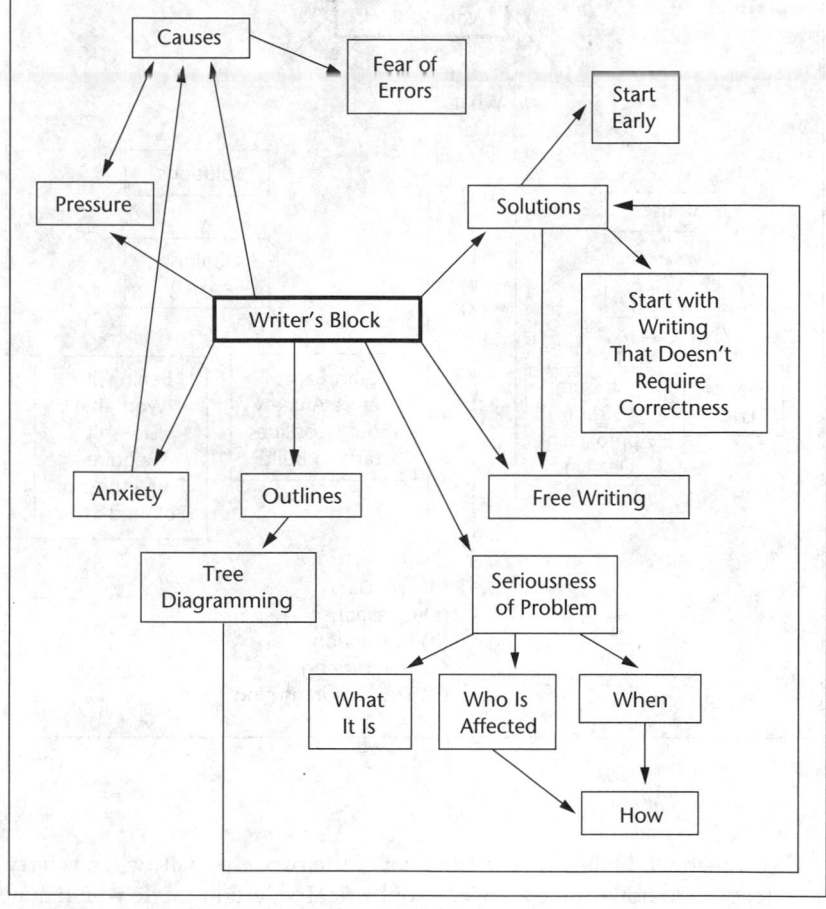

for a day or two. Then, coming back to the project relatively fresh, you will be able to decide more quickly and reliably whether what you have written needs cutting, expansion, or restructuring. After you are satisfied with the form and the essential content, it will be time for polishing style and fine-tuning your argument.

Remember: an essay you write over a week or ten days will almost always be better than one you produce in a single marathon effort, even though you invest the same number of hours in total.

Audience

As you revise your essay, you will have two main concerns — making your argument clear and forceful, and maintaining one consistent appropriate

Figure 2 Writer's Block: Second Tree Diagram

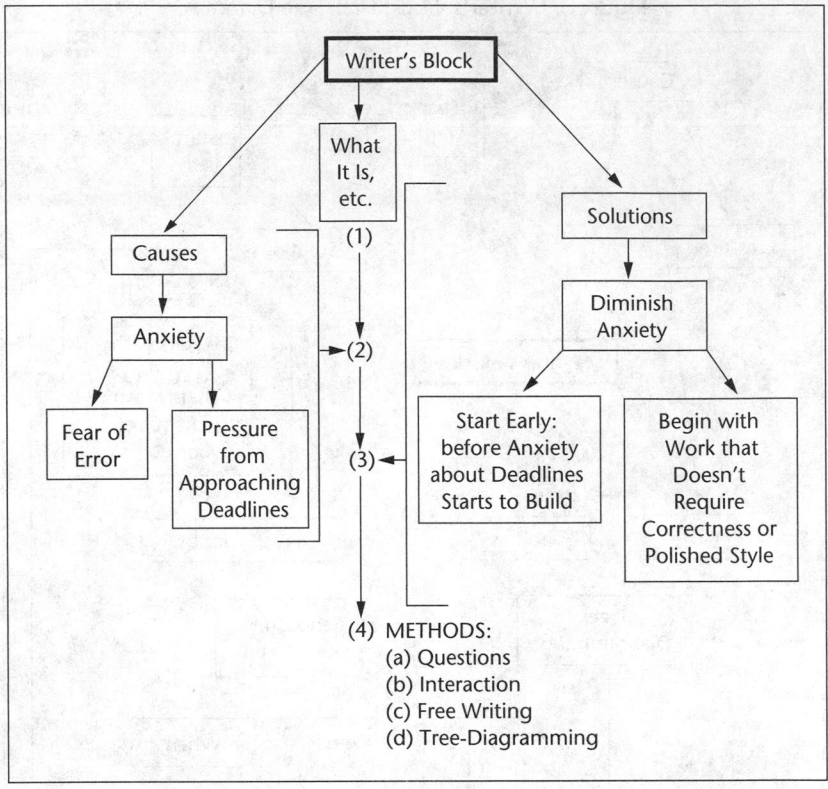

style throughout. Style can be the trickier of the two, especially when you try to affect it. Do not assume an overly sophisticated, erudite style which may not be appropriate even for literary critics. You will find that an unnatural style will be very difficult to maintain for an entire essay. A much easier and more reliable approach is to let your audience and your relationship with it control your style automatically, as they would your voice if you were speaking.

What audience do you write for? The answer is less obvious than you might think. While you probably want most to impress the instructor who will eventually give your work a grade, you may well find that writing with another audience in mind makes this easier. Consider the unnaturalness of explicating literature for someone who knows a great deal more about it than you and who has probably encountered views similar to yours many times before. Will this situation inspire you with confidence? Or is it more likely to make you adopt an apologetic tone and be slightly dismissive about your ideas? How do you feel about writing for someone who can be expected to note technical errors and lower your grade in consequence? Will this audience encourage a confident, forceful style? Hardly.

It makes more sense to write for an audience you can persuade and enlighten, one at about your own level of ability. An audience made up of the better students in your class is a sensible choice. You know this audience well, you can assume it will be familiar with the works you are considering, and you can be confident that it will find your insights fresh and interesting. Writing for an audience of equals will also make it easier for you to adopt a natural, unpretentious style — your own.

In addition to helping you find an appropriate style, writing for an audience of equals will also help you decide what needs to be explained and what does not. For example, since your audience has read and understood the surface meaning of the works you are writing about, you will not need to summarize plot or review other obvious facts. When you need to make specific references to plot or character in support of your developing argument, you will keep these references brief — reminders, rather than revelations. On the other hand, you cannot assume that your audience has seen reasoning similar to yours before, and you should therefore make your line of thinking and the connections between evidence and the conclusions you draw from it more explicit than you might if you were writing exclusively for your instructor.

Openings

Inexperienced writers often get into trouble by working on the assumption that the parts of an essay should be finished one at a time from first to last. This assumption is wrong on two counts. First, if you have the time, it is almost always easier to improve all the parts of an essay at about the same rate as you work through a series of drafts. Second, when lack of time makes a series of drafts impossible and you have to finish sections in sequence, it is usually easier to write the rest of the essay before you put the finishing touches on the opening.

If you are like most student writers, you have more difficulty with openings than with any other part of your essays. Your opening paragraphs may be wordy, vague, and repetitive, even though they receive more attention line for line than other sections. The problem is poor timing. While good essays generally require several drafts, inexperienced writers working under pressure hope to arrive at a final version in as few drafts as possible. In this hope, they attempt to produce a final, polished version when they have only an incomplete or very rough draft to revise, and they naturally start with the opening, struggling to introduce what they will say before they are sure of precisely what this will be. The time-consuming tinkering with wording and groping for ideas that ensue can take more time than revising the whole essay less meticulously. Even worse, having put so much effort into the opening, they are reluctant to make necessary changes once they finish the rest of the essay. The result: a vague, inflated introduction followed by a hastily composed argument that had to be dashed off because of all the time wasted in introducing it. There is nothing wrong with including an opening paragraph containing a clear thesis statement in your first draft; in fact it helps to keep your argument on topic. But, having done that, you will usually find it easiest to leave the opening rough until the rest of your essay is polished to its conclusion.

At this point, you will have a much more certain idea of what you want to introduce in the opening, and you will find writing it much easier in consequence.

Keep in mind as you complete your opening that it should actually accomplish something — excite your reader's interest, persuade your reader of the value of your approach, prepare your reader to grasp what follows. You can achieve these aims only when you yourself fully understand where your essay is going.

Revising for Correctness

While your first concerns throughout most of the writing process should be to make sense and express yourself in an appropriate, consistent style, you cannot afford to ignore correctness — following the accepted conventions of grammar, punctuation, and spelling. While correctness cannot in itself guarantee success, carelessness or incompetence in handling basic writing will certainly ensure failure.

Fortunately, whether they believe it or not, most students who are penalized for errors know enough about grammar and punctuation to write correctly. Attitude more than ignorance is the cause. If you tend to make a lot of mistakes, do not let discouragement or frustration exaggerate your weakness. Convincing yourself that you lack the ability to write correctly is simply an excuse for not investing the time and the work required to master correctness. Seriously confronted, the job of revising for correctness will become easier and less time-consuming with practice.

TEN COMMON MISTAKES TO AVOID IN WRITING ABOUT LITERATURE

Occasionally, even when you start early and work conscientiously, you will still get into difficulty in writing an essay about literature. More often than not this stems from one of the common errors below. While being on guard against these mistakes cannot guarantee success, it will greatly increase your chances.

1. Taking On Unrealistically Ambitious Projects
Be realistic in choosing topics. Avoid topics that will take more space, time, specialized knowledge, or research than you can put into them. If you are not sure whether your plans are manageable, check with your instructor.

2. Plagiarizing by Mistake
Be careful not to drift into plagiarism by keeping sloppy records of your research. Record complete information for references immediately upon

(continued)

---

encountering a source you may want to refer to later. When taking notes, make a clear distinction between recorded information, paraphrases, and quotations.

3. Retaining Irrelevant Material from Early Drafts

If sections of an essay seem loosely connected with each other or with the controlling thesis, try to put the essay in order by supplying clear transitions showing the reader how each part relates to the whole. If you find it difficult to justify a section, cut or shorten it. The ideas that could produce two or three good essays will usually make one bad one.

4. Attempting to Polish Style Too Early

Do not attempt to perfect style while you are still unsure of what you want to say. Be especially wary of polishing openings before you have a clear idea of what will follow.

5. Writing about Yourself Rather than Your Topic

Concentrate on your topic rather than your feelings, doubts, or difficulties as you write. Avoid such redundant insertions as "it seems to me that" and "I think that"; your reader will know you are doing the thinking that goes into your essay without constantly being reminded.

6. Summarizing Plot and Explaining the Obvious

Avoid boring your reader by summarizing what happens in literary works and reviewing obvious facts at length. Assume an audience of intelligent readers familiar with the works you are analyzing and supply only the information this audience will need to evaluate your argument.

Do not be influenced by the summaries provided in various publications termed "notes." These summaries do not constitute serious criticism and should not be imitated.

7. Confusing Verb Tenses

Keep the sequences of verb tenses within long sentences as simple as possible, and avoid shifting tenses unnecessarily. Using the conventional present tense to describe characters, circumstances, and events in literary works will help greatly.

8. Inflating Style

Inflated style is no substitute for good ideas. Impress your readers with the clarity and sense of your thinking rather than the sophistication of your presentation. Strive to write in your own voice; keep your sentence structure as straightforward as you can without being choppy and repetitive;

(continued)

use only those literary terms that you understand. If you work with a thesaurus, use it to find the most accurate and readily understood terms available rather than as a shortcut to pretentiousness and obscurity.

9. Failing to Follow Conventions of Manuscript Form

Follow the accepted conventions for presenting your work on the page and acknowledging sources. It helps to remember that these conventions are not merely decorative; rather, they are an essential code for communicating information efficiently and accurately.

10. Proofreading Inattentively

Proofread when you are rested, preferably after a good night's sleep, rather than immediately after you finish an essay. Proofread in a place free from distractions, and give the job the full attention it requires. The half hour or so you take to proofread an essay properly will often have more effect on the grade than any other half hour of work you invest in the project.

Time is the key factor. To write correctly you must know your limitations and allow yourself time to compensate for them. If you find yourself penalized for errors regularly, understand why. Is it carelessness in the final stages of writing? Or do you lack the background in the basics of writing? If you know what you are doing but make careless mistakes, you need merely improve your proofreading skills and find an appropriate proofreading time, which is to say a time when you will not be too tired to concentrate or likely to be distracted. If your problem is more serious and you are uncertain of what is correct in some cases, budget the extra time you will need to check. Checking your own work is a good way to learn, and you will probably find once you confront the problem of errors that you know more than you think you do. Like most students who are penalized for errors, you probably make the same types of errors again and again, although you handle most elements correctly. Take note of the types of things that go wrong and concentrate on these. Make a checklist of things to watch for. Review the relevant rules as you approach the final stages of writing. Ignorance, in this case, is no excuse: all the information you need about grammar and punctuation can be found easily in writing handbooks, and spelling can, of course, be checked in a dictionary — provided you allow yourself time to do the work.

Once you are satisfied that your own writing is correct, turn your attention to another aspect of your essay that requires care. Most instructors consider the format and accuracy of quotations and references to be just as important as the correctness of your own writing, so check these carefully before submitting your essay. Have you provided all the requirements, such as a title and title page, that are mentioned in the assignment? Are all your quotations recorded exactly? Have you consistently followed the correct format in supplying notes and bibliographical references? Taking care with such details shows that you are serious about your work; allowing even a few mistakes can call the accuracy of all your work into question.

One further word of warning, however: remember that timing is just as important as taking time in correcting your essays. It is as serious a mistake to let your concern with correctness preoccupy you during the earlier stages of writing as it is to neglect correctness later on. Worrying about errors early along will distract you from the important work of forming ideas, and it may also encourage you to adopt an overly cautious style aimed more at avoiding errors than communicating. So leave the job of checking for correctness till the end of your project, and then take it seriously.

*****

While you cannot avoid the basic fact that writing well about literature involves hard work, you can, by following the advice supplied here, avoid wasting the work you do and ensure that your hard work yields the good results it deserves. But be sceptical: this advice is a basis, not a formula, for success. Keep in mind that writing is a personal endeavour and that no one method will work best for every person and every occasion. Treat this and all advice on writing critically, measuring its usefulness against your experience of what works best for you as you continue to grow as a writer.

GLOSSARY OF LITERARY TERMS

accent The stress that makes a syllable more emphatic or prominent in pronunciation than neighbouring syllables.

act A main division of a drama.

action What happens in a drama; the physical activity represented on the stage, but also the mental activity stimulated in a reader or audience.

alliteration The repetition of consonant sounds, particularly at the beginning of words close to one another.

allusion A reference to characters, places, events, or objects from history, religion, mythology, or literature, which the reader is supposed to recognize and connect to the subject of the work in which the allusion appears.

ambiguity The presence of multiple meanings in a word or phrase, whether intentional or accidental.

amphibrach (amphibrachic) A poetic foot of three syllables, only the middle one being accented. See FOOT and Table 1, "The Metrical Feet," in the Introduction to Poetry.

amphimacer (amphimacric) A poetic foot of three syllables, the first and last being accented; also called a cretic. See FOOT and Table 1, "The Metrical Feet," in the Introduction to Poetry.

anapest (anapestic) A poetic foot of three syllables, only the last being accented. See FOOT and Table 1, "The Metrical Feet," in the Introduction to Poetry.

antagonist Any character who opposes another; most often applied to one opposing the main character (the protagonist).

apostrophe An address to an absent or dead person, to an object, or to an abstraction.

archetype A character type, symbol, plot, or theme that appears frequently in works of literature and therefore seems to have universal meaning.

aside Words delivered by one character to another or to the audience, and understood not to be heard by other characters on the stage.

assonance Repetition of similar vowel sounds.

ballad A form of narrative poetry used continuously since medieval times, consisting of four-line stanzas usually alternating iambic tetrameter and iambic trimeter and rhyming *abcb*, often characterized by repetition and repeated refrains. Ballads are usually classed as either popular or literary ballads. Popular ballads were transmitted orally and were frequently intended to be sung; they originated with anonymous authors among the folk, or common people of rural society. Literary ballads are conscious imitations of these popular ballads and are intended to be read or recited, not sung. Because they are often composed by individuals familiar with literary traditions, however, they may employ complex symbolism lacking in the popular ballads.

blank verse Lines of unrhymed iambic pentameter.

blocking The planning of movement on the stage for a production of a drama.

caesura A pause within a poetic line, created by punctuation, by the phrasing of ideas, or by the manipulation of metre.

carpe diem A Latin phrase, meaning "seize the day," often used to describe poems that urge the enjoyment of the moment because time is fleeting.

character A person in a work of literature or one of the *dramatis personae* of a play; also the moral, psychological, and intellectual traits of such a person. A *round* character possesses the complexities, contradictions, and subtle depths of personality associated with actual human beings. A *flat* character, in contrast, seems relatively two dimensional: the character is presented briefly and has little depth of personality. Both kinds may be *dynamic*— a character who changes, for better or worse, during the course of a literary work — or *static*, a character who undergoes no development.

characterization The techniques used to depict the traits of a character in a literary work. See CHARACTER.

chorus In ancient Greek drama, a group of characters who comment in unison upon and sometimes take part in the action of a drama.

classic A work considered to be the best of its class.

classical literature The literature of ancient Greece and Rome.

classicism The application of artistic principles supposedly derived from the classical literatures of Greece and Rome, including formal control, proportion, simplicity, unity, and rationality. Classicism emerged on the Continent and in England among the humanists of the fifteenth and sixteenth centuries. See NEOCLASSICISM.

climax The crucial or high point of tension, understanding, or recognition in a plot and the turning point of the action.

closed couplet See COUPLET.

comedy A literary mode, especially in drama, that ends happily, with the resolution of difficulties, the restoration of fortunes, and the unity of the community, often symbolized by one or more marriages. Comedy can celebrate or satirize the values of a society or individual, but it affirms life through its presentation of good fortune, positive pleasures, meaningful societal values, and individuals as significant parts of society.

complication The problem near the beginning of a story or drama that causes the conflict.

conceit An elaborate or extended comparison, whether simile or metaphor; known as Petrarchan conceits (after Petrarch, the poet who popularized them in his sonnets) when they are conventional, as with the comparison of a lover to a ship, and as metaphysical conceits (after the metaphysical poets of the seventeenth century) when they are elaborate or ingenious comparisons of things not traditionally linked, as with the comparison of separated lovers to a compass.

conflict The opposition of forces within a character, or the struggles either between characters (protagonists) and other characters (antagonists) or between characters and natural or supernatural forces.

connotation The implications of a word; that is, the feelings, ideas, or associations suggested by a word in addition to its denotation, or dictionary meaning.

consonance Repetition of consonants within or at the end of words.

contextual symbol See SYMBOL.

convention A technique or feature included frequently in specific types of literature or in literature from a particular historical period. The Petrarchan conceit is a conventional feature in some Renaissance poetry; the use of heroic couplets is a conventional technique in eighteenth-century poetry.

conventional symbol See SYMBOL.

couplet Two adjacent lines of poetry that rhyme; called a closed couplet when the pair is end-stopped by significant punctuation and contains a complete thought; called a heroic couplet when the rhymed lines are in iambic pentameter.

cretic See AMPHIMACER.

dactyl (dactylic) A poetic foot of three syllables, only the first being accented. See FOOT and Table 1, "The Metrical Feet," in the Introduction to Poetry.

dactylic rhyme See RHYME.

denotation The dictionary meaning of a word, which depends significantly on context, without reference to its implications and associations.

dénouement See RESOLUTION.

deus ex machina Literally, "the god out of the machine"; the descent of a god, represented by an actor lowered to the main level of the stage in a mechanical device, to intercede and conclude an ancient Greek drama; by extension, any contrived and improbable ending.

dialogue The direct presentation of the spoken words of characters in a story or play.

diction The choice of types of words, specific words, and levels of language. Levels may be formal (lofty language such as that used in epics and in the speeches of nobles in Shakespearean drama), informal (the speech and idiom of daily life), or colloquial (the speech and idioms of particular social classes or groups, such as the Cockneys in England).

dimeter A term of poetic measurement indicating a line containing two feet. See FOOT, METRE, and Table 2, "Line Lengths," in the Introduction to Poetry.

double rhyme See RHYME.

dramatic monologue A form of poetry in which a character speaks to a definite but silent listener and thereby reveals his or her own character.

dramatis personae Literally, "the characters of the drama"; a descriptive list of characters prefixed to a drama; see CHARACTER.

dynamic character See CHARACTER.

elegy In classical Greece, a poem on any serious theme that was written in a couplet form known as elegiac metre; since the Renaissance, used to refer to a lyric that laments a death.

end rhyme See RHYME.

end-stopped line A line terminated with a relatively strong pause, usually indicated by the presence of a comma, semicolon, dash, or period; the opposite of enjambment.

enjambment The running over of meaning from one line to another unhindered by punctuation or syntactical pauses; the opposite of an end-stopped line.

epic A long narrative poem recounting in elevated language the deeds of heroes; settings are vast, sometimes extending beyond earth, and episodes may involve the gods or other supernatural beings.

epilogue The concluding, summarizing section of a drama in which all the strands of the plot are drawn together; sometimes the epilogue is an actual addition.

epiphany A religious term meaning a "manifestation" or "showing forth"; western Christianity celebrates the Feast of the Epiphany on January 6 to mark Christ's manifestation of divinity to the Magi; James Joyce applied the term to short fiction to describe the moment when events show forth their meaning, bringing illumination or revelation to a character.

exeunt The plural form of the Latin *"exit"*; literally, "they go out"; a stage direction signalling the exit of all characters in a scene; sometimes expressed as *"exeunt omnes"* ("all go out"); when names or categories follow the term, as in *"exeunt* Lords," only the named group leaves the stage.

exposition The presentation, usually at or near the beginning of a narrative or drama, of necessary background information about characters and situations.

expressionism An early-twentieth-century artistic movement that emphasized the inner world of emotions and thought and projected this inner world through distortions of real-world objects; unlike impressionism, expressionist literature and drama distorts and abstracts the external world, creating works that are symbolic, anti-realistic, and often nightmarish in vision; in prose, stream of consciousness narration is one of its major techniques.

eye rhyme See RHYME.

feminine rhyme See RHYME.

figurative language Language that uses figures of speech (such as metaphors or similes) so that it means more than the simple denotation of the words and, therefore, must be understood in more than a literal way.

flashback An interruption of the chronological sequence of events to present an event that occurred at an earlier time.

flat character See CHARACTER.

foot The basic metrical unit in poetry, consisting of one or more syllables, usually with one stressed or accented; a basic pattern of stressed and unstressed syllables commonly identified by names derived from Greek poetics, the most common being the iamb, the trochee, the dactyl, the anapest, and the spondee. See METRE and Glossary entries for each kind, or see Table 1, "The Metrical Feet," in the Introduction to Poetry for a list.

foreshadowing The presentation of incidents, characters, or objects that hint at important events that will occur later.

free verse Poetry that is free of regular rhythm, rhyme pattern, and verse form; often called *vers libre*.

Freytag's Pyramid A structural diagram, resembling a pyramid in shape, devised by the nineteenth-century German playwright and critic Gustav Freytag to illustrate the rising and falling action of a five-act drama:

```
                   3. Climax
     2. Rising Action      4. Falling Action
   1. Exposition                    5. Resolution
```

genre A classification of literature into separate kinds, such as drama, poetry, and prose fiction; a major literary form that sometimes contains other related forms, which are known as subgenres.

heptameter A term of poetic measurement indicating a line containing seven feet. See FOOT, METRE, and Table 2, "Line Lengths," in the Introduction to Poetry.

heroic couplet See COUPLET.

heroic quatrain See QUATRAIN.

hexameter A term of poetic measurement indicating a line containing six feet. See FOOT, METRE, and Table 2, "Line Lengths," in the Introduction to Poetry.

hyperbole A figure of speech depending on exaggeration, the overstatement of the literal situation, to achieve dramatic or comic effects.

iamb (iambic) A poetic foot of two syllables, the second being accented. See FOOT and Table 1, "The Metrical Feet," in the Introduction to Poetry.

image See IMAGERY.

imagery At its most basic, the verbal creation of images, or pictures, in the imagination; also applied to verbal appeals to any of the senses.

imperfect rhyme See RHYME.

internal rhyme See RHYME.

irony A figure of speech that creates a discrepancy between appearance and reality, expectation and result, or surface meaning and implied meaning; traditionally categorized as verbal irony (a reversal of denotative meaning in which the thing stated is not the thing meant), dramatic irony (in which the discrepancy is between what a character believes or says and the truth possessed by the reader or audience), and situational irony (in which the result of a situation is the reverse of what a character expects).

Italian sonnet See SONNET AND SONNET, PETRARCHAN.

leitmotif A recurring word, phrase, situation, or theme running through a literary work. Also see MOTIF.

line length See Table 2, "Line Lengths," in the Introduction to Poetry for a list; consult this Glossary for descriptions of individual kinds.

lyric A form of poetry that is relatively short and that emphasizes emotions, moods, and thoughts, rather than story.

masculine rhyme See RHYME.

metaphor A figure of speech that makes a comparison by equating things, as in "His heart is a stone."

metaphysical conceit See CONCEIT.

metaphysical poets Seventeenth-century poets who linked physical with metaphysical or spiritual elements in their poetry.

metonymy A figure of speech that substitutes one idea or object for a related one, such as saying "the Crown" when referring to the monarchy or the government.

metre A measure of the feet in a line of poetry, and thus a term expressing the number of feet in a line and the pattern of the predominant feet in that line; the rhythmic pattern of a line. See Table 1, "The Metrical Feet," in the Introduction to Poetry.

Miltonic sonnet See SONNET, MILTONIC.

modernism An artistic movement of the early twentieth century that deliberately broke from the reliance on established forms and insisted that individual consciousness, not something objective or external, was the source of truth; modernist literature may be structurally fragmented; its themes tend to emphasize the philosophy of existentialism, the alienation of the individual, and the despair inherent in modern life.

monometer A term of poetic measurement indicating a line containing one foot. See FOOT, METRE, and Table 2, "Line Lengths," in the Introduction to Poetry.

mood A general emotional atmosphere created by the characters and setting and by the language chosen to present these.

motif An image, character, object, setting, situation, or theme recurring in many works. Also see LEITMOTIF.

motivation The psychological reason behind a character's words or actions.

myth A traditional story embodying ideas or beliefs of a people; also a story setting forth the ideas or beliefs of an individual writer.

narration The recounting, in summarized form, of events and conversations.

narrative poem A poem that tells a story.

narrator The person telling a story, either a fictional character or the implied author of the work; see POINT OF VIEW.

naturalism A literary movement based on philosophical determinism, the belief that the lives of ordinary people are determined by biological, economic, and social factors; naturalists tend to use the techniques of realism in order to present a tragic vision of the fate of individuals crushed by forces they cannot control.

near rhyme See RHYME.

neoclassicism The principles of those writers who emerged with the restoration of Charles II to the throne of England in 1660 and who sought to restore classical restraint in all areas of life. The literature of the Neoclassical Period, which extends until about the 1798 publication of Wordsworth and Coleridge's *Lyrical Ballads*, was highly formal (frequently being based on the heroic couplet), praised reason over emotion, and often used satire and irony to criticize deviations from decorum and propriety. See CLASSICISM.

oblique rhyme See RHYME.

octameter A term of poetic measurement indicating a line containing eight feet. See FOOT, METRE, and Table 2, "Line Lengths," in the Introduction to Poetry.

octave An eight-line stanza in any metre or any rhyme scheme; any eight-line unit of poetry, rhymed or unrhymed; the initial eight lines of a sonnet united by the rhyme scheme.

ode A long, often elaborate, lyric poem that uses a dignified tone and style in treating a lofty or serious theme; regular forms not frequently used in English include the Greek Pindaric ode, which was divided into three repeated types of stanzas (strophe, antistrophe, and epode), each with its own metrical pattern, and the Horatian ode, which retained a single pattern throughout every stanza.

off rhyme See RHYME.

onomatopoeia Words that imitate the sounds that they describe.

oxymoron An ironic figure of speech containing an overt contradiction, as in the word *oxymoron* itself, which means "sharp stupidity" in Greek, or in such phrases as "fearful joy" or "paper coin"; see IRONY and PARADOX.

paradox An apparent contradiction that, upon deeper analysis, contains a degree of truth.

parody A humorous imitation that mocks a given literary work by exaggerating or distorting some of its salient features.

pentameter A term of poetic measurement indicating a line containing five feet. See FOOT, METRE, and Table 2, "Line Lengths," in the Introduction to Poetry.

persona Literally, the mask; the speaking personality through which the author delivers the words in a poem or other literary work; the fictional "I" who acts as the actual author's mouthpiece in a literary work.

personification The attribution of human traits to inanimate objects or abstract concepts.

Petrarchan conceit See CONCEIT.

Petrarchan sonnet See SONNET and SONNET, PETRARCHAN.

plot The arrangement of actions in a drama or story, often in a sequence according to cause and effect.

point of view The angle of vision or perspective from which a story is told. The point of view may be first person (in which the narrator is a character within the story), third person (a character or an implied author outside the story), or, very rarely, second person (in which the narrator, as in "choose-your-adventure" books, addresses the reader as "you"). Narrative point of view also involves questions of knowledge and reliability. Narrators may be omniscient, knowing both external events and internal thoughts and motivations, or they may be limited to some degree, knowing only some external details. Reliable narrators (a category that includes omniscient narrators) tell the truth completely. Unreliable narrators have personal limitations, such as youth or lack of education, that make them misunderstand what they narrate.

prologue The preface or introduction to a play, often containing a plot summary.

protagonist The main character of a drama or story.

pyrrhic A poetic foot of two syllables, neither of which is accented. See FOOT and Table 1, "The Metrical Feet," in the Introduction to Poetry.

quatrain A four-line stanza in any metre or any rhyme scheme, except the heroic quatrain, which is in iambic pentameter and rhymes *abab*; any four-line unit of poetry, rhymed or unrhymed; four lines of a sonnet united by the rhyme scheme.

quintet A five-line stanza in any metre or any rhyme scheme; any five-line unit of poetry, rhymed or unrhymed.

realism The attempt to represent accurately the actual world; a literary movement that developed in reaction to the artificialities of romantic literature and melodramatic drama and that tended to focus on the lives of ordinary people, to use the language of daily speech, and to develop themes that offered social criticism and explored the problems of mundane life.

resolution A portion of a story or drama occurring after the climax that reveals the consequences of the plot and resolves conflicts.

rhyme (rime) The repetition of identical or similar final sounds in words, particularly at the end of lines of poetry. Single, or masculine, rhymes repeat only the last syllable of the words; double, or feminine, rhymes (also sometimes called trochaic rhymes) repeat identical sounds in both an accented syllable and the following unaccented syllable; triple, or dactylic, rhymes repeat identical sounds in an accented syllable and the two following unaccented syllables. End rhyme occurs when the rhyming words are at the end of their respective lines; internal rhyme occurs when one or both of the rhyming words are within a line. Most rhyme involves the exact repetition of sounds; near rhyme (also known as slant, off, imperfect, or oblique rhyme) depends upon the approximation, rather than duplication, of sounds: it repeats either the final consonant (but not the preceding vowels) or the vowels (but not the following consonants) of the words. Eye, or sight, rhyme depends on the similar spelling of words, not their pronunciation, as in *gone* and *lone*.

rhythm The flow of stressed and unstressed syllables; the patterned repetition of beats.

rising action The progression of events and development of the conflict of a story or play up to the point of the climax.

romanticism A literary movement that began in England sometime around the 1798 publication of Wordsworth and Coleridge's *Lyrical Ballads* and was a reaction to the restraint and order of neoclassicism. The Romantics praised emotion over reason and celebrated the imagination; their literature used a diction that was less formal and elevated than that of the classicists (see CLASSICISM), employed themes based on the supernatural, nature and nature's influence on human beings, and the power of the liberated imagination. "Romantic" and "romanticism" are applied to works that exhibit emotional and imaginative exuberance or that use such themes, whether or not written during the Romantic period.

round character See CHARACTER.

satire A literary form that uses wit and humour to ridicule persons, things, and ideas, frequently with the declared purpose of effecting a reformation of vices or follies.

scansion The analysis and marking of the metres and feet in a poem; see METRE and FOOT; see also Table 1, "The Metrical Feet," and Table 2, "Line Lengths," in the Introduction to Poetry.

septet A seven-line stanza in any metre or any rhyme scheme; any seven-line unit of poetry, rhymed or unrhymed.

sestet A six-line stanza in any metre or any rhyme scheme; any six-line unit of poetry, rhymed or unrhymed; the final six lines of a Petrarchan sonnet, which are united by the rhyme scheme.

setting Emotional, physical, temporal, and cultural context in which the action of the story or play takes place.

Shakespearean sonnet See SONNET and SONNET, ENGLISH.

sight rhyme See RHYME.

simile A figure of speech making a direct comparison between things by using *like* or *as* or similar words, as in "His heart is like a stone."

single rhyme See RHYME.

slant rhyme See RHYME.

soliloquy The thoughts and impulses of a character, voiced aloud on stage and shared with the audience.

sonnet A lyric form of fourteen lines, traditionally of iambic pentameter and following one of several established rhyme schemes; see SONNET, ENGLISH; SONNET, MILTONIC; SONNET, PETRARCHAN.

sonnet, English Also called the Shakespearean sonnet; a sonnet consisting of three quatrains and a couplet, rhyming *abab cdcd efef gg*; when the quatrains employ linked rhyme (*abab bcbc cdcd ee*), known as the Spenserian sonnet.

sonnet, Miltonic A variation of the Petrarchan sonnet that eliminates the pause at the end of the octave; thus, the *volta*, when it occurs, usually appears in the middle of the ninth line.

sonnet, Petrarchan Also called the Italian sonnet: the first eight lines (the octave) state a problem, and the final six lines (the sestet) frequently begin with a *volta*, or turn, such as *but*, *yet*, or *however*, and resolve or comment on the problem; originally limited to five rhymes, with the rhyme scheme of the octave usually being *abba abba* (thus dividing into two quatrains), and the rhyme scheme of the sestet varying, but generally being either *cde cde* (thus dividing into two tercets, or three-line units) or *cdcdcd*.

Spenserian sonnet See SONNET, ENGLISH.

spondee (spondaic) A poetic foot of two syllables, both of which are accented. See FOOT and Table 1, "The Metrical Feet," in the Introduction to Poetry.

stanza A division of a poem into a group of lines; traditionally, a grouping of lines according to rhyme scheme, number of lines, or metrical pattern that frequently is repeated in each stanza; a unit of two or more lines that are grouped together visually in any poem by being separated from preceding and following lines. See Table 3, "Names of Stanzas and Line Groupings," and Table 4, "Notable Fixed and Complex Forms," in the Introduction to Poetry.

static character See CHARACTER.

stream of consciousness A narrative presenting the flow of thoughts and emotions of a character.

structure The arrangement of elements within a work; the organization of and relationship between parts of a work; the plan, design, or form of a work.

style A writer's selection and arrangement of words.

suspense The anxiety created by a situation in which the outcome is uncertain.

symbol A figure of speech that links a person, place, object, or action to a meaning that is not necessarily inherent in it; a word so charged with implication that it means itself and also suggests additional meanings, which are the product of convention (the culture traditionally associates a particular image with a particular meaning) or of context (the placement of the image in a work and the details and emphases within that work add suggestiveness to the image, making it symbolic).

synecdoche A figure of speech in which a part stands for the whole or the whole stands for the part, as when the term "hands" signifies "sailors."

tercet A three-line stanza in any metre or any rhyme scheme, but usually called a triplet when all three lines rhyme; any three-line unit of poetry, rhymed or unrhymed; three lines united by the rhyme scheme in the sestet of a Petrarchan sonnet.

tetrameter A term of poetic measurement indicating a line containing four feet. See FOOT, METRE, and Table 2, "Line Lengths," in the Introduction to Poetry.

theme The central idea or meaning of a work; a generalization, or statement of underlying ideas, suggested by the concrete details of language, character, setting, and action in a work.

tone The speaker's attitude toward the subject matter or audience, as revealed by the choice of language and the rhythms of speech.

tragedy A literary work, especially a drama, presenting the failure and downfall of a character. Tragedy is a serious form demonstrating moral choice, error of judgement, and, in many cases, heroic death, as well as the enlightened understanding resulting from such considerations. Tragedy tends to deal with right and wrong, life and death, and the remorselessness of the universe in relationship to the puniness of human beings.

trimeter A term of poetic measurement indicating a line containing three feet. See FOOT, METRE, and Table 2, "Line Lengths," in the Introduction to Poetry.

triple rhyme See RHYME.

triplet A tercet; usually applied to one in which all three lines rhyme.

trochaic rhyme See RHYME.

trochee (trochaic) A poetic foot of two syllables, the first being accented. See FOOT and Table 1, "The Metrical Feet," in the Introduction to Poetry.

understatement A figure of speech, the opposite of exaggeration, that intensifies meaning ironically by deliberately minimizing, or underemphasizing, the importance of ideas, emotions, and situations.

unity The cohesiveness of a literary work in which all the parts and elements harmonize.

vers libre See FREE VERSE.

volta The turn of thought in a poem, especially after the octave of a Petrarchan sonnet.

zeugma A device in which one word is grammatically linked to two words (usually a verb to two objects or two subjects), with the linkage being logically appropriate in a different way for each word, as in Pope's "Or stain her honour, or her new Brocade."

CREDITS

Anonymous Medieval Lyrics "Western Wind" from *Early English Lyrics*, 1967, published by October House.

Anonymous Medieval Popular Ballads "Sir Patrick Spens" from *The Oxford Book of Ballads*, edited by Arthur Quiller-Couch (London: Oxford University Press, 1910).

Arnold, Matthew "Dover Beach" from *Arnold: Poetical Works*, edited by C.B. Tinker and H.F. Lowry (Oxford: Oxford University Press, 1950).

Atwood, Margaret "Progressive Insanities of a Pioneer," "The Animals in That Country," "Further Arrivals," "Variations on the Word *Love*," and "A Women's Issue" from *Selected Poems 1966–1984*. Copyright © 1990 by Margaret Atwood. Reprinted with the permission of Oxford University Press Canada. "you fit into me" from *Power Politics*, copyright © 1996 by Margaret Atwood. Reprinted by permission of House of Anansi Press. "Siren Song" from *You Are Happy* (Toronto: Oxford University Press, 1974). Reprinted with the permission of Oxford University Press Canada. "Helen of Troy Does Counter Dancing" from *Morning in the Burned House*. "The Resplendent Quetzal" from *Dancing Girls and Other Stories*. Used by permission of the Canadian Publishers, McClelland & Stewart, Toronto.

Auden, W.H. "The Unknown Citizen," "In Memory of W.B. Yeats" and "Musée des Beaux Arts" from *Collected Poems of W.H. Auden*, edited by Edward Mendelson (London: Faber and Faber, 1976). Reprinted by permission of Faber and Faber Limited.

Behn, Aphra *The Rover* reprinted from *The Works of Aphra Behn* (6 vols.), edited by Montague Summers (London: Heinemann, 1915).

Birney, Earle "Vancouver Lights," "Anglosaxon Street," "Bushed," and "The Bear on the Delhi Road" from *Collected Poems of Earle Birney*. Used by permission of the Canadian Publishers, McClelland & Stewart, Toronto.

Blake, William Songs of Innocence: "The Lamb," "The Little Black Boy," "The Chimney Sweeper (1789)," "Holy Thursday (1789)," and "Nurse's Song (1789)"; and Songs of Experience: "The Tyger," "The Chimney Sweeper (1794)," "Holy Thursday (1794)," "Nurse's Song (1794)," "The Sick Rose," and "London" from *The Complete Poetry and Prose of William Blake*, revised edition, edited by David V. Erdman (New York: Doubleday, 1962).

Bradstreet, Anne "To my Dear and loving Husband," and "Upon the burning of our house, July 10, 1666" from *Poems of Anne Bradstreet*, edited by Robert Hutchinson (New York: Dover Publications, 1969).

Brand, Dionne "Blues Spiritual for Mammy Prater" copyright © 1990 by Dionne Brand from *No Language Is Neutral*. Reprinted by permission of Coach House Press.

Browning, Elizabeth Barrett "*From* Sonnets from the Portuguese: XLIII (How do I love thee?)," "Hiram Powers's Greek Slave," and "A Musical Instrument" from *The Complete Works of Elizabeth Barrett Browning* (New York: T.Y. Crowell, 1900).

1192

Browning, Robert "My Last Duchess," "The Bishop Orders His Tomb at Saint Praxed's Church," and "'Childe Roland to the Dark Tower Came'" from *Robert Browning: The Poems, vol. 1*, edited by J. Pettigrew (New Haven: Yale University Press, 1981).

Byron, George Gordon, Lord "She Walks in Beauty" and "On This Day I Complete My Thirty-Sixth Year" from *The Poetical Works of Byron*, edited by Robert F. Gleckner (Boston: Houghton Mifflin, 1975).

Chopin, Kate "The Story of an Hour" from *The Complete Works of Kate Chopin, vol. 1* (Baton Rouge: Louisiana State University Press, 1969).

Clarke, Austin C. "The Motor Car" from *When He Was Free and Young and He Used to Wear Silks* (1971, House of Anansi). Published in Canada by Harcourt Canada.

Clarke, George Elliot "Salvation Army Blues" from *Lush Dreams, Blue Exile: Fugitive Poems, 1978–1993* (Lawrencetown Beach, NS: Pottersfield Press, 1994). "Blank Sonnet" from *Whylah Falls* (Vancouver, BC: Polestar Book Publishers, 1990).

Cohen, Leonard "A Kite Is a Victim," "For E.J.P.," "Suzanne Takes You Down," and "Closing Time" from *Stranger Music: Selected Poems and Songs* (Toronto: McClelland & Stewart, 1993). Used by permission of the Canadian Publishers, McClelland & Stewart, Toronto. "A Kite Is a Victim" originally published in *The Spice-Box of Earth*, 1961.

Coleridge, Samuel Taylor "Kubla Khan" and "The Rime of the Ancient Mariner" from *Coleridge: The Complete Poetical Works, Volume 1*, edited by Ernest Hartley Coleridge (Oxford: Oxford University Press, 1912).

Conrad, Joseph "An Outpost of Progress" from *The Medallion Edition of the Works of Joseph Conrad, vol. 1* (London: Gresham Publishing, 1925).

Crane, Stephen "The Open Boat" from *The Open Boat and Other Stories* (London: Heinemann, 1898).

Crawford, Robert "Anne of Green Gables" and "Mary Shelley on the Broughty Ferry Beach" from *Talkies* (London: Chatto and Windus, 1992). Used by permission of The Random House Group Limited.

Cummings, E.E. "in Just- spring" copyright 1923, 1951, © 1991 by the Trustees for the E.E. Cummings Trust. Copyright © 1976 by George James Firmage. "next to of course god america i" copyright 1926, 1954, © 1991 by the Trustees for the E.E. Cummings Trust. Copyright © 1985 by George James Firmage from *Complete Poems: 1904–1962*, edited by George J. Firmage. Reprinted by permission of Liveright Publishing Corporation. "l(a" Copyright © 1958, 1986, 1991 by the Trustees for the E.E. Cummings Trust.

Dawe, Tom "The Bear" from *Hemlock Cove and After* (Portugal Cove, NF: Breakwater Books, 1975). Reprinted with the permission of Breakwater Books, St. John's. "The Naked Man" from *Island Spell* (St. John's, NF: Harry Cuff Publications, 1981). Reprinted by permission of the author.

Dickinson, Emily "I'm Nobody! Who are you?," "The Soul selects her own Society —," "A Bird came down the Walk —," "I heard a Fly buzz — when I died —" and "I started Early — Took my Dog —" from *The Poems of Emily Dickinson*, edited by Thomas H. Johnson. (Cambridge, MA: The Belknap Press of Harvard University Press, Copyright © 1951, 1955, 1979, 1983 by the President and Fellows of Harvard College.) Reprinted by permission of the publishers and the Trustees of Amherst College.

Donne, John "Song (Go, and catch a falling star)," "The Bait," "A Valediction: Forbidding Mourning," "The Canonization," "The Flea," "Holy Sonnet X (Death be not proud)," and "Holy Sonnet XIV (Batter my heart)" from *John Donne: The Complete English Poems*, edited by A.J. Smith (Harmondsworth: Penguin, 1971).

Dumont, Marilyn "Letter to Sir John A. Macdonald" and "The Devil's Language" from *A Really Good Brown Girl* (London, ON: Brick Books, 1996).

Eliot, T.S. "The Love Song of J. Alfred Prufrock," "The Hollow Men," and "Journey of the Magi" from *Collected Poems 1909–1962* (London: Faber and Faber, 1964). Reprinted by permission of Faber and Faber Limited.

Faulkner, William "A Rose for Emily" from *Collected Stories of William Faulkner*. Copyright © 1930 and renewed 1958 by William Faulkner. Reprinted by permission of Random House, Inc.

Frost, Robert "After Apple-Picking," "An Old Man's Winter Night," "Stopping by Woods on a Snowy Evening," "Acquainted with the Night," and "Design" from *The Poetry of Robert Frost*, edited by Edward Connery Lathem. Copyright 1936, © 1956 by Robert Frost. Copyright © 1964 by Lesley Frost Ballantine. Copyright 1923, 1928, © 1969 by Henry Holt and Company, Inc. Reprinted by permission of Henry Holt and Company, Inc.

Gallant, Mavis "My Heart Is Broken." Copyright © 1957 by Mavis Gallant. Reprinted by permission of Georges Borchardt, Inc. for the author.

Gilman, Charlotte Perkins "The Yellow Wallpaper" from *The Charlotte Perkins Gilman Reader, Volume 1* (New York: Pantheon, 1980).

Gom, Leona "Metamorphosis" from *The Collected Poems* (Victoria, BC: Sono Nis Press, 1991).

Gray, Thomas "Elegy Written in a Country Church-Yard" from *The Complete Poems of Thomas Gray*, edited by H.W. Starr and J.R. Hendrickson (Oxford: Clarendon Press, 1966).

Halfe, Louise Bernice "My Ledders" and "Body Politics" from *Bear Bones & Feathers* (Regina: Coteau Books, 1994). Copyright © Louise Bernice Halfe, 1994.

Heaney, Seamus "Death of a Naturalist" from *Death of a Naturalist* (London: Faber and Faber, 1969). "The Singer's House," "The Harvest Bow," and "Casualty" from *Field Work* (London: Faber and Faber, 1980). Reprinted by permission.

Hemingway, Ernest "A Clean, Well-Lighted Place" from *The Complete Short Stories of Ernest Hemingway*. Copyright 1933 by Charles Scribner's Sons. Copyright renewed © 1961 by Mary Hemingway. Reprinted by permission of Scribner, a division of Simon & Schuster.

Herbert, George "The Altar" and "Easter Wings" from *The Poetical Works of George Herbert* (Oxford: Oxford University Press, 1941).

Herrick, Robert "To the Virgins, To Make Much of Time," and "Upon Julia's Clothes" from *Herrick's Poetical Works, Volume 1* (Boston: Houghton Mifflin, 1854).

Hollingshead, Greg "The Naked Man" from *The Roaring Girl* (Toronto: Somerville House Books, 1995). Reprinted by permission of the author.

Hopkins, Gerard Manley "Pied Beauty," "God's Grandeur," and "The Windhover" reprinted from *The Poems of Gerard Manley Hopkins*, edited by W.H. Gardiner and N.H. Mackenzie (Oxford: Oxford University Press, 1967).

Housman, A.E. "Loveliest of trees, the cherry now," "When I was one-and-twenty," and "To an Athlete Dying Young" from *Collected Poems*. Reprinted by permission of The Society of Authors as the literary representative of the Estate of A.E. Housman.

Howard, Henry, Earl Of Surrey "Love that doth reign" from *The Poems of Henry Howard, Earl of Surrey*, edited by F.M. Padelford (Seattle: University of Washington Press, 1928).

Hughes, Ted "Pike" and "Hawk Roosting" from *Selected Poems 1957–1967*. Copyright © 1972 by Ted Hughes. Reprinted by permission of Faber and Faber Limited.

Jonson, Ben "Song: To Celia" and "On My First Son" from *Ben Jonson: Selected Works*, edited by Harry Levin (New York: Random House, 1938).

Joyce, James "Araby" from *Dubliners*. Copyright 1916 by B.W. Huebsch. Definitive text copyright © 1967 by the Estate of James Joyce. Reprinted by permission of Viking Penguin, a division of Penguin Books USA Inc.

Keats, John "On First Looking into Chapman's Homer," "When I have fears," "Ode to a Nightingale," "Ode on a Grecian Urn," "To Autumn," and "La Belle Dame sans Merci: A Ballad" from *The Poetical Works of John Keats*, edited by H.W. Garrod (Oxford: Clarendon Press, 1958).

King, Thomas "Borders" from *One Good Story, That One*, copyright © 1993 by Thomas King. Published in Canada by HarperCollins Publishers Ltd. Reprinted with permission.

Klein, A.M. "Heirloom" and "Portrait of the Poet as Landscape" from *Complete Poems*, edited by Zailig Pollock. Copyright © 1990 by University of Toronto Press. Reprinted by permission of University of Toronto Press Incorporated.

Lampman, Archibald "Heat," "In November" (1895), "Winter Evening," and "The City of the End of Things" from *The Poems of Archibald Lampman, 2nd edition* (Toronto: G.N. Morang, 1900).

Larkin, Philip "Next, Please," "Church Going," and "Toads" from *The Less Deceived*. Reprinted by permission of The Marvell Press, England and Australia.

Lau, Evelyn "What We Do in the Name of Money" from *You Are Not Who You Claim* (Vancouver, BC: Beach Holme Publishing, 1990). Reprinted with permission of Beach Holme Publishing. "Nineteen" © by Evelyn Lau, from *Oedipal Dreams* (Toronto: Coach House Press, 1992). Reprinted by permission of the author. "Family" Extracted from *Choose Me* by Evelyn Lau. Copyright © Evelyn Lau 1999. Reprinted by permission of Doubleday Canada, a division of Random House of Canada Limited.

Laurence, Margaret "The Loons" from *A Bird in the House*. Used by permission of the Canadian Publishers, McClelland & Stewart, Toronto.

Lawrence, D.H. "Snake" from *The Complete Poems of D.H. Lawrence* (London: Heinemann, 1964, 1972).

Layton, Irving "The Birth of Tragedy" and "Keine Lazarovitch 1870–1959" from *A Wild Peculiar Joy*. Used by permission of the Canadian Publishers, McClelland & Stewart, Toronto.

LePan, Douglas "A Country without a Mythology" from *Weathering It*. Used by permission of the Canadian Publishers, McClelland & Stewart, Toronto.

Livesay, Dorothy "Bartok and the Geranium" and "The Three Emilys" from *Collected Poems: The Two Seasons* (Toronto: McGraw-Hill Ryerson, 1972). Copyright © and reprinted by permission.

MacEwen, Gwendolyn "A Breakfast for Barbarians" from *Magic Animals: Selected Poetry of Gwendolyn MacEwen* (Toronto: Macmillan, 1974). "Dark Pines under Water" from *The Shadow-Maker* (Toronto: Macmillan, 1969). Reprinted by permission of the author's family.

MacLeod, Alistair "The Boat" from *Island.* Used by permission of the Canadian Publishers, McClelland & Stewart, Toronto.

Mansfield, Katherine "Bliss" from *Bliss and Other Stories* (New York: Alfred A. Knopf, 1931).

Maracle, Lee "Too Much to Explain" from *Sojourners and Sundogs: First Nations Fiction* (Vancouver, BC: Press Gang Publishers, 1999). Reprinted by permission of Polestar/ Raincoast and the author.

Marvell, Andrew "To His Coy Mistress" and "The Garden" from *The Poetical Works of Milton and Marvell, with a Memoir of Each, Vol. 4* (Boston: Houghton Mifflin, 1880).

McGrath, Elizabeth "Fogbound in Avalon." Reprinted by permission of the author; © 1980. Originally published in *The New Yorker.*

Milton, John "Lycidas," "How soon hath Time, the subtle thief of youth," "When I consider how my light is spent," and "On the Late Massacre in Piedmont" from *The Poetical Works of John Milton,* edited by D. Masson (London: Macmillan, 1891).

Mistry, Rohinton "Squatter" from *Tales From Firozsha Baag* (Toronto: McClelland & Stewart, 1987).

Mitchell, Ken *The Shipbuilder* © Ken Mitchell. First produced for stage in 1979. Published by Fifth House Publishers, 1990. Reprinted by arrangement with Bella Pomer Agency Inc.

Mouré, Erin "Miss Chatelaine" and "The Producers" from *Furious* (Toronto: House of Anansi, 1987). Copyright © 1997 by Erin Mouré. Reprinted by permission of House of Anansi Press Ltd.

Munro, Alice "The Wild Swans" from *Who Do You Think You Are?* (Toronto: Macmillan, 1978). Reprinted by permission of The Writer's Shop.

Namjoshi, Suniti "Look, Medusa!" and "Poem Against Poets" from *The Blue Donkey Fables* (London: The Women's Press, 1988).

Nourbese Philip, Marlene "Meditations on the Declension of Beauty by the Girl with the Flying Cheek-bones" from *She Tries Her Tongue, Her Silence Softly Breaks* (Charlottetown, PEI: Ragweed Press, 1989). "Blackman Dead" from *Thorns* (Toronto: Williams-Wallace, 1980). Reprinted by permission of the author.

Nowlan, Alden "The Bull Moose" from *Selected Poems* copyright © 1983 by The Estate of Alden Nowlan. Reprinted by permission of House of Anansi Press.

Ondaatje, Michael "Elizabeth," "Letters & Other Worlds," "The Cinnamon Peeler" and "To a Sad Daughter" from *The Cinnamon Peeler* (Toronto: McClelland & Stewart, 1984). Copyright © 1984 by Michael Ondaatje. Reprinted by permission of the author.

Oodgeroo Noonuccal (Kath Walker) "We Are Going" from *My People,* 3rd edition, The Jacaranda Press, © 1990. Reproduced by permission of John Wiley & Sons, Australia.

Owen, Wilfred "Anthem for Doomed Youth," "*Dulce et Decorum Est,*" and "Strange Meeting" from *The Complete Poems and Fragments,* edited by Jon Stallworthy (London: The Hogarth Press, 1983).

Page, P.K. "The Stenographers," "Stories of Snow" and "The Landlady" from *The Hidden Room* (The Porcupine's Quill, 1997). Copyright © P.K. Page. Reprinted by permission of the author.

Plath, Sylvia "Daddy" and "Lady Lazarus" from *Ariel* (London: Faber and Faber, 1966). Reprinted by permission of Faber and Faber Limited. "Mirror" from *Crossing the Water* (London: Faber and Faber, 1971). Republished in *Collected Poems*, edited by Ted Hughes (London and Boston: Faber and Faber, 1981).

Pollock, Sharon *Blood Relations* from *Blood Relations and Other Plays*. Reprinted by permission of NeWest Publishers Limited, Edmonton.

Pope, Alexander "The Rape of the Lock; An Heroi-Comical Poem" from *The Rape of the Lock and Other Poems*, edited by Geoffrey Tillotson (London: Methuen, 1962).

Pound, Ezra "The River-Merchant's Wife: A Letter," "In a Station of the Metro," and "Ancient Music" from *Personae*. Copyright © 1926 by Ezra Pound. Reprinted by permission of New Directions Publishing Corporation.

Pratt, E.J. "The Shark," "From Stone to Steel," and "The Truant" from *E.J. Pratt: Complete Poems*, edited by Sandra Djwa and R.G. Moyles. Copyright © 1989 by University of Toronto Press. Reprinted by permission of University of Toronto Press Incorporated.

Purdy, Al "The Country North of Belleville," "Lament for the Dorsets," and "Wilderness Gothic" from *Being Alive: Poems 1958–1978*, McClelland & Stewart, Toronto. "Trees at the Arctic Circle" from *North of Summer: Poems from Baffin Island* (Toronto: McClelland & Stewart, 1967). Reprinted by permission.

Rich, Adrienne "Aunt Jennifer's Tigers" and "Diving into the Wreck" from *The Fact of a Doorframe: Poems Selected and New, 1950–1984*. Copyright © 1984. Copyright © 1975, 1978 by W.W. Norton & Company, Inc. Copyright © 1981 by Adrienne Rich. "What Kind of Times Are These" and "In Those Years" from *Dark Fields of the Republic: Poems 1991–1995*. Copyright © 1995 by Adrienne Rich. Reprinted by permission of W.W. Norton & Company, Inc.

Roberts, Sir Charles G.D. "Tantramar Revisited," "The Potato Harvest," "The Winter Fields," and "The Herring Weir" from *The Collected Poems of Sir Charles G.D. Roberts* (Wolfville, NS: The Wombat Press, 1985). Copyright © by Mary Pacey and Lady Joan Roberts. Reprinted by permission of The Wombat Press.

Roethke, Theodore "Root Cellar" by Theodore Roethke first appeared in *Poetry*, copyright © 1943. Reprinted by permission of Doubleday Broadway Publishing Group. "My Papa's Waltz" from *The Collected Poems of Theodore Roethke*, copyright 1942 by Hearst Magazines, Inc. Reprinted by permission of Doubleday Broadway Publishing Group. "The Waking" from *The Waking Poems: 1933–53* (New York: Doubleday, 1954). Used by permission of Doubleday, a division of Bantam Doubleday Dell Publishing Group, Inc.

Ross, Sinclair "The Lamp at Noon" from *The Lamp at Noon and Other Stories*. Used by permission of the Canadian Publishers, McClelland & Stewart, Toronto.

Rossetti, Christina "Song (When I am dead)," "The World," and "Goblin Market" from *The Poetical Works of Christina Georgina Rossetti*, edited by William Michael Rossetti (London: Macmillan, 1908).

Roth, Philip "The Conversion of the Jews" from *Goodbye, Columbus.* Copyright © 1959, renewed 1987 by Philip Roth. Reprinted by permission of Houghton Mifflin Co. All rights reserved.

Rule, Jane "Inland Passage" from *Inland Passage* (Toronto: Lester and Orpen Dennys, 1985). Reprinted by permission of Key Porter Books.

Scott, Duncan Campbell "The Forsaken" and "Night Hymns on Lake Nipigon" from *The Poems of Duncan Campbell Scott* (Toronto: McClelland & Stewart, 1926). Used by permission of John G. Aylen, Ottawa, Canada.

Scott, F.R. "The Canadian Authors Meet," "Trans Canada," "Laurentian Shield," and "For Bryan Priestman" from *The Collected Poems of F.R. Scott*, edited by John Newlove. Reprinted with the permission of William Toye, Literary Executor for the Estate of F.R. Scott.

Shelley, Percy Bysshe "Ozymandias," "Ode to the West Wind," and "To a Skylark" from *The Poetical Works of Percy Bysshe Shelley* (London: Macmillan, 1899).

Soyinka, Wole "Telephone Conversation" and "Procession I: Hanging Day" from *A Shuttle in the Crypt.* Copyright © 1972 by Wole Soyinka. Reprinted by permission of Hill & Wang, a division of Farrar, Straus and Giroux, LLC. "I Think It Rains" Copyright © 1967 by Wole Soyinka. Reprinted by permission of Melanie Jackson Agency, L.L.C.

Stevens, Wallace "Thirteen Ways of Looking at a Blackbird" and "The Idea of Order at Key West" from *Collected Poems of Wallace Stevens.* Copyright © 1954 by Wallace Stevens. Reprinted by permission of Alfred A. Knopf, a division of Random House, Inc.

Tan, Amy "Two Kinds" from *The Joy Luck Club.* Copyright © 1989 by Amy Tan. Reprinted by permission of G.P. Putnam's Sons, a division of Penguin Putnam Inc.

Tennyson, Alfred, Lord "The Eagle. Fragment," "The Lady of Shalott," "Ulysses," and "Tithonus" from *The Poetic and Dramatic Works of Alfred, Lord Tennyson*, edited by W.J. Rolfe (Boston: Houghton Mifflin, 1898).

Thomas, Dylan "And Death Shall Have No Dominion," "The Force That through the Green Fuse Drives the Flower," "Fern Hill," and "Do Not Go Gentle into That Good Night" from *Dylan Thomas: The Poems* (London: J.M. Dent, 1971). Reprinted by permission of David Higham Associates and the Trustees for the copyright of Dylan Thomas.

Thompson, Judith *Sled* (Toronto: Playwrights Canada Press, 1997). Copyright © 1997 Judith Thompson. Amateur or professional performance rights for *Sled* must be obtained from Great North Artists, 350 Dupont Street, Toronto, ON, Canada M5L 1Y9.

Vanderhaeghe, Guy "What I Learned from Caesar" from *Man Descending* (Toronto: Macmillan, 1982). Reprinted by permission of McClelland & Stewart, Inc., The Canadian Publishers.

Walcott, Derek "A Far Cry from Africa" and "Ruins of a Great House" from *Collected Poems 1948–1984.* Copyright © 1986 by Derek Walcott. Reprinted by permission of Farrar, Straus & Giroux, LLC. "The Virgins" from *Sea Grapes* (New York: Jonathan Cape). Reprinted by permission of The Random House Group Ltd.

Walker, Alice "Everyday Use" from *In Love & Trouble: Stories of Black Women*, copyright © 1973 by Alice Walker. Reprinted by permission of Harcourt Brace & Company.

Webb, Phyllis "Marvell's Garden" and "Treblinka Gas Chamber" from *Selected Poems: The Vision Tree*, edited by Sharon Thesen (Talon Books, Vancouver) copyright © 1982, 1985 and reprinted by permission of the author.

Welty, Eudora "Why I Live at the P.O." from *A Curtain of Green and Other Stories*, copyright 1941 and renewed 1969 by Eudora Welty. Reprinted by permission of Harcourt Brace & Company.

Whitman, Walt "When Lilacs Last in the Dooryard Bloom'd" and "One's-Self I Sing" from *Leaves of Grass, Comprehensive Reader's Edition*, edited by Harold W. Blodgett and Sculley Bradley. Copyright © 1965 by New York University. Reprinted by permission of New York University Press.

Wilde, Oscar *The Importance of Being Earnest*, reprinted from *The First Collected Edition of the Works of Oscar Wilde, vol. 3*, edited by R. Ross (London: Dawson of Pall Mall, 1969).

Williams, Tennessee *Cat on a Hot Tin Roof* copyright © 1954, 1955, 1971, 1975 by Tennessee Williams. Reprinted by permission of New Directions Publishing Corp.

Williams, William Carlos "Tract," and "The Red Wheelbarrow" from *Collected Poems: 1909–1939, Volume 1*. Copyright © 1938 by New Directions Publishing Corp. Reprinted by permission of New Directions Publishing Corp.

Wordsworth, William "Lines Composed a Few Miles above Tintern Abbey," Sonnet: "It is a beauteous evening, calm and free," Sonnet: "London, 1802," Sonnet: "The world is too much with us," and "I wandered lonely as a cloud" from *The Poetical Works of Wordsworth*, new edition, revised, edited by Ernest de Selincourt (Oxford: Oxford University Press, 1953).

Wyatt, Sir Thomas "My galley charged with forgetfulness" from *The Poetical Works of Sir Thomas Wyatt and Henry Howard, Earl of Surrey, with a Memoir of Each* (Boston: Houghton Mifflin, 1880).

Yeats, William Butler "Easter 1916," "The Second Coming," "Sailing to Byzantium," "Leda and the Swan," "Among School Children," and "Crazy Jane Talks with the Bishop" from *The Poems of William Butler Yeats* (London: Macmillan Publishing Company, 1961, 1933).

INDEX OF AUTHORS

INDEX OF TITLES
AND FIRST LINES*

---

* includes first lines of poetry selections only; first lines of drama and short fiction selections are not included.